HISTORY OF CHRISTIAN PHILOSOPHY IN THE MIDDLE AGES

THE RANDOM HOUSE

Lifetime Library

HISTORY OF
Christian Philosophy
in the Middle Ages

BY ETIENNE GILSON

Director of Studies, Pontifical Institute of
Mediaeval Studies, Toronto

RANDOM HOUSE · NEW YORK

Fifth Printing

NIHIL OBSTAT

VINCENT L. KENNEDY
Censor Deputatus

IMPRIMATUR

✠ JAMES C. CARDINAL McGUIGAN, D.D.
Archbishop of Toronto

September 29, 1954, the Feast of St. Michael
the Archangel

Published in New York by Random House, Inc., and simultaneously in
Toronto, Canada, by Random House of Canada, Limited.

Library of Congress Catalog Card Number: 54-7802

Manufactured in the United States of America

FOREWORD

THE aim and scope of this book is to provide general readers and students with an introduction to the history of Christian philosophy from Justin Martyr in the second century after Christ up to Nicholas of Cues whose work stands on the border line of a new historical period. We call Christian philosophy the use made of philosophical notions by the Christian writers of those times. Although it intends to convey some measure of literary information, the emphasis of this book is on philosophy itself; it is primarily concerned with the history of philosophical ideas even though, as is generally the case in the middle ages, philosophy is only found in a theological context.

The text itself represents, we hope, a sufficient introduction to the significant developments that took place during the fourteen centuries under consideration. The notes should provide teachers and advanced students with the first technical information they need in order to conduct their courses or to start their own research work. Special bibliographies, indicated in our own, will take them to the relevant sources of information.

The indebtedness of the author to his predecessors cannot be adequately expressed. Our bibliographies will say it better than any literary formulas. Another feeling of indebtedness is still less easy to convey. This *History of Christian Philosophy in the Middle Ages* has been entirely taught and written at the Pontifical Institute of Mediaeval Studies, in Toronto. Without the specialized library created twenty-five years ago by the insight and generosity of the Congregation of Saint Basil, we could not have attempted to write it. Without the patience and zeal of so many students whose personal reactions have always been constructive, we would not have dared to teach it. Without the constant good will of colleagues whose erudition has always been at our disposal, this book would have been still more imperfect than it is. We beg to extend to all, fellow historians, students and colleagues, the heartfelt expression of our gratitude.

E. G.

CONTENTS

PART THREE

From Augustine to Boethius

PART FOUR

From Scotus Erigena to Saint Bernard

PART FIVE

Arabian and Jewish Philosophy

PART SIX

Early Scholasticism

PART SEVEN

Theology and Learning

PART EIGHT

The Golden Age of Scholasticism

PART NINE

The Condemnation of 1277

PART TEN

Fourteenth-Century Scholasticism

PART ELEVEN

The Modern Way

NOTES

HISTORY OF CHRISTIAN

PHILOSOPHY IN THE

MIDDLE AGES

THE RANDOM HOUSE

Lifetime Library

INTRODUCTION

To THE theologians and philosophers of the middle ages,[1] what we now call the "canonical writings," [2] that is the books of Holy Scripture considered as divinely inspired, have been a constant object of meditation and of intellectual elucidation. Since all of them had been written under the inspiration of the Holy Ghost, they all could be attributed to the same author. Whatever its date, each of them was considered as relating a part of the same history. "In the beginning God created heaven and earth" (Gen. 1, 1), and within six days he finished them with all the beings which they contain. Among them was man, whom God created male and female, in his own image (Gen. 1, 27). After the creator had completed his work, "He saw all the things that He had made, and they were very good" (Gen. 1, 31). On the seventh day God rested from all the work he had done and, for this very reason, he blessed that day and sanctified it (Gen. 2, 3). Man was then put into a paradise of pleasure, to dress it and to keep it, under no other obligation than not to eat of a certain tree, which was the tree of "the knowledge of good and evil." Having transgressed God's order, Adam was cast out of paradise and condemned to toil up to the end of his life. As to Eve, she would henceforward bring forth children in sorrow and be under her husband's power (Gen. 3, 16). This curse has ever since remained upon mankind as a whole and, during the middle ages, its effects have been studied by theologians as the "consequences of original sin."

Yet, even after the fall of man, God did not leave his creature without help. Having chosen to himself a particular people from among the nations, God revealed to the Jews his own name, Yahweh, that is, "I AM WHO AM" (Ex. 3, 14). Since he is, and is He Who Is, there is but one God and there are no other gods before him. Because he has created heaven and earth, the world is His and no man can own any part of it except through some delegation of God's supreme ownership and in view of his own ends. The creator is so completely the master of his creation that he directs the general course of its history according to his own designs (Ecclus. 43-50); moreover, he can freely modify even the course of nature by working miracles according to his own will. He is the Lord, who governs the world by his providence, rules man as a supreme lawgiver and enforces his commandments by rewards and punishments. Nothing escapes him. I AM is a powerful and living God, who holds the world within his hand. Omnipresent to creation, he knows every being, every man, every act and every thought of man: "I am the Lord, who search the heart and prove the reins: who give to every one according to his way and according to the fruit of his

3

devices" (Jerem. 17, 10). Man, then, cannot possibly ignore such a God whose existence and glory shine everywhere in his creation: "The heavens shew forth the glory of God, and the firmament declareth the work of his hands" (Ps. 18, 2). For indeed, just as he is power, God is wisdom. He has ordered all things "in measure, and number, and weight" (Wisd. 11, 21) so that his art "reacheth from end to end mightily and ordereth all things sweetly" (Wisd. 8, 1). Last, not the least, God is love, for He loves all things that are and hates none of the things which He has made: "And how could anything endure, if thou wouldst not, or be preserved, if not called by Thee? But thou sparest all, because they are thine, O Lord, who lovest souls" (Wisd. 11, 26-27).

This same God of love, so clearly announced by the Old Testament, is also the God of the Gospel. A man, by the name of Jesus, had been born under miraculous circumstances. Proclaiming himself the son of God, the Messiah announced by the Prophets of Israel, he had fully justified his claim by many miracles as well as by his doctrine, "preaching the good news of the Kingdom and healing all manner of sickness and every infirmity among the people" (Matt. 4, 23). And, indeed, the kingdom of heaven was at hand, but only for those who would do penance and observe the two great commandments of the ancient law (Deut. 6, 4 and Levit. 19, 18): "Hear, O Israel: the Lord thy God is one God. And thou shalt love the Lord thy God with thy whole heart and with thy whole soul and with thy whole mind and with thy whole strength. This is the first commandment. And the second is like to it: Thou shalt love thy neighbor as thyself. There is no greater commandment than these" (Mark 12, 29-31). All our duties toward other men are implicit in the second of these commandments (Rom. 13, 9). Love, therefore, is the fulfilling of the law (Rom. 13, 10), and since "God is charity, he that abideth in charity, abideth in God and God in him" (I John 4, 16). The whole teaching of the Gospels revolves around this central notion: that we should believe in the name of the son of God, Jesus Christ, and love one another as he has given commandment unto us (I John 4, 11). And not only commandment, but example, for there is no greater love than to give one's life for those whom one loves. The death of Jesus on the cross, a scandal to the Jews and foolishness to the Greeks, has redeemed man from the malediction of original sin, and his resurrection remains as the promise of our own, for "if there be no resurrection of the dead, then Christ is not risen again" (I Cor. 15, 12). Two stories are here blending into one, for the God of the Old Testament is the Father almighty: "The earth is the Lord's, and the fulness thereof" (Ps. 23, 1. Cf. Ecclus. 17, 31 and I Cor. 10, 26), and just as, by his power, he has created heaven, and earth, and man (and all that he had made was good), so also he has restored his work impaired by the sin of man, planting the cross in the middle of the earth as a miracle of love. Indeed, the Incarnation and the death of Christ on the cross are here at the very center of world history, and this is why Christianity, itself centered upon the living person of Christ, is less a speculative view of reality than a way of life. It is not a philosophy; it is a religion.

This remark applies to the gospel of Saint John, including its celebrated prologue which, at first sight, seems to be full of philosophical notions: "In the beginning was the Word, and the Word was with God, and the Word was God" (John 1, 1). This notion of a divine Word or *Logos* certainly denotes a Greek philosophical origin, probably a Stoic one. Likewise, when Saint Paul spoke of Christ as of the "power" (*energeia*) or the wisdom (*sophia*) of God (I Cor. 1, 24) he certainly was making use of two Greek philosophical notions. There are in the canonical writings some terms of philosophical origin, and since they were there, it is no wonder that they became, later on, a source of theological and philosophical speculation. All historians agree about this fact, but, chiefly on account of religious differences, they do not agree on its historical interpretation.

A first position can be symbolized by the name of Adolf Harnack. It can be found, fully developed, in his well-known lectures on *The Essence of Christianity*. According to A. Harnack, "the most important event which ever happened in the history of Christian doctrines, took place at the beginning of the second century, on the day when Christian Apologists laid down the equation: *"The Logos is Jesus Christ."* This "invasion" of the teaching of Christ by a Greek element was the beginning of a progressive hellenization of Christian thought whose successive stages Harnack has attempted to determine. In this view, the whole body of Christian dogmas appears as a construction of Greek inspiration erected upon the soil of the Gospel.[3]

A second position, which is generally held by Catholic historians, does not deny, nor even minimize, the important part played by Greek philosophy in the formulation and interpretation of the Christian dogmas, but it stresses the fact that what was thus formulated and interpreted always remained the authentic teaching of Christ, which has come to us whole through the Catholic theological tradition. In this second view, not a single Greek philosophical notion, taken precisely as philosophical, has ever become a constitutive element of Christian faith as such.[4]

An important consequence of this opposition is that the same history, relating the same facts, can be told in two different ways, not on account of any divergences about the nature of historical method, but because two conflicting views of the essence of Christianity are here at stake. According to A. Harnack, Christianity should be limited to the actual teaching of Christ as it is found in Matthew, Mark and Luke. It should never have become "a religious philosophy." According to the second view, Christianity did not become "a religious philosophy" at all, but, precisely because it always remained a religion, and the very same religion, it did become an abundant source of theological and philosophical speculation.

In this matter our first choice is bound to be a decisive one, and it should be made on the strength of the very facts under consideration. Obviously, there is no trace of any *systematic* use of philosophy in canonical writings. This point is conceded by all. Secondly, even where philosophical terms appear in these writings, their ultimate import is not a philosophical one; they are meant to convey, in words familiar to their readers, the essentially religious message of the Christian revelation. To say that, in the gospel of Saint John, Christ became the *Logos* of the philosophers, would be to misread his text. On the contrary, Saint John said that, at the time of the Incarnation, "the Word was made flesh and dwelt among us" (John 1, 1). Philosophically understood, this would have been a very strange proposition. To tell philosophers that what they themselves called the *Logos* had become incarnate in the person of a man named Jesus, who had lived and died among us, would have been, in the words of St. Paul, to preach to them "foolishness." When Saint John wrote these lines, nothing happened to Christ, but something decisive happened to the *Logos,* namely, that he became Christ, the Son of God.[5] This is so true that, if the Greek *Logos* had not undergone this unexpected religious transfiguration, very few philosophers would still remember him. In A. Puech's own words: "As far as we know, this was the first time when Christianity borrowed something from Hellenism, and, already, it was borrowing much less a constitutive element of faith than a notion to be used in the philosophical interpretation of faith." Similarly, when Saint Paul wrote that Christ was "wisdom," he was not intending to reduce the person of Christ to the abstract notion of *sophia;* rather, he was saying that what the philosophers had vainly expected from their so-called wisdom, the Christians had just received from Christ, and again, this was not a philosophical statement; it was a religious one. These first contacts between Christianity and the Greek world should therefore be considered as the beginning of a long story which, after so many centuries, is not yet come to an end. If the essence of the Christian message had been "corrupted" into a philosophy as early as the second century, Christianity would have soon ceased to exist as a religion and, consequently, there would be no history of Christian philosophy to relate. In point of fact, it is not philosophy that kept Christianity alive during fourteen centuries, rather, it is Christianity that did not allow philosophy to perish. This second interpretation of the history of Christian speculation is the only one which accounts for the very existence of its object.

PART ONE

THE GREEK APOLOGISTS

CHAPTER I

THE GREEK APOLOGISTS

STRICTLY speaking the first non-canonical writing is the Apostles Creed. It is so called because it lays down the essential tenets of the Christian faith taught by the twelve apostles.[1] Wholly apostolic in its contents, it was primarily intended as a profession of Christian faith to be made by any convert who wanted to be baptized. It therefore contains no trace of philosophical speculation. The doctrinal elaboration of Christian faith begins with the "ecclesiastical writers" and especially with those among them whom we call the "Fathers of the Church."

A Father of the Church is an ecclesiastical writer whose works and person exhibit the four following characteristics: doctrinal orthodoxy, sanctity of life, approval by the Church, antiquity (approximately second to third centuries). Among the Fathers of the Church, four Greeks and four Latins enjoy an eminent authority, owing to their deep interpretation of Christian faith, the purity of their doctrine and the sanctity of their lives. These are the eight great Doctors of the Church, namely, among the Greeks: Gregory Nazianzenus, Basil, John Chrysostomus and Athanasius; among the Latins: Ambrose, Jerome, Augustine and Gregory the Great. Besides these Doctors of the Church *par excellence,* a number of other theologians have been given this title, at various times and on various occasions, during the history of the Church, but it has always been for similar reasons. Unlike that of Father of the Church, the title of Doctor of the Church does not require the mark of antiquity. Thomas Aquinas is not a Father of the Church; Augustine is both a Father and a Doctor.[2]

The early Fathers of the Church are called "Apostolic Fathers,"[3] because they professed to have been the disciples, either of some among the Apostles or of some among their immediate disciples. At any rate, their teaching truly was a continuation of the apostolic predication. In some cases, like that of Saint Ignatius of Antioch, even the style recalls the Epistles of Saint Paul. This is the reason why there is not much more speculation in these writings than there had been in the canonical writings. Christian theology and Christian philosophy truly begin with the generation of the Apologists.[4]

1. ARISTIDES AND QUADRATUS

The Apologists were the first Fathers of the Church to write Apologies in favor of the Christian religion. Technically, an "apology" was a formal statement made before a judge on behalf of a defendant. Most of these writings have been as many attempts to obtain from pagan emperors the official recognition of the rights of the Christians to practice their religion publicly. The Apologists could not avoid refuting the main objections or accusations directed by the pagans against Christianity; yet, in the mind of their authors, their apologies were not supposed to be complete expositions of the Christian faith, nor should they be read as such. On the contrary, Apologists have sometimes intentionally concealed the most secret parts of the Christian doctrine, or, as they would say, of the Christian "mysteries." The silence of an Apologist on a certain point of doctrine does not necessarily mean that he was not interested in it.

The first Christian apologies were written in Greek because Greek was the first language of the Church, even in Rome; but ever since the time of Thales, it had also been the language of philosophy, and this is the reason why, as soon as men of Greek culture became Christians, they initiated between Christianity and philosophy a dialogue which has not yet come to an end. Aristides, who wrote one of the first two Christian apologies,[5] introduces himself as a "Christian philosopher." He affirmed the superiority of Christian faith over philosophy on two grounds: faith had brought to men both a higher idea of God and more perfect rules of human conduct. These two main points, God and man, will always remain the central objects of Christian philosophical speculation.

The second oldest apology was that of Quadratus (Kodratos). Its text is lost.[6] Recent attempts to identify it with the anonymous *Letter to Diognetes* cannot be considered successful. The lost apology must have been written between 117 and 138, under the reign of Emperor Hadrian. The general problem discussed by the letter to Diognetes refers to a later date (*ca.* 250-300) at a time when the increasing number of Christians began to raise the problem of their relation to the non-Christian world.

After saying for what reasons an early Christian refused both the pagan worship of idols and the rites of the Jews, the author of the *Letter to Diognetes* declines to divulge the mysteries of Christian worship, but his short apology contains an unforgettable description of the Christians themselves and of the wholly new nature of Christian society. The Christians live in the world without belonging to the world. They dwell on earth, but their homeland is in heaven (Philip 3, 20). The radical otherworldliness of the Christian society, which we today call the Church, has immediately found its perfect expression in this text. The *City of God*, of Saint Augustine, will later on develop some of its fundamental positions, especially this important one that, although they be not *of* this world, since they are *in* it, the Christians are far from being indifferent to it. Rather, they are to the world what the soul of a man is to his body. Invisible, and yet scattered throughout the world as a soul is omnipresent to its body, the Christians love the world and quicken it from within; and just as the soul, which loves its body, is hated by its body, so also the Christians love the world, but they are hated by the world. In other words, as the soul, which is held in the body as in a jail, holds its body together, so also the Christians, who are imprisoned in the world, hold the world together. Both the body and the world will pass away, but the soul and the Christians will not pass away.[7] Each and every word of this remarkable text is as true today for a Christian as it was in the second century after Christ: the Christians still consider themselves as not being *of* this world, that is, of the society of men as organized apart from God and in view of purely temporal ends; but they also believe that, did they keep faith with it, their true mission would be, while they are *in* the world, to quicken it from within and to lead its citizens to eternal salvation.

2. JUSTIN MARTYR

Justin himself [8] has told the story of his conversion, in a narrative somewhat arranged to literary purposes, but whose substance exhibits the marks of historicity. At any rate, what it says forcefully expresses the reasons which a man of Greek culture could have, around A.D. 130, for becoming a convert to Christianity. Religious interests had always been part and parcel of Greek philosophical speculation. To the Stoics and to the Epicureans in particular, but hardly less to the Platonists, philosophy was a "way of life" as much as a doctrine. In the second century a philosopher was often as easily recognizable on the street as are, in our own days, a clergyman or a priest.[9] He did not live, nor talk, nor even dress like other men, and, as often as not, he actually did believe that the most important business of a philosopher was to seek after God. For such men then, to become a convert to Christianity was to pass from a philosophy quickened by a deeply religious feeling, to a religion capable of a philosophical view of the world. Such, at least, was young Justin's notion of philosophy. It was evident to him that "the philosophers turn every discourse on God"; that "questions continually arise to them about His unity and providence," and, in short, that it is "truly the duty of a philosopher, to investigate the deity." [10]

Justin himself had hoped that the philosophers would lead him to God. He first applied to a certain Stoic, but this man was not really interested in the question and he knew nothing about it. Justin then went to a Peripatetic who, after a few days, invited him to agree on a certain fee, in order that their intercourse "might not be unprofitable." This alone made Justin feel sure that the man was no philosopher. A Pythagorean, who came next, assured him that he could not reach the Good unless he first learned Geometry, Astronomy and Music, but Justin would not or could not afford to spend so much time in studying these sciences. The last philosopher whom he tried, a Platonist of high repute, seemed finally to give him full satisfaction. "The perception of immaterial things," Justin says, "quite overpowered me, and the contemplation of ideas furnished

my mind with wings, so that in a little while I supposed that I had become wise; and such was my stupidity, I expected forthwith to look upon
God, for this is the end of Plato's philosophy." [11]

Obviously, what Justin was looking for in philosophy was a natural
religion; no wonder then that he later exchanged Platonism for straight
religion. In the solitude where he had retired in order to meditate, he happened to meet an old man, of venerable appearance, who asked him questions about God, the nature of human souls and their transmigrations from
bodies to bodies after death. Justin answered him as a Platonist could do,
but the old man made him see how inconsistent his answers were, for indeed, if human souls should forget God after having once seen him, their
so-called beatitude would be but misery: as to those souls which are not
worthy to see God, if they remained chained to their bodies in punishment for their sins, since, by reason of their very unworthiness, they could
not be aware of any punishment, in what sense would they be punished?
Justin then attempted to vindicate the cosmogony taught in the *Timaeus,*
but the old man answered that he had no more use for the *Timaeus* of
Plato than for the Platonic doctrine of the immortality of the soul. The
soul is not immortal in its own right. Plato is wrong where he says that
the soul *is* life. The soul *has* life only because it receives it from God. So
the soul lives because God wills it to live and as long as he wills it. Deeply
impressed by this discovery, Justin asked the old man where he could find
that doctrine, and being answered that it was not to be found in the
books of the philosophers, but in Holy Scripture, he felt at once burning
with the desire to read it. "Straightway," Justin says, "a flame was
kindled in my soul; and a love of the Prophets, and of those men who
are friends of Christ, possessed me, and whilst revolving his words in
my mind, I found this philosophy alone to be safe and profitable. Thus
and for this reason, I am a philosopher." [12]

This dramatized version of Justin's intellectual story shows for what
reasons, as early as the second century, Christianity could appear to some
philosophers as the best answer to the questions asked by philosophy. As
compared with the Platonic doctrine of transmigration of souls, the
teaching of Christian faith looked much more rational than philosophical
reason itself. In short, reason was on the side of the Christians, not of the
philosophers. One could hardly exaggerate the importance of this experience. After eighteen centuries of speculation, what the early Christians
were conscious of having learned from the Bible has become to us so
essentially metaphysical that we cannot imagine a time when no philosopher had yet taught the existence of one God, who created heaven and
earth, and granted to each human soul personal immortality in view of
eternal life. Let us remember Leibniz, for instance: there is not one of
these notions which he will not demonstrate in his philosophy; yet, the
Christians of the second century were fully aware of the fact that no

philosopher had known them before the Christian revelation. Since a doctrine founded upon the teaching of inspired men and prophets was answering philosophical questions better than any philosopher had ever done, its followers felt justified in claiming for it the title of philosophy and in calling themselves philosophers. Such, at least, was the case of Justin: he had achieved philosophical wisdom on the very day he had become a Christian.

There remains, however, a difficulty. Was Justin sincere in what he was saying? Was he sincerely interested in philosophy or was he merely pretending to be, the better to win philosophers to Christianity? Since we are dealing with an Apologist, it cannot be doubted that, by addressing the philosophers in their own language, Justin hoped to make them accept the truth of Christian faith, but there are strong reasons to think that Justin was quite in earnest when he presented the Christian faith as a divinely inspired answer to the questions of the philosophers.

We have learned (John 1, 9), Justin says, that the Word enlightens every man who comes into this world; but we also know, from the same source (John 1, 14), that the Word is Christ; whence there follows, by strict scriptural reasoning, that even before the coming of Christ, all the philosophers who followed the light of reason (*logos*) have shared in the light of the Word (*Logos*), that is, of Christ. "We have been taught that Christ is the first-born of God, and we have declared above that he is the Word of whom every race of men were partakers; and those who live reasonably (i.e., according to *logos*) are Christians, even though they have been thought atheists as, among the Greeks, Socrates and Heraclitus, and men like them." [13] From this point of view, Greek philosophy and Christian revelation appear as two moments of one and the same revelation of the same divine Word who, after speaking to such Greeks as Socrates, or to such Barbarians as Abraham, finally took shape, and became man, and was called Jesus Christ. This same thesis, presented in the *First Apology,* is restated in the *Second Apology,* in terms which betray a Stoic influence. The Word is there likened unto a "seminal reason," that is a germ, or a seed, of which all men are partakers in different degrees, so that each philosopher spoke the truth according to his share of this seed and his ability to perceive its implications. This seed is not the Word himself, but a participation or an imitation of the Word, according to his grace; yet, this is enough to justify the Christians in claiming for their own all the truths which have ever been known by all the philosophers. If Socrates was right in fighting the false gods of the Greek mythology, the reason for it was that he had "partially" known Christ. Hence Justin's famous statement: "Whatever things were rightly said among all men, are the property of us Christians." [14]

Justin has left us, in his two *Apologies*, some indications concerning his own speculative interpretation of Christian faith,[15] but these are less important than the spirit which pervades his whole doctrine. Justin remains, still today, the patriarch of a spiritual family, whose wide-hearted Christian faith remains open to all that is true and good, and which seeks to discover it wherever it is to be found, in order to assimilate it, to purify it and to perfect it in the light of Christian faith. This is a family of many members who have not all been saints. But some of them were saints. Before Saint Thomas More, Justin has shown that the profession of faith of a Christian humanist can sometimes be signed with his own blood.

As a rule, such men provide historians with ample matter for scholarly disagreement. The twofold aspect of their thought invites the stress of either one at the expense of the other. Thus, for instance, after summing up the position of the Apologists by saying that, according to them, "the contents of Revelation should be rational," A. Harnack asks this leading question: "but was the rational in need of a revelation?" [16] To which it should be answered, first, that the whole meaning of Justin's work is here at stake. Clearly, in his own mind, the rational bequeathed by the Greeks stood in urgent need of a Revelation. Secondly, the precise point at stake, in the mind of Justin, was not that Revelation should be made rational, but that it was, and more so than philosophical reason itself had ever been. Unless he prefers to tell history as it should have happened, a historian has to accept facts just as they are, that is, most of the time, with their disconcerting complexity. In this case, the fact is certain that a philosopher did find in Christianity a philosophical satisfaction which he had not been able to find in philosophy. Yet, he knew very well that, taken in itself, Christianity was something else, and more important than, a substitute for philosophy. In the terse sentence of Eusebius of Caesarea: "Justin, in philosopher's garb, preached the word of God." [17]

3. TATIAN

Historical events are sometimes whimsical enough to fall into a pattern and to simulate order. After Justin, Tatian,[18] whose severity introduces the long lineage of those Christian writers to whom nature and, consequently, philosophy will always look suspicious, if not evil. At the end of his *Address to the Greeks,* Tatian has called himself "a disciple of the barbaric philosophy . . . born in the land of the Assyrians" and, afterwards, a convert to Christianity, to whose doctrines he adhered immovably, as "to that mode of life which is according to God." [19] In reading Tatian, one should never forget that to him, "barbaric philosophy" meant the philosophy of the non-Greeks; that is, Christianity. In this sense, the *Address* is a manifesto in favor of the Barbarians and of their religion, against both the Greeks and their philosophy. Whether or not he succeeded in killing two birds with one stone is a matter for personal appreciation.

Tatian's first argument against the Greeks is that they have borrowed from the Barbarians all their most celebrated inventions. "Be not, O Greeks, so very hostilely disposed toward the Barbarians, nor look with ill will on their opinions! For which of your institutions has not been derived from the Barbarians?" [20] The Greeks have learned astronomy from the Babylonians; geometry and history from the Egyptians; alphabetic writing from the Phoenicians; plastic arts from the Tuscans. As to philosophy, the lives of their philosophers clearly show what the Greeks have made of it: Diogenes died by gluttony; Aristippus was a profligate; Plato was sold by Dionysius "for his gormandizing propensities," etc.[21] Moreover, their very doctrines are full of absurdities. For instance, Aristotle has set a limit to Providence by subtracting from God's governance all sublunary things. In ethics, the same philosopher has taught that those who have "neither beauty, nor wealth, nor bodily strength, nor high birth, cannot achieve happiness." [22] Tatian's main argument, however, is one which had already been used by Jewish writers in their polemics against the Greeks (Josephus, *Against Apio*, I; Philo, *Allegories*, I, 33): even in philosophy, Tatian says, the Greeks have borrowed from the Barbarians! What is best in their doctrines is what they have found in the Bible. Since "our philosophy," "our barbaric philosophy," is older than the systems of the Greeks, the philosophers have derived from it what is true in their own systems. They have added nothing to it except their own errors.[23]

Obviously, Tatian was widely different from his master Justin; yet, in a sense, their fundamental intention was the same. After studying what we would today call Greek "culture," including its philosophies, laws and religions, Tatian too "happened to meet with certain barbaric writings, too old to be compared with the opinions of the Greeks, and too divine to be compared with their errors." To him, too, Christian revelation had appeared as an intellectual revelation no less than as a faith. Moreover, it was to him the promise of a political liberation. At the distance in time where we now stand from these events, it is not easy for us to realize that, in Asia, Christianity had then been hailed by some as an Eastern culture and pitted against that of their Western invaders, which was "philosophy." The "Barbarians" found themselves endowed by Christian revelation with a view of the world immediately accessible to all, and yet vastly superior to the philosophical conclusions of the Greeks. Even political and national interests were here at stake. Dimly, but intensely, Tatian realized that by ascribing to one Being and Lord the government of the whole universe, Christianity would some day "put an end to the slavery that is in the world, and rescue us from a multiplicity of rulers and ten thousand tyrants." [24] If political liberation of man through theocracy is but a dream, it is at least an old one, and there are a few sober minds in which it is not yet dead.

At the time of his *Address to the Greeks*, written before he joined the sect of the Encratists, the doctrine of Tatian closely resembles that of his master, Justin. It is not always easy to decide whether Tatian merely makes Justin more outspoken, or if he betrays him by overstressing some of his points.[25] At any rate, it is significant for the history of Christian thought that this arch-enemy of Greek philosophy died out of the communion of the Church, whereas he who had claimed for Christianity the benefit of all that was good and true in Greek culture had died a martyr and a saint.

4. ATHENAGORAS

The *Intercession for the Christians* was written by Athenagoras[26] under tragic circumstances. Since the reign of the Antonines, the Roman Empire had been enjoying a well-ordered administration under the authority of wise emperors, and yet, under the wisest among them, Marcus Aurelius, the Christians were cruelly persecuted. The persecutions of Carthage and of Lyons took place during the last years of his reign, and far from feeling moved by the generosity of their sacrifice, Marcus Aurelius could calmly write of the Christian martyrs: "What a soul is that which is ready to be released from the body at any requisite moment, and be quenched or dissipated or hold together! But the readiness must spring from a man's inner judgment, and not result from mere opposition (as is the case with the Christians). It must be associated with deliberation and dignity and, if others too are to be convinced, with nothing like stage-heroics." [27] Marcus Aurelius forgets that the stage had not been set by the Christians themselves, and this is why Athenagoras undertook to justify them against three main accusations: atheism, cannibalism and the practice of incest. Very brief on the last two charges, he is, on the contrary, very insistent on the first one. Athenagoras defends the Christians against the accusation of atheism by proving their monotheism, and it is while justifying their refusal to worship the national gods of the empire (which was the true meaning of the accusation) that he had to take a position with respect to Greek philosophers.

His position is very moderate. Unlike Justin, Athenagoras is not interested in those philosophers who have not known Christ; but, unlike Tatian, he does not say that the Greeks have borrowed their philosophy from the Old Testament.[28] Athenagoras simply remarks that, on a certain number of points, there is a factual agreement between the teachings of philosophy and those of the Christian revelation. In order to make this point, he attempts to prove that Plato, Aristotle and the Stoics have been monotheists, after which he asks why this same monotheism, which was considered as harmless in these philosophers, should suddenly become a crime in the case of the Christians.[29] Obviously, Athenagoras is forgetting the fate of the monotheist Socrates. At any rate, he is not trying to ascribe monotheism to Plato out of any sympathy for Plato himself, but because it would have been advantageous to the Christians to persuade such a philosopher as Marcus Aurelius that Plato had already taught the oneness of God.[30] Athenagoras would have been pleased to find a genuine agreement between faith and philosophy as well as between Church and State,[31] but one detects little warmth in his attitude toward Greek thought. A careful lawyer, he uses Greek philosophy to the best interest of his cause, but he does not seem to like it. One may even wonder if he entertained any illusions as to the depth of this alleged agreement. In his mind, the vague intimations of monotheism which could be found in Greek philosophers did not compare with the clear-cut doctrine of the Christians on this point. It never was for the Greeks more than a sort of "conjecture," due to the "sympathy" which obtained between their souls and the divine spirit.[32] In fact these philosophers never achieved an exact knowledge of God, because they tried to achieve it by themselves instead of expecting it from God. Now God alone can instruct us about God. On the contrary, the starting point of the Christians is their faith in the word of God. Naturally, it is not forbidden to them either to speculate upon the contents of their faith, or even to confirm it by rational arguments, especially while dealing with pagans, who do not believe in Holy Scripture.[33] Athenagoras has not only laid down this general principle of what was later on to be called "scholastic theology"; he has also given an example of what such a rational speculation about faith could be, by attempting the first technically developed demonstration of the oneness of God.[34] His proof can hardly be said to be convincing. It implicitly locates in space the same God whom Athenagoras holds elsewhere as spiritual. The notion of a spiritual omnipresence of God to the world is probably what was dimly present to his mind, but he nowhere formulates it in the course of his argumentation. Or perhaps he was trying to use, with the stoic philosopher Marcus Aurelius, the language of stoic materialism. At any rate, Christianity has certainly not yet found, with Athenagoras, the accurate philosophical language of which it already felt the need.

The theology of Athenagoras offers no marked progress over that of Justin nor of Tatian,[35] but his attempt to justify by rational argumentation the Christian faith in the resurrection of the dead deserves our attention. The readers whom Athenagoras has in mind either doubt the resurrection or do not know it. In order to convince them, he begins by establishing that the resurrection is not impossible to God, because he who has created man, and has given him life, can give life back to man after he has lost it.[36] Moreover, just as God can achieve the resurrection, he can will it, because to do so is neither unjust in itself nor unworthy of God.[37] These preliminary conclusions aim to prove that faith is not opposed to reason, or, in other words, that it does not involve any rational impossibility. This is what Athenagoras expresses in his own way, where he says that one should distinguish two moments in any apology for Christianity; the arguments *for* truth, which we have just seen; and the arguments *about* truth, which it remains for us to see.[38]

The first of these two moments is not always necessary, and it is never sufficient. On the contrary, the second moment is always necessary and, with respect to salvation, it is sufficient. In order to see this, let us ask successively: why has God created the soul; what is the nature of man; and what is man's future destiny?

Because God acts according to reason and does nothing in vain, he has created man for an end. Not, however, to his own use, for God stands in need of nothing; nor for the sake of some other creature, because a being endowed with reason and judgment can be created but for its own sake.[39] There are then only two conceivable reasons for the creation of man: the wisdom and the goodness of God which shine in his works, and the perpetual existence of such a being as man, who is able to know, through reason, the goodness of God and his wisdom: "For whatever has been created for the sake of something else, when that has ceased to be for the sake of which it has been created, will itself also fitly cease to be . . . but that which was created for the purpose of existing and living a life naturally suited to it, since the cause itself is bound up with its nature, and is recognized only in connection with existence itself, can never admit of any cause which shall utterly annihilate its existence." Now, in man, soul and body are two parts, each of which discharges its respective function: either to move (the soul) or to be moved (the body). Since man's end is to live, the resurrection of his body after death is required for the achievement of his end.[40]

The second argument rests upon the nature of man. God has not created souls, but men, that is, beings made up of souls and bodies. The preceding argument, then, has not established the end of the soul, but the end of man. This requires that the destiny of these two component parts of man be the same: generation of *man,* nature of *man,* life of *man,* actions and passions of *man,* end of *man.* For indeed, if there is a sort of "society," or "harmony," or solidarity, between the two component parts of man, the end of each one of these parts must needs be identical with that of the whole. In short, what has received understanding and reason is not the soul; it is man. Consequently, in order that reason may subsist, it is necessary that man himself should subsist; and since the human body dies, human reason could not subsist if there were no resurrection.[41]

The third and last argument is likewise demonstrative, but only if the two preceding ones have already been conceded. At any rate, it is more convincing when it comes after them. Their common starting points are the creation of the first men by God, and the final cause of their creation. Now, since God is just, he should judge men according to their merits. Let us not say "souls," but "men." It is not proper that the soul should be rewarded or punished alone, for deeds, either good or bad, which it had wrought in union with its body. Consequently, the resurrection of the body is required by the ultimate end of man.[42]

The historians of Christian thought have not always done full justice to the importance of this new development. Geffcken[43] sees Athenagoras as just one more among the rhetoricians of his times. In his excellent *History of the Scholastic Method*, M. Grabmann does not even quote him, at the place which he nevertheless deserves, between Justin and Irenaeus. Duchesne[44] sees in the treatise of Athenagoras on resurrection a simple appendix to his apology. On the contrary, M. Baumgartner[45] aptly remarks that its importance is considerable, and indeed it is, on two accounts: first, Athenagoras has clearly realized the distinction of the two moments which will remain distinct even in the demonstrations of the scholastics: proof of the rational possibility of faith; direct confirmation of the truth of faith by philosophical arguments. Next, Athenagoras has clearly seen that the main concern of Christianity was not with the soul, but with man. The significance of this second point could hardly be overstressed. It accounts for the fact that, despite all contrary appearances, a truly Christian philosophy cannot possibly be a "spiritualism." It also helps in understanding the deeply Christian reasons why, in the thirteenth century theologians will deem it advisable to substitute for the Platonist doctrine of the soul its Aristotelean definition as a form of the body. What has often been considered as a pagan invasion of theology has been, on the contrary, the belated fulfilment of one of the deepest aspirations of early Christian faith. This first intimation of the philosophical import of the Christian belief in the resurrection of bodies will not develop its full implications before the times of Saint Thomas Aquinas.

5. THEOPHILUS OF ANTIOCH

Theophilus of Antioch[46] has been severely judged by some historians, and, in a way, not without reason. His apology *To Autolycus* is truly the work of "a Tatian without talent";[47] yet it still is interesting to read as a witness to the attitude of early Christians toward philosophy.

Like his predecessors, Theophilus starts from the faith in one God, creator[48] of heaven and earth, orderer of the universe which he rules by his providence, and lawgiver who prescribes to men both justice and piety. His personal contribution to this already-established tradition is his effort to define accurately the notion of creation. Although the notion itself seems to have been clear in the minds of Justin and of Athenagoras, the vagueness of their formulas authorizes some hesitation as to their exact meaning. On the contrary, Theophilus is quite clear on this point. By saying that God has made man, he means to say that God has made man out of slime, which itself was nothing before it had been made by God.

Both the notion and the formula of the creation *ex nihilo* are there, and, for the first time, in words which preclude all hesitation on the meaning of the doctrine.[49] Theophilus emphasizes that this production of the very being of things is what makes creation different from the work of an artisan shaping things out of some pre-existing matter.[50] The fact that Theophilus reproaches Plato with having taught the eternity of matter clearly shows that he is opposing the doctrine of the *Timaeus*.[51] The God of Theophilus is not a Greek "maker" of the world; he is its creator.

As to the way in which the world has been created, our Apologist does not think that the philosophers have anything useful to say. They have done little more on this point than to contradict one another. On the contrary, the "men of God" have told us the truth about the formation of the world and the origin of things. Their remarkable agreement is due to the fact that they have been inspired by the Holy Ghost and endowed by him with the spirit of prophecy. The Greek Sybils sometimes agree with them because they have derived their inspiration from the same spirit.[52] To write commentaries on Holy Scripture then is the only fitting method to deal with the origin of things. This is what he himself has attempted to do, at least in an elementary way and without any originality. But he was thereby initiating the long and brilliant tradition of the speculative commentaries on the book of *Genesis* (or *In Hexaemeron*, i.e., commentaries on the work of the six days) which are among the most precious sources of information about the philosophical positions of their authors.

Addressing Autolycus, "an idolater and scorner of Christians," Theophilus opposes to the visible false gods of the pagans the invisible God of the Christians. Visible to souls only, he cannot be known by such as are involved in the darkness of sin. Even to the others, God is unnamable and indescribable; all his names are borrowed either from his attributes or from his works. "God" means: the "establisher" and mover of all things. "Lord" means: the ruler of the universe, etc. He can be known through his works, for "as any person, when he sees a ship on the sea rigged and in sail, and making for the harbor, will no doubt infer that there is a pilot in her who is steering her; so we must perceive that God is the pilot of the whole universe though he is not visible to eyes of flesh, since he is incomprehensible." After developing, in Bk. I, 5-6, this argument drawn from the purposiveness of created things, Theophilus criticizes the immoralities of mythology and the absurdities of idolatry. Theophilus says why he believes in the resurrection and how the fulfillment of the prophecies determined his own conversion. The second Book of the apology begins with a lengthy criticism of pagan fables, including the opinions of the philosophers and of the poets, whom he contrasts with the prophets. According to these, the world has been created by God, through his Word.[53] Theophilus then follows the Biblical narrative of the work of the six days,[54] adding to it, as he goes along, allegorical interpretations of his own.

The third book, not without sometimes returning to the preceding problems, gives a summary of Christian ethics (Chs. 9-15) and, naturally, re-establishes by learned calculations that Holy Scripture is more ancient than the writings of the Greeks, of the Egyptians or of "any other historians." Since it is also more true, we should not hesitate between the errors of the pagans or the wisdom of God.

6. IRENAEUS

The doctrinal positions of Irenaeus[55] are known to us chiefly through his treatise in five Books against the heresies (*Adversus Haereses*). This received title does not correctly translate the original Greek title, which announces an exposition and refutation of the self-styled *Gnosis*, that is of the doctrine which called itself "knowledge," though it was but error. Gnosticism was a general movement divided into many schools, or sects, whose members it would not always be correct to call "heretics," because most of them did not pretend to be Christians. True enough, they knew Christianity, and some of them have even attempted to integrate with their own doctrines elements borrowed from Christian faith, but instead of starting from faith in order to achieve some understanding of its object, the Gnostics openly aimed to turn faith into a "knowledge," or wisdom, accessible to reason alone. The substitution of knowledge (*gnosis*) for faith (*pistis*) is, so to speak, the hallmark of Gnosticism. Still less than Deism, its more sober seventeenth-century counterpart, Gnosticism belongs in the history of Christianity.

Already before Irenaeus, Justin Martyr, Miltiades and Theophilus of Antioch had written against such Gnostics as Marcion, Hermogenes and the Valentinians,[56] but Irenaeus remains for us the first theologian who ascribed to himself the task of making clear that no man could possibly be, at one and the same time, both a Gnostic and a Christian.[57] This was essentially the same problem as the one which Justin had tried to solve, with this sole difference, that, this time, the name of philosophy was Gnosticism. Justin had told the philosophers: Christianity is our philosophy. Irenaeus tells the Gnostics: Christianity is our own *Gnosis*. In both cases it would be an equal mistake to imagine that these Apologists were reducing Christianity to either a philosophy or to an additional Gnostic sect. The contrary is true. "The true *Gnosis*," Irenaeus says, "is the teaching of the twelve Apostles." [58] He has never said anything else, and when Clement of Alexandria will speak of a Christian *Gnosis*, he will mean exactly the same thing.

This, however, does not mean that it was not permitted to speculate on the teaching of the Twelve. It was not only permissible to do so; it was praiseworthy. But to speculate about mysteries is not to substitute speculation for mysteries. In fact, we are surrounded with mysteries, of which Irenaeus strikes a list which many a mediaeval writer will remember. We do not know the cause of the rise of the Nile; the dwelling place of the migratory birds; the reason for the flow and ebb of the ocean; the origin of rain, lightning, thunder, clouds, snow, hail and vapors in the sky; the reason for the phases of the moon, for the formation of metals or stones, nor the causes of their differences and of those which distinguish the different kinds of waters. Since we do not know everything about nature, how could we know everything about God? What was God doing before the creation? He alone knows the answer. What is the origin of the world? Or of life? To pretend we know it, as the Gnostics do, is to lack the proper feeling for what lies beyond the reach of human knowledge. In rationalizing mysteries, the Gnostics are bound to conceive divine things by analogy with human realities. For instance, the generation of the Word, which remains strictly inconceivable to us, becomes in their doctrines a sort of animal generation. No one is above his master. Let us therefore reserve to God the knowledge of the divinity. Obviously, the immediate purpose of Irenaeus was to destroy the very notion of a *Gnosis* conceived as the integral rationalization of the Christian mysteries, but his insistence on the deficiency of natural knowledge introduced, if not for the first time, at least with a force which was then new, what will remain, up to the time of Montaigne's *Apology for Raymond Sebond,* the favorite theme of a certain type of Christian apologetics.[59]

The whole doctrine of Irenaeus is directed against Gnosticism. In order to account for the presence of evil in the world without making God responsible for it, some Gnostics, Marcion for instance, had distinguished between two Gods. First, the God of the Old Testament, orderer of a matter which he had not created and which is the source of evil in the world. The presence of a matter to be shaped and framed accounts for the fact that the Maker of the world did not completely succeed in his undertaking. The defection of some angels, followed by the fall of man, have partly thwarted his intentions, and even then, he has found nothing better to do than to impose upon man severe laws and to enforce them through terrible sanctions. Far above this God of the Jews, was the *Foreign God,* thus named because he had remained unknown to men, and to the Maker of the world himself, up to the day when Jesus Christ had come in order to reveal him. Unlike the preceding God, who was a judge, this God is essentially goodness. All powerful, omniscient, he rules by his providence the world made by the God of the Jews, so much so that he has assumed a human shape in order to suffer for the salvation of men. Against such doctrines, Irenaeus maintains that there is only one God, who is both the God of the Old Testament and that of the New Testament, revealed to men by Holy Scripture, known by a universal intimation of the human mind, and demonstrable even to pagans from the consideration of his works as well as of their order.[60] Besides, Irenaeus says, even the Gnostics acknowledge the fact that their Maker of the world must turn his sight toward God in order to produce his work. They know that Plato has posited three principles: God, Exemplars and Matter. Why then multiply unnecessary intermediaries between God and the world? The more satisfactory answer to the problem of the origin of things is to admit that God himself has given to himself the plan and order of the universe.[61]

Created out of nothing,[62] and by a free act of the divine will,[63] the world has no other cause than the goodness of God, which is rather a motive than a cause.[64] On this point again, the radical Christian optimism of Irenaeus opposes Gnosticism under all its forms. The created world is not the outcome of an apostasy, nor of a defection, nor of an ignorance or of a mistake; rather, it has sprung forth from the generosity of its creator. Besides, anybody can read this in the Bible: "And it was so done. And God saw all the things that he had made, and they were very good." [65]

Like the rest of the world, man has been made good, but since he was created out of nothing, he was not perfect.[66] His imperfection appears from the fact that he is finite and limited, but also from the necessity which there is for him ceaselessly to change in order to reach his end, and to achieve progressively his own perfection. Hence the idea, often expressed by Irenaeus, that man is in a state of infancy, or of childhood, and that he needs to grow in order to achieve his spiritual maturity.[67]

Concerning human nature, Irenaeus opposes the threefold distinction of men into "spiritual," "animal" and "material." According to him, man is essentially a living and rational being,[68] that is to say, the whole make-up of his soul and body. A soul is not a man, it is a man's soul. On the other hand, since it is *his* soul, it is strictly individual and it belongs exclusively to him. So far, Irenaeus has been announcing some of the recognized positions of future scholastic theology and philosophy, and he continues to do so when he says that, because human nature is indivisible and the soul inseparable from the body which it animates, both shall later on receive the rewards or the punishments which man will have deserved in this life. Yet, his very notion of the soul is still wavering. Where, in order to refute transmigration, Irenaeus says that, since a soul assumes the shape of its body, it cannot possibly fit another body, he obviously ascribes a certain materiality to the soul.[69] The only text where he speaks of "immaterial souls" means that souls are not shaped out of the same coarse matter which is that of our body.[70] This is very different from conceiving souls as pure spirits.

What remains true is that, although he conceived the soul as material, Irenaeus ascribed to it some characteristics which should have led him to conceive it as spiritual. For instance, he refused to distinguish the soul from its faculties and operations. Perceiving, knowing, reasoning were to him the very substance of the soul.[71] Among these faculties, two are both outstanding and inseparable, namely, reason and freedom. It is through these that man was made in the image and resemblance of God, and it is through these that he deserves either rewards or punishments.[72] On this point, Irenaeus has sometimes been accused of having been a Pelagian before Pelagius,[73] but, first, there is no Pelagianism in saying that man could neither merit nor demerit if he were not free; secondly, Irenaeus constantly quotes, in favor of his thesis, such texts of Saint Paul as Rom. 5, 4-7; 4, 13; Eph. 13, 25, 29; 2, 4, 8; I Corinth. 6, 9-10. and Saint Paul was no Pelagian; last, but not least, we should once more remember what readers this Apologist had in mind. The Gnostics were teaching that God had created two different sorts of men: the one good and the other evil, so that each of us is born the one or the other and cannot change his nature. Should this happen to be true, the Maker of the world would be responsible for the existence of evil, including moral evil. Since he refused to ascribe creation to an inferior maker of the world, there was, for Irenaeus, no other way of exempting God from all responsibility for the existence of evil than to stress the responsibility of the human will. Now there is no responsibility without liberty. Assuredly, his solution of the problem was not complete, but his own object was not the problem, it was to overthrow its Gnostic solution.[74]

On the whole, Irenaeus appears to us, from these of his works which we know, as a writer who, through Polycarp, was still in contact with the apostolic generation of the early Christians. Like them, he liked to speculate on the circumstances of the end of the world,[75] which he could foresee in a not entirely unpredictable future. In the meantime, faith was enough to lead men to their ultimate end, provided only Christians kept intact the purity of its tradition and protected it against the wild speculations of the Gnostics. Once more it seemed manifest to the eyes of a Christian Apologist that reason was on the side of the defenders of faith.

7. HIPPOLYTUS

The history of the life and works of Hippolytus[76] is one with that of their progressive rediscovery by his historians. Many of his writings have been lost, among which a treatise *On the Universe,* directed against the Greeks, and more particularly against Plato. But we still have his *Refutations of All Heresies,* usually called *Philosophumena* (i.e., philosophical reflections), which enables us to form an opinion concerning Hippolytus' general attitude toward philosophy and philosophers.

The first Book of the *Philosophumena* is an exposition of the doctrines of the philosophers, whom Hippolytus distributes into three classes: the "naturalists," the "moralists" and the "dialecticians." The "naturalists" are practically those whom we today call the "presocratics." The "moralists" are Socrates and Plato, who, nevertheless have combined the three sorts of philosophy. The founder of the third class, that of the dialecticians, was Aristotle. The Stoics, namely Chrysippus and Zeno, belong to this third class. Hippolytus then lists separately: "Epicurus," who "maintained an opinion almost exactly contrary to all these. So did Pyrrho the Academic who asserts the incomprehensibility of all things. There are also the Brahmans among the Indians, the Druids among the Celts, and Hesiod." The reason for this interest of Hippolytus in philosophers was that, according to him, their most extravagant opinions were at the origin of heresies. His was the first Christian effort to set forth their doctrines before attempting to refute them. Thus did it come to pass that, in our own times and against his own expectations, Hippolytus was included by H. Diels among the Greek "doxographers." [77] Despite their shortness, his summaries of philosophical doctrines are not without interest. In fact, they represent a knowledge of Greek philosophy, which, scanty as it is, was far superior to that of most of his Christian successors.[78]

Besides fighting the Greek philosophies, Hippolytus has attacked many pseudo-sciences, widely spread in his own times, and which he considered as important sources of Gnosticism. He criticizes astrology on the twofold ground that the exact time of conception is never known and that, even if we knew it, accurate astronomical observations at the very moment of conception would still be impossible. Hippolytus successively criticizes in the same spirit the so-called "mathematicians," who calculated the future of a man from the numbers answering the letters composing his name; then the "physiognomists" and the "magicians," whose faked miracles he teaches us how to imitate: how to produce thunder, earthquakes and stars; how to print inscriptions on the spleen of victims; how to make a skull placed on the soil talk, etc. All this display of knowledge was intended to refute the accusation of ignorance so often directed against Christians.[79] As to Hippolytus' own doctrine, it simply reproduces the notions concerning God and man which he had inherited from his predecessors.[80] It does so with an unprecedented precision of language, and the Tenth Book of the *Philosophumena* is an attempted doctrinal synthesis far superior to the disconnected statements of the early Greek Apologists.

The Greek Apologists have been little interested in philosophy for its own sake; their main concern rather was to show the superiority of Christianity over philosophical wisdom. Yet, even before it achieved self-awareness, Christian speculation had already begun its work. The fundamental notions of the oneness of God; of the creation of the world through the Logos; of the divine providence; of man conceived as the subsisting unity of his body and of his soul; of a future life promised to him either in reward or in punishment of his virtue or of his vices; all these notions, to which many points of lesser importance might be added, were henceforward to remain part and parcel of the Christian view of the world. Their influence will remain recognizable throughout the whole history of Western philosophy, up to our own days.

On the other hand, it cannot be said that the second-century Apologists achieved an always complete and correct formulation of all these notions. Clear on the idea of one God, creator of heaven and earth, they exhibit a common tendency to subordinate the Logos to the Father, and even, for two of them, to conceive him as begotten by a free act of the Father, in view of the creation of the world and, so to speak, as its "beginning." Concerning the nature of man, they have hesitated between conceiving the "spirit" (*pneuma*) as a natural energy or as a grace, which has led them to speak of the soul as material and naturally mortal. It is generally difficult to say whether the death of the soul, of which they speak, is a spiritual or a natural one. It would be an error of perspective, however, to speak indiscriminately of heresies at a time when, on these precise points, no theological orthodoxy had yet been officially defined. As early as the beginning of the third century, Hippolytus already listed thirty-two heresies, beginning with that of Dositheus and ending with that of Noetus, but what he called a heresy was an error on the substance of faith itself, not a divergence of opinion concerning its speculative interpretation. What we have witnessed, while reading the second-century Greek Apologists, was the first effort of Christian faith still struggling for a clear awareness of its speculative implications.

PART TWO

EARLY CHRISTIAN SPECULATION

CHAPTER I

THE ALEXANDRINES

THE ORIGINS of the catechetical school of Alexandria are still obscure. The city itself had been for a long time a sort of clearing house for the religions of the Roman Empire. It had kept up the ancient religion of Egypt and was still dominated by the temple of Serapis; the Roman cults had added themselves to the Egyptian tradition without attempting to suppress it; an important Jewish community was living there, but it had become so thoroughly Hellenized that the Old Testament had been translated into Greek for the use of its members. Philo the Jew,[1] whose exegesis of Scripture was full of Platonic and Stoic elements, wrote his works in Greek, and he was, for the first Christian theologians of Alexandria, just about what Moses Maimonides was to be later on to the scholastic theologians of the thirteenth century: a model to imitate and, if possible, to excel. For indeed there was also a Christian community in Alexandria, and even a school, before the time when Pantaenus, a converted Stoic, became its head master (*ca.* 180-190). Pantaenus himself does not seem to have written any books, but it was in his school [2] that Clement of Alexandria received the better part of his formation.

I. CLEMENT OF ALEXANDRIA

The *Exhortation to the Greeks* is closely related to the works of Justin, Athenagoras and Tatian, not indeed by its content, but by its spirit. The main intention of Clement is less to defend the Christian faith against its opponents, than to teach it to unbelievers, or, at least, to persuade them to accept it. Clement exhorts the pagans to renounce the worship of idols and to turn their minds to the true God. Have not Greek philosophers and Greek poets already shown the necessity of a religion more spiritual than idolatry, and of beliefs more intelligent than mythology? But the revelation of the true God is to be found in the words of the Prophets only. Since God himself has offered truth to us, would it not be a crime not to accept it? The pagans object that it would be wrong for them to forsake the faith of their ancestors and to betray the traditional worship of their country, but this is not at all the question. The only problem for man is to know what is true, in order to accept it; and what is right, in order to do it. No man feels bound in conscience to feed during his whole life on the food of his infancy, nor to dress in his old age as he used to do when he was still a child; there is no more reason for any man to persevere indefinitely in error after recognizing it as such. Clement then enumerates

29

the benefits conferred upon mankind by Christ, and invites the Greeks to turn to him as to the only master of truth.[3]

Let us suppose that our pagan has become a convert; he now has to reform his moral conduct. This is a new progress which he will achieve under the guidance of the *Instructor*. The Word is this instructor. All men are sinners, but the Word has become their instructor in order to set limits to the spreading of sin. We say "instructor" rather than "teacher," because a teacher merely enlightens the mind, whereas an instructor, or a pedagogue, educates the whole soul and betters it by teaching man to live right. In this sense, the Word is the instructor, or the tutor, of all men without distinction. Against the Gnostic thesis which reserved for a spiritual aristocracy the privilege of the knowledge that saves, Clement maintains that, since all are baptized, all Christians are equally able to achieve salvation. In the sight of God even the most learned among the Christians are but children, while, inversely, the most humble among the Christians are just as much the children of God as the most learned ones. So, when he speaks of a Christian *Gnosis,* Clement does not have in mind a selected group of super-Christians whose religion would be superior in perfection to that of the common flock of the faithful. On the contrary, he means to say that all the Christians are the true Gnostics. No doubt, some Christians know more and better than the other ones, but they are not more Christian than those who know less, or who know it less well. On this central point, Clement has always maintained the teaching of the Gospel: "This is the will of my Father that sent me: that every one who sees the Son, and believeth in him, may have life everlasting, and I will raise him up in the last day" (John 6, 40). Nothing then is required for salvation but faith, for if his faith is in itself full and perfect, a Christian lacks nothing. This point shall be remembered by Clement's reader when, after thus assuring the perfect sufficiency of faith, our theologian will indulge in the free speculations of a philosopher.

The "instructor," then, is the Word, who teaches every man that comes into this world; but how does he give this education? The Gnostic Marcion had distinguished from the Father, whom he conceived as a loveless judge, the Word, whom he conceived as a tutor full of love but indifferent to justice. On the contrary, the Christians know that there is only one single God, and that, consequently, the goodness of God cannot be separated from his justice. Goodness comes first in the conduct of the divine instructor, but he knows, when necessary, how to subject his pupil to a wholesome discipline. Having established these principles, Clement writes a short treatise on practical ethics for the use of the Christians living in Alexandria. This part of his work is full of charming and picturesque information on the life of his compatriots.[4] By and large, Clement advocates simplicity, moderation and tastes suitable to ages, characters and social conditions.

This wise notion of moral life answered the needs of a big city like Alexandria, where Christians were to be found in all social classes, but we should not overlook its genuinely Christian spirit. Its very moderation intended to make clear that, because true Christianity lies in the soul, it is compatible with all forms of external life, provided these be conformable to reason. In his *Who Is the Rich Man That Is Saved? (Quis dives salvetur)*, Clement upholds the view that any wealthy man can be saved, provided only he be not a slave to his wealth, but its master. Even wealth can be turned to good account by using it in a Christian way. A Stoic like Seneca had already taught pagans the art of preserving spiritual liberty in the midst of material affluence. The same attitude is here inspired by a purely Christian spirit. Christianity teaches the poor that, because spiritual wealth is the only true one, they can be more wealthy than the rich men of this world, for indeed a man can wallow in money, and still be a spiritual pauper. Now, spiritual poverty is true poverty. The wholly Christian moderation of Clement's ethics expresses his deep conviction that the matter of our acts is not the deepest cause of their morality.[5]

The Word has converted and educated the Christian; he now can teach him, that is, enlighten his intellect. The *Stromata* of Clement (or *Miscellanies*) invite us to hear the Word as teacher of speculative truth. In this work, Clement was obviously trying to justify his personal interest in philosophy against the objections of some Christians of Alexandria who wanted nothing beyond bare faith.[6] Naturally, since they objected to philosophy, these men would have no part in any kind of theological speculation. To them, philosophy was Gnosticism, that is a scarecrow from which every Christian should turn away as from human reason rebelling against God.

The chief object of the *Miscellanies* is to show, on the contrary, that philosophy is in itself a good, because it has been willed by God. Already in the Old Testament, God himself has called certain men "wise of heart" because he had filled them "with the spirit of wisdom" (Exod. 28, 3). These words apply to two different classes of men: first, to the artisans, for everybody knows how perfect are the touch of the potters, the smell of perfumers, the hearing of musicians, the sight of intaglio engravers; but these words apply no less well to those men whose avocations require special intellectual gifts. Intellectuals have a specially developed sense of their own. This particular sense is "understanding." It takes a special intellectual gift to understand the figurative speech of the poets, the artful sentences of the orators and the syllogisms of the dialecticians. Intellectual gifts come from God, and not only these gifts themselves but also the courage it takes to educate them and to put them to good use. Philosophy, then, is one of the works of God, and, as such, it is good.[7]

To this, the enemies of philosophy sometimes object that it must be bad, since God has replaced it with faith. But this is to misunderstand the place of philosophy in history. Before Christ, there was the Jewish Law, which had certainly been willed by God. The Old Testament has prepared the New Testament. Yet the latter has not abrogated the former; rather, it has completed it, so that there has been a continuity even in the progress of the divine revelation. Unlike the Jews, the Greeks had neither law nor faith, yet, they were not altogether without help, since they had natural reason to judge them, as Saint Paul says (Rom. 2, 14-15), and to prepare them to receive Christianity. Clement is here introducing the theme of the "preparation of the Gospel" by the Greek poets and philosophers, especially Plato. Eusebius of Caesarea will fully develop this idea. The philosophers, Clement says, have been the prophets with respect to Greek natural reason. True enough, God was not speaking directly to the philosophers; unlike the prophets, the philosophers received from God no special revelation; yet, since natural reason itself is a divine light, it can be said that, through it, God was guiding the philosophers toward truth. To deny this would be to deny that the divine providence takes care of historical events, including their very order. God has certainly created reason to some useful purpose. If he has willed the existence of philosophers, it was because, like a good shepherd, he wanted to put his best sheep at the head of his flock. This, at least, should be easily understood by those who reproach the Greek philosophers for having stolen their ideas from the Old Testament. It cannot be maintained, at one and the same time, that philosophy is evil in itself and that it has been borrowed from Revelation by the Greeks. In fact, Jewish law and Greek philosophy have been two rivers, at whose confluence Christianity sprung forth, like a new source, powerful enough to carry, along with its own waters, those of its two feeders.[8] This ambition to include the totality of truth accessible to man had already been affirmed by Justin Martyr; it will still inspire the scholasticism of the thirteenth century.

Necessary to the Greeks before the coming of the Lord, philosophy remains useful to the Christians, provided they keep it in its proper place. From the very beginning of the *Miscellanies* (1, 5), Clement establishes this point by means of Biblical comparisons borrowed from Philo and which were to become the common property of the thirteenth-century theologians. In warning to keep away "from the stranger who sweeteneth her words" (Prov. 7, 5), Scripture gives us to understand that we should make use of profane learning without mistaking philosophical widom for the Christian wisdom which it but prepares. Just as the liberal arts "contribute to philosophy, which is their mistress, so also philosophy itself co-operates for the acquisition of wisdom. For philosophy is the study of wisdom, and wisdom is the knowledge of things divine and human, and of their causes. Wisdom therefore sways philosophy, as philosophy sways preparatory intellectual culture." Philo has thus become, through Clement, the inspirer of the famous formula: "philosophy is the handmaid of theology"; he has also provided theologians, and popes, with its scriptural justifications, including the symbolical interpretation of Abraham, Agar and Sarah.[9] The proper function of philosophy in Christian education is to exercise the mind, to awaken the intellect and to sharpen the acumen; yet it remains a "preparatory training for rest in Christ."

It would be an exaggeration to speak of a "philosophy" of Clement of Alexandria, the more so as he himself considered philosophical wisdom as lacking unity. Like the Bacchants, who had torn to pieces the body of Pentheus, the philosophers have broken up the natural unity of truth. Each philosophical sect still holds a piece of it and pretends to have it whole. The first task of a Christian philosopher is to eliminate from philosophy all that is false. The only completely useless sect is that of Epicurus, against whom Clement has directed all the texts of Saint Paul on the foolishness of worldly wisdom. With respect to the other philosophical sects, Christian wisdom acts as a selective principle which eliminates error and singles out truth, in order to preserve it. The two supreme masters in philosophy are Pythagoras, a man illuminated by God, and Plato, whose doctrine is a constant invitation to piety.[10]

The importance of Clement does not lie in the few philosophical ideas which can be found scattered throughout his works,[11] but, rather, in his deep and remarkably successful elucidation of the relation of philosophy to Christian faith. There is only one true philosophy, whose source is "the philosophy according to the Hebrews" or, in other words, "the philosophy according to Moses." Since the Greeks have drawn from it, we ourselves can draw from it under its two forms, Holy Scripture and Greek philosophy. Assuredly, the doctrine of Christ is sufficient unto salvation, but philosophy can help us in leading men to Christ and in inquiring into the meaning of faith after accepting it. A "Christian *Gnosis*," is precisely Christian faith blossoming into intellectual knowledge as a tree bearing flowers and yielding fruits. There are not three classes of men: the pagans, the believers and the Gnostics; there are but two: the pagans and the faithful, including those, among the latter, who are the only Gnostics worthy of the name because they are the only men to philosophize in the infallible light of faith.[12]

In the *Miscellanies* (vi, 15), Clement has expressed the same idea under the form of an apologue. There are wild olive trees and there are cultivated olive trees; that is, there are pagan men and there are Christian men. The pagan man is like unto a wild tree, which, until it has been engrafted by a gardener, yields no oil. God is this gardener, who grafts faith on to wild natural reason. Now there are four different ways to do this. First, by inserting the graft between the bark and the wood, as we do in instructing ignorant pagans who learn the elements of faith and go no farther. Secondly, a gardener can cleave the wood of the wild tree and insert in it a shoot from a cultivated tree; thus does faith enter a philosophical mind and grow in it. A third way of engrafting consists in removing the bark and the sap-wood from both the wild tree and the cultivated shoot, and then in tying them together; this is what we do with heretics or with uncouth men, when we bring them by force to the Christian truth. But the fourth and the best mode of engrafting is a still more powerful one. A bud is removed from a cultivated tree, together with the surrounding piece of bark; the trunk of the wild tree is then stripped of its own bark, over an equal surface; lastly, the graft is applied to the trunk, tied round and done over with clay without injuring the bud. Such is the kind of engrafting which gives birth to the true "gnostic." The eye of faith, so to speak, then replaces the eye of natural reason. Unless, on the contrary, we prefer to say, with Saint Paul, that reason has been transplanted into faith and thus made partaker "of the fatness of the olive tree" (Rom., 11, 17); but it seems better to understand these words of the grafting of faith on to the souls, which share in the Holy Spirit according to their respective capacities. Souls then bear fruit in both knowledge and virtue. The fear of God, the sorrow for our sins, the hope to share in God's eternal life, together with patience and temperance, spring forth in us from their common root, which is charity. How could it be otherwise, since God is love, and since faith is but the life of God in us? The perfect Gnostic is one with the perfect Christian.

The doctrine of Clement has received many different interpretations. Cognat stresses its genuinely Christian character; C. Merk thinks that the doctrine is formally Christian, but that its content is borrowed from Plato and the Stoics through Philo; J. Winter is of the opinion that, in it, Christian elements and Greek elements react upon one another in a quasi-chemical way, so as to produce an assimilation of kindred elements in an elimination of the incompatible ones; A. Harnack judges imprudent any attempt to establish exactly up to what point the doctrine of Clement was determined by the Gospel, and up to what point it was determined by philosophy, but he adds immediately that Clement has turned the Christian tradition into a religious philosophy of Hellenistic inspiration; reacting against Harnack, and also against Hatch, Hort maintains that Clement has simply obeyed the necessity which dominated the whole history of the Christian revelation ever since the times of the Apostles and even of the Evangelists; E. de Faye seems at first to go back to the position of Harnack, in thinking that Christianity and philosophy sway about equally the doctrine of Clement, but he presently adds that philosophy has contributed to it the rational element only, the religious one being entirely provided by Christianity; G. Bardy demurely observes that the Gnostic of Clement is not separated from his Christian by an unbridgeable gap, to which he adds this important remark: "Between them, the difference is more one of degree than one of nature." [13] As can be seen, all these interpretations agree on the presence of the two same elements in the doctrine of Clement, and although they do not quite agree about their respective proportions, they practically all recognize the fact that Christianity was the dominant element of his thought. His insistence on calling *Gnosis* a Christian faith deepened by intellectual speculation should not make us forget that the faith of his Christian Gnostic is, precisely *qua* faith, identically the same as that of the most humble of the Christians. Only, like Justin, Clement was an Apologist. He himself has described his *Miscellanies* as fish bait to catch philosophers (vii, 18). He wanted to tell them, in their own language, how truly Saint Paul had spoken of the "treasures of wisdom (*sophias*) and knowledge (*gnoseos*) that are hidden in Christ Jesus." It would be equally wrong to deny that Clement was very fond of philosophy and to forget that, because it was fully integrated with his religious life, what he called philosophy was to him the understanding of his religion.

2. ORIGEN

Origen studied philosophy under Ammonius Saccas, himself born of Christian parents. The doctrine of Ammonius, who never wrote any books, is known to us only from some notes preserved by Priscian. It is however certain that we should consider him as the founder of neoplatonism.[14] His influence on Origen and, through him,[15] on the later development of Christian thought, can hardly be exaggerated. He is said to have taught that God had made the world out of nothing and by an act of his will, but Origen himself must have learned this from his Christian parents. On the contrary, Ammonius's view of the world as a hierarchical society of spiritual substances, each of which is in charge of a certain body,[16] was an important contribution to the theology of Origen. The second of these points will be discarded by almost all the later Christian theologians, but the first point will be no less unanimously accepted. Origen has eliminated the materialism maintained by some of his Christian predecessors; from now on, and practically without exception, all the Christian writers will conceive human souls as so many spiritual substances entrusted by God with the care of their respective bodies. Thus, and for the first time, a sort of philosophical structure was inserted into the general framework of the Judeo-Christian view of the world.

The *Principles* of Origen were written for those who, although persuaded that Christ is the Son of God, and that they should learn truth from himself, still felt hesitant on important points related to the nature of God or of his creatures.[17] The only way to settle these difficulties is to begin by stating the "principles," that is to say, the fundamental tenets of the Christian faith, by which alone all its interpretations can be judged. Like his master Clement, Origen remains a theologian whose starting point is the same Christian faith as that of the simplest among his fellow Christians. To him, Greek philosophy is neither good nor bad in itself; it can become either one according as we make a good or a bad use of it.

Therefore, let Scripture be our starting point; but how is Scripture itself to be interpreted? Many parts of the Jewish Law have become obsolete since the new dispensation. Either they now are meaningless or they have an allegorical and spiritual meaning. For instance, the Jews had been forbidden to eat such birds as "the eagle, and the griffon, and the osprey, and the kite, and the vulture, according to their kind" (Levit. 11, 13-14): what can this mean to a Christian? If he takes it literally, nothing. In fact, it must have signified something higher even to the Jews. Why should God have told Moses to gather the people together at the well, and to give them water to drink? Was it really necessary to ask so great a prophet to take care of such a modest business? The Jews would have certainly gone to the well by themselves in order to drink even though nobody had told them to do so. There always is an allegorical meaning hidden in such texts: "the cheapness of the letter refers us to the preciousness of the spiritual interpretation." [18]

Origen did not attempt to lay down a set of rules for the exegesis of Scripture, but he seems to have followed a small number of elementary principles which remain the same throughout their countless applications. The literal truth of the Bible is above all discussion. There is always a literal sense in its text, and since its author is God, this literal sense is always true. This literal meaning is a twofold one; the "corporeal" sense and the "allegorical" sense. The first one is the grammatical sense, as it appears from the construction of the sentence and the meaning of the words. In some cases, this first sense is also the ultimate one. For instance: "God created heaven and earth" is a true statement, and what it says is true exactly as it says it. But when Scripture speaks of the face or of the hands of God; or when it says that the first three days were real days, in spite of the fact that neither the sun nor the moon had yet been created, the true literal meaning must needs be allegorical. In such matters, the general rule is that the material or "corporeal" sense of Scripture should be discarded every time it entails something impossible, absurd or unworthy of God.[19] In point of fact, Origen has made an almost continuous use of the allegorical interpretation of Scripture, and this has made it possible for him to introduce in his commentaries a large number of ideas borrowed from Philo and from Ammonius Saccas.[20]

A. *God*

Origen was the first ecclesiastical writer to establish on a philosophical basis the immateriality of God. There are four material elements: water, earth, air, and fire, plus a fifth one which is constitutive of celestial bodies: the Quintessence (i.e., the "fifth essence"). Matter is, by nature, the subject of change, and since what changes ceases to be what it was, change entails corruption; consequently, if God were material, he would be corruptible, that is imperfect. Now God is perfect (otherwise, being like all the rest, he would not be God); hence he is incorruptible and therefore immaterial.[21] True enough, it is not easy for us to conceive an immaterial reality. Because our reason now dwells in a jail of flesh, it is, so to speak, weakened by its constant intercourse with matter. Yet the fact that we cannot imagine God is no reason why we should not think of him as of a purely incorporeal being.

What is his nature? God is thought and absolute spiritual unity. On account of his spirituality, he is simple (i.e., a "simple intellectual nature"). There are in him no divisions, nothing that can be said to be "higher" or "lower." Such is the import of his "oneness" and of his "unity." The Lord is "one God," Scripture says; hence, philosophers should say that he is the absolute One, that is the "monad" (*monas*), or the only God there is; but we should also say that he is the *"henad"* (*henas,* from *hen,* one. Plato, *Phileb.* 15 A), that is the absolute unity and, as such, the source and origin of every intellectual nature, or mind. Through Ammonius Saccas, Plato was here helping the Christian Origen to interpret Scripture, and, at the same moment, he was inspiring the metaphysics of the pagan Plotinus. The notion of God as an "incorporeal being" gives their full meaning to the words of Saint Paul, that "the invisible things of him from the creation of the world, are clearly seen" (Rom. i, 20). Indeed, these cannot be seen otherwise. Just as we cannot see light in itself, but only in what it enables us to see, so also "the works of divine providence and the plan of this whole world are sorts of rays, as it were, of the nature of God, in comparison with his real substance and being. As, therefore, our understanding is unable of itself to behold God himself as he is, it knows the Father of the world from the beauty of his works and the comeliness of his creatures."[22] Yet, even this indirect knowledge of God is not easy to acquire. What idea of an *incorporeal* being can we derive from *corporeal* beings? To posit God as incorporeal is, at the same time, to posit him as unthinkable. If God is pure spirit, he is neither the world, nor part of the world, nor immanent in the world. Again, such a God can no more be a "whole" than he can be a "part," for indeed an incorporeal being has no parts, hence he cannot be a whole. What is pure intellection, absolute simplicity and essential incorporeity is not only beyond matter, it is beyond intellection, at least so far as our own intellection is concerned. And how could it be otherwise? In fact, God is beyond "being" itself.[23] The technical justification of the so called "negative theology" was here entering the history of Christian thought, and it was there to stay.

An absolute and immaterial being, conceived as above even being, must needs be perfect. On this point, Origen has clearly seen that God's essential perfection made it impossible for him to be the cause of evil,[24] but he seems to have found it difficult to reconcile the two notions of divine power and of divine perfection. The reason for this is that the notion of "infinite" was hard to conceive for a mind of Greek formation. To the Greeks, an infinite was an *apeiron,* that is something without a determining limit (*peras*), hence an "indeterminate." Now pure indetermination escapes the grasp of the intellect. In the present case, what would be the power of God if it remained indeterminate? It would be the power to do no one thing in particular, that is, the power to do nothing. In Origen's own words: "We must say that the power of God is finite, and not, under pretence of praising him, take away his limitation. For if the divine power be infinite, it must of necessity be unable to understand even itself, since that which is naturally illimitable is incapable of being comprehended. He made things therefore of such a size as to be able to apprehend and keep them under his power, and control them by his providence; so also he prepared matter of such size (i.e., in such quantity) as he had power to ornament." [25] This clearly shows what a tremendous effort was going to be required from Christian philosophy before it could achieve a complete awareness of the metaphysical import of the Christian revelation. Origen had read in the Bible that God has ordered all things in measure, and number, and weight, that is according to strictly determined reasons, but he had not read there that God was infinite, that is, the very infinity of being itself. All Christians have always believed in the same identical God of Holy Scripture, but it has taken them a long time to realize that, in the God of their faith, infinity was a perfection.[26]

B. *The Logos*

We have noted, in the Greek predecessors of Clement, a tendency to subordinate the Word to the Father. The same tendency is noticeable in Origen. Jesus Christ, who came into the world, was born of the Father before all creatures, but since he was made flesh and became visible, he cannot be said to be equal with the Father. This is the reason why Origen says that God is higher than Christ and consequently that Christ is by no means comparable to the Father. By the same token, Origen refuses to consider Christ as the Good in itself. To him, the only absolute Good is God the Father, of whom Christ is but an image.[27]

It is difficult to say how Origen understood the relations of the first two persons of the Trinity, because the original text of the *Principles* is lost, except some fragments, and this is one of the points where its Latin translator, Rufinus, has tried to bring the doctrine of Origen somewhat nearer to orthodoxy. According to the translation, Origen taught that the Word has always been with the Father, or, conversely, that the Father has never been without the Son. Since he is the Son of God, the Word (*Logos*) is God, but, in order to subordinate the Son to the Father, Origen called

God the Father "the God by right of self" (*autotheos*), with article, whereas the begotten Son, who is God but as an image and resemblance, was simply called "God," without article. Yet, while the Son is only "God," because he is not *the* God *par excellence,*" he is *"the* Word" because he is *"the* Logos *par excellence."* In other words, the Word is to what comes after him, what the Father is to him. We would perhaps not betray his intention in saying that, according to Origen, the Word is divine, but not God.[28]

Whatever his relation to the Father, the Word is Reason itself. As such, he is the seat of the Ideas and contains in himself the intelligible world after whose pattern the world has been created. The resemblance with Plotinus' doctrine of the *Nous* (i.e., the Intellect which is the first being emanated from the One) is so striking in this part of the doctrine of Origen, that it can be safely traced to their common master, the silent Ammonius Saccas. Even the Stoic notion of the *Logos,* conceived as a sort of energy pervading the world of matter, finds its counterpart in the cosmology of Plotinus.[29]

This first massive injection of Platonism into Christian theology has been very fruitful. Origen has imposed the notion of a purely spiritual being and implanted the conviction that immateriality is the highest type of reality. Other Origenian positions were no less definitive acquisitions. The doctrine of the divine ideas is one of them. An excellent text shows that Origen could be nearly right, even in cases when he was dangerously wrong. In this passage, he was wrong in saying that the Word is but the Image of the true God, but he was right in adding that the Word is the absolute Similitude of the Father, through which all the other beings share in the divine resemblance.[30] In judging Origen, let us not forget that he was doing pioneering work in theology. Moreover, being before anything else an exegete of Holy Scripture, he was as often in danger of missing the spiritual meaning of the sacred texts as of neglecting their literal and obvious meaning. Despite his many theological errors, Origen has always been considered one of the great names in the history of Christian thought.

C. *The World*

The creation of the world *ex nihilo* (from nothing) had been taught by Philo and restated by the Christian predecessors of Origen, but the first Apologists had not yet found the right words to distinguish with perfect clarity between the notion of creation and that of the simple shaping up of some pre-existing matter. In short, their explanations still hesitated between the Creator of the Bible and the Demiurge of the *Timaeus*. Origen clearly saw what prevented the pagans from accepting the notion of creation. To the mind of a philosopher, the formation of the world by a god working on a pre-existing matter seemed easier to understand, and therefore more rational, than its creation from nothing. Hence Origen's efforts to establish that the shaping up of a pre-existing matter by God was even less conceivable than its creation. Let us suppose a pre-existing matter; it must have at least an aptitude to receive the forms and shapes that will turn it into a *cosmos;* whence could an uncreated matter hold this aptitude? Neither from nothing, nor from God. We should then imagine some providence anterior to both matter and God, in order to account for this pre-existing adaptation of matter to the ordering power of God, which is absurd. But let us take this pre-adaptation of matter for granted: if it has no cause, it exists by chance, whence there follows that it is only by chance that creation was possible and that God deserves the titles of creator, father, benefactor of the world and such like. Last but not least, if matter has always existed without being created, its very existence has neither reason nor cause; it is irrational and, in fact, less easy to understand than its creation by God.[31]

The world then has been created, but it has always been created. In short, it is eternal. The story told by Genesis should be interpreted in an allegorical way. This is what Philo had already done and Origen follows him on this point. Two main reasons invited him to do so. First, the Christians profess to believe in God almighty, creator and ruler of the world. Now, how could God be the ruler of the world if he had no world to rule? Secondly, let us suppose a God who, being able to create the world, does not create it; we shall have to assign a reason why, all of a sudden, he will display the sudden outburst of energy which creation requires. In a perfect God, such a change would be the more inexplicable as it would be a progress, for indeed it would add the dignity of creator to his already complete perfection. The eternity of the world is therefore more intelligible than its creation in time. Nevertheless, to say that creation is eternal does not entail that the very world we now are in has always existed, nor that it shall always exist. On the contrary, since we know that this present world will some time be destroyed, we must conclude that, just as it will be followed by other ones, it has been preceded by other ones. The eternity of the world then means, that the series of these successive worlds is itself eternal.[32]

Unlimited in time, creation is, on the contrary, limited in space. Origen seems to have been led to this conclusion by the already quoted text of Scripture, which says that God has created the world according to number, weight and measure. Since, on the other hand, the divine power has to be finite in order to be perfect, the created world itself must needs be finite in order to receive order and beauty.[33] For indeed, the world is perfect. The better to refute the Gnostics who considered creation as too imperfect to be more than the work of a Demiurge inferior to the supreme God, Origen maintains that God has made each creature perfect in its own kind.[34] This is true despite the present condition of the world. For instance, man has been created as a soul united with a body, but, at the time of creation, the relation of souls to bodies was very different from what it now is. Had man persevered in his pristine condition, he would rapidly acquire the sciences and virtues which are naturally his. All men would; for God who is just, has created them all equal. There is no reason to distinguish men, as many Gnostics do, into "material," "animal" (i.e., "psychic," from *psykhè*, or *anima:* soul) and "spiritual." All men are equal and of the same nature. The justice of God is such that, in the beginning, all beings must have shared in intelligibility. This does not mean that God created pure spirits only, nor even that all creatures equally shared in rationality at the time of creation, but since all have been created by the same Word, who is the Image of the Father, they must have all shared in the resemblance of the Father, and, to that extent, they must have all partaken of his spirituality. This is clearly affirmed by Origen in his *Principles,* at least with respect to man: "As He Himself, then, was the cause of existence of those things which were to be created, in whom there was neither any variation nor change, nor want of power, He created all whom He made equal and alike, because there was in Him no reason for producing variety and diversity." The reason why the world did not remain in its pristine condition is that, although it had been made good by God, its goodness was not an essential goodness of nature, but the accidental and precarious goodness of a received gift. The only way for a man to turn a received gift into a personal property is to accept it. Freedom was precisely this power either to accept the gift of God, or to turn it down. God alone, because he *is* the Good, has not to choose goodness in order to have it, and since the good is his own nature, he cannot possibly lose it. On the contrary, all the creatures endowed with reason by God did have to make a choice, and it was their free choice that introduced inequalities into the world. By the same token, freedom has brought about the present hierarchical structure of the universe, where each kind of creatures still occupies the degree of perfection it has freely chosen.[35]

One may well ask Origen how he can prove the reality of this primitive act of free choice? His answer is that there is no other way to account for the present structure of the created world. Since the goodness of creation necessarily follows from the nature of God, what of evil there is in things must be traced to some unfortunate initiative on the part of creatures. At any rate their present inequality is obvious. Some beings are inert and receive their motions from without, such as the stones. Some have an internal principle of growth, which moves them from within and yet is not properly a soul; such are, for instance, the plants. Other beings have souls that move them from within according to what is presented to them by their imagination; these are the animals. Among them, men move themselves according to their intellectual knowledge of the nature of things; they are free, because freedom is nothing else than the power of choice, born of reason. Unlike animals, men can judge their sensitive and imaginative representations, approve or disapprove of their objects. Experience shows that our desires cannot overcome our will without the consent of the higher portion of the soul. Men make themselves to be what they are by choosing and organizing their acts according to the prescriptions of reason.[36]

This is to say that every soul has a personal history which, in the doctrine of Origen, is a curious one. Its successive stages differ from those recognized by the Gnostics. Among the spirits created by God, some have chosen to remain spirits. But, instead of remaining a *spirit (nous)* spirits have chosen to become souls (*psykhè, anima*). These have made the wrong choice and their history is that of their fall as well as of their effort to return to their pristine condition. For a spirit (*nous*) to become a soul is to tie itself with a body; it is, so to say, to become incarnate. Men are spirits that received human bodies in punishment for the wrong choice made by their free will. Let us note, however, that in the history of each one of the successive worlds, each soul can make this choice only once. Moreover, the resulting change in the condition of a certain spirit does not constitute for it a "metempsychosis"; the fall of a spirit into the condition of a soul is not the transmigration of a soul from a body to another body. Despite some doubtful texts, Origen does not seem to have ever admitted that spirits could fall into the bodies of irrational animals.[37]

If this be true, God is by no means responsible for the presence of evil in the world, but the change that took place in the condition of some spirits accounts for the fact that, after being a father, God had to become a judge. The apparent opposition, stressed by the Gnostics, between the goodness of God and his justice does not find its justification in the existence of two Gods, one for each of the two Testaments, but, rather, in the two successive conditions of those among the spirits which have chosen to become souls. Moreover, even the justice of God remains an aspect of his goodness. His so-called punishments are, in fact, so many remedies devised by him in order to bring the fallen spirits back to their primitive state of purity and sanctity.[38]

The diversity of beings is due to the "variety in the falls of those who, separating themselves from unity, did it in several different ways." [39] When beings broke away from unity each of them did it of its own accord and without bothering about the other ones. Hence a planless multiplication of diversity which, had it been permitted to proceed indefinitely, would have resulted in an infinite confusion. The justice of God has remedied this disorder by organizing individual wills into a planned whole. Hence the part played by matter in the history of the world. It had been a bad thing for spirits to fall from unity; yet, since they were doing it, it was a good thing for them to fall into matter, because matter stopped their fall. In this sense, matter has been a first remedy to the consequences of original sin.

The second remedy is the end of the world, or, rather, the successive ends of the successive worlds. When God sees that evil becomes too cumbersome, he destroys the existing world and creates another one. This does not happen at fixed times, but when God's providence wills it. How these ends of the world take place, and what becomes of the souls after each one of these destructions, are two problems which have particularly detained Origen's attention. As a Christian, Origen believed in the resurrection of bodies. As a philosopher, he thought, with Athenagoras, that it is as easy for God to resurrect a dead body as to make a tree grow from a seed or a man from a human germ. In Saint Paul's own words, the resurrection of the dead "is sown in corruption, it shall rise in incorruption" (I Cor. 15, 42). Concerning the future destiny of human souls, Origen seems to have hesitated between two solutions of the problem. In a first group of texts, he speaks of eternal punishments without any attenuation or limitation in time; in other texts, he suggests that it is better to let men believe that, and since he generally teaches that God's punishments are remedies to evil, one may well wonder what would be their use if they should never come to an end. In some passages, Origen suggests that the world shall end by a universal restoration of things into their primitive perfection.[40]

There is little doubt that this was what he wanted to believe; only, his own doctrine made it difficult for him to hold such an optimistic view. As has been said, Origen maintains that the world is eternal, in this sense at least that there is an endless succession of worlds. But then there should also be an indefinite succession of falls and of restorations. Origen was bound to get in difficulty with Christian orthodoxy on both accounts, and anybody who reads him in the passages faithfully translated by Saint Jerome, can easily see it.[41] Only a Saint Augustine could have absorbed such a dose of neoplatonism without harming Christian orthodoxy.[42] Yet, Jerome would not have translated the *Principles* if he had not been convinced of their importance; Saint Bernard of Clairvaux would not have quoted Origen in his own homilies on the Canticle of Canticles if he had not seen in him a master of the spiritual life. All his interpreters unanimously agree that he was wrong; they no less unanimously agree that he was great.

CHAPTER II

THE LATIN APOLOGISTS

THE first language of the Western Church was Greek. Even the Christian community of Rome used Greek as a liturgical language up to the middle of the third century. This is the reason why the first Christian writings in Latin appeared somewhat later than the Greek apologies.

I. TERTULLIAN

Tertullian,[43] one of the most famous Latin Apologists, opens the long series of the Christian writers born in Northern Africa. Up to the time of Augustine, practically all the great names in the history of Christian literature will be African.[44] During the same period, Rome herself will produce little or nothing.

A much better stylist than Tatian, Tertullian resembles him in many ways. Although he himself was to die out of the Church, he strongly opposed the Gnostics. His treatise *On Prescription Against the Heretics* shows that the situation was then different from what it had been at the time of Justin and Tatian. Instead of addressing the emperors on behalf of the Christians, he addresses the heretics; his apologies are in favor, not of the Christians, but of Christianity.

There are heresies, and we know that they must exist (II Pet. 2, 1) in order to try faith and to oblige it to manifest itself in its purity (I Cor. 11, 19). Yet, just as fevers may kill bodies, heresies may kill souls. The heresies are fostered by philosophy, which is the wisdom of the world. In point of fact, the heretics (Gnostics) and the philosophers ask the same questions: What is the origin of evil, or of man? Wretched Aristotle, who "invented for these men dialectics, the art of building up and pulling down; an art so evasive in its propositions, so far-fetched in its conjectures, so harsh in its arguments, so productive of contentions, embarrassing even to itself, retracting everything, and really treating of nothing."

After this invective, which many Christian enemies of dialectic will repeat and enlarge up to the times of Petrarch and of Erasmus, Tertullian opens a new line of argument which all the anti-dialecticians of the middle ages will eagerly follow after him. Had not Saint Paul warned us not to let anyone cheat us "by philosophy and vain deceit"? (Col. 2, 8) And yet, Saint Paul had been at Athens! He had become acquainted with the false wisdom of philosophers! What indeed has Athens to do with Jerusalem? What concord is there between the Academy and the Church? "The true school for Christians is the porch of Solomon where the Apostles used to teach" (Acts, 3, 1). Away then "with all attempts to produce a mottled Christianity of Stoic, Platonic and dialectic composition! We want no curious disputation after possessing Christ Jesus, no inquisition after enjoying the gospel!" [45] God himself has said: "Seek, and you shall find" (Matt. 7, 7), and, indeed, the philosophers do seek, but the Christians have found, which means that their search should cease. They have their own rule of thought, which is the Christian faith itself [46] as it is found in Scriptures. True enough, the heretics too argue from Scripture, but they have no right to do so. The rule of faith has been entrusted by Christ, not to the heretics, but to the Apostles, who themselves have transmitted it to the apostolic churches, especially to the eminently apostolic church of Rome. Scriptures, then, are the lawful possession of the Catholic churches alone which, having owned them at a time when heresies did not yet exist, can exclude heretics from their use on the ground of legal proscription.

Tertullian has expressed his opposition to philosophy, and to any kind of philosophical thinking in matters of faith, in brilliant formulas which have made more for his celebrity than all the rest of his works. For instance, in the fifth chapter of his treatise *On the Flesh of Christ,* he did not hesitate to write: "The son of God died; it is by all means to be believed, because it is absurd. And He was buried, and rose again; the fact is certain, because it is impossible." Nobody has even written the often quoted formula: I believe because it is absurd (*absurdum*): Tertullian himself has written: *credo quia ineptum;* and it must be conceded that, in this case, *ineptum* really means "absurd." The only question then is: what does this statement mean? Perhaps simply that faith is more certain than human reason, and that, since only what is incomprehensible to reason can be an object of faith, a crucified God is absolutely certain (by faith) in virtue of its very incomprehensibility. If this is what Tertullian intended to say, there was nothing original in his purely verbal paradox. If, on the contrary, his double "because" must be taken literally, posterity did not betray Tertullian in ascribing to him the celebrated *credo quia absurdum*. This, however, should then be added, that when taken in this sense, such a formula does not define the spirit of Christian theology, but its very negation. Ever since the time of Athenagoras, theologians have been most anxious always to establish at least the *rational possibility* of the Christian faith. In this sense, they have all believed because it was *not* absurd to believe. As to Tertullian himself, even if we remember that he was a rhetorician, it is hard to admit that he ever intended to place the criterion of truth in absurdity. [47]

Like Tatian, and for the very same reason, this enemy of philosophy died out of the communion of the Christian Church. His own philosophical ideas are elementary, ill-digested and, apart from his materialistic conception of the world, without particular significance. [48] The secret of his deep and lasting influence is to be found in the history of theology rather than of philosophy. He still remains one of the greatest exponents of the Catholic notion of faith conceived as a living tradition.

2. MINUCIUS FELIX

Scholars have not yet been able to decide whether the *Octavius* of Minucius Felix[49] was written before or after the *Apology* of Tertullian. The question is not without interest, for indeed the one of these two works which was written first has certainly inspired the other, at least in part. The Ciceronian turn of mind of Minucius Felix does not invite consideration as a likely source of ideas. He had few of them, whereas they are plentiful in the works of Tertullian. At any rate, even if Minucius Felix had borrowed from Tertullian some of his arguments, the general tone of his apology would remain quite personal and entirely distinct from that of his predecessor. It has been remarked that while Tertullian had strongly claimed, for the Christians, the right to practice their religion freely in a pagan empire, he would have been perhaps less favorable to the liberty of pagan worship in a Christian empire. After his conversion, Tertullian seems to have completely forgotten what reasons he had once had to be a pagan. This is something which Minucius Felix has never forgotten. Among all the Apologists of the second and third centuries, Minucius Felix is the only one who has shown us the two sides of the question.

Minucius reports an imaginary conversation, or, at least, an artistically reconstructed one, held in his presence, at Ostia, by the pagan Cecilius Natalis and the Christian Octavius. The two main arguments directed by Cecilius against Christianity are those which Cicero himself might have used. First, there was in the blunt dogmatism of Christian faith something unpalatable to the cultured pagan mind. At the end of his dialogue *On the Nature of the Gods,* Cicero had concluded his ample theological inquiry by these modest words: "When we parted, it seemed to Velleius that the opinions of Cotta were more true, and, to me, that there was more likelihood in those of Balbus." Such being the attitude of men of parts and well trained in the doctrines of Plato, Aristotle, Zeno and Epicurus, we can easily imagine their impatience with the Christians. It was annoying, for aristocrats of Greco-Roman culture, to hear illiterates answer all questions concerning God, the origin of the world, the nature of man and his destiny. Moreover, there were national reasons, for a wise and pious Roman citizen, to keep faith with the gods of the Empire. Had not these gods led it to world leadership? No doctrine could be certain enough to justify national apostasy. The only wise thing to do was to adhere to the commonly received Roman religion and to keep up its traditions.

In answering these objections, Octavius observes that there is no reason why truth should remain the exclusive property of the happy few instead of belonging to all. It is not easy to imagine the feeling of liberation which pervaded the minds of many men when they were told, for the first time, that the ultimate truth about man and the world had been revealed to all. What philosophy had not been able to give to the most learned intellects, that is, a complete explanation of the world, Christianity was offering to the millions. A single God, creator and providence of all was then revealing to man the secret of his origin and of his destiny. The end of the world, the immortality of the soul, the rewards or punishments that await all men in future life—these are so many truths which the pagans have worked hard to discover and which the Christians glory in having received from God. At the end of this conversation, Cecilius graciously consents to declare himself convinced and to embrace the religion of Octavius. Whereupon, Minucius Felix concludes: "We departed, glad and cheerful: Cecilius, to rejoice that he had believed; Octavius, that he had conquered; and I, that the one had believed, and the other had conquered."

3. ARNOBIUS

A great figure of the early Latin Christian church, Saint Cyprian[50] was more interested in practical and moral problems than in philosophical or theological speculation. Arnobius,[51] on the contrary, was a second-rate Christian writer, whose religious information was weak to the point of being questionable. Yet he remains an interesting witness to the remarkable progress achieved by the opponents of Christianity in their criticism of the new religion. Besides repeating the old accusations of immorality and atheism, the pagan apologists had learned to draw more serious objections from Christian doctrine itself. Be it only for this, the *Adversus Gentes* of Arnobius still deserves to be studied. For instance, in Bk. II, 63-65, Arnobius' opponent asks why, if Christ was sent by God that he might save men from destruction, he has not been sent earlier, to all without exception, and why God does not now compel us to believe in his salutary doctrine? These were no longer calumnies but real objections.

Against his adversaries, Arnobius defines the Christians as the worshippers of the supreme King of the world under the guidance and leadership of Christ.[52] To him, Christ is essentially the teacher by whom the truth about the supreme God has been revealed to us. There is only one God, Lord of all that is, whom we must obey and love. Of course, this fundamental truth implies many other ones;[53] yet, on the whole, this is the sum total of the new religion.

What impresses Arnobius most in the Christian revelation is that it is for all a pressing invitation to intellectual modesty. This conviction is the real source of his alleged "scepticism." The personal experience of his conversion was still vivid in his mind when he wrote his apology. While deriding the fables of pagan mythology and the ridicules of pagan worship, Arnobius could not possibly forget that, not so long ago, he himself had worshipped sacred stones anointed with olive oil and begged favors from senseless sticks of wood.[54] And he had done this at a time when Christian truth was already offering itself to him in its luminous simplicity! But, precisely, this agreed with God's intentions. The fact that faith brings to them more truth than their intellect can investigate should help men to realize what they are: shapeless animals addicted to vain opinions, which comprehend nothing and cannot even see what lies before their eyes. This Arnobian man is an ancestor of the genuinely Christian family which comprises Montaigne and Pascal. We call them sceptics, but their scepticism is less a negation of the natural power of reason to know truth than a reminder of its limits. It stresses the fact that, even outside of revelation, there are many mysteries for human reason.

Arnobius has tried practically all the arguments used by his successors in favor of such a position.

The first one is a list of problems which the human mind can neither shun nor answer. This list is found in *Adversus Gentes*, Bk. II.[55] The first argument introduces a second one, which is the mainspring of the demonstration: since we believe so many mysteries of nature, why should we not believe the mysteries of faith? All men live by beliefs. Travelers believe that they will go back home; patients believe that their physicians will heal them; the philosophers who think that all is water believe that Thales was right; others believe what has been said by Plato, Aristotle, Chrysippus, Zeno or Epicurus. Even those who think that man knows nothing believe Carneades on this point. You believe in Plato, Arnobius says, or in Numenius, or in somebody else; we believe in Christ. An always valid argument indeed, but, at the same time, always a weak one. One cannot prove that an extraordinary belief is true by enumerating other extraordinary beliefs.[56]

A third theme, equally familiar to the so-called "Christian sceptics," is their vilification of man and their correlative extolling of animals. Arnobius uses it in connection with the immortality of the human soul. The early Christian Apologists had hesitated to teach, with Plato, that the soul was immortal by nature, because they realized that, in his doctrine, the immortality of the soul was inseparably tied up with its pre-existence. For them, to posit the soul as a spiritual substance, immortal by nature, was to turn it into a god. It was to relapse at once into polytheism: Tatian and others had therefore refused to attribute to the soul a *natural* immortality. Arnobius goes further still. In order to silence those who pretend to share in the immortality of God, he maintains that men are not souls, but animals. True enough, men are rational animals and they would excel over the brutes if they knew how to use their reason, but since they don't, they are little better off with reason than the animals which simply follow nature. Beasts are provident as we are, they shelter themselves from the cold as we do, and one cannot help thinking that, had they hands as we have, they would build themselves houses as we do.[57]

Even granting that man has succeeded in acquiring some knowledge, he should not brag about it. Men have not been endowed by nature with the gift of science; they have toiled for it under the pressure of necessity. Plato was wrong in imagining that human souls bring science down from heaven when they join their bodies. Arnobius proves this point by means of a "mental experiment" to which other philosophers will resort after him. Let us imagine a child living in complete solitude up to the age of twenty or thirty. What would he know? Nothing. Yet, if what Plato says in his *Meno* were true, that is if our souls came to this world from another one where they knew all, such a man should be able to discover by himself what we have to learn from other men. Plato says that in order to remind him of what he knows, it is enough to ask him well-ordered questions. But how can he be questioned? Since he knows no language, he would not understand the first word of our questions! To completely establish his thesis, Arnobius imagines an underground room of moderate and always constant temperature, perfectly soundproof and empty of all objects. Let us place there a new-born baby, preferably of Platonic or of Pythagorean breed; let it be nursed by a naked and always silent nurse who, after suckling it, leaves it alone and stays away from it. Later on, she feeds the child, then the young man, always the same identical food cooked in the same identical way. The question is, what knowledge would a man have acquired after forty years of such a life? Obviously, none.[58] The sensualist philosophers of the eighteenth century will make good use of this philosophical tale; the French materialist La Mettrie will resort to it in order to prove that our whole knowledge consists in sense perception.

Firmly convinced of the divinity of Christ, Arnobius had but vague notions concerning the dogma of the Trinity. The supreme God, of whom he speaks so often, seems to preside over many other gods. Christ is the God who teaches us the truth about the supreme God and thus saves our souls from final destruction. These souls are not created by the supreme God, but by a member of the heavenly royal court. Of themselves they are beings of intermediate dignity in this sense, that they are immortal if they know Christ, and mortal if they ignore him. The souls that do not know Christ are finally annihilated (*in nihilum redactae*), so completely wiped out that nothing is left: *nihil residuum faciens*.[59] Obviously, Arnobius is no Doctor of the Church, but the very shortcomings of his apology are instructive. Christianity must have exercized a powerful attraction about the end of the third century to have thus conquered minds who knew practically nothing about it, except that it implied an absolute faith in the divinity of Christ.

4. LACTANTIUS

A pupil of Arnobius at Sicca, and like him a rhetorician, Lactantius was a more moderate Apologist than his master.[60] If he has written it, the pamphlet on *How the Persecutors Die* is sufficient proof that this quiet man was not incapable of violence, but, in his certainly authentic writings, the tone of Lactantius is different. Peacefully going his own way, he criticizes the pagans when necessary, but so as to show them the truth which he loves and to make them feel what a blessing it is to be a Christian. 'Tis a pity the refreshing candor of his heart sometimes affected his intellect.

Chapters have been written on "The Blunders of Lactantius" and, indeed, his plain common sense is sometimes deaf to the voice of reason. The *Divine Institutes* contain a justly famous chapter (III, 24), where Lactantius castigates the foolishness of those who believe in the Antipodes. His mistake would be without importance, if he himself had not singled out this question as a decisive proof of the danger there is in arguing logically from false premises. Because they saw that the sun and moon always rose from the east and set to the west, some inferred that the world was round like a ball. Now, if the earth is a globe, it must necessarily be concluded that there are antipodes, that there is a side of the earth where rains fall upwards to the ground, where crops and trees grow downwards and where men walk with their feet higher than their heads. This, Lactantius concludes, is a joke. He did not know on whom the joke was.

One would vainly expect from Lactantius scientific, philosophical or theological discovery. Simply, he was a man happy to be a Christian. And indeed, what is happiness, if not the knowledge of truth? Since he had found truth in the Christian faith, Lactantius felt happy and he wanted everybody else, especially the philosophers, to share in his happiness. In the past, he saw nothing but the absurd fables of mythology and the endless contradictions of great minds which even their genius had not rescued from ignorance; in the future, he saw a golden age of certitude, of light and of peace: "Therefore the only hope, the only safety for man is placed in this doctrine, which we defend. All the wisdom of man consists in this alone, the knowledge and worship of God. This is our tenet, this our opinion." [61] This, Lactantius could add, is our happiness, for he had betaken himself to Christianity "as to a most safe harbor: to that pious, true and divine wisdom in which all things are ready for utterance, pleasant to the hearing, easy to understand, honorable to be undertaken." [62]

When he speaks of the pagans, Lactantius thinks mainly of the ancient philosophers and orators, particularly Cicero, "who was not only a perfect orator, but also a perfect philosopher." Yet, what did Cicero know concerning the divinity? A glance at his book *On the Nature of the Gods* provides the answer. Where, perchance, Cicero thinks he knows something on the subject, he is wrong; Seneca is worse, for indeed, "who could be right where Cicero is wrong?" In inquiring into the cause of these errors, Lactantius comes by a felicitous idea which is perhaps his most important contribution to Christian apologetics. The weakness inherent in pagan thought, Lactantius says, was that it separated wisdom from religion. Pagan worship entailed no philosophy, and philosophers could find nothing in their religion but incoherency, absurdity, immorality. The great novelty of Christianity was, on the contrary, that it united wisdom and religion. Such is also the leading theme of the *Divine Institutes*. Lactantius announces it from the very first chapter of his work: I have wished, he says, "that both the learned may be directed to true wisdom, and the unlearned to true religion" (I, 1). Again: "And I thus briefly define the sum of this knowledge, that neither is any religion to be undertaken without wisdom, nor any wisdom to be approved of without religion" (I, 2). The pagans, Lactantius adds, "accept false religions for want of wisdom, or else false wisdoms for want of religion" (III, 11). The only remedy to this evil is the acceptance of monotheism which opens the door to both true philosophy and true religion: "Since, therefore, philosophy and the religious system of the gods are separated, and far removed from each other; seeing that some are professors of wisdom through whom it is manifest that there is no approach to the gods, and that others are priests of religion, through whom wisdom is not learned; it is manifest that the one is not true wisdom and that the other is not true religion. . . . Where, then, is wisdom joined with religion? There, indeed, where the one God is worshipped, where life and every action is referred to one source, and to one supreme authority: in short, the teachers of wisdom are the same who are also the priests of God. . . . Therefore religion is contained in wisdom, and wisdom in religion" (IV, 3). When Lactantius wrote these lines, he accurately prophesied what was to remain the condition of philosophy during the whole middle ages, when practically all the philosophers were priests.

This optimism[63] strikes a new note in the history of Christian apologetics. In the first years of the fourth century, Lactantius was conscious of following an already established tradition. He knew his Latin predecessors and he intended to continue their work. Moreover, after living under the persecution of Diocletian, he had been able to dedicate his *Divine Institutes* to Constantine, whose favorable attitude toward Christianity was opening a new political era in the history of the Church, and, consequently, in the history of Christian thought. Christianity was no longer on the defensive; the day of the Apologists was over and the times were ripe for the constructive work of the Fathers of the Church.

CHAPTER III

THE CAPPADOCIANS

IN THE political history of the Church, the main event to be noted in the fourth century was the edict of toleration issued in favor of the Christians by the Emperor Constantine the Great, at Milan, 313. In the history of Christian thought, the main event was a consequence of this edict, namely the convocation of the Council of Nicaea by Constantine in 325. One of its main objectives was to judge the doctrine of Arius whose theology made the Son to be a creature of the Father.[64] Many Christian writers had subordinated the Son to the Father either in origin or in dignity. The text of the Sapiential books provided arguments for such an attitude; for instance, Ecclus. 24, 5, whose orthodox exegesis was to be determined by Athanasius in his *Contra Arianos,* II, 4. But Arius was saying something different. In teaching that the Son was not substantially one with the Father, he had turned a mere groping for correct expression into the affirmation of a definite theological error. The part of the creed of Nicaea which affirms the consubstantiality of the Son with the Father[65] has always remained the correct formulation of the Christian faith on this point.

At the time of the Council of Nicaea, Eusebius of Caesarea was continuing the traditional work of the Apologists in his *Preparation for the Gospel* and his *Demonstration of the Gospel.* Full of erudition, but misled by a wrong chronology, Eusebius has hesitated between praising Plato for having paved the way to the teachings of the Gospel, and blaming him for having tacitly borrowed his doctrine from Moses.[66] Immediately after the Council the main preoccupation of the theologians was to expound and to justify its conclusions against the Arians. The two great names connected with this work are those of Athanasius among the Greeks[67] and of Hilary of Poitiers among the Latins.[68] But it was at the school of Caesarea, in Cappadocia, made illustrious by the teaching of Origen that the spirit of philosophical speculation entered the theologies of the three great Cappadocians: Gregory Nazianzenus, Basil of Caesarea and Gregory of Nyssa.

I. GREGORY NAZIANZENUS

Gregory Nazianzenus,[69] also called Gregory the Theologian (329-389), found an adversary of high quality in the person of the Arian Eunomius (d. *ca.* 395). Arianism was a philosophical heresy, in this sense at least that to conceive a begotten son as inferior to an unbegotten father appeared as more rational than to ascribe to Father and Son the same degree of perfection. In fact, the philosophy of Plotinus who, together with Origen, had been a pupil of Ammonius Saccas, clearly subordinated the *Nous* to the One and the World Soul to the *Nous*. Eunomius himself conceived God as the supremely one *ousia*, that is entity. Being absolutely simple, this divine essence excludes all plurality of attributes. The only thing that can be said about it is that it *is*, purely and simply. Accordingly, this God is characterized by the very necessity of his being.[70] He is, so to say, the essentially "unbegotten." By definition, the Son, or Word, cannot be God in the same sense as the Father. On the contrary, since he is "begotten," the Word is entirely different (*anomoios*) from the Father and in no way consubstantial with him. Like the Demiurge in Plato's *Timaeus*, the God of Eunomius has made a god by adoption, and he has made him eternal; he has made him partaker of his own divinity and of his own glory, but the Father himself has not been able to create this contradiction in terms: an essentially begotten being that is consubstantial with an essentially unbegotten being. Eunomius is sometimes reproached with the "sophisms" which he committed in order to reconcile his position with orthodoxy, but this is perhaps to misunderstand his real intention. A Christian theologian is interested, before anything else, in defining the object of his faith. If that which he believes is a mystery, his primary intention is to define this mystery such as it is, or, more precisely, to describe exactly the particular mystery which it is. Arius and Eunomius were trying to do something else, namely, to reduce the object of Christian faith to terms intelligible in the light of reason; they wanted to submit faith to the exigencies of logic. If to be a son is to have been begotten, then even the only begotten Son of God must be posterior and inferior to him.

This invasion of the field of faith by dialectical reasoning accounts for the fact that Gregory Nazianzenus forcefully stresses the primacy of faith.[71] He does not renounce his right to make use of rational arguments, but he wants to use them in accordance with the teaching of Christian faith.[72] To ask, as Eunomius does, how God may have begotten a Son equal to, and consubstantial with his Father, appears to Gregory as a somewhat naïve question. The Father, Eunomius says, must have begotten either an existent or a non-existent, and so on. Is not this to imagine the generation of the Word by God after the pattern of the generation of a child by a man? It is futile. Faith is for us an invitation to bow to mystery, and the use which we make of philosophical terms in order to define it is not intended to replace it with understanding.

2. BASIL THE GREAT

The name of Saint Basil,[73] or Basil the Great, is inseparable from that of his intimate friend, Gregory Nazianzenus. Both were excellent Greek writers, the one, Gregory, more eloquent, the other, Basil, more philosophically-minded and, owing to his medical studies, better equipped to deal with scientific problems. Still today, humanists take pleasure in reading his short treatise: *To Students, On How to Make Good Use of the Study of Greek Literature.* The problem was to know how to educate young Christians in a country whose culture was wholly Greek, that is, pagan, in letters as well as in ethics and in philosophy. Basil has solved the problem by giving the model of a well-written treatise, adorned with quotations from pagan writers and yet inspired of a wholly Christian spirit. Since there were two sides to the problem, the treatise of Basil can be interpreted either as a warning against Greek literature, or, on the contrary, as an invitation to study it. In fact, it was both. Greek could be studied in the works of the Greek writers only, and all the classical Greek writers had been pagans. The same problem arises in all countries where the standard classical literature is not Christian in its inspiration. In solving it, Basil warns his readers against the immorality and the impiety of many master-pieces of Greek literature, but he also underlines what some of them can contribute to the culture of literary taste and even to the formation of virtue. Not only are the precepts of the ancients often profitable, especially if, instead of merely reading them, we follow them, but some of their examples deserve to be imitated, when they show us how to cultivate our soul and how to free it from the body. This elegantly written essay will naturally be welcomed by the fourteenth- and fifteenth-century Christian humanists. All of them will interpret it as an invitation to study Greek letters, and Leonardo Bruni will translate it into Latin, as his complete justification for having previously translated Plutarch and Plato from the Greek into Latin.

The controversy of Basil against the Arianism of Eunomius follows the same general lines as that of his friend Gregory Nazianzenus, but it is perhaps easier to discern in his own case the meaning of their common objections against the application of dialectics to the mystery of the Trinity. Their precise point was that to submit a mystery to dialectical treatment was a self-contradictory undertaking. If a man considers dialectics as the supreme rule of human thought, he has no business to be a theologian, nor, for that matter, a Christian. Basil puts his finger on the weak point of Eunomius' dialectics, where he observes that the fact that God is essentially "unbegotten" does not imply that to be "unbegotten" is the very essence of God. This purely privative term does not fittingly designate the positive fullness of the divine entity. True enough, according to Eunomius, all the names given to God are synonymous, since, ultimately, they all signify nothing else than his ineffable being. But Basil maintains, on the contrary, that although no name adequately describes the nature of God, every one of his names points out either something that he is not, or something which he positively is. Incorporeal is a name which falls into the first one of these two classes; creator, just, judge, fall into the second class. Now the name which best designates God is "being" (*ousia*), and what it points out is "the very being of God" (*auto to einai tou theou*), which is by no means a negation. The starting point of a theologian, then, should not be the unbegotten nature of God, but his "being" (*ousia*), which, because it is common to the three divine persons, insures their consubstantiality.[74] Obviously, we are here witnessing the conflict of two contradictory attitudes, for Eunomius wanted to reduce the object of faith to the exigencies of dialectical reasoning, whereas Basil wanted to use dialectics in order to define with precision the object of Christian faith.

Philosophically speaking, the main work of Basil is the group of his nine *Homilies in Hexaemeron*. These homilies, which had been preceded by the now lost commentary of Origen on the book of Genesis, are the prototype of a long series of similar writings of other Fathers of the Church or to mediaeval theologians. There is one included in the *Summa Theologiae* of Thomas Aquinas. An *In Hexaemeron* is an explanation of the text of Genesis, i, 1-26, which describes the creation of the world. Its author uses the sacred text to develop his own philosophical or scientific views on related problems, that is, to show that the biblical account of the origin and nature of things makes philosophical sense. Like most of these writings, the nine *Homilies* of Basil contain less the systematic exposition of a philosophy than a medley of notions related to the problems which the text of Scripture happened to suggest to his mind.

God has created nature in time, or, rather, together with time, including matter itself. Nevertheless, God has not created a matter common to all beings. Each class of beings has its own matter according to its own nature. In a passage which curiously anticipates some modern criticisms of the notion of substance (I, 8), Basil observes that if we eliminate from a certain being all its properties in order to reach its matter, we shall ultimately reach, not matter, but nothingness. Let us remove from a material thing its color, its temperature, its weight, its odor and all its other sensible qualities, nothing will be left that we might call its matter. As to the general structure of the world,[75] it is in Basil what it will remain up to the end of the fourteenth century. Through its Latin imitator, Saint Ambrose, this *Hexaemeron* will become the common property of the Latin world.

3. GREGORY OF NYSSA

Gregory of Nyssa[76] was educated under the direction of his brother, Saint Basil, but his own work is more than a simple reflection of the thought of his elder. Among his writings, three deserve to detain our attention: his treatise *On the Formation of Man*, widely known in the middle ages under the title *De hominis opificio;* two commentaries *On the Canticle of Canticles* and *On the Eight Beatitudes*, whose influence on the mystical theology of Saint Bernard will be decisive; and the *Dialogue with Macrina on the Soul and the Resurrection*. We must nevertheless first apply to his own *Hexaemeron* for a general introduction to his conception of the world.

A. *Cosmology*

At the beginning of his *In Hexaemeron*, Gregory states his intention not to contradict Basil, but to follow a somewhat different order. In fact, the positive and literal method of interpretation of Holy Scripture prevails in this work. Speaking "in a summary way" (*en kephalaio,* rather than "in the beginning"), Moses says that God created heaven and earth, that is: 1) matter, which is the whole made up of all sensible qualities, each of which, taken apart, is an ideal notion, a pure object of thought; 2) all beings, animate or inanimate; 3) all their powers, causes and occasions. To "say" and to "create" are for God one and the same thing. His Word is "reason," wisdom; consequently, there is a "reason" (or intelligible essence) inherent in every created thing. The cause of all is an illuminating power which created light and fire; after spreading throughout matter, light and fire collected themselves on high and separated themselves from the rest, which became darkness. Thus the earth was "invisible" under the "firmament." Whether it be one of the four higher heavens, or a fifth heaven surrounding the other ones, as the "philosophers out of the pale" say it is, the "firmament" is not a solid body; it has a subtle and indestructible nature, akin to that of fire, and which can be said to be practically incorporeal. Beyond this external limit of the material world are the purely intelligible realities. All that is in motion, is moved in a circular way by a nature perceptible to the mind alone. From this point on, "following its own order, the nature of things added to the principles their necessary consequences." In short, the "order" or explanation which Gregory claims for his own, consists in showing that, when Moses said that God created heaven and earth, he described "in a summary way" the creation of all beings, whose natures necessarily follow from these two principles.[77] The commentary of Gregory on the work of the six days is a cosmogony, which, presupposing the creation of the four elements by God, deduces the nature of things from the elemental properties of fire, air, water and earth. The work of Gregory excels that of Basil by its more systematic elaboration.

B. *Anthropology*

Gregory's doctrine of man is chiefly found in his *De hominis opificio* (On the Formation of Man). Man has been created after all the rest because all the rest has been created for him. Unlike other creatures, he was created in the image of God. This can be gathered from the shape of his body, but still more from his soul (*psykhè*), to which man owes his truly royal dignity. Man is masterless (*adespotos*); he does everything of his own accord; he governs himself, so to speak, with supreme authority; in short, he is a king. Man is not a king unto himself only, but with respect to the whole world. He is in the image of God, because he is a king as God is a king. The beauty that shines in God also shines in man, whose destiny it is to share in an ineffable beatitude through virtue, and thus to become still more similar to his Creator.

Creation is divided into two regions, the visible world and the invisible world. Man belongs in the visible world by his body, in the invisible world by his soul; he is, therefore, their connecting link. Man is the summit of the visible world in that he is an animal endowed with reason. Beneath him are the animals, which have but sense perception, motion and life; then the plants, which have not a perfect soul, since they only grow and feed; then come the inanimate bodies, which have in themselves no vital principle, but without which life would be impossible. Man has not several souls, but his nature ("reason," *logos*) contains all the lower degrees of life: he lives like the plants; he feels like the beasts and he understands because he is man.[78] The main difficulty about man is to account for the union of soul and body. Gregory does not think that the problem can be completely cleared up, but some difficulties at least can be removed.

One of the great merits of Gregory on this point is that he gave a precise interpretation of the Pauline distinction between flesh, soul and spirit. To him this was a moral rather than a physical distinction. The "flesh" is what is pursued by men in quest of carnal pleasures; the "soul" is what is followed by men who wish to acquire virtue and to shun vice; the "spirit" is what leads men to perfect life according to the laws of God. Taken in its philosophical meaning, the soul itself is in us the cause of rational knowledge, and since such knowledge expresses itself in speech, even the body of man had to be that of a talking animal. The soul, or rather the intellect (*nous*), has built itself the bodily instrument it needs in order to know and, by knowing it, to gather within itself the whole world. Its amazing vastness, which enables it to include in its own simplicity the endless variety of things, renders the soul almost as incomprehensible as its model, which is God.

Some philosophers place the soul in the brain; others place it in the heart, and all quote reasons in support of their opinions. Yet, an incorporeal nature cannot be contained in a definite space. Even the fact that organic diseases affect the functioning of our intellectual faculties, does not prove that the soul is *in* the corresponding organs; simply, the soul exercises its powers in a more or less perfect way according to the physical condition of its bodily instruments. Since God is incorporeal, incorporeal being is possible; and since the soul is created in the image of God, it must be incorporeal like its model. Again, just as the existence of God can be proved from the sight of his creation, so also the existence of the soul can be proved from the consideration of man, who is a sort of "smaller world" (*mikrokosmos*), governed by the soul as the greater world (*macrocosmos*) is ruled by God. In short, the union of the soul with its body is that of a created, living and intellectual being, with the bodily organs which it uses as its instruments.

Gregory rejects the pre-existence of souls, because he clearly sees that to admit it necessarily leads to the platonic doctrine of transmigration. On the contrary, he strongly maintains that the union of each human soul with its own body is absolutely indestructible, so much so that, even between death and resurrection, the elements of a dead body are never completely separated from its soul. Leibniz will later on uphold the same position.

Like all the works of God, man has been created good, but the fact that creatures are made out of nothing introduces into their natures an element of mutability. This applies even to man and his free will. Capable of choosing between good or evil, man has chosen evil. But it would be more correct to say that man has made an evil choice, for indeed evil is not a positive reality which one could choose; it is a moral error committed by a created and fallible being. In this sense, it can be said that man has become the "demiurge" of evil. The immediate consequence of this fall of man was to blur with a sort of rust the image of God shining in him. Made in the resemblance of his creator, man has become unrecognizable. His similitude to God was turned into a dissimilitude, and not of the soul only, but of the body as well. Because his sin has consisted in preferring the material part of creation to what in it was divine, man's body was affected by the error of his soul; it became mortal, and mankind would have disappeared with the death of Adam had not God created male and female in order to insure the perpetuity of the human race. The division in sexes is not a consequence of the fall of man, but, rather, of the pre-vision of the fall by the omniscience of God. Without the original sin, men would have multiplied in a purely spiritual way, like the angels; the animal mode of reproduction which man now shares in common with the brutes marks one more degree in his further elongation from God by the loss of the divine resemblance. It is but one of the many consequences of original sin which the return of man to God shall wipe out.[79]

For indeed, this return will take place. In a sense, it will include even the body, which is possible since matter is but a concretion of intelligible qualities. But the soul must initiate the whole process of the progressive rehabilitation of the divine image in man. Covered with rust as it is, it has not been completely deleted. Yet, it has to be partly re-created, and this cannot be done by anyone else than its creator. Since the harm originated in human love turning away from God to creatures, the only possible remedy is a progressive returning of man to God through the holy love of which the *Canticle of Canticles* is the perfect expression. Faith is the first moment of this return, but charity engages him who believes in an effort of moral purification and of spiritual contemplation which is Christian life itself. The result of this effort is a purification of the soul, that is, a reviving of the divine resemblance which had been blurred by sin. A Christian is well advised to follow the advice of Socrates: "Know thyself," for indeed, to know oneself as an image of God is to know God. When this resemblance nears its supreme degree, mystical life begins to yield its most precious fruits: God is in the soul, and the soul is in God. The essentials of this doctrine will provide the framework of the mystical theology of Saint Bernard of Clairvaux. On the contrary, the eschatology of Gregory was too deeply influenced by that of Origen not to become obsolete. In order to insure the complete and final triumph of the Good over evil, Gregory admits that the whole world, purified at last from all pollution, will recover its pristine perfection, without even excepting, after the sufferings required for their purification, the reprobates and the devils. In the ninth century, John Scot Erigena will follow him even on this point.[80]

C. *Theology*

There is in man a "spoken word" (i.e., *logos*) which is an expression of his thought (*nous*). Since we were made in the image of our creator, God too should be conceived as a supreme Thought, that begets a Word. This divine Word is the perfect expression of his Father; not, indeed, a fleeting word like those we utter, but an eternally subsisting and living Word. Since he lives, the Word has a will, and since his will is divine, it is an all powerful and perfect will. Just as our mental words imitate the eternal generation of the divine Word, so also the inseparability of words from thought imitates in us the inseparability of the divine Word from the Father. And just as our breath proceeds from the unity of body and soul, so also does the Holy Ghost indivisibly proceed from both the Father and the Son. Natural reason here bears witness to the truth of the highest among all the Christian mysteries, and it confirms the superiority of the Christian notion of God over those held by the Jews and the pagans. The Jews know the unity of the divine being, but they ignore the plurality of the divine persons; on the contrary, the pagans know the plurality of the divine persons, but they ignore the unity of the divine being; the Christians alone know both, and this is why they know the whole truth. This attempt to rediscover by a dialectical process the truth of the Christian dogma of the Trinity has been aptly compared to the similar efforts of Saint Anselm and of Richard of Saint Victor.[81] In fact, like Anselm and Richard, Gregory attributes a certain reality to essences: if we can understand that Peter, Paul and Barnabas are three distinct persons sharing in the same essence of man, we should also understand how three divine persons may share in the unity of a single divine nature. There is, however, a difference: we correctly say that Peter, Paul and Barnabas are three men, whereas we correctly say of the Father, the Son and the Holy Ghost that they are one single God.[82] The authority of the Council of

Nicaea has obviously drawn a dividing line between orthodoxy and heresy on these questions.

4. NEMESIUS

The Christian writers of the middle ages often got mixed up in two "Gregories." In some cases they blended into a single Gregory the two persons of Gregory Nazianzenus and Gregory of Nyssa; in other cases, they distinguished the men but confused their works; and there were still other cases in which a mediaeval writer attributed to one of them works which neither of them had written.[83] The last remark particularly applies to a very important treatise *On the Nature of Man* (*De natura hominis*), often attributed by mediaeval theologians to Gregory of Nyssa. Its author was Nemesius, a name easily misread for "Nyssenus," the more so as nothing was known about the man. Even today all we know about him is that he wrote this book, *ca.* 400, and that he probably was a bishop of Emesa, in Phoenicia,[84] about the first years of the fifth century.

Like Gregory of Nyssa, Nemesius attributes an exceptional importance to the knowledge of human nature and particularly of the human soul. This science feeds on the liberal arts, but, in turn, it feeds them. It is like the trunk of a tree from which, as so many branches, the other sciences spring forth. Hence the title of the treatise: *Premnon physicon*, that is: the trunk of physical sciences (ed. Burckhard, Prol., p. 3). Made up of body and soul, man is placed on the border line of the world of spirits and of the world of bodies. This is but one particular instance of the universal continuity of order in things which is the most manifest proof of the existence of God (I, p. 7; p. 9, 1-21, p. 10, 1-8). This intermediate situation is also the key to man's destiny; he can save himself or lose himself according as he turns to spiritual goods or to material things. A proper understanding of man's nature here becomes an absolute necessity.

Two notions of the soul offer themselves to our choice: that of Plato and of many other philosophers who consider it a substance; that of Aristotle and of Dicaearchus who alone deny that the soul is a substance. Nemesius takes sides with Plato and maintains against Aristotle that the soul is a substance complete in itself, and not a simple part of the compound "man" (II, pp. 24-25). The soul is "an intelligible substance, able to move itself according to a certain numerical law" (II, p. 24). "The soul therefore can in no way be the perfection of the body, but it is an incorporeal substance which is to itself its own perfection" (II, p. 39). "Plato says that man is not both soul and body, but, rather, a soul using a body." Plato has understood human nature better than Aristotle. If we think that we are our souls, we shall turn to the goods of the soul, which are virtue and beatitude, rather than to the goods of the body (I, p. 6).

All these texts of Nemesius will be quoted by theologians of the thirteenth century, particularly Albert the Great.

Nevertheless, Nemesius is aware of a serious difficulty: if we say that man is a soul using a body and, so to speak, putting it on like a garment, what unity can we attribute to man? A man and his garment do not make up a unity. The answer to this difficulty is provided by Ammonius Saccas (i.e., Plotinus). Unlike corporeal substances intelligible substances can unite without undergoing any transmutation. It is manifest that soul and body are united since the soul shares in the modifications of the body (*quod autem uniatur, compassio demonstrat*). It is no less evident that the soul remains distinct from the body since it separates from it in sleep and ecstasy. Besides it is immortal. Consequently, the soul unites with the body after the manner of intelligible substances, that is, without undergoing any alteration (III, pp. 53-55). The soul is in the body as God is in us (III, 55, 1.23-26). While Nemesius follows Plato concerning the soul, he follows Aristotle concerning the body (IV, p. 61). All those who accept the teaching of Scripture know that God has created all things from no pre-existing matter. Apollinaris says that God has made things out of the "abyss." But, in Genesis, Moses does not mention the abyss as made before things. Rather, we read in Job: "He who made abyss." This word "abyss" simply points out the complete absence of forms in the matter first created by God. Besides, words do not make any difference: God is the creator of all and all things were created by him from nothing (V, p. 70).

The human soul has three powers, or faculties: 1) the imaginative (*phantastica*), an irrational faculty of the soul acting by senses and whose object is the "imaginable" (*phantaston, id est imaginabile*); 2) the phantasy (*phantasia, id est imaginatio*), also an irrational faculty of the soul, or rather, the impression caused in it by an imaginable; 3) the phantasm (*phantasma*), an objectless impression of the soul which no imaginable answers in reality. However, after discussing this Stoic classification, Nemesius concludes that these distinctions are nominal rather than real. He seems more interested in distinguishing the sensible, a corporeal change, from sensibility itself, which he defines the cognition of this change. But he does not say how this discerning of the sensible changes undergone by the five senses is achieved by sensibility (V, pp. 72-73; VII, p. 74); his main interest, however, seems to be the physiological description of the senses and the localization of the imagination in the frontal lobes of the brain.

Memory properly so-called is the power of conserving and reproducing past cognitions. It is localized in the middle ventricle of the brain. To reproduce a past memory is to remember. In a wider sense, memory may signify, as is the case in Plato's doctrine, the cognition of all that which we find naturally contained in our intellect. For instance, the universal certitude that there is a God may be considered the remembering of an Idea (XIII, p. 88).

There are two parts in the human soul, a rational part and an irrational part. According to some philosophers, including Plotinus, the intellect is superadded to the soul, so that, in this view, man is composed of three elements: body, soul and intellect. Apollinaris, bishop of Laodicea,[85] shares this opinion. On the contrary, according to Aristotle, whom Nemesius seems to interpret after Alexander of Aphrodisias,[86] the intellect is naturally in potency in man, but it only becomes in act under an influence from without. In this view, the intellect is not superadded to man in order to complete his essence, but in order to cause his knowledge and contemplation of nature. Aristotle considers that few men, and only among those who philosophize, have this intellect in act (I, pp. 5-6). Personally, Nemesius himself prefers the doctrine of Plato, according to whom man is essentially a soul united with a body and endowed by nature with intellectual cognition.

What we called the irrational soul is not really a soul, but a part and power of the soul (*partem et virtutem*, XVI, p. 93). It itself divides into two parts: one that obeys reason, and one that is not controlled by reason.

The part of the irrational soul which can be controlled by reason divides into the appetitive power and the irascible power. Under these two aspects, the soul is the seat of passions, that is, of modifications caused in our appetitive and irascible powers by the presence of a good or of an evil (XVII, pp. 94-95). The fundamental appetitive passions are pleasures and pains. Following Epicurus, Nemesius classifies pleasures as: both natural and necessary, natural but non-necessary, neither natural nor necessary. Above animal passions are the purely spiritual pleasures, that is, the joys of contemplation. But a joy is not a pleasure; nor is it a passion; it is an action (XVIII, p. 29). Such pains and affections as fear or anger are but particular cases of animal passion as we described it. As to the irrational part of the soul that does not obey reason, it includes the nutritive, generative and vital functions (described ibid., pp. 135-146).

More complex is the classification of the human acts. Their distinction by Nemesius into voluntary and involuntary, inspired of Aristotle, has been influential in the middle ages. Any reader of Thomas Aquinas is aware of the fact (Pegis, *Basic Writings*, II, 1175). Before distinguishing voluntary and involuntary acts, let us define "act." It is, Nemesius says, "a rational operation" (XXIX, p. 109). So far as we can see, he gets somewhat mixed up in this part of his classification, since, while defining acts as essentially rational, he acknowledges the existence of acts that are involuntary, and, consequently, as it seems, irrational. However, the involuntary (*involuntarium*) comprises all the acts imposed from without by violence or occasioned from within by ignorance (XXIX, p. 109). The voluntary (*voluntarium*) is the exact reverse of the involuntary. Whereas the principle of the involuntary act is exterior to the agent, the principle of the voluntary act is interior to it; and whereas the involuntary sometimes follows from our ignorance of the true circumstances of the act, the voluntary implies their detailed cognition. In short, an act is voluntary when its principle is in a subject aware of all the circumstances of the act (XXX-XXXI, pp. 110-113). All that is neither voluntary nor involuntary (for instance, digesting or assimilating) belongs in the purely negative category of the non-voluntary. What could not possibly be voluntary is not even involuntary; it is foreign to the order of the will.

The analysis of the voluntary act, in the doctrine of Nemesius, follows the broad lines of the doctrine of Aristotle. Taken in its whole complexity, such an act includes a deliberation of reason (*consilium*), a rational judgment (*judicium*), and finally a choice (*proairesis, praeelectio,* preference). This choice is a mixed act, where deliberation, judgment and desire blend together. It is none of these elements separately, it is their very unity. A choice, therefore, can indifferently be called either a deliberating desire, or a desiring deliberation (XXXIII, p. 119).

Deliberation itself is not about the end, but about the means. It is necessarily required when, because the attainment of the end is possible, but doubtful, the choice of the means is open to discussion. This implies that deliberation is always about the non-necessary and the non-impossible; its object must be both possible and contingent (XXXIV, pp. 122-124). Last, not the least, deliberation attests the existence of free choice; if he deliberates, a man is the principle of the acts about which there is deliberation (XXXIX, p. 125). This is to say that human reason is the very root of freedom. Man is such as he should be and God has created him such as he had to be: mutable because he is a created being, but capable of choosing the objects of his volitions. Our acquired habits, either good or bad, hang on our acts, and since our acts hang on our own free choice, we carry the responsibility of a life that is truly our own work (XLI, pp. 131-135).

O. Bardenhewer has remarked that the work of Nemesius "belongs really to the history of philosophy," which is true, provided only we keep in mind that, between the *De natura hominis* of Nemesius and the *Hexaemeron* of Saint Basil, the difference is less in nature than in degree. It is also true to say, with the same historian, that Nemesius "chiefly discusses psychological questions and is strongly influenced by neoplatonist thoughts," but one should add that the cause of his psychological interest is a purely Christian one and that he draws from Aristotle and from the Stoics, even from Galenus and Hippocrates, as freely as from Ammonius Saccas and Plotinus. His doctrine is a Christian eclecticism, which freely borrows from all philosophical doctrines, under the guidance of Christian faith. Epicurus himself, when it suits Nemesius' purpose, is freely put to use. His influence, however, will benefit Platonism more than any other doctrine, especially with respect to the definition of the soul, and, consequently, of man.[87] In the minds of the mediaeval doctors who will mistake him for Gregory of Nyssa, unknown Nemesius will become a powerful Christian authority to be quoted against the Aristotelian definition of the soul which makes it to be the form of an organized body and of its organs. Even the history of philosophical ideas is full of accidents.

PART THREE

FROM AUGUSTINE TO BOETHIUS

The Greek Christian writers were able to read the Greek philosophers in their own language. Most of the Latin Christian writers had to use Latin translations in order to draw from the perennial source of metaphysical speculation. For this reason, the work of the Latin translators was extremely important, but it should not be forgotten that certain classical Latin writers, such as Cicero and Seneca, transmitted to their readers some information concerning Greek philosophy. Moreover, the Latin Fathers, and even their mediaeval successors, knew and used a certain number of treatises, either translated from the Greek or directly influenced by Greek thought, dealing with the origin of the world and the destiny of man. Since several of them became known to the middle ages, one should at least be warned of their existence and acquainted with the strange titles under which they were sometimes quoted.[1]

CHAPTER I

VICTORINUS AND AUGUSTINE

I. MARIUS VICTORINUS

THE Christian writings of Marius Victorinus have not yet been critically edited, nor, therefore, properly studied.[2] In the present condition of the texts, no safe interpretation of his doctrine is possible. It is certain, however, that having translated neoplatonist writings, including some *Enneads* of Plotinus, Marius Victorinus himself became as much of a neoplatonist as it was possible to be without ceasing to be a Christian. In comparison with Victorinus, Augustine seems much less concerned with introducing neoplatonism into Christian theology than with limiting its invasion. The theology of Victorinus shows what would have happened if the genius of Augustine had not kept neoplatonism within the strict limits of Christian faith.

Victorinus had found a remarkable adversary in the person of the Arian theologian Candidus.[3] In his treatise *On the Generation of the Divine Word,* Candidus had clearly shown that, to a mind imbued with the Platonist notion of being, the dogma of a begotten God was unthinkable. In *Timaeus* 27 D, Plato had opposed that which is always a being, because it is never begotten, and that which, because it always is being begotten, never is a being. If God *is* being, then he cannot possibly *become* in virtue of any generation; consequently, if the Word is begotten, he cannot possibly be God. Candidus fails to see how this evidence could be questioned: God is immutable, hence he cannot be begotten; God is entity (*ousia*), hence he cannot receive it; again, since God is existence, he cannot possibly come to be. In short, God is being only, so that what he is, is to himself the cause why he is. If this be so, God neither begets, nor is begotten. The Word is not the upshot of a generation, but of a production. He is the first and the principal work of God. This was exactly the same Arian doctrine which Gregory Nazianzenus had opposed in the writings of Eunomius.

The answer of Victorinus to Candidus, at least as we now read it in his treatise *On the Generation of the Divine Word,* is as confused as the objections of Candidus were clear. Yet our theologian has done his best to achieve a correct philosophical statement of the Christian dogma on this point. Since the difficulty originated in the Platonist identification of being with immutability, Victorinus resorted to the doctrine of Plotinus, according to whom even "being" was inferior to unity. Of course, since he had become a Christian, Victorinus was bound to identify the One with God the Father. Having performed this metaphysical operation, he could feel justified in saying that since the One comes before being, God is much less "being" than "pre-being." As such, that is as anterior to all that "is," God is the cause of all. In a text that closely follows Plotinus, Victorinus asks: "What should we say of God: that he is being, or that he is non-being? Assuredly, we shall call him being, since he is the cause of all that is. But the Father of that which is, is not being so long as that of which he is the Father does not yet exist. On the other hand, it is neither permissible to say, nor even possible to conceive, that non-being be the cause of being, for indeed the cause is always superior to its effect. God then is supreme Being, and it is precisely *qua* supreme that he is said to be non-being; not in this sense that God lacks the being of all that is, but in this sense that the Being which is also non-being should be distinguished from the universality of that which merely is. As compared to what has to be begotten (in order to be) God is non-being; as cause of the generation of that which is, he is being." [4] Everything then comes from God, either by way of generation (the Word), or by way of production (the world).

In a language obscure and loaded with Greek terms, Victorinus distinguishes that which truly is, that which merely is, that which is not truly non-being, and that which is not. That which truly is, comprises the "intellectible realities" (*intellectibilia*), that is: Spirit (*pneuma*), Intellect (*nous*), soul (*psykhè*), thought (*noema*), learning (*paideia*), virtue (*aretè*), discourse (*logos*), etc; in the same class but above these, are "existentiality," "vitality," "intellectuality" in themselves. That which merely is comprises the "intellectual realities" (*intellectualia,* as distinct from the *intellectibilia*). These do not subsist in themselves; they are found in human souls whose nature it is to know intelligible objects, though they are distinct from, and subjected to, these objects. Once it has been awakened in a soul, the intellect (*nous*) illuminates and informs it. This is the reason why the soul is a substance (*sub-stantia*): it "understands" because it "stands under" the intellect, or *nous,* by which it is illuminated. When it receives this light, the soul grasps that which truly is, that is the intelligible realities, and, to the same extent, it becomes one of the things that truly are; by knowing, it becomes a "being." [5]

The things that are not truly *non-beings* are those which, because they are generated in matter and perceptible to sense, are less realities than images of true realities. Such are the heavens, and all those things made up of matter and form which constitute the universe. Such things are, at one and the same time, both being and non-being. Even the soul is non-being inasmuch as, being in potency to the light of the intellect, it is on the side of matter. There is matter everywhere there is potentiality, qualitative indetermination and, consequently, possibility of change. The soul is substance to the extent that it understands itself in the very act of knowing intellectible objects; it is matter to the extent that it is in potency to self-knowledge. Let us note, however, that matter itself is not one of those things which truly are not. To be pure potentiality still is to be something, and to be pure indetermination is not to be absolutely nothing. True non-being is that which cannot possibly be, because it is self-contradictory and impossible.[6]

Granting this fourfold division of being, where are we to place God? Beyond these four classes. God is above all existence, above all life, above all knowledge, above being and above the being of all beings. Incomprehensible, infinite, invisible, without intellect, without substance, unknowable, God is nothing of that which is, because he is above all that is. In short, God is non-being; not, however, in this sense that God truly is not, but in this sense that, for him, to be being only is to be the cause of being.[7]

God then is that non-being which contains, hidden in itself, the universality of being. Now the very manifestation of what was hidden is its "generation." The first "being" hidden in the "pre-being," is precisely the Word (*Logos*), who, eternally present in the Father, has been begotten by him. In a surprising metaphysical exegesis of Exod. 3, 14, Victorinus applies to Christ the answer made by Yahweh to Moses: "Thus shalt thou say to the children of Israel: HE WHO IS, hath sent me unto you." [8] So far as we understand him, Victorinus means to say that God, who is "pre-being," has eternally begotten the Word, who, like the *nous* of Plotinus, is being, purely, simply and absolutely.

A modern reader may well wonder where Victorinus could see the difference between his own position and that of Arius. Yet there was one. Candidus considered the Word a creature, whereas, in the mind of Victorinus, the Word was not created from nothing, but begotten by the Father as his self-manifestation. This is the reason why, to him, the Word was truly God. Christ is, *qua* Logos, the external revelation of Being, which, hidden in God the Father, reveals itself in God the Son. In this sense, that is, as cause of the Son who is God, it can be said that God is cause of himself. Assuredly, it is hard to understand how, just as the Son is in the Father, so also the Father is in the Son. For indeed the Father and the Son are not only together, they are one, but, Victorinus says, this is precisely where the mystery of the Trinity lies. We are not asked to understand this, but simply to believe it.[9] Victorinus certainly wished to express, in philosophical terms, the very object of Christian faith, but he had read too much of Plotinus to overcome the temptation of subjecting being to the One. Others, after him, will enter the same way and stumble upon similar difficulties. At any rate, Victorinus will remain in history as a forerunner of Dionysius, Maximus the Confessor, Scotus Erigena and Eckhart.[10] The significance of Augustine, in the history of Christian thought, precisely consists in the fact that, a reader of Plotinus and Victorinus, he nevertheless maintained, together with the primacy of being, its identity with the One and with the Good in the essence of the Christian God.

2. AUGUSTINE

Predominant in the theological writings of Victorinus, hardly visible in those of Saint Ambrose,[11] philosophical speculation was to reach a new peak in the thought of Saint Augustine.[12] It is natural that historians should disagree on the part played in his religious evolution by the reading of some of Plotinus's works. Here, as in many other cases, doctrinal interests interfere with objectively historical interpretation. Yet, all historians agree that the technical formulation of his doctrine betrays a marked neoplatonist influence. His own narrative in *Confessions*, VII, 9, 13, more than confirms the reality of the fact. The general nature of this influence has been accurately summed up by his worthy successor, Thomas Aquinas, in a terse sentence: "Whenever Augustine, who was imbued with the doctrines of the Platonists, found in their teaching anything consistent with faith, he adopted it; and those things which he found contrary to faith he amended." [13] It would be hard, indeed, to say something more accurate about an exceedingly complex case, and to say it in fewer words.[14]

A. *God*

Like most Christian theologians, Augustine conceives God as "being." The well-known text of Exod. 3, 14, which runs through the whole history of Christian thought, is accepted by him in its literal meaning. This alone was enough to separate him from Plotinus. According to Plotinus, the absolutely first principle was the One, which he posited above even being. Now, in the mind of a Christian, there is nothing above God, and since we know from Scripture that God is HE WHO IS, we also know that the absolutely first principle is being. Naturally, Augustine admits that God is the One, but he does not subordinate being to the One; rather, he identifies the One with Being.[15] Because of this fundamental divergence, no two metaphysical statements can have the same import in the doctrines of Augustine and of Plotinus.

For the same reason, the trinitarian doctrine of Augustine, who follows the decisions of the Council of Nicaea (325), is nowhere the same as that of Plotinus. The trinity of Plotinus comprises three universal causes: the One, who is above being; the Intellect, who is both *nous* and being, but is not the Word, or *Logos;* the World Soul, who is the lowest of these three universal causes. The One is above the Intellect and the Intellect is above the World Soul. In Augustine's Trinity, there is equality of the three persons, and unity in essence, that is in being. A theology of the One differs on every point from a theology of Being; a doctrine where the first three universal causes do not share in the same being (*ousia*), is in every respect other than a doctrine where the three divine persons are one single being, one single God.

This fundamental divergence obliged Augustine to attribute a new meaning to the doctrinal elements which he was borrowing from Plotinus, but, at the same time, Plotinus remained present to the mind of Augustine while he was correcting him. For instance, in Plotinus being only appears after the One, with the Intellect (*nous*) who fully deserves the title of Being; whereas, in Augustine, God the Father is Being in his own right. Yet, as a consequence of this doctrinal difference, Augustine applies to God the Father the Plotinian notion of being, conceived as entity itself (*ousia*), always identical with itself, that is, both eternal and unchangeable. Eternity and immutability will always remain the two main attributes of God in the doctrine of Saint Augustine.[16] Even in the middle ages, an Augustinian can always be recognized at once from the fact that, to him as to his master, the highest and the most proper of all the divine names is the eternal and immutable Being.

This fact has important philosophical implications. In a doctrine where God is, before anything else, eternity and immutability, the main metaphysical problem is the relation of becoming to being, of change to immutability, or, in other terms, of time to eternity. In Plotinus, the main metaphysical problem had been the relation of the manifold to the One; in Thomas Aquinas, it was going to be the relation of participated acts of being to the supreme act of *Esse;* in Augustine, it always is the relation of what is ceaselessly becoming "other" in time to what remains immutably the same in eternity.[17] No single proposition can be translated from the metaphysical language of one of these three doctrines into the language of another without undergoing a radical transposition.

Among the many attributes of God, two are particularly important for us. In himself and for himself, God is eternity; with respect to men, God is both light and beatitude.

Saint John says that the Word is the light that enlightens every man that comes into this world (i, 9). Philosophically speaking, this means that the Word is the living and eternal thought of the Father. In other words, he is the self-knowledge of the Father, and, as such, his perfect image and resemblance. In fact, being a perfect expression of the Father, the Word is Resemblance itself, and the model of all other minor resemblances. This is to say that the perfect resemblance of absolute "being" is the model of all that which is, or can be. The Word then contains within himself, or, rather, he *is* all the intelligible patterns, or "reasons," of all that which is capable of existence. These eternal intelligible patterns, or models, are called the divine Ideas. Augustine knows that, taken in this sense, the word Idea comes from Plato; but it was Plotinus who had conceived the second divine principle, that is the Intellect (*nous*), as the seat of the divine Ideas. After Augustine, this notion of the divine Word, conceived as full of the Ideas after whose pattern God has created the world, will become the common property of practically all the Christian theologians. This is why historians sometimes consider "exemplarism" as a typical feature of the Augustinian school in the thirteenth century. For instance, Saint Bonaventure will say, against Aristotle, that nobody who ignores the Ideas can be a metaphysician. But Thomism is no more conceivable than Bonaventurianism without the doctrine of the divine Ideas. To Thomas Aquinas as to Augustine, the Ideas are the very Wisdom of God, which is the "worker of all things" and "reacheth everywhere by reason of its purity" (Wisd. 7, 21 and 24). In short, the Word is the light of the world, because He is the source of its intelligibility, of its order, and of its beauty.[18]

The Word is more particularly the light of human minds. Plato, and after him Plotinus, had clearly seen that, in a world where things are but images, true knowledge is impossible unless the knowing intellect relates things to their models, which are the divine Ideas. This is the reason why Augustine says that Plotinus agrees with Saint John in teaching that: "In the beginning was the Word, and the Word was with God, and the Word was God . . . He was the true light which enlighteneth every man that cometh into this world" (i, 1 and 9). It is not easy to ascertain up to what point Augustine did actually find this in Plotinus, but that he himself thought he had found it there is beyond doubt.[19]

Just as God is light and life by his Word, he is beatitude by the mutual love of the Father and of the Son, that is, by the Holy Ghost. For indeed beatitude is the love of absolute truth, which itself is the absolute knowledge of absolute being, that is, of the supreme Good. Because God is essentially this, he is Beatitude itself and the only possible cause of beatitude for us. Men can be happy only in adhering with their whole heart to the immutable Truth and Wisdom, whose stability alone can redeem them from perpetual becoming in time. For man, as for God, to be happy is "truly to be," that is, if not to be immutable and eternal, at least to become partaker of God's immutability and eternity.[20]

B. *The World*

The main sources of information on the cosmogony of Augustine are his commentaries on the work of the six days (*De Genesi*) and the last three books of his *Confessions* (XI-XIII).

The world has been created by God out of pure love for the intellectual creatures which he wanted to associate to his own beautitude. God spoke, and, since his word was both his will and his power, the world was. In saying that the world was created out of nothing, we mean to say: without any pre-existing matter; yet, obviously, creation presupposes the existence of God. The world only is because God is and because, by a free decision of his supreme goodness, he has willed its existence. To look beyond this for the cause of creation is foolishness: it is to look for the cause of that which has no cause. For the will of God has no cause; it *is* the Cause; and since this cause is the will of a perfect Good, all that God wills must needs be good.[21]

According to Scripture (Ecclus. 18, 1), God has created all things at once. The six days of creation are a metaphor intended to help our imagination. By a single instantaneous act, God has created out of nothing all the beings which then were, and, in them, all those that have come to be ever since the first instant of creation, as well as all those that still are to come up to the end of the world. The created world was big with their "seminal reasons," that is with the seeds, or germs, of future beings, and since to create mutable beings was tantamount to creating time, it can be said that the succession of all future times was created at once, together with the totality of all future beings, in the very instant of creation.[22]

By "heaven" and "earth," Scripture means to designate matter, both visible and invisible, that is, the very mutability of spiritual substances, or angels, and that of corporeal substances, or bodies. As in all created beings, there is in angels an element of mutability, which is matter, but the sweetness of beatific contemplation at once withdrew them from change, so that, changeable by nature, they became immutable in fact. Their mode of duration is neither eternity, which belongs properly to the immutable essence of God; nor is it time, which is the duration of beings whose nature is subject to change; it is *aevum*, that is, the mode of duration proper to mutable natures that do not change[23] because they have achieved their perfection.

Besides this spiritual matter, which it calls "heaven," Scripture mentions the "earth." Whereas "heaven" designated a matter immediately stabilized under its forms, "earth" designates a formless matter, where forms will succeed one another up to the end of time. This matter of corporeal beings does not exist without some form; nor was it created by God prior to forms; rather, corporeal matter is to form in the same relation as inarticulate sound is to articulate voice. Matter is turned into a being by its form as a meaningless sound is turned into a meaningful word by human speech. Its anteriority to form is one of nature, not of time. Taken in itself, matter is neither a being nor a pure nothingness. Farther removed from God than any other creature, it is something that is nearly nothing.[24]

The forms of created beings are so many images of, or participations in, the divine Ideas. From this point of view, each and every thing has a twofold existence, the one in itself, the other in its divine Idea. In God, the thing is God, just as a work of art is but the artist himself inasmuch as it exists in his mind. In itself, the created thing is but an imitation of its model in God, just as a work of art is but an approximation of what the artist had in mind when he made it. This remark applies not only to species, but also to each and every individual. For instance, each and every individual man has his own Idea in God.[25]

The work of the six days describes in a figurative way the many effects caused by the simple creative act of God. Taken as a whole, the universality of beings exhibits a hierarchical structure, determined by their respective degrees of perfection. Since all creatures are images of the divine Ideas, there is not one of them in which the perfection of their common cause does not find its expression. Every created being is determined by an intelligible formula (*ratio*) which defines what it has to be according to its nature; so it has shape, form, order, measure, beauty. Even change and becoming in time can be expressed in intelligible terms by means of numbers. Now, to relate certain beings to other beings by numerical relations is to reduce change to a rule that does not change; in a sense, it is to redeem becoming from time by revealing in it an element of constancy and of true being. Likewise, to grasp several different beings as included within a certain order is to know them as one; consequently, it is to reduce their multiplicity to unity, that is, once more, to true being.[26] This unity of order between the diverse parts of each being, as well as between the diverse beings which make up the universe, concurs with the laws of their succession in time to give the world its beauty. World history then appears as the progressive unfolding of an immense poem, where every single word contributes to the meaning of the whole while it itself derives from it the fullness of its own signification.

C. *Man and Knowledge*

We know from Scripture that God created man a compound of soul and body. Augustine has always maintained that man was neither his soul apart nor his body apart, but the whole which results from their union. Yet, following Plotinus (*Enn.*, I, 1, 3), who himself had followed Plato on this point (*Alcibiades*, 129 E), he has also defined man: "a soul that uses a body." Taken literally, this formula would mean that man is essentially his soul.[27] Augustine himself never took it quite literally, but, rather, as a forcible expression of the transcendent superiority of the soul over the body. Even taken in this limited sense, the Plotinian notion of man has deeply influenced the noetic of Saint Augustine.

All corporeal beings are extended in space and measurable according to the three dimensions. The soul has neither extension nor dimensions in space; hence it is incorporeal. Besides, the soul knows this by immediate self-knowledge. It knows that it exists, that it lives and that it knows. In short, the soul is aware of living the life of an intelligence. Even where, in some philosophies, the soul mistakes itself for a body, it is not truly certain to be a body, but it is certain that it thinks. Let the soul therefore conceive itself as being that which it is sure to be, namely a thinking being. I know that I am because I know that I think and that I live. Even the most extreme scepticism cannot possibly deny this, and since I know myself directly as a knowing being, this is exactly what I am.[28]

Having described man as a soul that uses a body, Augustine finds it hard to understand their union. Since it is immaterial, the soul cannot spread throughout the body, but it exercises in it a permanent act of "vital attention." [29] Nothing of what happens to the body escapes the vigilance of the soul. This active watchfulness is what is pointed out in saying that the soul is the "life" of its body. But this is only possible because the soul is life in itself. Consequently, when the body dies and disintegrates, the soul continues to live. To survive its body is simply for the soul to continue to be what it is. A substance which, like the body, receives its life from without, ceases to be as soon as it becomes unable to receive it; a substance which, like the soul, is life in virtue of its own nature, cannot possibly lose it. The soul then is a spiritual and living substance which is immortal by the very fact that it is a soul.[30]

No superior substance can be acted upon by an inferior substance; so the body cannot act upon its soul. Sensations are not passions undergone by the soul; on the contrary, they are its actions. The human body undergoes actions exercised upon its sense organs by other bodies; since the human soul is constantly exerting a "vital attention" upon all the modifications undergone by its body, these corporeal modifications do not escape its watchfulness. As soon as it is aware of one of them, the soul instantaneously makes up, out of its own substance, one of the spiritual images which we call sensations.[31] This doctrine is in full agreement with the definition of man as a soul using its body; all that which is in the body comes to it from the soul, all that which is in the soul comes to it from within.

This appears still more clearly in the inner structure of the sensations. Each of them is a response of the soul to a corporeal motion that lasts a certain time and obeys a numerical law. In matter, each successive moment of these motions ceases to exist as soon as it is replaced by the succeeding one. On the contrary, every sensation has a certain duration. In order to hear a word of several syllables, I must still remember the first syllable while hearing the last one. In order to hear even a single syllable, I must remember its beginning while hearing its end. Its duration may be very short, yet it has one. If this be true, memory is at work in all our sensations. Now, what is memory, if not one of the clearest manifestations of the spirituality of the soul? Without it, what happens in matter would vanish into nothingness as soon as it happens. A certain redemption of matter from multiplicity and from time is achieved by memory even in the simplest of sensations.[32]

From the point of view of their cognitive value, it should be noted that, in the doctrine of Augustine, sense cognition is not perfectly safe. First, its proper function is to warn the soul of some changes that take place in the body rather than to represent to it the nature of things. Secondly, this nature of material things is itself a changeable one. For these two reasons, no pure truth can be expected from sensations. During the time when he had adhered to the moderate scepticism of the New Academy, Augustine had become acquainted with the main arguments of the sceptics against the truth value of sensations. In his *Contra Academicos,* and later on in his *De Trinitate,* Augustine forcefully maintained the validity of sense knowledge against all these sceptical arguments (sensory illusions, dreams, mental diseases). Yet, wholly sufficient to all practical purposes, these certitudes do not measure up to the standards of pure and unshakable truth. Like Plato, Augustine himself considered intelligible truth the best safeguard there was against scepticism. His doctrine of the divine illumination, to which we now have to turn always remained for him the decisive moment in his own liberation from scepticism.

Since the soul is the cause of its sensations, it is still more obviously the cause of its intellectual cognitions. Yet, on this point, Augustine has often stressed the fact that there is more in intellectual knowledge than in either the thing or the mind. Fully rational knowledge is true knowledge. Now, true knowledge exhibits certain characters which are both distinct and intimately related. Truth is necessary: whether we say that seven plus three are ten, or that wisdom is a knowledge that confers beatitude upon those who possess it, we do not simply know that it is so; we say that it cannot be otherwise. Since truth is necessary, it is immutable, for indeed that which cannot be other than it is, cannot possibly change. Thirdly, since truth is immutable, it is eternal, because that which cannot change cannot cease to be. Now, where could our mind discover these characters of truth? Not in things, for all of them are contingent and, since they all begin and end in time, none of them is either immutable or eternal. Nor can our mind discover these characters in itself, since, like all created things, it is contingent, mutable and enduring in time. The only way to account for these characters of truth in the human mind is to admit that, every time it forms a true judgment, our mind is so to speak in contact with something that is immutable and eternal. But to say "immutable" and "eternal" is tantamount to saying God. The existence of immutable truths in mutable minds is the proof of the existence of God. In other words, the demonstration of God's existence can be considered as included in the epistemology of Saint Augustine.

This proof is confirmed by the common nature of truth. All minds can see the same truth in the same way. Now, since I cannot see it in the mind of any other man, nor make any other man see it in my own mind, there must be a cause which makes us all see it at the same time and in the same way. God is the inner master who teaches the same truth to all the minds that seek after it. He is, so to say, the Intelligible Sun which enlightens the minds of all men. Those who turn away from sensations and purify their souls from vices can raise their minds up to a contemplation of truth that is a sort of intellectual contact with God, but even in the simplest judgment, provided only it be a true one, there is a sufficient foundation for a proof of the existence of God.[33] However different in their details, all the Augustinian itineraries of the soul in quest of God are substantially the same: they go from the exterior to the interior, and from the inferior to the superior; *ab exterioribus ad interiora, ab inferioribus ad superiora.*

D. *Ethics*

Like his anthropology and his noetic, the ethics of Augustine is one with his metaphysics and his religion. Ethical knowledge is a particular case of the divine illumination which itself is an effect of the divine Ideas. The definitions of the circle or of the sphere are eternal and necessary truths, which judge our thought and by which, in its turn, our thought judges particular circles and spheres. But moral truths are just as immutable, necessary and eternal as speculative truths. In their case too, each man sees them in his own mind, and yet they are common to all. All men agree that wisdom is that knowledge by which happiness is obtained; whence they all infer that they should strive to acquire wisdom. Many rules of wisdom are clear: to respect justice; to subordinate the inferior to the superior; to deal with equal things in an equal way; to give everybody his due, etc. All these rules, and many others that could be quoted, are in us so many imprints of an Idea, or of an Intelligible Law, which is for our mind a light. There is therefore a moral illumination of the virtues as there is a speculative illumination of scientific cognitions. In other words, the same metaphysical explanation accounts for the physical illumination of bodies by numbers, for the speculative illumination of minds by science, and for their moral illumination by virtue.[34]

The moral rules whose light shines in us make up the "natural law," whose awareness in us is called "conscience." But moral conscience and the knowledge of virtues are not enough to achieve moral life. Man is not an intellect only, he is also a will, and so long as his will does not conform to the prescriptions of moral truth, there is no morality. The model of the order which should obtain in ourselves, lies before us in nature. The wisdom of God has put everything in its own place and established between things all the relations that befit their natures. This physical "justice" is the ideal pattern after which our own actions should be performed. The four cardinal virtues of prudence, fortitude, temperance and justice are particular expressions of the "eternal law," that is, rules of conduct applicable to the particular problems of moral life. Inversely, the common origin of moral vices is the unjust move of a will that refuses to conform to the prescriptions of the eternal order. More specifically, vices are the disorderly motions of wills which prefer the enjoyment of material goods to enjoyment of intelligible truth. In short, just as God has made the mind a receiver of intellectual illumination, he has made the will the receiver of a moral illumination, through the intellectual illumination of the mind. To be an intellect is not to be wise; to be a will is not to be just, but man can become both wise and just by sharing, as a finite creature can do, in the blessed life of God.[35]

An obvious metaphysical optimism pervades the whole doctrine of Augustine. He never admitted that matter was evil, nor that the soul of man was united with the body in punishment for his sin. Having overcome the gnostic dualism of the Manicheans he never relapsed into it. On the other hand, Augustine never ceased to repeat that the present relations of soul and body were no longer what they used to be. The body of man was not created as a prison for his soul, but this is what it has come to be in consequence of Adam's sin, and the main problem of the moral life is for man to escape from this jail.

Sin, that is, the transgression of the divine law, resulted in a rebellion of the body against the soul. Hence arise both concupiscence and ignorance. Instead of controlling its body, the soul is controlled by it. Turned as it is toward matter, man feeds upon the sensible and since, as has been said, his soul draws sensations and images from its own substance, it exhausts itself in furnishing them. There comes a time when, drained by that loss of substance, the soul becomes unrecognizable, even to itself. It then takes itself to be a body. It is that error, not the body, which is the soul's tomb and the evil from which it has to be liberated.

In his fallen state, man cannot save himself by his own strength. Since it was a creature of God, free will was good; but since it was but a creature, it could not be perfectly good.[36] In other words, the fall of man was not necessary, but it was possible. Now, although he fell by his own free will, the free will of man is not sufficient to raise him again. This was, in Augustine, more than an abstract conviction. The decisive moment in his personal history had been the discovery of sin, of his inability to overcome it without God's grace, and the experience of his success in doing so with divine help. This is the reason why, from the very beginning of his career, and even before knowing Pelagius, he wrote against him as if he had known him.[37] The anti-Pelagian controversies which began about 412, only encouraged him to stress still more forcefully the necessity of grace. True enough, one cannot sustain disputes of this kind for more than twenty years without occasionally overstressing certain points. Having to answer endless objections against the necessity of grace, Augustine had no reason to stress the rights of nature and of free will. His central position has always remained the same: it takes both grace and free will to achieve moral righteousness because grace is an aid granted by God to man's free will. If grace destroyed free will, there would be nothing left to receive its aid. The effect of grace, therefore, is not to suppress free will, but rather to help it to achieve its purpose. This power of using free choice (*liberum arbitrium*) to good purposes is precisely liberty (*libertas*). To be able to do evil is a proof of free choice; to be able not to do evil is also a proof of free choice; but to be confirmed in grace to the point of no longer being able to do evil is the supreme degree of liberty. The man most completely strengthened by grace is also the freest: true liberty is to serve Christ.[38]

This plenary liberty is not accessible to us in this life, but to draw near it during this life is the means of obtaining it after death. Man lost it by turning away from God to the body; man can regain it by turning away from bodies to God. The fall was a movement of cupidity; the return to God is a movement of charity, which is the love of that which alone deserves to be loved. Expressed in terms of knowledge, this conversion to God consists in the effort of human reason to turn from the sensible to the intelligible. As immersed in sensible objects, reason is called "inferior reason"; as striving to break away from sensible objects and to rise up to the contemplation of the divine Ideas, it is called "superior reason." Both Plato and Plotinus already knew that such was the end of man; they themselves seem to have sometimes attained it for a split second in some fits of ecstasy. They knew the goal, but they did not know the way. Because they know both the goal and the way to it, the Christians who philosophize eminently deserve the title of philosophers. For indeed since the goal of philosophy is happiness, to be happy through the enjoyment of wisdom is truly to be a philosopher. Only the Christians are happy, because they alone possess the true Good which is the source of all beatitude, and, with Christ's grace, they will possess it forever and ever.

Only the Christians possess it, but all Christians possess it together. What is called a people, a society, or a city, is a group of men united in the pursuit and love of some common good. All men, pagans and Christians alike, live in temporal cities whose members are united by their common desire for the temporal goods that are necessary to temporal life. Peace, that is, tranquillity born of order,[39] is the most lofty of these desirable goods, because it includes all the others. But besides being members of these temporal cities, Christians make up another one, whose citizens are the men who, living by the same faith, are united by their common love of the same God and by their common pursuit of the same beatitude. Considered as organizing themselves in view of earthly goods and apart from God, all temporal cities can be considered as forming together a single "Earthly City," whose history begins with the earliest days of mankind; considered as organizing themselves into a Church, whose aim and scope it is to lead them to eternal beatitude, all Christians integrate a single "Heavenly City," which can justly be called the "City of God." The citizens of this City are recruited from among all the Christians who, having lived in any temporal city, at any place and in any time, have been, are or will be united together by their common love for the supreme Good. Ever since the origin of mankind, these two cities have been blended together, because even Christians need to live in temporal cities in order to avail themselves of the temporal goods that are necessary for life; but Christians only use these goods; they do not enjoy them as the ultimate objects of their love. So Christians will go on living a spiritual life of their own in the very middle of temporal cities up to the end of the world, when the Earthly City and the Heavenly City will ultimately separate and be constituted apart on the day of God's judgment.[40]

The progressive building up of the Heavenly City was the true end of God in creating the world. Present at the very moment of creation and carried on unceasingly ever since, this divine design gives universal history its meaning. The monumental treatise of Augustine, *The City of God,* has precisely for its object to retrace in bold outline a theology of history for which all historical events are so many moments of implementing a plan which has been foreseen and willed by God. World history is the temporal manifestation of a mystery which is that of divine charity always at work to restore a creation disordered by sin. The predestination of the chosen people to beatitude is the highest expression of this very charity. Why some are to be saved and not others, is the secret of God; in meditating upon this mystery, let us remember at least this, that ever since the fall of Adam, no single man has any *right* to be saved; salvation is a work of love, not of justice, and the mystery is much less why all men are not saved, than why some of them are. One thing at least is sure; God never condemns a man without a fully justified equity, even if the equity of his sentence remains so deeply hidden from us that our reason cannot even suspect what it is.

The work of Saint Augustine has always remained a landmark in the history of Christian thought. Anselm of Canterbury will pride himself on saying nothing that Augustine had not said before him; in the thirteenth century, the so-called "Augustinians" will strive to maintain his main philosophical positions against the rising tide of Aristotelianism, and even their opponents will proclaim their intention to restate his doctrine in a more accurate way. Historians have often quoted Augustine as a typical instance of what has been called "the Platonism of the Fathers."[41] That Plato has influenced Augustine, through Plotinus, is beyond discussion, but his doctrine cannot be reduced to those of either Plato or Plotinus. Any attempt to interpret Plotinus in the light of Augustine, and vice versa, would be doomed to failure; the two doctrines do not aim to reach the same goal; they disagree on the first principles and the consequences which they deduce from these two distinct sets of principles are not the same. The truth is that, in interpreting his Christian view of the world by means of a modified Plotinian technique, the philosophical speculation of Augustine met some serious obstacles, almost all connected with his initial notion of the soul and of man. The next philosophical reinterpretation of Christian thought will be the work of Thomas Aquinas. But even Thomas Aquinas would have considered himself a true disciple of Augustine. In point of fact, few men have had better reasons for doing so.

CHAPTER II

END OF THE GREEK PATRISTIC AGE

THE end of the fourth century abounds in interesting figures such as Macarius the Egyptian,[42] Synesius[43] and Theodoret of Cyrus,[44] but the works which now bear the name of Denis the Areopagite far surpass in importance all the Greek theological writings of that time. This collection of theological treatises, often called *Corpus Areopagiticum,* is one of the main sources of mediaeval thought. The theologian who wrote them was supposed to have been a disciple of the Apostles and even an intimate friend of some of them. In point of fact we know nothing about the person of this theologian, not even that his name was Denis. The date of his works is uncertain.[45] We shall, however, continue to call him Denis the Areopagite, or simply Denis, being well understood that this name simply designates the otherwise unknown author of the *Corpus Dionysiacum.*

I. DENIS THE AREOPAGITE

The treatise richest in philosophical data that has come to us under the name of Denis is an essentially theological work. Starting from the fact that Holy Scripture gives God a variety of names it establishes in what sense these names apply to God. Hence the title of the treatise: *On Divine Names (De divinis nominibus).* The author begins by affirming his intention to say nothing about God that is not found in, or cannot be proven by, Holy Scripture. For God alone knows himself; he alone, then, can make himself known to those who seek him with humility. Even in Scripture God speaks of himself in terms borrowed from creatures that represent him in various ways. Since creatures are participations in the supreme Good, which is God, every one of them represents him according to its own degree of perfection. The problem, then, is for the theologian to determine what can be known and said of God, whom we do not know, starting from his creatures which we know. This can be successfully done only with the help of Scripture, where so many names are given to God. Still, even these names require some interpretation.[46]

In a lost treatise on the *Theological Foundations,* Denis had proven that God is absolutely incomprehensible to the senses and to reason; consequently, since we cannot know him directly, we cannot name him directly. The only way correctly to name him from the names of creatures involves a threefold operation. First, we affirm that God is what Scripture says he is: One, Lord, Powerful, Just, etc. This first moment, which is common to both the simple believers and the theologians, constitutes what is called the "affirmative theology." But the theologians know that such notions as oneness, lordship and power, cannot possibly apply to God in the same sense as to creatures; hence, for them, the necessity of denying that God is any one of those things in the only sense which we can give to their names. If to be "one" means to enjoy the sort of unity which belongs to sensible beings, then God is *not* one. We have no positive notions of his oneness, lordship, power, etc. This second moment constitutes what the theologians call the "negative theology." These first two moments are then reconciled in a third one, which consists in saying that God deserves these names in a sense which, because it is incomparably higher than that in which it applies to creatures, is inconceivable to human reason. This Denis calls "superlative theology." God is "Hyper-Being," "Hyper-Goodness," "Hyper-Life," and so on. Denis has given a striking example of negative theology in his short treatise on *Mystical Theology*. The conclusion of this work is a series of negations, followed by a series of negations of these negations, for God is above all negations and all affirmations. What is affirmed about God is beneath him. His not being light does not mean that he is darkness; his not being truth does not mean that he is error; rather, because God is the inaccessible Cause of all things, he transcends both what can be affirmed or denied of him from our knowledge of his effects.[47]

In the *Divine Names,* God appears as deserving, before any other name, that of "the Good." The reason for this is clear: we can approach him only through his creatures, and it is by right of supreme Good that God has created them. In this sense, the God of Denis closely resembles the Idea of the Good described by Plato in his *Republic* (VI, 509), which is "not only the author of knowledge to all things known, but of their very entity, and yet is not entity, but far exceeds entity in dignity and power." Like the visible sun which, without having either to reason or to will, but from the sole fact of its existence, begets all those beings which its energy makes to grow, so also the divine Good, of which the visible sun is but a pallid likeness, bursts forth into natures which, after springing forth from him, strive to return to God.[48]

The world of Denis can be best described as a circulation of the good, from the Good and toward the Good. Denis himself speaks of it as of an "illumination" which, developing by degrees and weakening as it proceeds farther and farther from its source, naturally begets a hierarchy. To be a member of a "hierarchy," as Denis understands it, is both to occupy a certain place on the universal scale of beings and to exercise a certain function. A being has the very nature defined by its degree of elongation from God; pure Intelligences are at the top, matter is at the bottom. Moreover, each and every member of this universal hierarchy receives the divine illumination which makes it to be, and to be what it is, only in order to transmit it, in turn, to a lower rank.

The divine light and the being which it confers are the illuminative cascade whose steps are described by the treatises *On Celestial Hierarchy* and *On Ecclesiastical Hierarchy*. This "illumination" must not be conceived as a simple gift of light to already existing beings, but as the gift of a light which *is* their very being.[49] From the being and substance of that which has neither life nor soul, through the life of plants and the unreasoning souls of animals, up to rational beings and intellectual substances, all that merits to any degree the title of "being" is a definite moment of this illuminative effusion of the Good. What we call creation, then, is the very revelation or manifestation of God through his works. Denis calls this manifestation a "theophany." This doctrine justifies the use which Denis makes of the "divine names." Itself a "theophany," the world should enable us to know something about God. In fact, since each being is good inasmuch as it is, its cause must needs be "the Good"; but God cannot possibly be good in the same way as his creatures are good; consequently we must deny that God is good; on the other hand, the reason why God is not good is not that he is beneath goodness; rather, he is above it; our negation then must become an affirmation: God is not good, because he is the "Hyper-Good."

The same method applies to the other divine names: Light, Beauty, Life and so forth. Among these names, Love plays a particularly important part because it is through the divine love that all beings which radiate from God strive to return to him as to their source. Love is in each being as an active energy which, so to speak, draws it out of itself, in order to bring it back to God. This is what we mean in saying that of its very nature, Love is "esctatic" (*exstare*). Its natural effect is to place the lover outside of himself and to transform him into the object of his love. From this point of view, the universal circulation of being, from the Good and toward the Good, is a circulation of the divine love. Its effect in this life, and its term in future life, is a certain divinisation (*theosis*) of the loving creature which its love assimilates to, and unites with, God.

In such a universe, which is but the manifestation of the Good, all that which is, is good. Following the teaching of Proclus (411-485), Denis maintains that, as a consequence of what precedes, evil is, of itself, non-being; its appearance of reality is due only to the semblance of good it affords. This is precisely how evil deceives us, for although it be without substance or reality, it exhibits an appearance of good. God, therefore, is not the cause of evil, but he tolerates it because he governs natures and freedoms without using compulsion. In a work now lost *On the Just Judgment of God,* Denis had shown that a perfectly good God can with justice punish the guilty, because they are guilty of their own free will.

To say that God is the "Hyper-Good" is to name him with regard to creation, of which his goodness is the cause; with regard to himself, the best name which we can borrow from creatures in order to designate him is "Being." God is HE WHO IS (Exod. 3, 14), and by that right he is the cause of all being. He even is being for all that is, in this sense that, existing eternally in himself, he is that by which all the rest exists by mode of participation. In the temporal images of God, being comes first of all and this first participation is the foundation of all the others. Because a thing has first to be in order to be something else,[50] this participation in being necessarily precedes all other participations.

Taken in God, all these participations are one in him, as the radii of a circle are one in their center, or as numbers are one in unity. As models or patterns of possible beings, their prototypes in God are called Ideas; as active and causal forces, these prototypes are also called "divine volitions" or "predestinations." [51] Let us note, however, that there is in Denis a marked tendency to subordinate the divine Ideas to God. The reason for it is that, according to him, even being is just a "divine name." Accordingly, it cannot be correctly applied to God without being first affirmed, secondly denied, and thirdly reaffirmed in a transcendent way. Strictly speaking, God is no more Being than he is the Good; he is "Hyper-Being." Now, inasmuch as the other participations presuppose a first participation in being, God, who is beyond being, is beyond all the other participations. This principle applies to the divine Ideas themselves. As Denis himself says in the *Divine Names,* Ch. V, 5: "It is through their participation in being that the various principles of being exist and become principles; but they exist first, and then they become principles." It is because the Ideas are the first manifestations of God that they come after God, and it is because they are participations in being that they come after "Hyper-Being." Ideas are so many divine rays scarcely removed from their center, and yet already distinct from it.[52]

For this reason, Denis often resorts to the terminology of Plotinus and of Proclus. Rather than call God Being, he prefers to call him the One. God contains all within himself in a pure unity innocent of all multiplicity, because he is not the sum total of multiplicity, but its source. The multiple cannot exist without the One, but the One can exist without the multiple. All that exists participates in the One; on the contrary, the One participates in nothing. Hence God is both perfect and self-sufficient. One in his incomprehensible Trinity, the One is the principle and the end of everything else, that from which everything flows and to which everything returns. Yet, like being, "one" cannot be properly affirmed of God unless it has first been denied of him. God is not a unity made up of three other unities, which is the only kind of trinity we are able to imagine. He is no more One than he is Being. In short, God has no name. Because he is nothing of what does not exist and nothing of what does exist, no being can know him as he is. To know him as above all affirmation and all negation, that is, to know that he cannot be known, is the mystical ignorance in which the supreme degree of knowledge consists. Other ignorances can be dispelled by acquiring the lacking knowledge; this one, on the contrary, consists in an excess of knowledge to which one is raised by going beyond all possible cognition. So long as, in contemplating God, a man comprehends what he contemplates, what he is really contemplating is not God, but one of his creatures. Ignorance is necessarily the highest form of knowledge, in a case where knowledge strives to attain an object that lies beyond being.[53]

This view of a world emanating from God and flowing back to its source will become the common property of all the Christian theologians. The doctrine of Denis called for many precisions and corrections or, rather, for a reinterpretation in terms of a metaphysics of being; yet, such as it was, it has provided Christian thinkers with a general framework within which their interpretation of the world could easily take place. Moreover, the authority of Denis could not be lightly dismissed. Up to the time when Laurentius Valla and Erasmus will raise the first doubts on the subject, the author of the *Corpus Areopagiticum* will be unanimously accepted as a disciple of Saint Paul and perhaps a witness to some esoteric teaching of Christ belatedly revealed to the rank and file of the Christians. The works of Denis were several times translated into Latin during the middle ages and turned to account or commented by John Scotus Erigena, Hugh of Saint Victor, Thomas Gallus, Robert Grosseteste, Albert the Great, Bonaventure, Thomas Aquinas, etc. Among his followers, some will embrace his Platonism with enthusiasm; others will strive to tone it down and to make it more acceptable to Latin minds; all will be indebted to him for some aspect of their own thought.

2. MAXIMUS OF CHRYSOPOLIS

Ever since the ninth century and throughout the whole late middle ages, the doctrine of Denis has remained inseparable from that of his commentator, Maximus of Chrysopolis,[55] commonly called Maximus the Confessor (580-662). In fact, the commentaries on Denis commonly attributed to Maximus partly belong to John of Scythopolis, whose annotations, written about 530/40, were blended with those of Maximus by Byzantine copyists. It has become practically impossible to distinguish between the respective contributions of John and of Maximus.[56] Let us then remember that, when we say Maximus Confessor, it would often be just as correct to say John of Scythopolis.

Full as he was of Denis's doctrine, his commentator has nevertheless presented it in his own way, and it is necessary to consider his interpretation in itself, because, on certain points, it has exercised its influence independently from that of Denis. God is not a being; rather he is beyond being and entity.[57] God is pure Monad, that is, not that numerical unity which engenders numbers by addition, but rather, the source from which the manifold springs forth without altering its absolute simplicity. Inasmuch as it begets multiplicity, the Monad initiates a movement. Owing to this movement of the Divinity (*kinesis théotètos*), its being and the nature of its being begin to appear to intellects capable of knowing such objects.

The first movement of the Monad gives rise to the Dyad by generation of the Word who is its total manifestation; then the Monad proceeds up to the Triad by the procession of the Holy Ghost. The first movement of the Monad stops there because its highest manifestation is now perfect: "For our cult does not appeal to a petty monarchy consisting of a single person" (like that of the Jews) "nor, on the other hand, to a monarchy confused and which loses itself in an infinity of gods" (like that of the pagans) "but indeed to the Trinity of the Father, the Son and the Holy Ghost who are naturally equal in dignity. Their riches is that very accord, that irradiation at once distinct and one, beyond which divinity does not diffuse. Thus, without introducing a nation of gods, we shall not conceive divinity as a poverty bordering on indigence." [58]

This first movement precedes a second one, by which God manifests himself outside himself, in beings that are not God. The Word, who is a perfect knowledge of the Monad, contains eternally within himself the very entity (*ousia*) of all that exists or is ever to exist. Each of these future beings is eternally known, willed, decreed in him, to receive existence in due time. God does not make a special decree each time a new being appears. All is eternally contained in the infinite foreknowledge, will and power of God. As objects of the prescience of God, these cognitions are called Ideas. Each Idea is a partial and limited expression of God's perfection. And not only its expression, but its manifestation. The eternal manifestation of God by the production of beings after the pattern of their Ideas is called creation. By an effusion of pure goodness, the divine Triad radiates those expressions of itself called creatures. The whole of creatures makes up a sort of hierarchy where each of them occupies a place determined by its proper degree of perfection. Some of them are as permanent as the world itself; others pass away and are replaced by those which come to take their places at the moment fixed for them by the wisdom of God.[59]

Among creatures, many have no other destiny than to imitate God according to their essences. These can be only what they are, but others are capable of determining to a certain extent what they will become, and, consequently, their own place in the hierarchy of beings. Such creatures

are capable, through the decision of their free will, of increasing or decreasing their likeness to God. According to the good or bad use which
they make of their knowledge and of their will, they embark upon the
road of virtue or of vice, of good or of evil, of reward or of punishment.
In fact, any voluntary increase in divine resemblance is accompanied by
an enjoyment of God which is its own reward; any voluntary non-partici-
pation entails, on the contrary, an exclusion from this enjoyment, and this
is their punishment.

Man is one of these beings. He is made of a body which, because it is
material, is divisible and perishable; and of a soul which, because it is
immaterial, is indivisible and immortal. Since the body cannot exist without the soul, it cannot have existed before it. Conversely, the soul cannot
have existed before its body. Those who concede the pre-existence of souls
to Origen are led to the error of believing that God only created the body
as a prison where the souls of sinners suffer punishment for their crimes.
The eternal will of God cannot have been determined by the future behav-
ior of mere creatures. Through his pure goodness, and for the good of
man, God has willed the body as well as the soul. It is therefore only
reasonable to admit that soul and body come into being simultaneously in
virtue of an eternal divine decree.

Originally created on the border line between pure spirits and pure
bodies, man was intended to be their connecting link. He was in touch
with both the multiplicity of matter by his body and with the unity of
God by his mind. His own function was therefore to gather up the multiple
into the unity of his intellectual knowledge, and thus to re-unite it with
God. In point of fact, man did just the contrary; instead of re-uniting the
multiple by bringing things back to God, he lessened unity by turning
away from the knowledge of God toward the knowledge of things. Now,
for any being, to be one and to be are one and the same thing. By thus
turning away from unity, man nearly relapsed into non-being. In order
to save man from impending destruction, That whose nature is entirely
immobile, or, in other words, That which moves only immovably within
itself, began to move, so to speak, toward fallen nature in order to create
it anew. The Word was made flesh to rescue man from perdition. God
restored human nature to unity by bringing together the natures of body
and soul in the person of Christ. For indeed Christ took on the whole
nature of man, except sin, in order to free him from sin. Moreover, by
being born of a non-carnal act of generation, Christ revealed that another
way of multiplying mankind was possible and that the division of the sexes
had only been made necessary because man had lowered himself to the
level of dumb beasts by misusing his liberty.

This union of human nature and of divine nature is the very redemption
of man. The end of our restlessness is to rejoin the immutability of God.
Now, for a mind, to move is to know. To move toward God then is to

strive to be assimilated to him by knowing him. But God is the good and one cannot know the good without loving it. In knowing God man begins to love him. Placed outside of himself in the object of his love man undergoes a sort of ecstasy; he rushes headlong with an increased velocity, nor will he stop until he is completely absorbed within his Beloved and, so to say, embraced by him on all sides. Free from fear as well as from desire man then wishes for nothing more than this very saving envelopment and the awareness of being thus embraced in God who embraces him. Man then is like unto iron liquefied by fire, or like air wholly illumined by the presence of light. Blessed ecstasy where human nature shares in the divine resemblance to the point of becoming that very resemblance so that, without ceasing to be itself, it passes into God. When this happens, man no longer lives; rather, Christ lives in man.

In thus moving toward God by knowledge and love, man is simply returning to his own Idea in God. Even while he himself is wandering away from God, his Idea remains there. Every man is a part of God (*moira théou*) to the extent that, by his Idea, his essence is eternally pre-existent in God. Ecstasy is an earnest of life to come when the divinization (*theosis*) of the universe will be achieved by the returning of all things to the eternal Ideas, essences, natures and causes from which they now are separated. Maximus foresees a time when the universe will be brought back to God by the returning of man to his Principle. For man is the center of creation, and since, by his defection, the other beings were exiled from their principle, his return to God will bring about the return of the whole world. The division of human beings into two distinct sexes will be the first to go; next, the inhabited earth will be metamorphosed by uniting with earthly paradise; the earth will then be like unto heaven because men will become like unto angels; finally, the difference between sensible and intelligible beings will be abolished. Having been the first ones to appear, intelligible beings will be the last ones to disappear, but they finally must vanish, in this sense at least that they will not eternally remain in their present state of separation. Ultimately, all things shall be reunited with their eternal essences, or Ideas. God will then be All in All, to everything, and forever.[60]

This synthesis of what Christian thought could retain of Origen's teaching will become the very framework of the doctrine of John Scotus Erigena. A world that is but the self-revelation of God; whose creation is but the act whereby God declares, as it were, the intelligible essences in which his Word is so rich; where these essences, or intelligible entities, fall away from their origin by an error of man's judgment and, owing to the incarnation of Christ, are brought back to their origin through man's knowledge and love—these were vast perspectives. In point of fact, after being purified of their excessive neoplatonism and translated into a metaphysics of being more suitable to the Christian notion of God, these views will dominate the Sums of theology and the Commentaries on the Sentences during the whole age of scholastic theology. The general plan of the scholastic theologies will always remain: God, the divine names, the creation of the world, the fall, the restoration of creation by the incarnation of the divine Word and the final return of creation to its creator. The long and slow maturation of Christian philosophical thought will take place, during centuries within the general framework set up by Denis, John of Scythopolis and Saint Maximus Confessor, while the development of speculative mysticism will draw its inspiration either from its doctrine of ecstatic love (Bernard of Clairvaux) or from its invitation to intellectual contemplation (Albert the Great). Both tendencies will unite in the mystical theology of Thomas Aquinas.

3. JOHANNES PHILOPONUS

The obvious influence of neoplatonism on Christian speculation should not make us forget the no less manifest resistance of Christian thinkers to the doctrines of the eternity of matter or of the transmigration of souls. Two Syrian teachers, Aeneas of Gaza[61] and Zacharius Rhetor,[62] bear witness to the survival of this controversy during the sixth century. Johannes Philoponus, who belongs to the same period,[63] is a more important representative of this permanent dialogue between Christianity and Platonism, but the very versatility of his mind makes it difficult to encompass his thought within anything like a definition.

As a theologian, Philoponus is known to have taught that there are in God three "partial essences," plus an essence common to the three divine persons. The treatise in which he maintained this "tritheistic" position, *The Arbiter,* is now lost. In another lost treatise *On the Resurrection,* Philoponus upheld the view that resurrected bodies will not be identical with our present bodies. We still have his commentary *On the Creation of the World,* in which he begins by forcefully stating that the biblical account of creation is neither a scientific nor a philosophical explanation of the origin of things, but an invitation to seek after God and to live in conformity with his laws. In his treatise *Against Proclus on the Eternity of the World,* which has also been preserved, Philoponus continues the classical controversy between Christians and neoplatonists on the precise meaning of the notion of creation.[64] His commentaries on Aristotle, especially that on the Third Book of *On the Soul,* are the only part of his work which has exercised a deep and lasting influence upon mediaeval thought.

Himself a Christian, Philoponus could not write commentaries on Aristotle without stumbling upon many difficulties. In point of fact, he sometimes found himself at grips with the very same problems which Saint Thomas was to solve later on in refuting Averroes. The controversy between Philoponus and Simplicius foreshadows that of Thomas with

Averroes in the thirteenth century and even that of Brentano with Zeller in the nineteenth century. Absolutely speaking, it has not yet come to an end.

According to Philoponus, all the interpreters of Aristotle agree in admitting that every man has a possible intellect of his own, but they differ on the agent intellect. Some say that the agent intellect is universal, since it is God. The reason they give is that since it is sometimes in potency the being of the human intellect cannot be that of an act; hence the only intellect that can be essentially act is God. This doctrine of God as universal agent intellect will be taken up and blended with the doctrine of Augustine on divine illumination by several theologians of the thirteenth century. Yet, Philoponus adds, others say that the agent intellect is not God, but a being both inferior to God and superior to man (*demiourgos*), which illumines our souls and confers upon them a light proportionate to their nature; still others, on the contrary, place within the soul itself the principle of intellectual knowledge. Consequently, the latter posit two intellects in every soul: the one, which is the "possible intellect," belongs to each soul in virtue of its own nature and is always present in it; while the other one, the "agent" intellect, acts intermittently every time it illumines the possible intellect. Philoponus notes that the supporters of this thesis quote Plato as an authority in its favor, but without valid reason. The fourth interpretation of Aristotle is the true one: every man possesses his own intellect, and it is the same intellect that is now in potency, then in act.[65] Was this interpretation of Aristotle correct? This is a debatable question. Aristotle's own text is obscure on this point and his interpreters have understood it in many different ways. At any rate, Philoponus has interpreted it in a way which permitted its reconciliation with the teaching of Christianity concerning man. Unless every human soul has its own intellect, personal immortality is impossible. In Philoponus' own words, this interpretation makes it possible to uphold the immortality of the rational soul at least, even though all the other parts of the soul were mortal. The Christian Philoponus was thus breaking away from the doctrine of Alexander of Aphrodisias on the oneness of the agent intellect common to all human souls, just as, in the thirteenth century, Thomas Aquinas was to break away from Averroes, and for practically the same reasons.

In kinetics, Philoponus gives proof of the same freedom of mind. In his commentary on Aristotle's *Physics* (*ca.* 517), he turns against the doctrine according to which the shock communicated to air by someone throwing a missile, accompanies it and thus keeps it going. Against this explanation of the continuation of motion, which will be maintained by most mediaeval philosophers on the authority of Aristotle, Philoponus upholds that when we hurl a ball, we impart to it a certain moving force, or "kinetic energy," which continues to propel it after it has left the hand.

This theory will be known, in the middle ages, as the doctrine of the *impetus,* or "impulse." We will see it upheld against Aristotle's doctrine in several mediaeval authors.[66]

4. JOHN DAMASCENE

The last great name in Greek patristics known to the scholastic theologians is that of John of Damascus, commonly called John Damascene.[67] His main work, *The Source of Knowledge,* contains a philosophic introduction[68] then a short history of the heresies[69] and, finally, in the third part, a collection of texts, taken from his predecessors and arranged in systematic order, about the fundamental truths of the Christian religion. This third part, translated *ca.* 1151 by Burgundio of Pisa (one of the two Latin translators of Nemesius), was to serve as a model for the *Book of Sentences* of Peter Lombard. It will be frequently quoted in the thirteenth century under the title *De fide orthodoxa,* that is, *On True Faith.*

John Damascene did not claim to do any original work in philosophy, but to organize a handy collection of philosophical notions useful to the theologian. Some of the formulas he put into circulation have had an extraordinary success. From the very beginning of *De fide orthodoxa* he affirms that there is not a single man in whom the knowledge that God exists is not naturally implanted. This statement will be often quoted in the middle ages, sometimes with approbation, sometimes with adverse criticism. John Damascene himself does not seem here to be speaking of an innate knowledge properly so-called, for he gives as the sources of this knowledge the sight of created things, their preservation and the order they observe; next, the Law and the Prophets; and finally the revelation of Jesus Christ. In addition, beginning with Chapter III, John Damascene undertakes to prove the existence of God, for although the knowledge of God may be implanted in us naturally, Satan's malice has so obscured it that the foolish person goes so far as to say, in his heart: God does not exist (Ps., 13, 1). God has proved by his miracles that he exists, and his disciples have done the same by the gift of teaching which they had received from him: "But we who have received neither the gift of miracles nor this gift of teaching (because we made ourselves unworthy of it by an excessive propensity to pleasure), we have to discourse on the subject with what little the interpreters of grace have told us about it."

That is why, working on the Pauline principle that we can know God only through his creatures, John Damascene established the existence of God by showing that all that is known to us is sense experience and is mutable; that nothing of what comes into being by way of change is non-created; that everything known to us in that way is created, and that consequently its non-created Creator exists. A second argument drawn from the preserving and governing of things confirms the first, and the proof reaches completion in a third argument which proves, contrary to Epicurus, that the order and distribution of things cannot be the result of chance. This God whose existence is thus proven is unknowable to us: "It is evident that God exists; but what he is, as far as his being and his nature are concerned, we are entirely unable to grasp or to know (*akatalèpton touto pantélôs kai agnôston*)." We know that God is incorporeal. He is not even made of that incorporeal matter which Greek scientists call the "fifth essence" (quintessence). Similarly, God is non-begotten, immutable, incorruptible and so on; but with such words we tell what God is not, not what he is. All we can understand about him is that he is infinite and consequently incomprehensible. As to the positive names we give him, neither do they tell what he is nor describe his nature, but only what is predicable of his nature. We say that the Incomprehensible and Unknowable, which is God, is one, good, just, wise and so forth; but the enumeration of these attributes does not enable us to know the nature or the essence of the one to whom we attribute them. In fact, like the Good of Plato, the God of John Damascene is beyond knowledge because he is beyond entity. John Damascene interprets in this sense even the name God is given in the oft-quoted text of *Exodus* (3, 14): "I Am Who Am (*ho ôn*)." Properly understood, this name designates his very incomprehensibility, since it signifies that God "possesses and gathers within himself the totality of being, like some infinite and boundless ocean of entity (*ousias*)" (I, 9). This formula, borrowed by John Damascene from Gregory Nazianzenus, was frequently to be taken up and commented upon during the middle ages, in particular by Saint Thomas Aquinas.[70] In its comprehensive plan which includes the study of the angels, the visible heavens, the stars, the elements, the earth and man,[71] the *De fide orthodoxa* already presents itself as a work distinctly scholastic in aspect, whose very technicality was to interest the theologians of the thirteenth century and to serve as a model for their *Commentaries on the Sentences* or their *Sums of Theology*. Not only was its plan to be their inspiration, but it was to be exploited as a ready mine of notions and definitions, many of which could be immediately taken up by theologians familiar with Aristotle. Chapters XXII-XXVIII of Book II, on will, on the difference between the voluntary and the non-voluntary, on free will considered in its nature and its cause,[72] have handed down to the middle ages a great many notions, most of them Aristotelian in origin, but probably collected by John Damascene from the works of Gregory of Nyssa or Nemesius. Although he does not rank as an outstanding thinker, John Damascene has been a useful transmitter of ideas. One must certainly acknowledge him to be one of the most important intermediaries between the culture of the Greek Fathers and the Latin culture of Western theologians in the middle ages, including the greatest among them, such as Saint Bonaventure and Saint Thomas Aquinas.

5. THE PLATONISM OF THE FATHERS

The general impression left by Greek patristics is that its dominating philosophical inspiration was Plato's and the neoplatonists'. This was assuredly not the only one. On the contrary, we have seen some early Fathers accepting a materialistic conception of the soul, and hesitating to admit its survival between the death of the body and its resurrection. Elements of Aristotelian or Stoic origin have sometimes been welcomed by Christian writers of Greek culture. Yet, historians have often spoken of the "Platonism of the Fathers," as if their theologies were simple adaptations of neoplatonism. The problem goes beyond the bounds of Greek patristics, as it arises with regard to Saint Augustine as well, but all the data are contained in the work of the Greek Fathers and the answer is the same in both cases.[73]

It is important first of all to be forewarned against an almost inevitable error of perspective. The very attempt to discern the philosophical elements which theologians have used in their work throws these elements into an exaggerated relief with respect to the very theologies from which they are taken. For the Fathers of the Church, neither the truth of the faith, nor the dogma defining it, depended in any way on philosophy. In their mind, faith was the essential. The formula "The Platonism of the Fathers" would lead to an absurd interpretation if it were meant to say that the Fathers were Platonists. They were essentially Christians, that is to say, teachers of a doctrine of salvation by faith in Jesus Christ, and not at all the disciples of a philosopher who conceived salvation as a natural reward for the philosophical exercise of reason.

If the formula is legitimate, it is in another sense. In point of fact, the Fathers of the Church openly adopted a definite position toward some Greek philosophies, and they judged them according as they could help them to achieve a rational interpretation of Christian faith. Now it seems difficult to deny that Plato offered himself as an ally of Christianity on several important points: the doctrine of a maker of the universe; of a provident God; of the existence of an intelligible and divine world of which the sensible world is only an image; of the spirituality of the soul and its superiority over the body; of the illumination of the soul by God; of its enslavement to the body and of the necessity for it to liberate itself; last, not the least, the doctrine of the immortality of the soul, and of a life beyond the grave where it will receive the reward or punishment for its acts. The list of these Christian-Platonic affinities could be lengthened, especially in the domain of theology properly so-called. The Fathers have discovered in Plato and in some neoplatonists, a more or less vague presentiment of the Christian Trinity, the Demiurge announcing the Father, the *Nous* corresponding to the Word, and the World Soul to the

Holy Ghost. Besides, the whole doctrine of Plato was animated with such a love of truth and of those divine realities which every true philosopher strives to attain that one could hardly imagine a philosophy that would come nearer being a religion without actually being one. The Greek Fathers have felt this, and this alone would explain their predilection for a doctrine which, while it was not their own, appeared to them as the most easily assimilable by Christian thought. In the course of this task of assimilation errors were the more to be expected as Christian dogma itself was then in the process of being formulated; the fact remains, however, that most of these acquisitions have been immediately definitive, and that even where it was calling for rectifications, Platonism has been a wholesome challenge for Christian speculation to seek a philosophical formulation of its own truth.

Through Ammonius Saccas and Plotinus, this influence of Plato has reached the Latins as well as the Greeks. The striking difference which obtains between the respective styles of thought of Greek theology and of Latin theology must therefore have another cause, and, as we seem to see it, this cause is a theological rather than a philosophical one. What dominates the theology of Augustine, and that of almost all the Latins after him, is the relation of nature to grace. Hence, in the Latin world, the interminable controversies on the relation of grace and free will. It goes without saying that the same problems arise in the Christian theology of the Greeks, but their data are not identically the same. The central notion in Greek theology is rather that of "image" than of nature. As is said in Scripture (Genesis, i, 27), God has created man "in his own image"; the effect of sin has been the loss of this likeness or, at least, its blurring, and the main problem which Christians have to solve is how to recover this divine likeness by restoring it to its pristine purity. This is what the Greeks call "divinization." For this reason, the notion of image plays, in Greek theologies, a part analogous to that performed by the notion of grace in Latin theologies. In comparing them, the main difficulty arises from the fact that, when a Greek speaks of man as of a being created in the image and likeness of God, it is not easy to know if, for man, to be "image" is his nature or if it is a grace added to it. When Pelagius somewhat clumsily identified nature with grace, he fell the first victim to the risky undertaking of directly translating the language of Greek theology into that of Latin theology. Centuries were to elapse before the time when, owing to the efforts of Saint Bernard of Clairvaux and of William of Saint-Thierry, this difficult task would be successfully completed in the field of mystical theology. As to the field of metaphysics proper, the subtle and somewhat laborious commentaries of Thomas Aquinas on *The Divine Names,* as well as on the *Liber de Causis,* make it abundantly clear that it is not easy to speak, at one and the same time, the language of the One and the language of Being.

CHAPTER III

END OF THE LATIN PATRISTIC AGE

THE great period of Latin patristics came to an end with Saint Augustine, but several writers continued his work sometimes not without originality and, at any rate, under a form which has often prepared the technical type of speculation that was to prevail later on among Western theologians. The twelfth century cannot be understood without Augustine, but some of its aspects would not be much more intelligible to us if we did not know Boethius, Martianus Capella[74] or Isidore of Seville. In fact, we must begin by still more modest names, Claudianus Mamertus and even Faustus of Riez.[75]

I. FAUSTUS OF RIEZ

The name of this theologian should be mentioned on account of his attitude toward the problem of the soul. In the fifth century, it was an anachronism. Answering a question about "what is corporeal and what is incorporeal in human things," Faustus recalls the distinction established by some highly learned Fathers between what is "invisible" and what is "incorporeal." All that is created seems to be matter and, therefore, corporeal. These Fathers affirm that "the nature of both angels and souls is corporeal for this reason that, at the beginning, it was circumscribed even by space." Faustus' opponent believed that the soul is without quantity because it is in no place, but Cassian had clearly stated that, although our souls be much thinner than our bodies, they are nevertheless corporeal. God alone is incorporeal and this is precisely the reason why he alone can be omnipresent to the whole of his creation without himself being contained in any place. On the contrary, the soul is contained within the various limbs and organs of the body which it animates. Since it is *in loco*, it is corporeal.

Against this position the ready answer is that the soul can get out of its body by remembering or imagining other places, but, precisely, when a soul imagines Alexandria or Jerusalem, it does not have to go there nor to be there, so to speak, bodily. These motions of the soul are not its very substance. The soul is the standing substance which begets all our fleeting thoughts, memories and imaginations. When we think of a faraway place, or of a friend who is not present, we beget within ourselves the corresponding image without sending our soul to another place. Even the glorious soul of our Redeemer did not leave the world when it ascended to heaven. To conclude, if the soul is "local," then it is "corporeal."

2. CLAUDIANUS MAMERTUS

The letter of Faustus of Riez seems to have circulated under the form of an anonymous treatise. At least it is under this form that Claudianus Mamertus read it and undertook to refute it.[76] Hence his *De statu animae,* which is a connecting link between the later *De anima* of Cassiodorus and the previous treatises of Saint Augustine on the same subject.

Claudianus refuses to accept the position of Faustus, that "all that is created seems to be matter." On the contrary, since all creatures are informed matter, matter itself is not yet a creature. He also denies that all that can be comprehended by its creator must needs be corporeal. If this were true, God could not comprehend himself.[77] Conversely, if the human soul were a corporeal being, included in space and perceiving in space, how could man ever contemplate God, who is a purely spiritual being? If it were correct to say, with Faustus, that the soul knows its objects within its own body, that is within a certain place, then God himself should be in a certain place inasmuch as he is known by the soul.[78] Besides, if it is agreed that man is made up of body and soul, how could his soul be a body? To say that the soul is corporeal is tantamount to saying either that the soul has no body, since itself is one, or that the body has no soul, since even the soul is body.[79] The truth is that the soul, which is incorporeal, animates its body without itself being contained in any place or subjected to any motion.[80]

Claudianus has tirelessly restated the same fundamental notions through many digressions, but he himself has felt the need to sum up his general conclusions at the end of his treatise. The world appears to him as divided into three different types of being:

God
{ the supreme good without quality
{ has motion without time or place
{ judges and is not judged

Spirit
{ great good with quality
{ has motion in time without place
{ judges and is judged

Body
{ good with quality and quantity
{ has motion in time and place
{ does not judge nor is judged.[81]

We have already remarked that Stoic materialism has been accepted by some Christian thinkers, for instance, by the early Apologists among the Greeks, or by Tertullian among the Latins; but we have also observed the progressive disappearance of this tendency under the influence of Plato and of Plotinus. The doctrine of Augustine has settled the problem in the minds of the Western theologians. Claudianus was merely following his example in refusing to the soul any other quantity than the wholly metaphysical one of science and virtue. The *De quantitate animae* of Augustine has inspired Claudianus and, directly or indirectly, all his Christian successors.

3. BOETHIUS

The initial intention of Boethius had been to translate into Latin all the writings of Plato and Aristotle.[82] He fell far short of achieving that immense project, but an important part of the Greek message which he intended to convey to the Latin world has ultimately reached its destination. Boethius has not only left to the middle ages the allegorical description of philosophy one still sees carved on the facades of several European cathedrals; he also bequeathed to his successors a definition of it as well as a classification of the sciences it governs. Philosophy is the "love of wisdom." Wisdom itself is a reality, namely, the living thought and cause of all things, which subsists in itself and needs only itself to subsist. By illuminating man's thought, Wisdom attracts him to itself through love. Philosophy, or the love of wisdom, can therefore be considered variously as the pursuit of Wisdom, the quest for God, or the love of God.

A. *Problems in Logic*

Taken as a genus, philosophy is divided into two kinds: speculative and practical. Speculative philosophy is in turn subdivided into as many sciences as there are classes of beings to study. Using terms already coined by Marius Victorinus, Boethius distinguishes three kinds of beings: the intellectibles (*intellectibilia*), the intelligibles (*intelligibilia*) and natural beings, or natures (*naturalia*). The "intellectibles" are those beings which exist, outside of matter. The "intelligibles" are intellectibles that have fallen into bodies, such as the human souls. "Natural" beings, or natures, are those whose forms are inseparable from matter and cannot subsist apart. The science that deals with the "intellectibles" is theology: Boethius does not suggest any name for the science of the intelligible beings, but perhaps we should not betray his thought were we to call it "psychology," that is, the science that deals with souls. There remain natural bodies, or "natures," whose science is "physiology" or, as we would say today, physics.

Describing the collection of disciplines which go to make it up, Boethius gives the name *quadrivium* to the group of four sciences which cover the study of nature: arithmetic, astronomy, geometry and music. The meaning he himself gives to the term is "the quadruple road to wisdom." These sciences are, in fact, roads to wisdom, and whoever is ignorant of them cannot claim to love it. Just as theoretical philosophy is divided according to the objects to be known, practical philosophy is divided according to the acts to be accomplished. It is made up of three parts: one which teaches how to conduct oneself by the acquisition of virtues; one which consists in having those same virtues of prudence, justice, fortitude and temperance hold sway in the state; and finally, one which presides over the administration of domestic society. Three other disciplines make up the *trivium:* grammar, rhetoric and logic. These are concerned less with the acquisition of knowledge than with its method of exposition.[83]

A difficulty arises, however, with regard to logic; is it an art, or is it a science? In other words, is it an instrument at the service of philosophy, or is it part of philosophy itself? Boethius is of the opinion that the two theses can be reconciled. As the art of distinguishing the true from what is false or only probable, logic has its own object and can therefore be considered as one of the parts of philosophy; but since logic is useful to all the other parts of philosophy, it can be said to be their instrument. Logic is like the hand, which is, at one and the same time, both a part of the body and an aid to the whole body.[84]

The logic of Boethius is a commentary on Aristotle's in which the desire to interpret it according to Plato's philosophy frequently shows through. This is explained by the fact that Boethius closely follows a commentary by Porphyry and, in turn, it explains the swarm of contrary opinions which were to arise in the twelfth century on the meaning of Aristotle's doctrine. For all professors will comment on the text of Boethius, but while some of them will retain what he had kept of Aristotle, others, on the contrary, will cling to anything of Plato's which Boethius had introduced into it. In this respect the crucial problem is that of the nature of general ideas, or "universals." Mediaeval philosophy has long been spoken of as though it had dealt almost entirely with the problem of universals. In fact, the problem of universals is a battlefield where the adversaries join battle only when provided with all their armament. Conflicting metaphysics have tested their strength in attempting to solve it, but they did not spring from the solutions they proposed for it.

A passage from Porphyry's *Isagoge* (Introduction to Aristotle's *Categories*) is rightly considered to be the point of departure of the controversy. After having announced that he will deal with genera and species, Porphyry adds that he is postponing until later his decision as to whether genera and species are subsistent realities in themselves or simple conceptions of the mind; furthermore, supposing they are realities, he declines for the moment to say whether they are corporeal or incorporeal; finally, supposing they are incorporeal, he declines to investigate whether they exist apart from sensible things or only as united with them. As a good professor, Porphyry simply avoids raising problems of advanced metaphysics at the beginning of a treatise in logic written for beginners. Nevertheless, the very questions which he declines to discuss will remain, for the men of the middle ages, as a standing challenge to choose between Plato and Aristotle without having at their disposition either Plato or Aristotle, at least up to the middle of the thirteenth century. Boethius was the first one not to imitate Porphyry's discretion and, in his desire to conciliate Plato and Aristotle, he has proposed two solutions.

In his two commentaries on the Introduction to Aristotle's *Categories*, Aristotle's answer naturally prevails. Boethius first demonstrates that general concepts cannot be substances. As an example, suppose we take the concept of the genus "animal" and that of the species "man." Genera and species are, by definition, common to groups of individuals; now, that which is common to several individuals cannot itself be an individual. It is impossible because the genus belongs entirely to the species (a man possesses animality completely), whereas if it itself were a being, the genus should be divided between its various specific participations. But let us suppose, on the contrary, that the genera and species represented by our general ideas (universals) are only simple notions of the mind; in other words, let us suppose that absolutely nothing corresponds in reality to the concepts we have of them; in this second hypothesis our thought thinks nothing in thinking them. Now, if every thought worthy of the name has an object, universals must be thoughts of something, so that the problem of their nature arises once more, and in the same terms.

Faced with this dilemma Boethius rallies to a solution he borrows from Alexander of Aphrodisias. The senses turn things over to us in a state of confusion or, at least, of composition; our mind (*animus*), which is able to dissociate and recompose this data, distinguishes between elements given to it in a mixed state and considers them separately. Genera and species are of this number. Either the mind finds them in incorporeal beings, where they are separated from matter and already distinct; or it finds them in corporeal beings, in which case it extracts from the body whatever the body contains that is incorporeal in order to consider it separately as a naked and pure form. That is what we do when, in sense experience, we draw abstract notions of man and animal from given concrete individuals. Perhaps someone will object that this is another case of thinking what is not; but the objection would be superficial, for there is no error in separating in thought what is united in reality, provided one knows that what one thus separates in thought is united in reality. For instance, there is nothing wrong in conceiving line separate from surface. The mistake would be in thinking of things as joined which are not joined in reality; the chest of a man and the hindquarters of a horse, for example. Nothing forbids us to think of genera and species separately then, although they do not exist separately. And such is the solution of the problem of universals; *subsistunt ergo circa sensibilia, intelliguntur autem praeter corpora:* "they subsist in connection with sensible things, but we know them separate from bodies."

Boethius therefore did more for the middle ages than to posit the problem of universals. He solved it, and the solution he proposed was indeed that of Aristotle, but he did not propose it as its own: "Plato," he added, "thinks that genera, species and other universals are not only known separately from bodies, but also that they exist and subsist outside them; while Aristotle thinks that incorporeals and universals are really objects of knowledge, but that they exist only in sensible things. I had no intention of deciding which of these opinions is true, for that rests with a higher philosophy. I clung to Aristotle's opinion, therefore, not because I favored it particularly, but because this book (i.e. Porphyry's *Isagoge*) happened to be written in view of the *Categories,* whose author is Aristotle." [85]

Examining Boethius a little more closely one could easily see that the question was indeed not completely settled in his mind. The whole Aristotelian theory of the agent intellect, which gives its full meaning to the notion of abstraction because it explains why one can think separately of that which does not exist separately, is absent from the text of Boethius. He simply tells us that the mind abstracts the intelligible from the sensible without giving us any information on the nature and condition of that mysterious operation. Besides, even if they subsist only in individuals, these universals must needs be something! It is no wonder then, that in Book V of the *De consolatione philosophiae,* where he expresses his own views, Boethius propounds a rather different doctrine. Any being whatsoever, for example a man, is known in various ways according as he is known by the senses, by imagination, by reason, or by intellection. The senses see only a figure in a matter; the imagination pictures the figure alone, without the matter; the reason transcends the figure and grasps in one general view the form of the species present in all the individuals; but the eye of intelligence sees still higher, for, clearing the wall of the universe, it contemplates that form, simple in itself, with a pure glance of the mind.[86]

These formulas, which are to unite in the *De Anima* of Gundissalinus with Platonic notions coming from other sources, bear witness to the fact that, for Boethius, the reality which corresponds to universals is that of the Idea. For him, as for Augustine, sensation is not a passion suffered by the soul in consequence of some action on some part of the body, but it is indeed the very act by which the soul judges the passions suffered by its body. Sense impressions invite us simply to turn to Ideas. Acquainted as we are with history, we cannot fail to see the fundamental Platonism of Boethius, but some of his mediaeval readers have hesitated over the true meaning of his thought. They have imagined him hesitating between Plato and Aristotle, listening first to the one and then to the other, without ever reaching a decision.

B. *Problems in psychology and theology*

In fact, the real Boethius of history did not waver. For him the most lofty knowledge was the science, not even of the intelligible, object of reason, but of the "intellectible," object of pure intellectual intuition. Now, to him, the "intellectible" *par excellence* was God. We have an innate knowledge of God which represents him to us as the Sovereign Good, that is to say, according to the same definition that Saint Anselm was to exploit, a being than which no better can be conceived. In order to establish the existence of this being Boethius relies upon the principle that the imperfect can only be a diminution of the perfect; the existence of the imperfect in any order whatsoever therefore presupposes the existence of the perfect. Now the existence of imperfect beings is obvious; the existence of a perfect being, that is, of a Good, the source and principle of all other goods, cannot be doubted. We could, if need be, dispense with proving that this perfect being is God, since the perfect is better than anything we can conceive. But let us ponder this fact: to admit that God is not the perfect would be to admit a perfect being prior to God and, consequently, his principle. Now God is the principle of all things; he it is, therefore, who is the perfect. Short of admitting an absurd regression to infinity then, a perfect and supreme being, who is God, must exist. Saint Anselm was later on to follow a similar line of thought in his *Monologion*.

Being perfect, God is beatitude. In a formula which became classic, Boethius defined beatitude: "a condition made perfect by the union of all that is good." God is therefore blessed, or rather he is beatitude itself; hence the corollary that men can become blessed only by participating in God and by becoming themselves gods, so to speak. "So to speak," for the beatitude of man will never be in him more than a participation in the beatitude of God.

Being the primary cause of the universe, as the order of things suffices to show, this God escapes the determinations of our thought. Being perfect, God is absolutely One. The Father is God; the Son, God; the Holy Spirit, God. The reason for their unity, Boethius says, is their non-difference (*indifferentia*), a formula William of Champeaux was later to use to explain how a universal notion can be both one and yet common to several individuals at one and the same time. Since God is perfectly one, Boethius adds, he evades all the categories. What one can say of him applies much less to God himself than to the manner in which he administers the world. For instance, we describe him as the immobile mover of things, or as exercising his providence over everything, and so on for all the divine attributes. When man has said all he can about God, he has not yet attained what God is.[87]

All these theological doctrines are stated in the *De consolatione philoso-*

phiae without the support of the Scriptures, which is not surprising after all, since it is Philosophy speaking. Let us however note the case, apparently unique, in Book III, prose 12, where Boethius says of the Sovereign Good that it "reacheth from end to end mightily, and ordereth all things sweetly." This is undeniably the citation of a well-known text from Wisdom (8, 1) which Saint Augustine had indefatigably quoted. If one takes into account the fact that in the Preamble to the *De Trinitate*,[88] Boethius openly quotes Saint Augustine as his authority, one hardly risks being mistaken in saying that where the doctrine of the *De consolatione philosophiae* coincides with that of Augustine, the coincidence is not fortuitous. Even when he is speaking only as a philosopher Boethius thinks as a Christian.

After the intellectible, which is God, comes the intelligible, which is the soul. Only two texts of Boethius deal with the origin of the soul, but these two confirm one another and what they say is rather curious. The first is found in Boethius' commentary on Porphyry, where he speaks of the state and condition of human souls who, after having all been with the first intellectible substances (*i.e.* the angels), have, however, degenerated at contact with the body, from intellectibles into intelligibles. As a consequence, souls are no longer fitting objects for intellectual intuition, nor are they capable of exercising it. All they can do is to recapture happiness, for a fleeting moment, each time they apply themselves to the intelligibles. If souls have all been with the angels, they must have been pre-existent to the body. The second text outlines the same position and links it with the same doctrine of the pre-existence of souls.[89]

We have described the hierarchy of cognitive activities with regard to universals. Boethius did not deal with this point to any extent, but he developed his own views on the will at some length. The very subject of the *De consolatione philosophiae* invited him to do so. Threatened with death, he could only find consolation in the thought of a divine providence, whose will one had to submit to if one wished to be happy whatever the adversities of fortune might be. Natural beings tend naturally toward their natural places, where their integrity will be preserved; man can and should do likewise, but he does so by means of his will. Will is the synonym for liberty. Will is free only because man is endowed with a reason capable of knowing and choosing. The better a man uses his reason, the freer he is. God and the superior intellectible substances enjoy a knowledge so perfect that their judgment is infallible; their liberty is therefore perfect. As to man, his soul is all the freer as it patterns itself on divine thought; it is less free when it turns away from God to the knowledge of sensible things, and still less so when it allows itself to be governed by the passions of the body it animates. To will what the body desires is the extreme degree of servitude; to will what God wills, love what he loves, is the highest form of liberty; it is therefore happiness.

The objection will perhaps be raised that the problem is still untouched; if God's foreknowledge is infallible, either our will cannot decide other than he has foreseen, and it will not be free, or else it can, and the infallibility of providence will prove at fault. This is the classic problem of "future contingents." A simple question of logic in Aristotle, who did not ascribe to God the foreknowledge of human acts, it raised for the Christians this most difficult metaphysical and theological problem: how is one to reconcile human liberty with the prevision of our acts by God? Boethius' answer consists in dissociating the two problems of prevision and liberty. God infallibly foresees free acts, but he foresees them as free; the fact that these acts are foreseen does not make them become necessary. Furthermore, God is eternal and eternity is the complete possession, perfect and simultaneous, of a life without end (*aeternitas est interminabilis vitae tota simul et perfecta possessio*); God lives, then, in a perpetual present. It is not so with the world, for it endures in time, and even if one were to admit, with Aristotle, that it had always existed, one would have to call it *perpetual* (perpetually changing), but not *eternal* (immobility of a complete presence). There is, then, before-ness and after-ness in events, but not in the totally-present knowledge that God has of them. He does not *foresee*, he *provides;* his name is not "foresight" but "providence." He therefore eternally sees the necessary as necessary and the free as free. When I see that the sun is rising, the fact that I see it is not the cause of its rising. When I see that a man walks, that does not force him to walk. In like manner the immobile and permanent view that God has of our voluntary acts does not in the least detract from their liberty.

Sparing as he is of precise details concerning the origin of the soul, Boethius is even less prodigal with those concerning its end. He emphasizes the sanctions immanent in moral life itself; the good become godlike from the fact that they are good, it is their reward; the wicked grow beastlike from the fact of their wickedness, it is their punishment. Interpreting in the moral sense the mythology of Plato's *Phaedrus,* Boethius teaches that, through living as he does, the miser becomes a wolf because of his rapacity, the crafty person becomes a fox, the lazy one is changed into a donkey and the libertine into a pig. Boethius has not the slightest doubt that there is a purgatory after death for guilty souls and torture for criminals, but it is not his intention to hold forth on the subject.[90]

C. *Problems in the philosophy of nature*

After psychology comes physiology, or the philosophy of nature. The one Boethius proposed in the beautiful poem of the *De consolatione philosophiae,* Book III, metr. 9, is nothing but a résumé in twenty-eight verses of the *Timaeus* annotated by Chalcidius. Prompted by the generosity inherent in the good, God adorns chaotic matter with forms after the pattern of Ideas; the doctrines of numbers, elements, of the world-soul and the liberation of the soul by contemplation are briefly but clearly sketched. This cosmological scenario has nothing original about it, but Boethius has gone more deeply into two of its points: the relation of providence to destiny and the metaphysical structure of beings.

Following the example of Chalcidius, Boethius subordinates what he calls destiny to providence. Considered in the directing thought of God, the order of things is providence; considered as the inner law, which regulates the course of things from within, it is destiny. These are two distinct realities, for providence is God and subsists eternally in his perfect immobility, while destiny, which is the law of the succession of actual things, unrolls with them in time. Destiny, the realization in time of the eternal decrees of providence, does not oppose providence, it only serves it. But neither does it detract from human liberty. In a series of concentric circles in movement, the center remains immobile; the more man turns from God and away from his center, the more he is swept along by destiny; but the closer he draws to God, the more immobile and free he is. Whoever remained firmly fixed in the contemplation of the supreme Intellectible would therefore be both perfectly immobile and perfectly free. There is, in all this, a curious escape from Stoicism by means of a sort of Christian Platonism.

The second problem closely studied by Boethius is perhaps the one in which his thought was to become most influential. He identifies, as do Plato and Augustine, being with good, and non-being with evil. For everything that is, then, to be and to be good are one and the same thing. But if things are good *substantially,* in what do they differ from good in itself, which is God?

Boethius' answer is contained in a formula so dense that it was to provoke numerous commentaries: *diversum est esse et id quod est.* What does that mean? Every individual being is a collection of accidents unique and irreducible to any other. Such a collection of determinations linked together (dimension, sensible qualities, figure, etc.) is that very thing which is (*id quod est*). "That which is" is therefore the result of the collection of the parts which make it up: it is all these parts collectively, but it is none of them taken separately. For instance, since man is made up of a soul and a body, he is body and soul at the same time, but he is neither a body nor a soul. And so, no single part of man is what man is (*in parte igitur non est id quod est*). That is the case with every compound being, since it is the collection of its parts, but is no one of them alone. In a simple substance such as God, the case is quite different; we might say that, by reason of his perfect simplicity, his being and what he is are one and the same thing.

It remains to be seen what that being (*esse*) of compound substance is, which is different from "that which is" in it. Since being in this case depends upon that which binds the parts of the compound into a whole, it is the constitutive element of the whole which is the "being" of the "that which is." Now, every compound is made up of parts reduced to unity by a determining element. The ultimate determined is matter, the ultimate determinant is form. For instance, man is composed of a matter organized as a body, and a soul which organizes that matter into a body. The soul is that by which man is what he is; it is the *quo est* of that *id quod est,* and, since it causes him to be, it is his being (*esse*). The being (*esse*) of a compound substance is therefore the form by which the whole substance is what it is. On the other hand, this constitutive form of a compound substance is not that whole substance; it is only the form of the whole. Taken separately, it *is* not. It is proper to these compound substances—and that is how all that is not God is different from God—that even their *esse* is not, or, in other words, that their *esse* itself is still only a *quo est*. From whence come the formulas upon which all the sagacity of mediaeval philosophers was brought to bear: *diversum est esse* (the form) and *id quod est* (the complete substance); *ipsum enim esse* (the form alone), *nondum est* (is not substance in itself), *at vero quod est* (but the substance), *accepta essendi forma* (having received the form which makes it a being), *est atque subsistit* (both is and is a substance). And again: *omne quod est* (substance) *participat eo quod est esse* (shares in the form which causes it to be), *ut sit* (and, thereby, is); *alio vero participat, ut aliquid sit* (but it shares in something else, in order to be such a being). Again: *omni composito aliud est esse* (in every compound the form is one thing) *aliud ipsum est* (the compound is another thing). Boethius was not yet asking the question of the relation which obtains between essence and existence, but rather that of the relation between substance and the principle of its substantial being, that is to say: what causes it to be a substance. The very precision of his formulas was to make it more difficult for his successors to go, beyond the level of substance, up to the level of existence, but they helped those who succeeded in doing so to formulate their own thought in strictly accurate terms.[91]

The world of natural bodies presented itself to Boethius as an aggregate, ordained by providence, of participations in divine Ideas. Since Ideas are pure forms, they cannot be joined to matter; but from these separate forms have come others which shape up matter and make up bodies. We should not call them forms, properly speaking. As Boethius puts it in his *De Trinitate,* Chapter II, these are simple images of forms properly so-called, which are the Ideas of God. These form-images, which resemble the *species nativae* of Chalcidius and anticipate the *formae nativae* of Gilbert of la Porrée, are in reality those active principles called natures, which are the inner causes of the movements of bodies and of their operations.

Boethius did not write a complete encyclopedia of the seven liberal arts, but he left *Elements of Music* (*De institutione musica*), *Elements of Arithmetic* (*De institutione arithmetica*) and a *Geometry* (*De geometrica*) which is a summary of Euclid. These school text-books were to represent for a long time about all that the middle ages knew on those subjects. The influence of Boethius was manifold and profound. His scientific treatises nourished the teaching of the *quadrivium;* his works on logic took the place of Aristotle's during several centuries; his theological tractates set the example, which was to obsess certain fine minds in the middle ages, of a scientific theology, systematically deduced from previously-defined terms.[92] His *De Trinitate* will dominate the theology of the twelfth-century schools of Chartres. As to the *De consolatione philosophiae,* we find it present and active in all epochs. Annotated for the first time by the Anonymous of Saint Gall, then by Remi of Auxerre and Bovo of Corvey, it was later to be commented on by William of Conches, Nicholas Trivet, Peter d'Ailly (about 1372), to mention only a few names, and Badius Ascensius was to do it again toward the end of the fifteenth century. Its literary composition, alternating between prose and verse, made no slight contribution to the success of the "chantefable." King Alfred translated it into English, Notker Labeo into German, and John of Meun into French; it was to enter into the composition of the *Roman de la Rose,* and was put to good use by Chaucer. Finally, as supreme homage to the Sacred Science, the last days of the middle ages were to give as a counterpart to the *Philosophical Consolation,* which presided over its origin, the *Theological Consolation* of John Gerson. To be sure, the importance of the philosophical element is overwhelming in the writings of Boethius, even in his theological tractates, but this is precisely the reason why he is rightly considered as one of the founders of scholasticism. His whole doctrine is an example of putting to work a precept which he himself has formulated: "Conjoin faith and reason, if you can." There again Boethius could have quoted Saint Augustine.

4. FROM CASSIODORUS TO GREGORY THE GREAT

The treatise of Cassiodorus[93] *On the Soul* belongs to a sort of literary genre. Theologians will write treatises *De anima* just as, later on, they will write treatises *De intellectu.* The work of Cassiodorus betrays the influence of both Augustine (*De quantitate animae, De origine animae*) and of his more immediate predecessor Claudianus Mamertus (*De statu animae*). Like Augustine and Claudianus, Cassiodorus affirms the spirituality of the soul. A finite substance, since it is mutable and created, the soul is wholly present in the entire body, yet it is non-material since it is capable of knowing, and it is immortal, since it is spiritual and simple.[94] This treatise was to be quoted frequently and still more frequently plagiarised in the process of time. As to the *Institutiones,* their Book II was often to be used as a manual in monastic schools, so much so that it was sometimes quoted as a separate work under the title of *De artibus ac disciplinis liberalium litterarum*. In fact, in itself alone it constitutes a sort of encyclopedia of liberal arts, or rather of what a monk should know of them in order both to study and to teach Holy Scripture in an intelligent and useful way. Cassiodorus justifies his undertaking by the authority of Saint Augustine in *De doctrina christiana*.[95]

Cassiodorus' encyclopedia owed its success to the elegant and easy style of its author; the one by Isidore of Seville[96] owed its success to the mass of definitions and notions on all subjects that it placed at the disposition of the public. His *Origins,* or *Etymologiae,* form a sort of encyclopedic compendium in twenty books, which both titles suit equally well. Isidore was persuaded—and he was able to persuade the mass of his readers—that the nature and the very essence of things were recognizable in the etymology of their names. True or false, often ingenious, and sometimes ridiculous, Isidore's etymologies were to be transmitted from generation to generation up to the end of the middle ages. Here is what the famous encyclopedia contained: Book I, Grammar; II, Rhetoric and Dialectics; III, Arithmetic, Geometry, Astronomy, Music (these first three books thus containing the whole of the liberal arts); IV, Medicine; V, Universal History from the Creation to the year 627 in the Christian era; VI, The Sacred Books and Offices of the Church; VII, God, the Angels, the members of the Church; VIII, The Church; IX, languages, peoples, States, families; X, Dictionary; XI, Man; XII, Zoology; XIII, Cosmography; XIV, Geography; XV, monuments, ways of communication; XVI, Petrography, Mineralogy; XVII, Agriculture and Horticulture; XVIII, The Army, War, Games; XIX, ships, housing, apparel; XX, Alimentation, household arts and agricultural implements. The success of the work is easily explained; Isidore's *Etymologies* occupied, in a mediaeval library, about the same place that the *Encyclopedia Britannica* or the *Larousse* occupy in a modern library. They were frequently consulted.

Other works by Isidore, moreover, made it possible to complete the outlines provided by some parts of his encyclopedia. The *De fide catholica* and the *Sententiarum libri tres* were manuals of theology; a cosmography was to be found in the *De ordine creaturarum,* a cosmography and a meteorology in the *De natura rerum,* a universal history in the *Chronicon,* a modern history in the *History of the Kings of the Goths and the Vandals*. A great deal of research work has been done on the sources of Isidore of Seville, but his were not the sources of a thought, they were the sources of a dictionary. Such studies are nevertheless very useful in that they show the residue of general knowledge amassed by classical Latin culture, which provided the initial outlay on which, for several centuries, Europe has had to live.

Lesser lights than Isidore contributed to enrich it. A man as completely forgotten nowadays as Martin of Bracara[97] nevertheless still retains some claim on our gratitude. This bishop was a moralist, he liked Seneca and was inspired by him, when he was not simply copying him in his *Senecae de copia verborum* (or *Formula vitae honestae,* or again *De quatuor virtutibus*), as well as in his treatises *On Anger* and *On Poverty.* The importance of such writings does not lie in any originality of thought, but rather in the fact that they transmitted to Western civilization some fundamental notions concerning the dignity of moral life and the absolute value of virtue. Nothing more was needed to keep this ideal alive in the hearts of certain men. That spark only awaited favorable ground for gathering new strength and setting everything ablaze. These modest writings particularly fostered the sentiment, so lively in the middle ages, of a community of culture which bound the Christians, over and above their own origins, to the best that classical antiquity had produced. Cassiodorus is seldom if ever read now, though that charming spirit still gives pleasure; Isidore is consulted only out of curiosity and for the verification of references; Martin of Bracara is no more than a name familiar to a few specialists; but those who know what role these supporters of a civilization in ruins played in their time still preserve a grateful memory of them.

In the sixth century the store of ancient Roman culture seems to have been almost used up. The Latin Fathers had prolonged its duration by exploiting it for the benefit of Christian thought, but by that time the Roman Empire in which it had originated, and which was its natural environment, completed its disintegration. Its last representative was Pope Gregory I, whose genius for organization caused him to be called Gregory the Great.[98] Born of a patrician family in Rome, he inherited as his birthright the traditional culture of his country, and his writings bear its imprint. The brilliant success of his works is nevertheless due to their perfect adaptation to the needs of the Church. He reformed the liturgy and singing of the Church—it is still called "Gregorian chant"—and wrote a *Liber regulae pastoralis* on the duties of a Christian pastor, which was to be translated into Anglo-Saxon by Alfred as early as the end of the ninth century, and so to become one of the earliest monuments of English prose. His *Dialogues,* which are really four books of hagiographic legends, and his two Books of *Moralia in Job,* an allegorical commentary on Scripture in which moral preoccupation predominates, were very widely read, exploited and quoted throughout the course of the middle ages. Although the influence of the Ancients was not absent from them, Gregory the Great must not be thought of as a literary humanist. Didier, Bishop of Vienne in Gaul, stirred by the spreading of ignorance around him, and perhaps not having anyone to do it for him, had himself taken the heroic part of teaching Latin grammar, which necessarily entailed some teaching of classical Latin literature. The thing evidently created a scandal, for

Gregory was informed of it. The vehement letter Gregory wrote to Didier is surprising by the violence of its reaction against classical studies. In it Gregory expressed the hope that it was merely a question of misinformation and that Didier's heart had not allowed itself to be carried away by the love for profane literature. How could Gregory believe that a bishop was teaching grammar (*grammaticam quibusdam exponere*)? The same lips could not extol Jupiter and Jesus Christ at the same time! It was a grievous thing, it was abominable that bishops should declaim what it was not decent even for a layman to read (*Et quam grave nefandumque sit episcopis canere quod nec laico religioso conveniat ipse considerare*).[99]

Gregory did not mean to say that it was immoral to learn grammar; his real thought, as expressed in his Commentary on the first *Book of Kings* (5, 30) was that the liberal arts should only be studied with a view to understanding Scripture, but that a study of them with that end in view was really indispensable. God himself offers us this knowledge as a plain to be crossed before climbing the peaks of Holy Writ. Gregory was no obscurantist, but let us admit that he lacked enthusiasm. The Preface to his *Moralia in Job* already states the problem, oft debated by mediaeval grammarians, of knowing what the standard of Latin usage was for a Christian: the grammar of the classical writers or the grammar imposed by the Latin text of the Bible? And Gregory resolutely decided in favor of the latter. That which is a solecism or barbarism for a master of Latin grammar should not frighten away a Christian annotating the Scriptures, since the sacred text itself authorizes these grammatically incorrect constructions.[100] We are to see this protest revived against the purists of their times by Smaragdus of Saint Mihiel and John of Garlandia. But the following remark by Gregory also merits contemplating: "since our exposition has its origin in Scripture, it is quite suitable for the child to resemble its mother." [101] Thus a Christian Latin naturally tended to replace classical Latin as early as the end of the patristic epoch. It is one of the numerous ironies of history that this adversary of *belles lettres* should be the one to start the immense movement of literary culture which was to invade the West progressively through the rise and spread of Anglo-Saxon civilization.

PART FOUR

FROM SCOTUS ERIGENA TO SAINT BERNARD

The origin of the ninth-century philosophical movement is the effort of Charlemagne to improve the intellectual and moral state of the nations he governed. Hence the name of "Carolingian Renaissance" which it has sometimes been given. In point of fact, this intellectual movement was the continuation, in France, of the missionary work initiated in Great Britain by Augustine of Canterbury (?-604) and which had found its most perfect expression in the writings of the Venerable Bede (673-735). This Anglo-Saxon culture of Latin origin has been the starting point of the restoration of Humanities in continental Europe. Among the many scholars whom Charlemagne invited to share in this important work, one of the British masters of the cathedral school of York played an outstanding part. His name was Alcuin (730-804). About 580, Gregory of Tours had written in the preface to his *History of the Franks:* "The cities of Gaul have allowed the study of humanities to decline, or rather to die out . . . One could not find anyone who, as a grammarian versed in dialectics, could recount events, either in prose or in verse. Most of them lamented this and said: Woe to our times, for the study of Letters has perished in us!" After the death of Alcuin, the situation was entirely different. His personal ambition had been, in his own words, "to build up in France a new Athens," or, more exactly, a Christian one. It is worth noting that, at the very beginning of the *Chronicle of Saint Gall,* the monk Notker could write (about 885): "Alcuin's teaching was so fruitful that the modern Gauls, or Frenchmen, became the equals of the Ancients of Rome and Athens." [1]

This statement, which was to reverberate through centuries, was a manifest exaggeration, but it was not a complete illusion. At any rate already during Alcuin's lifetime, a modest revival of philosophical interest can be observed. Fredegisus (d. 834), compatriot, disciple and successor of Alcuin as abbot of Saint Martin of Tours (804-834) has left us an *Epistola de nihilo et tenebris,* in which he maintains that nothingness and darkness are something, and not simply the absence of something. His argument rests upon the assumption that any word with a definite meaning signifies something; a man, a stone, a tree, for example; therefore, nothingness refers to something, that is, to some actually existing thing.[2] This grammatical argument, based upon the definition of the noun, had a theological implication in the mind of Fredegisus. The "nothingness" at stake in his treatise was that from which God has created the world (*ex nihilo*), that is to say, a sort of common and undifferentiated matter from which he moulded everything. This trace of Platonist influence would probably be confirmed if we could read another treatise of Fredegisus now lost, and which is known to us only through its refutation by Agobard (769-840), Bishop of Lyons: *Liber contra objectiones Fredegisi abbatis.*[3] Agobard attributed to Fredegisus the doctrine of the pre-existence of souls, and he linked it with his doctrine of matter in the following way: "I find fault with you for having said of souls which are to be united with bodies: *The soul, when it comes to the body,* as though it were known from what region the soul arrives, or perhaps as if you knew in what region that unknown matter, from which you say that souls are created, lies." Agobard himself maintains, on the contrary, that the soul is created at the same time as the body.

Some other elementary efforts to introduce philosophy into theological discussions might be quoted as belonging to the late ninth century,[4] but the fact which dominates that period is what Heiricus of Auxerre was later on to call, in the prologue to his poem on *The Life of Saint Germain,* a migration of almost all of Ireland, with its troupe of philosophers, reaching the shores of France in defiance of the sea. These Irish, several of whom we shall meet later on at Rheims and at Laon, seem in most cases to have been excellent masters of the liberal arts, but content to follow the accepted curriculum of classical studies. In the midst of these grammarians and dialecticians lacking in metaphysical ambitions, the so-called *Corpus areopagiticum* falls as a meteor from another world, and the Irish Scotus Erigena welcomes it with enthusiasm. A neoplatonic fermentation immediately takes place, so active indeed that, five centuries later, John Gerson will deem it still dangerous.

CHAPTER I

JOHANNES SCOTUS ERIGENA

THE personality of John the Scot (Johannes Scotus Erigena) dominates his era, and his doctrine occupies so unique a place in the history of Western thought that it deserves our close attention.[5] It offered to the Latins the possibility, one might almost say the temptation, of entering once and for all the way initiated by the Greek theologians, Denis and Maximus the Confessor. Had this invitation been accepted, a neoplatonist philosophy would no doubt have prevailed in Western Europe up to the end of the middle ages. The fact that Erigena's example was not followed is, on the contrary, a sure sign that what we today call Europe was already groping its way toward a different type of metaphysical speculation.

I. FAITH AND REASON

Erigena's doctrine has received divergent interpretations. Görres, for instance, accuses him of having confused philosophy with religion, an error, which, however, he considers as suitable for a pantheist. On the contrary, B. Hauréau calls him "a very free thinker," thus awarding him the highest eulogy at his disposal.[6] The true meaning of Erigena's doctrine results from his conception of the relations which obtain between faith and reason.

Man has been in three successive states with regard to truth. Between original sin and the coming of Christ, reason was clouded by the consequences of error and, pending the complete revelation of truth by the Gospel, it could only construct a physics in order to understand nature and to prove the existence of God who is its cause. As early as that epoch, however, the Jewish revelation began its work, until it reached its height with Christ. From that moment forth, reason entered a second stage, in which it still is. Since it now receives truth from an infallible source, the wise thing for reason to do is to accept this truth as God reveals it in Holy Writ. Faith must now precede the exercise of reason. Yet, far from suppressing it, faith engenders in us a twofold effort, first, to make it pass into our acts so as to purify our moral life, next, to explore it rationally through the exercise of contemplative life. A third and last state will later on replace the present one. In the beatific vision, faith will disappear and be replaced by the direct sight of Truth. Just now, however, human reason is a reason taught by a divine revelation and this remains equally true whether the reason at stake be that of a philosopher or that of a theologian. From this point of view, philosophy is exactly in the same situation as religion.

The first consequence of this fact is that, for him who is aware of it, faith becomes the condition of intellectual knowledge. Scripture says it: "If you will not believe, you shall not understand." [7] Faith goes first and, in its own particular way, it grasps the object of intelligence before intelligence itself. Peter and John run to the tomb; Peter is the symbol of faith, John is the symbol of intelligence, and the tomb is Holy Writ. Both run to it, both enter, but Peter goes in first. Let our faith do the same; let it go first, and since divine revelation expresses itself in Scripture, let our acceptance of what Scripture teaches precede the effort of our reason. A strange rationalism indeed, whose first affirmation it is that faith is the only way which leads to intellection!

Yet, as has been said, faith is nothing more than a sort of principle from which, in a creature endowed with reason, the knowledge of his Creator begins to develop.[8] The woman of Samaria, in the Gospel, precisely represents human nature in search of truth and trying to discover it through reason alone. Now, she encounters Christ on her way and, strangely enough, he asks her to give him a drink, as though faith were asking reason to quench its thirst or, in other words, as though the Creator and Redeemer of nature were asking the very nature, created and redeemed by him, to seek him through reason.[9] Nor is this as paradoxical as it appears to be. First, if reason did not intervene to discern the spiritual meaning hidden in the letter of Scripture, its interpretation would lead to strange mistakes. Next, it is in the very nature of faith to kindle in minds disposed to that kind of speculation, an intellectual light which is that of philosophy itself. This is why Erigena considers philosophy and religion as equivalent terms, as indeed they are, in a doctrine where faith begets the desire for intellectual knowledge and where the object of intellectual knowledge is the very contents of faith. In short: "Light shines in the darkness of believing souls, and it shines more and more while, starting from faith, it tends towards the sight of God." [10]

Since the substance of faith is given to us in Scripture, a philosophical exegesis of the word of God is the only sound method to follow. By and large, the *Division of Nature* (*De divisione naturae*) of Erigena is nothing else than a rational interpretation of biblical texts pursued by a reader of Saint Ambrose and of Saint Augustine among the Latins, of Origen, the two Gregories, Denis and Maximus Confessor among the Greeks. No man has more constantly resorted to theological authorities in order to justify his own positions. The authority against which he sometimes revolts is neither that of God nor that of the Fathers of the Church. What Erigena maintains on this point is that, when all is said and done, the source of authority itself is reason. When God speaks, we have to believe him, because what God says is true, whether we understand it or not. When a man speaks, even if his authority is universally recognized by other men, what he says is true only if reason approves of it.

This position is a simple application of the principle, admitted by all mediaeval theologians, that God alone is infallible. Let us not, therefore, imagine John the Scot as a rationalist in the modern sense of the word. True enough, since he considered philosophy as a meditation on the substance of faith, it can be said either that he never had any philosophy, since all that he says presupposes faith, or that he never had any theology since, according to him, to theologize and to philosophize in the proper way are one and the same thing. The very least that can be said on this point is that Erigena consistently refused to distinguish between these two orders of speculation. Yet we should also remember that most of the Fathers would have approved his saying that, after Christ, the righteous use of reason, in all matters pertaining to God and to man, presupposes the acceptance of divine revelation. When we read Erigena's famous statement: "It is therefore certain that true religion is true philosophy, and, conversely, that true philosophy is true religion," let us not forget that he is merely repeating Augustine.[11] On the whole, his own position is simple; it even is a traditional one, and the bluntness of some of his formulas is mainly responsible for the misrepresentation of his thought by several of his historians.[12]

2. NATURE AND ITS DIVISION

The method reason uses to achieve the understanding of what man believes is dialectics, whose two fundamental operations are *division* and *analysis*. Division starts from the unity of the highest genera and progressively distinguishes their less and less general species, until it arrives at individuals, which are the terms of division. Analysis follows the opposite course. Starting from individuals, and going back up the steps division came down, it gathers them up on its way and reinstates them into the unity of the supreme genera. These two operations are complementary moments of one and the same method. In fact, they may be considered as a single movement which, after descending from the unity of the highest genus to the multiplicity of individuals, reascends to the original unity from which they came.[13]

It is a typical feature of this doctrine that division and analysis are not simply abstract methods of decomposing or recomposing ideas, but the very laws of nature are those which have just been defined. The explanation of the universe has to follow the ways of division and analysis because these are constitutive of its structure. Erigena's doctrine is not a logic. It is a physics, or rather, as he himself says, a "physiology" (IV, 1; 741 C). To understand the book of Genesis is to know "nature" (III, 29; 705 B); science is found in a proper understanding of revelation.

What is nature? The Greeks often used its name (*phusis*) as synonymous with being (*ousia*). Yet, their exact meanings are not identical. Being (*ousia*) designates the essence of that which, in any being, can neither become, nor be increased or decreased. Nature (*phusis*) properly signifies being inasmuch as it can be begotten in place and time (*Div. nat.*, V, 3; 867 A). Thus understood, nature extends to all that which is able either to be or even not to be. It divides itself into four main distinctions: first, nature which creates and is not created; secondly, nature which is created and creates; thirdly, nature which is created and does not create; fourthly, nature which does not create and is not created (I, 1; 441-442. II, 1; 526 A C. III, 23; 688 C-689 A). In reality, the four parts of this division are reducible to two. Since the second and third are created, while the first and fourth are uncreated, we are faced with only two main divisions: the Creator and the creature. And indeed, nature which creates and is not created is God considered as the principle of things, whereas nature which is not created and does not create is God considered as having ceased to create and entered in his rest. On the other hand, the second division corresponds to archetypal Ideas, which create things but themselves are created by God, and the third includes those very things which are created by Ideas but themselves create nothing. In short, God is posited as creator or origin in the first division, and as end in the fourth, creatures all being included between this principle and end (II, 2; 527 B. III, 1; 621 A. V, 39; 1019-1020).

Let us now consider the division of nature insofar as it includes what is not. In a doctrine which, directly or not, derives its inspiration from Plato's *Sophist*, the concepts of being and of non-being have only a relative value. All being is the non-being of what it is not; moreover, there are cases when what is said not to be is more real than what we usually call being. For indeed being can be reasonably defined: that which can be perceived by the senses or understood by the intellect. Consequently, whatever escapes the grasp of these two cognitive powers can rightly be called non-being. Applying this definition, Erigena distinguishes five types of non-being. First, that which escapes our senses and our understanding on account of its very perfection; for instance, God, or even the essences of things, which we know only through their accidents. Second, within the hierarchical order of beings, the affirmation of the inferior is the negation of the superior, and conversely, so that what a being is implies the non-being of what it is not. Third, potential being is the non-being of what it will be once it is actualized. Fourth, beings subject to generation and corruption are not, at least in comparison with the immutable Ideas, which are their models. Fifth, in the case of man one can say that he is insofar as he carries the image of God and that he is not insofar as he loses this image through his fault (I, 3-7; 443-447).

It is important to understand correctly the nature of this division. To a large extent, the pantheistic interpretations of Erigena's doctrine rest upon what is perhaps a misinterpretation of the word "division." We should not imagine "nature" as a whole of which God and creatures would be parts; or as a genus of which God and creatures would be species. God is not all things, nor are all things God. To say so would be to say a monstrosity (III, 10; 650 D). In point of fact, it would be to say that the One is multiple, which is absurd. The division of nature signifies the act by which God expresses himself and makes himself known in a hierarchy of beings which are other than, and inferior to, him.

When we want to determine the nature of a being, we must resort to the categories. The categories of Aristotle apply to creatures, that is, to those beings which *are,* because they can be perceived by sense or conceived by the intellect. All such beings are included in some genus and in some species. Now, as has just been said, God is neither a genus nor a species. He is so far above all particular beings that no category applies to him (I, 15; 463 C). This is but another way of saying that, strictly speaking, God is ineffable. In order to talk about him, we must use the method advocated by Denis. It follows three successive stages. First, that of "affirmative theology," which speaks as though the categories validly applied to God: God is substance; God is good (quality); God is great (quantity), etc. Next, the method of "negative theology," which corrects the affirmations of the preceding one: God is neither substance, nor quality, nor quantity, nor anything that enters any category. Let us note that affirmation and negation are equally justified, for it is true that God is everything that is, since he is its cause, and it is likewise true that God is nothing of what is, since he is above being. Hence the third moment of the method, which is that of the so-called "superlative theology." It says that God is not included in any particular category, because he transcends them all. For instance, the whole truth about God is neither that he is substance, nor that he is not substance; the whole truth is that God is "supersubstantial." Yet, we must admit that even the whole truth about God, at least as we can express it, remains a predominantly negative one. In saying that God is beyond substance, we say what he is not much more than what he is. So also, in saying that God is beyond being (*est qui plus quam esse est*), we are not saying what he is. What is he? We do not know. Since God is beyond all categories, he is superior to any affirmation and to any negation.[14]

3. THE DIVINE IDEAS

The second division of nature includes those created beings which are themselves creators. Philosophers have known both their existence and their nature, but they have given them many different names, such as "Ideas," "prototypes," "predestinations," "divine volitions," etc.[15] Whatever their name, these beings are the archetypes, or original patterns, of created things. Erigena himself uses different terms to express the way in which these beings are produced by God. He says, for example, that Ideas are "preformed," "established," "formed," or "made," but the meaning of these various expressions is always that of "created." Precisely because they are "beings," the Ideas are not God;[16] hence they must needs be creatures of God.

Created by the Father in the Word, Ideas subsist in him from all eternity. Since they have had no beginning in time, they can be said to be co-eternal with God. Yet, the title of "eternal" properly belongs to that only which has no beginning nor principle in any sense of the word; in short, God alone is eternal, and since Ideas are creatures of God, they cannot be said to have true eternity. This is why Erigena teaches that Ideas are, in a sense, eternal, and even co-eternal with God, but not quite, because they depend upon God for their eternal existence.[17]

This doctrine of the eternal creation of Ideas in God will be often criticized, and even condemned, by later theologians. And indeed, how can it be admitted that creatures are subsisting in God from all eternity? Yet, we should remember that, in Erigena's doctrine, God is above being. Like the God of Denis and of Plotinus, he is the One. Now, just as all numbers are eminently included in the perfect simplicity of the One, so also all Ideas are in God without altering his absolute unity. This is so true that the divine Word himself may be considered as the supreme Idea (*idea*), the reason (*ratio*) and the form (*forma*) of all things visible and invisible. He is moreover their cause, since all that is to develop in time is eternally in him as in its principle. In short, the Word of God is the reason and the creative cause, both perfectly simple and infinitely multiple, of the created universe (III, 1; 624 A C). The Word of Erigena seems to have inherited the main attributes and functions of the *nous* of Plotinus. He is a unity which, itself simple, contains the seeds of future multiplicity.

Let us admit, however, that this doctrine of Ideas involves a considerable difficulty. If the archetypes of things are creatures, they are necessarily finite, but, if they are finite, how can they be identified with the Word? Erigena himself has been obscurely aware of the problem, so much so that he has made several attempts to eliminate it.[18] Yet, when all is said and done, the main data from which it arises cannot be eliminated. Whether we call them "creatures" or not does not alter the fact that, in Erigena's doctrine, the Ideas are "made" by God; that, for this very reason, whereas the Word is strictly co-eternal with the Father, the Ideas are not: "I believe absolutely that the Son is wholly co-eternal with the Father; as to the things the Father makes (*facit*) in the Son, I say they are co-eternal with the Son, but not quite co-eternal" (II, 21; 561 C). In short, the reason why they should not be called creatures is not that they are not made, but that they are being made from all eternity. How else could Erigena posit Ideas as the second division of nature, that which both creates and is created? Obviously, his own thought is moving on another plane than that of the metaphysics of being. The true reason why what appears to us as self-contradictory did not raise insuperable difficulties in his own mind can only be made clear by an analysis of his notion of creation.

4. CREATION AND REVELATION

In a metaphysics of being, the word "creation" signifies the giving of being, to what we call creatures, by a supreme Being, whom we call their creator. In a metaphysics of the One, the word "creation" signifies the manifestation of unity through plurality. In the doctrine of Erigena, several different metaphors are used to convey this meaning. Creatures can be said to be, with respect to God, in the same relation as numbers are to absolute Unity; or they can be compared to light beams radiated from some intelligible Sun; or else they can be said to be in the same relation to God as the radii of a circumference are to its center. Whatever the image, the meaning is the same. The God of Erigena is like unto a principle which, incomprehensible in its simplicity, reveals itself at a stroke in the multiplicity of its consequences. This self-manifestation of God is the true meaning of creation in Erigena's doctrine. This is why he often calls it a "theophany," that is to say, an "apparition of God." For God to create is to reveal himself, and since to create is to reveal, to say that God reveals himself is tantamount to saying that he creates himself.[19] In other words, just as revelation is creation, creation is revelation.

This remark first applies to the so-called creation of Ideas. Their creation is the first of all theophanies. In Ideas God begins to emerge from the most hidden secret of his nature and he reveals himself to himself. And indeed, since God is beyond being, he is non-being; as such, God is unknowable not only to us, but to himself, unless he begins to reveal himself to himself under the form of the only objects accessible to intellectual knowledge, namely beings. This is why we had to say that, in producing Ideas, God creates himself, because, instead of remaining in his own inaccessible transcendency, God then "begins to be in something" which is his self-manifestation.

From this moment on, the multiplication of beings continues without interruption until it reaches individuals. Creation properly so-called is the work of the Father, and it consists in producing Ideas in the Word. Strictly speaking, creation is from then on complete: "the cognition of that which is, is that which is." In other words, for Ideas, to be known and to be are one and the same thing. Nor should we imagine that this creation of Ideas has to be followed by another one, which will be the creation of things. All beings are already implicitly contained in the Ideas as in their universal causes. All that still remains to be done in order to produce the world as we see it is to let the Ideas externalize their content, from the universal to the particular. By a continuous process of division which follows a down-ward hierarchical order, genera follow from Ideas; then, from genera follow the sub-genera, then the species, and, lastly, the individual substances. This emanation of the multiple from the One is the work of the third person of the Holy Trinity, the Holy Ghost. He is the fecundator and distributor of divine largesse. And so every creature, reproducing in its own way the image of God, is defined by a constitutive trinity: essence, which corresponds to the Father; active virtue, corresponding to the Son; operation, corresponding to the Holy Ghost.[20]

5. CREATION AND ILLUMINATION

The notion of creation conceived as a revelation introduces into the Erigenian universe another theme, that of "illumination." There were scriptural reasons to stress this notion. In a text of paramount importance to mediaeval thinkers, and which Erigena himself has often quoted and commented, it is said that: "Every best gift (*datum*), and every perfect present (*donum*), is from above, coming down from the Father of lights" (James, i, 17). Moreover, Saint Paul had said: "All that is made manifest is light" (Ephes., 5, 13). Thence comes, in many mediaeval doctrines, the two-fold illumination of grace (*donum*) and nature (*datum*). Thus conceived, nature is a light given by the Father of lights. In other words, all created beings are lights: *omnia quae sunt, lumina sunt,* and their very essence consists in being so many reflections of the divine light. Made up of that multitude of tiny lamps that things are, creation is only an illumination intended to show God.[21]

This conception of the creative act entails a correlative notion of the nature of created things. A manifestation of the divine light, the world would cease to be if God ceased to radiate. Each thing is therefore essentially a sign, a symbol, wherein God makes himself known to us. In Erigena's own words: "There is nothing, in visible and corporeal things, that does not signify something incorporeal and invisible" (V, 3; 865-866). This statement could be said to be the charter of mediaeval symbolism, not only in theology and philosophy, but even in the decorative art of the cathedrals. The universe is a revelation comparable to Holy Scripture. Let us look at things: each and every one of them is a word spoken to us by the Word.

The hierarchical illumination, or theophany, which constitutes the universe, divides itself into three worlds: that of purely immaterial substances, namely angels, that of corporeal and visible substances, and between the two, sharing in the natures of both and linking them together, this universe in reduction, man. God is present in all these beings as in his participations. Let us remember, however, that the word "participate" is here a misleading one. No creature is, in any sense, a "part" of God. In the doctrine of Erigena, "participation" signifies "distribution." Exactly, it signifies the hierarchical distribution of the graces and of the natures which enter the structure of the universe (III, 3; 631 A). Here, as in many other cases, Erigena speaks Latin, but he thinks in Greek. The notion which, in his mind, answers the word *participatio,* is the Greek notion of *metousia,* which does not mean "to share being in common with," but, rather, "to have being after," and as a consequence of, another being (III, 3; 632 B).

The so-called "pantheistic" formulas of Erigena should always be read in the light of this precision. When he says, for instance, that God is, in all things, whatever they are, or that God is the entity of all things (*est enim omnium essentia*), we should never forget that, to him, God is in each and every thing as the sun is in each and every light. But even this is not quite true, for indeed, whereas both the sun and its radiations are light, God himself is in beings as what is beyond being. Erigena has always understood in this sense the famous formula of Denis: "the being of all things is the Deity which is above being" (*esse omnium est superesse deitas*). The most extreme formulas of Erigena should be read in this sense, not in order to palliate them, but because this is the meaning they had in his own mind. We are used to considering creation as a relation between beings and Being; consequently, when we read in Erigena that "God and creature are one and the same thing," we naturally label him as a pantheist. No error could be more excusable, yet, in point of fact, Erigena only means that each and every creature is essentially a manifestation, under the form of being, of what is above being. The *esse* of a being is but a light radiated by the *superesse,* which is God.[22]

If correctly understood, the very notion of "hierarchy" implies both the relation of beings to the Divinity and the distance they are from their source. The word itself does not simply mean a system of ranks and orders, but, exactly, a system of "sacred" ranks and orders. Just as the nature of a being is to be a light which shows God, its degree of perfection corresponds to the very amount of *superesse* which it reveals. The most perfect creatures, which we call angels, owe their dignity to the fact that they are the most perfect manifestations of God under the form of beings. Angels, then, occupy the summit of the universal hierarchy of beings. Incorporeal beings, they have, nevertheless, spiritual bodies, simple and not perceptible to sense. Unlike man, they enjoy an immediate cognition of the Divinity. This does not mean that the angels see God face to face. No one has ever seen God; no creature will ever see him directly and in himself, that is, in his unmanifested transcendency. What angels see by immediate and direct sight are the first "theophanies," or manifestations of, God. Of course, since, in a sense, the theophanies of God are God, to see them is to see God. It even is to see his whole being, since, beyond these theophanies he is the supreme non-being. The fact remains, however, that the angels do not even see the archetypal Ideas, which would be for them to see the divine Word; they contemplate the first theophanies of the Word manifesting himself out of himself. Nothing could help us more to realize how, despite its misleading language, this doctrine is anxious to keep God above all finite being. Even the blessed, in the beatific vision, will not be able to see the innermost secret of the divinity. Strangely enough, while some theologians will accuse Erigena of confusing God and creatures, others will accuse him of completely separating creatures from God.[23]

6. THE HIERARCHY OF BEINGS

The divine theophanies do not communicate themselves to the angels equally; on the contrary, they are distributed according to a hierarchical scale, the most perfect angels receiving the first theophanies and transmitting them gradually downward. Here again, let us mind our expressions: this hierarchical transmission is not something added to the nature of angels and of their ordered hierarchy; it is their very nature and hierarchy. Every angel is part of the universal theophany; it is a particular theophany, and its place in the world order is determined by its relations to all the higher angels which illuminate it from above, and all the angels below which it itself illuminates. Its very being and essence can thus be defined by the amount of intelligible light which it both receives (or *is*) and transmits to others. Its individual nature is that of a unique moment in the universal manifestation of God.[24]

Thus distinguished and hierarchized, the angels make up an "order" whose intrinsic beauty is that of the universe. For, indeed, what is true of angels is equally true of all other creatures. All of them participate in the divine illumination through the intermediary of the angels, and the amount of perfection which constitutes its own being is, for each and every creature, exactly proportional to the degree of illumination which it represents. Such is precisely the case of man. Still less than the angels from whom he receives his illumination is man capable of illuminating himself by his own means. Just like air, which is only shadows as long as the light of the sun does not penetrate it, man is capable of wisdom only insofar as the light of the divine theophanies reaches him through the hierarchy of angelic substances. Because he is made up of mind and body, man is the lowest of all beings whose nature is capable of intellectual illumination.

To conceive correctly the nature of man, however, we must consider him in two different conditions; first, such as he was created by God; next, such as he now is in consequence of original sin (IV, 9; 780 B).

In his primitive condition, man was much more like an angel than he now is. True enough, man had a body, but mankind was not then divided into sexes. The division of human beings into males and females, together with the animal mode of reproduction which attends it, is, in Erigena's own words, an additional device contrived by God as one of the remedies to original sin.[25] The same remark applies, within each one of the two sexes, to the multiplication of individuals differing in figure, kind of life, customs and thought (II, 7; 533). Basically speaking, the true man is the Idea of man in God. In this Idea, all possible individual human beings were eternally contained and it is through their own fault that they have now become separated from it. Strictly speaking, these two divisions are more the results of original sin than they are this sin itself. The tragic side of the picture is that, once it got started, nothing has been able to stop this process of separation through multiplication. There is no stopping point for creatures in their wandering away from unity.

Nor is this all. In separating himself from God, man so to speak carried with him, in his fall, all the beings of inferior nature whose Ideas were contained in his own, and which, since they were there as intelligible realities, enjoyed a much more perfect type of being than the one they now have in their present state of separation. If the nature of this change seems difficult to conceive, let us remember that, according to Erigena, the Ideas occupy a sort of intermediate position between God and creatures (III, 20; 683 B), so that, having real being, they can be considered as the very same realities migrating, so to say, from their condition of unity in God to their condition of multiplicity in the present universe. Far from being more real now than they used to be in the unity of their Ideas, creatures have in fact degenerated. The physical triangle which we imagine is only a drawn representation of the intelligible triangle which geometry defines in the purity of its universal essence. Of these two, which is the truer triangle? Obviously, the intelligible pattern which includes in its unity an infinite number of material ones. The true triangle then exists in the thought of the geometer only, and the same is the case with all geometrical figures (IV, 8; 774 C-775 A). In the same sense, all bodies are less truly real in themselves than they are in their own Ideas in God.[26]

To this conclusion the ready objection is that the very materiality of corporeal beings cannot possibly exist in a mind; consequently, material beings can exist in a mind inasmuch as they are known, but not in themselves and with their material nature. But this is an illusion. If we consider material bodies, their specific forms appear to us as intelligible; their quantity is also submitted to intelligible laws; even their sensible qualities are made up of intelligible elements whose confusion begets what we call corporeal matter, but which we can analyse again into purely intelligible components. The genesis of sensible matter, then, can be explained completely by principles that do not fall under the perception of the senses. In point of fact, matter itself is neither sensible nor imaginable, it is conceivable by thought only. To sum up, matter is twice intelligible: in itself as the receiver of its sensible qualities, and in its sensible qualities themselves, which are a confused mixture of intelligible elements.[27]

If this be true, there is no metaphysical reason why material beings could not have been created by God, under the form of their respective Ideas, in the mind of man (IV, 8; 773 D-774 B). The fact that Genesis places the creation of man after that of all other creatures does not raise any difficulty; for indeed the creation of Adam should not be mistaken for the creation of man-in-himself. Adam, who was *a* man, has been created last, but the Idea of man has been created in the Word from all eternity. Now we should not imagine the Idea of man in God like man after original sin, full of error and ignorance. God desired man to be possessed of the knowledge of all beings, and since we said above that things exist more truly in thought than in themselves, it is clear that they were created by God, before the formation of the sensible world, in the knowledge that the archetypal man had of them. Without original sin, we still would be able to know things by their Ideas in us, prior to, and independently of, our sensible perception of them.

Such is the world of Erigena. It is a universe made up of bodies that are only "coagulated" intelligible qualities (*coagulatis videlicet illarum qualitatibus*) and which exist much more truly in their divine Ideas than in themselves. Just as all things come from the Word, where they should have eternally subsisted as in their native country, they are now striving to return to him.[28]

7. THE RETURN TO GOD

Although the multiplication of the world of bodies is a consequence of original sin, we should not imagine that the sensible world is a place of penitence where man has to expiate his crime. God has created it by an act of compassion, and as a place where sensible things would lead fallen man back to the intelligible realities from which he voluntarily separated himself. Even here, Christian optimism does not lose its rights.[29]

In the first place, let us note that there is no being that does not carry about itself the mark of God, so that all beings invite man to turn his thoughts toward their creator. This is particularly true of man himself. Material bodies are only imprints of God, but man has been made unto God's image and likeness. Scripture says so, and the fact can be verified by comparing the trinity of sensation, reason and intellection in man with the trinity of the divine persons. In itself, the soul is one and simple, and although it exercises various operations, it is entirely intellection, entirely reasoning, and so on with sensation, memory and life.[30] Its simplicity must not be forgotten even when, as we now have to do, we analyse its various operations.

The first operation of the soul is a pure intellectual activity. In this truly mystical contemplation, which transcends sensations, images and even the discursive operations of reasoning, the intellect is entirely turned toward God. The second operation of the soul is inferior in dignity to the first. It is a consideration of God in the soul itself. Its object is God and his attributes, no longer in his transcendent perfection, but as creator of the universe. In other words, the object of this contemplation is God as revealed in his "theophanies." The third operation of the soul is a complex motion which, starting from some impression made by an external object on one of our sensory organs, produces the internal image of it which we call sensation. The soul always remains one and wholly present in each one of these proceedings. It is a "pure thought" which progressively "divides" itself more and more as it descends from the contemplation of divine unity to reasoning and even to sensation; conversely, it still is a "pure thought" when, starting from the multiplicity of sense knowledge, it reassembles individuals through reasoning, into their species and genera, and ultimately brings them back to the unity of God.[31]

Considered in this light, the soul not only imitates God in his Trinity, it revolves around him. Nay more: the soul never leaves God, for what it knows of him when it turns to him by means of pure thought, it does not forget when it descends to the genera, the species and individuals. All knowledge is the work of the one and triune intellect, acting through reason with the help of consubstantial sense,[32] that is, of sense knowledge which is consubstantial with it. The multiplicity of operations of thought comes from it, subsists in it, and returns to it, as comes from God, subsists in God and returns to God the multiplicity of beings which constitutes the universe.

In order that this return may be accomplished, the same movement of love which spread out the hierarchy of beings must bring it back to unity. This recalling of things to God appears first as a sort of lack of internal necessity in beings themselves. Erigena calls it their formlessness, and he conceives it as a confused aspiration of matter toward form, of non-being toward being and, consequently, of multiplicity toward unity. Under the urge of this obscure thrust, the flood of beings acts like a river which, after being lost in the sands, would return to its source through the secret pores of the earth. This universal return is linked with that of man, and it begins at the point of maximum dispersion that the human being can attain, that is to say, death. As a result of sin, man has become like the beasts, subject to passions, to disease and to corruption. At the time of death the soul separates itself from the body, which, in turn, divides itself into its constitutive elements and disperses in earth; but precisely because the circulation of beings is an uninterrupted stream, the final moment of "division" is one with the first moment of "analysis." Just as, on a voyage, the point of arrival of the trip out is the starting point of the return trip, the death of man is the initial stage of his return to God.[33]

The second stage will be the resurrection of bodies which will be the joint effect of both nature and grace. The sexes will then be abolished and man will be as he would have been if God had not foreseen his fall at the time of creation. In the course of a third stage, the body of each individual will return to the soul from which it was separated by way of division. This reunion itself will require several return stages: the body will become life again; life will become sense; sense will become reason and reason will become pure thought. A fourth stage will return the human soul to its primary cause or Idea and, together with the soul, the body it has reabsorbed. By this movement, all those beings whose intelligible forms subsist in the intellect of man will be brought back to God. The fifth and last moment of this universal "analysis" will bring the terrestrial sphere back to Paradise. As this movement will propagate itself from sphere to sphere, nature and all its causes will let themselves be progressively permeated by God as air is by light. From that time and on, there will be nought else but God, and this will be the end of the great return, "when nothing else will be left but God." [34]

This first process of return already implies the work of grace, since, without the resurrection of Christ which is the pledge of our own resurrection, the universal movement toward God would be impossible; but it is completed by a second which is the work of grace alone. Good or bad, all men will once more inevitably recover the perfections with which they had been endowed by their creator. If then a new grace is added to the preceding one, it will no longer be for the purpose of restoring all natures, but to raise some of them to a truly "supernatural" state. Such will be the effect of beatifying grace, which will lift the chosen souls according to three stages. Having become pure thought again, that is, a pure Intellect, man will first attain plenary knowledge of all the intelligible beings in which God makes himself manifest; then he will be raised from this knowledge of Ideas to Wisdom itself, which is the self-subsisting plenary manifestation of God; the third and last degree will be the loss of even pure thought in the transcendent darkness of that inaccessible Light wherein are hidden the causes of all that is. What we call "beatific vision" will therefore take place beyond vision. It will not be the seeing of a light, but, rather, being engulfed in Light.[35]

Let us not believe, however, that this return of human nature and all other natures to God, that is, in Erigena's own words, their "deification," will result in their annihilation. Quite the contrary; since, as has been said, things are more real in their Ideas than in themselves, all nature will then recover the plenary reality which is its intelligible reality in God. Air does not cease to be air because the sun's light illumines it; red-hot iron is still iron, even though it seems to be transformed into fire; so, the body will still be a body when it is spiritualized, and the human soul will still be what it is in becoming transfigured to the light of God. In short, there will be no blending or confusion of substances, but a reunion, without mixture or composition, where all properties will immutably subsist.[36]

All this eschatology accounts for the chosen without difficulty, but what is to be done with the damned? In a universe where matter shall be dissolved into its intelligible elements, there is no place for a material hell. Like Origen, Erigena considers the notion of a material Gehenna to be a remnant of pagan superstition that the real Christians should get rid of. At least in the *De divisione naturae,* for the *De praedestinatione* seems to speak otherwise, Erigena considers the Valley of Josaphat (Joel, 3, 2), the cankerworms and the pools of sulphur, so dear to preachers, as childish imaginings, and he defends himself with great verve against those who attack him on this point. Where there is no corporeal matter left, how could there be valleys, worms or pools? Moreover, corporeal or not, should these punishments be considered eternal? To answer "yes," is to concede the final victory of sin, evil and the devil, in a creation which Jesus Christ has redeemed by his sacrifice. Unless we consent to the defeat of God by the devil, we must, on the contrary, affirm the final victory of good over evil. And the two problems are solved at the same time. With the reabsorption of matter into the intelligible, all trace of evil will one day disappear from nature. This done, the supernatural distinction between the chosen and the condemned will remain whole and will persist eternally, but each one will be beatified or punished in his own conscience.[37] Beatitude is eternal life, and since eternal life is to know truth, knowledge of truth is eternal beatitude. Conversely, if there is no other misery than eternal death, and if eternal death is ignorance of truth, there is no other eternal punishment than ignorance of truth, and who is truth, if not Christ? "Nothing then is to be desired but joy of the truth, which is Christ, and nothing is to be shunned but his absence, which is the one and only cause of all eternal sadness. Take Christ from me and nothing good will be left me, no torment can terrify me; for the deprivation and absence of Christ is the torment of any rational creature. That, and nothing else, at least in my opinion." [38]

It is easy to imagine the stupefaction of Scotus Erigena's contemporaries before that immense metaphysical and theological epic, hardly believable, and yet guaranteed at practically every point by the authority of Denis, Maximus Confessor, the two Gregories, or any one of the many ecclesiastical writers whom the astonishing erudition of its author enabled him to invoke. This "barbarian, placed on the outskirts of the world," of whom Anastasius the Librarian spoke with surprise to King Charles the Bald, aroused many misgivings. To us, he appears as the Latin discoverer of the immense world of Greek theology, that is to say, of a hitherto unknown mental universe whose wealth he had no time to sort out nor to assimilate.[39] Condemned and recondemned to destruction, his writings have nevertheless survived and they even seem to have exercised a kind of underground activity. No one, after him, has ever dared to take up as a whole a doctrine so little suited to the sober teachings of the Latin tradition, but it was to remain as a sort of permanent temptation against which, from century to century, doctrinal authorities were never to cease struggling, without ever succeeding in killing it.

CHAPTER II

SAINT ANSELM OF CANTERBURY

THE movement initiated by Scotus Erigena did not survive its author. Even apart from the aberrant character of some of its features, the doctrine did not find a political and social environment favorable to the development of a philosophical school. Soon after the death of Charlemagne (814), the Normans had begun to invade and to plunder the Loire valley, in France, up to the monastery of Tours (838). In 845, they sailed the river Seine up to Paris and plundered the famous abbey of Saint Germain des Prés. Paris was attacked a second time, in 885, by Rollo, their chieftain, who finally settled with his warriors in what we now call the province of Normandy (911). Moreover, the decadence of the Carolingian dynasty in France after the death of Charles the Bald (877) was attended by a political disorder no less harmful to cultural life than the Scandinavian invasions. The revival of philosophical production in France was not to take place before the restoration of the royal power by Hugh Capet (987). This is not to say that intellectual life died completely during the tenth century. It survived in some Benedictine monasteries, owing to the personal endeavors of obscure men whose good services should not be forgotten.[40] Yet, when all is said and done, there is for historians of philosophy little to reap on the desolate ground which extends from the death of Erigena up to the early eleventh-century theological controversies between "dialecticians" and "anti-dialecticians." In point of fact, they all were dialecticians, but they disagreed on some applications of dialectics to Christian faith.[41] The conflict which then arose between the defenders of a strictly monastic ideal of Christian life and those of a wise use of secular culture found its first satisfactory solution, between the walls of a monastery, in the writings of Saint Anselm of Canterbury.

I. REASON AND FAITH

Saint Anselm[42] is clearly conscious of his attitude with regard to the relation of reason to faith. The *Monologium* was written especially at the request of certain monks of Bec who desired a model for meditation on the existence and essence of God, in which everything would be proved by reason and where absolutely nothing would be based on Scriptural authority.[43]

Two sources of knowledge are at the disposition of Christians, reason and faith. Against the excesses of some dialecticians, Anselm affirms that one must first become firmly established in faith, and, consequently, he refuses to submit Holy Scripture to dialectics. Faith is for a Christian the given point from which he is to start. The facts that he is to understand and the realities that his reason shall have to interpret are given to him by revelation; one does not understand in order to believe, but on the contrary, one believes in order to understand: *neque enim quaero intelligere ut credam, sed credo ut intelligam.*[44] Understanding of faith, in short, presupposes faith. But, inversely, Saint Anselm takes sides against the irreducible adversaries of dialectics. For him who begins by being firmly established in faith, there is no objection to striving to understand rationally what he believes. To object to this legitimate use of reason, of which the Apostles and Fathers have already said all that has to be said, is to forget, first, that truth is so vast and profound that mortals can never succeed in exhausting it; that the days of man are numbered, so that even the Fathers were not able to say everything they would have said had they lived longer; that God has never ceased and never will cease to enlighten his Church; last, not the least, it is to forget that between faith and the beatific vision to which we all aspire there is here below an intermediary which is the understanding of faith. To understand one's faith is to draw nearer to the very sight of God. The order to be observed in the search for truth is therefore the following: first, to believe the mysteries of faith before discussing them through reason; next, to endeavor to understand what one believes. Not to put faith first is presumption; not to appeal to reason next is negligence. Both of those faults must therefore be avoided.[45]

Such being the rule, it remains to be known just how far reason can actually go, in the interpretation of faith. One must believe in order to understand, but can everything one believes be made intelligible? Is faith which seeks knowledge assured of finding it? It can be said that, practically, Saint Anselm's confidence in reason's power of interpretation is unlimited. He does not confuse faith and reason, since the exercise of reason presupposes faith; but everything happens as though one could always manage to understand, if not what one believes, at least the necessity of believing it. Saint Anselm did not shrink from the task of proving the necessity of the Trinity and the Incarnation.

In order to realize Saint Anselm's exact position on this point, we must bear in mind certain definite conditions under which he took up his task. He had an excellent knowledge of Augustine, but none at all of Plotinus, whose metaphysics alone would have enabled him to continue the work of his master along the same line. In the eleventh century philosophy proper was reduced to Aristotle's dialectic. No physics, no anthropology, no metaphysics, no purely rational ethics were known to the men of that period. To understand the sacred text was therefore first of all to seek understanding of it with the help of what resources a dialectician had at his disposal. Saint Anselm therefore did, with the philosophical technique then at hand, what Saint Thomas was to do over again in the thirteenth century after the discovery of the entire works of Aristotle. Arguing as a pure dialectician, Anselm proposed not to render the mysteries of faith intelligible in themselves, which would have been to suppress them, but to prove by what he called "necessary reasons" that rational inquiry well-conducted necessarily ends in supporting them. That was a high ambition, but it must not be forgotten that however strongly he might trust the power of reason, Saint Anselm never imagined that it would succeed in understanding mystery. To prove by logically necessary reasons that God exists, that he is one single God in three Persons, and that the incarnation of the Word was necessary to save mankind, is not to understand the secrets of divine nature or the mystery of a God made man for our salvation.[46] To understand a mystery would be much more than to understand its necessity.

2. THE EXISTENCE OF GOD IN THE *Monologium*

The *Monologium,* where nothing is established on the strength of revelation, but on that of reason alone, rests entirely upon its demonstrations of the existence of God.[47] Taken in themselves, these demonstrations presuppose the acceptance of two principles: first, a principle which is given to us in experience as an observable fact, namely, that things are unequal in perfection; next, a sort of immediate intellectual evidence, namely, that things which possess a perfection in a higher or a lower degree, derive it from the same perfection taken in its supreme degree. In other words, the mainspring of these demonstrations will be that the relative always is a participation in the absolute, whose existence is therefore required by that of its participations.

The starting point of the first proof is the given fact that there is goodness in things. This fact cannot be denied, for indeed we desire things, and we only desire them because we judge them to be good. It is therefore a natural question, and almost an inevitable one, to ask: whence come all those things we consider good? Now, on the one hand, we experience by sense and we know through reason that there are many different types of goods; on the other hand, we know that these goods must have a cause, but we may well wonder whether each good thing has its own particular cause or whether there is not a single cause for all these goods. Now it is absolutely certain and evident that all that possesses a perfection to a greater or less degree owes that perfection to the fact that it participates in one single and same principle. Everything which is more or less just is so because it participates more or less in absolute justice. Therefore, since all particular goods are unequally good, they can only be good by their participation in a single and same good. But this good by which everything is good can be only one great good. All the rest is good by it and it alone is good by itself. Now nothing of what is good by another is superior to what is good by itself. This sovereign good then surpasses all the rest to the point of having nothing above itself. That is to say, what is sovereignly good is also sovereignly great. There is, therefore, a primary being, superior to everything that exists, and it is him whom we call God.[48]

We can broaden the basis of this proof. Instead of arguing from the perfections noted in different beings, one can argue from the perfection they have in common, although in varying degrees, and which is being. As a matter of fact, everything which is has a cause; the only question arising with regard to the totality of things is, then, to know whether it is derived from several causes or from one single cause. If the universe has several causes, either they lead back to a single cause, or they exist by themselves, or they produce one another. If they lead back to a single one, it is evidently that sole cause which is the cause of the universe. If they exist by themselves, it is because they possess in common at least the faculty of existing by themselves, and it is this common faculty which causes them to be; they can therefore still be considered as coming under one same cause. There would be left only the third hypothesis, according to which these causes cause one another; but it is self-contradictory to admit that a thing exists in virtue of that to which it gives being. That is not true even of the terms of a relation, nor of the relation itself. The master and the servant are relative to one another, but each one does not exist in virtue of the other, and neither is the double relationship which unites them generated by itself, but it comes from the two real subjects between which it obtains. Thus, therefore, one single hypothesis remains acceptable; namely, that everything which exists, exists in virtue of a single cause, and that cause which exists by itself is God.[49]

The third proof bears on the degrees of perfection which things possess. It is enough just to cast a glance over the universe to note that the beings which constitute it are more or less perfect. This is an established fact to which no one can take exception. One could not be a man oneself and question whether horses are superior to trees, or men superior to horses. Now, granted that natures are superior to one another, one must admit either an infinity of beings, so that no being is so perfect that there is not one still more perfect; or else a finite number of beings, and consequently one being more perfect than all the rest. Now, to admit the existence of an infinite number of things is an absurd supposition. Therefore, there necessarily exists a nature that is superior to all and inferior to none. True enough, still another supposition is possible. One might imagine that several natures, equal in perfection, occupy the peak of the universal hierarchy. But this hypothesis is no less absurd than the preceding one, for if these several natures are equal, they must be so in virtue of what they have in common; now, if what they have in common is their essence, then they have a common essence and are only one single nature, whereas, if what they have in common is something else than their essence, then this common element is another nature, superior to them and in which they participate.[50] This proof rests upon the impossibility of not ending a series by a single term, when the series is a hierarchy which includes a finite number of terms.

3. THE PROOF OF THE *Proslogion*

Anselm had always desired to find proofs of the existence of God as simple and as immediately evident as possible. The three demonstrations of the *Monologium* seemed to him, though valid, still too complicated. After protracted investigations he finally discovered a new one, whose only presupposition was the knowledge of the word "God" and of the only meaning that can be ascribed to it. As it is presented in the *Proslogion*, this proof is one more application of the general rule: "faith seeking understanding." In point of fact, such was the title which he himself had first given to his treatise and which he changed later on to that of *Proslogiom*.

We know at least the word "God"; we even believe that God exists, and that he is what we believe him to be, namely, a being than which no greater can be conceived. The question is to know whether or not what we believe to be true is true. In other words, can what we believe to be true be demonstrated in the natural light of reason?

This is not evident. In fact, some deny the existence of such a being. According to the testimony of Holy Scripture, "The fool has said in his heart, there is no God" (Ps. 13, 1). Yet, if we say: a being than which no greater can be conceived, even the fool understands what we say, and what he understands exists in his understanding, even if he does not understand it to exist in reality. It is indeed possible for a thing to exist in an intellect without that intellect knowing that the thing exists in reality. When a painter pictures to himself the work he is going to paint, he has it in his intellect, but he is not conscious of its existence, as he has not yet painted it; when he has painted his picture, on the contrary, he both has his work in his intellect and is conscious of its existence, since he has already made it. We can, therefore, convince the fool himself that, at least in his mind, there is a being than which none greater can be conceived, because, when he hears these words, he understands them and what he understands is in his intellect. Now that which is such that nothing greater can be conceived cannot exist only in the intellect. For indeed, to exist in reality is greater than to exist in the intellect only. If, then, that which is such that one can conceive nothing greater exists only in the intellect, that than which nothing greater can be conceived is that than which something greater can be conceived, which is contradictory. The being than which none greater can be conceived then necessarily exists both in the intellect and in reality.[51]

The principles on which this argument rests are as follows: 1) a notion of God given by faith; 2) to exist in thought is to be truly; 3) the existence of the notion of God in thought requires logically that one affirm that he exists in reality. Here again, indeed, we start from a fact, but from a fact which belongs to a special order, that of revelation. The whole abstract dialectic which unfolds here goes from faith to reason and returns to its point of departure, reaching the conclusion that what is proposed by faith is rationally intelligible. Moreover, our starting point is a notion. A certain idea of God exists in thought: there we have the given fact; now this existence, which is real, logically demands that God exist also in reality: there we have the proof. It comes about through a comparison of the thought being and the actual being which compels our reason to posit the second as superior to the first. As early as the middle ages, the decisiveness of that proof has been questioned, and during the very lifetime of Saint Anselm it met a shrewd contradictor in the person of the monk Gaunilon. Gaunilon raised two main objections. First, that we have no distinct notion of God from which to infer his existence; next, that one cannot rely upon existence in thought to prove existence outside of thought. As a matter of fact, to exist as an object of thought is not to have a true existence; it is simply to be conceived. Now, one can conceive a quantity of unreal or even impossible objects, which even though they are in thought, certainly have no existence outside of thought. They are only notions in the understanding which conceives them, and not at all realities. Why should it be otherwise with the idea of God? If we conceive the idea of the Blessed Isles, lost somewhere in the Ocean and full of inaccessible riches, it will not follow that these lands, conceived as the most perfect of all, also exist in reality. To which Saint Anselm replies that the passing from existence in thought to existence in reality is possible and necessary only when it is a question of the greatest being one can conceive. The notion of the Blessed Isles obviously contains nothing which forces thought to attribute existence to them. It belongs to God alone that one cannot think he does not exist.[52]

This demonstration of the existence of God is assuredly the triumph of pure dialectic operating on a definition. It derives its strength from a deep awareness of what is indeed unique in the notion of *being* taken in the absolute. Even those who object to the proof as such will no doubt acknowledge that Saint Anselm took the right view of things in underlining the irresistible force with which the notion of absolute being, that is to say, of a being than which no greater can be thought, calls as it were for the affirmation of its existence by the thought that conceives it. An indication that this was a valid intuition can be seen in the vitality of which Saint Anselm's argument has given proof in the course of succeeding centuries. There have always been philosophers to take it up and refashion it in their own way, and its implications are so manifold that the sole fact of having rejected or admitted it almost suffices to determine the doctrinal group to which a philosophy belongs. Saint Bonaventure, Descartes, Leibniz and Hegel took it up again, each in his own way, whereas Saint Thomas Aquinas, Locke and Kant rejected it, each in his own way. What all those who accepted it have in common is the identification of real existence with intelligible being conceived by thought; what all those who condemn its principle have in common is the refusal to consider any problem of existence aside from an empirically given existent.

4. ATTRIBUTES OF GOD AND CREATION

Once the existence of God has been proven by any one of these proofs, it is easy to deduce his principal attributes. Since God is that which cannot not exist, he is Being *par excellence,* that is, the plenitude of entity. We, therefore, give him the title of *essentia,* and this term, which signifies "plenary entity," can be applied properly to God alone. That is why we have been able to prove that he exists even from the simple notion that we have of him: to say that *essentia* is not, would be to say that that whose very nature is to be, is not. On the contrary, nothing of what is not God is being in the full sense of the term; then all the rest, which is not God, and which nevertheless exists, must necessarily derive its being from God. How can one conceive this dependence of the universe with regard to God?

Notice first that to exist through oneself and exist through someone else are two different ways of existing; one does not possess being in the same way in both cases. In God, who alone exists through himself, essence and being are identical; his nature is, just as light shines. Just as the nature of light is not separate from the brilliance it diffuses, so divine nature is not separate from the being it enjoys. It is quite another thing with beings that derive their existence from others; their essence is not such as necessarily implies existence and, in order that their nature may exist, being must be conferred on it by God. It remains to be seen how God confers it.

Only two hypotheses are possible: either God is the productive cause of the universe, or he is the very matter from which the universe is made. If we admit the latter hypothesis, we implicitly admit that everything is

God. For indeed, God is total being; if, therefore, the world was made of any particular matter, this matter must necessarily be identical with God's being. In order to avoid this absurd consequence, we must admit that the world has been created from nothing. The doctrine of creation *ex nihilo* is the only one which does not reduce God and the universe to one single being. Let us further add that it is not quite clear just how divine being could have served as a matter for the universe. God is sovereign good, and he would have to undergo a sort of corruption in order to have this imperfect and limited universe engendered from his substance. This leaves, therefore, only the first hypothesis we mentioned to begin with: the universe came into being without any pre-existing matter; it did not exist, and now, through God's power alone, it does exist. This appearance of the world, following its non-being so to speak, and taking place through a decree of divine wisdom and will, is precisely what is meant when we say that God created the world from nothingness.[53]

Absolutely to deny the world any kind of existence before the very instant of its creation would be, however, to exaggerate and to make its very appearance unintelligible. At the time when the universe had not yet been given the actual being it received from God, it already existed as model, form, image or rule in the thought of its creator; only, in that form it had no other reality than that of the creative essence itself. The Anselmian doctrine of divine Ideas is the exact opposite of the Erigenian doctrine of created Ideas. It is certainly true to say that, according to Saint Anselm, creatures are pre-existent in God; it is even true to add that, in God, they are and they subsist more truly than in themselves, but the reason for this is precisely that in God they are nothing else than God. Already present in his thought, creatures only came out of it through the effect of his word, or his Word; God "said" them and they were. This creative Word naturally had nothing in common with the words our mouths utter, nor with the same words when we do not utter them but think them inwardly; if one consented to resort to miserably deficient images, this Word would appear more like that inner view we have of things when we imagine them or when our reason thinks their universal essence. Uttered words, either spoken or thought, are peculiar to each nation; the inner words by which we imagine beings or think essences, are common to all nations: it is truly a universal language by which all minds communicate. So it was a word, or a Word, of this kind, a prototype of the very world whose existence it preceded, which was, in divine thought, the model of things created, the means of their creation, and which remains even now that by which God knows them.[54]

Thus, everything which is not the essence of God was created by God, and just as he gave to all things the being they have, he sustains and preserves them to allow them to persevere in being. That is to say that God is everywhere present, sustaining all by his power, and that wherever he is not, nothing is.[55] If, therefore, we wish to say something of a being so completely transcendent to all created beings, we must attribute to him names which designate a positive perfection, and only such. Even this attributing is legitimate only under two conditions. In the first place, these names must be attributed to him absolutely and not relatively to creatures. Declaring divine substance superior to all creatures is not characterizing it, for if the universe did not exist, divine perfection, absolute in itself, would not suffer any change or diminution. In the second place, it is not legitimate to attribute all positive perfections indifferently to God, but only those which, absolutely speaking, it is better to be than not to be. We give God only those qualifications which attribute to him what is most perfect in each genus. For instance, we shall not say that God is a body, for we know something superior to the body, namely spirit; on the other hand, since we know nothing superior to spirit in the genus being, we shall say that God is spirit. Thus, in attributing to God all that, absolutely speaking, it seems to us better to be than not to be, we prove that God is, and that he is, indivisibly, living, wise, powerful and all-powerful, true, just, blessed, eternal. All these perfections are brought together in God without altering his perfect simplicity. Since he is by himself, and since existence is identical with essence in him, he has neither beginning nor end. He is in all places and in all times, without being confined to any place or any time. He is immutable, and his essence remains identical with itself, without receiving any accident. A substance and individual spirit, God does not, however, allow himself to be restricted to that category of substance which fits only created beings. He alone *is,* in the full meaning of this word, and other beings, compared to him, *are not.*[56]

5. KNOWLEDGE AND WILL

Among creatures, man is one of those in which the image of God is most easily found imprinted on his handiwork by the creator. When man examines his conscience he discovers in his soul vestiges of the Trinity. Of all creatures, only the human soul recollects itself, understands itself and loves itself, and by that memory, that intelligence and that love it constitutes an ineffable Trinity.[57] The knowledge we acquire of things requires the co-operation of the senses and the intellect, but Saint Anselm is not precise about the manner of that co-operation and is content to take up again, without going into them too deeply, some Augustinian expressions on God's illumination of the soul. As to the object of general ideas, Saint Anselm is vigorously opposed to the nominalist tendencies of Roscelin,[58] and through reaction against the attitude of his adversary, he insists upon the reality of genera and species to the point of making it a condition necessary for theological orthodoxy. According to him, if one cannot even understand how several men, collected together in their species, can form a single man, he will much less easily understand how one single God can be three distinct persons. This reality attributed to the object of general ideas is one of the elements which turned Saint Anselm's thought to the discovery of the ontological argument and permitted him to argue directly on the degrees of perfection in his proofs of the existence of God. If the objects of general notions are real, each degree of perfection is a degree of reality, and the idea of the most perfect being that can be conceived brings us straightway to the highest degree of reality. The passing over from idea to being was bound to tempt Saint Anselm's thought, because, for him, the objects of ideas were already beings.[59]

These indications are completed by a theory of truth considered in its most metaphysical aspect. The truth of a cognition derives from its "rectitude," that is to say, it is, as it should be, the correct understanding of what its object is. But that is only one particular form of truth. Like the knowledge that understands it, the object known has its own form of truth, and that again is a "rectitude": everything is true insofar as it is what it should be according to its idea in God. A will is true if it is upright; an action is true for the same reason. In short, truth is the conformity of what is, to the rule which fixes what it should be, and as this rule is always, in the last analysis, the divine essence, the *De veritate* concludes that there is only one truth of all that is true, namely, God.[60]

This notion of truth conceived as a "rectitude" dominates the ethics of Saint Anselm as well as his epistemology. The will (*voluntas*) is first of all one of the powers of the soul: just as it sees through its sight, the soul makes decisions through its will. In a second sense, the word "will" points out an "affection," that is, a disposition of this power, or instrument of the soul, to operate in a certain way. For instance, the love of the parents for their children. In a third sense, "will" signifies the work done by this instrument or power of the soul, namely, volition.

Let us consider apart the second sense, that is, the "affections" or dispositions of the will. There are two main ones: an inclination toward the useful (*commodum*) and an inclination toward justice (*justitia*). The first is inseparable from the will: we always will something because it looks to us useful and, consequently, desirable. The second is separable from the will. Of course, if it is a question of desiring justice because of its usefulness, many men will be found to love justice. But the true love of justice is the one which loves it for the sake of justice itself.[61] This is the most noble of all our "affections," dispositions or inclinations. In fact, it is the only one which can lead us up to true beatitude.[62] This is not all. Besides the will, its inclinations and its acts, the soul is endowed with a power of execution which enables it to do what it wills to do, and even to will what it would like to will. This is its capacity to act (*aptitudo ad faciendum*). The verb "to act" here signifies: to exercise any act that can be signified by any verb. In short, any kind of acting or doing, as well as of not acting or not doing.[63]

Free choice (*liberum arbitrium*) includes two elements: *arbitrium*, that is, an arbitration whereby a judgment of reason says what should be done; then the *liberum*, that is, freedom, or liberty, which is the power of choosing and doing according to the rule of justice. Hence two important consequences: first, that since inclination toward justice is separable from the will, moral liberty can be lost; next, that the power of sinning is no part of liberty. This answers the oft-asked question: how is it possible for man to sin? When he sinned for the first time, man did so in virtue of his choice, which was free, but not in virtue of his liberty, since he used it in order to abdicate his freedom from sin. Let us take an example. Here is a free man, whom nothing obliges to serve any other man. Now, precisely because he is a free man, he has a choice between remaining free and serving somebody else. His choice is free, in this sense that it rests with him to do either one. If he chooses to serve, he does so in virtue of his own free choice; nevertheless, he is not behaving like a free man, since he is abdicating his freedom. Just so in the case of a sinful free choice: it is a free choice, but instead of using its freedom of choice, it chooses to give it up.[64]

The present condition of man is therefore different from what it was before sin. His primitive freedom of choice was his power of preserving justice, that is, as has been said, the inclination or affection of a will which wills justice for the sake of justice itself.[65] Since this was an inclination separable from the will, it could be lost. Its loss has been the loss of "rectitude." Since we have it no longer, our freedom of choice cannot consist in preserving it. Since we did not give it to ourselves, we are unable to recover it by our own forces. Nevertheless, we did not lose our free choice, we have lost our power to use it in a free way. We are like a man whose eyes are sound but who finds himself in utter darkness; he cannot see, not because he has lost sight, but because there is no light in which he could see. So also, we still have our free choice, but we have lost the power of using its freedom, because we have lost it in losing the inclination of the will toward justice, which is the very essence of liberty.[66]

This subtle doctrine is a reinterpretation of the classical distinction introduced by Augustine between "free choice" and "liberty." Strictly speaking, however, Anselm's own problem is that of the "liberty of choice." Where there is rational knowledge and judgment, there is choice; where there is inclination of the will toward justice, and power to act following this inclination, there is liberty. In God, liberty is uncreated and self-subsisting, so that it cannot possibly be lost. In man, liberty is a God-given and a created power which is separable from the will that has received it. After losing it, man still has his power of choice, but not his power to exercise it as a true liberty. Liberty is given back to free choice through grace. The loss of liberty becomes final only in the will of the reprobates after death. As to the blessed, they do not lose their freedom of choice, but grace in them is so abounding that they can no longer lose their liberty.[67]

The theology of Anselm is so full of rational speculation that one of his historians has labeled it a "Christian rationalism." [68] Its ambivalence is due to the fact that, expressing the inner life of a faith that seeks understanding, it is both overflowing with a religious feeling which sometimes borders on mysticism and full of a dialectical passion which translates faith into terms of rational necessity. Hence its twofold influence in the fields of theology and of philosophy.

In theology, Anselm has been called the father of scholasticism. There is a justification for giving him this title. Not indeed that he was the first one to make use of philosophy in matters of theological speculation, but he was the first to pursue the ideal of a theology whose dialectical rigor turned it into a kind of science. In this sense he was the forerunner of the thirteenth-century scholastics whose ambition it will be to build up, within faith, a science of faith. On the other hand, the same dialectical passion for "necessary reasons," the same consistent application of logical reasoning to abstract notions and definitions, the same insistence on reducing the gist of Augustine's doctrine to a well-knitted whole of demonstrated conclusions, forcefully evoke to the mind the later doctrinal synthesis of Duns Scotus. Even the Scotist statement that, if the Supreme Being is possible, then he exists, has been anticipated by Anselm, many centuries before it was to be reinterpreted by Leibniz.

In philosophy, Anselm's name remains inseparable from the so-called "ontological argument," that is to say, from the endless controversy which will divide metaphysicians during several centuries. Thomas Aquinas will reject it against Bonaventure; Locke will reject it against Descartes, while Hegel will favor it against Kant.[69] Obviously, to know whether a metaphysician is for or against some sort of "ontological" argument is not enough to know his philosophy, but it enables one to make a good guess about some fundamental aspects of his metaphysics.

CHAPTER III

PLATONISM IN THE TWELFTH CENTURY

THE twelfth century witnessed the development of a Platonist movement whose center was the school of Chartres.[70] This was a cathedral school, like that of York where Alcuin had received his education, not an abbatial school like those of St. Martin of Tours, of Fleury sur Loire or of Auxerre. Its renown went back to the teaching of Fulbert, Bishop of Chartres

(d. 1028), but the first master whose philosophical positions are somewhat known to us is Bernard of Chartres, chancellor of the school, who died between 1124 and 1130. From what we know of him, chiefly through John of Salisbury, his teaching was characterized by a strong insistence on the humanities and, in philosophy, by a distinctly Platonist trend. This does not mean that Bernard had a first-hand knowledge of Plato, but that he drew mainly from neoplatonist sources.[71] What is often called the Platonism of the twelfth century was almost entirely derived from secondary sources: fragments of Plato's *Timaeus* in the translation of Chalcidius; the commentary of Chalcidius on the same; Macrobius, Apuleius and Boethius. Special mention should be made of Seneca, whose influence was restricted to a rather narrow field, but contributed to the diffusion of some important metaphysical notions, especially concerning the doctrine of Ideas. The first important theologian whose philosophical positions are known to us is Gilbert of la Porrée (1076-1154), a disciple of Bernard of Chartres and his successor as chancellor of the schools.[72]

I. GILBERT OF LA PORRÉE

The middle ages traditionally ascribed to Gilbert the treatise known by the titles of *De sex principiis*, or *Liber sex principiorum*.[73] It is a metaphysical interpretation of Aristotle's treatise on logic, the *Categories*. Logically equivalent, the categories of Aristotle are not so for the metaphysician. When we say: substance, quantity, quality, etc., it is obvious that, in reality itself, substance is something very different from color, figure, size, etc. Dividing the ten categories into two groups, the author of this treatise listed together, on the one hand, substance, quantity, quality and relation, and on the other hand, the last six categories (*sex principia*): place, time, situation, habit, action and passion. To him, categories are not merely types of logical predication; they are forms. The first group of four comprises "inherent forms"; the second group of six comprises "accessory forms" (*formae assistentes*). It is to be noted, with Hauréau, that Abélard also calls the two categories of "place" and "time": *principia adjacentia*, but the chronology of their respective writings is too uncertain for us to draw any conclusion as to possible relations between them.

Taken in itself, the distinction was an important one. This treatise calls "inherent" the forms or principles which are either substance itself or inherent in substance itself irrespective of its relations with other substances. Such is manifestly the case with quantity and quality, the quantity of a substance being its own quantity and its qualities its own qualities. At first glance, the contrary seems true of relations, yet, taken in itself, relation is the natural aptitude of a substance to be one of the two terms of a relation. As such, it is inherent in the substance, since it is of the essence of a substance to be apt to become one of the terms of a relation. In thus binding relation to substance, this treatise initiated a controversy which was never to cease during the middle ages: is relation real, or is it a mere *ens rationis?* As to the six remaining principles, it is clear that each of them is only an accessory determination of substance. Situation is the one most closely related to substance; place and time come next; then action and passion; finally *habitus* (permanent possession), which is the most extrinsic of the six, since its possessor is often another being than the thing possessed.

Gilbert's most important contribution to the history of metaphysics, however, is to be found in his commentaries on Boethius' theological tractates. The one he wrote on Boethius' *De Trinitate* became the origin of the difficulties which, from 1146 on, exposed him to the censure of Saint Bernard. In order to understand his position, let us first distinguish with him "substance" from "subsistence." A "substant" is an actually existing individual being. Such a being is called a substance, because it stands under (*sub-stat*) a certain number of accidents. Because they are substances, individuals are causes and principles of the accidents which share in their being. Subsistence (*subsistentia*) is simply the property of that which, in order to be what it is, has no need of accidents. Thus genera and species are subsistences, for, taken in themselves, they have no accidents, but, precisely because they are not real supports of anything else, they are not substances. Because they, too, do not need their accidents in order to subsist, all substances are subsistences, but because some of them do not actually support any accident, all subsistences are not substances. Thus, genera and species *subsistunt tantum, non substant vere*. How do they subsist, and how can substances arise from them? [74]

At the origin of sensible substances is what the Greeks called Ideas, and what the Latins call forms. These Ideas are not simply "subsistences," but substances. They are even pure substances (*substantiae sincerae*), in the sense that they subsist outside of matter, and without ever mingling with it. The first among these pure substances are four in number: fire, air, water and earth. We are not speaking here of the tangible elements we call by these names, but of their ideal models. Taken in themselves, they are simple. In order to explain the production of things, we must take into consideration three terms: raw matter, and two primary forms which are the *ousia* (being) of the Worker and the Ideas of sensible things. When we say "forms" we do not mean that God himself becomes the form of matter. Even Ideas never descend into matter. The forms properly so-called which are joined to the matter of sensible bodies are in some way copies (*exempla*). They come from their model (*exemplar*), by a kind of deduction which consists in their conforming to it (*quadam exempli ab exemplari suo conformativa deductione venerunt*). Forms that are in bodies are therefore not Ideas, but images of these pure and eternal substances, Ideas. We are near to the time when the "begotten" forms of Chalcidius will become the substantial forms of Aristotle in the mind of thirteenth-century theologians.

These forms are what we conceive as "universals." Joined to their matter, they constitute individual substances which, as has been said, are both "substants" and "subsistents." Taken in themselves, forms are not substances, but they are the subsistences in virtue of which there are substances. They are the "substantial forms" of substances. They must furthermore be spoken of in the plural, even with regard to a single individual, for each individual is determined by a generic subsistence, a specific subsistence and its substantial properties. Now human reason is capable of considering separately and abstractly what is given as a whole in reality. It considers first an engendered form (*forma nativa*), abstracts it mentally from the body in which it is found, compares it with other engendered forms which it resembles and with which it constitutes a group (*collectio*), and thus attains the first specific subsistence (i.e., concept of the species). Carrying on the same work on a group of kindred species, reason conceives the subsistence of the genus. The mutual resemblance of several species is what makes them form a more general "collection," which is called a nature, a genus, a universal. All that is then left for thought to do is to transcend all engendered forms in order to attain their models, the primary Ideas which subsist eternally. John of Salisbury gave a résumé of Gilbert of la Porrée's position in this concise formula: "He attributes universality to engendered forms, and he labors over their conformity." As a matter of fact, generalization consists, for Gilbert, in finding in things of the same species and in species of the same genus, that natural conformity which they derive precisely from the *deductio conformativa* which engenders forms from eternal Ideas.[75]

Gilbert's doctrine is more elaborate than that of Bernard of Chartres, and its technical solidity has insured its influence despite the rather obscure language in which it is expressed. This influence is recognizable by the persistence, up to the thirteenth century and beyond it, of a certain tendency to reduce real beings to their intelligible essences, which are their forms, and to think of them in this abstract way. There is in this a certain "formalism" of thought (a tendency to explain everything by a series of determinative forms), which, reinforced by Avicenna's influence, will come into full bloom in the doctrine of Duns Scotus. Gilbert of la Porrée himself had inherited it from Boethius, whose theological opuscules he annotated.

For Boethius, the being of a thing was first of all the thing itself which is (*id quod est*), but he distinguished, in each being, the thing which is from the principle by which it is what it is. Let us, then, call that which is the *id quod est*, and call *quo est* that by which a being is what it is: by so doing we shall end up at the formulas of the *De Trinitate*. Each and every given being is determined by its *quo est* to be what it is. Considering the eminent rôle this determining principle plays in the constitution of a being, it can be said that, properly speaking, the *quo est* is the very being (*esse*) of what is. This is so true that in an absolutely simple being like God, the *id quod est* and the *quo est* coincide. That is why God is truly what he is. On the contrary, all other beings are made up of what they are and of that by which they are what they are. Reserving the title of being (*esse*) for the *quo est*, we will speak of any compound being as not being wholly what it is: *in parte non est id quod est*. For example, a man is not entirely what he is because, made of a body and a soul, which is its form, man is not entirely either body or soul.

Received by Gilbert of la Porrée, these notions took on a new importance in his work. They corresponded, in fact, to what was most Platonic in the Aristotelian conception of being, and Gilbert only accentuated its Platonism. At the top of everything that is, he places God, who is the essential entity *par excellence* (*essentia*) and from whom all the rest of what is derives its own *essentia,* that is to say, its very entity. It can therefore be said that divine entity is the being of all creatures: *divina essentia, quam de Deo praedicamus, cum dicimus, Deus est, omnium creaturarum dicitur esse.* On the other hand, nothing of what God creates is pure and simple being, it is always a determinate kind of being. On these grounds, every created being is compound. It is broken up first into being (*esse*) and into what is (*id quod est*). The being of a thing is what makes it to be what it is. For example, *corporeality* is the being of the body, the body itself, which subsists by corporeality and of which corporeality is the principle of subsistence, is what is. In the same way *humanity* is the being of the subject man; man himself is what is. Creative work then consists, for God, in producing a form, called in Greek *ousia,* in the image of a divine Idea: for example, the corporeality of humanity. This generic form, or essence, determines then, the conjunction of a certain matter (*materia, hyle*) with its particular form (its own essentiality). Divine entity (*essentia*) seems then to communicate itself to creatures by conferring being (*esse*) upon them through their generic essence: to be a body is to be corporeality, as to be a man is to be humanity. Thus constituted in being by the essence which makes it subsist (*subsistentia*), the creature is a substance (*substantia*). Properly speaking, since it is not "what is," but "that by which" substance is, essence itself *is* not. Since what is not cannot participate, essence as such cannot participate in actual being. Yet, we call it being (*esse*) on account of the fact that it determines the generation of the substance which itself is being. Thus *corporeality* itself does not participate directly in anything, but the corporeal substance it engenders can participate, in addition to corporeality, in color, hardness, length, thickness, solidity and so on. All created reality therefore fully merits here the epithet "concrete," for it is a concretion (*concretio*) of various forms, united in a substance whose very being is the generic essence which causes it to subsist.[76]

This philosophical attitude with regard to created reality is so fundamental in Gilbert that he cannot completely detach himself from it when he tackles the theological problem of divine being. We have seen him affirm first that God is absolute entity (*essentia*) and that he is nothing but that (*simplex atque sola essentia*). Even though a man (*id quod est*) is not identical with his humanity (*quo est*), God, his essence and his divinity are one single and same thing. This did not hinder Gilbert from expressing himself on several occasions as though thus to affirm the simplicity of God amounted to saying that what God is (*id quod est Deus*) is God by nothing else than by his *quo est*. This *quo est* Gilbert even named: it is divinity (*divinitas*).[77] Hence the theological attacks of which he was the object at the Council of Rheims, in 1148, but which did not result in his condemnation. The philosophical significance of this purely formal distinction between God and divinity is that it announces the invasion of theology by a conceptual realism that was to blossom in Duns Scotus. Attributing a sort of reality to each of the intelligible essences conceived by our understanding, Gilbert portrayed finite beings as composed of a subject and of abstract determinations which, by qualifying it, cause it to be what it is. His disciples were so numerous that they are usually considered as a distinct doctrinal family, that of the *Porretani*. Among the best known let us mention Raoul Ardent, John Beleth and Alan of Lille. But that is not what is most important. The more one studies the middle ages, the more one notices the polymorphism of the Platonic influence. Plato himself does not appear at all, but Platonism is everywhere; let us say rather that there are Platonisms everywhere: the Platonism of Denis and of Maximus the Confessor, which passes on through Scotus Erigena and whose presence we have just observed in Bernard of Chartres; Saint Augustine's Platonism, which permeates the thought of Saint Anselm; the Platonism of Boethius, which dominates the work of Gilbert of la Porrée, while awaiting those of the *Liber de causis* and of the philosophy of Avicenna that we are soon to meet. This Platonic kinship between widely different doctrines explains certain otherwise incomprehensible alliances they have sometimes contracted with one another. Gilbert's place in this complex ensemble is clearly defined: he encouraged the diffusion of that particular form of Platonism we might call the realism of essences, and which the philosophy of Avicenna was soon so powerfully to reinforce.

2. THIERRY OF CHARTRES

Gilbert's successor as chancellor of the schools, Thierry of Chartres, Bernard's younger brother, was also one of the personalities most representative of his environment and his time.[78] The subject matter of his teaching is known to us thanks to his *Heptateuchon,* a collection of texts and manuals related to the seven liberal arts. Donatus and Priscian formed the basis of the teaching of grammar; Cicero and Marcianus Capella were used for rhetoric; Boethius and part of Aristotle's *Organon* for dialectics; Boethius, Capella, Isidore of Seville, Columellus, Gerbert, Hyginus, Ptolemeus, figure, at least by fragments, as the basis for arithmetic, geometry, astronomy and music. Thierry's teaching then covered not only the *trivium,* but also the *quadrivium.* An ancient tradition even claims that Abélard was his pupil in mathematics. Thierry left Chartres in 1134, came to Paris to teach, then returned to Chartres in 1141. When Gilbert of la Porrée was named bishop of Poitiers (1142), Thierry succeeded him as Chancellor of Chartres. He was still living in 1148, the date of his presence at the Council of Rheims. The exact date of his death is not known, but it was before 1155.

Thierry defended with no less courage and obstinacy than his predecessors their common ideal of classical culture. Less of a dialectician than Gilbert of la Porrée, his interest seems rather to have been in cosmogony. His *De septem diebus et sex operum distinctionibus* is an *Hexaemeron,* that is to say, a literal interpretation of Genesis I, according to the data of physics: *secundum physicam et ad litteram.*

The sacred books says: "In the beginning God created heaven, and earth," raising two questions: that of the causes of the universe, and that of the order of the days of creation. The causes are four in number: the efficient, which is God; the formal, which is the Wisdom of God arranging the form of future work; the final, which is divine benevolence (*benignitas*), and finally the material, which consists in the four elements. Creation properly so-called bears on these four elements: earth, water, air and fire. Scripture designates them by the names *heaven* and *earth.* God created them from nothing, by pure goodness and love, in order to produce beings who should participate in his beatitude.

As to the order of days, God created matter in the first instant, each element taking the place suitable to its nature, and all four arranging themselves in concentric spheres: earth, water, air, fire. This last, which is of an extreme lightness, tends naturally to move. Since it envelops everything, it cannot move forward, so it immediately sets about moving in a circular way. Its first complete revolution constitutes the first day, in the course of which fire begins to illuminate air and, through it, water and earth. Such was the work of the first day. But fire not only lights up, it also heats. Passing through water its heat engendered vapors. These rose above the zone of air and hung there, suspended, so that air found itself gripped between the liquid water beneath it and the vaporized water above it. That is what Scripture says: *et posuit firmamentum in medio aquarum.* In this case air deserves the title of firmament (*firmamentum*), since it firmly supports the layer of vapors rising above it; but it can also be called by that name because it presses in from all sides upon the earth it surrounds, and thus gives it hardness. Such was the work of the second day.

By vaporizing one part of the water, heat lessened the quantity of the liquid element, uncovered parts of the earth, thus allowed islands to appear, and, by heating them in turn, made them capable of producing plants and trees. This evaporation of liquid can be experimentally verified in a caldron. Or a table may be covered with a layer of water and a fire superimposed over it; the water will be seen to lose its depth and dry places will appear upon it, leaving parts of the table uncovered. Such was the work of the third day.

During the fourth day the vapors suspended above the air condensed and formed the bodies of the stars. This is obvious, for the stars are visible; now, taken in themselves, neither pure fire nor pure air is visible; they become so thanks only to their mingling with one of the thick elements, that is, with earth or water; but earth is too heavy to be lifted up to heaven; that leaves only water whose condensation could produce the body of stars. Besides, they say that the stars subsist on effluvia, and since a body can assimilate only bodies similar to itself, the body of stars can be only condensed water.

Once created and revolving under the firmament, the stars increased the heat by their very movement and brought it to the degree of vital heat. This affected first of all the water settled on the earth's surface and generated aquatic animals and winged creatures in it. This took place during the fifth celestial revolution; it was, therefore, the work of the fifth day. The vital heat next affected the earth, and there produced the animals of the earth, including man, made in the image and likeness of God; and this was the work of the sixth day. Then God entered into his rest, which means that no being appearing after the sixth day was created, but was produced either by the elements acting as has just been described, or by a germ (*ratio seminalis*) introduced by God into the elements in the course of the six days' work.

Thierry was aware of the difficulties which arise when one tries to make the *littera,* that is to say the Bible, agree with the *physica,* that is, Chalcidius's Commentary on the *Timaeus.* However, he thought he could overcome them by identifying heaven and earth with the four elements. His attempt is of interest to the history of science because it is the work of a man who did not know Aristotle's physics. He does not imagine each element as endowed with fixed qualities or situated in one particular place. For him, the particles of all the elements are interchangeable. Earth is not hard by nature, since it can liquefy and ignite. Its hardness does not even come from the fact that it is tightly pressed by the weight of air and fire, for these elements are imponderable. The true cause of its hardness is the incessant movement of air and fire which, hugging the earth and water on all sides, gives them solidity and hardness. Moreover, lightness is indistinguishable from movement itself; now everything that moves depends upon a fixed point and, if it is a question of a circular motion, upon a center. Air and fire therefore need this center, earth, to support their revolutions. That sacred philosopher (*philosophus divinus*) Moses was right then in saying that God created heaven (fire and air) and earth (water and earth), but it must be understood in the sense that he created mobile particles whose movement caused the firm center they needed in order to move. The mechanistic character of this explanation is the more remarkable as it seems to apply to living beings. Instead of a theory of natural places, as in Aristotle, we have here a kinetic explanation of the elements: the lightness of air and fire is only their movement, and this movement, at the same time that it causes the rigidity of the earth and the heaviness of the water, demands them as support of its revolutions. Thus we understand why God should create them together, and that is what Thierry understands by demonstrating "what Moses calls heaven and earth and how the physicists explain that they were created together."

There were then, in the twelfth century, linked with the Platonist movement, mechanistic tendencies which will reappear in the fourteenth, when the Aristotelianism of the thirteenth has run its course. The famous theory of the impulse transmitted to mobile bodies (*impetus*) seems to Thierry of Chartres a completely natural explanation of the state of bodies in movement: "When a stone is thrown, the impulse of the projectile (*impetus projecti*) comes from the fact that the one who throws it rests on something solid, and the more firmly he leans, the more powerful is his throw (*tanto jactus projicientis est impetuosior*)." This interpretation agrees with his mathematical trend of thought. In order to understand Genesis, theology needs the sciences of the *quadrivium:* arithmetic, music, geometry and astronomy. Now their common element is number, whose principle is unity; unity is therefore the fundamental notion on which every rational explanation depends.

Taken in itself, unity is stable, immovable, eternal; number is variable and movable, since it changes by the addition or subtraction of unities. Now the domain of the creature is that of change; creation is therefore the domain of number as the divine nature is that of unity. To go back to the principle of number, which is unity, is to go back from the creature to the creator. Things exist only through God and, in this sense, God is the *form* of everything that is. He is its form because he causes the creature to be what it is. Therefore God is not involved, as form, in the matter of beings, but "the presence of divinity in all creatures is their total and only being, so that even matter owes its existence to the presence of divinity." Since God is unity, to say that God is *forma essendi* for creatures amounts to saying that the form whereby they are is unity: *Unitas igitur singulis rebus forma essendi est.* It is obvious from this that unity is required for the conservation of beings, whereas their decomposition into multiple parts is the cause of their destruction. Just as unity is a constituent of being, so it is a constituent of truth; for where there is unity, there is equality; now a thing is true, that is to say truly itself, only insofar as it is equal to its own essence. Thus, by equality, unity begets truth. Since the first and absolute unity is God, its perfect equality is also God. To express both that identity and equality in God theologians have used the term *person:* the substance of Unity is identical with the substance of the Equality it begets, but the begetting person (Father) is distinct from the person begotten (Word). For their part, being particularly sensitive to the close connection between the notions of equality and of truth, philosophers have called that Equality of the One either Thought, or Providence, or Wisdom, and quite rightly, since all things are true through divine truth, as, being numbers, they subsist by the unity of God. There are, then, two ways of formulating the same doctrine. The philosophers have had an inkling of the truth that Christians know.

Nothing can show more clearly than this doctrine how the neoplatonism of certain theologians cleared the way for Arabian neoplatonism, particularly that of Avicenna. The principle by which Thierry explains why one unique Word was begotten is that Unity can only beget a unity equal to it (*Unitas enim per se nihil aliud gignere potest nisi ejusdem unitatis aequalitatem*). This theologically correct formula anticipates the neoplatonist principle which, as interpreted by Avicenna, will determine the dividing line between philosophy and theology in the fourteenth century; from one, only one can proceed. Moreover, Thierry of Chartres laid down in all its clarity the principle of any ontology in which the One is superior to being, because he is its cause (*Cum autem unitas omnium rerum primum et unicum esse sit*). This is no pantheism; things are not the One, they are manifold; besides, things cannot be God's being, since God is above being, being the One. What Thierry says is that beings, which are not the One, are only beings through the One, who is none of these beings. Such a doctrine powerfully encouraged the growing influence of Proclus, which we shall see reach its maximum intensity with the speculative mysticism of Eckhart or the metaphysics of Dietrich of Vrieberg.

3. CLARENBAUD OF ARRAS

Bernardus Silvestris[79] and William of Conches[80] do not compare in importance with Thierry of Chartres or with Gilbert of la Porrée, but Clarenbaud of Arras[81] deserves careful consideration. He is a typical instance of what might be called the Chartres complex: the overwhelming influence of Boethius, the presence of an elementary Platonism borrowed from Chalcidius, the doctrine of God as the form of all being, an aggressively realistic interpretation of universals, last, not the least, a classical culture which enables him to express himself with some elegance. After the technical impersonality of Gilbert, the lively personal reactions of Clarembaud create a welcome diversion.

Philosophy divides itself into three parts: theoretical (or speculative), practical, logical. Theoretical philosophy itself comprises physics, which deals with forms in matter; mathematics, which deals with physical properties considered in an abstract way, that is, apart from matter; and theology, which deals with forms naturally separated from matter. Man knows physical beings through "reason," which deals with forms in matter and uses a material instrument situated in the brain; he knows immaterial beings, or forms, through his "intellectibility," which is the only one divine element there is in human nature.

The main object of theological knowledge is God, who is form and, therefore, act. For indeed, form is act. In other beings, form is the act of something else, which is potency, or, in Clarenbaud's own terminology, "possibility" (i.e., potentiality). Absolute possibility is matter; absolute act is God; consequently, God is not the act of some matter, or possibility; he is not "act of," but act. Pure and absolute actuality is necessary; hence it is immutable and therefore eternal. God is eternity. This enables us to understand the meaning of the divine name: *Ego sum, qui sum* (Exod. 3, 14). It means that God is the "form of being" (*forma essendi*), that is "entity itself," participating in nothing. *Deus essendi forma est:* God is pure form, pure act, pure entity, pure and simple being.[82]

Pure being is also pure unity. All that is, only is because it is one. As soon as we enter the field of multiplicity, we are outside of God. The pure act of being is everywhere precisely because, being absolute form, everywhere there is form, God is present. It is extremely important to understand Clarenbaud correctly on this point. To say that God is *"forma essendi"* is to say that "just as wherever there is whiteness, the form of white is there, and just as wherever there is blackness, the form of black is there, so also wherever something is, the form of being is there. Now, everywhere, something is; consequently, the form of being is everywhere. But God is the form of being; therefore God is everywhere by essence. Hence it can be seen how this working form (*opifex forma*) is both true form and being itself, that is to say, the prime entity; it is, and being comes from it, precisely for this reason that all that is participates in the simple entity itself." [83] In short, in a doctrine where being is act, and where act is form, all that is owes its being to the absolute act and to the absolute form, which is God. In this precise sense God is the form of all things.

Since there is otherness, it must needs proceed from unity. All things are one in God, but the divine Ideas, then the forms born of these pure and eternal substances, are at the origin of the multiplication of beings. Clarenbaud follows Boethius and Gilbert on this point. But he does not follow the "bishop of Poitiers" (i.e., Gilbert) on the problem of individuation,[84] no more than in his interpretation of the dogma of the Trinity.[85] His opposition to Gilbert is particularly interesting to note on the problem of the relation which obtains between genera and individuals. The nature of the universals was at stake in this controversy. Gilbert maintained that each man is man through his own humanity, whereas Clarembaud maintains that all men are men through one and the same humanity: *unam et eandem humanitatem esse qua singuli homines sunt homines*.[86] His "realism" of universals is therefore more accentuated than that of Gilbert. On the whole, Clarembaud seems to have been a much less adventurous metaphysician than his master Thierry of Chartres. The influence of his other master, Hugh of St. Victor, may at least partly account for his moderation, but the theological misadventures of Gilbert and of Abélard, which he quotes, would have been enough to warn him against unnecessary flights of metaphysical imagination.

4. JOHN OF SALISBURY

The manifestation most typical of the refined spirit of Chartres was John of Salisbury (about 1125-1180). The works of this Englishman, educated in France, who died bishop of Chartres, anticipate the Renaissance by both the quality of their style and the delicacy of their inspiration. In the *Polycraticus* and the *Metalogicon,* the long humanistic effort of Chartres finally blossomed into charming works. Nothing can give a more vivid impression of the diversity of the middle ages than to linger over the writings of that twelfth-century bishop who was a good writer, a man of parts and a fine scholar.[87]

John of Salisbury would not have agreed to distinguish wisdom from eloquence as William of Conches did. The type of culture he consciously desired to have revived was the *eloquentia* of Cicero and Quintilian, that is to say, the complete intellectual and moral formation of an upright man, but a man capable of expressing himself well. On philosophical grounds properly so-called, he time and again quotes as his authority the sect of Academicians. The great man whose style he strove to imitate and whose thought he admired was not Plato, nor Aristotle, but Cicero. Not that he in any way professes a complete skepticism, but, as Cicero himself did, he begins by setting aside a certain number of acquired truths and he abandons all the rest to the sterile play of interminable controversies. To doubt everything would be an absurdity. The animals give proof of a certain intelligence; now man is more intelligent than the animal; therefore it is false that man is incapable of knowing. We can, in reality, derive certain knowledge from three different sources: the senses, reason, and faith. He who has not a minimum of confidence in his senses is inferior to animals; he who does not believe in his reason at all and doubts everything arrives at a point where he does not even know whether he doubts; he who refuses his assent to the obscure but certain knowledge of faith sets his face against the foundation of all wisdom. It is, therefore, ridiculous to be uncertain of everything and nevertheless to claim to be a philosopher. Nevertheless, it must be acknowledged that the modesty of Academicians is, in most cases, the wisest example we could follow. In almost all disputed questions one must be content to reach probabilities. The philosophers wanted to measure the world and submit the skies to their laws, but they had too much confidence in the forces of their reason; they fell down therefore the moment they arose and, when they thought they were wise, they began to talk nonsense. Just as the men who raised the tower of Babel against God fell into confusion of language, so the philosophers who undertook against God that kind of theomachy that philosophy is, fell into confusion of systems. And therefore they are now scattered into the infinite multiplicity of their insanities and their sects of error, all the more miserable and deserving of pity as they were not aware of their very misery.

The Academicians, on the contrary, avoid these errors by their very modesty. They recognize their ignorance and know enough not to affirm what they do not know. Their moderation is precisely the quality which commends them to our esteem and should lead us to prefer them. One must hesitate in all matters where neither the senses, nor reason, nor faith give us incontestable certitude, and the list of such questions is a long one. We should reserve judgment on the substance, the quantity, the faculties, the efficacy and origin of the soul; on destiny, chance, free will, matter, movement, elements, the infinity of numbers, and the indefinite divisibility of quantity; on time and space; on the origin and nature of speech; on sameness and otherness, divisibility and indivisibility, the nature of universals, the origin and end of virtues and vices, whether one possesses all the virtues if he has one of them, whether all sins are equal and equally punishable; on the causes of phenomena, the ebb and flow of the sea, the floods of the Nile, the increase and abatement of humors in animals according to the moon's phases; on nature's various hidden secrets, on evil spells; on nature and its works; on the true nature and origin of those things which our reason cannot grasp, for instance: have angels bodies, and of what nature? Or what is God? Many more questions of this sort are still unsolved for scholars. True enough, ignorant people know all the answers, but the modesty of the Academicians teaches us to reserve judgment.

It does not follow, however, that we should neglect to study these questions under the pretext that their definite solution must finally elude our grasp. Quite the contrary. It is ignorance that makes philosophy dogmatic, and it is erudition that makes the Academician. When one knows only one single system or one sole solution to some problem, he is naturally inclined to accept it. How could one choose, since he has no choice? Freedom of mind is proportional to knowledge, and that is why John of Salisbury took sides with the defenders of humanism, against the Philistines of his own time, the so-called "Cornificians."

A typical instance of the problems which John of Salisbury deemed insoluble is that of universals. Precisely because they could not answer it, the philosophers seized upon this difficult question, discussed it at length and, as they used words at random, they gave the appearance of maintaining different opinions and left their successors a wealth of controversial material. At the present time, John says, there are at least five solutions to this problem, a problem so old that the world itself has aged in striving to solve it, a problem over which more time has been lost than the Caesars have spent in conquering the world, and more money than ever filled the coffers of Croesus. According to some, universals exist only in the sensible and the singular; others conceive forms as separated after the manner of mathematical beings; others make of them either words or nouns; and, finally, still others identify universals with concepts. In fact, we know neither the nature nor the mode of existence of universals; but we can say, if not what their real condition is, at least the way in which we acquire them. The Aristotelian doctrine of abstraction enables us to solve this second problem, more modest than the first. To seek the real mode of existence of universals considered as things is an infinite and almost fruitless task, but to try to find what they are in the intellect is an easy and useful pursuit. What happens is that, considering the substantial resemblance of numerically different individuals, we obtain species; if we next consider the resemblances which obtain between different species, we have the genus. Our intellect achieves universals, then, by stripping individual substances of the forms and accidents by which they differ. Although they do not exist individually, universals can at least be thought individually, and although they do not exist separately, they can be conceived separately.

The nature of John of Salisbury's attitude is clear. This humanist has a taste for common sense and simple solutions, and a horror of mere hodge-podge and verbalism. John of Salisbury needs to feel sure of something before allowing himself to affirm it. Confronted with the logomachy of his contemporaries in the question of universals, he suspends his judgment after the fashion of Academicians, but not at all because of any taste for uncertainty. When he can see a reasonable way out of some labyrinth, he does not hesitate a moment to take it. Besides, John of Salisbury knows that philosophical speculation is no idle game. If the true God, he says, is the true Wisdom, then the love of God is the true philosophy. The complete philosopher therefore is not he who is content with a theoretical knowledge, but he who lives the doctrine he preaches; to follow the true precepts one teaches is truly to philosophize. *Philosophus amator Dei est:* in that appeal to love and piety lies the completion and consummation of this conception of life. John was a mind more delicate than powerful, but so fine, so rich and so perfectly cultured that its presence ennobles and graces in our thought the image of the twelfth century.

CHAPTER IV

PETER ABÉLARD

THE history of mediaeval philosophy cannot be reduced to that of the controversy concerning the nature of universals. Yet there is much to say in favor of such an interpretation. Up to the time when Avicenna, Averroes and Aristotle provided them with complete philosophical explanations of nature, the men of the middle ages had practically no other strictly philosophical problem to discuss than that of universals. Boethius had offered two solutions of it, the one according to the metaphysics of Plato, the other according to the metaphysics of Aristotle; but while Boethius himself knew both metaphysics, the men of the early thirteenth century knew neither one. What they could guess of them, through Chalcidius and Boethius on the one hand, and through the logic of Aristotle on the other hand, was not enough to provide their choice with a complete justification. At any rate, not one of these logicians has been able to reconstruct the psychologies and the metaphysics which, in the doctrines of their Greek predecessors, fully justified their epistemological conclusions.

This is the reason why, at the end of the twelfth century, John of Salisbury could denounce the striking sterility of these purely dialectical discussions. Each professor had figured out an answer to the problem. This answer was generally a word. After coining it, or accepting it, its defender would stick to it and fight for it with dialectical weapons. When he revisited the schools of Paris after an absence of twelve years, John says that he still found there the very same professors saying the very same things. None of them had either learned or unlearned anything—a striking illustration indeed of what happens to philosophy when it attempts to live by logic alone. Other centuries than the twelfth would be well advised to remember the lesson.

The oldest of these logicians mentioned by John of Salisbury was Roscelin,[88] whose doctrine, he says, died with its author (*Metal.*, II, 17). According to contemporary testimonies, he used to teach that general concepts were *voces,* that is to say, words. This is what most historians call his "nominalism." Yet he does not seem to have said that concepts are "names" (*nomina*), but words. In order to designate it by an appropriate name, one would have to coin a new one, such as "wordism." By "word" (*vox*), Roscelin understood a *flatus vocis,* that is, an emission of voice, or, in other words, the very sound uttered by a man when he speaks. His position makes sense when read in its historical context. All his contemporaries agreed that some reality answered our concepts. Most of them placed it in the actual being of genera and species. Following Aristotle's doctrine in the *Categories,* Roscelin maintained, on the contrary, that actual existence belongs to individuals only. Hence his conclusion: since individuals alone exist, the only other actually existing reality there is in a concept is that of the emission of voice that expresses it. In short, there are individuals on the one side and, on the other side, words designating these same individuals. True enough, words have a meaning, but their meaning is not an actually existing being.[89]

The contrary position, which we have already seen represented by Anselm of Canterbury, ascribed to genera and species a reality of their own. We find it maintained by Adelhard of Bath and by William of Champeaux,[90] the latter an exact contemporary of Roscelin and also, unhappily for him, one of the masters under whom Abélard had studied logic. His doctrine was that of the "community" of universals. According to him, Abélard says, a species was a thing simultaneously present in all its individuals, totally present in each and every one of them, and yet essentially common to all. In short, the essence of a species was the same in all its individuals, whose differentiation William explained by the variety of their accidents. This position was well known.[91] Yet, attacked on this point by his pupil Abélard, William gave up his former tenet that a species was "essentially" the same in all its individuals. Instead, he taught that species were there in a state of "undifferentiation" (*indifferenter*). This was another classical expression usually applied to the condition of the three persons with respect to the unity of divine essence. As will be seen, Abélard objected that this second position was a mere restatement of the first one, couched in different words. We lack the original texts which would probably enable us to understand William correctly. From what we know, he seems to have maintained, with Gilbert of la Porrée, that each individual man was man through his own "manness," or *humanitas,* and yet that the essence "man" was to be found in each individual, although in a state of indetermination with respect to individuality.[92]

By far the most famous among these masters was Peter Abélard.[93] His brilliant and aggressive personality would have been enough to make him conspicuous in his own century, but there was in his works a lasting quality which makes them still readable to men of our own times.[94] At any rate, his writings on logic exhibit those exceptional gifts of clarity and of vigor which made his teaching so successful. His lectures were commentaries on the *logica vetus*,[95] that is to say chiefly on Boethius' interpretation of Aristotle. He did not know the most important parts of Aristotle's *Organon;* he was in complete ignorance of Aristotle's *Physics* and *Metaphysics;* it is still more regrettable that he did not know Aristotle's treatise *On the Soul*, whose knowledge would have been priceless to him. In fact, Abélard worked on the same material as all the professors of logic we have already mentioned, and he dealt with the same problems, but he handled them in a highly personal way.

I. LOGIC

Like all his contemporaries, Abélard came up against pure philosophy in connection with the problem of universals and, like all of them, he got into trouble on account of its theological implications. The questions raised by Porphyry were first to know whether universals exist in reality or only in thought; next, supposing they exist in reality, whether they are corporeal or incorporeal; thirdly, whether they are separate from sensible things or whether they are involved in them. To these three questions of Porphyry, Abélard adds several other ones, for instance: what is there, in things, which enables us to give them common names? Again, if there are no such things as actually existing universals, what do common names designate? Last, not the least, if the particular things signified by universals were destroyed, would their names still mean the notion we have of these particular things? For instance, would the word "rose" still mean our concept of roses in general if all the roses to which it applies had ceased to exist?

But let us deal first with the questions asked by Porphyry himself: do universals exist in reality or only in thought? Some philosophers maintain that universals are things (*res*), but their position can be understood in two different ways. A first possible interpretation is that of Boethius: all individuals possess in common the essence of their species, but they differ from one another by the "collection" of accidents which is proper to each of them (size, color, shape, etc.). Thus, for instance, the essence of man is the same substance in both Plato and Socrates, but Socrates differs from Plato by his size, the shape of his nose, etc. In this hypothesis, a universal points out the substance which is one and the same in all the individuals that belong to a certain species. The same remark applies to the genus containing several species, for instance, the genus animal. In short, universals do not subsist in themselves, but they do subsist, wholly the same, in individuals where they are particularized by accidents. But, Abélard says, this is impossible. If the same substance, "animal," exists really and wholly in two of its species, for instance "man" and "horse," the same "animal" which is rational in the species man is non-rational in the species horse. Thus one and the same thing is both itself and its contrary, which is impossible. Another solution must be sought.[96]

The second possible interpretation is closer to the truth. It consists in saying that individuals are distinguished from one another, not only by their accidents, but by their very essences, so that nothing of what is found in one is found in the other. No individual has either its matter or its form in common with any other individual. In other words, as Gilbert of la Porrée had taught it, each individual man is man through his own "humanity." Thus far, all is clear. Unfortunately, they insist on maintaining the universality of essences and, in order to avoid the preceding difficulty, they say that although individuals are not the same "essentially" (since each of them has its own essence), they are the same "indifferently" (since the essence of one of these individuals is not different from the essence of another one within the same species). This seems to have been what Abélard calls the second position of William of Champeaux. In point of fact, William himself may not have been conscious of any fundamental change in his position; he was simply explaining it in saying that the kind of unity that belongs to genera and to species rests upon the similarity, or non-difference, between species within their genus, and between individuals within their species. At any rate, Abélard drove his master, William, out of this second position. For indeed, if that non-difference is understood in a purely negative sense, it must be granted that Socrates does not differ in any way from Plato as a man, which they both are, but it must be added that neither do they differ in any way as stones, which they are not. If, on the contrary, that non-difference is understood in a positive sense, then they do not differ as men, which is to go back to the first position.[97] How could Plato and Socrates be different men if, *qua* men, they are not different?

The common source of these difficulties is the illusion that universals are real things, if not in themselves, at least in individuals. Abélard is not here denying the reality of Plato's Ideas, but the reality of the genus in its species or that of the species in its individuals. His reason for denying it is simple: by definition, a universal is what can be predicated of several things; now, a thing cannot be predicated of other things; each thing is only itself and is only what it is. Hence Abélard's decisive conclusion: since universality cannot be attributed to things, it remains to ascribe it to words alone. Grammarians distinguish between universal terms and particular or singular terms. A particular term is predicated of only one single individual, for instance: Socrates; a universal term is predicable of a plurality of individuals, taken one by one, to which it applies by reason of their nature. Universality then is only the logical function of certain words.

Was Abélard reverting to the position of Roscelin? Scarcely. If Roscelin were right, universals would be nothing more than *flatus vocis,* that is to say, the very sounds we make in pronouncing words. Then every grammatically correct construction of words would be logically valid, and logic would be reduced to grammar. Now, in point of fact, a construction may be grammatically valid and logically absurd, for it is grammatically just as correct to say: man is a stone, as it is to say: man is an animal, but only the second proposition is logically valid. From whence arises a new problem: why are certain predications logically valid, while others are not?

This is tantamount to asking: why can the same noun be rightly attributed to several individuals? Abélard's answer is that, of themselves, things lend themselves to the predication of universals. It must be so. On the one hand, universal notions cannot be drawn from nothing; on the other hand, universals have no independent reality of their own; consequently there must needs be, in things themselves, what it takes to justify the validity or invalidity of our logical predications. What, in things, justifies our logical predications is their "state" (*status*), that is to say, the manner of being proper to each one of them. The mistake made by those who attribute any subsisting reality whatever to universals is to confuse "humanity," which is nothing, with "to be a man," which is something. Predication would not be possible if several beings were not found to be in the same "state." For instance, were there only one single individual which was man, horse, and so forth, no universal notion could be predicated of them. But that is not the case. Two or more beings are alike in this that each of them "is a man," or "is a horse," that is to say, is after the manner of a man or of a horse. We are not here assuming that such beings have in common any "essence"; in Abélard's own words: "We appeal to no essence." The common cause of imposition of the word "man" on several individuals is, that these all are in the same status. Now, the status of man is "to-be-man," which is not a thing distinct from man, but its very being.[98]

After the nature of universals, let us consider their formation. We have sensory organs and we perceive objects, a tower, for instance; an image of each object is formed in us and it remains in our mind independently of the object whereby it has been caused. We can still picture to ourselves the tower we have seen, even after it has been destroyed. These images produced in us by objects are something else than the artificial ones which we make up in our dreams, or when we imagine a city we have never seen. They also are something else than what we have in mind when we think of "a tower" in general. Our representation of a singular is a vivid image, precise and definite in its details. My inner picture of Peter applies to Peter only; when I imagine the tower of Cluny, what I have in mind applies to that tower only, and to no other one. On the contrary, our inner representation of man in general, or of a tower in general, is feeble, confused and somewhat indeterminate; it retains only the elements common to the similar individuals from which it is taken. This, of course, is the reason why it applies to several individuals. A universal is therefore only a word designating the confused image extracted by thought from a plurality of individuals which, because they are of like nature, are in the same status. Abélard does not seem to have ascribed to our general concepts any other nature than that of common and confused images of similar objects.

For the very same reason, these universals cannot be called "ideas." Properly speaking, an "idea" is the simple act by which an intellect represents distinctly to itself the plurality of individuals contained in a species or in a genus. Such, as the grammarian Priscian rightly remarks in his *Institutiones,* XVII, 6, 44, is the knowledge which God has of things. There are ideas in the divine mind because God knows the species and genera before their creation by his power, but there are no such ideas in the mind of man, except, of course, in the case of artificially made things. An artisan has an idea of what he is about to make. That is the way men make swords or build houses, but this does not apply to natural beings, which are the works of God, not of man. No wonder then that we find it so hard to go, beyond images, up to the pure intellection of the natures of things. Sense images prevent us, most of the time, from achieving acts of pure and simple intellection.[99]

From this analysis, it follows that, in the case of man, intellection (*intelligentia*) bears upon real objects and is a cognition of particular beings; on the contrary, when we form the notions of things we have not actually seen, we have an opinion rather than an intellection. Thus, for instance, after imagining a city we have never seen, we realize, after visiting it, that it is different from what we had imagined it to be. So also, when we conceive abstract forms which do not fall under our senses, such as "rationality," "paternity," etc., we have opinion rather than intellection; on the contrary, when we say "man," or "tree," we have intellection rather than opinion, because such names are intended to signify the natures of actually existing things. That we do not thoroughly understand these natures does not alter the fact that such names point out either confusedly known species or distinctly known individuals.[100]

In this doctrine, universals are in fact only "the meaning of words": *nominum significatio.* The process by which we form them is called "abstraction." Matter and form are always given to us together in reality, but our intellect has the power to turn its attention toward form alone or toward matter alone. This act of attention constitutes abstraction. There is no error in thus conceiving things. The intellect is not mistaken in thinking either form or matter separately; it would be mistaken in thinking that either form or matter existed separately, but then the mistake would lie in a false composition of abstracts, not in their abstraction. Their abstraction is nothing else than the manner in which our attention is brought to bear upon things, when we consider separately what does not exist separately. Knowledge posits as existing together what does exist together; opinion or error links together in thought what is not linked together in reality.

We are now in a position to answer Porphyry's questions. First, do genera and species exist, that is, do they designate really existing things, or simple objects of intellection? By themselves, they exist only in understanding (*in intellectu solo et nudo et puro*), but they signify real beings, to wit, the same particular things that particular terms designate. Let us take note of this conclusion whose importance will become outstanding in the fourteenth century: the only reality signified by general terms is that which particular terms signify: there is no more in "man" than in "Socrates"; there is probably less. Second question: are universals corporeal or incorporeal? Inasmuch as they are nouns, universals are corporeal, since their nature is that of uttered words, but their aptitude to signify a plurality of similar individuals is incorporeal; in short, nouns are corporeal, but their meaning is not; they are, Abélard says: *incorporea quantum ad modum significationis*. Third question: do universals exist in sensible things, or outside them? There are two kinds of incorporeals: those which exist outside the sensible, like God and the soul, and those existing within the sensible, like the forms of bodies. Insofar as they designate forms of this latter kind, universals subsist in sensibles, but insofar as they designate forms as separated from the sensible by abstraction, they are beyond the sensible. Abélard believes that one can thus reconcile Plato and Aristotle, for Aristotle says that forms exist only in the sensible, which is true; but Plato, the "investigator of physics," says that these forms would preserve their nature even if they no longer fell within the grasp of our senses, which is equally true. Fourth question: would universals still exist without corresponding individuals? As names signifying individuals they would cease to exist, since there would be no individuals for them to signify; however, their significations would still subsist, for if there were no more roses, it could still be said: there are no roses.[101]

Abélard seems to have remained the pupil of Roscelin much more than he himself imagined. We do not mean to say that his doctrine and that of his master are the same. Obviously, Abélard never reduced universals to the physical reality of the words which designate them. But, to begin with, let us remember that, even in Roscelin, this doctrine applied to a very definite object. It answered the question: what is actually existing in universals? Now, on this precise point, Abélard does not seem to be of a different opinion. Insofar as essences are concerned, no actual being answers them in reality. The word "man" is an actually existing reality, the essence "man" has no existence of its own. On this point, Abélard is as precise as it is possible to be: obviously, universals do not signify things as singular, but neither do they signify them as agreeing, for the simple reason that "there is no thing in which they agree." The logician who refuses to appeal to any essence in order to solve his problem is, in fact, primarily concerned with the philosophy of grammar rather than with metaphysical speculation. His own problem is that of the "imposition of nouns." His reflections on the question are prompted by the remarks of Priscian at least as much as by those of Boethius. In point of fact, Abélard does not hesitate to reproach Boethius with transferring to names what is true of things only and, conversely, to ascribe to things properties that belong to the words whereby they are signified. From this point of view, Abélard's logic can be said to be a logical speculation about grammar, rather than a metaphysical interpretation of logical problems. This is not to say that his logic is a "speculative grammar";[102] it is a logic, but his main interest is to define, so to speak, the meaning of meaning much more than to determine what is meaningful in the nature of things.

2. ETHICS

It is the privilege of such minds that they revivify every thing they touch. Their misfortune is to be the first victims of their own discoveries. After the simple scholar, professor of logic, we meet the monk, professor of theology. A sure instinct once more leads him to the central problem of ethics: that of the foundation of the morality of acts. Abélard, in his *Scito teipsum, (Know Thyself)*,[103] starts from the distinction between vice and sin. Vice is an inclination to consent to what is not right, that is to say, not to do what should be done or not to abstain from doing what should not be done. Of itself, vice is not a sin but an inclination to sin, against which we can struggle, and which is thus for us an occasion for merit. Let us add that, since we have defined it negatively (not to do, or not to abstain from doing), sin itself is devoid of substance: it is non-being, rather than being. It does not consist even in the inclination of the will, for our natural tendency can be to do evil; we accomplish no less good by it if, even while it lasts, we work against it. Neither does sin consist in the result of the act itself, taken, so to speak, in its materiality. Sin consists exactly in not abstaining from what should not be done, that is, in consenting to it. To

consent to evil is to despise God, and the intention to do so is the very
essence of sin.[104]

What is true of evil is also true of good. To behave well is to act with
the intention of respecting the divine will. We must therefore distinguish
between the goodness of the intention and the goodness of the deed (*opus*)
just as between the malice of the intention and the malice of the deed.
There is no more connection between them than between a father and his
son. The son of a good man may be bad; and similarly, the effect of a
good intention may be bad, and the fact that the intention from which it
proceeds is good changes nothing of its nature. Like evil, good is therefore
placed, between the spontaneous inclination of the will and the very deed
(*opus*) the act produces, in the intention governing that act. That is why
the act itself has no other moral value than that of the intention dictating
it. It is not, however, with the act (*operatio*) exactly as it is with the
deed resulting from the act. An intention which of itself is good can have
as its effect a deed bad in itself, or inversely; but the moral act which a
good intention dictates is always a good act, just as the one a bad intention
dictates is always bad. Thus, for good as for evil, the morality of the act
is identical with the morality of the intention.[105]

But what is a good intention? It is not simply an intention which
seems good. It is one that really is good. In order to do well, it is not
enough to believe that what one does is pleasing to God; it must also be
what God wills that man should do. This correction, so wise, involves
Abélard in serious difficulties. He is quite well aware that the personal
impression of having a good intention is not sufficient; otherwise the
persecutors of Christ and the martyrs could be morally justified. Furthermore, nothing is just without faith. But then, how could men have good
intentions prior to the preaching of the Gospel? Even while it was being
preached Christ was proclaiming the truth to certain cities and leaving
others in error. Even now, a good many unbelievers would be inclined to
become converted if they knew the Gospel, but they do not know it. How
could their intentions and their acts be good?

As a logician following the consequences of his principles, Abélard maintains that it is the intention that decides. Those who do not know the
Gospel obviously commit no fault in not believing in Jesus Christ. How
can one sin against a law of which one is ignorant? It may be, certainly,
that the works of such men are in fact bad, but how can they be held
responsible, since they cannot know it? A man aims with his bow at a
bird he sees, and kills a man he did not see; the deed is bad, the act itself
is not. Christ's persecutors accomplished an evil work in putting him to
death, but if they believed themselves bound by conscience to do it, they
would have sinned more grievously by sparing him. All that would have
been quite all right, had Abélard not come up against this additional theo-

logical difficulty: no matter how we qualify their acts morally, those who die without having known the Gospel are damned. How is that to be explained? If they are in ignorance of the Gospel and transgress its laws, it is surely not their fault! And here is Abélard's answer: "This unbelief in which these men die is sufficient for their damnation, even though the cause of that blindness, to which God abandoned them, is not apparent to us." Thus, for once, master Peter stopped short, but we shall see that it was not for long.[106]

3. THEOLOGY

The *Sic et non* appears to date from the years 1121-1122; in his *Theologia christiana,* which follows shortly after (1123-1124), Abélard ran up against the same difficulty, but now on a plane where it could be solved at least partially. The principle that unbelief excludes unbelievers from the kingdom of God remains intact, but who are the unbelievers? What about the pagan philosophers, for example; do they deserve this name? Reaching back across the centuries to join the most liberal theses of Saint Justin, Abélard makes sure that those of them who led a more chastened life received from God a certain light of truth. They knew that there was only one God; some of them, as is apparent from reading Saint Augustine, had a presentiment of the dogma of the Trinity, or even the mysteries of the Incarnation and Redemption. Since God revealed the essential of the saving truths to the Jews by the Prophets, and to the pagans by the philosophers, they are not to be excused if they did not listen to the teaching of their masters; on the contrary, those of them who did listen were certainly saved. Abélard considers that many pagans and some Jews were saved, and among the pagans, the Greeks first, then the Latins who followed their doctrine. It is enough, moreover, to see how the philosophers lived to be assured of it. What we know of their lives testifies that they followed the natural law, which the Gospel only brought to its perfection. Hence we cannot be surprised at the harmony of their lives with what the Gospel enjoins and of which the saints have set the example. After having brought in several witnesses to prove his point, Abélard concludes: "We find that their lives, as well as their doctrine, express to the greatest degree evangelical and apostolic perfection, that they deviate but little or not at all from the Christian religion, and that they are united with us not only by their ways of life, but even in name. For we call ourselves Christians because the true wisdom, that is, the wisdom of God the Father, is Christ; we therefore truly deserve the name of philosophers if we truly love Christ."[107] Since the contrary was obviously also true, how could we refuse the true philosophers the title of Christians? Perhaps they were Gentiles only by nationality, but not by faith: *Gentiles fortasse natione, non fide, omnes fuerunt philosophi.* One cannot agree therefore that those to whom God revealed the secrets of his faith and the deep mysteries of the Trinity, as Saint Paul himself testifies, have been condemned to unbelief and damnation. John the Baptist and many others were saved without the sacraments: why not philosophers? It is rather we who should be ashamed of the lives we lead when we see how those admirable men knew how to live, without the revelation of the Gospel or the help of grace. Abélard is here freely indulging in his general tendency to look upon grace as a blossoming of nature, or inversely, as in the *Dialogue between a Philosopher, a Jew and a Christian,* to conceive Christianity as the total verity which includes all others within it. In this latter work, which was interrupted by his death, we see the Christian exerting himself to convince the Jew and the pagan, not by denying the truths that they themselves lay claim to, but by bringing all of them into the richer and more comprehensive truth of Christian faith.

Abélard had a clear mind and a generous heart. Christian revelation was never, for him, an impassable barrier dividing the chosen from the condemned and truth from error. Abélard knew secret passages from one side to the other and he liked to believe that the Ancients he loved had already found them. He himself passes from faith to reason with a frank audacity that William of Saint-Thierry and Saint Bernard of Clairvaux condemned as intellectual pride. *Nil videt per speculum, nil in aenigmate;* all was clear to him, even mystery. As we have said, the sincerity of his faith was not in question, but the philosophers' reason looked in him too much like his faith, for his faith not to look too much like his reason. One cannot read Abélard without thinking of those educated Christians of the sixteenth century, Erasmus for example, to whom the distance from ancient wisdom to the wisdom of the Gospel will seem so short. But Abélard is not a prefiguration of the sixteenth century; he is a man of the twelfth century, nourished on antique culture as it was known in his time, carrying farther than others a generous confidence in the catholicity of the true, and expressing it with the dialectical obstinacy which, whatever the subject they treat, characterizes all his works.

Abélard's influence was momentous. It cannot be said that the most eminent qualities of Abélard were the sole cause of his glory and influence, but it is certain at least that the end of the twelfth century is indebted to him for an ideal of technical strictness and exhaustive justification, even in theology, which was to find its complete expression in the doctrinal syntheses of the thirteenth century. Abélard imposed, so to speak, an intellectual *standard* which no one thenceforth cared to lower. The history of mediaeval theology would show this much better than the history of mediaeval philosophy, for if he himself was somewhat unfortunate in this domain, the illustrious disciples who took up and continued his work witness to the fecundity of the new spirit he had brought to it.[108]

CHAPTER V

SPECULATIVE MYSTICISM

SAINT BERNARD of Clairvaux,[109] a leader of men, an ecstatic blessed with high personal mystical experiences, was also one of the founders of Western speculative mysticism. In circumstances which we do not know yet, he became acquainted with Latin translations of works of Gregory of Nyssa and of Origen. He was acquainted with the treatises of Denis as well as with their commentaries by Maximus Confessor, perhaps even with the works of Erigena. The central place occupied by Bernard in the history of theology, although its real significance has not yet been clearly defined, is due to the fact that, in his mind, the Latin theology of Augustine found itself confronted, for the first time since Erigena, with the Greek theology of Gregory and Denis. Only, instead of being carried away by his discovery, Bernard achieved a synthesis of the two traditions. There is no trace of a clash between them in his mind. If there was one, we know nothing about it. What we know is the finished product; that is, a new theology which unites the Greek theology, based upon the relation of image to model, with the Latin theology based upon the relation of nature to grace. All the Greek theology of "resemblance" is dominated and justified in Bernard's own theology by his sharp-cut ontological distinction between God, "causal being" of all that is, and the finite images that are his created effects. Naturally, there still was much to be done after Bernard of Clairvaux, but, precisely, he laid down the foundations for the synthesis of the two theological traditions which were to be pursued by his thirteenth-century successors. The belated Erigenians condemned in 1241, and those who were to renew the same attempt in the fourteenth century, simply failed to realize the true meaning of the work of the abbot of Clairvaux.

Bernard maintains that the knowledge of profane sciences is of small value compared with that of sacred sciences, and he watches closely the philosopher theologians of his time. His own philosophy is "to know Jesus, and Jesus crucified." His sentiments regarding dialecticians are revealed in the struggle he carried on against Abélard and Gilbert of la Porrée, whose general tendencies and excessive indulgence in reasoning in theology disturbed him profoundly. Saint Bernard certainly did little to bring about the rise of the great scholastic philosophies; he maintained a suspicious attitude with regard to contemporary attempts preparing it, but his very elaborate doctrine of mystical love initiated a speculative movement which was to develop in the course of centuries to follow.

The way that leads to truth is Christ, and Christ's teaching is humility.

Work is one thing, the fruit of work is another. The work first thrust upon us, if we would know, is to humble ourselves. Humility may be defined as the virtue by which man, knowing himself exactly for what he is, is humbled in his own eyes. This virtue is suitable for those who have in their hearts degrees and, as it were, steps to raise themselves progressively up to God. Those who follow Saint Benedict's way of life know from his Rule that the degrees of humility are twelve in number, but this saint gives them to us to mount rather than to count. In attaining the acme of humility we also attain the first degree of truth, which is to recognize our own misery; from this first degree we soon reach a second, charity, because in recognizing our misery we sympathize with our neighbor in his own; and from this second degree we pass easily on to the third because, in compassion alike for our misery and the misery of others, we bewail our faults and our blemishes, detest them, aspire to justice and thus purify our heart to render it capable of contemplating heavenly things.

Those are the three degrees of truth surmounting the twelve degrees of humility; we lift ourselves up to the first by the effort of humility, to the second by the feeling of compassion, to the third by the fervor of contemplation. In the first, truth is severe; it is pious in the second, and pure in the third. Just as there are degrees of humility, there are also degrees of pride; to go up the one is to descend the other, and to raise oneself up in the way of good is to go down the scale of evil. The culminating point of human knowledge is reached by man in the ecstasy in which the soul is in some way separated from the body, becomes empty and loses itself to enjoy a sort of deification.[110]

This intercourse is a fusion and a sort of deification of the soul by love: "Just as a tiny drop of water which falls into a great quantity of wine seems to become diluted and disappear, taking on the taste and color of the wine, just as red-hot glowing iron becomes like fire and seems to lose its original form, just as air flooded with sunlight seems to be transformed into that luminous clarity itself to such a point that it seems no longer to be illuminated but light, so should all human affection in saints finally dissolve and become liquefied in order to flow whole in the will of God. How, in fact, could God be all in all things if there remained in man something of man? His substance will no doubt continue to be, but under another form, another power and another glory." [111] The last sentence could be turned round without betraying Saint Bernard's thought, for although man can thus pass into God when grace accomplishes that perfect resemblance and conformity between human will and divine will, man's substance remains no less infinitely distinct from divine substance. Charity alone can bring about that marvel of a perfect union in a radical distinction of beings. Harmony of wills, but not confusion of substances (*non substantiis confusos, sed voluntate consentaneos*), that is what this communion and harmony in love means. And it is also the supreme limit man sometimes thinks he reaches for an instant in this life, through ecstasy, and which he attains forever only in the beatific vision. However, even then, the union of man with God is in no way comparable to that of the Son with the Father, which is not a union, but unity itself.[112]

Several causes account for the influence of Saint Bernard: the prestige of his saintliness and the authority of the religious reformer; the eloquence of his style. Two other causes should, however, be noted separately: his doctrine was based on a personal experiencing of ecstasy, and he gave a fully elaborated interpretation of that experience. In the long series of his sermons on the *Canticle of Canticles,* Bernard clearly affirmed that the ecstatic union of the soul with God was a familiar experience for him. He also added that it was incommunicable. Whoever has not experienced it cannot know what it is, and whoever has experienced it is incapable of describing it. And even if he could, we should be no further along, for ecstasy is strictly individual, and the experience of one person would teach us nothing of what another's might be.[113] But one can speculate on its causes and on the conditions which make it possible.

In an act of pure charity, for he is Charity, God created man in his image and resemblance. This image is found mainly in the will, that is to say, in free will. Created by an act of divine love, man's will is essentially a divine love, a charity. We may therefore say that, as God naturally loves himself, man's will naturally loves God. The fact that man loves himself is no obstacle. If man loves himself as God loves him, there is perfect accord between his will and divine will; there is, therefore, perfect resemblance between man and God. That is what Saint Bernard calls union with God. It is therefore not a question of a community of essence which would unite human being with divine being, but of a community by way of resemblance which is based upon a perfect accord of wills. To love God for himself, as God loves himself, is to have attuned our will to his; it is, therefore, while continuing to be ourselves, to be indistinguishable from him.[114]

Taken in its essence, sin consists in the act by which man wills himself for himself, or wills for himself the other creatures of God, instead of willing for God both himself and the rest. This "proper will" made man dissimilar to God, but the effect of the grace of Redemption is to restore man to the divine resemblance he lost. The Christian life is therefore identical with the mystical life, and the latter in turn can be considered as a re-education of love. To love God for himself is to love him with a disinterested love, that is, as Saint Bernard explains in his *De diligendo Deo,* with a love which finds in itself its own recompense. To be sure, God will repay love, but since love excludes any view to recompense, it is contradictory to love God in view of a recompense and to love him without being repaid. Once brought to that purity of intention, the love man has naturally for himself is no longer opposed to the love of God for

God, for man himself has again become the image of God. Being no more than a love of God for God, the love man has for himself takes on the exact shape of the love with which God loves him and coincides in intention with it. If, then, God so wills, he can take the soul as a bride, love himself in that image of himself as he loves himself in himself. Ecstasy is nothing else than the extreme point of this union of wills and this coinciding of a human love with the divine.[115]

William of Saint Thierry[116] is somewhat overshadowed by Saint Bernard's glory, but history is beginning to do him justice. He deserves it, for this friend of Saint Bernard's was his exact contemporary, and the close agreement of their doctrines is not an identity. His most famous work is the *Epistola ad Fratres de Monte Dei* (often called the *Golden Letter*), but at least two other writings should be read together with that one: *On the Contemplation of God,* and *On the Nature and Dignity of Love.* William's doctrine, like Saint Bernard's, develops entirely within the framework of monastic life. Secular schools teach profane love according to the *Ars amatoria* of Ovid; the cloisters should be religious schools where divine love is taught. William's doctrine, then, will also be a science of love, but it differs from Saint Bernard's in the more important role the Augustinian doctrine of memory plays in it. The love of God has been naturally inserted by him into the heart of his creature. Human love should therefore tend naturally toward God in virtue of its own weight, but original sin turns it aside and the aim of monastic life is to bring the love of man back to his creator. The method to follow in order to achieve this result requires first an effort to know oneself. The soul knows itself by knowing itself as created in the image of God to the extent that it is a mind (*mens*). In mind itself is found a sort of secret point where God has, so to speak, left his imprint so that we may always remember him. Like Saint Augustine, let us call this innermost recess of the mind "memory." We shall then say that our secret "memory" begets our reason, and that will proceeds from both of them. This created trinity represents in us the creative Trinity, memory corresponding to the Father, reason to the Word and will to the Holy Ghost. Born of a memory which itself is but the stamp of God upon man, this reason and this will should have no other object than God. The effect of divine grace is to straighten out the faculties of the soul disordered by sin, so that the love with which we love God shall coincide with the love he has for himself in himself and with which he loves himself in us. The more the soul recovers its resemblance to God which belongs to it by right of birth, and which it should never have lost, the better it knows God by knowing itself: the resemblance of the soul to God constitutes its knowledge of God.

After Saint Bernard and William of Saint Thierry the great Cistercian mystical thrust loses its force, and their continuators turn rather toward religious moralism. Some of them, however, gathered into their work philosophical elements whose influence was to endure. That is particularly the case with Isaac, abbot of the Cistercian monastery of Etoile from 1147 to 1169 (hence his name, Isaac Stella), and with the monk Alcher of Clairvaux. To tell the truth, their works are less examples of speculative mysticism than expressions of a speculation oriented toward mysticism.

Isaac[117] has left us, as did other Cistercians following the example set by Saint Bernard, a series of Sermons on the *Canticle of Canticles,* but he seeks God less through ecstasy than by metaphysics. This is certainly the case for a group of eight of these sermons (XIX-XXVI) in which Isaac lifts thought up to God by a dialectical analysis, equally firm and subtle, of the notion of substance. This interesting bit of metaphysics is the perfect type of a theology based on the notion of God as pure essence. These pages are a remarkable testimony to the profound penetration of spirituality by the metaphysics of that epoch. Moreover, they confirm the diffusion, toward the middle of the twelfth century, of a sort of abstract Platonism, for which the dialectical manipulation of essences constituted the rational explanation of reality.

The most celebrated and influential work Isaac wrote is his *Letter on the Soul,* written at the request of Alcher of Clairvaux. This epistle, which is a real treatise on the soul, owes its success to the scrupulously careful classification of the faculties it contains. There are three realities: the body, the soul and God; we do not know the essence of any one of them, but we know the body less certainly than the soul, and the soul less certainly than God (P.L. 194, 1883 B). Made in the image of God, the soul has been defined by a philosopher as the "similitude of all things. Situated between God and the body, it agrees in something with both of them, and by its very intermediary situation, it has a base, a middle and a peak. The soul's base, or imagination, is related to the summit of the body, which is sensibility; the peak of the soul, intelligence, is related to God. Between these two extreme faculties rise, one above another, all the other faculties according to an ascending order beginning with the body: corporeal sense, imagination, reason, intellect, intelligence. Reason is that faculty of the soul which perceives the incorporeal forms of corporeal things: "It abstracts (*abstrahit*) from the body what is grounded in the body, not by an action but by a consideration, and, although it sees that this actually subsists only in the body, it perceives, however, that it is not a body. In fact, the very nature of the body, by which every body is body, is no body. And yet it subsists nowhere outside of the body, and the nature of the body is found only in the body, even though it is neither a body nor the likeness of a body. Reason therefore perceives what neither sense nor imagination perceive; namely, the natures of things corporeal, their forms, differences, properties, accidents, all things which are incorporeal but which do not subsist outside the body except in thought alone, for second substances (i.e., abstract notions) subsist only in first substances (i.e., concrete individuals)." Isaac certainly did not consider universals to be things, nor does he say that they are only words, but the *consideration*, which is not an *action*, to which for him abstraction is reduced, leaves him still far from what Saint Thomas Aquinas's doctrine will be. He differs from it still more by what he borrows from Boethius regarding intellect and intelligence. By *intellectus* he means that faculty of the soul which perceives the forms of things that are truly incorporeal, the soul, for example; and by *intelligentia,* the faculty of knowing the sole supreme and pure incorporeal, which is God. All Platonist themes converge on this point of his doctrine. *Intelligentia* comes to it from Boethius. Through Augustine, this "intelligence" inherits from Plotinus its aptitude to receive divine illumination and thus to return to the very source of light. Through Erigena, it inherits from Maximus Confessor the theophanies which come down to it from God while, inversely, images come up to it from the body. This syncretism shows how what Abélard had taught on the nature of rational knowledge could be reconciled with the mystical aspirations of a Cistercian soul.

If, as is commonly agreed, the treatise *On Spirit and Soul* (*De spiritu et anima*) is the work of Alcher of Clairvaux,[118] and an answer to the treatise of Isaac, it must be acknowledged that it was a poor reply. Historically speaking, it remains an interesting document in that it lists many definitions of the soul and classifications of its faculties borrowed from all the Latin sources accessible to its author. Lactantius, Macrobius, Augustine, Boethius, Bede, Alcuin, and even such contemporaries as Hugh of Saint Victor and Isaac himself are present in this compilation. Everybody could find there the particular type of psychology that suited his own taste. Moreover, this philosophical patchwork had the good fortune to be received as the work of Saint Augustine, an error which, of course, conferred upon it exceptional authority. Even Albertus Magnus attributed it to Augustine, but Thomas Aquinas did not make the same mistake. "This *De spiritu et anima*," Thomas says, "is not the work of Augustine; they say it was written by some Cistercian, nor should one worry very much about what is said in it" (*Qu. disp. de anima,* 12, ad 1m.). Obviously the monks of Citeaux were drifting away from the lofty speculations of Saint Bernard and following the general trend of their own times. Even those among them who were truly imbued with his spirit, like the charming Aelred of Rievaulx,[119] could not continue with his work. First, they had no mystical experience to compare with that of their master; next, they seem to have sought their inspiration in Bernard himself rather than in the direct meditation of his Greek sources. In this domain like in all other ones, the Latin tradition remains metaphysically sterile; mediaeval speculation peters out as soon as the Greek stream ceases to flow.

The second home of speculative mysticism in the twelfth century was the

Parisian abbey of the Augustine Canons of Saint Victor, founded by William of Champeaux. Hugh of Saint Victor (1096-1141), born in Saxony, educated first at the abbey of Hamersleben, then at Saint Victor where he taught until his death, was a high-ranking theologian.[120] A comprehensive and lucid mind, he strove to reassemble in his works the essential in sacred and in profane sciences, but in order to turn them to the contemplation of God and to love. When he spoke of dialectics and of profane studies carried on in view of themselves, Hugh of Saint Victor could express himself in terms no less severe than those of Saint Bernard and William of Saint Thierry. The novices he addressed were not to imagine that they had entered Saint Victor to be educated there as though in a school of liberal arts. They were there to follow the path to moral and contemplative perfection. Nevertheless, we should not apply to him too simplified formulas, such as, for example: "Hugh was *only* a mystic." One can be a very exalted mystic without knowing how to read or write; one can be a very exalted mystic, more or less educated, without identifying one's knowledge with one's mystical life; one can be a highly learned mystic, anxious to turn knowledge itself into mystical contemplation. Hugh of Saint Victor belonged to this latter group, and that is why his doctrine is not without interest for the history of mediaeval thought. As he conceives it, the life of a monk is filled with a series of hierarchical exercises: reading or teaching, meditation, prayer, action, and finally contemplation, in which, gathering in a way the fruits of what has gone before, one tastes in this very life what will one day be the reward of good works. Since this reward is to be the eternal joy of divine love, contemplation in this life cannot be separated from love. In short, contemplation here presupposes the acquisition of science. One has to acquire it in order to transcend it. Learn everything, Hugh says, and you will then see that there is nothing useless (*Didasc.*, VI, 3). As a matter of fact, his treatise *On Sacraments* is a theological Summa, and his *Didascalion* is intended to teach what should be read, in what order it should be read, and how to read it. The knowledge resulting from reading and contemplation, that is, the only part of learning that can be transmitted to others, is what Hugh offers us in this *Art of Reading*.

The sciences are reduced to four, which contain all the others: theoretical science, which seeks to discover truth; practical science, which ponders the discipline of morals; mechanics, which directs our practical activities; logic, which teaches us the science of speaking well and of discussing. Theoretical or speculative science includes theology, mathematics and physics; mathematics itself is divided into arithmetic, music, geometry and astronomy. Practical science subdivides into individual, domestic and political ethics. Mechanics in turn subdivides into seven sciences: weaving, the making of arms, navigation, agriculture, hunting, medicine and theater. Logic, which is the fourth part of philosophy, divides into grammar and the art of discourse, this latter comprising the theory of demonstration, rhetoric and dialectics.

Among these sciences seven are particularly worth studying, namely, the seven liberal arts which compose the *trivium* and *quadrivium*. The ancients possessed them so perfectly, and were therefore so wise, that they wrote more things than we can read; our scholastics on the contrary, do not know how or do not care to keep the just measure in acquiring knowledge; no wonder then that we have so many students and so few scholars.

The seven liberal arts are inseparable; nobody can achieve wisdom by learning some of these arts and neglecting the others. These fundamental sciences are so closely connected that, if one happens to be lacking, the others are not sufficient to make a philosopher. True knowledge is acquired by means of abstraction. According to Hugh, to abstract is simply to consider separately a certain element of the real. For instance a mathematician abstracts when he considers separately point, line or surface, although these be always given together in reality.[121]

As a mystic, Hugh appeals to no exceptional experiences or revelations. He rather seeks allegorical interpretations of natural things and leads the soul to inner peace and joy through contemplation. In theology proper, his *De sacramentis* anticipates the general plan of the future *Summae* of the thirteenth century. The whole history of the world is organized around its two critical moments, creation and the Incarnation. Hugh does not hesitate to resort to philosophical demonstration in order to establish the reasonableness of faith. Following Augustine (*Soliloq.*, II, 1, 1), he posits as first knowledge that of our own existence. We cannot be ignorant of the fact that we exist. More exactly, the soul cannot ignore the fact that it exists and that it is not a body; since we know that we did not always exist and that we have had a beginning, there must be an author of our being, who is God. A more notable feature of his doctrine is that, according to Hugh, God does not will things because they are right; rather, things are right because God wills them.[122]

A disciple and successor to Hugh, Richard of St. Victor made no original contribution to metaphysical speculation. He owed his later influence to his mystical works: *On the Preparation of the Soul to Contemplation* (or *Benjamin minor*) and *On the Grace of Contemplation* (or *Benjamin major*). Their consistent scriptural symbolism was to exert a deep influence on a certain type of spirituality, particularly that of Saint Bonaventure, in the thirteenth century. The same remark is true of a third Victorine, Thomas Gallus (d. 1246), whose writings are still largely unknown but whose influence on the speculative theology of the thirteenth century is clearly visible in the doctrine of Saint Bonaventure.[123]

CHAPTER VI

ALAN OF LILLE

ALAN OF LILLE,[124] born about 1128, became a well-known master of theology, but renounced the world and entered the monastery of Citeaux, where he died in 1202. One of the most striking features of his writings is their peculiarly polemical character. Rather, it is the peculiar nature of the adversaries against which the polemic of Alan is directed. Thus far, we have seen theologians fighting among themselves, for instance, on the correct use of dialectics in theological matters, or on such questions as the relation of "God" to "divinity." These were personal controversies, between theologian and theologian, and when they had to be settled by a local council, they ended in a personal condemnation. Incidentally, let us note that there is not a single known case of any philosopher condemned to any corporal punishment for having maintained any philosophical opinion up to the time of the Council of Prague. At any rate, Alan of Lille appears as witness to a new situation. In the last third of the twelfth century, Jewish communities had become numerous and prosperous enough in Western Europe to turn Judaism into a living force and a serious opponent. But a more radically new situation was created by Mohammedanism. The founder of Islam had died in 632, but although the Arabic invasion of Spain, and even of France (battle of Poitiers, 732) had created violent contacts between Christianity and the new religion, very little was known about the Koran before the last third of the twelfth century. The Venerable Peter, abbot of Cluny,[125] was the first to provide the Western world with a translation of the Koran. From that time on, Christianity found itself confronted with two living religions, that is, with something quite different from doctrinal divergences between individual Christians. At the very same moment when the Crusades created contacts between the Christians and the most highly civilized peoples of their times, sects were arising within Christendom itself, such as, for instance, the Albigenses, whose doctrine was much less a heresy than a religion, and which created a political problem by breaking up the religious unity of the Western world.[126] The treatise of Alan *On Catholic Faith against the Heretics* marks the moment when, after centuries of uninterrupted conquests, Christianity will once more find itself on the defensive. We are now entering the era of the treatises "against the Gentiles," the best known of which will be written, in the thirteenth century, by Thomas Aquinas.

The position of Alan, however, is rather different from that of his illustrious successors. He still is dealing with religions or religious sects rather than with pagan or non-Christian philosophies. He does not know the work of his contemporary, Averroes, nor that of Avicenna, who had died about 1037. In order to face the new peril, Alan simply undertook a revision of theological methods and attempted a direct demonstration of the main philosophical truths which pave the way to Christian faith.

His personal conception of theology is dominated by a few remarks of Boethius. At the beginning of his treatise *Quomodo substantiae,* Boethius had spoken of his *Hebdomades ("ex hebdomadibus nostris")* as of another one of his works. As the title of the *Quomodo substantiae* was rather long, and since it claimed to elucidate one of the questions discussed in the *Hebdomades,* it became customary to call it the *De hebdomadibus.* Now, explaining what he had tried to achieve in his *Hebdomades,* Boethius had clearly defined the ideal of a sort of mathematically demonstrated theology. There, Boethius says, just as is usually done in mathematics, and even in other disciplines, I laid down terms and rules whereby I could make all my following points. Not knowing Greek, Alan inferred from these words that the term *hebdomades* signified "maxims" or "axioms," in which he was not right but, after all, not far wrong, for indeed this mysterious title probably signified two or more sets of seven axioms each. At any rate, Alan concluded from Boethius's suggestion that theology could and perhaps should be constructed deductively from previously defined terms and axioms. In point of fact, no thirteenth-century theologian ever attempted to build up a complete theology following this method. And no wonder, since, to the whole extent that they presuppose the free will of God Christian mysteries cannot possibly be deduced.[127]

Another influence played an important part in this development. In his treatise *On Catholic Faith* (I, 30), Alan quotes what he calls the *Aphorisms on the Essence of Supreme Goodness,* a work better known by the title of *De causis.* Let us note its first appearance in our history; it is not going to be the last one. The origins of the *De causis* are still obscure, but that of its content is clear. It comes from the *Elementatio theologica* of Proclus and, through Proclus, it goes back to the *Enneads* of Plotinus. The aphoristic form of the *Liber de causis* is obviously the model which Alan has attempted to imitate in his own *Maxims of Theology* or *Rules of Sacred Theology.*[128]

The "maxims" of theology are "common conceptions of the soul," that is to say, according to the Stoic definition of such conceptions, immediately evident propositions, practically innate, which cannot be proven by other propositions but, on the contrary, serve to prove them. The absolutely first theological maxim is that the "monad" is that by which every thing is one: *Monas est qua quaelibet res est una.* This formula is enough to assure us that Alan is moving in the orbit of Plotinus. His theology of the One is a "monadology." Naturally, the Monad, or pure Unity, which the first maxim posits, is none other than God. With such a starting point, the only way for Alan to justify the fundamental tenets of

Christian theology is to translate all relations of superior to inferior in terms of relations between "same" and "other," sameness being on the side of unity and otherness on the side of plurality. The three main orders of beings form a decreasing hierarchy according to the increasing amount of otherness and of multiplicity which enters their texture. The highest of these three orders is the "supercelestial" one, which is the absolute Unity, that is God. The second one is the "celestial" order, that of angels, in whom the first otherness appears because, created by God, it is subjected to mutability. The third order is the "subcelestial" one, that is, the world of bodies and of plurality in which we live. There is some unity everywhere there is some being, and all unity there is in plurality ultimately comes to it from the Monad: "The Monad alone is; in other words, God alone is, that is, he whose being is simple and immutable; as to the rest, it is not, because it never remains in the same condition."

Since it is perfectly simple, the Monad engenders unity. What it begets is another self, the Son, and it is still another self which proceeds from the Father and the Son: the Holy Ghost. Alan was not conscious of overstepping the frontiers of philosophy in proceeding to this deduction of the Christian dogma of the Trinity. On the contrary, he thought that the pagan author of the *Asclepius* had glimpsed the truth on this point when he wrote: "The supreme God made a second God; he loved him as his only son and called him the son of his eternal benediction." Had he only said "engendered" instead of "made," his formula would have been perfect! But Alan found the absolutely perfect formula in another "hermetic" book, namely the *Book of the Twenty-Four Philosophers,* which he ascribed to Hermes Trismegistos:[129] *"Monas gignit Monadem et in se suum reflectit ardorem";* which he interprets in the following manner: the Monad can engender only a Monad, and it reflects its own ardor upon itself, its own ardor being the Holy Ghost (*Max. theol.,* 3).

By engendering a unity which is another self, the Monad manifests itself as a principle and an end which itself has neither principle nor end. As principle and end, the Monad can be called a circle, since the end of a circle is in its own beginning. On the other hand, since everything is by the Monad, it is a circle that encompasses all; hence this new maxim: "God is an intelligible sphere, whose center is everywhere and the circumference nowhere" (*Max. theol.,* 7). The success of this maxim has been astounding. Rabelais has ascribed it to Hermes Trismegistus, to the dismay of his commentators who could not find it there (III Bk., ch. 13); it reappears in Petrus Ramus, Pierre Charron, Blaise Pascal (who, naturally, interprets it in his own way); Voltaire ascribes it to Timaeus Locrensis. Any one of them might have found it in a dozen different books, but its true origin, as far as we know, is a modest pseudo-hermetic treatise of the twelfth century, the *Liber XXIV philosophorum.*

All that is simple is, at one time and indivisibly, both its being and what it is: *omne simplex esse esse suum, et id quod est, unum habet.* Obviously borrowed from Boethius, this maxim means that the Monad does not divide itself into *esse* and *quod est.* Since it is simple, it is immaterial and, consequently, it is form. Hence it is the form of all, in this sense at least that everything derives its being from form: "Since God is said to be form because he informs all things and gives them their being, it is correct to say that all that is, is in virtue of form." In this sense, God (i.e., the Monad) is the being of all that is, inasmuch as he is its cause, but since there is nothing in which God participates, nothing is the being of God. In other words, the divine form is *formalissima* (supremely form); form of all, it is informed by nothing.

On the strength of these principles, Alan minutely determines the rules of language to be observed in speaking of God; then he defines divine omnipotence (note *reg.*, 69, concerning the important question of knowing whether the real is possible), the relations of future contingents to providence and the necessity which results from their prevision, the nature of natural good, of voluntary good and evil, which leads him to the problems of sin, grace, Christ and the sacraments. Alan concludes with a set of rules concerning causality, and determines in what sense each of them is valid, either in theology, in philosophy, or in both sciences at once. The last of the rules is that there is a cause, namely Unity, the affirmation of which is implied in that of every other thing: *haec causa est unitas; omnem enim proprietatem unitas comitatur.* For instance, to say that Socrates is man in virtue of humanity is to say that his own unity is that which belongs to humanity; likewise, to say that Socrates is white, is to attribute to him the kind of unity which is proper to whiteness, and so on with all the other properties of the subject, except perhaps individuality, which is one in virtue of its own unity.[130]

Alan, however, owed his fame to two works of a totally different kind, the *Anticlaudianus* and the *De planctu naturae.* The first one is hardly readable today. At the beginning of a poem entitled *Rufinus,* the poet Claudian had called up all the Vices to pervert the prefect Rufinus and thus assure his ruin; in his own poem (*Anticlaudian*), Alan assumes, on the contrary, that Nature is planning the birth of a perfect man and calls upon all the sciences and all the virtues to form him. Hence comes the title *Anticlaudianus.* The academic commonplaces of the twelfth century fill the work, not forgetting the unavoidable "Noys" who, by order of the creator, prepares for Nature the Idea, or model, of the perfect human mind that is to be created.[131]

The *De planctu Naturae* derives its title from its beginning, which is a "lament of Nature" deploring the crimes committed against her by the Sodomites. Inferior to its model, the "Consolation" of Boethius, the *De planctu naturae* is still interesting to read and the allegorical figure of Nature, which dominates the whole work, is not without a certain gran-

deur. Moreover, it expresses the Christian idea of nature common to practically all mediaeval theologians, except, of course, the extreme representatives of strict other-worldliness (*contemptus saeculi*). Just as in Boethius
and in Bernardus Silvestris, Nature represents here the inexhaustible fecundity from which springs the pullulation of beings. It is the source of universal life, and not only the cause of beings but their rule, their law, their
order, their beauty and their end. Nature could not be too highly praised
in her works, which are, through her, the works of God. Alan has poetically
expressed, by that allegorical figure, what may be called the "Christian
naturalism" of the twelfth century.[132] However proud of herself she may
be when she describes her works, Nature becomes humble the moment she
turns to their Author: "His operation is single, mine is manifold; his work
is self-sufficient, mine is self-undoing . . . He makes, and I am made; he
is the workman whose work I am: I am the work of this worker; he works
with nothing, I beg for a matter with which to work; he works in his own
name, I work in the name of God."

This subordination of nature to God entails that of the sciences of
nature to the science of God: "To learn that my power is impotence with
respect to divine knowledge . . . consult theological science whose faith-
fulness has more right to your approval than the steadfastness of my
reasons. According to the teaching of faith, man owes his birth to my
action, but his rebirth to the authority of God." Theology and Nature
sometimes think differently, but they do not contradict each other. Besides,
their methods are not the same. Nature goes from reason to faith, theology goes from faith to reason: "As for me, Nature says, I know in order
that I may believe, theology believes in order to know; I consent by
knowing, it knows by consenting." Like the Demiurge of the *Timaeus,*
Nature works without losing sight of divine Ideas.[133] The spirit of Chartres,
whose influence is everywhere present in his writings, is here bearing its last
fruits.

Among the works attributed to Alan of Lille is a remarkable treatise
which historical research first ascribed to Nicholas of Amiens,[134] but which
more historical research has recently restored to its traditional author,
Alan of Lille. In his *Art of Catholic Faith,* Alan carries methodological
exigences to their limit. He knows that unbelievers do not heed any arguments based on authority, and that the testimony of Scripture leaves them
completely indifferent; the only way to deal with such opponents is to call
upon reason. That is why, he says, "I have carefully put in order the
probable reasons in favor of our faith,—reasons of a kind that a clear-
sighted mind could scarcely reject, so that those who refuse to believe the
prophecies and Scripture find themselves brought to it at least by human
reasons." Alan, however, does not think these reasons capable of totally
penetrating and completely illuminating the content of faith, but he wishes
at least to arrange these reasons for believing in a convincing manner and

that is why he presents them in the form of definitions, distinctions and propositions linked together according to an intended order. The general plan of the work is the one which the *Book of Sentences* of Peter Lombard was spreading among theologians: God, the World, the Creation of the Angels and Mankind, the Redeemer, the Sacraments and the Resurrection. But in the very detail of the exposition, Alan gives proof of originality. His work is based on definitions, postulates and axioms. The definitions fix the meaning of the terms: cause, substance, matter, form, etc.; the postulates are undemonstrable truths; the axioms, propositions such that one cannot hear them stated without accepting them. From these principles Alan unrolls the chain of his propositions and syllogistic demonstrations somewhat as a *theologia more geometrico demonstrata.*

Alan pretty well succeeded in giving his work a Euclidean aspect. One incontestable advantage of his method is that it does away with useless developments. Divided into five very short books, his theology starts out with a series of definitions: cause, substance, matter, form, movement, etc.; Alan next posits three postulates and seven axioms (Prolog.), after which he begins to construct his theorems according to the ordinary rules of geometry. The first four theorems are: The cause of a cause is cause of its effect; every cause of a subject is cause of its accident; nothing can compose itself or cause its own existence; no matter can exist without its form, nor can any form exist without its matter. The fifth theorem can serve as an example of what Alan calls a demonstration: *"The composition of form and matter is cause of the substance.*—For indeed substance consists of matter and form, consequently matter and form are the cause of the composition of substance (by the first postulate: there is a component cause of all composition). Again, neither the form can exist unless it is composed with matter, nor can matter exist unless it is composed with form (as has been proved in the fourth theorem); therefore form and matter have actual existence because of their composition; therefore their composition is the cause of their existence. But their existence is the cause of the substance; therefore (by the first theorem) the composition of form with matter is the cause of the substance (since all that is cause of a cause is cause of its effect)" (V, 599 C).

There is something pathetic in the case of a man exhibiting such a passionate confidence in the power of reason to convince the infidels. Alan was not wholly unaware of the fact. The Moslems, he says, attack Christians by force of arms, but I cannot answer them in the same way. Jews and pagans have been converted by miracles, but, he says modestly, I have not received the grace to do that. True enough, there is left the authority of the Scriptures, but what good is it against infidels who challenge it and heretics who pervert it? What is needed, then, is a rational technique universally valid, to convince whatever enemies of faith there may be; in short, an "Art" of the Catholic faith, that is, a method of rational justification of the Christian faith, as thorough as such a justification can possibly be. Alan of Lille dedicates his *Art* to Pope Clement III, as Roger Bacon is to dedicate his *Opus Majus* to Pope Clement IV. This same ambition to enlarge the Church to world dimensions without counting on force nor expecting everything from faith alone, was to inspire the *Ars Magna* of Ramon Lull at the end of the thirteenth century. The *Ars catholicae fidei* of Alan of Lille is its modest prefiguration.

PART FIVE

ARABIAN AND JEWISH PHILOSOPHY

It is a fact of considerable importance for the history of mediaeval philosophy that its evolution should have been at least two centuries behind that of Arab speculation. In abstract historical time, Alkindi appears as a contemporary of Scotus Erigena, and Avicenna had already elaborated a complete philosophical system, from logic to metaphysics and natural theology, at a time when Western theologians were still laboring in interpreting Christian faith by means of dialectics alone. When we speak, with a not wholly unjustifiable pride, of the achievements of Western culture, we should never forget what the East has contributed to it. Our religion is Christianity, and its birthplace, Palestine, is in Asia, not in Europe. Our whole philosophy comes from Greece, which lies on the borderline between Europe and Asia and, for this very reason, has always been open to Asiatic influences. Through Egypt, even Africa has been influential in shaping Western culture. Last, not least, mediaeval Europe did not inherit Greek philosophy directly, but indirectly, through the channel of Syrian, Persian and Arabic scholars, scientists and philosophers. Some elementary notions concerning the history of Arabian philosophy are therefore necessary for a correct interpretation of the history of mediaeval thought.

CHAPTER I

ARABIAN PHILOSOPHY

In 529 A.D., Emperor Justinian ordered the closing of the philosophical schools in Athens. Had it been taken earlier, this decision would have deprived the Christian Church of the works of Saint Basil, of Saint Gregory Nazianzenus and of Saint Gregory of Nyssa, not to mention less important theologians. By that time, however, Greek thought had already begun to gain ground in Asia, and this fact initiated the circling movement which was to bring back Plato and Aristotle to Western Europe via Syria, Persia, Egypt, Morocco and Spain.

In the beginning, Greek philosophy was imported into Asia by Christians who had studied it in Athens before the closing of its schools. The Christian school of Edessa, in Mesopotamia, founded in 563 by Saint Ephrem, taught the philosophy of Aristotle together with the medicine of Hippocrates and of Galen. On the other hand, when the Syrians became converts to Christianity, they had to learn Greek in order to read Holy Writ. Greek theology followed and, together with it, the Greek culture which was included in it. When this school of Edessa was closed, its professors went on into Persia and made the schools of Nisibis and Gandisapora famous. In Syria, the schools of Risaina and Kinnesrin had harbored the philosophy of Aristotle; philosophical and scientific works had been translated from the Greek into Syriac, which explains why even such an epoch-making event as the founding of Islam by Mohammed (571-632) did not stop the spreading of Greek philosophy. The Mohammedan era begins in 622 (*hegira*), date of the flight of Mohammed from Mecca to Medina. During the following years, Islam replaced Christianity in Western Asia. In 750 the dynasty of the Abbassides califs was founded by Aboul-Abbas, whose successors were to reside in Baghdad from 762 up to 1258. The Baghdad califs (i.e., *successors* of the Prophet) soon called upon the services of Syrian scholars, who continued their teaching and their work under the auspices of these new masters. Arabic then became a scientific language. Euclid, Archimedes, Ptolemy, Hippocrates, Galen, Aristotle, Theophrastus and Alexander of Aphrodisias were translated, either directly from Greek into Arabic, or indirectly from Greek into Syriac, then from Syriac into Arabic. On the whole, the Syriac scholars have transmitted Greek learning to the Arabs, pending the time when it should pass on from the Arabs to the Jews and to the theologians of the Christian West.[1]

The bulk of this philosophical tradition was constituted by the works of Aristotle, but two treatises, essentially neoplatonic in character, where ascribed to him at a very early date. This blending of Plato and Aristotle, already apparent in the Greek commentator of Aristotle, Alexander of

Aphrodisias, was to become a decisive factor in the evolution of mediaeval thought. History of philosophy, which aims to attribute to each philosopher his own doctrine, and no other one, is a comparatively recent discipline. Mediaeval scholars would seldom hesitate to ascribe to a philosopher the works of someone else, provided only they could find a way to reconcile their statements. The so-called *Theology of Aristotle* has long passed for an authentic production of the master. In point of fact, its content was borrowed from Plotinus' *Enneads,* Books IV–VI.[2] The second treatise, namely the *Liber de causis,* or "On Causes," which we have already seen quoted by Alan of Lille, was largely excerpted from the *Elementatio theologica,* or "Elements of Theology," of Proclus.[3] The most important consequence of this fact is that the Arabian philosophers have circulated, under the name of Aristotle, a mixture of Aristotle and Plotinus, who himself was very far from representing the pure doctrine of Plato. The Arabs have never felt the need to choose between these two philosophies. As a matter of fact, they never imagined that they were two philosophies. As has rightly been said: "They believed that there was only one philosophy, whose two masters were Plato and Aristotle." [4]

Like Christian faith, Islamic faith soon felt the need of an intellectual interpretation, be it only in order to correct the literal interpretation of the Koran upheld by the fundamentalists of those times. The early contacts of Islam with Greek philosophy gave rise to a philosophico-religious speculation which is represented by the "mutazilite" school. The "mutazilites" stressed the need of resorting to reason in the interpretation of revelation. They were especially concerned with establishing the absolute unity of God, to the point of refusing any distinction between his essence and his attributes. Moreover, they insisted on the justice of the divine will and refused to admit that good and evil were only such because God had willed them to be either good or evil. Last, not least, they fought against all anthropomorphic representations of God by consistently applying the negative method (*tanzih*), which consists in denying of God all the determinations that apply to his creatures. These positions had far-reaching applications. For instance, to submit the will of God to an intrinsic law of justice was implicitly to admit the existence of an objective good and of an objective evil which reason is able to discover and to which men have to conform their acts. In short, these Moslem theologians were endowing man with moral liberty.

The mutazilites were succeeded by another group, that of the "mutakallimoun," (from *halàm,* discourse) whose members were exactly those whom Thomas Aquinas was to call the *loquentes in lege Maurorum,* that is to say, the Moslem theologians. The "mutakallimoun" represent a theological reaction against the somewhat unorthodox activity of the "mutazilites." We shall have to recall later on the doctrine of Al Ash'ari who, after many years of teaching as a "mutazilite," publicly renounced his former attitude and built up a complete justification of the absolute freedom of God. His second doctrine finally became the orthodox theology of Islam, and it is still being taught today in some Mohammedan schools. This repudiation of Greek philosophy by orthodox theologians had for its consequence that some Arabic thinkers, without losing touch with religion, began to pursue philosophy for its own sake. In striking contrast with what was to happen in Western Europe, where the greatest contributions to philosophy were to be made by theologians, the greatest contributions to philosophy by Mohammedan thinkers have been made by philosophers. Such men as Alkindi, Alfarabi, Avicenna or Averroes, who were neither theologians nor even what the West would have called clerics, were not to be seen at the universities of Paris, of Oxford, nor, in fact, anywhere in Europe during the middle ages. On the other hand, no Moslem theologian ever succeeded in reinterpreting Greek philosophy in the light of the Koran, as Thomas Aquinas or Duns Scotus was to reinterpret Greek philosophy in the light of the Gospel. A curious consequence of this situation was that, since Islamic theology was progressively separating itself from Greek philosophy, up to the point of repudiating it, the great Christian theologians were to become the pupils of the Mohammedan philosophers much more than of the Mohammedan theologians. This is the reason why, dealing as we are with the speculation of Arabic thinkers as with one of the sources of mediaeval scholasticism, we have to pay more attention to the philosophers of Islam than to its theologians.[5]

I. ALKINDI AND ALFARABI

The first great Arabian philosopher among those whom the Christian world was to know is Alkindi, who lived in Basra, then at Baghdad, and died in 873.[6] He was an encyclopaedist, whose writings cover almost the whole field of Greek learning: arithmetic, geometry, astronomy, music, optics, medicine, logic, psychology, meteorology and politics. The middle ages knew but a small part of this extensive work. His treatise "On the Intellect" (*De intellectu*) deserves particular attention because it belongs in a well-defined family of philosophical writings. The origin of this family is the section of the *De anima* of Alexander of Aphrodisias that deals with the nature of the intellect, isolated from its context and published as a separate work under the title *De intellectu et intellecto* (i.e., "On Understanding and the Understood"). The object of this *De intellectu* was to clarify the meaning of the distinction introduced by Aristotle between the possible intellect (which receives intellection) and the agent intellect (which produces intelligible objects). In Aristotle himself, such a treatment of the problem of universals implied a complete theory of the soul and of human nature of which, up to the end of the twelfth century, the Latins knew nothing. All they knew about the problem was its logical position, as they had found it defined in the introduction of Boethius to the *Isagoge* of Porphyry. The *De intellectu* of Alkindi could not fail to interest Latin translators because, in describing the operations of the intellect, it threw light on the nature of abstraction, the operation which produces universals. Two points deserve to be noted in Alkindi's treatment of the question. First, he claims to discourse in it on the intellect, "following the doctrine of Plato and of Aristotle" (*secundum sententiam Platonis et Aristotelis*). Secondly, he considers the agent intellect, or "intellect always in act," as an Intelligence, that is, as a spiritual being, or substance, distinct from the soul, superior to it, and acting on it so as to turn a soul intelligent in potency into a soul intelligent in act. Arab philosophy therefore admitted from the beginning, under the influence of Alexander of Aphrodisias, that there is only one agent intellect for all mankind, each individual possessing but a receptive power which the action of the agent intellect carries from potency to act. In other words, all our concepts flow into our individual souls from a purely spiritual being, or Intelligence, which is one and the same for all mankind.

The second great name in Arabian philosophy is Alfarabi,[7] who studied and taught at Baghdad, and died in 950. In addition to translations of, and commentaries on, Porphyry's and Aristotle's logical works, Alfarabi wrote treatises *On the Intellect and the Intelligible* (*De intellectu et intellecto*), *On the Soul, On Unity and the One*, etc. The same tendency, which prevailed in Alkindi, to deal with Platonism and Aristotelianism as with a single philosophy, is still at work in Alfarabi. Moreover, now is the time for us to remember that, although these men were philosophers, not theologians, they had a religion, namely Islam, which was not without influence on their philosophical speculation. What is more important still, their religion had something in common with Christianity. The Prophet had been careful to distinguish between the "infidels," properly so called, and those whom the Koran calls "the men of the Book," or of the Bible, that is the Jews and the Christians. Like the God of the Old Testament, the God of the Koran is one, eternal, all-powerful and creator of all things; before the Christians, the Arabian philosophers came up against the problem of reconciling the Greek conception of a necessarily existing universe, ruled by a strictly intelligible necessity, with the Biblical notion of a freely created world ruled by a free and all-powerful divine will.

Shortly before the time of Alkindi a Moslem theological school had strongly stressed the rights of the God of the Koran and of the Old Testament. According to Al Ash'ari (d. 936), the third reformer of Islam and the founder of the school of the Ash'arites, everything is created by the sole *fiat* of God, nothing is independent of his power, and good as well as evil only exist in virtue of his all-powerful will.[8] The metaphysical elaboration of this religious belief led Ash'ari and his disciples to a curious conception of the universe, which Thomas Aquinas was to know, at least in a summary way, through Moses Maimonides and which he was to refute on the strength of his own philosophical notion of God. According to the Ash'arites, the world was made up of moments of time and points of space, connected together by the sole will of God, and whose combinations were therefore always liable to be altered by free interventions of the divine power. A matter composed of disjointed atoms, enduring in a time composed of disjointed instants, accomplishing operations in which each moment was independent of the preceding one and without effect on the following moment, the whole structure subsisting, holding together and functioning only by the will of a God who prevents it from relapsing into nothingness and quickens it by his efficacy—such was the world of the Ash'arites. These theologians have achieved a true "Moslem philosophy," in this sense at least that their conception of the universe was in deep agreement with the Koranic conception of God. A world as wholly innocent of intrinsic necessity as that of the Ash'arites was completely un-Greek; it was a perfectly plastic matter permanently open to the free interventions of Allah's all-powerful will. Because the God of the Old Testament was common to Christianity and to Islam, a similar tendency will sometimes affirm itself in the history of Christian philosophy. It can be recognized by the fact that it criticizes the Greek notion of "nature" as a thoroughly "pagan" notion, inseparable from those of natural necessity and of natural law, impossible to reconcile with the absolute freedom of the all-powerful Christian God. In the French seventeenth century, Malebranche's Occasionalism will be another attempt to reconcile the notion of a created world empty of all intrinsic efficacy with the Greek notion of natural and necessary laws.

No such thing is found in Alfarabi, but that great logician was also a profoundly religious spirit, and it is at least probable that this same sentiment inspired his epoch-making distinction of essence and existence in created beings. It marks a date in the history of metaphysics. Alfarabi, as M. Horten so aptly remarks, showed himself capable of adapting the overwhelming richness of Greek philosophical speculation to the nostalgic feeling for God that the Orientals have, and to his own mystical experience. Indeed, he himself was a mystic, a Sufi: "His notion of contingence is a turning point in philosophical evolution; essence and existence are distinct, that is to say, natural beings are contingent; they are not necessarily bound to existence; consequently, they can either possess it or be deprived of it and lose it. Since they are endowed with existence and form . . . natural beings must have received existence from some cause to which it belongs essentially and which, for that very reason, cannot lose it, that is, from God."

In order to formulate this distinction technically, Alfarabi resorted to a logical remark made by Aristotle: the notion of *what a thing is* does not include the fact *that it is*. Carrying that observation from the logical to the metaphysical plane, Alfarabi declares, in his *Gem of Wisdom:* "We admit that essence and existence are distinct in existing things. The essence is not the existence, and it does not come under its comprehension. If the essence of man implied his existence, to conceive his essence would also be to conceive his existence, and it would be enough to know what man is, in order to know that man exists, so that every representation would entail an affirmation. By the same token, existence is not included in the essence of things; otherwise it would become one of their constitutive characters, and the representation of what essence is would remain incomplete without the representation of its existence. And what is more, it would be impossible for us to separate them by the imagination. If man's existence coincided with his corporeal and animal nature, there would be nobody who, having an exact idea of what man is, and knowing his corporeal and animal nature, could question man's existence. But that is not the way it is, and we doubt the existence of things until we have direct perception of them through the senses, or mediate perception through a proof. Thus existence is not a constitutive character, it is only an accessory accident." [9]

This important text marked the moment when the logical distinction introduced by Aristotle between the conception of essence and the affirmation of existence became the sign of their metaphysical distinction. The new doctrinal position thus defined is made up of three moments: a dialectical analysis of the notion of essence, which shows that the notion of existence is not included; the affirmation that, since it is so, essence does not entail actual existence; the affirmation that existence is adventitious to essence. In order not to confuse this important metaphysical move with later ones, it should be noted that the primacy of essence dominates the whole argumentation. Not for an instant is there any doubt that existence is a predicate of essence, and because it is not essentially included in it, it is considered an "accident." We are still far away from the Thomistic position, which will deny both that existence is included in essence and that it is accidental to it. With Thomas Aquinas, existence will become the "act" of essence, and therefore the act of being; we are not yet there, but we are on the way to it.

From this point of view, the mental universe of Alfarabi appears as similar to that of the thirteenth-century Christian theologians. It depends on a primary cause in its existence, in the movement which animates it and even in the essences which define the beings of which it is composed. Moreover, the source, or cause, of *what things are* is also the source, or cause, *of the knowledge we have of them.* In his *De intellectu et intellecto,* which frequently appears in mediaeval manuscripts after those of Alexander and of Alkindi, and before that of Albertus Magnus, Alfarabi distinguishes four meanings of the word "intellect": 1) the intellect in potency with regard to the knowledge it can acquire; 2) the intellect in act with regard to that knowledge while acquiring it; 3) the acquired intellect (*intellectus adeptus*), that is, the intellect considered as already possessed of that knowledge; 4) and finally, the agent intellect, a subsisting spiritual being, who presides over this sublunary world and confers both forms on its matter and actual knowledge on all its intellects. We should not imagine this separate substance as eternally busy providing either this piece of matter with a certain form, or that intellect in potency with some actual cognition. The agent intellect is immutable in his action as he is in his being. Eternally radiating all the intelligible forms, he does not care in what matters nor in what intellects they may happen to be received. When a certain matter has been conveniently prepared by prior forms to receive that of "man," a man is born; when an intellect has been conveniently prepared and trained to receive the intelligible form "man," it conceives the essence of man. The diversity of effects produced by the eternally uniform action of the agent intellect is simply due to the fact that the matters and intellects which come under it are not all, nor always, similarly disposed to receive it. Let us add that this Intelligence is not the supreme cause. Other Intellects rise in tiers above it according to a hierarchical order, and all are subordinated to the First, who resides in his inaccessible solitude. Man's ultimate end is to be united, through intellect and love, to the separate agent intellect, who is the immediate immovable mover and the source of all intelligible knowledge for the world in which we live.[10] The Prophet supremely realizes this union.

Alfarabi was also interested in political philosophy and he dreamed of a world-wide society including all the nations of the earth. Yet, according to him, this terrestrial city could not be in itself its own end; perfect as one may assume it to be, it would remain only a step toward the superterrestrial city and its bliss. On leaving this world, the troops of the living go to join the troops of the dead and are intelligibly united with them, each uniting with those whom he resembles, and by this ceaselessly renewed union of soul to soul, the joys of the dead are fostered, increased and indefinitely enriched. The doctrine of Alfarabi, no less striking by the force of its expression than by the originality of its thought, deserves to be studied for itself. Avicenna probably owed him much more than we imagine; yet, as a matter of fact, and be it only by reason of his remarkable literary fecundity, Avicenna has exercised a much stronger influence on the evolution of mediaeval philosophy than Alfarabi, not only in Mohammedan countries but even in the Christian world.

2. AVICENNA

The influence of Avicenna on mediaeval philosophies and theologies is only one of the many aspects of the all-pervading influence of Aristotle. Yet, his own interpretation of Aristotle's doctrine was so personal on many points that it can be considered as the source of a distinct doctrinal stream, as easily recognizable at first sight as that of Averroes. By his religious inspiration and his mystical tendencies, Avicenna was destined to remain, for the Christian theologians of the middle ages, both a great help and a perilous temptation. His whole system was a striking example of the possibility of a *natural* and *philosophical* explanation of the world crowned by a no less natural and philosophical doctrine of salvation. On account of its neoplatonic elements, the influence exercised by the doctrine of Avicenna will often combine with that of Saint Augustine, but, before using it to their own purpose, all Christian theologians will have to overcome, and if possible to refute, his Greek conception of a universe both caused and ruled according to the laws of intelligible necessity.[11]

A. *Logic*

The Logic of Avicenna has been very incompletely translated into Latin, and still more incompletely published in the 1508 edition. Yet the translated fragments were extremely important, the more so as some of them provided a basis for the psychology and the metaphysics of our philosophers.

The aim and scope of philosophy is to know the truth about all things as far as it is possible for the human understanding to know it. The universality of all things divides itself into two classes, those which are what they are in virtue of their "natures" and those which are dependent on our free choice and will. The first class is the object of speculative philosophy, the second class is the object of "active" or practical philosophy. Speculative philosophy aims to know what things are, that is to say, truth; practical philosophy aims to know how we should act, that is to say, the good.

Among the objects of speculative philosophy, some are tied up with motion or change; some are not. Among those which are tied up with change, some only exist because it is possible for them to undergo it, as, for instance, the essence of man (*humanitas*), or squareness, and the like; others, on the contrary, don't require change as a condition for their existence. Among those which cannot exist apart from change and motion, two more classes should be distinguished: that of those beings which can neither exist nor be conceived apart from their own matter, such as the form of man or of any other animal; and the class of those beings, or things, which cannot exist without their own matter, but which can be understood apart from it, such as, for instance, squareness. As to those objects whose existence and intelligibility are independent of change, they are general properties of being, such as identity and diversity, unity and multiplicity, causality and so forth.

Truth is related to those objects which can be separated from change by our understanding, and it is of two kinds. First, necessary truth, which answers necessary beings such as God or the separate Intelligences; secondly, non-necessary truth, that is to say, truth about objects whose existence is only possible, or, at least, not impossible. If we consider intelligible objects in their state of separation from matter, then our knowledge of them will apply to essences, irrespective of the matters in which these happen to subsist; if, on the contrary, we consider them in the matters wherein they happen to subsist, then, again, their consideration becomes a twofold one. For indeed, we can consider them together with their own particular matter, for instance the unity of air, the plurality of the elements, etc.; or else we can consider them apart from any particular matter, as we do, for instance, when we speak of aggregation or of segregation with respect to bodies in general.

The division of philosophy follows that of its objects. Its first part deals with those objects which are involved in motion and whose existence depends on that of their proper matters: it is called "natural science." Its second part deals with those objects which exist in matter, but which our understanding can consider apart from matter: it is the science of number, the intellectual "discipline" *par excellence* (i.e., mathematics). The third part deals with those beings which are separate from motion and from matter both in themselves and in our understanding; we call it *scientia divina*, that is "divinity."

Our quest for truth deals with essences, that is to say, with the natures of things. Essences are to be found in three different conditions: in themselves, in concrete things, or in our intellect. Considered such as they are in themselves, they constitute the proper object of metaphysics; considered such as they are in singular things, they constitute the proper object of natural science, or physics; considered such as they are in our intellect, they constitute the proper object of logic. In other words, the proper object of logic is to study what happens to essences in consequence of the fact that they are in our intellect. Many things happen to them, in consequence of this fact, which would not happen if they only existed either in themselves or in the singular individuals which make up the objects of physics. Concepts, judgments, propositions, reasonings, inquiries in order to discover unknown truths by means of already known ones would simply not exist if there were no intellects to perform such operations. These all are about the essences of things, but they do not belong to these essences as such. The essence of man, for instance, is not a concept, nor a definition; it is that of which our intellect can form the concept or the definition. Obviously, we need a science dealing with all these intellectual determinations added to essences by the various operations of the mind. We need it because it provides us with an instrument which, if we use it correctly, will preserve us from error in our quest for truth. In itself, this instrument is a science. It is the science of how to go from what we already know to what we still do not know. There have been many discussions as to whether logic is an instrument of philosophy (an art), or one of its parts (a science). Such discussions are futile because there is no contradiction between these two possibilities. In fact, logic is both an instrument of philosophy and a part of philosophy. It is that part of philosophy whose proper object it is to study and to direct the operations of the mind.

In its content, this logic follows the general lines of that of Aristotle, not however without interpreting some of its theses from the point of view of the metaphysics of Avicenna himself. Its starting point is the distinction between simple apprehensions (*intentiones*, i.e., concepts), and composite enunciations (i.e., judgments). "Man" is a simple apprehension; "man is an animal" is a complex enunciation. Simple apprehensions do not imply any assent; we just conceive them. Complex enunciations are always attended by assent (*credulitas*), in this sense that we are bound either to believe them as true or to disbelieve them as false. Because such enunciations are either affirmations or negations, they are attended by truth or by error. Assent is therefore distinct from simple intellection. I understand the simple apprehensions of "whiteness" and of "accident"; unless I do, I cannot unite them in any judgment; but I cannot say that "whiteness always is an accident" without assenting to the truth of this proposition. If it is neither true, nor probable, nor false, an enunciation does not deserve its name; it is just words.

The true function of nouns is to signify concepts. When we use a noun to signify what a certain essence is, this noun is a predicate. Predication does not say that the essence of the subject is the essence of the predicate. For instance, in saying that "a triangle is a figure" I do not mean to say that the essence of the triangle is the essence of the figure. I only mean to say that, such as I am considering it just now, the thing called "triangle" is the thing called "figure." Predicates are of three different sorts. Some are "essential," that is to say, constitutive of a certain essence or quiddity. For instance, "figure" is an essential predicate of "triangle," because it is of the essence of a triangle to be a figure. Other predicates are inseparable accidents, or concomitants; such determinations follow from the essence, or quiddity, although they do not constitute it. For instance, it is of the essence of the triangle to be constituted by three sides, but the fact that its angles are equal to two right angles is only a concomitant inseparable from its essence. In this sense, as Aristotle had already said, it is an "accident" (*Metaph.*, IV, 30, 1025 a 30-33). Other concomitants, or accidents, are separable; for instance, whiteness with respect to triangle. The Avicennian application of this distinction to "existence," introduces into the logic of Aristotle a metaphysical notion of being borrowed from Alfarabi. Aristotle had only said that since a demonstration can prove only one thing at a time, the reasoning which proves the essence of a thing does not also prove its existence; in short, "what man is, is one thing, and the fact that man exists is another thing" (*Post.*

Anal., II, 7, 92 b 8-11). From this Avicenna infers that "existence," or "to be," is a "separable concomitant," and, in this sense, an "accident" of essence. This doctrine will be criticized by Averroes as betraying an undue influence of the religious notion of creation upon the philosophical notion of being. It will also be criticized by Thomas Aquinas as not expressing correctly the true relation of an essence to its own existence. At any rate, these are striking examples of the mutual implication of logic and metaphysics in mediaeval philosophies.

However we interpret it, the metaphysical distinction of essence and existence is answered in logic by the two kinds of questions which we can ask concerning any thing: "What is it?" and "Is it?", that is: "Does it exist?" To the question "What is it?" the answer is given by the definition, which includes the genus, the specific difference, and then all the other differences which are required for the complete description of a certain essence. Logic is concerned with essence much more than with existence which, being accidental to essences, cannot be established by necessary deduction. In a way, whether the thing exists or not, and whether it exists or not with such and such a determination, is the first question to ask. We must answer the question: "Does God exist?", or "Does the void exist?" before arguing about the nature of God or that of the void. About what does not exist, there is nothing to say (cf. Aristotle, *Post. Anal.*, II, 1, 89 b 39-90 a 5). Yet, when all is said and done, logical reasoning deals much more with the causes of existence and the essences of existents than with the bare fact of existence. Given that something exists, or that it exists in a certain definite way, why does it exist? Or why is it that which it is? Such are the main questions which logical methods of reasoning enable us to answer.

In Avicenna's own interpretation of logic, two points deserve particular attention: his realistic interpretation of the nature of definition and his interpretation of the modality of judgment which concerns possibility. Naturally, the special importance of these two points is due to their metaphysical implications.

The first point is tied up with his fundamental notion of the absolute character of essences. Because each of them is just what it is, that is, neither singular (or physical), nor universal (or logical), its definition points out a distinct and absolute intelligible entity. Hence this corollary, that, just as all that which is contained in the definition of its essence belongs to a thing, nothing that is not included in its definition can be considered as belonging to it. In other words, a thing is nothing of that without which it can be distinctly conceived. A justly famous application of this rule is to be found in the Avicennian definition of the human soul; since it can conceive itself without including its body in its own definition, then it is really other than its body. Where there are two completely distinct notions, there are two really distinct entities.

The second point follows from the same notion of essence. Since existence is never included in the definition of any essence, but is added to it as a separable concomitant, to ascertain the identity of an essence is to define a pure "possible." What is logically impossible is impossible in reality, but what is logically possible, and even necessary, does not necessarily exist. If it does exist, its mode of existence has to conform to the logical necessity of its essence. If a man exists, his existence must needs be that of the essence "man," but that is all. The actual existence of things is given in sensible intuitions, together with the judgments involved in sense experience: for instance, the sun exists, fire is burning, etc. A first datum of experience is made up of judgments following a succession of self-repeating sense perceptions. Logicians are not concerned with the reason why sense experience is self-repeating; its regularity, or constancy, is presupposed by their argumentations. The other datum of logical reasoning is intellectual intuition, whose evidence is so compelling that we cannot not assent to it. For instance, given the way the moon shines at each one of its different phases, we evidently see that its light comes from the sun. Here again, sense perception of what actually is must needs come first; logical reasoning only teaches us how to discover the truth about it.

The logic of Avicenna is full of concrete observations, which make it different from the more abstract treatises usually written by Latin logicians. It betrays the fact that its author himself had made practical use of its methods in his physics as well as in his metaphysics. Even in those parts of it whose exposition would largely amount to a re-exposition of the logic of Aristotle such as, for instance, the doctrine of syllogism, its reader perceives the constant presence of a scientist and of a philosopher whose personal experience quickens from within his explanations and his conclusions.

B. *Physics*

The physics of Avicenna bears the title of *Sufficientia,* because it intends to deal with physical truth in a sufficient way (*liber sufficientiae*) and without wasting time in refuting errors. His own treatises should therefore "suffice" for those of his readers who want an elementary introduction to this science. The subject matter of physics is the sensible body inasmuch as it is subjected to change. The objects of physical inquiry are the accidents which follow from the essence of such bodies and, consequently, are "essential" to them. Hence their denomination of *essentialia.*[12]

Following the doctrine of Aristotle, Avicenna considers all natural bodies as made up of two principles, or causes: form and matter. The term matter applies to that which, in the body, makes it to be susceptible of generation and of corruption. The term "form" applies to what makes a body to be that which it is. For instance, in a wooden bed, wood is the matter, and the shape which turns wood into a bed is its form.

The first and most universal of all physical forms is that which makes matter to be a body (*corpus*). It is called the form of corporeity (*forma corporeitatis*). This form is to be found in all bodies, together with other forms. It gives them extension according to the three dimensions of space. The influence of Avicenna can often be detected in a thirteenth-century scholastic theology, owing to the presence of this form of corporeity. In doctrines where "corporeity" remains present under the higher forms (animality, rationality, etc.), the form of corporeity entails the plurality of forms in physical beings. Each being then is made up of a matter plus at least two forms, that of corporeity and, for instance, that of animality. In any case, as Avicenna says, the form of corporeity is prior to all the other forms of physical genera and species, which can never be separated from it (*Sufficientia*, I, 2).

Matter never is without the form of corporeity, but it always has other forms. Taken in itself, it is called *hyle* (matter); taken as endowed with its specific form (*forma specialis*), or with its accidental forms (whiteness, position, etc.), it is called a subject (*subjectum*); taken as common to all physical beings, it is called element.

Apart from these intrinsic principles, bodies have two extrinsic ones. The efficient cause impresses the forms into their matters and it thus constitutes composite beings that act by their forms and undergo by their matter the actions of other forms. The final cause is that on account of which forms have been impressed into their respective matters. Since, in physics, these principles of nature are considered in their absolute generality, they can be said to be the common natural principles, that is, the principles common to all natural beings. For this reason, Roger Bacon and other scholastics will call the physics of Avicenna the *communia naturalium*.

Privation is often quoted as another physical principle, and rightly so, but it should not be understood as something superadded to matter; it is matter itself considered as lacking any one of the formal determinations which it is able to receive. Thus understood, privation is the very aptitude of matter to receive. It is its receptivity. This aptitude is not a desire; it is the mere possibility, inherent in a subject, to receive further formal determinations and perfections.

The efficient principle common to all natural beings is called "nature." Nature is the intrinsic force, or energy, in virtue of which natural beings perform their motions and operations, without choice and in a necessary way. Souls are natures; forms are natures; in short all internal energies are natures, or spring from natures (I, 5). Every natural being, then, has a matter, a form which determines its essence, a nature which causes its motion, and accidents which are its extrinsic determinations. In simple

beings, the nature is the form itself; but it is called form inasmuch as
it determines the species, whereas it is called nature inasmuch as it is
the cause of natural motions and operations (I, 6).

In the strict sense of the word, motion is locomotion, that is, the passing of
a body from a place to another place, but philosophers usually give it a
broader meaning, namely, change under all its various forms. For instance,
change of place (*locus*), of position in the same place (*situs*), of quality
(color, temperature), of quantity (size, weight). Whatever its particular
nature, motion always is the progressive actualization of a certain potentiality. In short, the general name for motion is change, becoming (II, 1).

Motion is either accidental, or violent, or natural. A body moves by
accident when it is involved in the motion of another body: in a water
jug, water moves accidentally when the jug is moved. Motion is violent
when it removes a body from its natural place (*locus proprius*): for instance, when a stone, or any naturally heavy body, is thrown upwards.
Motion is natural when it flows from the very nature of the physical
body: for instance, for fire, which is naturally light, to move upwards;
or for water, which is naturally cold, to cool off after being heated. In
some animated bodies, whose forms are souls, there is another principle
of motion, entirely different in kind, which is appetition, or will. Like
nature, the will is an internal principle of motion and rest for the being
in which it is.

As has been seen, the notion of physical motion is inseparable from
that of natural place. There is a great deal of disagreement among physicists concerning the notion of place (*locus*). Some of them identify it
with space (*spatium*), but how can we conceive the space that is contained in a jug otherwise than as contained within the place occupied
by that jug? Others identify place with void, or emptiness, which they
conceive as the universal container of all things. But there is no such
thing as absolute void, which would be absolute nothingness. What we
call an empty jug, is a jug full of air, which itself is a body. According
to Aristotle, and to truth, the "place" of a thing is the internal surface of
the body that surrounds it.

The "natural" place of a body is the place toward which it tends in
virtue of its own nature, and wherein, once it is there, it naturally rests.
The qualities which differentiate natural places are related to their different altitude with respect to the center of the earth. The notions of "up"
and of "down" are essential in this respect. Whatever its natural place,
a physical body is rightly said to be *in* it. Incidentally, this is the reason
why, taken as a whole, the universe itself has no place. Above the external
limit of the highest celestial sphere, which is made up of purest fire, there
is nothing; that is, there is no thing to surround it and, consequently,
there is no *locus* in which it can possibly be contained (II, 8; II, 9).
Like that of Aristotle, the physics of Avicenna is therefore dominated by

the notion of quality, not, like our own modern physics, by that of quantity. Accordingly, it is less interested in measurements than in classifications.

Besides their specific forms, elements differ by their elementary qualities, which are accidental forms. These are four in number: cold, warmth, dryness and moistness. Each one of the four elements has two elementary qualities. Fire is warm and dry; air is warm and moist; earth is cold and dry; water is cold and moist. Elementary qualities can be changed, at least up to a point. Water is moist and cold, but its coldness can be replaced by warmth; it then becomes warm water. For the same reason, elementary qualities can pass from one physical body to another. They can also increase or diminish, so that, at least from the point of view of their qualitative intensity, they are susceptible of some sort of measurement. On the contrary, forms themselves can neither increase nor diminish: water can be more or less cold; it cannot be more or less water.

The distinction of the four elements can be recognized by that of their natural places. Bodies that tend toward the same place and rest in it after getting there are of the same nature. Of course, two distinct bodies cannot occupy the same place at one and the same time, but earth is always tending downwards on account of its natural heaviness, just as fire is always tending upwards on account of its natural lightness, and this is what we mean by saying that the distinction between earth and fire can be recognized from the difference between the natural places toward which they tend. (II, 9).

The Avicennian interpretation of the composition of material substances was to become the focus of lively discussions among the scholastics. Aristotle had said that the component forms of a compound substance remain in it in potency. Avicenna interprets Aristotle's position as meaning that the substantial forms remain unchanged in the compound. This, of course, implied the doctrine of the plurality of substantial forms, whose development will always remain more or less closely related to the influence of Avicenna. As to the elementary qualities, Avicenna considered them as undergoing a sort of weakening, or "remission" (*remissio*). The compound resulting from these altered, or "broken" qualities was a "complexion," in the primitive meaning of this term signifying a combination of qualities determining the nature of a body. The degree of perfection of each body is proportional to the complexity and to the equilibrium of its component elements. For instance, man is the most perfect among all sublunary beings because the composition of the human body is more complex and its complexion better balanced than that of any other body. Consequently it receives a more perfect form, which is the human soul. This doctrine implies that new physical beings are born every time the complexion of certain matters makes them fit to receive appropriate forms. It also implies that there is a cause that gives to conveniently prepared matters the forms they are fit to receive. In other words, there must be a "giver of forms." Its nature will presently be ascertained in astronomy.

C. *Astronomy*

Sublunary bodies naturally move along straight lines; celestial bodies naturally have circular motions, and since each of them always follows the same path, they never meet. Hence they are simple. On the other hand, since all straight motions toward natural places of rest are caused by natures, they require no other explanation; on the contrary, since circular motions consist in perpetually changing direction in order to reach the next place on the same circle, they must have a different cause. Now, the only causes there are, besides natures, are wills. Consequently, the celestial bodies must be moved from place to place by souls endowed with wills. But since these souls are moving their bodies regularly and perpetually, there must be a cause for the stability of their purpose. This cause can be no other than an Intellect or Intelligence which, because it desires its perfection, makes the souls revolve their bodies around it, always, and always in the same way. When he has resolved to go from A to B, a man still has to imagine and to will each one of the successive steps that are required for him to cross the distance. So also, each celestial body is an animal, whose soul imagines and wills each one of the successive motions that are required to satisfy its eternal longing for a pure Intelligence. There is therefore, for each celestial being, a body informed by a soul, plus a separate Intelligence which is the cause of its motion. Love is the prime moving force of this physical universe.

To will is to desire some end. What then is the end and scope of the eternal motions of the celestial bodies? The cause of an eternal motion must needs be infinite in power, and since nothing material can be infinite, this cause can neither be a body, nor subsist in a body. Hence it is wholly immaterial and, consequently, a purely intelligible substance. We have called it an Intelligence, or an Intellect, that is, a being wholly separate from matter and from all the determinations which belong to matter. Such spiritual beings have nothing to fear, nor to gain, from what is below them. They are not pursuing any end inferior to themselves and, therefore, there is no reason why they should take care of this sublunary world. Even if they would, they could not act upon matter, on account of their very immateriality. This is to say that Intelligences are causes of astronomical motion in an indirect way only, as final causes. Separate Intelligences are beautiful in virtue of their pure intelligibility. As such, they are objects of desire for the souls of the celestial bodies. Enraptured by the beauty of its own separate Intelligence, each one of these souls strives to imitate it by making itself as similar as possible to the essence of this divine being. Contemplation then is for celestial souls the cause of their love, and since they are the forms of the celestial bodies, they cannot fail to impart to these bodies the perfection which they themselves derive from contemplation. Now, as has been said, celestial bodies are simple. Being wholly actuated by their souls, they are in potency to nothing, with the sole exception of place, because even a celestial body can occupy only one place at one and the same time; consequently, each part of a celestial body remains in potency to the places which it does not occupy. The only way for its soul further to actualize its body therefore remains to actualize it with respect to place, that is, to move it circularly, so that each one of its points may occupy successively all the places which it cannot occupy simultaneously. Hence the existence and nature of astronomical motion. In the light of this explanation, the number of the separate Intelligences must equal that of the celestial spheres whose movement they cause. We shall have to confirm this point later on. Incidentally, since they are specifically distinct, and yet immaterial, the multiplication of these intelligences within the same species is impossible. Each of them is a whole species in its own right.

Time is the measure of motion considered from the point of view of "before" and "after." If there were no motion, there would be no time, but as soon as there is motion, there must needs be time. The becoming of time resembles the progressive motion of a physical body between two points on a straight line. Like the line itself, time is divisible into shorter or longer parts of duration. The regular motion of celestial bodies is both its own time-measure and the common time-measure of all the other motions (*Sufficientia*, II, 10; II, 11).

To sum up, the universe of Avicenna is made up of concentric spheres. At the center, the earth, surrounded by the regions of water, then of air, then of fire. Above the earth comes the lowest of the celestial spheres, namely the sphere of the moon, and so on up to the highest of all celestial spheres, beyond which there is nothing.

The origin of this spherical and finite world is the only ultimate explanation there is for its structure. Since there are several heavens, specifically distinct in their natures, and all in potency with respect to place, there must be a cause of their being as well as of their motion. In order to be first, this cause has to be one. Now, it is a principle that, from one cause, only one effect can follow: *ex uno autem non provenit nisi unum* (Algazel, p. 117, lines 33-34). The problem therefore arises to know how the multiplicity of the celestial bodies and of the sublunary beings can follow from a single cause. In other words: how does multiplicity flow from unity? The last word about physics will be said by metaphysics.

D. *Psychology*

Among beings, there are animals, that is, animated beings able to feel and to move at will. This aptitude does not come to them from their bodies; hence there must be in them a principle other than corporeity.

We call soul "all that which is a principle from which emanate diversified actions due to a will" (*De anima*, I, 1). This external determination of the soul does not tell us anything about its essence. To know that animated bodies have a mover is not to know what this mover is. Since it causes motion, a soul is a force, an energy; moreover, it also is a "perfection," in this sense that it perfects the genus by adding to it its specific determination. Lastly, it is the particular kind of perfection which we call a "form," in this sense at least, that it is the form of the matter which it makes to be a living body. The soul is therefore a force, a form and a perfection.

There remains to be seen which one of these determinations designates the very essence or nature of the soul. The problem is a crucial one, because it entails a choice between the Platonic conception of the soul as a spiritual substance and the Aristotelian conception of the soul as a form of the body. Now, while Avicenna does not hesitate to say that the soul is the form of its body, he also maintains that this defines a *function* of the soul, not its *nature*. What the soul is with respect to the body, and what it does there, is not what it is in itself. True enough, the word "soul" or *anima*, signifies something that "animates" a body; but precisely, "this word, *anima*, has not been given to it as pointing out its substance"; it points out its relation to a certain body. When we say that a certain man is a "worker," we point out what he does, not what he is, for indeed, before being a worker, he is a man. So also, in the case of the soul, the word *anima* designates a being which exercises an animating function, but whose nature, or essence, still remains to be determined in itself (I, 1).

In order to realize the nature of the soul let a man imagine himself as suddenly created in an adult condition. His face is veiled so that he cannot see. He is floating in an empty space, so that he cannot feel the resistance of the air. His limbs are disjointed, so that he cannot feel them. Our question is: Could such a man affirm his own existence? Most certainly. Such a man would know that he exists, although he could not affirm the existence of his limbs, nor of his inner organs, nor of his blood, nor of his brains. All of these would appear to him as extrinsic to his essence, which he would consider as having neither length, nor breadth nor thickness. Nay, supposing it were possible for him, at that moment, to imagine his hands, or any other one of his organs, this man would never conceive them as parts of his being nor as belonging to his essence. Now, it is one of the fundamental rules of Avicenna's logic that "what is affirmed is other than what is not affirmed" (*quod affirmatur aliud est ab eo quod non affirmatur*). Since, therefore, such a man could conceive his own essence without conceiving his body, his body is other than his own essence. True enough, this is but an image; yet it should help us to understand that the entity of the soul is other than that of the body, since we have no need of knowing our body in order to know our soul. It is this essentially incorporeal being which exercises in us the animating functions of a soul (I, 1).

This is to say that, taken in itself, the soul is a substance (I, 3) endowed with a plurality of powers from which flow many diverse operations. Specifically distinct operations presuppose specifically distinct powers. These distinct powers are: 1) the nutritive power and the generative power, common to both plants and animals; 2) the powers of perception, imagination and voluntary motion, which belong to animals only, not to plants; 3) the aptitude to know intelligible objects, to invent the arts, to speculate about natural beings and to distinguish good from evil, which is proper to man (I, 4). In short, there are three kinds of souls: 1) the vegetative soul, which is the prime perfection of a natural and organic body exercising vital functions; 2) the sensitive soul, which is the prime perfection of a natural and organic body inasmuch as it perceives particular objects and moves at will; 3) the human soul, which is the prime perfection of a natural and organic body, inasmuch as it enables it to perform deliberate actions, and to acquire science through meditation, because, of itself, this soul can apprehend universals (I, 5). Such is the reason why the powers of the human soul are divided into active powers and speculative powers.

The active power of the human soul has dominion over its body, which it moves to particular acts according to its own judgments. On the contrary, the contemplative power of the soul is dominated by intelligible objects to which it is subjected. Accordingly, our soul has two faces, one which looks downward to the body, and another which looks upward to the intelligible beings from which it receives its principles. The active power of the rational soul begets ethics; its contemplative power begets wisdom. Where the contemplative power of the soul finds naturally intelligible objects, it is easier for it to apprehend their forms; where, on the contrary, these objects are given to us in matter, our intellective power must disengage them from it by a process of abstraction which will be described later on (I, 5).

The speculative power of the soul is given different names according as it is differently disposed with respect to its intelligible objects. Considered as being in absolute potency to an intelligible which it has not yet received, it is called "material intellect" (*intellectus materialis*), not at all in this sense that it is corporeal, but simply because it is, with respect to the intelligible object, in the same relation of pure potency to act which is that of prime matter with respect to all forms. Considered as being already possessed of cognitions which it could use, but which it is not actually using, the same speculative power is called "habitual intellect" (*intellectus in habitu*). In a way, it is in act, for indeed it is able to know in act if it chooses to do so; for instance, a man who knows a certain principle is virtually able to know its consequences; yet he knows them implicitly, that is, as virtually contained within their principle. Likewise, a man who has learned something has an habitual knowledge of it even while he does not turn his mind to it. It is an acquired aptitude to consider the first principles and to proceed from them to their consequences. Avicenna defines it, "the intellect which understands every time it wants to understand, without having to work in order to acquire knowledge." In act, if we compare it with the "material intellect," the "habitual intellect" remains in potency if we compare it with the following one, which is called intellect in act (*intellectus in effectu*) because it does actually know, and knows that it knows. At that moment, the intelligible form is effectively present in it. But this intelligible form comes to it from without, and because intellectual cognition is granted to the intellect by a spiritual substance which is above human nature, we also call it a "given intellection": *intellectus accommodatus,* that is, an intellection given to us from outside (*accommodatus ab extrinsecus*). The exact meaning of this expression will be made clear later on (I, 5).

Generally speaking, to know is to abstract, and the degrees of knowledge follow the degrees of abstraction. The common object of all cognitions is form, but since forms are given to us in matter, we must separate them from their material determinations in order to grasp them. Sense perception is the lowest degree of abstraction: it consists in grasping forms without their matter (when the eye sees blue, it does not become blue) but such as they are actually given in it. Imagination implies a higher degree of abstraction: it perceives material forms even while they are not materially present to the knowing subject: I cannot perceive the form of a tower that is not there, but, if I have seen it before, I can imagine it. A third and slightly higher degree of abstraction belongs to the power of the soul which Avicenna calls "estimative." It is just about what we call instinct. The estimative perceives sense objects as good or as harmful and, consequently, as to be desired or to be avoided. Now, obviously, desirability and undesirability are not sensible qualities. They are not accidental properties of matter like size, color or weight. Yet, we perceive them in matter and we ascribe them to material beings.

The highest degree of abstraction is that of pure intellection. It perceives intelligible forms as separated from all material determinations. For instance, when I conceive "man," that is, human nature in itself, irrespective of any human being in particular, I am grasping a pure form, stripped from all material determinations in size, color, time, place, etc. Ultimate intellectual abstraction is made possible by the fact that, as has been seen in logic, the nature of any essence is wholly indeterminate with respect to either singularity or universality; "humanity" is neither that of Socrates in particular, nor that of all human beings in general; it is just humanity. The highest degree of abstraction consists, precisely, in grasping essences just as they are in themselves and in their state of complete indetermination (II, 2).

Avicenna then proceeds to the psycho-physiological description of the external senses: touch, taste, smell, hearing (II, 3-6); sight (III, 1), including a demonstration of the non-corporeal nature of light beams (III, 2), a completely developed theory of colors (III, 3-4) and a critical discussion of other theories (III, 5-7); a special chapter is devoted to the optical illusion which, in some cases, makes us see two objects where there is only one (III, 8).

After the external senses come the internal ones, and, in the first place, "common sense" (*sensus communis*). We both hear and touch, but touch does not know that it does not hear, nor vice versa. "Common sense" enables us to distinguish colors from sounds and from smells; in short, it is the common receiver of all external sensations and offers them in a state of distinction to the light of our intellect (IV, 1). Common sense is a distinct sensitive power, localized in an inner organ to be found in the brain. In Avicenna's own words: "It is the center of all other sense powers; all the nerves derive from it; all sensations are transmitted to it and it truly is that which feels" (IV, 1).

Two further internal senses, imagination and fantasy, can be conceived as making up, together with common sense, a single power of the soul. Yet, although the forms with which these internal senses deal are the same, what receives them (common sense) is not what preserves them (imagination and fantasy). Imagination is localized in the anterior part of the brain; it is, so to speak, the treasure chest of sensations, whereas the treasure chest of those qualities of usefulness or harmfulness whose perception has been ascribed to the "estimative," is localized in the posterior part of the brain. In man, who is endowed with intellectual knowledge, the power answering the "estimative" of animals is called "cogitative," because it is not a blindly instinctive reaction, but rather an already quasi-rational appreciation. All these powers obviously belong to one and the same soul, as can be seen from the fact that we cannot both perceive, imagine and remember with equal force at one and the same time. Still less can we pay close attention to sense perceptions while speculating about intelligible objects.

Just as they have perceptive powers, animals have a motive power, which is the will. The will (*voluntas*) is more than desire (*desiderium*). It comprises two parts, namely, the "irascible," which aims to suppress what is harmful or dangerous; and the "concupiscible" (*virtus concupiscibilis*), which moves the muscles and the body toward desirable objects. Desire, then, is only one of the powers of the will (IV, 4).

Thus far, Avicenna has been dealing with the nature and powers of the soul in general. The human soul differs from other souls in this, that it is able to form universal and intelligible notions (*intentiones*) and to proceed from the known to the unknown through judging and reasoning (V, 1). The "theoretic" intellect (*intellectus contemplativus*) is therefore a power proper to the human soul. It judges of truth and error; of the possible, the necessary and the impossible; of what is good, evil or merely permissible. Its principles are immediately evident propositions; the proper type of cognition which it achieves is "science," that is, a distinct and absolutely certain knowledge. Science is only possible with respect to intelligible objects. In dealing with matters known through sense perception and imagination, the theoretic intellect goes seldom beyond probability, or opinion. We call opinion the type of conclusion that is attended by the fear that the other position might well be true (*Opinio vero est conceptio ad quam acceditur cum formidine alterius partis*, V, 1. Cf. Thomas Aquinas on faith, *Sum. theol.*, IIa-IIae, 1, 4, Resp.).

Just as the "theoretic" intellect deals with matters of speculation, the "practical intellect" deals with matters of action. Borrowing its universal maxims from the theoretic intellect, the active intellect applies them to particular problems of human conduct. In working out this application, it often resorts to merely probable maxims or to the authority of famous men. Consequently, its conclusions lack the solidity which characterizes science. It is entangled in particular facts, images, desires and passions. For this very reason, the practical intellect needs the co-operation of the body and of the corporeal powers of the soul in all its operations. The theoretic, or speculative, intellect may also need the co-operation of its body and of the corporeal powers of the soul, but not necessarily nor always. It is self-sufficient (*sufficit enim ipse sibi per ipsum*, V, 2). Let us add that none of these powers is the human soul; the human soul is that which has all these powers. In itself, it is a solitary substance: *substantia solitaria* (V, 2), whose existence and spiritual nature can be demonstrated.

It is manifest that there is in man a power of grasping intelligible objects by receiving them. It is no less obvious that the subject of such a power cannot possibly either be a body, or exist in view of a body. Were it extended in space, the immaterial forms could not be received in it without themselves becoming extended, divisible and therefore material. Intelligible forms could not even be received in some indivisible point of a corporeal soul, because a point is the extremity of a line, which itself is always extended in space. Consequently, the subject of the rational power which knows intelligible forms must needs be immaterial (V, 2).

Another proof that the human soul does not know by means of a corporeal instrument is the fact that it knows itself, and knows that it knows. It even knows that it needs no corporeal instrument in order to know; it understands by itself: *intelligit per seipsam non per instrumentum* (V, 2); it always understands its own essence; in short, it is not a body; it is not immersed in a body, nor indebted in any way to a body for its own being. These arguments confirm the mental experiment described at the beginning of the book: a soul can always know its own essence as distinct from that of the body. Several thirteenth-century Augustinian theologians will adopt the same position, including the mental experiment imagined by Avicenna.

In saying that the rational soul does not need a corporeal instrument in order to produce knowledge, we do not mean to say that it derives absolutely no help from its body. First, the animal powers help the rational soul in providing it with the sense knowledge of particular beings, that is, in Avicenna's own language, with the knowledge of "singulars." This enables the rational soul to separate universals from singulars, that is to say, to achieve abstraction. Secondly, once it is possessed of these abstract universals, the rational soul can unite or separate them in judgments, and these judgments themselves in syllogistical reasonings. The sole difficulty is to find the necessary middle terms; when it does not find them, our intellect just waits. Thirdly, the rational soul can gather knowledge by turning to experience; if we see that a certain predicate regularly attends a certain subject, we know that it can be affirmed of the subject. This method takes a long time, but it yields good results. Fourthly, sense perception enables us to hear statements which we believe because they sound probable; we can accept them, at least provisorily, pending the time when they will be submitted to closer examination. In all these cases, sense experience is but a starting point. Once it is strengthened and perfected in knowledge, the rational soul performs its operations absolutely alone: *sola per se operatur actiones suas absolute*. It is like a man who needs a horse in order to go to a certain place; after getting there, he dismisses the horse and does what he has to do without giving the beast another thought. Above all, let us not forget that in case the means we use in order to get there should prevent us from reaching our destination, the reason we had to reach it would be an excellent one for us not to resort to such means (V, 3).

Since all human souls have the same definition, they all belong in the same species and are, specifically speaking, one soul. There is no difference of essence or form between any two souls; indeed, like that of all essences, their form is one: *forma earum una est*. Their multiplicity is due to the diversity of the bodies which they animate. This is a sure proof that the human soul never subsisted in itself before entering corporeal bodies. Had it ever subsisted alone, there would be only one human soul. Consequently, human souls have always been in bodies, from all eternity (V, 3).

Since souls are individual and numerically distinct by reason of their bodies, which are accidental to their essences, they begin to exist in time at the very moment when a matter fit to be animated by them begins to exist. The body of each soul is both its domain and its instrument. The soul is created with a natural inclination to take care of its body. Because of this natural affection, the soul renounces, so to say, all the other bodies, but, in turn, it finds in this body the origin of its own perfection. After the death of its body, the rational soul remains numerically distinct, because it then receives from its creator a principle of individuation other than corporeal matter. What this principle is, we know not. We know for sure, however, that the soul sometimes perceives its own singular essence, when its becomes aware of affections that are proper to itself. Perhaps these affections, which the soul acquires in its capacity of "intellect in act," are enough to render it numerically different from other souls. Whatever the reason for it, the intrinsic individuality of each separate soul is certain (V, 3). As to its survival, it is equally certain. Just like its body, the soul is a substance: *est utrumque substantia.* Now, between two substances, there can be no other union than an accidental one. If it is accidental, and not substantial, for soul and body to be united, then the destruction of one of them entails that of their relation, not that of the other substance. The survival of the soul is therefore possible. Moreover, since the substance of the soul is simple, it cannot contain in itself the cause of its own disintegration. In point of fact, the existence of the soul hangs on immutable and indestructible causes, namely, its own essence and the divine power by which it is being preserved (V, 4).

The psychology of Avicenna aims to identify the human soul with the human intellect. It describes the soul as a self-sufficient intellectual substance, which needs a body in order to actualize itself, but not in order to subsist after it has achieved its self-actualization. No wonder then that the *Liber sextus naturalium* ends by describing the progressive acquisition of intelligible knowledge by the rational soul.

Human intellects always are partly in potency and partly in act. The only Intellect that is wholly in act is a separate substance. This *Intelligentia in effectu* is full of the pure intelligible forms which are the principles of our own knowledge. Its relation to us is that of the sun to our own sight. Without the sun and its light, our eyes would see nothing; without the Intelligence in act, our intellects would be blind to all intelligible objects. In both cases it is a question of illumination. While our rational power considers the singulars present to our imagination, it becomes illuminated by the light of the Intelligence acting in us. Under its light, these singulars are stripped from matter and its accidental determinations. This is what is called "abstraction." The effect of abstraction is to lay the essence of a singular bare of its individualizing determinations, and, consequently, to impress it in the rational soul. There is here no transferring of form from imagination to intellect. Neither does our intellect need to compare several forms in order to make sure that their essence is the same. A single form is enough to manifest a certain essence in its totality, provided only the separate agent Intellect makes us see it in its intelligible purity. The proper contribution of rational souls to the acquisition of intelligible knowledge consists in their effort to adapt themselves to the light of the intelligible sun. "Abstraction" emanates in it from the separate Intelligence in act as soon as our soul is in a fitting condition to receive it: *aptatur anima ut emanet in eam ab Intelligentia agente abstractio* (V, 5). The word "abstraction" here does not point out an operation of human reason, but the intelligible form which it receives from the divine giver of forms. "Our cogitations and considerations," Avicenna says, "are motions which render our soul fit to receive the emanation" (V, 5). This emanation itself precisely is abstraction.

In order to understand itself, that is, both its existence and its essence, the soul does not need to strip itself from matter, for indeed souls are intelligible in their own right. With respect to other things, the question arises how our intellect can know them. Some say that our intellect "becomes" the things which it understands. But this does not make sense. How could something be both itself and something else? When the soul knows itself, it does not have to become it: it is itself; when the soul knows another form, it does not "become" it, it simply receives it. The soul is like a mirror (*et est anima quasi speculum,* V, 6). It conserves in its memory the images of singular things, but not the intelligible forms which it has received from the separate Intelligence. The meaning of "the soul understand" simply is: the understood form is present in the soul. This form has no distinct existence of its own outside of the Intelligence which gives it and of our intellect which receives it. There is therefore no intellectual memory where it could be stored while we are not receiving it. Insofar as we are concerned, as soon as it ceases to be known, it ceases to exist in us. For our own intellect, to learn is not to accumulate knowledge in our memory; it is to acquire the perfect aptitude to conjoin itself with the Intelligence in act, so as to receive from it the simple intellection from which other forms will follow in an orderly manner in us, owing to the reflections of our soul (V, 6).

A part of his physics, the psychology of Avicenna is inseparable from his metaphysics, but it is also the work of a physiologist and of a physician, or rather, to use his own expression, of a surgeon. Being one, the soul appears to him as ruling the body through the agency of only one organ, which is not the brain, but the heart. This relation is a reciprocal one: it is through the heart that, in turn, the soul is dependent on the body. The heart is the source of the animal spirits and of all the forces which flow from it into the limbs. The function of the brain is rather to prepare the spirits which enable the body to feel and to move. These and many other scientific notions (V, 8), borrowed from Avicenna, will reappear later on in Albert the Great and his thirteenth-century successors.

E. *Metaphysics*

Different sciences deal with different types of beings: mobile beings, living beings, animated beings. The science that deals with being as such, or being *qua* being, is metaphysics. Moreover, particular sciences deal with particular effects of the four causes; but there must be a cause of all causes and, consequently, of all effects. Until we know this cause, all that is said about natural causality remains merely probable. The science of ultimate causes, or cause, is metaphysics (*Metaphysica*, I, 1).

Metaphysics is an abstract science, in that it considers its objects apart from matter and from sensible qualities. This type of metaphysical consideration implies what Avicenna calls "estimation" (that is, *expoliatio a sensibilibus*, I, 2). The notion of being is the most general among these abstractions. It is an absolutely prime notion, and since it cannot be deduced from any other one, metaphysics has to take it for granted, that is, to start from it in order to examine its properties and its consequences: "Being *qua* being is common to all the rest; so it must be posited as the subject of this science (i.e., metaphysics), and there is no need to ask *if* it is (*an sit*), nor what it is (*quid sit*), as though another science were necessary to establish these points." Now, since no science can establish the existence nor the nature of its own subject matter, metaphysics can do nothing more on this point than to grant both the existence of being and its nature: *oportet concedere tantum quia est et quid est* (I, 2). Moreover, to posit being as the first principle does not mean that there is a principle of being, otherwise, being would have to be its own principle, which is absurd. What we really mean to say is that there is a principle of all that which can be an object of discourse. Metaphysics is called "prime science," precisely because it deals with the first principle; being and its cause. It is also called "wisdom," because it is the noblest of all sciences, in that it establishes the existence of the noblest of all causes, namely, God. Inasmuch as it is able to know something about God and the other separate Intelligences, metaphysics is called *divina scientia*, that is, divinity (I, 2).

Abstract as it is, metaphysical knowledge is not a merely logical speculation. It does not deal with concepts of second intention (*entia rationis*) but with actual being itself, abstractedly considered in its essence and apart from any material determinations. It is therefore a "real" knowledge, or, in other words, a cognition of actual reality. The most immediately given aspects of reality are three in number: being (*ens*), thing (*res*) and necessary (*necesse*). These are the first notions that fall into the soul, the first impressions which it receives and which it cannot derive from any anterior ones. Consequently, such notions can be pointed out; they cannot be explained. Any attempt to demonstrate them would result in a vicious circle, since, being first, they would be involved in their own demonstration. A being is something that is; a thing is an object of which something true can be said (I, 6); in other words, a being is a being and a thing is something. As to "necessary," let us observe that the intelligibility of each and every thing is given together with it. For indeed, apart from the fact that it is, which it has in common with all other beings, a thing is that which it is, and it cannot possibly be anything else. That which a thing is, is its "quiddity." It is also called its "certitude," because its quiddity is the very truth that can be known and said about it. What is neither a being, nor a thing conceivable through its quiddity, is strictly nothing. As such, it can neither be known nor thought. On the contrary, every being is necessarily that which it is. Necessary and possible then are immediately given primitive notions, whose definitions are bound to be circular ones. Some say that "possible" is what is neither necessary nor impossible. Others say that "necessary" is what is neither impossible nor merely possible. In both cases the notions are implied in their own definitions. This does not mean that we do not evidently perceive their import. We understand the necessity of necessary being as a sort of intensity (*vehementia entis*) (I, 7); we can describe it by opposition to the mere possibility of being, but we cannot clear it up by means of a definition in which its own notion is not involved.

What is necessary by itself has no cause; what needs a cause in order to exist is merely possible. This is evident, for that which has a cause only exists in virtue of that cause; consequently, it is not necessary by itself. On the other hand, while it exists, what is in itself merely possible cannot exist in virtue of its mere possibility; consequently, in itself, it remains possible. There is therefore a necessary connection between these notions: to be necessary by itself is to be causeless; to be possible in itself is to require a cause in order actually to exist.

Let us now consider any possible being while it receives existence from its cause. As has been said, it remains possible in itself; yet, while it is being caused, it cannot not exist. Its caused existence is necessary in virtue of its cause. Such a being then is both possible in itself and necessary by another (I, 7; VIII, 4). Even then, it remains without intrinsic necessity.

There can be only one necessary being. If there were several necessary beings, their essences would have to be either the same or different. If their essences were the same, there should be in them something to make them individually distinct, and this something should be external to their essences. What is external to an essence is accidental to it. Consequently, the cause why these necessary beings would have distinct existences would be accidental to their essences, so that, without it, they would not exist. Hence, they would not be necessary by themselves. On the other hand, two essences cannot be both different and necessary. For indeed, in order to be different, one of them must have something which is not to be found in the other one, and since this is part of necessary being, how can the other one be necessary? Therefore, there can be only one absolutely necessary being (I, 8).

That which an essence is, is its truth. The being that is necessary by itself is true by itself; beings that are necessary by their causes are true by their causes. Thus, considered in themselves, possible beings are false (i.e., not true). Consequently, all that which is, besides the unique being that is necessary by itself, is false in itself. The truth of the necessary being is the only one which is necessarily true, because its essence cannot be otherwise than it is. Similarly, what is possible in itself but necessary by another can also be false in itself but true in virtue of another, which is its cause. In all cases, truth can only be ascertained by comparing the thing with itself and by affirming it to be what it is because it cannot be itself and something else at one and the same time, and no third position is conceivable between affirmation and negation (I, 9).

In describing the intrinsic properties of being and its divisions, Avicenna generally follows the doctrine of Aristotle, not however without sometimes adding to it or interpreting it in his own way. The general frame of Aristotle's metaphysics is faithfully preserved. Being is either by essence, in which case it is substance, or it is not by essence, in which case it is accident (II, 1). Corporeal substance is not composed of indivisible parts (atoms); it is continuous and extended in space according to the three dimensions. The form which enables it to receive the dimensions is the "corporeal form" (*forma corporealis*). This is true of the physical body; but the body studied by science (*corpus disciplinale*) does not include the actual existence of its matter nor of its dimensions; it is the form of the physical body, together with its figure and dimensions, existing in the soul only. Each body is in act by its corporeal form and in potency by its matter (*hyle*). Matter is nothing else than pure receptivity; in itself, it is absolute potency; one and the same in nature wherever it is found, it receives all its determinations and specifications from without, that is from its forms (II, 2). For the same reason, it cannot be separated from form (II, 3). Since corporeal matter has being through its form, it can be said that form has priority over matter in the order of being (II, 4). True enough, corporeal forms need matters in which to subsist, and these matters are prepared for them by extrinsic causes whose nature we shall have to determine later on; yet, taking the composite substance in itself, even what matter contributes to it hangs on the being which it receives from the form. The form, then, can truly be said to be the cause of the composite substance, including even its very being.

Substances are qualified by their accidents, whose study is one with the description of the categories: quantity (unity and number), quality, etc. Avicenna had devoted to their analysis treatises II and III of his *Meta-*

physics. Then comes the study of some general properties of being, such as anteriority and posteriority, act and potency, perfection and imperfection (Tr. IV), immediately followed by the extremely important treatise that deals with the problem of universals.

Universal signifies that which is actually predicated of several things, for instance, man; or that which could be predicated of several things, in case they did exist, for instance, heptagonal house; or that which is predicated of only one thing, because there happens to be only one, although there is nothing in its nature to prevent it from being multiplied, for instance, the sun. In short, "universal" is what it is not impossible to predicate of many. On the contrary, "singular" is that which cannot be conceived as predicable of many; for instance, this one man whom we call Plato. It is possible to predicate universal concepts of individual beings because each being has a nature, whose quiddity is neither universal nor singular but, so to speak, indifferent to both singularity and to universality. For instance, humanity, or human nature, is neither singular nor universal; of itself, it is just *humanitas*. Universality then is something superadded to natures, quiddities or essences, by the human intellect. A nature becomes universal when it is rendered predicable of many by some operation of the intellect (V, 1). The logical doctrine of nature finds in this problem its metaphysical application.

Just as indeterminate nature can be universalized by the intellect, it can be singularized by its accidents. Individual men, or horses, are distinct beings on account of the particular determinations of their natures by quantity, quality, etc. This does not mean that there actually exists natures, or essences, that are neither singular nor universal. What we call nature is nothing else than the form of the species (man, horse, etc.), stripped by the intellect of its individualizing differences, and conceived in a state of complete abstraction (V, 1; V, 2).

This doctrine provides a basis for a metaphysical interpretation of the traditional doctrine of the definition by the genus and the specific difference (V, 3, 4, 5, 6). The following treatise deals with the different types of causes and their definitions. Avicenna follows the Aristotelian division of the four causes: material, formal, efficient and final. Final causes are the most perfect of all and their science is the highest wisdom (VI, 5).

Despite his insistence on the realness of common natures, or essences, Avicenna had no intention of returning to the universe of Plato. All arts, he says, begin by being somewhat crude and immature, but they progress with time, until they finally reach their perfection. Such was the case with the ancient philosophy of the Greeks. In the beginning, philosophy was rhetorical and aimed to persuade; then the Greeks sucessively mastered dialectics, natural science and theology. But this could not be achieved without effort, and the main difficulty they had to overcome was to pass over from the sensible to the intelligible. Plato, and his master

Socrates, imagined that *humanitas,* that is, human nature, enjoyed a separate existence, so much so that it would still continue to exist in itself even if all men were annihilated. Others ascribed this state of separation, not to forms, but to their mathematical principles. Many other solutions of the problem have been put forward in antiquity (VII, 2), but Avicenna forcefully rejects any hypothesis ascribing to forms, or to their constituent elements, any kind of separate existence (VII, 3). All the elements distinguished by metaphysical analysis in the structure of any being are included in its own concrete reality.

F. *Theology*

Theology is the crowning part of metaphysics. Its first task is to establish the existence of a primary cause, namely, the First. This problem provides Avicenna with an occasion to define the meaning of the word "cause" when applied to the causality of God. Among the examples of active causality quoted in his *Metaphysics* (V, 2, 1013 a 29-32) Aristotle had included the relation of the maker to the thing made; to him, this seems to have been just one particular case of the type of causality which he attributes to "that from which change or stability first begins." And indeed his metaphysics, like his physics, was chiefly concerned with causality as the origin of coming to be or, on the contrary, of necessary being. Under the same religious pressure which Averroes was to denounce as having corrupted his Aristotelianism, Avicenna was prompted to distinguish, within "that from which change first begins," between the causality of the mover and the causality of the maker. The notion of efficient cause, always more or less confusedly present to the mind of the Christian theologians describing the divine act of creation, finds itself integrated by Avicenna with the Aristotelian doctrine of the four causes. This metaphysical initiative was to have far-reaching consequences in the history of Christian philosophy.

The new type of causality distinguished by Avicenna is that of the "agent cause" (*causa agens*). Its proper effect is the very being of the thing caused. What is here meant by being, is existence. The agent, Avicenna says, "is the cause that gives to the thing an existence (*esse*) distinct from its own" (*Metaph.* VI, 1). This metaphysical causality is very different from the physical causality investigated by the scientists: "The theologians do not understand by agent the principle of motion only, as the natural philosophers do, but rather, the origin of existence (*principium essendi*), and its giver (*et datorem ejus*), as the creator of the world is." What we call a natural agent cause, that is, the cause that makes natural things to be, is the origin of a change (*acquirens esse naturalibus est principium motus*), whereas the properly so-called agent cause is the origin of existence itself. The fabricator is not truly the agent cause of the fabricated product, nor the father of the son, nor the fire of the heat; they are not the cause of their existence, nor, strictly speaking, of their being (*non sunt verae causae existentiae . . . nec etiam sunt causae sui esse,* ibid. VI, 2). The maker is, by his motion, the cause of another motion, whose term is the generation of effect. In the order of causality, the cause of existence, or "agent cause," stands alone.

From the point of view of metaphysical terminology, the Latin translation of Avicenna's *Metaphysics* has spread, together with the corresponding notion, the formula *causa agens;* the Latin translation of Algazel's abridgement of Avicenna's work has popularized the formula *causa efficiens* (*Metaph.* I, 5, p. 37). Already in Avicenna, and still more in Algazel, the notion of efficient causality exhibited a tendency to invade even the order of natural causality. The distinction between natural efficient causes and voluntary efficient causes (Algazel, p. 38) is a clear sign of this tendency. In the thirteenth century, the Christian philosophers or theologians will freely use the two formulas as equivalent: *causa agens* and *causa efficiens*. Some of them, for instance Peter of Auvergne, will explicitly raise the question whether the action of the "efficient cause" is identical with the natural causality exercised by "that from which change first begins." The awareness of the problem will grow together with the progressive realization of the true meaning of the physics of Aristotle in which, so far as we know, no provision had been made for an efficient causality half way between the necessity of true entity, that has no cause, and the cause of change whose term is that of natural generation. Thomas Aquinas will freely write *causa movens seu efficiens* as though the two expressions were obviously equivalent. His remarkable formula, in the opuscle *On the Principles of Nature,* is significant in this respect: "There must therefore be, over and above matter and form, an acting principle of being (*esse*); and it is called efficient cause, or mover, or agent, or that from which change begins." The transformation brought about by the metaphysical initiative of Avicenna is visible in the statement made by Thomas Aquinas in his commentary on the *Metaphysics* (V, 1, 1) that to be cause "entails a certain influx into the being (*esse*) of the caused." The metaphysical complex resulting from the combination of Avicenna's notion of efficient causality as origin of existences, with the Proclean universe described in the *Book on Causes,* will become very common about the end of the thirteenth century. The upshot will be a universe neoplatonic in structure but permeated throughout with the efficient causality proper to the creating God of the Old Testament. Averroes was not far wrong in denouncing the influence exercised upon the metaphysics of Avicenna by biblical revelation.

In order to establish the existence of a cause of the universe, Avicenna proves that, in all orders of causes, there must be a first one. In other words, since all orders of causes are finite, each of them hangs on a first principle; now, the first principle of one order of causes is the same as the first principle of the other orders; consequently, this first principle is distinct from all the rest; it is the necessary being and all the rest finds in it its origin.

The mainspring of the demonstration is the proposition that essential causes are simultaneously given together with their effects (VI, 2). By "essential causes," Avicenna designates causes whose efficacy produces the very being of their effects. Arguing from principles similar to those of the *Liber de causis*, Avicenna shows that in any causal series of three terms, there must be a cause that is not caused, a cause that is being caused, and an effect that does not cause. The fact that there is only one intermediate cause, or many, between the first cause and the last effect, is irrelevant to the problem. In all such cases, the existence of the last effect is necessary by reason of the first cause, whose efficacy accounts for the whole series of causes and effects. Incidentally, let us note that this kind of causation, which consists in giving being to something that had not yet received it, is called "creation." Consequently, to prove the existence of a first cause is also to prove that the universe is created. Creatures are beings whose essences owe their actual existence to a first necessary being. This is the reason why, when the production of actual being is at stake, the existence of any effect implies that of a first cause in virtue of which it exists. The whole argument is a proof of the existence of God, based upon the given fact that merely possible beings do actually exist.

The only way to refute this conclusion would be to maintain that the series of intermediate causes is infinite. But this can be said, not thought. Every series of causes and effects has at least one extremity, namely, the very being whose cause we investigate. Hence it is finite. Now a finite series of causes and effects cannot contain an infinite number of terms. The only series whose terms are infinite in number are those of non-essentially ordered causes which succeed one another in time indefinitely. An infinite series of thus accidentally ordered causes is possible, but this is another problem with which we are not now concerned (VI, 1). The connection there is between this argument and the Avicennian notion of beings possible in themselves but necessary by their causes is obvious.

The same demonstration applies in the orders of formal cause and of final cause and since, in all three orders, the first cause is necessary, it must be one and the same cause (VI, 4), for indeed any difference between them would require a cause, so that none of them would be the necessary being. The First is individualized and separated from the rest by its very necessity (VIII, 5). For the same reason, the necessary being is perfect, since it is all that it is possible to be and can neither acquire nor lose any part of its being (VIII, 6). In point of fact, the First is "more than perfect," since it is not its own being only, but also that of all other beings, inasmuch as it is their cause. Everything that is flows from the abundance of its perfection. Because the necessary being is pure goodness, He desires all perfection: that is, He desires all being inasmuch as it is being. Even the smallest amount of being is good in itself; so God desires it; but evil has no essence, no being, and, consequently, God does not desire it. Thus, the world of Avicenna is caused by a necessary being which necessarily wills all that which can possibly be, because all being is good inasmuch as it is being. Hence the ceaseless actualization of all possible beings (*possibilia per se*) by the supreme Necessary, which is God.

Thus understood, the First is a pure separate Intelligence, eternally knowing itself as necessary being; in fact, it is neither itself nor any other being; it is, absolutely. In the First, even the knowledge of possible beings is one with the knowledge of its own necessity. The intelligible order of all "possibles in themselves" is one with the First's self-knowledge, so that their passing away in time is always present to its eternity (VIII, 6). The multiplicity of the intelligible forms does not plurify its essence. The will of the First is not disturbed by any desire to find out what it should will; in it, self-love necessarily includes the love of all the rest. In the First, everything is one, because it is part of its essence. Since the nature of the First is to be all that which is possible, and since all that which is possible flows from its essence, the necessary being knows all, and causes all, without itself being related to anything. To repeat, the First is, absolutely.

Let us now consider the order according to which possible beings flow from the First. Since its essence is simple, its will necessarily follows its knowledge. It is one with it. In the self-knowledge of the necessary being, the order of the possibles is an order of principles and consequences. The essence of God is immense. He knows that all intelligibles flow from his essence inasmuch as they are known to him. He also knows that beings flow from his being inasmuch as he is the principle of all beings. Moreover, he knows that the order according to which things flow from his own necessity is the very order of their intelligible essences and perfections in his mind, so that, from the mere fact that he knows it, this order "flows, and becomes, and is" (VIII, 7). This becoming, which is creation, is necessary, as its cause itself is. Any decision to create would have introduced in God a change incompatible with his essential necessity. Hence creation is eternal (IX, 1). Our sole problem then is to know how becoming is eternally flowing from the first and necessary being; it is the problem *de fluxu entis*.

Becoming, or change, is motion, and all motion takes place in view of an end. The ultimate end is the necessary being, whose perfection is eminently desirable. The cause of the first created motion must therefore be the love experienced by a knowing being for the supreme perfection of the

First. The effect of this love must be a desire to resemble the supreme being by imitating its perfection. Thus, the first being that flows from the first cause must be a pure separate Intelligence, equal in everything to its cause, save in this only, that it comes second, not first. Being an intellect, it is a subsisting and perfect cognition of its cause. On the other hand it knows itself as a being possible in itself, but necessary in virtue of the necessity of its cause. This first duality is the origin of number and of all further multiplicity.

The first caused Intelligence first knows God, and this act of knowing is the second separate Intelligence. Then it thinks itself as necessary in virtue of its cause, and this act of knowing is the soul of the heavenly sphere which surrounds and contains the universe. Then again the first caused Intelligence thinks itself as possible in itself (since it has a cause) and this act of knowing begets the body of the said sphere. The reason for this is that matter is possibility. The second Intelligence operates in the same way. By knowing the First Intelligence, it begets the third one; by knowing itself as necessary in virtue of the second Intelligence, it begets the soul of the second sphere; by knowing itself as possible in itself, it begets the body of the same sphere, which bear the constellations of the zodiac. There then follow, according to the same pattern, the fourth Intelligence with the circle (soul and body) of the planet Saturn; then the fifth Intelligence (Jupiter), the sixth Intelligence (Mars), the seventh Intelligence (the Sun), the eighth Intelligence (Venus), the ninth Intelligence (Mercury), and the tenth Intelligence (the Moon). Astronomers know of nine heavenly spheres only; if and when new astronomical spheres are discovered, an equal number of separate Intelligences shall be added to this description. Incidentally, these Intelligences are the same beings which theologians call Angels. Christian theologians will unanimously object that, according to Scripture, the number of Angels is much greater than that of the heavenly spheres (Dan. 7, 10).

Below the sphere of the moon is the sublunary world, with its four elements, its common matter and the unending succession of its forms. This is the reason why sublunary beings are ceaselessly coming to be and passing away. The various influences exercised upon matter by celestial bodies have for their effect that certain portions of matter are fittingly disposed to receive certain forms. Below the separate Intelligence that presides over the sphere of the moon, there is another one ceaselessly radiating all possible forms and causing them to exist in proportionate matters, or to be known by intellects. In this sense, it can be called the "giver of forms." Every time one of these forms happens to find a matter fittingly disposed to receive it, the corresponding sublunary being comes to be; when its matter ceases to be so disposed, the same being loses its form and, consequently, ceases to exist. With respect to human souls, it is the separate agent Intellect. What of contingency there is in the universe of Avicenna is due, not to some intervention of the First Cause, but to the matter which enters the structure of the sublunary world, and whose intrinsic imperfection often prevents the form from fully achieving its natural end (IX, 3-5).

The world of Avicenna is not ruled by a particular providence intending the welfare of each individual being. Yet, since it necessarily follows from a perfect cause, it is good, at least on the whole, and even particular imperfections are there in view of the common good. Floods are bad, but the presence of water in the world is in itself a good thing. Fires are dangerous, but fire itself is excellent and, by and large, the world is better with it than without it. There is providence, then, in this sense that the universe is as good as it can possibly be (IX, 6). Besides, since evil is but the privation of the good, just as blindness is but the privation of sight, it has really no cause. And let us not forget that, frequent as it is, evil is much less common than good; otherwise, since non-being would overcome being, there would be no world.

The ultimate end of man is what it had to be in a universe thus conceived. The religious law given by the prophet Mohammed announces the resurrection of bodies, but this is a matter of faith; it cannot be demonstrated by philosophy. The same revelation promises fleshly pleasures to the good and corporal punishments to sinners, as sanctions to be received after death in future life, but philosophers know better. They are expecting a much higher felicity, which consists in the union of their possible intellects with the supreme truth. The perfection and blessedness of the rational soul is to become an intelligible world, that is to say, a contemplation of the universal order of beings known in its intelligible necessity. Those who begin to philosophize during the present life do not cease to seek for knowledge after the death of their bodies. They then continue to do what they have done up to then, only they do it much better than was possible for them while they still were in their bodies. Like paralytics suddenly cured of their disease, souls relieved from their bodies can at long last achieve what had always been the end of their desire. Such is their ultimate end and supreme beatitude, to be conjoined with the lowest separate Intelligence, which is for man the source of all light. Naturally, moral life is a necessary preparation for this reward (IX, 7). And not only moral life, but also political life, including the respect of the religious law established by the Prophet. For indeed, prophecy and revelation teach the same truth as philosophy, only they teach it under a form accessible to the imagination of all men. In the prophetic mind, revelation and philosophical knowledge are one. Religious cult and philosophical speculation are therefore tending toward the same end (X, 3).

The deeply religious inspiration of the doctrine is obvious. Even apart from this, it contained many elements which could not fail to interest the thirteenth-century Christian theologians. A universe of essences distinct from their existence was a good technical description of a created universe. A human soul substantially distinct from its body, immortal in virtue of its own substantiality and open to the illuminations from on high in virtue of its total immateriality, was eminently suitable to those theologians who, while anxious to maintain the tradition of Saint Augustine, desired to re-state it in the language of Aristotle. Last, not least, a universe whose cause was the Necessary Being, a pure existent without essence or quiddity, was exactly what was needed by men whose God was much less the Prime Mover of Aristotle than the WHO IS of the Old Testament. All these positions will be re-interpreted by the Christian theologians of the thirteenth century. On the other hand, the same Christian theologians could not fail to realize the fact that the God of Avicenna, although ontologically separated from merely possible beings by his own necessity, still remained tied up with them in a necessary way. From the very fact that the Neces-sary Being is, the Avicennian universe of finite beings necessarily follows and, except that accidents occur owing to the presence of matter, it must necessarily be that which it is. Where there is no free choice in God, there is none in man. Avicenna has thus confronted Christian theologians with the problem of reinstating liberty in a world created by a necessary being. We shall see, in due time, how the greatest among them successfully per-formed this task.

3. AVERROES

However careful he was to leave to revealed theology an open door, Avi-cenna did not succeed in placating the theologians. Obviously, he was a philosopher before anything else. Among the theologians who opposed his doctrine, one at least must be mentioned because, instead of weakening it, he strengthened its influence. Al Gazali (Algazel), who died about 1111, wrote several important works (*Restoration of Religious Knowledge, De-struction of Philosophers*) none of which was familiar to the mediaeval Latin world. On the contrary, the scholastics have known well his treatise *On the Intentions of the Philosophers,* wherein he contented himself with exposing the doctrines of Alfarabi and of Avicenna, which he intended to refute later on. As a consequence, the scholastics have considered him as a faithful summarizer (*abbreviator*) of the men he wanted to refute[13] and the history of his influence in the Latin world coincides with that of Avicenna's. The steady theological opposition met by Moslem philosophers did not stop the development of philosophy, but it may have been one of the reasons why it migrated from the East to Spain, where it was repre-sented by Avempace, Ibn Thofail and especially by Averroes.

Avempace (Ibn Badja, d. 1138), an Arab living in Spain, equally versed in the sciences and philosophy, left treatises on logic, a book *On the Soul,* the *Guide for the Solitary* and a work *On the Connection of the Intellect with Man* (quoted by Albert the Great under the title *Continuatio intel-*

lectus cum homine). This title clearly suggests what was then the chief problem for the philosophers: to establish contact between rational individuals and the separate agent Intelligence from which they draw their beatitude. *The Guide for the Solitary* was a sort of soul's itinerary toward God, or rather toward the agent Intelligence by which man communicates with the divine world. This doctrine therefore assumed that it was possible for man to work his way up progressively from the knowledge of things to the knowledge of a substance separated from matter. Ibn Badja thought that such was the case. The aim of a science is to know the essences of its objects. From the essence of each object, we can abstract another; and if this latter had one we could extract it in turn; but as one cannot go on to infinity, it must come to a knowledge of an essence which has not in itself any other essence. Such is the essence of the separate Substance, on which our knowledge depends. Note that in such a doctrine the knowledge of any intelligible whatever straightway reaches a separate substance. These reasons, which assimilate the knowledge of an essence abstracted from the sensible to that of an intelligible substance, appeared frivolous to Saint Thomas Aquinas; however Avempace will have the honors in a chapter of the *Contra Gentiles* (III, 41): *Hoc autem quaestionem habet,* Saint Thomas is to admit: that is a question. From time to time, in Albert the Great, Thomas Aquinas and still others, we also come across a certain Abubacer. He is Abou Bekr ibn Thofaïl, born in Cadiz about 1100, died in Morocco in 1185, a man of encyclopaedic knowledge, like all those Arabs whose learning so far exceeded the knowledge of the Christians of their times. Abubacer's doctrine, like that of Ibn Badja, seems to have been known by the Christians of the thirteenth century particularly through the criticism directed against it by Averroes in his *De anima*. For them he was the philosopher who had identified the possible intellect of man with imagination (*phantasia*). Once suitably prepared, the latter could receive intelligible forms, so that no other "intellect" was required. The Latins were not acquainted with Abubacer's philosophical novel, the *Hayy ben Yaqdhân,* in which he showed how a man living in solitude can rise progressively, through the study of the sciences and the contemplation of the true, up to the knowledge of God and to bliss.[14]

The greatest name in Arabian philosophy, along with Avicenna, is Averroes (*Averrois,* Ibn Rochd), whose influence spread, in many directions, throughout the duration of the middle ages, then in the epoch of the Renaissance and up to the very threshold of modern times. He was another Spanish Arab. Born in 1126 at Cordova, he studied theology, jurisprudence, medicine, mathematics and philosophy. For several years he held the office of a judge, while writing a considerable number of personal works on medicine, astronomy, and philosophy. Some of his commentaries on Aristotle, which earned him, during the middle ages, the title of "Commentator," have come down to us in three different accounts. The Arabian originals of these works are now partly lost, but we know them through their Latin translations. They bear the names of great and lesser commentaries, the shortest of them being paraphrases or "epitomes." Averroes died in 1198 at the age of seventy-two.[15]

A. *Philosophy and Religion*

One of Averroes' most influential efforts was his attempt to determine the mutual relations of philosophy and religion. He was well aware of the presence of a large number of philosophical and theological sects, whose perpetual dissensions were permanent danger for philosophy as well as for religion. In fact, it was essential to safeguard the rights and liberty of philosophical speculation; but on the other hand, one could not dispute the fact that theologians had some reason to be uneasy in seeing the free discussion of texts from the Koran spread through all quarters.[16] Averroes attributed all the difficulty to the fact that access to philosophy was authorized for minds incapable of understanding it; he saw the remedy in an exact definition of the various levels of comprehension of Koranic texts accessible to different minds, and in the prohibition given to each mind to go beyond the degree accessible to it.

The Koran is truth itself, since it results from a miracle of God, but, as it is intended for mankind as a whole, it must contain what will satisfy and convince all minds. Now there are three categories of minds, and three corresponding kinds of men: first, men of demonstration, who demand demonstrative proofs and insist on attaining knowledge by going from the necessary to the necessary by the necessary: second, dialectical men, who are satisfied with probable arguments: third, men of exhortation, for whom oratorical arguments suffice which call upon the imagination and the passions.

The Koran is addressed simultaneously to these three kinds of minds, and that is what proves its miraculous character; it has an exterior and symbolic meaning for the uninstructed, an interior and hidden meaning for scholars. Averroes' main point is that each spirit has the right and the duty to understand and interpret the Koran in the most perfect way of which it is capable. The one who can understand the philosophical meaning of the sacred text should interpret it philosophically, for its most lofty meaning is the true meaning of revelation, and each time there appears any conflict between the religious text and demonstrative conclusions, it is by interpreting the religious text philosophically that harmony should be re-established.

Two consequences follow immediately from this principle. The first is that a mind should never seek to raise itself above the degree of interpretation of which it is capable; the second is that one should never divulge to inferior classes of minds the interpretations reserved for superior classes. The error into which philosophers have fallen consist precisely in the untimely communication of superior knowledge to inferior minds; as a result of this we have seen arise hybrid methods which mix oratorical art, dialectics and demonstration and are the inexhaustible source of heresies. It is advisable therefore to re-establish in all its exactness the distinction of the three orders of interpretation and teaching: at the peak, philosophy, which gives absolute knowledge and truth; immediately below that, theology, the domain of dialectical interpretation and of mere probability; and at the bottom of the scale, religion and faith, which should be left carefully to those for whom they are necessary. Thus are brought together and graded the three degrees of intellection of one single and same truth.

In such a complex position, conflicts of jurisdiction are inevitable. What is to be done when, on a definite point, philosophy teaches one thing and faith another? What did the Commentator himself really think? The answer is hidden in his most secret conscience. Averroes never broke away from the Moslem community; he never allowed himself the slightest attack against religion, and his very doctrine forbade him to do anything that might weaken a religious faith necessary to the social order; he recognized the reality of prophecy and put the Prophet at the peak of human knowledge, since, in the Prophet's mind, religion and philosophy coincide. Yet, when all is said and done, there is no doubt that Averroes considered philosophical truth as the highest type of human truth. When philosophers and simple believers affirm the same thing, for instance, that there is a supreme felicity for man, the philosophical notion of this beatitude is vastly superior to what revelation says about it. In the doctrine of Averroes, there is absolutely nothing that philosophy does not know better than simple faith, and those who assimilate his position to that of Thomas Aquinas, which has been done, should also remember that, according to Averroes, theology is the worst type of speculation precisely because it is neither faith nor philosophy, but, rather, a corruption of both.

Taken in itself, the work of Averroes was a conscious effort to restore in its purity the philosophy of Aristotle and of his legitimate successors. True enough, it retains a good deal of the Platonism which Alexander of Aphrodisias, among others, had injected into the authentic doctrine of Aristotle; it excludes those aspects of the Platonic tradition which could easily harmonize with religion (e.g., the cosmogony of Plato's *Timaeus*). The thirteenth-century scholastics were not to overlook this aspect of his thought.

Strangely enough, very few men have been more influential than Averroes in shaping the popular notion of mediaeval philosophy which is now currently received as historical truth. In fact, it was Averroes' firm and absolute conviction that philosophical truth and the philosophy of Aristotle were one and the same thing. The formulas in which he expressed his admiration for the Stagirite are well known, and in fact they deserve to be known, for the exclusive cult of Aristotle which they express is a distinctive mark of the Averroistic school, and not, as is sometimes imagined, of the whole middle ages: "The doctrine of Aristotle is the supreme truth, because his intellect was the limit of the human intellect. It is therefore rightly said that he was created and given to us by divine providence, so that we might know all that can be known." (*Aristotelis doctrina est summa veritas, quoniam ejus intellectus fuit finis humani intellectus. Quare bene dicitur, quod fuit creatus et datus nobis divina providentia, ut sciremus quidquid potest sciri.*) These are rather strong expressions. The sound advice given us by an Oriental historian of philosophy in this regard should probably be kept in mind: do not take literally the hyperbole of oriental praise. The mediaeval Latins who took Averroes' statements at their face value should have been given the same warning.[17]

B. *Epistemology and Metaphysics*

Averroes played no other role in logic than the very important one of being a keen and faithful interpreter of authentic Aristotelianism. In anthropology and in metaphysics, he circulated an Aristotelianism of a definite type, which was to contend with Avicenna's in the minds of the Latins throughout the course of the thirteenth and fourteenth centuries. Metaphysics is the science of being as being, and of the properties pertaining to it as such. By the term "being," the very substance which is must be understood. All substance is a being; all being is either a substance, or an accident which participates in the being of the substance. There is therefore no ground for considering separately the problem of existence, still less for imagining, like Avicenna, that it is an "accident" of essence. To be a real being is also to exist. Substance is the individual thing itself. This is the primary meaning of the term; but substance is even more the quiddity, or real essence, which determines each substance to be what it is. Thus one with concrete reality, the being of each thing is proper to it; consequently, being cannot be predicated univocally. On the other hand, all that which is, is a being of some sort: a substance, or an accident, or a quantity, or a quality, etc. Now, each of the categories of being has this in common with the others, that it designates something which is. Being, therefore, cannot be predicated equivocally (in totally different meanings). This is why Aristotle says that being is "analogous," which means that, whatever they are and in whatever manner they are, all the categories are related to being. The object of metaphysics then is the study of all that is, insofar as it is. Its method is that of logic, not, however, used as a simple collection of the rules of correct thought, but as a means of exploring the real nature of being and its properties.[18]

In order that our logic may apply to the real, sensible things must also be intelligible. In fact, they are, and this clearly proves that their primary cause is the thinking act of an Intellect. If it were otherwise, whence would their nature derive its aptitude to be known by us? Their intelligibility is essential to beings; but what is essential exists only through a necessary efficient cause. If it is essential to sensible things to be virtually intelligible, then they originate in the cognition of an intellect, just about as man-made things originate in the minds of artisans. If we can understand the nature of manufactured objects, it is because they themselves come from some thought, that is, from intelligible forms present in the intellects of those who made them. It is the same with natural things. The Platonists were wrong in believing in the existence of separate Ideas, but not in thinking that the sensible things hold their intelligibility from some intelligible beings.

It would be a mistake to think that universals exist in themselves, outside of individuals. To ascribe reality to a universal is to assume, either that each individual possesses only a part of it, so that Zaid and Amr would each represent a different part of the concept "man," which is absurd; or else, it is to assume that the universal is entirely present in each individual, which amounts to positing it as both one and multiple at the same time, which is no less absurd. It must be assumed therefore that a universal is not a substance, but the work of the understanding: it is the intellect which gives universality to forms. The purpose of science is not to know universal realities; it is to know particular things in a universal way, by abstracting from singular things the natures that their matters make individual.[19]

Thus conceived, the universal is "that which can be predicated of several individuals." As such, it cannot itself be an individual, yet this does not entail that the knowledge we have of it is without object. Individuals are not simple. Form is the act and essence of what is; matter is potency actualized and determined by form; individual substance is a compound of the two. What thought attains in conceiving the universal is form, and it expresses that form in definition. The name of the thing designates the whole thing, but form is entitled to it essentially.[20]

Made up of form and matter, therefore of a determinant and a determined, all sensible substance is both potency and act. Through act, it is; through potency, it can become. To change in quality, quantity or place is to pass from potency to act; it is to be in motion. It is proved in physics that everything in motion is moved by a mover and that, as the thing moved is moved only because it is in potency, the mover moves only because it is in act. Let us take any number of beings in movement; they will necessarily be distributed into three classes; the first, and lowest, will include those which are moved and do not move; the second, and intermediary, will contain those which both move and are moved; the highest will include the beings which move without being moved. All this, says Averroes, is a matter of course. The intermediary beings can be multiplied as much as one wishes. Their number has nothing to do with the question, provided only it be not infinite. But it is not, for if it were, there would be no primary causes, and consequently no movement; now there is movement; the number of the intermediary causes is therefore finite, and their action implies the existence of a class of primary causes, which move without being moved.[21]

To move without being moved is to be an act without any potentiality, a pure act. Therefore pure acts exist, and since their actuality is perfect, they are continually causing movement. Now there is no movement without a moving body. In order that the motor action of these pure acts may be continual, movement and things moved must also be so. The world, therefore, has certainly always existed, and will continue always to exist. In short, the duration of the world is eternal. That is not all. Since they are free from potentiality, these Acts are also free from matter. They are thus immaterial substances. How many of them are there? We shall posit as many as are necessary to explain the primary movements, which are the causes of all the others in the universe. Unfortunately, astronomers do not agree as to the number of these movements, but it is commonly assumed that there are thirty-eight of them; five for each of the superior planets (Saturn, Jupiter, and Mars), five for the Moon, eight for Mercury, seven for Venus, one for the Sun (if it is considered as moving in an eccentric orbit, not in an epicycle), and one for the sphere that envelops the world, that is, the firmament. There is perhaps a ninth sphere, but that is not certain. If there are thirty-eight movements, there are thirty-eight movers.

How do these movers, being immobile themselves, move? This way: in order to move, they have nothing to do but exist. The movement of each sphere arises in it from the desire it feels for the pure Act on which it depends. Of its own accord it moves toward this Act. To understand this movement, we must remember that the movers are immaterial acts, that is to say, Intelligences, and that it is their thought that the corresponding sphere desires. Each celestial body must therefore possess, if not senses and an imagination as Avicenna mistakenly believed, at least an understanding, and this understanding experiences an intellectual desire for its immobile mover. Conceiving the thought of this Intelligence as the good which gives it its perfection, it desires to put itself in the most perfect state of which it is capable; and as movement is better for it than immobility, for movement is the life of a body, it moves perpetually.

The pure Acts which thus move the celestial bodies give them not only movement, but the form from which each one receives its essence. If it ceased to be moved by its separate Intelligence, each planet would lose its form, just as there would be no souls for us were the agent Intelligence to cease to act. The Movers are therefore also, in a certain sense, eternally causing the celestial bodies, since the forms of these bodies are nothing but the ideas which they have of their respective movers. Moreover, since the separate movers are the good which celestial bodies desire, they are also their ultimate ends, and, therefore their final causes. These Intelligences are consequently the motive, efficient and final causes of the celestial bodies, that move out of love for their intelligible perfection.

Let us now consider these movers in their mutual relations. The spheres they move form a hierarchy from the Moon up to the Firmament, according to their size and the velocity of their movement. Their Movers must therefore form a hierarchy in the same way. All these separate principles must as a consequence end in a first principle, which is the prime separate Mover. This hierarchy of dignity only expresses the hierarchy of their connection in the order of causality. In fact, all are principles, since they form the genus of principles. Now, in a genus, beings form a hierarchy according to their more or less perfect way of realizing the genus. In the genus "hot," beings are more or less hot according to their more or less close proximity to fire, which is the cause of heat for all that is hot. Similarly, in the genus of principles, there must be a primary term with respect to which the degree in which each one of them is principle is measured. There is therefore one absolutely first Principle, the ultimate end desired by all the rest, the cause of the forms and of the movement of all the rest. It is the immobile Prime Mover, the first separate Intelligence, whose unity insures the unity of the universe, and consequently its very being. This is what God himself teaches, when he says in the Koran (XXI, 22): "If there were in these two worlds any gods besides Allah, the two worlds would cease to exist."

The Prophet furthermore gives us a useful piece of advice, in saying: "Know thyself, and thou wilt know thy creator." For indeed, to know how these Intelligences stand with regard to one another, one cannot do better than examine the relation of intellect to intelligible in human understanding. Our intellect is capable of reflecting its act upon itself, in which case the intellect and its intelligible are identical. This is all the more true for separate Intelligences: each of them is identically knowledge and what it knows. But an effect cannot know itself without knowing its cause, and inversely, if a being knows another than itself by knowing itself, it is because it has a cause. In knowing itself, each of these separate Intelligences therefore knows itself and its cause at one and the same time, except the first one of all which, having no cause, knows only itself. As its essence is absolutely perfect, the knowledge it has of itself forms a thought equally perfect, with nothing above it that it may know, with nothing below it that it should know. Not to know what is below him is not, in God, a shortcoming. Since he knows all reality by knowing himself, not to know, in a less perfect way, what he already knows in the most perfect way by knowing himself, cannot, in him, be any lack.

Intelligible Substances endowed with knowledge and desire, these Intelligences are also living and capable of bliss. As it lives of its own life, the first one is blissful in its own beatitude; the others only have joy and bliss through it, in proportion to the degree of what they know, and consequently of what they are. For the First is the supreme Unity, transcendent to all the multiplicity linked with movement which it causes. God is therefore the cause of the existence of the motive Intelligence of the highest sphere, the sphere of the Fixed. That Intelligence itself is, in the proper sense, the mover of the whole universe and to it are subordinate the following Movers, in a hierarchical order upon which we have no definite data, but of which it can be assumed that it coincides with the order assigned to the spheres by astronomy. From God would emanate the mover of the heaven of the Fixed and the mover of Saturn's sphere; from the mover of Saturn's sphere would emanate the intellect of that planet, the mover of Jupiter's sphere, plus the four other movers necessary to cause its various movements, and so on up to the Moon's sphere, whose own Mover brings into all being the agent Intelligence, the unique cause of intellectual knowledge for all mankind.[22]

In the center of that universe are the four elements, caused by the most rapid movement, which is that of the sphere of the Fixed. Physics explains how the qualities of these elements and the movement of the celestial spheres bring to life plants and other living beings. The forms of these beings are given them by the agent Intelligence (or agent Intellect), the source of order for prime matter, itself devoid of all form. It will perhaps be asked why these forms should exist in matter, since they already exist in the agent Intelligence. They are in God, no doubt, and there they are even in a more noble state than in matter; yet, inferior though it may be, the existence of these forms in matter is a second mode of existence added to the first mode, and which is better than nothing.

Such is the place of man, whose soul is one of these forms, and whom the awareness of his own insufficiency turns toward his cause, which he strives to join through knowledge and desire. This union is certainly possible in a universe, where the agent Intelligence is the same for all mankind. It produces intelligible knowledge in individual souls as the sun produces seeing in the eyes through its light. Averroes agrees with Avicenna on this point, but he goes beyond him in another. Avicenna attributed at least a possible intellect to each individual, a solid kernel of personality capable of surviving death: Averroes grants to individuals a passive intellect (*intellectus passivus*), a simple "disposition" to receive the intelligible forms which come to it from the separate Intellect. This "passive intellect" is "imagination." Entirely corporeal, imagination perishes with the body. In order to cause cognition in man, the agent Intellect must illumine this passive intellect (or imagination); the contact of these two intellects gives rise to a third one, the material intellect (*intellectus materialis*). This name is misleading concerning the nature of the thing in question, for the "material" intellect is in no way corporeal; it is pure intellectual potentiality. The scholastics have made no mistake on this point. They all say that, according to Averroes, not only the agent Intellect, but even the "possible intellect" is one for all mankind. Nevertheless, this second formula could be misleading in its turn by making it seem that Averroes makes of the possible intellect a second separate substance distinct from the agent Intellect. This would not be exact. Averroes teaches that the contact of the separate agent Intellect with the passive intellect (disposition) of the individual engenders a receptivity with regard to the intelligible. This receptivity is only the agent Intellect particularizing itself in a soul as the light of the sun in a visible body. This is the reason why this possible intellect is truly separate; it belongs no more to the individual than the light which illumines it belongs to the body. Man's immortality, then, cannot be the immortality of an intelligible substance capable of surviving the death of the body. All that is eternal or capable of perpetuation in the individual belongs to the agent Intellect by full right and is immortal only by its immortality.[23]

The Latin philosophers of the middle ages will react differently to this complex doctrine. Up to the end of the thirteenth century, some theologians, like Albert the Great himself, will feel particularly interested in the description it gives of the process of abstractive knowledge: sensible things, sensations, presence of sensible species in a power of the soul, purification of these species by an agent intellect, reception of the thus-purified form in a possible intellect, and, consequently, actual cognition. The fact that Averroes had posited the agent Intellect as a separate substance was irrelevant to the problem; since, according to Augustine, God is illuminating the human mind in all its true cognitions, it was easy to ascribe an *intellectus agens* to each human soul and to add to it the light of a separate illuminating substance, which is God. In the beginning, some scholastics, for instance William of Auvergne, will read Averroes himself as if he had already held this position. Later on, others will realize the true meaning of his doctrine, but, like Albert the Great up to the end of his life, they will maintain that the description of abstraction given by Averroes was a substantially correct one, with the sole difference that the whole process takes place within the human soul and that, over and above the individual agent intellect of each man, philosophy should posit a higher active and separate Intellect; namely, God.

CHAPTER II

JEWISH PHILOSOPHY

THE starting point of philosophical speculation among the Arabs or, at least, in the Arabic speaking world, was Greek philosophy. The Moslem faith in the Koranic revelation was certainly not without an influence on philosophical thought, yet, on the whole, a history of Moslem theology would rather appear as that of a conflict between philosophers and theologians. Hence the curious fact that Moslem philosophers have exercised a much deeper influence on Christian theology than Moslem theologians. For deep-seated religious reasons, there has been a sort of continuity from Avicenna and Averroes to the scholastic theologians, not from the As'harites or Gazali to Christian speculation. On the contrary, the starting point of Jewish speculation was an essentially religious one, namely, the Old Testament, together with the commentaries accumulated in the rabbinic collections, especially the *Talmud*. This is the reason why Christian theologians will always feel a kind of affinity with their Jewish predecessors, especially on such fundamental points as the oneness of God, his absolute freedom and the notion of creation.[24]

Only a small portion of the Jewish philosophical and theological literature became known to the scholastics, and this is the only one with which we shall deal. It was not always the more original part of this literature. For instance, such a man as Saadia Gaon, who did pioneering work in practically all fields, plays no part in our own history,[25] whereas we must at least mention a second-rate writer, namely Isaac Israeli,[26] because the Latins have known, used and quoted time and again his modest *Book of Definitions,* which does not even represent the more valuable aspect of his own speculative activity.

I. SOLOMON IBN GABIROL

Such is not the case with Solomon Ibn Gabirol (*ca.* 1021-1058), a Spanish Jew, whose important philosophical treatise, *The Source of Life,* was known to the scholastics in a Latin translation probably made by John of Spain and Dominic Gundisalvi. His Latin names are many; for instance, Avencebrol, Avicembron or Avicebron. Some among the scholastics have mistaken him for a Christian writer and, therefore, quoted him as a Christian authority.[27] This is one more evidence of a religious affinity between Jewish and Christian thinkers due to their common acceptance of the same revelation. The Moslems did not reject the Old Testament, but Jews and Christians alike rejected the Koran.

The *Source of Life* is a long dialogue divided into five Books, full of dialectical demonstrations, of which Gabirol does not hesitate to accumulate, in some cases, up to more than sixty to establish one and the same point. This heaping up of dialectical proofs will become one of the most common features of scholastic demonstration. Despite its neoplatonic garb, the doctrine is imbued with the Jewish spirit, and it was through this, that it later fascinated so many Christian thinkers.[28]

This philosophical dialogue begins by establishing a thesis whose influence was to be profound and durable, especially among the Franciscan

thinkers of the thirteenth century. With the exception of God, all substances, even those that are called simple substances, are composed of
matter and form. If it is agreed to call "hylomorphic" any composition
of this kind, it may be said that Gabirol's "hylomorphism" became, for
a number of Christian theologians, the surest recipe for radically distinguishing creatures from the creator. According to this doctrine, just
as corporeal substances are composed of a corporeal matter and a form,
so spiritual substances, said to be simple because they have no body,
are also composed of a spiritual matter and a form. This spiritual matter is, in them, the principle of their individuation and of the change
to which, unlike God, all creatures are subject. There is, then, a universal
entity (*essentia*) composed of the universal form and of universal primary
matter, which exists of itself only in potency, but exists in act by the
various forms in which it is clothed.[29] Thus, the matter of all bodies exists
as such by the form "corporeity," which actualizes it and which it bears.[30]
What distinguishes one particular body from another particular body is
one or more complementary forms, in virtue of which it is determined as
simple mineral, as plant, animal or man. There is, then, in every composed
being, a "plurality of forms" (as it was later to be called), all created beings interlocking, so to speak, according to the degree of generality of the
forms which determine them.[31] Nine principal degrees can be distinguished
in that order according to which beings subsist in one another. First, all
reside and subsist in the knowledge of God; second, universal form in
universal matter; third, simple substances in one another; fourth, simple
accidents in simple substances; fifth, quantity in substance; sixth, surfaces
in solids, lines in surfaces and points in lines; seventh, colors and figures in
surfaces; eighth, parts of homogeneous bodies in one another; ninth, all
bodies in one another, and that is their common mode of existence known
by the name of their place.[32]

One cannot fail to recognize the Plotinian nature of a universe in which
all beings are what they are in virtue of forms overlapping one another
and in which each being participates; yet, from another aspect no less
important, Gabirol's cosmology appears profoundly Jewish, and that, as
one might expect, at the moment when it becomes a cosmogony.[33] Instead
of directly flowing out of a supreme Thought by way of dialectical development, Gabirol's world, with all its structure of forms dovetailing one
another, flows from the Prime Maker through a will. As long as he is
describing the *what* of things, Gabirol can remain faithful to Greek tradition; when he starts to posit their *why,* biblical tradition becomes upper-
most in his thought, and it is the God of Genesis, plus perhaps the god of
the *Timaeus,* who becomes the sole acceptable principle of explanation.
There are three principles of being: matter and form, the Prime Entity,
and the Will, which is their mediator. It is difficult to state precisely
whether this Will is identical with God, of whom it would be only the

outer manifestation, or whether it should be considered a hypostasis, that is, a spiritual substance itself emanated from God. Gabirol does not claim that this principle is entirely intelligible. On the contrary, it suggests a great mystery, namely, that all beings are held by the Will and dependent upon it, because, by it, each of the forms of beings is drawn in matter and imprinted there. In fact, it is the Will which holds them and fixes them to the limits and extremities where they stop, and it is by the Will that forms are regularly disposed and legalized, while being dependent to it and held by it.[34]

It is easy to see why such a doctrine should appeal to so many Christian thinkers. It described a philosophically intelligible world, suspended to a supreme Will analogous to the will of the God of Scripture, in short, a neoplatonic universe which would have been willed by Yahweh.[35] In a world of this kind, where beings are more intelligible and intelligent the more incorporeal and simple they are, man occupies an intermediate position from which, thanks to his intellect, he can climb back, from form to form, up to the very creative Will. Sensible forms have nothing more to do, to lead thought in it, than to awaken in the human soul the intelligible forms with which it is pregnant and which only await that stirring in order to develop. Sensible forms are to the soul what the written book is to the reader. This formula, which we shall find brilliantly commented on by William of Auvergne, Saint Bonaventure and Ramon Lull, was to develop all its consequences in the *Liber creaturarum* by Ramon Sibiude which Montaigne has translated. Gabirol therefore put into circulation a cosmogony, a cosmology and a noetic whose influence on Christian thought was to be considerable, more especially as, by all the Platonism it implied, it lent itself to many possible combinations with the influences of Denis and of Saint Augustine. For this reason, although it can be rightly maintained that the true origin of the scholastic doctrine of the plurality of forms is found in Gabirol's work, it will become part and parcel of the Augustinian complex.

Jewish speculation still numbered several representatives in the twelfth century who would be worth studying for themselves alone, but who exerted no direct influence on Christian scholasticism. It should, however, be noted that a whole series of proofs of the existence of God is worked out in their writings. Ibn Pakuda (about 1080) proves this thesis starting from the fact that the world is compound; Ibn Caddiq, of Cordova (1080-1149), proves in his *Microcosm* the existence of God by the contingence of the world. Ibn Daoud, of Toledo, whom we shall meet later on, demonstrates it by dwelling successively on the necessity of a primary mover and the distinction between the possible and the necessary. Against all this movement which tends toward a rational interpretation of religious tradition, a theological and nationalist reaction was to be expected. Juda Hallevi (born in 1085) was its promoter. His famous book, *Kozari*, advocates a theology that will be purely Jewish and as little philosophical as possible. He does not believe in the God of the scholars and philosophers, but in the God of Abraham, Isaac and Jacob, who delivered the children of Israel out of Egypt and gave them the land of Canaan. This reactionary attempt is often compared to Al Gazali's among the Arabs, but Hallevi is, in addition to being a theologian, a magnificent figure of a nationalist and an exalted traditionalist. Not content to extol Israel, he wished to die in the land of his fathers, left Spain, was forced by contrary winds to land in Egypt, left Cairo in spite of his compatriots' efforts to hold him, and started on his way to Damietta, Tyr and Damascus. Here we lose trace of him, and legend has it that he died, killed by an Arab, at the very gates of Jerusalem, singing his hymn to Zion.[36] This reaction, however, was neither to stop nor even to slow up the development of Jewish philosophy; on the contrary, it attained its culminating point as early as the twelfth century, in the work of Moses Maïmonides.

2. MOSES MAÍMONIDES

Moses ben Maimon, born the 30th of March, 1135, at Cordova, died December 13, 1204. He owes his philosophical fame to his *Guide for the Perplexed*. This book does not deal primarily with metaphysics, but with Jewish theology. The work is addressed to minds already trained in philosophy and the sciences, but uncertain and undecided as to how to reconcile the conclusions of the sciences and philosophy with the literal meaning of the Scriptures. Hence its title of *Guide for the Perplexed*, and not the "misguided," as it has sometimes been translated.[37] Its inspiration, like the inspiration of the Arabian philosophers in whose footsteps Maïmonides followed, is both neoplatonic and Aristotelian, but accentuating a movement already outlined in Ibn Daoud, he firmly puts Aristotle in the first rank. This accounts for the undeniable influence he exerted on the Christian philosophers of the following century, and especially on Saint Thomas Aquinas. If Maïmonides had not taught a doctrine of the soul that was strongly influenced by Averroes and which led him to a very special conception of immortality, it could have been said that their philosophies were in harmony with one another on all the really important points.

According to the Jewish doctor, the science of the divine Law and philosophy are forms of knowledge of a distinct nature, and the nature of metaphysics must be respected by those who expect from it a rational confirmation of religious faith.[38] Only thus will philosophical speculation show that the Aristotelian proofs in favor of the eternity of the world are not conclusive; that the creation of the world is not impossible from the point of view of reason and that consequently, in the absence of a decisive proof in one direction or the other, it is permissible to accept the Mosaïc doctrine of creation in time. In opposition to Ibn Gabirol Maïmonides admits that pure Intelligences are free from matter, and that there is a matter in celestial bodies different from that in terrestrial bodies. The existence of the Intelligences is established, the nine superior ones presiding over the nine spheres, and the tenth being the agent Intellect, which exerts its influence directly upon all men. Below the last sphere is the sublunary world, the place of the four elements, subject to the action of the superior spheres. Composed of a body and a soul which is its form, man is endowed with five faculties: nutritive, sensitive, imaginative, appetitive and intellective. Personally, he possesses as his own only the passive intellect, and under the influence of the agent Intellect (tenth Intelligence emanated from that of the lunar sphere), an acquired intellect is constituted in him.[39] Each man thus acquires a sort of intellectual capital, varying according to the degree of his merit, and which is reunited to the agent Intellect after death. It rests with each one of us, therefore, to save as much as possible of himself by enriching his intellect through the practice of philosophy. Spinoza, who knew Maïmonides, was to remember, in his *Ethics,* Book V, prop. 23, that doctrine of immortality.

We have said that the world was not eternal, but created by God in time; but we added, on the other hand, that this thesis was not demonstrable; one could not then depend upon it to establish the existence of God, and this truth remains to be proved as though the world had existed from all eternity. Maïmonides proves the existence of a primary mover, the existence of a necessary being, and the existence of a primary cause.[40] The existence of God is therefore established whether the world was created *ex nihilo* in time, or whether it existed from all eternity.[41] That is exactly the attitude Saint Thomas was to adopt with regard to the same problem. Maïmonides, on the contrary, absolutely refuses any essential attributes of God except negative ones. We know that God is, we do not know what he is, and our only resource, if we wish to speak of him, is to accumulate negative attributes. To deny any imperfection concerning God, at least makes us know what his is not. In that doctrine is found the Jewish desire to safeguard the strict and total unity of God.[42] If the essence of God eludes us, the effects of his action in the world are, on the contrary, manifest to all eyes. God is evidently the final cause of the world, as he is its efficient cause. His providence extends over the whole of things as well as to the slightest details, and what evil there can possibly be in the world is explained either by the limitation inherent in the state of the creature, or by the disorders of the creature itself which is often the author of its own evils.[43]

Despite Maïmonides's penetration and even profundity of thought, the *Guide for the Perplexed* does not resemble the Christian theologies of the following century. It does not have their systematic order. In fact, Maïmonides never considered his work as a systematic exposition. Nevertheless, his influence on the Christian thought of the middle ages has been considerable. A Jewish theologian, Maīmonides shared with the Christian theologians their faith in the Old Testament; he therefore had to solve before they did the problem of making it harmonize with true philosophy, and they profited by his example, even when they did not follow him. What many of them retained of his teaching was the fact that, on a number of points, philosophy alone is incapable of attaining the truths contained in revelation. This might well be the most important lesson they learned from him. The criticism directed by Maīmonides against the "kalam," that is, Moslem theology as he knew it, rested on his conviction that theologians have no right to call "philosophical" pseudo-rational arguments whose sole merit it is to agree with the teaching of religious faith. In this respect, Maīmonides has been both an inspiration and a model to Thomas Aquinas.[44]

If we compare the Jewish twelfth century with the Christian, we shall immediately perceive what superiority Jewish thought owed to its close intercourse with Arabian philosophy. In Avicenna, and especially in Averroes, the Jewish philosophers found a whole technical equipment of concepts borrowed from the Greeks, which it only remained for them to utilize. What would have come of it had the powerful mind of an Abélard found itself, through the play of circumstance, the heir to the treasures accumulated by Greek speculation? But Abélard had to use all his lucidity and penetration to reconstruct, from incomplete documents, a substitute for the Aristotelian theory of abstraction. On the one hand, all philosophy already given; or, the other hand, a dialectic turned into an incomplete or uncertain metaphysics. We now are approaching the time when Christian scholasticism is in turn to find itself confronted with those riches hitherto unknown to it. Will it have enough vitality to assimilate them, or will it, on the contrary, unable to dam their flood, allow itself to be swamped by them? Such is the significance of the truly dramatic movement and conflict of ideas which developed at the heart of Christian thought during the first half of the thirteenth century, and whose historical importance is such that even today we continue to feel its repercussions.

PART SIX

EARLY SCHOLASTICISM

CHAPTER I

GRECO-ARABIAN INFLUENCES

THE development of Western theological speculation was decisively influenced by the discovery of Arabian philosophy and of the philosophy of Aristotle. Literary history has made substantial progress in the knowledge of the transmission of Arabic and Greek philosophical literature to the Latin world. The history of philosophy can only take stock of the provisory conclusions proposed by specialists on these questions.

The Spanish city of Toledo was one of the most important centers of diffusion of Greco-Arabian philosophy in the twelfth century. The catalan Ramon of Sauvetât, bishop of Toledo (1126-1151), promoted the translation into Latin of works of Aristotle, Alfarabi, Avicenna, Gazali and Gabirol. Despite the progress made by historical research, some confusion still reigns concerning the names of the translators. An author of personal works, Domingo Gonzalez is usually called, in scholastic writings, Dominicus Gundissalinus. His own personality is clearly distinguishable, but some hesitation remains concerning the identities of two other translators: John of Spain (Johannes Hispanus), and Avendehut, or Avendehat, that is Ibn Daoud, or the son of David. It seems, however, that these were two distinct writers and that there never was any author named Johannes Hispanus-Ibn Daoud.

Another scholar, Gerard of Cremona (d. 1187), translated from Arabic into Latin several works of Aristotle: the *Posterior Analytics* with the commentary by Themistius; the *De naturali auditu* (physics), the *De coelo et mundo* (cosmology), the *De generatione et corruptione* (biology), and the *Meteors* (Bk. I-III). Moreover, Gerard translated several treatises by Alexander of Aphrodisias: *De tempore* (On time), *De sensu* (On sensations), *De intellectu* (On the Intellect). One of his most influential translations (if it is his) was that of the *Book of Causes* (*Liber de causis,* or *Liber bonitatis purae*), a compilation of extracts from the *Elements of Theology* of Proclus. Alfred of Sareshel (Alfredus Anglicus) and his compatriot Daniel of Morley contributed to the spread of this new learning. The number of properly scientific writings translated from Arabic into Latin was considerable, especially in the fields of astronomy and optics. Let us add that, outside of Toledo, the work of translating Aristotle directly from the Greek original into Latin began as early as the twelfth century. Henricus Aristippus was one of those who initiated this vast undertaking.

The translations whose influence was immediately felt were those of original philosophical works of Arabic or Jewish origin. Johannes Hispanus is credited with the translation of Avicenna's *Logic;* Dominicus Gundissalinus, helped in his work by Johannes Hispanus (John of Spain) and the Jew Solomon, translated the *Physics* of Avicenna (*Sufficientia*), his *Cosmology* (*De coelo et mundo*), his treatise *On the Soul* (*Liber sextus naturalium*), and his *Metaphysics*. To the same translators, we owe the *Logic, Physics* and *Metaphysics* of Algazel (Gazali), as well as the *Source of Life* (*Fons vitae*) of Avencebrol (Ibn Gabirol). John of Spain also translated a treatise *On the Difference of the Spirit and of the Soul* (*De differentia spiritus et animae*), attributed by its mediaeval readers to the Syrian Costa ben Luca (Constabulinus). Gerard of Cremona translated several treatises by Alkindi (*On the Intellect* and *On the Five Essences*), and perhaps Alfarabi's *De intellectu* (*On the Intellect*).

The thirty-two propositions which form the *Liber de Causis* have exercised a twofold influence on the following centuries. From the point of view of literary form, they have favored the development of the aphoristic style of which Boethius and Alan of Lille had already given striking examples. Every time a philosophical or theological opuscule consists of concise aphoristic statements, often alliterative, and attended or not by a short commentary, the influence of the *Book of Causes* can be at least suspected. From the point of view of the doctrine itself, this treatise has largely contributed to reinforce the influence of Gabirol on at least two points: hylomorphism and the plurality of forms.

The universe is a series of causes and effects. The Prime Cause is the cause of all the other causes and, consequently, of all their effects. Since its energy contains all the rest, it is more truly the cause of any effect than the proximate cause of that effect itself is. Its energy is constant and it is unaffected by the presence or absence of its effects. If rationality be removed from man, life remains; if life be removed, being remains. The Prime Cause is the cause of being, which is the cause of life, which is the cause of rationality; so its causal energy is more intensely at work in man than that of life, and more intensely in life than that of being. In short, the remote cause is always more intensely the cause of a thing than the proximate cause of that thing (pr. 1).

The first created thing is being (*prima rerum creatarum est esse*, pr. 2). It is the simplest of all things, being only composed of finite and infinite. This being is an Intelligence, full of an infinity of intelligible forms, whence an infinity of individuals follow. These forms can be diversified without being separated. The Intelligences that flow from the first one receive from it intelligible forms and transmit them to the inferior Intelligences. Some of these forms join matter and become souls (pr. 4). Intelligences are causes from the very fact that they are Intelligences; all things are intelligible in an Intelligence, even corporeal things, because this Intelligence is the cause of their being (pr. 7).

The Prime Cause is neither an Intelligence, nor a soul, nor a nature; it is above these because it creates them; but it creates the prime Intelligence without any intermediary, whereas it creates souls, natures and the other things through this Intelligence. Since it is created, this Intelligence itself has both matter and form; this soul too has matter and form, and so also has nature. The Prime Cause alone has no matter, because it is being only (pr. 8). It rules creatures without mixing up with them (pr. 19).

All Intelligence is full of forms; higher Intelligences contain more universal forms, lower ones contain less universal forms. The more universal the forms, the more united they are (pr. 9). All Intelligence understands its own essence and its own being (pr. 12). It achieves self-knowledge in completely returning upon itself (pr. 13).

The Prime Cause exists in all things, but things receive the Prime Cause according to their own capacities. The different ways in which its efficacy is received do not arise from the Prime Cause, but, rather, from the receivers of its efficacy (pr. 23). Composite substances are incorruptible (pr. 26; cf. pr. 27). Simple substances stand in virtue of their own essences; they do not endure in time and are more noble than temporal substances (pr. 28). Between eternal substances and temporal substances, there are intermediate ones which are eternal by their substance and temporal by their operations (pr. 30). These intermediate substances are both being (by their substance) and becoming (by their operations). Whatever they are, all substances only have unity on account of their cause, which is the only true One (pr. 31). After that of the One, every unity is created and acquired from it as from a Cause which grants unity without having to acquire it.[1]

The first Western philosopher to undergo the influence of the Toledan translations was one of the translators, Dominicus Gundissalinus. His name has been obscured by those of the great scholastics of the thirteenth century, and it must be conceded that he has largely drawn from his own translations in writing his own works; yet, when all is said and done, we cannot read them today without realizing at once that Gundissalinus has initiated the new style of philosophical speculation, and therefore of theological argumentation, which was to blossom in the following century. His treatise *On the Division of Philosophy*[2] adds to the *quadrivium* of the early middle ages the newly discovered sciences of physics, psychology, metaphysics, politics and economics which he himself had found in the works of Avicenna. This revelation came to Western theologians as the discovery of a new mental universe. Still more important is the treatise of Gundissalinus *On the Origin of the World* (*De processione mundi*), in which he describes the creation of the universe as a man who himself has translated the *Metaphysics* of Avicenna and the *Fons vitae* of Ibn Gabirol.[3] This short treatise is full of philosophical themes which will become part and parcel of scholasticism: technical proofs of the existence of God as a Prime Mover and a necessary being; the technical definition of the notion of creation, etc. He also borrowed from Avicenna for his treatise *On the Immortality of the Soul*,[4] which William of Auvergne was soon to put to good use. His still shorter tractate *On Unity*,[5] so full of Boethius that it was attributed to him, blends the Platonism of this Latin writer with those of the school of Chartres, and of Gabirol's *Source of Life*. This booklet is full of striking formulas: *unitas est qua quaeque res una est, et est id quod est* (unity is that by which every thing is one, and is what it is); again: *quidquid est ideo est quia unum est* (all that which is, is, because it is one); and again: *omne esse ex forma est* (all being comes from form). All these principles were common to all the Platonisms, Christian or otherwise, which were to seize upon the scientific world of Aristotle, to take possession of it and reorganize it from within.

The word "complex" has been aptly suggested to describe such doctrinal positions. A doctrinal complex is a more or less organic whole, made up of interrelated theses which are frequently found united despite the diversity of their respective origins. For instance, the Greek notion of entity (*ousia*), is common to practically all theologians before the time of Thomas Aquinas; it comes to them from Plato and Plotinus through Saint Augustine, but it often expresses itself in the language of Boethius (*quod est* and *quo est*), and, after Denis the Areopagite, it sometimes blends with the metaphysics of the One. Still later on, the brand of Platonism proper to Avicenna will add a new feeder to the common Platonic stream. The treatise of Gundissalinus *On Unity* is such a syncretic combination of elements united together by their common neoplatonist inspiration.

What the Latins needed more than anything else was a cosmology, that is, a scientific and metaphysical description of the structure of the universe. All they had at their disposal, before reading Avicenna, was a partial knowledge of the *Timaeus*. True enough, the *Celestial Hierarchy* of Denis presupposed a complete doctrine of the emanation of beings from the One, only its mediaeval readers could not guess it. As soon as they began to read Avicenna, what the Latins retained first was his metaphysical cosmology. All the Platonism diffused through the twelfth century found in it a system of the universe which gave its view a scientific consistency. There is no known instance of a Christian writer accepting the doctrine of Avicenna wholesale and as an absolute philosophical truth. In other words, there does not seem to have been a Latin Avicennism as there is going to be a Latin Averroism in the second half of the thirteenth century, and still more evidently later on. Many Christians have followed Avicenna as far as they could get along with him, but when it came to positing a separate Intelligence as the cause and the ultimate end of man, they had to part company. The Christians owed it to their faith either to push beyond this separate Intelligence to go as far as God, or else to identify it with God. They tried both.

The treatise of Dominicus Gundissalinus *On the Soul* (*De anima*) is an interesting example of this curious syncretism.[6] It is a compilation of texts borrowed literally from the Latin translation of Avicenna's psychology (*Liber sextus naturalium*). This summary of Avicennian psychology faithfully follows its model, not however without introducing notions borrowed from other sources, like the treatise *On the Difference between Soul and Spirit,* attributed to Costa ben Luca (*Constabulinus*). The Avicennian demonstration of the immortality of the soul suits Gundissalinus perfectly; he accepts without protest the existence of the separate Intelligence which is the sun of human souls, but, once having reached this point, he has to burst the roof of the Avicennian universe in order to join the Christian God. To achieve this result, Gundissalinus borrows from Chalcidius and from Boethius the psychological notion of human "intelligence" (*intelligentia*), a mystical power of knowledge similar to the one that carried Saint Paul up to the third heaven. And this is a Christian notion. The very structure of his *De anima* reveals the nature of the problem. One can edit its text, from beginning almost to end, noting page after page the Arabian sources its compiler has plagiarized, but the system breaks down in the last chapter. Since he was a Christian, the author had to write this chapter himself, and he did so with the help of Chalcidius, Boethius and Isaac Stella, all of them Christian writers. The treatise of Gundissalinus thus exemplifies a doctrinal "complex," in which the natural tendency of all Platonisms to blend together makes it possible for Avicenna's psychology to be crowned with the Christian rapture of Saint Paul. Its dual definition of the soul, conceived as being in itself a substance, but a form with respect to its body; its description of the various degrees of perfection of the human intellect; its final decision to substitute the Christian God of the *Soliloquies* for the separate Intelligence of Avicenna; all these features of the synthesis attempted by Gundissalinus will reappear in Roger Bacon, in Albert the Great, and under an even cruder form in the *Scientia de anima* of Peter of Spain, the future Pope John XXI. Whether they drew it from Gundissalinus himself, or directly from Avicenna whose treatise he had translated for them, Gundissalinus remains their predecessor.

Another work of similar nature is the curious *Book of Avicenna on Primary and Secondary Substances (Liber Avicennae in primis et secundis substantiis)*, or, more briefly, *De fluxu entis.* The work is certainly not Avicenna's, for, although the author of this compilation has made use of the Arabian philosopher, shreds of Avicenna are roughly sewn to shreds he has torn from Saint Augustine, Denis the Areopagite, Gregory of Nyssa and Scotus Erigena. The unknown compiler borrows from Erigena the doctrines of the theophanies, of the relative coeternity of divine Ideas, of their creation by God, of God's creation of himself in the Ideas, and of the reduction of a body to its incorporeal elements.[7] As to Avicenna, the author of the *De fluxu entis* borrows from him the main point in his cosmogony, that is to say, the system of emanation of separate Intelligences, with the soul and body of the celestial sphere which result from each of them, going from the Primary Cause to the sublunary world and human souls. This compilation has been attributed to Gundissalinus; it may, as a matter of fact, be poor Gundissalinus. Must we speak of a "Latin Avicennism" in regard to this work? To the extent that the formula signifies that the *De fluxu entis* strongly undergoes the influence of Avicenna, it is valid; but it may become misleading, in that it suggests that its author accepted purely and simply the doctrine of Avicenna as "Latin Averroism" was to accept the doctrine of Averroes. The compiler follows Avicenna here only because, for him, what Avicenna says completes what Christians like Erigena, Denis and Saint Augustine had already said. As in Gundissalinus, the God enlightener of Augustine's *Soliloquies* is here identified with Avicenna's agent Intelligence, whose intelligible forms come to us from without, *extrinsecus;* but one could just as well say that the opposite is true. We shall often meet, in the thirteenth century, that same subordination of Avicenna's noetic to the Augustinian doctrine of the divine illumination.

Christian thought then first bent under the Arabian thrust; submerged in this philosophical context, the biblical notion of creation disappears under the luxuriant metaphysics of the emanation of the world. It is hard to say to what extent the same influences were responsible for other doctrines, this time distinctly aberrant, which were then elaborated in Christian circles. Perhaps we should only see in these doctrines an expression of possibilities, for a long time latent, which were then made explicit by a resolute application of the methods of dialectics to the new cosmological problems. We know these doctrines only by rather short fragments, or even, as is the case with the doctrine of Amaury of Bène[8], by condemned propositions which were extracted from it and by their refutations. Their internal structure remains unknown and it is therefore impossible for us to see them under their authentic aspect, but they are so characteristic of their time that we cannot afford to ignore them.

Amaury of Bène (diocese of Chartres), a professor of logic and theology at Paris (d. 1206 or 1207), was accused during his lifetime of teaching dangerous theses, but the first official condemnation of his doctrine that we know of took place in 1210. There existed at that time a group of "Amauricians" (*amauriciani*) whose doctrines were the object of ecclesiastical censure. According to a gloss by Henry of Suse (*Ostiensis*), Amaury had taught that God was all things (*dixit quod Deus erat omnia*). This formula was far from being a new one. If it was taken to mean, as Saint Bernard meant it, "causal being," nothing could be better; but if it was taken in the sense that the being of God is essentially the same as the being of things, it was out-and-out pantheism. We do not know how Amaury understood it, but we know that he was accused of meaning it as Erigena did, who was accused of taking it in the second sense. In fact, the arguments attributed to him greatly resemble many of those of the "dialecticians" of the twelfth century, arguing syllogistically on the basis of dogmas and marveling at the consequences they thus arrived at. Saint Paul said: *et erit Deus omnia in omnibus;* let us argue: God is immutable, therefore he is already what he will be; therefore he is already all that which is. Saint John said of God: *quod factum est in ipso vita erat;* let us argue: all that which is in God is God, now all that God made, is life in him; therefore God is all that lives. Combining in turn this conclusion with the theme *de unitate,* an Amaurician called Bernard argued thus: all is one, since all that which is, is God; consequently, insofar as I am, I cannot be burned, nor executed, since, insofar as I am, I am God. It is very difficult for us to discern the real thought of Amaury behind the theses of such disciples, and even behind those attributed to him. Was it a question of metaphysico-dialectical paradoxes and verbal extravagances, that he could not have admitted without at the same time admitting something of their meaning; or must we think that Amaury really identified God and creature? We simply do not know. The fact that he seems to have taken up the Erigenian doctrine of theophanies and denied the possibility of the beatific vision, would not even prove anything against the pantheism of which they accuse him, for we do not know how he interpreted Erigena, and there are reasons why we should be on our guard, when we see how he interpreted Saint John and Saint Paul. The only sure facts are that his formulas were condemned as false, and that they were dangerous to handle at a time when, taken up by the Catharians or the Albigenses, they ran the risk of reaching the crowd. It is in any case interesting to note that, in his *Chronicle,* Alberic of Trois-Fontaines tried once more, in 1225, to clear Erigena of all responsibility in those events: "He incurred condemnation because of the new Albigenses and false theologians who, misunderstanding formulas, perhaps pronounced formerly in a good sense and understood in the same sense by the Ancients, perverted them and made use of them to confirm their own heresies." Erigena was perhaps blameworthy on his own account, but it is certainly because of other doctrines than his that he was condemned in 1210.

Similar problems arise concerning David of Dinant,[9] the author of a treatise *On the Divisions* (*De tomis, id est de divisionibus*) perhaps identical with the *Quaternuli* condemned in 1210. The work is now lost, except for a fragment equivalent to about fifteen pages which recently came to light, and important quotations or analyses contained in the works of Albert the Great, Thomas Aquinas and Nicholas of Cues. As the title of his treatise suggests, David's doctrine, like Erigena's, consisted in "dividing" reality. It divided it into three indivisibles: body, soul and separate substances. The first indivisible, of which the body is constituted, he called *hyle* (matter); the first indivisible of which the soul is constituted, he called *Nous,* or Thought (*mentem*); as to the first indivisible in eternal substances, he called it God. But, explains Saint Thomas, to whom we are indebted for this information, David added that these three indivisibles are one and the same thing, from which there follows the conclusion that all is essentially one (*Et haec tria esse unum et idem: ex quo iterum consequitur esse omnia per essentiam unum, In II Sent.,* 17, 1, 1). Saint Thomas' text is not a quotation; we therefore do not know for a certainty whether this last conclusion was deduced by David himself, but it is not impossible.

The notions of "divisions" of reality, *hyle* and *Nous,* are old acquaintances of ours. They can enter into the formation of the same "complex" with that other principle that everything which is, is one inasmuch as it is. What there was new in David's doctrine consisted rather in this: instead of unifying everything through the divine being, he seems to unify everything, including God himself, through being. This master brought the habits of a logician over into metaphysics. The point of departure of his argumentation seems to have been the fact that our intellect is capable of conceiving both God and matter. Now, to conceive a thing is to assimilate it. Ordinarily, the intellect assimilates objects by abstracting their forms, but since neither God nor primary matter has forms, our intellect cannot grasp them in that way. It must, then, grasp them because it itself is identical with them. Thus God, intellect and matter are one and the same thing. Now, matter alone can be the reality common to these three terms. David's argumentation to this effect rests on the principle that neither God nor matter has form. For indeed, beings determined by forms are substances, which fall under the categories. In order to grasp beings which, like God and matter, escape categories, it is necessary to attain what is anterior to being actuated by form; but then one meets nothing but being in potency, and since being in potency is indeterminate by definition, it is one. Now pure potentiality and matter are identical: therefore God and matter are identical. Of course, David does not mean by this that everything is *body:* a body is made up of matter determined by form; but he does mean to say that if one goes beyond body to rejoin its principle, one finds a pure potentiality, matter, which eludes all the categories, and that, if one wishes to grasp divine nature, it must also be posited as anterior to all the categories, therefore as a pure potentiality, that is, again as matter. Consequently God and matter are identical. Nothing was easier than to arrive at this conclusion by arguing logically on the "God non-being" of Denis and Erigena. God is non-being, matter is non-being, therefore God is matter or matter is God. The fragments we have at our disposal do not show definitely that this was the road David followed; besides he may have taken his inspiration from sources we know nothing about. Albert the Great says that his doctrine goes back to the doctrine of Xenophanes, as Alexander of Aphrodisias makes it known in a treatise entitled *De Noi, hoc est de mente, et Deo et materia prima (On the Nous, that is on the Mind, on God and on Prime Matter).* A promising title, indeed, and one that Albert probably did not invent, but no work bearing that title is known, and the exactitude of this information cannot be verified.

David of Dinant shows well how the former Latin Platonism gave way before Alexander of Aphrodisia's Aristotle and his doctrine of the human intellect as pure potentiality (*intellectus materialis*): neither in his case nor in the case of Amaury of Bène is there absolute proof of Arabian influences, but a curious work has been recently discovered,[10] in which the mixture of all these influences is complicated by a strictly religious element. In this anonymous treatise, which apparently dates from the end of the twelfth century and comes from a Spanish quarter, we follow the voyage of souls after death, those of the chosen rising progressively from perfection to perfection and from Intelligence to Intelligence right up to God; those of the condemned, on the contrary, descending by inverse degrees of misery, and going back over the series of spheres, in the wrong direction, until they come to their incarceration in the shades of Hell. Whatever the sources of this mythical tale may have been, some of the philosophical ideas inspiring it certainly came from the *Dream of Scipio,* and consequently from Macrobius, while others come from Gabirol's *Source of Life.* The author is certainly Christian, not only because his work abounds in Scriptural quotations, but also because he manifestly professes the dogma of the Holy Trinity. It may even be added that, because he was a Christian, he was interested in the notion of being. In one and the same sentence, he identifies the relation between creature and creator with the Avicennian relation of possible to necessary, and precisely at the same time, contrary to Avicenna, he says that God produces all the rest by himself and without intermediary—thus avoiding, almost a century ahead of time, one of the errors that Etienne Tempier was to condemn in 1277. For this God is not only pure Light, he is also the "absolutely necessary being, and all that comes after him has an admixture of possibility and of contingency, but he himself has none, and he produces everything by himself, without any intermediary whatsoever." Yet, this same Christian quietly writes, toward the end of his treatise, that the ten felicities and the ten general miseries he has just discussed, were known, as he is firmly convinced (*ut vehementer credo*), by the lawgivers illumined by God, such as Moses, Mohammed and Christ, who was greater than the two others: *"legumlatores justi, sapientissimi, alios salvare curantes, super quos cecidit lumen Dei et ejus cognitio et ejus verbum super linguas eorum, sicut Moyses et Mahometh et Christus qui fuit potentior his duobus et sermone virtuosior."* This marked preference for Christ does not prevent the sentence from sounding strange. Who may have written this? We do not know.

The inevitable conflict between Arabian philosophy and Christian theology took place about the beginning of the thirteenth century, in the University of Paris, which had just been established. In the year 1200, all the masters and students in the cathedral schools of Paris got together in a single body, recognized by King Philip Augustus and by Pope Innocent III, whose statutes the Pope's legate, Robert of Courson, sanctioned in 1215.[11] The University of Paris (*Universitas magistrorum et scholarium Parisiis studentium*), the most famous of the great mediaeval universities, was thus established. It was there that, from the first years of its activity, translations of the scientific treatises of Aristotle and his Arabian commentators made their first appearance, not, of course, in the world of scholars, but in the classrooms. The best proof that these treatises were immediately used by some Parisian masters of the Faculty of Arts is that, as early as 1210, their teaching was interdicted.

It is advisable first to consider separately and to explain for itself this attitude of ecclesiastical authority.[12] The plane on which it moves was less that of philosophical speculation than of theological prudence and rectitude. Faced with that mass of new conceptions, and in order to give itself time to discriminate, it began by prohibiting. As early as the year 1210, the provincial Council of Paris, under the presidency of Peter of Corbeil, archbishop of Sens, forbade under penalty of excommunication, the teaching in Paris, either publicly or privately, of Aristotle's writings on natural philosophy or their commentaries.[13] In the statutes of the University of Paris sanctioned by Robert of Courson in 1215, the study of Aristotle's logic, which had long been taught, was still authorized, but the *Metaphysics*, all the books on physics and natural science with whatever expositions that could be made of them, were forbidden, together with the doctrines of David of Dinant, Amaury of Bène and a certain Mauritius of Spain, whose identity had not yet been established. It is worthy of note that this text, and others of the same epoch, confounded Aristotle's cause with that of two suspicious philosophers, as though he shared with them the errors for which their doctrines had been condemned.[14]

While the teaching of Aristotle was still forbidden at Paris, it remained authorized, not only in England, but at Toulouse, and the masters in that city did not hesitate to avail themselves of that liberty and to advertise it.[15] But even in Paris, there was little hope of preventing masters, who were permitted to teach half of Aristotle's philosophy, from taking an active interest in the other half. How could the logic of Aristotle be separated from his psychology? Moreover, the physics of Aristotle and Avicenna provided the Parisian masters with principles so vastly superior to anything they had ever known that their discovery amounted to a revelation. In fact, the Latin world was then discovering the universe of Greek science. For the first time and at one fell swoop the men of the middle ages found themselves face to face with a purely philosophical explanation of nature. The fundamental principles of this explanation they found in many treatises on astronomy, physics and biology, all based upon a logic which mediaeval schools had already been teaching for centuries. How could the logic of Aristotle be right, and all its applications be wrong? Besides, if it was forbidden to teach error, it was not forbidden to oppose it, and in order to oppose it, it was necessary to know it. No wonder then that even masters as strict as William of Auvergne, for example, found it necessary to become acquainted with the newly discovered doctrines of Avicenna. Even while the books ceased to be taught, they continued to be read.

As early as April 13, 1231, Pope Gregory IX renewed the interdiction against teaching Aristotle in terms which reveal that an evolution had taken place in the interval. It was still forbidden to teach Aristotle's *Physics,* but only until it had been submitted to censorship and purged of its errors. Ten days later the pope appointed a sort of commission, of which William of Auvergne was a member, precisely to carry out this task of revision in order to make Aristotle's natural philosophy utilizable in teaching.[16] There is no evidence that the work of the theologians charged with this task brought about any positive results: only Thomas Aquinas was to achieve this task after 1260. From 1231 on, however, Aristotle's writings on physics and metaphysics permeated everywhere and did not cease to gain ground.[17] The translations made directly from the Greek text were brought to a successful issue by translators such as William of Moerbeke (1215-1286), who was to be a veritable collaborator for Saint Thomas; above all, so many masters were commenting, interpreting, assimilating the doctrine of the Greek philosopher, that in 1366 pontifical authority was to make it compulsory for the candidates for the degree in arts to have studied those very treatises of Aristotle's it had for so long a time forbidden.[18]

The influence of these pontifical interdictions has been twofold. In the Faculty of Arts of the University of Paris, it slowed down considerably the study of the philosophy of Aristotle up to about 1240. As has already been said, there is evidence that they never ceased to be privately read, but their interdiction prevented the works of Aristotle from being objects of public and continous teaching. The result of this situation is visible. The teaching of logic went on uninterruptedly from the last years of the twelfth century up to 1250, but there is no written evidence of any philosophical activity in the fields of natural science or of metaphysics, at the University of Paris, prior to about 1240. From that time on, there must have been some teaching in those fields, otherwise such works as the *Summa de anima* of John of la Rochelle (d. 1245) or the Commentary of Saint Bonaventure on the *Sentences* (*ca.* 1250) would have been impossible. After 1250 there will be warnings, but no more interdictions.

In the Faculty of Theology the influence of the pontifical interdictions was felt in a different way. Everything points to the fact that they fully achieved their true end. The very liberty granted to the Faculty of Arts between 1245 and 1277 is a sure sign that, in the Faculty of Theology, the spirit of these interdictions had been respected. Their import was that theology should be taught such as it had always been, without any admixture of worldly wisdom. In this, the desire of the theologians themselves wholly concurred with the injunctions of the popes. On July 27, 1228, Gregory IX had invited the masters to teach "theology in its purity." On April 13, 1231, the same pope had invited the same masters not to pretend to be philosophers. Concretely speaking, this meant that professors of theology should content themselves with teaching straight theology, and never handle problems that could not be settled by resorting to revelation or to the writings of the Fathers of the Church. The order was obeyed, and, as it seems, willingly. Even those among the masters who felt it necessary to assimilate as much as possible of the new learning carefully avoided letting it sway their theological teaching. Hence the general trend, still perceptible up to the end of the thirteenth century and beyond, to favor some philosophical doctrines which, because of their neoplatonic inspiration, could be more easily reconciled with the teaching of Saint Augustine.[19] The conservative trend which will prevail in the schools of theology, and eventually oppose even the wholesome innovations of Thomas Aquinas as late as 1270, finds here one of its surest historical explanations.

CHAPTER II

UNIVERSITIES AND SCHOLASTICISM

THE word "university" (*universitas*) first meant the whole group of masters and students residing in some town, for instance Paris,[20] which, about the beginning of the thirteenth century, must have been a city of about 150,000 inhabitants. Once fully constituted, its university consisted of four Faculties: Theology, Law, Medicine and Arts. The Faculty of Arts was, so to speak, the gate to the others. The supremacy of the Faculty of Theology was not contested.[21] The students themselves were divided into four organized bodies called "nations": French, Norman, Picard and German. The "nations" themselves were divided into "provinces." Since the university had grown out of the cathedral schools of Paris, the bishops of the city continued to control it in many matters through the Chancellor of the cathedral, himself one of the masters in theology belonging to the chapter of Notre Dame. The university progressively asserted its independence with respect to the Chancellor. Each faculty had its own rector. The rector of the Faculty of Arts, chosen by the four nations, was also the rector of the university. His main functions were to convene the meetings of the Faculty of Arts, or the general meetings of the university, and to act as their president.

The two main methods of teaching were lectures and disputations. Lecture should be understood in its etymological meaning of "reading." The masters were all expected to read prescribed authors before their students and to explain these texts by appropriate commentaries. In the Faculty of Arts of the University of Paris, most of the reading material was provided by the writings of Aristotle, the list of the prescribed readings varying, however, according to the fluctuations of the church's attitude toward the Philosopher. At the end of the thirteenth century, practically all his writings were on the prescribed list. In the Faculty of Theology, the prescribed readings were Holy Scripture and the *Book of Sentences* of Peter Lombard. Concerning the latter text, the master would often invite his students to read it and content himself with discussing specially selected topics suggested by the book. As time went on, the commentaries became less and less continuous, until they ultimately assumed the form of a series of "questions."

A Disputed Question (*quaestio disputata*) was a formal exercise which occupied an important place in the regular teaching of the universities. A thesis was chosen by the masters; objections could be raised against it, either by himself or by his students, not excluding occasional guests. A younger teacher (*baccalarius*) then upheld the thesis by appropriate arguments and answered the question (*respondens*). The master had always a right to intervene in the discussion and the final conclusion was his. On his next lecturing day, the master could take up again the subject matter of the preceding dispute. He would then restate the thesis, make a choice of arguments against it, announce his own decision, justify it himself as if he were the *respondens* and finally refute the objections. If he wrote it himself, this lecture became a *Quaestio disputata;* if one of the listeners wrote it for him, it became the "reportation" of a Disputed Question. Since the master was free to determine the number of these disputes, he could decide to hold enough of them, within a year or even more, so as to discuss completely the different aspects of one and the same question. Hence the remarkable series of disputed questions found, for instance, in the works of Saint Thomas Aquinas (*Quaestiones disputatae de veritate, etc.*), or of Matthew of Aquasparta (*Quaestiones disputatae de fide, humana cognitione, etc.*).

Apart from these disputes, held in the class of a certain master at his own convenience and for his students, there were public disputations. Each master was free to hold them or not, and they were such an ordeal that not all masters cared to do so. These public disputes had to take place about the second week of Advent and the third or fourth weeks of Lent. Anybody could submit a question on any subject; hence their name of "Quodlibetic Questions" (*Quaestiones de quolibet,* or *quodlibe-*

tales). Naturally, the master could turn down certain questions as unsuitable for discussion. The dispute then followed the usual routine, with this difference however, that any number of masters could intervene in the discussion. In some cases, their number was large. Over and above these lectures and disputes, there were academic sermons preached by masters before the university; in some of these sermons, general questions pertaining to theology, sometimes even to philosophy, could be debated at length and the history of philosophy or of theology has often to learn from them.

If we consider the course of studies and the conferring of degrees (which, like universities, seems to be a mediaeval innovation), it appears that, despite numerous local variations and many irregularities in Paris itself, the complete and typical career, in the eyes of the university people of the middle ages, was that of the Parisian master. According to the statutes of Robert of Courson in 1215, at least six years of study and twenty-one years of age were required for anyone teaching the liberal arts, and at least eight years of study and thirty-four years of age for theology. A student in arts first passed his baccalaureate (B.A.), then his licentiate's degree, following which he gave his first lecture and received the title of master of arts (M.A.). If he then wished to become a theologian, he passed three more baccalaureates: biblical (*baccalarius biblicus*), sententiary (*baccalarius sententiarius*), complete bachelor (*baccalarius formatus*). After this, the young theologian had to beg, and to obtain from the Chancellor, leave to teach theology. If and when it had been granted, he could give his first lecture (*principium*) and thus receive the title of master in theology. The number of the chairs of theology being limited (twelve in 1254) not all masters could have one. A master provided with a chair was a full professor (*magister regens*). The Dean of the Faculty of Theology of Paris was the elder among those of the full professors who were secular priests.

The teaching methods of the universities exercised a deep influence on the technique of theological and philosophical thinking. It became more and more technical according to the rules of the dialectics of Aristotle. The "question" (*aporia*) is the typical expression of this method. All the main products of this school teaching are either isolated disputed questions or aggregates of disputed questions ordered according to some organic plan. Naturally, variations were always possible. From time to time, a mediaeval master could write a continuous opuscule, or treatise, in the more traditional form used by the Fathers of the Church. Yet, by and large, the "question" remained, up to the end of the middle ages, the favorite mode of exposition of personal thought for the masters of the university. It was the living cell of school teaching.[22]

Since the reading of certain books was compulsory in both faculties, the commentaries of the master could be written by him and circulated under his name. Hence the second main form of expression common during the middle ages, namely, the "commentaries." Some of them are of great importance. Like those of the "Commentator" *par excellence,* Averroes, they sometimes inform us about the personal intentions of their authors. Yet, as shall be seen later on, the main intention of a commentator was not to express his own thought, but to clear up the meaning of a certain author as it was expressed in one of his writings.

Anyone who has seen one of these writings will recognize at once any other work written by a master of the late middle ages. Hence their common epithet, partly arbitrary like all appellations: "scholastic." And indeed, most of them owe their particular style to the teaching methods used in mediaeval schools. Scholasticism is the common denomination for the "scholastic philosophy" of the Faculty of Arts and for the "scholastic theology" of the Faculty of Theology. There is no harm in attempting to define the "essence" of scholasticism, supposing it has one, but to do so is beyond the proper capacity of a historian.[23]

The early beginnings of some European universities go back to schools which already existed before the end of the twelfth century; these universities were sometimes called, in the middle ages, traditional universities (*ex consuetudine*). No exact chronology is possible in the story of their transformation. The oldest ones were Bologna, Paris, Oxford and Orléans. After 1200, the dates of the foundations become much more precise, because they mark either the beginning of new universities or the official transformation of older schools into universities, that is, organized corporations of masters and students. Cambridge seems to be the first case of schools which did not become a university but were created as such (1209). A few years later, Padua followed the same example (1222). It was to become an extremely influential center of Aristotelian studies; it was there that Albert the Great was first initiated to secular learning. A new type of teaching institution appeared when, instead of growing out of older schools or of spontaneously establishing themselves, they were created by various kings or princes, sometimes on the instigation of the Church. Among the better known ones, let us mention Naples (Frederic II, 1224), Toulouse (Count of Toulouse, 1229, on the request of Popes Honorius III and Gregory IX, against the Albigenses), Salamanca (Alfonso IX, *ca.* 1220). After 1300, the movement reached Germanic countries (Holy Roman Empire), Prague (1347), Vienna (1365), Heidelberg (1386), Erfurt (1389), Cologne (1388, transformation by the City of an old thirteenth-century *studium* already made illustrious by Albert the Great). During the fifteenth century, the same movement continued to extend eastwards to Leipzig, Rostock, Greifswald, Freiburg in Breisgau, Upsala, etc.

The structure and history of each one of these institutions is peculiar to it. Nevertheless they all followed the general pattern of scholastic teaching as it was given at Paris; their masters were interchangeable and, like the scholastic Latin they used, their spirit was practically the same. All these universities shared in the doctrinal unity of the Catholic Church. Nevertheless, they seem to have undergone a twofold evolution. In the beginning, these universities were made out of masters and students, that is, of men. They had no special buildings, no libraries, no endowments, no personnel. Especially from the fifteenth century on, they progressively established themselves on a more solid material basis. Spiritually speaking, they underwent a still deeper change. Instead of remaining Church institutions, they progressively became national ones. This change became unavoidable from the time when many centers of learning were created, in different European countries, by local authorities or local princes whose protection mediaeval schools had to buy at the price of their academic freedom. Yet, the same tendency seems to have spontaneously germinated in the University of Paris itself, especially in its Law School, as early as the thirteenth century, on the occasion of the political difficulties arising between the Holy See and the French kings. The transition from the old universalist University of Paris to our modern type of nationalistically-minded modern universities, has been a slow and steady one. Without despairing of the future, those of us who still believe in the absolutely universal value of intellectual culture, and of truth, must look for their golden age in the past.

CHAPTER III

EARLY THIRTEENTH-CENTURY THEOLOGIANS

GUNDISSALINUS' effort to assimilate the teaching of the Arabian philosophies but recently discovered had clearly revealed the difficulty of the undertaking and what risks Christian faith ran in it. Pope Gregory IX's warning to the theologians of Paris (July 7, 1228), to teach a theology pure of worldly learning (*sine fermento mundanae scientiae*), without any mixture of philosophical figments (*non adulterantes verbum Dei philosophorum figmentis*), was practically impossible to follow in a university where these figments had to be taught. To back up and return simply to the old liberal arts seemed desirable to many, but was averred impossible. Since nothing could stop the flow of philosophical studies, the theologians attempted at least to dam it up.

I. PARIS: W. OF AUVERGNE

Little is known even yet of the first efforts in this direction. The earliest seem to date from the end of the twelfth century, such as the *Commentary on the Sentences* by Peter of Poitiers[24] who taught theology in Paris from 1167 up to his death in 1205, and who makes at least one allusion to Aristotle's *Metaphysics,* or like the theological Summa by Simon of Tournai (d. about 1203) who already knew the *Physics.*[25] There again, however, it was a question of works that were almost exclusively theological, in which philosophical problems were only touched upon in passing, and that very rarely. Not so with the *Summa aurea* by William of Auxerre, who died in 1231, shortly after having been appointed by Gregory IX a member of the committee in charge of correcting Aristotle's works.[26] Recent research has enhanced the originality he showed in treating certain moral problems, such as free will, the virtues, natural law. Another theologian, Philip the Chancellor, author of a still unpublished *Summa de bono* is said to have written the first treatise on the transcendental properties of being: the one, the true and the good.[27] This essentially philosophical problem is included by Philip in an essentially theological work. The use he makes of Aristotle and the Arabian philosophers clearly shows that, from that moment, a theologian could no longer ignore their writings.

The publication of the still unpublished works of these theologians may one day bring about some changes of perspective, but the name which so far dominates all others in the first third of the thirteenth century is that of William of Auvergne.[28] Born about 1180 at Aurillac, professor of theology at Paris, consecrated bishop of Paris by Gregory IX in 1228 (whence comes his other name, William of Paris), he died in 1249, leaving a considerable theological work. Among his writings, some are particularly interesting for the history of philosophy; namely, the *De primo principio* (about 1228), the *De anima* (1230), and the *De universo* (between 1231 and 1236). In more than one way, William was a precursor, yet, at the same time, his general attitude was that of a Christian reaction against the philosophical universe of Avicenna. As is usually the case, William had to borrow from his adversary some of the weapons he needed in order to fight him.

William's writings follow the patristic style of continuous exposition.[29] Lively, witty, sometimes sarcastic, he also was a good story-teller, as we know from the story that "li evesques Guillaume de Paris" told Saint Louis, who in turn told it to Joinville, from whom we have it, about the master of theology who could not believe in the Blessed Sacrament "such as holy Church teaches it." In short, he was a Frenchman, and one feels tempted to say that, for this very reason, he still belongs in the twelfth century. For it would be too much to say that the twelfth was a French century, but it is true that two Frenchmen dominated it, Abélard and Bernard of Clairvaux, the first of those couples of hostile brothers that often appear in the history of French thought, some of whom put their passionate hearts to serve intelligence, the others their lucid intelligences to serve the love of their hearts. Certainly William of Auvergne was not in their class, but he was the last of their race that a history of theology or philosophy in the thirteenth century cannot avoid mentioning. An institution of the Catholic Church, the early University of Paris was a sort of clearing-house for the intellectual transactions of Christendom. It was therefore natural that strangers should be there, and it could even be understood how so many illustrious foreigners happened to teach there, but it is difficult to explain why there should not be one great French name among them. Alexander of Hales, Roger Bacon and Ockham were English; Duns Scotus was Scottish; Albert the Great and Eckhart, German; Bonaventure and Thomas Aquinas were Italian; Henry of Ghent was a Fleming, and if we call to mind Siger of Brabant and Boetius of Dacia, it must be agreed that France did not even produce the unorthodox great, inevitable in similar surroundings. At ease in the rarefied atmosphere of logic, confident as long as she can rely upon the experience of the inner life, those immense dialectical constructions disconcert her, and it is probably not by chance that the last great French work of the thirteenth century, the *Magisterium divinale* of William of Auvergne (1231-1236) should be the critical reflection of a traditional theologian upon the philosophy of Avicenna that had just been discovered.

On this point at least, William belongs to the century of Albert and Thomas. The non-Christian physics, psychologies, metaphysics and moral philosophies were there, which the Christian doctors could no longer afford not to know. Now too many of them did remain in ignorance of these sciences, or at least knew them only slightly, which did not prevent them from discussing them, thus making ridiculous both themselves and the Christianity they were defending. William could not excuse this. When he spoke of it he could be as brutal as Albert the Great was soon to be, but as a general rule, he avoided them: "Here is my advice: in philosophical matters, you are always to refer to philosophers and to them only, and you will avoid disputes, disagreements and altercations with incompetent people, without worrying about their opinions, for they are like daydreams and delirium." This theologian clearly saw that one cannot efficaciously combat ideas of which one is in ignorance, and that one can triumph over philosophy only as a philosopher, exactly as Albert and Thomas Aquinas were later to do.

William of Auvergne, moreover, gave evidence of a true sense of values. If Gabirol's doctrine of the divine will made William exaggerate ever so slightly the greatness of that philosopher, he clearly saw the importance of Avicenna and the major interest that his distinction of essence and existence offered for a Christian theologian. The term "being" (*esse*) has two meanings. It signifies essence first, or substance, taken in itself and stripped of its accidents: *substantia rei et ejus esse et ejus quidditas*, that is to say, the being that the definition signifies and explains by telling what essence is; but it also signifies what the verb *is* designates, when one says it about anything whatsoever. Taken in this second sense, not only does *esse* not signify the essence the definition expresses, but it is foreign to it. The rule, however, has one exception, which is God. In its existential meaning, *esse* does not enter into the definition of any being; if one imagines any being, such as a man, a donkey or anything one wishes, one can conceive it without its existing. The only exception has to do with Him whose existence is said to be his being; for his essence cannot be conceived without its existing, since itself and its existing are absolutely the same thing. William of Auvergne therefore enters resolutely here into the way of the distinction of essence and existence, which starts from Alfarabi and Avicenna to reach its goal in the metaphysics of Saint Thomas Aquinas.[30]

This principle is the very basis of William's proofs of the existence of God in his *De Trinitate* (or *De primo principio*). Any being is such that its essence includes or does not include existence. Any being is, therefore, such that it exists by itself or by others. Now it is inconceivable that there should be beings only by others, for any being which is such has a cause of its existence, which should itself be by itself or have a cause, and so on *ad infinitum*. There is room then for only three hypotheses: either to admit that the series of beings by others is infinite, which is inconceivable to reason as actual infinity itself is, and furthermore explains nothing, since the existence of beings by others is precisely what one is attempting to explain; or admit a circular series of beings causing one another, which is absurd since one is thus admitting that these beings indirectly cause themselves; or else admit the existence of a being by itself, which possesses existence by essence, and which is God.[31]

As William conceives him, God is absolutely simple, precisely because in him existence (*esse*) is separable from essence neither in reality nor in thought. That is also why God is not definable. One can easily speak of his existence, but if one asks with regard to him the question *quid sit*, there will be no answer; there is, then, no "quiddity": *non habet quidditatem nec diffinitionem*. The only name which can be suitable for him is the one he gave himself in Exodus (3, 13-14), WHO IS, that is, Being. One may, however, ask oneself, as William does, exactly what meaning the notion of being takes on here. What it seems to allude to for him in the first place is the "necessity of being," or Avicenna's *necesse esse*, rather than the pure existential actuality Saint Thomas first has in view. By this is meant that, leading up to Scotism rather than to Thomism, William considers this first notion as making us attain God only as being, not as God. By the notion of *ens*, which Avicenna says is the first object of the understanding, God is immediately imprinted on our intellect. William therefore speaks like the Bible, but perhaps he is thinking here especially of Avicenna's *necesse esse per se,* which the Thomist God will still be, but only in consequence of the pure and infinite actuality of his *esse.*[32]

Just as William of Auvergne stays close to Avicenna and Maimonides (*Guide,* I, 63) in his interpretation of the identity of the divine essence and existence, he does not clearly go beyond them in the distinction of created essence and existence. He clearly sees that this distinction is of quite another nature than the distinction of matter and form, which is already very important; moreover, he does not conceive it only as an ideal distinction posited by reason alone, but as a real distinction, which is no less important, but his foreshadowing of Thomism is restricted to this. For William, for Maimonides and their common master Avicenna, existence is a sort of addition to essence, whence follows this other difference that existence seems to combine with essence as a *quo est,* added from without to the *quod est* whose act it is. If William is urged to explain what he means by the *esse* of the creature, his answer will not be slow in coming: it is a participation in the divine *esse.* In expressing himself thus, he purposely breaks away from Avicenna, for whom the existence of a thing is a participation only in some other being anteriorly emanated from the First; but he links up created essence so directly to God that its own existence is volatilized, the creature being nothing more than an essence all of whose existing is reduced to a simple "existing through God." Of course, God is the being by whom all things are, and not at all the being they are (*esse quo sunt, non autem quod sunt*). Making use of a typical formula whose full import will only appear in Albert the Great and Eckhart,[33] William compares with the relation of soul to body the relation of divine *esse* to created essences. God is the being of all things as the soul is the life of its body; and that is exactly why the existence of beings is always in some way accidental to them. Since the unique supreme essence, which is God, is the unique existing by which all exists—which in no way takes away from the essential diversity of things—it can be said of the existing by which they are that it is not essential to them, but, in a way, superadded (*esse quo sunt non est eis essentiale, sed quasi accidit*). Beyond Gilbert of la Porrée and the masters of Chartres, William is half-way between the ontology of Boethius and that of Thomas Aquinas.

William of Auvergne's technique here is clearly far behind his profound intuition, which it betrays in its very effort to express it. He has the keenest sense of the primordial importance of the act of existing. Some texts opportunely gathered together and excellently interpreted by A. Masnovo, insist as strongly as possible on that profound and primitive love of existence which torments beings, makes them sacrifice everything for it and in them is only the love of the supreme *Esse,* which is God. If, by "accident" an unimportant appendix is understood, one cannot consider it an accident. Existence is worth more than an accident, *and even than substance,* since in losing it, one loses everything. What this doctrine lacks is a clear conception of the autonomy proper to each act of being.[34]

This ontological indigence of created being affects the whole cosmogony and cosmology of William of Auvergne. No matter how closely he follows Avicenna, any Christian theologian disagrees with him on the question of creation, but William's reaction goes far beyond what one could normally foresee. Naturally, he is opposed to the Avicennian thesis of an eternal emanation of possibles governed by the necessity of the divine understanding. The will of God is eternal but free; his decisions are eternal, but it does not follow that their effect is also eternal. God has eternally and freely willed that the world should begin in or with time. Created from nothingness, the world was created after nothingness. It is true that Avicenna considers this position absurd. If, says this philosopher, the fact that a being exists in no way affects the cause on which it depends, it is because that being already existed; now everybody agrees that God is in no way affected by the existence of things; therefore things have always existed. But William turns the argument round: it is true that the existence or non-existence of the world does not prevent God from remaining identically the same; now God freely created the world in time; nothing then makes it impossible for the world to be created in time without God himself being in any way affected. Now it is not only in their existence that creatures depend on God, but in their natures and operations as well. All that they do depends on the divine will. God did not create them to leave them to themselves; the power of nature is the sole will of the creator: *potestas naturarum sola voluntas est conditoris.* The Aristotelian and Avicennian notion of natures operating in virtue of an eternal necessity and according to the law of their essences is therefore ejected from philosophy. Between created nature and its working is interposed the free will of the creator, on whom the creature depends at every moment in its operating just as it depends on it in its being. Their efficacy, then, comes to things from the superabundance of their source. Created natures are undoubtedly such that they can receive that efficacy; a house has to have windows, if one wishes to gather in light; but who will maintain that a window has a right to light? In the universal distribution of divine efficacy, God alone is really Cause; creatures are only the channels through which it circulates, when God so wills, and as he wills, until he is pleased to stay its course. This pulverisation of natures and their causal efficacy brings us back into line with the thesis *de potentia absoluta* which goes from Peter Damian to William of Ockham. To what extent William of Auvergne is speaking here as a theologian defending the liberty of the Christian God against the necessity of the Greek nature can easily be seen by the arguments he uses. William cites many miracles already alleged by the anti-dialecticians of the twelfth century as manifest proofs of the liberty of God with respect to nature, but he also finds in Gabirol's cosmogony the means of justifying philosophically the Christian notion of a free creation. That is why he gives him first rank among philosophers: *unicus omnium philosophorum nobilissimus.*[35]

William's cosmology, strongly influenced by Plato's *Timaeus*, makes a place for that World-Soul which had appealed to so many minds in the twelfth century. After refusing to conceive the separate Intelligences as so many creative substances interposed between God and things, he eliminates them even as simple motive substances. The Avicennian notion of souls of the spheres, themselves moved by their desire for the Intelligences, seems to him impossible and even ridiculous; that was to assign to these intelligible substances functions comparable to those of a donkey harnessed to a mill-wheel. William's main preoccupation here is to suppress the intermediaries accumulated by Avicenna between the human soul and God, who should be our sole principle and end.

The soul is the form of the body (Aristotle); a wholly simple spiritual substance, it is free of all composition. Those who represent it as a potential whole or a virtual whole simply show by so doing their puerility and their imbecility. The soul therefore remains one and undivided, no matter what operations it may accomplish. In the human soul as in God, essence is the immediate cause of its operations of knowledge and of will; no distinct faculty of the soul is interposed between it and the operations it accomplishes. This thesis will be opposed by Saint Thomas Aquinas, but it has exerted a profound influence in both England and France on the theologians of the fourteenth century who, because they refused to distinguish the faculties from the essence of the soul, spoke of a cognitive function of the will.[36]

In William of Auvergne himself, this position justifies a radical criticism of the Aristotelian and Avicennian theories of knowledge. Since the soul is one and indivisible, one cannot attribute to it two intellects distinct both from one another and from its essence, namely, the possible intellect and the agent intellect. If we wish to speak of an intellect, let us conceive it as the very essence of the soul exercising its knowing activity; above all, let us make it clear that this intellect cannot be an agent intellect. The philosophers who affirm the necessity of an agent intellect to explain that the first principles become intelligible to us in act make a superfluous hypothesis; the principles are as naturally intelligible to the soul as light is naturally visible to sight. If there is a light of the soul which makes it capable of knowing, that can only be God. At any rate, it is essential not to imagine, as Avicenna does, a separate agent intellect and illuminator of the soul which is other than God.

In explaining how the soul acquires its knowledge, William begins by acknowledging the extreme difficulty of the problem, but he sets to work courageously to solve it. Whether it be a question of the principles of knowledge or of our general ideas (universals), the difficulty is the same:

they are universal forms of knowledge, and universals cannot exert any action on the soul, for the simple reason that they do not exist. In both cases a really existing and an active cause must be found which imprints in the soul either the general ideas, or the principles. The active cause of the general idea is nothing but the individual object perceived by the senses, and the operation which draws the universal from the particular is abstraction. This operation implies two moments. The point of departure is sensation, which apprehends the individual object distinctly, with all its individuating differences; sensation leaves in the imagination only an already abstract image, in the sense that it is less precise and is bereft of the individual marks of the object. Seen at close range a statue represents Hercules; seen from afar, it represents nothing but a man; our images are all vague like the perceptions of objects seen from far off. That first imaginative abstraction provides the intellect with an occasion for receiving the intelligible forms which come to it from another cause. Were we to believe Aristotle and Avicenna, that cause would be a separate substance, the agent Intelligence, but "according to the doctrine of the Christians, which is necessarily most true in everything and throughout, and perfectly free of all falseness and error, we must affirm that the human soul is naturally placed at the border line of two worlds and adapted to both. One of these worlds is the world of sensible things to which it is tightly bound by its body; but the other is the creator, who is in himself as the model and mirror in which the first intelligibles are reflected universally and with perfect limpidity. That is where all the rules of truth are; primary rules, I say, and known in themselves, and similarly the rules of morality as well as the universality of the hidden intelligible objects that the created intellect cannot attain without the gift and the grace of divine revelation. It is therefore the creator who is eternal truth, an eternal model of most transparent expression and expressive representation, in short, as I have said, the spotless and most pure mirror in which everything becomes visible. This mirror, then, as I have said, is intimately joined to, and very present in, human intellects, before which it is naturally placed, and which consequently can read in it, without any intermediary, the principles and rules of which we have spoken. It is then in it, as in a living book and in a mirror productive of forms, that the intellect reads by itself these two kinds of rules and principles, so that the creator himself is the book proper and natural to the human intellect." [37]

That was getting back to Saint Augustine as to a safeguard and protection against the noetic of Avicenna. In the human soul, as William of Auvergne conceives it, everything comes from within, on the occasion of the stimuli that the body undergoes from without, and under the internal action of the divine light. This doctrine of knowledge postulated a universe already filled with intelligible forms directly readable by the intellect. Such is precisely William of Auvergne's universe. Species are not only real in it, as they were for William of Champeaux, they are reality itself. A man, like Socrates, is essentially for him the species "man," whatever else is added to it being only individual accidents (*Quare totum esse ipsius est ipsa species, videlicet haec species homo, sicut dicitur vel praedicatur de ipso cum dicitur, Socrates est homo*). The human soul is therefore in the presence of intelligibles by its thought, as it is in the presence of sensibles by its senses, and the intelligibles are the causes of the sensibles. If the intelligible essences of earth and fire did not exist in the sensible world, there would be neither earth nor fire. William can then crowd the whole of Platonism and an Aristotelianism, interpreted according to Avicenna, into a vast synthesis: "Aristotle said of the agent Intelligence that it is in a way the intelligible sun of our souls and the light of our intellect, in which it makes appear in act the intelligible forms which Aristotle posited as being in it in potency. It makes them pass from potentiality to act, as the sun does for the colors visible in potency when, by its irradiation, that is, by the perfection of its light, it makes the colors which are in potency in colored bodies pass into act. The cause which obliged him to posit this Intelligence was Plato's positing of forms, or of the world of species, which is also called the archetypal world, world of principal forms, world of species, and intelligible world, or world of the intelligibles. Aristotle, in fact, has had to concede that position of Plato's. On what reasons or what proofs Plato relied to posit it, this knowledge has not reached me. I shall therefore give the reasons he seems to have had or could have had. To this I say, then, that the intellect must be believed about intelligibles no less than the senses about sensibles (*Ad hoc dico igitur quod non minus credendum est intellectui de intelligibilibus quam sensui de sensibilibus*). Since the testimony or attestation of the senses obliges us to posit the world of sensibles, that is, the sensible itself and the world of particulars or singulars, with far greater reason should the intellect oblige us to posit a world of intelligibles, which is the world of species or universals" (*De universo*, II, 14).

It is clear that William has not been able to re-discover, even through Augustine, the Platonist dialectic which justifies the existence of the Ideas. He does not seem to have read the *Phaedo* (translated in the twelfth century by Henry Aristippus), when he wrote those pages. His own doctrine is a sort of intuitionism of the intelligible which duplicates that of the sensible, and which is understood as an illumination by the archetypal world, reason and model of the universe, whose real name, for Christians, is the Word, Son of God and true God. The Augustinian complex of the thirteenth century is almost completely represented by the doctrine of William of Auvergne. When William died, in 1249, Saint Bonaventure was already lecturing on the *Sentences* and his "exemplarism" was no philosophical novelty.

There is almost no other truly original work of French origin to mention, in addition to the vast doctrinal synthesis drawn up by the bishop of Paris at the beginning of the century, except the curious treatise which bears the title of *Memorial of Difficult Things (Memoriale rerum difficilium)*.[38] Nor is it absolutely certain that its author was French. It was attributed first to the Polish philosopher and scholar, Witelo (Vitellion), under the title of *On Intelligences (De intelligentiis)*, but since the work was quoted by authors before Witelo's time, this attribution has now been abandoned. Two manuscripts name as its author a Parisian master, Adam Pulchrae Mulieris; one of the two even says: *"Ade pulcherrime mulieris."* If we discount the superlative, it still seems that this *De intelligentiis,* or *Memoriale rerum difficilium,* might be the work of a certain Adam Belle-femme (or something like that). Very little else is known of this Parisian theologian who, if we are to judge by the content of his work and the quotations from it, must have written it about the year 1230. Richard of Furnival mentions the work (about 1246); it is quoted in Gerard of Abbeville's *Quodlibeta* and even had the honor of being mentioned by Saint Thomas Aquinas (*De veritate,* II, 1, Praeterea; *Quaest. quodlib.,* VI, 11, 19, *Sed contra*) under the title of *De intelligentiis.*

It is an interesting application of the Dionysian theme of hierarchical illumination, which inspired, after Gundissalinus, Alan of Lille and Nicholas of Amiens, but Adam added to it another theme, which Clemens Baeumker called the "metaphysics of light," and whose main representative is Robert Grosseteste. Without denying the possibility of an influence of Grosseteste, it must be said that the *Memoriale* is clearly distinct from the works of the Oxford master by its technique as well as by its content. Adam starts with a primary substance, infinite and the origin of all others, which is an Intelligence. It is anterior to all the rest in order of definition, for the rest can only be defined with respect to it; it is anterior to them also in the order of knowledge, for it is the first intelligible; and finally, it comes first in the order of existence, for it is the actual cause of the existence of all other beings. This primary being is light. Saint John affirms this in his Gospel, and Augustine declares that "light" is the proper name for God (*De Genesi ad litteram,* IV, 28, 45). We know, on the other hand, that what is not God, exists only through its participation in God; from which it follows that, since God is light, all that is, is only insofar as it participates in light; or, what amounts to the same thing, that a thing retains as much of the divine being as it has light: *Unumquodque quantum habet de luce, tantum retinet esse divini.*

Light is therefore the form or perfection of all that exists (*perfectio omnium eorum quae sunt in ordine universi est lux*). By essence, it is self-diffusive and self-multiplying (*diffusiva sui, multiplicativa suiipsius*). This is the proof that light is the source of life, which also possesses that propagative force and consequently partakes of the nature of light (*est enim vita actus entis diffusivi sui esse in aliud. Quod est hujusmodi, lux est proprie vel naturam lucis habens*). Propagation or manifestation, it is all one. Augustine had already said, after Saint Paul (Ephes., 5, 13), that all manifestation is light; moreover, light is not only life, but also "exemplary force," as is seen from the fact that the forms of things only appear in light. Once these principles are posited, one can deduce a hierarchy of distinct substances, ranging from the noblest to the humblest according to whether their light is more or less separated from matter: God, the pure Intelligences, human souls as movers of their bodies, bodies in which light shades off into heat, and in which it causes life and movement, until it peters out in inert matter.

The *Memoriale* is, if not exactly a *de fluxu entis,* at least a picture of the universal illumination to which Denis, Augustine, Gundissalinus and Gabirol all contributed something. The main current of Parisian speculation took, about 1230, a different direction. Not that the light-metaphysics disappeared then from Paris; on the contrary, it is clearly visible in Saint Bonaventure. Traces of it are generally to be found everywhere the Augustinian doctrine of the necessity of God's illumination of the soul for the cognition of truth is maintained.

2. OXFORD

It is an accepted view that while logic was dominant in France, scientific studies were flourishing in England. There is a sense in which this is undoubtedly true. Ever since the end of the twelfth century there had been in England men endowed with scientific interests and aptitudes, the like of whom could not be found in France during the early years of the thirteenth century. But the Parisian masters in theology were not slow in making some use of Aristotle. The *Summa aurea* of William of Auxerre (1215-1220), Roland of Cremona (1229-1232), Philip the Chancellor (*Summa de bono,* 1230-1236) William of Auvergne (*De universo* and *De anima,* 1231-1236) all bear witness to their awareness of the fact that there was such a thing as pagan philosophy. At that time, no such theological development seems to have taken place in England. Yet, as will be seen, Robert Grosseteste was pursuing there an entirely different type of theological work, which put to good use all the resources of optics and of mathematics.

The explanation for this difference is to be found in the work of Adelard of Bath, of Daniel of Morley, of Alfred of Sareshel and several other late twelfth-century English scholars who spread the new Arabic learning in their country. Although the scientific value of some of their writings seems to have been somewhat overrated (for instance, in the case of Alexander Neckam) they certainly created a tradition of learning far superior in these matters to anything that could then be found on the continent.[39]

When we consider scholars and writers no longer interested in the pursuit of learning, but schools and teaching activities, the picture looks somewhat different. Concerning the new logic (*logica nova*) already known in the late twelfth-century French schools, it seems that it did not reach the English schools before the first decade of the thirteenth century. As to the scientific works of Aristotle (*libri naturales*) there is some indirect evidence that they were taught at Oxford shortly after being taught at Paris, but not before. The treatise of John Blund, *Treatise on the Soul*, is material evidence of the teaching activity of these early masters in the field of natural science. Unfortunately, the date of the treatise is unknown. We are better informed concerning the commentaries of Adam of Buckfield, who taught at the Oxford faculty of arts as early as 1243, at a time when Roger Bacon was studying in Paris. Written after the pattern of the commentary of Averroes, or, as in the case of the *De anima* under the form of questions, the commentaries of Buckfield are the sure proof that, about the middle of the century, the teaching of Aristotle at Oxford had reached its full maturity. These glosses cover all the works of Aristotle, minus logic, ethics and *De animalibus*. The short fragments already published deal with the problem of the unity of the human soul. In the soul of man, are the intellective, sensitive and vegetative souls one and the same substance, or are they three different substances? Adam's answer is that they are different. The intellective soul does not arise from the potentiality of matter, as is the case with the two others; it is directly created by God. Created apart, it is a substance apart.

This position calls for two remarks. Adam argues from the fact that "the intellective soul is something divine and created, coming completely from without, even according to Aristotle, whereas the vegetative and the sensitive souls come from within and are educed from the principles of matter." This remarkable statement shows that Adam was interpreting the doctrine of Aristotle concerning the separate agent Intellect as an explanation of the origin of the intellective soul. Paradoxically enough, his opponent on this point becomes Saint Augustine, whose followers maintain that the three souls are not three substances, but one in their root and essence. Their unity is that of form and matter, for the intellective soul is, in a way, the act and perfection of the other two. In this curious case, the supporter of the plurality of forms in man is arguing from the position of Aristotle-Averroes against supporters of the unity of the form arguing from the position of Augustine. But the problem of the substantial unity of the soul is only one aspect of the question. Let us note that Richard of Cornwall will later reproach Buckfield with following the "philosophers" rather than the "Saints." [40]

A. *Robert Grosseteste*

Robert Grosseteste (1175-1253) was almost exactly contemporary with William of Auvergne (1180-1249) and their careers are strikingly parallel.

Both were secular priests, professors, bishops, and both represent, the one in England and the other in France, the early thirteenth-century theologico-philosophical movement which blended together Denis, Boethius, Avicenna and Gabirol. On the other hand, their works are very different in style. While William was writing his *Magisterium divinale,* that is, a sort of *summa theologica,* Robert was writing a series of short opuscules which look like the work of a better-informed master of Chartres, anxious to use the latest scientific information in support of revealed truth. Roger Bacon will bitterly regret not to find in Paris this alliance of neoplatonism and of mathematical physics, especially optics, which might have become the source of a theology very different from what we call scholasticism. The influence of Grosseteste on the continental movement of ideas can often be detected, especially where what has been called the metaphysics of light blends together optics and philosophical considerations concerning the nature and source of intelligible light. This, of course, goes back to the "intelligible sun" of Plato, but in an indirect way only.[41]

Robert Grosseteste, Bishop of Lincoln (hence his other name, *Lincoln-iensis*), was invited by his study of Arabic treatises in optics to ascribe to light a central role in the production and constitution of the physical world. This is particularly obvious in his treatise on light and on the origin of forms (*De luce seu de inchoatione formarum*), where, in agreement with his general notion of the usefulness of positive science in all domains,[42] he resorts to physics in order to account for the formation of the universe.

In the beginning, God created, simultaneously and out of nothing, both matter and form. For reasons we are to see, it is enough to assume that God created first a material point endowed with its form. A single material point was enough because its form was light. Now light is a very subtle corporeal substance, whose exceeding thinness and rarity approaches the incorporeal, and which of its own nature perpetually generates itself and is at once spherically diffused around a given point.[43] In Grosseteste's own words: "Light of its very nature diffuses itself in every direction in such a way that a point of light will produce instantaneously a sphere of light of any size whatsoever, unless some opaque object stands in the way" (Riedl transl., p. 10). Another reason why its diffusion should stop, besides meeting an opaque obstacle, is that it attains the extreme limit of its possible rarefaction; its propagation then comes to an end of itself. This form is the active principle of all things and of all their operations.

Form is inseparable from matter and matter cannot be deprived of form. This accounts for the fact that two substances lacking all dimensions, namely, a point of matter and a point of light, can nevertheless beget the three dimensions which attend corporeity. We know that, given a point of light, a sphere of light is produced instantaneously; since matter and form are inseparable, the self-diffusion of a light point must needs produce a material sphere, that is, the very universe we contemplate.

By fine-spun reasoning, Grosseteste thinks he can prove that the result of this infinite self-multiplication of form and matter must needs be a *finite* universe. His main argument is that "the multiplication of a simple being an infinite number of times must produce a finite quantity." For indeed an infinite quantity exceeds a simple being, not only by infinity, but by infinity times infinity.[44] At any rate, light, which is simple, must extend matter, which is equally simple, until it reaches the limit of its propagation. Thus is formed a finite sphere, wherein matter is at the ultimate limit of rarefaction on the edges, becoming thicker and denser, on the contrary, the nearer it is to the center. After this first movement of expansion which sets the limits of the universe, central matter remains capable of further rarefaction. This is the reason why corporeal substances are endowed with activity.

When the whole possibility of the rarefaction of light (*lux*) is exhausted, the exterior limit of the sphere constitutes the firmament, which in turn reflects a light (*lumen*) toward the center of the world. It is the action of that reflected light (*lumen*) which successively generates the nine celestial spheres, the lowest of which is the sphere of the Moon. Below this lowest celestial sphere, inalterable and immovable, are spread in order the spheres of the elements: fire, air, water and earth. The earth concentrates within itself the actions of all the superior spheres; that is why the poets call it Pan, that is, the Whole; for all the superior lights are gathered in it and the virtues of all the spheres can be "educed from it into act and operation." It is Cybele, the common mother from whom all the gods can be procreated.[45]

Robert Grosseteste's principal merit is not, perhaps, to have imagined this cosmogony of light; he must be lauded still more for having chosen that conception of matter because it allowed the application of a positive method to the study of natural sciences. Before his pupil, Roger Bacon, and with a clarity which leaves nothing to be desired, he affirms the necessity of applying mathematics to physics. There is an extreme utility in considering lines, angles and figures because, without their help, it is impossible to know natural philosophy: *utilitas considerationis linearum, angulorum et figurarum est maxima quoniam impossibile est sciri naturalem philosophiam sine illis.* Their action makes itself felt in the whole universe and in each of its parts: *valent in toto universo et partibus ejus absolute.*[46] That is why Grosseteste wrote his opuscule *On Lines, Angles and Figures.* In it he defines the normal mode of propagation of natural forces, which follows a straight line, either directly or according to the laws of reflection and refraction. As to figures, the two it is indispensable to know and to study are the sphere, because light multiplies spherically; and the pyramid, because the most powerful action that a body can exert on another is the one which starts from the whole surface of the agent to concentrate on one single point of the patient. The essential part of physics would therefore lead to the study of the properties of figures and the laws of movement as they exist in the sublunary world. All natural effects can be explained by means of geometry; that is, by means of lines, angles and figures; it is the triumph of geometry.[47]

Grosseteste did not limit his hypothesis to the explanation of the material world and the inorganic kingdom; he extended it to the phenomena of life and the order of knowledge itself. God acts upon the world through light; now man is like a little world (*microcosmus*), where the soul occupies the same place that God does in the great one.[48] It is therefore also by light that the soul acts in the senses and in the whole body. Faithful to Augustine's teaching, Grosseteste affirms that the soul can act upon the body, but that, since the less noble cannot act upon the more noble, the body cannot act upon the soul. How then can the soul act upon the body? The problem is especially hard to solve with regard to the superior part of the soul, intelligence (*intelligentia*), which is not the act of a body and needs no corporeal instrument in order to act. It was precisely in order to solve it that Grosseteste introduced light as the intermediary between the purely spiritual substance, the soul, and the grossly material substance, the body.

In a doctrine in which light is the primary energy, the primary form and the bond of all substances, the theory of knowledge is inevitably oriented toward the Augustinian doctrine of illumination. A spiritual light exists which is to intelligible things as the corporeal light is to sensible things. To know a thing, is to know the formal cause which is in it, that is to say, the form by which that thing is what it is.[49] The operation by which we know that form is abstraction. By its nature, intelligence (*intelligentia*) which is the superior part of our soul, is not the act of the body and needs no corporeal organ for its operation. Were it not dulled by the mass of the body, it could know sensible forms directly, as the angels and God know them. As a matter of fact, it cannot, except in some choice souls which the love of God liberates, even in this life, from all contact with the images of corporeal things, and, naturally, among the blessed after death. In an analysis which recalls Plato's *Meno,* Grosseteste explains next how the soul, having become torpid, so to speak, in the body, awakens little by little to the intelligible, under the repeated shock of sensations, analyses the complexity of objects, divides color from size, shape and mass, then the shape and size from the mass, and so on, until it thus gets to know the corporeal substance which bears these various accidents. If we have thus to put up with sensations, it is because our soul, blinded by the love it has for its own body, can see only what it loves. In casting off its love of the body, the soul is, on the contrary purified, open to the influence of divine Ideas and it discerns by their light the truth of things, which are so to speak their reflections.[50]

The arrival of the Franciscans at Oxford took place in 1224; their first master in theology at that university was Adam of Marsh, whose learning Roger Bacon has several times highly praised, but whose writings have not yet been discovered. Adam seems to have taught there about 1247-1250; he died between 1259 and 1269. The fourth Franciscan master at Oxford was Thomas of York, author of a still unpublished *Sapientiale* whose very nature remains in doubt. From what we know of it, it seems to be a sort of philosophical compilation, or mosaic work, whose elements are connected by personal transitions and whose general pattern is a distinctly visible one. Thomas borrows from Alfarabi, Avicenna, Averroes, Gabirol, Maïmonides; on the Christian side, he resorts to Augustine, Anselm, Nicholas of Amiens, and William of Auvergne. His general view of the world includes a complex theory of matter: absolute universal matter conceived as pure potentiality (Augustine, Gabirol and, later on, Richard of Mediavilla); Aristotelian matter, subjected to form and seat of privation; the matter of heavenly bodies, in potency with respect to place but without privation. He subscribes to hylomorphism; he maintains the separate substances as givers of forms, or, more exactly, as the beings whose influence extracts forms from matter. With William of Auvergne, he gives a psychological description of the process of abstraction and explicitly upholds, over and above this operation, the inner illumination of the soul by God; the notion of God is innate in man and his existence can be established by the argument used in Anselm's *Proslogion* or in Augustine's *De libero arbitrio*.[51] An excellent picture of the average philosophy of its own time and an inexhaustible source of historical information, because Thomas usually quotes his sources, the *Sapientiale* seems to be an impersonal exposition of philosophical interests.

B. *Pseudo-Grosseteste*

The only reason we have to deal here with the *Summa philosophiae* we are about to examine is its wrong attribution to Grosseteste.[52] It does not belong to him; it has been written at a much later date and although it often agrees with the doctrine of the bishop of Lincoln, the reason for this is that the philosophical positions it represents are practically common to all his contemporaries, except, naturally Thomas Aquinas.

The *Summa philosophiae* is divided into treatises as Avicenna's *Metaphysics* is. The first is a curious history of philosophy, whose data are borrowed principally from Aristotle, Augustine and Isidore of Seville. Starting from Abraham, who was the inventor of monotheism and taught the Egyptians arithmetic and astronomy, it goes up as far as the thirteenth century, working through the Greeks, the Latins (where we meet Plotinus), the Arabs and the Moslem or Christian Spaniards (Algazel was a Christian), to end with contemporary philosophers. All the ancient philosophers up to the time of Theodosius made enormous blunders with regard to God, the human soul and the life to come. As to the philosophy of nature, very few of them, except the peripatetics and Boethius, had the right opinions. It is interesting to observe, moreover, that the Christian Latins who came after Boethius and before the end of the twelfth century do not figure in this history. The author does, however, quote several of them in the course of his work, but in his eyes they were not philosophers, they were theologians. In the historical perspective he adopts the Latin Occident has only just discovered philosophy, and what he says about it amounts to this: "There are still many other remarkable men in philosophy whose names, even though I have examined their philosophy, I do not know or do not mention without some particular reason (*quorum . . . nomina tamen vel ignoramus vel non sine causa reticemus*). I consider furthermore that John the Peripatetic (John of Salisbury?) and Alfred (Anglicus?), or, among the more modern, the Minorite Brother Alexander (of Hales) and the Preacher Brother Albert of Cologne should be counted among the most remarkable, without necessarily considering them authorities." To say that even the best of the moderns were not "authorities," was to refuse to place any of the Occidentals on the same level as an Averroes, an Avicenna, or a Boethius—still less a Plato or an Aristotle. These latter two he sees under a more precise aspect than one would expect. Plato seems to him to prevail over Aristotle "by the clarity of his mind, the subtlety of his intellect, the beauty of his language, and the art of arranging facts and regulating morals," but Aristotle is incomparably superior to him in scholarship and more safe in philosophy: *incomparabiliter studiosior et in philosophia certior*. Their methods were also different: Plato does not criticize his predecessors; he sets forth truth directly, asserting rather than proving: *auctoritate magis philosophica quam argumentatione;* Aristotle argues, demonstrates and refutes by syllogistic arguments, thus putting order into the confused knowledge that existed at that time in logic, science, morals and metaphysics. He made of it—and nothing was more admired in the middle ages—a body of doctrine, an organized knowledge, in short an "art": *regulas . . . confuse prius traditas in artem artificiosamque doctrinam et, ut aestimatur, completam, primus redegit, nonnullaque proprio studio adjecit.* One wonders why almost all the Greek and Latin Ancients preferred the philosophy of Plato, up to the time of the Arabs. It is unlikely that the obscurity of Aristotle's style should have made his works impenetrable to so many minds curious to know and therefore penetrating. What is certain, however, is that Plato was very well versed in everything that pertained to human problems, very eloquent and, especially, completely devoid of arrogance. On the contrary, Aristotle's eagerness to attack and contradict made him appear extremely arrogant, and if we add to that a negligence in style and refinement of argument, it is not surprising that he was not popular. We must not put too high a value on the greatness of genius, when it seems to have found fault with the wisdom of its forerunners, or, because of envy, to have appropriated it as if it were its own creation. These touches of moralism are frequent in the author of the *Summa*.

The classification of authors he proposes is extremely interesting. In addition to the philosophers he has just spoken of, he divides them into two classes: the theosophists, the theologians. The theosophists (*theosophi*) are the inspired authors, Moses and the prophets for example; their authority is incomparably greater and their teaching more certain than that of any man. This theosophy (wisdom of God) was fully revealed in Jesus Christ, whose birth was foretold by the prophets and the Sibyl, and whose miracles, power of reading hearts, and celestial teaching, that is to say, moral example, prove his divinity: "And the Saracens are unpardonable in that they made equal to Jesus Christ himself, a Mohammed sunk in crime, a thing which some will do with other false prophets until the end of time."

We call theosophists in the proper sense those who expound theosophy; in the broader sense, those who deal with it or teach it, and those who listen to them. Theologians properly so-called are divided into three orders. The first includes those whom the brilliance of their knowledge and the saintliness of their life have caused to be inscribed by the Sovereign Pontiffs in the catalogue of saints (Denis, Athanasius, Basil, Cyprian, Ambrose, Jerome, Augustine, *etc.*). The second comprises the theologians whose doctrine is equally true and similarly universal, but approved to a lesser degree by the same Pontiffs (Origen, John of Damascus, Alcuin, Anselm, Bernard, Hugh and Richard of Saint Victor); and finally the third, composed of a number of very famous names such as Peter Lombard, Gilbert of la Porrée, William of Auxerre, and many modern writers, in short, those that are called "makers of Summaries" (*multique moderniores scriptores, quos summarum vocant confectores*). This classification shows what was entirely new, for a witness of the thirteenth century, in the theological method of Alexander of Hales and Albert the Great.

The authority of the "theosophists," compared to the philosophers' authority, is as science to opinion. In fact, at the time of their divine inspiration, the theosophists are infallible. When they spoke as men not inspired they could make mistakes like simple philosophers, but not when God inspired them. Even then, the authentic meaning of their words cannot easily be understood without the help of the theologians of the first two orders, whose authority is more certain than the authority of the philosophers in everything that concerns the soul, the angels and creatures in general. The theologians themselves, in fact, were not without a knowledge of philosophy; moreover, they were endowed with more divine grace than the ordinary run of believers. Furthermore, the fact that these theologians were sometimes mistaken in matters of natural science unimportant for salvation, or that they had no knowledge of them, is no disadvantage; nor should it be concluded from this that they were always mistaken, even in these matters, wherever they disagreed with the teachings of the philosophers. This should be admitted only when the philosophers' theses are proved to be true by necessary syllogisms, or, at least, rest upon a scarcely contestable probability. It is a well-known fact that all the philosophical knowledge accessible to man is implicitly contained in Scripture as in its root. The *Summa philosophiae* here follows Roger Bacon's track.

So far, it has been a question only of theologians of the first two orders; those of the third had their own task to fulfil. They compared the philosophy of the theologians of the first and second orders more exactly with the philosophy of this world and amalgamated them with the teaching of revelation, when subject or reason required it (*Jam vero theologi tertii gradus supradicti et ordinis, philosophiam primorum et secundorum theologorum philosophiae mundanae certius comparaverunt et utramque, cum causa vel ratio exigeret, theosophiae sententiae commiscuerunt*). In fact, the theosophists often mention notable properties of things, but it was not their custom to explain the essences of things or their causes. It is not then superfluous but very necessary care on the theologians' part, if they add to their own interpretation of truth what the theosophists for some secret reason omitted. Thus, every person who asks enlightenment on these points will be satisfied.

The author of the *Summa philosophiae*, therefore, exactly analysed the work of the theologians of his time, and lucidly discerned the reasons which had led them to that synthesis of revelation, of the doctrines of the Fathers, and of Arabian or Greek philosophy, that today we call scholastic theology. The Catholic faith has no need of human reason, but it may have recourse to philosophy to protect itself against unbelievers and to show those who are badly informed that it is not devoid of reason. It was necessary to contend against heretics (Manicheans, Arians, Nestorians, Pelagians, Moslems and others), whose errors would have multiplied rapidly had they not been theosophically and philosophically refuted. That is why our author considered excellent the work carried on by his contemporaries: "Modern theologians make philosophy usefully serve theosophy as well as the theology of the theologians of the first two orders, and even of those in the third order." Since Peter Lombard was a theologian of this third order, the *Commentaries on the Sentences* are thereby justified.

The second Treatise bears upon truth, and begins by establishing that it is necessarily eternal and without cause, whence it follows that there exists a being that is truly eternal and that there can be only one such being whose existence is necessary and whose non-existence is impossible: (*Erit igitur veritas aeterna substantia increata, omnino unica, cujus esse est necesse omnino esse et impossibile non esse*). Then, starting from finite truth as it is formally in our thought and materially in things, it is again established that the existence of this mutable truth implies the existence of a created immutable truth, and finally the existence of an uncreated immutable truth.

The necessity for the principle of contradiction depends on this uncreated truth. In fact, there are two kinds of truth: the incomplex truth, which is the very entity of each being, taken in its indivision from its existence (*indivisio entis et esse*), and the complex truth which is the adequation of the thing and of the intellect affirming or denying a predicate of a subject. The contrary of these two truths, therefore, would be the divisibility of the being and its existence, and the non-adequation of the thing and the intellect. Between one of these two kinds of truth and its contrary, the contradiction is absolute and the opposition is consequently infinite. Even an intellect of infinite comprehension cannot apprehend a greater distance than the distance between contradictorily opposed terms. If, then, there is a Prime Being, there will also obviously be a contradiction eternally founded on its opposition to non-being. It will therefore be eternally true of an incomplex truth that its being is supremely distant from non-being, and of a complex truth that two opposite contradictory terms absolutely cannot be simultaneously true. Such is the eternal basis of the truth of the philosophical principle of contradiction.

After truth, science (*Tract.* III). Borrowing from Algazel a formula he was frequently to use, the author of the *Summa* begins by establishing its *anitas*. "Anity" is the term corresponding to "quiddity"; it is therefore the answer to the question: does the thing exist (*an sit*)? If it is agreed that there is truth, it is necessarily agreed that there is knowledge, that is, the result of the union of an intelligible and an intellectual power. Once acquired, this result is a stable disposition (*habitus*) which enables the intellect actually to distinguish the true from the false with regard to the intelligible in question. Aristotle has correctly classified the sciences, but theosophy must be placed at their head, and Aristotle's classification can be completed by Alfarabi's, which Algazel followed. The sciences differ from the arts in that a science takes into consideration the causes of its truth, while an art is more a way of working according to an already established truth. All those who deal with a science and occupy a prominent place in it, have a right to the title of philosopher; those who shine in any art whatever should be called masters; note, however, that the title of philosopher is given to those who excelled in metaphysics, and that we call sages, or theologians, those most eminent in theosophy.

The fact that all art has a matter, which no one doubts, necessarily implies that there is matter in nature (*Tract.* IV). The question of matter's "anity" having thus been settled, let us go on to the question of its "quiddity." Absolutely primary matter is a substance devoid of form, but nevertheless knowable in its relation to form. Matter is necessarily a substance, since it is an essential part of all composed substances; and it is knowable only in connection with form, since that which is only in potency is knowable only in virtue of the relation of potentiality to act. Now form stands on the side of act. Primary matter is unique and is characterized by two properties: to be universally in potency with regard to all form, to be related to form by that inclination to receive it that is called privation. Primary matter successively undergoes all the determinations of form. As a universal potentiality, it is first determined by a universal form, which is that of substance. Substance is in turn determined by a series of oppositions within its own line, from that primary and universal form up to individuals. The first of the determinations of substance as such is the well-known couple of contraries (*binarium famosissimum*), corporeal and incorporeal. Matter is therefore of itself incorporeal; it is body only by the form "corporeity." Taken in its pure potentiality, it is what Plato calls *hyle,* that is, *silva;* it must not, however, be confused, as sometimes happens, with what Moses calls earth or water—terms which point out a matter already determined by the form of substantiality plus the elementary forms of either earth or water. Plato was the first Greek to attain the notion of primary matter thus understood, and it escaped Aristotle's attention. It follows, in fact, from Plato's doctrine, that even though every order of substance may have its own matter, the sky and the elements for example, there is a common primary matter which, as pure potentiality with regard to all form, is common to all compound beings, celestial or terrestrial bodies, corporeal or spiritual substances. The author of the *Summa* accepts, then, in this sense, the universal composition of matter and form taught by Gabirol (hylomorphism).

The form which constitutes substance in determining matter is called substantial form. From the mere fact that substance is constituted as such, it is individual by full right; it is therefore the substantial form which, in constituting its substance, individuates matter (*quia materia in actu poni non potest nisi per formam eam perficientem, ipsius individuationis actualitas a forma vere causatur*). Incidentally, this is the reason why the distinction introduced by Boethius between the *quod est* and the *quo est,* should not be understood as a real distinction, but as a distinction of reason. Taking the creature in itself, its *quod est* (that is, what it is), is sufficiently and completely determined by its matter and its form. Its "being" thus understood is not distinct from what it is. True it is that the creature has a *quo est,* that is to say, a cause by which it is, but this cause is the uncreated being which cannot enter into composition with anything else: (*Absurdum est autem creaturam, id est D E vel A B C, componi ex eo quod quodlibet eorum est, et ex suo quo est, id est esse increato, cum impossibile sit illud in compositionem venire*). The *Summa* therefore rejects the distinction of essence and existence understood in this sense; and it further rejects it in the sense in which the *quo est* is not God, but an act of existing created by God, which would be the act of essence (cf. Thomas Aquinas). The essence, or quiddity, is the *quod est*. If it is "that which is," it is. The being that it is, is exactly the same being as that by which it is, considered now as being, now as essence. Here, then, there is neither composition nor distinction (*Tract.* V, cap. 5).

In order to find the origin of forms we must go back to the Ideas which, according to Plato, exist in three ways: in the divine thought, in the Intelligences, and in the species of natural things (cf. Grosseteste). Aristotle contradicted Plato on this point and ruined, as far as was in his power, the Platonic identification of species and Idea, but the very arguments he directed against this thesis show how right it was. There is nothing contradictory in positing forms as singular in themselves and universal in the intellect, at one and the same time. At any rate, it is certain that the Ideas existing in the divine thought are creative of natural things. Augustine and Plato agree on this; true, Aristotle denies it; but all Antiquity held this position as venerable except Aristotle and his dear fellow-travellers (*exceptis Aristotele et suis carissimis complicibus*). It is easier to criticize than to understand, and we may be sure that if Plato had followed after Aristotle, he would have refuted all Aristotle's objections. The *Summa* at least attempts to do so and concludes that Aristotle once more yielded to his mania for contradicting Plato.

God, and God alone, is the creative Cause of the actual existence of natural forms and of souls, for he is the primary, eternal, uncreated and creative force (*virtus*). He is also the primary and uncreated Form and the primary and uncreated Life. As Life, he is Intelligence and Will, Cause of all intellect and all will. Philosophers have committed very great errors about the relation of the will and the intellect of God to the divine essence; on the other hand, instructed by the theosophists and by God himself, the theologians rightly profess that there is supreme unity and simplicity in the divine substance. The consequences of this truth in philosophy are important, precisely as concerns the correct way of understanding the divine Ideas. These should be conceived under two aspects: with relation to the intellect which is considering them, and to the will which actualizes their possibility into real effects. Now it is clear that the knowledge which the uncreated intellect has of itself is both co-eternal, one with its own essence and uncreated; hence it is a unique uncreated Idea; but this unique Idea contains within itself all the species according to which the divine will produces beings, even primary matter. In this *Summa*, as in Erigena, the multiplication of the Idea is therefore the work of the will; on the contrary the *Summa* expressly and especially rejects Erigena's doctrine, to which he adds Avicenna's and even Gilbert of la Porrée's, who, our author states, for reasons better known to himself posited Ideas as being neither creatures nor the creator, but betwixt and between (*mediam inter crea-*

torem et creaturas et necque creatorem neque creaturam; Tr. VII, c. 16).
This error, he says, originates in Plato, who conceived Ideas as creative,
while there is nothing creative but the will of God.

We thus come to a tripartite distinction of the Idea. First there is the
Idea properly so-called, simple, which results from the self-awareness of
the uncreated intellect. Next come the essences, or species, which are born
in God of his voluntary and loving contemplation of the Idea. These can
still be called Ideas, but this time they are rather contemplations (*the-
oriae*), as Denis says, that is, the views of things to be made, which are in
the divine intellect, but belong principally to the uncreated will taken as
will. The *Summa* clearly distinguishes these two levels: (*Aliud est enim
idea, aliud cujus est idea causa vel ratio, et sic patet ideam originalem*
(the Unique Idea), *quae est ex conversione seu reditione intellectus increati
super se, omnino alterius modi esse ab idea rei cujuscumque fiendae*).
Beneath these archetypes, or views of things to be made, come the theophanies, which are intelligible impressions born of the supreme Good, actively
caused by him, passively received in the most noble of his creatures, those
endowed with an intellect.

Intelligent beings not joined to bodies are called Intelligences. These
Intelligences are innumerable; they differ both in species and in individuality. Modern theologians (cf. Thomas Aquinas) who maintain that, in the
Intelligences, each individual is a species are mistaken. Their error comes
from the fact that, like Aristotle, they are unaware of the existence of the
primary intelligible matter posited by Plato. The only matter they know
is extended matter, in which they see the principle of individuation and,
since no extended matter can be attributed to separate Intelligences, these
theologians logically conclude that the angelic species are not multipliable
into individuals. In reality, even separate Intelligences are composed of
quo est and *quod est,* as are all creatures; but since this composition is
only of reason, one must attribute to them, besides, the composition of
primary matter and of form, which, by the same token, makes it possible
to conceive their species as multipliable into individuals. Thus Intelligences
are real individuals and real persons numerically distinct from one another,
forms received in a matter and not pure forms or species.

No wise man of antiquity was in any doubt about the "anity" of the
human soul, but they did not all agree on its definition. The metaphysicians considered it in itself and, consequently, they defined it as a complete
individual substance, whereas the naturalists considered it in what it had
in common with all animal souls; accordingly, they defined it as the act
of the body which has life in potency. In reality, the human soul is both,
or rather, it lies between the two. Our soul is indeed an incorporeal
and intelligent substance, but capable of being joined to a body and to
be separated from it. Some "modern philosophers" (*moderni philosophantes*) deny that it is made up of true matter and form, but their reason

for this is the same as the one concerning the angels, and, in both cases, it brings them to the same conclusions. Incapable as they are of pushing beyond the notion of extended matter to the notion of an absolutely primary matter, these men refuse to include matter in the essence of spiritual beings, and so are led to deny that souls can be individual substances apart from their bodies. The proof that they are mistaken is that the separate soul is a thing completely in act and a true primary substance, essentially independent of its body, even though it preserves at the time its natural inclination to depend upon the body whose form it was. The *Summa* then binds the soul to the body only by a natural inclination, which is a propensity of its essence rather than its essence. Even though compound, such a soul is naturally immortal, because there is no internal clash, but on the contrary perfect harmony, between the matter and form of which it is composed.

Any spiritual substance of such a structure is in potency by its matter, in act by its form. Such is already the case in separate Intelligences, which are endowed with a possible intellect by which they receive the intelligibles, and an agent intellect by which they apprehend them. It is all the more so in human souls. Each man has his own possible intellect and his own agent intellect. These are two completely distinct faculties, for it would be contradictory to admit that the same substance—in this case the soul—can be, at the same time and in the same connection, both in potency and in act with regard to all the intelligibles. The agent intellect is like light; the possible intellect is like a transparent but dark medium; the natural forms are like colors which become visible in the air when the light illumines them; similarly, the natural forms become intelligible in the possible intellect by the light of the agent intellect. There is then no intellectual knowledge that does not presuppose sensible knowledge, and Aristotle is right on this point; but Plato is not wrong when he says that to know is to remember, for, if the intellect had no innate knowledge of natural forms, how would it recognize them in the sensible? That is why Plato compares the object of knowledge to a slave in flight: if his master did not already know him, he would not recognize him when he saw him again. The certain knowledge of natural things and principles therefore exists in the soul from the moment of its creation, and it is that which our agent intellect represents progressively to our possible intellect by the agency of sensible knowledge and imagination.

Such are the main metaphysical positions of the *Summa philosophiae*, the rest of the work (*Tract.* XII-XIII) being devoted to psychology (sensitive and vegetative souls), then to the study of light (*Tract.* XIV), to astronomy (*Tract.* XV), to the properties of the nature of every body (*Tract.* XVI), to the four elements (*Tract.* XVII), to meteors (*Tract.* XVIII) and to minerals (*Tract.* XIX). The same qualities of order and sobriety in the exposition of doctrines prevail to the end of the work without anything revealing the identity of the author. With regard to the influence of the stars on human events, he tells of having formerly seen, in Germany, an old astrologer who had read in the stars for him what the ends of the Emperor Frederick II and King Saint Louis would be. Some lines farther on he speaks of his master in terms which first suggest Roger Bacon, then Robert Grosseteste; (*magister meus in naturalibus et mathematicis peritissimus et in theologia perfectisimus vitaque et religione sanctissimus*). But it has been rightly observed that the author greatly admired Alexander of Hales and Albert the Great (XII, 17), a sentiment he cannot have inherited from Roger Bacon, and which constitutes perhaps the strongest objection that can be raised against the English origin of the work. Now Albert the Great seems to have written treatises on geometry, optics and astronomy (D. J. Meersemann); the *Summa* could therefore be connected with Albert's teaching, even though it deviates from it on some very important points. On the other hand, the author's reference to another of his works, entitled *De luce,* naturally brings to mind Bartholomew of Bologna, which would suggest Italy. Whoever the author and whatever its true origin may have been, this work expresses with remarkable clarity the reaction of a representative of the early Oxonian tradition against the novelties introduced into theology by Saint Thomas Aquinas. The traditional character of its inspiration explains its attribution to R. Grosseteste, but its historical setting belongs in the second half of the thirteenth century, about the year 1270 or even later on, at the moment when the representatives of the tradition began to oppose the distinction of being and essence taught by Saint Thomas Aquinas. This *Summa* is a remarkable exposition of what might be called the philosophical *koinè* of the times, that is to say, despite many individual variations, the doctrinal complex common to the majority of the thirteenth-century theologians.

PART SEVEN

THEOLOGY AND LEARNING

The discovery of the new learning brought about different reactions according to the character and intellectual dispositions of the Christians who first realized its importance. Most of them went on with their theological work, criticizing the new doctrines, or using them to a certain extent with a minimum of effort to assimilate their true meaning. A few others, led by a deep-seated fear of seeing Christian theology outdistanced by pagans and infidels in the main fields of secular learning, considered it their duty to catch up with the "philosophers" and to put the Christians on a footing of equality with their opponents. It would not be true to say that these men were not interested in achieving a synthesis of secular learning and theology, but they seem to have felt that learning had to be acquired before being used, that it was a good thing in itself and that Christians could never have too much of it. Naturally, such men as Grosseteste, Roger Bacon and Albert the Great were also convinced that, ultimately, the acquisition of secular learning would help to spread the Christian truth, but their writings bear witness to a properly scientific interest. We wish to stress this point because, since we are not dealing with the history of science, the significance of such works as the zoology of Albert the Great will necessarily be missed. The representatives of this tendency should not be considered a separate class of theologians. It can be said, however, that they conceived the work of the theologian in a way distinctly recognizable and one which bears the mark of their passionate interest for the conquest of secular learning.

CHAPTER I

ALBERT THE GREAT

ALBERT THE GREAT,[1] born at Lauingen in 1206,[2] entered the Dominican Order in 1223 while he was studying philosophy at Padua; taught at Cologne (1228); then at the University of Paris (1240-1248) where Thomas Aquinas studied under him (1245-1248); then again at the Dominican *studium* in Cologne (1248-1260). In 1260, he was consecrated Bishop of Ratisbon (Regensburg) much to the displeasure of his General Minister Humbert of Romans. After resigning his bishopric (1262), and without ceasing to carry out various official missions, he resumed his teaching at Cologne, where he died Nov. 15, 1280; Albert then was 74 years old.

I. ALBERT AND SECULAR LEARNING

The long and studious life of Albert covers the whole thirteenth century. Open to all intellectual interests and to the most various influences, yet an original investigator in all fields, especially in biology and zoology; at the same time, as independent a mind as there ever was, and yet a holy Christian soul, Albert has left us a gigantic literary production which defies analysis, not only because of its bulk but also, and perhaps still more, on account of its nature. At the same time that he was a theologian, and precisely in order to carry out his theological work, Albert was a scholar in the full sense of the term. The amount of philosophical and scientific information heaped up in his writings is amazing, so much so that it is not always easy to discern between what he was merely reporting, or storing up in view of later applications or interpretations, and what he himself subscribed to or taught as doctrinal truth. His theological writings, however, provide many clues as to what was his own position on many points.[3]

As has already been said, the arrival of Greco-Arabian learning confronted the Latin world with an entirely new problem, namely, how to interpret it in a Christian way? It has likewise been seen that the first Christians who dealt with the problem did not at once realize its deepest implications. When their attitude was not a wholesale rejection of the new learning as harmful to faith, they simply attempted to reconcile the psychology and the metaphysics of Avicenna with the traditional teaching of the Fathers, especially Saint Augustine. The personal contribution of Albert to the evolution of the problem was a decisive one. With Roger Bacon, he seems to have been the first among the Latins fully to realize the significance of the event. Albert saw that the mental universe of Greco-Arabian learning was specifically other than the patristic world of Christian faith. This implied the clear awareness of the twofold fact that theology was specifically distinct from philosophy and that faith was a mode of cognition specifically other than natural reason.

The consequences of these distinctions were manifold. Instead of inferring from them that Christians should take no interest in philosophy, Albert concluded that the first task for them was to achieve a complete mastery of philosophical and scientific learning under all its forms. This rediscovery of the philosophical world, which the Christians had lost sight of ever since the second century, marks a turning point in the history of Western thought.

A second achievement of Albert should be carefully distinguished from the preceding one. The fact that he clearly realized the distinction of philosophy and theology did not entail that he himself wanted to elaborate a philosophy of his own. His approach to philosophy was that of a scholar. Because he wanted to know it, he learned it from the philosophers themselves, his main contribution to their work consisting in a systematic reordering of all the material accumulated in their writings. Philosophy always remained for him something to be learned from books as science had to be learned from facts. Hence, particularly in his philosophical encyclopaedia, his was a passionate effort of objective understanding and interpretation, rather than of personal creation. Even in theology, Albert has used philosophy rather than changed it. Unlike his pupil Thomas Aquinas, he has left philosophy practically as he had found it in the philosophers. For this reason, his own philosophical positions are a free blending of Aristotle, Avicenna, Alfarabi, Gabirol, and, on the Christian side, Augustine and Denis. From the point of view of its form, his encyclopaedia much more resembles the Avicennian style of continuous doctrinal exposition (*per modum expositionis*) than the Averroistic and Thomistic commentaries on Aristotle (*per modum commentarii*). As Roger Bacon was to say, Albert wrote as an "author." His avowed intention was to rewrite, for the benefit of the Latins, all the treatises of Aristotle and even to add to this philosophical *corpus* those treatises which it was necessary to compose in order to complete it, either because Aristotle had not had the time to write them, or else because they had been lost.[4]

On the whole, the philosophical work of Albert represents an older style of thought than that of Thomas Aquinas. Assuredly, when a writing career extends over such a long time, an evolution is always possible, or probable, but only detailed research work can establish that it took place. In the present state of our knowledge, there is no reason to think that the general doctrine taught by Albert in his early *Summa de creaturis* differs on any important point from his late doctrinal positions as we find them defined in his unfinished *Summa theologica*. It goes without saying that further historical research may make it necessary to revise this conclusion. With all this, the intellectual style of Albert remains intensely personal. One cannot open his works without meeting him personally with his enthusiasms, his likes and dislikes, and occasionally with his angers against those who sin against the light of reason. He certainly did not like those lazy men who, in order to justify their laziness, were spending their time looking for errors in the writings of those who work. "Such men killed Socrates, expelled Plato from Athens . . . and, by their intrigues, they compelled Aristotle himself to leave Athens." Just as gall embitters the whole body when it evaporates, these galling people embitter the whole body of scholars and prevent them from enjoying the sweetness of their common quest of truth (Borgnet, VIII, pp. 803-804). Even among those who believed in the value of studies, he did not like the dialecticians who, as the Latins love to do, considered any distinction a solution (*hi more Latinorum, qui omnem distinctionem solutionem esse reputant,* B. VI, p. 6). What Albert himself is seeking is real scientific knowledge, that is, the knowledge not of words, but of things: "As to me, I detest such logical consequences in sciences dealing with things, because they lead to many errors" (ibid.). There is little in Albert of the objectivity of Thomas Aquinas in abstract discussion; nothing is more familiar to him than the "I" and, in this sense, he is as concretely and humanly real to us as Roger Bacon.

2. THE FOUR COEVALS

According to the classical Gloss on Scripture, God first created four coevals (*coaequeva*), namely, matter, time, the empyrean heaven and angelic nature (*Summa de creaturis,* Borgnet, vol. XXXIV, p. 319).

Matter comes first in the order of generation because it is the subject of the forms of all the beings to be generated. In another sense, the first created thing is "being," (Proclus) because, in the order of knowledge, being is the first principle to which our cognition of any being is ultimately reducible. But since we are speaking here of the generation of things in reality, prime matter is the first "principle," or origin, of all things (ibid., p. 321). The proper nature of matter is to be in potency with respect to all forms; as such, it is not intelligible apart from some form whose subject it is. Its first form is the substantial form of the element which, for this reason, is ultimate in nature and, consequently, is a principle in the natural order (ibid., p. 323).

As the universal subject of generation and corruption, matter is simple. Whether it is also one is a difficult question. Some say that there is one and the same matter for all substances, both corporeal and incorporeal: it is with quantity in corporeal substances, without quantity in incorporeal substances. Others say that we should distinguish between generable things, in which there is composition of matter and form, and non-generable things, in which the *quo est* is, as Boethius says, the form of the *quod est*,[5] that is, the form of the whole whose act it is.[6] At any rate, since generically distinct beings cannot have the same matter, spiritual substances and non-spiritual substances, which do not belong in the same genus, cannot have the same sort of matter. Nay, matter cannot even be the same in incorruptible heavenly bodies and in generable and corruptible beings (ibid., pp. 332-335). On this point, let us note that we have not been dealing with the logical notion of matter. Speaking an abstract logical language, all that is determinable by form is matter, so that matter is everywhere one and the same. But we are dealing with concrete reality. Now, speaking *realiter,* we still have to distinguish between the point of view of the theologian and that of the philosopher. To theologians, matter is that which the creator turns into distinct and shapely beings through the work of the six days; such is the point of view of Genesis, and, thus considered, matter is one. To philosophers, matter is the subject of change, and, consequently, different sorts of change require different sorts of matter (Aristotle). There is no contradiction in saying that all matters are one and the same with respect to the work of creation, and that matters are generically different with respect to the generically distinct sorts of forms which they receive.

The second "coeval" is time. This word points out the kind of duration that is proper to each different type of being. In other words, for any given being, the measure of its duration differs according to the nature of its being. God is an immutable being; his measure is eternity (ibid., p. 339), that is to say, a perpetually present "now." Speaking in a more technical way, eternity is the limitless duration proper to the uncreated *esse* of God, which is the act of the divine essence (*actus essentiae divinae;* ibid., p. 344). In this sense, God is eternity itself, or, in other words, eternity is nothing else than the divine entity itself, conceived as the measure of its own duration (ibid., p. 352).

God alone is eternal, but if we take eternity in a looser sense, beings simply without an end are also called eternal. Yet, this is an improper sense of the term. The kind of duration proper to mutable beings whose change has neither beginning nor end in time is properly called "aeon." Such beings are not eternal, but, so to speak, "aeviternal," that is, living an everlasting life. Besides, let us not forget that, since the world has been created in time, even everlasting beings have had a beginning; aeon and time began to be at the very same moment (ibid., p. 361).

Time is the type of measure that is proper to generable and corruptible beings. It is the measure of motion or change (i.e., becoming). Here again, the "now" is the substance of duration, only it is a fleeting "now" that is being ceaselessly superseded by another one. Time is known by the soul only, but it exists in things, because the process of their passing from potency to act is a successive one and, consequently, of its own nature, it implies a before and an after that are susceptible of measurement. Here again, the language of the theologians is not that of the philosophers. To theologians, time is the measure of any change, either divisible or indivisible, either spiritual or corporeal; in short, it applies to all created beings, including angels, in whose case time has neither before nor after. To philosophers, time is the measure of continuous motion, or change, which always includes a before and an after. Here again the difference in point of view entails no contradiction (ibid., pp. 369-370). Philosophical time is a fleeting "now," that is, the mode of duration proper to being that is becoming (ibid., pp. 373-374). Just as every sort of substance has its own kind of matter, every sort of duration has its own kind of time; mutations in intellective faculties and in wills are measured by their own time; mutations in heavenly bodies are not in the same time as the mutations of sublunary beings. True enough, these are extrinsically measured by astronomical time, but their duration is not the same (ibid., p. 384).

The empyrean heaven is the third of the coeval beings. Heaven's nature is not the same as that of the elements. Created by God, it can cease to exist at his will. Its form gives to heaven being, permanency, shape and movement. Because its operations initiate the series of generations and corruptions in the whole universe, it is a universal cause. Such is the reason why "some say that there is a *natura naturans* and a *natura naturata;* naturing nature is God, and his work is heaven; the work of natured nature are the generable and corruptible beings" (ibid., p. 402). Heaven is composed of matter and form, but the nature of its matter is not known; we only know that it is in potency with respect to place (ibid., p. 404). Over and above the astronomical heavens, there is the heaven of the Trinity, immaterial in nature because it is identical with God himself or, more precisely, with the surpassing excellence of his power, which contains and surrounds all created beings (ibid., p. 417). The empyrean heaven is the noblest of all simple bodies; it is the abode of angels and its nature is that of light (ibid., p. 421). It is immobile. Then comes the crystalline heaven (or "aqueous"), endowed with a uniform movement and whose matter is similar to, but essentially different from, what we call water. It is the heaven which God created when, on the second day, he divided the waters that are above the firmament from the waters that are beneath it (Gen., i, 6). The reason for positing such a heaven is that, between the empyrean which is immobile in its perfection, and the firmament which achieves its perfection through various movements, there must be a heaven which achieves its perfection through a single uniform movement (ibid., p. 427).

The next heaven is the firmament, which comes eighth counting up from the sphere of the moon. It is called firmament from the firmness, or solidity of its nature. It contains many stars whose lights, being diverse in nature, cause life in inferior beings. Astronomers like Al Bitrogi (Anavelpetra) and philosophers like Averroes do not agree on the cause and nature of its movement (ibid., p. 429). What is certain, however, is that the stars are the causes that move the elements in view of all generations and corruptions; the manifold nature of generations therefore requires the different motions of the different stars, together with their conjunctions, interferences and other relations, which are the subject matter of astrology (ibid., p. 435).

Each one of the nine moving spheres has a mover; in fact, it has three of them: First, God, who is the prime mover of the world, extrinsic to it and immobile. In this sense Ptolemy says that "nothing moves the heaven, save only God." Moses Maīmonides likewise proves by many reasons that the mover of heaven is external to it; that it is neither a body nor existing in a body, but is beyond both bodily divisibility and bodily indivisibility. Such a prime mover, to which Aristotle alludes in his *Metaphysics*,[7] is necessarily the only one there is, as has been proved by Maīmonides and Boethius. The second mover is the form of each heaven taken as a whole and irrespective of its division into different parts. According to some philosophers (Avicenna) these forms of the spheres are their souls, but the saints deny that the spheres have souls, and that they are "animals," at least in the proper sense of the word. If, however, we desire to reconcile the philosophers with the saints, we can say that each sphere is moved, if not by a soul, at least by a separate Intelligence, whose nature is aptly described in the *Book of Causes*. These are pure Intellects and Wills, directly participating in the divine perfection of the Prime Mover, which is God. Inasmuch that it is a mover, each separate Intelligence exercises a moving power, which can be called a soul in a loose and improper way (ibid., pp. 443-444). The third mover of the sphere is a material form, divisible according to the dimension of each heaven and proportioned to it. This form of the sphere is the immediate cause of its circular motion, or, rather, the cause which keeps it moving in a circular way. Whatever their causes, it is a fact that these astronomical motions exercise a verifiable influence upon generable and corruptible beings. Human souls, however, which are in matter but not tied up with it, are not determined by this influence; otherwise, there would be no room left in the world for liberty or free will (ibid., p. 450).

The fourth coeval being is the angelic nature. Angels are composite natures, made up of their *quod est* and of their *quo est*. This does not entail any composition of matter and form. Where there is hylomorphic composition, form is not predicated of the whole, because it is the form of matter only. In non-generable and incorruptible beings, which have no matter, the form is that of the whole and, consequently, it is that which a being is. In this sense, Socrates is "that which is," just as Raphael is "that which is." Consequently, in such cases, the form of the composite is predicated of the composite itself; for instance, man is the being of Socrates and angel is the being of Raphael. Naturally, this is not to say that the form of the whole is a universal imbedded in a body; on the contrary, it is the form through which something is a being, and from which a universal can be abstracted by the operation of our intellect (ibid., pp. 463-464). Angelic beings are subsisting Intelligences, endowed with an innate knowledge of intelligible realities and able to reason about such knowledge, at least to the extent that its object is not the direct contemplation of God. In angels, discursive knowledge is not needed in order to remove any ignorance; it rather is sheer enjoyment of intellectual power (ibid., p. 469). Endowed with free will, like men, angels are nevertheless different from human souls. Their Idea in God is not the same. Angels are in no way tied up with matter; a soul is apt to be united with a body, not, indeed, as a form unable to subsist outside of matter, but as a form and substance ruling and steering its body as a pilot steers his ship (ibid., p. 501).

3. MAN

The last born of creation, man is a composite being. Three points deserve attention with respect to man: his soul, his body and the union of both.

The existence of the soul is manifest from the fact that some beings have within themselves a principle of motion and rest that is different from a mere nature; the difference is particularly evident when this principle is a will. To define the essence of the soul is much more difficult than to prove its existence. On this point, Albert proceeds to an extensive inquiry. A whole question is devoted to the definitions of the soul propounded by the Fathers (*de diffinitionibus sanctorum*), then a second chapter is wholly devoted to the definitions of the soul propounded by Aristotle and his successors, that is, the "philosophers."

However we define it, the human soul is an incorporeal substance united with a body.[8] As its prime act, it gives to its body being; as a second act and motor of the body, it causes its operations (Borgnet, XXXV, p. 16, ad 1m.). Albert has always maintained these two points: first, Plato was right in defining the soul as an "incorporeal substance moving a body"; secondly, Aristotle was right in defining the soul as "the form of an organized body that is susceptible of life." The two definitions can be reconciled, but, as was to be expected, Albert borrows from Avicenna the principle of their reconciliation. Considered in itself and from the point of view of its essence, the soul is an incorporeal substance; considered with respect to its body, the soul is its act and its mover. Another way to say the same thing is to say that there is a certain incorporeal substance, which, inasmuch as it is the act and the mover of a body, is called "soul" (ibid., p. 34).

Having thus insured the substantiality of the soul, Albert now feels free to stress its union with the body. Some say that the soul is prime act inasmuch as it is the form and perfection which gives being to the body and that it is second act as cause of its operations. But this is not true. The operations themselves *are* the second act. On this point, Averroes was wrong and Avicenna was right (ibid., p. 39). The soul, precisely *qua* soul, is a substance from which emanate operations that are tied up with the body; as an incorporeal substance, it causes second acts in which no bodily organ has any part.

There is only one soul in each animal. This soul is neither God nor matter (*hyle*) as David of Dinant erroneously taught it (ibid., pp. 67-73); it has not been created in a kindred star whence it came down on earth: this story told by Macrobius sounds equally fabulous to both theologians and philosophers (ibid., p. 82). Souls are not even created by separate Intelligences, or angels, but directly and immediately by God (ibid., pp. 82-84).

There are three powers in the human soul: vegetative, sensitive and rational, but these are in man one single substance, a single soul and a single act (ibid., p. 93). The only composition there is in the soul as an incorporeal substance is that of its *quo est* and of its *quod est;* this problem is the same as that of the simplicity of angels and it receives the same solution (ibid., p. 102); as the act of the body, the soul is one, and its distinct powers do not divide its essence; rather, the soul unites them in its own unity.

After a lengthy and detailed study of all the biological functions of the soul, then of the five senses, their organs and their objects, Albert examines the nature of sense knowledge in general. It consists in receiving the sensible species without matter (ibid., p. 303). By and large, his psychology of the internal senses (*sensus communis, etc.*) follows that of Aristotle as interpreted by Avicenna. To these problems, Albert adds a complete exposition of those related to sleep, to the reasons why plants do not sleep, and why all animals do sleep, but not always. Dreams, their causes and their nature, are subjects which he considers with an almost passionate interest (ibid., p. 421). He wants to know why some people never dream, while others have many dreams; or why some people remember their dreams, while others do not; or why what we imagine in dreams, especially about their end, often announces some future events, etc. One of his questions deals with this subtle problem: Is the science one has in dreams speculative or practical? The answer is: neither. It is not speculative because it does not follow from any demonstration; it is not practical because it does not follow from deliberation or choice. As Socrates says in his *Apology*, such cognition is not human, but divine (ibid., p. 439-440).

Albert's approach to the problem of the intellect is typical of his general attitude. Naturally, he has first exhausted all the literature available on the subject. He knew the classifications of Aristotle, Alexander of Aphrodisias, Alkindi, Alfarabi, Avicenna and Averroes, but he also realized, with great acumen, that they did not all apply to the same problem. For instance, he clearly saw that the division of Avicenna and that of Aristotle did not add up, because Aristotle intended to divide the human intellect into its essential parts (the agent intellect and the possible intellect), whereas Avicenna intended to distinguish the various stages which attend the acquisition of learning. His *intellectus in habitu, intellectus adeptus,* and so on, do not fit the Aristotelian distinction of intellect in potency and intellect in act. The same remark applies to the division of Averroes, which is taken from the degrees of perfection of the intellect (ibid., p. 451). These penetrating remarks justify the extensive use which he himself occasionally makes of several different divisions and classifications of the human modes of intellection.

His own position is well defined. The agent intellect is *in* the soul (ibid., p. 455). The possible intellect also is *in* the soul.[9] The agent intellect is not a habit (*habitus,* i.e. the permanent possession of certain intelligible cognitions, cf. Themistius); nor is it a separate Intelligence pouring intelligible forms into our possible intellect: "The human agent intellect is conjoined to the human soul, it is simple, it has no intelligibles, but it produces them in the possible intellect from the phantasms, as Averroes expressly says it in his commentary on the *De anima*" (ibid., p. 466). A remarkable statement indeed, for Albert knew full well that the intellects of Averroes were separate substances, which he himself has just said they are not. But the fact that they are in the human soul does not alter the nature of their functions. Once it has been corrected, the doctrine of Averroes becomes true; it is more satisfactory than any other one.

The agent intellect flows from the soul inasmuch as the soul is act; it flows from its *quo est.* The possible intellect flows from it inasmuch as the soul is potency; it flows from its *quod est* (ibid., p. 470). The proper action of the agent intellect is that of an efficient and formal cause whose effect it is to draw the possible intellect from potency to act (ibid., p. 476). Naturally, in saying that the intellect knows, we mean to say that "man" knows through his intellect. Yet, the agent intellect is the efficient cause of intellection. It operates in the possible intellect a "transmutation" from potency into act (ibid., p. 478). There are, however, degrees in this transmutation, and this is the point where Alfarabi and Avicenna have something useful to say. With respect to *science,* the possible intellect is susceptible of three degrees (not powers or faculties): first, as being in potency to all intelligibles, the possible intellect is *hylealis,* that is, it resembles prime matter to the extent that it is a completely indeterminate possibility; secondly, the same intellect can be considered as already possessed of the knowledge of the principles (*habitus principiorum*) which are necessary for the acquisition of science (*intellectus in habitu*); thirdly, the same possible intellect can be considered as already possessed of science and able to turn to it at will (Avicenna's *intellectus in effectu*). With respect to the *intelligible* as such, the possible intellect is susceptible of two relations only: before knowing it and after knowing it (ibid., pp. 481-482). It is to be noted that, in this text, the highest degree of intellection listed by Avicenna (*intellectus accommodatus*) is intentionally left out, probably because, implying as it does actual communication with a separate Intelligence, it does not pertain to psychology but to metaphysics, and even to theology, since the true separate agent Intelligence is God.[10]

Let us now consider the whole intellect as already possessed of its knowledge and actually proceeding from there to its various operations: studying, learning, teaching, inventing; it is then called the speculative intellect (*intellectus speculativus*). Speculation is the very life of the intellect, as Aristotle has said: "Science is in the soul what the soul is in its body" (ibid., p. 489). In fact, the intellect and its science are one, just as substance and its accidents are one. Nay, both intellect and science are one with the known thing; not, of course, with its being, but with its intelligibility (ibid., pp. 491-492).

Since each man has his own agent intellect (ibid., p. 493), we need not believe, with Avicenna, that man must turn to a separate Intelligence every time he wants to consider some intelligible; yet, on the other hand, Avicenna was right in saying that the rational soul has no "memory" properly speaking, in which to store up its already acquired intelligibles. The possible intellect itself is this so-called memory. Just as it receives them, it keeps them, but the only way for it to consider them again is to apply to its own agent intellect (ibid., p. 498).

All this doctrine implies that intelligibles are given to the soul under the form of "species." What the agent intellect produces in the possible intellect is an intelligible species in act. What makes a species to be intelligible? The answer given to this question in the 1230 *Summa de creaturis* (i.e., *De homine*) is a twofold one. By nature, every intelligible is simple. It has the simplicity of things separated from matter and its concomitants. But matter itself can be understood in two different ways. First, it may mean the subject of motion and change, that is, the subject of becoming. Secondly, it may mean any singular being as determined to singularity by individuating properties, or accidents, which restrict its form and confine it to be that of one single being. With respect to the present problem, this second sense of matter is the correct one. Matter is the whole individual being, including all its individuating determinations; in other words, it is that which the thing actually is: the *quod est*. Form is the form of the whole (*forma totius*); in other words, it is what makes it to be the kind of a being it is: the *quo est*. The two meanings are very different. Considered as the subject of change or motion, matter is a part of the thing; it is in potency to a form which, being another part of the thing, is not the whole. Consequently, in this case, neither matter nor form are "that which the thing is" (*quod est*). In the second case, matter is that which the thing is (*id quod est res*), because it is the individual itself, "and since its form is that of the whole, and not of a part, it is predicated of the whole thing," including even its individuating accidents. The proper effect of abstraction is precisely to consider the form of the whole apart from its individuating accidents. For instance, our intellect does not abstract "soul" from "man," which would be to separate a part from its whole; but our intellect abstracts "man" from this and that particular man, and it does this by disregarding their individuating accidents, so that nothing remains except the form of the whole only, that is "man." In Albert's own words: "When it is said that an intellect abstracts from matter, this should be understood of the matter which is the particular" (*intelligitur de materia quae est particulare*). Albert is obviously following in the wake of Boethius' tradition (ibid., p. 501), confirmed in his mind by the Avicennian doctrine of the *natura communis*. Once thus abstracted from singularity by the intellect, these forms themselves become in the mind so many "particular substances," and the intellect gives them universality by retaining their "common nature" only (*accipiendo naturam communem in ipsis*, ibid., p. 502). In this doctrine, the intelligible species is the intelligible essence of the thing; abstraction is the intellectual grasping of that which, in the thing, is intelligible, namely, the *species intelligibilis, quae est species rei* (p. 512). Albert seems to be reading Aristotle in a Boethian context.[11]

Given his definition of the soul as a spiritual substance, Albert can easily prove its immortality. Some arguments are merely probable, some are necessary. Among the latter, those of Avicenna are particularly cogent. The soul is not a corporeal energy; the human intellect is not the act of any kind of body; the soul is not there in view of the body; the reverse is true. In short, the rational soul is a "substance existing by itself," and since it has subsistence apart from the body, it survives it. The Avicennian definition of the soul, which Albert himself recalls on this occasion (p. 530), plays a decisive part in the discussion of the problem. As Avicenna says at the beginning of his *Liber sextus naturalium*: "This name, *anima*, does not designate the essence of the thing which it names, nor is it taken from the category in which it is contained (i.e., substance); it is taken from an accident which happens to it; and this is the reason why the name of the soul (*anima*) is derived from the verb, to animate (*anima dicitur ab animando*)" (p. 530).

This same definition implies that, besides being the act of its body, the substance soul is its mover (*movens corpus*). This leads us to the notion of "practical intellect." The intellect is called "practical" inasmuch as, through cognition and rational disquisition, it directs the will and the acts of man. Doing and making are under the sway of the practical intellect (ibid., p. 540). As substances, the practical intellect and the speculative intellect are one; they are the same intellect now turning to the good, now turning to truth. The practical intellect first turns toward the good in general, which is the prime mover in the order of actions and operations; then it turns toward good things which can be done or made, in which case it deals with singulars; thirdly, it moves desire toward these particular goods apprehended as desirable ends. Goodness is, in the practical order, what truth is in the speculative order (ibid., p. 544).

Taken in its proper sense, the will is the natural appetite of a rational soul. Its objects are threefold in kind: first, within the soul, it sways all the other powers: I have the will to know, or to speak, or to walk; outside of the soul, the will applies to what can keep up and protect nature; thirdly, concerning that which, outside of the soul, is not strictly required to maintain nature, it may tend toward impossible things (in which case it is irrational), or else it may tend toward possible things. Among these possible things themselves, some are such that we can do little or nothing about them, because they are not wholly in our power, for instance: to be a king, or to be a well man; but others are such that they can be brought about by ourselves alone, if we choose to do so, and these are the proper objects of the rational will (ibid., p. 551). In this sense, the will includes all the various "appetites," because it is an inclination of the soul toward the good apprehended by the intellect, either in general or in particular (ibid., p. 559).

Free choice, which is to be found in man only, is called *liberum arbitrium* from man's liberty to decide, by way of "arbitration," what is good and what is evil according to the rule of reason. The liberty of desire consists in its power either to yield to the judgment of reason, or else to turn away from it (ibid., pp. 569-570). Many different definitions of free choice have been suggested; this is not surprising, because its nature is a twofold one. As an arbitrating power, it belongs to reason; as free, it belongs to the will; but to be an act of arbitration is its very substance, to be free is incidental to it: free choice is chiefly free because it is a choice, made either by reason, or by the will, or by both reason and will (ibid., p. 579).

In all this part of his doctrine, Albert closely follows the patristic tradition, including the classical distinction between free choice (*liberum arbitrium*) and liberty (*libertas*), which he inherits from Augustine through Anselm of Canterbury (p. 583). Free choice is the power to do what one pleases, without being under the sway of some higher power; liberty, which must be defined with respect to the end, is the power to preserve the rectitude of the will, desired for rectitude's sake. Other definitions of free choice can be explained and, to that extent, justified, by the various points of view from which they are taken.

Moral conscience (*synderesis*) is a special power of the soul in which, according to Augustine, the universal principles of right or wrong are inscribed. Just as, in the speculative order, we know the principles without having to learn them, so also, in the practical order, we are naturally possessed of universal principles of moral conduct according to which we judge what is good or evil in moral acts. These principles are the universal laws of justice; positive law is their application, by way of rational inquiry, to the particular problems of human conduct (ibid., p. 593). The intrinsic unity of moral conscience does not suffer from the multiplicity of its applications. Taken in its proper sense, conscience (*conscientia*) is, in each particular moral problem, the conclusion which practical reason draws from two premises: a "major," which is the *synderesis*, or habitual cognition of the first practical principles, and a "minor," which is the particular judgment of practical reason (ibid., p. 599).

Having thus completed his description of man, Albert concludes this part of his work by describing man's dwelling: first earthly paradise, in which man was created; next the universe, in which man still is. The world is not eternal: natural reason cannot prove that it has had no beginning, because all the so-called demonstrations of the eternity of the world postulate the existence of movement and of matter, which is the subject of change (ibid., p. 651). Naturally, there is a simpler way to refute what philosophers say on this point; it is to say that they are wrong, and that they do not understand what they say, nor what they affirm (ibid., p. 654). Albert himself prefers to give philosophers a philosophical answer; he has no patience with the saintly simplicity of some theologians.

There is only one world. Some say, with Empedocles, that an infinite number of worlds are succeeding each other. Others say that there is an infinite number of worlds actually existing outside of one another. Some say, like the Manicheans, that there is a world of light and a world of darkness. And there still are the Pharisees, who prophesy that after the end of this world there shall be another one in which, inhabiting a Jerusalem of gold, they themselves shall rule all the nations, having the kings for their servants and the queens for their nurses. We, on the contrary, maintain that outside of this universe, there is neither place nor time, but blessed life only, and not a life blessed on account of its place, but on account of its object, because God is not commensurable with the dimensions of this world (ibid., p. 656). Finite in its size, complete in its parts, the world is ordered in its structure in view of man and of God. Yet it is not an animal; there is no such thing as a world-soul (ibid., p. 660); its intrinsic order is enough to insure its unity.

4. GOD

Natural science deals with specifically distinct types of being: quantitative being, mobile being, living being, knowing being. There is a "transphysical science" (*scientia transphysica*) which deals with being as such and with the properties of being taken precisely *qua* being (*Metaph.*, ed. Borgnet, vol. VI, p. 3). It is the noblest and the highest of all sciences accessible to natural reason. Its unity is analogical; that is to say, all the various objects which it studies fall under its consideration inasmuch as they *are* beings, or, in some way, *related to* being (ibid., p. 7). Metaphysics is a purely speculative knowledge, and because it considers the most universal of all objects, which includes all principles and all causes, it is called wisdom. In its capacity of wisdom, it is "prime philosophy" and its ultimate purpose is to ascertain the prime cause of all that is.

It is not easy to form an accurate estimate of Albert's own metaphysical positions. By and large, his paraphrase of Aristotle's *Metaphysics* certainly represents what he himself held to be metaphysically true; but an inventory of this Aristotelian heritage would teach us very little about his own contribution to the solution of metaphysical problems. Unfortunately, there is no *Summa philosophica* to tell us what Albert himself considered to be of vital importance to a Christian theologian in such matters. His *Summa theologiae,* to which we shall have to apply for information, certainly contains his last word on all the questions with which it deals. Even when he tacitly borrows from his predecessors, what Albert takes up becomes his own; yet, when all is said and done, it is to be regretted that no work comparable to the *Summa de creaturis* exists to inform us concerning Albert's metaphysical treatment of the notions of being and of the cause of being, which is God.[12]

Even in this late work, Albert maintains a notion of theology older than, and different from, that which had recently been developed by his pupil Thomas Aquinas. Following Augustine, he includes piety in the very essence of theological learning, and, consequently, in its very definition (*Summa theologiae,* ed. Borgnet, vol. XXXI, p. 11). To him, *theologia scientia est ad pietatem,* that is, a learning that leads man to salvation through piety. It owes its unity to the relation there is between all its parts and the ultimate knowledge which it aims to attain, that of the supremely enjoyable divine reality. Unlike metaphysics, theology does not deal with being *qua* being and its properties, but with the Being who is the ultimate end of man and with what man must know in order to reach this end (ibid., p. 19). Thus understood, theology is a separate science. In other sciences, the subject is being itself or some aspect of being known in the light of natural reason; in theology, the subject is the supremely enjoyable (the *fruibile*) known in the light of revelation. Of course, philosophical matters have often to be considered by the theologian, but, to him, they are always interpreted in relation to the ultimate enjoyable reality (ibid., pp. 20-21).

The word *esse* is not easy to translate in the technical language of Albert the Great. As has already been said, he distinguishes between "being" (*ens*), or that which is, and *esse,* or that which makes a thing to be what it is (*quo est*). Truly and properly, being cannot be attributed to those things which we know, whose whole is other than their form. There is only one being whose whole is identical with its form, or *esse:* it is God (ibid., p. 126). Such is the reason why, as Anselm rightly says, God can neither not be, nor be thought not to be. In other words, God can only be conceived as an existing being. This is what Anselm says in his *Proslogion,* and where Avicenna proves that God is the necessary being, he is proving, by the same token, that God cannot not exist and that he cannot be conceived as non-existing (ibid., pp. 126-128).

As compared with what truly and properly is, namely, God, all other beings only are by accident; in other words, their *esse* (or *quo est*) is accidental to their being (or *quod est*). On this point, Albert expressly invokes the authority of Avicenna, plus that of a spurious work of Aristotle, who, indeed, never taught any such doctrine (ibid., p. 130). In fact, Albert is keeping faith with the Boethian notion of being. There is no indication that, even at the end of his life, he became a convert to the Thomistic notion of *esse.* To him, as indeed to many of his successors up to our own times, the distinction of *esse* and *quod est* remained a technical expression of the fact that created beings require a cause of their existence. Hence his reference to "the Philosopher in the *Book on Causes":* "The first created thing is being (*esse*) and nothing was created before it" (ibid., p. 130). This is why God is the only being that cannot be conceived as non-existing (ibid., p. 131). Albert uses Avicenna in all these argumentations.

The simplicity of God follows from the preceding conclusions. Since, in him, to be and to be what he is are one and the same thing, God is perfectly simple (ibid., p. 134, 4 and 5): *"In prima causa, quae Deus est, ut dicunt Avicenna et Algazel, omnino et omnimodum idem est esse, et quod est, et quo est"* (ibid., p. 139). This is, therefore, a philosophical as well as a theological truth. Since only God is simple, all other beings are composite. The sole fact that the creature comes second proves that it is not simple, for to be second is to add something to what is first. Here, however, the "composition" is not necessarily denoting a composition of things. Since, for instance, a created being includes its relations to the causes of its existence, it is not in the highest degree of simplicity (ibid., pp. 147-148); consequently it is a composite being.

The immutability of God is another consequence of his simplicity; for indeed God is substantially all that which he is; he can therefore change neither in his substance nor by reason of any accidents (ibid., p. 150). Since God alone is his own substance, he alone is immutable. As Boethius says in his *De hebdomadibus,* something can be added to that which is; but to being, nothing. Being, the *Liber de Causis* says "flows from the Prime Being, through all that which is caused or created, like a continuous stream" (ibid., p. 154-155). The duration proper to this absolutely changeless Being is what we already called eternity. Eternity is not an endless time; we call it a duration because, to us, it looks like an indefinitely extended existence, but in itself it does not endure; even an eternal time would not equal eternity (ibid., p. 177). It simply is the mode of existence proper to simple, immutable and pure *esse*.

Proceeding with his determination of the divine being, Albert successively establishes that God is one, true and good. His demonstration can hardly be called a deduction. Inasmuch as the entity of God can neither not be, nor be conceived as not being, it is one; there is only one such essence, because there is only one necessary being. Inasmuch as the divine entity is simple and without any admixture of foreign elements, it is what it is; now, as Augustine says in his *Soliloquies*, "truth is that which is"; consequently, the divine being is true (ibid., p. 204). Not only is God truth, he is the immutable truth itself and the cause of all other truths. These are threefold in kind: the truth inherent in each thing by reason of its form, or quiddity, which is a corruptible truth in corruptible things and an incorruptible truth in incorruptible things; the truth that is to be found in the mind, especially in the first principles by which we judge all truths, and this second truth is necessary in itself but mutable inasmuch as it is a created one; thirdly, the truth which, in the divine mind, is the model of the truth which is in things and the rule of the truth which is in created minds. We do not see this divine truth, but it is in us the model and the rule according to which we judge all truths (ibid., pp. 211-212).

Just as God is one and true, he is good, because a being which is eternal, immutable and can neither acquire nor lose anything, is necessarily the supreme good. He is good in himself and for himself; he is likewise good for us, as the ultimate final cause of all beings and the supreme object of universal desire (ibid., p. 237, n. 1 and p. 238). His goodness is substantially identical with his beauty (ibid., pp. 241-242). We call God the supreme good (*summum bonum*) from the point of view of his causality, because he is the supreme and universal cause of all goodness in things; having virtually, eminently and simply all goods within himself, it can be said, with Plato, that he is their "form" and that they are his "images" (ibid., p. 261). As supreme good, then, God is supreme cause. As Boethius says: the good is what comes from the Good (ibid., p. 264).

Considered as cause of all that is, God is called creator.[13] This word points out the divine essence itself as the principle of beings which, taken in themselves, are not the causes of their own existence. A creature can be defined: what is caused to be (ibid., pp. 541-542). God makes things be, "He is the efficient cause of all by his universally agent intellect,[14] since he himself is the prime intellect, to which alone it belongs to act absolutely and in all universally possible ways" (ibid., p. 552). Now, since every intellect acts according to some form that is in it, the universal agent intellect must also be the formal cause of all that is. Thirdly, since the good alone is self-diffusing, or, to use the language of Denis, since its essentially "ecstatic" nature does not allow the good to stay in itself, but urges it to communicate itself, God is the final cause of all that is. For the final cause of a being is always its good (ibid., pp. 551-552). In God, these three causalities are identically one with the very essence of God; in God considered as formal cause, the divine Ideas are identical with the self-knowledge of God (ibid., p. 561). In short, although the exceeding perfection of God compels us to use many different names in order to describe him as best we can, all that we say of him ultimately points to his essence and to the relations of created beings to their cause (ibid., pp. 579-580). Concerning the name which God himself claimed for his own, I AM WHO AM (Exod. 3, 14), the *Summa* of Albert expresses itself as though the *Summa* of Thomas Aquinas had never been written. What interests Albert is to know whether this name, WHO IS, is essential or personal. And the answer is: essential; for indeed, when he heard it, Moses did not apply it to one divine person rather than to another. God said to Moses: "He who is God through his true essentiality has sent me unto you." Besides, this question has been well answered by the Ancients: Praepositinus (of Cremona), William of Auvergne and Alexander of Hales (ibid., p. 586). Obviously, even in 1270, shortly before the death of his genial disciple, Thomas Aquinas, Albert the Great remained an intellectual contemporary of the men of his youth.

The same remarks apply to the parts of Albert's theology that deal with the science, the power and the will of God. It has often been said that, in his old age, the master had become the disciple of his disciple. We do not feel prepared to deny it, for the simple reason that, on some particular points, Albert may well have modified some of his positions after reading the works of Thomas Aquinas. He sometimes criticizes him. By and large, however, everything goes as though Albert had quietly followed his own chosen way without making any visible effort to assimilate the recent discoveries made by Thomas. Further inquiries may invite other historians to modify these conclusions; they are given here *salvo meliori judicio*.

These remarks are not a dogmatic judgment of the work of Albert the Great. Their intention is not to stress the intrinsic superiority of the doctrine of Thomas Aquinas, but, rather, to suggest the *nature* of the work of Albert. Like that of Roger Bacon, it represents a tremendous will to conquer learning, a result which it probably was necessary to achieve before attempting a new understanding of faith by means of this accumulated learning. Albert's speculative views on the relations of faith and reason are not here at stake. We are only attempting to describe what, by and large, he has actually done. On this point, our personal impression is that of M. Grabmann: "In sacred doctrine, Albert does not resort to argumentation in order to cause this science to invent new truths by rational argumentation from principles; rather, he attributes to theology argumentation in a polemic sense, in view of refuting as erroneous the conclusions opposed to the principles of theology." This may not be the whole truth, but we think it is the core of what can be truly said concerning Albert's own theological work.

CHAPTER II

ROGER BACON

ROGER BACON was born about 1214, probably somewhat later (1220?) at an unknown place, but certainly in England. The history of his studies is full of obscurities. Whether or not he studied under Robert Grosseteste at Oxford (1229-1235) still remains a matter for speculation. The date of his arrival at Paris is unknown. Since he himself says that he had seen (*vidimus oculis nostris*) both Alexander of Hales and William of Auvergne, Bacon must have been in Paris before the death of Alexander (1245). This was probably the time when he himself was "reading" to students the books of Aristotle in the Faculty of Arts, which he says he did more often than any other Parisian master. He must have studied theology, but under what masters he did so is not known. As will be seen, he had his own ideas about theology, but the fact remains that he has not written any commentary on the *Sentences,* nor any *Summa theologiae.* The integration of secular learning with Christian wisdom, which remained his constant aim and purpose, does not seem to have required, in his own mind, anything like a systematic body of scholastic theology, not even under the form conceived by Albert the Great. Had he had to teach theology, the *Principal Work* (*Opus principale*) which Bacon always intended to write, would not have fitted the commonly received theological curriculum of thirteenth-century universities. Yet, Christian wisdom always remained his first and foremost interest.

Bacon went back to Oxford about 1247; up to about 1257, he seems to have devoted himself to scientific studies, perhaps, this time, under the inspiration of Grosseteste who was interested in identically the same type of learning. His entry into the Franciscan Order seems to have taken place about 1257, after these ten years of intensive study, but of teaching inactivity, which he himself explains by the poor condition of his health. After his return to Paris, Bacon engaged in the great task of reforming the teaching of Christian wisdom. His *Longer Work* (*Opus majus*) remains the less incomplete exposition of his ideas. When his old Parisian acquaintance, Guy Foulkes, became pope under the name of Clement IV (1265-1268), Bacon sent him a copy of his book which is still extant in the Vatican Library. The pope seems to have received it in 1267. The *Shorter Work* (*Opus minus*) and the *Third Work* (*Opus tertium*) are two shorter, but still more urgent, appeals for a reformation of Christian learning.

After the death of Clement IV (1268), Bacon pursued his scientific activities; The *General Mathematics* (*Communia mathematica*) and the *General Physics* (*Communia naturalium*) seem to belong to this later part of his life. For reasons that remain obscure (they may have been related to his interest in astrology), Bacon became an object of suspicion in his Order. The condemnation of his doctrine by Jerome of Ascoli, Minister General of the Franciscan Order (1274-1279), refers to "certain suspected novelties, on account of which he was condemned to prison." We know that he had been freed before 1292, when he composed his last work, the *Compendium of Theological Studies* (*Compendium studii theologiae*). The date of his death is not known. The career of Roger Bacon practically covers the whole thirteenth century. One of the first masters to "read" Aristotle at Paris, he died after both Thomas Aquinas and Albert the Great. Yet, on the whole, his intellectual attitude links him with Robert Grosseteste and his circle more closely than with anybody else. The new type of scholastic theology which developed during his own lifetime always remained to him, except for his objections to it, as if it had never existed.[15]

I. THE PHILOSOPHER

A mere glance at the philosophical works of Roger Bacon is enough to convince the reader that they were written under the predominant influence of Avicenna. The style is Avicennian; the titles are Avicennian (*Communia naturalium*); last, not the least, Bacon himself explicitly says that, to him, Avicenna was the leader and the prince of philosophy after Aristotle (*Avicenna dux et princeps philosophiae post eum, Opus majus,* Bridges, III, 14). Naturally, Bacon never doubted that, in following Avicenna, he was following Aristotle himself; he should remain to us a representative of those to whom, precisely, Avicenna was Aristotle, which, on some important points, Avicenna was not.

A. *Physics*

Like Albert the Great, Roger Bacon intended to compose an encyclopedia of all sciences, written in a free and direct way (*per modum expositionis*), without adhering to the text of Aristotle, nor even always to the order of his books. He wrote a grammar dealing with the various scientific languages necessary to the Latins; then he disposed of Logic; physics came next in order, to be followed by metaphysics and ethics, which is the end of learning because the cognition of truth is ordained to the doing of the good as to its ultimate end. Since the name "physics" means nothing else than "science of nature" (*physis*), it includes the science of the soul (*psychology*) together with that of other living beings. Bacon intends to deal with these sciences in a free way, without wasting his time on philosophical positions which, like those of Anaxagoras, Democritus, Empedocles, Melissus or Parmenides may have been interesting in their own times, but, today, sound perfectly sterile and ridiculous. Moreover, we should remember that more scientific knowledge could be contained in a single treatise the size of his *De coelo et mundo,* for instance, than there is in all the books of Aristotle. The moderns, who write on a single one of Aristotle's treatises commentaries longer than his complete works, are simply displaying their ignorance. They do not know what is necessary and what is not. The reason for this is simple: these men have never learned the sciences about which they write; they have never taught them in some famous school (*in studio solemni*); they have not even learned them under anybody, and thus, becoming masters without having been pupils, they spread their own errors among the rank and file of their students (II, 11). Again, these men do not know mathematics, without which natural science cannot be acquired. In writing these things, Bacon had two men in mind, two masters famous in his own times (*duo moderni gloriosi*), the Franciscan Alexander of Hales and the Dominican Albert the Great. His remark, that Albert was presuming to teach natural science without having first learned it from any master in any university, may have been true, although we do not know what he had been taught at Padua. As will be seen, according to Bacon, man is essentially a "taught" animal. At any rate, the personal ambition of Bacon was only to retain the very substance of scientific knowledge, and, so to say, its "marrow" (*substantia medullaris,* II, 13), beginning with the fundamental notions of matter and form, whose union makes up all substances.

Matter is an essence essentially different from all forms, either substantial or accidental. It is a common substance. This point is denied by those who imagine that, to conceive matter as a common substance is to conceive it as numerically the same in all composite beings, which is absurd. What is everywhere one and the same, and therefore numerically one, is the "essence" of matter, not its "being." In other words, matter has the same nature in all composite beings. To confuse this doctrine with that of David of Dinant, who taught that since matter is common to all beings, it is infinite like God, and, therefore, is God, is precisely to confuse essence and being. Moreover, it is to forget that the passive receptivity of matter with respect to all forms may well be said to be infinite, but not at all in the same sense as the active potency of God is infinite; there is no resemblance whatever between the passive potency of matter and the active potency of God (II, 55).

Bacon is clear on the point that, considered in its essence, matter is one (X, 60). His conception of what the essence of matter actually is cannot be understood unless one remembers his significant attack against "all" his contemporaries, whom he accuses of positing matter as "numerically one in all things" (*Opus tertium,* Brewer ed., pp. 120-121). This seems to imply that, in Bacon's own mind, matter was much more like the universal intelligible entity posited by Gabirol than the element of the physical composite posited by Aristotle. At any rate, the matter of which he speaks seems to be nothing else than the possibility (i.e., non-necessity) inherent in all beings that are not the necessary being, or God. Since this lack of necessity is common to all finite beings (XI, 57-58), they all are composed of matter and form. Since, on the other hand, each species of beings has its own specifically distinct sort of matter, the problem is to find out the cause for their distinction.[16]

Considered in itself, the notion of universal potentiality is identical with the notion of the matter of any substance in general; it is the matter included in the most general of all genera (*genus generalissimum*, II, 90); this universal genus, therefore, is that of substance in general. All that is a substance first has the matter of substance and the form of substance. In order to be made either a corporeal substance or an incorporeal substance, it must receive the form of either one of these two types of substances. The same remark applies to each one of the successive degrees of determination acquired by concrete beings. Every single being is made up of a hierarchy of matters determined by a corresponding hierarchy of forms. Moreover, every higher matter is as form to the lower ones, just as every lower form is as matter with respect to the higher ones. This twofold series of matters actuating, or perfecting, other matters, and of forms actuating other forms, plays an important part in the doctrine of Roger Bacon (II, 58-60).

The three general species of matter are: spiritual matter (Intelligences and souls), the matter of celestial bodies, the matter of sublunary bodies. Spiritual matter is not subjected to quantity nor change; the matter of celestial bodies is subjected to motion; the matter of sublunary bodies is subjected to both motion and change. Consequently these constitute three specifically distinct types of matter. Incidentally, this confirms what has been said of matter and its divisions. Naturally, just as these matters are specifically distinct, their forms are specifically distinct. The division of beings by their forms is more manifest than their division by their matters, but the matter of a celestial body differs essentially from the matter of a stone by reason of its specific differences in the *genus* matter (II, 64). This is an important point in physics because, if matter were everywhere one and the same in all physical bodies, as all modern philosophers assure us it is, there could be no distinct physical substances and, therefore, neither generations nor corruptions (II, 65).

Natural beings are composed of form, matter and privation, which is, in matter itself, a craving, or blind desire, for the destruction of the old form and to the acquisition of a new one. (II, 72). Strictly speaking, privation is not a third principle; it is matter itself, in the restlessness born of its potentiality. As Alfarabi says, it is not of the essence of matter; rather, it is its accident (II, 79).

A physical form acts upon matter by educing it from potency to act.

The rank and file of theologians and philosophers make a big mistake in imagining, in matter, a kind of active potency which, under the stimulus of an external agent, actuates itself, and becomes form. The potentiality of matter truly is its craving for perfection which, as Aristotle says, it loves as the female loves the male and as the ugly loves the beautiful (II, 84). This is the Baconian meaning of Augustine's doctrine of the "seminal reasons." A seminal reason, Bacon says, "is the very essence of matter which, being incomplete, can be brought to completion, as a seed can become a tree." In itself, it is a seed; inasmuch as it craves to be perfected and actuated, it is a "seminal reason." This aspiration inherent in matter is the seminal reason itself (II, 85). In this sense, natural forms come to matter from both within and without. From within, because their coming fulfils the desire of an imperfect being; from without, because they are given to it by an external agent (VII, 131-132). Bacon is substituting the "mutability" attributed by Augustine to matter for the "seminal reasons." He is parting company with the Philosopher as well as with the Saint.

Since physical beings are made up of matters actuated by forms, Bacon can be counted among the supporters of the plurality of forms; but "form" has not the same meaning in his doctrine and in those of Aristotle, Averroes or Thomas Aquinas. Those who teach the oneness of substantial form imply that where there is a substantial form, there also is an actual being. Consequently, they refuse to posit a plurality of substantial forms in any being for the simple reason that, were it made up of several substantial forms, a being would be made up of several beings. Such is not the case with Roger Bacon. Following the tradition of Denis, he considers each substantial form as preserving within its own being all the inferior forms included in its own essence. When the advent of a higher form has been prepared by that of the lower ones, or when a higher form essentially includes lower ones, these lower forms remain present in the higher one, where they continue to exercise their operations. Yet when all is said and done, the unity of the composite being is safe, because the supreme form of the composite holds all the other ones within its own unity.[17] The Scotist school will call these included forms "formalities."

Although its structure parallels a system of more or less general concepts, this universe is not made up of universals. Forms are more or less universal, but they themselves are not abstract universals. The proof of this is that their degrees of nobility do not follow their degrees of universality. Physical beings, which are the subject matter of natural science, are ruled by their natures. Now, as Avicenna says in his *Metaphysics* (tr. VI, ch. 5), nature is twofold in kind. There is universal nature, that is, the virtues and forces of the celestial bodies, which can be considered as one single nature because they cause all generations and corruptions in this sublunary world. And there is particular nature, which is the ruling virtue of each particular species as well as of each one of the individuals it contains. From the point of view of the operations of nature, the more universal goes first: nature proceeds from substance to body, then to animal. But from the point of view of nature's intention, the particular goes before the universal: nature does not stop at producing animal, it produces horse, or rather "horses," that is, not only a species, but completely determined individuals. What is true in philosophy is equally true in theology. Each individual is more noble than its own universal (*singulare est nobilius quam suum universale*, II, 95). Now, Bacon says, since I deal with all matters in view of theology (*quia omnia quae tracto sunt propter theologiam*, II, 95), let us observe that God has not made this world for man in general, but for individual persons; God has not created mankind; he has redeemed, not man in general, but singular persons; he has not prepared beatific vision for universal man, but for a certain number of personally chosen men. All this shows that "the singular is better than the universal." This is what Aristotle says in the First Book of his *Posterior Analytics:* Farewell, *genera* and *species!* How could they bring about anything? They are monsters (II, p. 95).

This is a point which Bacon intends to enforce because he knows that the rank and file are against it. Ignorant persons, he says, love universals (*homines imperiti adorant universalia*, II, 86). Hence their ceaseless questions about what turns species into individuals. This is the big and insoluble problem of the principle of individuation. In fact, it is a foolish question. Since the intention of nature is to produce individuals, nature itself, which makes individuals, is the cause of individuation. When such people ask us what can be the cause of individuation, since neither the species nor something added to the species can cause it, we should ask them in turn what is the cause of universality, since neither the individual nor something added to the individual can cause it! Theirs is a silly question, because it supposes that an individual can be caused by nothing else than a species, plus something. Singulars are made up of singular constituents just as universals are made up of universal constituents. God makes things as they should be: a man according to his nature and a donkey according to its own, a universal nature if many individuals are to agree in it and a singular nature if it is to be that of only one single individual. There is indeed a great deal of nonsense in this problem they raise about individuation (II, 101).

This is a good example of how a doctrine can be at the origin of several other ones. The plurality of forms, as Bacon conceives it, anticipates the similar position of Duns Scotus. At the same time, his insistence on the singularity of all that is real will find an echo in many early fourteenth-century doctrines, most of them opposed to Scotism. The remark of Bacon, that what stands in need of an explanation is not singularity, but universality, will be taken up by the "Thomist" John of Naples as well as by the "nominalist" William of Ockham.

On nature, the four kinds of causes, chance and other classical problems, Bacon does not seem to have contributed much that was new. As has been said, his whole effort was to simplify problems, leaving out what was useless or had become obsolete in the philosophy of Aristotle. Seen from his own modern times, many things said by the Philosopher appeared to him superfluous (II, 10). Moreover, the translations of his writings were often faulty. Even the masters who had publicly "read" his works in famous schools, when they went over their own notes, could not help wondering if natural philosophy could be learned from Aristotle, following his method and even with the help of his commentators. So, Bacon says, they turn to scientific studies and to mathematics, as well as to the writings of those who wrote on natural philosophy, such as Pliny, Seneca and many other ones; thus, indeed, they succeed in learning what they have failed to learn from Aristotle (II, 12-13). Obviously, the main intention of Bacon went beyond that of Albert the Great, which had been to make Aristotle's doctrine intelligible to the Latins. One of the reasons for this was the difficulties he himself encountered in understanding it, as well as his partial dissatisfaction with Aristotle's neglect of mathematical method. He expressly states that the natural philosophy of Aristotle had begun to be taught about 1245, at the earliest, and this by few masters who had written nothing (*a paucis viris a quibus scripta non sunt facta*, II, 12). He himself seems to be one of those men who, after learning and teaching Aristotle's natural philosophy, had turned their minds to the study of sciences and of other authors in the hope of finding there what they had failed to find in Aristotle. And this effort, too, has left its mark on the physics of Roger Bacon.

The more interesting part of his work is his theory of the multiplication, or propagation, of species. It is directly inspired of Robert Grosseteste and of the optics of the Arabs. The very notion of "species," in its meaning of physical or spiritual emanations flowing from beings and reaching other beings, is one of the most confused we find in mediaeval philosophy. Grosseteste and Bacon have attempted to give it a scientific meaning. Physics is about actions exerted by causes. As undergone, an action is called a passion. Now, let us call "species" the first effect produced by any efficient cause; that is, the medium through which it acts upon another being. A typical case of "species" is light, by which the sun illumines air and causes objects to become visible. Light is the "species" of the sun. It may be given other names: Virtue of the agent, Similitude, Image. Whatever the name, it is a "species," like heat, odors, tastes, etc. The notion of species, therefore, extends to all physical forces because it points out the medium of all natural actions. Optics revealed to Bacon, as to Grosseteste, the possibility of a universal science of the propagation of species and therefore the possibility of a geometrical explanation of all natural operations. By extending to the objects of the five senses what optics had established concerning the object of sight, they hoped to achieve a mathematical interpretation of all natural phenomena. The generalization of the notion of species was necessary to their purpose. This being done, the science of the propagation of species (*de multiplicatione specierum*) could be considered as applicable to all physical facts.

There was, however, a difficulty. It was not easy to fit this quantitative type of explanation in a qualitative physics of Aristotelian forms. But the world of Bacon was not quite the same as that of Aristotle. It was a universe full of efficient causes. To him, the efficient cause of the species is the form, and the purer the form, the more efficient it is. By a special disposition of universal nature, that is, ultimately, by the will of God who intends the welfare of the universe, the highest natures are held, in virtue of their very perfection, to multiply their own influence (*species*); in fact, they do practically nothing else (II, 21). The absolutely highest of all beings, namely, God, produces no species; he creates *ex nihilo*, for his species, or Image, is a similitude naturally born of the Father: the Son of God, identical with him in substance. But all creatures, imitating their creator as best they can, communicate to others, not indeed their substance, but a being specifically similar in nature to their own. The species is the medium of this communication. It is not the active form itself: the species of fire is not fire, but it is its resemblance, that is, something like it: *propter quod non vocantur res, sed similitudines rerum* (II, 23). This awkward notion, which Descartes will severely criticize as being neither clear nor distinct, permitted Roger Bacon to write the sketch of what we would today call a sort of general physics, that is, a mathematical exposition of the laws according to which all forces propagate themselves, first along straight lines (II, 24-26); then following the laws of refraction (II, 28-32); then again in a circular or pyramidal way (II, 36-39), etc. This part of his physics, which Roger Bacon wrote several times under more or less different forms, was incorporated by him to his *Opus majus,* itself the sketch of his *Principal Work,* the great doctrinal synthesis of which he dreamed during his whole life, and never wrote.

B. *Man*

The problem of the human soul is studied by Bacon according to the same method and in the same spirit. His guide remains the same: Aristotle interpreted by Avicenna. He knows that the famous *De spiritu et anima* is not the work of Saint Augustine, but he still thinks that they who, "among other men have been and still are rather good scholars" (III, 282-283), always deserve to be consulted. In the doctrinal milieu where he lives, the traditional conception of the soul as a complete spiritual substance remains the natural one; the only question is for him, as it was for Albert, to maintain this substantial independence of the soul without destroying the substantial unity of man.

The intellective soul alone is immediately created by God; the vegetative and the sensitive souls are just like the other forms which efficient causes draw out of the potency of matter. That the intellective soul is created is a Christian truth, but it also is a philosophical one: *Tota philosophia clamat quod solus intellectus creatur* (III, 283). The agreement between philosophy and theology is perfect on this point, since "all the theologians of England and all the philosophers teach it" (III, 282). The rank and file of the Parisian philosophers, whose errors on this point Bacon reports and refutes, are therefore sinning against both theology and philosophy (III, 284-286).

An important consequence of this position is that, since it is created apart from the other powers animating the body, the intellectual soul is an individual substance composed of its own matter and of its own form; it is an individual in the full sense of the term: a *hoc aliquid* (X, 269). This does not entail that the human soul is a separate Intelligence. Its *unibilitas*, i.e., its natural aptitude to be united with a body, renders it specifically different from pure Intelligences (X, 87). Thus, of its own nature, it is both an individual substance and the immediate act, or perfection, of a physical body. The soul is not the separate mover of its body; it is its mover inasmuch as it is its act.

Since it is an individual substance, the intellectual soul is completely definable apart from its body; but since *unibilitas* is part of its specific definition, it is of the essence of the soul to be the act and perfection of its body. The difficulty is inherent in the problem itself. The soul of the Christian man must be both individually immortal, like a Platonic soul, and the form of its organic body, like an Aristotelian soul. We should not be surprised to find Bacon using both languages. Rather, we should note that the difficulty is less apparent in his doctrine than it was in that of Albert the Great. To him, this probably was one more of those cases when a higher substantial form gathers within its own perfection the lower forms together with their operations.

In accordance with this general position, Bacon holds that rational souls are composed of matter and form, like angels (III, 291), for indeed the question is the same in both cases (*eadem enim est quaestio de angelis et de animalibus rationalibus*, ibid.). The Aristotelian doctrine of the categories compels us to accept this conclusion, for indeed, all that is, is either substance or accident; if angels and souls were not substances, they would be accidents, which is absurd. Now all substances are made up of matter and form; consequently angels and souls are composed of these same principles of being (III, 292-293). Here, like everywhere else, the subject of generation progressively achieves more and more perfect degrees of composition until it receives its highest degree from its highest form. Now, it is a Baconian principle that composite beings are made up of composite beings. The highest form of man must therefore be composite like the preceding ones. The only difference is that, in the case of the rational soul, instead of resulting from an operation of nature (generation), the highest form is directly created by God. This explains the relation of the soul to its body in the doctrine of Roger Bacon. "Since the rational soul is the ultimate perfection of the human embryo, which is composite, this soul must needs be composite, so that its form may perfect the form of the embryo, while its matter completes the matter of the embryo" (III, 293).

The powers of the soul are in it as parts are in a whole. Some say that they are accidents of the substance "soul"; others say that they are something intermediate between substance and accident; in fact, they are "virtual" or "potential" parts, as Boethius says. Such parts are not material fragments of a corporeal whole, but spiritual parts. Their distinction follows from that of their essences, which itself can be inferred from the diversity of their operations. "The soul is one substance composed of several parts, like the body. These parts are different in essence, like those of the body; nevertheless, the whole which results from these parts is one by essence, and it is truly one, because, just as, in the body, there results a form of the whole uniting all the parts in its essential unity, so also, in the soul, there results from many parts a substantial nature in which these parts have an essential unity" (III, 297).

All the problems related to free choice revolve around this question: are reason and will really distinct in the soul, or is their distinction a mere distinction of reason? Bacon holds that the soul is one single substance whose diverse operations are given various names, although, in reality, they cannot be isolated from each other. The same soul both knows and loves, because it knows in order to love, just as, in order to have something to love, it first needs to know (III, 299). This is what theologians seem to forget in dealing with the notion of free choice. Augustine rightly says that it is a power of both reason and will (*facultas rationis et voluntatis*). Now, if we make reason and will to be two essentially distinct powers of the soul, free choice cannot be considered an essentially distinct power. Otherwise, its own essence would be made up of two other distinct essences, which is impossible. Consequently, free choice itself is a power of the soul whose operations are diverse but reciprocally ordered (III, 302). This answer gives Bacon full satisfaction, including that of once more carping at theologians who, because they do not first ascertain the fundamental notions they use, multiply questions almost to infinity.

In a thus conceived human soul, the operations of the intellect cannot be considered apart from the dual aspect of the substance from which they flow. As has been said, the intellective soul is both a substance and a form.

Considered as the form of its body, it performs its operations in conjunction with the body, negotiates with phantasms and, so to speak, uses them in order to know. As form, the intellective soul is the act of its body, inseparable from it and, consequently, mortal like it. On the contrary, considered as a substance, the soul is not passive, but active (*agens*); its intellectual operation does not belong to it *qua* form of a body, but as separated from it; it does not consist in negotiating with phantasms but, rather, in completely turning itself to its own essence, where it contemplates the intelligible models of things. As a spiritual substance, the soul is naturally immortal (VII, 15-16). Now, this is the part of the soul which is an active intellect (*intellectus agens*). Although created in conjunction with a body, which is a matter subjected to change and mutability, the intellective soul can contemplate exalted realities through innate models confusedly known. We call it agent intellect because it does not need sense knowledge. It remains in the soul after death. The possible intellect, however, that is, the inferior reason which negotiates with sensible things, and of which it is said that there is in it nothing that has not first been in the senses, does not seem to remain in the separated soul after death (VII, 109-110). The blending of the Augustinian distinction of *ratio inferior* and *ratio superior*, with the Aristotelian distinction of *intellectus possibilis* and *intellectus agens* is here apparent.[18]

This, which Bacon has never recanted, does not contradict what he says elsewhere concerning an agent intellect separated from the soul. On the one hand, Bacon has always maintained that the duality of the soul (as absolute substance and as form) entailed the duality of its intellectual powers (XII, 157); on the other hand, like Albert the Great, Bacon never denied that, over and above the active intellect that is part of the soul, there was a universally acting intellect, wholly separated from the soul and from all that is, namely God. This is the separate agent intellect which Bacon has always maintained as the source and cause of all reality and intelligibility. The two positions were compatible in a doctrine where the agent intellect in man was just the aptitude of the soul, *qua* spiritual substance, to turn to pure intelligible realities.[19]

Leaving aside the divine agent intellect, whose consideration belongs in metaphysics, let us return to Bacon's statement that our own intellect finds in itself an innate confused cognition of the intelligible models (*exemplaria*) which in God, are principles of both knowledge (Ideas) and operation (forms). Our own active intellect does not know these models in a distinct way, as separate Intelligences do, but in a confused way: "*exemplar . . . innatum et . . . confusum in intellectu animae scilicet agente*" VII, 111). This is what enables our own agent intellect, whose intelligible models (*exemplaria*) are created, to illumine the phantasms and, after purifying them from material conditions, to impart them to the possible intellect (VIII, 81). Hence, Roger Bacon had a notion of abstraction which practically identified it with an illumination of the phantasms by the light of the innate intelligible models created in the soul's agent intellect. That this agent intellect belongs to the soul *qua* substance is in perfect agreement with Bacon's psychology. The seat of these innate intelligibles must needs be separated by its very nature from corporeal matter. Although it speaks the language of Aristotle, this doctrine rests upon a notion of the soul derived from Plotinus through Augustine and Avicenna. Set forth by Gundissalinus, elaborated by William of Auvergne and considered by Bacon as common to practically all theologians, it runs throughout the whole thirteenth and fourteenth centuries. Despite the opposition of Saint Thomas Aquinas, it still will remain a fitting object of reflection, as late as the fifteenth century, for the Franciscan William of Vaurouillon.[20]

C. Being

Metaphysics is the science of being, which is the first and the most universal of our notions. Being is neither equivocal nor univocal; it is analogical. This means that its notion is attributed to all that is, neither as signifying a mere community of name (*canis*, "dog," may mean either an animal or a constellation), nor as signifying a real community of being ("animal" is identical in all animals), but as a name which points out either the same thing or the same notion (according to cases) attributed according to an order of priority or of posteriority. In short, being is analogical because it belongs to all that is, not equally, but by priority or posteriority (XI, 91-92).

Being can be considered as a thing abstracted from other things; for instance, mathematicians abstract mathematical things from sensible things. Being can be considered as a notion abstracted from concrete reality; for instance, in physics, or natural science, "man" or "horse" are abstracted from the particular beings that bear these names. Being can be considered as a notion abstracted from other notions, which is the case in logic, where second intentions are at stake: "species" is a second intention superadded to "man" or "horse." Being can be considered in its universality, that is, neither as restricted to singulars or to species, nor as abstracted from actual beings, and this is the kind of being studied by the metaphysician (XI, 89), whose proper function it is to determine the relations of priority and of posteriority of all things with respect to being. After studying these relations, the metaphysician is led to examine the notion of absolute Being, as neither abstracted nor restricted by any determination, but as separated from the rest by its own perfection, namely, God. Metaphysics then receives the name of theology.

Bacon refuses to introduce any real distinction between being and its properties. Being is substance, and thing, and one, precisely inasmuch as it is being. These notions point out various modalities in our own ways of conceiving being, but no distinct reality. For instance, to say that "being is one is to say that, inasmuch as it is, a being cannot be separated from itself" (XI, 95). "Man," "a man," "this man," are so many expressions that signify the same metaphysical being *qua* being (XI, 96).

After considering the properties of being, metaphysics deals with its causes, not, however, without some qualification.[21] All sciences deal with all the four causes, but each science is especially in charge of one of them, to which it relates the other three. Natural science principally deals with matter; mathematics with form; ethics with ends, and metaphysics with the efficient cause (XI, 105). Accordingly, the metaphysician demonstrates by the efficient cause, which is will (XI, 108). Naturally, this does not prevent him from resorting to forms and to ends in his demonstrations, for, indeed, the final cause is the noblest of all, and it is through its formal cause that the nature of a thing is best known (XI, 110). Yet, when all is said and done, all the demonstrations of the metaphysician ultimately lead him to the supreme efficient cause, which is God.

Being is either universal or singular. Universal beings are caused partly by creation, partly by nature. To create first means to produce something *ex nihilo*, and this is, for all things, the first way of coming into existence. In a second sense, to create means to distinguish and to order already existing singular things. Thirdly, the same term means to unite already distinguished and ordered beings, and this uniting is achieved in universals. The universal is "one in many"; it extends to many singulars. Let us observe, however, that only singulars are created in the proper sense of the term because they are the only completely determinated and subsisting beings. As to universals, they are created in, and together with, singulars; they are "concreated, not created" (XI, 143). For the same reason, universals are not "natures" in the proper sense of the term; they are not tied up with any determinate individual; rather, they are everywhere in a state of indifference to individuals (XI, 144). In things, a universal is an essence that is one in many; in the soul, it is an "intention," or notion, that is found, not *in* singulars, but outside them (XI, 144-145). From the point of view of actual and natural existence, the true being of universals is in singulars; from the point of view of spiritual and cognitive existence, their true being is in the soul (XI, 145). As such, that is, in the soul, to be a universal and to be predicable are two different notions, but in reality they are one and the same thing (XI, 152). All the problems raised by Porphyry and by Boethius in their *Isagoge* are successively dealt with by Roger Bacon, in the same order, not even forgetting the problem added by Abélard: is it possible for universals to subsist after the destruction of all singulars? (XI, 156-158). The object of metaphysical cognition, however, is not the universal as such, which, since universality is predicability, belongs to the order of logic; it is the being of essence considered in itself; for this is metaphysical being

(XI, 160): namely, the essence, or quiddity, which is the complete reality of every being (X, 207-208).

In investigating being and its causes, metaphysics has to posit a non-caused cause whose proper effect is *esse,* being (XII, 89-95). God is the first eternal efficient cause; acting by his will, he is the source whence all beings flow according to their natural order (VII, 57). He is one and eternal; great by his power, which is identical with the infinity of his essence; generous, as one who gives without needing to receive anything (VII, 57-61). Since he is perfect, God is endowed with knowledge: not, however, a knowledge derived from things, but one which is their cause (VII, 78 and 84-85). Although his knowledge is identical with his essence, God knows not only himself, but all beings (VII, 88), whose ideal forms are eternally contained in him. His cognition of other things is achieved through that of their formal principles, or exemplars (VII, 93), in which they are known more truly than in themselves (VII, 95). Possible beings are as well known to him as actual ones. Let us note that, since possibles are included in their eternal exemplars, they are not mere non-beings (VII, 98).

The word "exemplar" signifies a form present in the mind of an artisan.[22] As a principle of cognition, it is called "Idea," or "species." As a principle of operation, it is called "form"; as a principle of both cognition and operation, it is called "exemplar" (VII, 111). In God, there is only one exemplar, neither created nor made, in whose unity the multiplicity of all possible beings is contained (VII, 112-115).

God is immobile; he moves all things because he is their ultimate end (VII, 139-140). He can move them all because he knows them all through his own substance, which is the Idea of all that is (VII, 148). It is therefore an error to posit, under the sphere of the moon, a separate substance such as the "giver of forms" of Avicenna, at least if we understand it as a natural and necessary cause of all motions and cognitions in the sublunary world. Like Albert the Great, Roger Bacon maintains that God is the agent intellect of all that is, so much so that, in comparison with him, man is merely "possible." No doubt, angels have in themselves intelligible forms, but these are not the very forms which are to be found later on either in matter or in our intellects (XII, 62). All forms ultimately come from the divine Ideas, through the will and power of God. Angels can help us in knowing; they even are, with respect to our intellect, active separate substances, because our own intellect has not enough natural light; in this sense, it is fitting that angels should irradiate our intellect, according to their will, in order to help us in acquiring merits (X, 37). Nevertheless, speaking in his own name as well as on behalf of the whole tradition, Bacon maintains that God is the prime and universal cause of all created forms, such as these are found either in actual existence or in human cognitions.

2. THE REFORMER

Even while explaining Aristotle at the Faculty of Arts, Bacon had in view the great theological synthesis (*Opus principale*) which it was his intention to write. He knew that a considerable amount of research work was required for it; that the common effort of many theologians, besides himself, was necessary to bring it to completion, but Bacon was alone, and he never ceased to complain about what he considered a general decadence of philosophical and theological studies in his own times. His obstinate energy in denouncing the prejudices, the ignorance and the laziness of his contemporaries, as he himself saw them, must have contributed to bring upon him their enmity. His treatise *On the Vices Contracted in the Study of Theology* (Steele, I) is a good specimen of what Bacon could write when in his controversial mood, but the *Longer Work* and the two shorter ones show that this was not with him a mood; rather, it was an obsession.[23]

There is one single perfect wisdom, and one science which dominates all the others, that is, theology; but two other sciences are indispensable to unfold it: canon law and philosophy. In other words, the whole body of human knowledge is included in Holy Scripture, which is wisdom, and from whose roots the truth of all the other sciences has sprung. Thus, an interpretation of Scripture by canon law and philosophy would yield a perfect knowledge of divine truth. "All wisdom has been given by one God, to one world, for one purpose," namely man's salvation.[24]

This unitarian conception of human learning, where philosophy, together with its many particular disciplines, is virtually included in revelation, gives its full meaning to the doctrine of God as agent intellect developed by Roger Bacon. First, there is no truth to be found outside of this divine wisdom; at least, whatever intimation of truth may be found elsewhere is sure to be found there in its state of perfection. Secondly, we know that even whatever truth the ancient philosophers have known has come to them from God, that is, from the divine light which illumined their minds.

Roger Bacon has two reasons to affirm this. Philosophers themselves agree that there is a possible intellect and an agent intellect. They also agree that the human "soul" (Bacon does not say "intellect") is "possible" because it is able to receive from on high an illuminating light. Moreover, Alfarabi and Avicenna agree that the active Intellect is no part of the soul; it is a separate substance essentially other than the possible intellect. Even Aristotle says, in his *De anima*, that the active Intellect is separated and unmixed. All those acquainted with philosophy also agree that such was the intention of Aristotle: "For when the University of Paris was convoked, I twice saw and heard its venerable president, Master William, bishop of Paris, of blessed memory, speaking in the presence of all, express the opinion that the active intellect cannot be a part of the soul; and

Master Robert, bishop of Lincoln, and brother Adam of Marsh, and elders of this type supported the same view" (Burke's transl., I, 46). Last, not the least, does not Augustine teach, in his *Soliloquies* and elsewhere, that the rational mind of man "is subject to God alone in its illuminations and in all principal influences," so much so that "we do not learn any truth except in the uncreated truth and in eternal laws." What all these famous theologians, and Bacon after them, were doing on this point, is clear: they were substituting the Christian Word of Saint John and Saint Augustine for the separate Intelligence of Avicenna.[25]

If what Bacon says is true, he is equally well founded in maintaining that philosophy is, in our minds, an effect of the divine illumination. Philosophy was revealed to men in the beginning; the patriarchs and the prophets received it from God, and not only the law of God, but all the disciplines that make up philosophy (*Opus majus*, II, 9). The pagan philosophers, who succeeded the prophets, inherited their wisdom, and Bacon tells at great length the fantastic tale of this transmission of divine learning from the Jewish prophets to the Greek philosophers. Its details are of no particular importance, but its conclusion is highly significant: "Therefore philosophy is merely the unfolding of the divine wisdom by learning and art. Hence there is one perfect wisdom which is contained in the Scriptures, and was given to the Saints by God; to be unfolded, however, by philosophy as well as by canon law" (*Opus majus*, II, 14; Burke, I, 65).

Bacon did not think he was the first one to know the rules of sound theological and scientific methods. The two predecessors he liked to mention were Robert Grosseteste and Peter of Maricourt. He liked Robert Grosseteste first because, without being in the least ignorant of Aristotle's books, the bishop of Lincoln had desired to learn from other authors and from his own experience; then because, with Adam of Marsh and others, he had learned to explain mathematically the causes of all phenomena, and shown that mathematics is necessary, not only to all natural sciences, but to theology itself: *per potestatem mathematicae sciverunt causas omnium exponere*.[26] But if he received from his English masters the taste and respect for mathematics, it was to a Frenchman that he owed the feeling, so vivid in him, of the necessity for experiments. His real master on this point, and the one he was forever praising, was Peter of Maricourt, the author of a treatise on the magnet which W. Gilbert quoted even in the early seventeenth century and which at that time was still the best work on magnetism.[27] Peter proclaimed, in his *Letter on the Magnet* the necessity of completing the mathematical method by the experimental method. It was not enough to know how to calculate and reason, one should also be clever with one's hands. With manual skill (*manuum industria*) one can easily correct an error that he would not discover after an eternity of trying by the sole resources of physics and mathematics. Roger Bacon seems to have been deeply impressed by that new method and by the learning Peter of Maricourt owed to it. He calls him the master of experiments: *dominus experimentorum,* and draws us a really striking portrait of this solitary scholar, of whom we know so little. Those, with a few other still more obscure names of isolated seekers, were the masters whose methods he claimed to take up again and whose effort he wanted to promote.

It is, therefore, important to stress first the role mathematics were to play in the constitution of science. One can learn nothing of the things of this world, either celestial or terrestrial, unless he knows mathematics (*impossibile est res hujus mundi sciri, nisi sciatur mathematica*). That is evidently true of astronomical phenomena, but since terrestrial phenomena depend directly on the stars, no man can understand what happens on earth if he is ignorant of what is happening in the heavens. Moreover, it is certain, and Robert Grosseteste had perfectly proved it, that all natural actions are propagated and performed in conformity with the mathematical properties of lines and angles. There is, therefore, no need to press this point.[28]

As to experiment, it is much more necessary, for the superiority of the evidence it brings with it is such that even mathematical evidence can sometimes be upheld by it. "There are, in fact, two ways of knowing: reasoning and experiment. Theory concludes, and makes us admit the conclusion, but it does not give that assurance free from all doubt in which the mind rests in the intuition of truth, so long as the conclusion was not arrived at by way of experiment. Many people have theories on certain subjects, but as they have not had experience of them, these theories remain unutilized by them and incite them neither to seek a certain good, nor to avoid a certain evil. If a man who has never seen fire were to prove by conclusive arguments that fire burns, that it spoils and destroys things, his listener's mind would remain unconvinced, and he would not keep away from fire until he had put his hand or some combustible object in it, to prove by experience what theory had taught him. But once having made the experiment of combustion, the mind is convinced and rests on the evidence of truth; reasoning, therefore, is not enough, but experiment does suffice. That is clearly evident even in mathematics, whose demonstrations are the surest of all." If someone possesses a conclusive demonstration in these matters, but without having verified it by experience, his mind does not follow it, is not interested in it, and he disregards the conclusion until an experimental proof makes him see the truth. Then only will he accept that conclusion with perfect tranquillity.

Experiment as Roger Bacon conceives it is twofold. The one is internal and spiritual, whose highest degrees lead us to the summits of the inner life and of mysticism; the other is external and we acquire it by means of the senses. It is the latter which is the source of all our veritably certain scientific knowledge and, in particular, of the most perfect of all sciences, experimental science.

Experimental science (*scientia experimentalis*), whose name seems to appear for the first time in the history of human thought under the pen of Roger Bacon, prevails over all the other kinds of knowledge by a triple prerogative. The first is that, as we have said, it engenders a complete certitude. The other sciences start from experiences considered as principles and deduce their conclusions from them by way of reasoning; but if they wish to have in addition the complete and particular demonstration of their own conclusions, they are forced to seek it from experimental science. This is what Roger Bacon proves at great length in a series of chapters devoted to the theory of the rainbow. The second prerogative of that science is that it can take up at the point where each of the other sciences ends and demonstrate conclusions that they could not attain by their own means. An example of discoveries that are found at the limit of the sciences without being either their conclusions or their principles is the increased length of human life, which will crown medicine, but which speculative medicine alone could not achieve. The third prerogative of experimental science is not relative to the other sciences, but consists in the proper power which enables it to peer into the secrets of nature, to discover the past, the future and to produce so many marvelous effects that it will secure power to those who possess it. This is what the Church should take into consideration, in order to be sparing of Christian blood in its struggle against the unbelievers. This science would enable us to foresee the perils that will attend the coming of Anti-Christ, perils which it would be easy for the Church to prevent, with the grace of God, if the princes of the world and the popes would favor the study of experimental science and carry on the search for the secrets of nature and of art.[29]

Roger Bacon's *Opus majus* does not present itself as an exposition of Christian wisdom, for the learning necessary to it still remains to be acquired. Bacon only intends to urge the pursuit of research, and especially the practice of experiment. This is the theme he goes over tirelessly: here reasoning does not prove anything, everything depends on experience (*Nullus sermo in his potest certificare, totum enim dependet ab experientia*). Beyond describing this method, of which he is sure, Bacon can give us only samples of its fecundity. This accounts for the encyclopedic character of his main work, in which we come across successively: the analysis of the conditions required for a serious study of scientific languages, an exposition of the mathematical method with examples of its application to sacred and profane sciences, a treatise on geography, a treatise on astrology and its uses, one on vision, a description of the experimental method and an ethical doctrine borrowed from Seneca and other ancient moralists. All these speculations attest a very extensive erudition, a lively taste for concrete facts and a sound appreciation of the conditions necessary to promote scientific progress. His errors themselves often betray a mind ahead of his time. For instance, his vivid interest in alchemy and in astrology, which he shared with many of his contemporaries, should not be considered as the mark of an abnormally adventurous spirit; Bacon simply knew more about these things than most of the theologians of his times, with the possible exception of Albert the Great. Had he been able to write it up, the theology he had in mind, although unusual in its form and in its method, would have been rather traditional in its content. More than the doctrine itself, the spirit that animated it gives it interest and assures it a lasting place in the history of ideas. Remembering the miserable conditions in which he lived, his poor health, the difficulties which hindered him not only from making experiments, but even from writing, one feels astonished at this unhappy genius who, alone in the thirteenth century, dreamed of a universal Republic of Christians, united under the authority of the popes, and directed, guided, saved by the truth of an all-comprehensive Christian Wisdom.[30]

CHAPTER III

MIDDLE THIRTEENTH-CENTURY LOGICIANS

THE progressive invasion of the University of Paris by the doctrine of Aristotle is a well-known fact, but we are still far from knowing with precision the details of this epoch-making event. One of the safest approaches to its correct understanding is to remember that, to the Parisian masters of the early thirteenth century, the discovery of the natural philosophy of Aristotle, either in his own works or in those of his Eastern disciples was that of a new and universally applicable method. The notion of "science," that is, of a necessary knowledge justified by strict demonstrations, together with the notion of "art," that is, of a systematic body of principles and consequences, progressively invaded the whole field of intellectual culture. According to the doctrine of the *Posterior Analytics*, I, 1, teaching (*doctrina*) was the communicating of an art, while learning (*disciplina*) was the acquiring of this art under the guidance of a teacher. These three notions progressively became inseparable. Teachers began to consider it their duty to reduce everything to an art, that is to say, to a set of conclusions deduced from principles. This evolution affected the whole field of studies, from grammar up to theology. The new conception of grammar which appears, not for the first time but with unmistakable clarity, in the doctrine of Roger Bacon, was the starting point of this evolution.

Few mediaeval philosophers have insisted as strongly as Roger Bacon on the importance of the *grammatica,* that is, the teaching and learning of languages, but he was interested in them for scientific rather than for literary reasons. Moreover, Bacon is an excellent witness to the change which the very notion of grammar was slowly undergoing in his own times. Taken in its traditional sense, grammar has for its object to teach the congruity of expression in any language. To know the grammar of a language is to know the rules, or the received usage, which have to be observed if one wants to speak that language correctly. Consequently, there are as many grammars as there are languages. On the other hand, the grammarians of the thirteenth century noticed that each language raised two sorts of problems, some proper to the language in question (Hebrew, Greek or Latin grammar), others common to all languages (what is a noun, a verb, an adverb, etc.). The first sort of problems could not become an object of science; the second sort of problems, on the contrary, could be taught in a scientific way on account of their generality. Hence the progressive constitution of what was to be called later on "speculative grammar" (*grammatica speculativa*), whose object it was to teach the general rules followed by the human intellect in expressing itself, namely, its various "ways of signifying" what it thinks (*modi significandi*). Thus conceived, grammar could become a science and be taught as a true learning because its object was universal and its conclusions deducible from principles. As Roger Bacon vigorously puts it: "Grammar is substantially the same in all languages, even though it may undergo in them accidental variations." He himself was keenly aware of the irreducible nature of particular languages and of the importance of their study; no language, he said, can be translated into another one without losing its proper qualities. Bacon did not want to suppress particular grammars; he merely conceived the possibility of a general one: the universal grammar of human language, taken precisely *qua* human.

This new conception of *grammatica,* which seems to go back to the twelfth century, is remarkably expressed in an anonymous text of that period: "He who knows grammar in one language, also knows it in another as far as the essentials are concerned. The fact that he cannot, however, speak another language, or understand those who speak it, arises from the difference of words and their formations, which is accidental to grammar." [31] In other words, one can know the essentials of Latin grammar without knowing a single word of the language of Virgil. This position accounts for the violent hostility of the mediaeval humanists to the logicians and dialecticians of their own times. Petrarch will be an outstanding witness to this reaction. Later on, Alexander Hegius, Erasmus's professor at Deventer, was to write a pamphlet *Against Those Who Believe that the Knowledge of the Modes of Significance is Necessary to Grammar.* Nothing less than literary culture was at stake. The poem of

Henry of Andelys, *The Battle of the Seven Arts*,[32] which seems to date from the second quarter of the thirteenth century, vividly describes the classical grammar of the mediaeval humanist as fighting a losing battle. In Henry's poem, the situation is remarkably clear. The Classics are in retreat; the students no longer are interested in anything but the "books on nature"; theology keeps aloof from the fight; yet, Henry concludes, the battle is not lost forever. After thirty years or so, new men will come and revive the study of grammar as it used to be taught and learned at the time when Henry of Andelys was born. Henry was not a bad prophet. Not thirty, but about sixty years later, the child Petrarch was to rediscover classical grammar in the school of a modest grammarian of Carpentras.

The history of the thirteenth-century doctrinal development is dominated by the fact that it had two distinct centers. On the one side, theology was teaching Christian dogmas as found in the Bible and in the *Book of Sentences* of Peter Lombard. This book itself resembled what we would call a course in "positive theology." It was an ordered compilation of texts borrowed from the Fathers of the Church, especially Augustine. These texts retained very little of the philosophical speculation inserted by Augustine himself in his own "Christian learning" (*doctrina christiana*). It is a notable fact that, up to the time of Saint Bonaventure, there is little evidence of direct utilization by the theologians of the philosophical elements contained in Augustine's theology. Anselm, for instance, who professed to attempt a re-exposition of Augustine's theological teaching, had borrowed from him no proof of the existence of God, no doctrine of the divine illumination, no doctrine of matter, of seminal reasons, etc. During the first half of the thirteenth century, in the works of Albert the Great and of Roger Bacon for instance, there is evidence of a direct acquaintance with the *Soliloquies* and other writings of Augustine. Augustine is then quoted in support of the fundamental doctrine of the divine illumination, which is practically inseparable from the notion of the human soul as a complete spiritual substance. It is not always easy to distinguish the influence of Augustine from that of Denis on the first point, nor of that of Avicenna on the second point; in fact, the two influences often combine in the mind of the same theologian. The theme *de fluxu entis*, on the universal flowing of beings and knowledge from God, is no less typical of this early theological position, and it is likewise difficult to say what it borrows from Denis, or what it borrows from Alfarabi and Avicenna, sometimes through Gundissalinus. Even Maximus Confessor and Erigena can occasionally enter this doctrinal complex. Albert the Great has sometimes quoted Erigena, under the name of Maximus, without being aware of what he was really doing. At any rate, it is important to realize that, in the minds of the representatives of this early theological attitude, since the doctrine of the divine illumination was to be found in Saint John, in Denis the Areopagite and in Augustine, it was straight theology. Similarly, since Augustine had taught that the soul is a spiritual substance united to a body, these two positions appeared to them as purely theological. They were part of the "Christian learning" and theologians would maintain them as such, as part and parcel of the theological tradition. This justifies those historians who deny the existence of a "philosophical" Augustinianism before 1250 or so; but it does not justify the denial of the presence, in early thirteenth-century theology, of Augustinian elements which, because they had been borrowed from Plotinus, or from Proclus, were no less philosophical in nature than in origin. The commentary of Grosseteste on the *Posterior Analytics* is a point in case, and it is representative of many others. When a theologian writes a commentary on the logic of Aristotle, and crowns his interpretation of the Philosopher with an Augustinian (or Dionysian) doctrine of the divine illumination, it is not easy to deny that, essentially, philosophical notions are at stake. In history, which deals with singulars, formal distinctions seldom apply. In fact the philosophical elements which Augustine had included in the science (*scientia*) which he used to call *doctrina christiana* (Christian learning), seem to have dominated the speculation of the early thirteenth-century theologians.

The other starting point was philosophy, especially logic, whose natural teaching center was the Faculty of Arts. Yet, from the very beginning, its masters were reminded that there was a Faculty of Theology whose decisions were final in many philosophical matters. Nor were the Masters of Arts unaware of the fact. Rather, like Roger Bacon, they would study philosophy in view of theology. Albert the Great, whom Bacon reproaches with teaching the philosophy of nature without having first learned it under a master and in a regularly constituted school, had no other intention in composing his gigantic philosophical encyclopedia. The fact that the meeting of philosophy and theology took place in the minds of theologians, or in theologically-minded intellects, makes it difficult, if not impossible, to divide doctrinal history following the lines of institutional distinctions.[33] To be a Master of Arts was to be, at least as a rule, a future master in theology. True enough, Bacon never taught in any faculty of theology; yet, his questions on the books of Aristotle are full of protests on behalf of the Christian tradition and of invectives against the rank and file of the theologians who, according to him, are constantly betraying it. Even in the minds of such men as William of Auvergne and of Albert the Great, who were fully aware of the speculative distinction between philosophy and theology, there was a continuous interplay of these two distinct disciplines. That, in some minds, and partly under the influence of the distinction between the two faculties, a tendency to specialize in philosophy should arise, was practically unavoidable, but it is hardly perceptible, about 1230, at the Faculty of Arts of the University of Paris.

The only Masters of Arts teaching philosophy as if there were no theology, in the first half of the thirteenth century, were the logicians, not at all because they themselves were not interested in theological problems (for many of them became theologians) but because, by reason of its abstract nature, logic afforded few opportunities to deal with properly theological questions. Since it dealt with beings of second intention, logic was not a *scientia realis;* because they were not handling reality, its teachers had a free hand. Moreover, the teaching of logic had been part and parcel of mediaeval learning ever since the discovery of Boethius, whose work had been continued by Abbo of Fleury, renewed by Abélard and perfected by his successors. Discussions about logic should be conceived as distinct from the metaphysical controversies about the nature of universals which had developed around the *Isagoge* of Porphyry. Logic *qua* logic was henceforward at stake, and the Faculty of Arts was the proper place to study it.

In his *Battle of the Seven Arts,* Henry of Andelys has named several logicians well known in his own times, but of whom we know very little. The armed forces of Dame Logic were under the command of Pierron of Courtenay, "a very learned logician," whose lieutenants were John le Page, Pointlane of Gamaches and Nicole (lines 51-56). We do not know who Pierron of Courtenay was, but both Pointlane of Gamaches (*Pungensasinum*) and John le Page (*Johannes Pagus, Pagius*) have been identified.[34] They had certainly been Masters of Arts and, consequently, professors of logic, but our documents also attribute to them commentaries on the *Sentences,* and consider them as theologians. Nevertheless, John le Page seems to have written a treatise in logic: *Appellationes seu syncategoremata,* a subject matter which called for few properly philosophical developments.

An extremely precious document discovered by M. Grabmann[35] enables us to form an opinion about the kind of teaching given at the Faculty of Arts in the second quarter of the thirteenth century (*ca.* 1240). The Introduction to this interesting treatise clearly defines its object: "The number and difficulty of the questions, especially those asked at examinations, are a burden all the heavier because they are exceedingly widespread and arise from various disciplines without having any order or continuity about them. With this in mind, we thought it would be useful to present a sort of résumé of those questions with their answers, and to explain what was most important to know, following a certain continued order and beginning with what philosophy is, whose name is common to all these disciplines." The author then begins with a series of definitions, the knowledge of which is still precious to those who read nowadays the philosophical or theological works of the middle ages. *Philosophia* designates the search for and discovery of causes, the outcome of the love of knowledge; *scientia* designates a *habitus* of the soul, that is, the firm possession of a certain knowledge; *doctrina* is the communication of knowledge by the master, in the schools, by means of teaching; *disciplina* expresses the spiritual link between the master and the pupil; *ars* signifies the method of exposition and the technique of a science; *facultas,* the last, emphasizes the facility of elocution and expression, the alertness of mind and the resources to be drawn from a science, somewhat as we give the name *facultates* to acquired wealth. Following these indications, the handbook classifies the various sciences, or branches of philosophy, which it divides into natural philosophy, whose principle is nature studied in its various degrees of abstraction (mathematics, physics, metaphysics); moral philosophy, whose domain is subject to the will; rational philosophy, whose principle is reason. Next come the indications of books, principally those by Aristotle, in which these sciences are set forth, and the questions habitually propounded at examinations. By far the larger part of the question bears on "rational philosophy," which is here divided into grammar, rhetoric and logic. In grammar, the classical textbooks of Donatus and Priscian are used and great importance is ascribed to speculative grammar. On the contrary, comparatively few questions deal with the philosophy of nature and metaphysics; a larger number deal with ethics. If this document represents the real situation obtaining at the Parisian Faculty of Arts between 1230 and 1240, we may safely conclude that, up to that date, the center of gravity of its philosophical teaching was speculative grammar, logic and ethics. The repeated interdictions to teach the other books of Aristotle, in 1210, 1215, and even as late as 1231, certainly exercised a delaying influence on the spread of the new philosophical learning. But another cause contributed to the same result. Professors of logic had been plentiful ever since the early twelfth century, whereas there were no masters prepared to teach biology, physics, astronomy, psychology or metaphysics. In these domains, there was no school tradition. The remarks made later on by Bacon, when he remembered the early efforts of "few" and often discouraged masters, who wrote nothing, to teach these difficult texts, throw a vivid light on the situation then obtaining. His own teaching of the philosophical and scientific writings of Aristotle did not begin earlier than 1240. Apart from always possible discoveries, there is little hope for us to gather precise information concerning the early attempts to teach the scientific books of Aristotle at the Faculty of Arts of the University of Paris.

Not so with logic. The *Introductions to Logic* by William of Sherwood, an English master in Paris during the first half of the thirteenth century (d. after 1267), seem only to have survived thanks to a unique Paris manuscript which has recently been edited.[36] The circulation of this introductory work seems, therefore, to have been somewhat restricted, perhaps because of the extraordinary success of the slightly later but

similar works by Lambert of Auxerre and Peter of Spain. William of
Sherwood's logic, divided into seven parts, takes up successively the
proposition, the predicable, syllogism, dialectic sources, the properties of
terms, sophisms and *syncatagoremata*.[37] The whole treatise is oriented
toward the two chapters dealing with dialectics and sophistics. A remark
by William himself throws a vivid light on the spirit of his work: "The
complete knowledge of the syllogism demands that it be known not only
according to its definition, but also according to its division . . . There
is a demonstrative syllogism, a dialectic syllogism, a sophistic syllgoism.
The demonstrative produces knowledge starting from the necessary and
absolutely certain causes of the conclusion; the dialectic starts with the
probable and ends with opinion; as to the sophistic, syllogizing beginning
with what has the appearance of the probable, or seeming to syllogize
starting from the probable, or doing both, its aim is glory and triumph in
discussion. Omitting the others, we shall confine ourselves to the dialectic
syllogism." [38] This is typical of the mediaeval taste for dialectics conceived
as the art of ending in probable opinions, halfway between the certitude
of scientific knowledge and the sham of sophistics.

Lambert of Auxerre's *Dialectics* (about 1250) seems to have been
widely known. Lambert was supposed to have been William's student. It
is a not unlikely hypothesis, but it is not even necessary to admit it to
explain the similarity of two textbooks written about the same period, in
view of the same examination and for the students of the same university.
At any rate, the spirit of the two works is the same. Lambert knows
very well that logic is the science of discerning the true from the false
by argumentation, and that because of its universal bearing it is the art
of arts, the science of sciences. To open it is to open them all, and to
shut it is to shut them all; in short, it is the science without which no
other is possible, with which all the others become possible. Thus understood, logic is superior to dialectics, that is, the one among its parts
which only deals with the probable, or even with what has only the appearance of the true syllogism. Lambert of Auxerre's logic is an art, that
is to say, a body of rules all tending to the same end, which is the knowledge of the principal object of a certain discipline. That art itself can be
reduced in method. This term, which Descartes was to make famous by
his *Discourse on Method,* seems to have attracted Lambert's attention
as early as the thirteenth century. Methods, he says, are to the corresponding arts what footpaths are to main roads, that is, short-cuts that lead
to the same place more directly and quickly. A method, therefore, is
always easier than the corresponding art (*facilius methodus quam ars*).
In this sense, dialectics can be considered the art of arts because its
method gives access to all other methods. Since it alone is qualified to
test the principles of all the other arts, it introduces us to the principles

of all the other methods. The publication of Lambert's treatise would fill up a regrettable gap in the history of thirteenth century logic.[39]

We are more fortunate in the case of the *Summulae logicales* of the Portuguese Peter Juliani, usually called Peter of Spain (Petrus Hispanus), pope at his death in 1277, under the title of John XXI.[40] An echo of the ideas just noted in Lambert is heard in the very first sentence of Peter of Spain: "Dialectics is the art of arts, opening the way to all methods . . ." etc.[41] The *Summulae* of Peter soon became what we would call a best-seller in mediaeval universities, and it kept its place on the list for about three centuries, which modern best-sellers seldom do. It was often annotated and commented upon by representatives of different philosophical schools, a sure sign that its logic did not seem to be tied up to any particular metaphysical doctrine.[42] Commentaries on these *Summulae logicales* have been written by Simon of Faversham, professor at Paris and at Oxford (d. 1306); by the Dominican Robert Kilwardby (d. 1279), who describes the treatise by Peter of Spain as an "introduction to dialectical art for students"; by the Carthusian Henry of Coesfeld (d. 1410); by John Hockelin, Ulrich of Tübingen, John of Bayreuth, Jean Letourneur (*Versorius*, d. about 1480), Lambertus de Monte (d. 1499); by the Albertist Gehrard Harderwyck (d. 1503); by numerous Scotists like Nicolaus de Orbellis (d. 1455), Peter Tateret (*Tartaretus*, rector of the University of Paris in 1494), Johannes de Magistris, and so forth, and even by such famous nominalists as Marsilius of Inghen and John Buridan. This variety in commentators makes it difficult to accept the hypothesis, attractive in itself, that the dialectical probabilism of the logicians of Paris was one of the causes (some have even said the main cause) of the philosophical probabilism of the fourteenth century.

At any rate, it is remarkable that in Peter of Spain himself the dialectical character of logic by no means had as its consequence either a probabilism or a skepticism of any sort in philosophy properly so-called. For he was not only a logician. In addition to his *Summulae logicales* and the *Syncategoremata*, we owe to him commentaries on the *De animalibus, De morte et vita, De causis longitudinis et brevitatis vitae* and *De anima*. His predilection for these treatises is understandable for this logician was at the same time a physician. His chief philosophical work is a treatise *On the Soul,* and perhaps a commentary on the *De anima* of Aristotle; both have recently been published. The fact that Peter remains best known for his *Summulae logicales* has unjustly overshadowed the importance of his contribution to philosophy.

The *Science of the Soul* [43] of Peter of Spain seems to be posterior to his *Summulae.* In the last lines of his treatise, he modestly calls himself "doctor in liberal arts, rector of the philosophical sublimity, honor of the medical faculty and past master in the science of the soul." This suggests at least a man well advanced in his career. The prologue to the treatise unmistakably recalls the pious and rhetorical psychology of the twelfth century. Created unto the image of God, the soul is obscured by the darkness of corporeal clouds. Forgetful of itself, of its natural conformity with the spiritual substances, and desirous to recover its pristine resemblance to God, this soul reveals at once its Cistercian origin (Alonso ed., p. 46).

As soon as he begins to deal with technical problems, Peter takes sides with the representatives of the Avicennian tradition. Since all that is, is either substance or accident, and since the human soul cannot be an accident, it is a substance. To be exact, it is a thing placed in the category of substance (*Res quae anima dicitur, in genere substantiae collocatur*, p. 58). Defined in itself, it is a substance participating in reason; defined with respect to its body, it is the formal principle, or act, that perfects it (p. 58). Being a spiritual substance, the soul has no matter. Besides, since it is a substance complete and individual in itself (*forma completa et hoc aliquid*) the soul needs no matter in order to subsist (p. 58). Nevertheless, it is not a separate substance. It belongs in the genus of substance by reason of its essence, or entity, which is that of a quasi-complete substance (*substantia quodammodo completa*), but it is united to a body, in which it exists and which it rules as the pilot steers his ship or as the prince sways his city (p. 59). In other words, the soul is the lowest of the spiritual substances according to the order of nature; for this reason, while it is conformable to the purely spiritual beings above itself it also is conformable to the world of corporeal beings by reason of the body it animates and in virtue of its aptitude to be united to it (pp. 74-75). Naturally, since it is a substance, it is immortal (pp. 389-402).

Without quoting anybody, not even Aristotle, Peter proceeds "by mode of exposition" to a complete description of the powers of the soul and of their operations. Like Albert the Great, Peter simply stores up secular learning under a Christian roof. When it comes to definite philosophical problems, Peter is even less precise than Albert. For instance, he knows that sensation is a particular case of "abstraction" from matter; in fact, it is the lowest one (p. 210). He also defines the sensitive soul as the perfection of the organic body and he sees in it "the origin of the apprehension of corporeal forms" (p. 102); but if we ask him what is the exact nature of sense perception, he gives no clear answer. From what he says, one would think that, on the whole, he agrees with Aristotle (p. 213), but since, in other passages, he expressly ascribes to us "innate" cognitions (p. 477), he could not very well conceive even sense knowledge in exactly the same way as Aristotle. A still more puzzling problem is raised by the passages where Peter speaks of *esse* as of "the proper act of essence, and the prime act of all, including all in its comprehension" (pp. 411 and 413). What does he mean by *essentia*? Is it "essence," or is it "entity"? And how should we understand *esse*? Does it mean "to be"? Or does it mean "being"? In reading that "in any living creature, its life differs from its substance" (p. 411), one has the uncomfortable impression of meeting already-known formulas, which have come from elsewhere and have lost their meaning during the journey.

This scarcity of doctrinal elaboration becomes still more apparent in the last part of the treatise, where Peter of Spain deals with the nature, powers and operation of the intellective soul. Since one of its functions is to receive intelligibles, it must have a possible intellect of its own. This intellect, which is open to all the intelligible forms as matter is open to all the material forms, emanates from the essence of the soul. Consequently, it is incorporeal in nature, and yet, it is bent upon the body and its lowest faculties (p. 430). At the time of death it ceases to exercise its functions, but it retains the incorruptible life given to it at its origin (p. 401).

As it has its own possible intellect, each soul has its own agent intellect. Neither one of these two intellects can be defined apart from the other. The possible intellect is "a power emanating from the soul, bent upon the body and the powers of the lower order, and immediately receptive of the impressions made by the intelligible phantasms, which the sensitive powers offer to it together with their appendages" (p. 430). The agent intellect is "a power of the intellective soul, illuminating by its light the intelligible species received from the possible intellect and the sensitive powers, purifying them from their material and accidental appendages, and educing them from possible intellection to actual intellection, in order that, having thus received its perfection, the intellectual soul may apply its most exalted power to the consideration of the highest objects" (p. 440).

Thus understood, the soul is placed, so to speak, on the border-line of two worlds. It extracts intelligible forms from material things, and, in so doing, it becomes like a mirror of the corporeal universe, but, at the same time, through the power of the agent intellect, "the Separate Substance presents to it both its own nature and the exemplars of things." One of the functions of the agent intellect then is "to transmit to the possible intellect the impressions which it receives from the Supreme Cause and from the Separate Substances" (p. 440). This intellect is no less distinct from the possible intellect than from the essence of the soul. Whereas the agent intellect of man is "immortal, separable, perpetual and unmixed, the possible intellect does not attain to these conditions" (p. 443).

Over and above these two human intellects, there is a separate agent Intelligence (*Intelligentia agens separata*). No abstractive cognition would be possible without its co-operation (p. 445). This Intelligence causes

knowledge in the intellect as the light of the sun causes sight in our
eyes (p. 446). This "active substance is the Intelligence of the last and
lowest order which, being intimately present to the intellectual soul, reveals to it, by its illumination, the intelligibles[44] so that its relation to
the intelligible forms is the same as that of light to colors" (p. 446).
These remarks apply only to the illumination of sensible forms, for indeed,
since the soul itself is a spiritual substance, it is directly and immediately
intelligible to itself: (*Anima vero se intelligit per presentiam suam nudam*,
p. 447; cf. pp. 459-462). This theme immediately combines with the
well-known doctrine of Avicenna, that since the intelligible forms cannot
be the material forms themselves extracted from their matters by the
agent intellect of man, they cannot be stored in it as in a sort of
intellectual memory. These forms simply emanate from the Separate
Intelligence into the soul each time the human intellect needs to conceive
them (p. 448; cf. pp. 459-462). The Separate Intelligence creates these
forms; all that the human intellect has to do is to receive, to distinguish
and to order them. Incidentally, let us note that just as our intellect
does not extract material forms from matter, the separate agent Intelligence does not drop into our souls the intelligible forms of which it is
full. Its action is one more particular case of the universal law of the
"multiplication of species" (Grosseteste, Bacon). What the Separate Intelligence does is to multiply images, or "similitudes," that is, "species"
of its own intelligible forms (p. 449). Intellectual cognition, then, is the
actual copulation of a naked intelligible form with the soul (p. 449).
Every time this happens, there is an act of intellection. Concerning the
various levels at which this spiritual union may occur, Peter tacitly
follows Avicenna's classification of the different degrees of intellectual
perfection: *intellectus materialis*, or *possibilis; intellectus adeptus; intellectus accommodatus et in effectu* (pp. 466-467). Once the soul has reached
this summit, it can turn upon itself and, in perceiving its own perfection,
it arrives at the term of its intellectual effort (p. 469).

Peter of Spain had never taught theology. In fact, about the only title
which he did not claim for his own at the end of his treatise was that of
a theologian. Roger Bacon, whom he resembled in more than one way, but
especially in his doctrine of the soul, had never taught theology either.
What they were both teaching appeared to them as straight science. As
Peter says, it is the science of the soul (*scientia de anima*). All this
doctrinal complex, whose main features dated from Gundissalinus in
the twelfth century, survived up to the end of the thirteenth century,
and it did not completely disappear even after the death of Roger
Bacon, Albert the Great and Peter of Spain. It was little more than a
syncretism, but it was an unmistakably philosophical one. In it, the
Plotinian doctrine of divine illumination, inherited and revised by
Augustine, combines with elements borrowed from Boethius, Alfarabi

and Avicenna, not to quote many other sources. Like all Christians, these men had predominantly theological interests, but their teaching was not a theological one. Even in the theological synthesis of Albert the Great, the scientific and philosophical elements which belong to this doctrinal complex are still found in their condition of crude ore, before its later theological processing. Whether we call this complex "Augustinian" or not is of little importance. What matters is the fact that it did exist and that one of its most typical representatives, Peter of Spain, happens to be the pope who, under the name of John XXI, was to provoke later on the condemnation of 1277.[45]

PART EIGHT

THE GOLDEN AGE OF SCHOLASTICISM

The second half of the thirteenth century can be called the classical period in the development of mediaeval scholasticism. It corresponds to the moment when, fully conscious of the nature of the task that lay ahead of them and provided with the material required to perform it, some theologians succeeded in building up complete theological syntheses, for instance, Saint Bonaventure and Saint Thomas Aquinas. It was their privilege to achieve their work at a time when, although anybody could see that a crisis was brewing, it had not yet taken place. There is, in the writings of these masters, and especially in their earlier ones, a sort of serenity born of the confidence felt by their authors that, if properly understood, philosophy was on the side of theology and reason in fundamental harmony with revelation. The commentary of Bonaventure on the *Sentences* was completed, at the latest, in 1255; Thomas Aquinas completed the Third Part of the Summa, up to qu. XC, in 1273; both died in 1274, three years before the doctrinal storm of 1277 which brought the summer of scholasticism to an end. Even the theological style of these fifty years can be said to be classical in its own order. The technique of the "question" has been perfectly mastered; the language of the theologians and of the philosophers has become both precise and supple and no writers have ever said more with a stricter economy of words. Historians have created a different reputation for them, but among those who judge the language of the great scholastics, how many can understand its meaning?

CHAPTER I

THE FRANCISCAN SCHOOL

ALEXANDER was born in England, at Hales, probably Hales Owen (Shropshire), slightly before 1186. He was about fifteen years old when he went to Paris in order to complete his first education. After the six years of studies required from future teachers, he became a "regent" at the University, at the age of twenty-one, in 1206-1207. From the Faculty of Arts, he went over to the Faculty of Theology where he became a "master," probably in 1220-1221. He was one of the first masters to teach a commentary on the *Sentences* of Peter Lombard, whose text had recently been approved by the Lateran Council (1215). After two years of interruption (1229-1231), Alexander resumed his teaching at the University of Paris (1231-1232) and entered the Franciscan Order about the beginning of the school year 1236-1237. He then was at least fifty years old. This decision gave to the Franciscans their first chair at the University and became the origin of the Franciscan school of theology at Paris. There is no decisive reason to think that Alexander did not carry his teaching up to the date of his death, August 21, 1245.[1]

I. ALEXANDER OF HALES AND JOHN OF LA ROCHELLE

The name of Alexander is linked to a monumental work of which Roger Bacon has said in his *Shorter Work* (*Opus minus*) that the Franciscans "attributed to him that great *Summa*, heavier than a horse, although it had not been done by him, but by others." Modern historians admit that Bacon was largely right. The so-called *Summa of Brother Alexander* certainly contains elements borrowed from his authentic works, but even these are often either abbreviated or enlarged; for the rest, it is a compilation, probably undertaken by John of la Rochelle and completed by later Franciscan theologians. It already existed about 1250, but what its composition may have been at that date is not known. Under its present form, it includes extracts from John of la Rochelle, Bonaventure, William of Meliton, etc. This does not mean that the *Summa* is of no historical interest. Despite its composite character, it has a unity of its own, due to the fact that its component fragments are all borrowed from Franciscan theologians belonging to the same doctrinal school. Owing to this unity of inspiration, it remarkably illustrates what may be called "the spirit of the thirteenth-century Franciscan school of theology at the University of Paris." Even as a collective work, it has a distinct signification.

Apart from the *Summa,* some authentic works of Alexander have now been published. In his glosses on the First Book of Peter Lombard,

327

Alexander appears to us as hesitating between two mental universes. On the one hand, he freely draws from Aristotle, and not only from his logical writings, but also from his *De anima, Physics, De coelo, De generatione et corruptione, De animalium generatione, De motu animalium, De juventute et senectute, De somno et vigilia, Metaphysics,* etc. In short, at the time when he wrote his own commentary on Lombard (1220-1225), Alexander had practically the whole doctrine of Aristotle at his disposal. On the other hand, his main theological authorities were Saint Augustine, Denis, Boethius and many eleventh- and twelfth-century theologians, such as Anselm, Alan of Lille (*Regulae*), Bernard of Clairvaux, Gilbertus Porretanus, William of Conches, the psuedo-hermetic *Book of the Twenty-four Philosophers,* Richard of Saint Victor, etc. There is little evidence of sustained controversies with his own contemporaries in the texts of Alexander which we know. His work seems to belong to a time when no collective theological effort was yet being made in order to assimilate the newly discovered Aristotelian world.

The "Distinctions" of Alexander on the *Sentences* already resemble the "articles" that will constitute the *Summa* of Thomas Aquinas. Their structure is simple: 1) statement of the question (*Quaeritur an . . .*); 2) a choice of objections against the intended answer (*Videtur quod non . . .*); 3) affirmation of the answer on the strength of a theological authority (*Sed contra . . .*); 4) justification of the answer (*Respondeo . . .*); 5) refutation of the objections. Not all the Distinctions of Alexander exhibit this perfect structure, but many do. The scholastic "Question," which is the organic cell of all the scholastic Commentaries on the Sentences, Disputed Questions, Quodlibetic Questions and *Summae theologiae,* is already present in the glosses of Alexander of Hales.

Like all his contemporaries, and some of his successors, Alexander had no clear idea of the true meaning of the philosophy of Aristotle. He repeatedly quoted the *Liber de Causis* as an authentic work of the Philosopher. His sketchy arguments in favor of the existence of God can hardly be called demonstrations (p. 40), although we should remember that these notes of a professor in view of his lectures do not represent their full oral development: "Every mobile, taken as such, presupposes some supreme immobile principle, otherwise one should proceed *in infinitum.*— Likewise, nothing of that which is can hold its being from itself; otherwise, being would have no term, and, from this the existence of a supreme being can be inferred." A no less short argument proves that, since nothing is good by itself, there must be a supreme good. Thus, Alexander says, "in reasoning, our intellect always strives to reach that which does not exist in virtue of something else" (p. 40). Even adding to these assertions other arguments borrowed from John Damascene and from Anselm of Canterbury (whose *Proslogion* he quotes as the *De personis logion,* that is, "on the divine persons"), we still remain very far from the speculations of Saint Bonaventure on the divine being. It is a curious fact that a man so full of Augustine, whom he never tires of quoting, does not think of resorting to the remarkable demonstrations of the existence of God which he had at his disposal.

The treatment of psychological notions, inserted in the commentary on the occasion of the doctrine of the image of God in man, is strictly Augustinian, or inspired of such pseudo-Augustinian sources as the *De spiritu et anima*. Against William of Auxerre, Alexander maintains that the powers of the soul are one with its substance. Not, however, with its essence, because, since essence is that by which the soul is what it is, its powers are not what makes the soul to be a soul; on the contrary, since substance is what makes a thing subsist in its indivisible unity, the soul cannot be complete without its powers or faculties (p. 65). This position of the problem will remain characteristic of the Franciscan school up to the time of Duns Scotus. The theological interest at stake was that, for a true Augustinian, it could not be "accidental" to the human soul to be a created trinity, that is, an image of God.

Alexander follows Augustine in his discussion of the problem of evil (pp. 68-73); Boethius on the distinction of *quo est* and *quod est* (p. 105, with shades of difference in interpretation); Augustine again concerning the notion of wisdom (p. 468), and, indeed, practically everywhere, without betraying any eagerness to go beyond the theological statement of his positions in order to elaborate properly philosophical interpretations of their meaning. To repeat, Alexander of Hales cannot be judged on the sole basis of this early commentary. Yet, since no other certainly authentic documents are at present available, we can only see him as the origin of a theological movement which rapidly went beyond its initiator. His first disciples probably knew, between the years 1220 and 1245, a more mature Alexander, whose teaching they incorporated into the *Summa fratris Alexandri* and into their own works. This supposition agrees better than the text of his commentary with the repeatedly-made statement of his immediate successors, including Saint Bonaventure himself, that they felt indebted to him for their whole theological teaching.

Such was, for instance, the case, with John of la Rochelle,[2] a disciple and younger colleague of Alexander at the University of Paris, who died a few months before his master, on February 8, 1245. In addition to several theological works (*Summa de virtutibus, Summa de vitiis, Summa de articulis fidei*) he left a *Summa de anima* which shows him to be imbued with a very highly developed philosophical spirit. He himself, in one of his sermons, alludes to the hostility of those who were at that time making every effort to stifle theological studies, and attributes it openly to the influence of Satan who does not want Christians to have cultivated minds.

As he conceives it with Avicenna, the rational soul is a simple substance, capable of vivifying the body and accomplishing multiple operations in it.[3] Simple in its essence,[4] the soul is multiple as to the several different powers whose operations it exercises either with the body or without it. In order to recognize them, it is sufficient to observe the distinction of their objects. From there one goes on to the distinction of their operations, and then to that of their natures. His classification of faculties follows almost exactly that of the Augustinian apocrypha *De spiritu et anima* and places at their peak, beyond the intellect which knows the created intelligibles (angels, souls), the intelligence (*intelligentia*) which knows the true and the immovable good, that is, God. The following ascending scale of faculties is thus obtained: the senses perceive the body; the imagination, the similitudes of bodies; reason, the nature of bodies; intellect, created spirits; intelligence, the uncreated Spirit.

Sensations result from the action exerted on the organs by bodies, thanks to the intermediary of physical media, which are the diaphanous for sight, air for hearing, vapors exhaled by objects for the sense of smell, saliva for taste, flesh for touch. The data from those particular senses are centralized by the "common sense," here described as in charge of preserving them and combining them to form the "common sensibles" (that is to say, common to several senses), such as size, movement, rest, number and so on. Common sense, which Avicenna calls *sensus formalis,* is an internal sense. In order to disengage abstract notions from common images, the intellectual faculty (*virtus intellectiva*) is required, which is bound to no particular organ, but is completely present in the whole body: *est in toto corpore tota.*[5] Abstraction does not consist in really separating the constitutive elements of the object, but in considering them separately, thanks to an appreciation (*aestimatio*) which distinguishes them from one another by grouping the resemblances and eliminating the differences, but without cutting them completely off from the sensible: "On the contrary, the intellective faculty apprehends the corporeal form, stripped of all the particularities of matter and of its very singularity, and it apprehends it thus itself, naked, simple and universal . . . In fact, if it were not thus stripped of all the rest by the consideration of the intellect, it could not be known as a common form predicable of all the individuals. These degrees in the order of abstraction from the body should therefore be distinguished: first, in the senses; secondly, in the imagination; thirdly, in the cogitative (*aestimatio*); fourthly, in the intellect."[6]

In spite of the influence of the *De spiritu et anima,* and of Avicenna's psychology, this doctrine represents rather well what was commonly to be retained of Aristotle's teaching; but John of la Rochelle wished in addition to reconcile the Greco-Arabian doctrine of the agent intellect with the Augustinian doctrine of divine illumination. He expressly recognizes, in each human soul, the Aristotelian distinction of the possible intellect (in potency with regard to intelligibles, like a tablet on which nothing is yet written), and of the agent intellect which is in our soul as the intelligible light of God himself, and always in act. Aristotelianism is thereby winning a decisive victory, since John of la Rochelle, like Albert the Great and Saint Thomas Aquinas, but contrary to William of Auvergne, is here attributing to every human soul, taken individually, an agent intellect proper to it, which is in it as the mark God left upon his handiwork. This intellect, John says, is the highest faculty of the soul: *intellectus agens, id est vis animae suprema,* and we need nothing else in order to know either the material beings external to us, or the faculties and operations of our soul, or even the primary principles of natural knowledge. From that moment, at least in all essentials, the bases of an Aristotelian and Thomist theory of knowledge are already laid down. The fact that John of la Rochelle seems nevertheless to admit one or several other separate agent intellects is not hard to explain. He simply desires to impart a Christian meaning to the Avicennian doctrine of the separate Intelligences. Each of them can be called an agent Intellect, since it is a spiritual substance, distinct from the soul, superior to it and capable of acting upon it to confer on it gratuitously and from without forms of knowledge that it could not acquire by its natural light. In this sense, God and the angels can be considered as so many separate agent Intellects, the angels to instruct man in what concerns the angels, God to instruct him in supernatural truths like the Trinity, which concern only God. These verbal concessions entail no modification of the doctrine. If we add that John of la Rochelle rejects Gabirol's thesis on the composition of matter and form in the human soul and in angels, we shall doubtless feel inclined to see in his psychology the manifest proof of the profound influence exerted by Aristotle, as early as the first half of the thirteenth century, even on some Franciscan masters, but Saint Bonaventure's doctrine was soon to rally his contemporaries, especially within the Franciscan Order, around the principles of Saint Augustine.

2. BONAVENTURE AND HIS SCHOOL

The spirituality of Saint Bonaventure has exercised a decisive influence on the choice he made of a set of philosophical positions as well as on his way of handling them.[7] First and foremost a theologian, he was clearly conscious of the new type of learning represented by what we today call scholasticism and he has left us one of its most perfect descriptions. Since the subject matter of theology is what a Christian must "believe," its formal reason is to be the object of a possible act of faith; let us call this, by nature, something "believable," or "credible." The proper task of theology, conceived as a discipline distinct from simple faith, then, is to render "intelligible" this "credible" by adding reason to it. As he says in the first question of the Prologue to his commentary on the *Sentences:* the subject matter of theology is the believable turned into intelligible owing to an addition of reasoning (*credibile, prout tamen credibile transit in rationem intelligibilis, et hoc per additamentum rationis*). To study what may be called the "philosophy of Saint Bonaventure" is first of all to abstract from his theological speculation the rational elements which he intentionally added to faith in order to achieve its understanding. Here again, as in the case of all his contemporaries, abstraction entails no separation. The connecting link between faith and reason is love. The human soul is destined to enjoy the infinite good which is God. This supreme good is now confusedly and obscurely grasped by man through faith; for a rational being, nothing is more desirable than to understand what he firmly believes and loves; thus, because theology is born of an effort to understand faith, a new rational speculation arises from it.

A. *God*

This theological speculation finds itself confronted with different objects. Some exceed the power of human reason and belong to theological speculation alone because they necessarily require faith at the origin of argumentation. When the starting point either is, or includes, an act of faith, philosophy can still be put to good use by the theologian, but his conclusions are irrelevant to philosophy. On the contrary, when natural reason can grasp a certain object, then, even though it may be offered to man as a "credible," this object retains the formal reason of "intelligible" as common to all objects of rational speculation. To express in concrete terms this general attitude, let us say that, in the mind of Saint Bonaventure, faith leads the way and reason is its fellow traveler. At a certain point, reason has to stop, because it ceases to see what faith is still able to grasp. Up to that point, however, reason is able to see, in its own light, something of what revelation offers us to believe. The larger part of these naturally knowable truths included in theological learning are related to God and to man, that is, to man and to his ultimate end.

Saint Bonaventure's doctrine can be characterized as an "itinerary of the soul toward God," or, rather, up to him. It teaches "how man goes to God through other things." Accordingly, his outlook on man and things will be dominated by a twofold tendency; first, to conceive the sensible world as the road that leads to God; next, to conceive man as a creature naturally open to the divine light and God as revealing himself to man through the whole gamut of his illuminations. The mystical trend of the doctrine is immediately apparent to the reader of Saint Bonaventure; it accounts for his effort to retain as much as he could of the doctrines of Augustine and of Denis even while speaking the language of Aristotle.

As has already been seen, he was not the first theologian to do so; nor was he to be the last one, but he has done it in a particularly systematic and consistent way.

It is possible to find God by considering his creatures, because the truth of things consists in their representing the primary and supreme truth. In this sense, all creatures are so many ways to God. Their resemblance to him is not a sharing in his own being; it is but a resemblance or imitation which can be a faithful one only to the extent that the finite can resemble the infinite. To describe it by a technical term, let us say that it is a resemblance of "expression," as a spoken word expresses its meaning. Considered from this point of view, therefore, what we call creatures, or things, constitute a sort of language, and the whole universe is only a book in which the Trinity is read on every page (*creatura mundi est quasi quidam liber in quo legitur Trinitas fabricatrix*).[8] And if one were to ask why God created the world on this plan, the answer would be very simple: the world has no other reason for being than to give utterance to God; it is a book which was written only that it might be read by man and be the unceasing reminder of its Author's love. Since the First Cause has made the world in order to manifest itself, the illuminative way will go back over the course of things in order to raise us up to the God whose expression they are.

Three principal stages will mark the moments of that ascension. The first consists in finding the *shadows* and *vestiges* of God in the sensible world; the second consists in seeking his *image* in our soul; the third goes beyond created things and brings us into the mystical delights of the knowledge and adoration of God.[9]

To find God again, thanks to the vestiges he has left in things, is to "enter into the way of God," and it is also to find in passing all the proofs of his existence one ordinarily derives from considering corporeal reality. But what characterizes Saint Bonaventure's attitude is that he scarcely stops over the technique of their elaboration; he urges us directly to perceive God present in the movement, order, measure, beauty and disposition of things; still better, he manifestly thinks that we can arrive at the existence of God no matter what we start with, so that, for a cleansed mind and heart, every object and every aspect of each object betrays the secret presence of its creator. That is why the dialectic of the *Itinerary* tends to multiply the points of view from which we perceive God rather than to constrain us to reach him through a small number of channels. It is a question, fundamentally, of not having scales on our eyes; when the scales fall from our eyes, we see God everywhere. The splendor of things reveals him to us if we are not blind; they proclaim him aloud and will awaken us if we are not deaf; one must, in fact, be dumb not to praise God in each of his operations and mad not to recognize the primary principle by so many indications.

And yet that is still but the first degree of the ascension, and all these clarities are still only shadows. The proofs through the sensible world that he gives us as blinding evidence seem to Saint Bonaventure to be nothing more than exercises of the mind when he thinks of the more decisive proofs offered us by that image of God, our soul. In considering the sensible world we can in fact find in it a sort of shadow of God, for all the properties of things require a cause: we can also see his traces in it by seeking in the unity, truth and goodness they possess the mark of their efficient, formal and final cause; but in both cases we turn our backs, so to speak, on the divine light whose reflection is all we seek in things. By seeking God in our soul, we turn directly to God himself; what makes us find in it not only a shadow, or a mark, but the very image of God, is that he is not only its Cause, but even its Object.

Notice that the idea of God is, in fact, implied in the simplest of our intellectual operations. In order fully to define any particular substance, higher and higher principles must be called upon until the idea of self-subsisting being is arrived at, for indeed, unless we know what being is in itself, we cannot fully know the definition of any particular being. Our intellect only manages, therefore, fully to grasp its objects thanks to the idea of being, pure, total and absolute; it is the presence in us of the idea of the perfect and the absolute which permits us to know the particular as imperfect and relative.

But let us go still further. Not only could our changing and uncertain intellect not apprehend without God's help the immutable and necessary truths, as Saint Augustine had already shown, but it even finds God directly each time we go deeply enough into ourselves. Our intellect is joined to the eternal truth itself; we have within us the image of God naturally infused. Just as we directly know our soul and its operations, so we know God without the help of exterior senses.[10] If, then, there seemed to be no evidence of the existence of God, that could only be for lack of reflection on our part. If concupiscence and sensible images do not interpose their veils between truth and us, it becomes evident that it is useless to prove that God exists.

It is easily conceivable that such a theologian should welcome Saint Anselm's ontological proof and incorporate it just as it was in his own doctrine. Perhaps one might even say that for the first time that argument takes on its full value, and places its reliance on a full knowledge of the conditions it presupposes, in the doctrine of the Seraphic Doctor. The fact is that in this case we are no longer affirming the presence of God because we are gaining knowledge of it; we know God, on the contrary, because he is eminently present to us: *Deus praesentissimus est ipsi animae et eo ipso cognoscibilis.*[11] If God's presence is the basis of our knowledge of him, it goes without saying that the very notion we have of God implies his existence. It implies it precisely because the impossibility of our thinking that God is not, is in us the immediate effect of the intrinsic necessity for his existence: *tanta est veritas divini esse, quod cum assensu non potest cogitari non esse.* It is, therefore, the intrinsic necessity of God himself which, constantly illuminating our soul, makes it impossible for us to think that God is not, or to maintain that without contradiction. To become aware of this fact is to see that the very notion of God implies his existence. Since he is being pure and simple, immutable and necessary, it is one and the same thing to say that God is God, or to say that he exists: *si Deus est Deus, Deus est.*[12]

It goes without saying that Saint Bonaventure does not thereby attribute to us a clear concept of the divine essence. What is found to be inseparable from, and profoundly imprinted upon, our own thought is the affirmation of the existence of God, and not to the slightest degree the comprehension of his essence. Saint Bonaventure was quite aware of the very precise objections which, ever since the time of Gaunilon, theologians had leveled at the ontological argument, but he considered them irrelevant. Hugh of Saint Victor had already said that God proportioned our knowledge of him in such a way that we could never either know *what* he is, or not know *that* he is.[13] Such also is the formula that Saint Bonaventure adopts, agreeing on this point with tradition.

We could go beyond this second stage of the "Itinerary of the soul toward God," and ask of mystical contemplation the ineffable joys of the divine presence, but in overstepping the limit of what can be expressed in words we would be leaving philosophy. Here, says Saint Bonaventure himself, we must concede little to word and pen, and grant everything to the gift of God, that is, to the Holy Ghost. Let us then leave these lofty regions and ask ourselves rather what conception of the human soul and of knowledge implied such proofs of the existence of God.

B. *The Soul*

The soul is essentially one, but its faculties, or powers, vary according to the nature of the objects to which it applies. This is possible because the soul itself is at one and the same time an intelligible substance complete in itself, to such a point that it can survive the death of the body, and the form of the organic body it animates. Insofar as it animates the body, it exercises its sensitive functions in the sensory organs. Sensitive knowledge includes first an action exerted by some exterior object and undergone by a sensory organ. Moreover—and Bonaventure here cedes to Aristotle the ground Augustine occupied—the soul itself spiritually undergoes that action, inasmuch precisely as it is the quickener of the body; but it immediately reacts, in bringing a judgment (*judicium*) to bear on the action it has just undergone, and it is this very judgment which is sensible knowledge. Bonaventure seems, therefore, to wish to reconcile the Aristotelian doctrine of sensation conceived as a passion undergone by the human compound with the Augustinian and Plotinian theory of sensation conceived as an action of the soul.[14]

Sensible images are the data from which the intellect gets its intelligible knowledge. Abstraction is the work of the possible intellect which, turning toward these images, carries out the necessary operations for retaining only the common and universal element of these particular data. It seems that Saint Bonaventure confines himself to the purely psychological plane of abstraction conceived as an effort of attention to classify and order sensible data according to the laws of reason. The possible intellect, for him, is not then pure potentiality, which would be confusing it with matter; it is an active faculty of the intellect which prepares intelligible notions and gathers them up. It is called "possible" because, of itself alone, it would not be equal to that task. Each human soul possesses, in addition to its own possible intellect, its own agent intellect whose function is to illuminate the possible intellect and render it capable of effecting abstraction. This implies that just as the possible intellect is not devoid of all actuality, the agent intellect is not exempt from all potentiality. A pure act, it would be the separate agent Intelligence which Avicenna describes, and which Bonaventure well knows, but which he does not want at any price.[15] Agent intellect and possible intellect are fundamentally two distinct functions of one and the same soul in its effort to assimilate what there is intelligible in the sensible.

This effort of abstraction, furthermore, is not always necessary; it is required only when our thought turns its "lower face" toward the body in order to acquire scientific knowledge of it, not when it turns its "upper face" toward the intelligible to acquire wisdom. In fact, the intellect must have recourse to sensible knowledge in order to know everything foreign to its own spiritual nature, that is to say, in order to know everything which is not itself and God. All the products of the mechanical arts and all natural objects are foreign to its own nature; the knowledge of the former is foreign to it as exterior, the knowledge of the latter is foreign to it as inferior, and for both of them the intervention of the senses is needed. But it is quite another thing when the intellect is turned toward the soul, which is always present to it, and toward God, who is still more present. It is not Aristotle who prevails this time, but Plato. From the moment we go beyond sensible objects to raise ourselves up to intelligible truths, we call upon an inner light which is perceived in the principles of the sciences and the natural truth innate in man. The soul itself, the principles of philosophy which it contains, and the divine light which makes us know them, spring from a loftier order of knowledge in which sensibility has no part. Saint Bonaventure here is not confusing two philosophies whose fundamental oppositions might be unknown to him; he is, on the contrary, in full awareness of what he is doing, attempting a synthesis of Plato and Aristotle. Let us be more exact, he believes he is promoting the tradition of a synthesis which the genius of Saint Augustine had already achieved. Aristotle knew how to speak the language of science, and he clearly saw, contrary to Plato, that human knowledge has not the intelligible world of ideas for its object; but Plato spoke the language of wisdom in affirming the existence of the eternal reasons and Ideas; Augustine, enlightened by the Holy Ghost, could speak both languages: *uterque autem sermo, scilicet sapientiae et scientiae, per Spiritum datus est Augustino.*[16]

If Saint Augustine had been able to realize this synthesis, it was thanks to his doctrine of the illumination of the intellect by the Ideas of God. Saint Bonaventure made that doctrine his and transmitted it to his school. It consists essentially in explaining the presence of necessary truths in human thought by the direct and immediate action of divine Ideas on our intellect. The usual formula of the problem, in Saint Bonaventure's works, consists in asking how the human intellect can attain an absolutely certain knowledge (*certitudinalis cognitio*). Such knowledge presents two characteristics: it is immutable as concerns the object known and infallible as concerns the subject knowing. Now, man is neither an infallible knowing subject, nor are the objects he attains immutable in nature. If, therefore, the human intellect possesses intellectual certitudes, it is because the divine Ideas themselves, which are immutable intelligibles, illumine the human intellect in its knowledge of such objects. The Ideas do not come in here as objects seen, for they are God himself, a sight of whom is inaccessible to us here below; they act upon the human intellect by immediate contact, but they exercise upon it a simply regulative action. Thanks to them, we see not only *what is,* but the agreement or disagreement of what is with *what should be.* Because the divine Ideas judge our intellect, it in turn becomes capable of judging things.

It would be unwise to reduce this complex doctrine of knowledge to a single formula. But one would not be very far from the mark in saying that Bonaventure explains all true knowledge of the intelligible by the action and presence in us of a weakened ray of the divine light. A weakened ray, we say, because Bonaventure always declares that we do not attain the eternal "reasons" or ideas as they are in God, but as their reflection, and confusedly: we see of them only what a creature can, *cum propria ratione creata.* But it is certain, on the other hand, that the divine Ideas, or eternal reasons, are indeed the immediate rule of our knowledge. It is not simply *by* the eternal reasons, but *in* the eternal reasons that we see the truth: Bonaventure is formal on this point, and his steady refusal to water down his doctrine rests upon his interpretation of Saint Augustine. His thought is so firm here and his conviction so unshakable that he accepts even the utmost consequences that could be derived from it. If all true knowledge implies that we attain the eternal reasons, and as we attain these reasons only confusedly, does it not follow that we have no perfectly well-grounded knowledge here below? This, answers Saint Bonaventure, must be conceded. We have certain and clear knowledge here on earth because the created principles that God has impressed in our minds, and by which we know things, appear to us clearly and unveiled. But that clear and certain knowledge is not complete; its ultimate foundation is still lacking, for, if the principles of knowledge are clear, the eternal Ideas, whose action regulates our intellect by submitting it to these principles, escape our notice here below, and yet they give the principles their truth value. If, therefore, one were to say that in this life we have no "plenary" knowledge, there would not be much objection to that: *si diceretur quod nihil in hac vita scitur plenarie, non esset magnum inconveniens.*[17]

Why this double aspect of human knowledge? It is because man finds himself in an intermediary position, doubtless infinitely nearer to things than to God, but between God and things nevertheless. One can consider truth as it is in God, in our soul, or in matter, and if we consider it in our soul we shall see that it has relation to the truth in God as well as to the truth in matter. An intermediate between two extremes, the soul turns by its superior part toward God, and by its inferior part toward things. From what is beneath it, it receives a relative certitude, from what is above it it receives an absolute certitude.

C. *The World*

Since we have relied upon creatures to raise us up to God, we have attained him immediately as creator. The question is now to know whether the world is eternal or whether it began in time. Aristotle and Averroes are of the opinion that the universe is eternal because movement itself is.[18] Saint Thomas was to consider that the proofs adduced in favor of the eternity of the world are not decisive, but that there are no decisive proofs in favor of creation in time either; and thus creation in time will only be retained as true on the strength of revelation. Bonaventure adheres more firmly than ever to tradition on this point, and refuses the least concession to Aristotle's thought. To him, it is contradictory to admit that the world may have existed from all eternity. If the universe continued to exist after an infinite time had already gone by, one would have to admit that the infinite could increase since new days are added to old; or that of two numbers equally infinite, like the number of the lunar revolutions and that of the solar revolutions, one is twelve times larger than the other; or that the world had no initial time-limit, and that consequently it could not arrive at its present time-limit since the duration to be run through would be infinite. Moreover, let us remember that an infinity of objects or individuals cannot exist simultaneously (since an infinite quantity cannot actually exist); now if the world were eternal, there would be an infinity of immortal souls, which is contradictory. We should therefore recognize, not only by faith but also by reason, that it is impossible to posit the created universe as co-eternal with God.[19]

With respect to the very structure of creation, let us observe first that in all created things essence is really distinct from existence.[20] In other words, since no creature is of itself sufficient reason for its existence, each one requires the efficacy of a creator; thus pantheism is set aside. But in addition all created beings are made up of matter and form, that is, of possibility and of act. In itself, matter is not necessarily either corporeal or spiritual, it becomes one or the other only according to the form it receives. God alone is pure act. In every finite being, its very finiteness must necessarily leave room for a further possibility of being, and this possibility is the very thing we call matter. Thus the angels and human souls, because both of them are substances, are composed of a spiritual matter and the form which determines it.[21]

If this be true, matter alone cannot constitute the principle of individuation. A thing is, only because it has matter, but it is what it is only because that matter is determined by a form. The union of matter and form is the true principle of individuation.[22] But in combining this theory of individuation with the theory of universal matter, we obtain two new consequences. The first is that it will not be necessary to agree with Saint Thomas that an angel, because devoid of matter, can only be an individual species rather than a true individual. The second is that we should have no difficulty in explaining the survival of the soul after the destruction of the body. Souls are not incomplete substances whose union with a body would constitute man, a complete substance. The soul is already a form complete in itself, composed of its matter and its form, independently from the body which it will in turn perfect. The soul possesses itself of the already constituted body and gives it its final perfection, but it achieves its own perfection in separating from it.[23]

Two other doctrines give to Saint Bonaventure's doctrine of nature its characteristic aspect. First the thesis of the plurality of forms. Every being assumes as many forms as it has different properties; in each thing, therefore, a multiplicity of forms is discovered which are graded in such a way as to constitute a unity. That is true of the simplest bodies and even of elements. A body always presupposes at least two different forms; one, which is general and common to all, is the form of light, in which all things share; the other, or others, which vary with different beings, are mixed forms or elements. Secondly, Bonaventure integrates with his doctrine, under the double pressure of reason and Saint Augustine, the Stoic notion of seminal reasons. Matter, which by itself would be completely passive, immediately receives a virtual determination by the substantial forms which remain latent in it until they later germinate and unfold. All the phenomena and all beings in the universe are thus accounted for by the development into forms of primitive seeds, or seminal reasons, whose primary cause is God.[24]

It appears from this summary that Saint Bonaventure's doctrine was not without reason designated by the name "Augustinism." Although he combined Ibn Gabirol with Saint Augustine, it was really from the philosophical elements present in Augustine's doctrine that the principles of Bonaventure's conception of God were borrowed, together with his conception of human knowledge and the nature of things. But, even after having redistributed between their numerous sources all the elements of that synthesis, the existence of a spirit of Saint Bonaventure and an attitude truly personal to him must still be recognized. One frequently imagines, in reading his *Opuscules* or even his *Commentary on the Sentences,* a Saint Francis of Assisi gone philosopher and lecturing at the University of Paris. The confident ease and deep emotion with which Brother Bonaventure discovers in things the very visage of God, closely resemble the sentiments of Francis, reading like an illuminated manuscript the beautiful book of nature. And no doubt, sentiments are not doctrines, but it happens that they engender doctrines. To that permanent emotion of a heart that feels itself near to God we owe the refusal to follow up to its very final consequences the philosophy of Aristotle, and the persistent maintenance of an intimate contact between creatures and their creator.

D. *The Bonaventurian School*

Representatives of this doctrinal complex are to be found everywhere in the second part of the thirteenth century, at Paris, Oxford and in Italy. These university centers were communicating at that time, as one did not leave Christendom in going from one to the other. Augustinians belonged to all the religious Orders, but most of them were Franciscan Brothers, and it is the members of this group that we are to study. Some of their names are still for us only the symbols of important works, largely unedited and consequently not well known, whose meaning will perhaps appear some day to be quite different from what we suppose it to be.

Such a surprise, however, is hardly to be expected with regard to Eustachius of Arras (d. 1291). This disciple of Saint Bonaventure gives the appearance, at least in the texts already published, of a resolute partisan of the doctrine of divine illumination.[25] To explain our knowledge of bodies, he admits that their substantial form can attain the intellect through the senses. This invites us to imagine that, in spite of his Aristotelian terminology, the substantial forms of which Eustachius speaks, differed only slightly from forms as Bonaventure conceived them.

Another disciple of Saint Bonaventure, Walter of Bruges (d. 1307), left a *Commentary on the Sentences* (Bks. I, II, IV) that is almost entirely unpublished, and important *Disputed Questions,* which give evidence of his fidelity to the principles of Saint Augustine. He himself declared that he trusted more to Augustine and Anselm than to the Philosopher, and this statement is in keeping with the few published texts we already have at our disposal. The hylomorphic composition of spiritual substances (souls and angels), direct knowledge of the soul by itself, the doctrine of divine illumination, the immediate certitude of the existence of God, are so many Bonaventurian theses that Gauthier must have taught at Paris about 1267-1269, and which belong—all of them—to the Augustinian complex.[26]

The work of Saint Bonaventure's famous Italian disciple, Matthew of Aquasparta,[27] is also largely unpublished, but it has been better studied than the works of Walter of Bruges. Matthew had a clear mind, and if not in his commentary on Peter Lombard which seems to be an immature work,[28] at least in his admirably constructed disputed questions, he often clarifies points which Bonaventure had left unsettled. Faithful as he is to his master, there are nevertheless many points on which Matthew goes his own way. For instance, he stresses the unity of the human composite more forcefully than Bonaventure had done.[29] On the whole, however, his doctrine is mainly a development of that of his great predecessor.

The end of human knowledge is not speculation, but love.[30] Matthew knows well the various doctrines of the intellect.[31] He himself thinks, with Aristotle, that the soul is created as a tablet on which nothing is written, but he looks for a conciliation between Aristotle and Augustine (p. 285) and he seems to find it (naturally enough) in Avicenna (p. 286), who, like Augustine, admits a certain activity of the sensitive powers. The soul itself makes its sensations; it progressively purifies the species from sense to imagination, and when the species is in its supreme state of purity, it is, so to speak, ready for the intellect. Averroes calls it "the intention understood in potency." The agent intellect then transforms it into the possible intellect and makes it to be understood in act.[32] And this, Matthew concludes, is what the Philosopher calls to abstract.

It cannot be doubted that Aristotle is here providing a new language for what nevertheless remains the doctrine of Augustine. The fact becomes evident in the texts where Matthew describes our cognition of purely intelligible objects (p. 49) when these are present to the soul and seen in the light of the divine illumination. On this point, his doctrine is an amplified restatement of that of Saint Bonaventure.[33] There is no better witness to its authentic meaning than Matthew of Aquasparta. So far as we can judge from the now-known texts, the rest of the doctrine moved within the same circle as that of his Franciscan colleagues, but it would not be wise, with the scanty information at our disposal, to be too assertive on this point.[34]

The remarkable interest some Franciscan theologians took in the Arabian *Perspectivae* (treatises on optics), notably in the one by Alhacen, is easily explained. The science of light, optics taught the laws of that sensible light which symbolized in their eyes the invisible light with which God illuminates every man who comes into this world. Nothing was more natural than to combine the science of light with a metaphysics of light and with the theology of divine illumination. Already developed by Grosseteste and taken up again occasionally by Saint Bonaventure, this synthesis occupies the whole of the *De luce* by the Franciscan Barthol-omew of Bologna, master of theology in Paris, regent of the theological school of Bologna after Matthew of Aquasparta, and whom history loses trace of after 1294.[35] Forty-one disputed Questions by him, recently published, are waiting for their historian. Among them, the questions bear-ing on the Primary Principle, creation and the soul are of direct interest to the history of philosophy.[36]

The *De luce* of Bartholomew joins the speculations inspired by optics not only to theology, but to spirituality. This work is essentially religious. Its scriptural theme is borrowed from Saint John (8, 12): "I am the light of the world; he that followeth me, walketh not in darkness, but shall have the light of life." For Bartholomew of Bologna, as for Roger Bacon, the Bible was the epitome of all truth. Why should it surprise us that the truth of optics should be in a way implied in the sacred text and that, consequently, science should spontaneously blend with theology? Of all the metaphors by which God designated himself, none more openly invites speculation than the comparison with light which, visible in itself, helps the feeble light with which nature endowed our eyes. The authors of treatises on optics distinguish *lux,* that is to say, the nature of light considered in its source; the ray (*radius*) which is light radially engendered in the center by the luminous source; *lumen,* or light spherically diffused from the center by luminous rays; *splendor,* that is to say, the gleam of shining objects made bright by light. In giving himself the title *lux,* and not that of ray (diffused light or gleam), God advises us that he is the very illuminative Source of all the intellectual creatures of the world, and not one of those engendered lights, which owe their being to his illumina·tion. However ingenious they may be, the justifications that the *De luce* proposes for this thesis belong less to philosophical speculation properly so-called than to that symbolical theology of which Saint Thomas said that it was not demonstrative. Because optics knows seven modes of participa-tion of material light, Bartholomew finds their seven corresponding modes of spiritual illumination in angelic and human intellects. To the various material conditions required by optics in order that a body may receive light, he makes as many spiritual conditions correspond, so that our intellect may receive divine illumination, in this life and in the other. The Franciscan spirituality and the methods of symbolical exegesis of Saint Bonaventure are predominant in this work, in which science and philos-ophy combine in a theology itself entirely turned toward spirituality. To Bartholomew of Bologna has sometimes been attributed the *Summa philosophica* ascribed to Pseudo-Grosseteste, of which we have already spoken. The only reason for doing so is that the unknown author of this

Summa refers to a treatise *De luce* as to one of his own works; but nothing proves that it is identical with Bartholomew's *De luce*. At any rate, and without considering this a decisive argument, one can at least note that the style and general inspiration of the two works are profoundly different.

The stability of the thirteenth-century Franciscan school is confirmed by the doctrine of Roger Marston, who taught successively at Oxford and Cambridge, then was minister of the Franciscan province of England from 1292 to 1298 and always remained a resolute supporter of the Augustinian doctrine of illumination. It should not be forgotten that, by subscribing to this doctrine, a theologian was committing himself to accept the philosophical notions of man, of the soul and of human knowledge that went with it.

Like Bacon, Marston distinguishes between the positions of the "philosophers" (Aristotle, Avicenna, Alfarabi, Averroes, etc.), the positions of the Saints (that is, essentially, Augustine), and the positions of the *philosophantes in theologia* whom he calls neither philosophers nor theologians but "those who philosophize in theology." Usually, on critical points, his personal position consists in showing that, although he himself feels perfectly satisfied with following Augustine, he sees no harm in using expressions borrowed from the "philosophers," provided they be given an authentically Augustinian meaning.

Conformably with this attitude, Marston restates the doctrine of Augustine on sensation conceived as an act of the soul, that is a "judgment" on sense impressions. Then he ascribes to the soul a twofold intellectual power, the possible intellect and the agent intellect. Then again he maintains that abstraction by the human agent intellect requires the light of a higher illuminating cause, which the philosophers consider a separate Intellect common to all men, but which the theologians call God. There is no harm in saying that God is the separate substance posited by the philosophers, provided it be well understood that its true name is God. For Marston, as for Matthew of Aquasparta and Saint Bonaventure, the difficulty was to know whether this illuminating influence of God was a natural light or a supernatural one, that is, a grace. Between nature and grace, no mean term is conceivable; yet Bonaventure himself had hesitated, and Matthew of Aquasparta had called it, now a "special influence," now a "somewhat general influence," of God. Marston himself considers that, unless the divine light makes an intellect see supernatural objects, its influence is "common," "inseparable" from the intellect, constantly created as the soul itself is, and, consequently, not supernatural.[37]

These internal difficulties deserve to be noted because, under their stress, the Augustinian complex was then beginning to disintegrate. At first sight, it looked inseparable from Christian truth; on second thought, it raised a very difficult problem, namely: was man really one as a composite substance, and was his intellectual knowledge a truly "natural" one apart from grace? In other words, was there such a thing as a strictly "natural light of the human intellect"? Pending the time when the clear awareness of these difficulties will give rise to the second Franciscan School, we are now meeting witnesses to the somewhat puzzled feeling experienced by the last representatives of the first one. There is no better example of this feeling than Peter Olieu (*Petrus Johannis Olivi*) who was born about 1248-1249 and died in 1298.[38]

Most of the themes constitutive of the Augustinian complex of the thirteenth century reappear in his doctrine, but some of them are maintained by Olieu in a half-hearted way, and, as he himself says, because they are part and parcel of the doctrine of his Order, that is, of the teaching commonly received among Franciscan theologians. Olieu maintains, together with the classical doctrine of the composition of matter and form in the human soul, that of the plurality of forms in composite beings. Combining these two positions, he added to them the conclusion that, although the various substantial forms of man all make up a single soul and a single form of their spiritual matter, the intellective soul of man is joined to its body only through inferior forms. In other words, although it constitutes substantially one being by its union with the body, the intellectual soul is not its immediate form. This had always been a possible consequence of the doctrine of the plurality of forms, but so long as it had not been explicitly deduced, the theologians had raised no objections. On the contrary, the plurality of forms became suspect when some masters began to draw from it consequences that seemed to put the unity of man in jeopardy. In 1311, that is, after the death of Olieu, the Council of Vienne condemned the proposition that the intellectual or rational soul "is not of itself and essentially the form of the human body." This decision, which Descartes was still to remember in the seventeenth century, seems to have contributed to the downfall of the doctrine of the plurality of the forms in the composite.[39]

Concerning human knowledge, Olieu follows the Augustinian doctrine of the active nature of sensation (because the corporeal cannot act upon the spiritual); he also follows the doctrine of divine illumination, which makes the certitude of natural knowledge rest upon the regulating influence of the divine light in us, but, on this point, he declares himself frankly puzzled. Peter knows full well the main objections directed against this doctrine. He therefore accepts it to the extent that it does not entail a sort of theological skepticism, that is, a mistrusting of the certainty of natural knowledge redeemed by the theological conviction that natural cognitions receive their necessity from a special influence of God. Although he himself does not see very clearly how this objection can successfully be met, he declares himself in favor of the doctrine of divine illumination because it is the traditional teaching of his Order.[40]

The doctrine of the solidarity of the powers of the soul (*colligantia*), which was no less common before him than the preceding one, is clearly explained by Olieu. He relates it to the hylomorphic composition of the soul. As has been said, the soul is a composite unit made up of several forms arranged in hierarchic order (vegetative, sensitive, intellectual) and bound together by their common relation to the same spiritual matter. Since their matter is the same, the action of one of these forms agitates, so to speak, this matter, whose commotion is felt by the other forms and perceived by their knowing powers. There is therefore no direct action of one faculty on the others, but there is a natural solidarity between the several forms of a common matter.[41]

Similar positions are found in the unpublished commentary on the *Sentences* written by Peter of Trabes (*Petrus de Trabibus*), another Franciscan recently rescued from the complete oblivion in which he spent several centuries. After accepting for some time the position which made God the "formal" cause of natural knowledge, Peter gave it up as unintelligible to him. He could find no way to hold this position without accepting, as its necessary consequence, that all men naturally see the very essence of God. Since the light of God is his very essence, man could not see the one without seeing the other. At the same time, Peter maintains that the reason why the intellectual soul is free from the body and able to operate without it, is that, although it is the ultimate perfection of man, it is not through it that the soul informs the body (*non tamen secundum eam informat anima corpus, tribuens ei et communicans actum ejus*). By accepting the new development added by Olieu to the traditional doctrine of the plurality of forms, Peter was exposing himself to the future condemnation of Vienne. This accounts for the fact that the doctrine of the unity of the substantial form taught by Thomas Aquinas, still considered a suspicious novelty in 1277, was going to gain ground progressively in the minds of many theologians.

Like Olieu, Peter complains that useless philosophical subtleties have been introduced into theology. For instance, is there only one possible intellect and only one possible agent intellect? First of all, is there any distinction between these so-called intellects? These terms are borrowed from the philosophers. Since Augustine got along very well without them in describing human knowledge, theologians could do without them in their turn. In fact, the human intellect is neither completely passive nor completely active; it is both at a time, so much so that, if it is to be called "possible," it should be conceived to be such with respect to the illuminating influence of God. Obviously, to Peter as to all the representatives of the same school, abstraction was more a psychological problem than a metaphysical one. As has been rightly noted by several of its historians, the continuity of the Franciscan tradition is remarkable on this point.[42]

E. *Disintegration and Revival*

Cardinal Vital du Four (*Vitalis de Furno*) remained forgotten up to very recent years,[43] although several of his Disputed Questions, wrongly included in the pseudo-Scotist treatise *De rerum principio,* created many difficulties for the historians of John Duns Scotus. The recent publication of these questions has cleared up the situation concerning Duns Scotus but it has created another problem concerning Vital himself. In reading these texts, in which Vital du Four freely draws from his own contemporaries or immediate predecessors (Matthew of Aquasparta, John Peckham, Roger Marston, Henry of Ghent and Giles of Rome), one should not forget that their author is not responsible for their publication. Besides, our compiler often gives the slip to those whom he seems at first to follow. In his writings, as in the *Summa* of Albert the Great, personal conclusions often follow from borrowed arguments.

The essence of real beings is identical with their existence. Actual existence is the very essence of the thing as related to its efficient cause. It is not this relation; rather it is the essence of the thing as subjected to this relation. As to the relation itself, it is an actual participation in the divine resemblance; this participation is one with the essence of the existing thing; it is not something distinct from the essence nor added in any way to it. Obviously, Vital intends to turn down the "act of being" conceived as distinct from the essence by Thomas Aquinas. Since an essence cannot exist without being individual, there is no reason to look further than existence in order to discover the principle of individuation. All essence is real from the very fact it exists, and it is singular from the very fact it is real. This doctrine of individuation by actual existence will be rejected by Duns Scotus.

All intellectual cognition bears first on the existing singular given in sense perception. Sensation is the apprehension of the existence of an external being, which is the lowest object of cognition it is possible to conceive. Yet, even at this early stage of the acquisition of knowledge, the intellect is already at work. In the sensation, it experiences the singular. What we call sensation is one with intellection because singular objects are simultaneously experienced by the senses and known by the intellect. Since this common act of cognition is numerically one, it is called sensation rather than intellection. The main concern of Vital on this point is not to prove that our intellect has a direct cognition of the singular; rather, it is to explain why this cognition, which is the joint act of two powers of the soul, is denominated from the sensation rather than from the intellection which it includes. The fact remains, however, that our whole knowledge rests upon this first existential contact, which Vital calls "an experiencing of the actuality of the thing, that is, a certain contact with the very actuality of the sensible thing." [44]

Since the intellective soul is tied to no corporeal organ, it can perceive both itself and its own acts by means of an internal sense. Vital is here maintaining the doctrine of Augustine on the intuitive knowledge that the soul has of itself and of its operations. If this inner sense did not exist, all science of the soul would be as impossible to us as the cognition of light is impossible to the blind. Moreover, this same internal sense makes it possible for us to receive the divine light. At the time of Vital, the problem of the nature of the divine illumination had reached a point of maturity which made it impossible for its supporters to content themselves with metaphors. Combining themes borrowed from Roger Marston and from Henry of Ghent, Vital states that the divine illumination cannot be described as an impression produced by God in the human intellect; if it were such an impression, it would participate in the mutability of the intellect that receives it; consequently, it would not confer on it the eternal immutability and necessity of truth. In order to avoid this consequence, Vital conceives the divine illumination as an intimate union of the soul with the light of God. This light insinuates itself in the mind more intimately than any species or any acquired knowledge; by its presence, it conforms our mind to truth known in its purity. God does this if and when he pleases, so that his intimate presence to the soul does for it all that which the sensible species and the sensible light can do for corporeal sight.[45] Mystical experience seems here to gain the upper hand.

Anxious as they are to maintain the doctrinal traditions of their Order, these later Franciscans modify them, if only by simplifying the problems. But the Augustinian complex seems to come to pieces even more clearly in the work of Richardus de Mediavilla,[46] who is commonly considered an Englishman, and, consequently, is called Richard of Middleton. Since he completed the Fourth Book of his *Commentary on the Sentences* soon after 1294, his work still belongs in the thirteenth century. He seems to have been a very free mind, with no rank prejudice, ready to welcome truth from wherever it came to him and to set out in new directions when need arose. Recent research shows us this Franciscan as almost won over to some of the fundamental positions of Thomist noetics: an agent intellect proper to every rational soul, which forms concepts by way of abstraction starting from sensible experience; no direct intuiting of the soul by itself; reduction of the divine illumination to the natural light of the agent intellect; no innate idea of God; a posteriori demonstrations of the existence of God, beginning with sensible experience: these are so many theses one would be more likely to meet in the writings of a Dominican influenced by Thomas Aquinas.[47] Let us note, however, that even there Richard "drinks from his own well," since he derives from these principles reasons to attribute the knowledge of the singular to the human intellect. We know these singulars, not only spiritual but even sensible, by one and the same intelligible species, in which our intellect first attains the universal, and then, by reflection, the individual. There can therefore be, in a certain sense, an intellectual knowledge of the singular.[48]

In metaphysics, Richard seems on the contrary to be held by theology within the limits of a more Bonaventurian notion of being. First, the pre-eminence of good over even being and truth: (*melior est ratio bonitatis quam ratio entitatis vel veritatis*), a principle inevitably entailing a certain pre-eminence of nobility ascribed to the will, not only in psychology, but also in ethics; then, rejection of the Thomist distinction of essence and existence, where Richard sees only a distinction of reason;[49] maintenance of the distinction of matter and form in every creature, spiritual or corporeal;[50] attributing a minimum of actuality to matter, since God can create a matter without any form. Over and above this matter, however, Richard grants another one, which is pure possibility, but not nothingness, and which can exist only concreated with form. Richard conceives it as transmissible from one form to the other by the action of natural agents. This way of conceiving form as bound to the pure possibility of matter dispenses him from admitting seminal reasons, but he maintains the plurality of forms, perhaps in substances that are inferior to man, certainly in the human compound, and he finds in the indivisibility of essence itself a sufficient reason for its individuation. This dual meaning of the term matter can be traced back, with some probability, to the notion of matter developed by Gabirol.[51]

Nothing, in so eclectic a doctrine, betokens an innovator in physics. The history of sciences, however, assures us that he was one. Breaking with the traditional notion of a finite universe, Richard of Middleton upholds the possibility of a universe, not actually infinite or actually infinitely divided, but capable of expanding or dividing beyond any actually given limit: "God can produce a magnitude or a dimension which increases without end, provided that at every instant the magnitude already actually achieved be in that instant finite: just as God can indefinitely divide a continuum into parts whose size ultimately falls below any limit, provided there never exists actually an infinite number of really divided parts." This was an unexpected consequence of the condemnation of Arabian peripateticism in 1277, and we shall find other examples of it in the domain of science as well as in theology. Because it was a protest against Greek necessitarianism, that condemnation emboldened a number of theologians to affirm as possible, on account of the omnipotence of the Christian God, scientific or philosophical positions traditionally deemed impossible on account of the nature of things. In inviting new mental experiments, the theological notion of an infinitely powerful God freed minds from the finite limits within which Greek thought had enclosed the universe. Among the new hypotheses formulated on the strength of this principle, some were to be confirmed later on by Western science, for sometimes different reasons and always by another method. Christian theology therefore facilitated, even in science, the opening of new perspectives.

Encouraged by Etienne Tempier's condemnation of the proposition "that the Prime Cause could not create several worlds," Richard maintains that the plurality of worlds is possible. Under the same influence, he maintains that God could impart to the farthest heaven, traditionally conceived as fixed, a movement of translation, and that there is no point in objecting that this movement would produce a void, whose existence was then judged to be impossible. The void, Richard in turn objects, would do away with the local distance between two bodies by suppressing the medium separating them, but these bodies would remain no less separate. After showing that these ideas were to reappear in Parisian scholasticism of the fourteenth century, P. Duhem concludes: "If we had to assign a date to the birth of modern science, we should undoubtedly choose that date of 1277 on which the bishop of Paris solemnly proclaimed that several worlds could exist and that the whole system of celestial spheres could, without contradiction, be endowed with a rectilinear movement." Nevertheless, in order not to form a distorted view of historical reality, let us also remember that the bishop of Paris never concerned himself with science; he simply declared that no philosopher, arguing from the intrinsic necessity of the world of Greek philosophy, had any right to impose limits on the free will and infinite power of the Christian God. From the very moment it became clear that God could have created another universe than that of Greek philosophy, theologians began to wonder if, in fact, he had not created another one. This was not a scientific liberation of science; it was theological liberation.

Whatever its origin may have been, Richard certainly was one of the first to take advantage of the newly acquired liberty, not only, as we have just seen, in cosmology, but also in kinetics. P. Duhem gives him the honor of having established, against Themistius and Aristotle, that the speed of a falling body does not depend solely on the distance from the center of the world, but also on the time elapsed and the space traversed. Other observations of Richard's, such as the introduction of an intervening rest between the rising of a projectile flying through the air and the moment of its fall, seem to have been frequently taken up again after him. These were new intellectual interests, of which Richard is one of the earliest witnesses and one of the most intelligent representatives.[52] As to his philosophy, his best historian values it exactly when he says that "Richard finishes an epoch. The last representative of the school of Saint Bonaventure, he attempted a synthesis prudently new, in which were to be integrated the great Bonaventurian theses driven home and perfected, and what seemed to him to be the best in Saint Thomas' Aristotelianism and theology. This attempt was short-lived." [53]

Other Franciscans, however, were entering similar ways at the same time, at least in philosophy, and paving the way for the new synthesis of Duns Scotus. Unless the Bonaventurian tradition had died off, no new Franciscan theology would have been possible. The work of the English master, William of Ware,[54] is still too little known for us to judge it but he seems to have played a part in this necessary preparation. His proofs of the existence of God derive their inspiration from both Aristotle and Augustine.[55] Like Richard, he abandons the Augustinian doctrine of divine illumination. Like Thomas Aquinas, he thinks that the soul must have been provided by God with the faculties necessary for the exercise of its natural function, which is intellectual knowledge. Traditional Augustinism could not give way on this central position without abandoning others which rested upon it. Accordingly, William of Ware abandons the hylomorphic composition of spiritual substances and rallies to the doctrine of the unity of form. On the contrary, he maintains the identity of the faculties of the soul with its essence, for theological reasons which become apparent where he says that "the powers of the soul are its very essence and are distinct from one another like the divine attributes." This identification leads him to stress the interaction between faculties so fundamentally one. Thus William says, agreeing in this with Augustine, that the impression of the species in the memory or the intellect would not suffice without the actual assistance of the will which unites them. It is no wonder then that he should have placed, in his general classification of the activities of the soul, what he calls the "speculative will" above the speculative intellect, and the practical will above the practical intellect.[56] This tendency to voluntarism is not enough to justify the tradition, which does not go back much further than the end of the fourteenth century, according to which William of Ware was Duns Scotus' master. One thing, however, is sure. With William of Ware, it is clear that the Bonaventurian positions are being questioned. Duns Scotus could appear without creating a scandal within the Franciscan Order. One might even say that, in a sense, his coming was being expected.

This does not mean that there were never more to be any hearts attuned to the mystical appeal of Bonaventurian exemplarism. An exact contemporary of Duns Scotus, Ramon Lull (1235-1315),[57] took up again the same theme and gave it a new vitality. His life would make an excellent subject for a novel, but he himself has reviewed it for us, with as much simplicity as exactitude, in his *Disputatio clerici et Raymundi phantastici:* "I was a married man, the father of a family, well-situated as to fortune, lustful and worldly. I renounced all that of my own accord, in order to be able to honor God, serve the public good and exalt our holy faith. I learned Arabic, and went several times to preach to the Saracens. Arrested, imprisoned and flogged for the faith, I worked for five years to rouse the chiefs of the Church and the Christian princes on behalf of the common weal. Now I am old, now I am poor, but my purpose is the same, and I shall persevere in it, God willing, even unto death." His life remained, therefore, entirely dominated by the same apostolic preoccupations which had inspired the work of Roger Bacon. The legend of Ramon Lull as an alchemist and to a slight extent a magician is in no way confirmed by the study of his life and works. It is true that, as at least two hundred works are attributed to him, very few persons can boast of having read them all; but many of them are very much alike, and since Lull often speaks of himself, one soon succeeds in picturing him as a great imaginative person (*phantasticus*) and even an illuminee (*Doctor illuminatus*), convinced that he holds his doctrine from a divine revelation, and who dedicates himself, with a slightly chimerical ardor, to the propagation of a homemade method of apologetics which will infallibly bring about the conversion of unbelievers.

Lull's famous *Art* is the exposition of that method. It consists essentially in circles on which are inscribed the fundamental concepts, in such a way that by combining the various possible positions of these circles with regard to one another, one can automatically obtain all the relations of concepts corresponding to the essential verities of religion. It must be confessed that when we today try to use those tables, we come up against the worst difficulties, and one cannot help wondering whether Lull himself was ever able to use them. If we confine ourselves to his own declaration, we must believe he was, the more so as we could not otherwise conceive the insistence with which he advocated the use of his *Art* against the errors of the Averroists and the Moslems.

The feeling of the necessity for an apologetic work intended to win over the infidels, so strong in Ramon Lull, was in no way personal to him and did not constitute a new fact. Ramon Martin in his *Pugio fidei*, and Saint Thomas with his *Summa contra gentiles*, had already pursued the same end. In the twelfth century, Alan of Lille's *Ars catholicae fidei* had already been a technique of apologetic demonstration, and closer to Lull, Roger Bacon's *Opus majus* also was the fruit of apostolic zeal for the propagation of faith through the power of Christian wisdom. But it can be said that, in Ramon Lull, that preoccupation was the very seed of the whole doctrine, especially his Arts. A method was necessary, but only one, to convict Moslems and Averroists of error. The Moslems deny Christian revelation while, on philosophical grounds, the Averroists refuse to take it into consideration. Philosophy and religion are therefore separated by an abyss, the one arguing only in the name of reason, the other arguing by a positive method (*positiva consideratio*), that is to say, in the name of revealed data which it posits first as fact, and from which it then deduces conclusions. Now it is evident *a priori* that it must be possible to establish agreement between the two sciences.[58] Theology is the mother and the mistress of philosophy; there must therefore be the same accord between theology and philosophy that one always finds between cause and effect. The best way to reveal their fundamental agreement is to start with principles which are recognized and avowed by all. This is the reason why Ramon proposes the list of notions which figure on his tables, as principles common to all disciplines, self-evident, and without which there could be neither science nor philosophy.[59] These principles are: goodness, greatness, eternity or duration, power, wisdom, will, virtue, truth and glory; difference, agreement, contrariety, principle, means, end, greater, equality, smaller. All beings are either implied in these principles, or develop according to their essence and their nature. Ramon Lull adds to his list—and therein lies the secret of the *Great Art*—the rules which allow the correct combining of these principles; he even invented revolving figures which made it possible to combine them more easily, and all the combinations that Lull's tables make possible precisely correspond to all the truths and all the secrets of nature that the human intellect can attain in this life.

The rules which control all the possible combinations of those principles are a series of general questions applicable to all that is, for instance: what, why, how, which, when, where, and others of the same kind. As to the operations which enable us to relate particular things to universal principles by means of rules, they assume logical and metaphysical notions which Lull seems to put on the same level as the rest and to consider as equally evident. In a dialogue in which we see Lull convince an exceptionally docile Socrates, the Greek philosopher accepts as naturally evident propositions from which immediately results a demonstration of the Trinity. For instance, Lull considers as one of the rules of his art that human intelligence can rise above the verifications of the senses and even correct them; he also asks Socrates to admit that reason can criticize itself, with God's help, and sometimes recognize in itself the reality of a divine influence, whose effects it feels even though it cannot understand it. Socrates willingly admits that the intellect transcends the senses and must sometimes even transcend itself in recognizing the necessary existence of things which it does not understand.[60] Lull's art largely consists in begging ahead of time the principles from which the expected agreement must necessarily follow. But the technical processes thanks to which he believed he could teach the uninstructed and convince the unbelievers contained the germ of an idea which had quite a future. Those revolving tables on which Lull inscribed his fundamental concepts are the first attempt of that "combinative Art" that Leibniz, who remembered his mediaeval predecessor, also failed to constitute. It is by no means certain that the project of Ramon Lull is dead.

The influence of the *Doctor Illuminatus* was felt along other lines, at least one of which deserves to hold our attention. It is an old Christian idea that God revealed himself in two books, the Bible and the Book of the World.[61] Scotus Erigena's "theophanic" universe, the *liber creaturarum* of William of Auvergne and Saint Bonaventure, in fact the whole symbolism of the Lapidaries and the Bestiaries, without forgetting the symbolism that decorated the porches of mediaeval cathedrals or shone in their windows, were so many testimonials of a general confidence in the translucency of a universe in which the least of all beings was a living token of the presence of God. If, as is commonly believed, he was associated with the Franciscan Order, Lull had not far to look to make acquaintance with this universe. Saint Francis of Assisi and Saint Bonaventure had lived in no other one. Let us recall Saint Bonaventure's words: "the created world is like unto a sort of book in which the Trinity which made it is read," and let us compare them with those in which, speaking of himself, Lull describes that illumination he had one day in the solitude of Mount Randa: "It seems as though a light had been given him with which to discern the divine perfections, as to some of their properties and their mutual relationships, with all the connections there are between them . . . By that same light, he knew that the whole created being is nothing but an imitation of God" (*eodem lumine, cognovit totum esse creaturae nihil aliud esse quam imitationem Dei*). Obviously the illuminations of the "Illuminated Doctor" and of the "Seraphic Doctor" coincide. It can also be seen how the vision of Ramon Lull became the very foundation of his doctrine: the Great Art is possible only if, all creatures being so many images of God, or at least his more or less remote imitations, their fundamental properties, and the mutual relations of these properties, enable us to know the nature and attributes of God. Inversely, if the Great Art is possible, the method which permits us to combine the perfections of creatures in all possible ways should yield at the same time all possible combinations of the perfections of God. Let us grant, however, that when it is used to this end, the science of things becomes theology, but this is what Lull had wanted it to be from the very beginning.

CHAPTER II

SCHOLASTIC THEOLOGIANS IN ENGLAND

THE doctrinal continuity of the Franciscan School initiated by Alexander of Hales and promoted by Saint Bonaventure should not be construed as meaning that each religious order had its own theology. First, the Franciscan Order has never dedicated itself to the promotion of only one theology; Bonaventure, Duns Scotus, even Ockham, have always found Franciscan supporters. Secondly, up to the rise of Thomism, a large number of common theological positions were upheld by both Dominicans and Franciscans, with, of course, particular variations in content as well as in spirit.

The Dominicans (Black Friars) arrived at Oxford in the summer of 1221. The first of them to hold an Oxford degree in theology was Richard Fishacre. He is also the first English Dominican master to have written a commentary on the *Sentences,* probably about 1240-1243.[62] It has been said of him, not without humor, that "it would certainly be an exaggeration to claim Fishacre as an ardent Aristotelian." In fact, the terms "Aristotelian" and "Augustinian" are so vague that they seldom can be used without some qualifications. In the particular case of Fishacre, however, the question arises whether Aristotle himself would have been able to understand the meaning of his main positions.

Fishacre admits the hylomorphic composition of angels and souls. Naturally he can prove it by Aristotelian arguments: there are individuals in the species angel and the species man; now Aristotle teaches that where there is no matter there are no individuals; therefore there is matter in angels and souls. Moreover, Aristotle affirms that an object exists without matter only in the thought of the maker; therefore a soul without matter could only exist in the thought of God. Concerning causality, Fishacre holds that the form of the effect must somehow pre-exist in matter (*aliquid formae latitans in materia*); this adumbration of effect is what Saint Augustine called a "seminal reason," and the cause had only to actualize it to produce its effect. For Fishacre as for Saint Bonaventure, a cause producing an effect that was in no way pre-existent in matter would be not only efficient, but creative: it would produce *ex nihilo.* The fact may occur, but it is a miracle. These "seminal reasons" were created by God in matter, each of them corresponding to a "causal notion" in God's thought. One feels a bit discouraged to see Fishacre attribute this doctrine to Aristotle: (*patet quod Augustinus est hujus ejusdem opinionis cum Aristotele*). His noetic took its inspiration from Augustine's, and perhaps from William of Auvergne. All cognition results not from an action of the object on the soul, but from the soul's aptitude for making itself similar to the object by "imitating it." As Saint Augustine and the Platonists say, this is possible because all truths are inscribed in the soul, where they are only dormant, so that they need only be wakened. Fishacre considers furthermore that here again Aristotle does not say anything different, but his Aristotelian exegesis is a desperate adventure.[63] Once such principles were admitted, nothing was easier for him than to develop under the form of proofs the latent knowledge of God that we possess. Not only does Saint Anselm's argument by the *id quod majus cogitari non potest* satisfy him completely, but he proposes one of his own vintage, which seems still more direct: "If a thing were absolutely simple, it would not differ from its existence, but would be its existence; for, if it were not that, it would have existence and something else in addition, and then it would not be absolutely simple. Consequently, if a thing were absolutely simple, it would exist; now the absolutely simple is absolutely simple: therefore it exists (*sed simplicissimum: ergo est*)." [64]

The Franciscans (Grey Friars) arrived at Oxford in 1224. Their first masters at the university were Adam of Marsh, then Thomas of York, of whom mention has already been made. The successor of Thomas of York was Richardus Rufus (Richard of Cornwall). He first read the *Sentences* at Oxford from 1250 to 1253; then at Paris, where he succeeded Saint Bonaventure, from 1253 to 1255; in 1256, he returned to Oxford.[65] Many studies have been devoted to the literary history of his works, but so little has been published that his doctrine remains practically unknown.[66] His historians have stressed the personal quality of his style and the sharpness of his tongue. He often apostrophizes his opponent. If the published fragments of his works fairly represent his general attitude, Richard intended to adhere to the theological teaching of Peter Lombard and, in many cases, he declared his unwillingness to take sides in philosophical discussion. This is what he did with respect to the substantial unity of the soul.[67] On the problem of hylomorphism, he likewise refused to choose.[68] We do not know if this was his usual attitude; any opinion concerning the character of his works should be suspended until after their publication.

I. ROBERT KILWARDBY

The successor of Fishacre in the Dominican chair of theology at Oxford was Robert Kilwardby.[69] After taking his degree of master in arts at the University of Paris, he succeeded Fishacre from 1248 to 1261, was elected Archbishop of Canterbury in 1272, created cardinal in 1272, and died at Viterbo in 1279. Chronologically speaking, he belongs in the same generation as Saint Thomas Aquinas; intellectually, he lived in a different doctrinal world. The fact is the more interesting as, at that date, it becomes difficult to account for the existence of different theological schools by the unequal progress they had made in the discovery of Aristotle. Kilwardby is credited with commentaries on the logic of Aristotle and on the following works: *Physics, On the Heaven and the World, On Coming to be and Passing away, On the Soul* and on the *Metaphysics*. These works, as well as his *Commentary on the Sentences*, have not yet been sufficiently studied.[70]

The very title of his treatise *On the Origin of Sciences* recalls the similar work of Gundissalinus. It is a classification of the sciences, inspired by Aristotle and developed as a general introduction to philosophy.[71] His personal positions, however, appear more clearly in his commentary on Peter Lombard and in several short treatises recently studied, *On the*

Imaginative Spirit, On Time, On the Unity of Forms, On the Nature of Relation, On Conscience, On Theology, in which Kilwardby speaks for himself. His very instructive letter to Petrus de Confleto (Peter of Conflans) is of great value to locate his own positions with respect to the main doctrinal currents of his time.

On March 7, 1277, Etienne Tempier had condemned a long list of propositions, in the hope of checking the Averroist movement and the spread of theologies which, like Thomas Aquinas', took their inspiration from Aristotle's method. Some days later (March 18, 1277), in his capacity as Archbishop of Canterbury, Kilwardby, in turn, condemned a much shorter list of thirty propositions, manifestly chosen with the same intention and in the same spirit.[72] Although it is ordinarily used in this connection, the term "condemnation" is not absolutely exact. The Dominican Archbishop of Corinth, Peter of Conflans, having reproached him for his action, Kilwardby answered that this condemnation "was not of the same kind as the condemnations of actual heresies, but that it was an interdiction to affirm such conclusions in the schools, either in concluding (disputed questions), or in lectures, or under any other dogmatic form." It should, however, be recognized that, in his own opinion, the Christian faith was at least indirectly at stake. He himself says, in fact, about the errors he was forbidding to be taught, that "some are manifestly false, some depart from philosophical truth, some border on intolerable errors, and some are obviously baneful as opposed to the Catholic faith." To which Kilwardby adds this historically instructive remark: "I have not acted alone in this prohibition: on the contrary, as you put it yourself, it met with the approval of all of the masters of Oxford; it was even the counsel (*suasio*) of many theologians and philosophers more competent than I which bound me to it."

Kilwardby probably exaggerates slightly. If one thinks of the early pro-Thomist reactions on the part of certain Dominicans of Oxford, such as Richard Clapwell, who followed that prohibition by very little, one cannot help thinking that, as early as 1277, Thomistic theology found at Oxford some sympathy. But that must have been, as they say, "among the young" who represented the present turned toward the future. The masters in full authority, who represented the present continuing the past, mistrusted these innovations. In 1277, the Archbishop of Oxford was slightly behind the teaching of Oxford and the Bishop of Paris was publicly denouncing as dangerous certain theses taught by the future Common Doctor of the Church, Saint Thomas Aquinas. It is human for the guardians of orthodoxy to confuse it sometimes with their personal way of conceiving it.

The sixteen propositions in natural philosophy prohibited by Kilwardby do, in fact, give us information on his own positions.[73] The third prohibits to teach at Oxford that "there is no active potency in matter." This was tantamount to enforcing the teaching of a doctrine of causality analogous to Augustine's "seminal reasons." Besides, it is what Kilwardby says in his Letter to Peter of Conflans, and what he had already upheld in his *Commentary on the Sentences,* where he identified the active power of the secondary cause, which moves because it is moved, with what is called "seminal reason" because it lies in matter like a seed. Just as that interdiction to teach the Aristotelian doctrine of matter affected all ontology and all physics, the whole of psychology and anthropology was affected by the twelfth proposition: "that the vegetative, the sensitive and the intellective are one simple form." To be forbidden to teach this, was practically to be obliged to teach the plurality of forms in the soul and, consequently, in man. Once more, this is what Kilwardby's Letter to the bishop of Corinth expressly maintains: "I know, however, that for one man there is one form, and that this form is not one in this sense that it is simple, but it is made up of many forms mutually related according to a natural order." Kilwardby's *Commentary on the Sentences* had already taught the same doctrine: "The constitution of an individual requires several forms in a single matter, as, in this one fire, there is the form of the substance, the form of the body and the form of fire (*igneitas*)." The seminal reasons and the plurality of forms, ordinarily suffice to locate a doctrine, but some recent soundings in his *Commentary* on Peter Lombard and in the other treatises confirm the diagnosis: hylomorphic composition of angels; divine illumination required as complement to our intellectual light, even for the knowledge of the sensible; simple distinction of reason between the soul and its faculties, all these positions belong to the Augustinian complex. Kilwardby gives evidence of personal initiative in his way of justifying these theses, especially on the points where patristic tradition was no longer enough to enlighten him. His solution of the problem of individuation would deserve to be studied closely for the philosophical and historical interest attached to it. He posits form as the active cause and matter as the passive cause of individuation, but the latter seems to him to be a complex fact which includes individuality itself. One should therefore say: first matter and form, then determination (*signatio*) of matter by form, and finally the resulting individual which is being in act. Form itself, he clearly states, individuates itself in making its matter individual, and actual existence seems to be the property of the individual thus constituted.[74]

It has already been noted, with regard to Richard of Middleton, that the rejection of the Aristotelian doctrine of movement occurs well in advance of the Parisian nominalism of the fourteenth century. The question is not without importance. We have seen P. Duhem date from the condemnation of 1277 the beginnings of modern science;[75] in another text, the same historian proposes another date, and a later one: "If one

wished, by a definite line, to separate the reign of antique Science from
the reign of modern Science, he would have to draw it, I think, at the
instant that John Buridan conceived that theory (of the *impetus*), at the
instant when they ceased to regard the stars as moved by divine beings,
when they agreed that celestial movements and sublunary movements
depended on one and the same mechanics." [76] Since this last point implies
the existence of a mechanics, it is, for the history of science, the principal
point; but it is not without interest to note that, at least in theology, the
Aristotelian doctrine of motive Intelligences was an innovation. According
to Aristotle, all movement presupposes a mover distinct from the mobile;
that is why he attributes separate Movers to the celestial spheres, and
Saint Thomas Aquinas follows him docilely on this point; but this novelty
shocked the theologians of the old school. In 1271, the general minister
of the Dominican Order, John of Vercelli, addressed to Thomas Aquinas
and Robert Kilwardby a list of forty-three questions, to which both gave
rather different answers. To John of Vercelli's fourth question: "Is it
infallibly proven that the angels are the movers of celestial bodies?", Saint
Thomas answered that, on the one hand, Christian Doctors taught that
God governs inferior things by means of superior things, and that, on the
other hand, the Platonist and peripatetic philosophers held to be conclusive
their proofs that celestial bodies are either animated and moved by their
souls (Avicenna), or, better still, are moved by angels (Averroes). This
was not exactly claiming that the thesis was infallibly proven, but to
say that the philosophers held it to be proven, that it was in agreement
with a general principle posited by the Fathers, and to add that none of
them, as far as one could remember, had ever denied it, was tantamount
to recommending it. On the other hand, while he expressed himself with
indulgence on the Avicennian thesis of the souls of spheres, Kilwardby
rejected the idea that celestial bodies may be moved by angelic spirits
which are neither their acts nor their forms. This opinion, he declares, "is
not philosophical, nor do I remember that any Saint approved of it as
true and certain." Thus, while Thomas Aquinas is content to have it
considered as proven by the philosophers without being denied by the
Fathers, Kilwardby declares it to be without any philosophical value and
notes that no Father accepted it as certainly true. His answer went more
closely into John of Vercelli's question, but that was because he himself
preferred a third opinion to the two preceding ones—an opinion he, moreover, does not present as personal. *Tertii ponunt* . . . a third group
acknowledges that, just as light and heavy bodies are moved by their own
weight and inclinations (*propriis ponderibus et inclinationibus*) toward the
places where they come to rest, in the same way celestial bodies move circularly in space because their natural inclinations, which are as their weight,
are to preserve corruptible beings and to keep them from rapidly disinte-
grating and perishing. As it has been justly remarked, "the inclination, the

tendency of their own weight seem surely to belong to the order of quality, and therefore remain under the spell of Aristotle's qualitative physics, while the *impetus* of Buridan is clearly oriented toward a quantitative interpretation and is open to mathematical measurement." [77] In other words, Kilwardby is not yet on the threshold of modern science, because he is not concerned with mechanics, but he certainly affirms the principle that the celestial movements and the sublunary movements may depend on one and the same mechanics. Conservatives sometimes get ahead of progressives simply by anticipating progress without moving from the spot.

2. JOHN PECKHAM

Kilwardby's successor to the archiepiscopal seat of Canterbury was John Peckham (d. 1292). He was a Franciscan[78] but one who used his authority to renew, October 29, 1284, the doctrinal condemnation pronounced by his Dominican predecessor, and censured, April 30, 1286, certain propositions of Richard Clapwell. His personal attitude is clearly defined in a letter dated June 1, 1285, to the Bishop of Lincoln: "I do not in any way disapprove of philosophical studies, insofar as they serve theological mysteries, but I do disapprove of irreverent innovations in language, introduced within the last twenty years into the depths of theology against philosophical truth, and to the detriment of the Fathers whose positions are disdained and openly held in contempt. Which doctrine is more solid and more sound, the doctrine of the sons of Saint Francis, that is, of Brother Alexander (of Hales) of sainted memory, of Brother Bonaventure and others like him, who rely on the Fathers and the philosophers in treatises secure against any reproach, or else that very recent and almost entirely contrary doctrine, which fills the entire world with wordy quarrels, weakening and destroying with all its strength what Augustine teaches concerning the eternal rules and the unchangeable light, the faculties of the soul, the seminal reasons included in matter and innumerable questions of the same kind, let the Ancients be the judges, since in them is wisdom, let the God of heaven be judge, and may he remedy it." [79]

This priceless testimony traces the origin of the evil it denounces back to about 1265. As a matter of fact, the commentaries of Saint Thomas on Aristotle date from the years 1269-1270, and since the dates proposed for the *Summa contra gentiles* vary between 1258 and 1264, in 1285 it was really less than twenty years before (*citra viginti annos*) that the novel theology Peckham deplores had been definitely constituted. It will be noted also that Peckham does not disapprove of philosophy, but of a certain indiscreet use of a false philosophy; that, in spite of the opposite case of the Dominican Kilwardby which he had had under his very eyes, the opposition of the two doctrines was concretely translated by him into an opposition of the two Orders: the Augustinism of the Franciscans and the Aristotelianism of the Dominicans; lastly, that when he wants to list some of the points upon which the two groups are opposed, the first three that come to his mind are, in the order in which he mentions them: the doctrine of divine illumination, the real unity of the powers of the soul with the essence of the soul, and seminal reasons.[80]

To attribute considerable importance to the problem of knowledge in the doctrinal struggles of the closing thirteenth century is not yielding to an illusion of perspective due to the influence of modern philosophy. Even without Peckham's declaration, the long list of disputed questions devoted to it would give information enough. The truth is that this problem did not owe its importance to any idealistic preoccupations, but to its metaphysical and religious connotations. It is above all a question of knowing whether or not man can get along without a special help from God for a knowledge of the true. On the answer given to this question depends the value of the Augustinian proofs of the existence of God by truth, with the doctrine of the inner Master and the spirituality inspired by it. That is why we see Peckham himself closely examining this problem in his Questions *De anima*. Careful to lose nothing of the true teaching of the philosophers, but especially to sacrifice nothing essential in Augustine's teaching, he grants to each man a created agent intellect, but, in full agreement on this point with Bacon and Albert the Great, he adds to it a still higher agent Intellect, which is God. His position is therefore not the position of Avicenna, for whom the sole agent intellect of the human species was not God, but a separate Intelligence; nor is it the position of Thomas Aquinas, for whom God is not in any sense our own "agent intellect"; but, if he had to choose between Avicenna and Thomas Aquinas, Peckham would prefer Avicenna; "Avicenna, who posited the agent intellect as a separate Intelligence, did better than those who posit it as but a part of the soul." [81] In reality, the only one who stated the truth in this case, if not the whole truth at least its essential, is Saint Augustine, whom nothing seems to have been able to dislodge from Oxford until toward the last few years of the thirteenth century.

Faithful to the Fathers, Peckham was also faithful to scientific studies, as can be seen from his *Perspectiva communis* (Optics), his *Tractatus spherae*, the *Theorica planetarum* and the *Mathematicae rudimenta*. In these, he was promoting the tradition of Roger Bacon and Robert Grosseteste.[82] The time-honored alliance between Platonism and mathematics, the fidelity to the tradition and spirituality of the Fathers, are certainly more frequently met together in thirteenth-century England than on the Continent. One would like to follow the history of this patristic culture; one would particularly like to know if it was by chance that Oriel College gave us Joseph Butler in the eighteenth century and, in the nineteenth, Henry Newman.

With the exception of Robert Grosseteste, who heads the list of famous Oxonians, the great English masters of the thirteenth century belong to one of the two great Mendicant Orders. The study of the English secular masters is still much less advanced than that of their Parisian colleagues. Very little is known of Robert of Winchelsea (d. 1313), the author of theological questions; of Henry Wile (d. 1329), who left Questions *De anima,* or of Gilbert Segrave (d. 1316), of whom Leland remarked that his works were often met, in Oxford libraries and elsewhere, but none of which have been identified. The only one of these English secular masters who recently came out of obscurity is Simon Faversham (d. 1306), whose Questions on the *Categories* and on Book III *De anima* were recently published.[83] These are the clear and concise notes of a professor well-informed on the Greek and Arabian commentaries of the works he discusses, and whom his moderate opinions do not involve in any adventures. He carefully avoids Averroism, betrays no inclination toward Augustinism, and generally stresses, in his Questions *De anima,* solutions analogous to Saint Thomas Aquinas'. Ever since about 1270, but still more markedly by the end of the thirteenth century, it becomes impossible to interpret the philosophical or theological positions of the mediaeval masters without taking Thomism into consideration.

CHAPTER III

THOMAS AQUINAS

I. THE THOMISTIC REFORMATION

No two doctrines of the masters we have studied so far can be said to be identical, but they all had in common a certain number of fundamental positions, or, at least, they all shared in common a limited number of possible doctrinal positions among which they made their choice.

Among these positions, one at least has been maintained by all the masters we have studied, and this without a single exception, since it includes even Albert the Great. It is the definition of the soul as a spiritual substance. This was the unanimous opinion of all. Taken in itself, the soul is a substance. Naturally, since man is one, this substance implies, in its very essence, some sort of relation to its body. Some would call it a "unibility," others a love or an inclination; still others preferred to say that soul is, secondarily, the act and perfection of its body, but not one of them would uphold the view that the very essence of this substance was to be the form of a body. The origin of their position is well known. It is the definition of man given by Plato in the *Alcibiades,* and inherited from him, through Plotinus, by Saint Augustine: man is a soul that uses a body. To the extent that all the masters we have studied are indebted to

Augustine, directly or indirectly, for their notion of the soul, they all are Augustinians.[84]

In the doctrine of Augustine himself, this position entails several other ones. In noetics, the active nature of sense perception conceived as an act of the soul rather than a passion; the possibility for such a spiritual substance to receive from God the complement of light it needs in order to form necessary judgments about purely intelligible objects; an intrinsic aptitude to know itself directly and by a sort of immediate experience. Among these corollaries, one at least has been maintained by all masters before Saint Thomas Aquinas, namely, the doctrine of the divine illumination conceived as a light required for the perfect cognition of necessary truth over and above the natural light of the changeable intellect of man. Even those among the theologians anterior to Saint Thomas who accept the distinction between the possible intellect and the agent intellect, not without interpreting it sometimes in curious ways, unanimously agree in positing, over and above the active intellect of man, a super-agent Intellect which is none other than the Interior Master of Saint Augustine or the Intelligible Sun of the *Soliloquies*. Peter of Spain, so far as we know, is the only one who, having expressed himself on the subject, neglected to add to the separate agent Intelligence of Avicenna the illuminating God of Augustine. The reason for this probably is that he was writing a *De anima,* not a metaphysics. All the others, William of Auvergne, Roger Bacon, John of la Rochelle, Albert the Great, Fishacre, Kilwardby and naturally the whole Bonaventurian school, have upheld, under some form or other, the doctrine of divine illumination as a divine light superadded, in true natural cognitions, to the natural light of the human intellect. To the extent that this was an authentically Augustinian doctrine, they all were Augustinians.[85]

Nor is this all. To posit the soul as a substance, either complete or quasi-complete in itself, leaves open this other question: what is the relation of this spiritual substance to the matter of its body?

Concerning matter itself, a large number of these masters, but not all, posit a universal matter of which they say two things: 1) since it has been created by God, it is not nothing: hence a tendency to attribute to matter a minimum of intrinsic actuality proportioned to the minimum of being it has; 2) since mutability is the distinctive mark of created being, matter should be identified with the pure possibility of change, that is, with the very mutability inherent in all that is. These two notions are authentically Augustinian in origin. On the first point, Augustine says that matter is "almost nothing" (*prope nihil*) and, consequently, not absolutely nothing. Keeping in mind the disciples of Mani, he stresses the fact that matter has been created by God; he calls it "the non-formed matter of things" which already "was" (*iam erat*): an "almost nothing" which necessarily is, since it is good (*Conf.,* XII, 18, 28-22, 31). On the second point, Augustine clearly teaches that God has created, in his Word, "the unformed matter of creatures both spiritual and corporeal" (*Conf.*, XII, 20, 29); this is the "mutability" created by God, which is present in all beings, either permanent like "the eternal household of God," or else transitory like corporeal beings. In some texts, however, Augustine went further than this. The statements of Augustine concerning matter are open to two interpretations: 1) matter was made "creatable," that is, transmutable into form; 2) matter was created as a pure mutability determinable by forms. In both cases, there was in Augustinian matter an incipient seeking toward form, the very "positive privation" which the Augustinians were to uphold against the mere absence of form attributed to matter by Aristotle. The Stoic doctrine of seminal reasons, accepted by Augustine, was not a necessary consequence of this position, but it harmonized with it. Even those converts to Aristotle who gave up the seminal reasons usually maintained in matter a sort of positive passivity very different from the total passivity of Aristotelian matter. At any rate, all the scholastics who either maintained the seminal reasons, or refused to deprive matter of all actuality, can be truly said to have kept faith with the deepest inspiration of Saint Augustine. To this extent they can be called Augustinians.[86]

Naturally, no early scholastic reproduced the doctrine of Augustine in its entirety. Many other influences combined with his own in order to give rise to the theological doctrines of the thirteenth century, but these fundamental positions are all Augustinian and they dominate the rest as the *forma totius* perfects, unifies and orders its whole. The objection that the term "Augustinian" should point out pure Augustinianism is perfectly tenable. Then there never was a single Augustinian, apart from Augustine himself; nor should we say that there ever was a single Aristotelian since the death of Aristotle, nor even a single Thomist since the death of Thomas Aquinas. As to the other objection, that there can have been no Augustinianism until there was an Aristotelianism to oppose it, it rests upon the assumption that no doctrinal position can be held as true so long as nobody opposes it as false, which is not evident.[87]

If the existence of any real Augustinianism in the middle ages can be rightly denied, it is on a different ground, and, this time, Aristotle is truly responsible for it. His logic spread in all the Christian schools a dialectical ideal of exposition which progressively invaded theology. Even Saint Anselm of Canterbury, who expressly affirmed that he had said nothing that could not be found in the writings of Augustine, used a dialectical mode of exposition that little resembled the free and supple digressions so frequent in the works of his master. Beyond this simple problem of intellectual style, there was a deeper one. What is a "doctrine," or a teaching? On this point, the Aristotelian notion of "art," and still more that of "science," progressively invaded the minds of the masters and their schools. Already in the twelfth century, we heard a grammarian affirming that, if a master does not assign the "causes" for grammatical constructions, he does not "teach." Since causes are principles, minds trained in logic would naturally infer that, in order to teach theology, the first thing to do was to lay down theological principles and to use them as the causes of theological conclusions. Such is the reason why, even before Thomas Aquinas, William of Auxerre had posited the articles of faith as the principles from which theological conclusions should be deduced. Thus understood, theology was becoming a science teachable in the same way as all the other arts or sciences, but, at the same time, it was becoming very different from the teaching of Saint Augustine. Instead of rooting itself in the personal experience of the theologian, theology assumed the shape of an objective exposition and interpretation of the saving truth, as impersonally teachable as any other art or science. In this respect, Thomas Aquinas has brought the work of his predecessors up to its point of perfection, but with regard to the very content of theology, he has done something entirely different. His intention was not to make theology still more learned than Albert the Great had already made it. It was first to eliminate from it all learning irrelevant to the exposition and intellection of the saving truth, then to integrate in theology the relevant learning even if, in order to do so, it was necessary to reform certain commonly held positions and to reinterpret certain philosophical principles. Insofar as Christian faith itself was concerned, Thomas Aquinas never intended to touch it. The magnificent elaboration of Christian dogma left by Augustine to his successors was likewise taken up by Thomas Aquinas and integrated by him in his new synthesis. On the contrary, always with a pious respect for his great predecessor, yet fearlessly, Thomas felt free to reinterpret and, wherever it was necessary, to replace with a truer philosophy the purely philosophical elements integrated by Augustine in his own theological synthesis. His reason for doing so was simple. Philosophy is not necessary for human salvation; it is not even necessary for theology to resort to philosophy, but, if it does, the philosophy it uses should be the true philosophy. When a theologian has good reasons to think that Augustine did not make use of the best possible philosophy, he should not hesitate to change it.

Because Thomas Aquinas did so, his reformation of theology entailed a reformation of philosophy. There is no reason not to call it an Aristotelian reformation, for indeed, on many points, Thomas Aquinas substituted for the doctrines borrowed from Plotinus by Augustine, other doctrines which he himself was borrowing from Aristotle. Two points, however, should be kept in mind. First, the philosophical reformation achieved by Thomas Aquinas is a moment in the history of theology before being one in the history of metaphysics. Secondly, even on the level of pure philosophy, his doctrine cannot be understood as a further stage in the progressive discovery of Aristotle by the Latins. Thomism was not the upshot of a better understanding of Aristotle. It did not come out of Aristotelianism by way of evolution, but of revolution. Thomas uses the language of Aristotle everywhere to make the Philosopher say that there is only one God, the pure Act of Being, Creator of the world, infinite and omnipotent, a providence for all that which is, intimately present to every one of his creatures, especially to men, every one of whom is endowed with a personally immortal soul naturally able to survive the death of its body. The best way to make Aristotle say so many things he never said was not to show that, had he understood himself better than he did, he could have said them. For indeed Aristotle seems to have understood himself pretty well. He has said what he had to say, given the meaning which he himself attributed to the principles of his own philosophy. Even the dialectical acumen of Saint Thomas Aquinas could not have extracted from the principles of Aristotle more than what they could possibly yield. The true reason why his conclusions were different from those of Aristotle was that his own principles themselves were different. As will be seen, in order to metamorphose the doctrine of Aristotle, Thomas has ascribed a new meaning to the principles of Aristotle. As a philosophy, Thomism is essentially a metaphysics. It is a revolution in the history of the metaphysical interpretation of the first principle, which is "being."

We are living in times so different from those of Thomas Aquinas that it is difficult for us to understand how philosophy can become theology and yet gain in rationality. This, however, is exactly what happened to philosophy in the *Summa theologiae*, when Thomas changed the water of philosophy to the wine of theology. Thomas always considered himself a theologian. Up to the last years of his life he kept faith with the teaching of Augustine forcefully restated in the injunction of Gregory IX to the theologians of the University of Paris. In his own view, he was not only a theologian, but a monk who had no right to indulge in philosophical activities except in the spirit of his religious vocation. "The philosophers," Thomas says, "made profession of studying Letters in view of acquiring secular learning, but what chiefly befits a religious is to study those Letters that pertain to the learning that is *according to godliness,* as is written in the Epistle to Titus, i, 1. As to the other branches of learning, they are not suitable objects of study for a religious whose whole life is dedicated to the divine service, except insofar as their study is related to sacred learning." [88] Whereupon Thomas immediately quotes Augustine in support of his assertion. Thomas intended to do exactly the same thing as all the other theologians of his time, only he did it differently. Then, naturally, the question arises: since he was a theologian, and such a strict one, how could he have anything to do with philosophy? His own notion of the nature of theology will be the answer to this difficulty.

2. THEOLOGY AND PHILOSOPHY

The question is often asked why a historian of philosophical doctrines should take an interest in the works of a theologian? One of the answers is that he should not, because theological speculation presupposes faith in revelation which the philosopher has not to take into account in his reasoning. Another answer is that he should, because, in the particular case of Thomas Aquinas, we are meeting a theologian so careful to distinguish between faith and reason that the philosophical elements included in his theology can be extracted from it and considered apart without undergoing any modification in nature or in content.[89]

These two opposite conclusions rest upon the same assumption, that in any theological reasoning one at least of the premises is accepted by faith. If this were true, either one of two consequences would necessarily follow. Since Thomas Aquinas was a theologian, all that he said was theological, and since theological conclusions rest upon premises accepted by faith, what Thomas has said is irrelevant to philosophy. Or else, since in many cases Thomas does not argue from any premise that can be said to be *de fide,* we are justified in concluding that, in these cases at least, he is speaking as a philosopher, not as a theologian.

The true nature of the distinction there is between philosophy and theology is a matter to be settled between philosophers and theologians. All that a historian can say is that, in the mind of Thomas Aquinas himself, their distinction was not as simple as it is sometimes supposed to be.[90] With all theologians, Thomas affirms that, supposing the free will of God to save mankind as a whole, it was necessary that the knowledge required for human salvation should be revealed to men. This is evident in the case of those saving truths which escape the grasp of natural human reason. But even when it was within the grasp of natural human reason, saving truth had to be revealed because, otherwise, most men would have remained ignorant of it. Few men are gifted for metaphysical or ethical studies; even those who have the necessary gifts have to wait up to the later part of their life before reaching conclusions in these lofty matters, and who knows at what age he will die? Above all, even those philosophers who live long enough to reach these conclusions, never or seldom do it without some admixture of error.[91]

A first consequence follows from these facts. To the extent that it pertains to the sacred teaching imparted to man through revelation (*sacra doctrina*) theology must deal with some philosophically knowable truths, namely, those whose knowledge is required for the salvation of any man; for instance, God exists, he is one, he is incorporeal, etc. Since they have been in fact revealed to men, these truths were revealable, but the formal reason of the "revealable" extends even beyond the limits of the actually revealed; it includes the whole body of human natural knowledge inasmuch as it can be considered by the theologian in the light of revelation and used by him in view of its end, which is the salvation of man in general. This leaves intact, within theology, the formal distinction between natural knowledge and supernatural knowledge, but it includes them both under a still wider formal reason since "revealables" comprise the whole body of natural cognitions considered as being at the disposal of the theologian in view of his own theological end which is the salvation of man.[92]

If this be true, the unity of theology is that of an organic whole whose parts are united under one single formal reason. Naturally, it first includes what God has actually revealed (whether it be naturally knowable or not). It also includes what the theologian deduces, as a necessary consequence, from the actually revealed truth (theologians often call this the "virtually" revealed). Moreover, it includes all the material provided by logic, the sciences of nature and metaphysics, to the extent that it is taken up by the theologian and incorporated by him into his work. He alone is judge of this extent. Just as it is the soul that builds itself a body, so also theology builds itself the philosophical body which it needs in order to promote the saving work of the sacred teaching.

This notion of theology and of its unity had to be cleared up on two accounts. First, because it was that of Thomas Aquinas himself, and since we are dealing with his doctrine, it is of great historical importance. Secondly, it is our only justification for considering the purely rational conclusions of Thomas Aquinas apart from the theological whole in which they belong. There is no philosophical writing of Thomas Aquinas to which we could apply for an exposition of the truths concerning God and man which he considered knowable in the natural light of human reason. His commentaries on Aristotle are so many expositions of the doctrine of Aristotle, not of what might be called his own philosophy. As a commentator, Thomas could add to the text something of his own, but this was not his principal intention. We may find fragmentary expositions of his own philosophical conceptions in some particular treatises, for instance in the *De ente et essentia*. Generally speaking, however, we must resort to his theological writings in order to find them fully developed, but following a theological order. This is the only mode of historical existence they have and, whatever order of exposition he might have chosen to follow in philosophy, the theology of Thomas Aquinas remains for us the only place where his own rational view of the world is to be found.

Although, taken in itself, it also escapes the competency of the simple historian, still another question may legitimately be asked: what point is there, for a history of philosophy, in considering philosophy in this theological condition? To this question, there are two historical answers. First, it is a fact that philosophical speculation did find itself in this condition during the middle ages. Secondly, it is another historical fact that, in the eyes of mediaeval theologians, its integration with theology was eminently favorable to the purification and progress of philosophical knowledge.[93] Whether the upshot was a truly favorable one or not is a point on which anybody is free to entertain his own opinion, provided he knows the history which he makes bold to judge; in any case, his conclusion can only be that of a philosopher, not of a historian.[94]

3. GOD

Like all theologies the doctrine of Saint Thomas[95] is dominated by his own notion of God. Like all Christian theologians, he knew that the proper name of God was I AM WHO AM, or HE WHO IS (Exod. 3, 14), but even for men who agreed on the truth of this divine name, there remained a problem of interpretation. Modern philology has a right to investigate the question; naturally, it will find in this text what can be found in any text by means of grammars and dictionaries alone. This is not negligible but, philosophically speaking, it seldom amounts to much. Even with such a limited aim in mind, the grammarians have already achieved amazingly different results. What we are concerned with is very different. Our own problem is to know what meaning the Christian masters have attributed to this famous text. Most of them agreed that it meant: I am Being. But what is being? To Augustine, "who was imbued with the doctrines of the Platonists," being was eternal immutability. To John Damascene, absolute being was an "infinite ocean of entity." To Saint Anselm, it was that whose very nature it is to be: *natura essendi*. In all these cases, the dominating notion was that of "entity" (*essentia*). In the mind of Thomas Aquinas, the notion of being underwent a remarkable transformation; from now on, and so long as we will be dealing with Thomas Aquinas, the deepest meaning of the word "being" will be the act pointed out by the verb "to be." Since, in common human experience, to be is to exist, it can be said that, in the doctrine of Thomas Aquinas, being has received the fullness of its existential meaning. In order to avoid all possible confusions with some modern uses of the word "existence," let us add that, in every being, "to be," or *esse,* is not to become; it is not any kind of projection from the present into the future. On the contrary, because it is act, "to be" is something fixed and at rest in being: *esse est aliquid fixum et quietum in ente.*[96] In short, this act is the very core of all that is, inasmuch precisely as what is, is a being.

As Thomas Aquinas understands him, God is the being whose whole nature it is to be such an existential act. This is the reason why his most proper name is, HE IS. After saying this, any addition would be a subtraction. To say that God "is this," or that he "is that," would be to restrict his being to the essences of what "this" and "that" are. God "is," absolutely. Because "what" a thing is usually receives the name of "essence," or of "quiddity" (its "whatness"), some say that since he is "being only" (*esse tantum*), God has no essence or quiddity.[97] Thomas Aquinas does not seem to have favored this way of expressing the purity of the divine act of being. He prefers to say that the essence of God is his *esse*. In other words, God is the being of which it can be said that, what in other beings is their essence, is in it what we call "to be." All the attributes of God are either deducible from this true meaning of his name, or qualified by it.

In our human experience, a "being" is "something that is," or exists. Since, in God, there is no something to which existence could be attributed, his own *esse* is precisely that which God is. To us, such a being is strictly beyond all possible representation. We can establish *that* God is, we cannot know *what* he is because, in him, there is no what; and since our whole experience is about things that *have* existence, we cannot figure out what it is to be a being whose only essence is "to be." For this reason, we can prove the truth of the proposition "God is," but, in this unique case, we cannot know the meaning of the verb "is." [98] Such is the Thomistic meaning of the classical doctrine of the ineffability of God.

Unknowable in himself, at least to us and in this life, God can be known by man imperfectly, from the consideration of his creatures. Two things at least are known of him in this way: first, that he is entirely unlike any one of his creatures; secondly, that he is in himself at least what he has to be in order to be their cause. For this reason, our knowledge of God is said to be "analogical"; we know that God is, with respect to the universe, in a relation similar to that which obtains, in our human experience, between causes and their effects. Such a cognition is not purely negative, since it enables us to say something true about God; it is not wholly positive, and far from it, since not a single one of our concepts, not even that of existence, properly applies to God; we call it "analogical" precisely because it bears upon resemblances between relations, that is, upon proportions.[99]

This notion of God as the absolute act of being flows from the demonstrations of his existence. To demonstrate it is both possible and necessary. It is necessary because the existence of God is not immediately evident; self-evidence would only be possible in this matter if we had an adequate notion of the divine essence; the essence of God would then appear to be one with his existence. But God is an infinite being and, as it has no concept of him, our finite mind cannot see existence as necessarily implied in his infinity; we therefore have to conclude, by way of reasoning, that existence which we cannot intuit. Thus the direct way apparently opened by Saint Anselm's ontological argument is closed to us; but the indirect way which Aristotle has pointed out remains open. Let us therefore seek in sensible things, whose nature is proportioned to our intellect, the starting point of our way to God.[100]

All the Thomistic proofs bring two distinct elements into play: 1) the existence of a sensible reality whose existence requires a cause; 2) the demonstration of the fact that its existence requires a finite series of causes, and consequently a Prime Cause, which is what we call God. Because movement is immediately perceptible to sense knowledge, let us start from the fact that movement exists. The only superiority of this "way" with respect to the other ones, is that its point of departure is the easiest to grasp. All movement has a cause, and that cause must be other than the very being that is in motion; when a thing seems to be self-moving, a certain part of it is moving the rest. Now, whatever it is, the mover itself must be moved by another, and that other by still another. It must therefore be admitted, either that the series of causes is infinite and has no origin, but then nothing explains that there is movement, or else that the series is finite and that there is a primary cause, and this primary cause is precisely what everyone understands to be God.

Just as there is motion in sensible things, there are causes and effects. Now what has just been said of the causes of movement can also be said of causes in general. Nothing can be its own efficient cause, for in order to produce itself, it would have to be anterior, as cause, to itself as effect. Every efficient cause therefore presupposes another, which in turn presupposes another. Now, in this order of causes, in which each higher one is the cause of the lower, it is impossible to go on to infinity, otherwise, there would be neither a first efficient cause, nor intermediate causes, and the effects whose existence we perceive could not possibly exist. There must therefore be a first efficient cause of the series, in order that there may be a middle and a last one, and that first efficient cause is what everyone calls God.

Now let us consider beings themselves. As we know them, they are ceaselessly becoming. Since some of them are being generated, while others are passing away, it is possible for them to be or not to be. Their existence then is not necessary. Now the necessary needs no cause in order to exist; precisely because it is necessary, it exists of itself. But the possible cannot account for its own existence, and if there were absolutely nothing but possibility in things, there would be nothing. This is to say that, since there is something, there must be some being whose existence is necessary. If there are several necessary beings, their series must be finite for the same reason as above. There is therefore a first necessary being, to whose necessity all possible beings owe their existence, and this is what all men call God.

A fourth way goes through the hierarchical degrees of perfection observed in things. There are degrees in goodness, truth, nobility and other perfections of being. Now, more or less are always said with reference to a term of comparison which is absolute. There is therefore a true and a good in itself, that is to say, in the last resort, a being in itself which is the cause of all the other beings and this we call God.

The fifth way rests upon the order of things. All natural bodies, even those which lack knowledge, act for an end. The regularity with which, by and large, they achieve their end, is a safe indication that they do not arrive at it by chance and that this regularity can only be intentional and willed. Since they themselves are without knowledge, someone has to know for them. This primary Intelligent Being, cause of the purpose there is in natural things, is the being we call God.[101]

Since God is first from all points of view and with respect to all the rest, he cannot enter into composition with anything else. The cause of all other beings can enter into composition with none of them. Consequently, God is simple. His simplicity itself has many consequences. Because corporeal bodies are in potency with respect to both motion and being, they are not simple; hence God cannot be corporeal. For the same reason, since he is pure act, God is not composed of matter and form. He is not even a subject endowed with its own form, essence or nature. Divinity is something that God *is,* not that he *has.*[102] But what is such a being which *is* all that he can be said to be, and *has* nothing? He is WHO IS. Since God *is* what other beings only *have,* there is in him no distinct essence to unite with the act of being. This unique being, the only one whose whole essence it is "to be," is so perfectly simple that it is its own being.[103]

If this direct argument seems too abstract to satisfy the intellect, let us remember the conclusions of each one of the five "ways." All particular beings owe their existence to the Prime Cause. Consequently, they receive existence. In other words, what they are (i.e., their essence) receives from God the existence which it has. On the contrary, since the Prime Efficient Cause does not receive its own existence (otherwise it would not be prime) there is no sense in which it can be said to be distinct from it. If there were such a thing as a pure and absolute "fire," it would not *have* the nature of fire, it would *be* it. Similarly, God is not really "being"; he is the very act of what we call "to be." He does not share in it, he is it. Naturally, since we have no experience of this unique being, our mind is unable to conceive it and our language has no perfectly fitting words to express it. From the very first moment we attempt to say what God is, we must content ourselves with saying that he is not in the same way as other things are. As has already been said, we do not know what it is for God "to be";[104] we only know that it is true to say that God is.

The metaphysician thus joins, by reason alone, the philosophical truth hidden in the name that God himself has revealed to man: I AM WHO AM (Exod. 3, 14). God is the pure act of existing, that is, not some essence or other, such as the One, or the Good, or Thought, to which might be attributed existence in addition; not even a certain eminent way of existing, like Eternity, Immutability or Necessity, that could be attributed to his being as characteristic of the divine reality; but Existing itself (*ipsum esse*) in itself and without any addition whatever, since all that could be added to it would limit it in determining it. If he is pure Existing, God is by that very fact the absolute Plenitude of being; he is therefore infinite. If he is infinite Being, he can lack nothing that he should acquire; no change is conceivable in him; he is therefore sovereignly immutable and eternal, and so with other perfections that can be fittingly attributed to him. Now, it is fitting to attribute all of them to him, for, if the absolute act of existing is infinite, it is so in the order of being; it is therefore perfect.[105]

Such is the cause of the many deficiencies of the language in which we express him. This God whose existence we affirm, does not allow us to fathom what he is; he is infinite, and our minds are finite; we must therefore take as many exterior views of him as we can, without ever claiming to exhaust the subject. A first way of proceeding consists in denying everything about the divine essence that could not belong to it. By successively removing from the idea of God movement, change, passivity, composition, we end by positing him as an immobile, immovable being, perfectly in act and absolutely simple; this is the way of negation. But one can take a second way and try to name God according to the analogies obtaining between him and things. There is necessarily a connection, and consequently a resemblance, between cause and effect. When the cause is infinite and the effect finite, it obviously cannot be said that the properties of the effect are found in it such as they are in the cause, but what exists in effects must also be pre-existent in their cause, whatever its manner of existing. In this sense, we attribute to God all the perfections of which we have found some shadow in the creature, but we carry them to the infinite. Thus we say that God is perfect, supremely good, unique, intelligent, omniscient, voluntary, free, and all-powerful, each of these attributes being reduced, in the last analysis, to an aspect of the infinite and perfectly single perfection of the pure act that God is.[106]

4. CREATION

In demonstrating the existence of God by efficient causality, we establish at the same time that God is the creator of the world. Since he is absolute and infinite, God has within himself virtually the being and perfections of all creatures. The way in which finite being emanates from the universal cause is called creation. With respect to this problem, three points should be noted. First, the notion of creation is not intended to account for the existence of this or that particular thing, but of the totality of what exists. In the second place, creation can only be the very gift of existence: there is nothing, neither thing, nor movement, nor time, and behold creature appears, the universe of things, of movement and of time. To say that creation is the emanation *totius esse,* is to say that to create is an act which, apart from the creator himself, presupposes nothing. It is *ex nihilo.* In the third place, if, by definition, creation presupposes no matter, it does presuppose, equally by definition, a creative being which, because it is itself the pure act of being, can cause finite beings to exist.[107]

Once these conditions are propounded, the possibility of a creation becomes conceivable, and we see that it must be free. In fact, the pure act of being would not lack anything if the world did not exist, and it is not increased by anything if the world exists. The existence of creatures is, therefore, radically contingent in relation to God, and that is what we mean in saying that, if it happens, creation is a free act. Now it can happen, for, if we posit God as pure act, not only of thought as Aristotle did, but of being itself, the three conditions required for a true creation are realized: it is the production of the very existence of all that is, it is a production *ex nihilo,* and the cause of that production is in the perfection of the divine act of being. The connection between creature and creator, as it results from creation, is called participation. It must be noted at once that, far from implying any pantheistic signification, that expression, on the contrary, aims at removing it. Participation expresses both the bond uniting the creature to the creator, which makes creation intelligible, and the separation which prohibits them from intermingling. To participate in the pure act or the perfection of God is to possess a perfection which was pre-existent in God, but it is not to be "a part of" what one participates in; it is to derive and to receive being from another being, and the fact of receiving being from God is the best proof that its receiver is not God.[108]

Thus creation is placed infinitely below the creator, so far below him that there is no real relation between God and things, but only between things and God. The world comes into being without any change happening in the divine essence; and yet the universe did not come out of God by a sort of natural necessity, but is manifestly the product of an intelligence and a will. All the effects of God are pre-existent in him, but since he is an infinite Intelligence, and his intelligence is his very being, all his effects are pre-existent in him according to an intelligible mode of being. God knows, therefore, all his effects before producing them, and if he happens to produce them because he knows them, it is therefore because he has willed them. The simple sight of the order and finality reigning in the world is sufficient to show that it is not blind nature which produced things by a sort of necessity, but an intelligent providence which freely chose its works.[109]

It is equally conceivable from this angle how a single being could directly and immediately produce a multitude of beings. Certain Arabian philosophers, especially Avicenna, believed that from one cause can come only one effect. From this they concluded that God must create a first creature which creates in turn another, and so on. But Augustine had long since given us the solution of the problem. Since God is pure intelligence he must possess within him all the intelligibles, that is to say, the forms which will later be the forms of things, but which, so far, exist only in his thought. These forms of things which we call Ideas, are pre-existent in God as the models of things to be created and as the objects of divine knowledge. In knowing himself, not as he is himself, but as he can be participated in by creatures, God knows Ideas. The idea of a creature is therefore the knowledge God has of a certain possible imitation of his perfection by a creature.[110] And so it is that without lessening the divine unity, a multiplicity of things can follow from God.

It would still remain to be seen at what moment the universe was created. The Arabian philosophers, Averroes in particular, claim they are interpreting the authentic thought of Aristotle by teaching that the world is eternal. In this doctrine, God remains the primary cause of things, but he is an infinite and immutable cause which, existing from all eternity, also produces its effect from all eternity. Others, on the contrary—and Saint Bonaventure was one of them—claim to demonstrate rationally that the world did not always exist. Agreeing with Albert the Great on this point, Thomas considers that both sides can call up likely arguments in favor of their theses, but neither hypothesis is susceptible of demonstration. Whatever may be the solution he wishes to establish, a theologian can seek the principle of his demonstration only in things themselves or in the divine will that created them; now neither in one case nor the other does our reason find the basis for a veritable proof. To demonstrate is, in fact, to start from the essence of a thing to show that a certain property belongs to that thing. Now if we start from the essence of things contained in the created universe, we shall see that all essence, taken in itself, is indifferent to all consideration of time. The definitions of the essence of heaven, of man, of stone, are intemporal like all definitions; they give us no information on the question of knowing whether heaven, man or stone are or are not, have always or have not always existed. We can therefore find no help in the consideration of the world. But we shall not find any more help in the consideration of the primary cause, which is God. If God *freely* willed the world, it is absolutely impossible for us to demonstrate that he *necessarily* willed it in time rather than in eternity. The sole basis for our opinion is that God made his will manifest to us by revelation upon which faith is founded. Since reason cannot conclude, and since God has informed us, we must believe that the world began, but we cannot demonstrate it and, strictly speaking, we do not *know* it.[111]

If the universe owes its existence to an intelligent cause, and moreover a perfect one, the result is that the imperfections of the universe cannot be imputed to its author. To create the world was to produce a certain amount of perfection and a certain degree of being; but evil is nothing properly speaking; it is much less a being than an absence of being; natural evil derives from the ontological limitation essential to any creature, and to say that God created not only the world but the evil in it, would be to say that God created nothingness. In reality, from its very first moment creation bridged an infinite gap between God and things, but it did not suppress it, because the gap cannot be suppressed. The resemblance of the world to God is inevitably deficient. No creature receives the total plenitude of divine perfection because perfections pass from God to creatures only by effecting a sort of descent. The order according to which this descent is effected is the very law which regulates the intimate constitution of the universe: all creatures are ordered according to a hierarchical scale of perfection, going from the most perfect, which are the angels, to the least perfect, namely, material things, in such a way that the lowest degree of each superior species borders on the highest degree of each inferior species.[112]

5. MAN

At the summit of creation are the angels. They are incorporeal and even immaterial creatures; Saint Thomas, therefore, does not grant to other theologians that every created thing is composed of matter and form. Yet, since they are creatures, even angels are not simple. In order to place the first degree of creation as close as possible to God, Saint Thomas is willing to grant angels the highest perfection compatible with the state of creature; now simplicity accompanies perfection; angels must therefore be conceived as being as simple as it is possible for a creature to be. This simplicity could obviously not be total, for if the angels were absolutely free of all composition they would be the pure act of being, that is God. Since the angels have received existence from God, they are therefore, like all creatures, composed of their essence and their existence. This composition is enough to place them infinitely below God, but the angels include no other one. They have no matter, therefore no principle of individuation in the ordinary sense of the word; each angel is less an individual than a species, forming by himself alone an irreducible degree in the descending scale that leads to the body; each of them receives from the immediately superior angel intelligible species that are the first parceling out of the divine light, and each of them adapts this illumination, by dimming it and breaking it up, to the immediately inferior angelic Intelligence.[113]

In this downgrade hierarchy of creatures the appearance of man, and consequently of matter, marks a characteristic degree. Man still belongs to the series of immaterial beings through his soul, but his soul is not a pure Intelligence as the angels are. It is an intellect because it is still a principle of intellection and can know a certain type of intelligible; but it is not an Intelligence, because it is essentially the act and form of a body. The human soul is an intellectual substance indeed, but one to which it is essential to be the form of a body and with it to constitute a physical compound of the same nature as all compounds of matter and form, namely, a "man." This is why the human soul is at the lowest degree of intelligent creatures; it is the furthest removed from all the perfections of the divine intellect. On the other hand, insofar as it is the form of a body, it dominates and prevails over it in such a way that the human soul marks the confines and a sort of horizon between the kingdom of pure Intelligences and the domain of corporeal beings.[114]

In a sense, this doctrine complicates the structure of man; in another sense it simplifies it. In Thomism, there is in man (as in all corporeal beings) a twofold composition. First, that of soul and body, which is but one more particular case of the general composition of form and matter in corporeal beings. Because it is a form, the human intellect makes matter become that of a human body and it makes man himself to be "what" he is. In the order of "whatness," which is that of essence and quiddity, form is supreme. There is no form of the form. The human intellect is the highest formal act in virtue of which a certain being is a man and because of which all its operations are human operations. Secondly, since it is a created being, there is in man a composition of essence and existence. True enough, it is through the form "soul" that existence comes to all the component elements of a human being, including the living cells of his body, but before giving existence, the soul receives it from its own created act of being. For this reason, each corporeal being, including man, is the seat of a twofold composition: that of matter with form, that of essence with its act of being.[115] In this structure, *esse*, the act of being, is the keystone of the whole. It is the act of even the form; consequently, it is the act of acts and the perfection of the formal perfections.[116]

At the same time he was complicating finite being, Thomas was simplifying it. The introduction of the composition of being and essence in angels, permitted him to eliminate their hylomorphic composition without attributing to them the absolute simplicity of God. On the other hand, in introducing the notion of the act of being, Thomas was eliminating the plurality of forms in the composite. So long as there is no *actus essendi* distinct from the form, there is no reason why a being should not include a plurality of substantial forms held together and ordered by the highest one. True enough, even in the doctrine of Aristotle, where there is no composition of essence and *esse*, there was a pressing invitation to attribute only one substantial form to each actually existing substance, but to understand in this way the unity of man was to condemn the human soul to perish with the composite of which it is the form. The Aristotelian unity of the substantial form could not apply to a soul immediately created by God in the body and separable from it. How can the human soul be the sole substantial form of its body if, as Thomas does in the *De ente et essentia*, it is to be counted among the separate substances: *"in substantiis separatis, scilicet in anima, intelligentiis et causa prima"* (ch. 5)? So long as there was no act of the substantial form, theologians were bound to hesitate a long time before eliminating the other forms. On the contrary, as soon as Thomas posited *esse* as the act of the form, it became possible and necessary to eliminate the other ones. It became possible because, after the death of its body, the intellective soul still remains a substance composed of its essence and its act of being; hence it still can "subsist." It became necessary because, since form was to be conceived as the proper receiver of its act of being, the composition of *esse* with several distinct substantial forms would have given rise to several distinct actually existing beings. The radical elimination of the *binarium famosissimum*, i.e., hylomorphism and the plurality of forms, was not due to a more correct understanding of the metaphysics of Aristotle but to the introduction, by Thomas Aquinas, of a new metaphysical notion of being.

To each manner of being, its manner of knowing corresponds. By becoming the immediate form of a body, the human soul loses its Augustinian aptitude to the direct apprehension of the intelligible. No doubt there still remains in us some faint glimmer of the divine rays; we still participate in the irradiation of which God is the source, since we end by finding in things the trace of the intelligible that was active at the time of their formation. The agent intellect each human soul possesses is the natural power by which we come nearest to the angels. Yet our intellect does not provide us with innate intelligible species; it cannot even directly receive them from the Separate Substances, nor from God; itself a form, it feeds on other sensible forms. Its highest function is the cognition of primary principles; these are pre-existent in us, at least virtually, and they are the first conceptions of the intellect. It is the perfection of the agent intellect to contain them virtually and to be capable of forming them, but it is also its weakness to be able to form them only in connection with our perception of sensible things. The origin of human knowledge is therefore in the senses; it results from a collaboration between material things, senses and intellect.

Itself a compound of a matter and form, man is only one among an enormous number of natures, that is to say, of material bodies each one having its form. The element which particularizes and individualizes these natures is the matter of each one of them; the universal element they contain is their form; knowing must therefore consist in isolating from

378 *The Golden Age of Scholasticism*

things the universal element they contain. Such is the role of the most characteristic operation of the human intellect—namely, abstraction. Sensible objects act upon the senses by the species they imprint on them; these species, even though they are already stripped of bodily matter, still bear the traces of the materiality and particularity of the objects from which they come. They are therefore, properly speaking, not intelligible, but they can be made intelligible by removing from them the marks of their sensible origin. Such is precisely the role of the agent intellect. By turning toward the sensible species and projecting upon them its light, it illumines and transfigures them so to speak; itself an intelligible being, it finds in, and abstracts from, the natural forms what is in them actually intelligible and virtually universal. Their analogy of structure establishes a sort of correspondence between human beings and things. The human soul is endowed with an agent intellect and with a possible intellect. The species of sensible things are presented to it in the organs of the senses, where they make singular beings known together with their individual properties. The sensible species are therefore only virtually intelligible, that is, in potency, not in act. On the other hand, there is in the rational soul an active faculty capable of making these sensible species actually intelligible, namely, the agent intellect; and in it there also is a passive aptitude for receiving species abstracted from their particular determinations, namely, the possible intellect. Abstract cognition is this abstracting of the intelligible forms by the agent intellect and their being received by the possible intellect.[117]

Abstracting is the first operation of the intellect; it produces simple apprehensions, or concepts. Since these do not affirm or deny anything, they can be neither true nor false. The second operation of the intellect, namely, judging, consists in uniting or separating simple apprehensions by means of a copula, namely, the verb *is*. A judgment is true when what it affirms, or denies, adequately agrees with reality. In the first place, there are things. Through sense knowledge and abstraction the intellect becomes assimilated to things such as they are. Through judgment, the intellect affirms that things are, when they are, or that they are not, when they are not. Judgments must therefore be either true or false. They are true when they agree with the essence of their objects, but since beings are so called because of the act of being (*esse*) which makes them to be, the truth of judgments ultimately rests on the *esse* of the thing rather than on its essence.[117]

Judgments combine into reasonings and, in turn, reasonings combine into demonstrations whose conclusions are scientifically known. In the doctrine of Thomas Aquinas, the logic of judgments and the art of demonstration remain, on the whole, what they had been in the logic of Aristotle. Likewise, Thomas has preserved the Aristotelian notion of "science" and of "learning," conceived as a body of conclusions deduced from principles by means of necessary syllogistic reasoning. This is so true that even his theology has taken up the general form of an Aristotelian science made up of conclusions deduced from principles. Only, in the case of theology, the principles are accepted on the strength of divine revelation, whereas, in scientific knowledge, properly so-called, the principles are accepted on the strength of sensible and of intellectual evidence. Moreover, it should be kept in mind that even though Thomas Aquinas made his own the Aristotelian technique of logical demonstration, he himself has interpreted it and used it in his own way, with the transcendent liberty of a theologian who keeps the whole body of human knowledge permanently available for the work of salvation. Thomas Aquinas has done more than assimilate the body of known philosophical truth; he has deeply transformed it through his new interpretation of the first principle, namely, "being."

6. THE END OF MAN

All form is naturally active. In a being devoid of knowledge, form is inclined only toward the complete realization of that being. In a being endowed with intelligence, the inclination can tend toward any one of the objects it apprehends, and this is the source of free activity and will. The proper object of the will is good as such; whenever the intellect presents some image of it, the will tends spontaneously to embrace it. Fundamentally, what the will seeks above all these forms of good it pursues, is the good in itself in which all these particular forms of good participate. If the human intellect could offer to us, as a known object, the Sovereign Good Himself, our will would cleave to it at once, and seize it with an immovable grip which would also be the most perfect liberty. But we do not directly see the supreme perfection; we are therefore reduced to trying, by an incessantly renewed effort of the intellect, to determine those among the forms of good offered to us which are bound to the Sovereign Good by a necessary connection. And therein—at least here on earth—consists our very liberty. Since unshakable adherence to the Sovereign Good is denied us, our will can never choose except between particular forms of good; how to determine the particular goods we should choose, and, knowing them, how to determine our acts in view of these ends, is the fundamental problem of morality.[118]

The motion of the will moving itself and all the other powers of the soul toward a certain object is its "intention." The proper object of intention is a certain end. If, in order to reach an end, it is necessary first to desire certain means, one and the same intention runs through our successive volitions of the different means; this intention wills the means in view of the end and, consequently, there is only one intention for the means and for the end.

Since human acts deal with singular cases and objects, a deliberation is always necessary to establish the appropriate means required in view of the end. This deliberation (*consilium*) terminates in a choice (*electio*) and in the consent, or approval, given by our will to that choice. This is, therefore, a complex operation in which the intellect and the will share in different ways.[119] Through repeating similar moral choices we progressively form moral habits (*habitus*) whose effect it is to facilitate the corresponding acts. When these habits are morally good, they are called virtues; when they are morally bad, they are called vices. The formation and development of the moral personality of each human individual is one with the acquisition of his own virtues and, unfortunately, of his own vices.[120] Since the problem is one of personal dispositions, of education and of self-discipline, the deliberate acquisition of moral virtues and of moral vices is the very history of every moral being.

Being a rational animal, man should rule his conduct according to the laws of reason. He does it by correctly using his intellect whose speculative function it is to know the true and whose practical function it is to know the good. Like the speculative intellect, the practical intellect has its own principles. The first one is that we should desire what is good and avoid what is evil. What is good, for a rational being, is what agrees with its rational nature and, consequently, with reason. Every act that is conformable to reason, is good; every act that disagrees with reason, is evil. Virtue, then, is a permanent disposition to act conformably to the prescriptions of practical reason. We need intellectual virtues in order to grasp the principles of human conduct (Intelligence), to deduce from these principles the correct conclusions (Science), and even to relate both principles and conclusions to the first principles and causes (Wisdom). All these are virtues of the intellect. Naturally, since morality is to be found in acts, there must also be moral virtues properly so-called, whose seat is the will. The three fundamental ones are justice, which regulates our acts every time the rights of other men are concerned; temperance, which represses passions; and force, which enables the will to comply with the commands of practical reason. An exceptionally important intellectual virtue, however, is prudence. It is the progressively acquired habit of correctly solving particular moral problems. For indeed each concrete particular problem is a distinct case, different from all other ones because particular circumstances are never twice identically the same. The prudent man is the one whose practical judgment is so sound that he can advise both himself and those who consult him in their practical moral problems.[121] He decides what it is best to do, given the circumstances of the case, judged in the light of the principles of speculative reason and of their rationally deduced consequences. From beginning to end "moral virtue holds its goodness from the rule of reason." [122]

These rules, however, do not merely say what seems to be right or wrong according to our own preferences. They are laws, that is to say, commandments of reason prescribing what is required for the common good. The eternal law is the dictate of the divine providence, and therefore of the divine reason, governing the perfect community which we call the universe. Inasmuch as man is subject to this eternal law of divine providence, there is in him an imprint of it which is called natural law. Moreover, inasmuch as he is a rational creature, man is subject to the eternal law in a particularly excellent way. He does not simply undergo it, as all natural beings do, he also knows it and wills it. In man, therefore, "the natural law is nothing else than the rational creature's participation of the eternal law." As to human laws, they are so many prescriptions of human practical reason, promulgated by men vested in authority and in charge of insuring the common good of cities. Since they are human, these laws too, when they are just, are so many participations of the divine law. Every moral fault, or every sin, is before anything else a violation of the law of nature, and through it, a violation of the laws prescribed to nature by the divine reason.[123]

Whether man knows it or not, his love for the good and his pursuit of happiness are, in fact, two unconscious expressions of a natural desire for God which nature alone is unable to fulfill. Thus the total destiny of man reveals itself as early as this life in his permanent and fecund anxiety for a beyond. There is for man a relatively supreme good toward which he should tend during his earthly life; the proper object of ethics is to let us know what it is and to facilitate our access to it. To know and dominate our passions, to eradicate vices, to acquire and preserve virtues, to seek happiness in man's highest and most perfect operation, that is to say, in the consideration of truth through the study of speculative sciences, this is the real beatitude, however imperfect, to which we can lay claim here below. But our speculative knowledge, even imperfect as it is, is sufficient to allow us to divine and confusedly desire what it lacks. It leads us to the existence of God, but it does not allow us to attain his essence. How could a soul which knows itself to be immortal because it is immaterial not place in an otherworldly future the end of its desires and its true Supreme Good? [124]

7. THOMISM AT THE CROSSWAYS

The doctrine of Thomas Aquinas surprised his contemporaries. He was not a promoter of scientific learning like Albert the Great or Robert Grosseteste. To him the scientific knowledge of nature was in Aristotle, whose doctrine he had learned, commented upon and accepted, on the whole, in logic, physics, astronomy, biology, psychology, metaphysics and ethics. Even in his theology, which he could not borrow from Aristotle, Thomas Aquinas had accepted the general notion of science, the empiricism and the intellectualism of the Philosopher. The Aristotelians of his time naturally considered him an ally, and indeed, he was one of them.

This is so true that the representatives of the traditional theology could not help resenting his attitude on many points. They had no objections to his using the notions of matter and form; Augustine had used them too, after Plotinus; but they did not like the Aristotelian definition of matter as pure potentiality: this made the efficient causality of secondary causes look too much like a creation. They also resented his application of the notion of form of the body to the definition of the human soul; how could the soul be an independent substance, if it was assimilated to other perishable material forms? The consequences of this new definition of the soul were doubly disturbing. In noetics, it entailed an empirical intellectualism, restricting the data of intellection to sense knowledge only and eliminating the supplement of light which the Augustinian soul used to derive, even in natural cognition, from the divine light. In metaphysics, it made it difficult to add to the proofs of the existence of God based upon physical creatures, those which Augustine had drawn from the existence of created intellectual effects, especially the divine nature of created necessary and immutable truth. Because the handmaid whose services were required by the new theology was no longer the same, the household was looking strangely different. The controversies about the unity or plurality of substantial forms, incidental to the new definition of the soul, were soon to manifest the importance of the philosophical and theological interests at stake in the discussion.

Nor was this all. In a way, the Aristotelians were about as much disturbed as the Augustinians by the new theology. On two points, at least, Thomas Aquinas was following his own way, which was neither that of Augustine nor that of Aristotle. For deep-seated reasons, these two points were those which had been defined many centuries ago by the *noverim me, noverim te* of Saint Augustine: God and man. To the pure Self-Thinking Thought of Aristotle, and to the Dear Eternity of Augustine, Thomas Aquinas had substituted the Pure Act of Being, or *Purum Esse.* This was the same Christian God as that of Augustine; his traditional attributes remained the same, but because the God of Thomas Aquinas was philosophically different from those of Aristotle, and even of Saint Augustine, the relation of the world to him was conceived by Thomas in a new way; in short, the notion of being was becoming a new one. At the same time as a new theology was making its appearance, a new metaphysics was being offered to the meditation of the philosophers. From this point of view, the philosophy of Aristotle was finding itself, with respect to the Thomistic notion of *esse,* in the relation of matter to form, and Aristotelian metaphysics, too, was receiving a new act of being. The consequences of this event can hardly be calculated. Turned into the "proper receivers" of the act of being, the Aristotelian forms were becoming Thomistic forms;

the unity of compound substances was becoming a Thomistic unity; the human soul could now become a substantial form without losing its own substantiality nor the immortality which it held from its actuation by its own act of being; directly related to God in his very *esse,* which is in him the first effect of the Prime Cause, the man of Thomas Aquinas knew himself as a subsisting and enduring individuality, known and willed by a God whose supreme act of being included in its unity the Ideas of all its freely created effects; the global governance of the Aristotelian world was thus being replaced with a particular providence without impairing the laws of nature or their normal necessity. It is no wonder that while the representatives of the traditional theology were feeling dubious about the Thomistic notion of man, those of the Aristotelian metaphysics should take exception to the Thomistic notion of being. Because Thomas Aquinas had tackled the fundamental problems in metaphysics, things began to move even before his death. The extraordinary flowering of philosophical speculation which we shall observe between 1277 and about 1350 can be considered, from more than one point of view, as an after-effect of this theological and metaphysical reformation.

PART NINE

THE CONDEMNATION OF 1277

The condemnation of 1277 is not an isolable complex of historical events but it is a convenient center of reference around which the exposition of many historical facts can be ordered. It was both a point of arrival and a point of departure. Many different factors contributed to it and, in a way, it itself became a dividing line, in this sense at least, that after it the attitude of many theologians toward philosophy underwent a perceptible change whose effects are visible in their works.

CHAPTER I

LATIN AVERROISM

As HAS already been said, the discovery of the Greek philosophical universe was for the Latins an epoch-making event. From a certain point of view, its history coincides with that of the progressive discovery of Aristotle. By Aristotle, we should understand the doctrine of Aristotle as interpreted by his various commentators, including such theologians as Albert the Great and Thomas Aquinas. Since, even today, historians still hesitate on the authentic meaning of Aristotelianism, it is no wonder that, in the thirteenth century, there was disagreement on its interpretation.

Roughly speaking, two main interpretations of Aristotle attracted the attention of the masters in philosophy and theology up to about 1260-1265, namely, those of Avicenna and Averroes. These were two different philosophies, and everybody knew it because Averroes himself had often blamed Avicenna for arbitrarily departing from the authentic teaching of the Philosopher. From about 1261 on, a third Aristotle entered the schools with the commentaries of Thomas Aquinas. Like the preceding ones, this new Aristotle presented himself as the true one. Inspired, to a large extent, by older commentaries, including that by the Christian John Philoponus, the new interpretation eliminated many elements which Avicenna and Averroes had added to the letter of the Philosopher; at the same time, it offered a version of his doctrine which, often as historically justifiable as the preceding ones, was better adapted to the demands of Christian theology. To speak of an Avicennian, an Averroistic or a Thomistic Aristotle is to point out three different interpretations of a fourth one.[1] There was, however, this difference between them, that the Avicennian interpretation of Aristotle was the philosophy of Avicenna and that the Averroistic interpretation of Aristotle was the philosophy of Averroes, whereas the Thomistic interpretation of Aristotle was not the philosophy of Thomas Aquinas. Included in his own philosophy, the Aristotelianism of Thomas Aquinas was not co-extensive with it.

From this point of view, the influence of Averroes would have raised no particular problem without the definite position it implied concerning the relationship of philosophy and theology. Aristotle, Avicenna and Averroes were all considered "philosophers" by the "theologians"; but, of the three, only Averroes had stressed the fact that philosophy should be kept apart from theology, and since he had blamed Avicenna for blending his so-called philosophy with religious beliefs, his Christian readers could not ignore his attitude on this point. Many Christian masters used Averroes as the best literal commentary on Aristotle at their disposal; their situation was that of a modern professor of history of philosophy trying to make his pupils understand a doctrine which he himself does not necessarily consider true. Some theologians resented the fact that theologically false doctrines could be taught, even to this pedagogical end. The simplest answer to this reproach was that of Richard Rufus: if you ask us to teach Aristotle, all we can do is to explain the meaning of what he has said, and it is no wonder that he sometimes disagrees with Christian faith since he was a pagan and a "philosopher," not a Christian nor a "theologian." But still another position was possible. A master in arts could think and say that the conclusions of Averroes, and consequently those of Aristotle, were philosophically correct. In other words, he could maintain that, so far as philosophy itself was concerned, the conclusions of Aristotle appeared to him as necessary rational conclusions. This, again, implied no opposition to theology, nor any inner doubt as to the absolute certitude of Christian faith, but it did imply the possibility of a conflict between philosophy and theology. For instance, if the eternity of the world is a necessary rational conclusion in philosophy, then to believe that the world has had a beginning is to accept as true, on the strength of revelation, something that contradicts one of the necessary conclusions of natural reason. Even if one did not add that the necessary conclusions of reason were necessarily true, one still created a conflict between philosophy and theology, revelation and reason.

Whether we call it, from its relation to theology, a "heterodox Aristotelianism," or, from its historic cause, an "Averroism," the designation points out the attitude of the masters of arts, who, identifying Averroes with Aristotle, and Aristotle himself with philosophy, maintained that necessary philosophical conclusions could contradict the teaching of Christian revelation. Even this conflict was not a necessary one. The general reaction of the theologians could have been one of indifference to the problem. Why not say, for instance, that in consequence of original sin, human reason has become so obscured that it can no longer see even natural truth in its own natural light? The fact is, however, that many theologians refused to despair of natural reason. They maintained that its necessary conclusions were necessarily true and they denied that what was necessary for reason could be false for faith. Philosophism was not a wholly new attitude: the so-called "dialecticians" of the twelfth century had already exhibited the same tendency; only, this time, Averroism was pitting the universe of the "philosophers" against that of the "theologians," and even though it expressly maintained that the universe of the theologians was the true one, it also maintained that the universe of the philosophers was that of natural reason. To this extent, the Averroists were initiating on some crucial points a separation of philosophy from theology, of reason from revelation.

One cannot write the history of this movement without ceaselessly naming Averroes. First of all, its representatives usually followed his interpretation of Aristotle, at least in a general way. Moreover, although his own doctrine of the relations of philosophy and theology was not their own, Averroes himself had expressly favored this separation. Prophecy was to him the sole case of a real coincidence of religious and philosophical truth. As to theology, he considered it a mixture of reason and faith, fatal to both. To the extent that, in various ways and in various degrees, some Latin masters cultivated a philosophy intentionally kept apart from theological influences, their philosophism was an Averroism. Such appellations are neither definitions nor descriptions. They merely point out some aspects of reality which, for reasons proper to each case, are considered historically significant.

If this be true, the spreading of the works of Averroes should not be confused with the Averroistic movement. The case of the English master Adam of Buckfield using Averroes to prepare his commentary on Aristotle is only one among many others.[2] The more puzzling cases in which famous masters, for instance Albert the Great, declared their fundamental agreement with certain doctrines of Averroes hardly reconcilable with the teaching of the Church, are not impossible to explain. It was for them a foregone conclusion that every man had his own intellect; having to choose between Avicenna who separated the agent intellect from the possible intellect, and Averroes who kept them together, some Christian masters felt closer to Averroes, who separated the two intellects from man but kept them together, than to Avicenna who left to man at least the possible intellect but separated it from the agent intellect.[3] True Averroism consisted in considering Averroes as being, on the whole, a faithful exponent of Aristotle and of truth.

There is no precise date for such events as the formation of a group or the birth of a school. The name, "Averroist," has been widely used during the fourteenth and fifteenth centuries. To use it today is certainly to apply a mediaeval name to a mediaeval reality,[4] but it is not easy to say at what moment the school of thought which this name points out first became recognizable as a specified entity. When Albert wrote his treatise *On the Oneness of the Intellect against Averroes* (1256),[5] he was opposing Averroes himself, not a group of Averroists. The *Summa contra gentiles* of Thomas Aquinas (*ca.* 1258) contains a refutation of the same position of Averroes, but it makes no mention of Averroists. The relevant chapters develop a straight philosophical and theological discussion. On the contrary, the 1270 condemnation of Averroistic errors taught at the University of Paris is a sure proof that, at that date, there already was an Averroistic movement.[6]

I. SIGER OF BRABANT

The Parisian master of arts whose doctrine was to become the center of the controversy is Siger of Brabant.[7] To call him an Averroist does not mean that his doctrine betrays no other influences than that of Averroes. On certain points, Siger followed Avicenna, or he combined Avicenna's doctrine with that of Averroes. A still more important source of Siger's metaphysics was the neoplatonist Proclus whose doctrine of causality blended in the mind of Siger with the cosmology of Averroes. The spirit of the two doctrines was very different. The *Elements of Theology* of Proclus, or the *Book of Causes* excerpted from the *Elements,* developed a cosmogony, that is, a system of causes intended to account for the existence and structure of the universe. The cosmology of Averroes was emphatically not a cosmogony; taking the existence of the world for granted, it intended to account for its sole intelligibility. Many reasons made their blending possible, but the spirit of the two doctrines was not the same and their combination in the metaphysics of Siger makes it difficult to interpret. One does not see clearly whether Proclus has gained the upper hand or Averroes still remained the undisputed master of the situation.

Metaphysics is the science of being *qua* being. Like Averroes, Siger takes sides against Avicenna on the question of knowing whether the existence of God should be proved in physics and his nature studied in metaphysics, or his existence should be proved in metaphysics and his nature studied in theology. This was an important problem. Avicenna had taught that the physicist does not deal with prime matter, but only with the proximate matter of the natural beings which he studies; consequently he cannot even ask the question of the cause of being *qua* being; only the metaphysician can ask it. Averroes had maintained, on the contrary (*In Phys.,* II, text. 22), that the physicist deals with prime matter for the simple reason that he is qualified to treat of the material cause; consequently, according to him, the demonstration of the existence of the First Cause had to start from some physically given being (*"Primus autem Motor impossibile est ut declaretur esse nisi per signum naturale"*). On this point, where Duns Scotus will agree with Avicenna, Thomas Aquinas and Siger agree with Averroes. The difference with Thomas Aquinas is that, since Siger leaves revealed theology out of his own consideration, metaphysics becomes in his doctrine identical with Wisdom. It is divinity itself: *scientia divina.*[8]

Being is analogical. God is pure and absolute being. His existence is demonstrated by starting from actually given physical being. Since it is impossible to posit a series of essentially ordered causes without positing a first one, the existence of a first cause can be proved in the three orders of efficient cause, formal cause and final cause. God is precisely the first cause in every order of causality. The material cause is naturally left out because matter is on the side of potentiality whereas Being is act.[9]

Since God is proved to exist as the first cause, his causality extends to all that exists. He is the cause of every individual, Socrates, etc., to the extent that Socrates is a being. This is so true that no cognition of a singular is complete until it is related to the cognition of the Prime Cause.[10] The fact that Siger posits God as the Prime Mover of all, and therefore as the prime efficient cause of all, leaves open many problems of interpretation. Is God efficient cause in the Avicennian sense of creative efficiency, or in the Averroistic sense of moving cause only? Almost certainly in the Averroistic sense of the term, which identifies the efficient cause with the moving cause. In order to lessen the difficulty, Siger stresses the fact that almost everybody agrees that God is the prime efficient cause of all without determining the precise sense in which "efficient cause" should be understood. In fact he himself must have understood it in a very broad sense in order to reconcile all the authorities which, according to him, agree on that point: Aristotle, Avicenna, Proclus and Christian faith.[11] In demonstrating this truth, however, Siger borrows more from Proclus than from Averroes[12] and before deciding in what sense God is the cause of everything we must wait for Siger's opinion about the notion of creation.

Taking the term in its most general meaning: the production of an effect by a cause, it can be said that God is the creator of all things. He has in himself the Ideas of all beings;[13] he also has the efficacy required to cause them; nothing is in the potentiality of matter that is not first in act in the Prime Mover.[14] So long as we do not go beyond this notion of a Prime Cause of all generations, there is no problem. On the contrary, the notion of creation from nothingness raises many difficulties. Since the point of view of the Philosopher was restricted to the problem of the generation of beings by eduction of forms from matter, the notion of an eduction of forms from nothingness never occurred to his mind. From the point of view of Aristotle, it is a contradictory notion. Consequently, there is no place for creation in his philosophy, nor should this fact be concealed. As the Christians understand it, creation is a miracle. It can be affirmed on the strength of revelation only.[15]

As has been said, the position of Siger is not easy to interpret. He certainly did his best to express himself in terms compatible with the teaching of Christian faith. His language is the same as that of Thomas Aquinas: God is the efficient cause of all. On the other hand, we have just seen that the notion of creation appears to him as self-contradictory; consequently, when Siger says that God is the efficient cause of all that is, he does not have in mind a creative efficient cause. Then what sort of an efficient cause is it? Referring to the remarkable analysis of the various interpretations of the notion of efficient cause given by Averroes, we must choose between attributing to him the doctrine of Avicenna (a mediation between philosophy and theology) or that of Aristotle as interpreted by Averroes, which reduces the efficient cause to the moving cause. No hesitation would be possible were it not for the use that Siger makes of Proclus. We feel inclined to think that, according to Siger, the divine causality remains what it was in Averroes, namely, that of the Prime Mover and nothing else, but more studies, and perhaps better texts, would be required to prove this conclusion, or to disprove it.

On the contrary, the position of Siger is perfectly clear concernnig the problem of the possibility of a creation in time and, consequently, of the eternity of the created world. According to revelation (Gen. i, 1) God created the world "in the beginning"; so there has been a beginning. According to philosophy, it is not impossible to conceive God as an eternal and necessary cause without positing at the same time the existence of *all* his effects, but it is impossible to conceive him as a cause without positing, together with him, the existence of *some* effects. Otherwise, how would he be cause? If this be true, there have always been some created beings. Consequently, the created world is eternal. Nay, since the world is eternal, the same species of creatures are bound to reappear, so to speak in a circular way, succeeding each other in the same order as before, and so on indefinitely. Of course, this is what philosophy says; we are doing nothing more than reporting it.[16]

In a universe thus conceived, every being can be said to have being more or less according to its more or less close proximity to the First.[17] To be and to be one are one and the same thing. On this point, Avicenna was wrong in imagining that oneness was a disposition added to being. It is being conceived as undivided from itself; in short, it is being in its very lack of division, that is, in its indivision. Consequently, when we say "thing," "one" or "being," we are really speaking of only one and the same reality. It is called "thing" (*res*) because it has entity conceived in a general way (*essentia in communi*); it is called an "animal" or a "man" from the essence that determines it to be what it is.[18]

In 1272, the problem of the nature of being had reached its point of maturity and it was becoming a controversial issue. Its origin was the distinction between essence and existence posited by Alfarabi and Avicenna under the form of a certain accidentality of existence with respect to essence. Averroes had denied this distinction, but it had been taken up by Maimonides among the Jews and, among the Christians, by William of Auvergne, Albert the Great and several others. In the mind of these masters, the distinction introduced by Avicenna had more or less coalesced with the older distinction of Boethius between *quod est* and *quo est;* instead of signifying, respectively, as it did in Boethius, the whole and its form, it was then made to signify being and its existence. The rise of Thomism added to the complexity of the situation. Thomas opposed the Avicennian notion of the accidentality of existence, but, at the same time, he kept existence distinct from essence, as its act. The new position adopted by Thomas was an answer to the objection raised by Averroes against Avicenna: existence cannot possibly be an accident. Avicenna was right:

existence is other than essence; Averroes was right: existence is not an accident; existence, Thomas said, is distinct from essence, not as its accident, but as its act.

This was a purely philosophical problem. All theologians agreed that finite beings held their existence from the creative power of God; how to express this fact in philosophical terms, and how to conceive the nature of finite being, were problems open to free philosophical discussion. This is exactly how Siger of Brabant took it. In his questions on the *Metaphysics,* he objectively reviews the several positions already taken on this problem; he freely criticizes them and, finally, he defines his own. If the date 1272, proposed for these Questions, is correct, Siger did nothing more than to maintain the authentic position of Aristotle and Averroes; he did not initiate any controversy of his own concerning the notion of being.

All the positions he opposes upheld the view that the existence (*esse*) of a thing was something added to its essence: (*esse est aliquid additum essentiae*). The first example of such a position quoted by Siger is that of Albert the Great commenting upon the *Liber de causis*.[19] Since, Albert says, things hold their existence from their first principle, they are not their own existence (*esse*). As Siger understands him, Albert is the ancestor of all those who reduce the distinction of essence and existence to be a technical expression of the fact that, by definition, creatures only are in virtue of their cause. God alone is *per se* or *a se;* since they are created, things hold their existence from without: they are *ab alio*.[20] To this, Siger answers that all that which is found in any being other than the First is equally caused by the First Principle. Existence is caused by the First, but so are essence and accidents. The reason alleged by Albert does not justify the conclusion that existence is distinct from essence as if existence were an effect of the First Principle in any other sense than essence itself is.

Another way to justify this distinction is to say, with Avicenna, that if the essence of a being includes its existence, it needs no cause; consequently, no caused being can be its own existence. This, Siger replies, contains an equivocation on the manifold meaning of the word "cause." To say that "it is by himself that man is man," is true in the order of formal cause, whereas to say that "man is man by something else" is true in the order of efficient cause. Consequently, the fact that every man exists by an efficient cause is no reason why we should attribute to him an existence (*esse*) distinct from his essence in the order of formal cause.[21] Still another way to justify the same conclusion would be to say, once more with Avicenna, that "being" and "thing" are two distinct notions. To which Siger makes a typically Averroistic answer: Aristotle denies it.[22]

The place attributed to the next position is worthy of notice. Siger inserts it between the first one (Albert: existence comes to the thing from without) and the second one (Avicenna: existence is distinct from essence within the thing). This third and intermediate position is that of Thomas Aquinas. "The existence (*esse*) of a thing, although it is something else than its essence, should not be understood as something superadded to it in the same way as an accident; it is constituted, as it were, by the principles of the essence." [23] Siger himself agrees with Thomas that existence is no accident of the essence. On the other hand, it cannot be part of the essence of the thing either as matter or as form. But, in substances, there is nothing else besides matter, form and accidents. To add existence to them is to posit a fourth nature in things.[24] This criticism brings out in full relief the novelty of the Thomistic answer to the problem: instead of repeating Aristotle, Thomas had indeed posited a fourth nature in beings (to use Siger's own words), namely, the act of being. At the same time, it typifies what was to be a very common objection to the new doctrine: what can this act of being possibly be? Many a so-called Thomist will wonder about it.

The personal answer of Siger to this question is no less remarkable than his criticism of the other positions. Let us note, in the first place, that in answering Thomas, Siger did not say that the conclusion was false; on the contrary, he expressly affirmed that it was true; only he disagreed with its formulation. And indeed, he himself will retain something of the language of Saint Thomas, but nothing of his position. In caused beings, Siger says, existence itself (*ipsum esse*) belongs to their essences; it is not added to their essences; the words being and thing do not signify two distinct notions. The refutation of Avicenna by Averroes is decisive on this point. Yet, it is true to add, with Boethius and other masters, that while essences are by themselves what they are, they hold their existence from the First Principle. "Now, many have posited that only in the First Principle does existence belong to essence. And there is some truth in this because existence (*esse*, to be) signifies essence in its greatest actuality." Thus, in Siger's own position, there is no act of being distinct from essence, but existing essence enjoys the full actuality which, according to Thomas, it owes to its existential act. In short, there is no "real composition of essence and existence"; actual existence belongs to the very essence of man: *"ad esse essentiale hominis pertinet actualitas essendi."* [25]

On this point, Siger was holding a purely philosophical position, between which and Christian faith no necessary connection obtained. Its philosophical origin is visible: Siger was taking sides with Averroes against Avicenna and extending the refutation of Avicenna by Averroes to more recent positions in which he saw modified restatements of the Avicennian distinction of essence and existence. His own position was so authentically Aristotelian that, on this point, many so-called Thomists will share his views out of sheer loyalty to the true inspiration of the Philosopher.

The Prime Cause is the cause of all things, but all things are not immediately caused by it. God is the cause of the whole being (*causa totius esse*). It is not easy to say if he understands this causation after the manner of Proclus, of Avicenna or, as is highly probable, of Averroes. The oneness of the Prime Cause is forcefully stressed in his questions on the *Metaphysics*, III, 7 and 12. The Prime Cause is called an "efficient cause" in the same work, III, 8. This is the place where Siger shows that the universal efficient causality of God can be established following several different ways, namely, those of Aristotle, Avicenna and Proclus. His own way to prove this is to show that since there is an excellent disposition of things, the world must be ruled by only one ruler; hence there must be only one efficient cause of all (p. 100). A second reason is the analogical nature of beings; what is possessed in an analogical way demands the existence of a single term of reference with respect to which it is analogical; so there must be only one single being with respect to which all the rest is said to be. This being is the efficient cause of all beings (pp. 101-102). A third and a fourth proof of the same conclusion are borrowed from the *Elements of Theology* of Proclus: 1) since all multitude derives from unity, all causes follow from one single cause; 2) the Prime Being is perfect, therefore he is perfectly in act, but no other being is pure act, not even the prime substances since, "not being their own existence, they are in potency with respect to non-being"; consequently, all that is not pure act presupposes the existence of one single Pure Act (p. 103). Obviously, Siger is mainly interested in proving the oneness of the first cause. Among his demonstrations, only the last one rests upon the very existence of beings and could entail a truly efficient causality, but, curiously enough, Siger ceases to speak of an efficient cause at the very moment he introduces Proclus. Siger's own thought seems to follow the general line of moving causes; he says that since this is the reason given by Aristotle, we should prefer it (p. 101); but he does not exclude the other reasons; he simply does not define the limits of their validity.

The same difficulty besets the interpretation of his doctrine of causes in general. Does Siger follow Avicenna's cosmogony? Or does he follow Averroes' cosmology? The point is not clear. In his treatise *On the Necessity and Contingency of Causes*, where he certainly expresses his own thought, Siger states that the First is the immediate and necessary cause of the first Intelligence.[26] This time, he is mainly interested in proving that there are limits to necessity in the world. The necessity of God's influence only extends to the order of the separate substances. There is contingency everywhere else because there is matter and, consequently, chance, accidental events and indetermination. This contingncy is a mere absence of intelligible determination; it has nothing in common with the free interventions of a divine will. Of course, miracles are always possible, but philosophy is not concerned with them. For the same reason, still speaking from the point of view of the philosophers only, the foreknowledge of God does not extend further than his causality. God does not know what he does not necessarily cause; contingent events, then, escape his cognition, even though, in an indirect way, they do not escape his causality.[27]

The problem of the intellective soul is of particular interest because, connected as it was with the problem of the possibility of personal immortality, it immediately caught the attention of the theologians. The question was not to know if the immortality of the soul was demonstrable; it was to know if there is in man a personal intellective soul whose immortality could be demonstrated. Following Averroes, Siger maintains that the possible intellect and the agent intellect constitue a separate substance. Subsisting in itself and outside of individual men, it is, so to speak, the intellective soul of the human species. On the other hand, since he was a Christian, Siger had to present his doctrines in terms best calculated not to hurt Christian feelings more than was unavoidable. This scruple was so sincere with him that he openly expressed it at least once; besides, this was a genuinely Averroistic scruple, since Averroes had recommended not to disturb religious beliefs on any philosophical grounds. Even the tendency exhibited by some Averroists to keep their doctrine to themselves or to teach it in secret was in keeping with the recommendation of Averroes, not to discuss philosophy with theologians.

Judging from the conclusion of his treatise *On the Oneness of the Intellect against the Averroists,* it seems probable that, in it, Thomas was answering an Averroistic writing which, so far, has not been discovered. It seems still more probable that Siger had written, partly in answer to this treatise of Saint Thomas, another treatise *On the Intellect (De intellectu)* of which some fragments have been preserved in the writings of Nifo, a late fifteenth-century Averroist.

After presenting these quotations of Siger by Nifo, Bruno Nardi sums up the main positions of this lost treatise as follows: "1) The possible Intellect is, in itself, the lowest of the separate substances, and there is only one for the whole human species; 2) The intellective soul of man results from the union of the possible Intellect, separate and eternal, with the cogitative, which is the highest of the faculties with which the sensitive souls of individual men are endowed; 3) In this union with singular souls the Intellect, one in itself, acquires an existence both individual and multiple, according to the number of the individuals; 4) Thanks to this union the intellective soul can be said to be a substantial form inherent in man and not only an assisting form; so that it is from it that man derives his specific being of rational animal; 5) The possible Intellect is pure potency without any substantial act; it is only thanks to the action of the agent Intellect that it is gradually actuated; 6) The agent Intellect is God; but he can be said to be part of the soul to the extent that he concurs with the human act of understanding and, at the end of his intellectual development, man unites himself with the possible Intellect as with its form; 7) The human intellect can succeed in knowing the separate substances and God through intentional union with their essence." [28]

In fragments of another lost treatise of Siger *On Happiness* (*De felicitate*), Bruno Nardi notes the following positions: "1) The supreme felicity of man in this life formally consists in the intellectual act by which the possible Intellect understands the essence of the agent Intellect, that is God; 2) Like the human intellect, the other separate Intelligences find their beatitude in the act by which they understand the divine essence; 3) For the human intellect as well as for the other separate Intelligences, the intellection by which God is understood is God himself." [29]

These doctrinal positions betray a desire to express the essentials of what Siger held to be philosophically established on the matter without hurting the feelings of the theologians more than was inevitable. His intention was to find a description of the human act of knowing which, while maintaining the separation of the Intellects, justified the attribution to every man of an intellective soul of his own, at least in this life.[30]

The same remarks apply to Siger's Questions *On the Soul*. Siger knew that other Christians had preceded him in the study of the problem, and far from despising them, he once called them "the two leading men in philosophy, Albert and Thomas" (*praecipui viri in philosophia, Albertus et Thomas*). Having read the paraphrase of the one and the commentary of the other, Siger could not ignore their respective interpretations of the Aristotelian doctrine of the intellect. These two men say that "the substance of the intellective power of the soul is separated from the body, since it operates by no corporeal organ." To this position, Siger opposes many reasons, the first of which probably was decisive in his mind: "If a substance is united with matter, its power cannot be separated from matter." After such an argument, no conciliation was possible. This conclusion of Siger went much beyond his usually announced intention merely to restate the teaching of Aristotle. On a point whose consequences were decisive concerning man's personal immortality, Siger was saying that neither Albert nor Thomas had succeeded in demonstrating the existence of individual intellective souls. Where the two best men in philosophy had failed, nobody else was likely to succeed. In short, as a *philosophical* demonstration, it was impossible. This conclusion was bound to provoke a theological reaction, for indeed, if man had no personal intellect, God would have to create one in order to render the soul immortal.

The philosophical position of Siger had its difficulties too. As we know it from these certainly authentic questions, it consisted in maintaining both that the intellective soul is the act and form of its body, and that, nevertheless, the intellect is separate. His answer to the problem was that the intellective soul is not united with the body of man by its very being, but that it unites with it in its operation. The intellective soul and the body are "one in operation because they concur in producing one single effect." Since, in order to produce an intellection, the agent Intellect has to operate in the body, the act of understanding should be attributed, not to the separate Intellect alone, but to the whole man. If this be true, no singular man has any individual intellective soul of his own, but the separate Intellect can still be called the perfection and form of the body, because that which operates in a body truly is its form and perfection. The definition of the soul given by Aristotle was a general one; its particular applications are manifold and, in this case, we have to say in what precise sense the separate Intellect is the form and perfection of the body. This is what Siger is doing in saying that the separate Intellect is the common perfection of every man. Naturally, Siger adds, this is "the intention of the Philosophers, particularly that of Aristotle; but the opinion of Aristotle may not agree with truth; it is also possible that revelation has given us, about the soul, information which cannot be proved by natural reasons." [31]

This general attitude can be judged from two different points of view. The first one is that of the contemporaries of Siger, especially the theologians. Thomas Aquinas seems to have spoken for the majority in a sermon delivered before the University of Paris: "Among those who labor in philosophy, some say things that are not true according to faith; and when told that what they say goes against faith, they answer that it is the Philosopher who says so; as to themselves, they do not affirm it, they are only repeating the Philosopher's words." Thus, Thomas goes on to say, according to these men, faith affirms things whose contrary can be demonstrated by natural reason. Now, since what reason demonstrates to be necessary, is necessarily true, the contrary is false and impossible. Consequently, according to these same philosophers, something can be true for faith and false for philosophy, and vice versa, which is impossible even for God to achieve. In other words the theologians reproached Siger for teaching, in fact, a doctrine of the double truth.

Seen from the point of view of Siger himself things look different. We do not know of a single text where he himself said that necessary philosophical conclusions were true when they contradicted Christian faith. On the contrary, he always maintained that, in such cases, truth was on the side of faith.[32] It is not easy to decide whether his language was prudent or sincere, because, in both cases, it had to be the same. Psychologically speaking, a sincere Siger would not be a unique case. There have been deeply religious souls, firmly attached to the Christian faith, but whose philosophical tenets had little to do with what they believed to be true. Such men could not think differently, but the transcendent certitude of their faith remained unaffected by what they held to attest the limitations of human reason. Contemporaries of Siger seem to have adopted this attitude. "Desiring to live worthily in the study and contemplation of truth as far as can be done in this life, we are undertaking to treat of natural, moral and divine things following the doctrine and order of Aristotle, but we are not making any attempt upon the rights of the orthodox faith made manifest to us in the light of the divine revelation by which the philosophers themselves were not enlightened; for, considering the ordinary and habitual course of nature, and not divine miracles, they have explained things according to the light of reason, without, by doing so, contradicting the theological truth whose cognition derives from a loftier light. When a philosopher concludes that a certain thing is either impossible or necessary from the point of view of the inferior causes accessible to reason, he is not contradicting faith, which affirms that things can be otherwise thanks to the supreme cause whose causal power can be grasped by no creature. This is so true that the holy prophets themselves, imbued with the spirit of prophecy but taking account of the order of inferior causes, have predicted certain events which did not take place because the Prime Cause disposed otherwise." Everybody is free to speculate about the state of mind that inspired such words, but there is risk in dogmatizing about it.[33]

2. BOETIUS OF SWEDEN

After Siger of Brabant, the best known among the thirteenth-century Averroists was Boetius of Sweden (*Boetius de Dacia*). The information concerning his life is scanty. We know for certain that he was born in Sweden at an unknown date; he still was present in 1283 at the pontifical curia in Orvieto; the date of his death is not known. His career was that of a master of arts at the University of Paris where he became personally involved, together with Siger, in the condemnation of 1277. The two masters left France together and fled to Italy.[34] Siger's writings, almost certainly anterior to the date of the condemnation, have not yet all been discovered or identified. Most of them were commentaries by mode of Questions on the works of Aristotle. Apart from the two opuscules recently published by Grabmann, the only known works of Boethius are related to logic, that is to say, unfortunately, to topics which afforded little occasion to express personal opinions on philosophical problems. It is impossible for us to verify the truth of the assertion contained in one of the list of the condemned propositions, that he was their main supporter: *principalis assertor istorum articulorum.*

The recent publication, by Grabmann, of the short treatise of Boetius

On the Sovereign Good, or On Philosophical Life (*De summo bono sive de vita philosophi*), clearly proves, by its very title, that Boetius identified beatitude with the life of the philosopher. From the very beginning of the treatise, however, a short sentence warns his reader that Boetius will not talk about the supreme good in itself, that is God, but about the supreme good accessible to man and only to the extent that it can be investigated by reason. This supreme good can only be found in the exercise of the best of man's powers, the intellect. A power truly divine, if there is in man anything divine, for "just as, in the whole universality of beings that which is best is divine, so also, that which is best in man, we call divine." The term "intellect" especially designates the speculative intellect, by which we know the true. For the knowledge of the true is the source of delight. Because the Prime Intellect (Pure Thought) has as its object its own divine essence, its life is a life of supreme delight. As for man, he finds his happiness both in the accomplishment of the good according to the prescriptions of his practical intellect, and in the cognition of the true by his speculative intellect. The truly wise man, therefore, accomplishes no act which does not make him happy and more capable of becoming so. All the actions of man which are not directed toward this sovereign good of man, including even the merely indifferent ones, are sin; those that are opposed to it are still more sinful. Pity, then, the crowd of cowardly ones who run in pursuit of the pleasures of the senses and fortune's goods, but honor those who are concerned with the study of wisdom. Honor them first because they live according to the natural order: (*Quos etiam voco honorandos, quia vivunt secundum ordinem naturalem*). Such are the philosophers (*et isti sunt philosophi, qui ponunt vitam suam in studio sapientiae*) whose whole action is the contemplation of truth.

Going up by his intellect from cause to cause, the philosopher is led progressively to the first cause of all, which has no other cause than itself, but is eternal, immutable, most perfect, and the one on which all the rest depend: "This Prime Principle is to this world as the father of a family is to his house, the commander to his army and the common weal to the City. And just as the army is one in the unity of its chief, and as the good of the army is in its chief intrinsically, and in the others only according to the rank, so also the unity of this world depends on the unity of this Prime Principle, and the good of this world is intrinsically in this Prime Principle, but it is in the other beings of this world only according to their participation in this Prime Principle and to their rank in relation to it, so that there is not, in any being in this world, any good which is not a sharing in the Prime Principle. Considering this, the philosopher wonders at this Primary Principle, and is filled with love for it, for we love the source from which we receive our good, and most of all that source whence comes to us our own supreme good. And so, knowing that all good comes to him from this Prime Principle, and that all this good is preserved for him only insofar as this Prime Principle preserves it, the philosopher comes into great love of this Prime Principle, according to the right reason of both nature and the intellect. Now each one finds his delight in what he loves, and his greatest delight in what he loves most, and since the philosopher supremely loves this Prime Principle, as has just been said, it follows that the philosopher finds his supreme delectation in this Prime Principle and in the contemplation of its goodness, and that this delectation is the only right one. That is what a philosopher's life is, and whoever does not lead it, does not live right. Now I call 'philosopher' any man who, living according to the right order of nature, has attained the best and ultimate end of human life. As to the said Prime Principle, it is God, the glorious, the sublime, who is blessed throughout the centuries. *Amen.*" [35]

The sequence of ideas in this little masterpiece is simple. Its aim is to define, in a strictly philosophical way, the supreme good accessible to man, and to identify it with the contemplation of good by reason. All his interpreters are in agreement on this point, and all agree that the work is perfectly clear, but in two diametrically opposed senses. Some, with P. Mandonnet, consider it evident that the author is thinking as an out-and-out pagan: "This is the purest, clearest and most resolute rationalism one could possibly find . . . The rationalism of the Renaissance with its loose thinking and its diluted speech, has produced nothing comparable to this, as far as I can judge"; for others, like D. Salman, there is nothing in this treatise contrary to faith.

Both of these theses can be upheld, and this is precisely the puzzling problem of Averroism. Boetius of Sweden does not oppose faith; rather, he seems to be unaware of it, except for two lines in which he expressly reserves its rights: "Who is more perfect in the beatitude than we know by reason possible in this human life, is also nearest to the beatitude that, by faith, we expect in the life to come." He still adds, further on, that this principle of which he speaks, "is the Prime Being according to the philosophers, and, according to the Saints, God the Blessed." This opuscule, therefore, reserves the possibility of a future life; its author does not deny the immortality of the personal soul. The true difficulty lies in the tone in which this treatise speaks of these things. The delight of reason that he extols is perceptible not only in his ideas, but in his style, in which a serene joy that Spinoza in turn was to inherit from Averroes breaks through, a joy which is perhaps only the quivering of the intellect in sight of its own light. Not only is it that Boethius does not take Christian faith into account, one does not feel that he is unhappy away from it. But who are we to probe the heart? The *De summo bono* clearly reveals its own meaning; as to the personal intentions of its author, they escape historical investigation.

New discoveries of hitherto lost writings will certainly throw more light on the history of the Averroistic group at Paris about 1270-1277. There is no reason to suppose that the unity of the group ever was a strict one; each one of its members probably attempted to find suitable expressions enabling him to maintain his own positions without openly clashing with orthodoxy. It is still more probable that many masters were more or less influenced by the movement without really joining it. Each mediaeval master is a distinct historical case. The list of names is growing longer and each new name adds something to our previous information. In fact, we probably have more information than we think, but it is not easy to use it because too many writings betraying some measure of Averroistic influence still remain for us anonymous. The name of James of Douai[36] is beginning to emerge from this still confused historical material. Recent inquiries[37] have brought back to light hitherto forgotten commentaries which show how manifold the influence of the first Averroistic movement has been. It was, however, to enjoy a long and a remarkable continuity up to the seventeenth century. Especially in Italy, the Averroists will consider themselves as belonging to a distinct doctrinal school, use the name of Averroes as the sign of their common heritage and trace their origin back to the Parisian group condemned in 1277 at the University of Paris.

CHAPTER II

THE THEOLOGICAL REACTION

THE repeated warnings of the popes, even after the early prohibition of the scientific treatises of Aristotle had been lifted, did not mean that, henceforward, philosophers should feel free to teach philosophy in complete disregard of theological teaching. Against the attitude of the "Averroists," a theological reaction was unavoidable. Its first known symptoms appear about 1266, and, as could be normally expected, on the side of Saint Bonaventure and his school.

In saying that the first symptoms began to be seen, we are not forgetting that the roots of the uneasy feeling which they betrayed can be traced to an earlier date. Bonaventure himself assures us of this point: "When I was a student, I heard it said that Aristotle posited the world as eternal, and when I heard the reasons and arguments quoted to that effect, my heart began to beat, and I asked myself: how is this possible? But now, all this is so public that no hesitation is permitted." [38] Since he began to lecture on the *Sentences* of P. Lombard about 1250, his testimony takes us back to about 1245. In his Commentary itself, although he expressed no animosity against an Averroistic movement which, at that date, did not exist, Bonaventure had reminded his readers not to trust philosophers beyond certain limits. In 1267, on the contrary, in his conferences on the Decalogue (*Collationes de decem praeceptis*), Bonaventure pointed out the three philosophical errors which were to remain at the very center of the Averroistic controversy: that the world is eternal, that there is only one intellect in all men, and that it is impossible for a mortal being to attain immortality.[39] The common root of these errors was found by Bonaventure in the excessive audacity displayed by some masters in philosophical inquiry (*hoc . . . provenit ex improbo ausu investigationis philosophicae*). The following year, in 1268, the lectures of Bonaventure *On the Gifts of the Holy Ghost* directly attacked a certain number of positions certainly held by the Averroists: that God cannot create all beings out of nothing; that a separate Intelligence can create another one; and especially the three main errors already denounced as destructive of Sacred Scripture, of Christian faith and of all wisdom, because God is for all things "the cause of being, the rule of knowledge and the order of life," namely: the eternity of the world, founded upon the circular nature of movement and time; the fatal necessity of events, founded upon the revolutions of the spheres; the oneness of the intellect, founded upon the oneness of the separate Intelligence. All this is false. The first error is against Scripture (Gen. i, 1); the second error is destructive of free choice; the third error eliminates the distinction of personal merits, since the soul of Judas becomes one with that of Christ.[40] Here again, let us remember that, in the second book of his Commentary on Peter Lombard, Bonaventure had correctly reported the arguments of Aristotle in favor of the eternity of motion and, naturally, he had already opposed them.[41] The fact that, instead of opposing Aristotle, he now was opposing the Parisian masters who upheld the positions of the Philosopher was an event of great historical significance; it implied no change in his own thought.

On December 10, 1270, for reasons perhaps not completely unrelated to the attacks of Bonaventure, the Bishop of Paris, Etienne Tempier, condemned thirteen philosophical propositions: 1) The intellect of all men is one and numerically identical; 2) This is a false or improper proposition: man understands; 3) The will of man wills and chooses in a necessary way; 4) All that which happens here below is subject to the necessity of celestial bodies; 5) The world is eternal; 6) There never was a first man; 7) The soul, which is the form of man precisely *qua* man, is corrupted when the body corrupts; 8) After death, the separated soul cannot suffer from corporeal fire; 9) Free choice is a passive power, not an active one, and it is moved with necessity by the desired object; 10) God does not know singulars; 11) God does not know other beings than himself; 12) Human acts are not ruled by the providence of God; 13) God cannot give immortality and incorruption to a mortal and corruptible thing.[42]

All these propositions can be traced to the doctrine of Aristotle as

Averroes had interpreted it. We do not know if, at that date, all of them had been professed by one and the same man. The Questions of Siger on the *Metaphysics* and on the *De anima* often reveal his effort to oppose to these errors a verbal denial while, in fact, he continues to maintain them, at least in an indirect way or with some attenuations. The Questions of Siger on the *Metaphysics* bear the mark of that effort, which is no less visible in his Questions *De anima*. Between 1269 and 1272, probably in 1270, Thomas Aquinas entered the field with his treatise *On the Unity of the Intellect against the Averroists*. Naturally, Thomas had already refuted the positions of Averroes in his *Summa contra gentiles* (1259-1264); as in the case of Bonaventure, the errors which Thomas was opposing were the same which he had always opposed, only, this time, he was opposing their teaching by some masters at the Faculty of Arts of the University of Paris.[43]

The 1270 condemnation did not stop the spreading of Averroism; consequently its opponents did not slacken their effort. In 1273, the lectures of Bonaventure on the work of the six days (*In Hexaemeron*) witness to the bitterness of his opposition. At this late date in his life, since he was to die in 1274, Bonaventure displays a verbal violence to which his readers are not accustomed. He still has nothing against Aristotle himself, whom he continues to quote together with Euclid and many other non-Christian writers whose doctrine he wishes to use, but the Christians who maintain in the name of philosophy positions contrary to faith arouse his vehement indignation. These are the masters of arts whose false doctrines are an attack against the teaching of Christ. In a justly famous passage, Bonaventure deduces all the fundamental errors of his adversaries from their common doctrine that God knows only himself. This is what Aristotle has taught in denying the Ideas; from which there follows that God has no cognition of singulars, that there is no truth about the future except in matters of necessity; that there is no divine providence, etc. Another error following from the first one is that the world is eternal, whence there follows, if one wishes to avoid the consequence that there is an infinity of souls, that the human intellect is common to all men and that, consequently, there are neither rewards nor punishments in another life. All these errors, and many others[44] clearly show what peril there is in the indiscreet abuse made of philosophy in theological matters. It may be that this peril cannot be completely avoided. After all, a saint like Bernard, who used to study nothing else than the text of Scripture, was doing pretty well without even the writings of the Fathers. No doubt, these writings are necessary, but since they are not easy to understand, there is peril in descending from Scripture to them; there is a still greater peril in descending from the writings of the Fathers to the *Summae* of the masters in theology which, in order to elucidate the difficulties contained in the works of the Fathers, often resort to philosophy; but the greatest of these perils lies in descending from the *Summae* to philosophy itself. The writings of the philosophers should only be studied in view of theology. This is not what some professors do. On the contrary, they secretly teach and copy the books of the philosophers, then they hide them like so many idols.[45] Defined in these terms, the problem was not a philosophical one. Simply, the use made of philosophy by some masters was meeting a stiff theological opposition.

Another symptom of this reaction, and a confirmation of its nature, is found in a treatise of Giles of Rome, written about 1270, *On the Errors of the Philosophers*[46] and in the fifteen questions addressed to Albert the Great by Giles of Lessines between May and December of the same year. The questions and the answers of Albert deal with the same problems which formed the subject matter of the Averroistic controversy: oneness of the intellect, eternity of the world, immortality of the soul, providence, free will, etc. Both questions and answers are those of masters of theology dealing competently with "articles set forth, in the schools of Paris, by men who are reputed to be the best masters in philosophy" (*magistri in scholis Parisius, qui in philosophia majores reputantur*). The time-honored distinction between "philosophers" and "theologians" seems to become an opposition during those years. This does not mean an opposition between philosophy and theology. Theologians themselves knew how to handle philosophy; Albert, for instance, criticizes the positions of the Parisian masters as contrary, not only to theology, but to sound philosophy as well. The true cause for some of these errors, Albert says, is philosophical ignorance: "Many Parisians have followed, not philosophy, but sophisms." [47] Defined in Albert's own terms, the conflict was between some philosophers and some theologians philosophizing, sometimes better than the philosophers themselves, in view of a theological end.

As was unavoidable, the Parisian unrest was felt at the pontifical curia. On January 18, 1277, Pope John XXI (Peter of Spain) wrote to Etienne Tempier, Bishop of Paris, expressly prescribing him to ascertain by whom and where the errors in question had been taught or written, and then to transmit to him, as soon as possible, all this information.[48] The fact that no answer of Etienne to the pope has ever been found is no proof that there was none. It is almost incredible that the Bishop of Paris could have left unanswered a letter from the pope. At any rate, nothing can be proved against the contention of most historians that, owing to the impetuosity of his character, the Bishop of Paris did not send to the pope the report on the situation he had been prescribed to send, but, instead of obeying this order, did something which the pope had not invited him to do, namely, to condemn 219 propositions, some of which, beyond the Averroists, touched Thomas Aquinas. To repeat, no proof can be alleged to the contrary, but before

giving this interpretation for a certitude, one would like to see its supporters envisage a curious implication of their hypothesis. On March 7,
1277, without consulting the pope even by messenger, Etienne Tempier is
supposed to have proceeded *motu proprio* to a doctrinal condemnation. A
few days later, the Dominican Robert Kilwardby, Archbishop of Canterbury, practically endorsed the condemnation without wondering if it met
with the approval of the pope (March 18, 1277). More extraordinary
still, John XXI does not seem to have resented this high-handed attitude
of the Bishop of Paris and of the Archbishop of Canterbury. Far from it,
since on April 28, 1277, about a month later, a second letter of John
XXI prescribed measures implementing the Parisian condemnation.[49] The
dates are certain; the facts are puzzling; in the light of present historical
evidence we find it equally difficult to understand how Tempier may have
acted without the previous agreement of the pope, and how he could
have obtained it. Hypothetical explanations are plentiful, none of them
is convincing.

Before listing the condemned propositions, Etienne Tempier had
warned Siger and Boethius that the usual excuse, which consisted in
maintaining that one and the same proposition could be considered simultaneously as false from the point of view of reason and true from the point
of view of faith, would not be accepted. This was the condemnation of
the thesis which has ever since been called the doctrine of the "double
truth." [50]

The 219 condemned propositions were not all Averroist. A few, essentially ethical, related to the treatise on courtly love (*Liber de Amore*) by
Andrew Capellanus;[51] some attacked Saint Thomas's philosophy;[52] several of them strongly resembled the theses upheld by the dialecticians of
the twelfth century; quite a large number of them attacked Avicenna no
less than Averroes; in short, it seems that this condemnation included
Averroism in a sort of polymorphic naturalism stressing the rights of
pagan nature against Christian nature, of philosophy against theology,
of reason against faith. Inasmuch as it placed philosophy above religious
belief, this naturalism could use the name of Averroes, who could himself claim kinship with Aristotle (*Metaphysics*, XI, 8, 1074*b*). Among
the propositions condemned, some are of unknown origin and may have
been spoken rather than written; for instance: that the Christian religion
hinders education (*quod lex christiana impedit addiscere*); that there are
falsehoods and errors in the Christian religion as in all the others (*quod
fabulae et falsa sunt in lege christiana, sicut in aliis*); that one does not
know more for knowing theology (*quod nihil plus scitur propter scire
theologiam*); that what the theologians say rests upon myths (*quod sermones theologi fundati sunt in fabulis*).[53]

Reduced to their abstract meaning, these positions amount to maintaining that true wisdom is the wisdom of the philosophers, not of the

theologians (*quod sapientes mundi sunt philosophi tantum*) and that therefore there is no state superior to the practice of philosophy (*quod non est exellentior status quam vacare philosophiae*). The wise man thus conceived finds in the rational sciences man's whole good, for from this knowledge flow the natural moral virtues described by Aristotle, and these virtues make up all the happiness accessible to man in this life, after which there is no other (*quod felicitas habetur in ista vita, non in alia*). No more infused supernatural virtues (*quod non sunt possibiles aliae virtutes, nisi acquisitae vel innatae*), no more of this Christian humility which consists in hiding one's own merits, nor of abstinence, nor continence, but on the contrary let us get back to those virtues that Aristotle reserves for an élite and which are not made for the poor (*quod pauper bonis fortunae non potest bene agere in moralibus*). These masters may have been wrong to remain so faithful to the *Nichomachean Ethics,* but they understood it very well.

Among the psychological or metaphysical theses, those already condemned in 1270 reappeared: the eternity of the world, unity of the agent Intellect in the human species, mortality of the soul, rejection of free will, and refusal to extend divine providence beyond the species to the individual; but the doctrinal act of 1277 traced all these errors to their very root, namely, the Aristotelian identification of reality, intelligibility and necessity, not only in things, but first and above all in God. If the world is eternal, it is because God cannot not produce it, and if the world is such as it is, it is because God cannot produce it other than it is. From the first principle, which is one, can only come a single effect, which is similar to it; God, therefore, cannot immediately and freely produce a plurality of effects (*quod ab uno primo agente non potest esse multitudo effectuum*), but the multiplicity of things presupposes a multiplicity of intermediary causes whose existence is necessarily required for their own. This 28th condemned proposition is to be carefully noted, for it is of capital importance for the understanding of the subsequent history of mediaeval philosophy and theology: the Primary Principle can be the cause of different effects here below only through the medium of other causes, because nothing which transmutes can effect transmutations of several sorts, without itself being transmuted.[54] To maintain this principle was radically to deny the liberty and omnipotence of the Christian God. The Jewish and Christian God was not only able to create at a single stroke the world with the multiplicity of beings it holds, he still could intervene in it freely at any instant, either directly to create in it human souls or to act miraculously and without the intervention of secondary causes; between Yahweh and the Greco-Arabian god from whom effects proceed one by one and according to a necessary order no conciliation was possible. Before the condemnation, Philip the Chancellor, William of Auvergne, Bonaventure, and others had already perceived their incompatibility; from 1277 on, all the theologians knew it.

The condemnation of 1277 is a landmark in the history of mediaeval philosophy and theology. There is no way to measure its influence, for the simple reason that it itself was the symptom of an already existing reaction against the excessive philosophical independence of some masters in philosophy and theology. The condemnation was not a starting point; it initiated nothing; it did not even issue any warning that was new; only, because of the solemnity of the two prohibitions, at Paris and at Oxford, the general atmosphere of the schools became different. Instead of carrying on its effort to conquer philosophy by renovating it, scholasticism acted on the defensive. At that very moment, its golden age came to an end.

Averroism itself was not stopped by the condemnations. In point of fact, it was to survive the middle ages. The teaching of Aristotle was not interrupted and theologians did not cease to resort to his philosophy in order to elaborate their doctrinal syntheses: Duns Scotus and Ockham will be full of it. On the other side, either because it had already lost some of its impetus, or on account of the condemnation, the ambition to build up a learned theology did not survive 1277, at least not in the same degree nor in the same spirit. Before this date, the greatest theologians had exploited the resources of science and of philosophical learning in a spirit of eager confidence; since they themselves were leading the movement, they had no reason to fear that faith could be threatened by philosophy in the mind of any Christians. Their very freedom in handling the doctrines of the philosophers is significant in this respect. Learned in philosophy as they were, none of them had considered himself a "philosopher." The importance of Siger and his group was not due to the fact that they had discovered any philosophy unknown before their times; simply, they were Christians who, within the Church, pretended to be, in doctrinal matters, nothing else than philosophers. Philosophism lies at the bottom of Averroism, as indeed it lies at the bottom of the positions of Averroes himself. In 1277, this fact became visible to all. It is no wonder then that a spirit of suspicion toward the "philosophers" began to replace, after that date, the spirit of friendly and confident collaboration with philosophy which had generally prevailed, from the beginning of the century, in the minds of the theologians.

In a general manner, the marks of this change in mood are visible in the theologies of the fourteenth century, especially those of Duns Scotus and Ockham. Seen from without, both of them exhibit a marked tendency to withdraw from metaphysical demonstration theological conclusions commonly held to be rationally demonstrable and to posit them as only knowable in the light of revelation. For instance, the immortality of the soul, a demonstrable truth for most theologians from William of Auvergne up to Thomas Aquinas, will cease to be considered as a philosophically demonstrable conclusion by Duns Scotus, by Ockham and even by the "Thomist" Cajetan. Obviously, the presence of Averroists pressing their arguments against the possibility, for the form of a body, to be at the same time a separable substance, or vice versa, was not unrelated to this new attitude.

A second mark of this change concerns the very substances of the post-1277 theologies, that is to say, of the theologies conceived by masters whose intellectual formation is posterior to 1277. The general trend of the condemnation had been against the Greek necessitarianism which Avicenna and Averroes had inherited from Aristotle. Ever since the time of William of Auvergne the masters of the thirteenth century had vigorously opposed it. Its refutation was included in all their theologies. During the first half of the century, however, the heresy of the Albigenses and their Manichaean dualism had been considered by most of the theologians as the immediate danger to face. Without getting overlooked, this peril certainly lost some of its urgency in the sight of the second generation of theologians, that of Albert, Bonaventure and Thomas, to which the rise of Averroism imposed another task. But even this second generation had to oppose the new peril with theological weapons forged at a time when it did not yet exist, at least under the form it took about 1270. Even Pope John XXI and Albert the Great had adopted certain positions at a time when these were still harmless because no Christian master had decided to teach them in their purity and with the whole series of their philosophical consequences. Arabian philosophy had been pruned and adjusted to faith, but its philosophical *sanatio in radice* had not been undertaken nor, consequently, achieved. The case of Thomas Aquinas is still more striking. He seems to have realized that, with respect to the rise of Aristotelianism and its problems, two attitudes were possible: either to adopt the language of Aristotle without conceding his fundamental principles, as Bonaventure was doing, or else to adopt both his language and his principles, but to transfigure their *philosophical* interpretation. This is what he himself undertook to do, or rather, this is what he spontaneously did. The result was that, when the Averroists began to make trouble, he was mistaken by some for one of them. And indeed, in the sight of those who could not understand the deeper meaning of his philosophical innovations, Thomas Aquinas was bound to appear, if not as an Averroist, at least as a fellow traveler.

Not so with the theologies conceived after 1277. Scotism and Ockhamism are dominated by the desire to insure the freedom of the Christian God with respect to the world of things. Greek necessitarianism is the Carthage they are eager to destroy. Their theologies are wholly dominated by the desire to eliminate the naturalism of the Greeks and the Greco-Arabian notion of a god who, precisely because his is a self-thinking thought, allows the world to flow from his intelligible perfection as necessary consequences follow from their principles. The very fact that the theology of Duns Scotus is often mistaken for a voluntarism is due to his desire not to teach a single one of the condemned theses, even in their Thomistic and legitimate meaning. To the necessitarianism of the Greeks, Scotus will oppose the contingency of the operations of God *ad extra* and, within man, the radical indetermination of the will. The omnipotent God of Ockham will be another devastating attack against the determinism of the Greeks. These will be post-1277 theologies in a more than chronological sense. The cause for these changes in orientation will not be the condemnation itself, but, rather, the philosophical situation which it intended to bring to an end. Between 1270 and 1310, however, a rather confused period will take place, during which the last representatives of the old theology will attempt to maintain at least the essentials of their traditional positions, while others, impressed with the results achieved by Thomas Aquinas, but still uncertain about the true meaning of his principles, will make abortive attempts to follow him up to a point, and sometimes even to adopt his very language without always grasping its deeper meaning.

CHAPTER III

PHILOSOPHICAL CONTROVERSIES

WE HAVE already noticed, in the doctrine of several theologians, the rise of a sporadic opposition to certain teachings of Thomas Aquinas. Marston, Vital du Four, Kilwardby, Peckham either discussed and rejected several doctrines unmistakably Thomistic in origin, or even attempted to obtain against them theological condemnations. This opposition seems to have begun about 1270, perhaps somewhat earlier, but it increased after the death of Thomas Aquinas (1274) and the 1277 condemnations added to its impetus. The movement was not a concerted attack. In fact, the objections to Thomism came from opposite quarters. Thomas was no Averroist, so he was criticized by Siger; but he owed Averroes a certain part of his own interpretation of Aristotle, so he was criticized by the Augustinians, to whom he appeared as yielding to Aristotle more ground than he should. Above all, Thomas had used the language of Aristotle in order to express strikingly un-Aristotelian thoughts, and it was not easy for his contemporaries to grasp at once the full import of his doctrinal innovations. The center around which the controversy will revolve is Thomism itself as seen from the different point of views of his supporters and of its opponents.[55]

I. THE "CORRECTIVES"

There were booksellers before there were printers. As soon as the works of Thomas Aquinas began to sell,[56] the adversaries of his doctrine realized that its spread could not be stopped. As an imagined remedy to this evil, some of them wrote corrections and criticisms to be appended to the text of his writings. Such was the origin of the so-called *Correctoria,* or "Correctives" to the doctrine of Thomas Aquinas. After their publication, these corrections were in turn corrected by supporters of Thomism, who sometimes labeled "corruptions" the "corrections" proposed by their adversaries. When they reached their complete development, such documents became very elaborate structures. One of their best specimens consists of doctrinal corrections by the English Franciscan William of La Mare,[57] corrected in turn by an English Dominican, Richard Clapwell or Thomas of Sutton.[58] Each article begins by restating the Thomistic position on a certain problem; then come La Mare's corrections of the position of Thomas, themselves followed by Clapwell's corrections of La Mare's corrections.

The purely theological character of the work is immediately manifest. William of La Mare has followed no plan. His corrections are a series of remarks on the *Summa* of Thomas Aquinas (47 articles of Part I, 12 of I-II, 16 of II-III), on the *Disputed Questions* (9 of *De veritate,* 10 of *De anima,* 1 of *De virtutibus,* 4 of *De potentia*), on the quodlibetic questions (9 questions), on the First Book of the *Sentences* (9 questions). Though by no means systematic, the choice of the subjects betrays a preference for the problems related to the nature of angels and of human souls. William often repeats himself and consequently Richard has to do the same thing. The absence of certain fundamental problems is noticeable; for instance, the nature of being is nowhere discussed for its own sake, in spite of the fact that most of the texts of Thomas under discussion directly or indirectly imply it. William has made no systematic inquiry into the principles of the doctrine; he has simply read Thomas, and finding himself confronted with theological positions different from his own, he has rejected them by mode of straight opposition without asking himself what could be said in favor of his adversary, nor even what was the authentic meaning of his doctrine.

On the existence and nature of God, William seems to have nothing to object to Thomas Aquinas, but he raises serious objections concerning the nature of the divine knowledge and concerning the creation of the world. Thomas had taught that not all things have their distinct idea in God; for instance, matter has no idea distinct from that of the composite, since it cannot exist apart; likewise, genera have no idea distinct from that of their species since they do not exist apart from it. On the first point, William objects that since matter has an entity of its own, it must have in God a distinct idea of its own.[59] On the second point, he objects that genera have a distinct entity of their own, consequently, they must have a distinct idea in God. His main argument on this point is borrowed from the embryology of Aristotle. For indeed, the embryo is an animal before being a horse, or a man. When an individual is on its way to becoming a horse, or a man, it is an individual in a certain genus (i.e., animal) before being an individual in a species (i.e., horse or man). This implies that the form of the genus can exist apart from the form of any species and, consequently, that each genus has its own idea in God.[60]

Nothing could show with more clarity the nature of these discussions and the reason for their speculative sterility. The question was about the divine Ideas; the objections of William rest upon two metaphysical notions entirely foreign to Thomism, and therefore to the Thomistic doctrine of the divine Ideas. The one is the Augustinian doctrine of the distinct entity of matter; the other is the neoplatonic doctrine of the formal entity proper to genera as well as to each distinctly conceivable degree of being. In short, the second argument introduces the doctrine of the plurality of forms which, better informed by Averroes of the doctrine of Aristotle, Thomas had progressively eliminated. There was no point in correcting Thomas Aquinas without first settling these problems, and there was little more point in correcting William's corrections by a mere restatement of the Thomistic doctrines of the co-creation of matter with the composite or of the unity of the substantial form.[61]

The same remarks apply to the criticism directed by William against the Thomistic conclusion that God knows future contingents as actually present. Anybody knowing the notion of eternity proper to Thomas Aquinas realizes at once that his answer could not be different. Yet, here again, another notion is brought to bear upon the problem, and it is one which we know well, namely, the eternity of the world. Behind the answer of Thomas, William rightly perceives an Aristotelian influence. There are only two ways for things to be present to God, either in the divine Ideas or in their actual existence. Now their actual existence presupposes their production in time from non-being to being. If, therefore, all that exists in time is eternally present to God otherwise than in its Idea, all must have eternally had actual existence in God. This is to posit the eternal existence of all things, "which is against our faith." [62] Yes, indeed, provided "actual existence" has the same meaning in the two doctrines. It has not, and for this reason the two arguments never meet.

In the light of what precedes, the position of William of La Mare concerning the nature of angels and souls is easy to foresee: hylomorphism and plurality of forms. Thomas had said that angels are not composed of matter and form.[63] In refuting this position, William does not resort to Gabirol as he probably would have done ten years before. Fully aware of the support which Augustine can provide for the doctrine of spiritual matter, he takes full advantage of the texts of the *Confessions,* XII, 6, and of the literal commentary of Augustine on Genesis, 5, 5, in which the saint had tentatively attributed matter to all mutable beings.[64] Confronted as he is with the doctrine of Thomas, that angels are composed of essence and existence (*esse*), William completely misses its meaning and translates it into terms of the only composition of being which he himself understands: the composition of potency and act, identified by him with the composition of matter and form. Since Thomas admits that angels have potency, and since, according to William, potency is always found in matter, angels must have matter.[65] For indeed, what does Augustine call matter in angels, if not their potentiality? Inversely, prompted by his zeal for the Thomistic truth, Clapwell (or Sutton) has the fancy to maintain, against William, that when Themistius and other philosophers spoke of some material disposition in angels, what they had in mind was the essence or quiddity of angels, which these philosophers called matter on account of its potentiality with respect to the *esse* (to be) that it participates. And indeed only God is his own *esse*.[66] Thus to ascribe to Themistius the Thomistic doctrine of a composition of essence and existence in separate substances was merely to add to an already desperate confusion.

The official adoption of William of La Mare's *Corrective* by the Franciscan Order, in 1282, contributed to turn the doctrinal controversy into an opposition between two religious Orders. At the same time, while these theologians were opposing Thomas Aquinas on behalf of the Augustinian tradition, others were preparing the Scotist doctrinal synthesis and restating under a new form the traditional positions of the pre-Thomistic theology. Besides, all the opponents of Thomas Aquinas were not Franciscans, nor were his supporters all Dominicans. But the main point is that his supporters did not always understand his doctrine much more correctly than his opponents. Confusion is of the very essence of controversy, and, in this case, it certainly was abounding.

John Quidort (*Joannes Dormiens*) is a case in point.[67] A Dominican and a supporter of Thomas Aquinas, he corrected the corrections of William of La Mare, but he did it in his own way. A Thomist, John also was an adventurous mind who had twice to face theological censure, in 1284[68] and in 1304.[69] The fact that he became a master in theology only two years before his death, when he was at least fifty years old, is a sure indication that he never was completely trusted. One should not forget, however, that the reason why some writers get in trouble is that they write about controversial matters, not that they have a controversial mind. At any rate, the Quodlibetic Questions of John and his commentary on the *Sentences* complete what we can learn from his answers to La Mare's *Correctorium* about his own doctrinal positions.[70]

Since he goes over almost the whole series of the questions raised by William, John often repeats in his own way what Clapwell or Sutton had said before him, and even leaving aside the theological questions irrelevant to philosophy we still have to make a choice.[71] The 27th article is a crucial one: can matter exist without form? John answers that it cannot. His main argument is that since being comes from the form, a matter without a form would be a matter without any being;[72] it would be this contradiction in terms: an act without any act. This conclusion leads John to the next question: is the soul composed of matter and form? John answers it in the negative on the ground that to posit the soul as composed of form and matter would be to contradict Augustine. There is indeed a potential element in the soul, but it is not matter. The essence of the soul is in potency with respect to many things; for instance to the accidents (species and forms) which it receives. John does not avail himself of this opportunity to explain the composition of essence and existence substituted for hylomorphism by Thomas Aquinas.[73] His allusion to this point, in his art. 9 about angels,[74] leaves the reader uncertain as to the meaning it had in John's own mind. One may well wonder whether he ever grasped the full import of the doctrine. The least that can be said is that, while John strongly denied the necessity of any finite existence,[75] his own distinction of essence and existence was rather different from that of Thomas Aquinas.[76]

On the problem of the unity of the form in the composite, John says that he has dealt with it at length elsewhere and that there is an infinity of reasons in favor of this conclusion. Both theology and philosophy are against the plurality of forms. The treatise *On Forms* to which he alludes, and to whose ch. 18 and 19 he refers, was a detailed study of the question.[77] What John says on the problem in his Quodlibetic Questions confirms his general agreement with Thomas Aquinas on this point.[78] Yet, the free nature of his Thomism would appear still more clearly if his Commentary had been published, especially the part of it which deals with the human intellect and human intellectual knowledge.[79] John always agrees with Thomas on each one of the positions attacked by William of La Mare; he never contradicts the letter of his conclusions but, to him, this seems to have been the main point.

The answer of Rambert of Bologna to the *Corrective* of William of La Mare is an incomplete work. The part which should have dealt with the plurality of forms is missing or was never written.[80] Moreover, the reader cannot help suspecting that some parts of it are disputed questions inserted by Rambert in his work rather than answers explicitly written against the objections of William. The admiration of Rambert for Thomas was sincere and his own intentions were no doubt excellent, but so long as he could find reasons in favor of Saint Thomas, the question whether these reasons were Thomistic or not did not arise. Rambert is excellent when Thomas is accused of holding views that are not his. For instance, concerning the divine knowledge of future contingents (art. 3), the nature of the divine Ideas (art. 4) or the possibility there is for God to make the universe better than it is (art. 5). Rambert is perfectly competent to correct all the misrepresentations, intentional or not, of the authentic positions of Thomas Aquinas. He steadily maintains all the conclusions of the Master and his answer of more than sixty pages on the demonstrability of a beginning of the world in time is by itself a complete treatise on the question (art. 6). Thomas himself never wrote such a long one to justify his own positions. On the other hand, one cannot help feeling that Rambert intentionally avoids the composition of essence and existence, especially when it would provide a clear-cut answer to the problem. One waits for it, but it never comes, except in art. 14: "If angels are incorruptible", and even there one may well wonder if Rambert understood it in the same sense as Thomas Aquinas. After rejecting the hylomorphic composition of spiritual substances, he proves their incorruptibility by the natural indestructibility of a form that is a "principle of existence (*principium essendi*) formally, if not effectively" (p. 174). In demonstrating the incorruptibility of this subsisting form, Rambert stresses the point that form is for all things the principle of their existence (*principium essendi*, p. 174); that, in angels, no part of the composite is corruptible, whence there follows that since angels are not composite beings (*cum ergo angelus non sit compositus*, p. 175), they cannot be corrupted. Naturally, Rambert himself realizes that his affirmation of the simplicity of angelic substances, true against hylomorphism, is calling for a complement. This was the place to recall that there is a composition of essence and existence in all creatures, but Rambert does not do so. Instead, he does something else. After reaffirming that form is "principle of existence," and of permanent existence for the forms which do not endure in time (including the human soul as to its *esse*) he observes that, anyway, the angelic substance is not simple as God himself is. It has accidents (p. 176), hence it is composed of act and potency; more important still, angels are composed of "substance and *esse*." In compounds of substance and existence, existence itself is act (*In his autem quae componuntur ex substantia et esse, esse est ipse actus*, p. 177).

Why is Rambert shunning the Thomistic formula "essence and existence"? We do not know. He says that, in compounds of matter and form, form is not the act of being, and this is the very position of

Thomas Aquinas, yet, in explaining it, Rambert always insists on the "composition of substance and existence" (p. 177) and the only proof of this composition which he gives is that, in finite beings, "the existence (*esse*) of created forms differs in something from the essence," for indeed "the form itself is not its own existence, otherwise God could not make its being to be" (p. 177). Rambert may well have said all he had to say on the question in this simple line: "To be composed of matter and form is not the same as to be composed of *quo est* and *quod est*" (p. 176). One could hardly guess, on the sole basis of what Rambert says, the true position of Thomas Aquinas on the question.

Historical research concerning this controversial literature has not yet said its last word.[81] A comparative study of the *Correctoria* is still required to ascertain the detail of their filiation. The interplay of the philosophical positions involved in these controversies creates complications which, in the present state of historical information, still appear inextricable. Two main controversies, however, are assuming an increasing historical importance; the one about the plurality of forms, the other about the nature of being.

2. THE PLURALITY OF FORMS

A general survey of the theological literature of the late thirteenth century reveals the presence of zones of tension. The problem of the plurality of forms was one of them. There was nothing new in it. A many-sided issue, it was particularly tied up with the problem of the human soul. All possible answers had been given to the question. Some had said that the human soul was a complex unity made up of three "substances," or of three "substantial forms"; among those who felt hesitant, some recognized only two forms: the rational soul and the "form of corporeity"; as early as 1230, we saw John Blund, a modest Oxford master, unequivocally uphold the view that the rational soul is the only substantial form in man. Various theological interests were involved in this philosophical problem: the substantial unity of man (soul and body); the immortality of the soul, or, at least, its possibility; the nature of Christ's body between his death and his resurrection (if there is no form of corporeity, whose body was it?), etc. The majority of these masters seem to have favored a certain plurality of forms in the composite, at least if two is a plurality.[82] As time went on, discussions about embryogeny complicated the problem, the more so as these discussions themselves implied a twofold element: the biological data borrowed from Aristotle and the theological belief in the direct creation of the rational soul by God. There was a discussion, but it was a peaceful one. Masters would then answer the arguments set forth by other masters, whom they had either heard or read, in a spirit of purely speculative inquiry. For instance, in his *Summa de bono* (about 1230), Philip the Chancellor had used on this point the example of the oneness of a light beam made up of two or three distinct light beams; it was taken up after him by several other masters each of whom reinterpreted it in his own way. This lively but peaceful discussion only flared up into a controversy when, after the theological reformation achieved by Thomas Aquinas, it became necessary for theologians to choose between two distinct theologies. Anybody could then see the full import of the problem. What was at stake was not merely a particular philosophical problem, but, rather, the notions of man and of the human soul, together with their theological implications.

The public occasion for the doctrinal rupture seems to have been the Disputed Question in which Roger Marston witnessed the open conflict there was between Thomas Aquinas, supporter of the oneness of the form, and John Peckham, supporter of the plurality of forms. The text of Marston is clear: "I was in Paris, and I heard it with my own bodily ears, at the inception of the Precentor of Péronne, before master Gerard of Abbeville, in the presence of brother Thomas Aquinas, of brother John of Peckham and of about twenty-four other doctors in sacred theology, when this opinion was solemnly excommunicated as contrary to the teaching of the Saints, particularly of Augustine and Anselm, as was made manifest by the opposition." [83] This incident must have taken place about 1270. That both Thomas and Peckham actively shared in the discussion, appears from a letter of Peckham (January 1, 1285) in which he recalls the fact that Thomas Aquinas, who then upheld the doctrine of the unity of the form, humbly declared to the assembly that he was submitting his opinions in this matter to the examination and criticism of the Parisian masters.[84] Knowing him as we do, nothing is less surprising than his attitude; nor does it surprise us that, having submitted his doctrine to the judgment of his colleagues, he stuck to it.

After 1270, the problem reappears in many Disputed Questions, but still in the form of a free discussion in which the orthodoxy of the opponents was not at stake. The incident related by Marston had a limited importance and the "excommunication" of which he speaks cannot have been more than a verbal one. No master presiding over a Disputed Question had any right to "terminate" it by a sentence of excommunication properly so-called. Not so in 1277. It is true that the Parisian condemnation contained no explicit allusion to the doctrine of the plurality of forms; the reason for this may be that, in Paris, the unity of the form had already found too many supporters; but eleven days later, in full agreement, as it seems, with the other Dominicans of Oxford, Robert Kilwardby explicitly condemned the oneness of the substantial form. The twelfth condemned proposition was: "That the vegetative, the sensitive and the rational (souls) are one simple form." For a while, the

University of Paris envisaged confirming this condemnation, but the death of John XXI (May 20, 1277) brought the procedure to an end.[85] It did not stop the controversy. On April 30, 1286, the successor of Kilwardby to the see of Canterbury, John Peckham, condemned in London the proposition "that there is in man only one form, namely, the rational soul, and no other substantial form." [86] A list of theological errors following from the condemned proposition preceded this eighth article. Since Christian faith was at stake, at least in the minds of certain ecclesiastical authorities, a heated controversy could hardly fail to embitter the philosophical discussion.

The traces of this controversy are to be found everywhere, in Commentaries on P. Lombard, Disputed Questions, Quodlibetic Questions, academic sermons, letters, official documents, etc. It may be convenient, however, to consider more particularly, on this occasion, men whose part in the discussion was significant. Giles of Rome is one of them.[87] The very title of his treatise *Against the Degrees and the Plurality of Forms* (1278) clearly states his own position. It also marks the culminating point of a personal evolution described by his historians.[88] Giles is far from having adhered at once to the doctrine of the unity of the substantial form as Thomas had taught it at the time of his own maturity. One of the main reasons for his hesitation seems to have been the predominantly theological character of the issue in the minds of his contemporaries. Personally, he began by siding with the supporters of the oneness of the substantial form in all animals, with the sole exception of man. And indeed, the main theological objections against the oneness of the form arose from problems related to the human soul and to the body of Christ. For this very reason, in his own treatise against the plurality of forms, Giles attempted to show that other theological difficulties arose from the hypothesis of their plurality. He even added to his theological demonstration a philosophical explanation of the notion of "body" which seems to represent his personal contribution to the controversy.[89] Giles distinguishes three usages of the term: 1) the mathematical body, which is three dimensional quantity; 2) the natural body, which is a substance, namely, an animated body; 3) what Giles calls the material body, that is, the human body taken as part of the substance man, conceived as composing with quantity and as deriving from it its own extension. Manifestly, Giles was trying to find in the accidental form of quantity a substitute for the form of corporeity so dear to the heart of many famous theologians.

Contemporary with the treatise of Giles, the *De unitate formae* (*On the Unity of the Form*) of Giles of Lessines[90] was very different from it. Giles was a man going his own way and anxious to justify his own conclusions on the strength of his own philosophical positions. Giles of Lessines intends to prove that the position of Thomas Aquinas is true.

His own treatise is an answer to the seventh and last article of the Letter of Kilwardby to Peter of Conflans (1278). Kilwardby should remain in our memory as the author of the most extraordinary objection ever formulated against the oneness of the form. If the oneness of the form were true, Kilwardby says, nothing would be composed except of matter and of one form. In other words, the doctrine was incredible; hence it was false.

Against this incredulity, Giles of Lessines restates the fundamental positions of Thomas Aquinas. There may be a succession of higher and higher forms during the generation and progressive formation of one and the same being, but when a higher form arrives, it replaces the preceding one and takes up its functions. The oneness of the substantial form insures the substantial unity of the being whose form it is; one single form can have diverse powers and exercise through them a multiplicity of operations. This justifies the attribution of only one substantial form even to man. The rational soul is able to exercise all the vegetative and sensitive operations in which its body participates. As to the theological difficulties, Giles shows that they can be answered.[91] He certainly represents, as exactly as possible, the new group of masters who, instead of merely supporting the conclusions of Thomas Aquinas, had assimilated the very substance of his doctrine and could justify his conclusions on the strength of his own reasons.

The treatise of John Quidort on the question has not yet been identified. There are two candidates for the title: the *Treatise on Forms,* printed among the works of Hervaeus Natalis (Harvey of Nedellec) and an anonymous, still unpublished *Treatise on the Unity of Forms.* According to recent research[92] these two writings added little to the controversy. As to the treatise of Thomas of Sutton *On the Plurality of Forms,* traditionally attributed to Thomas Aquinas and often printed among his opuscules, it has been studied with sympathy so long as it was considered authentic; now that its spurious character has been established, it is considered as teaching a "deterioration" of the doctrine of Thomas Aquinas. Which, indeed, it does, but Thomas of Sutton has been so little studied that what now appears as a weak interpretation of Thomas Aquinas might well be explainable by some personal positions of its author.[93] Sutton may have been one of those supporters of the conclusions of Thomas Aquinas who did not necessarily agree on all points with his reasons.[94]

The case of Godfrey of Fontaines is more interesting.[95] First of all, he is an irrefutable witness to the fact that, in his own mind as in that of his contemporaries, this philosophical controversy was dominated by theological interests: the nature of man and especially the being of Christ.[96] Had it not been for these difficulties, he would have favored the unity of the form; even in man the oneness of the form, that is, of the rational soul, appeared to him as probable;[97] yet, on account of the aforesaid theological difficulties, he contented himself with affirming that, "in beings other than man, there can be only one form." [98] This was not exactly skepticism. Rather, Godfrey did not clearly see how what he held to be a true philosophical conclusion could be reconciled with theological truth. It seems clear that, in the minds of men like Godfrey, the spreading of Thomism was held in check by the condemnation of 1277.

Other causes were then contributing to the same effect. There were at least two different conceptions of the oneness of the substantial form: that of Aristotle, according to whom substances were made up of matter and of form; and that of Thomas Aquinas, according to whom substances were made up of matter, of form and of their act of being. Taken in itself, this Thomistic composition of essence and *esse* (act of being) could be understood, or misunderstood, in many different ways. One of the reasons why some supporters of the conclusions of Thomas Aquinas did not accept his own reasons in favor of this thesis was that they tried to justify it without accepting the composition of essence and existence, or, at least, without realizing the true meaning of this composition. In order to follow these controversies, it is useful to keep in mind the equivocal meaning of the notion of form which was the subject matter of the discussion. Not only, as Giles of Rome clearly saw, a Platonic form is not an Aristotelian form, but an Aristotelian form is not a Thomistic form. In other words, the substantial form whose oneness is affirmed by one philosopher differs in kind from the substantial forms whose plurality is affirmed by another philosopher. Moreover, the form whose oneness is affirmed by Aristotle and Averroes differs in kind from the form whose oneness is affirmed by Thomas Aquinas. Because the nature of these forms is not the same, their oneness cannot be ultimately justified by the same reasons. The fact that all the masters who shared in this controversy were talking the same Aristotelese should create no illusion in our minds; they were all using the same language but they were not all talking about the same things.

3. EXISTENCE AND ESSENCE

Thomas Aquinas had taught the doctrine of the composition of *esse* (to be, act of being) with essence in created things. His own position implied, 1) that even in immaterial substances there is a composition of their essence with their act of being; 2) that in corporeal substances there is a twofold composition: *a*) that of matter and form, *b*) that of the form itself with a still higher act, which is the act of being (*esse*). Since being was commonly held to be the first principle, to disagree about it entailed an explicit or implicit disagreement about all the rest. Consequently, a master who expressly refused the composition of essence and *esse* can hardly be considered a Thomist. Yet many masters who have ignored or rejected this fundamental position are considered Thomists by their historians. Since there is no yardstick to measure Thomism, at least no universally recognized one, all that we shall mean in saying that a doctrine is not Thomistic will be that its author disagreed with Thomas Aquinas on the exact meaning of the first principle.

Many controversies have obscured the issue. First of all, we commonly attribute to Thomas a "distinction" of essence and existence, whereas he usually spoke of their "composition." Secondly, although he often said that essence and existence are united in the thing (*re*) Thomas never understood this as a composition of two *res,* or things. They are united in the reality, but reality is not made up of realities. Thomas was trying to make it clear that this composition was not a mere composition of two abstract notions, but, rather, of two elements inherent in the metaphysical structure of actual being. A careful reading of *Contra Gentiles,* II, 54, reveals the essentials of what Thomas had to say on the question. After him, however, the interpretation of his doctrine led to many controversies. Those who refused all distinction of essence and existence within being can safely be considered as having opposed Thomas Aquinas, but not all those who upheld a certain distinction of essence and existence can be safely considered his supporters. In order to avoid, so far as possible, unnecessary controversies, we shall try to describe the positions of those who shared in the dispute without attempting any doctrinal classification.

Three notions dominated the debate. First, the notion of creation. All theologians accepted it and, to the extent that every created being is not the cause of its own existence, they all agreed that there was a real distinction between the essence of a being as known to the mind of God and the same essence turned by the creative power of God into an actually existing being.

Secondly, they all knew the distinction introduced by Boethius between *quod est* (that which is) and *quo est,* or *esse* (the form which makes it to be what it is). In its Thomistic reinterpretation, this had become a composition of: *a*) the whole substance, *quod est; b*) the form, *quo est; c*) the act in virtue of which both substance and form are a being, *esse.* In immaterial substances, however, the whole substance is a form, so that its composition is that of a *quod est* (the form which it is) and of a *quo est:* its act of being, *esse.* Confusions often arose from the use of the terminology of Boethius in its Thomistic meaning (*Cont. Gent.,* II, 54).

Thirdly, all theologians knew the doctrine of Avicenna: *a*) the quiddity of no essence includes its existence; *b*) since what is not essential is accidental, existence is accidental to essence; it "happens" to it: *ei accidit.* Incidentally, they also knew that Avicenna had been vigorously opposed on that point by Averroes, who had reproached him with teaching thereby a theological doctrine of creation in philosophical garb.

Against these forces working in favor of a composition of essence and existence in finite beings, there was only one obstacle, namely, Aristotle himself. The composition of matter and form dominates the natural philosophy of Aristotle, but the composition of essence and existence is not Aristotelian. In fact, Averroes opposed the composition of essence and existence as found in Avicenna, and even among the scholastics whom we now call Thomists, some parted company with him on this crucial point. They favored Thomas so long as he himself agreed with Aristotle; when it came to choosing between Thomas and Aristotle, they preferred Aristotle to Thomas. On the other hand, the composition of essence and existence has found resolute supporters who understood it in a way quite different from that of Thomas Aquinas. Just as in the case with the plurality of forms, the problem of the nature of being exhibits an exceeding complexity after 1270.

The interplay of these doctrinal positions must nevertheless be known in order to understand their history. When Chossat wrote that the true founder of the composition of essence and existence was not Thomas Aquinas, but Giles of Rome,[99] Grabmann crushed him under an avalanche of thirteenth-century masters who had all attributed this doctrine to Thomas Aquinas.[100] Both were right, but not from the same point of view. Chossat was well founded in saying that Giles of Rome had invented a *real distinction* of essence and existence which is not found in Thomas Aquinas; and Grabmann was right in saying that many contemporaries of Thomas had credited him with a doctrine of the real composition of essence and existence, but Thomas and Giles did not understand this composition in the same way.

We are still far from knowing the theology of Giles as it deserves to be known, but the publication of his *Theorems on Existence and Essence*[101] permits a first estimate of his own notion of being. It is an excellent witness to the embarrassment felt by the first readers of the *Summa theologiae.* Thomas had said that "beings" were made up of metaphysical constituents which, since they enter the constitution of being as such, should not themselves be understood as "beings," and much less as "things." But human intellects naturally feed on things; so the first reaction of these masters was to ask themselves: is the composition of essence and existence a composition of "things"? Because, if it is, then it is a "real" composition (real: *res:* thing), whereas, if it is not, the composition at stake cannot be said to be a "real" one. Incidentally, this statement of the problem changed the emphasis from the composition of essence and existence to their distinction. For indeed, in Thomas Aquinas, "things" are compounds of essence and existence, neither of which is a thing. If we separate them, there is no being. On the contrary, if their composition is supposed to be "real," in the sense that it is a composition of two things, then to prove their distinction is the only way to prove that they are things.

Such was the proper ground of Giles of Rome. He knew the doctrine of Avicenna, according to whom, in created beings, existence happens to essences. Since existence is "received" by essences, there must be a real difference between them. Hence the questions asked by Giles: "Can essence and existence be two things? How does existence flow from essence, and, if it does, in what sense is it its act?" [102]

The problems raised by Giles presupposed the existence of the conclusions of Thomas Aquinas. They likewise presupposed a certain alteration of the authentic perspective of Thomas himself. In the mind of Giles, the proper aim and scope of his own inquiry was to account for the possibility of such beings as creatures. This was not an empty question. Giles had clearly seen that Aristotelian substances do not bear in their structure the mark of having been created; Thomistic substances certainly do bear that mark. On this point, Giles was right, but he does not seem to have seen that, in Thomas Aquinas, the answer to this problem was a corollary to a previous transmutation of the notion of being and, consequently, of God. This event had taken place in the metaphysical heaven of the first principles. Giles himself tackled the problem of created nature at the lower level of the structure of actually given created beings.[103] The consequences of this move were epoch-making in the history of Thomism: Giles seems to have been the first theologian to attempt dialectical *demonstrations* of the distinction of essence and existence. He is still having successors.[104]

The hallmark of this distinction, such as Giles understands it, is his often-recurring expression: existence is a "thing" (*res*).[105] This was not an inadvertence with him; on the contrary, it was the very point he was enforcing. A second characteristic feature of his doctrine is the distinction which he introduces, within finite being itself, between the substantial being conferred by the form and the being of existence conferred by *esse*.[106] Giles seems to have intended to prove thereby that existence was as much of a thing as essence itself was. This was necessary from his own point of view, since he wanted a "real" distinction between two things. His demonstrations of the distinction are a third and a no less typical feature of his own position.[107] His intentions are clear, but the nature of the "thing" which he calls existence is less clear at the end of his demonstrations. Giles does not seem to have mistaken it for another essence, but more studies on his Platonism are perhaps needed to find an answer to this question.[108]

Thomas of Sutton OP.,[109] who defended the doctrine of Thomas Aquinas against Henry of Ghent before defending it against Duns

Scotus, is an interesting witness to the controversy *ca.* 1298. His own conclusion is that the position of some "great Doctors" who uphold that "in creatures, the composition of essence and existence is a real one" is a true and necessary position. However, his own language recalls Giles of Rome more than Thomas Aquinas. According to Sutton: "Essence and existence differ in reality." This position is true for the reason that "All that is not included in the notion of an essence, if it is something real in the being to which this essence belongs, makes a real composition with the essence and differs really from it." This conclusion is borrowed from Avicenna, or, at least, from a well-known principle posited by Avicenna and often applied by Thomas Aquinas, but from which Giles of Rome had attempted to draw a demonstration of the real distinction of essence and existence.[110] Sutton defends it against the objection that existence is essence conceived in its relation to its efficient cause (Vital du Four, Henry of Ghent). This, Sutton objects, does not say what existence must add to essence in order to found this relation.[111] On the other hand, Sutton rejects the thesis of Giles, that "real composition" in creatures is required in order to render creation possible. The thesis is false, at least as Giles formulates it, because before it has existence, essence is not even possible; it is nothing at all. The true reason why the distinction should be posited in order to insure the possibility of creation is that, unless it be really different from existence, essence cannot possibly be created from nothing.[112]

Sutton's own conception of existence is no less intimately related to the problem of creation than that of Giles. There is a contradiction in the notion of a created being whose essence includes its own existence.[113] Outside of God, every being participates in being, not as species participates in genus (which is included in its notion) but as matter participates in the form, which is really distinct from the matter that participates in it.[114] Sutton understands the being of existence as an absolute; it is something real (*aliquid reale*); it is the very reality which answers the question *an est;* it is a positive and an absolute reality (*reale positivum et absolutum*), etc.[115] The doctrine of Sutton is that of a disciple of Thomas Aquinas influenced by the language of Giles of Rome. This was hardly avoidable. When engaged in a controversy, a man does not always express his ultimate convictions; he often uses the language of his adversaries. Despite some questionable formulas[116] there is no reason to suppose that Sutton really misunderstood the authentic position of Thomas Aquinas. At the same time that Sutton was accepting it in England, Bernard of Trillia was defending it in France against the objections of Henry of Ghent.[117] Although it was not always supported in Thomas Aquinas' own language, the real composition of essence and existence found at once resolute defenders.

Godfrey of Fontaines had a remarkable insight into doctrinal positions.

Dealing with being and essence, he went straight to the text of Avicenna's *Logic* on the three possible conditions of essence: universal in the intellect, singular in matter, or taken in itself and as indifferent to both. Hence his own question: is the essence of created being indifferent to both being and non-being? His answer is in the negative, because the relation of essence to existence can be understood in two ways, according to none of which essence can be considered indifferent to existence. If essence is another thing than existence, then essence can have no actuality of its own apart from existence; it is not indifferent to it. If essence and existence are considered identical, with only a distinction of reason, or of notion (*ratione vel intentione*), then essence is still less indifferent to existence, since, in this case, they must either be posited together or disappear together. Incidentally, this leads Godfrey to another conclusion: there is no eternal quidditative being of creatures unless God, as efficient cause, first wills their existence. An eternally created world is possible, but things depend on God as on their efficient cause before depending on him as on their formal cause. Even an eternal world would depend on God as on its free efficient cause producing it from all eternity.[118]

This is to say that there is no being of essence without a being of existence.[119] In texts probably directed against Thomas Aquinas, Godfrey denies that the being of a compound thing is the "actuality of the form." There is therefore no real distinction of essence and existence. Existence means the same thing as "essence" or "thing." All these distinctions are mere abstractions which consider apart various aspects of the same reality. Godfrey gives no evidence of having truly grasped the position which he rejected under the influence of Aristotle and of Averroes, but he has seen with remarkable clarity that the distinction of essence and existence did not follow with necessity from the notion of creation.[120] So many supporters of the distinction have made this philosophical mistake that even one of its most resolute adversaries should be praised for having denounced it.

It is not easy to say how many masters supported the distinction of essence and existence, understood in its Thomistic sense, because this would presuppose a universal agreement about the true Thomistic meaning of the doctrine. This universal agreement does not exist. On the contrary, there is no doubt that most of the contemporaries and immediate successors of Thomas Aquinas attributed to him a doctrine of the composition of essence and existence, and even of their real composition, in this sense at least, that it was more than either a distinction between modes of signification or a distinction between mere notions in the mind. To distinguish, among his opponents, those who rejected his true doctrine and those who only rejected what they believed it to be, would be an ambitious undertaking.[121]

The same problem arises with respect to the history of the early Thomistic school. The influence of Thomas Aquinas, *as a philosopher,* was deeply felt even in the Faculty of Arts of the University of Paris. This is beyond a doubt. We saw Siger counting him, with Albert, as one of the two leaders "in philosophy" and there is irrefutable historical evidence that he was not alone in this opinion.[122] The difficulty is to know how far, beyond admiring the genius and the doctrine of Thomas, these masters went in accepting his principles and his conclusions. From what has been seen, to accept his conclusions was not always to accept his principles. John Quidort has certainly supported a distinction of essence and existence against the adversaries of Thomas Aquinas, but was his notion of being the same as that of Thomas? As has been noted, the problem becomes still more puzzling if one wonders what the word "Thomism" may mean when applied to doctrines in which the Thomistic composition of essence and existence is rejected. For indeed, the meaning of the first principle itself is then at stake, and how can one agree with a doctrine if one disagrees with it on the meaning of the first principle? Yet to limit ourselves to some of the most famous names among the universally recognized Thomists, Giles of Lessines seems to have hesitated on the composition of essence and existence;[123] Harvey of Nédellec (Hervaeus Natalis), who defended Thomas against Duns Scotus, rejected the composition;[124] Peter of La Palu (Petrus de Palude), classically considered a Thomist among the Thomists, did not accept the crucial notion of being ceaselessly restated by Thomas.[125] These oppositions did not arise from any rivalry between religious Orders: all these men were Dominicans, all were defenders of Thomas Aquinas, and in 1279 a General Chapter, held at Paris, had forbidden those who disagreed with his doctrine to speak against it. Leaving aside, as metahistorical, the question whether such men were true Thomists, one still can wonder at the reasons behind their opposition.

The problem is susceptible of several different answers according to the different groups of opponents. The unanimous opposition of the traditionalists in philosophy and theology should probably be examined separately and explained by reasons proper to that school. The data of the problem are different within the Dominican Order. Even there, there remained, after Thomas Aquinas, representatives of the traditional theology, but the official approval of the doctrine by the Order is a sure sign that, to say the least, it did not meet there with any systematic opposition. The cause for this opposition even within the Order of Saint Dominic itself was probably the influence of Aristotle. The cases of such masters as Godfrey of Fontaines or Peter of Auvergne are clear: they would follow Thomas as far as he himself went along with Aristotle, but no further. It is remarkable that, as we heard it said by the Thomist Bernard Lombardi,[126] all the secular masters at the University of Paris, from about 1277 up to the first third of the fourteenth century, unanimously opposed the Thomistic composition of essence and existence. Here again, each case should be examined separately. Henry of Ghent, whom we shall have to study, may have had other reasons to oppose the doctrine than Peter of Auvergne.[127] The Averroists had a very good reason to oppose it: they were following the opposition of Averroes to Avicenna on this point. But one had not to be an Averroist in order to realize the non-Aristotelian character of the doctrine. Minds trained in the long study and meditation of Aristotle's ontology would naturally find it hard to make the Philosopher posit an act of the form. The same feeling may have prevented some of the followers and defenders of Thomas from crossing this metaphysical frontier. In their own way, these men too were initiating a tradition. Their Thomism without composition of essence and existence, that is, minus the act of being, has never ceased to live, and even to prosper, after the end of the thirteenth century. It is a Thomism of substance, in which what Thomas had made of Aristotle survives, minus what Thomas had added to the metaphysics of the Philosopher. The influence of this brand of Thomism in the history of theology and of Christian thought has been a deep and a lasting one. At the end of the sixteenth century, its opposition to the Thomism of the act of being has given rise to controversies whose historical consequences have been manifold. It is not dead yet. Its fascinating history is still waiting for its historians.

The masters of the thirteenth century were not aware of the generality of the problem. They themselves were making history, not writing it. Yet, just as the twelfth century had found in John of Salisbury an unconcerned and amused witness to its doctrinal controversies, the thirteenth century found its critical observer in the person of Henry of Bate, born at Mechlin in 1246, died in 1317.[128] A poet and a musician who was not above dancing, Henry got caught in the school routine of his own times and there is scarcely a branch of learning which he had not cultivated. Like John of Salisbury, he lived with the princes whose secretary he was, which allowed him to learn without having to teach. The first two parts of his *Mirror of Divine Things and of Some Natural Ones* invite one to hope that the other twenty-one parts will also be published.

FOURTEENTH CENTURY SCHOLASTICISM

The division of time into astronomical years does not affect the evolution of ideas. The masters living at the end of the thirteenth century carried their doctrinal positions into the fourteenth century without realizing that a new era was at hand. The only school whose history came to a close at about the same time as the century was that of Saint Bonaventure. We saw it disintegrate under the pressure of its own internal difficulties. Naturally, it never was completely deserted and his own brand of Augustinianism has had revivals even after the end of the middle ages. Nevertheless, the Franciscan masters writing about the last years of the thirteenth century seem to prepare another doctrinal synthesis; several of their doctrinal positions will be taken up by Duns Scotus.

The traditional theology created by William of Auxerre, William of Auvergne and Philip the Chancellor, including its Aristotelian language and its often Augustinian inspiration, was kept alive by the first disciples of Albert the Great, and it received a new reinforcement from the spread of the doctrine of Proclus whose influence, already perceptible in the thirteenth century, gathered strength about the beginning of the fourteenth century and never ceased to grow up to the time of Nicholas of Cues.

CHAPTER I

ALBERTISTS AND NEOPLATONISTS

ALBERT THE GREAT himself outlived several of his best disciples. The doctrine which he bequeathed to them was not the half-way house on the road to Thomism which some of his historians think it was. On one point at least, Albert has kept intact an essential element of what Mandonnet has called "philosophical Augustinianism," namely, the definition of the human soul as an independent substance. The Thomistic conception of the soul as a spiritual substance endowed with sensitive powers and, consequently, needing a body in order to achieve its own substantiality, never convinced Albert the Great. On the contrary, we owe him one of the most perfect descriptions of the traditional position adopted by the theologians on this point: "If we consider the soul in itself, we shall agree with Plato; if we consider it as a form giving life to the body, we shall agree with Aristotle." [1] For the same reason, Albert bequeathed to his disciples a complex of doctrines in which psychological elements borrowed from Alfarabi, Avicenna and Toletanus (Gundissalinus) combined with the Augustinian doctrine of divine illumination. Ever since the beginning of his career, Albert had taught that the possible intellect and the agent intellect required a complement of light for the cognition of truth. In his mind, there was a secret affinity between the Intelligible Sun of Augustine's *Soliloquies*, the Father of Lights of St. James (i, 17) and of Denis, the Giver of forms of Avicenna, and this affinity was by no means an illusion. From the beginning of his long career up to its end Albert had always maintained the themes of the flux of being (*de fluxu entis*) and of the light-metaphysics (*de luce*). The true meaning of the doctrine of Albert is much less visible in the teaching of Thomas Aquinas, whose inspiration was quite different from the theological doctrines of his German continuators. Their school seems to have grown quietly, in the relative doctrinal peace of Cologne, away from the Averroistic turmoil of Paris.

One of Albert's first disciples was Hugh Ripelin (Hugh of Strasbourg), probable author of a *Compendium of Theological Truth* or *Compendium theologiae* (1268), which was a huge success in the fourteenth century, and was often attributed to Albert the Great. The mistake is easily accounted for by the numerous borrowings from the master by the disciple.[2] Much more important is the work of Albert's favorite pupil, Ulrich of Strasbourg (Ulrich Engelbrecht, Engelberti), who died before his master did, in 1277.[3] His work included a Commentary on Aristotle's *Meteors,* a *Commentary on the Sentences,* and a Summa *On the Supreme Good,* of which only Book I has been published. It is an essentially theological work, whose first two books are a sort of commentary of the *Divine Names*. Like all theologians, Ulrich thinks that theology is the science of faith, that is to say, the science by which what one believes by faith becomes the object of intellection. Faith suffices for salvation, but it does not suffice for theology itself, at least if theology is to be a science. Taking up in his own way the idea of Alan of Lille and Boethius, Ulrich notes that all science presupposes rules (*regulae veritatis*), that is, principles to which one can refer to settle discussions. All principles are not equally primary, and the only ones that are absolutely so are those which are immediately evident. As the science of faith, theology also presupposes, therefore, primary and universal principles by which all the articles and the whole body of Christian truth shall be proved. These principles are four in number: God is the supreme Truth and the cause of all truth; primary Truth can neither be mistaken nor mislead us, and consequently everything that his testimony certifies is true and should be believed; we should believe in everything that is said by those through whom God proves that he is the one who is speaking to us; Scripture is true precisely because God gave it to us that way. Unlike these rules, the articles of faith are not immediately evident (*per se nota*), but we prove them by these primary principles; thus, in the light of faith and of these principles, the articles of faith become objects of scientific cognition.[4]

To affirm that God is the supreme Truth and the Cause of all truth, is to grant that the existence of God can itself be known with a certitude nigh to immediate evidence.[5] Like Albert the Great, Ulrich of Strasbourg takes up the Avicennian doctrine of the states of the intellect, up to those where it contacts, through the hierarchy of separate Intelligences, the divine light.[6] The universe in which his thought moves is the universe that Albert the Great had inherited from the Arabs. All forms are imprinted in things by the motive Intelligences of the celestial spheres; these Intelligences themselves owe their instrumental causality to the fact that they "are informed" by the light of the primary Cause, to whom they are indebted for being, and for being causes. The multiplication of forms in beings has its primary source in God, in whom are the Ideas. Thanks to the divine light, these Ideas are received by the motive Intelligences of the spheres, from which they go (*prodeunt in res extra*) to constitute the things of which they are the forms. The parallel illumination of beings and intellects by the divine Ideas remain intact in Ulrich's doctrine.[7]

The same neoplatonic influence makes itself felt in his ontology. For him, as for the author of the *Book of Causes*, being is the first of created things. By *esse*, Ulrich means not abstract being, but the primary form, which is the origin of all its successive determinations, and in which they are finally resolved. That first "being," or primary form,

presupposes nothing before it, save its creation by God, but the sole fact
that it needs to be created suffices to distinguish it from the First, for
the being of the First is "pure being," whereas the first created "being,"
precisely because it is created, is mixed with non-being. It can even be
said of this "being" that it is composed of finite and infinite. In its
relation to the cause by which it is, that is, to the Primary Principle, it
is finite, for it is the simple intellectual intuition of its cause, and, so to
say, a conception standing in the light of the intellect which produces
it; in its relation to what comes after it, the first created *esse* is infinite
in potentiality, for it is divided into what is by itself and what is by
another (substance and accident), and this division is then multiplied
to infinity, which could not happen were this *esse* not infinite in potentiality. Any such composition is entirely absent from the uncreated Being.
This "being," which is divine thought actualized, is really a form produced by the divine intellect, and in this sense Ulrich calls it an Intelligence, a term which in this case signifies both an intellectual substance
and an intellection. This ontology is in perfect agreement with a cosmology of universal illumination, where all forms come from God through
the first creature—which is itself an intellection—as through the diffusion of a light: "The prime cause is pure, formal and intellectual light,
and since it causes by its own essence (for otherwise it would not be
the prime cause) his effect must needs be the diffusion of this light and
of this formality." We find here the mingling of all the neoplatonic
themes once more calling forth one another: universal hierarchical procession by way of knowledge, divine illumination, identification of being
and form. There is not one of these themes whose equivalent could not
be found in Albert the Great.[8]

I. DIETRICH OF VRIEBERG

It is a sort of rule, in the history of philosophy, that the elements of
a doctrinal synthesis exhibit a tendency to extricate themselves and, so
to speak, to return to their natural places. Aristotelianism almost completely triumphed in the thirteenth century as a philosophical technique. Everyone, or almost everyone, borrowed its terminology, its
fundamental notions and many of its conclusions, but toward the end
of the century the neoplatonic elements borrowed by Albert from Avicenna and Denis decisively took the upper hand. In physics, the Aristotelian elements (notions of motion, space, time, etc.) remained stable,
but in metaphysics and noetic, Plotinus gained ground. This seems to
have happened at least in the mind of the Dominican, Dietrich of Vrieberg (Theodoricus Teutonicus de Vrieberg), a scholar, philosopher and
theologian, who died shortly after 1310.[9]
Dietrich seems to have studied and taught first at the Dominican

convent at Vrieberg, in Saxony, whence he was sent to Paris in 1276 to complete his studies. This time we are not dealing with a pupil of Albert the Great, but with one of those thinkers of Eckhart's generation in whose minds the influence of Proclus can be felt. This influence had been active ever since the *Liber de causis,* whose doctrine was taken from Proclus, had been translated into Latin, perhaps by Gerard of Cremona, about 1180. We saw Alan of Lille quote it, as early as the end of the twelfth century, under the title of *Aphorisms on the Essence of the Supreme Goodness.* The eighteenth of May, 1268, William of Moerbecke, finished at Viterbo the translation of Proclus' *Elements of Theology,* the direct source of the *Book of Causes.* In 1281, he translated three other works by Proclus (*Ten problems about Providence, On Providence and Fate, On the Nature of Evils*), as well as Proclus' Commentaries on Plato's *Timaeus* and *Parmenides.*[10] The influence of these translations was immediate and considerable, especially in theological and philosophical centers where Albert the Great's influence dominated. Dietrich of Vrieberg, Eckhart and Berthold of Mosburg all show the stamp of it: three Germans like Albert and, like him, three Dominicans.[11]

The classical alliance of the light-metaphysics with mathematical interests and the study of optics is still found in the mind of Dietrich. The geometrical construction of his answer to the problem of the rainbow was not entirely correct, but he was the first to see that the rainbow results from a simple reflection and a double refraction, to recognize that each tiny drop generates a complete solar spectrum, and to explain how the various colors, coming from different little drops, are reassembled in the eye. Dietrich, besides, correctly determined the order of colors in the refracted rays and the solar spectrum, and finally demonstrated, by a correct geometrical construction, that the required condition is valid for all the drops situated at the same angular height with regard to the axis which goes from the sun to the eye, and for them only, so that the rainbow must always be an arc of a circle, which attains its maximum when the sun is at the horizon.

Dietrich's scientific work continues the tradition of Roger Bacon and Witelo. Myopic paleographers who wonder how the people of the middle ages could write and read their own manuscripts will be pleased to know that, in his *De intellectu et intelligibili* (p. 193*), Dietrich speaks of men who use crystals to help sight (*ut patet de illis qui vident per berillum et similia*). They were already using magnifying lenses, perhaps even glasses. "Bacon had dreamed of the telescope, which was not to be discovered until about 300 years later; artisans were beginning to back mirrors with lead; Bacon had studied the effects produced by the focuses of concave mirrors, to which Witelo had given a parabolical form; sailors were beginning to navigate by the compass, as Dietrich himself mentions it in his *De tribus difficilibus articulis,* and Vincent of Beauvais and

Thomas of Cantimpré were popularizing the science of nature. As to what Albert the Great had done for the study of botany and zoology, in his careful personal observations, in his radical opposition to a multitude of foolish legends, that alone would be sufficient to assure him the rank of a very great scholar in the history of science. Taking all this into consideration, it must be granted that this century, to which we are indebted for the greatest philosophers and theologians of the middle ages, two of the foremost popes politically, and the greatest saints as well as the greatest poet in Italy, also deserves the glory of having been a highly important period for the history of science." [12] This seems to be true. We might add that if Aristotle's influence encouraged the revival of botany and zoology, Plato's was almost constantly exerted for the benefit of geometry and optics. Ultimately, Denis and Alhacen's Optics get the best of it; the metaphysics of light, noetic of light and physics of light seem mutually to call upon and confirm one another. A verification of this view is to be found in Dietrich's treatise *On the Intellect and the Intelligible*.

The work is full of Proclus, whose doctrine of Intelligences it combines with Avicenna's and with all that one can relate them with in Augustine's texts. All the Platonisms once more run into one another. The activity of the Intelligences, or Intellects, is a sort of internal effervescence of those intellectual substances described by Proclus, and at whose summit he places the One. From this source, as a consequence of the mutual transfusion which takes place within it, being seems to overflow out of the One, which creates it out of nothing and governs it.[13] According to this Dionysian view of the world, things flow from God by way of creation, so that what Proclus says can be expressed in terms borrowed from Augustine: "According to Augustine's interpretation *Super Genesim ad litteram* (II, 6, 13), where we read: God said, let there be light, or, let there be the firmament, we should understand: the Word, in Whom it was, engendered it that it might be. From which it appears that this One, Whom Proclus put in first place and above all things, has the fecundity of an intellect." The following hierarchy of beings is therefore obtained: God, who is unnamable and above all causes; his first "signification," which is the One, or the Word, and whose inner "ebullition" causes a "transfusion," which is the creation of being, the whole of this doctrine being confirmed indifferently by Proclus or Augustine.[14]

Creation, thus understood as an intellectual emanation, must therefore be conceived after the mode of activity proper to all agent intellects. All philosophers agree on this emergence of beings originating in the primary cause. Plato, Aristotle, the Platonist Proclus, Avicenna, of whose doctrine Algazel wrote a digest, unanimously teach that things flow from God following this order: the primary Intelligence, from which comes the second Intelligence, the soul of the first firmament and the first firmament, and so on down to the world of man. All this agrees with the Christian doctrine of creation since, as the *Book of Causes* says, God alone creates. In fact, to create is to produce without presupposing any anterior cause; the fact that things proceed one from the other does not imply that one creates the other (*procedere enim rem a re non est unam creare aliam*); one can therefore grant the procession of all things starting from a first created, without putting the Christian notion of creation in jeopardy.[15]

Dietrich's psychology and noetic are included in his cosmogony. Our agent intellect is presented as a particular case of the problem of agent intellects. Any intellect, as such, is the image (*similitudo*) of the total being, or being as being, and it is so by essence. That is why the intellect is capable of producing any intelligible. Essentially active, it is the causal principle of the very substance of the soul, in which it is as the heart in the animal. In fact, it is the cause of the known intelligible form, whose intellection is the whole substance of the possible intellect, as Alexander of Aphrodisias and Alfarabi say in their treatises *De intellectu et intelligibili*. Taken in itself this possible intellect is only a pure potentiality, without any positive nature, whose intelligible form is a simple accident. The agent intellect is, therefore, the sole substantial act that can be discerned here and, as it cannot be the form of the soul, it must be its cause. It goes without saying that this cause of the soul acts only in virtue of the primary Cause, whence flows all causality.[16]

Each agent intellect is an individual substance. It must be a substance because it is capable of discursive rational knowledge, which cannot pertain to mere intelligible species as such, and also because it constitutes a compound unity with the substance of the soul of which it is the cause. It is essentially one being with the essence of the soul. Abstraction, at least as it is ordinarily conceived, is not enough to explain intellectual knowledge. As a matter of fact, it is quite true that there are first things, then sensible impressions, particular images and their elaboration by the cogitative power in universal intentions; but all this belongs in the sensible order and the act of the agent intellect is needed to raise cognition up to the truly intelligible order. The agent intellect can only work that transmutation because it is permanently turned toward God. We must not forget its nature: just like all other things, our intellect proceeds from the divine Ideas as an image and likeness of total being, and this is why the virtual knowledge of everything is contained in it. Its primary cognition of things is not discursive, but intuitive; it does not consider one object after another, but rather, in a single intuition, it knows its principle, acquires being and knows the totality of beings.

Despite the Aristotelian terminology which he uses, Dietrich is really restating Plotinus. As he conceives it, the agent intellect is not a power flowing from the essence of the soul; it is the cause of the essence of the soul. In his treatise *On the Intellect* [17] Dietrich expressly identifies this Plotinian agent intellect with the hidden recess of the mind (*abditum mentis*), or the more hidden depth (*abstrusior profunditas*) mentioned by Augustine in his *De Trinitate*. We are already moving in the Plotinian world of Eckhart, in which intellect comes before being, because it causes it. In his treatise *On the Beatific Vision*, the second of the three writings of which his work *On the Three Difficult Articles* is composed, Dietrich develops this point in a series of propositions which clearly define his position with respect to the doctrine of divine illumination: 1) the hidden recess of the soul mentioned by Augustine, which is also the agent intellect, is a substance; 2) this same hidden recess of the mind, or agent intellect, is always standing in the light of an Intelligence in act and always understanding in act; 3) it is owing to this intellection that the hidden recess of the mind understands its own essence; 4) the intellect is by essence an exemplar and a similitude of being, in that it understands being and all things; 5) an intellect which is such by essence and is always in act, as the agent intellect is, knows all other things by its own essence, in the same way as it knows itself, and by the same simple act. Commenting upon this last proposition, Dietrich expressly concludes that the agent intellect is by essence the pattern of all being *qua* being, and, consequently, that it is in itself all being. By knowing itself, it knows all. In his own divine way, God does the same thing.[18]

However much he had borrowed from the neoplatonists, Augustine had never taught what Dietrich was making him say. Since he was living in the world of Proclus, this Dominican could still less be expected to agree with the Thomistic notion of being. In his own treatise *On Being and Essence*, Dietrich began by noting that he who is wrong about universal notions cannot help being wrong about particular ones.[19] Even without this warning, we would have been able to guess that his ontology was different from that of Thomas Aquinas.

This influence of Proclus was to be felt long after the beginning of the fourteenth century. Berthold of Mosburg, a contemporary of Eckhart, has left a vast *Exposition on the Elements of Theology of Proclus*, still unpublished, in which Dietrich of Vrieberg and Ulrich of Strasbourg are quoted among many others, and which Nicholas of Cues was in turn to quote, with praise, in his treatise *On Learned Ignorance*.[20] These masters form a continuous chain which runs from the immediate disciples of Albert up to the immediate forerunners of the Renaissance; Proclus is their connecting link.

2. MASTER ECKHART

The ontology of form, which had developed from Boethius and Gilbert of la Porrée to Albert the Great, naturally tended to rejoin the neoplatonic metaphysics of the One which had engendered it. This tendency had always been counterbalanced by the Christian identification of Being with God, which made it difficult to raise the One above being. One of the outstanding achievements of Saint Augustine had precisely been to substitute the God of Exodus, that is, Being, for the One of Plotinus. This barrier seems to have finally given way, under the pressure of Proclus, in the doctrine of John Eckhart.[21] Born in 1260 at Hochheim, near Gotha, he belonged to the Dominican Order. In 1302 Eckhart took his licentiate degree and taught at Paris. Toward the end of his life, his adversaries undertook to have some of his doctrines condemned, but he died in 1327, before the condemnation of March 27, 1329, which censured twenty-seven of his propositions.

Eckhart was equally familiar with the doctrines of Aristotle, of Albert the Great and of Thomas Aquinas. He constantly used their language and freely drew from their writings, but not always to say the same things.

What was to remain Eckhart's main tendency to the very end comes to light as early as his Questions on being, which seem to date from about 1313-1314. In the first of these Questions he asks himself whether, in God, being and knowing are identical, and he answers, in direct opposition to Thomas Aquinas, that God does not know because he is, but that he is because he knows (*est ipsum intelligere fundamentum ipsius esse*). One could not more definitely subordinate the plane of being, and Eckhart does it in full agreement with the neoplatonism of the *De causis,* whose celebrated formula he adopts as his own: The first of created things is being. Instead of altering its meaning as Thomas Aquinas had done in his own Commentary, Eckhart welcomes it in all its force: "as soon as we come to being, we come to creature." If one reaches the order of creation by arriving at the order of being, one is above the order of being as long as one clings to God. Since being is proper to creatures, it is in God only as in its cause: it is not there formally. Eckhart knows very well that in this case he is running afoul of the text from Exodus (3, 15): I AM WHO AM, but as the negative theology of Maïmonides here reinforces the ontology of Proclus in an unexpected manner, he has the means of interpreting it. If God, he observes, had wished to say that he was being, he would have been content to say: I AM; but he said something else. If we meet by night someone who wishes to hide and to remain unknown, and if we ask him: who are you? he answers: I am who I am. That is what God did in his answer to Moses: consequently, being does not belong to God.

In these Questions, then, Eckhart considers God as One who has the privilege of being pure of all being (*puritas essendi*), and One who, by reason of that very purity with regard to being, can be its cause. Aristotle had said that sight must be colorless in order to see all colors; similarly, God must be innocent of being in order that he may be the cause of being. Therefore, God is something higher than being: *est aliquid altius ente.* He possesses everything ahead of time in his purity. His plenitude and his perfection are the roots and causes of all, and this is precisely what God meant when he said: I AM WHO AM. This something anterior to being is here identified with the act of intellection. For indeed, in the beginning was the Word (John, i, 1), therefore intellection itself is the foundation of being. Now the Word said of himself: "I am the Truth" (John 14, 6), that is to say, Wisdom. However he may have expressed himself later on the subject of being, Eckhart never varied on this point: insofar as God is Wisdom (*sapientia*), he is free of everything else, even including being.[22]

This point should never be forgotten in interpreting the later works in which Eckhart so frequently repeats that God is being (*esse est Deus*) and that he is being in its purity and its plenitude: *esse purum et plenum;* not that he had really changed his mind, but that he expressed himself differently. As early as the epoch of the Questions, Eckhart is seen identifying God with the act of intellection. Of the triad: to be, to live and to understand, it is the third that he places in first rank, no longer simply, as Augustine had done in his treatise *On Free Will* (II, 3, 7), because its presence implies the presence of the other two and not inversely (stones are but do not know), but because the divine act of intellection cannot be the cause of being if it is not itself being in some way or other. Now it seems indeed that Eckhart never varied on this point. Throughout his doctrinal career he obstinately maintained that God the Father is Intellection, as he appropriated Life to the Son and Being to the Holy Spirit. By that last solution he put himself in conformity, as far as was possible for him to do so, with the Christian tradition, and he found his own way to say that God is being and being is God; but in order to find it, he had to put being third in the eternal processions of the Trinity, which enabled him to reserve the first place for Intellection. If any real change in Eckhart's thought had to be observed on this point, it would consist rather in the final subordination of Intellect itself to a still higher term, the One.[23]

In a sermon of Eckhart that Nicholas of Cues has owned, read and annotated, this thought is expressed with all the clarity one could hope for in such matters.[24] Saint Paul had recalled, in the *Epistle to the Galatians* (3, 20), that God is One, and his unity was to remain for Eckhart the appropriate mark of God. Now, in this sermon, he develops insistently the thesis that unity belongs properly only to the intellect. Material beings are not perfectly one, because they are composed of matter and form; immaterial and intelligent beings are not strictly one, because they are intelligent-beings, that is creatures whose being is not their intelligence. Only the pure Intellect can be pure unity; it is therefore one and the same thing to say that God is wholly Intellect and that God is one.

We thus obtain the superior terms of Eckhart's ontology. At the peak, of course, the Christian Trinity. With all the theologians, Eckhart distinguishes the unity of essence and the three divine persons, but, if one is careful of the terms he uses, he will notice that the very root of divine being is less the essence itself than its "purity," which is unity. This is the summit and the center of all: the immobile unity, the repose, the solitude and the desert of the Deity. The *deitas* thus understood lies beyond the three divine persons. But we have seen that the "purity" of the essence, which is its unity, is by the same stroke Intellect, since the Intellect alone is perfectly one. To posit the purity of the divine essence is therefore to posit the Intellect, which is the Father, and with which we pass from the repose of the One to the inner seething of divine generations and processions, the preambles of creation. It is thus that the pure Unity of essence manifests its paternal fecundity: germinating, breathing, creating all being. It is therefore quite true to say, with the symbol of Athanasius, "One Father," but it must be understood here with Eckhart: for indeed he is father because he is One and, inversely, he is One because he is father: the unity is the paternity: *et unitas paternitas est.* In fact, the Unity of essence is the same Unity of Intellect, which engenders Life, or the Son (*Quod factum est in ipso vita erat*), and from which comes being, or the Holy Ghost. Thus we find in the Trinity the Augustinian triad and in the same order: to know, to live, to be; but let us not forget what its root is: "Thy God, God is One, the God of Israel, the Seeing God, the God of those who see." [25] The two key terms that Eckhart retains from this text are "one" and "seeing": unity and intellect, and he commends two interpretations of them. God teaches us first that because he is One, he is Being (*hoc ipso quod unus, ipsi competit esse*); and next, that nothing other than God is truly one, because nothing other than he is of itself intellect wholly (*se toto intellectus*). Scripture leads us to God-Intellect and, by him, to the Unity, pure of all being, which is the very desert of the Deity.

If God is Being because he is One, and if nothing other than God is one, nothing other than he is being. The technical justification for this conclusion is found in the notion of analogy proper to Eckhart and which is explained in the preface to his commentary on Ecclesiasticus published by Denifle (p. 588). Participated perfections, such as being, good, true, just, light and so forth, are imparted to creatures wholly from without, and they never become rooted in the beings that receive them. Even while they are participating in their source, the analogues have nothing of the form they receive positively rooted in them: *analogata nihil in se habent positive radicatum formae.* For instance, while God is creating my being, this being remains in God *positive et radicaliter;* created being *semper ex se non est, sed ab alio.* Being is, so to speak, imputed to beings by God without ever becoming their own being, about in the same way as, in Luther's theology, justice will be imputed to the just without ever becoming their own justice. Man never truly is, rather he is always being produced and created, in the same way as the Lutheran Christian will never be just, but, rather, will always remain in the condition of being justified. The creature is therefore a pure nothingness, in this sense at least, that of itself, it is not. What characterizes the creature taken in itself, is its nullity (*nulleitas*); it only is as a manifestation of the divine fecundity and to the extent that it shares in the nature of the intellect and the intellectual (*Quantum habet unumquodque de intellectu sive de intellectuali, tantum habet Dei, et tantum de uno, et tantum de esse*). This accounts for the very curious and profound psychology of Eckhart whose object it was to permit the return of man to the One through intellectual knowledge. Such had already been the object of Plotinus' dialectic.

For Eckhart, as for Augustine, Avicenna and Albert the Great, the soul is a spiritual substance. The name, *anima,* does not designate its essence but, rather, its animative function. Besides the three Augustinian faculties: memory, intellect and will, which are not God but created together with the soul, Eckhart recognizes in the soul an element more secret and properly divine, which he designates by different images, such as the "citadel" or the "spark" of the soul. It is in fact a spark of the divine Intellect, one and simple as this Intellect itself is. One of the propositions attributed to Eckhart and censured in 1329 was: "There is in the soul something which is uncreated and uncreatable, and that is its intellect." It is not surprising that such a formula should have caught the attention of the theologians to whom the Plotinian doctrine of the presence of the One in the soul, or rather of the permanent dwelling of the soul in the One, was not familiar. It seems on the contrary to be absolutely central in Eckhart's doctrine, and to account for several of those other propositions concerning the mystical life which were condemned together with it. In order to unite with God, man only has to lock himself up in that "citadel of the soul," where he is no longer distinguished from God, since it is a sharing in the One. This notion of the mystical union presupposed two conditions. First, the reality of this unity of man and God: "The Father begets me His one and only Son. All that God does is one; that is why He begets me His Son without any distinction"; secondly, the conquest by man of a state of separation and detachment from all that is not God. This state is the inner citadel of the soul, which alone is free by reason of its very unity. Once there, man loses interest in all the rest: "The external act is not, properly speaking, either good or divine, and it is not, properly speaking, God who brings it about or who begets it"; on the contrary, all that is proper to divine nature, is equally proper to a just and divine man; that is why this man brings about all that God brings about, and has created together with God heaven and earth, and he is the generator of the divine Word, and God could not do anything without such a man.[26]

In master Eckhart, all the neoplatonism that Thomas Aquinas had so carefully ballasted with Aristotelianism and that Albert the Great had subordinated to the natural theology of being, tends to reassert itself in its original purity. This doctrine would have been only a speculative curiosity without the profound spiritual life that animated it. Since the soul clings by its innermost depths to the Deity, it can certainly never be outside God, but it can either become attached to itself and thus withdraw from him, or, on the contrary, it can become attached to what there is most profound in itself and thus become reunited to him. In order to achieve this union, man must bend all his effort to find God beyond the creature. The first condition necessary for his success is to remember our previous conclusion that, in themselves, that is to say independently of what they have of divine being, creatures are only a pure nothingness. That is why the love of creatures and the pursuit of pleasure leave in the soul only sadness and bitterness. The only creature that can lead us directly to God is the soul itself, which is the most noble of all. By becoming conscious of its own limits, and voluntarily denying them, the soul gives up everything that makes it a certain determined and particular being. Once the shackles binding it and the partitions separating it have fallen, the soul perceives in itself only the continuity of its being with the Being from which it derives. In rejecting himself for love of God, man finds himself. The detachment, the abandonment of self to God by which the soul achieves complete liberty in reaching its pure essence, is its highest virtue. And the highest degree of that highest virtue is called Poverty, for after reaching this degree of perfection, man knows nothing, he can do nothing, he owns nothing. The soul has lost itself in losing the sense of all determination by its return to God. Whence it follows that all the traditional prescriptions of morals are secondary or useless. Prayer, faith, grace, sacraments are only the preparations and the means of raising oneself to a higher view. Necessary as they are when the soul begins to become detached from itself and things, they become useless from the moment a sort of new birth of God is accomplished in the soul. Man can then renounce all things, and even God, since there is for man no need to desire what he already possesses; by that supreme virtue, man blends with God in the beatitude of their common unity.[27]

3. TAULER AND RUYSBROECK

Eckhart's thought was not simple; its language was not free, and it is no wonder that his historians do not always agree on the sense of its doctrine. Some see in it a Christian mysticism, others a Platonic and Plotinian dialectic, and probably they all are right. There is no incompatibility between dialectic and speculative mysticism. One would perhaps be not very far from the truth in representing Eckhart as a soul devoured by the love for God, favored perhaps with an intense feeling for the divine presence and anxious to express it by means of dialectic. At any rate, his successors seem to have understood him in that way. For Eckhart left disciples, and it is probably not by chance that these disciples count also among the masters of Christian spirituality. If an authentically Christian spiritual life had not been the nourishing soil of Eckhartian speculation, the doctrinal condemnations directed against it would have put an end to its history. But that is not what happened. The names and works of John Tauler (1300-1361), of Henry Suso (1300-1365)[28] and of John Ruysbroeck (1293-1381) testify to the lasting influence of Eckhart's doctrine on souls whose spiritual life was certainly very noble. There must have been in Eckhart something of what a Tauler has found in him.

Of Tauler's works we have a collection of Sermons in which is expressed a mysticism whose study directly concerns the history of theology. Let us note, however, the persistence of psychological themes familiar to the readers of Albert the Great and his successors. The principal one is his doctrine of "the ground of the soul," which he also calls the "summit of the soul," formulas which recall the *abditum mentis* and the *apex mentis*. As a matter of fact, what Tauler thus designates has no name, for this depth of the soul is only the intimate connection of the soul with God, and since God is unnamable, this secret retreat of the soul is also unnamable. Situated beyond all the faculties, interior to the very essence of the soul, a perpetual silence and repose reign there, without images, without cognition, without action; it is a pure receptivity with regard to the divine light and an essential possibility of mystical contemplation. Tauler himself describes the origin of this doctrine in an important passage: "Many doctors, ancient or modern, have spoken of that inner nobility hidden in the depths of the soul—Bishop Albert (the Great), master Dietrich (of Vrieberg), master Eckhart. One calls it a *spark* of the soul, another a *center* or a *summit,* a third the *principle* of the soul. As to Bishop Albert, he calls this nobility an image in which the Holy Trinity is represented and resides. This spark flies up to the summits where its true place is, even beyond this world, where intelligence cannot follow it, for it does not rest until it returns to that Center from which it originates and where it used to be in its uncreated state."[29]

Tauler's mysticism aims to provide an opportunity for a soul created by God to return to its uncreated idea in God. This Erigenian and Dionysian theme is here clothed in formulas borrowed from doctrines it had, itself, inspired. Between the center (or ground) of the soul and its faculties properly so-called comes the *Gemüt,* that is, a stable disposition of the soul which conditions, in good or evil, the exercise of all its faculties. If the *Gemüt* turns to the depth of the soul, and consequently toward God, all the rest is and functions as it should. On the contrary, let the *Gemüt* turn away from the center of the soul, all the soul's faculties turn away from God. In short, the *Gemüt* is the permanent attitude of the soul toward its own "center." [30]

This structure of the soul favors its communications with God, not only in the order of the supernatural life, but even at the level of natural knowledge. Any man who enters into contact with his own innermost depths knows God there immediately and more clearly than his eyes see the sun: "Proclus and Plato arrived at that point and have given a clear judgment of it to those who could not manage to find it themselves." On this occasion, Tauler recalls the texts in which Augustine grants that certain philosophers were able to raise themselves high enough to perceive for an instant the divine light, but it is also probable that he himself has just read Proclus in William of Moerbeke's translation. One of Tauler's commentators has shown[31] that one of the Sermons in which Tauler quotes Proclus is closely inspired, in its description of the contemplation of the Christian soul and its own core, by a passage from the treatise *On Providence* where Proclus undertakes to conduct his disciple beyond Aristotle, as far as Plato and his doctrine of divine enthusiasm. While freely using the teaching of the philosophers, Tauler strongly advises his readers not to attempt to enter into such contemplation before having had apprenticeship in the Christian virtues. Such is the condition necessary for all true knowledge of God. This is why, taking up literally the formulas of the Prologue of the *Itinerary of the Soul toward God* by Saint Bonaventure, Tauler declares that the only road that leads to this end is the life and passion of Jesus Christ.

These facts must be borne in mind in order not to imagine these speculatives as Platonic philosophers in monastic garb. They were Christians who, especially preoccupied with supernatural contemplation, naturally found in Platonism a language and an intellectual technique better adapted to their needs than those of Aristotle's empiricism. The remark still more validly applies to another mystic[32] in whom these philosophical notions have left hardly perceptible traces, John Ruysbroeck (1293-1381). This Brabantine contemplative had a genius for fine titles: *The Adornment of Spiritual Nuptials* and *The Book of the Twelve Nuns* remain in the memory even of those who have never seen the books. Ruysbroeck describes in them the twofold movement by which God comes to meet the soul in the gifts he confers upon it, and by which, in its turn, the soul "goes out" to meet God. Here, the initiative comes from God (*Ipse prior dilexit nos*), but Ruysbroeck does not fail to emphasize the freedom of the act by which will responds to grace. If the good will of the man who answers the call of God is still not sufficient, it is up to God to complete his work. The *Adornment of Spiritual Nuptials* is the careful analysis of these exchanges, according to the word of the Gospel of which that work is only a technical commentary: *Behold, the bridegroom cometh, go ye forth to meet him* (Matthew, 25, 6).

Ruysbroeck's mysticism is far from being a doctrine of pure passivity under the gifts of grace. On the contrary, it is a doctrine of life, and even of triple life: active, affective and contemplative, by which man finally becomes engulfed in the beatitude of the divine life. It would not be exact to say that Ruysbroeck had given up speculation, but Ruysbroeck's speculation certainly does without philosophy. In his mystical doctrine, as in Saint Bernard's, by which it was to a certain extent inspired, traces of neoplatonism are all that is left of philosophical speculation. *The Adornment of Spiritual Nuptials* (II, 2) distinguishes three unities in man, interior to one another though less and less perfect: the unity which, like all creatures, man has in God; the unity of the superior powers of man in his mind; the unity of the inferior powers of man in his heart. These three unities are explained in the same way: the multiple is one, and is in the one, only because it has its origin in it. The work of grace in man consists precisely in reconducting these three unities to the summit of the primary and highest unity, not, naturally, without the co-operation of the will. Beyond the moral virtues of the active life, the internal exercises of the spiritual life, and even the supernatural contemplative life in general, Ruysbroeck rejoins the mystical experiences of Saint Bernard and Richard of Saint Victor, which are, for him as well as for them, the foretaste of the beatific vision:—experiences unifying in the highest degree, for God is supremely Unity. As such, God does not cease to dwell in the essence of the soul and, moving it supernaturally from within as the Primary Mover moves the primary mobile (II, 50), he reunites the soul with himself through grace: a wholly divine initiative this time, for only he whom God thus wills to unite with him is fit for such a gift.

Such "encounters" cannot be described, but Ruysbroeck at least attempted to account for their possibility by presenting this union as a restoration of man to his "essential existence" in divine thought. By the eternal generation of the Word, "all creatures are born eternally before having been created in time. Thus God saw them and knew them in Himself, distinctly, according to the Ideas which are in Him, and as different from Him; not, however, different in all ways, for all that is in God is God. This origin and this eternal life which we possess in God and which we are outside of ourselves, is the principle of our created being in time; and our created being is attached to our eternal being and is identical with it, according to its essential existence." We are eternally, through that being which we are in the Wisdom of God, both identical with him and other than him. The peak of the contemplative life attains its eternal model in God, in whose image it was created, and thus contemplates all things, through a simple view, in the unity of the divine light (III, 5). There are, in Ruysbroeck's thought, reminiscences of Maximus the Confessor, and perhaps of Erigena. John Gerson became anxious about this and conducted an offensive against Ruysbroeck which was perhaps not fundamentally unjust, but which had at least the defect of presenting speculative elements integrated to a mystical doctrine as a metaphysics of the divine Ideas which Ruysbroeck never intended to maintain. If we were more certain of possessing Ruysbroeck's text free from any retouching, we should be better able to tell whether Gerson had not slightly dramatized the situation, and to what extent he had done so. However this may be, Gerson was assuredly not led astray on the importance of the work, which was to have a profound effect on the history of Christian spirituality in the course of the centuries to follow.

The first apologist against Ruysbroeck's adversaries, John of Schoonhoven (d. 1432), defended and propagated the doctrine of his master; whether he himself accepted it whole is a question which it would not be prudent to answer as long as some of his works remain unpublished. Without ceasing to be speculative, the mystics of the fifteenth century became less and less philosophically-minded. The treatise of the Benedictine monk, John of Kastl, *On Adhering to God,* long attributed to Albert the Great and printed among his works[33] was written about 1410. Themes borrowed from Augustine, Eckhart and Tauler reappear in it under the form of mere reminiscences. The Bonaventurian doctrine of the cognition of truth in the divine light is occasionally exploited in the *Spiritual Philosophy* of the same author. The publication of his treatise *On Uncreated Light* makes him appear reminiscent of the doctrine of Eckhart on the nothingness of creatures. The vein of scholastic speculation which still gave to the doctrine of Eckhart a sort of theological consistency seems to be nearly exhausted in the fifteenth century. The distrust of scholasticism spread by the modern school of devotion (*devotio moderna*) and of which the universally known *Imitation of Christ* unmistakably bears the mark,[34] is only one among the many signs announcing the end of mediaeval scholasticism. At the same time, the return to the devotion of the Fathers of the Church and, by the same token, to the type of classical culture which had created its language, attests the continuity of Christian intellectual culture at the very moment when one of its deepest expressions seems to reach its end.

CHAPTER II

THE SECOND AUGUSTINIAN SCHOOL

I. HENRY OF GHENT

THE philosophical doctrine of Saint Augustine had largely been a neo-platonist answer to the semi-skepticism in which he himself had lived for some time between his repudiation of Manichaeism and his conversion to Christianity. His *Contra Academicos,* written shortly after his conversion, was a refutation of the skepticism of the New Academy; in order to refute the arguments of the skeptics, he had been obliged to state them; in stating them, he transmitted them to his mediaeval readers. Against his own intention, Augustine thus provided his disciples with a supply of skeptical arguments which they had to take into consideration, be it only in order to refute them in their own way. Moreover, the Augustinian refutation of these arguments rested upon the acceptance of a Platonic conception of human knowledge which granted to the skeptics at least part of their own arguments. One of the most often-quoted conclusions of Augustine, after 1255, was that "no pure truth can be expected from sensation." [35] So long as a master adhered to the doctrine of the divine illumination, he could distrust sense knowledge without falling into skepticism; his certitude came to him from on high, not from sensations. When the doctrine of the divine illumination began to give way and was replaced with the empiricism of Aristotle, it became necessary to find another protection against the arguments of the skeptics. A direct justification of the trustworthiness of sense cognition became necessary. Duns Scotus will provide such a justification in the very question in which he will do away with the Augustinian doctrine of the divine illumination, at least as Bonaventure and Matthew of Aquasparta had understood it. [36] It is worthy of note that just as the Academy of Plato had brought about the skepticism of the New Academy, so also the Platonic elements carried by Augustinianism always exhibited a tendency to spread a certain skepticism with respect to the validity of sense cognition. There always was a danger that this skepticism might outlive its Platonic refutation, and in the fourteenth century it did.

This is one of the surest threads which run from the Franciscan school of Saint Bonaventure to the theology of Henry of Ghent. [37] This secular master in theology, who took an active part in the condemnation of 1277, taught at the University of Paris from 1276 up to 1292 and died in 1293. His influence was considerable, so much so that it is hardly possible to read Duns Scotus without having at hand the writings of Henry of Ghent. His doctrine was truly his own; yet, in the very first article of his *Summa theologiae,* Henry begins by questioning the validity of natural knowledge, and as some of his Augustinian predecessors had done before him, he partly denies it.[38] The reason for this denial is simple. Henry maintains that absolutely pure truth cannot be known by man without a divine illumination; but he also thinks that, although man can receive this illumination in his present natural condition, God gives it when he pleases and to whom he pleases. In short, it is a free gift of God. Absolutely speaking, then, "man can know pure truth about no thing by acquiring its knowledge through purely natural means, but only by an illumination of the divine light; even when he attains this light in his purely natural condition, man does not attain it by purely natural means, because it freely offers itself to whom it wills." [39] This mistrust of natural knowledge, corrected by a theology, conditions the whole attitude of Henry of Ghent with respect to the doctrines taught by the philosophers. The philosophical probabilism of Ockham certainly follows from his own noetic, but one should keep in mind that all the probabilisms, or skepticisms of the fourteenth century are not necessarily Ockhamist in origin.

Henry of Ghent conceives metaphysics as the science of being. The notion of being escapes definition but its meaning is immediately known to all. Being is that which is. Conceived as that which is, we call it "thing." With Avicenna, Henry considers the notion of "necessary" as given together with those of being and of thing. In order to avoid the consequences deduced by Avicenna from the notion of "necessary being," Henry substitutes, for the couple necessary-possible, another one, very similar to it, whose two terms are: "that which is being itself" and "that which is something to which being belongs, or may belong." In short: what *is* being and what *has* being, or may have it. The first kind of being is by itself, it is uncreated; the second kind of being is by another, it is created. This general division dominates the metaphysics of Henry of Ghent. It simplifies the problem of the demonstration of the existence of God, for it can assuredly be proved from creatures (Rom., i, 20), but it is easier to prove it directly, by starting from the very notion of being which is the primary object of the human intellect. It then suffices to observe that, seen under one of its two primary aspects, being offers itself to the intellect as "that which is being itself" or, in other words, as that whose essence is identical with its existence. This Being, which is being only, but which is the totality of being, can indifferently be called the Good, or the True; it is both precisely because it is the essence to which being belongs in virtue of what it is.

Incidentally, let us note in the theology of Henry of Ghent the new meaning attributed to the divine "infinity." Like all his predecessors, Henry considers infinity a negative notion. It essentially points out the non-existence of any limits set to the divine being or to the divine perfection. But Henry has stressed the fact that, negative as it is in its mode of signifying, the notion of infinity points out a most positive perfection of the divine being. We are here witnessing a complete reversal of the Greek idea of infinity conceived as the condition of that which, being left unfinished, lacks the determinations required for its perfection. Henry conceives infinity as the positive power whereby the divine being transcends all possible limitations. The passage of his *Summa* II, art. 44, qu. 2, in which Henry extends this notion of infinity from God to creatures marks an important date in the history of the notion. The world, Henry says, is finite, but its finitude does not result in it from any perfection. On the contrary, "the word *infinite,* not only in God but in creatures as well, principally signifies that something is being posited, or affirmed"; and again, "in God as well as in creatures, the word *infinite* really imports an affirmation, although it expresses it under the form of a negation or of a privation (of limits)." This positive interpretation of the notion of infinity will play a decisive part in the theology of Duns Scotus.

The second aspect of being, conceived as that to which being belongs, or may belong, covers the universality of actual or possible finite beings. Henry applies his notion of being to God as well as to creatures so that, in a sense, one could say that he is using it univocally, but the notion of univocity does not seem to have occurred to his mind. At any rate, he does not resort to this terminology and it seems doubtful that he would have approved of it. In his doctrine, the term "being" may mean either one of these two types of being, but it does not apply to both at one and the same time. Henry grants to Avicenna that the notion of being *qua* being is anterior to the notions of created or uncreated being. It is anterior to both since we only can conceive them as beings, but Henry does not seem to admit, as Duns Scotus will, that there is a notion of being applicable to both.[40]

This is one of the points of his doctrine which Duns Scotus will criticize, and for very interesting reasons which help in ascertaining the true meaning of Henry's own position. If we do not begin by positing a univocal notion of being, applicable to both God and creatures in the same sense, but only to the extent that they are beings, we cannot help establishing an order of priority between the first two aspects of known being. If we do, "being by itself" necessarily comes first. This entails the consequence that the notion of necessary being, or of being by itself, becomes both the first known object (*primum cognitum*) and the universal notion in which and by which we know all the rest (*ratio cognoscendi*). While it facilitates the demonstration of the existence of God this position creates difficulties on another point. In a doctrine in which all infallible truth is known in the divine light and for which the first object known in this light is divine being itself, to see truth in the light of God grows perilously near to seeing God in the light of God.[41]

In order to distinguish God from his creatures a Christian philosopher can always resort to the notion of creation. Between the creator and his creatures the divine Ideas provide a connecting link. Assuredly, they themselves are God. The divine Ideas are not created in any sense of the term; having no subsistence of their own, they have no other actual being than that of God. Nevertheless, since an Idea represents a possible creature, it can be said to be distinct from God at least to the extent that it is in him a distinct object of cognition. Let us say then that God first knows his own essence in itself; secondly, in the very act by which God knows his own essence, he knows all creatable things according to the being they have in his own knowledge of them; thirdly, God knows the being which possible creatures have in themselves and as distinct from his own being.

The being proper to the creature considered in itself is its "essence." This essence of each possible creature, taken together with the content which defines it, is an Idea. It represents a possible imitation of the divine essence. As such, this ideal essence has a being of its own; otherwise it would not be the idea of a possible creature; it would be the self-knowledge of God *qua* God. Its being, however, is not an actual being added to that of God. It is the being that belongs to a known essence precisely inasmuch as it is known. The being of an essence taken precisely *qua* essence is what Henry calls "being of essence" (*esse essentiae*). This famous doctrine will be severely criticized by Duns Scotus, although he himself will find it hard to imagine a better one. Our two theologians were writing at a time when, as will be seen later on, there was a controversy about the nature of the divine Ideas. Both were firmly resolved to avoid the error of Erigena and his doctrine of the creation, or quasi-creation, of the Ideas by God. On the other hand, since both agreed to identify being with essence, they could not avoid duplicating all distinctions between essences with corresponding distinctions between beings. Distinct essences then, to the extent that they are distinct, must be distinct beings. The "being of essence" [42] posited by Henry is the kind of being which belongs to the object of a known Idea; to use his own expression, whose history was going to be a long one, it is an "ideated" (*ideatum*). Duns Scotus will turn down this solution of the problem. His preference will go to a "secondary," "relative," or "diminished" being of the divine Idea which some of his best disciples will be at a loss to interpret. One of them, William of Alnwick, will declare his inability to distinguish it from the *esse essentiae* it was intended to replace. And no wonder; the two doctrines were haunted by the Dionysian conception of the divine Ideas as "theophanies." Henry and Scotus were trying to avoid it without renouncing the Platonic notion by which it had been engendered. [43]

From the point of view of theology, the Ideas are "relations of imitability within the divine essence"; from the point of view of philosophy they are, before anything else, "the essences of things in the divine knowledge."

Avicenna has excellently described the nature of these essences, but Henry cannot subscribe to the way Avicenna conceives the passing over to actual existence of the essences included in the intellect of God. In the doctrine of Avicenna, God has a will, but his will cannot not consent to the consecutions of Ideas which eternally unfold themselves in the divine mind. While God is thinking the intelligible order of all the possibles, they come to be according to the same order; the eternal speculation of God is eternally being actualized by his will. In Henry's doctrine, the will of God freely consents to the creation of certain possibles by the power of God. The fact that God freely chooses from amongst an infinity of possibles does not affect the content of their essences; it simply turns their being of essence into a being of existence, which is the proper effect of creation.

In God, the act of creation is in no way distinct from the divine being itself. In creatures, creation is nothing more than their relation to the cause of their actual being. What we call existence is nothing else than being itself taken as an effect of this causal relation. There is therefore no such thing as a distinction or composition of essence and existence. In a study especially devoted to the history of this post-Thomist polemic, the controversy between Henry of Ghent and Giles of Rome concerning the metaphysical structure of finite being would perhaps occupy the central place. It lasted for several years and, naturally, it never achieved any measure of agreement.[44] To Henry of Ghent, an existent is simply a possible being actualized by its cause. Once actualized, it is an individual in its own right; each created form is in a fully constituted subject (*suppositum*) which is distinct from all the other ones in virtue of its very unity. A being is distinct from the others because it is one; it is one because it is not divided from itself; consequently, every actual being is individual in virtue of a "twofold negation": a negation which denies of every being all difference with respect to itself, and a negation which denies of any being all identity with any other one.[45] As can be seen, Henry answers the problem of the cause of individuation by a description of its effects.

The lowest of all creatures is matter. Following the Augustinian tradition Henry refuses to reduce matter to pure potentiality. Since it can be created, matter has its own Idea in God. Consequently it has its own "being of essence," and since creation is the actualization of an essence by its cause, once it is created, matter has its own being of existence. This is so true that God could create it apart. The complete being of a compound of matter and form is therefore made up of the partial beings of essence and of the partial beings of existence which enter the composition of the whole.[46] From Duns Scotus on, many theologians will live in a universe similar to that of Henry of Ghent. Each distinct essence has its distinct existence:[47] such will be their common metaphysical world.

Man is a compound of matter and form; the form of man is his soul, but the intellective soul of man is not the immediate form of his body. In order to become the form of a body, the soul must first have a body to inform. This body itself has its own form which is the "form of corporeity." With many of his contemporaries, Henry feels willing to accept the oneness of the substantial form in all beings, except in man. His reason for making this restriction is that, since the intellective soul is directly created by God, its arrival in no way interferes with a purely natural form such as that of the embryo. Besides, there is no moment when the natural form exists without the supernatural one; God creates the intellective soul at the very instant when the material form of the body is about to inform it.[48]

Placed in a world of actualized essences, and itself a spiritual substance comparatively free from its body, the intellective soul needs to resort to sense knowledge in order to conceive intelligible objects, but its abstractive operation is simpler here than it is in other doctrines. Sensible species are necessary because there must be an intermediary between a material body and a spiritual soul, but since images themselves are already immaterial, no intermediary is necessary between them and the intellect. Consequently, Henry suppresses intelligible species. In the light of the agent intellect, the intelligible quiddity carried by the image appears as formally universal and is directly received in the possible intellect.[49] Backed, as it is in this doctrine, by an Augustinian "memory" which insures its contact with the Prime Cause of all intelligibility, the agent intellect described by Henry of Ghent is an Augustinian mind in Aristotelian garb.[50]

The same remark would apply to the doctrine of the radical spontaneity of the will developed by Henry. To him, the will is a self-moving power of the soul. The known object does not move the will in any way; it is but a *causa sine qua non:* without its presence, man would have nothing to will; but it is not the cause why we will.[51] This cause *sine qua non* was not wholly to satisfy Duns Scotus, but his own answer to the question will not be substantially different from that of Henry. Duns Scotus too, and on the same Augustinian grounds, will maintain the radical spontaneity of the will.

Henry of Ghent was a secular master in theology. There was behind him no religious Order to adopt his doctrine. No school rallied around his teaching. Nevertheless, Henry was read, attacked, defended, so much so that his Questions and his *Summa* were printed in the sixteenth, seventeenth and eighteenth centuries. In the sixteenth century, the Order of Servites found itself without an official Doctor to adopt; Henry of Ghent was not engaged; so they decided that he had been a Servite and adopted him. We certainly owe to this incident the ancient editions of his works which make it easier for us to read him.

The history of the kind of Augustinianism represented by Henry of Ghent has not yet been studied.[52] Moreover, there have been so many cross currents in the fourteenth century that a similarity between doctrines, or doctrinal attitudes, does not always betray an actual influence. The Franciscans could return to the pre-Scotist Augustinianism of Saint Bonaventure without consulting Henry of Ghent. About such men as Francis of Marchia, who might represent an interesting moment in our history, we know next to nothing. He seems to have influenced the English Franciscan John of Rodington[53] who maintained the Augustinian thesis that divine illumination is necessary for absolutely certain knowledge (*certitudinalis cognitio*). Like Henry of Ghent, Rodington asks if man can have any certain knowledge of any truth by purely natural means. After listing the arguments of the skeptics against the truth value of sense cognitions, he concludes that all senses are deceptive, but that our intellect is able to correct their errors. Yet, our intellect itself is liable to be mistaken. In fact, it is always possible for it to be deceived because it is always possible for God to make a thing appear to be another one. This does not mean that, by and large, natural cognitions cannot be probable or even evidently certain while we are keeping them in sight; but if we only know unshakable truth in the light of the divine Ideas, and if these divine Ideas only appear to a few men illuminated by God, there are few rational conclusions whose certitude is absolute. This is the reason why those who know such unshakable truths are rightly considered prophets rather than philosophers. All this is maintained by Rodington on the authority of Saint Augustine. Rodington is not a skeptic; he does not consider the arguments of the skeptics as ultimately valid; they would be valid, however, were it not for the fact that, in some cases, an unshakable cognition of truth is possible in the light of the divine illumination.[54] The practical conclusions of Rodington are interesting. It is a good thing to study, provided one does it well, that is to say, without trusting too much one's own intellect, in a right intention and without attributing too much to philosophers and to philosophy. Because they have philosophized without a Mediator, namely Christ, the philosophers have not attained truth (Augustine, Bonaventure). Let us beware of excessive curiosity, put our trust in God, and always remember that, "without a special illumination, no perfect work can be done, no object whatever can be perfectly known." [55]

Still more disillusioned about philosophy was the Augustine theologian, Hugolin Malabranca of Orvieto,[56] a contemporary of John of Ripa and the author of a still unpublished commentary on the *Sentences*. He considers philosophy a mixture of errors. Far from being a science, philosophy only makes use of false proofs, or, at the very best, of simply probable proofs. One of his more interesting remarks is that, too often, theologians are using philosophical proofs that are not adapted to their object. Even when Aristotle says "God is," his formula has not the same meaning as it has in the thought of a theologian, for the theologian understands "God" as signifying the Trinity, and "is" as signifying the infinite. The whole psychology of Aristotle rests on the hypothesis that the soul is primary matter; all that he says about the soul therefore becomes false simply through the falsity of that supposition. And what about his ethics? It is false for the most part, and where it is not false, it is without value, for Aristotle knew only the semblances of virtues and did not know the true rules of good. From which Hugolin draws this conclusion: "Ethics is superfluous to the faithful." The faithful have their faith, and that is all they need. It has been rightly pointed out[57] that this criticism of philosophers is directly connected with the Augustinian thesis of the divine illumination. Referring expressly to Saint Augustine, whom he makes talk in a strange language, Hugolin makes God the agent intellect which illumines and assists "formally" our intellect. This enables him to explain that, in spite of everything, philosophers have from time to time said things that were right. Doubtless they were able to take their inspiration from the Bible, but the best explanation is that they received a special illumination from God who revealed to them those truths. Note that Hugolin here follows Henry of Ghent, as he does, moreover, in what he says of the light proper to theologians (*lumen theologicum*). The work of the doctor from Ghent, whose stamp we shall find on the teaching of Fitz Ralph, was therefore perhaps never as completely abandoned in the fourteenth century as was commonly supposed.

2. JOHN DUNS SCOTUS AND HIS SCHOOL

John Duns, called Scotus from his country's name, was born in 1266 at Maxton, in the county of Roxborough (Scotland). Sent to the convent of Dumfries in 1277, he joined the Franciscan Order in 1281. John studied at Oxford shortly before 1290, was ordained a priest at Northampton March 17, 1291, and studied at Paris (1293-1296). After his return to Oxford he began to teach theology (1297-1301). His first teaching at Oxford is represented by the *Lectura Oxoniensis,* still unpublished, but whose final redaction by the master is known under the title of *Opus Oxoniense.* In 1302 the young master returned to Paris and, in order to pass his Parisian doctorate, he publicly "read" for the second time the same text. As a result of this teaching we have a second redaction of his Commentary, known by the title of *Reportata Parisiensa.* Banished from France in 1303, with many others who, like himself, had taken the part of the Holy See against Philip the Fair, Duns Scotus returned to Paris in 1304, there became doctor in theology in 1305, and was sent to Cologne in 1307, where he died November 8, 1308. In addition to his two Commentaries on Peter Lombard, we have from his pen a series of writings on logic, important *Questions on the Metaphysics, Quaestiones quodlibetales* and a treatise *De primo principio*. Even if the less important works were not taken into consideration, the immensity of the effort accomplished by a master dead at the age of forty-two would still be overwhelming.[57]

A. *Metaphysics and its object*

His premature end certainly deprived us of writings where we would find the complete expression of his thought, and whose absence is cruelly felt. On some important points we are sometimes reduced to knowing only his conclusions, without being able to say how he justified them. On the other hand, the general inspiration of his philosophy is clear, and we can assign to it, without risk of any very grave error, a definite place in the history of mediaeval philosophies. With Avicenna, and against Averroes, Duns Scotus considers that the object of theology is God, whereas the proper object of philosophy, or rather of the metaphysics crowning it, is being as being. Even our theology does not bear upon God as God, but upon God as knowable by the most perfect of the concepts we can form of his nature, namely, that of "infinite being." The metaphysician only deals with being *qua* being. Moreover, even being *qua* being partly escapes the intellect of the metaphysician. Strictly speaking, being as such is an absolute, without any determination which restrains it to a certain mode of determined being. Now it happens that man has to draw his knowledge from the sensible. The human intellect, therefore, knows about being only what it can abstract from sense data. We have no direct intuition of being, both material and immaterial, in its entire indetermination and generality. All our metaphysics is therefore an abstract science of being as being, constructed by an intellect attaining only one of its aspects, which is not even the highest.[58]

Such being the situation, the only way to find for metaphysics an object endowed with a sufficient unity is to posit a notion of being so abstract and indeterminate that it may apply indifferently, always in the same sense, to everything that is. That is why metaphysics cannot intend to attain that act of existing (*ipsum esse*) which, according to Saint Thomas, is the core of every being. Existents are, in the last analysis, irreducibly distinct from one another; they cannot provide metaphysics with an object truly one. In order to save the unity of its object, and consequently its own possibility, metaphysics must consider the notion of being at its ultimate degree of abstraction, where it becomes applicable in one and the same sense to all that is. This is what we mean when we say that being is "univocal" for the metaphysician.

The univocity of being imposes a certain method in the demonstration of the existence of God. Some deem it necessary to start from the existence of sensible things to infer from it the existence of their cause. Assuredly, if we start from physical bodies, we will finally succeed in proving the existence of their primary cause, but whether it be that of their movement or even of their existence, it will remain a physical cause. This is what happens in the philosophy of Aristotle, where the Prime Mover, primary cause of the universe, is itself included in it. In other words, if it is the function of physics to prove the existence of God, the God whose existence physics can demonstrate does not transcend the physical order; as a keytone is gripped in the arch, this God is gripped in nature, even if it holds together only through him. To attain a primary principle which causes the world in its very being, one cannot build upon *sensible being,* but on *being.*

The univocal notion of being as being is therefore the condition of the very possibility of a science transcendent to physics and the indispensable point of departure for metaphysics. It is an abstract notion, and the first one of all, since, as Avicenna says, being is what falls first in the intellect. It is therefore a universal notion, but the metaphysician does not envisage it from the point of view of its universal predicability. The nature and conditions of the predicability of our concepts are logical properties; their study does not concern metaphysics, but logic. On the other hand, since the metaphysician disregards the individuating conditions of sensible beings, he does not consider them as a physicist either. The kind of being considered by the metaphysician is neither a particular physical reality, nor a universal taken in its logical generality; it is the intelligible reality which the very *nature* of being as being is. Avicenna had clearly established that, of themselves, "natures" are neither universal nor singular. If the nature of a horse was singular in itself, there could only be one horse; if it were universal in itself, no individual horses could exist; consequently, as Duns Scotus likes to repeat with Avicenna, natures are just what they are. The same is true with regard to the nature of being: it is everything that being is, and nothing but that.[59]

Taken in its logical predicability with respect to all that is, being is the emptiest of forms; no matter how it is considered, no *real* knowledge can come from it. On the contrary, the being of the metaphysician is a reality; it is rich in possibilities, and being wrapped up in it is not to get into a deadlock. Being as being has properties, the first of which are its modes. The modes of a nature, or essence, are its possible intrinsic determinations. Let us take an example. Here is a luminous ray; it can be varied in color; the colors which diversify it add to its nature of luminous ray, which is only that of light itself; they are therefore extrinsic determinations for it, they are not modes of light as light. On the contrary, if we increase or diminish its intensity, a certain light will become more or less luminous without anything being added to its nature or subtracted from it: intensity is therefore a mode of light. There are likewise modes of being, that is, as the very name indicates, "manners of being," which are only being itself, diversely modified, but modified as being. The two primary modes of being are the finite and the infinite. This first division of being includes all the others. It is, in fact, anterior to the Aristotelian distinction of being into the ten categories, for every category is a determination, therefore a limitation, so that the being to which the categories apply enters by full right into the finite modality of being. For the metaphysician, to demonstrate the existence of God is to prove that the "infinite being" is, or exists. Limited by the very nature of its object, which is being, metaphysics could not claim to go any further, but it can go that far.[60]

B. *The existence of God*

To achieve this the metaphysician will proceed in two phases: he will prove first that a Primary exists in the order of being, then that this Primary is infinite. Note in passing that this way of defining the problem is sufficient evidence of Avicenna's influence, whose customary manner of designating God is to call him *Primus*. This doctrinal affinity will last as long as the problem will be to prove that there is a First in the order of being. Among the many modalities of being considered as being is the couple possible-necessary. Proving the existence of a primary being will therefore be done also in two stages: proving the necessity there is for thought to posit a first necessary being, then proving that this first necessary being is an existent.

Such demonstrations cannot be made *a priori*, that is to say, starting solely from the definition of God, as Saint Anselm wished. It might even be said that it is more impossible in Duns Scotus's doctrine than in any other, since the Scotist argumentation must bear solely upon the notion of being, not on the notion of God. These demonstrations will therefore be *a posteriori*, that is to say, going up from effects to their cause; but the effects from which they start will not be the contingent beings given in sensible experience. Not only would the proofs based on them not permit us to get out of physics; they would not even allow us to get out of the contingent. The necessity of the prime cause of contingent effects is but a hypothetical necessity, because it rests upon the actual existence of beings which might not exist. The solid base on which the proof will be built up must therefore be some modality of being considered as being, not the contingent existence of some existent.[61]

The first proof is based on these complementary properties of being, "causality" and "producibility," or aptitudes for producing and being produced. Let us start from the fact that some being is producible: how will it be produced? It can only be produced by nothing, by itself, or by another. It cannot be by nothing, for what is nothing causes nothing. It cannot be by itself, for nothing is cause of itself. It must therefore be by another. Suppose that it be by A; if A is absolutely first, we have our conclusion. If A is not first, it is a secondary cause, therefore it is caused by another. Let us suppose that this other cause is B: the reasoning will be the same for it as for A. Either, therefore, the reasoning will continue thus *ad infinitum,* which is absurd, since then nothing would be producible for lack of a primary cause, or it will stop at an absolutely primary cause, which is what had to be demonstrated.

The same argumentation makes it possible to prove that it is necessary to posit an ultimate final cause, which itself has no final cause, but is the final cause of all the rest. Thirdly, it can be proved by the same method that being itself requires a supreme degree of perfection and eminence. The next step consists in proving that what is First in one of these three orders coincides with what is First in the two others. The Prime Cause, the Ultimate End and the Prime Being must be posited as one and the same First. This is a necessary metaphysical conclusion. There still remains for us, however, to prove the actual existence of this Prime Being. A truly metaphysical demonstration must rest upon the very nature of the being at stake. In the present case, our intellect is grasping the nature of a primary cause; it is therefore positing a prime uncausable cause as being at least possible. Two hypotheses remain open to us concerning it: it exists or it does not exist. These two hypotheses are contradictory and of two contradictory propositions one must be false. Let us suppose, then, that this uncausable cause does not exist. Why should it not exist? Would it be in virtue of a cause of its non-existence? But the primary cause has no cause. Would it be that, possible in itself, it would be incompossible with another? But then neither this other nor itself would be possible: now it is possible by definition. In reality, if an uncaused primary cause is possible, it is possible by itself. In other words such a being is the only conceivable cause of its very possibility. Hence the conclusion of Duns Scotus: if a Prime Being is possible, it exists.

This is not a "physical" argument, but it is no "logical" argument either. It deals with intrinsic properties of the very nature of being *qua* being as conceived by the metaphysician. The possibility of that whose being is causable does not necessarily bring with it its actual existence, but that which excludes all cause, either extrinsic or intrinsic, with regard to its own being, cannot not exist: *excludendo omnem causam aliam a se, intrinsecam et extrinsecam, respectu sui esse, ex se est impossibile non esse.* As has been said, if primary being is possible, it exists. The conceptual character of these arguments should not hoodwink us concerning their nature. Duns Scotus knows that one can start from the empirical fact that there is movement produced and effects caused; he also knows that one can validly conclude from these factual data in favor of the existence of a prime cause; but that, to him, is not metaphysics. Starting from existences is starting from the real, certainly, but from what there is contingent in the real. As for me, says Duns Scotus, I prefer to propose premises and conclusions drawn from the possible; for, if one concedes those taken from act, one does not thereby concede those taken from the possible, while, if one grants those taken from the possible, those taken from act are granted at the same stroke. And the reason for this is simple; one can conclude from the necessary to the contingent, but not inversely; now, the proofs drawn from actual existence are conclusive enough, but they remain contingent, whereas the proofs drawn from possible beings give necessary demonstrations.

The infinity of this Primary, which exists, is still to be established. The same roads lead to this new conclusion. A primary and consequently uncaused cause is not limited by anything in its causality; it is therefore infinite. More, first in the order of perfection, this necessary being is intelligent; it is even the Primary Intelligent, therefore the supreme Intelligent, that knows all that can be known; there is therefore an infinity of intelligibles in the primary intelligence and consequently the intellect which embraces them all simultaneously is actually infinite. Finally the infinity of the First is proved to us by the natural inclination of our will toward a supreme good and of our intelligence toward a supreme truth. Our will would not incline toward an infinite good as toward its real object if the nature of this infinite good were contradictory and could not exist; the possibility of such an attraction in the will implies that its center of attraction is at least possible. It is the same with regard to intelligence. Not only, as a matter of fact, does the idea of an infinite being not seem to us contradictory, but it seems to be the very type of the intelligible. Now it would be extraordinary if no one were to perceive the least contradiction in this primary object of thought even though our ear immediately discovers the slightest dissonance in sounds. It is even because the idea of infinite being seems to us so perfectly intelligible that Saint Anselm's argument preserves some value; it would not be perfectly intelligible were it not first a really infinite being answering our intellection. It is therefore certain that the Prime Being whose existence we have affirmed in the conclusion is an infinite being.[62]

C. *Infinity and Contingency*

After proving its existence, metaphysics has said most of what it can say about the Infinite Being. To study its nature belongs to the theologian. Like Saint Thomas, Duns Scotus considers our philosophical knowledge of the divine attributes relative and frail, but he considers it to be better founded on reality than is generally supposed. This is a point to be kept in mind by those who compare Duns Scotus' thought with Descartes'. These two philosophers have in common an acute feeling for the importance of the infinity of God; but while Descartes concludes from it the negation of all distinction, even of reason between the divine attributes, Duns Scotus considers the distinction generally admitted between these attributes insufficient. The fact is, the tendency to bring out the transcendence of the creator with regard to the creature is balanced in the mind of Duns Scotus by another tendency to stress the entity of forms. All the divine attributes are one because, each of them sharing in the infinity of the divine being, they all are infinite. This is the pre-Cartesian aspect of the Scotist God, but there is in him another aspect which is as anti-Cartesian as possible. Duns Scotus maintains that there is in God at least a virtual foundation for the distinction that we posit between his different attributes, namely the "formal" perfection corresponding to the names by which we designate them. Since "natures" have an intelligible entity of their own, there is a formal distinction between the natures answering the various attributes of God, and this plurality of formal entities does not break up the absolute unity of Infinite Being.[63]

Having thus posited a necessary being as the first cause of all that is, Duns Scotus finds himself at the same starting point as Avicenna, but when it comes to explaining the relation of finite beings to the infinite being, he separates from the Arabian philosopher. For Avicenna, the possible emanated from the necessary by way of necessity; for Duns Scotus, whose doctrine in this case becomes a radical anti-Avicennism, the possible comes from the necessary by way of liberty. The God of Duns Scotus is a necessary being because he is infinite being. Now, between infinite being and finite beings, all ontological relations are radically contingent. In a doctrine which is based on univocal being and not upon analogical acts of being, a dividing line other than the act of being must be drawn between God and creatures. The role played in Thomism by the existential purity of the divine Act of Being, is played in Scotism by the divine will. The infinite essence of God is the necessary object of God's will. There is, in the God of Duns Scotus, no voluntarism with respect to God. There is no trace of voluntarism in him even with respect to the essences of creatable beings. Even in the moral domain God is in some way bound by the first two commandments of the Decalogue, which are the expression of the natural law and correspond to an absolute necessity. In Scotism, divine liberty is emphatically not the enlightened despotism of the Cartesian Lawgiver whose will freely promulgates even necessary and eternal truth. In Scotism, the will of God intervenes to bridge the ontological gap there is between the necessary existence of Infinite Being and the possible existence of finite beings. In the universe of Avicenna, because the First was necessary, all the rest enjoyed a conditional necessity; in the universe of Duns Scotus, because the First is infinite, all the rest is contingent. Between the necessary and the contingent the only conceivable link is a Will.

In a curious text wherein Duns Scotus describes a hypothetical generating of essences in God, we see that, at the first moment, God knows his own essence in itself and absolutely; in the second moment the divine intellect produces the stone conferring upon it an intelligible being, and God knows the stone (*in secundo instanti producit lapidem in esse intelligibili, et intelligit lapidem*); in the third instant, God is compared to this intelligible and a relation is thus established between them; in the fourth moment, God in some way reflects on that relation and knows it. It is therefore clearly a posteriority of finite essences in relation to the infinite essence of God which is here at stake. Since God's essence is the only necessary object of God's will, there is not one of these finite essences whose existence should be necessarily willed by God. God creates if he wills to do so, and only because he so wills. To ask the reason why God willed or did not will such and such a thing is to ask the reason for something for which there is no reason. The sole cause for which the necessary being willed contingent things is his will, and the sole cause for the choice he made is that his will is his will; there is no getting beyond that. The only conditions this liberty observes are to will essences such as they are, to choose only compossible essences among those that are to be produced, and to preserve unchangingly the laws which have once been decreed. With the exception of the principle of contradiction and of the intrinsic necessity of the intelligible forms taken in themselves, the will of God is therefore absolute master of the decision to create or not to create, as well as of the choice and combination of essences to be created. With respect to what is not God, the divine will is not necessarily ruled by the good; it is on the contrary the choice of the good that is subject to the will of God. If God wills a thing, that thing will be good; and if he had willed other moral laws than the ones he established, these other laws would have been just, because righteousness is within his very will, and no law is upright except insofar as it is accepted by the will of God. One could not go any further without ending in Cartesianism; but in order to go further, one should first reject the very essence of Scotism, which lies here in the formal distinction there is between the intellect of God and his will.[64]

D. *Species and individuals*

The duality of tendencies which leads Duns Scotus strictly to subordinate existences to God while accentuating the distinction he maintains between formal entities affects his conception of essences themselves. We have seen that, while maintaining the divine Ideas, Scotus stresses their ideal posteriority with regard to the thought of God.[65] In this sense Duns Scotus was less of a Platonist than Saint Thomas had been. But once the essences are posited in the divine intellect, Duns Scotus attributes more proper and distinct entity to forms than Saint Thomas had done. His realism of forms is first expressed in his famous theory of "formal distinction," which had always been present in the doctrine of the plurality of forms. Duns Scotus conceives this distinction as intermediary between a mere distinction of reason and a real distinction. It must not, however, be confused with the Thomist distinction of reason *cum fundamento in re*. The basis for the formal distinction of Scotus is the actual presence, in reality, of formally distinct entities. Since Scotus does not accept the real composition of essence and existence,[66] he can attribute several formal entities to any being without disrupting its actual unity. The "formalities" thus conceived are therefore both really distinct formal entities in the thing, and really one as sharing in the actual being of the whole subject whose parts they are. This, moreover, is in agreement with the way in which, in Scotism, the formation of concepts is explained. Scotist concepts answer this distinction between forms in the unity of concrete subjects. The universal, as we conceive it, clearly results from the abstraction our intellect works on things; but, Duns Scotus observes, if the universal were a pure product of the intellect without any foundation in things themselves, there would be no difference between metaphysics, which bears upon being, and logic, which deals with beings of reason. Better still, to the extent that it deals with concepts, all science would be simply logic: *omnis scientia esset logica*. It is to avoid this consequence that Duns Scotus considers essence as equally indifferent to the universal and to the individual, but as containing virtually both of them. The distinction introduced by Scotus between formal entities has therefore its foundation in things; the intrinsic indetermination of essence provides us with the very material out of which the agent intellect draws its universal concepts, but which the metaphysician rediscovers intact in the very structure of reality.[67]

It must therefore be admitted that the real is in itself neither pure universality nor pure individuality. The very fact that we can abstract general ideas from it shows that it is not pure individuality. If species had not already a certain unity, although inferior to the numerical unity of the individual, our concepts would not correspond to anything. Inversely, the same common nature of the species is still found in individuals, but, this time, determined by their principle of individuation. In accounting for the possibility of individuals, Duns Scotus still had to start from the "nature" or "common essence," neither universal nor particular, which the metaphysician considers. Solving this problem, therefore, inevitably consisted for him in adding an individuating determination to the essence. That determination could not be a form, for all form is common to the individuals of one species; it must therefore be added to form from within. In fact, says Duns Scotus, it is its ultimate actuality. The famous "hecceity" of the Scotists is the ultimate act which restricts the form of a species to the singularity of its individuals.[68]

E. *Intellect and Will*

Duns Scotus' desire to guarantee as completely as possible the originality of the individual is closely related to his conception of the pre-eminence of will and to his doctrine of liberty in man. For him as for Saint Thomas, it is certainly the will that wills and the intelligence that knows, but the fact that the will can command acts of understanding seems to him to decide in favor of the primacy of the will. No doubt we only will what we know, and in that sense the intellect is the cause of the will; but it is only its occasional cause. On the contrary, when the will commands the intellect, it is clearly the will that causes intellection, even though that act taken in itself is an act of the intellect. And if we consider an act of will taken in itself, it is certainly true that the knowledge of the object willed is anterior to the volition in time, but it is nevertheless the will which is the primary cause of the act. The cognition of the object by the intellect is but the accidental cause of our volition.

This affirmation of the primacy of nobility of the will over the intellect in man announces a more voluntarist than intellectualist conception of liberty and that is precisely what we find in Duns Scotus' doctrine. Just as he had insisted upon the radical indifference of the divine will with respect to the existence of created finite beings, so he endeavors to attribute solely to the human will the total causality of the voluntary. It is the will alone, Scotus says in a striking formula, which is the total cause of volition in the will: *nihil aliud a voluntate est causa totalis volitionis in voluntate*. It is true that we have to know an object to will it and that it is the good that we know to be in that object that makes us will it; but it is equally true that if we know that object rather than another, it is because we will to know it. Our cognitions determine us, but we first determine the choice of our cognitions. Even when the decision of the act seems irresistibly drawn by the knowledge we have of an object, it is first of all the will which has desired that knowledge, and, in the end, it is the will alone that bears the total responsibility for the decision.[69]

Thus Duns Scotus' thought, which at first glance may seem closely related to Saint Thomas', is on the contrary distinguished from it in more than one respect, and it is not empty subtleties or simple pettifogging words that separate the two doctors. Both theologies make use of the same stock of concepts borrowed from Aristotle's philosophy, but the edifices constructed with those common materials are very different in style.

They differ first, if not by the idea their authors have of philosophical demonstration, at least by the value they attribute to it. It is not in this case a question simply of sorting out what is accessible to reason and what must be reserved for revelation, but of what one has the right to call demonstration within the very domain reserved for reason. It is understood that the Trinity or other dogmas of this kind cannot be rationally demonstrated. But in what is ordinarily considered as demonstrable, there must also be a distinction between the demonstration taken as it is possible in itself and the demonstration taken as it is possible for us in the present state of our human condition. For some reason or other, our intellect which, by its very nature, should be capable of intellectual intuition, finds itself restricted to abstractive cognition. Even the whole range of being *qua* being is no longer accessible to it. Since the sole kind of being which it directly grasps is sensible being, the philosophers naturally mistook sensible being for being itself, with the consequence that they attributed to being itself characters which are proper to sensible being only. Hence, we find in the mind of Duns Scotus a general appreciation of the work of the "philosophers" which affects his own doctrinal positions. The science of sensible being naturally leads to a metaphysical doctrine of universal necessity, whereas the consideration of being *qua* pure being leads to a metaphysics of the radical contingency of finite being. Theologians have, for the same reason, been liberated by theology from the limited outlook which was naturally that of the philosophers. The liberation of metaphysics is achieved in Scotism by the new task imparted to it by the theologian: to demonstrate by philosophical reasons the existence of the Infinite Being.

The philosophical consequences of this new situation were manifold. After Scotus, a new importance is attributed to the notion of infinite. In theology, there appears a marked tendency to withdraw from the competency of the metaphysician all the problems whose ultimate answer hangs on the infinity of the divine being. Philosophers can know that there is an infinite being, but concerning the essence of God precisely *qua* infinite, only the theologians have something to say and this only to the extent that revelation provides a starting point for their speculation. Because he considers finite beings in the light of Infinite Being, the theologian knows that God is absolutely omnipotent; that he is free to create or not, and to act through secondary causes or not; that he is omnipresent to all creatures and free to set up any moral code he pleases so long as it deals with rules of human conduct whose relations to his own essence are not necessary ones. Nothing of what depends on the free decisions of this absolutely free God is philosophically deducible. The very condition of some natural beings falls under this rule. What does not belong to them strictly in virtue of their essences cannot be deduced from their nature; consequently, it is no object of philosophical demonstration. The immortality of the human soul is a point in case. Philosophical reasons may show it to be probable, and even more probable than its contrary, but they cannot demonstrate it as a necessary conclusion.[70]

F. *Early Scotism*

Even if we did not know its dates, we could guess that the doctrine of Duns Scotus was conceived after the condemnation of 1277. One should not imagine Scotus writing with the text of the condemned propositions at hand and calculating his doctrine in view of avoiding them. Only, as has been said, the honeymoon of theology and philosophy had then come to an end. Too many philosophers had stressed their incompatibility on some crucial points; too many theologians had expressed their doubts as to the exact meaning of the conclusions held by Aristotle, Avicenna and Averroes, not to create a general impression of uncertainty as to the nature and limits of the services which theology could expect from philosophy. Hence, after 1277, the strengthening of the tendency, which had been there long before that date, to rely upon revelation and faith more than upon philosophical reasoning in order to ascertain the truth of theological conclusions. From now on, there will not be less philosophy in theology than there had been before. On the contrary, there are few theological problems which the theologians of the fourteenth century did not handle in a dialectical way, but, precisely, an always larger number of their conclusions became purely dialectical and their theology learned to content itself, in matters of rational justification, with mere probability.[71] Whether or not the famous *Theorems* are an authentic work of Duns Scotus is a problem for literary history to decide.[72] Whatever its decision, these *Theorems* exist and they bear witness to the state of mind we are attempting to describe.

An almost complete divorce between the supernatural theology of the theologians and the natural theology of the philosophers is brought about in the *Theoremata* on the strength of philosophical principles similar to Duns Scotus' and exactly the opposite of those which are to motivate the same divorce in William of Ockham. Far from being an Ockhamist, the author of these *Theorems* was a partisan of the Avicennian doctrine of the "common nature" and of the univocity of being in the Scotist sense of the term. *Theorema IV* affirms in principle that to every universal there corresponds a certain degree of real entity, shared in common by all that is contained under this universal.

The only God whose existence the author of the *Theorems* can prove by strict philosophical reasoning is the Prime Cause of a physical universe, operating through secondary causes which, like itself, obey the laws of a purely intelligible necessity. It is a far cry from that impersonal being to the living God of Scripture (*non potest probari Deum esse vivum*). Neither can one prove that he is unique, nor consequently that the universe depends on a single cause, nor even that after having produced the universe, that same cause still continues to exist. If that is so, it cannot be proved that God is present everywhere by his essence, or that God is all-powerful, at least in the absolute sense that he can immediately and by himself alone cause what he causes through the agency of secondary causes. In short, the philosophers who examined these problems with the help of reason alone were never able to rise to the Christian notion of a free God. They stopped at a necessary primary cause, necessarily and eternally producing a primary and unique effect, which effect in turn necessarily produced several others, in virtue of the mixture of necessity and possibility included in each of them. From the primary being to our sublunary world, everything is interlinked by a series of necessary causal relations, which do not entail the presence of the Primary in the distant consequences of his act, but on the contrary, exclude the possibility of his intervening by a free and immediate act, as the Christian God can always do. There was, therefore, about the time of Duns Scotus, a criticism of natural theology wholly independent from the principles of William of Ockham. And no wonder. If the conclusions of philosophy were identical with those of Aristotle, how could philosophy prove the existence and nature of the Christian God?

However, it was not in the direction of this criticism of natural theology that Scotism was later to evolve. The disciples of the Subtle Doctor applied themselves to the task of completing the master's theological synthesis and to defending it against its opponents. For some of them, like Antonius Andreas (d. 1320), whose writings are still mingled with those of Scotus himself, it is difficult to determine their personal contribution.[73] Literary history has not yet done its work on this point. For others, such as the Provençal Franciscan Francis of Meyronnes (d. after 1328), their originality is already more easily discernible.[74] Among his numerous writings should be mentioned the commentaries on Porphyry's *Isagoge,* on the *Categories,* on Aristotle's *Perihermenias* and *Physics;* a *Commentary on the Sentences, Quodlibeta* and a series of treatises, almost all of them important for the study of his philosophical thought: *On the Univocity of Being, On Transcendentals,* etc. Francis of Meyronnes knew Duns Scotus personally, and was his student during the master's sojourn in Paris from 1304 to 1307; he undoubtedly remained his disciple, but a disciple who himself took on the aspect of a master. A celebrated Scotist of the fifteenth century, William of Vaurouillon (d. 1464), after having recalled, in the oratorical style of the time, the famous "triad of Doctors": Thomas Aquinas, Bonaventure, Duns Scotus, immediately adds a second: Francis of Meyronnes, Henry of Ghent and Giles of Rome. In this same text William of Vaurouillon criticizes Francis for his peculiar habit of always dividing and arguing on four points, even when three were enough. Three good points, William says, are better than four bad ones.

Faithful to the univocity of being and to the formal distinction, those two bastions of Scotism, Francis interpreted in his own way the theory of the "intrinsic modes of being," which occupies so central a place in Scotus' theology. In full agreement with his master's ontology, Francis identifies being with entity (*essentia*) to which he attributes an extensive series of intrinsic modes. The essence of God is first posited as entity (*essentia*); in the second moment, it is posited as "this particular entity"; in the third moment, as this here "infinite entity"; in the fourth moment, as the actually existing infinite entity. Existence, therefore, in God as in all the rest, is nothing other than an intrinsic mode of essence. Taken literally, this position entails the curious consequence, that the essence of God, taken purely as essence, does not immediately include existence. This does not mean that God is not by his own essence (*ens per se*) but that his existence is a modality of his essence, not that very essence taken as such. That was going astray from Duns Scotus along an authentically Scotist road. On the other hand, Francis of Meyronnes abandoned his master on two important points. He absolutely refused to admit that divine Ideas were not formally identical and absolutely co-eternal with God. Francis expressly went back to Saint Augustine on this point, and William of Vaurouillon, as a good upholder of Scotist orthodoxy, was to reproach him sharply for this infidelity to Duns Scotus. This first point was, moreover, linked in his mind to a second one. Francis of Meyronnes refused to make of the Idea a simple "secondary object" of divine knowledge, because he himself attributed more reality to it than that of a simple object of cognition (*ens cognitum*). As he conceived it, the divine Idea seemed to possess a "being of essence" analogous to the one Duns Scotus had criticized in Henry of Ghent.

One sentence from Francis of Meyronnes, to which P. Duhem has drawn attention, shows what evolution was then taking place in the general conception of the universe. It is found in his *Commentary on the Sentences*, lib. II, dist. 14, q. 5: "A certain Doctor says that, if the earth were in movement and the heavens at rest, that arrangement would be better. But this is disputed because the diverse movements of the celestial bodies could not be accounted for." The movement of the earth was therefore already no longer considered by everyone to be an absurdity, but obviously Francis of Meyronnes remained faithful to the old doctrine, and it is a pity he did not name the unknown Doctor.

The essential features of Scotism are found in another member of a group of Franciscans whose work dates from the fourteenth century. In his *Commentary on the Sentences*, John of Bassoles (d. 1347) upholds the reality of genera and species, in the sense Duns Scotus meant it,[75] that is to say, not as universals (for universality, or predicability as such, is the work of the intellect), but as distinct realities constitutive of essences (*Genus et differentia dicunt distinctas realitates in eadem essentia ejus quod est per se in genere*). Animality and rationality signify two different "things." Such formulas imply that Bassoles maintained a formal distinction between the metaphysical constituents of beings. In natural theology, John of Bassoles follows on certain problems a line of thought curiously similar to that of the *Theorems*. This is particularly true with respect to the existence of God. The reasons for positing an absolutely primary being are "highly probable and more so than any reasons that can be quoted to the contrary," but they are not perfect demonstrations, for one can deny with likelihood that a progress of causes to infinity is impossible. There have been, therefore, about 1330, disciples of Scotus who admitted the thesis of the *Theorems*. The unicity of God, his absolute omnipotence, his ubiquity, his intimate presence in all things are, for Bassoles, so many objects about which faith alone assures us with certainty.

Similar positions are found in the *Commentary on the Sentences* by Landolph Caracciolo (d. 1351), and in the one by his follower Hugh of Castro Novo, whose date has been fixed as before 1317. About the same time (in 1320), Francis of Marchia (Fr. of Pignano, or of Esculo) annotated Peter Lombard's text in Paris, and taught that it is impossible strictly to demonstrate the immortality of the soul, either *a priori* or *a posteriori*. On this point, however, he was simply approving a well known conclusion of Duns Scotus.

Among the original minds standing out in that group, was the Franciscan William of Alnwick (d. 1332), whose remarkable *Questions on Intelligible Being* have been published.[76] It would be difficult to quote a more perfect specimen of dialectical discussion. At the end of the work, the question is literally exhausted. It is true that the reader is also. But at least he knows what to adhere to, and if he remains insensible to the technical perfection of such an intellectual style, one can only feel sorry for him. The problem discussed by Alnwick is that of the degree of reality one should attribute to the being of the object known, precisely insofar as it only is an object known in the mind. His conclusion is that, although Duns Scotus attributed a sort of relative being to the object of cognition (*esse cognitum*), no precise meaning can be found for that thesis. The fact of "being known" does not imply, in the being that is known, any reality more distinct from it than the fact of representing Caesar implies in the statue of Caesar. On the side of the intellect, the being of a stone, considered as known by it, is none other than the being of the intellect that knows it. Applied to the problem of divine Ideas, this conclusion leads William of Alnwick to deny that they have, in the divine understanding, a relative intelligible being (*esse secundum quid*) which would be, if not created, at least produced. This liberty of judgment justifies the title of "independent Scotist" its editor gives him. There is little doubt that when their writings are better known, some other Scotists will deserve the same qualification.[77]

Another name, legitimately connected with Scotism and whose importance is ever increasing, is the name of the Franciscan John of Ripa, so called after the monastery of Ripatransone.[78] We are indebted to him for a *Commentary on the Sentences* and for *Determinations* (1354) written in a very personal philosophical and theological style. His name is mentioned, as that of a master whose positions are worthy of discussion, in Peter of Ailly (1350-1420), John Gerson (1363-1429) and John of Basel (before 1365). The only parts of his work that have as yet been studied bear upon the theological problem of the divine knowledge of future contingents, but it is known, through recent research, that Gerson attributed to him four of the twelve propositions condemned in 1362 under the name of Louis of Padua. According to this testimony, John of Ripa taught that the divine Ideas are distinct, not only by a distinction of reason, as Henry of Ghent granted, but by a stronger distinction, so that the one would not be the other, and that *ex parte rei*. The four propositions condemned in 1362 for which Gerson makes John of Ripa responsible are the following: Something is God according to his real being, that is not God according to his formal being; That something intrinsic to God is contingent; That the volition by which God wills *a* to be, is no less distinct from the volition by which God wills *b* to be, than he is really distinct from prime matter; That every volition by which God wills *a* to be is immensely distinct, formally speaking, from the will by which he wills *b* to be. If they do not sum up a doctrine, these four points at least attest a perceptible influence of Duns Scotus, whose formal distinctions have given rise to endless controversies between Thomists and Scotists. John Gerson includes Ripa among the *formalizantes,* and, indeed, the four propositions at stake seem to rest upon Scotist "formalities"; distinction between what God is according to his real being and what he is (i.e., his divinity) according to his formal being; formal subsistence in God of future contingents as such; formal distinction of divine volitions; distinction *ex parte rei* between God and his Ideas. In what measure the personal thought of John of Ripa was inspired by Duns Scotus', developed it, or deformed it, are questions to which no answers are possible until the *Commentary* and the *Determinations* are published.

One of the first and main witnesses of John of Ripa's authority is Peter of Candia (d. 1410), a Franciscan of Cretan origin,[79] who once took advantage of it to come to the defence of his compatriot Plato (*cum Plato fuisset Graecorum peritissimus, et ego qui sum suae regioni vicinus, jure patriae debeo pro compatriota pugnare*). It was an occasion for him to state that, according to Plato, the Ideas are forms existing outside of things, in the divine thought, where they share in its identity, even though they completely retain there their irreducibly distinct formalities (*habentes identicum concursum, suas tamen formalitates indelebiles penitus retinentes*). True enough, Peter adds, Aristotle was also a Greek, and he said the contrary; but, since it comes to choosing between two friends, let the truth prevail! Moreover, Peter concludes, if I wished to defend all my compatriots, I should often have to contradict myself, for quarrels are frequent between neighbors.

Such is the customary tone of this pleasant Greek: easy, witty and of a courteous irony in discussion. A bachelor in theology at the University of Oxford, master in theology at the University of Paris (1378-1381), successively bishop of Piacenza and Vicenza, then archbishop of Milan, he was finally elected pope June 26, 1409, and took the name of Alexander V. Such careers seldom go without some diplomacy, and we have just seen that Peter of Candia was not lacking in it, even as a theologian. His *Commentary*, in which proper names abound, shows him arbitrating on each question the differences that brought to grips Ockham and his disciples, Duns Scotus and his partisans, without forgetting John of Ripa, whose doctrine on future contingents he describes as restating that of Scotus in greater detail. We have seen him make of Plato a *formalizans* in spite of himself, and the way he conceives the distinction of Ideas in God would bring him close to the Scotist school. But did Peter of Candia ever belong to any school? That would be admitting that he took philosophy more seriously than he himself says he did. Faced with the conflict then raging between Scotism and Ockhamism, Peter sees clearly just how the doctrines of these two masters differ from each other, and even sometimes from those of their followers. Speaking of the Avicennian doctrine of the "common nature" (*equinitas est tantum equinitas*), he observes with great perspicacity that the opposition between Ockham and Scotus on this fundamental point is especially in their methods (*in modo investigandi*), Ockham proceeding as a logician and Duns Scotus as a metaphysician (*unus namque procedit logice et alius metaphysice*). This adaptability of mind is not of a doctrinarian. But even if subsequent research ever discovers in Peter anything in any way resembling a system, there is at least one point where his thought would refuse to be unified. Duns Scotus had taught that the ultimate differences of being are contained in it only virtually and denominatively, which Peter of Candia in turn upholds at the beginning of his *Commentary;* but, in the course of this same *Commentary*, he next maintains that the ultimate differences of being are formally and essentially contained in it; upon which he himself draws attention to the fact that he is contradicting himself and knows it: "If I here maintain the contrary, it is not because I consider one position to be truer than the other, but in order to illustrate several ways of conceiving the problem, for the convenience of those who desire to eat sometimes bread and sometimes cheese." Yet, the whole meaning of the Scotist univocity of being was there at stake, with the metaphysics and theology it justifies. This pope should perhaps remain in the history of ideas as one of the first witnesses of a speculative lassitude, signs of which were beginning to multiply toward the end of the fourteenth century.

CHAPTER III

DISINTEGRATION OF SCHOLASTIC THEOLOGY

"SCHOLASTICISM begins to get interesting after Thomas Aquinas." Quoting this remark of Hans Meyer, P. Bayerschmidt adds that, "by his inspired conception of philosophy and theology, Thomas Aquinas put to his time questions which touched the spirit of the West like a magic wand and stimulated it to push research to the utmost." This is perfectly true, only it does not mean that, in making his contemporaries and successors think in a deeper metaphysical way, Thomas Aquinas succeeded in winning them over to his own doctrinal positions.

In a letter of May 20, 1346, to the masters and students of the University of Paris, Pope Clement VI blamed some of them for "disregarding and despising the time-honored writings of the Philosopher as well as of the other ancient masters and commentators whose text they should follow so far as it does not contradict the Catholic faith." The atmosphere was then very different from that of the early thirteenth century. The philosophical authority of Aristotle was so firmly established about 1350 that even the popes made it a duty for the Parisian masters to follow his doctrine. The importance of this peculiar Aristotle was, historically speaking, not only considerable but, in a sense, decisive. Augustinianism, Averroism, Scotism, Ockhamism have opposed Thomism from without, but ever since 1270, this "Aristotle not contrary to faith" had begun to oppose Thomas Aquinas within the so-called Thomistic school itself. In the fourteenth century, after a short period of hesitation, all the Dominicans became Thomists in virtue of the fact that they were Dominicans, but some of them were also good Aristotelians and their effort to keep faith with this double allegiance resulted in the birth of an Aristotle that was neither Averroes, nor Thomas Aquinas, nor even Aristotle himself, but, precisely, an "Aristotle not contrary to faith." This attempt to purify Thomism from Thomas Aquinas by replacing the metaphysics of the Angelic Doctor with that of a moderate Aristotelianism was headed for a brilliant future; its triumph will last as long as that of Cajetan. In the fourteenth century, it brought about the disintegration of Thomism in the Dominican school and the disintegration of Scotism in the Franciscan school. In short, it caused the disintegration of the thirteenth-century scholastic theology.

This hesitation is noticeable, at the beginning of the fourteenth century, even among certain Dominicans that the discipline of the Order should have rallied to the fundamental positions of Saint Thomas. Of this number was James of Metz, who twice glossed the *Sentences*, between 1295 and 1302, and whose Commentary still exists in two drafts.[79] In neither one does he make up his mind to take sides on the distinction of essence and existence. James of Metz knows Giles of Rome's arguments, but they are not enough to decide him. On the other hand, he solves the problem of individuation against Saint Thomas. It is form which gives matter its unity; then how could matter individuate form? There is individuality only where there is substance; individuality, therefore, presupposes substantiality, and as it is form that constitutes substance, it is also form that constitutes individuality. Consequently, two angels are two distinct individuals, and not two species, even though they are free of all matter. For the same reason, souls separated from their bodies preserve their individuality. Concerning intellectual knowledge, James of Metz admits the necessity of species for the knowledge of material objects, but not for the knowledge of God and immaterial beings. He does not claim to be the inventor of this expedient, but adopts it and even felicitates those who found it, thus to satisfy the exigences of both Aristotle and Augustine: *Et sic salvant multa, scilicet recursum ad phantasmata et dicta doctorum.* Where the intervention of sensible species is necessary, the agent intellect must confer on the material impression resulting from it (*phantasma*) a spiritual virtue which permits it to act upon the intellect. The agent intellect and the phantasm then act in concert on the possible intellect. The act of knowing thus produced constitutes the mental word (*verbum mentis*). The mental word in this case is not, therefore, as it is in Saint Thomas, an effect of the act of knowing, but that act itself. The infidelities of James of Metz to the Thomist doctrine were too serious (they were even more so in theology) not to draw down reproach upon him. The Dominican Harvey Nédellec (*Herveus Natalis*) composed, between 1302 and 1307, a *Correctorium fratris Jacobi Metensis* which is of equal interest in determining the exact thought of James of Metz and of Harvey himself, which is not always Saint Thomas' thought. The scholar to whom we are indebted for about all we now know of James of Metz has therefore good reason for saying of this doctor: "He was not a Thomist and did not wish to be one." Neither was he an anti-Thomist, but rather a man whose thought originated in another source than Thomism—Henry of Ghent on at least one point—but especially, the same historian assures us, Peter of Auvergne. If this is true, we are witnessing an important historical filiation: Peter of Auvergne, James of Metz, Durand of Saint-Pourçain.[80]

I. DURAND OF SAINT-POURÇAIN

This latter Dominican master, whose *Commentary on the Sentences* caused him so much difficulty within his Order, was nonetheless a considerable ecclesiastical personage. Charged by Pope John XXII with a diplomatic mission, he was rewarded for it by being given the bishopric of Limoux (1317), a truly singular title, since no one had borne it before him, and no one was to bear it after him. He soon abandoned it, moreover, for that of Bishop of Le Puy (1318), then of Meaux (1326), and died in 1334. Durand's only wrong in the eyes of his Order seems to have consisted in not being a Thomist, and to have shown this, at a time when Saint Thomas was already the Order's official Doctor. Of the three successive drafts of his *Commentary on the Sentences,* the first is the one in which his thought is most clearly shown and which earned him a first warning from the Order; he then wrote a second draft of his work, expurgated of doubtful propositions, but the first one continued to circulate, and a commission presided over by Harvey Nédellec censured 91 articles taken from that work (1314). Durand defended himself in his *Excusationes,* but Harvey answered with the *Reprobationes excusationum Durandi,* and still pursued him with tenacity by attacking a *Quodlibet* disputed by Durand at Avignon during Advent in 1314. As none of his retractions appeared to be sufficient, the general Chapter of the Order held at Montpellier (1316) asked that someone remedy his errors; whereupon Peter of la Palu and John of Naples drew up a list of 235 articles upon which Durand deviated from Saint Thomas, but Durand came back partly, in the third draft of his *Commentary* (1317-1327), to his first positions, which he had probably never repudiated in his heart. After having been the object of so much censure, he had the consolation of belonging later (1326), as Bishop of Meaux, to the commission which censured 51 articles taken from William of Ockham's *Commentary on the Sentences,* but he was again to be censured himself, in 1333, and that time by a pontifical commission, for his treatise *De visione Dei,* on the view of God the holy souls have before the general judgment. He was, moreover, an independent spirit, watchful of his philosophical liberty. He believed that in everything that was not an article of faith, one should rely upon reason rather than on the authority of any doctor, no matter how famous and revered he might be; one should attach little importance to human authority when it contradicts the evidence of reason (*et parvipendatur omnis humana auctoritas, quando per rationem elucescit contraria veritas*). With such a principle, and when one is not spontaneously in harmony with the official doctor of his Order, one's death is not regretted by everyone. Hence the gracious epitaph which, so they say, was proposed for the tomb of the Bishop of Meaux: "Here lies the hard Durand beneath the hard tombstone, Whether he is saved or not, I don't know, nor do I care:

> Durus Durandus jacet hic sub marmore duro,
> An sit salvandus ego nescio, nec quoque curo.

One of the philosophical problems on which it can always be hoped that a theologian has expressed himself, is the problem of the nature of relation and of its connection with relative being.[81] The theological problem of the relation between divine beings at the heart of the Trinity made a study of it imperative. Henry of Ghent had solved the problem, after some hesitation, by his theory of the three modes of being. Being, real or possible, can be only, either in itself (substance), or in another (accident), or connected with another (relation); that is to say, *in se sistendo, in alio inhaerendo, ad aliud inclinando,* and this is why the being of relation is reduced for Henry to the being either of substance or of accident. A relation, therefore, is always for him, in what real being it has, a substance or an accident taken in their tendency toward another being. The only real accidents being quantity and quality, relation, in Henry of Ghent, comprises substance, quality or quantity taken in their various tendencies toward something else. This is how Aristotle's ten categories are justified in his opinion: substance; quality and quantity (accidents); then relation, which subdivides itself into six categories (action, passion, place, time, situation, manner of being). This fundamental distinction of the three modes of being, and consequently of the categories, is found again in James of Metz, who concludes from it, as does Henry of Ghent, that relation has no real being other than that of the relative. The same doctrine is finally found in Durand of Saint-Pourçain. Starting from the distinction of the three *modi essendi,* and establishing that their distinction is real, and not at all a distinction simply of reason, but that these modes are nevertheless not things, he concludes that relation is a mode of being distinct from its ground, but does not make a composition with it like one thing with another thing. There is therefore a real distinction between the subject and its relation, even though the relation is only the subject itself in its internal exigence for a connection with others. Most relations are only in thought (resemblance and difference, equality and inequality, etc.); only one is real, that is to say, consists in the real demand for another being; it is, causality.[82]

The notion of man, as Durand describes it in the last redaction of his commentary, does not differ widely from that of Thomas Aquinas, although he conceived it in such a way that some important divergences were bound to follow in the field of noetic. According to Durand, the relation of the intellective soul to the body only necessitates its recourse to sense knowledge because of its present union with the body.[83] On this point, he may have undergone the influence of Duns Scotus.

The striking differences between Durand and Thomas appear in noetic. Since it is the form of its body, the soul needs to resort to the sensible which is its proportionate object; that is why the soul does not know itself by its essence. Thus far, Durand agrees with Thomas, but he conceives the operations of the soul otherwise than the official Doctor of the Dominican Order. According to Durand, sense perception and intellection are not something real added to the sensitive or to the intellective powers of the soul and making a real composition with them; moreover, the efficient cause of these acts is not their objects, but, rather, it is the creating or generating cause of the sensitive power and of the intellective power. The object of a sensation or of an intellection is but a cause *sine qua non.* This general position, with its touch of occasionalism, betrays an Augustinian influence, but the noetic of Durand is not exactly that of Augustine. His reasons are drawn from his interpretation of Aristotle, of which it can be said that it follows a certain pattern common enough in his own time, although it is not easy to put a label upon it.

Whatever his motives, Durand had reached, in the first edition of his commentary, a definite position on this point. He was opposing the doctrine which identified intellection with the passive reception of an intelligible form by the possible intellect. To him, intellection did not consist in "having a form" but in exercising an act. Those who imagined that an added form is required for the perfection of the intellect were mistaken. The intellect, Durand said, is not more perfect while it understands than it was before. Since, in understanding, the intellect acts according to its nature, to understand adds nothing to its nature. There can be no real composition between the primary act of a form (its nature) and its secondary act (its operation).[84]

The noetic of Durand is inseparable from his notion of being. Like that of the "Thomist" John of Naples, it marks a decisive step on the road to an interpretation of Aristotle, certainly tenable, but which was to develop in Ockham unexpected consequences. All Aristotelians agree that actual being is singular and that universals are the work of the intellect, but, in the thirteenth century, most of them had considered the form as a sort of universal found in the thing (*universale in re*) which provided the universals found in the mind with a foundation in reality. According to Durand, on the contrary, all that which exists is singular by itself and the principle of individuation lies in the very nature of the thing. Since it exists, a thing is an individual, because, since they exist, both its form and its matter are individual. Now, if everything that exists outside of the intellect is individual, there is nothing universal in reality. This elimination of the *universale in re* recalls the doctrine of Abélard. Durand considers the genus, or the species, as indeterminate expressions of the individual, which is determinate. The universal does not pre-exist to intellection; it results from a mere consideration of the intellect leaving out the individuating conditions of the thing. Needless to add that in such a doctrine the first known object is not the universal, it is the singular. And this too is something which Aristotle had said: either the universal is nothing, or it comes after the thing.[85]

What Durand calls abstraction is not the metaphysical operation described by Thomas Aquinas; rather, it is a psychological operation of which we are conscious, at least in many cases, and by which, in all cases, we substitute an indeterminate representation of the thing for its determinate presentation by sense perception. Only two conditions are required for sensations as well as for intellections: a sense power or an intellect on the one side, a sensible or an intelligible object on the other side. These powers and these objects are what they are by reason of their Cause, and nothing more is required. Impressed species are a superfluous hypothesis; even if they existed, they could cause no cognition. As has been said, even the object itself is not the cause of cognition; it is a cause *sine qua non,* not an efficient cause. Likewise, no agent intellect is required; since there is nothing universal in things, we need no intellect to abstract it: one cannot abstract what does not exist. All that is needed to account for the possibility of intellectual knowledge is a possible intellect, singulars given in sense perception and their proper consideration by the possible intellect. By leaving out what distinguishes one individual from another, this intellect forms a universal.[86]

The stormy doctrinal career of Durand was mainly troubled by Dominican tempests. The principal list of errors for which he was blamed were "Thomistic errors," that is to say, errors against the doctrine of Thomas Aquinas. A Dominican had no right to commit them at that date.[87] What is surprising is that his judges only found 235 points on which Durand had deviated from Thomistic orthodoxy.[88] In fact, Durand was not born to be a Thomist because his mind inhabited another intellectual country, which it is not easy to describe and still less to classify. Moreover, in interpreting him in the light of the consequences deduced by Ockham from similar principles, we probably attribute to Durand intentions foreign to his mind. Durand agreed with John of Naples on the crucial point that universality is exclusively in the mind; yet, John of Naples was one of his fiercest adversaries.[89] Durand agreed on the same point with Ockham; yet, at the time when he was a bishop of Meaux, Durand was one of the judges who condemned a list of fifty-one articles extracted from the works of Ockham.[90] Historical events seldom obey the strict laws of dialectical necessity.

2. PETER AURIOL

Peter Auriol (*Petrus Aureoli*) born near Gourdon (France), a Franciscan master in theology at the University of Paris, Archbishop of Aix-en-Provence in 1321, died in 1322, is a witness to the resistance opposed by Aristotelianism to classical scholastic theology.[91] The author of a *Tractatus de principiis* and of a *Commentary on the Sentences,* he attacked particularly Saint Bonaventure, Saint Thomas and Duns Scotus, thus giving evidence of the same indifference that Roger Bacon showed to Order and party spirit in matters of doctrine. His criticism, like Durand of Saint-Pourçain's, was the natural attitude of a constructive mind using opposition to find out its own positions. The Franciscan, James of Ascoli (*de Esculo*), has been quoted as one of the sources of Auriol's noetic, but we are studying a time when it is not easy to distinguish between influences and spontaneous agreements.[92]

Following classical Aristotelianism, and in opposition to Duns Scotus, the Franciscan Auriol refuses matter any actuality. God himself could not create matter apart from any form. Inversely, and the point is an important one, Auriol believes that form can neither exist nor be conceived apart from matter. It is of its essence to be the act of a matter, there can therefore be no form where there is no matter to inform. That, he assures us, is the doctrine of Aristotle and Averroes, and he intends to adhere to it. This principle makes it extremely difficult for him to solve the problem of the union of the soul and the body without dangerously clashing with Christian dogma. On the one hand, the council of Vienne had just decreed (1311-1312) that the substance of the rational or intellective soul is truly and in itself form of the human body; on the other hand, for Peter Auriol, all form is inseparable from its matter. Crediting the council of Vienne with his own conception of form, he concludes from this that one is forced to believe in virtue of this "new decretal" that the soul is the form of the body "in the same manner as other forms or other souls." Taken literally, and understood in this sense, this formula would make inconceivable not only the immortality of the soul, which is in fact not evident, but even the simple fact of intellectual knowledge, that everybody can verify.

To get out of this difficulty, Auriol observes first that the Fathers of the Church are of a different opinion from the council; many of them seem to say expressly that the soul is a substance distinct from the body as one nature is distinct from another nature. The recent decision of the council must be accepted; but if the council obliges us to believe that "the soul is form of the body in the same way as other forms," it does not oblige us either to understand it, or to believe it can be understood. After all, why should a council define a philosophical verity accessible to reason alone? One is bound to believe the dogma of the Trinity, not to be able to understand it. Let us say then, since the council will have it so, "that the soul is the pure actuation and formation of the body, in the same way that other forms are, and that, just as one need not try to find out why a unity results from wax and its figure, so there is no need to seek the cause of the unity of the soul and the body, and that therefore the soul is a pure act and perfection of matter as the figure is of the wax." It must be believed, but it cannot be proved.[93]

If that is so, there is a second thesis which should be believed without being understood—the immortality of the soul. The strangest thing is that, this time, it is the decision of the council of Vienna that makes it most difficult to admit that it can be proved. If the soul is form of the body, it is born and perishes with it. Assuredly, since God can miraculously preserve accidents separate from their substance, he can preserve the soul without the body. But it is a miracle, and, although one can advance reasons for its being credible, one could not prove it.[94]

The situation is much more awkward with respect to intellectual knowledge, for this is an observable fact, therefore it is possible; and yet it should not be so, at least if one agrees that the soul is form of the body. All form which is the act of a matter is incapable of thinking. Here there is no other resource than saying under what conditions intellectual knowledge is philosophically possible, without affirming that it is so in reality. Two facts, then, dominate the discussion of the problem. In order for intellectual knowledge to be possible the human soul must, on the one hand, be an intelligible substance really distinct from the body, as one nature from another nature; on the other hand, since our knowledge starts from the sensible, the body and soul must reach, at least on this point, a sort of indivision. Auriol's response consists precisely in saying that the union of soul and body is limited to what must be admitted in order to understand that intellectual knowledge is possible. He therefore posits, between the intellective soul and the body of every man, a relation similar to the "continuity" imagined by Averroes between every man and the separate agent Intellect. At the same time, Auriol realizes that, where the substantial unity of man is at stake, the problem cannot be solved by attributing to them a common operation. Auriol therefore affirms that the union of the imaginable with the intelligible in the object of knowledge expresses the real union there is between imagination and intellect in the knowing subject. In the soul, therefore, there is "a solidarity similar to that of the objects," due to the fact that our intellect, created on the borderline of separate Intelligences and sensible forms, is incapable of grasping the intelligible without the help of the imagination. The human soul, then, has need of these two modes of knowing, and one can concede that the intellect is the form of the body, in the limited sense at least that the natural determination of the one by the other is required for the possibility of one and the same act, intellection.[95]

Once established on these grounds, Peter Auriol is naturally led to restore certain psychological and noetic theses of the Augustinian school, and even to reinforce them for two main reasons. First, he can no longer simply assert them: he must maintain them against Thomism and Scotism, criticizing the latter when necessary; next, since philosophy may lead in this to solutions that theology does not approve, it must clearly define the nature of its own method and the value of its own conclusions. What can one know in philosophy? One can know what the understanding can know starting from experience. All the rest is pure imagination. Thomist psychology had been led to construct a whole mechanism of sensible species, of phantasms and intelligible species, in order to explain how an intellect, which is the form of a body, can abstract the intelligible from the sensible. We have no experience of all that, and moreover the Fathers never spoke about it: it must therefore be resolutely suppressed. It is a principle of Aristotle's that nature does nothing in vain; Christians admit that this principle is true of the works of God himself; there is therefore no reason for multiplying beings needlessly in that way.[96]

Suppose we start with the faculties. The intellect and the will are only the soul itself in these various operations. Their unity, moreover, is such that one cannot conceive the operations of the intellect without the influence of the will, at least as regards their execution. It is the soul that desires to know and that, as intellect, turns toward sensible impressions (*phantasmata*) to get from them intelligible notions. Taken in itself the act of cognition is less mysterious than it is said to be. What is given us in sensible experience is individual. This is a fact, and it has not to be explained by any principle of individuation whatever: *omnis res est se ipsa singularis et per nihil aliud*.[97] God can, if he so wills, produce a plurality of individuals none of which exhausts the type of the species; we see that he so wills, and that settles the question. To explain that intellection is possible, it also suffices to admit that cognition is "the known thing itself considered as term of the intuition of the intellect." At first glance, Peter Auriol seems to admit an immediate grasping of the thing known by the knowing subject; in fact, he excludes intelligible species, but he conceives cognition as mediate in another way.

Things have a form, and some of these forms possess a certain quality called resemblance. That *similitudo*, which is not itself a being but a simple quality of beings, is the only real foundation there is for universals. These universals exist only in the intellect. In order to produce them the intellect assimilates that resemblance in its capacity as agent intellect, and it is assimilated to it in its capacity as possible intellect. This operation is what is called *conceptio*, and its result is the *conceptus*. By "conception," the intellect is made similar to the thing; the concept is the very being of the thing, but as a mental appearance resulting from the formal assimilation of the intellect to what it knows. The concept then—to express it in modern terms—has only a phenomenal being (*esse apparens*), that is, the being of an object of knowledge; to that extent, it is distinct from the thing known; on the other hand, it is the thing known itself, in the only way in which it can be present in an intellect, and, in this sense, it has "intentional" being (*esse intentionale*). The concept of the rose, as Auriol says in an example Ockham was soon to criticize, is the rose itself as known; it is therefore certainly things themselves that we know, in the phenomenal being they have in the intellect; this "objective cognition" is the concept.[98]

To base our knowledge of the universal on the resemblance of the real forms to one another, was to return to Abélard's position, the main consequences of which do in fact reappear here. Particular knowledge, which bears only on reality properly so-called, that of the individual actually existing, is the superior type of knowing. General knowledge, which only attains that qualitative resemblance present to the intellect in the concept, bears only upon one aspect of what is, not on something that may be. There is therefore only the knowledge of the singular which attains the real itself: *notitia individui demonstrati*. Now that knowledge is inaccessible to the intellect, which can grasp only the universal; but there can be an attempt to get as close to it as possible. The only difference there is between our more or less general concepts, those of genus and of difference, for example, is the result of the more or less distinct and perfect impression produced by one and the same object on one and the same intellect. The objective diversity of concepts comes, therefore, in the last analysis, from the formal diversity of impressions made by things on the intellect, but this diversity can itself result from different circumstances, such as the distance at which the object is perceived, the quality of the imagination or intellect themselves, finally the will, which in the adult plays so considerable a rôle, since he depends upon it to fix or not fix the intellect on such or such a subject. This, moreover, is the reason why sensible knowledge, more in bondage to the object than intellectual knowledge, is proof against many errors, into which the intellect allows itself to be led by the will.[99]

The name of "conceptualism" has been proposed for this doctrine, and it has at least the merit of fixing in the memory the rôle the concept plays in it; on the other hand, its nominalist tendencies have been emphasized, and rightly so, at least if one defines nominalism as a tendency to eliminate from reality all element of universality. Nevertheless, the "resemblance" maintained by Auriol in the nature of things has often led him to use a language almost as realistic as that of Avicenna. True enough, there was no being of essence behind his natures, but his doctrine of universals still attributes to them a foundation in qualitative reality.[100]

3. HENRY OF HARCLAY

A similar mistrust with respect to "real essences" appears in Henry of Harclay. Born in the diocese of Carlisle about 1270 or slightly later, ordained a priest in 1297, he studied at Oxford, and taught theology there in his turn, became Chancellor in 1312 and led the struggle against some Dominicans who claimed to teach theology without being masters of arts. Soon named Bishop of Lincoln, he was to make two trips to Avignon, to plead his cause, and died there during his second voyage, in 1317. If he had administrative difficulties with the Dominicans, it was with the Franciscan Duns Scotus that he had philosophical contentions.[101] The Avicennian realism of the *natura communis,* which played such a big part in Scotism, could not fail to rouse protestations; Henry of Harclay was one of the opponents. The fear of Scotus' realism started him out on the road that Ockham alone finally dared to follow through to its end.

Duns Scotus had conceived the individual as constituted of a common nature, in itself indeterminate to universality and to singularity, but individualized by the ultimate actuality of its form, hecceity. These two principles, radically distinct since hecceity is individual by full right and will not enter into the constitution of a species, are, however, intimately united. Henry of Harclay infers from this, that "nature" and "hecceity" are inseparably united. The hecceity of a form cannot be united with another form than its own. Scotus would no doubt have accepted this conclusion from the point of view of actual existence, but in maintaining that it is not contradictory that nature, taken in its essential indetermination (Avicenna), can be united to various hecceities. On the contrary, if Harclay's first point is conceded, it must also be granted that, of these two elements, the one cannot be more common than the other. If the "humanity" of Socrates is inseparable from his "Socrateity," his "humanity" cannot be found in Plato, because of his "Socrateity"; therefore *nature* cannot be more common than *hecceity.* Form, therefore, demands to be individualized. Henry confirms this by an argument already directed by James of Metz against individuation by matter. James of Metz, Scotus and Henry agree that quantified matter cannot individualize substance, since the appropriation of a certain matter to a certain substance presupposes, on the contrary, that this substance is already constituted. But, Henry adds, the same argument is valid against individuation by hecceity, for if we say that the substance of Socrates determines the quantity of Socrates, so that the latter cannot be found in the substance of Plato, we must say, in the same way, that the substance of Socrates determines the "nature" of Socrates, so that the latter can never be found in the substance of Plato. Thus, the "humanity" (or manhood) of Socrates is not a common nature, it is individual by full right.

This conclusion dominates the discussion of the problem of universals. Aristotle had taught (*De anima,* I, 1), that the notion of animal is either nothing or posterior to the individuals from which it is formed by the intellect. Averroes had concluded that the definitions of genera and species are not definitions of real things outside the soul, but of individuals, and that it is the intellect that produces universality in them. Duns Scotus in turn had accepted this conclusion; only, he had attributed to natures, and consequently to species (but not to genera) if not universality, at least that "commonhood" of which we have so often spoken, and which lends itself indifferently to universality or to singularity. Natures thus conceived are not things (*res*), but realities (*realitates*); not beings (*entia*), but entities (*entitates*), and they are real enough for their formal distinction by thought to be possible. Wishing to come back to the true position of Aristotle, Henry, on the contrary, upholds that it is the same thing which, singular if one considers it from a certain point of view, is universal in another connection. Taken in itself, any real thing outside the soul is intrinsically singular, but this singular thing is naturally capable of affecting the intellect so as to be conceived either confusedly or distinctly. The confused concept is the one by which the intellect neither distinguishes nor knows Socrates as distinct from Plato. Thus understood, any concept more general than that of Socrates (man or animal, for example), signifies only Socrates, but as confusedly conceived. Henry of Harclay comes back spontaneously then to Abélard's position, and this is precisely the reason why Ockham will still consider him a realist. To the extent that he is distinctly conceived, says Henry, Socrates is Socrates, purely and simply; as confusedly conceived, Socrates is man, purely and simply; thus, in reality (*in rei veritate*), Socrates is man, animal and body. All this is really one (*ista omnia sunt unum realiter*), and there is in it more or less generality according to our various ways of considering it. For Ockham, this was not to be the ultimate solution of the problem: "All those that I have seen," he was to say, "agree in saying that nature, which is in a way universal, at least in potency and incompletely, is *really* in the individual; although some say that it is really distinct from it; others, that it is distinguished from it only formally; and finally, others, that it is not distinguished from it at all in reality, but only according to reason from the point of view of the intellect." Ockham's criticism emphasizes remarkably what of realism Henry's position still retained: "It is false that a thing is singular under one concept and universal under another, for a thing which is in itself singular is not in any way nor under any concept universal." In short, the universal of Henry of Harclay will remain to Ockham, "a fiction answered by something similar in reality." This is what Ockham will not have at any price. According to him, no universal exists in any way outside of thought nor belongs in any sense to the quiddity or essence of any substance. Harclay therefore remains, like Auriol, this side of the line which, for Ockham, separates realism from true terminism. One would perhaps better understand the reason for this if one knew the text of his still-unpublished Questions on the divine Ideas. William of Alnwick has reproached Henry for having distinguished Ideas, in God and of God, in a way that amounted practically to making creatures of them. Harclay's doctrine is one of those whose internal economy escapes us and about which much is still to be discovered.

The position occupied by the Franciscan William Farinier (d. 1361) in his *Quaestiones de ente* has been described as resembling that of Harclay's. According to him, there is no common nature nor Scotist hecceity, there only are singular substances immediately distinct from one another.[102] William even says that they are "totally different," like Plato and Socrates for example, but that the intellect can consider them either in themselves and as individuals, or as universals, or as indifferent to singularity and universality (Avicenna). Naturally, the possibility of these various aspects of one same being is still to be explained. Like many others before him, William Farinier in this case falls back on the old conformity (*conformitas*) of the twelfth century; there is between one fire and another fire more natural "imitation" than between fire and water. Assuredly, but this precisely is the whole question. All these thinkers make a desperate effort to solve a metaphysical problem by means of empirical verification: it is no wonder that they have not succeeded.

4. THE CARMELITE GROUP

It seems, however, that this psychologism satisfied many masters at the beginning of the fourteenth century. We find it in several of the foremost theologians belonging to the Carmelite Order who taught at the University of Paris. Gerard of Bologna (d. 1317), the author of *Quodlibets*, of *Disputed Questions* and of a *Summa theologica*, belongs to that generation of theologians whose eyes were opened to the true Aristotle by the condemnation of 1277.[103] He knows that the Philosopher was a polytheist, that his supreme god was neither creator nor provident, and that the intellect, for him, was not the form of the human body. In short, Gerard thought that, by and large, the Aristotle of Averroes was the true Aristotle. His own doctrine bears the mark of the various influences he has undergone, especially that of Godfrey of Fontaines, who had convinced him of the radical passivity of the intellect and the will; but we see him teaching the same doctrine of universals which, perhaps by reaction against the Scotist realism of the "common nature," reduced abstraction to a confused cognition of the singular, and the universal to the singular confusedly conceived. We shall find this thesis again in Guy Terrena. Note that, as is the case with Gerard of Bologna, this thesis is often attended by two others: the rejection of the distinction of essence and existence, and the refusal of individuation by matter. These masters conceive individual substance as a block, constituted in being by its form, and which our knowledge can seize in a more or less precise way, but whose structure it has not to break up in order to grasp it under the form of a concept.

This general tendency is freely displayed in the writings of the Catalan Carmelite Guy Terrena (*Guido Terreni*, d. 1342), the author of Commentaries on Aristotle (*Physics, De anima, Metaphysics, Ethics, Politics*), of a *Commentary on the Sentences* and of *Disputed Questions*.[104] Relying on a text from John Damascene (*De fide orthodoxa*, I, 8), which may have played a part in that controversy, Guy Terrena refuses common nature any reality: Plato and Socrates have each not only their proper individuating differences, they even have their own humanity. He agrees on this point with Henry of Harclay's thesis, for whom "Socrates and Plato are really distinct in humanity as they are in Socrateity and Platoneity." Guy does not even hesitate to uphold this thesis for genera. *Animal* is one thing when applied to a donkey, and another thing when attributed to man, for the simple reason that, in one case the thing predicated is a donkey, while in the other case it is a man. In such a doctrine, as in Ockham's, the various propositions: Socrates is man, Socrates is animal, Socrates is substance, signify simply that Socrates is Socrates.

Nevertheless—and this is where Guy differs from Ockham—what answers universals in reality is a certain resemblance between substances which, considered as real, are individually distinct from one another. This resemblance is not a thing, but it is a "real relation" grounded in the nature of things. Speaking of the concept of genus, Guy bases it upon a certain conformity in sensations. When we predicate animal of man, what the word stands for is not the same as when it is predicated of a donkey, because our concepts are different by reason of a certain conformity in the corresponding sense perceptions (*propter aliquam conformitatem in sentire*). Referring to the Commentary of Themistius *On the Soul*, Guy speaks again of "the unity born of a sort of thin resemblance of diverse things, from which one single concept is gathered." A donkey is not very much like a man; yet both are sentient beings; this thin resemblance is enough to permit the formation of the concept "animal," which includes them both. Yet, when all is said and done, to say that Socrates is a substance, or an animal, or a man, is nothing more than to say: Socrates is Socrates. To predicate the genus of the species is not to predicate something more general of something less general, it is to predicate the particular more confusedly conceived of the particular less confusedly conceived. In this sense, the cognition of the general finally bears upon the singular.

These masters can hardly be said to form a school. The remarkable concordance of their conclusions follows from a general position adopted by men belonging to various Orders and bearing in history many different labels. So long as forms had been conceived as retaining, even in singulars, their own metaphysical actuality, no such doctrines could possibly arise. The dividing line passes between the doctrines in which form requires a distinct principle of individuation in order not to become an

Idea (Thomas Aquinas), and the doctrines in which substantial forms are individual by the very fact that they are (James of Naples). Among those who crossed the divide, some went hardly beyond it while others pushed further on, but they all were on the straight road to Ockhamism. In a doctrine where the form is a singular *qua* existing, the universality of concepts has no foundation in reality; abstraction, such as Thomas had understood it, then loses its object and the concept is almost fatally destined to become a natural "fiction." Ockham will consider his own noetic as wholly different from that of his predecessors, and indeed nobody before him dared to follow the principle up to its ultimate consequences, but the principle was already there and the road to Ockhamism was open before Ockham himself entered it.

PART ELEVEN

THE MODERN WAY

It is customary to divide the doctrines taught during the second part of the fourteenth century into two classes, according as their authors were following the "old way" (*via antiqua*) or the "modern way" (*via moderna*). The initiator of the modern way is no less commonly considered to be William of Ockham and the essential feature of his new way is called "nominalism." In other words, the nominalism of the new way is considered as having opposed everywhere the realism of the old way in the main universities and schools of Europe. Although this traditional picture of the situation calls for some corrections, it seems to keep its value as a general statement.

It is no less true that the new interpretation of logic by Ockham played an important role in this evolution. Logic had always been taught in mediaeval schools.[1] There had always been masters to interpret it as dealing with mere names (nominalism), while others maintained that names signifying genera and species pointed out a certain reality in things (realism). This, however, was not in itself a logical question; it was a metaphysical problem related to the nature of being.[2] In order to justify nominalism in philosophy, a master in logic had to assert that logic itself was a philosophy. Some of them adopted this attitude, but, in so doing, they made a philosophical move, not a logical one. A typical instance of this metaphysical interpretation of logic is found in the doctrine of William of Ockham.[3]

CHAPTER I

WILLIAM OF OCKHAM

WILLIAM OF OCKHAM was born shortly before 1300 at Ockham (Surrey). He entered the Franciscan Order, studied at Oxford (1312-1318) and commented on the *Sentences* at the same university (1318-1320). In 1324, he went to Avignon, where he had been summoned to answer a charge of heresy. There was a long examination of the doctrine, but no formal condemnation of the theological propositions at stake.[4] While at the pontifical court of Avignon, Ockham met Michael of Cesena, General Minister of the Franciscan Order, who also was in difficulty with the pope. He then took sides with Michael against Pope John XXII on the question of the temporal power of the Church, a move which was to decide the orientation of his intellectual activities up to the end of his life. Michael and William escaped from Avignon about the end of May, 1328, and went to Pisa where they found protection at the court of the Emperor Louis of Bavaria who also was opposing the pope on the same ground. In 1320 Ockham accompanied the emperor to Munich where he wrote a series of political treatises in defense of the rights of the princes and in favor of his own conception of the relations of Church and State. He died *ca.* 1349-1350. The main sources for the study of his philosophical doctrines are his treatises on logic, his Questions on the *Sentences* and the *Quodlibeta septem.*

Like Thomas Aquinas and Duns Scotus, Ockham was first and last a theologian using certain philosophical doctrines in order to elaborate his own understanding of Christian faith.[5] The dissolving influence exercised by his doctrine in the history of mediaeval scholasticism is due to the fact that, professing as he did a radical empiricism in philosophy, he had to reduce the understanding of faith to a bare minimum. An Ockhamist intellect is as badly equipped as possible for metaphysical cognition, and since where there is no metaphysical knowledge theology can expect little help from philosophy, the consequence of Ockhamism was to substitute for the positive collaboration of faith and reason which obtained in the golden age of scholasticism, a new and much looser regime in which the absolute and self-sufficient certitude of faith was only backed by mere philosophical probabilities.

1. INTUITION AND ABSTRACTION

Aristotle, Averroes, Thomas Aquinas had all agreed that principles are twofold in kind. Some are intellectually evident, others are immediately given sensible certitudes. Ockham innovated nothing on this point, but his interpretation of this classical distinction was a very personal one. First of all, in order to attribute evidence to sense perception, he distinguished the notion of "evidence" from those of science and of wisdom. There is science of the general only; since sense perception bears upon singular objects, to attribute evidence to it entails that there can be evidence even where there is no science.[6] In Ockham's own doctrine, the evidence of sense perception belongs to it by reason of the fact that sensation is an intuition.[7] The Scotist distinction between intuitive knowledge and abstractive knowledge has been taken up by Ockham, but he has turned it against Duns Scotus and reinterpreted it in his own way.[8]

Verbally speaking, the distinction is the same in Scotus and in Ockham, but its nature is different because it does not apply to the same sort of metaphysical being.[9] It does not even apply to the same sort of cognitions. In the doctrine of Scotus, the intelligible always precedes intellection; it is its cause. Between Scotus and Ockham, Durand of Saint-Pourçain had stressed the fact that the cause of cognition was not its object, but the cognitive power itself and, ultimately, the Prime Cause of this cognitive power. On the strength of this position, Ockham correctly deduces the consequence that Duns Scotus had been wrong in defining intuitive knowledge as the type of cognition which is caused by the existence and presence of its object. In his own doctrine, to be intuitive or abstractive is a character that belongs to a cognition in virtue of its own nature. There are cognitions that are intuitive in themselves while others are abstractive in themselves. Cognitions are intuitive or abstractive by reason of their respective natures, not by reason of their objects.

The proof of this is that there can be intuitive cognition of a thing which does not exist (*notitia intuitiva, tam sensitiva quam intellectiva, potest esse de re non existente*). Of course, this is a miracle, but even a miracle cannot bring about a self-contradictory effect. God can create an intuition of something that does not exist because an intuition is the kind of cognition it is irrespective of its object. This conclusion in noetic is backed up by another one in metaphysics. As shall be seen, all that which actually exists is a singular. Now a world of singulars, in which nothing general exists, is also a world of completely separated individuals each of which can exist apart from any other one. Consequently, the object of an intuitive cognition is one thing, its intuitive cognition itself is another thing. God could destroy one of them without destroying the other one. We shall have to remember this point in discussing the Ockhamist notion of causality. Its immediate consequence, with respect to human knowledge, is that to conceive an intuition and its object as two independent realities is to justify the possibility of an intuition of the nonexistent.[10]

The proposition which dominates this metaphysics is that "every positive thing existing outside of the soul is by that very fact singular." We have witnessed the spreading of this position in the theological schools, and even, in the case of John of Naples, in the school of Thomas Aquinas.[11] Ockham did not invent it, but he was the first master to follow its consequences up to their bitter end.

2. SIGNS

The singular is that which is only one, and not many. A singular can be a sign pointing out a plurality but, even then, it itself remains a singular. To the extent that they are such signs in the mind, universals are singulars whose universality does not lie in their being but in their signification only. These signs are twofold in kind, natural or conventional. The only difficulty there is in understanding Ockham is related to his fundamental notion of "natural sign."

A natural sign is in fact a concept. It is what a human intellect has in mind when, even before designating it by an uttered word, it knows a thing. The proof of the fact that such signs are natural is that they are the same in all human minds. Men do not all speak the same language, but they all have the same notions in mind. For instance, there are in different languages countless different words, or names, to say "dog," but wherever there are dogs, there is a name for them because, whatever their countries, races, and languages, all men form the same notion when they see a dog. Such notions are signs because the mental image of a dog applies to practically any dog. Natural universals are precisely these notional signs; they are cognitions in the soul (*tale universale non est nisi intentio animae*), anterior to, and independent of, any verbal expression. On the contrary, their verbal expressions, namely, words or names, are not natural signs; their institution is a conventional one. Hence the plurality of spoken languages whereas, precisely because they are facts of nature, natural universals are the same in all human minds.[12]

Since it is a sign predicable of many, a natural universal has no other reality than that of an act of the intellect. It is real because it is in the mind an accident and, more precisely, a quality. It is something made (*fictum*) because it is a product caused by the mind. This *fictum*, however, is no "fiction" in the usual sense of the term. It is no more arbitrary than smoke, for instance, which is naturally caused by fire and, for this very reason, is universally known to be a sign of fire. Groaning is a natural sign for pain and laughter for joy. The mental notions, or signs, naturally caused in us by their objects are likewise natural products of the intellect acting in a determined way in the presence of their objects and, consequently, apt to signify their causes. Such being the nature of the universal, there is nothing real about it. It can still be called a concept because it is *conceived* by the mind, but the concept is nothing else than the universal which, in turn, is nothing else than a singular mental act

naturally apt to signify many. It may signify singular things outside of
the mind, or it may signify other acts of the mind; in no case does it
signify anything that is not singular. When he wrote his commentary on
the *Sentences*, Ockham left his reader free to choose between two conceptions of the nature of concepts in the mind: the one which interprets the
concept as a resemblance of the thing made by the intellect, a sort of an
imitative representation of the thing; the other which identifies the concept
with subjective intellection, or "intention," which is, in the mind, a real
singular quality, naturally pointing out a plurality of possible objects.
This second interpretation agreed much better than the first one with the
general inspiration of Ockham's doctrine, and it is no wonder that he
finally preferred it.[13]

Against the reality of universality, Ockham accumulates all the classical
arguments borrowed from Aristotle and Averroes. These were the common
property of all. What is proper to Ockham is his reduction of the universal
to the act of understanding.[14] "The intellection, by which I understand
man, is the natural sign of man, just as groaning is the sign of sickness,
of sadness or of pain, *and such a sign can stand for men in mental propositions, just as a word can stand for things in vocal propositions.*"[15]
Ockham knows full well that very few posit universals as substances
existing outside of the mind and really distinct from the individuals in
which they are, but he also knows that, in fact, many entertain this
illusion under various forms. He has no use for the Scotist nature
"formally distinct" from individuals; to Ockham, outside of the soul,
every distinction is a real distinction. He does not believe in "something
common" that makes Socrates resemble Plato more than a donkey; of
course Socrates resembles Plato more, but Socrates and Plato do not
resemble each other by their resemblance; they resemble each other by
what they are, purely and simply: *sufficit quod per seipsis plus conve-
niunt*.[16] What creates the contrary illusion is the old belief that "relations"
are things, whereas, in truth, a relation is nothing but a noun which
can enter the structure of a mental proposition.[17] No logician has been
more conscious of the logical implications of his philosophy. The destruction of concrete universality introduces to us the Ockhamist doctrine of
the suppositions.

3. SUPPOSITION AND SIGNIFICATION

"Supposition" is the positing of something for something else: *dicitur
suppositio quasi pro alio positio*. Ockham retains the classical distinction
of the three suppositions: material, personal and simple, only he warns
us not to trust these names: personal supposition does not supposit for
a person, simple supposition does not supposit for something simple,
material supposition does not supposit for matter.

Material supposition raises no problem: it does not signify at all; in "man is a noun," *man* supposits for itself considered as a spoken or written word. On the contrary, Ockham has a great deal to say on the two other modes of supposition.

"Personal supposition," by far the more important one, occurs when the term supposits (stands for, acts as a substitute for) the signified thing. This "signified" may be a thing outside of the soul, or a concept in the soul (*intentio animae*), or a word (spoken or written); in short, it may be anything provided it be some thing. The fundamental rule is that: "Every time the subject or the predicate of a proposition stands for the thing signified, so that it is used as significative, the supposition always is personal." As can be seen, Ockham is once more busy exterminating real universality. In "every man is an animal," the term "man" supposits for any individual man, not for something common to all men. Ockham's predecessors had often said that supposition is personal when the term supposits for a thing (*res*). Ockham's own definition of it is that, in personal supposition, the term points out the very thing which it signifies. This may seem to be an insignificant correction, but it was not. In the mind of Ockham, it meant that personal supposition was the only case when a "supposition" was, at the same time, a "signification."

"Simple supposition," precisely, is not a signification. Just as material supposition supposits for the term itself (and not for something signified by the term), so also "simple supposition" supposits for the intention, or notion, in the mind, and not for what this notion signifies. In other words, in saying "Man is a species," I am saying: "Man is, in my mind, the concept which *is* the species man." Naturally, I can use the term "man" as signifying men, but then I am leaving the order of simple supposition and entering again the order of personal supposition. The common error opposed by Ockham is the belief that in simple supposition the term supposits for something signified. It does not stand for any thing, except the concept itself, which is indeed a thing in the soul, but, if taken precisely *qua* thing, does not signify any other thing.[18]

The Ockhamist doctrine of supposition is of a piece with his doctrine of signification and of universals. Since the only significative supposition is the *suppositio personalis*, every signification is about singulars. How could it be otherwise? Outside of singulars, there is nothing. Since only the singular exists, all concepts are bound to be about singulars confusedly or distinctly known. A confused concept is a mental sign which does not allow us to distinguish its object from other similar objects. "Man" is a confused concept because it does not distinctly represent the singular "Socrates" nor the singular "Plato." So "man" does not signify, since it has no reality to signify except my own concept of man; but if I see Socrates, I form a distinct concept of him and, consequently, the term which stands for such a concept really stands for a concept that signifies something; it is a case of personal supposition. A consequence of this doctrine is that, since only singulars can be signified because only singulars exist, to predicate the general of the particular is to predicate the singular confusedly known of the singular distinctly known. "Socrates is man" signifies that Socrates distinctly known is Socrates confusedly known. The next problem then is to know how these significative concepts, which make personal supposition possible, can be produced by the soul.

4. INTELLECTION

All philosophers agree that knowledge presupposes a knowing subject and an object known, but many of them feel obliged, for various reasons, to introduce an intermediary between the knowing intellect and the things it knows. They call it a "species" and the problem of relating this species to both intellect and objects becomes a source of abundant difficulties.

The existence of species is generally affirmed either to explain the assimilation of the object known to the intellect, or to explain how the object can be represented to the intellect, or to explain how an object makes the intellect pass from potentiality into act, or, finally, to explain the union of agent and patient in the act of cognition. Now there is no ground for affirming the existence of species for any of these reasons. First, no species could serve as an intermediary between matter and soul nor, consequently, explain the assimilation of a material object to the intellect that knows it. If it is assumed that the material object cannot be the partial cause of an act of intellection, this object cannot contribute to the act of intellection by producing an intelligible species, which is spiritual, in the possible intellect, which is also spiritual. If, on the contrary, it is maintained that the intellect requires the presence of a material object in order to produce the intelligible species, we shall also certainly have the right to say that it requires the presence of a material object to produce intellection.

On the other hand, is the species required in order to give the intellect a sort of image of the object? But this is obviously absurd, for if the species is anterior to the act of cognition, its function cannot be to represent anything. Or should we introduce this intermediary in order to explain how the object moves the intellect from potency to act? But why this intermediary? When two objects face each other, one of which can exert an action and the other undergo it, all the conditions necessary for the production of the act are given. There is then no reason in any kind of intuitive knowledge, either intellectual or sensible, for imagining any intermediary between the thing known and the intellect that knows it. It is the thing itself that is immediately seen or apprehended. There is no more reason for introducing an intermediary between the thing seen and the act by which it is seen than there is for introducing one between God the creator and the things he creates. Just as the existence of God suffices to explain the existence of the creature, so, by the sole fact that there is a thing and an intellect, the thing is seen or known.

The same conclusion might be arrived at by direct demonstration. The necessity of a cause must never be affirmed, unless one is constrained to do so by evident reason or by experience. Now it is clear that experience teaches us nothing of these so-called species. Experience is always reduced to an intuition that cannot be questioned; when an object is white, we see something white, we do not see the species of "whiteness"; experience therefore does not authorize the affirmation of its existence. On the other hand, we have just seen that there are no necessary reasons to affirm it, and, indeed, there cannot be any. No reasoning can demonstrate that there is a cause unless we learn its reality from experience. When a cause is truly necessary to the production of a given object, experience enables us to affirm its existence. If experience does not make it possible to prove the existence of a certain cause, that cause is not truly necessary, and no reasoning in the world could establish any necessity for it.[19]

Thus the object and the intellect are sufficient to explain sensible intuition; and they are equally sufficient to explain the abstract knowledge flowing from it. Sensible intuition leaves the trace of its passing on the intellect. After a sensible intuition, the intellect is capable of a corresponding abstract cognition, while before intuition it was not. Whether it be conceived as a sort of mental picture of the thing, or, as Ockham finally concluded it was, as the very act of cognition subjectively present in the soul, its sole reality is the reality of the soul which produces it. As there are similar things, common images are formed, which are valid for all these objects. This community, made of its very confusion, is what universality boils down to. Universality, therefore, is self-producing in thought, under the natural action of individual things, without the intellect having to produce it; it is "nature" which produces universals in us, in a way that is occult and whose effects only are known to us: *natura occulte operatur in universalibus*.[20]

5. BEING AND CAUSE

Now let us apply this instrument of knowledge to the traditional problems that natural theology propounds, and ask ourselves what kind of answers it permits us to give. It is easily foreseen that most of the answers will be either negative or doubtful. When one is forbidden to go beyond experimental proofs, he does not go very far in metaphysics. Now Ockham's intentions leave not the slightest room for doubt; in tackling philosophical and theological problems he certainly intends not to bate a jot of his demands in matters of proof. In this, Ockham does not differ from any other great theologian. His intentions are the same as those of his predecessors. Only, his philosophy is not the same; so he cannot rationally demonstrate many conclusions which they considered justifiable by rational demonstrations in the light of natural reason.

The first cause for this difference lies in the impact of Ockham's doctrine of universals on his own notion of being. He defines univocity in the same terms as Duns Scotus, from whom he borrows them;[21] only, in his doctrine the notion itself becomes a different one. In logic, there is a univocal predication of being, and since there is no intermediate position between univocity and equivocity in logic, if logical being were not univocal, it would be equivocal, which would make all logical quidditative predication impossible.[22] On the contrary, if we try to use it as carrying a "signification," then all predication of being becomes equivocal because it is predicated of irreducibly distinct singular beings.[23]

The univocity of Ockham is therefore the very reverse of the univocity of Duns Scotus. In Scotism, it was the metaphysical univocity of a concept rooted in the formal entity of a common nature; in Ockhamism, it is a logical univocity in the predication of names. In a doctrine in which every concept ultimately points out a singular, there is no such thing as a univocal entity, nor, for that matter, an equivocal one; the only univocity that belongs to being is the univocal predicability of the term which supposits for its concept.[24] The problem is not to defend the Ockhamist univocity of being against the reproach of pantheism. There can be no pantheism in a doctrine where nothing real is univocal with anything else;[25] it rather is to know what the cognition of being can teach us in a doctrine where being has no univocal or analogical quiddity.

Similar remarks apply to the Ockhamist notion of cause. There is no criticism of the notion of causality in the doctrine of Ockham. To him, causality is given in sense intuition together with substances and their qualities. Only, for the same reasons as above, this is all we know about causality. Since no real thing participates in the nature of any other real thing, the simple intuition of a thing cannot give us any knowledge, either intuitive or abstractive, of the nature of another thing which we have not perceived before by sensation or intellection.[26] How do we know that a thing is cause of a certain effect? Simply by observing that when that thing is present what we call its effect habitually follows. By repetition of such sensible experiences we form corresponding propositions concerning causes and effects. There is nothing like an intrinsic physical causality, or, at least, if there is one, we do not perceive it. Nor is there any principle of causality present in our minds, which compels us to relate physical events as effects to causes. Simply, we see causes and effects and we learn their order from nature by sense perception. The naïve empiricism of Ockham is as obvious here as it was in the case of sense knowledge. It is fundamentally the same case. After all, since singulars are so many absolute things, there would be no contradiction for the absolute power of God in making effects subsist without their causes, forms without matter, accidents without substances. Since creatures are pure singulars, there can be between them no intrinsically necessary relations of causality.[27]

In applying to the being of things the kind of reasoning we have learned from experience, we can prove that this being has an efficient cause, which is God. Only, in order to avoid the difficulties raised by some philosophers concerning the possibility of an infinite series of causes— difficulties which it is difficult or impossible to remove—it is safer to prove God as the efficient cause of the conservation of the world than as the cause of its creation (see Descartes). There can be no infinite series of conserving causes; now, the prime conserving cause is the prime efficient cause. This is a point on which all philosophers agree and there is no doubt about the truth of their conclusion, but we still have to ascertain what it means.

After proving that there is a prime efficient cause, philosophy cannot add very much to this first certitude. This time, we are affirming a cause of which we have neither sense experience, nor proper univocal concept, nor analogical concept. What can we infer from the nominal definition of such a Prime Cause? Very little, if anything. Since it is impossible to infer from the simple concept of a being to the simple notion of another being, we cannot infer from creatures to their cause. Since creatures are finite, we cannot prove by evident demonstration that their cause is infinite.[28] We cannot evidently prove that there is only one such cause,[29] nor that it is free, nor that it is the first efficient cause of *all* things. The ultimate reason for these restrictions to the competence of natural theology is to be found in the refutation of Duns Scotus placed by Ockham at the very beginning of his *Sentences*. In establishing that there can be no abstractive cognition where there has not first been an intuitive cognition, Ockham eliminates at once the possibility of any quidditative concept properly applicable to God, especially the Scotist concept of "infinite being." All that metaphysics can prove is the existence of one or several gods like those of Aristotle, finite rather than infinite, and partial causes of some beings in a way which can hardly be determined with certainty.[30]

Even concerning man, many things cannot be proved. We have intuitive knowledge of our own feelings, as well as of our voluntary acts and intellectual operations, but there is no intuition or scientific demonstration of the existence of an immaterial soul which, although it be the form of our body, is immortal. All this is ultimately held on the strength of faith.[31] It is worthy of note, however, that the science which Ockham considers as one of the safest and best established we may naturally acquire is ethics.[32]

6. THE SPIRIT OF OCKHAMISM

Considered under its purely theological aspect, this doctrine is dominated by the first words of the Christian creed: "I believe in one God, the Father almighty." Ockham only resembles Duns Scotus, his pet adversary, in their common desire to overcome the obstacle raised against Christianity by the philosophical necessitarianism of Aristotle, Avicenna and Averroes. The God in whom Ockham believes is Yahweh, who obeys nothing, not even Ideas. Duns Scotus had submitted to the free will of God the choice of the essences to be created; instead of letting God be free to choose between essences, Ockham suppresses them. Abélard had made Ideas the privilege of the divine mind; Ockham suppresses universals even in God. It is because there are no universal Ideas in God that there is no universality in things. The so-called Ideas are nothing but the very things producible by God. God needs no Ideas in order to know; by the very fact that God is God, he knows all.[33]

Many different labels can be tagged upon such a doctrine; its result, at any rate, is clear. The predecessors of Ockham had often disagreed as to the sense in which it could be said that theology was a science; ever since the time of William of Auxerre, all had agreed that it was a science. Ockham denies that theology is a science, because no science can rest upon faith.[34] No wonder then that he does not worry very much about what natural reason can, or cannot, prove, in matters of faith. It would be a grave misinterpretation of his thought to imagine that there was in his mind any conflict between faith and reason, or revelation and philosophy. Ockham is perfectly safe in what he believes, only he does not *know* what he believes, nor does he need to know it.[35] It is enough for him that probability stands in all cases on the side of faith and of revelation. The practical effect of his theology was to nullify, in many minds, the effort of what might be called the classical scholasticism of the thirteenth century, including Henry of Ghent and Duns Scotus. Of the rational understanding of faith attempted by Bonaventure, Albert the Great, Thomas Aquinas and their contemporaries, very little, if anything, was left after Ockham. This is the reason why we described Ockhamism as marking the end of the golden age of scholasticism. Faith was intact, but to follow Ockham was to give up any hope of achieving, in this life, a positive philosophical understanding of its intelligible meaning.[36] In philosophy itself, this apprentice sorcerer has, not at all created, but unleashed and encouraged forces which he himself could not possibly control after setting them free. In this sense, it can be said that the doctrine of Ockham marked a turning point in the history of philosophy as well as of theology. In theology his doctrine was paving the way to the "positive theology" of the moderns. In philosophy, it was paving the way to modern empiricism. In both cases it really was a *via moderna:* a modern way.

The import and significance of the theology of Ockham was immediately grasped by his contemporaries. The anonymous treatise *De principiis theologiae,* which provides a synthesis of Ockhamism impossible to find in the writings of Ockham himself, is an almost ideal example of what can be the intelligent and faithful rendering of the thought of another man.[37] From this point of view, the *De principiis* is more useful to consult than the later *Collectorium* of Gabriel Biel,[38] a much too personal mind simply to follow the doctrine of another master. However deep and sincere his admiration for Ockham, Biel often disagrees with him; but where he does, he says so, and he usually disagrees along genuinely Ockhamistic lines. This accounts for the place of honor he has always occupied in the school.

Another treatise, still attributed to Ockham by some historians, but whose authenticity is doubtful, is a free application of Ockham's dialectic to theological matters. The *Centiloquium* is neither a summary like the *De principiis,* nor a commentary like the *Collectorium* of Gabriel Biel. It follows its own way, listing a series of one hundred propositions whose philosophical or theological significance is not always obvious.[39] If it was written by Ockham, the *Centiloquium* is the least interesting of his works.

CHAPTER II

NOMINALISM

The expressions "nominalists" and "realists" (*nominales, reales*) had been in use as early as the twelfth century. In the thirteenth century, Albert the Great had spoken of the "nominalists" as of men who placed community in the intellect only (*De praedicabilibus,* II, 2). But there have been few nominalists in the thirteenth century. After Ockham, this ancient appellation was used to designate his disciples. Hence a new doctrinal alignment.[40] Despite their constant controversies, Thomists and Scotists were lumped together and made up the class of the "realists," or partisans of the "ancient way" in philosophy and theology (*via antiqua*); the nominalists, or terminists (*nominales, terministae*) were also called the moderns (*moderni*), not because they intended to abandon Aristotle, but because they were following a new way (*via moderna*) in interpreting it. As early as September 25, 1339, the doctrine of William of Ockham was the object of a censure by the Parisian Faculty of Arts, whose terms suggest that the doctrine was being studied at Paris in private groups (*conventiuncula*) and that it was even beginning to be taught. On December 29, 1340, some nominalistic theses were prohibited [41] by the same faculty, but these measures no more stopped the spread of Ockhamism than the thirteenth-century interdictions to teach Aristotle had prevented Aristotelianism from invading the mediaeval schools.

1. WODHAM, HOLKOT, RIMINI

The doctrine of the English Franciscan Adam Wodham (d. 1349) bears obvious traces of Ockham's influence.[42] After studying under him at Oxford, he himself taught theology at London, then at Oxford in 1340. His own commentary on the *Sentences,* revised by Henry of Oyta, was published by John Mair (Johannes Maior) at Paris, in 1512. In a Preface which he wrote for the logic of Ockham, Adam complains about the fact that many (*plurimos*) among his contemporaries were neglecting the study of logic and teaching many errors, or unintelligible propositions, on account of their ignorance. Among the logicians who succeeded Aristotle, Adam places first the venerable and incomparable Doctor, as eminent in genius as any man can be in this life thanks to the divine light from on high, "brother William Ockham, a Minor by his Order, but a major by the perspicacity of his genius and the truth of his teaching." He assures us that Ockham had ruled him "with an iron rule." His works are too little known to permit an estimate of the influence exercised by Ockham upon Adam's own thought. A character in the new play, the *protervus,* certainly born in the schools of logic, is assuming more and more importance. He is not exactly the devil's advocate, because the devil's advocate does not always believe in the arguments of the devil whose mouthpiece he is. The *protervus* (hence, *protervire, proterviens*) is an obstinate dialectician who never gives up so long as he has one argument left with which to oppose any conclusion in philosophy or theology. Against a conclusively proved thesis, no objection should remain possible. What can still be opposed by the *protervus* remains a mere probability.

The Ockhamist separatism of theology and philosophy is visible in the *Commentary on the Sentences* of the Cambridge Dominican Robert Holkot (d. 1349). Like every theologian, Robert observes that the mystery of the Trinity is incompatible with the exigencies of logic,[43] but he concludes from this the existence of another logic, proper to theology, which the philosophers have not known. Aristotle did not see that the same can be both one and three. Besides, very few of the rules set up by Aristotle in the *Prior Analytics* are valid in all cases. There is not even one. This does not imply that, even in theology, either reason or logic should be renounced; but it does signify that theologians should set up a logic of faith (*oportet ponere unam logicam fidei*). This logic of faith is rational in its own way, even though its principles are different from those of natural logic. Robert Holkot seems to conceive the possibility of a non-Aristotelian logic, valid at a level of intelligibility higher than that of philosophical reason. This was returning to the position of Peter Damiani in the eleventh century, and it is not surprising that the argument from the absolute power of God (*de potentia Dei absoluta*) plays a decisive rôle in the two doctrines. Holkot sets no limits to the will or causality of God. Thus, God does not approve sin; he is therefore not its author; yet since he is the immediate cause of volition included in sin, it follows that, although God is not responsible for sin, he is its cause (*sequitur necessario quod Deus sit immediate causa peccati*). God then wills the existence of sin (*voluntate beneplaciti*) and he can even, *de potentia absoluta*, command man to hate God.

The latter principle operates, in Holkot even more than in William of Ockham, as a powerful agent of disintegration of natural theology. This is visible in the *Quodlibet I*, studied by C. Michalski. There are no evident propositions but those in which the predicate is included in the concept of the subject; now, since all our knowledge is borrowed from sensible experience, we have no concept of God; we cannot, therefore, form any evident proposition applicable to God. More generally speaking, no philosopher has ever demonstratively proven the existence of any incorporeal being whatever, since, for lack of sensible experience, we have no concepts of it. The remark applies to angels as well as to God: "Everything the philosophers have written on the subject of such beings in their books, they received from the founders of religions, or else from those of their own predecessors in whose minds there still remained a vestige and shadow of the knowledge of God from our first parents: (*in quibus relinquebatur quoddam vestigium umbrosum cognitionis Dei a primis parentibus*)."

Such a text clearly shows how true it is that Ockhamism was, by one of its most authentic aspects, an anti-Averroist theological reaction. The cosmos of Aristotle and Averroes held together only by its separate Intelligences and its immobile Primary Mover; it breaks down as soon as the possibility of demonstrating the existence of separate substances begins to be questioned. Besides, what the philosophers say about angels shows well enough that they did not know much about them. Aristotle does not know what the angels are for, unless perhaps to move the celestial bodies, and since he proves their existence only on the strength of the eternity of movement, which is a false supposition, what he says about it cannot pass for a demonstration. It is just the same concerning God. Never did a philosopher demonstratively prove the proposition, "God is," with the meaning the word "God" has in the mind of a Catholic believer. It is still more impossible to prove conclusively the attributes of the God of Christian faith. God is good, intelligent, infinitely powerful: so many propositions for the demonstration of which any concept of God is lacking (*conceptum Dei nullus acquiritur naturaliter sed tantum per doctrinam*). Averroes knew it right well, that shocking ribald one who despised equally all the religious laws, Moslem and Jewish no less than Christian (*ribaldus ille pessimus, Commentator Averroes, omnium legum contemptor*). And the Church also knows it, for what the Nicaean Council enjoins is that we believe that God created heaven and earth: if it were possible to demonstrate it, we should not be told to believe it.

Gregory of Rimini (d. 1358), of the Eremite Order of Saint Augustine, commented on the *Sentences* at Paris for about ten years beginning with 1341 and was elected General of his Order in 1357.[44] His name is well known in the history of theology because of his doctrine of predestination, but we still know little about his philosophical positions. It has become customary to relate him to the nominalist movement, and in fact he does appear to have come under its influence; but like many others in the fourteenth century, Gregory of Rimini perhaps only accepted certain Ockhamist conclusions for personal reasons and without any connection with the principles of Ockham. The master quoted by this Eremite of Saint Augustine in matters concerning the problem of knowledge is none other than Saint Augustine, "who has investigated human knowledge more diligently and penetratingly than anybody else whose writings have come to us." His work therefore raises the curious problem of possible collusions between nominalism and a certain Augustinianism. There may have been secret communications between them (Durand, the *ficta* of Ockham). At any rate, it is worthy of note that Gregory should have been able to confirm by so many quotations from Augustine some theses one would otherwise feel tempted to explain by the spreading influence of Ockham. He insists on the primacy of intuitive knowledge both internal and external, does away with species as intermediaries in the intuition of present objects, but maintains them for the representation of absent objects. If, as has been pointed out by Würsdorfer, a certain "psychologism" is at work in these theses, might it not be the psychologism of a reader of Saint Augustine using a scholastic language?

Gregory's curious position with regard to the object of knowledge and science shows how difficult it would be to explain it from the point of view of a single school. He affirms that universal cognition (*notitia universalis*) does not bear upon really existing universals, but upon signs which designate groups of individuals, and this closely resembles Ockhamism; yet, in support of this thesis, Gregory quotes texts from Augustine on the mode of formation of our general notions. Whether he is an Ockhamist hiding behind Augustine, or an Augustinian making the best of certain Ockhamist conclusions, we know him too little to decide.

In any case, what Gregory says of the object of scientific knowledge suggests that we still have a great deal to learn about him. For him, as for any Aristotelian, not excepting Ockham, science deals with the universal and the necessary, but Gregory concludes from this that the object of science cannot be external reality, which includes only contingent singulars. God alone is necessary; if then geometry and physics had external things for their objects, they would not be sciences. The sole conceivable object of science is therefore what he calls "what the conclusion signifies" (*significatum conclusionis*), which is in fact that to which the mind in possession of the proof gives its assent. Since it is a "being in the soul," this "signified" has no other than mental reality. It is therefore, in a sense, a non-being (*nihil*), but it does not follow from this that science has no object. Whether Gregory was resting the purely mental object thus ascribed to knowledge on some Augustinian illumination, or whether he was allowing it to float between being and non-being, is one more problem history leaves unsolved, or rather, still unpropounded.

2. JOHN OF MIRECOURT

The Ockhamist movement was to recruit its most brilliant partisans and develop its virtualities in the University of Paris, but not without giving rise to strong opposition. One of the first victims was the Cistercian John of Mirecourt,[45] who commented on the *Sentences* at Paris in 1345, and forty of whose theses were condemned in 1347.[46]

Although his own conclusions often agree with Ockham's, John of Mirecourt joins them by ways that are his own, and his thought is completely personal in style. He distinguishes two orders of evidence. The first is the intellectual evidence of the first principle, which is the principle of contradiction. It is impossible for thought not to see it or not to admit it; its evidence is therefore infallible, and all infallible evidence participates in it as in its ultimate justification. The second order of evidence is that of experience, which is internal or external. Internal experience is the direct cognition each one has of his own existence, and consequently of the existence of something in general. Taking up again a remark already made by Saint Augustine (*De Trinitate*, X, 10, 14), John of Mirecourt points out that, since in order to doubt, one must be, no one can doubt his own existence without affirming it. In this case, there is confirmation of an evident internal experience by the necessity of the principle of contradiction; that is why such a knowledge is evident and infallible. External experience is also evident, because it also is immediate (*res ipsa extra est illa quae primo intelligitur*). There is no reason to introduce between the thing and the intellect any species or representative mental object. First, if such an intermediary is posited between object and intellect, a second must be posited between it and intellect, and so on *ad infinitum*. Furthermore, how is such an intermediary to be conceived? It can be neither a substance nor an accident; it is therefore a fiction. There is no image of man by which man is known (*idolum hominis mediante quo intelligitur homo*); in short, the external object is intuitively known (*cognoscitur intuitive*).

This intuitive cognition is evident; yet this empirical evidence of sense perception is not unconditional like that of the first principle, because it is still at the mercy of a divine miracle. As Buridan was to point out, science requires nothing more. John of Mirecourt considers this "natural evidence" as proof against the fear of any possible error, so long at least as God merely exerts his general influence and accomplishes no miracle.

This fundamental distinction enables us to classify cognitions according to their degree of certitude. The human intellect knows with absolute certainty everything whose evidence is reduced to that of the principle of contradiction: if God is, God is; or again, if man is, then animal is. In all cases where we simply affirm that a thing is what it is, the conclusion is evident; it follows from a simple application of the primary principle to the subject of the proposition. As to the propositions which bear upon the external world, they are also evident, but theirs is the purely empirical evidence which we called "natural." It is no longer the unconditional evidence of the primary principle, but it is enough to assure us that there is white, black, a man, and that a certain cause produces a certain effect. In all these cases, it is certainly as it seems, and it cannot be otherwise, so long as the natural causes act naturally and without the miraculous intervention of God. All our philosophical knowledge shares this kind of evidence with our science of the external world. It does not go beyond that, for God can cause any sensation whatever in us without the corresponding object existing; but it does go that far, for, apart from the possibility of some miracle, we cannot possibly perceive what is not. John of Mirecourt, therefore, moves in a universe, the empirical knowledge of which presents all the guarantees necessary and sufficient for a natural science to be possible. He even asked himself if one could not conceive the sensible universe as uniquely composed of substances without accidents. Were it not for the Christian dogma, he thinks, many would doubtless have long since admitted that it was so.

The theological articles condemned in 1347 by the theologians of Paris, under the presidency of their Chancellor, the Florentine and friend of Petrarch, Roberto de' Bardi, show some of the consequences following from these principles. The rôle of the divine will is emphasized there with extreme force. The Ockhamist argument "by the absolute power of God" once more brings about a revival of some of Saint Peter Damiani's positions. Naturally, their philosophical justification is a new one. John maintains that God can arrange that the world never existed, or more exactly that "it is neither evident nor imposed by faith, that God could not so make it that the world never existed"; to which he adds that the contrary is no more evident, for he could not drive "the partisans of the contrary either to contradict themselves, or to deny faith, experiences or demonstrated conclusions." Of course, he concludes, "I know that it follows from faith that this should be false." This probably was a verbal precaution. How could a man accept by faith a thesis which he maintains does not necessarily follow from faith? Commenting on the fifth of his condemned propositions: "For me, it is neither evident, nor evidently proven, nor resulting from faith, that it should be impossible for God so to arrange it that the world never existed," John simply remarks: "My conclusion on this subject appeared to me to be true, because I did not wish to flatter myself that I had a knowledge I did not have."

The consequences of this attitude would not have been really serious, had John of Mirecourt not pursued them on the grounds of future contingents and the predetermination of human acts. All that is, in whatever manner it is, God wills that it should be thus. Even if the thing is contingent, it is God who makes it to be so, and he does it efficaciously (*Qualitercumque sit, Deus vult efficaciter sic esse*). Taking up in his turn the expression *voluntas beneplaciti*, not in its classical sense of "divine approbation," but in the strong sense of "efficacious will of God," he in turn concludes like Holkot, that God efficaciously wills sin. Without wishing expressly to affirm it, John of Mirecourt concedes then "that God makes it that some one sins and is a sinner, and that he wills (*voluntate beneplaciti*), that such a man be a sinner and that evil happens." Certainly, God cannot do evil, nor make evil happen, immediately and by himself alone; but it is certainly in virtue of his efficacious will (*velle efficax*) that sin is committed. God makes the sinner sin, and that it be he who sins (*facit ipsum peccare et quod ipse peccet*). Holkot had already admitted that there are three cases in which the inner liberty of the will disappears: those in which the will yields to the violence of affliction, or of joy, or to the tyranny of habit; John of Mirecourt also admits that there are temptations which one cannot resist short of a miracle, and that, if the miracle does not take place, intercourse with another man's wife is then no longer adultery, and so on with other sins. Are we to recognize an influence of Thomas Bradwardine's theological determinism on these doctors? The dates actually given for Bradwardine's work authorize the hypothesis, but it should not be forgotten that all these positions betray an intricate complex of diverse doctrinal traditions.

3. NICHOLAS OF AUTRECOURT

Important as the work of John of Mirecourt may be, the history of philosophy is still more immediately interested by that of Nicholas of Autrecourt, a fellow of the house of Sorbonne between 1320 and 1327, master of arts and bachelor in theology, condemned to burn publicly, the 25th of November 1247, before the assembled University of Paris, his letters to Bernard of Arezzo and his treatise *Exigit ordo executionis*.[47] Nicholas' starting point is a doctrine of human knowledge which, based on principles analogous to those of Ockham, makes them yield their most extreme consequences. He admits only one single order of absolutely certain cognitions, those that are immediately evident. Now immediate evidence can have only two sources, experimental verification or the affirmation of the identity of a thing with itself. Aside from the experimental verification of what is, and the affirmation that what is is, is what it is and nothing else, there is for man no certitude properly so-called. The significance of the doctrine of Nicholas is made clear by the consistent application he makes of it to the philosophical notions of cause and substance. Ockham had already distinguished these two criteria of evidence, but he had not judged sense evidence in the light of intellectual evidence. Consequently, while limiting the inferences that can be drawn from experienced causality, he had never denied the validity of such inferences. On the contrary, Nicholas judges the relation of causality itself in the light of the principle of contradiction, and since relations between natural beings cannot be reduced to relations between terms in a treatise on logic, the world does not appear to him as wholly intelligible.

The first principle, by which all certain knowledge is established, is the principle of contradiction: contradictory propositions cannot be simultaneously true. This principle is first, because no other principle comes before it; on the contrary, it precedes all the others. Six corollaries follow from this position. First: the certitude of all knowledge based on the first principle is absolute; so, what is demonstrated by the natural light of reason is absolutely demonstrated, and nothing can make contradictory propositions be simultaneously true. Second: there are no degrees of evidence, and all that is evident is equally evident. Third: except for the certitude of faith, there is nothing certain but the primary principle or what is reducible to it. Fourth: any true syllogistic conclusion must be directly or indirectly reducible to this primary principle. Fifth: in any consequence immediately reducible to the primary principle, the consequent should be identical with all or part of the antecedent; otherwise, it would not be immediately evident that the antecedent and the consequent are compossible. Sixth: in any consequence reducible to the first principle, the antecedent is identical with the consequent, in whole or in part, no matter how many the intermediaries.

Let us apply these rules to the relation of causality. It follows first that, from the fact that one thing is, it cannot be evidently concluded that another exists. This conclusion is manifest, for, either the thing whose existence is inferred is other than the thing given, or it is the same. If it is the same, there is no inference; if it is another, there is no compulsory reason why we should affirm or deny it, since the principle of contradiction guarantees simply that one same thing cannot be itself and its contrary at one and the same time. The first principle, final guarantee of certitude, never allows us to conclude from one thing to another; hence it follows that the bond which unites the cause to the effect is neither necessary nor evident.

It has been said of Nicholas of Autrecourt that he was the Hume of the middle ages, and the comparison of the two names is inevitable. Expressing it in modern terms, both thinkers say that the relationship of cause to effect is not analytical. But Nicholas of Autrecourt still admits that a real relation of cause to effect is given with evidence in sense experience. Unlike Hume, he does not reduce the real relation of causality to our psychological habit, born of sense experience, of associating the notion of a thing with that of another one. On the other hand, like Hume, he strongly stresses the distinction there is between analytical relations of ideas and empirical cognitions about matters of fact.

The same reasoning applies to final causes and to the notion of perfection. Just as the efficient cause cannot be inferred from the sole notion of any being, so one cannot affirm from one thing that it is the final cause of another. It is never either necessary or contradictory for a thing to be or not be the end of another thing. Consequently, there is no intellectual necessity to posit any final cause, and there is no impossibility to affirm any such cause. What is true of purposiveness is true of the degrees of perfection that philosophers discover in things. In order to affirm that one thing is more perfect than another, two different things must be compared; if the things compared are really different, they are not properly comparable. It should therefore not be said of such things that they are more or less perfect, but only that they are different. If they are different, they are equally different and consequently they are also equally perfect. Each of them is what it is and what it should be, given its place in the whole universe. The judgments by which we claim to hierarchize things only express our personal preferences, not any degrees of perfection in things.

Nicholas of Autrecourt affirmed these theses, whose consequences were to be decisive with regard to natural theology, on the strength of a definite conception of human knowledge. The source of our knowledge lies in sense experience, and the principle of contradiction is the criterion of truth solely because it extends the immediate evidence of primary intuition through a more or less long series of intermediaries. To gain experience of a thing is to establish that it is; to reason about that thing with a compelling certitude is to affirm that it is what it is. There can therefore be a direct and certain knowledge of causality, but it endures as long as the sensible experience in which we perceive the co-existence of cause and effect. After this experience, what remains is the intellectual probability that the same effects will be reproduced if the same conditions are again given. In order to have that simply probable cognition of a relation of cause to effect, it is necessary to have had previously the evident cognition of it.

Because it was evident to me that my hand became warm when I held it close to the fire, I now consider it probable that my hand will become warm when I hold it to the fire again. When all is said and done, this inference remains a simple probability. Even if all the conditions are given so that the phenomenon may be produced, the principle of contradiction does not guarantee that the phenomenon will occur. The proposition: if you put fire near straw and there is no barrier, the straw will burn, is not evident; it is only a probability based on experience.

Our affirmation of substances rests upon the relation of causality. Given the physical properties of certain bodies, or the intuition of some psychological operations, the existence of a material or spiritual substance to explain them is immediately assumed. In so doing, we are once more concluding from one thing to another. It is not contradictory to do so, and it is no more contradictory not to do so; the inference from accident to substance expresses a simple possibility. If we wish to stick to given facts, we shall affirm the existence of a substance every time it is given us in experience at the same time as an accident; but we have no right to use this principle: all accident demands a substance, in order to conclude from the existence of an experienced accident to that of a non-experienced substance. Nothing authorizes us to affirm anything else than what we know by our five senses and by formal experiment (*nec illud valet ad ostendendum rem aliam esse ab objectis quinque sensuum et ab experientiis formalibus nostris*).

This is the reason why we should be cautious in inferring the existence of a substance. The only substances whose existence we can affirm are our soul and what we verify by means of our senses. Except our soul and the objects we know by our five senses as well as by formal experience, we have no right to affirm the existence of any substance. If there were others, we could only know them either by immediate experience and without reasoning, or by means of reasoning. Now if we had intuitive experience of them, even peasants would know what they are; but if we wished to infer their existence from what we perceive, we should have to conclude from the fact that one thing is to the existence of another thing, which is impossible. Hence it follows that, sensible objects being posited, no one has ever been able to conclude from them with evidence to the existence of these other things called substances (*Ex regula supra dicta sequitur, quod numquam fuit alicui evidens, quod positis istis rebus apparentibus ante omnem discursum, essent quaedam aliae res, utpote aliae quae dicuntur substantiae*). And if no one has ever had an evident knowledge of these alleged substances, it follows likewise that we cannot even have a probable knowledge of them, since all present probability presupposes a past evidence. Nicholas of Autrecourt therefore keeps only the name of substance, since he identifies it with the content of inner or outer experience; substance is all that which, and nothing but that which, we perceive. He saw perfectly well, in particular, that the application of the principle: all accident resides in a substance, is a pure tautology. If accident is defined "what exists in a substance," it evidently follows that if there is an accident, there is also a substance; but with such a method one could just as well prove anything at all. Let us suppose, for example, that the word "man" signifies something inseparable from donkey, the necessary inference would follow: there is a man, therefore there is a donkey. Nicholas of Autrecourt pushes his criticism so far that he denies the existence of psychological faculties themselves. Reasoning such as this is not evident: there is an intellection, therefore there is an intellect; there is a volition, therefore there is a will (*istae consequentiae non sunt evidentes: actus intelligendi est, ergo intellectus est; actus volendi est, igitur voluntas est*). Let us see the metaphysical consequences of such a doctrine.

Nicholas of Autrecourt was fully conscious of them. By such a doctrine of knowledge, he was closing the ways that lead metaphysicians to the existence of God. From the fact that one thing exists we cannot conclude that another exists; so we cannot conclude from the world's existence, the existence of God. Inversely, from the non-existence of one thing we cannot conclude that another does not exist; so we cannot conclude that if God did not exist the world would not exist. Note, moreover, that since a knowledge which has never been experimentally evident cannot even become probable, Nicholas of Autrecourt could not even consider as probable the existence of a primary cause. One must therefore not be too surprised that he should have considered these two propositions to be two different ways of saying the same thing: God exists and God does not exist. What is true of causality is true of purposiveness and perfection; the proofs of the existence of God by finality and the degrees of perfection are not evident; such conclusions will join the mass of truths which can only appeal to faith.

By casting doubt upon the reality of substances, Nicholas was led profoundly to modify the Aristotelian conceptions of matter and the soul. If one cannot demonstrate that there is in a piece of bread more than its sensible properties, it becomes impossible to explain phenomena through the intervention of substances and forms. This is why Nicholas gives up Aristotle's physics and rallies to Epicurean atomism. There is only one kind of movement in nature: local movement. The generation and corruption of bodies does not mean that different forms succeed one another in the same subject, but simply that atoms combine so as to form certain bodies and break away from one another when these bodies disintegrate. Light itself is explained by a corporeal movement which attends the presence of luminous bodies, and its transmission, contrary to general belief, demands a certain time. As to the soul, it consists in a certain spirit called the intellect and in another, called the senses. When the atoms which constitute the human body disintegrate, the intellect and the senses continue to exist. There is, therefore, an assured immortality, and there are even rewards and punishments awaiting the good and the wicked, but here is the form under which they are conceived. In the just, the intellect and the senses are excellently disposed; they are, on the contrary, poorly disposed in the wicked and the unjust. It must then be admitted that the senses and the intellect of the just will be found an infinite number of times in the same state of perfection when they reunite with the same combination of atoms which constitute their body. For the body will build up and disintegrate an infinite number of times. When, on the contrary, the soul of a wicked person recovers its body, it rejoins it in the poor disposition in which it was at the moment it left the body. Perhaps one might equally assume that when the two spirits of a just man, that is, his intellect and his senses, leave his body, they are immediately united with another body composed of more perfect atoms. These conclusions, Nicholas says, should not trouble anyone, for no matter how astonishing they seem, they are more probable than many others in which we have long believed. And perhaps still another doctrine will come along and make this one improbable in its turn. Let us cling then, in the meantime, to the law of Christ, and believe that rewards and punishments are meted out as the sacred law tells us.

Like many critical spirits, Nicholas of Autrecourt wanted to limit knowledge in order to strengthen its foundation. We think of him as of a sceptic as though one of his dominant preoccupations had not been to avoid scepticism. In placing intuitive knowledge at the origin of all our certitudes, he intended to make sure of at least a few which no doubt whatever could at any time unsettle. Granting that experience, and only experience, permits us to attain existences, we are at least certain of the objects of our five senses and of our psychological operations directly perceived by inner intuition. If this is not posited as certain, we are no longer sure of the existence of the world nor of ourselves. We finally end up at the scepticism of the academicians: "And it is in order to avoid all such absurdities," Nicholas concludes, "that I have maintained, in my disputes in the Sorbonne, that I have an evident certitude of the objects of the five senses and of my psychological operations."

Thus empiricism is the sole assured refuge against scepticism and it is the adverse position, on the contrary, that leads to it. How can a man declare himself certain of conclusions as hidden as the existence of a primary mover and others of the same sort, while doubting these actual primary truths which are the most certain of all? But men have turned away from things only to put their confidence in books. The certitudes we have with regard to natural phenomena are very few, but men could soon acquire them if they applied their intellect to things instead of applying it to Aristotle and Averroes. "And as the knowledge of things could be acquired in a short time starting from natural appearances, it is astonishing that certain people study Aristotle and Averroes up to the age of decrepitude, neglect moral problems and care for the common welfare, for the study of logic, and that if some friend of truth arises to sound the trumpet to awaken these sleepers from their slumber, they become indignant and, so to speak, take up arms in a struggle to the death against him." This rebellious mood of Nicholas of Autrecourt, probably shared by some of his contemporaries, is but one of the many symptoms of a then widely spread dissatisfaction with the predominantly dialectical culture of the mediaeval schools.

Nicole Oresme has quoted from a *Commentary on the Sentences* of a certain Richard Billingham,[48] who seems to have considered the existence of all substance as a mere probability. He seems to have started from the Aristotelian doctrine, generally accepted by mediaeval masters, that we know substance only through accidents. One might as well say, concludes Billingham, that we do not know it at all and that in consequence we have no reason to affirm that it exists. Now what is true of so-called sensible substance is much more true of those separate substances of which everyone agrees we have no experience. According to Billingham, says Oresme, substance is no more perceived than the mover of heaven; and, he adds, this time speaking in the plural as of a group: "So they say that the existence of any substance is not absolutely evident; it only is probable." This is one more empiricism about which it is not evident whether or not it owes anything to Ockham's influence. The Franciscan, Brinkel,[49] whom we find quoted by Peter of Candia and John of Basel (bishop of Lombez in 1389), is a still more instructive case, for there is a *Logic* of his in which the doctrine of the *suppositio* does not agree with Ockham's; he nevertheless maintained that God is not demonstrable starting from his effects, because it is impossible to conclude from finite effects an infinite cause; this had been one of the main objections leveled at Scotus by Ockham.

4. JOHN BURIDAN

At the University of Paris the terminist movement seems to have been dominated by John Buridan[50] of Bethune, whose long career and personal merits sufficiently explain his influence in France and abroad. Rector of the University of Paris in 1328, he received that dignity again in 1340; we find him still active in 1358, perhaps even in 1366, after which he disappears from history to go over into legend. He was a logician, the author of *Summulae logicae* which had the signal honor of being inscribed, in 1398, with the *Summulae* of Peter of Spain, on the program of authors to be read at the Faculty of Arts at Cologne. His works are those of a master of arts: Questions on the *Physics*, the *De anima*, the *Metaphysics*, the *Ethics* and the *Politics*; according to recent research, he was a master of arts who lent himself to Ockham's influence, but not without discernment. Besides, he was one of a group of masters who, December 29, 1340, signed a decree forbidding the teaching of several of Ockham's theses, and, in fact, he had his personal answers to many of these questions.

Ockham had sharply distinguished the order of concepts, with their significations, from the order of words, with their predications. This duality seems to have become for Buridan a fruitful object of reflections. While maintaining a strict nominalism in logic, he attempted a rehabilitation of the concept. His language at least, in which the word "essence" plays such a large part, at times recalls Avicenna's. One and the same essence, that of Socrates for example, can be conceived by two different concepts, one of which applies to several individuals, the other of which is proper to one of them. The first kind of concept is designated by common names, the second by proper names. Whether the name is proper or common, it is a name of primary intention (*nomen primae intentionis*), that is to say, according to Aristotle's language, a name which signifies a real being, and not a simple notion of the intellect. As Buridan himself says, man, horse, Socrates, white, etc., are names of "primary intention," the only difference between them being that the proper name designates the individual as the concrete subject (*individuum pro subjecto*), while the common name designates the individual taken in its form (*individuum pro forma*). Common names and proper names, then, signify the same reality under two different aspects. On hearing this, Ockham would have looked for his "iron rod."

We pass from real knowledge to logic when, instead of positing concrete beings as objects of thought, we consider that indifference to individual subjects which is the modality proper to common names and their concepts. From that moment on, our thought no longer bears upon individuals (Socrates, this man), but upon a species or a genus, that is, on a universal. The universal itself can be grasped in two ways. First, as signifying singular things in a universal way; next, as signifying the very universal mode under which our concept of man seizes men. This is no longer the universal taking the place of the subjects it connotes (*universale pro subjecto*), but the universal taken in its very universality (*universale pro forma*). This is a distinction it was doubtless worthwhile to know in order to pass examinations in logic, between 1328 and 1358, in the Faculty of Arts of the University of Paris.

Logic thus understood does certainly bear, as Aristotle would have it, on concepts of concepts, or concepts of second intention, but science itself bears upon concepts of the first degree, those which designate the individuals in themselves or in their forms. In the order of real cognition, all the categories ultimately signify the real thing that they determine in various ways. This is true even of the category of relation: "the paternity of Socrates" and "Socrates is a father," or "the resemblance of Socrates" and "Socrates is similar to Plato," formulas in which *paternity, father, resemblance* and *similar* signify nothing other than the thing itself, which is Socrates taken in his various relations.

Science, therefore, always deals with concrete subjects, and it studies them in the light of the first principle, but it does not deduce them from it. The principle of contradiction applies to all the real given in sensible experience, but sensible experience also is a principle. That is why Buridan rejects Nicholas of Autrecourt's conclusions, or as he puts it so well, the conclusions of those who think "that it is absolutely impossible to demonstrate any conclusion whatever, in which one applies to any subject whatever the verb *is*." The defenders of this thesis deny that one can demonstrate that some thing is, by means of the sole first principle, for the simple reason that there is no middle term more evident than the term *is*. Any attempt of this kind would be a *petitio principii;* for example: *b* is, now *a* is *b*, therefore *a* is. This, they say, is assuming under another form precisely what had to be demonstrated. Their conclusion would be correct if, as they demand, all demonstration were to be reduced to the evidence of the first principle; but this is not exact, for we find the principles of many of our demonstrations in sensation, in memory, or in the experience which results from accumulated sensations. Moreover, if the first principle never suffices to prove that a thing exists, it makes it possible to demonstrate the existence of one thing starting from the existence of another: man does not exist without a heart, now this man exists, therefore his heart exists. In order that the reasoning be conclusive, it is enough to prove that man cannot live without a heart. By similar reasoning Aristotle demonstrated the existence of the Prime Cause, or of primary matter, and all real knowledge is due to it.

Such an attitude is in accordance with what we know from other sources of the interest Buridan took in problems of natural philosophy.[51] There again the work had been begun before him, and even before Ockham, whose personal reflections and method had, however, taken him rather far along. Because beings should not be multiplied unnecessarily, the *Venerabilis Inceptor* had attributed the same matter to celestial and terrestrial bodies; since all phenomena are explained just as well with one single matter as with two, we should assume only one. The same desire to account for phenomena in the simplest way had led him to criticize the universally accepted doctrine of the movement of bodies. According to Aristotle, any motion presupposes a mover distinct from the mobile. If the movement at stake is natural, the very form of the mobile body accounts for its movement; if it is a "violent" movement, that is to say, a movement forced from without on the mobile, the case is more complex and the phenomenon more difficult to explain. It is easy to understand that a natural movement endures in time, for the cause of the movement is interior to the mobile and always there to keep it moving; such is the case with a stone that falls because it is naturally heavy, or with fire which flames up because it is naturally light. But if it is a question of violent movement, like that of a stone going up because it is thrown into the air, it is hard to understand why the movement continues after it has left the hand that has thrown it. For, as soon as the stone has left the hand, the violent mover no longer acts upon it, and since the stone moves in a direction contrary to its natural tendency, nothing explains its continuing to move. It was in order to solve this problem that Aristotle had imagined a movement of the surrounding air, thanks to which the mobile would necessarily be projected farther and farther. When the hand throws the stone, it moves at the same time the air surrounding the stone, the part of the air thus disturbed moves the next part and so on, each of these parts of air pulling along with it the moving body. Aristotle seeks, in short, a continuous air wave by which the persistence of movement in a mobile separated from its mover can be explained.

William of Ockham opposed this explanation, and his own solution to the problem was so radically simple that his disciples themselves did not always dare to follow it. It is evident first that the cause of the movement of a body is no longer in the body which set it in motion; if in fact we destroy the hand or the machine which set it in motion the mobile will nevertheless continue to move. Neither can one uphold the view that the air disturbed by the mover continues to push the mobile on ahead, for if two archers draw against one another and the two arrows meet, one would have to assume that the same air moves at this point in two opposite directions. In short, the cause of movement is not a virtue inherent in the mobile for, in that hypothesis, the virtue conferred upon the body in movement could only come from the body moving it. Now, if I slowly move my hand toward a stone, that stone remains motionless; it has therefore received no virtue from my hand. If I move it suddenly toward the stone, the stone is going to move, but the only conceivable effect that the local movement can produce is to put the mover and the mobile into contact, and one cannot see how any virtue whatever could be engendered from the simple fact of this movement. The simplest solution of the problem is to say that a body in movement moves precisely because it is in movement and there is no need to assume any mover distinct from the mobile. Thus William of Ockham foreshadows the notion, and perhaps even, as we shall see, the law of inertia, and when he hesitates to prove the existence of God on the strength of the principle that all that moves is moved by another, he had a physical reason for maintaining that a body can move itself. Movement being given (and it is eternal), there is no need to invoke anything else than its existence to explain its continuation.

John Buridan did not wish completely to give up the notion of a form, or virtue, interior to the mobile, just as in logic he had wished to preserve essences. The true cause of this apparent timidity may have been a proper respect for the physical reality to be explained. Taking up again a former notion that a Greek commentator of Aristotle, John Philoponus, had already defended against Aristotle himself, he explains the continuation of movement in the mobile by a sort of impulse, *impetus,* that the mover imparts to the body moved. To claim that the air maintains the movement is an obvious error, and experience proves it, for such an explanation does not make it possible to understand why a top continues to spin by itself nor why a grindstone that one has stopped moving does not stop turning even if one cuts it off from the air around it by means of a piece of cloth. Suppose on the other hand a boat loaded with straw, covered with canvas, that one suddenly stopped hauling; if at that moment the canvas is lifted off and consequently the surrounding air also, the boat should cease moving, or else one should see the air bend the straws forward; now the boat still moves on for a rather long time and the pieces of straw are bent toward the back by resistance of the surrounding air; it is therefore not the movement of the air that maintains the movement of the boat.

To solve the problem Buridan proposes the following hypothesis: at the moment that the mover moves the mobile, it imparts to it a certain impulse; this impulse, or *impetus,* is proportionate on the one hand to the velocity with which the mover moves the mobile, and on the other hand, to the quantity of matter of the body which receives it. It is this impetus which maintains the movement in the mobile until the resistance of the air and the weight, which oppose the movement, finally prevail. The impulse imparted to the mobile, therefore, continually diminishes, the movement of the stone continually slows down, and finally it yields to gravity which makes it fall back to its natural place. This explanation accounts for all the phenomena that Aristotle's solution could not explain. It explains why one can throw a stone farther than a pen: a thick body contains a lot of matter in little volume (*sub pauca magnitudine seu quantitate*) and the impetus to which a body is susceptible is proportionate to its density. We also understand why the natural fall of heavy bodies is continually accelerated. At the beginning of the movement, gravity alone moves the body, but from the moment it begins to move it imparts a certain impetus to the weighty body, that impetus acts upon the body at the same time that gravity does, and the movement is accelerated; but the more the velocity increases, the stronger the impetus becomes; the natural fall of a heavy body must therefore develop according to a continually accelerated movement. To generalize this explanation remarkably simplifies our astronomical conceptions. As Kilwardby had already concluded from a similar principle, the Intelligences in charge of maintaining the movement of celestial orbs then become completely useless. Assuming that God conferred on celestial orbs a certain *impetus* at the moment of their creation, that he preserves it in them as he universally preserves all things, and that no resistance either inner or outer neutralizes that initial impetus, there is no reason why the movement of celestial orbs should not continue by itself. And, Buridan concludes: "I do not give all this as demonstrated, but I only beg their Honors the Theologians to explain to me how all that can happen."

The clarity with which Buridan describes the data defining the movement of a body is remarkable. The expressions he uses are sometimes so precise that it is difficult to resist mentally substituting for them the equivalent algebraic formulas: "If he who hurls projectiles moves with an equal speed a light piece of wood and a heavy piece of iron, these two pieces being otherwise the same in volume and shape, the piece of iron will go farther because the impetus imparted to it is more intense." John Buridan got very close to the notion of the *impeto* in Galileo and the *quantity of movement* in Descartes.

It is curious, but after all satisfactory for the philosopher, to note that the author of such remarkable theories should owe his popularity to imaginary love affairs with Joan of Navarre and to the famous donkey that has not yet been found anywhere in his writings.

5. ALBERT OF SAXONY AND ORESME

The breadth and depth of the experimental movement becomes more manifest still in John Buridan's disciple, Albert of Saxony.[52] This philosopher, likewise designated under the names Albert of Helmstedt, or of Ricmestorp, Albertutius or Albertus parvus, studied and taught at the University of Paris. He was rector of that university in 1357, and in 1362; we find him again in 1365 in the position of first rector of the University of Vienna, which had just been founded; in 1366 he was made Bishop of Halberstadt and died in 1390. Albert of Saxony, of whom we have numerous works dedicated to logic, physics, mathematics and morals, openly claimed kinship with his "revered masters of the noble faculty of arts of Paris." It was they, he tells us, who taught him the doctrines contained in his commentary on the *De coelo et mundo*. We find in them the theory of the *impetus* and its application to the problem of the movement of celestial orbs; but among the new conceptions that Albert of Saxony developed in a personal way, his theory of weight must occupy first rank. We have seen John Buridan make use of the notion of "gravity" without giving any precise definitions of it; for him heavy bodies fall because they are to rejoin their natural place which is the earth. But what is the natural place of the earth itself? Albert of Saxony finds himself faced with two answers. Some, who with Aristotle consider that a body's place is the inner surface of the body immediately surrounding it, affirm that the natural place of the earth is the inner surface of the sea or of the air that cover it; others, on the contrary, consider that the natural place of the earth is the center of the world. Albert of Saxony settles the question by distinguishing two centers in each heavy body, its center of magnitude which corresponds practically to what is today called the center of volume, and its center of gravity. In a body whose gravity is not perfectly homogeneous, these two centers do not coincide. Now the earth has no uniform gravity; those of its parts covered by the waters are less exposed to the sun's rays and consequently less dilated than those which are uncovered. Hence the center of magnitude of the earth does not coincide with its center of gravity and it is not the center of magnitude of the earth which is the center of the world. Therefore it is its center of gravity. Now all the parts of the earth, and each of the heavy bodies, tend to have their center of gravity become the center of the world. A plane passing through the center of the world must also pass through the center of gravity of the earth, for if it remained outside of this center, it would divide the earth into two unequal parts the heavier of which would push the lighter until the center of gravity was at the center of the world and the equilibrium was established. This tendency, moreover, is invariable; it remains the same, whether one considers it in potency, when the heavy body is in its natural place, or whether one considers it in act, when the heavy body resists the effort put forth to push it out of its place, moves to rejoin it or weighs upon the body that hinders it from arriving at it. By this theory of weight, Albert of Saxony exerted his influence on the whole development of statics up to the middle of the seventeenth century. Moreover, in discussing the problem of the connection between speed, time and distance, he maintained that the speed of the mobile is proportionate to the space passed through; he also seems to have conceived as possible the proportionality of speed to time, but the least that can be said is that he could not decide which of the two solutions was the right one. He therefore did not solve the problem correctly, but he raised it and certainly prepared for the discovery of the true solution.[51] We shall see the question make new progress in the writings of another Parisian master, Nicole Oresme.

Born in the diocese of Bayeux, Nicole Oresme[53] studied theology at the University of Paris; we know that he was already there in 1348. Grand master of the College of Navarre in 1356, he was master of theology in 1362, Bishop of Lisieux in 1377 and died there July 11, 1382. He was a scholar of the first order and a truly universal mind. His works were written now in Latin, now in French. We are indebted to him for the French translation of the *Politics* and *Ethics* of Aristotle, a *Book on Politics*, a *Book called Economics* and especially a treatise *On the Origin, Nature and Mutation of Moneys* which assures him first place in the domain of political economy in the fourteenth century. His most important works remain, however, the Latin and French writings he devoted to the problems of physics and astronomy; among others, *On the Deformity of Qualities,* the *Treatise on the Sphere,* the *Commentary on the Books of Heaven and Earth,* and those he left on the *Physics* and the *Meteors* by Aristotle.

Nicole Oresme has played an important part in three great discoveries. He clearly anticipated the law of falling bodies, the diurnal movement of the earth and the use of co-ordinates. Concerning this last point, Oresme considers that "all intensity that can be acquired in a progressive way must be represented by a straight line raised vertically from each point of the space or of the subject affected by this intensity. The proportion between two intensities of the same nature is always found between the lines which represent them and inversely."

In the order of mechanics, and starting from the same principles as Albert of Saxony, Oresme discovered that the space traversed by a body animated by a uniformly varied movement is proportionate to time. He applied rectangular co-ordinates to the study of the fall of bodies and defined with precision the conditions required for its correct representation. In studying the variation of intensity of the particular quality called "a uniformly accelerated speed," Oresme shows that it can be represented as equivalent to a uniform speed. The distance covered by a mobile endowed with a uniformly varied movement is equal to the distance covered in the same time by a mobile animated by a uniform movement, and having a speed equal to that which the first mobile attains at its mean instant. Oresme, therefore, went well beyond John Buridan; he discovered truths which, by a continuous series of intermediaries, were to go right up to Galileo.

Just as he anticipated certain discoveries of Descartes and Galileo in physics, Oresme anticipated Copernicus in astronomy. In his *Treatise on Heaven and Earth* he maintained that experiments would be required to demonstrate that the sky is moved and that the earth is not; that this thesis, which cannot be proved by experience, cannot be proved by reason either; next he gives "several fine persuasions to show that the earth is moved in a daily movement and the sky not," and finally Oresme concludes by showing "how such considerations are profitable for the defense of our faith." It would doubtless be excessive to trace back to Nicole Oresme alone the honor of this discovery. The theory of the diurnal movement of the earth was known by everyone in the Faculty of Arts at the University of Paris at the time our philosopher was a student there. Albert of Saxony declares that one of his masters upheld exactly the same thesis as Nicole Oresme, namely, that one cannot demonstrate that it is not the earth which is in movement and the sky at rest. As early as the first years of the fourteenth century, we saw the Scotist Francis of Meyronnes record the opinion of "a certain doctor," according to whom the doctrine of the movement of the earth would be more satisfactory than the contrary doctrine (*dicit tamen quidam doctor, quod si terra moveretur et coelum quiesceret, quod hic esset melior dispositio*). But we must get to Oresme before we find more than a simple mention of this thesis and see its possibility demonstrated by arguments whose "clarity and precision," in P. Duhem's judgment, "greatly surpass what Copernicus wrote on the same subject."

6. EXTENSION OF THE PARISIAN SCHOOL

Just as the Faculty of Arts of Paris had given the University of Vienna its first rector in the person of Albert of Saxony, it gave the new University of Heidelberg its rector in Marsilius of Inghen (d. 1396). A pupil of Buridan in Paris,[54] he himself had taught there before becoming rector of Heidelberg. Like that of his master, his terminism does not involve him in any philosophical scepticism. Marsilius distinguishes between mathematical demonstration, unfit to prove the existence of God, and metaphysical demonstration which can prove it, as Duns Scotus did, for example. It can also be proved metaphysically that God is unique, the efficient and preserving cause of all things; but it cannot be proved by natural light alone that creation *ex nihilo* is possible. Faith alone enables to affirm an immense and free God who can immediately produce a multiplicity of beings, including matter itself. Ockham and Buridan had already taught that natural reason cannot prove the infinity of the moving power of God. Marsilius, therefore, was only following his master on these points.

Henry of Hainbuch (Henry of Langenstein), a colleague of Marsilius at Paris, taught philosophy there beginning in 1363, then theology from 1376 to 1383; we find him in 1384 at the University of Vienna where he died in 1397.[55] His *Questions on the Sentences* date from his teaching in Vienna. His work includes a vast Commentary on the first three chapters of Genesis, treatises on physics (*De reductione effectuum specialium in virtutes communes, De habitudine causarum et influxu naturae communis respectu inferiorum*), on astronomy (*De improbatione epicyclorum et concentricorum*), on economics (*De contractibus emptionis et venditionis*, plus an *Epistola* on the same subject), without counting numerous writings motivated by the schism of 1378, and even treatises on asceticism (*De contemptu mundi, Speculum animae*). Like Henry of Hainbuch, his Parisian colleague and friend Henry of Oyta (Henry Totting of Hoyta, d. 1397) ended his days on the Faculty of Theology of Vienna, after having taught at Paris and at Prague. We are indebted to him for questions on the *Isagoge*, three *Treatises on the Soul and its Powers*, a work on economics (*Tractatus moralis de contractibus reddituum annuorum*) and a *Commentary on the Sentences*. His writings are sometimes confused with those of another Henry of Oyta (Henry Pape of Oyta), who was also teaching at Prague in 1369.[56] Most of the works of Henry of Hainbuch and Henry of Oyta are still unpublished, but the few soundings already taken invite classification in the Parisian school of Buridan.

In the thirteenth century, Paris had cultivated logic and forsaken the sciences, while Oxford was cultivating the sciences, but without forsaking logic. In the fourteenth century, it seems that the interest in scientific problems was greater in Paris than at Oxford. P. Duhem even believed that Oxford had at that time degenerated into a logicism that had corrupted its mathematics, and that this logicized mathematics had, in turn, provoked the decadence of Parisian scholasticism in the fifteenth century. Apart from the fact that this makes Oxford look too much like the villain in the play, we should beware of such historical generalizations. P. Duhem's original and intelligent pioneering work perhaps runs the risk of causing us to imagine the University of Paris in the fourteenth century as peopled by physicists completely absorbed in statics, kinetics and astronomy. As a matter of fact, Buridan, Albert of Saxony and Oresme continued at Paris the work of the masters of arts of the thirteenth century, without giving up logic in the slightest degree; only they went more and more deeply and originally into the problems raised by the scientific works of Aristotle. It was in their pedagogical framework, as immutable for the philosophers as the *Commentary on the Sentences* was for the theologians, that they introduced new ideas, which were sometimes only the revival of very old intuitions that had long been in desuetude. It may be that the Oxonians of the fourteenth century were less original than their colleagues in Paris, or simply that their own originality has not yet been detected. The idea of logicizing mathematics was not, itself, without its own possibilities, although the place for it should have been Cambridge. However that may be, there is no marked difference between the writings of the Parisian masters and the work of Swineshead [57] for example (Richard, Roger or Robert), the author of a *Commentary on the Sentences,* a treatise *On the Motion of Heaven,* logical *Insolubilia,* and a *Book of Calculations* which earned him the surname of *Calculator* in the course of the two centuries that followed. Swineshead agrees that the affirmation of a being unique and superior to all others is more probable than the contrary, but that a *protervus* that wished to maintain the possibility of an infinite series of causes would easily answer the contrary arguments of Aristotle. And it is the same for the infinite power of God. One could link with Swineshead the Oxonian William Heytesbury (d. 1380), and a good many others, but of them we must admit that they are little more than names to us.[58]

CHAPTER III

THE SECOND AVERROISM

COMBATED and condemned in the thirteenth century, Averroism nevertheless did not cease to gain ground and recruit partisans in the course
of the fourteenth, but they were of several sorts. First there were, as
always in these clashes, cool-headed men to find that things had been
needlessly made tragic. Had Averroes really said all he had been made to
say? Richard Fitz-Ralph (Siraph), Bishop of Armagh (*Armacanus*) and
primate of Ireland (d. 1360), was not at all convinced he had.[59] The
famous thesis of the unity of the agent intellect is not from Aristotle,
nor from any other philosopher; if it was an invention of Averroes, both
natural reason and Aristotle's doctrine were against it; even the doctrine
of Averroes himself in other parts of his work was against it. In fact,
Averroes has it clearly understood that this separate agent Intellect is
not the material and possible intellect, but its form; it is therefore
obvious that, according to Averroes, the agent Intellect is God (*Unde
patet quod intellectus agens secundum Commentatorem est Deus*). It is
surprising that intelligent men make him say such things, which are
contrary to what he thought. Since the thesis of Averroes thus understood
agrees with Robert Grosseteste's and Saint Augustine's, Fitz-Ralph adopts
it. It seems to him, therefore, that the agent Intellect is the primary form,
that is, God himself, as joined with the thought (*mens*) of man in such
a way as to prepare it to receive the intellections in the bodily faculties
of man (*intellectus agens . . . est forma prima, scilicet Deus ipse quate-
nus sic conjungitur menti hominis, ut praeparet ipsam ad recipiendam
passionem ab intellectionibus in virtutibus materialibus homnis*). Fitz-
Ralph's Augustinism seems to be inherited from Henry of Ghent, but
not without modifications. As he interprets it, Henry of Ghent conceived
divine illumination as conferring actual knowledge on human thought;
Fitz-Ralph considers that it only confers habitual knowledge. The divine
light increases in the mind through the exercise of speculation, while
perturbations naturally caused in the soul by its body proportionately
decrease. There are few possible doctrinal combinations that the middle
ages did not try at least once.

From the list of Latin Averroists should be struck the name of the
Carmelite John Baconthrop (*Johannes Baco,* d. 1345-48), who has, however, traditionally been called "the prince of the Averroists." [60] This
legend was recently destroyed, and in its place we see nothing more
than a theologian of moderate opinions, almost timid, who does not
hesitate to record at full length the opinions of Averroes, but without

conceding any one of them, and rather anxious to refute them. Not only does he consider Averroes as the worst of heretics, but he sets himself strongly against Latin Averroists on the subject of the agent intellect, which seems to him an error against the faith and even against philosophy. Another Englishman of the first half of the fourteenth century, Thomas Wilton,[61] seems to have a better right to the title of Averroist. At least, Baconthrop, in his *Commentary on the Sentences,* reproached him with favoring the Averroistic interpretation of the possible intellect. Some texts of his reveal him strongly impressed by several of Averroes' conclusions, which he carefully presents as admitted by certain "modern theologians." It cannot be demonstrated against Averroes, by natural reason alone, that God knows anything but himself, or that the rational soul is multiplied with human bodies, or, consequently, that it is the form of the body. It remains to be seen to what extent Thomas Wilton himself was involved in these theses, or if he only "recited" them.

I. JOHN OF JANDUN

It was not in England, so it seems, that the movement took on its full force. It was there only an imported product recently arrived from Paris. On the contrary, a continuous vein of Averroism runs between the Parisian Faculty of Arts and the schools of Northern Italy, whose masters were to maintain Aristotle's doctrine against the supporters of modern physics with much more tenacity than the orthodox theologians themselves. The only way to be convinced that Averroism, in spite of its daring and revolutionary aspect, was essentially conservative is to take a general survey of its history. There is perhaps no example in the history of philosophy of a school as closed on itself and of a doctrine so little permeable to influences from without. The only concessions agreed to by Latin Averroism of the fourteenth century have been to Christian dogma; a certain number of masters can be pointed out who made every effort to lessen the divergence between Averroes and the data of revelation; but the attempts to open Averroism to the influence of the Ockhamist movement were rare and, so far as we can see, insignificant. The significance of Averroism lies in the history of Western culture. Philosophically speaking, it is Averroism, and not scholasticism in general, that deserves to be called a repetitious and obdurate Aristotelianism. It forgot nothing; it learned nothing.

As early as John of Jandun,[62] however, another characteristic of the doctrine was perceptible, which it is necessary to stress. In studying Siger of Brabant we noted how difficult it was to interpret his attitude concerning the relations of faith to reason. He expressly states that truth is on the side of faith and nothing authorizes us to think that he does not believe what he says. With John of Jandun, on the contrary, a political adversary of the papacy, and one of the refugees at the court of Louis of Bavaria, there are motives to suspect that he places truth on the side of reason and simply cares nothing for faith. This master of the Faculty of Arts of Paris (d. 1328) modestly declares that he will content himself in his commentaries with aping Averroes. Elsewhere, it is true, we see him point with pride to his personal contribution to the demonstration of such and such a thesis, but, by and large, he remains the faithful disciple of the Commentator. His works are less interesting by the content of his Averroism than by the nuance of mocking incredulity he gives it. John of Jandun naturally upholds the eternity of movement and the world, the oneness of the agent intellect for all the human species, the unlikelihood of personal immortality as well as of the resurrection and of a future life. Those are the ordinary threads of which all Averroist writings are woven, but the way in which he constantly proclaims his submission to the teachings of the Church is really curious.

John of Jandun claims he has no other masters than natural reason and experience, but since he immediately identifies their conclusions with the conclusions of Averroes, his doctrine is almost entirely a commentary on a commentary, plus the defense of Averroes' authority against objections.[63] Averroes, for him, is the "most perfect and glorious friend and defender of philosophical truth"; Saint Thomas he considers also not without merit, but John thinks he had, in common with other Latin commentators, the defect of having become more interested in theology than in philosophy as he grew older. It is, therefore, to reason incarnate in Averroes that one must cling while, at the same time, maintaining intact the rights of faith. Faced with one of the contradictions between faith and his philosophy, John notes it, adding simply that if anyone can solve it he is lucky, but that he, John of Jandun, realizes that he is quite incapable of doing so. "I believe," he writes for example, "and I hold firmly that this substance of the soul has natural faculties which are not the acts of corporeal organs, but which have their immediate root in the essence of the soul; these are: the possible intellect, the agent intellect and the will. These faculties are of an order superior to the order of corporeal matter and exceed all its capacities . . . And even though the soul is in matter, it nevertheless remains an act in which corporeal matter does not participate; and all these attributes of the soul belong to it really, simply and absolutely, according to our faith. I also believe that the immaterial soul can suffer from a corporeal fire and be united with the body after death on the order of God the Creator. I am not prepared to demonstrate all this, but I think these things must be believed by simple faith, as well as many others that must be believed without any demonstrative reason solely on the authority of Holy Scripture and miracles. Furthermore, that is why our faith is meritorious, for the Doctors teach that there is no merit in believing what reason can demonstrate." It takes an ear trained to the language of mediaeval theologians to appreciate the humor, in this context, of this quotation.[64]

When he speaks elsewhere of creation *ex nihilo* John of Jandun likewise enjoins us to believe it even though it seems to him absolutely incomprehensible. From the point of view of natural reason he evidently cannot conceive another process of becoming than generation from a pre-existing matter. Creation proper, which makes being follow nothingness, is to him an unintelligible thing. It is no wonder, then, that the pagan philosophers knew nothing about it: "Nor is this surprising, for creation cannot be known from sensible things, nor proved from notions that agree with them. And that is why the ancients, who derived all their knowledge from reasons based on sensible things, did not manage to conceive such a mode of production; all the more so since creation so rarely happens, that there has only been one, and a great deal of time has elapsed since then (*praecipue quia raro contingit iste modus, et nunquam fuit nisi semel, et est valde longum tempus praeteritum postquam fuit*)." The irony that we cannot help perceiving in this passage invites us to give to so many of the little disquieting formulas we meet in John of Jandun's writings a similar meaning: "I believe that this is true, but I do not know how to prove it; good for those who do: *sed demonstrare nescio; gaudeant qui hoc sciunt.*" Or again: "I say that God can do it; how, I do not know; but God knows: *modum tamen nescio; Deus scit.*" It is therefore possible that John of Jandun's Averroism was a learned form of religious incredulity. Yet, strictly speaking, there is no way to prove this. Was he sneering at Christian faith itself? Or was he sneering at the simplicity of the theologians who pretended to demonstrate what they can only believe? We do not know.

2. MARSILIUS OF PADUA

It was also at Paris, and at the same time as John of Jandun, that Marsilius of Padua (d. between 1336 and 1343) taught the liberal arts.[65] He became a collaborator of Ockham and a refugee at the court of Louis of Bavaria, but what we now know of his Averroism does not go beyond an application of the theoretical separation of reason and faith in the philosophical order to the strict separation of the spiritual from the temporal in the political order. Dante had reached similar conclusions in his masterly treatise *De Monarchia,* but his own intentions were entirely different. A resolute partisan of the co-ordination of strictly distinct and independent orders, Dante was more interested in a universal monarchy than in the philosophy of Averroes. Nor could the philosopher and physician, Peter of Abano,[66] professor at Padua from 1307 on, be considered a true Averroist. It is, however, certain, by the testimony of Petrarch, that Averroism spread very early in Italy, attended by a radical religious incredulity, as early as the first half of the fourteenth century. Moreover, we are assured of the existence of at least two Italian masters who accepted Averroism at that time. The astronomer and philosopher, Taddeo of Parma,[67] whose Question *On Elements* is dated from Bologna, 1321. His *Theory of the Planets* was written in the same city, for the students in medicine, in 1318, and his *Questions on the Soul* conform to the Averroist standard we know. Dealing with the question: whether the intellective soul is the substantial form of the body and gives it being, Taddeo states that he will proceed in the following manner: "First, I shall take up the opinions of others and refute them; second, I shall take up the opinion I believe to be the opinion of Aristotle and the Commentator; third, I shall brush aside certain difficulties; fourth, I shall relate (*recitando*) the opinion to which one should adhere by faith." His conclusion therefore leaves us faced with the uncertainty inherent in any Averroist position concerning the intimate convictions of its author: "Let each one, however, note well that, in these writings, I have not spoken in asserting, but in reporting (*non dixisse asserendo, sed solum recitando*). The truth of the thing is, in fact, that our intellective soul is the substantial form and perfection inherent in the human body, infused into it, by way of creation, by the First Principle, Who is blest world without end. *Amen.*" All this, even the final doxology, is Averroist.

The second of these Italian Averroists, Angelo of Arezzo,[68] a pupil of the Aristotelian commentator Gentile da Cingoli,[69] left us works on the *Isagoge* of Porphyry and Aristotle's *Categories*. It is worthy of note that Angelo managed to stuff his Averroism into treatises on logic, where nothing really obliged him to put it. The texts quoted by M. Grabmann leave no room to doubt that he taught the unity of the possible Intellect for the whole human species (*intellectus possibilis separatur a corpore tamquam perpetuum a corruptibili*). Naturally, what he himself thought about it cannot really be known: "according to the intention of the Commentator and of Aristotle the intellect is numerically one in all men; although this be against faith." Literally, the phrase signifies that Aristotle's opinion and Averroes' is contrary to faith. Who could deny it? Similarly, discussing the question whether the number of men is infinite, Angelo answers that according to Aristotle it is, since the Philosopher states that the world is eternal, from which it follows that there was no first man and there never will be a last one. But, he immediately adds, "since this is false and against faith, don't admit it." And here is his way out of this contradiction without getting away from philosophy: instead of asking the question for the whole duration of the world, let us ask it only for the number of men actually existing. The problem then becomes easy to solve, for Aristotle demonstrates that the actual infinite is impossible; it is therefore impossible that there be an infinite number of actually existing men. Is this still another "foxy evasion"?

It is quite possible. In any case, it is an expedient, and one which could not put him in order with theology, since he obviously refuses to ask the question for a universe of unlimited duration. Like all the Averroists, Angelo of Arezzo does not present the thesis of the philosophers as true, but as false. It is not in his works that we can hope to find the famous doctrine of the "double truth" expressly formulated and admitted.

The attitude that formula points out was none the less at work in all domains, even that of political philosophy. A famous treatise of Marsilius of Padua, the *Defensor pacis* (1324) is as perfect an example of political Averroism as one could wish for. Starting from the classical distinction of the two ends of man, Marsilius distinguishes two corresponding modes of life: the temporal life, which the princes regulate according to the teachings of philosophy, and eternal life, to which the priests lead man with the help of revelation (I, 4, 3 and 4). The needs of the temporal life are satisfied by various orders of artisans and civil servants indispensable to that end. The priests also have a rôle to play in the city, but the philosophers have never been able to prove which rôle by demonstrative reason, and moreover there is none that is evident: "All nations are, however, agreed on this point, that it is important to institute a sacerdotal class to honor God and worship him, and this for the comfort that may result from it in this world or the other one" (I, 5, 10). In fact, most religious sects promise that the good shall be rewarded and the wicked punished in another life. These beliefs are admitted without proof (*absque demonstratione creduntur*), but they are very useful for they incite the citizens to live peacefully and respect the rules of private morality, to the greatest benefit of the social order. The ancient philosophers did not believe in the resurrection of the body nor in an eternal life, but they imagined and taught that doctrine (*fixerunt et persuaserunt*) to encourage men toward virtue. To maintain more easily law and order, such was the result they proposed finally to obtain (I, 5, 11). This led to the organization of temples, cults, and a class of masters charged with the teaching of these doctrines. Priests were chosen with great care: men already free from passion, studious, respected and of non-mercenary character. After having thus described the pagan priests, Marsilius calmly adds that all the religious sects were false, except the Jews and the Christians: "We have nevertheless spoken of their rites, the better to show the difference from the true priesthood, which is that of the Christians, as well as the necessity for the sacerdotal class in communities" (I, 5, 13).

Nothing could be clearer. The priests are there to teach the Gospel, first with a view to eternal salvation, and, accessorily, to facilitate the task of the police. All goes well then, as long as the priesthood pursues its own ends, but all goes badly as soon as it mixes in the temporal. It is a pernicious plague and destructive of peace. For the Church is the spouse of Christ, and it includes, in addition to the clergy, all the faithful. The priests have a universal right of judgment in it, but no right of coercion in the temporal. Similar to the physician, the priest informs, counsels, prescribes, but never constrains. The only judge who has, in addition to the power of judging, the power of constraining, is Christ. True enough, the superiority of sacerdotal power over temporal power is usually admitted. It is more noble, they say, and the power whose action is more noble cannot be subjected to the one whose action is less noble. Doubtless, but it is so only in the Christian religion, and after all, what do we know about it? All this reasoning rests on the hypothesis that the Christian religion is the most perfect of all, and faith alone assures us of this: *quod tamen sola fide tenemus*. Thus deprived of all authority to intervene in the temporal, the Church is therefore relegated to the sphere of the supernatural and of what prepares us for the future life. As to the City, it administers itself according to the art of the workers and the counsel of the philosophers. The complete separation of philosophy and theology is here attended by a complete separation of Church and State. The disruption of mediaeval Christendom is from this moment an accomplished fact.

The history of Averroism does not come to an end with the fourteenth century. On the contrary, it solidly entrenched itself in Italy, whence its influence radiated throughout the rest of Europe. The Hermite of Saint Augustine, Paul of Venice (d. 1429) seems to have mainly followed John of Jandun.[70] But the citadel of Averroism always remained Padua. Some of its masters were rather moderate in their views; for instance, Cajetan of Tiene (Cajetanus Thienaeus, d. 1463) endeavored to lessen the gap between the doctrine of Averroes and the teachings of Christian faith.[71] Nicoletto Vernias, a monk of the Order of the Theatines, who taught at Padua from 1471 to 1499, was more radical in his views and maintained, at least in his earlier writings, the oneness of the agent Intellect.[72] In proceeding further, we would decidedly overstep any conceivable boundaries for the middle ages. Let us therefore simply recall the names of Peter Pompanazzi (d. 1525) and of Cesar Cremonini (d. 1631), whose writings are inseparable from the history of Western culture at the time of the Renaissance. These men are usually considered "modern." In fact, their main concern was to defend the Averroistic interpretation of Aristotle against that of Alexander of Aphrodisias. The true founder of modern philosophy was not to be an Averroist. When Descartes died, in 1650, he left us his *Discourse on Method* and his *Metaphysical Meditations*, and these are really the first outstanding monuments of modern philosophy, but Descartes had first learned scholastic philosophy at La Flèche. He was a pupil, not of Averroes, but of the Jesuits.

CHAPTER IV

JOURNEY'S END

READING a history of Christian philosophy in the middle ages leaves an impression of linear evolution which, although unavoidable, is deceptive. Every one of the great doctrinal innovations which took place, in theology as well as in philosophy, perpetuated itself throughout the following centuries. The doctrines accumulated by the successive masters, backed by their Orders, exploited by their schools and continually distorted in the heat of endless controversies, finally created what cannot be described otherwise than an extreme doctrinal confusion. The broad distinction between the two "ways," the ancient way and the modern way, introduced some sort of order in the late mediaeval schools, but a fourteenth-century document from Ingolstadt gives a vivid picture of the real confusion hidden behind these two apparently clear terms. On the one hand, there was the old way (*via antiqua*), that is, "the common doctrine of Aristotle . . . and of his Commentator Averroes and . . . of Albert the Great, St. Thomas Aquinas, Giles of Rome, Alexander of Hales, Scotus, Bonaventure, Richard of Mediavilla, Peter of Tarantasia, Peter of La Palu, and other realists (*aliorumque realium*); on the other hand, there was the modern way (*via moderna*), that is, the doctrine of certain "renovators called Nominalists" (*doctrina quorumdam renovatorum qui Nominales dicuntur*), namely "William Ockham, Buridan, Peter of Ailly, Marsilius of Inghen, Adam Dorp, Albert of Saxonia and the other Nominalists." [73] The fifteenth century was to witness continuous struggles between these two parties, here quarreling over possession of the same university, as was the case at Paris, elsewhere sharing it peacefully, or still elsewhere winning over the university to the benefit of one side by the radical exclusion of the other.

I. JOHN GERSON

This doctrinal confusion finds its saddened and powerless witness in the person of John Gerson (d. 1492). A pupil of the nominalist Peter of Ailly,[74] whom he succeeded in 1395 as chancellor of the University of Paris, Gerson[75] was not, properly speaking, a philosopher; but he was a theologian competent in philosophical matters and eminently capable of intervening efficaciously in philosophical controversies when the interests of theology demanded it. The nominalists of the fourteenth and fifteenth centuries were constantly claiming him as one of them. They even used his fame and his authority as an irrefutable argument in favor of the orthodoxy of nominalism. Was not realism the very basis

of the heresies of John Hus and Jerome of Prague, and who had silenced
these heretics at the Council of Constance, if not the champions raised
up by God for his cause, Peter of Ailly and John Gerson? In fact, Gerson
had never adhered to nominalism except against a certain realism and,
more precisely, against what, in realism, ran the risk of leading to the
doctrines of Scotus Erigena, of Wyclif, of Jerome of Prague and John Hus.
It was not the philosophical aspect of the problem that held his attention.
Gerson did not propose a system but a remedy for the evil which the clash
of systems was for the Church. This remedy, he believed he would find not
in any philosopher whatever, but in a certain notion of theology.

The evil that needed curing is remarkably described by Gerson in his
Fifty Propositions on the modes of signification (1426). This treatise has
as an epigraph a phrase taken from Saint Matthew: "An evil and adul-
terous generation seeketh a sign." Any theologian could immediately
complete the text: "and a sign shall not be given it, but the sign of
Jonas the prophet" (Matt. 12, 39). An opportunely chosen text in truth,
for the generation Gerson had before his eyes was particularly avid for
signs, but incapable of using them as should be done. When he cast his
eyes on his own university, the chancellor discovered there only a general
confusion of the orders of knowledge, each one using the mode of signification proper to a certain discipline and made for a certain object, in order
to solve problems raised by another discipline and another object. He saw
the masters of grammar, whose object is the congruity of discourse, solve
their problems by methods proper to logic, whose object is the truth or
falsity of propositions, while masters of logic claimed to solve by those
same methods the problems of metaphysics, a science which does not bear
upon propositions but upon things. And he saw that grammarians, logicians
and metaphysicians believed they could solve the problems of theology
by all these methods at once, as though theology had not its own methods
and its own object, which is the word of God. Taking up the particular
problem of the relations between logic and metaphysics in another treatise
of the same year, 1426 (*De concordia metaphysicae cum logica*), Gerson
gave proof of a perspicacity that was truly admirable, for what he wished
to cure was really the evil of the century, the twofold and complementary
vice of treating of logic as a metaphysician or of metaphysics as a logician.

For anyone wishing to know exactly how this perspicacious witness himself drew up the balance sheet of the fourteenth century, nothing can
replace the two lessons by Gerson *Against Vain Curiosity in Matters of Faith,*
the first of which is dated November 8, 1402, the very year of the *Treatise
on the Roman de la Rose,* and which the second must have closely followed.

The theme of these two lessons is taken from Mark, 1, 15: *Repent and
believe the gospel,* and what Gerson gets out of it is a pitiless criticism of
the methods of the scholastic theology of his time. All preaching should
first announce penitence, with which we turn from vice, and especially

pride. In turning from penitence, pride turns from faith, especially among
the university men (*praesertim apud scholasticos*). That evil mother, pride,
has two evil daughters, curiosity and the desire to be different, to which
we add envy, which is their sister, and of whom are born in turn the spirit
of contention, of dispute, of obstinacy, the defence of error, the love of the
literal, the refusal to renounce one's opinions or the opinions of one's spiritual family, scandal and scorn for the simple ones, and the horror of everything that is humble. That vain curiosity which formerly deceived the
philosophers, it may be feared may also deceive the theologians of our
time. Natural knowledge has its limits, let us not seek to go beyond them.
What can reason alone know of God? That he is the One than whom no
greater can be conceived, the Being who has all that is better than its
opposite. Such is the philosophy that Paul, and his pupil Denis call the
wisdom of God. Let us say rather: his revelation, for it is an idea innate
in all that God is the Being than whom one can conceive no greater. This
wisdom, or revelation, is impressed on all of us as the light of God's face, as
the magnificent and luminous little sketch by the divine Bonaventure puts
it, the *Itinerarium mentis in Deum:* "booklet beyond all praise," Gerson
continues, "and I can never be astonished enough at the fact that the
Minorite Fathers and Brothers should abandon such a Doctor—so great
that I do not know whether the university has ever had another equal to
him—to turn toward I know not what newcomers, for whom they are ready
to come to blows with fists and feet. After all, it is up to them to see
whether the others are useful to them, and we shall speak of this farther
on."

Thus, after having begun his lecture as a sermon by Saint Francis of
Assisi, we find Gerson back with Saint Anselm and Saint Bonaventure,
with an innate idea of God that does not exclude the proofs of his
existence. By which it is evident first that Gerson's nominalism has its
limits, and these limits become more and more apparent the further we
penetrate into the reasons he has for adopting it on a definite point. The
ravages of pride in theology begin where one wishes to attain demonstration on matters which arise from the will of God. As soon as one commits
this error, all is lost. If a philosopher is asked: is the world eternal? let
him answer: I know nothing about it; that depends upon the will of God,
therefore it is for God to answer your question. Instead of that, what do
they say? That, according to the philosophers God does not act freely, but
rather through a natural necessity and a sort of property that his own
goodness has of diffusing itself. This, Gerson concludes, is what seems to
me the main root of all error in those who philosophize in that way (*Haec
est, fateor, tota et praecipua radix errorum in istis philosophantibus*). It
would be impossible to bring into clearer light the profound theological
reason for so many famous adhesions to nominalism. What is here retained
of Ockham, and what, moreover, constituted really the very root of his

work, is his criticism of the radical Platonism of the natural theologies which confound the Christian God with the Good conceived as more or less analogous to a nature, when it is first of all a free will. All the evil comes from that, and it is obvious enough how pride turns it to account. If God is a nature, were he even the *Bonum diffusivum sui* so often spoken of, we can raise problems concerning him with the certainty of being able to solve them. All we have to do is to deduce the properties of such a nature according to the logic of reason. What a convenient God for philosophers to handle, but how different from the free God of Scripture! For if God is not a nature but a freedom, any question concerning him admits only of an unforeseeable answer. One can no longer deduce what he must have done; since he did what he wished to do, one can only believe what he did. And in order that this can be known, it must even be God who said so. To believe him is an act of humility, and humility is only obtained by penitence: *Repent and believe the Gospel.* All Christian wisdom really lies in this.

This radical opposition to Platonism explains Gerson's adhesion, and the adhesion of many others with him, to certain theses characteristic of Ockhamism, and his opposition to all realism of Ideas which, introducing into God necessary essences, would limit from within his supreme liberty. "God does not will certain actions because they are good," Gerson affirms, "but they are good because he wills them." If there are in him no rules for good previous to his very will, it is because he is free of all the *formalitates* so valued by the *formalizantes.* How dangerous it is thus to mistake logic for metaphysics! Essences are only abstractions, the results of operations which the mind must accomplish in order to distinguish its objects; to make things of them is therefore to transform logic into metaphysics, and soon into theology. That was the danger presented by the work of Duns Scotus and the *formalizantes.* By introducing into God metaphysical forms, or quiddities, or ideal reasons, the free and simple God of faith has been destroyed.

It was from this center that Gerson's criticisms started against various philosophers and theologians he does not refrain from naming. These men, whom he considers in 1402 as forming only a minority, are in his eyes the heirs of a Platonism that comes down to them through Avicenna and Algazel, and which each one interprets in his own way: Duns Scotus already named, Ramon Lull, John of Ripa, Bradwardine; more moderate ones and less dangerous, like Henry of Oyta; but also the most to be feared because they turned the Ideas of God into so many creatures: Scotus Erigena and Amaury of Bène condemned in 1210, who engendered Wyclif, who engendered John Hus and Jerome of Prague. Whatever may have been its origin, all this realism is contrary to peripateticism as well as to Catholicism (*peripateticae et catholicae scholae contrarium*), and the error on which it rests is simple: it consists in believing that all that the intellect knows universally, abstractly or separately, exists universally, abstractly and separately, in things and in God.

Reduced to its simplest expression, Gerson's position was reviving at more than a hundred years' distance the Bonaventurian spirit which had inspired the condemnation of 1277. To borrow too much from pagan philosophers is a dangerous practice in theology, for it is contrary to the spirit of penitence, and therefore also of humility and faith. It is the old error of Origen who drank too freely from the golden cup of Babylon, that is to say, as Gerson explains in his second lesson, not of just any philosophy—far be it from him to think of condemning philosophy as such!—but of pagan philosophy. And returning immediately to one of the key propositions among those that Etienne Tempier had condemned, he fixes his criticism on the neoplatonic naturalism of Avicenna, Algazel and several other unbelievers, whose principle it was that from the one as one can come only the one, whence they concluded that the second Intelligence alone was caused by the first. Such is the erroneous principle which, penetrating into Christian theology itself, caused such havoc. For lack of having strongly enough repudiated it, distinctions were introduced in God, not real distinctions in truth, for they never dared go as far as that, but distinctions taken from the nature of things which greatly resemble real distinctions. The thing that Gerson finds so sound about nominalism is that it makes such an error impossible. Whether Ockham's doctrine itself was or was not born of that spirit, this is what Gerson himself discovers in it and the principal lesson he seems to have retained from it.

Considered under this aspect, the nominalism of the fourteenth century therefore prepared a reform of theology conceived as a discipline of faith, based on tradition and linked up to the tradition of the Fathers. The criticisms of scholastic theology in the fifteenth and sixteenth centuries will say nothing against it that Gerson has not already said. Not that he condemned the scholastic method as such. Quite the contrary, Gerson considers it necessary for the interpretation of the doctrine of the Fathers; and the work of the great Doctors of the thirteenth century, especially Saint Bonaventure's, is in his eyes of the greatest importance. But, when he looks at his own times, the situation seems to have become quite different: one considers himself a theologian solely because he has learned philosophy; the Bible and the Fathers are scorned (*spreta Biblia et aliis doctoribus*); one has forgotten that, according to Augustine's statement, the language of theology is not free like that of philosophy, but has its rules (*nobis autem ad certam regulam loqui fas est*), and that the terms used by the Fathers must be respected; questions are uselessly and arbitrarily multiplied; questions not only arbitrary but absurd are asked about God (the Son can produce another Son because he is the same power as the Father; the Father and the Son are not love; the

Holy Spirit was produced before being sovereignly perfect, etc.). To remedy this evil, Gerson dreams of a simplified theology, the same everywhere, taught in each cathedral school by one single master, perhaps in one school only for all France, perhaps in one single school for the whole Church. In his dream-world the philosophers will no longer presume to deal with theology, the theologians will refrain from speculating about everything, and finally the Franciscan and other Orders will cease to rise in a body as soon as anyone dares question the opinions of one of their members. It is not the philosophers, but faith, hope and charity which will heal the hearts and dress the wounds of the Church. To imitate Jesus, that we should imitate Jesus made wisdom for us by God (*Jesum imitari, imitandus est Jesus factus nobis a Deo sapientia*), such is the Franciscan theme which the Chancellor of Paris put back into circulation and which others after him never tired of taking up. With the final years of the fourteenth century, the powerful theological reform initiated in the thirteenth century visibly lost much of its creative force. In a distant past, the Platonist *Consolation of Philosophy* by Boethius had watched over its origins; in 1418, the *Consolation of Theology* by Gerson was foretelling its end.

Seen from without, the situation exhibited no disquieting symptoms. The number of the universities was constantly growing; intellectual life was as intense as it had ever been, but it was degenerating into a mere commentary on what had been created before. The school of Thomas Aquinas was organizing itself under the impulse of Capreolus, the first interpreter of Thomism who attempted to achieve an understanding of the doctrine, not only against its opponents but even, which was less easy, against some of its supporters.[76] The fifteenth century witnessed a no less remarkable development of the Scotist school: Petrus Tartaretus, who taught at Paris about 1490; Mauritius de Portu (d. 1513), Franciscus Lychetus (d. 1520) still remain for us important helps in the interpretation of Duns Scotus.[77] As was inevitable, controversies were keeping alive the classical misunderstanding which had opposed the metaphysics of univocal being to that of analogical being, and vice versa, as if real contradictions on the consequences had been possible in controversies in which the principles themselves had not the same meaning. A great deal of intellectual energy was wasted by both schools on these disputes. Yet, at the same time that the nominalists were showing that both Thomism and Scotism were wrong, a curious revival of Albertism was taking place as if to bring the doctrinal disorder to its point of perfection.

Such as it is represented by John of Maisonneuve, one of the Parisian initiators of the movement, the new Albertism was anxious to maintain the rights of the Fathers of the Church on all points concerning which there was disagreement between their words and those of the philosophers.

Following the example of Albert, John wants to uphold the positions of the Fathers "without toning them down" (*sine quacumque moderatione*). For instance, the Fathers do not agree with the philosophers concerning the separate Intelligences, the angels, and the matter of the celestial bodies, which the philosophers consider as endowed with souls.

In his own treatise *On Being and Essence*[78] John of Maisonneuve develops at length a conception of being which makes essence to be the source of actual being. In actually existing beings there is no real distinction between essence and existence. From this point of view, the new Albertism was a reaction against the Thomism of Thomas Aquinas himself and a return to the positions of the common theology which had dominated the first half of the thirteenth century and had survived, owing to Albert, up to its end. John maintains that there is a plurality of individuals in every angelic species, each angel differing from every other one, within the same species, because of his *quod est* (Boethius), or *hyleachim* (spiritual matter, *Book of Causes*, Prop. IX). These doctrines are traced by Meersseman to the *De causis et processu universitatis* of Albert the Great. Far from following a strictly philosophical direction, this Albertism was one of the moments of a theological reaction common at that date; it was reacting in particular against certain of the philosophical innovations of Thomas Aquinas.

At the same time, logic was still flourishing in the schools; the philosophical teaching of the faculties of arts was developing along its traditional lines, not, however, without adding a new stress on the scientific problems connected with the *Physics* of Aristotle as well as on the notion of infinity which, theological and metaphysical in its origin, was assuming a greater and greater scientific importance.[79] The next generation of historians will know better than we do how a new universe progressively extricated itself from the wreckage of the qualitative physics of Aristotle. On one point at least we can already credit the fifteenth century with a positive philosophical achievement. Caught in the middle of these controversies, and no less tired of them than John Gerson, a man free from school work and from teaching responsibilities attempted to re-establish intellectual unity, not by reconciling the opposition, but by transcending the contradictions.

2. NICHOLAS OF CUES

The outstanding figure of Nicholas of Cues[80] towers above his century. Born at Cues, on the Moselle river, in 1401, Nicholas studied law at Padua, then theology at Cologne and he was for a time an archdeacon at Liège. An active member of the council of Basel (1437), he never ceased afterwards to occupy official positions in the Church. His services as a pontifical legate were rewarded by the cardinalate (1448).

Nicholas was then given the bishopric of Brixen (1450) and died August 11, 1464. His work is an intimate blending of theology and philosophy in which it is almost impossible to draw any dividing line between them other than in words. Moreover, it is a philosophical synthesis spontaneously adapted to the needs of its own times. Nicholas of Cues did not content himself with exhorting his contemporaries to achieve unity, as Gerson had done, he himself attempted to create it for them, or, rather, to make them see that unity was at hand, and they themselves were in it, only they did not know it. Naturally, there was a price to pay for achieving such a result. Any hope of reconciling rival sects was vain so long as Aristotelian dialectics was considered the normal instrument of philosophical thinking. The remedy to the harm done by Aristotle's *Organon* could not be found in the *Organon*. Every attempt to find it there had simply resulted in the creation of one more Aristotelian sect eager to join in the fight carried among themselves by the existing Aristotelian schools. If there was a way out of Babel, Plotinus alone could provide it. Only, the kind of unity which Plotinus normally provides brings no satisfaction to minds less anxious to realize how deeply they really are one than to define the individuating marks which make them to be different.

Metaphysical doctrines of Plotinian inspiration have no particular point of entry. Each and every one of their points is a center or can be used as if it were one. Moreover, to approach the doctrine of Nicholas in the sole light of its Plotinian inspiration exposes his reader to overlook what was new and original in it. The dominating notion is that of infinity, which is a typically Christian notion when it is understood, as is here the case, in the sense of an infinite fullness of positive being. The Anselmian definition of God, whose elements were already present in Boethius, had introduced the notion of a being "than which no greater can be conceived." Henry of Ghent had stressed the positive nature of infinity. Duns Scotus had posited the concept of "infinite being" as the very object of our theology, and had attributed to it an importance which it had never had before in the minds of theologians. Scotus had even distinguished between the notion of infinity in causal power, which he granted to Aristotle, and the notion of infinity in being, which he held to be proper to the Christian God. This notion of infinity which, understood in this sense, had never entered a Greek mind, is at the core of the metaphysics of Nicholas of Cues.

From the very beginning of his treatise *On Learned Unknowing* (*De docta ignorantia*) Nicholas recalls that every inquiry concerning truth consists in relating some notions to anterior ones or to posterior ones, which we call principles and consequences. It is all a question of relations and proportions. Now, precisely, since it is out of proportion with anything, the infinite as such is unknown (I, 1). The originality of this position is that it takes the notion of infinity seriously, that is, otherwise than as meaning a finite reality exceedingly greater than the other ones. Between the true infinite and anything finite, there is no proportion.

First of all, the infinite is a maximum; as an absolute maximum, it is one (since nothing can be either added to, or subtracted from it); since it is unity, it is entity (because unity and being are convertible); if the absolute maximum is one, it is all; if it is all, all things are in it and all things are by it; it is wholly uncontracted (restricted to the form of any particular being). For the same reason, since it is all, nothing else can oppose the infinite; it has therefore no contrary; in consequence, this maximum is also a minimum. In short, the infinite is the absolute and perfect coincidence of contraries (I, 2).

Nicholas was fully aware of the import of this new notion, especially in regard to its methodological consequences. In this order, the new notion of infinity entailed nothing less than a revolution. All the mediaeval philosophies and theologies had been swayed by the Aristotelian principle of contradiction. Anybody inviting Thomas Aquinas, Siger of Brabant, Duns Scotus, Ockham or Nicholas of Autrecourt to argue from this principle, or in conformity with it, was assured of a favorable answer. Nicholas of Cues sees in this universal agreement on the absolute validity of the principle of contradiction the common illusion, not of nominalism only, but of Aristotle and all his followers. In his *Apology for Learned Unknowing,* he expressly protests against the "present predominance of the Aristotelian sect, which considers the coincidence of opposites a heresy, whereas its admission is the starting point of the ascension to mystical theology" (p. 6). In short, the new doctrine demanded the rejection of the dialectics of Aristotle. In Nicholas' own mind, there was nothing new about this demand. He was inviting his contemporaries to return to Hermes Trismegistos, Asclepius and Denis the Aeropagite. Many had done this before him, but nobody had realized that to do it completely entailed the rejection of the Aristotelian dialectics of the principle of contradiction. Nor did Nicholas imagine that many would listen to his advice. Speaking of the Aristotelians, Nicholas remarks that it takes a sort of miracle, something like a religious conversion, to see one of them reject Aristotle in order to rise up to something better (*Apol.*, p. 6). Philosophically speaking, Nicholas was positing contradiction and its progressive overcoming as the proper way toward truth. Instead of carefully avoiding it as fatal to philosophical thinking, Nicholas exhorted his readers to enter the thickness of a reality whose very essence, since it is permeated with the presence of the infinite, is the coincidence of opposites. Before finding another philosophy remotely resembling this one, at least in its attitude toward the principle of contradiction, one would have to wait for the nineteenth century and for the method of Hegel.

In Nicholas of Cues, however, the philosopher is not in quest of a supreme concept virtually including all concept; his intention is to drown all conceptual distinctions in the unity of mystical intuition. Not to achieve perfect conceptualization, but to overcome it, is his own ideal. This result can be achieved provided we remember that finite and sensible beings, such as they are given to us in concrete experience, are, in a way, so many moments included in the unfolding of the Infinite, which is God. But this statement calls for some precisions.

Among the adversaries of the doctrine, John Wenck pointed out at once that the teaching of the *Learned Unknowing* was headed for a confusion of God and creatures, that is, for what we today call pantheism.[81] In fact, what Nicholas says becomes pantheistic as soon as one forgets the nature of infinity. In the doctrines of Denis, Maximus Confessor and Scotus Erigena, there could be no confusion of being between God and creatures for the simple reason that God is above being. Since God *is not,* no creature can share in his *being.* For the same reason, in Nicholas' own doctrine, the finite cannot possibly be the infinite. To participate in the infinite is to be finite. If it did not somehow share in what is the cause of all, the finite would be nothing at all. Moreover, in this doctrine, there is no sense in asking such questions. So long as he has not yet reached the contemplation of God, the dialectician may well ask them; but then he is arguing about something he does not know. If, instead of attempting to triumph in what he says about a knowledge which he has not, the same dialectician strove to acquire it, he would realize that, when that knowledge is there, nothing can be said about it (*Apologia*, pp. 7-8). All this business about confusing God with creatures ceases to make sense once the finite order of contradictory notions has been overcome. It does not apply to the Infinite which is not the sum total of all finites plus a great many possible ones, but, rather, the ineffable coincidence of the maximum and the minimum.

The true method that leads to learned unknowing is therefore possible, but it is entirely different from the usually received ones. Far from confusing God with creatures, it first posits that finite and infinite are incommensurable; as has been said, there is no "proportion" between them. Where there is no proportion, no precise cognition is possible; the precise relation of equality, or of adequacy between intellect and thing, which philosophers require for the possibility of truth, is necessarily relative to the degree of unity that belongs to the thing. Whether it be an individual, a species, a genus, a moment in time or a place in space, no two finite beings are so similar or equal that an infinite number of higher degrees of similitude or equality between them does not remain possible. However equal, the measure and the measured remain always different. Where there is absolute unity, neither measure nor things to be measured are left. Consequently, precise truth is impossible. "The quiddity of the things, which is the truth of beings, is inaccessible in its purity; all philosophers have investigated it, but nobody has discovered it such as it is; and the deeper we shall steep ourselves in this ignorance, the nearer we will find ourselves to truth" (*Apologia,* I, 3). In order to make clear the peculiar nature of the presence of the infinite to finite realities, Nicholas often resorts to examples borrowed from geometry. Had he followed this line of thought as a mathematician, he would have found himself very near the modern notion of the mathematical infinite, but his own intention only was to show that all things are to the maximum as the infinite line is to finite lines. When he comes to the concrete applications of his principle, Nicholas falls back upon Denis rather than upon mathematics (op. cit., I, 16-17). For indeed the problem then is: what is it, for a finite being, to participate in unity, and therefore in being? It is to be posited in a being whose measure is defined by its distance from the maximum (I, 18). God is this maximum; since, precisely *qua* maximum, he is the minimum, God is the simultaneous mutual implication (*complicatio*) of all things, even the contradictory ones (*Deum esse omnium complicationem, etiam contradictoriorum,* I, 44). In the first place, this accounts for the possibility of the divine providence. Secondly, it shows the reason why, according to Denis, negative theology is the only kind of language that fits the absolute transcendency of the maximum (I, 26). Thirdly, it invites us to reform our usual notion of the universe.

Philosophers say that the world is finite. If we call universe all that is not God, they are right. Only God is infinite; so the universe is finite; but since, on the part of God, an infinity of larger and larger created worlds remain possible, we had better say that the world is neither infinite nor finite; it is "infinite in a privative sense," that is to say, in this sense that its matter cannot extend beyond its limits. Its being is "contracted" by the condition of its nature. This is the only way there is for us to conceive some sort of proportion between the universe and God (II, 1).

For God, to create all things is to be all things (II, 2, p. 66). For creatures, to be created is to participate in God, not by taking up a "part" of him (since the infinite has no parts and is out of proportion with the finite, p. 67), but by imitating him as images reflect an object in a mirror. In this case, however, there is not even a mirror. To the extent that language is here possible, creatures are just images. If he ever read this, Berkeley must have felt interested (*sicut imago speciei in speculo— posito quod speculum, ante aut post, per se et in se nihil sit;* II, 2, p. 67).

Let us then posit the maximum. It involves everything by mode of reciprocal implication. It involves even motion, which is a serially ordered rest (*quies seriatim ordinata*). Keeping in mind that this ordered rest is in the maximum by mode of implication, we can conceive actual motion as its explication: *motus igitur est explicatio quietis.* Time is nothing but an ordered presence, for the now is present, the past has been present, the future shall be present. So past and future are the explication (unfolding) of the present, just as the present is the implication of all present times, either in what we call past or in what we call future. In a similar way, "God is implicating all things in this sense that all things are in him; he is explicating all things in this sense that he is in all things" (II, 3, p. 70). This is about all we can know concerning this problem, namely, that creation is an unfolding or explication of God. The how of this escapes us. For indeed, since God is all, the creature is nothing. Remove God from creature, there is nothing left. If we say that God is *in* the creature, then the plurality of things arises from the fact that "God is in nothingness." And indeed, a creature is not to God even what an accident is to a substance. How could we comprehend the presence of God in what is not in any way a being? It is impossible. Creatures are to God in the same relation as its images are to our own face when they multiply in a series of mirrors (II, 3; pp. 71-72). Only let us remember that, in the case of creatures, there is not even a mirror.

As can be seen, this is the very type of a universe in which "everything is in everything." The old saying of Anaxagoras, *"quodlibet esse in quolibet"* suits Nicholas of Cues perfectly (II, 5). The whole universe is in everything in a contracted way and since Nicholas adds that every actually existing thing "contracts" within itself the universe, it is hardly a joke, after saying that "everything is in every thing"; to add: "and inversely." It would be somewhat intricate, to follow Nicholas in his description of the "various degrees of contraction of the universe" (II, 6). This part of his theology is ultimately related to one of the most obscure parts of the doctrine of Nicholas, the notion of matter. Seldom clear, this notion is particularly difficult to define here because, if God is everything, he must also be matter, a conclusion which Nicholas only avoids by establishing that, strictly speaking, absolute matter does not exist.

What could absolute matter be? Nothing more than absolute possibility. Now absolute possibility is God. God is not absolute possibility by privation of all forms, as was the case with matter in ancient philosophies; he is the infinite possibility of all things because, in himself, all things are himself in act. Now, among the possibles, absolute possibility is least capable of actual existence. Even the ancients, when they defined matter as absolute possibility, regularly added that, for this very reason, it was practically nothing. Infinitely actual inasmuch as they are God, the possibles are almost nothing inasmuch as they are themselves. Outside of the pure possibility which is identical with the pure actuality of God (coincidence of opposites) pure possibility without actuality of its own cannot exist. Every particular possibility, then, is contracted by an act. God is the cause of this act and since it has a cause, the existence of every contracted possibility is contingent. Consequently its act too is contingent. In short, just as its act is contracted by possibility, possibility is contracted by its act (II, 8). There is no such thing as absolute matter in things because God alone is the coincidence of absolute actuality and absolute possibility.

After studying the school of Chartres and on entering the new Aristotelian world of the thirteenth century, it looked as though we had left behind us a mental universe gone beyond recall. One cannot even imagine how completely out of date a lecture by Thierry of Chartres would have sounded at the thirteenth-century Faculty of Arts of the University of Paris. In fact, it would have been impossible. Yet, at the end of the fifteenth century, Aristotelianism itself was in turn reaching the term of its course. It was going in circles. Then Nicholas went back to Chartres. The critical edition of his *Learned Unknowing* abounds in references to Thierry of Chartres, to Gilbert of la Porrée, to Clarenbaud of Arras, John of Salisbury and others whose inspiration was akin to his own doctrine. Nicholas went still farther back into the past, to the sources of these latter sources: Chalcidius, Macrobius, Asclepius, Hermes Trismegistus were names familiar to him, and since their Platonism agreed with the doctrine of Denis the Aeropagite, Nicholas could not doubt that they were substantially right. At the end of an age which is commonly described as having been swayed by Aristotle, this cardinal of the Holy Roman Church calmly decided that the logic of Aristotle, inspired by the present condition of man, was no fitting instrument to investigate a universe created by the infinite God of Christianity. Instead of a logic made to separate, Nicholas wanted a logic made to unite, for indeed, no other one could successfully apply to a universe in which everything is in everything. Aristotle himself had known this truth (*Metaph.*, III, 5, 1009a, 27) but he had discarded it as one of those antiquated positions which philosophy outgrows in the course of its progress. But to Nicholas, who was reading it almost twenty centuries after Aristotle had reported it, the doctrine of Anaxagoras appeared as full of life, still well worth exploring and teeming with possibilities. Ideas never die; they are ageless and always ready to revive in the minds which need them, just as ancient seeds can germinate again when they find a fertile soil.

3. GREEK PHILOSOPHY AND CHRISTIANITY

The fourteen centuries of history whose development we have attempted to summarize were dominated by two distinct influences, Greek philosophy and Christianity. Every time educated Christians came in contact with Greek philosophical sources, there was a blossoming of theological and philosophical speculation. Ancient Rome had produced no philosophy.

The Ciceronian tradition, which never disappeared from the horizon during the middle ages, played an extremely important part in the history of Western civilization, and, through Petrarch, it became a decisive factor in bringing about the revival of classical humanism, but one does not see any philosophical doctrine whose origin could be traced back to any Roman writer. Cicero, Seneca, even Lucretius have been busy popularizing ideas of Greek origin; they did not add anything important to their sources. The philosophical sterility of ancient Rome seems to be a fact. It accounts for this other fact, that the men of the middle ages never found in the Latin classics more than secondary sources of information incapable of initiating a new philosophical movement.

The ignorance of the Greek language, very general in the West after the fall of the Roman Empire, had for its result a severance of the Latins from the perennial source of Greek thought in the Western world. From the fourth century on, the role of the translators became extremely important. Practically every notable event in the history of Western thought in the middle ages is tied up with the presence of a man who had studied in Greece, or who knew Greek and had translated some Greek philosophical writings, or who had had access to such translations. Marius Victorinus translated Plotinus into Latin: we are indebted to him for making possible the doctrine of Saint Augustine. Then nothing happened up to the time of Boethius, but Boethius translated the *Organon* of Aristotle and he knew the Platonism of Alexandria; hence the whole history of mediaeval logic and even, owing to the theological opuscules of Boethius, a large section of the Latin theologico-philosophical speculation in the West up to the end of the twelfth century. Then again nothing happened until the Greek writings of Denis the Aeropagite exploded in the ninth century Latin world. The immediate result was the *Division of Nature* by Scotus Erigena, a doctrinal synthesis to which nothing compares between the ninth and the twelfth centuries. Even the works of Saint Anselm of Canterbury, whose dialectical genius is beyond discussion and whose philosophical gifts are evident, betray a certain metaphysical dryness probably due to the fact that, apart from logic, his main source in philosophy was Augustine instead of being the Greek source of Augustine. After Anselm, the twelfth century school of Chartres draws its inspiration from Chalcidius and other Platonic sources; Abélard feeds on the Greeks through Boethius; Bernard of Clairvaux opens the great tradition of Western speculative mysticism on account of his familiarity with the Greek theology of Gregory of Nyssa. Last, not the least, the arrival of Aristotle's encyclopedia at the end of the twelfth century, read either in itself or in its interpretations by Avicenna and Averroes, initiates the flowering of Christian speculation which we call scholasticism. The Philosopher *par excellence* was a Greek; the author of the *Elements of*

Theology was a Greek; seen from this point of view, the philosophical speculation of the middle ages appears as a sort of appendix to the history of Greek philosophy.[82]

But there is another side to the picture. Something happened to philosophy during the fourteen centuries which we call the middle ages. The easiest way to see what happened to it is to remember the general view of the world propagated by the last Greek philosophers and to compare it with the interpretation of the world common to the founders of modern philosophy, namely, Descartes, Malebranche, Leibniz, Spinoza and Locke. In the seventeenth century, the commonly received philosophical notions of God, of the origin of the world, of the nature of man and of his destiny are strikingly different from those which the middle ages had inherited from the Greeks. Strict monotheism, an undisputed truth in the minds of all the metaphysicians of the thirteenth century, is only one of the points in case. In its content, the metaphysics of Descartes was much more a continuation of the metaphysics of the scholastics than of the Greeks. He himself was a Christian and it is no wonder that his philosophy continued, in a most original way, the tradition of the Christian theology of the middle ages. True, Descartes called it a philosophy, and it certainly was one, but the upshot of his *Meditations on Prime Philosophy* was to confirm by a new method all the main conclusions already established in metaphysics by Augustine, Anselm, Bonaventure, Thomas Aquinas and Duns Scotus: the existence of one single God, infinite in being and in power, free creator of heaven and earth, conserving the world by his all-powerful will and acting as a Providence for man whose soul can be proved to be spiritual in nature. With Descartes, Malebranche and Leibniz, the point of departure of modern philosophy coincides with the point of arrival of mediaeval theology. Even Spinoza cannot be fully accounted for without taking into account the speculation of the middle ages. To overlook what happened to philosophy in the thirteenth century is to deprive the history of Western thought of its continuity and, by the same token, its intelligibility.

This duality of nature explains the existence of two historical perspectives on the development of mediaeval speculation. Some historians prefer to follow its philosophical axis. The literary history of the progressive rediscovery of the Greek philosophical sources then becomes of paramount importance; from the end of the twelfth century on, Aristotle figures as the leading character in the play; Averroes and his followers then become, despite their occasional errors, the representatives of philosophy *qua* pure philosophy in the middle ages, or, at least, of the purely philosophical spirit from the thirteenth century up to the beginning of modern times. This is not only a perspective legitimate in itself, but one which answers an incontrovertible reality. It coincides with the very perspective adopted by the first modern philosophers on mediaeval speculation.

It identifies it with Aristotelianism in its various mediaeval and more or less Christianized versions. It fully justifies the famous statement of O. Hamelin that Descartes comes immediately after the Greeks as though there had been nothing else in between. It is likewise tied up with an irreducible opposition to the notion of Christian philosophy in the past as well as in the present, with a corresponding tendency to make philosophy as independent from theology as possible and, consequently, to introduce into the theology of the scholastics a separation between rationally demonstrable conclusions and those whose premises, or at least one of them, rests upon faith.

A second perspective, no less historically justifiable, follows the axis of theology. It is the one which we have followed in this history, not on the strength of any preconceived ideas, but because of two facts. First, unless we consider the rediscovery of Greek philosophy as a philosophical creation of the mediaeval mind, all the original contributions made by the middle ages to the common treasure of philosophical knowledge have been made by theologians. Augustine, Denis, Anselm, Thomas Aquinas, Duns Scotus and Ockham have all been theologians; even when they wrote purely philosophical treatises, the deepest expression of their philosophical thought is found in their theological works; not one of them has ever imagined that there was no place for purely rational speculation in theology; in fact, their theologies are full of it, and to take mediaeval scholasticism just as it was should also be considered a historically justifiable perspective. True enough, it is an incomplete one, but no harm is done so long as this abstraction does not mistake itself for a separation in reality.

This second perspective has its drawbacks too. The fact that most modern theologians restrict the qualification of "theological" to conclusions among whose premises one at least is held as true by faith only, gives a paradoxical aspect to the history of doctrines which saw no difficulty in maintaining a position on strictly rational grounds and yet in considering it theological. It is not easy to persuade our contemporaries that they should look at mediaeval scholasticism from a mediaeval point of view; they may even have good reasons for refusing to do so, only these reasons cannot be historical ones. Now the only truth which history is supposed to look for is that of historical reality. Like every other truth, it has a right to be fully respected, and while no historian can be simple enough for confusing his own conclusions with historical truth itself he himself cannot help stating it as he sees it. The progress of historical research and interpretation will finally put everything in its proper perspective, no honest effort will have been lost and, since truth is one, there is nothing to lose and everything to gain in striving to respect it in all its orders and under all its aspects.

The philosophical appreciation of the results achieved by the Fathers of the Church and by scholastics does not fall under the competence of their historian. The least that a historian can say about this, however, is that apart from their ignorance of the facts, there is no excuse for those who describe the middle ages as a long period of philosophical stagnation. It might have been one. The Catholic Church could have condemned all philosophical speculation, including the very study of philosophy, as opposed to Christian faith. The Christian priests and monks could have been forbidden by the Church to indulge in such studies, to open schools and to teach doctrines that had been taught by pagans at a time when the gospel had not yet been preached to the Gentiles. The popes could have condemned all efforts to achieve any understanding of faith by means of philosophical speculation. Only no such thing happened during the middle ages; in fact the very reverse took place between the times of Justin Martyr and those of Nicholas of Cues. It is not a good thing to judge fourteen centuries on the ground of their historical misrepresentation.[83]

The intrinsic value of this Christian philosophy in the middle ages is a point for every philosopher to decide in the light of his own judgment. Most of them have their own opinion about it, but this opinion is not always founded upon a first-hand knowledge of the doctrines at stake. Now there is an excellent excuse, if not for judging what one does not sufficiently know, at least for not sufficiently knowing it. Life is short and the history of philosophy is growing longer every year. But if any Christian master felt the same indifference with respect to the history of scholasticism, he would be less easily excusable, because this is his own personal history or, at least, that of his own personal philosophical tradition. This tradition is not a dead thing; it is still alive and our own times bear witness to its enduring fecundity. There is no reason why this fecundity should come to an end. On the contrary, it can be expected to exhibit a new vitality every time it will re-establish contact with its authentic methods and its true principles, whose permanent truth is independent of time. The only object of the history of Christian philosophy, apart from being a history like all the others, is to facilitate access to the perennial sources of Christian speculation.

If, on the whole, this history has not completely misrepresented its object, it can be said that the treasure of Christian philosophy in the middle ages exhibits an amazing wealth of still incompletely exploited ideas. But even leaving them aside, this history should convey to its readers an invitation to establish personal contact with at least three main schools of thought which no Christian philosopher can afford to ignore. Augustine will introduce him to a metaphysical method based upon the data of personal introspection; Duns Scotus will introduce him to a metaphysical universe of essences; Thomas Aquinas will tell him what happens to such a universe when existence is added to essences as a further metaphysical dimension. Had they bequeathed to us nothing more than these three pure philosophical positions, the scholastics would still remain for all Christian philosophers the safest guides in their quest for a rationally valid interpretation of man and the world.

At this point, our philosophical problem arises once more: how can a speculation be rational and philosophical if it is tied up with religious beliefs? Here again, history as such has no competence to answer the question. It knows, however, that far from sterilizing philosophical speculation, this alliance of two distinct orders of thought has given philosophy a new life and brought about positive philosophical results. The history of the influence of Christianity on the development of modern philosophy, quite independently of scholasticism and sometimes even in reaction against its methods, would be another field of investigation. From what little is already known of it, it appears that objectivity in judgment and freedom from settled intellectual prejudices are not the exclusive property of pagan philosophers, that reason is not always found at its best on the side of what is commonly called rationalism, and that, at any rate, the range of intelligibility is incomparably wider than that of reason. This is a lesson which only the frequentation of the true philosophical master minds can teach us. Why should we feel afraid of living in their company? No real master will ever invite us to listen to himself, but to the truth of what he says, such as we ourselves can see it in our own minds. In these matters, nothing can replace personal experience, and none can be more precious than this one if it is true to say, with Thomas Aquinas, that the "highest felicity of man consists in the speculation through which he is seeking the knowledge of truth."

NOTES

I

BIBLIOGRAPHICAL SOURCES

Most periodicals interested in mediaeval studies run bibliographical bulletins. Since no single bibliography can hope to be complete they all are worth consulting. Two publications should be set aside, however, as the only ones that are devoted to critico-bibliographical information.

Bulletin de théologie ancienne et médiévale, Abbaye du Mont César, Louvain, Belgium.

Bulletin Thomiste; Institut d'études médiévales, 831 avenue Rockland, Montréal 8 (P.Q.) Canada.

Covering wider fields but well informed about the history of mediaeval philosophies and theologies:

Revue philosophique de Louvain, Louvain (Belgium)
Revue des sciences philosophiques et théologiques, Etiolles (S. et O.), France.
Scholastik, Freiburg, i. Br. (Germany).
Franziskanische Studien, Paderborn (Germany).
Archivum Franciscanum Historicum, Rome.
Gregorianum, Rome.
Traditio, New York.

Bulletin covering the whole field of mediaeval studies in the United States and Canada:

Progress of Medieval and Renaissance Studies in the United States and Canada, ed. S. Harrison Thomson, Boulder, Colorado (Bulletin 22, 1952).

Bibliographical index of philosophical publications, including works on patristics and scholasticism:

Répertoire bibliographique de la philosophie, Louvain, Editions de l'Institut supérieur de philosophie; published since 1949; vol. 5, 1953.

II

LIST OF ABBREVIATIONS

ADGM. *Aus der Geisteswelt des Mittel-
alters,* Festgabe M. Grabmann,
Münster i. W., 1935 (Beiträge,
Supplement, III).

AFH. Archivum Franciscanum Historicum. Quaracchi (Italy).

AFP. Archivum Fratrum Praedicato-
rum. Rome.

AHDL. Archives d'histoire doctrinale et
littéraire du moyen âge. Paris.

AJT. American Journal of Theology.

ALKM. Archiv für Literatur und Kirchengeschichte des Mittelalters.

AN. The Ante-Nicene Fathers of the
Church.

APA. Acta Pontificiae Academiae Romanae S. Thomae Aquinatis.
Rome.

AST. Analecta sacra Tarraconensia.
Barcelona.

Beiträge. Beiträge zur Geschichte der Philosophie des Mittelalters. Münster i. W.

BET. C. P. Farrar and A. P. Evans,
*Bibliography of English Transla-
tions from Medieval Sources,*
New York, 1946.

CF. Collectanea Franciscana. Rome.

CUP. *Chartularium Universitatis Parisiensis,* by H. Denifle and E.
Chatelain, 4 vols., Paris, 1889-
1897.

CSEL. Corpus scriptorum ecclesiasticorum latinorum. Wien.

DHGE. Dictionnaire d'histoire et de
géographie ecclésiastique. Paris.

DTC. Dictionnaire de théologie catholique. Paris.

DTF. Divus Thomas, Fribourg (Switzerland).

DTP. Divus Thomas, Piacenza (Italy).

FS. Franziskanische Studien. Paderborn (the American journal will
be quoted by its full title: *Franciscan Studies*).

GCFI. Giornale critico della filosofia
italiana. Florence.

GCS. Die griechischen christlichen
Schriftsteller der ersten drei Jahrhunderte. Leipzig.

GDP. Fried. Ueberwegs *Grundriss der
Geschichte der Philosophie;* II,
*Die patristische und scholastische
Philosophie,* 11 ed., by B. Geyer,
Berlin, 1928.

GLOLIT. P. Glorieux, *La littérature
quodlibétique . . . ,* 2 vols.,
Paris, J. Vrin, 1925, 1935.

GLOREP. P. Glorieux, *Répertoire des
maîtres en théologie de Paris au
XIII siècle,* 2 vols., Paris, J.
Vrin, 1933, 1934.

HLF. Histoire littéraire de la France.

HTR. The Harvard Theological Review.
Cambridge (Mass).

JPST. Jahrbuch für Philosophie und
spekulative Theologie (now continued by DTF.).

JQR. The Jewish Quarterly Review.

JTS. Journal of Theological Studies.
London.

MAN. M. Manitius, *Geschichte der lateinischen Literatur des Mittelalters,* 3 vols., Munich, 1911,
1923, 1931.

MAP. Mélanges Auguste Pelzer. Louvain, 1947.

MG. M. Grabmann, *Mittelalterliches
Geistesleben* 2 vols. Munich,
1926, 1936. A third volume is
announced.

MM. Mélanges Mandonnet; études
d'histoire littéraire et doctrinale
du moyen âge. 2 vols. Paris,
1930.

MS. Mediaeval Studies. Toronto.

MSR. Mélanges de science religieuse.
Lille (France).

NPN. A Select Library of the Nicene
and Post-Nicene Fathers of the
Church.

NRT. Nouvelle revue théologique.
Tournai (Belgium).

NS. New Scholasticism. Washington.

OTT. A. G. Little-F. Pelster, *Oxford Theology and Theologians* c. A.D. 1282-1302, Oxford, 1934.

OW. Origenes Werke, 12 vols., in GCS.

PBA. Proceedings of the British Academy. London.

PEM. O. Lottin, *Psychologie et morale aux XIIe et XIIIe siècles,* 7 vols., Louvain, 1942, 1948, 1949, 1954.

PG. Migne, Patrologiae cursus completus, Series Graeca, 162 vols., with Latin transl., Paris. 1857-1866.

PJ. Philosophisches Jahrbuch der Görresgesellschaft. Fulda.

PL. Migne, Patrologiae cursus completus, Series Latina, 221 vols., Paris, 1844-1864.

RAM. Revue d'ascétique et de mystique. Toulouse.

RB. Revue Bénédictine. Maredsous (Belgium).

RFNS. Rivista di filosofia neoscolastica. Milan.

RHE. Revue d'histoire ecclésiastique. Louvain.

RHEF. Revue d'histoire de l'Eglise de France. Paris.

RHR. Revue d'histoire religieuse. Paris.

RMAL. Revue du moyen âge latin. Lyon.

RNSP. Revue Néo-Scolastique de philosophie. Louvain. From vol. 44 (1946) bears the new title: Revue philosophique de Louvain.

RPL. Revue philosophique de Louvain; see RNSP.

RSPT. Revue des sciences philosophiques et théologiques. Le Saulchoir (France).

RSR. Revue des sciences religieuses. Strasbourg-Paris.

RT. Revue Thomiste. Saint-Maximin (Var).

RTAM. Recherches de théologie ancienne et médiévale. Louvain.

SA. Studia Anselmiana. Rome.

Sitzungsberichte. Sitzungsberichte der Bayerischen Akademie der Wissenschaften, philosophisch-historische Abteilung. Munich.

SPCK. Society for the Propagation of Christian Knowledge. London-New York.

SRHC. Scholastica ratione historico-critica instauranda, Rome, Antonianum, 1951.

TMS. The Modern Schoolman. Saint Louis.

TQ. Theologische Quartalschrift. Stuttgart.

TR. Theologische Revue. Münster.

TSK. Theologische Studien und Kritiken. Gotha.

UNIV. Lynn Thorndike, *University Records and Life in the Middle Ages,* Columbia University Press, New York, 2 ed., 1949.

ZKG. Zeitschrift für Kirchengeschichte. Stuttgart.

ZKT. Zeitschrift für katholische Theologie. Innsbruck.

ZNW. Zeitschrift für neutestamentliche Wissenschaft und die Kunde der älteren Kirche. Giessen.

ZTK. Zeitschrift für Theologie und Kirche. Tübingen.

The titles of the Reviews and Journals are quoted in full when they are seldom quoted, or when their title consists of one single word (Angelicum, Scholastik, Speculum, etc.), or else when their initials could be confused with those of another title; for instance, *Franciscan Studies* is quoted in full in order to avoid confusion with *Franziskanische Studien.*—The bibliography has been carried up to April 1, 1953.—The numbering of the notes is continuous within each Part of the book. The Indexes of proper names found at the end will provide cross references for both authors and their modern historians.

NOTES

INTRODUCTION

[1] On the appellation: "middle ages," G. Gordon, *Medium Aevum and the Middle Age,* Oxford, Clarendon Press, 1925. The earliest Latin forms are: *media tempestas* (1469), *media etas* (1518), *medium aevum* (1604). English forms in the Oxford Dictionary; "middle age" (1621), "middle ages" (1722), "mediaeval (1827).—General introduction to the study of the period: H. O. Taylor, *The Mediaeval Mind. A History of the Development of Thought and Emotion in the Middle Ages,* 2 vols. 5 ed. Harvard Press, 1949. P. Duhem, *Etudes sur Léonard de Vinci, ceux qu'il a lus, ceux qui l'ont lu,* 3 vols., Paris, 1906-1913; *Le système du monde; histoire des doctrines cosmologiques de Platon à Copernic,* 5 vols., Paris, 1913-1917.—F. B. Artz, *The Mind of the Middle Ages. A.D. 200-1500,* New York, 1954.—Political background: C. W. Previté-Orton, *The Shorter Cambridge Medieval History,* Cambridge University Press, 2 vols. 1952.—Social background, *The Cambridge Economic History of Europe,* 2 vols. Cambridge University Press, I, 1941; II, 1952.—Connecting link between general history and doctrinal history, Chr. Dawson, *Religion and the Rise of Western Culture,* New York, 1950. L. Génicot, *Les lignes de faîte du moyen âge,* Tournai-Paris, 1951.

[2] The "canonical writings" are those which the Fathers of the Church have considered as divinely inspired. They constitute what we shall call the Bible, or Holy Scripture. The Bible will be quoted from the so-called "Douai version," which includes the "sapiential books." The fact that these books were written in a Hellenistic environment explains precisely why the Fathers found in them so many invitations to philosophy.

[3] A. Harnack, *Das Wesen des Christentums,* 1900. Discussion of this position (A. Harnack, E. von Dobschutz) in M. Grabmann, *Die Geschichte der scholastischen Methode,* Freiburg i. Br., 1909, I, 55-68. J. de Ghellinck SJ., *Patristique et moyen âge,* Paris, Desclée, III, 3-102.

[4] I, LITERARY HISTORY. O. Bardenhewer, *Geschichte der altkirchlichen Literatur,* Freiburg i. Br., 4 vols., 1913, 1914, 1923, 1924 (Catholic). Ad. Harnack, *Geschichte der altchristlichen Literatur der ersten drei Jahrhunderte,* 3 vols., 1893, 1897, 1904 (Protestant).—II, DOCTRINAL HISTORY. O. Bardenhewer, *Patrologie,* Freiburg i. Br., 3 ed. 1910; Engl. transl. from the 2 ed. German edition, *Patrology,* Herder, St. Louis, 1908. French revision by P. Godet and C. Verschaffel, *Les Pères de l'Eglise, leur vie, leurs oeuvres,* 3 vols. Paris, 1905. F. Cayré, *Patrologie et histoire de la théologie,* 3 vols., 4 ed. Paris, 1945; Engl. transl., *Manual of Patrology and of History of Theology,* 2 vols. 1936. Bertoldo Altaner, *Patrologia,* Roma, Marietti, 1944 (Italian transl. and revised ed. of the German ed. of 1938). Joannes Quasten, *Patrology,* I, Westminster (Maryland) 1950; II, 1953.,—III, GREEK FATHERS. A. Puech, *Les apologistes grecs au IIe siècle de notre ère,* Paris, 1912. Same author, *Histoire de la littérature grecque chrétienne,* 3 vols. Paris, 1928-1930. G. Bardy, *The Greek Literature of the Early Christian Church,* St. Louis, Herder, 1929.—IV, GENERAL HISTORY OF EARLY CHRISTIAN THOUGHT. B. Geyer, *Die patristische und scholastische Philosophie,* Berlin, 1928 (vol. II of Ueberweg's *Grundriss der Geschichte der Philosophie;* fundamental). A. Stöckl, *Geschichte der christlichen Philosophie zur Zeit der Kirchenväter,* Mainz, 1891. B. Romeyer, *La philosophie chrétienne jusqu'à Descartes,* 3 vols., Paris, 1935, 1936, 1937. E. Gilson, *La philosophie au moyen âge des origines patristiques à la fin du XIVe siècle,* Paris, 2 ed., 1944 (written from

the point of view of the history of mediaeval culture).—V, BIBLIOGRAPHICAL INTRODUCTIONS, L. J. Paetow, *A Guide to the Study of Medieval History*, 2 ed. by D. C. Munro and G. C. Boyce, London, 1931. L. Halphen and J. B. Mahn, *Initiation aux études d'histoire du moyen âge*, Paris, 1940. J. W. Thompson, *Reference Studies in Medieval History;* 3 vols., I, *The Dark Ages (180-814)*; II, *The Feudal Age (814-1291)*; III, *The End of the Middle Ages (1291-1498)*, University of Chicago Press, 2 ed., 1925-1926.—VI, ENGLISH TRANSLATIONS. Clarissa P. Farrar and Austin P. Evans, *Bibliography of English Translations from Medieval Sources*, Columbia University Press, 1946.

⁵ The Word, or Logos, is not named in the received versions of the Creed (note, however, *lumen de lumine*, which refers to John, I, 9). It was named in the Creed of Caesarea (perhaps written by Eusebius) whose text was discussed at the Council of Nicaea (325), but the text adopted by the Council, as well as the liturgical version still in use in the Catholic Church, does not name the Word. The direct and immediate object of the Christian faith is "the only-begotten son of God," namely Jesus Christ. On the strength of St. John's canonical authority, all Christians believe that Christ is the Word because, being the Son of God, he is the Word incarnate.—On the Creed of Caesarea, DTC., I (1923) 1796. On the Word in the *Fides Damasi*, Denzinger, *Enchiridion Symbolorum*, 20 ed., 1932, 12, n. 15.

PART ONE

THE GREEK APOLOGISTS

¹ Very short in the beginning ("I believe that Jesus Christ is the Son of God," Acts, 8, 37) the Creed progressively integrated the fundamental points of Christian faith (J. Quasten, *Patrology*, I, 24).—Texts and documents in F. Kattenbusch, *Das apostolische Symbol*, 2 vols. Leipzig, 1894, 1900. J. N. D. Kelly, *Early Christian Creeds*, London, 1950. Simpler collection in H. Lietzmann, *Symbole der alten Kirche*, 4 ed. Berlin, 1935.—History of the problem: J. de Ghellinck, *Patristique et moyen âge . . .* I, *Les recherches sur le Symbole des Apôtres*, Paris, 1946; *Les origines du Symbole des Apôtres après cinq siècles de recherches*, NRT., 67 (1945) 178-201. P. Th. Camelot, *Les récentes recherches sur le Symbole des Apôtres et leur portée théologique*, Mélanges Lebreton, Recherches de Science Religieuse, 38 (1951) 149-163; *Le Symbole des Apôtres. Origines, développement, signification*, Lumière et Vie, 2 (1952) 61-80.—Liturgical, B. Capelle OSB., *L'introduction du symbole à la messe*, Mélange de Ghellinck, II (1951) 1003-1028.

² The name "patrology" first appears with the Lutheran theologian Joh. Gehrhard, *Patrologia*, 1653 (J. Quasten, *Patrology*, I, 1). It designates the history of the Fathers of the Church, of their writings and of their doctrines. "Patristics" (1847) is practically synonymous with patrology. In fact, no patrology can be written without adding to the Fathers of the Church all the ecclesiastical writers. The present tendency is to include in it even the sects and heresies directly related to the Christian Church.—General bibliographies in GDP., pp. 3-140 and 636-672. F. Cayré, *Manual of Patrology*, I, pp. XXI-XXVII. J. Quasten, *Patrology*, I, 5-9, 12-22. B. Altaner, *Patrologia*, 7-22.—On the need for a new Patrology, historical but not including doctrinal history, B. Altaner, *Der Stand der patrologischen Wissenschaft und das Problem einer neuen altchristlichen Literaturgeschichte*, Miscellanea Giovanni Mercati, I (1946) 483-520.—On the notion of theology, M.-J. Congar, OP., art. *Théologie*, DTC., 15 (1946) 341-502.

³ APOSTOLIC FATHERS. Greek, F. X. Funk, *Patres Apostolici*, Tübingen, 2 ed. 1901. Greek and English by Kirsopp Lake, *The Apostolic Fathers* (Loeb class. libr.) 2 vols. New York, 1925. English only in AN., I, Buffalo, 1885 (Protestant); Glimm, Marique & Walsh, *The Apostolic Fathers*, New York, 1947 (Catholic). C. C. Richardson, *Early Christian Fathers*. Selections from Clement, Ignatius, Polycarp, Diognetus, Justin, Athenagoras, Irenaeus, London, 1953 (this is the first volume of a new Protestant collection: *The Library of Christian Classics;* 13 vols. of selec-

tions will be devoted to the Catholic writers of the middle ages, and 13 to the writers of the Reformation). BET., 329-336.

The present collection comprises: I, *The Teaching of the Lord to the Twelve Apostles,* or *Didache,* or *The Two Ways* (on account of ch. 1-6), anonymous, dates between 70 and 180.—II Saint CLEMENT, Bishop of Rome (92-101), *Letter to the Corinthians* (read ch. 20); spurious: *II Letter to the Corinthians, Epistles to the Virgins, Recognitions, Homilies, Decretals, Apocalypse of Clement* (or *of Peter*), *Apostolic Constitutions.*—III, Saint IGNATIUS of Rome (martyr *ca.* 107): seven Letters to the *Ephesians, Magnesians, Trallians, Philadelphians, Smyrnians, Romans, Polycarp;* read *To the Romans* in A. C. Pegis, *The Wisdom of Catholicism,* New York, 1949, 3-7.—IV, Saint POLYCARP (martyr in Rome *ca.* 155-156): *Letter to the Philippians.*—V, the group called THE ELDERS or PRESBYTERS (between 70-150): collected reports on some teachings of the Apostles.—VI, PAPIAS, bishop of Hierapolis in Phrygia (*ca.* 125), *Exposition of the Oracles of the Lord;* these fragments are known through Eusebius.—VII, Saint BARNABAS (pseudo-), *Letter,* author and date unknown: influenced by the *Didache.*—VIII, HERMAS, *The Shepherd, ca.* 140-155: five visions with commentaries.—BIBLIOGRAPHY, F. Cayré, *Manual of Patrology,* I, 31-96. J. Quasten, *Patrology,* I, 29-105. B. Altaner, *Patrologia,* 53-63.

[4] HISTORY OF THE TEXTS: Ad. Harnack, *Die Ueberlieferung der griechischen Apologeten des II Jahrhunderts in der alten Kirche und im Mittelalter,* Leipzig, Hinrichs, 1883 (*Texte und Untersuchungen,* vol. I). Osc. v. Gebhardt, *Zur handschriftlichen Ueberlieferung der griechischen Apologeten,* Leipzig, Hinrichs, 1883 (same volume). General bibliography in J. Quasten, *Patrology,* I, 189-190.

[5] ARISTIDES. His Apology was addressed to Emperor Hadrian (117-118). Fragments in Edg. Hennecke, *Die Apologie des Aristides. Recension und Rekonstruktion des Textes,* Leipzig, 1893 (Texte und Untersuchungen, IV). Engl. transl. by D. M. Kay, AN., IX, 263-279. Cf. BET., 365-367. The existence and order of things requires a maker and an orderer, that is God (cf. Rom. 1, 20). Immobile, perfect, incomprehensible and unnamable,

God encompasses by his power the world he has created. Neither the elements nor the stars are divinities. There is only one God, whom all the races of men must equally worship, be they Barbarians, Greeks, Jews or Christians. This Judeo-Christian notion of God will always remain that of all the Christian theologians up to the end of the middle ages. Cf. Hermas, *The Shepherd (Vision V,* Mandate I, 1): "First of all, believe that there is one God, that He created all things and set them in order; that He caused all things to pass from non-existence to existence, and that, though He contains all things, He is Himself uncontained" (transl. J. M.-F. Marique, SJ., *The Apostolic Fathers,* 259). The notion of creation from nothing goes back to Macc. II, 7, 28; that of an all containing yet uncontained God is, in germ, the later notion of an "infinite" God. —On Aristides, see A. Puech, *Histoire de la littérature grecque chrétienne,* II, 126-130. J. Quasten, *Patrology,* I, 191-195, bibliography, 194-195.

[6] QUADRATUS. F. Cayré, *Manual,* I, 113. B. Altaner, *Patrologia,* 66.

[7] LETTER TO DIOGNETES. Text in F. X. Funk, *Patres apostolici,* 390-413; Engl. transl. L. B. Radford, SPCK., N.Y. 1908. G. G. Walsh, *The Fathers of the Church,* N.Y. 1946, I, 355-367; also The Newman Press, Westm., Maryland, 1948. On its possible identification with Quadratus: D. P. Andriessen, *L'Apologie de Quadratus conservée sous le titre d'Epitre à Diognète,* RTAM., 13 (1946) 5-39, 125-149, 237-260, 14 (1947) 121-156. Against this identification, I. Marrou, *A Diognète,* Paris, 1951 (important Introduction). Some historians consider as certain that ch. 11-12 are not by the same writer as the rest of the work: F. X. Funk, *Das Schlusskapitel des Diognetes briefes,* TQ., 85 (1903) 638-639. O. Bardenhewer, *Patrology,* 68. Widely different dates have been assigned to this writing. Even the probability in favor of the III century is not a certitude. P. Thomsen once attempted to prove that the Letter was the work of a Byzantine scholar of the XII/XIII cent. More recently, Connolly has attributed it to Hippolytus (JTS., 1935, 347-353 and 1936, 2-15).—BET., 1463-1464.

[8] JUSTIN MARTYR. Born at Flavia Ne-

apolis (Nablous) of pagan parents; a convert to Christianity before 132; died a martyr in Rome under prefect Junius Rusticus (163-167). Wrote a *First Apology* to Emperor Hadrian (152); *Dialogue with Trypho* (155); *Second Apology*, to Marcus Aurelius (*ca.* 161); *On the Resurrection* (fragments, date unknown).—EDITIONS. Greek and Latin transl., PG., vol. 6. Otto, S. Justini . . . *Opera quae feruntur omnia*, 3 ed., 5 vols., Jena, 1876-1877. Greek text only, A. W. Blunt, *The Apologies of Justin Martyr*, Cambridge, 1911. Greek and Latin, G. Rauschen, *S. Justini Apologiae duae*, Bonn, 1911. Greek and French, G. Archambault, 2 vols., Paris, 1909. English transl. AN., (Buffalo), I, 159-272 (*Apologies* and *Dialogues*); 294 299 (*On the Resurrection*); 305-306 (*Acta S. S. Justini et Sociorum*). A. L. William, *The Dialogue*, SPCK., N.Y., 1930. T. B. Falls, *Saint Justin Martyr: The first Apology, The second Apology, Dialogue with Trypho, Exhortation to the Greeks, Discourse to the Greeks, The Monarchy*, N.Y. (Christian Heritage), 1949.—BIBLIOGRAPHY. C. Clemen, *Die religionsphilosophische Bedeutung des stoisch-christlichen Eudemonismus in Justins Apologie*, Leipzig, 1890. J. Rivière, *S. Justin et les Apologistes du IIe siècle*, Paris, 1907. Pfättisch, *Der Einfluss Platons auf die Theologie Justins des Martyrers*, in Forschungen zur christl.-Literatur und Dogmengeschichte, Paderborn, 10, 1910. A. L. Feder, *Justins des Martyrers Lehre von Jesus Christus dem Messias und dem Menschengewordenem Sohne Gottes*, Freiburg i. Br., 1906 (important). A. Puech, *Les Apologistes . . .* , 46-147 (important). M. J. Lagrange, OP., *Saint Justin, philosophe et martyr*, Paris, 1914. C. C. Martindale, *St. Justin the Martyr*, London, 1921. E. Goodenough, *The Theology of Justin Martyr*, Jena, 1923 (bibliography, 295-320). G. Bardy, *Saint Justin et le Stoicisme*, RSR., 13 (1923) 491-510; 14 (1924) 33-45. G. Bardy, art. *Justin (saint)*, DTC., 8 (1925) 2228-2277 (bibliography). A Casamassa, *Gli Apologisti e i Polemisti del II secolo*, Roma, 1935. W. von Lövenich, *Das Johannes—Verständnis im zweiten Jahrhundert*, Giessen, 1932 (Justin, Gnosis, Irenaeus: important). J. Champonier, *Naissance de l'humanisme chrétien*, Bulletin G. Budé, 1947, 58-68. M.-M. Sagnard, OP., *Y a-t-il un plan du Dialogue avec Tryphon?* Mélanges de Ghellinck, I (1951) 171-182.—BET., 2323-2330.

[9] See Tatian, *Address to the Greeks*, 25; AN., (Edinburgh), III, 30.

[10] *Dialogue with Trypho*, I; AN., (Buffalo) I, 194. Cf. "Philosophy is, in fact, the greatest possession and most honorable before God, to whom it leads us and alone commends us; and these are truly holy men who have bestowed attention on philosophy" (*Dialogue*, 2; AN., I, 195). Yet, philosophical knowledge should be one, and not divided into sects as has been done by schools (*Dialogue*, 2, 195). Above all, philosophy should not be the privilege of the happy few but, owing to revelation, it should be accessible to all (*I Apology*, 60; I, 183. *II Apology*, 10, 191-192). Note that Justin's Christianity is absorbing Greek philosophy, not inversely.—G. Bardy, *La conversion au Christianisme durant les premiers siècles*, Paris, 1947, pp. 127-129.

[11] *Dialogue*, 2; AN., I, 195. Justin had really been a Platonist before his conversion: *II Apology*, 12; AN., I, 192.

[12] *Dialogue*, 8; AN., I, 198; we are quoting from this translation.

[13] *I Apology*, 46; AN., I, 178.—Philosophers partially share in the *Logos;* the Christians partake of the whole Logos: *I Apology*, 5; *II Apology*, 5, and 8.—General interpretation of Justin's attitude in B. Seeberg, *Die Geschichtstheologie des Justins des Märtyrers*, ZKG., 58 (1939) 1-81.

[14] *II Apology*, 10; AN., I, 191, and 13, I, 193. For instance, the Christians can claim for their own what Plato has said in the *Timaeus* concerning creation, providence, the Son of God "placed crosswise in the universe," etc.; or what the Stoics have said of the future destruction of the world by fire; or what the philosophers and poets have said of rewards or punishments in future life. In such cases, the Christians "seem to say the same things," but they say them better. Besides, let us not forget his own statement: "We claim to be acknowledged, not because we say the same things as these writers said, but because we say true things" (*I Apology*, 23; AN., I, 170).

EXHORTATION TO THE GREEKS. Of unknown origin; printed among the works of Justin (PG., 6, 241-312); probably written about the beginning of the III century (O. Bardenhewer, *Patrology*, 53).

Its author claims that the Greek poets and philosophers have borrowed from Scripture whatever truths they may have taught; see *Exhortation,* 13; PG., 6, 265-268. Plato has learned monotheism from the text of Exod. 3, 14; Plato has artfully concealed his borrowings in order to avoid the fate of Socrates: *Exhortation,* 20-22; PG., 6, 276-281.—ON MONARCHY, that is on the government of the world by one single God, is a short treatise also published among the works of Justin (PG., 6, 311-325). It lists a series of texts of Greek poets in favor of monotheism.

[15] GOD. There is only one God. Everything is named after its cause; since God has no cause, he is "anonymous," i.e., unnamable (*I Apology,* 63; AN., I, 184. Cf. E. R. Goodenough, 130-131). To call him Father, Creator, Lord or Master is less to say what he is in himself than what he does for us (*II Apology,* 6; AN., I, 190). Invisible in himself he has made himself known by sending to men "a God other than the one who has made everything; other, I mean, as to number, but not as to the notion." Such is the *Logos* or Word, through whom all the rest was made, and who is Christ. Thus there is unity in divinity, but there is numerical distinction between God the Father, unchangeable and eternal, creator of all; and Christ, the son of God, whom we hold in the second place; and the prophetic Spirit, whom we hold in the third place (*I Apology,* 13; AN., I, 166-167). In spite of the fact that he is God in the second place (*I Apology,* 60; AN., I, 183), the Word is the ruler "than whom, after God who begat him, there is no ruler more kingly and just." In a text strongly influenced by Proverbs, 8, 22-26 (cf. Ecclus. 24, 14), Justin describes the Word as, "He who alone is called Son, the Word who, before all creatures, was with Him and was begotten when, in the beginning, the Father made and ordered all things through Him" (*Dialogue,* 61; AN., I, 227. Cf. 62 and the interesting text 129, AN., I, 264). The Word has been "established," or "constituted" by the Father before all creatures, as a fire kindles other fires without itself losing of its substance, or as thought utters itself in spoken words without separation from itself.—MAN. Being good, God has shaped the world in view of man (*I Apology,* 10; AN., I, 165) and he governs it by his providence. Man is made up of body,

soul, and spirit (*pneuma,* cf. Gal. 5, 17). God alone is incorruptible, "but all things after Him are created and corruptible," even the soul. "The soul partakes of life since God wills it to live," but it is not immortal by nature: "For to live is not its attribute as it is God's," but a man does not live always, and the soul is not always conjoined with the body, since, whenever this harmony must be broken up, the soul leaves the body, and man exists no longer; the soul itself does not cease to exist unless the spirit of life be removed from it; then the soul ceases to be; it returns to the place whence it was taken (*Dialogue,* 6; AN., I, 198).—ETHICS. This death of the soul by loss of its immortal spirit should probably be read in the light of Rom. 8, 2-13. It has moral implications. Through his *Logos,* God has endowed all men with reason and knowledge. Hence men are capable of good and evil, responsible for their acts and in no way subject to necessity. This is what the Stoics failed to understand, thereby injuring both man and God: "For if they say that human actions come to pass by fate, they will . . . have looked on God himself as emerging both in part and in whole in every wickedness; or (said) that neither vice nor virtue is anything, which is contrary to every sound idea, reason and sense" (*II Apology,* 7; AN., I, 191). Some men live according to the *Logos* (for instance Socrates), some do not. The Christians should live according to the two great commandments (Matt. 22, 37) as implemented by the precepts of the Gospel (*Dialogue,* 93; AN., I, 246).

[16] A. Harnack, *Lehrbuch der Dogmengeschichte,* 3 ed., Leipzig, 1894; I, 463.

[17] Eusebius, *Eccles. History,* IV, 11; quoted in AN., I, 194, note 2.

[18] TATIAN.—Born in Assyria *ca.* 120; studies rhetoric and sophistic; a convert to Christianity; studies in Rome under Justin Martyr; after his master's death Tatian opens a school of his own; *Address to the Greeks* before 172; joins the sect of the Encratists (from the Greek *enkrateia:* temperance) which advocated a strict asceticism: meat, wine, even marriage were considered almost sinful. Date of death unknown. Two of his works have come to us: I, *Diatessaron,* a synopsis of the four Gospels: A. A. Hobson,

The Diatessaron of Tatian and the Synoptic Problem, Chicago Univ. Press, 1904; II, The Address to the Greeks, PG., 6, 803-888. Greek only, Edw. Schwartz, Leipzig, Texte und Untersuchungen, IV, 1-43. Engl. transl., B. P. Pratten, in AN., (Edinburgh edition, 1867) III, 5-45. French transl. and commentary, A. Puech, Recherches sur le Discours aux Grecs de Tatien . . . , Paris, 1903.—BIBLIOGRAPHY. H. Dombrowski, Die Quellen der christlichen Apologetik des zweiten Jahrhunderts; I, Die Apologie Tatians, Leipzig, 1878. J. Geffcken, Zwei Griechische Apologeten, Leipzig, 1906. R.-C. Kukula, Tatians sogenannte Apologie, Leipzig, 1910. J. Lebreton SJ., Histoire du dogme de la Trinité, Paris, 1928, II, 485 491. V. A.-S. Little, The Christology of the Apologists, 1934. G. Bardy, art. Tatien, DTC., 15 (1946) 59-66.—BET., 3568-3572.

[19] Address, 42; AN., 3, 45. "Barbaric philosophy" will be used by Clement of Alexandria without any trace of hostility toward the Greeks: Stromata, V, 12 (PG., 9, 117 B). Many references to similar texts in O. Staehlin's edition of Clement, IV, 792-793.

[20] Address, 1-2; AN., III, 5-7.

[21] Address, 7, AN., III, 7-8; 25, 30-31. Compare this chapter with HERMIAS, Satire on the pagan philosophers, PG., VI, 1167-1180; Otto, Hermias . . . , Jena, 1872, 2-31.—L. Alfonsi, Una parodia del Teeteto nello "Scherno" di Ermia, Vigiliae Christianae, 5 (1951) 80-83.

[22] Address, 2; AN., III, 7.

[23] Address, 35; AN., III, 40. The teaching of Moses older than that of Homer, Address, 31-40, AN., III, 35-44; and even older than that of all the other writers: 41, III, 44-45. This argument will be taken up again by Clement of Alexandria, Eusebius, Augustine, etc., up to the XVIIth century: "Literary history knows no other example of such an enormous hoax," P. Lagrange OP., Saint Justin, 132-133. It probably was less a hoax than a self-delusion.

[24] Address, 29; AN., III, 33-34.

[25] GOD. There is but one God, pure spirit, hence invisible to human eyes. He is principle (i.e., cause) of all that is, including matter. God is not cause of matter as immanent in it, but as above it. If there is a World Soul (Stoics), it is not God, it is a creature of God. God himself has no cause, but, being the cause of all that is, he can be known from his works (Rom. i, 20. Cf. Address, 4; AN., III, 8-9). Before the creation, God is alone, but, being omnipotent, he is all the things that are in his power. Such is the Logos who, because he is in God, subsists with God (John, i, 1). By God's will, the Logos comes forth, and not in vain, as do our own "words" which vanish as soon as they are uttered. On the contrary, the Logos then becomes "the first-begotten of the Father," and, as first-begotten, he is "the beginning of this world" (cf. John, i, 1-2). The generation of the Word is not an "abscission"; nor does it separate him from his Father; nor is the Father himself lessened in any way by this generation. The Father begets as a fire lights up many other fires without losing of its own substance; or as, by uttering my own "words," I can impart my thought to others without losing it. Rather, through my "word," I reduce to order the confused material that is in other minds: "And as the Logos, begotten in the beginning, begot in turn our world, having first created for Himself the necessary matter, so also, I, in imitation of the Logos, being begotten again (i.e., through baptism), and having become possessed of the truth, am trying to reduce to order the confused matter which is kindred with myself." Matter is "brought into existence by the Framer of all things alone" (Address, 5; AN., III, 9-10). ANGELS. First creatures of the Logos, the Angels are not gods, nor do they possess goodness in virtue of their essences; rather, they achieve goodness through their wills and, in consequence, they are justly rewarded or punished. Tatian speaks, in abstract terms, of orders issued by the Word, and of the rebellion of the first Angel against his laws. Other Angels then recognized this rebel for their god, but the Logos excluded them all from his intercourse, and they became devils.—MAN. Having followed the devils, men became mortal in punishment for their sin (Address, 7, AN., III, 11-12). Tatian is here chiefly concerned with making clear, against the Stoics, that the origin of evil is the free

will of creatures, and not fatality. On the contrary, the doctrine of universal necessity has been taught to men by the devils and, once accepted by men, it has acted for them as a real fatality. Man is made up of body, soul and spirit (cf. I Thess. 5, 23). The Soul permeates all beings (stars, angels, men, beasts, plants, waters), but it assumes different natures according to the different species of beings which it animates; according to Holy Writ, the soul is material (Levit. 17, 11: "Because the life of the flesh is in the blood"). Above the soul is the spirit (*pneuma*), immaterial, wherein the image of God in man resides. The soul is not immortal by nature, but it is capable of immortality. If it does not know truth, it dies with the body; yet it will be resurrected at the end of the world, so as to receive, in punishment for its sins, together with its body, death in immortality (i.e., an eternal death). If, on the contrary, the soul has acquired the knowledge of God by following its spirit, it will not die eternally, even though it has been temporarily dissolved. In itself, the soul is the "darkness" which does not comprehend the light. Left to itself, "it tends downward toward matter and dies with the flesh." But the Light, that is the Logos, shines in the darkness (John, i, 5), that is in the soul. If the spirit (*pneuma*) follows the Light, it leads its soul toward the Spirit of God (i.e., the Holy Ghost), and, through wisdom, it acquires life in immortality (i.e., eternal life). Cf. *Address,* 13; AN., III, 18-19. This requires a conversion (*metanoia*), or turning of the spirit that is in us, to the divine Spirit whom sin has expelled from our soul. God then dwells again in man as in his temple. If a man is not thus made an image of God by the presence of the divine Spirit in him, articulate language is the only difference that remains between him and a beast (*Address,* 15; AN., III, 20-21). Let us note that, in Tatian as in Justin, the doctrine of the spirit, or *pneuma,* seems to be an interpretation of the teaching of Saint Paul. The "Spirit in our spirit" probably means the Holy Ghost in us, that is grace, and the death of the spirit may simply mean a spiritual death. Let us not make the doctrine of Tatian more precise than it was in his own mind. Besides, the history of the notion of "immortality" has not yet been properly studied. In the early Christian writers,

Christianity sometimes appears as being essentially a promise of immortality. Salvation is redemption from death. Scriptural sources of the doctrine, Wisd. 15, 3. I Cor. 15, 54 (where immortality follows the resurrection). I Tim. 6, 15-16 (i.e., Christ). Similar remarks could be made concerning the notion of "spirit" ("spirit of life") which has long retained connotations partly psychological, partly religious: Rom. 8, 2. I Cor. 2, 11, etc.

[26] ATHENAGORAS; life unknown. The title of his apology calls him "a Christian philosopher of Athens," but since the oldest known ms. of the work belongs to the X century, this title may be quite recent. Main writings: I, *Intercession for the Christians* (in Greek: *presbeia,* i.e., *Legatio pro Christianis*), dedicated to the emperors Marcus Aurelius and Commodus, probably in 177; II, *On the Resurrection of the Dead* (announced at the end of the *Intercession*). Editions: PG., 6, 889-1024. Otto, *Athenagorae philosophi Atheniensis Opera,* Jena, 1857 (bibliography: preceding editions, XXX-XLIII; transl., XLIII-XLVIII). Greek only, Ed. Schwartz, in Texte und Untersuchungen, IV, Leipzig, 1891. French transl., G. Bardy, Athénagoras, *Supplique* . . ., Paris, 1943. Engl. transl., AN., Edinburgh, II, 375-456. BET., 409-411.— BIBLIOGRAPHY. Literary history: A. Harnack, *Geschichte der altchristlichen Literatur,* 1893, I, 256-258. O. Bardenhewer, *Geschichte der altkirchlichen Literatur,* 1902, I, 267-271. Doctrinal history: F. Schubring, *Die Philosophie des Athenagoras,* Berlin, 1882 (Progr.). J. Lehmann, *Die Auferstehungslehre des Athenagoras,* (Inaug.-Diss.), Leipzig, 1890. A. Eberhard, *Athenagoras,* Augsburg, 1895 (Progr.). L. Arnould, *De Apologia Athenagorae,* Paris, 1898. K. F. Bauer, *Die Lehre des Athenagoras von Gottes Einheit und Dreieinigkeit* (Inaug.-Diss.), Bamberg, 1902. L. Richter, *Philosophisches in der Gottes-und Logoslehre des Apologeten Athenagoras aus Athen,* Meissen, 1905 (monotheism; cosmology; logos and pneuma; relations between Athenagoras and Justin, Philo, Plotinus and the Stoics; Athenagoras and Plato's cosmology). L. Chaudouard, *La philosophie du dogme de la résurrection de la chair au IIe siècle,* Lyon, 1905. J. Van Beck, *Athenagoras Geschrift De resurrectione mortuorum,* Leiden, 1908. A. Puech, *Histoire de la littérature grecque chrétienne,* II, 196-203.

Another apology dedicated to Marcus Aurelius was that of MELITO, Bishop of Sardis (d. *ca.* 195). Title: *To Antoninus* (Eusebius, *Eccl. Hist.*, IV, 26). The work is lost. Melito may have been the first to make use of an argument whose importance was to grow steadily up to the time of Augustine: "Our philosophy (i.e., Christianity) first grew up among the Barbarians, but its full flower came among your nation in the great reign of your ancestor Augustus, and became an omen of good to your empire, for from that time the power of the Romans became great and splendid. You are now his happy successor, and shall be so along with your son (i.e., Commodus), if you protect the philosophy which grew up with the empire and began with Augustus . . ." etc. (transl. by K. Lake, Loeb collection, 390-391.—C. Thomas, *Melito von Sardis,* Osnabrück, 1893. A. Puech, *Histoire de la littérature grecque chrétienne,* II, 189-195. Fragments in PG., 5, 1207-1232.—BET., 2738-2739.

[27] Marcus Aurelius, *The Communings with himself,* transl. by C. R. Haines, London-N.Y. 1916 (Loeb Class, Libr.); p. 295. The allusion to the Christians may be an interpolation, but there is little doubt that Marcus Aurelius had them in mind when he wrote these lines.

[28] A. Puech, *Les Apologistes grecs . . . ,* 179-180.

[29] Athenagoras, *Intercession . . . ,* 7; AN., II, 382. Cf. A. Puech, *Les Apologistes grecs,* 182.—The title used by AN., is *A Plea* (var. an *Embassy*) *for the Christians.*

[30] Athenagoras, *Intercession . . . ,* 6; AN., II, 380-382. The reference to Plato is: *Timaeus,* 28 C: "To find out the Maker and Father of this universe is difficult; and, when found, it is impossible to declare Him to all." True enough, Plato speaks of other gods (sun, moon, stars), but he holds them as created by the Father and Maker (*Timaeus,* 41 A). "If, therefore, Plato is not an atheist for conceiving of one uncreated God, the Framer of the universe, neither are we atheists who acknowledge and firmly hold that he is God who has framed all things by the Logos, and holds in being by his Spirit" (transl. B. P. Pratten, AN., II, 381). The information that fol-lows about the God of Aristotle is very inaccurate. As to the Stoics, Athenagoras says that, since matter is "permeated by the Spirit of God" (*sic*), "they multiply the Deity in name, yet in reality they consider God to be one" (AN., II, 382). Yet, a "Spirit of God" who is an "artistic fire," is an unusual theological combination.

[31] A. Puech, *Les Apologistes grecs . . . ,* p. 184.

[32] Athenagoras, *Intercession . . . ,* 7; AN., 382. The nature of this "affinity," or "sympathy" is not defined. It is of Stoic origin.

[00] What Athenagoras calls "the argumentative grounds of our faith," *Intercession . . . ,* 8; AN., II, 383.

[34] If the world is spherical, and if the Creator is above the world, where could another god be? Neither in this world, which belongs to its creator, nor about it, for the same reason. Or would this second god be about another world? But the first God occupies all. Clearly, a God who could be nowhere, nor do anything, simply could not exist. *Intercession . . . ,* 8; AN., II, 383-384. Otto's edit. (pp. 36-42) refers to John Damascene, *De fide orthodoxa,* I, 5.

[35] God is one, "uncreated, eternal, invisible, impassible, incomprehensible, illimitable" (note this intimation of God's infinity) "who is apprehended by the understanding only and the reason, who is encompassed by light, and beauty, and spirit, and power ineffable, by whom the universe has been created through his Logos, and set in order, and is kept in being."—"The Son of God is the Logos of the Father, in idea and in operation; for by him and through him were all things made, the Father and the Son being one." The generation of the Son, one with the Father in power and spirit, is eternal. God had the Logos within Himself from the beginning (John, i, 1); but the Logos "came forth to be the idea and energizing power of all material things (cf. Proverbs, 8, 22-31). As to the Holy Spirit, "which operates in the Prophets," he is "an effluence of God, flowing from Him, and returning back again like a beam of the sun." *Intercession . . . ,* 10; transl. Pratten, in AN., II, 385-386.

[36] Athenagoras, *On Resurrection*, 3; AN., II, 426-427.

[37] Athenagoras, *On Resurrection*, 10; AN., II, 434-435.

[38] Athenagoras, *On Resurrection*, 11; AN., II, 436.

[39] Athenagoras, *On Resurrection*, 12; AN., II, 437-439. Otto (p. 234, note 24, refers to Clement of Alexandria, *Paed.*, I, 3.—On divine providence, *On Resurrection*, 19; AN., II, 448.

[40] Athenagoras, *On Resurrection*, 15; AN., II, 442, B. P. Pratten's transl.

[41] Athenagoras, *On Resurrection*, 18; AN., II, 446-448. Note, ch. 16 and 17, the arguments in favor of the resurrection drawn from the analogy of death and sleep and from the successive changes which take place in man. These are given as merely probable.

[42] Athenagoras, *On Resurrection*, 21; AN., II, 450-452.

[43] Geffcken, *Zwei griechische Apologeten*, 162.

[44] L. Duchesne, *Histoire ancienne de l'Eglise*, I, 211.

[45] In GDP., II, 68. Also Schubring, *Die Philosophie des Athenagoras*, 4. L. Richter, *Philosophisches* . . . , 4-5—It is significant that, writing an apology addressed to non-Christian readers, Athenagoras does not make use of what was the typically Christian argument: the resurrection of Christ.

[46] THEOPHILUS, probably the sixth Bishop of Antioch (Eusebius, *Hist. eccl.*, IV, 20). Born a pagan, near the rivers Tigris and Euphrates ("for these border on our own regions," *To Autolycus*, II, 24; AN., III, 90); a convert to Christianity; then a bishop of Antioch (169); date of death unknown. The only extant work of Theophilus is his apology *To Autolycus* (about 181), in three books. On his lost works, O. Bardenhewer, *Patrology*, 67. Greek text and Latin transl. in PG., 6, 1123-1168. Also Otto, *Theophili episcopi Antiocheni ad Autolycum libri tres*, Jena, 1861 (on older translations, XXXIII-XXXVI).

Engl. transl. alone by M. Dodds, in AN., Edinburgh edit., from which we will quote, vol. III, 53-133 (Buffalo edit., vol. II, 89-121). French transl. and notes, J. Sender and G. Bardy, Paris, 1948 (Sources chrétiennes). History of the text, Harnack, *Geschichte* . . . , I, 496-502. Bardenhewer, *Geschichte* . . . , I, 302-310.—BIBLIOGRAPHY: Cook, *Theophilus ad Autolycum*, II, 7; in Classical Review 6 (1894) 246-248. O. Gross, *Die Weltenstehungslehre des Theophilus von Antiochia* (Inaug.-Dissert.), Jena, 1895. Same author: *Die Gotteslehre des Theophilus von Antiochia* (Prog.), Chemnitz, 1896. O. Clausen, *Die Theologie des Theophilus von Antiochien*, Zeitschrift f. wissensch. Theologie, 46 (1903) 81-141, 195-213. A. Pommrich, *Des Apologeten Theophilus von Antiochia Gottes-und Logoslehre*, Leipzig, 1904. A. Puech, *Histoire de la littérature grecque chrétienne*, II, 204-213. Fried. Loofs, *Theophilus von Antiochien Adversus Marcionem* . . . , Leipzig, 1930. E. Rapisarda, *Teofilo di Antiochia*, Torino, 1936. R. M. Grant, *Theophilus of Antioch to Autolycus*, HTR., 40 (1947) 227-256.—BET., 3619-3620.

[47] A. Puech, *Les Apologistes grecs*, 227. Cf. p. 213: "It really seems that Theophilus has condemned philosophy without having understood a single word of it." And, indeed, see the remarks on Socrates and Plato (III, 2-3) or on Epicurus and the Stoics (III, 6).

[48] *To Autolycus*, III, 9; AN., III, 114.

[49] The formula "from non-being" occurs several times: I, 8; II, 10; II, 13.

[50] *To Autolycus*, II, 4; AN., III, 67.

[51] *To Autolycus*, II, 9; AN., III, 74.

[52] *To Autolycus*, II, 36; AN., III, 102-104.

[53] In *To Autolycus*, II, 10; AN., (trad. M. Dodds) III, 74-76. Theophilus applies to the generation of the Logos, the Stoic distinction between the "internal word" and the "uttered word." The internal Logos is eternally "compresent" with the Father (II, 10). He is essentially thought and forethought; in this sense, he prepares the creation (II, 22; AN., III, 88-89), but God utters his Logos as first-born of the creation (cf. Coloss. i, 15); God,

then, having his own Word internal within his own bowels, begot him, emitting him along with his own Wisdom before all things (cf. Prov. 8, 27). He had this Word as a helper in the things that were created by him, and by him he made all things" (M. Dodds, AN., III, 75). The Logos of God is both his creative energy and his ordering power (II, 13; AN., III, 79-80). What Theophilus calls wisdom is not clear. It seems to be in the same relation to the Holy Ghost as the uttered word to the internal Word (I, 7; AN., III, 58, and II, 10; AN., III, 75. Cf. O. Gross, 33). It is highly probable that, in Theophilus' theology, wisdom is identical with the Holy Ghost. Gross, who refuses this identification, is thus led to the conclusion (pp. 50-51) that Theophilus has not known the doctrine of the Trinity conceived as the unity of the Father, the Son and the Holy Ghost. But then, why should wisdom come to the Prophets under the inspiration of the Holy Ghost? See II, 9; AN., III, 74.

[54] On resurrection, *To Autolycus*, I, 7; AN., III, 58. Cf. I, 13; AN., III, 62-63, and II, 14; AN., III, 81. Theophilus does not go beyond the level of vulgarization. The same is true of his few remarks on the soul, which is "called immortal by most persons" because God has breathed life into the face of man (II, 19; AN., III, 85). In fact, man was made by God neither immortal (for then man would have been a god), nor mortal (otherwise God would have been cause of his death). God has made man free to incline either to "the things of immortality" by keeping the commandment of his creator, and to be rewarded by immortality; or to incline to mortal things by disobeying God, and thus to be "the cause of death to himself" (II, 27; AN., III, 92-93). There seems to be no clear distinction, in the thought of Theophilus, between the religious and the physical notions of immortality.

[55] IRENAEUS. Born *ca.* 126, in or near Smyrna (Asia Minor). In his childhood, Irenaeus had often heard Polycarp whose discourses to the people he was never to forget (Eusebius, *Eccl. Hist.*, V, 20); was a priest in Lyons at the time of Marcus Aurelius' persecution; mission to Pope Eleutherius in Rome (177); succeeds Photinus as Bishop of Lyons;

date of death unknown. A later tradition makes him die a martyr under Septimius Severus (193-211). Writings listed by Eusebius, *Ecc. Hist.*, V, 20. The best known is an early Latin translation of the Greek original: *Against Heresies* (Latin: *Adversus Haereses*. Greek: *Exposition and refutation of the so-called Gnosis*). Text in PG., 7, 433-1224. Engl. translations, AN., (American edition, Buffalo, 1885) I, 315-567; F. R. Montgomery . . . *Against the Heresies*, SPCK., 1916. The only other known writing of Irenaeus is his *Demonstration of the Apostolic Preaching*, text in *Patrologia orientalis*, XII, 659-731; Engl. transl., J. A. Robinson, SPCK., 1920. On the text of the *Against Heresies*, Harnack, *Geschichte* . . . , I, 263-288. O. Bardenhewer, *Geschichte* . . . , I, 399-430.—BIBLIOGRAPHY. I General: H. Ziegler, *Irenaeus, der Bischof von Lyon, ein Beitrag zur Enstehungsgeschichte der Altkatholischen Kirche*, Berlin, 1871 (detailed doctrinal study). A. Dufourcq, *Saint Irénée* (Les Saints) Paris, 3 ed. 1904 on the doctrine, 95-167). A. Dufourcq, *Saint Irénée* (La Pensée Chrétienne), Paris, 1905. P. Beuzart, *Essai sur la théologie d'Irénée,* Paris, 1908.—II, Specialized studies: L. Duncker, *Des hl. Irenaeus Christologie* . . . , Göttingen, 1843. H. G. Erbkam, *De S. Irenaei principiis ethicis,* Regiomonti (i.e., Königsberg) 1856. V. Courdaveaux, *Saint Irénée,* RHR., 21 (1891) 149-175; criticized by F. Cabrol. *Le dogme de saint Irénée et la critique de M. Courdaveaux,* Science catholique, 5, 1891. J. Kunze, *Die Gotteslehre des Irenaeus,* Leipzig, 1891 (God, the Creator, Logos, Trinity). L. Atzberger, *Geschichte der christlichen Eschatologie innerhalb der vornicäischen Zeit,* Freiburg i. Br., 1896, 219-263. E. Klebba, *Die Anthropologie des hl. Irenaeus. Eine dogmenhistorische Studie,* Münster i. W., 1894 (biblical anthropology, speculative anthropology, man, reason, liberty, grace, future life in Irenaeus). Gry, *Le millénarisme dans son développement,* Paris, 1904. F.R.M. Hitchcock, *Irenaeus of Lugdunum,* London, 1914. A. d'Alès, *La doctrine eucharistique de saint Irénée,* RSR., 13 (1923) 24-46; *La doctrine de l'esprit en saint Irénée,* RSR., 14 (1924) 497-538. G. N. Bonwetsch, *Die Theologie des Irenaeus,* 1925. B. Reynders, *Optimisme et théocentrisme chez saint Irénée,* RTAM., 8 (1936) 225-232. E. Peterson, *L'immagine di Dio in S. Ireneo,* Scuola Cattolica, 69 (1941) 46-54. Th.-A

Audet, *Orientations théologiques chez saint Irénée. Le contexte mental d'une "gnôsis alethès,"* Traditio, I (1943) 15-54. W. Hunger, *Der Gedanke der Weltplanheit und Adameinheit in der Theologie des hl. Irenaeus . . . ,* Scholastik, 17 (1942) 161-177. J. Daniélou, *Saint Irénée et les origines de la théologie de l'histoire,* RSR., 21 (1947) 227-231. L. Lawson, *The Biblical Theology of St. Irenaeus,* London, 1948.—Engl. transl., BET., 2146-2150.

⁵⁶ The two works of Justin: *Against Heresies* and *Against Marcion* are lost: O. Bardenhewer, *Geschichte . . . ,* I, 227. —MILTIADES, contemporary with Tatian, author of a treatise on Christian philosophy, had also composed a lost refutation of Valentine: Tertullian, *Adv. Valent.,* chapt. 5. Cf. O. Bardenhewer, *Geschichte . . . ,* I, 262.—Theophilus of Antioch had written a treatise against Hermogenes and another one against Marcion (O. Bardenhewer, *Geschichte . . . ,* I, 286-287), both are lost and we have no information about their content. On the anti-gnostic Christian literature prior to Irenaeus, O. Bardenhewer, I, 481-495.

⁵⁷ On the history of Gnosticism, A. Harnack, *Geschichte . . . ,* I, 141-231. O. Bardenhewer, *Geschichte . . . ,* I, 343-376. On the doctrine A. Harnack, *Lehrbuch der Dogmengeschichte,* I, 211-271. A. Hilgenfeld, *Die Ketzergeschichte des Urchristentums urkundlich dargestellt,* Leipzig, 1884. W. Bousset, *Hauptprobleme der Gnosis,* Göttingen, 1907. E. de Faye, *Gnostiques et gnosticisme. Etude critique des documents du gnosticisme chrétien aux IIe et IIIe siècles,* Paris, Leroux, 1913; 2nd. ed., 1925. H. Leisegang, *Die Gnosis,* Leipzig, Kröner, 1924; 2nd. ed., 1936. E. Buonaiuti, *Frammenti Gnostici. Introduzione, traduzione e commento,* Roma, 1923; English transl. *Gnostic Fragments,* Will & Norgate, London, 1924. General introductions: O. Bardenhewer, *Patrology,* 72-81. F. Cayré, *Manual of Patrology,* 100-105. G. Bareille, art. *Gnosticisme,* DTC., 6 (1925) 1434-1467. L. Duchesne, art. *Gnose,* Dict. apologétique, 2 (1924) 298-312; borrowed from *Histoire ancienne de l'Eglise,* vol. I, same author. M. Sagnard, *La gnose valentinienne et le témoignage de saint Irénée,* Paris, J. Vrin, 1947. J. Quasten, *Patrology,* I, 254-277.

⁵⁸ *Contra Haereses,* IV, 33, **8**. **PG.,** 7, 1077-1078. Cf. III, 24; 965-967. II, 27, 2; 803. II, 26, 1; 800. II, 28, 1; 804. Cf. *Démonstration de la prédication apostolique,* in *Recherches de science religieuse,* 1917, 368-369. For the formula: "True knowledge is the doctrine of the Apostles . . ." etc.; see AN., Buffalo edition, I, 508. In the following notes, *Contra Haereses* refers to the treatise *Against Heresies,* also called in Latin *Adversus Haereses.*

⁵⁹ *Contra Haereses,* II, 25, 3-4; AN., I, 396-397. II, 28, 2-3; AN., I, 399-400. (In A. Dufourcq, *Saint Irénée,* 112-113). That the Maker of the world has to turn to divine models: II, 16; AN., I, 379-380.—The doctrine of the Trinity is much more precise in Irenaeus than in his predecessors: the Creator should not be separated from his Word nor from his Wisdom, who is the Holy Ghost (*Contra Haereses,* IV, 20, 1. Cf. IV, 28, 1 and II, 25, 3). Through his Word, God has made all things visible and invisible (I, 22, 1. II, 2, 4. II, 8, 3. II, 30, 9. III, 8, 3, with reference to John, i, 3). No trace left of a generation of the Word as the "beginning" of creation. From the beginning the Word "reveals" the Father, and this is his eternal function: II, 30, 9 and III, 8, 3. Obviously, the need to fight Gnosticism has invited Irenaeus to stress the unity of the divine persons in the Trinity.

⁶⁰ *Contra Haereses,* II, 9, 1; AN., I, 369. Cf. IV, 6, 6; AN., I, 469.

⁶¹ On this point, Irenaeus says, Plato has seen the truth better than the Gnostics: *Contra Haereses,* III, 25, 5; AN., I, 459. Because the Creator is the Good, the world is good and ruled by divine providence: II, 6, 1; AN., I, 365. II, 26, 3; AN., I, 397-398. III, 25, 1; I, 459. The references to Plato naturally are: *Timaeus,* 28-30 (Cf. Hippolytus, *Philosophumena,* I, 16)—"Plato vero rursus materiam dicit et exemplum et Deum." II, 14, 3; AN., I, 377. Cf. PG., 7, 731 C.

⁶² *Contra Haereses,* I, 22, 1; AN., I, 347. II, 10, 4; AN., 370.

⁶³ *Contra Haereses,* II, 5, 4; AN., I, 365.

⁶⁴ *Contra Haereses,* III, 25, 5; AN., I, 459-460. Cf. Plato, *Laws,* IV, 715-716.

[65] Gen. 1, 31.

[66] *Contra Haereses*, IV, 38, 1; AN., I, 521. On the nature of man before original sin, E. Klebba, *Die Anthropologie des Irenaeus*, 15-88.

[67] In this, he is following S. Paul: I Cor. 3, 2: Cf. *Contra Haereses*, IV, 38, 2; AN., I, 521.

[68] *Contra Haereses*, V, 3, 2; AN., I, 529-530. Cf. E. Klebba, 92, on the Stoic sources of the definition: "an animated and rational creature."

[69] The soul and the spirit are parts of man: V, 6, 1; AN., I, 531. This text shows that, in the mind of Irenaeus, the "spirit" has become an entirely religious notion and, more precisely, the supernatural element included in human nature by the "Spirit of God" when the Creator made man in his own image.—On the materiality of souls, *Contra Haereses*, II, 34, 1; AN., I, 411: "By these things, then, it is plainly declared that souls continue to exist, that they do not pass from body to body, that they possess the form of man, so that they may be recognized . . ." — The body is an instrument for the soul, not a cause of oblivion: II, 33, 3-5; AN., I, 410-411; yet, the soul itself is so certainly material that Irenaeus does not hesitate to use this comparison: "Just as water when poured into a vessel takes the form of that vessel, and if on any occasion it happens to congeal in it, it will acquire the form of the vessel in which it has thus been frozen, since souls themselves possess the figure of the body; for they themselves have been adapted to the vessel, as I have said before." *Contra Haereses*, II, 19, 6; AN., I, 386.

[70] Cf. *Contra Haereses*, V, 7, 1; AN., I, 532: "for souls are incorporeal when put in comparison with mortal bodies . . ." Yet, the soul is the breath of life breathed by God into the face of man. As such, it is "incorporeal" and, since it is "life," it cannot die. Death can happen neither to the soul, "for it is the breath of life; nor to the spirit, for the spirit is simple, and not composite, so that it cannot be decomposed, and is itself the life of those who receive it." The flesh, then, is what is mortal; but it can be resurrected: V, 7, 2; AN., I, 533.

[71] These are but various movements of the soul: *Contra Haereses*, II, 29, 3; AN., I, 403. Cf. II, 13, 1-2; AN., I, 373.

[72] *Contra Haereses*, IV, 4, 3; AN., I, 466. Cf. IV, 37, 1; AN., I, 518-519; and IV, 37, 4; AN., I, 519.

[73] For instance, Beuzart, *Essai sur la théologie d'Irénée*, p. 64.

[74] *Contra Haereses*, IV, 37, 2-6; AN., I, 519-520. The text IV, 37, 5, is particularly interesting: "And not only in works, but also in faith, has God preserved the will of man free and under his own control . . ." etc.

[75] Like all creatures, man is exposed to dissolution (*Contra Haereses*, II, 34, 3; AN., I, 411); as has been said, the soul is life, but not, as in Plato, because this is its nature; the soul is life because it has received life from God, and it continues to live so long as God wills it to live (II, 34, 4; AN., I, 412). In point of fact, God wills it to live eternally (many texts: II, 33, 4. II, 34, 2-4. V, 7, 1. V, 13, 3). Between bodily death and resurrection, the soul goes to an invisible place, where it waits for the resurrection of its body. (*Contra Haereses*, V, 31, 2; AN., I, 560). This will take place at the end of the world, after the coming of Antichrist, when the universe will have lasted for 6000 years. See the elements of this curious calculation, *Contra Haereses*, V, 28-30; AN., I, 556-560. The essential parts of these texts are found in A. Dufourcq, *Saint Irénée*, 245-265.

[76] HIPPOLYTUS, probably a pupil of Irenaeus; opposed the doctrine of Pope Zephirinus on the Trinity. According to Hippolytus, Zephirinus did not distinguish enough between the Father and the Son (modalism); inversely, according to Zephirinus, Hippolytus exaggerated the distinction (ditheism). After the death of Zephirinus, Hippolytus seceded from the Christian community of Rome and remained isolated under the pontificates of Urbanus and of Pontinianus. Arrested at the same time as Pontinianus and deported with him to Sardinia, he is said to have recognized the authority of Pontianus and invited his own partisans to do the same. Both died in jail and are considered martyrs. Of the writings listed

by his historians, two are of direct interest to us: the *Philosophumena,* PG., 16, 3017-3454; Bk. I in Herm. Diels, *Doxographi Graeci,* 1879, 551-576. English transl. in AN., VI (Engl. ed.), and F. Legge, London, SPCK., 1921, 2 vols; the second one is the treatise *Against Noetus,* PG., 10, 803-830; English transl. in AN., (English ed.) VI, 51-70. Another easily accessible work of Hippolytus is *The Apostolic Tradition,* English transl. by B. S. Easton, Cambridge Univ. Press, 1934, and G. Dix, SPCK., London, 1937. BIBLIOGRAPHY. —History of the texts, A. Harnack, *Geschichte . . .* , I, 2, 605-646; O. Bardenhewer, *Geschichte . . .* , II, 605-646.— On the doctrine, A. Stöckl, *Geschichte der christlichen Philosophie,* 98-103. A. d'Alès, *La théologie de saint Hippolyte,* Paris, 1906 (excellent); *L'édit de Calliste,* Paris, 1914. A. Donini, *Ippolito di Roma,* 1925. The commentary of A. Siouville to the *Philosophumena,* 2 vols., 1928, should also be consulted without forgetting that the authenticity of the *Philosophumena* is not *absolutely* certain. B. Capelle, *Le Logos, Fils de Dieu, dans la théologie d'Hippolyte,* RTAM., 9 (1937) 109-124. P. Nautin, *Hippolyte et Josipe,* Paris, 1947; *Note sur le catalogue des oeuvres d'Hippolyte,* RTAM., 9 (1937) 109-124, 347-359. B. Capelle, *Hippolyte de Rome,* RTAM., 17 (1950) 145-174. R. M. Grant, *The Problem of Theophilus,* HTR., 43 (1950) 179-196. B. Capelle, *A propos d'Hippolyte de Rome,* RTAM., 19 (1952) 193-202. P. Nautin, *Le dossier d'Hippolyte et de Méliton,* Paris, Editions du Cerf, 1953. J. Quasten, *Patrology,* II, 163-210.—English transl., BET., 1960-1964.

[77] Revised text of *Philosophumena,* Bk. I, in H. Diels, *Doxographi Graeci,* Berlin, 1879. Hippolytus never intended to write a "history of Greek philosophy." He was a Christian unveiling the "secrets" of philosophico-religious sects, whose methods of progressive doctrinal initiation he curiously describes in *Philosophumena,* I, Prologue (see Legge's transl. I, pp. 33-34).

[78] For instance, the notice on Plato (*Philosophumena,* I, 16; Legge's transl. I, 51-55), for which Hippolytus has drawn from Alcinous' *Introduction to Plato's doctrines,* mentions, among other points: the three principles of the universe (God: maker, orderer and providence; matter: a "recipient and a nurse"; the model, i.e.,

the ideas, after which God has made all things). Matter is coeternal with God and, consequently, so also is the universe. According to some, Plato posited only one God (*Laws,* IV, 7); according to others, he said that there were several gods (*Timaeus,* 16), begotten but unperishable by the will of the God of gods. As to the human soul, Plato first says that it is immortal by nature, because it is life (*Phaedo*) then he says that it has been created by God and made immortal by the divine will (*Phaedrus,* 51-52). At any rate, Plato admits rewards and punishments after death, and also the transmigration of souls from bodies to bodies, although some deny that he ever taught this. The chapter ends with an exposition of Plato's ethics: primacy of the four main virtues: Prudence, Temperance, Justice and Fortitude; "happiness is likeness to God as far as possible"; "any one is like God when he becomes holy and just with intention"; in our own lives, a part hangs on destiny, but another part hangs on our own choice; since evil has no reality of its own, it is not caused by God; it is an absence of goodness and of being.—On Aristotle, I, 17; Legge's transl. I, pp. 55-57. On the Brachmans, I, 21; transl. I, 60-61. On "the Druids among the Celts," I, 22; transl. I, 61-62.

[79] Hippolytus, *Philosophumena,* I; PG., 16, 3017-3018. Chapters on Pythagoras (I, 2; 3021-3028) and Plato (I, 9; 3041). No philosopher compares with Plato (IV, 3; 3066 D). Shorter chapter on Aristotle (I, 20; 3045), completed further on where he tries to show that Basilides borrowed from Aristotle the principles of his own *Gnosis* (VII, 14-19; 3295-3301).—Against Astrology: IV, 3-5; 3059-3067 (seems to borrow from Ptolemy, IV, 12; 3075).—Against the "mathematicians," IV, 14; 3078-3082.—Against the "physiognomists," IV, 15-27; 3082-3090.—Against the magicians; IV, 28-42; 3090-3103.—On the reproach of ignorance directed against the Christians, IV, 45; 3109.

[80] GOD. One single God, sole creator of all things; nothing is coeternal with him, not even chaos. He was alone in himself before the creation, but he had the foreknowledge of all that was to be made (*Philosophumena,* X, 32; 3446-3447). This God begot the Word, "not

a word in the sense of a voice, but the indwelling Reason of the all. He begot him alone (i.e., begot, *not* created) from the things which are. For the Father himself was what is; from whom was the Word, the cause of the begetting of things coming into being, bearing within himself the will of his begetter, not ignorant of the thought of the Father. For from the time of his coming forth from him who begot him, becoming his first-born voice, he holds within himself the Ideas (note one of the first appearances of the Platonic doctrine of the divine Ideas in the history of Christian thought) conceived in his Father's mind. Whence, on the Father ordering the world to come into being, the Word completed it in detail, pleasing God" (*Philosophumena*, X, 33; 3447; Legge's transl., pp. 173-174). Hippolytus seems to imply that the Word was made at God's will (*Contra Noetum*, X; PG., 10, 847. Cf. "For had God willed to make thee a God, He could: thou hast the example of the Word," *Philosophumena*, X, 33; Legge's transl., p. 174). The Father and the Word are two "persons," but a single power (*Contra Noetum*, VII; PG., 10, 813 A). He himself has said it (John, 10, 30): "I and the Father are one"; he says *are*, not *am*. By being thus begotten as a distinct person, the Word has completed his self-manifestation as Son of God and Christ. Before his incarnation, he was perfectly "word," but he was not yet perfectly "son" (*Contra Noetum*, X; PG., 10, 818. Cf. XV; PG., 10, 824, and the interpretation of Döllinger, summed up in A. Stöckl, *Geschichte der christlichen Philosophie zur Zeit der Kirchenväter*, 101-102. Same interpretation in A. d'Alès, *La théologie de saint Hippolyte*, p. 30. There are then

three moments in the revelation of the Word: his eternal coexistence with God; his generation as a distinct person before the creation; his incarnation.—WORLD. Because it is created from nothing, it is not God (*Philosophumena*, X, 33; PG., 16, 3347 C and 3450 B). The first four creatures are the elements (principles of all the future beings) fire, spirit (*pneuma*), water and earth. In his lost treatise *On the Universe,* Hippolytus established that some creatures are made of a single element; others are made of two, three or four elements. Creatures made of only one element are simple, indivisible and immortal; the others can be dissolved, and their dissolution is called "death" (*Philosophumena*, X, 32; PG., 16, 3447 AB). Being made of a single element, the first beings are neither male nor female: for instance, the angels, who are made up of fire, are not male and female; even the stars, which are made up of fire and *pneuma* (air), do not seem to be male and female. The division into sexes appears as soon as water enters the composition of beings (*Philosophumena*, X, 32; PG., 16, 3447 C and 3450 A). Since God is good he has created no evil; but man has been created free and, consequently, capable of doing evil. Evil is but a possible consequence of our liberty (*Philosophumena*, X, 33; PG., 16, 3450 B). This explains why God has promulgated his laws; animals do not obey laws, but whips. The divine laws were given to the world by Moses and the Prophets, speaking under the inspiration of the Holy Ghost, and they were finally manifested by the Logos himself, God incarnate in the person of Christ (*Philosophumena*, X, 33; PG., 16, 3450-3451).

PART TWO
EARLY CHRISTIAN SPECULATION

CHAPTER I. THE ALEXANDRINES

[1] PHILO THE JEW, also called Philo of Alexandria d. *ca.* 40 A.D.—E. Bréhier, *Les idées philosophiques et religieuses de Philon d'Alexandrie,* Paris, J. Vrin, 2 ed., 1925. E. R. Goodenough, *An Introduction to Philo Judaeus,* New Haven, 1940. H. A. Wolfson, *Philo. Foundations of Religious Philosophy in Judaism, Christianity and Islam,* 2 vols. Harvard University Press,

1947.—P. Wendland, *Philo und Klemens Alexandrinus,* Hermes, 31 (1896) 435-456.

[2] CLEMENT OF ALEXANDRIA, born *ca.* 150; a convert to Christianity he studied in different cities and finally settled in Alexandria where the teaching of Pantaenus gave him full satisfaction. Ordained a priest, he succeeded Pantaenus as head-

master of the school (*ca.* 200). During the persecution of Septimus Severus, he fled to Caesarea in Cappadocia (*ca.* 202). Died before 215. Main works: *Protreptikos,* or *Exhortation to the Heathens; Paidagogos,* that is *The Instructor; Stromata,* or *Miscellanies* (litt. the *Tapestries*); an important homily on Mark, 10, 17-31: *Which Rich Man Will Be Saved?*—Greek and Latin texts in PL., VIII-IX. Critical edition of the Greek text by O. Stählin in GCS., I, Clemens Alexandrinus, *Protrepticus und Paedagogus,* Leipzig, 1905; II, *Stromata, I-VI,* 1906; III, *Stromata VII-VIII, Excerpta ex Theodoto, Eclogae propheticae, Quis dives salvetur, Fragments,* 1909. English transl. by W. Wilson, *The Writings of Clement of Alexandria,* in AN., 2 vols. Edinburgh, 1868, 1869 (minus the *Quis dives* . . .). Selections: J. A. Hort & J. B. Mayor, *Clement of Alexandria, Miscellanies Bk. VII,* London & New York, 1907 (Greek and English). G. W. Butterworth, *Clement of Alexandria,* London & New York, 1919 (*Protreptikos, Quis dives salvetur*). S. Q. Wood, *Christ the Educator,* New York, 1954. French selections, G. Bardy, *Clement of Alexandria,* Paris, 1926.—BIBLIOGRAPHY, J. Quasten, *Patrology,* II, 5-36. De la Barre, art. *Clément d'Alexandrie,* DTC., 3 (1923) 137-199. J. Patrick, *Clement of Alexandria,* Edinburgh & London, 1914. R. B. Tollinton, *Clement of Alexandria. A Study in Christian Liberalism,* 2 vols. London, 1914.—Greek sources: C. Merk, *Clemens Alexandrinus in seiner Abhängigkeit von der Griechischen Philosophie,* Leipzig, 1879. J. Bernays, *Zu Aristoteles und Clemens,* Gesammelten Abhandlungen von J. B., Bonn, 1885, I, 151-164. P. Wendland, *Quaestiones Musonianae. De Musonio stoico Clementis Alexandrini aliorumque auctore,* Berlin, 1886. A. Schreck, *De fontibus Clementis Alexandrini,* Augsburg, 1889 (Progr.-Gymnas.). A. Aabl, *Der Logos. Geschichte seiner Entwicklung in der Griechieschen Philosophie und der christlichen Literatur,* 2 ed. Leipzig, 1899, pp. 384-427. Ch. P. Parker, *Musonius and Clement,* Harvard Studies, 12 (1901) 191-200. F. L. Clark, *Citations of Plato in Clement of Alexandria,* Proceedings of the American Philological Association, 33 (1902) pp. XII-XX. Hort & Mayor, excellent pages in the above-listed edition of the *Miscellanies,* pp. XXII-XLIX. J. Gabrielsson, *Ueber die Quellen des Clemens Alexandrinus,* Uppsala & Leipzig, 2 vols., I, 1906; II, 1909.

M. Daskadalis, *Die eklektischen Anschauungen des Clemens von Alexandria und seine Abhängigkeit von der Griechischen Philosophie,* Leipzig, 1908 (Inaug.-Dissert.).—Religion and Philosophy, G. Mondésert, *La pensée religieuse de Clément d'Alexandrie à partir de l'Ecriture,* Paris, 1944. Th. Camelot, *Foi et Gnose, Introduction à l'étude de la connaissance mystique chez Clément d'Alexandrie,* Paris, 1945. Fr. Quatember, *Die christliche Lebenshaltung des Klemens von Alexandrien nach seinem Pädagogus,* Wien, 1946. J. Moingt, *La gnose de Clément d'Alexandrie dans ses rapports avec la foi et la philosophie,* RSR., 37 (1950) 176-194, 537-564; 38 (1951) 82-118. More general: J. Lebreton, *Le désaccord de la foi populaire et de la théologie savante dans l'Eglise chrétienne au IIIe siècle,* RHE., 19 (1923) 481-506; 20 (1924) 5-37. W. Wagner, *Wert und Verwertung der Griechischen Bildung im Urteil des Klemens von Alexandrien,* Marburg, 1902 (Inaug.-Dissert.). Th. Rütter, *Ueber die Stellung des Klemens Alexandrinus zur Philosophie,* Theologie und Glaube, 4 (1912) 740-749.—Psychologie: P. Ziegert, *Zwei Abhandlungen über T. Fl. Klemens Alexandrinus. Psychologie und Logoschristologie,* Heidelberg, 1894, 75-176. G. Verkuyl, *Die Psychologie des Klemens von Alexandrien im Verhältnis zu seiner Ethik,* Leipzig, 1906 (Inaug.-Dissert.). W. Scherer, *Klemens von Alexandrien und seine Erkenntnisprinzipien,* Munich, 1907. Lhande, *Les trois âges. Essais de Psychologie religieuse et domestique sur Clément d'Alexandrie,* Etudes, 24 (1910) 466-482, 615-630, 780-789. J. Hering, *La préexistence des âmes chez Clément d'Alexandrie,* Paris, 1923.—Ethics: K. Ernesti, *Die Ethik des Titus Flavius Klemens von Alexandrien* . . . , Paderborn, 1903. W. Capitaine, *Die Moral von Clemens von Alexandrien,* Paderborn, 1903. J. Van der Hagen, *De Clementis Alexandrini sententiis economicis, socialibus, politicis,* Utrecht, 1920 (Inaug.-Dissert.).—General history of the school: Ch. Bigg, *The Christian Platonists of Alexandria,* Oxford, 1886. W. Bousset, *Jüdisch-christlicher Schulbetrieb in Alexandria und Rom,* Göttingen, 1915. H. R. Nielz, *Die theologischen Schulen der morgenländischen Kirchen* . . . , Bonn, 1916. R. B. Tollinton, *Alexandrine Teaching on the Universe,* New York, 1932. G. Bardy, *Aux origines de l'école d'Alexandrie,* Recherches de sciences religieuses, 27 (1937)

65-90. *Pour l'histoire d'Alexandrie,* Vivre et Penser 2 (1942), 80-109. W. Völker, *Der wahre Gnostiker nach Clemens Alexandrinus* (Texte und Untersuchungen, 57), Leipzig, 1952.—Engl. transl., BET., 990-997.

[3] *Exhortation,* ch. XII, AN., I, 106-110.

[4] Relation of the *Exhortation* to the *Instructor,* in *Instructor,* I, 1; Stählin, I, 89-91 and AN., I, 113-114.—The Instructor as educator and physician: I, 5-6; St. I, 96-121. On faith as the perfection of knowledge, I, 6; St. I, 107, line 14. The Instructor as a judge: I, 8-9; St. I, 126-142 (AN., 155-173) and I, 12; St. 148-150 (AN., 181-183).—Practical rules of moral conduct (eating, drinking, laughter, clothing, cosmetics, etc.) Bk. II, and Bk. III, ch. 11 (AN., I, 313-331).

[5] *Quis dives salvetur,* ed. Stählin, III, 159-191.

[6] *Miscellanies,* I, 1; St. II, 13, lines 1-14 (AN., I, 349-351).—On the meaning of *Miscellanies* (or *Stromata),* see VII, 18; Stählin, III, 78, 1. 19—79, 1. 8 (AN., II, 489).

[7] Faith is sufficient, I, 9; St. II, 28. VI, 10; St. 471, 30-472, 7. VIII, 1; St. III, 80, 1. 4-5, where Christianity is said to be the only philosophy worthy of the name (AN., I, 379-383; II, 349-351; 490-491). —Christian hostility against philosophy, I, 2; St. II, 13, 1. 14-16 and 14, 1. 13-19 (AN., I, 360-361).—Philosophy and arts given to man by God, I, 4 (AN., I, 364-365), and VI, 17; St. II, 513, 1. 23—514, 1. 5 (AN., II, 399-401).—The words of Matthew, 7, 7, and of Luke, 11, 9, as an invitation to philosophize: VIII, 1; St. III, 80, 1. 9-10 (AN., II, 490).—Philosophical aptitudes are a gift of God, I, 4; St. II, 16-17 (AN., I, 365).—Philosophy was to the Greeks what the Law had been to the Jews: VI, 5; St. II, 451-453 and VI, 7; St. 459-463 (AN., II, 326-328 and 335-339).—J. T. Muckle, *Clement of Alexandria on Philosophy as a Divine Testament for the Greeks,* The Phoenix (Journal of the Classical Association of Canada) 5 (1951) 79-86.

[8] "And, in general terms, we shall not err in alleging that all things necessary and profitable for life came to us from God, and that philosophy more especially

was given to the Greeks, as a covenant peculiar to them, being, as it were, a stepping-stone to the philosophy which is according to Christ . . . ," *Miscellanies,* VI, 8 (AN., II, 342).—The "philosophy according to Christ" is sometimes called by Clement "the Barbaric philosophy," that is the philosophy of the Barbarians as opposed to the philosophy of the Greeks: *Miscellanies,* V, 14; St. II, 389, 23. II, 13; St. II, 36, 10. He also uses "Barbaric theology": II, 13; St. II, 36, 29. More references in the Index to Stählin's edition, vol. IV, 792-793.

[9] Philosophy the handmaid of theology: *Miscellanies,* I, 5; St. II, 17-21 (AN., I, 366-370). Same doctrine in Philo: H. A. Wolfson, *Philo,* I, 2; 87-163.

[10] The collaboration of faith and reason is possible on account of the unity of human thought. The world is saturated with a "prudence" (*phronesis*) which, in the human soul, receives different names according to its different operations. As seeking to know the first causes, it is "intellection" (*noesis*); as trying to demonstrate the intuitions of the intellect, it becomes Knowledge, Science, Wisdom; as accepting the teaching of God without striving to understand it, it is "faith" (*pistis*); as applying itself to sensible things, it begets "true opinion," "experience" and the practical arts: *Miscellanies,* VI, 17; St. II, 511, lines 25-512, line 6 (AN., II, 397).—Faith as criterion of philosophical truth, *Miscellanies,* II, 4; St. II, 120, lines 26-27 (AN., II, 9). Faith begets "wisdom, understanding, intelligence, knowledge," according to pseudo-Barnabas. How philosophy is perfected by faith, *Miscellanies,* VI, 7; St. II, 459, line 25—460, line 4 (AN., II, 335-339). On true gnosis as an intellectual comprehension of all, including what seems incomprehensible, *Miscellanies,* VI, 8; St. II, 465, 1. 18—467, 1. 6 (AN., II, 343-344).

[11] NOETIC. God prescribes to man to seek in order that he may find (Matt. 7, 7; Luke, 11, 9). To find is to know; in order to know, we must define terms (*blictri,* which means nothing, is no object of demonstration; *Miscellanies,* VIII, 2; St. III, 81, 1. 12 (AN., II, 491); the starting point is nominal definition, whence we proceed to real definition; all demonstrations bring about assent on points dis-

puted from points already conceded (*Miscellanies,* VIII, 3); this is achieved by way of sylogisms, but discussions would have no end if they did not hang on the evidence of the first principles. To relate conclusions to the first principles is "analysis"; to infer conclusions from principles by syllogistic reasoning is "demonstration" (*Miscellanies,* VIII, 3; St. III, 84, l. 9-14; AN., II, 493-494). On this part of the doctrine, Chr. de Wedel, *Symbola ad Clementis Alexandrini Stromatum librum VIII interpretandum,* Berlin, 1905; and W. Ernst, *De Clementis Alexandrini Stromatum libro VIII qui fertur,* Göttingen, 1910.—CAUSES. Clement follows the Stoic classification of the four causes: procatarctic, which are the best occasions of some event, as beauty is the cause of love; synectic, which suffice by themselves to cause their effect; the assisting, or "co-operating" causes, which share in the production of the effect; the causes "*sine qua non,*" which are necessary conditions for the production of effects, for instance: time. Clement reduces this Stoic classification to that of Aristotle in efficient, material, formal and final causes. (*Miscellanies,* VIII, 9; St. III, 95 and 98; AN., II, 508. Cf. Von Arnim, *Stoicorum veterum fragmenta,* II, 354-356). The notion of causality entails that of relation. Nothing is cause of itself, because nothing can, at one and the same time, exercise a certain action and undergo it (*Miscellanies,* VIII, 9; St. III, 99, l. 13-24; AN., II, 511-512).—GOD. God is known by a sort of natural anticipation (*prolepsis*) which seems to have been common to most philosophers. A divine influence suggested to them the notion of one single God, cause and end of the universe; Plato and many others bear witness to the fact (*Exhortation,* ch. 6; St. I, 51-55; AN., I, 69-72. The natural character of this "anticipation" is well marked in *Miscellanies,* V, 13; St. II, 383, l. 21-24, and AN., II, 270-273).— The nature of God is ineffable because it is above all determinations and categories. One must first go beyond sensations, and then, by means of "analysis," go up from given experience to the prime intelligible Cause of all. This analysis proceeds by successive abstractions: from bodies dimensions are abstracted; from dimensions the point in space is abstracted; from the point in space, the point is abstracted; what is left is an intelligible unit beyond space, time, name

and knowledge; *Miscellanies,* V, 11; St. II, 374 (AN., II, 261-267), and V, 12; St. II, 380 line 10—381, line 13 (AN., II, 267-270). God is one because he is beyond unity and beyond the "monad" itself; we only have a negative knowledge of him: *Exhortation,* I, 8; St. I, 131, lines 18-19, and *Miscellanies,* V, 12; St. II, 377-381 (AN., I, 76-79 and II, 270: "For the One is indivisible; wherefore also it is infinite, not with reference to its inscrutability, but with reference to its having no dimensions and not having a limit." Note this early reference to the infinity of God). This impossibility fully to declare God is attested by Plato, *Timaeus* 28 C, *Epist.* VII 341 C, and by Exod. 19, 12-24. Yet we know that God is being and we can ascribe to him some attributes (references in A. de la Barre, DTC., III, 156-158). The self-knowledge of God is his Word (*Logos*), coeternal with the Father, begotten and yet without a beginning: *Miscellanies,* V, 14; St. II, 395 (AN., II, 282). Cf. W. Capitaine, *Die Moral . . . ,* 87-102.—CREATION is the common work of the Father and the Word, performed in and by the Word: *Exhortation,* X; St. I, 71, lines 23-29 (AN., I, 91; 98-99). Even matter is created from nothing; Plato and the Stoics borrowed this truth from Moses, together with the distinction of two worlds, the intelligible world and the sensible world made after the model of the intelligible world. Greek philosophy simply follows the "Barbaric philosophy" on this point: *Miscellanies,* V, 14; St. II, 386, line 21—388, line 11 (Stählin gives references to Philonian sources), AN., II, 275 ff.—God created the world by his pure goodness, which is that of a free will: *Exhortation,* IV; St. I, 48, lines 14-19 ("His bare volition was the creation of the universe." AN., I, 65). Cf. *Miscellanies,* VII, 7; St. III, 31, line 31-32, line 8 (AN., II, 436). Time was created together with the world; creation did not extend over a period of six days, but things appeared successively in consequence of the single and simple act of the divine will by which they now subsist: *Miscellanies,* VI, 16; St. II, 504 (AN., II, 390); this point, however, is not as clear in the text as we make it. —MAN. After angels, man is the most perfect creature of the world; he is good in what he is and he is able to become better; the soul should use its body precisely to this end. No pre-existence of souls; yet souls are immortal according to Plato who borrowed the doctrine from Pythagoras, who had borrowed it from the Egyptians. *Miscellanies*, IV, 26; St. II, 321, l. 16-22 (AN., II, 216), and VI, 2; St. II, 443, l. 11-13; AN., II, 318-319; all this shows "the selfish plagiarism of the Greeks, and how they claim the discovery of the best of their doctrines, which they have received from us." Clement's notion of the soul is obscure and has been given diverse interpretations (W. Capitaine, 127 ff., G. Verkuyl, 9-30. W. Scherer, 7-14. Fr. Winter, 55-58). The soul is more simple and more subtle than water, so much so that it can be said to be incorporeal; in fact, even the souls of brutes are invisible: *Miscellanies*, VI, 6; St. II, 458, l. 6-9 (AN., II, 334), and VI, 18; St. II, 516, l. 11-14 (AN., II, 402: "For souls are invisible; not only those that are rational, but those also of the other animals").— Man has been created in the image of God, which is natural to all, but also in his likeness, which is not natural to all. This likeness is a supernatural gift which we must cultivate with the help of both free will and grace: *Miscellanies*, II, 22; St. II, 185-188 (AN., II, 74-78). Cf. II, 19; St. II, 168, l. 9-12 (AN., II, 58-59). See W. Capitaine, 224-257, and A. de la Barre, DTC., 3 (1923) 171-176.—Gnostic wisdom is the life of Christian faith at its point of perfection: *Miscellanies*, VI, 14; St. II, 487, l. 24-29. Cf. AN., II, 369, where Clement distinguishes the actions of the Gnostic, which are right, from those of the simple believers which are "intermediate" (as not having been "made right according to knowledge"), and from those of the unbelievers, which are sinful.

[12] *Miscellanies*, IV, 21; St. II, 305, l. 18-23; l. 25-26; l. 28-31 (AN., II, 199-202). Cf. *Miscellanies*, IV, 22; St. II, 308, l. 5. V, 1; II, 326, l. 8-9 and 16-20. VI, 12; II, 480, l. 12-20 and 481, l. 6—484, l. 28. VI, 15; II, 491, l. 18—492, l. 12. This chapter contains the description of the four modes of ingrafting: cf. AN., II, 373-374.—Not every Christian is a "Gnostic," because not all have knowledge, but all true Gnostics are Christians; the true Gnostic is the Christian perfect in knowledge: *Miscellanies*, IV, 21; St. II. 305, l. 25-26 and 28-31 (AN., II, 199). Had he to choose between the knowledge of God and eternal salvation, he would choose knowledge, because "the knowl-

edge itself suffices as the reason for contemplation": *Miscellanies*, IV, 22; St. II, 308, l. 23-33 (AN., II, 202-203). The love of God, who is the only true object of love, considers no other gain than the "knowledge" of its object (AN., II, 207). —The true Gnostic is impassible (*apatheia*), as his "Instructor" himself is, because the possession of true knowledge eradicates all desires: *Miscellanies*, VI, 9; St. II, 468, l. 15-22 (AN., II, 346-347). —On this subtle point, R. B. Tollinton, ch. XIV, vol. II, pp. 72-101, where the esoteric character of the Christian Gnosis is traced to Saint Paul and to Barnabas: p. 73.

[13] Cognat, *Clément d'Alexandrie, sa doctrine et sa polémique*, Paris, 1858, 359. —C. Merk, *Clemens Alexandrinus in seinen Abhängigkeit von der griechischen Philosophie*, 1879, 90.—Winter, *Studien zur Geschichte der christlichen Ethik*, Leipzig, 1882; I, 16.—A. Harnack, *Lehrbuch der Dogmengeschichte*, 3 ed. Freiburg i. Br., 1894, 600-601.—Hatch, *Influence of Greek Ideas and Usages upon the Christian Church*, 1890, 106-109.—F. J. A. Hort and J. B. Mayor, *Clement of Alexandria Miscellanies Bk. VII*, Introduction, pp. XXII-XLVII.—E. de Faye, *Clément d'Alexandrie*, Paris, 1898, 316-318.—G. Bardy, *Clément d'Alexandrie*, 32; more severe judgment, p. 275.

[14] ORIGEN. See Eusebius, *Historia ecclesiastica*, VI, 2, 7. Born in Egypt of Christian parents, 185. His father Leonidas died a martyr, 202. Taught at the school of Alexandria, 202-215. Taking Matt. 19, 12 in a literal sense, he made himself "eunuch for the kingdom of heaven" (see, however, his spiritual interpretation of the text, *Origenes Werke*, X, p. 358). Studied under Ammonius Saccas, in whose school he perhaps knew Plotinus. Under the persecution of Caracalla (*ca.* 216) left Alexandria and went to Palestine where he taught up to *ca.* 230. On his way to Athens, he stopped at Caesarea where he was ordained a priest without the consent of his own bishop, Demetrios (Bishop of Alexandria). Eusebius and Jerome suggest some jealousy on the part of Demetrios and of the head of the Alexandria school, Heraclas. The obstacle to the validity of his ordination, however, was clear (Matt. 19, 12). Origen was deposed and returned to Caesarea where he conducted a flourishing school. One of his most famous

pupils was Saint Gregory Thaumaturgus (*Paneg. in Orig.*, ch. 7-15; BET., 1812). The condemnation of some of his doctrines by his successor Heraclas does not seem to have lessened his authority. Arrested, incarcerated and several times tortured during the persecution of Decius (235), but not put to death, he died at Tyre (*ca.* 254) 69 years old.

WRITINGS. Greek text and Latin transl., PG., 6-7. Greek or Latin text only, GCS., 10 vols., Leipzig, Hinrichs, 1899-1941: especially important for the history of philosophical notions: *Against Celsus*, vols. I, II; *On the Principles* (*De principiis*) in the Latin transl. by Rufinus, vols. VI, VII. On the liberties taken by Rufinus with the text, G. Bardy, *Recherches sur l'histoire du texte et des versions latines du "De principiis" d'Origène*, Lille, 1923. —English transl. in AN., X and XXIII: *The Writings of Origen;* I, *De principiis* and *Contra Celsum* I; II, *Contra Celsum*, II-VIII. R. R. Tollinton, *Selections from the Commentaries and Homilies of Origen*, SPCK., New York, 1927. *Contra Celsum*, transl. by H. Chadwick, Cambr. Univ. Press, 1953 (useful notes). BET., 3020-3026.—French transl., Origène, *Homélies sur la Genèse*, ed. L. Doutreleau, Paris, 1944; *Homélies sur l'Exode*, ed. P. Fortier & H. de Lubac, Paris, 1947. *Homélies sur les Nombres*, ed. A. Méhat, Paris, 1951.

BIBLIOGRAPHY. E. R. Redepening, *Origenes. Eine Darstellung seiner Leben und seiner Lehre*, 2 vols. Bonn, 1841, 1846. J. Denis, *De la philosophie d'Origène*, Paris, 1884. Stöckl, *Geschichte der christlichen Philosophie*, 115-150. A. Harnack, *Lehrbuch der Dogmengeschichte*, 4 ed. (1909-1910) I, 650-697, *Der System des Origenes;* same author, *Der kirchengeschichtliche Ertrag der exegetischen Arbeiten des Origenes*, 2 vols. Leipzig, 1918, 1919. E. de Faye, *Origène, sa vie, sa pensée*, 3 vols. Paris, 1923-1928. J. Cadiou, *Introduction au système d'Origène*, Paris, 1932; same author, *La jeunesse d'Origène, Histoire de l'Ecole d'Alexandrie au début du IIIe siècle*, Paris, 1933: Engl. transl. minus most references to texts by J. A. Southwell, *Origen. His Life at Alexandria*, St. Louis, 1944. J. Daniélou, *Origène*, Paris, n.d. (1948). J. Quasten, *Patrology*, II, 37-101.

Many particular studies, among which: F. G. Gass, *De Dei indole et attributis Origenes quid docuerit*, Breslau (Inaug.-Diss.) 1838. Krüger, *Ueber Origenes' Ver-*

hältnis zu Ammonius Saccas, Illgensh. Zeitschrift, 1843, 46 ff. F. Borkowski, *De Origenis Cosmologia*, Greifswald, 1848. P. Melhorn, *Die Lehre von der menschlichen Freiheit nach Origenes Peri Arkhôn*, ZKG., 11 (1878) 234-253. H. J. Bestmann, *Origenes und Plotinus*, Zeitschrift für kirch. Wissenschaft und kirch. Leben, 1883, 169-187. M. Lang, *Ueber die Leiblichkeit der Vernunftwesen bei Origenes*, Leipzig, 1892 (Inaug.-Diss.). L. Klein, *Die Freiheitslehre des Origenes in ihren ethisch-theologischen Voraussetzungen und Folgerungen im Zusammenhang mit der altgriechischen Ethik*, Strassburg, 1894. Davies, *Origen's Theory of Knowledge*, AJT., 11 (1898) 276 ff. W. Capitaine, *De Origenis Ethica*, Münster i. W., 1898. A. Aall, *Der Logos* . . . , 424-445. W. Schüler, *Die Vorstellungen der Seele bei Plotin und bei Origenes*, ZTK., 10 (1900) 167-188. W. Fairweather, *Origen and the Greek Patristic Theology*, New York, Scribner's, 1901. J. Lebreton SJ., *Les degrés de la connaissance religieuse d'après Origène*, RSR., 12 (1922) 265-296. A. Miura-Stange, *Celsus und Origenes, das Gemeinsame ihrer Weltanschauung* . . . , Giessen, 1926. A. Lieske, *Die Theologie der Logosmystik bei Origenes*, Münster i. W., 1938. M. Villain, *Rufin d'Aquilée. La querelle autour d'Origène*, Recherches de science religieuse, 27 (1937) 5-37, 165-195. H. Chadwick, *Origen, Celsus and the Stoa*, JTS., 1947, 39-49. E. F. Lako, *Origen's Concept of Penance*, Québec, 1949. K. Rahner, *La doctrine d'Origène sur la pénitence*, RSR., 37 (1950) 47-97, 252-286, 422-456. H. de Lubac, *Histoire et esprit. L'intelligence de l'Ecriture d'après Origène*, Paris, 1950. E. van Ivanka, *Zur geistesgeschichtlichen Einordnung des Origenismus*, Byzantinische Zeitschrift, 44 (1951) 291-303.

[15] F. Heinemann, *Ammonius Sakkas und der Ursprung des Neuplatonismus*, Hermes, 61 (1926), 1-27.

[16] Cadiou, 194: "la théorie qui attribue un corps à tous les esprits"; that is: the theory according to which every spirit is in charge of a body.

[17] *De principiis*, Preface, which contains an important statement concerning points then under discussion among Christians; in AN., transl. Fred Crombie, I, 1-7 (AN., I, 1-5). Here are the main points. All Christians agree that there is only one God, creator of the world, the "God of

the Apostles and of the Old and the New Testaments; one Lord, Jesus Christ," born of the Father before all creatures "by whom all things were made and who became a true man, was truly born, and truly died, without ceasing to be the God which he was"; that "the Holy Spirit was associated in honor and dignity with the Father and the Son," but, on this point, the Church does not clearly say whether he has been made, or begotten as a son. —Concerning the soul, all Christians agree that it shall be eternally rewarded or punished; that there will be a resurrection of the dead; that rational souls are free and must fight against the fallen angels in order to live right, so that men are masters of their own destinies and not subjected to necessity; but the teaching of the Church does not say clearly whether the soul is transmitted from the seed (traducianism), or whether it is born with the body, or bestowed upon it from without.—Concerning angels, especially devils, the Church teaches that they exist; and most Christians are of the opinion that the devils are fallen angels; but what they are and how they exist is not defined with sufficient clarity. Concerning the world, the Church teaches that it was made and will be destroyed; but it does not define what there was before this world, nor what there will be after it.—Finally, all agree that beyond their literal meaning, the Scriptures have a spiritual one that is not known to all, "but to those only on whom the grace of the Holy Spirit is bestowed in the word of wisdom and knowledge." For instance, the word *asomaton* (i.e., incorporeal) is not found in Scripture. To most men it means a body so thin and subtle that it cannot be touched (for instance, air). To philosophers it means a being whose nature is different from that of bodies. Is this notion to be found in Scripture under another name? Is God himself corporeal or, on the contrary, incorporeal in the philosophical sense of the term? The same questions apply to Christ, the Holy Spirit and rational souls, but their answers "are not clearly indicated in our teaching." Let us remember that Justin, Tatian, Athenagoras, Irenaeus, etc., had found no incompatibility between Christian faith and the materiality of souls. Tertullian conceived even God as corporeal. Origen is aware of making a philosophical decision in teaching, with Plato, the existence of purely spiritual (i.e., in-

corporeal) beings. He gives its full meaning to the text of Saint John (4, 24): "God is spirit." Cf. *De principiis*, I, 1, 1; in *Origenes Werke* (quoted as OW.), V, 17.

[18] *Homilia XII in Numeros,* OW., VII, 2, p. 93.

[19] *De principiis,* IV, 2; OW., V, 305-323 (AN., I, 291-314). In Prat, *Origène,* 140-163.

[20] On the sources of Origen, see E. Denis, *De la philosophie d'Origène,* 59-60. E. de Faye, *Origène,* III, ch. 4, pp. 52-64.

[21] *De principiis,* I, 1, 6; OW., V, 21, and AN., I, 12. In this sense, as a simple spiritual nature, God is both thought and what is being thought; in other words, the thinking being and the object of its thought are one. See OW., V, 21, note to 13 ff.

[22] *De principiis,* I, 1, 6; OW., V, 20-21, quoted from AN., I, 12.

[23] *Contra Celsum,* VII, 38; OW., II, 188 (AN., II, 460).—The text of *Contra Celsum,* VI, 64; OW., II, 134 (AN., II, 407) where God is said to be "beyond substance," in both dignity and power, is literally inspired by Plato, *Republic,* VI, 509 B.

[24] The reason for this is that, just as the nature of sugar is to sweeten, the nature of the Good is to produce good things. So the power of doing evil is contrary to the very nature of God and, consequently, to his omnipotence: *Contra Celsum,* III, 70; OW., I, 262 (AN., II, 149).

[25] *De principiis,* II, 9, 1; OW., V, 164, l. 5-6 (AN., I, 126, note 2).

[26] The history of the Christian notion of "infinity" has never been studied for its own sake. The title of H. Guyot, *L'infinité divine depuis Philon le Juif jusqu'à Plotin* (Paris, 1906), is misleading. All the texts which he quotes from Scripture (pp. 37-42) justify the Christian theologians who were to say that God is infinite, but no Biblical text says it in so many words. As to Philo himself, H. Guyot admits that the word "infinity" does not occur in his writings as applied

to God (p. 55). In short, Philo never spoke of the infinity of God. After Clement, Origen has posited the principle from which other theologians were to deduce the infinity of God, namely, his incorporeity (what is not in *space* has no *limits*), but he himself has not drawn the inference. He has not even asked the question. His remarks on the finitude of God apply to the determination of God's will-power, not to a limitation of his being.

[27] *Comm. on Saint John,* XIII, 3; OW., IV, 229, l. 9-10: "Christ is life; and He who is higher than Christ, is higher than life." Cf. John, 14, 28: "the Father is greater than I."—This text of John is explicitly quoted in the same *Commentary,* XIII, 25 (OW., IV, 249), where Origen says that Christ did not want to accept for himself the unqualified, true and perfect appellation of "good." To which he adds, still speaking of Christ: "He does in no way compare with the Father. For indeed he is an image of his goodness, an effulgence (*apaugasma*), radiating, not from God, but from his glory, and from his eternal light; a beam, not of the Father, but of his power . . ." etc. This commentary goes far beyond the text of Saint John and obviously not in the right direction.

[28] *Comm. on Saint John,* II, 3; OW., IV, 55-57. There is only one true God, but many other gods have been made by the true one and are gods by participation only. There is, however, only one Son of the Father, the one we call *the* Logos. The Holy Ghost comes in the third place. On the third person of the Trinity, see J. Denis, *De la philosophie d'Origène,* 115-124.

[29] On the "reasons" in the Word: *Comm. on Saint John,* I, 19 (OW., IV, 24, l. 4-10). Also I, 34 (IV, 43, l. 16-34). *De principiis,* I, 2, 2 (OW., 32-33; and in AN., I, 18-19).—Against a self-subsisting world of Ideas, *De principiis,* II, 3, 6 (AN., I, 87). On the Word as cause of the created world: *Comm. on Saint John,* II, 10 (OW., IV, 64-65). *Contra Celsum,* VI, 10 (AN., II, 402-403).—On the Word as light of the world: *Comm. on Saint John,* VI, 38 (OW., IV, 146-147; cf. E. de Faye, *Origène,* III, 127, and 130-137).

[30] *Comm. on Saint John,* II, 2-3 (OW.,

IV, 54-57. Origen had read in Ps. 49, 1: "The God of gods, the Lord hath spoken." Hence there are other gods, those whom, precisely like the first-born of the whole creation, we call "gods," in order to distinguish them from "the God" (i.e., the Deity by right of self: *autotheos*). Yet the Logos has this prerogative, to be always with "the God," so as to appropriate to himself the divinity and to be its transmitter to the other gods. So the Logos (Word) is the Image after which all other images are made. Origen defines the life of the Word as a continuous contemplation of the Father. Note the preponderance of the notion of image, or similitude, which almost completely eliminates the Stoic notion of uttered or spoken word.

[31] See Eusebius, *The Preparation for the Gospel,* VII, 20. This fragment of Origen's commentary on Genesis has been preserved by Eusebius alone. English transl. by E. H. Gifford, vol. III, pp. 334-335.

[32] *De principiis,* III, 5, 3; OW., V, 272-273 (AN., I, 255-256). In this view, the world has had a beginning in time, but so have many other worlds before it. On the fact that there will be other worlds after it, Isaiah, 66, 22: "For as the new heavens, and the new earth, which I will make to stand before me, saith the Lord . . ." etc. The great master of allegorical exegesis often has texts whose letter supports the most adventurous of his views.

[33] *De principiis,* II, 9, 1; OW., V, 164-165 (AN., I, 126-127). Cf. Wisd. 7, 15-30.

[34] *Comm on Saint John,* XIII, 37; OW., IV, 261-263.

[35] Quoted in our text: *De principiis,* II, 9, 6; OW., V, 169-170 (AN., I, 132-133). —The primitive equality of all souls is certain in Origen's doctrine; the rest is less clear. Do the spirits created by God remain the same through the infinite series of successive worlds? Probably yes, since spirits are eternal and world history is a cyclical one. Are all creatures intellectual or rational? Probably yes, since they all are in the image of God (*Hom. in Jerem.,* 2, 1). Were these spirits created unrelated to matter? Certainly not; God alone is completely separated from matter; all the other spirits have

to make use of bodies; those among the spirits which dedicated themselves to God deserved their present rank and function (Raphael: curing and healing; Gabriel: conducting wars; Michael: attending to the prayers of men); the spirits that applied themselves to their bodies are now, so to speak, immersed in them. The history of the present structure of the world is less that of its creation by God than that of the fall of the spirits created by him. Beings have become what they now are, like men become sailors, carpenters or grammarians. Any man can become a sailor, but he could have become something else. Beings have become what they now are in virtue of their free will.

[36] *De principiis,* II, 9, 2; OW., V, 165-166 (AN., I, 128). *Contra Celsum,* V, 21 (AN., II, 289-290).

[37] On the diverse types of beings: *De principiis,* III, 1, 2-3; OW., V, 196-198 (AN., I, 157-160).—The present souls are spirits that "have grown cold out of a better and more divine condition"; in short, souls are frozen spirits: *De principiis,* II, 8, 3; OW., V, 157 (AN., I, 123).—On the reasons for his denial of the fall of human souls into animal bodies, see his commentary *On Saint John,* III, 41, and the explanations of Denis, *De la philosophie d'Origène,* pp. 207-210. The main reason is that, according to Origen, neither animals nor plants have souls properly so called.—On souls, *Entretien d'Origène avec Héraclide et les évêques ses collègues sur le Père, le Fils et l'âme,* ed. by J. Scherer, Le Caire, 1949, pp. 145-175.

[38] *De principiis,* II, 5, 1; OW., V, 132-133 (AN., I, 97-98).

[39] *De principiis,* II, 1, 1; OW., V, 106-107 (AN., I, 72). This text, which implies that even beasts have become diversified on account of a primitive "apostasy," or voluntary desertion from the divine One, makes it difficult to understand why animals should not have souls, nor, consequently, why human souls could not enter animal bodies. See, in AN., I, 72-73, the English transl. of this obscure text.

[40] In favor of eternal punishments, *Contra Celsum,* VIII, 51; OW., II, 266 (AN., II, 534-535).—Usefulness of the belief in eternal punishments, *Hom. in Jer.,* 19, 4. (on these texts, Prat, *Origène,* pp. 99-103).

[41] *De principiis,* III, 6, 3; OW., V, 284. See, in AN., I, 266, note 1, the transl. by F. Crombie of the Latin version by Saint Jerome: "Nor is there any doubt that, after certain intervals of time, matter will again exist, and bodies be formed, and a diversity be established in the world on account of the varying wills of rational creatures, who, after (enjoying) perfect blessedness down to the end of all things, have gradually fallen away to a lower condition, and received into them so much wickedness, that they are converted into an opposite condition, by their unwillingness to retain their original state, and to preserve their blessedness uncorrupted. Nor is this point to be suppressed, that many rational creatures retain their first condition even to the second, and third and fourth worlds, and allow no room for any change within them; while others, again, will lose a little of their pristine state, that they will appear to have lost almost nothing, and some are precipitated with great destruction into the lowest pit. And God, the disposer of all things, when creating his worlds, knows how to treat each individual agreeably to his merits . . . ; so that he who surpassed all others in wickedness, and brought himself completely down to the earth, is made in another world, which is afterwards to be formed, a devil. . . ." Inversely, in *De principiis,* III, 6, 3 (AN., I, 266-267) Origen says that the end of the world and its consummation will come when sinners will have been punished in proportion to their crimes. Then, God will be "all in all" (I Cor. 15, 28), that is, the end of things will be restored in the beginning, and beings will be re-established in the condition "in which rational nature was placed, when it had no need to eat of the tree of the knowledge of good and evil; so that when all feeling of wickedness has been removed, and the individual has been purified and cleansed, He who alone is the one good God becomes to him *all,* and that not in the case of a few individuals, or of a considerable number, but He Himself is *all in all.* And when death shall no longer anywhere exist, nor the sting of death, nor any evil at all, then verily God will be *all in all.*" All these

themes will reappear in the doctrine of John Scotus Erigena (IX cent.).

[42] Origenism survived in the school of Alexandria in the teaching of DIDYMUS THE BLIND (*ca.* 310-395): PG., 39, the whole volume. Another Origenist was EVAGRIUS PONTICUS (*ca.* 345-399): fragments in PG., 40; 1219 ff. His *Gnosticus,* perhaps a witness to the survival of Clement's influence, is unfortunately lost. See Bardenhewer, *Patrology,* 307-310.

PART TWO

CHAPTER II. THE LATIN APOLOGISTS

[43] TERTULLIAN, born at Carthage *ca.* 160; converted to Christianity *ca.* 190-195; married (cf. *Ad uxorem*) and yet, according to Saint Jerome, a priest (*De viris illustribus,* 53). At a later date, he joined the sect of the Montanists (206) and left the Church (213), but he broke away from Montanism and founded the church of the Tertullianists. He died about 240. Works in PL., 1-2. Fr. Oehler, *Tertulliani quae supersunt omnia,* Leipzig, 1853-1854. Critical edition in CSEL., Wien; vol. 20, 1890: *De spectaculis, De idololatria, Ad nationes, De testimonio animae, Scorpiace, De oratione, De baptismo, De pudicitia, De jejunio adversus psychicos, De anima;* vol. 42, 1906: *De patientia, De carnis resurrectione, Adversus Hermogenem, Adversus Valentinianos, Adversus omnes haereses, Adversus Praxean, Adversus Marcionem libri quinque;* vol. 69, 1939: *Apologeticum;* vol. 70, 1942: *De praescriptione haereticorum, De cultu feminarum, Ad uxorem, De exhortatione castitatis, De corona, De carne Christi, Adversus Judaeos.*—A new edition of all the Latin patristic texts, up to Bede, is announced under the title: *Corpus christianorum;* vol. I, *Tertulliani Opera,* Part 1; M. Nijhoff, The Hague, 1953. The complete collection will comprise 175 volumes. English transl., *The Writings of Tertullian,* AN., vols. 11 (Edinburgh, 1869); 15 (1870); 18 (1870). A. Souter, *On Baptism, Against Praxeas, On the Resurrection of the Flesh,* SPCK., N.Y., 1920. Same author, *The Apology,* Latin and English transl., Cambridge Univ. Press, 1917. R. Arbesman, E. J. Daly, E. A. Quain, *Tertullian, Apologetical works,* N.Y. Fathers of the Church, Inc., 1950 (*Apology, The Testimony of the Soul, To Scapula, On the Soul*).— BET., 3592-3601.

BIBLIOGRAPHY. P. Monceaux, *Histoire littéraire de l'Afrique chrétienne,* I, 178-461. G. Esser, *Die Seelenlehre Tertullians,* Paderborn, 1893. A. D'Alès, *La théologie de Tertullien,* Paris, 1905. J. P. Waltzing, *L'Apologeticum,* Louvain, 1910 (Introduction). P. de Labriolle, *La crise Montaniste,* Paris, 1913. R. E. Roberts, *The Theology of Tertullian,* London, 1924, J. Morgan, *The Importance of Tertullian in the Development of Christian Dogma,* London, 1928. J. Lortz, *Tertullian als Apologet,* Münster i. W., 2 vols. 1927, 1928. C. de L. Shortt, *The Influence of Philosophy on the Mind of Tertullian,* London, 1933. G. Bardy, *La latinisation de l'Eglise d'Occident,* Irenikon, 14 (1937) 3-20, 113-130; same author, art. *Tertullian,* DTC., 15 (1943) 130-171. V. Morel, *Disciplina. Le mot et l'idée représentée par lui dans les oeuvres de Tertullien,* RHE., 40 (1944-1945) 5-46.

[44] P. Monceaux, *Histoire littéraire de l'Afrique chrétienne depuis les origines jusqu'à l'invasion arabe,* 7 vols., Paris, Leroux, 1901-1923; still fundamental.— More general in outlook: R. Payne, *The Fathers of the Western Church,* New York, 1951.

General remark concerning the Latin Patrology of Migne. Although its texts do not measure up to the requirements of modern philology, it remains an extremely precious collection of mediaeval texts from the origins up to the end of the twelfth century. Before using it, consult P. Glorieux, *Pour revaloriser Migne. Tables rectificatives,* Mélanges de Science Religieuse, 1952, Supplement.

[45] *On Prescription against Heretics,* 7; tr. P. Holmes, AN.; vol. 15, 9-10.—J.-L. Allie, *L'argument de prescription dans le droit romain, en apologétique et en théologie dogmatique,* Ottawa, 1940 (cf. Revue de l'Université d'Ottawa, 6 (1937) 211-225; 7 (1938) 16-28). J. K. Stirnimann, *Die Praescriptio Tertullians im Lichte des römischen Rechtes und der Theologie (Paradosis 3),* Freiburg (Switz.) 1949.

[46] *On Prescription,* 13; AN., 15, 16-17; contains the so-called "Symbol of Tertullian," in fact, one of the oldest redactions of the Christian Creed.—The same juridical spirit pervades the *Apology* of Tertullian (*Apologeticum*), whose purpose it is to prove that, legally speaking, if the Christians are innocent of the crimes with which they are commonly charged, they should be tolerated; now, in fact, they are innocent of those crimes; hence anti-Christian laws should be abrogated. H. F. Hallock, *Church and State in Tertullian,* Church Quarterly Review, 119 (1934-1935) 61-78.

[47] A. d'Alès (*La Théologie de Tertullien,* 33-36) rightly speaks of the "rational character of Christian faith" in Tertullian's doctrine; the reason which Tertullian derides is that of the philosophers, who are, "so to say, the patriarchs of the heretics" (*On the Soul,* 3; AN., 15, 416. *Against Hermogenes,* 8; AN., 15, 67). But one cannot speak of the "philosophical" character of Christian faith in Tertullian. Tertullian resorts to reason in defending faith, but reason has for him no other function than to understand Scripture: "Whoever gives ear will find God in them; whoever takes pains to understand, will be compelled to believe" (*Apolog.* 18; AN., 11., 88). He does not mean: to understand their rational meaning, but rather to understand their Greek version by "the seventy-two interpreters."—On the importance of the notion of "tradition" in the early history of Christian thought, D. Van den Eynde OFM., *Les normes de l'enseignement chrétien dans la littérature patristique des trois premiers siècles,* Gembloux (Belgium) 1933.

[48] GOD is naturally known by a "naturally Christian soul" (*Apolog.,* 17; AN., 11, 87), in this sense that it bears the mark of its creator. He is one, and a spirit, but even the spirit is material according to Tertullian. To be a "spirit" is not to be "immaterial." Cf. "Quis negabit Deum corpus esse, etsi Deus spiritus est?" ("Who will deny that God is body, even though he be spirit?" *Adversus Praxeam,* 7; AN., 15, 346). There is no getting around this text; besides, it perfectly fits Tertullian's doctrine of the materiality of the soul. The Word is likewise a "spirit," begotten by the Father. Before the creation, the Word was the internal thought, or discourse, of the Father (*ratio, sensus, sermo, logos*); also his Wisdom (Prov. 8, 22); before producing the world, God uttered his Word, as the instrument of his works (*Adv. Prax.,* 4-6; AN., 15, 339-344). There is, in God, unity of substance, but trinity of "persons" (note the appearance of the term *persona,* in *Adv. Prax.,* 18; AN., 15, 372). The Word is uttered, begotten under his perfect form, when God says: "Be light made" (Gen. i, 3). Cf. *Adv. Prax.,* 12; AN., 15, 357; *Adversus Hermogenem,* 18; AN., 15, 79-81. Little is said about the Holy Ghost, who proceeds from the two other Persons, yet is not clearly conceived by Tertullian as distinct from the Son (*Adv. Prax.,* 26; AN., 15, 392-395). —MAN is body and soul, but the soul itself is nothing if it is not a body, more fluid and subtle than the external body through which it spreads and whose form it takes: *nihil enim, si non corpus.* Being material like the body, the soul can benefit by the food we eat. Some object to this that the food of the soul is wisdom, which is immaterial, but there are plenty of perfectly robust Barbarians! The Stoics are right in teaching that both souls and the arts by which souls are nourished are likewise material (*On the Soul,* ch. 6-9; AN., vol. 15, 420-430). Yet the soul is simple (ch. 10); its only multiplicity is that of its functions; it is "spirit," not because it is not a body, but because it breathes, or "respires"; it is called *animus* (mind, *Nous*), inasmuch as it knows (ch. 12; AN., 15, 423); despite what Plato says to the contrary, sense knowledge is quite reliable (*On the Soul,* 17; AN., 15, 444-449) and the distinction introduced by him between the intellect and the senses is responsible for certain errors of the Gnostics (*On the Soul,* 18; AN., 15, 450). Created by God, the soul is transmitted to the child as a fragment of the soul of the father and, thereby, it carries with itself, from generation to generation, both the image of God (hence, the "naturally" Christian soul) and original sin. Transmigration, of course, is an absurdity. Recapitulation of the doctrine of the soul in *On the Soul,* 22; AN., 15, 462.—The best edition of *On the Soul* is J. H. Waszink, *Q. S. F. Tertulliani De anima. Edited with Introduction and Commentary,* Amsterdam, 1947. On the doctrine, *Die Seelenlehre Tertullians,* Paderborn, 1893. H. Koch, *Tertullianisches III-IV,* TSK., 104 (1932) 127-159; 105 (1933)

39-50. H. Karpp, *Sorans vier Bücher "Peri psukhès" und Tertullians Schrift De anima,* ZNW., 33 (1934) 31-47; influence of the physician Soranus of Ephesa. A. J. Festugière OP., *La composition et l'esprit du De anima de Tertullien,* RSPT., 33 (1949) 121-161.—On the general history of the notion of *pneuma,* G. Verbeke, *L'évolution de la notion de pneuma du stoïcisme à saint Augustin,* Louvain, 1945.—On the problem of evil (against Gnosticism), V. Nauman, *Das Problem des Bosen in Tertullians zweiten Buch gegen Marcion. Ein Beitrag zur Theodizee Tertullians,* ZKT., 58 (1934) 311-363.

⁴⁹ MINUCIUS FELIX. Life unknown. Lactantius (*Divinae institutiones,* V, 1, 22) places him before Tertullian; Jerome (*De viris illustribus,* 35 and 58) places him after Tertullian. O. Bardenhewer sums up the now commonly received opinion in saying that "it is Tertullian who made use of Minucius, and not Minucius who used the writings of Tertullian" (*Patrology,* 71). This would place the *Octavius* before 197.—Text in PL., 3, 239-375. Critical editions by Halm, CSEL., II; J. P. Waltzing, Louvain, 1903 (with French transl.); Kerr and Randall, in Loeb Classical Library, N.Y. 1931 (Latin and English, in the same volume as Tertullian's *Apology* and *De spectaculis*). English transl. only in AN., 13 (vol. 2 of St. Cyprian's writings), Edinburgh, 1869. R. Arbesmann, in The Fathers of the Church, X; N.Y., 1950 (select bibliography, p. 319).—BIBLIOGRAPHY. H. J. Baylis, *Minucius Felix and His Place among the Fathers of the Latin Church,* London, 1928. M. Schuster, *Minucius Felix und die christlische Popular Philosophie,* Wiener Studien, 52 (1934) 163-167. H. Diller, *In Sachen Tertullian-Minucius Felix,* Philologus, 90 (1935) 98-114, 216-239 (places Tertullian before Minucius Felix; the *Apologeticus* and the *Adversus nationes* of Tertullian as sources of the *Octavius*). F. Wetke, *Der Octavius des Minucius Felix ein christlicher Logos Protreptikos,* Commentationes Vindobonenses, 1 (1935) 110-128. J. J. de Jong, *Apologetiek en Christendom in den Octavius van Minucius Felix,* Maastricht, 1935. R. Beutler, *Philosophie und Apologetik bei Minucius Felix,* Weida i. Thür. (Inaug.-Dissert.), 1936. A. S. Pease, *Caeli enarrant,* HTR., 34 (1941) 103-200 (classical sources of the teleological argument in Minucius Felix and his successors). L. Alfonsi, *Appunti sull'Octavius di Minucio Felice,* Scuola Cattolica, 70 (1942) 70-73. J. Quasten, *Patrology,* II, 155-163.—BET., 2756-2764. The point of view of the pagan apologists, so fairly represented by Minucius Felix, has not always been appreciated by Christian historians; for instance, P. G. N. Rhodes, *The Pagan Apologists,* The Pre-Nicene Church, Pref. by C. Lattey SJ., London, Burn Oates, 1935, pp. 123-142. An exceptionally objective interpretation of the pagan side of the question is found in P. de Labriolle, *La réaction païenne,* Paris, 1934.

⁵⁰ SAINT CYPRIAN (about 200-258), a convert to the faith and a Bishop of Carthage, died a martyr on Sept. 14, 258. O. Bardenhewer says of him: "He does not go far afield in theoretical discussion, but appeals to the Christian and ecclesiastical sentiments of his hearers, and bases his argument on the authority of Sacred Scripture" (*Patrology,* 192). AN., 8 and 13, Edinburgh, 1868, 1869.—The best general introductions to his life, works and doctrine are: P. Monceaux, *Histoire littéraire de l'Afrique chrétienne,* II, 201-386. A. d'Alès, *La théologie de saint Cyprien,* Paris, 1922. Protestant interpretation in W. Benson, *Cyprian, His Life, His Times, His Work,* London, 1897.—BET., 1139-1157.

⁵¹ ARNOBIUS, born about 260; professor of rhetoric at Sicca, where he was a sort of local celebrity. About 296, Arnobius announced that he had become a Christian and he wrote his *Adversus Gentes* (or *Adversus nationes*) in order to convince his bishop of his sincerity. Yet the work does not seem to have been completed before 303. Of its seven Books, the first two contain an apology for the Christian religion, the last five being a criticism of pagan beliefs and worship. Died about 327. Works in PL., 5, 713-1290. A. Reifferscheid, in CSEL., vol. IV, Wien, 1875. English transl. by H. Bryce and H. Campbell: *The Seven Books of Arnobius Adversus Gentes,* in AN., 19, Edinburgh, 1871; also G. E. McCracken, Ancient Christian Writers, vol. 7, Newman Press, 1949.—BIBLIOGRAPHY. K. B. Francke, *Die Psychologie und Erkenntnislehre des Arnobius,* (Inaug.-Diss.), Leipzig, 1878 (on the immortality of the soul, 26-40; on human knowledge, 41-82).

A. Röricht, *Die Seelenlehre des Arnobius,* Hamburg, 1893. E. F. Schultze, *Das Uebel in der Welt nach der Lehre des Arnobius* (Inaug.-Diss.) Jena, 1896. P. Monceaux, *Histoire litt. de l'Afr. chrét.,* III, 241-286, Paris, 1905. P. de Labriolle, *Hist. de la litt. lat. chrét.,* 252-267. F. Gabarrou, *Arnobe, son oeuvre,* Paris, 1921 (bibliography, pp. 74-77). Same author: *Le latin d'Arnobe,* Paris, 1921. E. F. Micka, OFM., *The Problem of Divine Anger in Arnobius and Lactantius,* C. U. A. Press, Washington, 1943 (on Arnobius, 39-77); bibliography common to Arnobius and Lactantius, XIV-XXII. A.-J. Festugière OP., *La doctrine des "uiri novi" sur l'origine et le sort des âmes, d'après Arnobe, II, 11-66.* Mémorial Lagrange, Paris, 1940, pp. 97-132. J. Quasten, *Patrology,* II, 383-392. —BET., 376, 1535.
On the then debated question whether a convert should continue to run a school after his conversion, G. Bardy, *L'Eglise et l'enseignement pendant les trois premiers siècles,* RSR., 12 (1932) 1-28.

⁵² *Adversus Gentes,* I, 27; AN., vol. 19, p. 20. Contrasted with the worshipping of animals by pagans: I, 28; AN., 20-22. The existence of God is, so to speak, an innate cognition: I, 32-33; AN., 25-26. God is the first cause, unbegotten, unnamable, unknown: I, 31; AN., 24-25. Cf. III, 17-19; AN., 162-163.—Enumeration of the truths about God and the origin of things which Christ has revealed to us: 1, 38; AN., 29-30. Cf. II, 60; AN., 129-130.—Even the absence of dialectics in the Scriptures (I, 58) and their uncouth language (I, 59) are no arguments against them (AN., 47-50). Cf. II, 6; AN., 67-68.

⁵³ *Adversus Gentes,* I, 39; AN., 31.

⁵⁴ *Adversus Gentes,* II, 7; AN., 69.

⁵⁵ *Adversus Gentes,* II, 8; AN., 71.

⁵⁶ *Adversus Gentes,* II, 9; AN., 71-72; and II, 11; AN., 74.

⁵⁷ *Adversus Gentes,* II, 16-19; AN., 82-86.

⁵⁸ *Adversus Gentes,* II, 20-24; AN., 86-91.

⁵⁹ *Adversus Gentes,* II, 60; AN., 129-130 (divinity of Christ).—II, 36; AN.,

104 (souls are created by a being inferior to the supreme God).—II, 14; AN., 80. This annihilation has been interpreted as an "everlasting destruction" in the spiritual sense of the word, which indeed it is; but it is also a physical destruction, for the soul is not incorporeal (II, 26; AN., 93) and the arguments directed against Plato in this text, imply precisely that, according to the teaching of Christ, instead of all of them being immortal, some souls will be destroyed. See II, 62; AN., 131: on the "gods . . . who are real" and those "who are merely said to be from hearsay."

⁶⁰ LACTANTIUS. Born in Africa, dates of birth and death unknown. A convert to Christianity (Jerome, *De viris illustribus,* 80) ; he studied under Arnobius at Sicca; taught rhetoric at Nicomedia and resigned his position during the persecution of Diocletian. Works in PL., 6 (*Divinarum institutionum libri VII* and an abridgment of same, called *Epitome divinarum institutionum;* 7, *De opificio Dei, De ira Dei, De mortibus persecutorum, De phoenice*). Excellent critical edition of the *Institutes* and *Epitome* by S. Brandt and Laubmann, CSEL., 19, Wien, 1890-1897. Engl. transl. by W. Fletcher, AN., 21-22, Edinburgh, 1871 and by E. H. Blakeney, London, SPCK., 1950. See BET., 2392-2394.—BIBLIOGRAPHY. P. G. Frotscher, *Der Apologet Lactantius in seinem verhältnis zur griechischen Philosophie,* Leipzig, 1895. R. Pichon, *Lactance. Etude sur le mouvement philosophique et religieux sous le règne de Constantin,* Paris, 1901. P. Monceaux, *Hist. litt. de l'Afrique chrét.,* III, 287-359. E. Amann, art. *Lactance,* DTC., 8 (1925) 2425-2444. E. F. Micka, *The Problem of Divine Anger . . . ,* XIV-XXII. G. Gonella, *La critica dell'autoritá delle leggi secondo Tertulliano e Lattanzio,* Rivista internazionale di filosofia del diritto, 17 (1937) 23-37. E. Schneweis, *Angels and Demons According to Lactantius,* Cath. Univ. of Amer. Press, Washington, 1944. J. Quasten, *Patrology,* II, 392-410.

⁶¹ *The Divine Institutes,* III, 30; AN., 21, 209.

⁶² *The Divine Institutes,* I, 1; AN., 3.— This "Christian Cicero," as he has been called, had no other ambition than to defend Christianity *ornate copioseque* (I, 1). See a short history of his pre-

decessors: Minucius Felix would have done well if he had wholly dedicated himself to the task; excellent, Cyprian is intelligible to the Christians only, the Pagans deride him; Tertullian is very obscure (V, 1; AN., 293-294). He himself is the first one to defend Christianity with distinctness and elegance of speech in view of pagan readers.—Practically all that he has to say about God is to be found in I, 3 and 8 (AN., 6-9 and 20-21). God is one, perfect, simple, indestructible, creator and providence, supremely powerful, supremely happy. "But because that which exists must of necessity have had a beginning, it follows that since there was nothing before him, he was produced from Himself before all things. Therefore he is called by Apollo "self-produced"; by the Sibyl "self-created," "uncreated," and "unmade" (I, 7; AN., 20). God has neither body nor sex; he does not need them for himself, since he is immortal, nor for the production of other beings, since he is almighty (I, 8; AN., 20-21). —On the generation of the Word: the "holy and incorruptible spirit of God," (IV, 6; AN., 220-222).—The nature of man is studied in *On the Workmanship of God* (i.e., *De opificio Dei*). God made man an eternal and immortal being (ch. 2; AN., 22, 52-53). Epicurus and Lucretius are raving when they deny that the limbs of the body have been made to a purpose (ch. 6). The senses are not false if they are sound; if they are deceived, the mind recognizes their error (ch. 9). The nature of the mind is incomprehensible. It is in the highest part of the head,

whence it spreads through the whole body as God through the world (ch. 16). The soul is not the blood; it "appears to be like light, since it is not itself blood, but is nourished by the moisture of the blood, as light is by oil" (ch. 17). In short, since the soul cannot be seen, it cannot be defined. The difference between *anima* and *animus* is obscure; that between the soul and the mind is inextricable; they differ however, since death extinguishes the soul whereas sleep is enough to extinguish the mind (ch. 18). The soul is produced by God alone, not by the parents (ch. 19). All these texts in AN., 22, 62-64; 69-70; 82-90. Philosophers have not yet agreed about the nature of the soul, and they never will.

[63] Lactantius has been accused of having taught a "subordinated dualism" in order, precisely, to account for the presence of evil in a world created by a perfect God. S. Brandt has suggested that the passages of the *Divine Institutes* (II, 9 and VII, 5) which teach that God has created evil, at least indirectly, are fourth century interpolations (see S. Brandt, *Ueber die dualistischen Zusätze und die Kaiseranreden bei Lactantius,* in Sitzungsberichte, Wien, 118, 8 and 119, 1, 1889). But this is not quite certain. By no means a Manichean, Lactantius seems to have conceived the devil somewhat in the same way as Goethe: "A part of that power which always wills evil and always brings forth good." Cf. *Institutes,* VII, 5; AN., 439-442. Let us note, however, that W. Fletcher too doubts the authenticity of this passage (AN., 21, 439, note 3).

PART TWO

CHAPTER III. THE CAPPADOCIANS

[64] ARIUS, born in Lybia *ca.* the middle of the III century, settled in Alexandria and became the pastor of a nearby parish *ca.* 310. He taught in a dogmatic way that if the Father has begotten the Son, the Son must have had a beginning in time and have been created out of nothing. To be "unbegotten" thus became for Arius the proper attribute of the true God (i.e., the Father). The notion of generation entailed in his mind that of a contingent beginning. Under the influence of Prov. 8, 22, Arius conceived the Logos

as the first of God's creatures, and as an image of the internal Logos which is in the Father from eternity. The technical formula of his doctrine was that the Son is not consubstantial (*homoousios*) with the Father, but, rather, wholly unlike the nature of the Father. See X. Le Bachelet, art. *Arianisme,* DTC., 1 (1923) 1779-1863 (bibliogr., 1862-1863).

[65] "We believe in one God, the Father almighty, maker of all things visible and invisible. And in one Lord Jesus Christ,

Son of God, the only begotten of the Father, that is of the substance of the Father; God of God, light of light, true God of true God; begotten, not made; consubstantial with the Father; by whom all things were made in heaven and on earth; who came down for us, men, and for our salvation; and was made flesh, and became man. . . ." The Nicaean creed was followed by this formal condemnation of the errors of Arius: "As to those who say: there was a time when the Son was not; when he was not because he had not yet been begotten; or, he has been made out of nothing; and as to those who say: he is of another substance (*hypostasis*) or being (*ousia*); or he is a creature, or changeable, or mutable, these men are anathematized by the Catholic Church." The term *homoousios* will be translated into Latin by: "unius substantiae" (i.e., of one substance), and, later on, by *consubstantialis,* i.e., "consubstantial."—I. Ortiz de Urbina, SJ., *El simbolo niceno,* Madrid, 1947. J. Tixeront, DTC., I (1923) 2178-2187.

⁶⁶ The works of EUSEBIUS OF CESAREA (269-340) are to be found (Greek text and Latin transl.) in PG., 19-24, which is their last complete edition. Separate editions: I, *The Preparation for the Gospel,* Greek and English transl., by E. H. Gifford, Oxford, 1903, 4 vols.; the vol. III, in 2 parts, contains the English transl.—II, *Proof of the Gospel,* English transl. only by W. J. Ferrar, SPCK., 2 vols., 1920.—III, *The Ecclesiastical History,* Greek text and Latin transl. by Kirsopp Lake (Loeb Class. Libr.) 2 vols., 1926, 1932.—Introduction to Eusebius: art. *Eusèbe de Césarée,* C. Verschaffel, DTC., 5 (1924) 1527-1532 (bibliogr., 1530-1532).—That the Greeks were plagiarists, *The Preparation for the Gospel,* Bk. X; for a comparison between the philosophy of Plato and the "philosophy of the Hebrews," especially that of the "all-wise Moses," same work, Bks. XI-XIII.—On the general attitude of the Church with respect to teaching in the IV century, G. Bardy, *L'Eglise et l'enseignement au IVe siècle,* RSR., 14 (1934) 525-549; 15 (1935) 1-27; influence of the edict of Julian; Basil, Chrysostom, Jerome and Augustine).

⁶⁷ ATHANASIUS, born *ca.* 295 at Alexandria, died a bishop of that city on May 2, 373. Ever since the Council of Nicaea,

where he had played a leading part, Athanasius was engaged in ceaseless battles against the Arians. He was five times exiled from Alexandria as a consequence of their attacks against him. By his *Adversum gentes libri duo,* he still belongs in the generation of the Apologists, but his main contribution to theology consists in his *Discourses Against the Arians* (PG., 26, 11-468; the IV *Discourse,* col. 468-526, is probably spurious). See F. Cavallera, *Saint Athanase,* Paris, 1908. X. Le Bachelet, art. *Athanase (saint),* in DTC., I (1923) 2143-2178. G. Müller, SJ., *Lexicon Athanasianum,* Berlin, 1952. R. Bernard, *L'image de Dieu d'après Saint Athanase,* Paris, 1952 (bibliography 149-152).—English transl., *On the Incarnation,* by a Religious of CSMV., London, Mowbray, 2 ed., 1953. Selected works in NPN., IV, Oxford and New York, 1892.—BET., 392-407.

⁶⁸ SAINT HILARY, born at Poitiers (*ca.* 315); baptized *ca.* 345; married (a daughter: Abra); Bishop of Poitiers *ca.* 353; like Athanasius, engaged in a relentless fight against Arianism, and, in consequence, was exiled to Phrygia (356-360), where he wrote his Latin treatise *De Trinitate.* After his return to Gaul (360), he contributed, with his friend Saint Martin of Tours, to the foundation of the monastery of Ligugé (near Poitiers), *ca.* 361. Died at Poitiers Jan. 17, 366. His main work is the *De fide adversus Arianos,* better known as *De Trinitate* (PL., 10, 25-472). See the interesting account of his conversion in *De Trinitate,* I, 1-10. Inspired by the craving for happiness, he soon reached the conclusion that God could not have given us life in order to take it away from us. God, then, should be very different from the pagan gods. In fact, he should be "one, eternal, all powerful and immutable." What was not Hilary's surprise when he read later on in the Bible (Exod. 3, 14): "I AM WHO AM"? This was the starting point of his conversion, which was completed by his reading of the Gospel of Saint John. A God who had become incarnate in order to give man eternal life was the very God Hilary had been looking for. Thus, and for this reason did he become a Christian. —On his interpretation of Exod. 3, 14, see *De Trinitate,* I, 6; PL., 10, 28-30.— On Hilary; X. Le Bachelet, art. *Hilaire (Saint),* in DTC., 6 (1925) 2388-2462. P. Smulders, *La doctrine trinitaire de S.*

Hilaire de Poitiers, Rome, 1944. E. Emmenegger, *The Functions of Faith and Reason in the Theology of St. Hilary of Poitiers*, Cath. Univ. of America Press, 1947.—BET., 1949-1950.

[69] GREGORY NAZIANZENUS (or the Theologian) was born *ca.* 330, near Nazianzus in Cappadocia, of a Christian family. He studied in the school of Caesarea (Cappadocia) at the same time as Basil, with whom he became later intimately acquainted when they both met again at the school of Athens (see Gregory, *Funeral Oration in praise of Basil the Great, Bishop of Caesarea in Cappadocia*, PG., 36, 519-522). He will always maintain the usefulness of this "external culture": *Funeral Oration*, 11; PG., 36, 508-509. He came back home *ca.* 357, was baptized and presently was ordained a priest by his father Gregory, Bishop of Nazianzus, against his own will. After the death of his father (374), Gregory retired to Seleucia. His friend Basil died in 379. The same year, Gregory went to Constantinople and was nominated as bishop of this city, but his nomination was opposed by some adversaries and he went back in 381 to his birthplace, Arianzum, where he died in 389.—WORKS. The most important part of Gregory's works are his 45 *Orations*. The five which he himself has called "the theological orations" (PG., 36, 25 C), that is 27-31 (PG., 36, 11-172), have caused him to be called Gregory the Theologian. His funeral oration for Saint Basil is full of information about the two saints (cf. the *Oration on Himself*, XXVI, in PG., 36, 265-280). Gregory has also left us 243 letters, mostly personal (see nevertheless the letter 243, on the Trinity), and some poems, among which the one *On His Own Life* contains biographical information.—Text in PG., 35-38. English transl. of the "Theological Orations" in NPN., vol. VII (Oxford-N.Y., 1894), pp. 280-328. *Funeral Oration on Saint Basil*, 395-422.—BIBLIOGRAPHY. K. Unterstein, *Die natürliche Gotteserkenntnis nach der Lehre der kappadozischen Kirchenväter Basilius, Gregor von Nazianz und Gregor von Nyssa*, (Progr.) Strassburg, 1902-1903. R. Gottwald, *De Gregorio Nazianzeno, Platonico*, Breslau, 1906. H. Pinault, *Le platonisme de saint Grégoire de Nazianze*, Paris, 1926. E. Fleury, *Hellénisme et Christianisme. Saint Grégoire de Nazianze et son temps*, Paris, Beauchesne, 1930. H. Dausend,

OFM., *Die St. Gregor von Nazianz-Stellen in den Werken des hl. Bonaventura*, FS., 3 (1916) 151-160. J. Plagnieux, *Saint Gregoire, de Nazianze théologien*, Paris, 1952.—On the attitude of the Fathers toward dialectics: J. de Ghellinck, SJ., *Un aspect de l'opposition entre Hellénisme et Christianisme. L'attitude vis-à-vis de la dialectique dans les débats trinitaires*, in *Patristique et moyen âge*, vol. III, 245-310.—BET., 1805-1809.

[70] EUNOMIUS, author of an *Apologetikos* (PG., 30, 835-868) written *ca.* 360; refuted by Saint Basil (PG., 30, 835-868). The first of the "Theological Orations" (XXVII) is directed against the Eunomians and their wrong way of philosophizing in theological matters (PG., 36, 11-26; in NPN., VII, 284-288.—BET., 1477.

[71] Gregory considers practically all subjects as open to free philosophical discussion, except one, which is precisely the nature of the Trinity. Eunomius is welcome to philosophize against all philosophers, and about any philosophical questions but one: "Philosophize about the world or worlds; about matter; about the soul; about natures endowed with reason, good or bad; about resurrection, about judgment, about reward, about the sufferings of Christ. For in these subjects to hit the mark is not useless, and to miss it is not dangerous. But with God we shall have converse, in this life, only in a small degree; but a little later, it may be, more perfectly" (PG., 36, 25; quoted from the English transl. in NPN., VII, 288).

[72] The question is not: should one philosophize? Rather, it is: Who should do it, when, and how? It does not belong to everyone to "philosophize about God," but to spiritual men only, whose minds have been purified by meditation (*Orat.* XXVII, 3); those whose faith is not strong enough are in danger of losing it because of their very inability to grasp arguments (XXVII, 4); moreover, we should not philosophize about God before any kind of audiences, especially not before systematically hostile hearers who are interested in our weak points only (XXVII, 5-6); in fine, the dialecticians who are mostly interested in dialectics for its own sake, would be well advised to turn to other subjects of discussion

XXVII, 8); see PG., 36, 11-24; or NPN., VII, 285-288.—God is difficult to conceive and impossible to define (cf. *Timaeus*, 28 E), as has been said by Plato, "one of the Greek teachers of theology"; in fact, God cannot be conceived by our minds, which are blinded by the obscurity of the world and of the flesh; it might not be the same with the separate Intelligences which, being nearer to God and "illumined with all his light," can perhaps see, "if not the whole, at any rate more perfectly and distinctly than we do; some perhaps more, some less than others, in proportion to their rank" (XXVIII, 4; PG., 36, 29-32, quoted from NPN., VII, 289-290).— In fact, Gregory himself has philosophized about nothing else than God, who is peace, as can be seen from the order of nature (XXVIII, 5). There must be a maker of beings in order to account for their existence (XXVIII, 6). God is not a body; hence he is un-limited, that is "infinite," or uncircumscribed (XXVIII, 7); just as he is unlimited in space, he is infinite in duration, so much so that we can liken him unto "some great ocean of being, infinite and limitless" (XXXVIII, 7-8; PG., 36, 32-36. Cf. XLV, 3; PG., 625). This comparison will be taken up by John Damascene, *De fide orthodoxa*, I, 9; PG., 94, 836 B and often quoted under his name by the theologians of the XIII century.—Since God is immaterial, he is simple (XXVIII, 7-8; PG., 36, 317-320); hence it is impossible to define him, or even to name him so as to make men know what he is; if he were "comprehensible in thought," he would be somewhat circumscribed (XXVIII, 9-10; PG., 36, 320-321).—Thus, to say that God is self-existent is not to know what he is; nevertheless, he can properly and positively be called "being" (Exod. 3, 14), and God. Of these two names, "being" is the more absolute one; "being is in its proper sense peculiar to God, and belongs to him entirely, and is not limited or cut short by any *before* or *after*, for indeed in him there is no past or future" (XXX, 18; PG., 36, 126-128). This remark confirms what Gregory has just said of the infinity of God, which he seems to have conceived as an infinity of duration, that is as the very eternity of God, rather than as an infinity of the divine entity.—On the progressive character of the revelation of the mystery of the Trinity: XXXI, 26-27; PG., 36, 161-164.

[73] BASIL THE GREAT, born *ca.* 331 at Caesarea, of Christian parents, in a wealthy family. First education at home, under his father Pontus, himself a rhetorician; then in a school at Caesarea, the "metropolis of Letters" (see Gregory Nazianzenus, *Funeral Oration in Praise of Basil*, 13; PG., 36, 512). A brilliant student: "Eloquence was his by work, from which he culled enough to make it an assistance to him in our own philosophy, since power of this kind is needed to set forth the objects of our contemplation. For a mind which cannot express itself is like the motion of a man in a lethargy. His pursuit was philosophy, and breaking from the world, by concerning himself, amid things below, with things above, and winning, where all is unstable and fluctuating, the things which are stable and remain" (*Oration in Praise of Basil*, 13; PG., 36, 512, and NPN., VII, 309). From Caesarea, Basil goes to Constantinople, then to the schools of Athens, where students were "mad after rhetorical skill" (*Oration*, 15; PG., 36, 513-515). On students' initiation (*Oration* 16; PG., 36, 516-517) and how, on this occasion, he became Gregory's friend (*Oration* 18; PG., 36, 517-520). Both recognized that "philosophy" (i.e., *our* philosophy) was their common aim (*Oratio* 19; PG., 36, 520). They knew but two ways, the one to churches, the other one to schools (*Oration*, 21; PG., 36, 524). On his study of the liberal arts, plus medicine: *Oration* 23; PG., 36, 525-528. Returns to Caesarea in 359. Goes to Egypt and visits the Eastern anchorites, but prefers the cenobitic life and founds a monastery near Neocaesarea, in the Pontic desert. Ordained a priest in 364. Elected in 370 as Bishop of Caesarea. Died on Jan. 1, 379. —WORKS. His main works are: *Refutation of the Apology of Impious Eunomius* (*ca.* 363); nine Homilies *In Hexaemeron* (PG., 29, 3-208); fifteen Homilies *On Psalms*, PG., 29-30; *To Young Men On Making Good Use of Greek Literature* (PG., 31, 563-590); Engl. transl. A. C. Pegis, *The Wisdom of Catholicism*, N.Y. 1949, 9-26. BET., 547-555, 1477, 1790; index, p. 467. —EDITIONS. Greek text and Latin transl. in PG., 29-32. English transl. of selected works of Basil, NPN., vol. VIII, N.Y., 1895. R. J. Deferrari, *St. Basil, The Letters*, 4 vols (Loeb Classical Library), 1926-1934. M. M. Wagner, *St. Basil, Ascetical Works*, N.Y., 1950.—BIBLIOGRAPHY. See O. Bardenhewer, *Patrology*,

283-286. P. Allard, art. *Basile (saint)* DTC., 2 (1923) 441-455. L. V. Jacks, *St. Basil and Greek Literature,* Cath. Univ. of America, Washington, 1922. Y. Courtonne, *Saint Basile et l'Hellénisme,* Paris, 1934. M. M. Fox, *The Life and Times of Saint Basil the Great as Revealed in His Works,* Cath. Univ. of Amer. Press, Washington, 1939 (bibliography, IX-XV).—On the social and economic doctrines of Saint Basil: A. Dirking, *Sancti Basilii Magni de divitiis et paupertate sententiae quam habeant rationem cum veterum philosophorum doctrina,* Münster i. Westf., 1911. S. Giet, *Les idées et l'action sociales de St. Basile,* Paris, 1941. G. F. Reilly, *Imperium and Sacerdotium According to St. Basil the Great,* Cath. Univ. of America Press, Washington, D.C., 1945.—On the teaching of the Fathers on these questions: Ign. Seipel, *Die Wirtschaftsetischen Lehren der Kirchenväter,* Wien, 1907., and Th. Sommerlad, *Das Wirtschaftsprogramm der Kirche des Mittelalters,* Leipzig, 1903.—Influence of Plotinus upon Basil's theology, P. Henry, *Les états du texte de Plotin,* Louvain, 1938. B. Pruche, *Basile de Césarée. Traité du Saint Esprit,* Paris, 1947, pp. 57-62; 92, n. 1; 137, n. 4; 212, n. 5. Cf. B. Pruche, *L'originalité du traité de saint Basile sur le Saint-Esprit,* in RSPT., 32 (1948) 207-221. B. Altaner, *Augustinus und Basilius der Grosse. Eine Quellenkritische Untersuchung,* RB., 60 (1950) 222-239.—On the Latin translation of Basil's *Hexaemeron* (used by Augustine, *De Genesi ad litteram,* I, 18), B. Altaner, *Eustathius, der lateinische Uebersetzer der Hexaemeron-Homilien Basilius des Grossen,* ZNW., 39 (1940) 161-170. Probable date of the translation, *ca.* 400.

[74] *Against Eunomius,* I, 10; PG., 29, 536.

[75] The nine homilies *On Hexaemeron* are the work of an educated Christian of the fourth century, but neither a scientific work, nor even an exposition of Basil's learning. We should read them as "homilies," delivered at the rate of one a day, before an audience of Christians including simple workers whom their daily salary hardly sufficed to maintain (*Hexaemeron,* III, 1; PG., 29, 53 A; NPN., 8, 65). Basil's method is different from that of Origen (III, 9; 73-76; NPN., 8, 70): few mystical interpretations; frequent moral interpretations, and these always

based upon the strict literal meaning of Scripture: "When I hear *fish,* I understand *fish;* plant, fish, wild beast, domestic animal, I take all in the literal sense" (9, 1; 188 B; NPN., 8, 101). Hence the large amount of positive information on plants, animals and natural phenomena which he has gathered in his sermons. On one point, however, there seems to be an influence of Origen (*De principiis,* II, 1, 3): Basil thinks that before the beginning of our world, there was another order of things suitable to the nature of pure Intelligences, and that God has added our world to it, as "both a school and a training place where the souls of men should be taught, and a home for beings destined to be born and die" (I, 5; PG., 29, 13; NPN., 8, 54).—On the sense of "beginning," as "first movement," or else as the instantaneous act of creation: I, 6; PG., 15 C.—Why the earth is immobile at the center of the world: I, 9-10; PG., 29, 21-25.—On the creation of matter: II, 1-3; PG., 29, 28-36.—Evil is not created, because it is not an entity, but the evil condition of the soul opposed to virtue: II, 4-5; PG., 29, 36-41.—On the firmament: III, 4; PG., 29, 60-61.—Against astrology; VII, 5-7; PG., 29, 128-133.—Optical proofs of the prodigious size of the Sun and Moon (because God made two "great" luminaries: Gen. i, 16): VI, 9-11; PG., 29, 137-148.—On animals, *Hom.* VII, VIII (against the transmigration of souls). Note, VIII, 4, the moral lesson drawn from the "king of bees" as to the best way to choose a king; NPN., 8, 97.—The history of social and economic doctrines should take into account three important *Homilies,* PG., 31, 261-328; and *Homily II in PS. 14,* PG., 29, 263-280 (on usury).

[76] GREGORY OF NYSSA (Gregorius Nyssenus), younger brother of St. Basil; birth date unknown; taught rhetoric; probably married; entered the ecclesiastical orders; made a bishop of Nyssa by his brother Basil (371); deposed and exiled by an Arian Council in 375; came to Nyssa in 394; date of death unknown. Works in PG., 44-46.—The main sources of information concerning his philosophical views are: *On the Formation of Man* (PG., 44, 125-256); *In Hexaemeron* (PG., 44, 61-124); *Dialogue with Macrina on the Soul and the Resurrection* (PG., 46, 12-160); *The Life of Moses* (PG., 44, 297-430); fifteen *Homilies on the Canticle of Can-*

ticles (PG., 44, 756-1120); eight *Homilies on the Beatitudes* (PG., 44, 1193-1301); *The Catechetical Oration against Pagans, Jews and Heretics,* PG., 45, 9-105); *Against Eunomius* (PG., 45, 237-1121). —English transl. in NPN., V, Oxford-New York, 1893 (includes *Against Eunomius, On the Making of Man, On the Soul and the Resurrection, The Great Catechism,* etc.). *Encomium of St. Gregory . . . on . . . St. Basil,* by J. A. Stein, Cath. Univ. of Amer., Washington, D.C., 1928. See BET., 219, 1045, 1788-1791.—French transl. of *La vie de Moïse* by J. Daniélou, Paris, 1941; *La crétion de l'homme,* by J. Laplace and J. Daniélou, Paris, 1943. —The first volume of the long desired critical edition of the Greek text has just been published: Gregorii Nysseni *Opera ascetica,* by W. Jäger, J. P. Cavarnos, V. W. Callaghan (*Opera,* vol. VIII, pars I) GCS., 1952.

BIBLIOGRAPHY. F. Hilt, *Des heiligen Gregor von Nyssa Lehre von Menschen systematisch dargestellt,* 1890. F. Diekamp, *Die Gotteslehre des heiligen Gregor von Nyssa,* 1896. H. Koch, *Das mystische Schauen beim hl. Gregor von Nyssa,* TQ., 79 (1898) 397 ff., L. Méridier, *L'influence de la seconde sophistique sur l'oeuvre de saint Grégoire de Nysse,* Rennes, 1906. C. Gronau, *De Basilio, Gregorio Nazianzeno Nyssenoque Platonis imitatoribus,* Göttingen, 1908. J. B. Aufhauser, *Die Heilslehre des Gregor von Nyssa,* Munich, 1910. A. Krampff, *Der Urzustand des Menschen nach der Lehre des hl. Gregor von Nyssa,* Trier, 1925. H. Lewy, *Sobria ebrietas,* Giessen, 1929. H. F. Cherniss, *The Platonism of Gregory of Nyssa,* Berkeley, 1930. J. Bayer, *Gregors von Nyssa Gottesbegriff,* Giessen, 1935. Endre van Ivanka, *Vom Platonismus zur Theorie der Mystik. Zur Erkenntnislehre Gregors von Nyssa,* Scholastik, 11 (1936) 163-195. S. Gonzalez, *El realismo platonico de S. Gregorio de Nisa,* Gregorianum, 20 (1939) 189-206. H. von Balthasar, *Présence et pensée. Essai sur la philosophie religieuse de Grégoire de Nysse,* Paris, 1942. J. B. Schöman, *Gregors von Nyssa theologische Anthropologie als Bildtheologie,* Scholastik, 1942, 31-53, 175-200, J. Daniélou, *Platonisme et théologie mystique. Essai sur la doctrine spirituelle de Grégoire de Nysse,* Paris, 1944 (bibliography, 334-335). J. T. Muckle CSB., *The Doctrine of St. Gregory of Nyssa on Man as the Image of God,* MS., 7 (1945) 55-84. T. A. Goggin, *The Times of St. Greg-*

ory of Nyssa as Reflected in the Letters and the Contra Eunomium, Cath. Univ. of Amer. Press, Washington, D.C., 1947. R. Leys, *L'image de Dieu chez Grégoire de Nysse,* Bruxelles, 1951. H. Merki, *Omoiôsis Theô. Von der platonischen Angleichung an Gott zur Gottähnlichkeit bei Gregor von Nyssa,* Freiburg i. d. Schweiz (Paradosis, 7) 1952 (bibliography xiii-xix). Jerome Gaïth, *La conception de la liberté chez Grégoire de Nysse,* Paris, J. Vrin, 1953. P. Floerl, *Le sens de la "division des sexes" chez Grégoire de Nysse,* RSR., 27 (1953) 105-111. W. Jaeger, see Part III, ch. II, note 42.

[77] Unless otherwise indicated the following references are to the *Homilies in Hexaemeron,* PG., 44.—On the meaning of *in principio,* 68 D and 69 D-72 C.—On the intelligible nature of sensible qualities, 212-213 (Cf. *Dialogue with Macrina,* PG., 46, 124 C-125 B).—All things created with their powers and causes, 69 C-72 C.—And their internal "reasons," 73 A. —Moses said nothing of air, 85-88.—On the firmament, 80 D.—On the intelligible heaven, 81 C D.—On the circular motion of the world, 84 D.—On the progressive development of created beings, 85 D.—Meteorology, 96—100.—On seas, 100 C-108 A.—On nature as a perpetual exchange of qualities between elements, 108 A-114 A.

[78] Man as an image of God, *De opificio hominis,* in PG., 44; III, 133 D. IV, 136 B D. V, 137.—Definitions of soul, *Dialogue with Macrina,* PG., 46, 29 B. —Only one soul in man, *In Hexaemeron,* PG., 44, 176 B.—Dignity of free will, *In Hexaemeron,* 15, PG., 44, 184 C.—Against the pre-existence of souls, *In Hexaemeron,* 28; PG., 44, 229-233.— Observations *de somno et vigilia, In Hexaemeron,* 13; PG., 44, 166-174.—On man's anatomy, *In Hexaemeron,* 30; PG., 44, 240-256.

[79] Flesh, soul and spirit, *De opificio hominis,* VIII; PG., 44, 148 A.—Body of a speaking animal, IX; PG., 44, 149-152.—Vastness of the soul, XI; PG., 44, 153-156. Soul and body, XII; PG., 44, 164 C. Cf. *Dialogue with Macrina,* PG., 46, 44 B-46 A.—Cause of the division in sexes, *In Hexaemeron,* PG., 44, 189 B-192 A. Cf. 206 A C.—Loss of the divine resemblance, *Dialogue with Macrina,* PG., 46, 86 D-87 C.—Restoration of the lost

resemblance, *Dialogue with Macrina*, PG., 46, 89 C-96 A.

[80] That resurrection is necessary to stop the progress of evil in the world, *In Hexaemeron*, 21; PG., 44, 201 C-204 A. —The soul is never completely separated from its body, *In Hexaemeron*, 27; PG., 229-233.—On the final abolition of evil when God will be "all in all" (I Cor. 15, 28), see *Dialogue*, PG., 46; 104 A-105 B. For a contrary interpretation, see *Scholion a*, in note to 103-104. But this second interpretation is not easily reconciled with 156 C-158 B, nor with *On the Dead*, PG., 46, 524-525; and still less with *The Catechetical Oration*, 35; PG., 45, 92 B C. Besides, it should not be forgotten that Gregory may have been influenced on this point by Origen, *Contra Celsum*, VIII, 72. The point, however, is not clear, and those who want to absolve him have a right to grant him the benefit of his obscurity on this point.

[81] There is, however, this important difference, that Gregory is very far from aiming to give "necessary reasons" in favor of Christian faith. On the contrary, he strongly objects to "dialectical" demonstrations of dogmas: *Dialogue*, PG., 46; 51 B C. No theologian was less inclined than he to mistake the speculation of a Christian about his faith with what he himself has called "the foreign philosophy" (*Dialogue*, PG., 46, 49 B), Cf. *In Hexaemeron*, PG., 44, 80 D: *è exôthen philosophia*.

[82] *On the Common Notions*, PG., 45; 177 D. Cf. *That One Should not Speak of Three Gods*, PG., 45, 117 A.—The theology of Gregory follows that of the Council of Nicaea. See, in his *Contra Eunomium*, I (PG., 45, 333-336) a general division of nature, both created and uncreated.—On participation, I, 337 C.— God is above duration in time and, consequently, above limitation: I; PG., 45, 364-365.—For the same reason, he is above limitation in space: I; PG., 45, 368 A.—Hence God's entity (*ousia*) is infinite and incomprehensible: III; PG., 601 B.

[83] Certain confusions have long been committed and they sometimes still occur between the following treatises: the *De opificio hominis* of Gregory of Nyssa; the *De natura hominis* of Nemesius; two homilies twice printed in Migne's PG.: 1) under the name of St. Basil, *Orationes de hominis structura* (PG., 30, 9-61); 2) under the name of Gregory of Nyssa, *In Scripturae verba: Faciamus hominem ad imaginem et similitudinem nostram* (PG., 44, 257-298). The author of these two homilies is still unknown (unlike Gregory, the author of the second sermon places the image of God in reason: *logismos*, PG., 44, 264 A). As if to add to the confusion, another treatise *De anima* is attributed in Migne to Gregory of Nyssa (PG., 45, 187-222); it is a fragment of the *De natura hominis* of Nemesius. The similitude of the two written names— Nyssenus, Nemesius—accounts for their frequent confusion in the manuscript tradition.

[84] The *De natura hominis* of NEMESIUS is to be found (Greek and Latin transl.) in PG., 40, 503-818. Two mediaeval Latin translations are known; I, Alfanus, Bishop of Salerno (1058-1085), edit. by C. Burkhard, *Nemesii Episcopi Premnon Physicon*, Teubner, Leipzig, 1917; II, Burgundio Pisano, a jurist of Pisa, edit. by C. Burkhard, *Gregorii Nysseni (Nemesii Emesini) Peri Phuseos Anthropou liber a Burgondione in Latinum translatus*, in a series of annual programs of the Karl Ludwig Gymnasium, Wien, 1891, 1892, 1896, 1901, 1902. Table of the chapters in 1891, pp. 12-13. This second translation is more complete and seems to have been more widely known than the preceding one.—BIBLIOGRAPHY. O. Bardenhewer, *Geschichte der altchristlichen Literatur*, IV, 279. D. Bender, *Untersuchungen zu Nemesius von Emesa*, Leipzig, 1898. B. Domanski, *Die Psychologie des Nemesius* (Beiträge, 3, 1) Münster i. West., 1900. W. Jäger, *Nemesios von Emesa, Quellenforschungen zum Neuplatonismus und seinen Anfängen bei Poseidonios*, Berlin, 1914 (influence of Poseidonios through the commentary of Origen on Genesis). H. A. Koch, *Quellenuntersuchungen zu Nemesius von Emesa*, Berlin, 1921 (stresses the influences of Poseidonios and Aristotle). E. Amann, art. *Némésis d'Emèse*, DTC., 11 (1931) 62-67. E. Dobler, *Nemesius von Emesa und die Psychologie des menschlichen Aktes bei Thomas von Aquin. Eine quellenanalytische Studie*, Freiburg i. d. Schweiz, 1950 (important for the study of Thomas Aquinas).—BET., 2922.

[85] APOLLINARIS, Bishop of Laodicea in Syria (*ca.* 390), is said by Nemesius to have erected the whole structure of his doctrine upon this foundation. In fact, it is at least true to say that, according to Apollinaris, Christ had assumed a human body and a human soul, but that, in him, what is in us the intellect (*nous*) or the spirit (*pneuma*), was divine. Apollinarianism was condemned by the second Ecumenical Council, at Constantinople, in 381. See, G. Voisin, *L'Apollinarisme,* Louvain, 1901.

[86] There have been materialists and spiritualists, but even within each group, philosophers do not agree. Among the materialists, the Stoics define the soul as an "ignited spirit"; Critias says it is blood; Hippo: water; Democritus: fire; Heraclitus: a moist exhalation. Among those who hold it to be incorporeal, some consider the soul as an immortal substance: Thales: a perpetually self-moving substance; Pythagoras: a self-moving number; Plato: an intelligible substance, able by itself to move according to certain numbers. Some, on the contrary, deny that the soul is a substance: Aristotle: the prime entelechy of the natural body, endowed with its organs and which has life in potency; Dicaearchus (who will become *Dinarchus* in mediaeval writings): the harmony of the four elements. —Against the materialists, Nemesius argues (with Ammonius Saccas, the master of Plotinus, and with Numenius), that since matter is of itself divisible *ad infinitum,* it needs a container, which must be an immaterial soul in potency. Cf. II; PG., 40, 536-541 A. The end of the chapter refutes the materialistic definitions one by one. Note (553 B), the remark that, in his *Demonstrations,* Galen denies having affirmed anything about the soul: those who invoke his authority to maintain that the soul is a "temperament" (*krasis*),

have no right to do so.—Aristotle, who calls the soul an *entelecheia,* practically says that it is a quality; for indeed, to him, the prime entelechy is the form of a matter, the second entelechy being its faculty (sight is a second entelechy with respect to the soul); but the soul is not a quality, it is a substance: II; PG., 40; 560 C-570 A.—All the Greeks who have upheld the immortality of the soul, have also taught its transmigration of souls from men to beasts and vice versa (II; PG., 40; 581-584), with the remarkable exception of Jamblichus (584 A); but a free human soul is incompatible with the body of an animal whose acts are all determined; besides, the admirable Galenus has shown that each animal species has a different species of soul. Besides, Christians need nothing else than Holy Scripture in order to know that the soul is immortal: II; PG., 40, 588-589. No particular text is quoted.

[87] Remarks of O. Bardenhewer in his *Patrology,* p. 306.—Because the Burkhard edition of the mediaeval translation is hard to find, we are adding the main references to the text of Migne, PG., 40: Man is a soul using a body, I, 504 A-505 B.—Man as final cause of created things, I, 511 B.—How man became mortal, I, 516 A.—Against Origen, III, 592-608.—The human body, IV, 608-612.—Its component elements, V, 612-632.—Parts of the soul which share in reason, VI-XV, 632-672.—Parts of the soul which do not share in reason, XVI-XXV, 672-704. —On passions, XVII-XXI, 676-692.—Voluntary, involuntary, non-voluntary, XXIX-XXXII, 717-729. — Deliberation, judgment, choice, XXXIII-XXXIV, 729-741.—Providence and liberty, XXXVI-XLIV, 745-817.—Incidentally, note curious remarks about certain nymphs or "demons," I, 524 C-525 A.

PART THREE
FROM AUGUSTINE TO BOETHIUS

CHAPTER I.   VICTORINUS AND AUGUSTINE

[1] The main writings of this group which a reader of mediaeval theologians may have to identify are as follows:

I. HERMES TRISMEGISTOS. A mythical author, supposed to be the Egyptian God Thot, identified by the Greeks with

Hermes and by the Latins with Mercury (see L. Thorndyke, *A History of Magic,* II, 288). Mentioned by Athenagoras; quoted by Tertullian (*De anima,* 33; *Adv. Valentinianos,* 15); list of works in Clement of Alexandria (*Stromata,* VI, 4);

is an important authority for Lactantius, who says that, in a mysterious way, Hermes has scrutinized practically the whole truth (*Institutes*, IV, 9. Cf. I, 6; II, 8; II, 10; VI, 25; VII, 13 and 18).—Editions of the *Corpus Hermeticum:* G. Parthey, *Hermetis Trismegisti Poemander*, Berlin, 1854 (Greek and Latin transl.). Walt. Scott, *Hermetica*, Greek and English transl., 4 vols. Oxford, Clar. Press, 1924-1936. A. D. Nock and A. J. Festugière, *Corpus Hermeticum*, 2 vols. Paris, 1945 (Greek and French transl.).—Included in the *corpus* is the Latin translation of an almost completely lost Greek original, entitled *Asclepius*, wrongly ascribed to Apuleius and often printed among his works (ed. Goldbacher, Wien, 1886; or Thomas, Teubner, Leipzig, 1921). Text in Nock and Festugière, II, 296-356. Quoted in mediaeval writings under several misleading names: *De hellera* (W. of Auvergne, *De legibus, ch.* 23); *Logostilios*, i.e., *Logos teleios, Verbum perfectum, Sermo perfectus* (W. of Auvergne, *De universo*, I, 26; Richard of Bury, *Philobiblion*, VII, 110).—On the doctrine of the *Corpus*, see R. Reitzenstein, *Poimandres. Studien zur griechisch-ägyptischen und frühchristlichen Literatur*, Leipzig, 1904. Jos. Kroll, *Die Lehren des Hermes Trismegistos*, Münster i. Westf., 1914 (Beitrage., 12, 2-4). A. J. Festugière, OP., *La révélation d'Hermès Trismégiste*, Paris, Gabalda; vol. I, *L'astrologie et les sciences occultes*, 1944; vol. II, *Le Dieu cosmique*, 1949; vol. III, *Les doctrines de l'âme*, 1953. On Hermetic astrological and "scientific" writings: L. Thorndyke, *A History of Magic and Experimental Science*, vol. II, ch. 45; N.Y., 1923.—An anonymous XII-cent. author has written a *Liber de propositionibus sive de regulis theologiae*, generally quoted as *Liber XXIV philosophorum* and also ascribed to the mythical Hermes. Text and study in Cl. Baeumker, *Studien und Charakteristiken zur Geschichte der Philosophie insbesondere des Mittelalters*, Münster i. W., 1928 (Beiträge, 25, 1-2) pp. 194-214 (also in *Hertling-Festgabe*, Freib. i. Br., 1913, pp. 17-40). D. Mahnke, *Unendliche Sphäre und Allmittelpunkt*, . . . Halle an d. Saale, 1937 (cf. PJ., 52 (1939) 49-58). H. Ostlender, *Scholastisches zu "dunklen Worten" in Dantes Vita nuova*, Mélanges de Ghellinck, II (1951) 889-903.

II. MACROBIUS. *Commentarium in Somnium Scipionis*, ed. by Fr. Eyssenhardt,

Leipzig, Teubner, 1868; 2 ed. 1893. W. H. Stahl, Engl. transl., *Macrobius: Commentary on the Dream of Scipio*, New York, Columbia University Press, 1952. A commentary by Macrobius (early IV cent.) on the dream of Scipio (Cicero, *De re publica*, bk. VI). Strongly influenced by Plato and Plotinus. The three main causes are the Good (*Tagathon*); then The Intelligence (*nous*), which contains the Ideas of all things; then the Soul (*psykhe*). The Good is also the One, and its unity remains unbroken up to the Soul which, although it still be one, contains the seed of multiplicity. For indeed, all souls are in the Soul as all numbers are implicitly contained within unity. These souls fall, so to speak, from the Soul into bodies, where a sort of drunkenness makes them forget their origin. Matter (*hyle*) thus becomes the cause why beings are separated from their first Cause. While falling, every soul successively crosses each one of the celestial spheres and acquires in each of them one of the powers which it will exercise in its body: in Saturn, reasoning and intellect (*ratiocinatio et intelligentia*); in Jupiter, active powers (*vis agendi*, or *praktikon*); in Mars, courage (*animositatis ardor*); in the Sun, sense perception and opinion (*sentiendi opinandique natura*); in Venus, desires (*desiderii motus*); in Mercury, speech (*hermeneutikon*); in the Moon, the vegetative powers, which are the lowest of the divine powers and the highest of the corporeal ones. In order to exercise them, the soul has, so to speak, to bury itself in its body (*soma*), which is also its grave (*sema*). Yet, even there, the soul still faintly remembers its origin and it can return to it through the pursuit of the four kinds of virtues: political (prudence, force, temperance and justice); purifying, which turn the soul from action toward contemplation; contemplative, which belong to the already purified soul; exemplary, which reside in the divine mind as the models and causes of all things. This will provide Saint Bonaventure with a formula for moral illumination. See P. Courcelle, *Les Lettres grecques en Occident de Macrobe à Cassiodore*, Paris, 1943, pp. 3-36. P. Duhem, *Le système du monde*, III, 62-87; 112-125.

III. CHALCIDIUS. End of the III or early IV cent., (quotes Origen, d. 254). Probably a Christian, known to the middle ages as the author of a fragmentary translation of *Timaeus* (17 A-53 C) and of a commentary on the same text (inspired from Posidonius). Edit. Joh. Wrobel, *Platonis Timaeus interprete Chalcidio,* Leipzig, Teubner, 1876. On the doctrine: B. Switalski, *Des Chalcidius Kommentar zu Platos Timaeus,* Münster i. W., 1902 (Beiträge, 3, 6). P. Duhem, *Le système du monde,* II, 417-426. There are three principles (*initia*): God, matter and the Idea. The use of *silva,* by a mediaeval writer, in order to designate matter, normally denotes the influence of Chalcidius. God is the supreme Good, beyond all substance and nature, perfect in himself, incomprehensible to us. Then comes Providence, whom the Greeks call Intelligence (*nous*), and from whom follows Destiny (*fatum*). This Christianized fate hangs on Providence and respects both natures and wills. Fortune and Chance are also subordinated to Providence. Then comes the World Soul, which permeates the world and quickens it from within (cf. Plotinus). The "intelligible world" is eternal and contains the models (*exempla*), or Ideas, according to which all sensible things are made. An Idea is an incorporeal substance, without color or shape, comprehensible by intellect or reason alone, and cause of the sensible beings which share in its likeness. God produces Ideas by conceiving them, so that the intelligible world is eternal in God.—Since the Ideas and God are one, the exact number of the principles is rather two than three, namely God and matter (*silva*). At the beginning was Chaos (Ovid, *Metam.,* I, 1-23), which the Greeks call *hyle.* The existence of matter can be proved by way of analysis (*resolutio*), that is by abstracting from bodies, elements and sensible qualities the reality which supports them all. Conversely, it can be proved by synthesis, that is by recomposing concrete reality from matter up. Matter itself is simple, indeterminate and eternal. It is pure potentiality, neither corporeal nor incorporeal, but able to be made to be either one.—Between matter and the Ideas are the forms of things (*species nativae*), which are images of the ideas and, by their union with matter, give rise to corporeal substances. The Idea is object of science; the form is object of opinion; matter can be neither known nor perceived, but a sort of indirect knowledge allows us to affirm its existence without knowing what it is. In man, the soul is not a form (against Aristotle), it

is a rational, self-moving and incorporeal substance. The influence of Chalcidius will help that of Nemesius in delaying the moment when the Aristotelian definition of the soul, as form of the body, will seem acceptable to Christian writers. Generally speaking, the knowledge of Chalcidius is required for a correct understanding of the XII-cent. school of Chartres.—J. R. O'Donnell, csb., *The Meaning of "Silva" in the Commentary of the Timaeus of Plato by Chalcidius,* MS. 7 (1945) 1-20.

[2] Marius Victorinus Afer was born in Africa *ca.* 280-300. After teaching there, he went to Rome *ca.* 340 and opened a school of rhetoric. A statue was erected to him on a Roman forum in 353. Author of many writings in philosophy as well as in the liberal arts. At first a fierce adversary of Christianity, he became a convert to the new religion *ca.* 355. His baptism made a deep impression on the future Saint Augustine. His difficulties had long been philosophical ones, for however much he loved the beginning of the gospel of Saint John, he could not accept that "the Word was made flesh and had lived among us" (Augustine, *De civitate Dei,* X, 29; PL., 41, 309). Even after subscribing to this article of faith, he continued to proclaim the uselessness of external rites. In Monceaux' words (III, 378): "Everything suggests that his conversion was purely, or mainly, an intellectual one." In 362, when the edict of Emperor Julian obliged him to choose between teaching or giving up Christianity, he gave up his school. Died *ca.* 363.— works. The works of Marius Victorinus which have been preserved fall into two categories: I, on liberal arts (pagan period), *Ars grammatica,* ed. by Keil, *Grammat. lat.,* vol. VI, Leipzig, 1874, 1-184.—*Explanationes in Ciceronis Rhetoricam,* a comm. in two Bks. on Cicero's *De inventione rhetorica;* crit. ed. by Halm, *Rhetores latini minores,* Leipzig, 1863, pp. 155-304; contains philosophical digressions and some jokes about the Christians, one of which will become a classical example among the dialecticians, Manegold of Lautenbach for instance: *si peperit, cum viro concubuit* (Cicero, *De inv. rhet.,* I, 29, 44).—*Liber de definitionibus,* crit. ed. by Stangl, *Mario-Victoriniana,* München, 1888, pp. 17-48; also in Migne, PL., 64, 891-910.— II, theological writings (Christian pe-

riod): *Liber de generatione divini Verbi* (358); four books *Adversus Arium* (359); a short treatise *De Homoousio recipiendo* (360); three hymns *On the Trinity* (*ca.* 360); three commentaries on Saint Paul's Epistles *To the Galatians, To the Ephesians, To the Philippians* ((after 360) all in PL., 8, 999-1036; 1039-1294; the text is often incorrect).—BIBLIOGRAPHY. The best introduction is P. Monceaux, *Hist. litt. de l'Afrique chrétienne*, III, 373-422. Cf. Koffmane, *De Mario Victorino philosopho christiano*, Breslau, 1880. Geiger, *C. Marius Victorinus Afer, ein neuplatonischer Philosoph*, I-II, Metten, 1887-1889. R. Schmid, *Marius Victorinus rhetor und seine Beziehungen zu Augustin*, Kiel, 1895. J. Wöhrer, *Studien zu Marius Victorinus*, (Progr.-Schrift) Wilhering, 1905-1912 (important). E. Benz, *Marius Victorinus und die Entwicklung der abendländischen Willensmetaphysik*, Stuttgart, 1932. A. H. Travis, *Marius Victorinus, a Biographical Note*, HTR., 36 (1943) 83-90. P. Hadot, *La notion de Dieu "causa sui" chez Marius Victorinus*, Institut catholique de Paris (ms. thesis) 1949. P. Séjourné, art. *Victorinus Afer*, DTC., 15 (1950) 2887-2954.

³ CANDIDUS, a friend of Victorinus, addressed to him two writings on the same subject: *De generatione divina* (PL., 8; 1013-1020) and *Epistola* (PL., 8; 1035-1040).

⁴ *Liber de generatione divina*, IV; PL., 8; 1021-1022. Victorinus is clear on one point: God is no one being in particular; he is not "something" (*aliquid*); so, as compared with beings, he is non-being. Beyond this point, his thought becomes obscure. In the *Liber de generatione*, he seems to say that, even in himself, the Father is non-being, because he is the One, which is an "ante-being." In his later treatise *Adversus Arium* (IV, 19; 1127 A B), he says that, although God is not "being" (*on*), he is *esse*, or *to einai*, that is, the force and the power to exist. Victorinus adds there that this power to exist is in God anterior to "one," "simple," "alone," "infinite," etc. It is "pre-existence rather than existence." But the whole context suggests that, in this important text, Victorinus has in mind the *Logos*, whom he always calls being; "Ergo si non *on*, nec *logos, logos* enim definitus est, et definitor" (1127 C). Cf. XX, 1127-1128, and XXI, 1128. His

negative theology should already be understood, like later on that of Dionysius, as preparatory to a "superlative" theology: *Adversus Arium*, IV, 23; PG., 8, 1129-1130.

⁵ *Liber* . . . , VII-IX; PL., 8, 1023-1025.

⁶ *Liber* . . . , X; PL., 8, 1025-1026.— That matter itself is "something": VIII; PG., 8, 1024 A B.

⁷ *Liber* . . . , XIII; PL., 8, 1027.

⁸ *Liber* . . . , XIV; PL., 8, 1027-1028. God, i.e., *prôon* (or "ante-being"), has begotten *on* (i.e., "being") as his self-manifestation (ch. XV). Thus, because he is the Word, Christ is being, the first being through which all that which is has received being (ch. XVI; PG., 8, 1028-1029).

⁹ *Liber* . . . , XVIII; PL., 8, 1030, and XX, 1030 C.—The Word, who is the very intelligence and will of God, consubstantial with him, has sprung forth from eternity by the will of God: XXIII: PG., 8, 1031-1032. Here (XXIX; PL., 8, 1034) and still more forcefully in his treatise *Adversus Arium*, Victorinus stresses the *Homoousios*. See his *De Homoousiô recipiendo*, PG., 8, 1137-1140.

¹⁰ The *Adversus Arium* makes a more generous use of Scripture.—See the Creed of Victorinus, I, 47, 1076-1077.—On the primacy of the One, I, 49, 1078. I, 50, 1078-1079.—God is *esse, vivere et intelligere*, I, 52, 1080-1081. IV, 8, 1118-1119. IV, 16, 1124. IV, 18, 1126 D. IV, 26, 1132.—God is non-being as not being *aliquid*, IV, 11, 1121.—The *Logos* as a spherical motion, a straight motion, etc., I, 60-61, 1085-1086. III, 2, 1099-1100. III, 10, 1106 D.—The *Logos* seed and power of all beings, III, 4; 1101-1102. IV, 2, 1114.—On man as made up of body and soul (the body having a soul of matter and a spirit of matter, while the soul has a *nous*, which makes it more divine than the souls of beasts): "The divine soul is in the material spirit (*in hylico spiritu*); the material spirit is in the material soul (i.e., in the soul of the material body); the material soul is in the carnal body, which has to be purified with all three, in order that it may receive eternal light and eternal life, which

is the work of faith in Christ," I, 62, 1087 B. Cf. IV, 11, 1121 B C.—On Ideas: source of the terms *existentialitas, vitalitas,* etc., from the Greek *ontolès, zoôtes,* etc., IV, 5, 1116: Cf. Plotinus, *Enneads,* III, 5, 9.—On the general history of some technical Latin terms in philosophy and theology, C. Arpe, *Substantia,* Philologus, 94 (1940) 64-67. J. de Ghellinck, *L'entrée d'essentia, substantia et autres mots apparentés dans le latin médiéval,* Archivum Latinitatis Medii Aevi. Bulletin Du Cange, 16 (1941) 77-112; *Essentia et substantia,* op. cit., 17 (1942) 129-133. E. Gilson, *Notes sur le vocabulaire de l'être,* MS., 8 (1946) 150-158.

[11] SAINT AMBROSE (340-397). Works in PL., 14-17. More important for the history of theology than for that of philosophical ideas. A comparison of his *Hexaemeron* with the similar work by Saint Basil, which he knew, shows how little interested Ambrose was in abstract speculation. He is interested in facts for the moral lessons they suggest (*Hexaemeron,* I, 6, 20. I, 6, 22-23. II, 2, 7. VI, 2, 8.). For instance, the Apostles were fishermen; then, morally speaking, man is a fish (V, 6, 15). He does not trust the philosophers (*De fide,* I, 5. I, 13. IV, 8; *De incarnatione,* IX, 89). Traces of Plotinus have been detected by P. Courcelle, *Recherches sur les Confessions de saint Augustin,* Paris, 1950, pp. 106-138: the God of Exod. 3, 14, is being itself, that is that which always is (*In Ps.,* 43, 19). God is entity (*essentia, ousia*), a word which means "always existing" (*De fide,* III, 15). Another group of Plotinian notions is found in *De Isaac et anima* (VII, 60-61, evil is non-being; VII, 65, on virtues and vices; VII, 78-79, on the spiritual flight of man toward his Father and true homeland); also in the *De bono mortis* (death is not an evil, I, 1 and IV, 13; the soul uses its body, VII, 27; the soul is life, consequently it is immortal, IX, 42, etc). All these philosophical notions will be taken up by Augustine; whether he was indebted to Ambrose for them is hard to say; what is certain is that Augustine learned from Ambrose to interpret Scripture in a spiritual sense, *Confessions,* VI, 4, 6 (cf. II Cor. 3, 6); Ambrose invited Augustine to read, not Plotinus, but Isaiah (*Conf.* IX, 5, 13). The fact that Ambrose wrote a *De philosophia* does not warrant any conclusion; the

treatise is lost, and we do not even know up to what point it was for, or against, philosophy.—R. Thamin, *Saint Ambroise et la morale chrétienne au IVe siècle. Etude comparée des traités "Des devoirs" de Cicéron et de saint Ambroise,* Paris, 1895. P. de Labriolle, *The Life and Times of St. Ambrose,* St. Louis, Mo., 1928. J. R. Palanque, *Saint Ambroise et l'empire romain . . . ,* Paris, 1933. L. M. Zucker, *S. Ambrosii De Tobia;* a commentary with an introduction and translation, Cath. Univ. of Amer., Washington, D.C., 1933. N. E. Nelson, *Cicero's De officiis in Christian Thought,* Ann Arbor (Mich.) 1933. Homes Dudden, *S. Ambrose, his Life and Times,* Oxford, 1935, 2 vols. (bibliography, II, 714-724). G. Ferretti, *L'influsso di S. Ambrogio in S. Agostino,* Faenza, 1951. Cl. Morino, *Ritorno al paradiso di Adamo in S. Ambrogio. Itinerario spirituale,* Rome, Tip. Pol. Vat., 1952. Th. Deman, *Le 'De officiis' de S. Ambroise dans l'histoire de la théologie morale,* RSPT., 37 (1953) 409-424.—BET., 178-191.

On the so-called "collectivism" of Ambrose and other Fathers, O. Schilling, *Der Kollektivismus der Kirchenväter,* TQ., 114 (1933) 481-492. S. Giet, *La doctrine de l'appropriation des biens chez quelques uns des Pères. Peut-on parler de communisme?* RSR., 1948, 55-91. Cf. M. B. Schwalm, art. *Communisme,* DTC., 3 (1923) 574-596.

[12] SAINT AUGUSTINE (Aurelius Augustinus), Nov. 13, 354-Aug. 28, 430, born at Tagasta (Hippo Regius, Souk Aras, Tunisia), son of Saint Monica who taught him the elements of Christian faith: existence of a divine providence of the world, Christ saviour of men, future life with rewards or punishments (*Conf.,* I, 9, 14. III, 4, 8. VI, 16, 26). Studied at Carthage (370); had a son from the woman with whom he was to live for fifteen years (372); in 373, he was initiated to the doctrine of Mani (215-276), who had taught a dualistic conception of the world and a Gnostic doctrine of salvation (to know in order to believe). While teaching Latin grammar and literature at Carthage, he wrote the now lost treatise *De pulchro et apto* and progressively lost his faith in the doctrine of Mani, which he gave up in 382. Augustine then became a disciple of the moderate skepticism professed by Cicero. He then went to Rome as a professor of eloquence (383). At Milan, he

heard sermons preached by Saint Ambrose and learned from them that there was a "spiritual meaning" hidden behind the letter of Scripture (II Cor. 3, 6; *Conf.* VI, 4, 6). The reading of a small number of neoplatonic writings (among which some *Enneads* of Plotinus) then revealed to him that true reality is intelligible reality, not the corporeal one. He also learned from Plotinus that God is the light that illumines our souls in order to liberate them from their enslavement to bodies, and that, since evil has no entity of its own, it cannot be one of the principles of the universe (against Mani). Yet, while showing the true goal of human life, Plotinus was providing no way to reach it. The reading of Saint Paul revealed to Augustine both the nature of the obstacle and the help required in order to remove it. The obstacle is sin, the help is the grace of God. Only a Christian can do what Plotinus says a man ought to do. Encouraged by the conversion of a then famous Platonist, Marius Victorinus, Augustine himself became a Christian (386) and was baptized by Saint Ambrose in 387 after a year of studious retreat at Cassiciacum. Monica died at Ostia in 387 while they were waiting there for a ship to take them back to Africa. Augustine returned alone to Carthage, then to Tagasta where he set up a sort of monastic community. He spent the rest of his life in his birthplace (Tagasta, or Hippo Regius) where he was ordained a priest (391) and whose bishop he became at the age of 41 or 42 (395 or 396). Augustine died in 430.

On Augustine's life and conversion, G. Bardy. *Saint Augustin,* Paris, 1940 (complete biography).—P. Alfaric, *L'évolution intellectuelle de saint Augustin,* Paris, 1919. Ch. Boyer, SJ., *Christianisme et néoplatonisme dans la formation de saint Augustin,* Paris, 1920; 2 ed., enlarged, Rome, 1953 (competent refutation of Alfaric). Jens Nörregaard, *Augustins Bekehrung,* Tübingen, 1923 (important). K. Holl, *Augustins innere Entwicklung,* Gesammelte Aufsätze zur Kirchengeschichte, III, Tübingen, 1928, 54-116. E. Haenchen, *Die Frage nach der Gewissheit beim Jungen Augustin,* Stuttgart, 1923. W. Theiler, *Porphyrios und Augustine,* Halle an d. Saale, 1933. P. Henry, *Plotin et l'Occident,* Louvain, 1934; conclusions in English in *Augustine and Plotinus,* JTS., 38 (1937) 1-23. J. Geffcken, *Augustins Tolle-lege Erlebnis,*

Archiv für Religionswissenschaft, 31 (1934) 1-13; same author, *Inhalt und Aufgabe der Philosophie in den Jugendschriften Augustinus,* Osnabrück, 1939. M. P. Garvey, *Saint Augustine: Christian or Neoplatonist?* . . . , Milwaukee, 1939. J. De Blic, *Platonisme et christianisme dans la conception augustinienne du Dieu créateur,* RSR., 30 (1940) 172-190. P. Muñoz, *Psicologia de la conversion en San Agustin,* Gregorianum, 22 (1941) 9-24, 325-352. J. M. Le Blond, *Les conversions de saint Augustin,* Paris, 1948. P. Courcelle, *Les lettres grecques en Occident de Macrobe à Cassiodore,* Paris, 1943, 137-209; same author, *Recherches sur les Confessions de saint Augustin,* Paris, 1950 (bibliography, pp. 259-278). B. Altaner, *Augustinus und Philo von Alexandrien,* ZKT., 65 (1941, 81-90; Augustine has used the *Quaest. et solutiones in Genesim* by Philo).—Origins of the literary genus "confessions": G. Misch, *A History of Autobiography in Antiquity,* 2 vols. Harvard Univ. Press, 1951.—On the structure of the *City of God:* H.-I. Marrou, *La division en chapitres des livres de la Cité de Dieu,* Mélanges de Ghellinck, I (1951) 235-250.

[13]Thomas Aquinas, *Summa Theologiae,* part I, qu. 84, art. 5, *Resp.,* in A. C. Pegis, *Basic Writings of St. Thomas Aquinas,* Random House, N.Y., 1945, vol. I, p. 804. Cf. *De spiritualibus creaturis,* art. X, ad 8m.

[14] WORKS of Saint Augustine: Migne, PL., vols. 32-47 (reproduces the Benedictine edition of the Maurists). For a comparative study of this edition with the Vienna edition (CSEL), see J. de Ghellinck, *Une édition patristique célèbre,* in *Patristique et moyen âge,* vol. III, pp. 339-484.—In critical editions (*Corpus scriptorum ecclesiasticorum latinorum*): *Confessiones,* vol. 33, 1896.—*Contra Academicos, De beata vita, De ordine,* v. 63, 1922.—*Retractationes,* v. 36, 1902.—*Epistulae,* 1-123, v. 44, 1895; 124-184, v. 44, 1904; 185-270, v. 57, 1911; Tables, v. 58, 1923.—*Speculum et Liber de divinis scripturis,* v. 12, 1887.—*De utilitate credendi, De duabus animabus, Contra Fortunatum, Contra Adimantum, Contra epistulam fundamenti, Contra Faustum,* v. 25, 1892.—*De Genesi ad litteram imperfectus liber, De Genesi ad litteram, Lectiones in Heptateuchon, Adnotationes in Job,* v. 28, 1895.—*De civitate*

Dei, I-XIII, v. 40, 1899; XIV-XXIV, v. 40, 1900.—*De consensu evangelistarum,* v. 43, 1904.—*De fide et symbolo, De fide et operibus, De agone christiano, De continentia, De bono conjugali, De sancta virginitate, De bono viduitatis, De adulteriis conjugiis, De mendacio, Contra mendacium, De opere monachorum, De divinatione daemonum, De cura pro mortuis gerenda, De patientia,* v. 41, 1900. —*Psalmus contra partem Donati, Contra epistulam Parmeniani, De baptismo,* v. 51, 1908.—*Contra litteras Petiliani, Epistula ad Catholicos de secta Donatistarum, Contra Crescentium,* v. 52, 1909.—*De unico baptismo, Breviculus collationis cum Donatistis, Contra partem Donati post gesta, Sermo ad Caesariensis ecclesiae plebem, Gesta cum emerito Donatistarum epis copo, Contra Gaudentium,* v. 53, 1910.— *De peccatorum meritis et remissione et de baptismo parvulorum, De spiritu et littera, De natura et gratia, De natura et origine animae, Contra duas epistulas Pelagianorum,* v. 60, 1913.—*De perfectione justitiae hominis, De gestis Pelagii, De gratia Christi et peccato originali, De nuptiis et concupiscentia,* v. 42, 1902.— The best Latin edition of the *Confessions* is that of M. Skutella, Teubner, Leipzig, 1934.

ENGLISH TRANSLATIONS. *The Works of Aurelius Augustinus,* ed. M. Dodds, Edinburgh, 16 vols., 1871-1876. Reprinted with suppressions and additions (*Soliloquies* in vol. VII) in NPN., P. Schaff, New York, Christian Literature Co., 14 vols., 1886-1890.—A new translation is included in the collection published by "The Fathers of the Church," New York; 10 vols. of Augustine already published (1952); the vols. 6 and 7 contain *The City of God.*—Several translations of the *Confessions,* among which the classical Pusey translation often reprinted since 1838. Extracts from *On the Free Will,* II, 1-17, in R. McKeon, *Selections,* I, 11-64. J. H. S. Burleigh, *Augustine: Earlier Writings,* London, 1953 (The Soliloquies, The Teacher, On Free Will, Of True Religion, The Usefulness of Belief, The Nature of the Good, Faith and the Creed, On Various Questions Bk. 1; vol. VI of the new Protestant series: The Library of Christian Classics).—An ample choice of translated texts is found in W. J. Oates, *Basic Writings of Saint Augustine,* 2 vols. Random House, New York, 1948. —BET., 426-485; Index, 466.

INTRODUCTIONS. E. Portalié SJ., art.

Augustin (saint), DTC., 1 (1923) 2268-2472 (the best introduction). J. Martin, *Saint Augustin,* 2 ed., Paris, 1923 (a large quantity of well-chosen references). E. Przyvara, *An Augustine Synthesis,* New York, 1936. E. Gilson, *Introduction à l'étude de saint Augustin,* 2 ed., Paris, 1943. A. C. Pegis, *The Mind of St Augustine,* MS., 6 (1944) 1-61. V. J. Bourke, *Augustine's Quest of Wisdom. Life and Philosophy of the Bishop of Hippo,* Milwaukee, 1945. F. Cayré, AA., *Initiation à l'étude de saint Augustin,* Paris, 1947. F. Copleston, *A History of Philosophy,* II, 40-90.—Cosmology, P. Duhem, *Le système du monde,* II, 393-494.—Cultural background, H.-I. Marrou, *Saint Augustin et la fin de la culture antique,* 2 ed. Paris, 1949.—Manichaeism, H.-C. Puech, *Le manichéisme, son fondateur* Paris, 1949.—Influence: M. Grabmann, *Der Einfluss des hl. Augustinus auf die Verwertung und Bewertung der Antike im Mittelalter,* MG., II, 1-24; *Des heiligen Augustins Quaestio de Ideis (De diversis quaestionibus 83, qu. 46) in ihrer inhaltlichen Bedeutung und mittelalterlichen Weiterwirkung,* MG., II, 25-34; *Augustins Lehre von Glauben und Wissen und ihr Einfluss auf das mittelalterliche Denken,* MG., II, 35-62.—Chronology of Augustine's writings: M. Zarb OP., *Chronologia operum Sancti Augustini,* Angelicum, 10 (1933) 359-396, 478-512; II (1934) 78-91.

[15] HE WHO IS (Exod. 3, 14) is being itself (*essentia,* entity); in its absolute sense, it only can be predicated of God, *De Trinitate,* V, 2, 3, PL., 42, 912; cf. E. Gilson, *Introduction,* Paris, 1943, 27-28; *Le Thomisme,* Paris, 1945, 75-76; *Philosophie et incarnation selon saint Augustin,* Montreal, 1947. A. M. Dubarle, *La signification du nom de Iahweh,* RSPT., 34 (1951) 17-21.—On the notion of God, J. Nörregaard, *Augustins Bekehrung,* pp. 142-156. Jak. Barion, *Plotin und Augustinus. Untersuchungen zum Gottesproblem,* Berlin, 1935.

[16] Being is equated with eternity and immutability in countless texts; for instance, *Sermo* VI, 3, 4; PL., 39, 61. *Confessions,* VII, II, 177; VII, 20, 26; IX, 10, 24; XI, 6, 8.—Among the other attributes of God, Augustin quotes: "supreme, excellent, supremely powerful, all-powerful, most merciful and most just, most secret and most present, most beautiful

and most strong, stable and incomprehensible; unchangeable and yet changing all things; never new, never old; renewing all things, but leading proud men to senility, and they do not know it; always acting, always resting . . . ," etc. *Conf.*, I, 4, 4; PL., 32, 662. Infinity is not usually mentioned by Augustine among the attributes of God, except in connection with the incorporeity of the divine being. That which is spiritual cannot be limited, because it is not in space; hence it is "in-finite": *Confessions*, VII, i. 1-2; PL., 32, 733-734.—F. Orestano, *L'idea dell' "infinito" nelle "Confessioni" di S. Agostino*, Sophia, 3 (1935) 3-13.

[17] See E. Gilson, *Philosophie et incarnation*, pp. 37-43. In Augustine, *Enarratio in Ps.* 101, 10-14; PL., 37, 1310-1315.— Augustine has certainly read the treatise of Plotinus *On the Three Substances which are Causes, Enn.* V, 1 (cf. *De civitate Dei*, X, 23; PL., 41, 300); and he was no less certainly aware of the radical difference which separated their two doctrines: "We do not speak of two or three principles, when we speak of God, no more than we are permitted to speak of two or three Gods," *De civitate Dei*, X, 24; PL., 41, 300-301.

[18] The central text of Augustine on this point, and one of the main sources of the mediaeval speculation about the divine Ideas, is *De diversis quaestionibus 83*, qu. 46, 1-2; PL., 40, 29-31. The words *idea, forma, species, ratio*, do not have absolutely identical connotations, but they are practically synonymous in the terminology of Augustine.—On the later influence of this doctrine: M. Grabmann, MG., München, 1936, v. II, pp. 25-34.

[19] See the famous and much controverted text: *Conf.* VII, 9, 13-14; PL., 32, 740-741.

[20] On beatitude as the love of truth: *Conf.* X, 23, 33; PL., 32, 793-794, and the whole *De beata vita*, especially IV, 34-35; PL., 32, 975-976.

[21] *De Genesi contra Manichaeos*, I, 2, 4; PL., 34, 175. *De diversis quaestionibus 83*, qu. 28; PL., 40, 18. *De civitate Dei*, XI, 24; PL., 41, 338. *Epist.* 166, 5, 15; PL., 33, 727.

[22] Creation instantaneous, *De Genesi ad litteram* IV, 33, 51; PL., 34, 318. *De Genesi ad litt. liber imperfectus*, VII, 28; PL., 34, 231. *De Genesi contra Manichaeos*, II, 3, 4; PL., 41, 197-198.—Seminal reasons, *De Genesi ad litteram*, VI, 6, 10; PL., 34, 343. *De Trinitate*, III, 9, 16; PL., 42, 877-878. Cf. *De Genesi ad litteram*, V, 7, 20; PL., 34, 328 and V, 23, 45; PL., 34, 338.—Unfolding of the world according to the rules of Wisdom, *De Genesi ad litteram*, IV, 33, 51; PL., 34, 318.—Time and eternity, *Confessions*, XI, 23, 29-30; PL., 32, 820-821: on this important problem, consult the works of Guitton and Marrou, note 23.

The notion of "seminal reason" has been often studied, especially in view of showing that it is quite unlike the modern idea of creative evolution. H. Meyer, *Geschichte der Lehre der Keimkräften von der Stoa bis zum Ausgang der Patristik*, 1914. H. Woods, *Augustine and Evolution, A Study in the Saint's "De genesi ad litteram" and "De Trinitate,"* New York, 1924. M. J. McKeough, *The Meaning of the rationes seminales in St. Augustine*, Washington, 1926. R. de Sinéty, *Saint Augustin et le transformisme*, Archives de Philosophie, VII, 2 (1930) 244-272; bibliographie, pp. 271-272. A. Darmet, *Les notions de raison séminale et de puissance obédientielle chez saint Augustin et saint Thomas d'Aquin*, Belley, 1934. G. Guinagh, *Saint Augustine and Evolution*, Classical Weekly, 40 (1946) 26-31.

A consequence of the doctrine of the seminal reasons is to reduce to a bare minimum the efficacy of secondary efficient causes. See the remarkable text of *De civitate Dei*, XXII, 24, 2; PL., 41, 789. The sower, the father, the mother do not count (*non est aliquid*). God is still operating and making the seeds evolve their latent forms according to the laws of numbers. This doctrine, taken up by William of Auvergne and by St. Bonaventure, will be criticized by Thomas Aquinas as depriving natural causes of their efficiency: *II Sent.*, 1, 1, 4; Mandonnet ed. I, 23-27.

[23] Spiritual matter, *De civitate Dei*. XII, 15; PL., 41, 363-365. *Conf.*, XII, 9, 9; PL., 32, 829.—On the duration proper to angels, *Conf.*, XII, 11, 12; PL., 32, 830 and XII, 13, 16; PL., 32, 839-840.

The two opposite poles of being are

God and matter. Since God is "immutability," matter is "mutability." To the extent that man is tied up with matter, he is engaged in mutability and therefore in time. The philosophical notion of salvation, in Augustine, is that of a redemption of man from time and his eternal stabilization in the eternity of God. The fact that memory transcends time explains its importance in the doctrine of Augustine. Likewise, by its necessity, intelligible truth is in man a token of eternity. All that, in time, escapes time, is an anticipated image of, or a sharing in, the divine immutability. The world history of the City of God is that of mankind itself in its pilgrimage toward the stability of eternal life. The psychology, the noetic, the theology of history and the spirituality of Augustine are so many aspects of one and the same effort of man to liberate himself of the anguish of time and of becoming. J. Guitton, *Le temps et l'éternité chez Plotin et saint Augustin,* Paris, 1933. M. Pontet, *L'exégèse de S. Augustin prédicateur,* Paris, 1945. E. Gilson, *Philosophie et incarnation,* Montréal, 1947. H.-I. Marrou, *L'ambivalence du temps de l'histoire chez saint Augustin,* Montréal, 1950.

²⁴ On matter: Scriptural text, Wisdom, 11, 18: "For thy almighty hand, which made the world of matter without form"; decisive in the mind of Augustine. This *"omnia fecisti de materia informi"* is the source of countless texts of Augustine where he comments upon the *de* and the *informi.* For instance, *De Genesi ad litteram,* I, 15, 29; PL., 34, 257. *Confessions,* XII, 8, 8; PL., 32, 829. Cf. XII, 6, 6; XII, 15, 22, etc. *De vera religione,* XVIII, 35. Augustine has never affirmed the existence of a spiritual matter as a demonstrated truth, and this is a point which Thomas Aquinas will not fail to note; but Augustine has repeatedly developed this notion as providing the best understanding of certain scriptural texts related to the creation of all things, visible and invisible. The book XII of the *Confessions* bears witness to this state of mind. Other biblical equivalents for matter: *coelum et terra, terra invisibilis et incomposita, abyssus* with *tenebris* or *aqua:* in *De Genesi contra Manichaeos,* I, 7, 11; PL., 34, 326.—J. Witzes, *Bemerkungen zu dem neuplatonischen Einfluss in Augustins "de Genesi ad litteram,"* ZNW., 39 (1940) 137-151. On the actu-

ality of matter, spiritual matter and the ensuing universality of hylomorphism considered as zones of tension between Augustinianism and Thomism in the last third of the XIII century, see B. Janssen SJ., *Der Augustinismus des Petrus Johannis Olivi,* ADGM., II, 881-882.

²⁵ *In Joannis evangelium,* I, 17; PL., 35, 1387. *De vera religione,* XXII, 42; PL., 34, 140. *De Genesi contra Manicheos,* I, 8, 13; PL., 34, 179. *Epist.* 14, 4; PL., 33, 80. *De Trinitate,* IV, 1, 3; PL., 42, 888.

²⁶ *De moribus Manichaeorum,* II, 6, 8; PL., 32, 1348. *De vera religione,* XXXII, 60; PL., 34, 149, and XXXIV, 63; PL., 150. *Conf.* XIII, 2, 2; PL., 32, 845.— Moral and sociological implications of the doctrine, *Conf.* XIII, 34; PL., 32, 866-867. — Implications concerning salvation, *Conf.* XI, 29, 39; PL., 32, 825.

²⁷ *De moribus ecclesiae,* I, 27, 52; PL., 32, 1332. *In Joannis evangelium,* XIX, 1, 15; PL., 35, 1553.—Augustine naturally defines "man" as the unity of soul and body (*De moribus ecclesiae,* I, 4, 6; PL., 32, 1313) and Thomas Aquinas will make the best of this aspect of Augustine's doctrine (*Sum. theol.* I, 75, 4, quoting Augustine, *De civitate Dei,* XIX, 3, 1; PL., 41, 625-626); he will remember the definition of the *Alcibiades* (*Sum. theol.* I, 75, 4) and relate it to the Plotinian doctrine of sense cognition (ibid.), but he will not stress his fundamental disagreement with the Augustinian definition of man as "a soul using a body" and, nevertheless, constituting with its body one single person, man. —The soul (*animus*) is defined "substantia quaedam rationis particeps, regendo corpori accommodata," *De quantitate animae,* XIII, 22; PL., 32, 1048. This definition will be widely spread by the XII-century pseudo-Augustinian treatise *De spiritu et anima,* I; PL., 40, 781. —Cf., "Ego interior cognovi haec, *ego, ego animus per sensum corporis mei,*" *Conf.* X. 6, 9. The body is the "exterior man," the soul is the "interior man," a spiritual substance capable of saying "I," *ego,* and of knowing by the senses of "its body." This soul truly animates its body and makes it able to feel (*qua vivifico sed etiam qua sensifico carnem meam*) but the true man is his soul, and God is above the head of the soul (*super caput animae meae,* X, 7, 11). The deeper part

of the soul, and therefore of man, is memory (*cum animus sit etiam ipsa memoria,* X, 14, 21); hence the typically Augustinian equation: man, soul, memory, and vice versa, "Ego sum qui memini, *ego animus*" (X, 16, 25). The unity of man does not prevent the threefold hierarchical order: body, soul vivifying body, God vivifying soul (X, 20, 29). The whole structure of the doctrine is at stake; on the strength of the Augustinian notion of man, the soul has to look inside itself in order to find God: "et ecce intus eras et ego foris, et ibi te quaerebam et in ista formosa, quae fecisti, deformis inruebam. Mecum eras, et tecum non eram" (*Conf.* X, 27, 38).

²⁸ *De Trinitate,* X, 10, 13-16; PL., 42, 980-982. Compare Descartes, *Meditationes,* II; ed. Adam-Tannery, vol. VII, pp. 27-28.

²⁹ *Epist.,* 166, 4; PL., 33, 722.—On the soul as intermediary between the Ideas and its own body, *De immortalitate animae,* XV, 24; PL., 32, 1033.

³⁰ *De immortalitate animae,* VII, 12; PL., 32, 1027. Cf. IX, 16; PL., 32, 1029, and XII, 19; PL., 32, 1031.—For a comprehensive study of the notion of man in Augustine, E. Dinkler, *Die Anthropologie Augustins,* Stuttgart, 1934.

³¹ *De quantitate animae,* XXIII, 41; PL., 32, 1058. *De quantitate animae,* XXV, 48; PL., 32, 1063. Cf. Plotinus, *Enneads,* IV, 4, 20.—These sense cognitions, and the corresponding intellectual notions, are expressed by words; on this point, K. Kuypers, *Der Zeichen-und Wortbegriff im Denken Augustins,* Amsterdam, 1934.

³² On memory, *De musica,* VI, 2-9; PL., 32, 1163-1177. Cf. the classical chapters of *Conf.* X, 8-19; PL., 32, 784-791.—The notion of memory plays an important part in noetic. Because he cannot accept the pre-existence of the soul, Augustine must reject the position of Plato, according to whom cognitions are innate, in this sense that to know an intelligible truth is to remember having seen it in a former life. Yet, since no intelligible knowledge comes from without, there must be some sense in which it is true to say, with Plato, that to learn is to remember. This sense is provided by the doctrine of the divine illumination.

Memory thus becomes the deepest hidden recess of the mind, in which God dwells by his light, and where he teaches us as our "internal Master." To learn and to know intelligible truth is, therefore, to remember, in the present, the everlasting presence of the divine light in us. This doctrine of memory will have important consequences in the speculative mysticism of the fourteenth century. See *De Trinitate,* XIV, 7, 9; PL., 42, 1043. XIV, 15, 21; PL., 42, 1052. XV, 21, 40; PL., 42, 1088.—On the Augustinian interpretation of Plato's reminiscence, *Retractationes,* I, 4, 4; PL., 32, 590.—On the self-knowledge of the soul, J. Geyer, *Die Theorie Augustins von der Selbsterkenntnis der menschlichen Seele,* ADGM., 169-187.

³³ *De magistro,* PL., 32, 1193-1220. *De libero arbitrio,* II, 2-12; PL., 32, 1241-1260. *Enarratio in Ps. 41,* 6-8; PL., 36, 467-469. The famous formula: "ab exterioribus ad interiora, ab inferioribus ad superiora," is found in *Enarratio in Ps. 145,* 5; PL., 37, 1887.—The noetic of Augustine and his proofs of the existence of God are inseparable because God is proved to exist as cause of truth in the human intellect. The many historians who have interpreted this part of his doctrine can be situated with respect to two extreme tendencies: 1) to stress the Plotinian aspect of the position; 2) to show that after all, there is a fundamental agreement between Augustine and Thomas Aquinas on this point. Those who attempt to steer a middle course are naturally blamed by the tenants of the two extreme tendencies.—Examples of the first position, J. Hessen, *Die Begründung der Erkenntnis nach dem hl. Augustinus,* Münster i. W., 1916 (Beiträge, 19, 2); same author: *Die unmittelbare Gotteserkenntnis nach dem hl. Augustin,* Paderborn, 1919. B. Kälin, *Die Erkenntnislehre des hl. Augustinus,* Sarnen, 1920; same author, *St. Augustin und die Erkenntnis der Existenz Gottes,* DTF., 14 (1936) 331-352. Examples of the second position, Ch. Boyer SJ., *L'idée de vérité dans la philosophie de saint Augustin,* Paris, 1921. F. Cayré, *Le point de départ de la philosophie augustinienne,* Revue de philosophie, 36 (1936) 306-328, 477-493. For an example of the usual sterility of discussions on this point, Année théologique, 5 (1944) 311-334. Interesting remarks in J. Pépin, *Le problème de la communication des consciences chez Plotin et saint*

Augustin, Revue de métaphysique et de morale, 55 (1950) 128-148.

[34] The divine Ideas of equality, order, justice and, generally speaking, of righteousness under all its forms are the immutable rules of action just as the other Ideas are for things the causes of their natures and of their intelligibility. In this sense, there is a moral illumination as well as an intellectual one. Augustine speaks of the "lights of virtues" (*lumina virtutum*) in several texts; for instance, *De libero arbitrio,* II, 19, 52; PL., 32, 1268. Cf. II, 10, 29, 1256-1257. On this part of the doctrine: *Contra Julianum Pelagianum,* IV, 3, 17; PL., 44, 745. *Sermo* 341, 6, 8; PL., 39, 1498.

[35] The principle which dominates this position is the identity of "number" and "wisdom", whence there follows that moral life should be "ordered" according to the light of the same "eternal law" which has created the physical world according to number, weight and measure. See *Epistola 140,* 2, 4; PL., 33, 539. Cf. *De libero arbitrio,* I, 8, 18; PL., 32, 1231, and I, 15, 32; PL., 1238-1239. *In Joannis evangelium,* 19, 5, 12; PL., 35, 1549-1550.

[36] *De libero arbitrio,* II, 18, 48; PL., 32, 1266, and II, 18, 49-50; PL., 32, 1267-1268. Cf. *Retractationes,* I, 9, 6; PL., 32, 598.

[37] PELAGIUS, born in Great Britain *ca.* 350/54, died between 423/29. The best introduction is: G. de Plinval, *Pélage, ses écrits, sa vie et sa réforme,* Payot, Lausanne, 1943 (bibliography pp. 9-11). Same author, *Recherches sur l'oeuvre littéraire de Pélage,* Revue de philologie, 60 (1934) 9-42. C. Martini, *Quattuor fragmenta Pelagio restituenda,* Antonianum, 13 (1938) 293-334. G. de Plinval, *Vue d'ensemble sur la littérature pélagienne,* Revue des études latines, 29 (1951) 284-294. The essentials of Pelagius' position are summed up in ch. 13 of his *Libellus fidei:* "We say that it is always in man's power both to sin or not to sin, so that we may always be declared to have free will" (in G. de Plinval, *Pélage . . . ,* p. 310, n. 3). His doctrine was an effort to eliminate grace as a distinct gift added by God to free will. In other words, according to him, free will was grace, because it was the very gift by which God had made man capable of achieving his own salvation.

[38] On the various meanings of the words *liberum arbitrium* and *libertas,* see E. Gilson, *Introduction à l'étude de saint Augustin,* ch. III, 3. This important historical problem, which announces the later controversy between Molinism, and even Jansenism, plus the various theologies of the Reformers, cannot be discussed without actually taking sides in the dispute. Despite what has been objected to it, we still are of opinion that a beginner in search of an honest introduction to the problem, will find it in the article of Portalié, DTC., I (1923) 2375-2408.

[39] *De civitate Dei,* 19, 13; PL., 41, 640-641.—On the definition of nations as associations of men linked together by a common love: *De civitate Dei,* 19, 24; PL., 41, 655.—On peace as the common goal of all societies: *De civitate Dei,* 19, 12; PL., 41, 637-638.—The whole doctrine summed up in one sentence: *De civitate Dei,* 19, 131; PL., 41, 640.

[40] Main source: *De civitate Dei,* XIX; PL. 41, 621-658.—On the problems related to the *De civitate Dei,* see J. N. Figgis, *The Political Aspects of St. Augustine's City of God,* London, 1921 (bibliography, pp. 118-122).—On the place of the doctrine in history: H. Scholtz, *Glaube und Unglaube in der Weltgeschichte,* Leipzig, 1911. J. H. S. Burleigh, *The City of God, a Study of St. Augustine's Philosophy,* London, 1944. H. Eibl, *Augustinus von Götterreich zum Gottesstaat,* Freiburg i. Br., 1951. E. Gilson, *Les métamorphoses de la Cité de Dieu,* Louvain-Paris, 1952. A. Lauras and H. Rondet, *Le thème des deux cités dans l'oeuvre de saint Augustin,* Etudes augustiniennes, Paris, 1953, 99-160.

[41] R. Arnou, DTC., 12, 2294-2390; bibliography, 2390-2392.—On the Platonist elements in Saint Augustine, see Portalié, in DTC., I, 2327-2331. E. Ugarte de Ercilla, *El platonismo de S. Agustin,* Razon y Fè, 95 (1931) 365-378; 96 (1931) 182-189; 98 (1932) 102-118. E. Hoffmann, *Platonism in Augustine's Philosophy of History,* Philosophy and History (R. Klibansky and H. J. Paton edd.) Essays presented to Ernst Cassirer, Ox-

ford, Clarendon Press, 1936, pp. 173-190. B. Switalski, *Neoplatonism and the Ethics of St. Augustine*, New York, 1946. R. M.

Bushmann, *St. Augustine's Metaphysics and Stoic Doctrine*, NS., 26 (1952) 283-304.

PART THREE

CHAPTER II. END OF THE GREEK PATRISTIC AGE

[42] MACARIUS THE EGYPTIAN (*ca.* 300/395) is the supposed author of homilies which very few still consider authentic. The 50 *Homilies* are printed in Migne, PG., 34, 449-822. Seven homilies belonging to the same group have been added by G. L. Mariott, *Macarii Anecdota*, Cambridge, 1918. Even the date which we accept (fifth century) is not certain.—God is immaterial, but angels, demons and souls are material. Souls are subtle and invisible beings endowed with organs similar to those of their bodies (*Hom.* 4; 480 A). Yet souls are immortal (*Hom.* 5, 26; 492 D). These notions are casual remarks, incidental to the main theme, which is moral and ascetic life. The same downright materialism is found in the treatise *De elevatione mentis*, ch. 6; 894 C D, which seems to be an excerpt from *Homily* 4, quoted above.—See O. Bardenhewer, *Patrology*, 266-268. E. Amann, art. *Macaire d'Egypte*, DTC., 9 (1927) 1452-1455. W. Jaeger, *Two Rediscovered Works of Ancient Christian Literature: Gregory of Nyssa* and *Macarius*, Leiden, E. J. Brill, 1954, pp. 145-230; Greek text of the new *Great Letter*, 233-301.—BET., 2598-2600.

[43] SYNESIUS (*ca.* 370/75, d. after 413), studied at Alexandria where he was introduced to neoplatonism by a young woman famed for her learning, Hypatia, with whom he always remained on friendly terms. In 409, as he was invited to become Bishop of Ptolemais (perhaps before being a Christian), Synesius accepted under two conditions: that he would be compelled neither to dismiss his wife, nor to give up his philosophical convictions even though they might clash with the teaching of other theologians. This was accepted and he was consecrated a bishop. Works in PG., 66; 1053-1626. His *Hymns* and *Letters* show a man strongly influenced by neoplatonism but animated by genuine Christian feelings. The God of Synesius is the "monad of monads," the "principle of principles," the "number of numbers," the "one and all" and "the one of all" (*Hymn* 3; PG., 66, 1596). God is both One and Triune, and from him minds are born. After descending into matter, each soul has to make an effort to extricate itself and to rise again up to its source, where it will be god in God. Pre-existence of souls, *Hymn* 3; 1603.—Liberation of the souls from matter, *Hymn* 5; 1607-1608. Cf. 1609).—The letter 57, PG., 66, 1384-1400 is revealing concerning his general attitude as a philosopher and a Christian. Cf. letter 103; 1475 A B; Letter 136; 1525-1528, and Letter 153, to Hypatia, especially 1536.—Bibliography. G. Bardy, DTC., 14 (1941) 2296-3002. C. Lacombrade, *Synésios de Cyrène, hellène et Chrétien*, Paris, Les Belles-Lettres, 1951.—BET., 3545-3548.

[44] THEODORET OF CYRUS (*ca.* 390-458). Works in PG., 80-84. Among his many writings is a curious treatise, entitled *Cure for Greek Maladies, or the Discovery of the Evangelical Truth Beginning from Greek Philosophy* (PG., 83, 783-1152). The general intention of the work is the same as that of Eusebius' *Praeparatio evangelica*, namely, to show that the teaching of Christianity has been foreshadowed by the best among the Greeks; the very best, was, of course, Plato. There is a harmony between "the old theology and the new," and we may say with Numenius, according to Eusebius' quotation: "Who is this Plato, if not a Moses that speaks Greek?" And no wonder, since Plato borrowed many doctrines from Moses. This whole treatise, in which the *Miscellanies* of Clement and the *Evangelical Preparation* of Eusebius are often put to use, concludes the series of the apologies written by Christians in order to convince pagans that Christianity was the fulfillment of Greek philosophy at its best. See O. Bardenhewer, *Patrology*, 370-376. G. Bardy, art. *Théodoret*, DTC., 15 (1946) 299-325. I. Mon-

talverne OFM., *Theodoreti Cyrensis doctrina antiquior de Verbo "inhumanato"* (*a. circiter 423-435*), Romae, Pontificium Studium Antonianum, 1948 (Studia Antoniana, I). M. F. A. Brok, *De waarde van de Graecarum affectionum curatio van Theodoretus van Cyrus als apologetisch Werk,* Studia Catholica, 27 (1952) 201-212.—BET., 3607-3608.

[45] DENIS THE AREOPAGITE (Dionysius Aeropagita, Pseudo-Denis, Pseudo-Dionysius) introduces himself as a disciple of Saint Paul, present at the death of the Blessed Virgin Mary; was identified with the Denis of Act. 17, 34; then with the founder of the abbey of S. Denis, near Paris.—In fact, there is no reason to suppose that the works attributed to him were written before the middle of the fifth century (Corn. de Bye, *De scriptis quae sub Dionysii nomine circumferuntur,* Acta sanctorum Octobris, Paris, Palmé, 1866; IV, 802-855). There is an abundant controversial literature on the origin of these writings.—The *Corpus Areopagiticum* includes: On the Celestial Hierarchy (*De divina hierarchia*), On the Ecclesiastical Hierarchy (*De ecclesiastica Hierarchia*), On Divine Names (*De divinis nominibus*); On mystical theology (*De mystica theologia*), and ten Letters. Text in PG., 3 and 4, with Lat. transl. Synoptic edition of the Greek text with four mediaeval Latin translations (Hilduin, Erigena, Joa. Saracenus, R. Grosseteste) by Ph. Chevallier, *Dionysiaca,* 2 vols., Paris, Desclée, 1937. French transl. by P. de Gandillac, *Oeuvres complètes du pseudo-Denys l'Aréopagite,* Paris, 1943. Engl. transl. of *On the Divine Names* and *The Mystical Theology* by C. E. Rolt, SPCK., 1920.—BET., 1000, 1287-1293.

BIBLIOGRAPHY. Up to 1908, O. Bardenhewer, *Patrology,* 535-541. Articles of J. Stiglmayr listed in GDP., 667-668.—J. Stiglmayr has proposed the end of the fifth century as a probable date: Scholastik, 3 (1928) 1-27; this conclusion is generally accepted, but not his identification of Denis with Severus of Antioch. A more recent attempt to place the Corpus in the second half of the fourth century has failed to carry conviction: J. Lebon, *Le pseudo-Aréopagite et Sévère d'Antioche,* RHE., 26 (1930) 880-915; *Encore le pseudo-Denys l'Aréopagite,* RHE., 28 (1932) 296-313. C. Pera OP., *Denys le Mystique et la*

theomakhia, RSPT., 25 (1936) 5-75.—On the doctrine, H. F. Müller, *Dionysios, Proklos und Plotinos,* Münster i.W., 1918 (Beiträge, 20, 3-4). E. van Ivànka, *Der Aufbau der Schrift "De divinis nominibus" des Pseudo-Dionysios,* Scholastik, 15 (1940) 386-399. The following scheme is suggested for this work: 1) the Good, 2) entity, life, wisdom (i.e., the triad of Proclus); 3) wisdom, power, peace (i.e., the "Constantinian" triad; cf. Gregory of Nyssa); 4) the notions borrowed from Plato's *Parmenides;* 5) the Perfect and the One. The relation of the *Corpus dionysiacum* to the theology of Gregory of Nyssa (*De perfecta christiani forma,* PG., 46, 251-286) is one of the most important conclusions of this article, pp. 395-396.— O. Semmelroth, *Gottes geeinte Vielheit. Zur Gotteslehre des Ps.—Dionysius Areopagita,* Scholastik, 25 (1950) 389-403. H. F. Dondaine, OP., *Le Corpus Dionysien de l'Université de Paris au XIIIe siècle,* Rome, 1952. O. Semmelroth, *Die Lehre des Ps.—Dionysius Areopagita vom Aufstieg der Kreatur zum göttlichen Licht,* Scholastik, 29 (1954) 24-52.

[46] *De div. nom.,* I, 5; PG., 3, 593.— Denis uses the expression: "the philosophy according to us" (i.e., to us Christians), and also the word "theosophy" (i.e., wisdom about God) to designate the knowledge of God which rests upon Scripture: *De div. nom.,* II, 2; PG., 3, 640 A.—On the names given by Scripture to God: *De div. nom.,* I, 6; PG., 3, 596.

[47] *De myst. theol.,* I, 2-3; PG., 3, 1000-1001.—Note, at the end of I, 3, how this theological method directly introduces to mystical speculation. All the themes that were to become classic in Christian mysticism (darkness of unknowing, contemplation above the passive stillness of reason, etc.) are already present.

[48] *De div. nom.,* IV, 3; PG., 3, 697. On the universal circulation of the Good, *De div. nom.,* IV, 4; PG., 4, 697-700. *De coel. hier.,* I., 1; PG., 3, 120-121.— V. Lossky, *La notion des "Analogies" chez Denys le Pseudo-Aréopagite,* AHDL., 5 (1930) 279-309.

[49] Doctrine summed up in *De div. nom.,* IV, 2; PG., 3, 696 (note, 696 C, a lost treatise *De anima*).—Why the common representation of angels should be purified, *De coel. hier.,* II, 2; PG., 3, 140.—

What is "hierarchy," *De coel. hier.*, III, 1; PG., 3, 164.—Its functions, *De coel. hier.*, III, 2; PG., 3, 165. *De eccl. hier.*, I, 3; PG., 3, 373-376.—On this notion, so important for the history of mediaeval thought, see R. Roques, *La notion de hiérarchie selon le Pseudo-Denys*, AHDL., 17 (1949), 183-222; 18 (1950-1951), 5-44.

[50] God as "Hyper-Entity," *De div. nom.*, I, 5; PG., 3, 593 B.—God, as cause of beings, is no being, *De div. nom.*, I, 5; PG., 3, 593 C.—God is infinite being, *De div. nom.*, V, 4; PG., 3, 817. Cf. III, 1; PG., 3, 680 B C.—Being is the first of all participations in God, *De div. nom.*, V, 6; PG., 3, 820.—In this sense, God is all, inasmuch as he is the cause of all, but he is no one of all beings, *De div. nom.*, V, 8; PG., 3, 824, B C.—God compared with the sun, *De div. nom.*, V, 8; PG., 3, 824 C.

[51] Following the example of Plotinus, Denis deals with the Ideas in the same texts where he deals with being, because to be and to be intelligible are one and the same thing. On Ideas, *De div. nom.*, V, 7; PG., 3, 821.—On their various names, *De div. nom.*, V, 8; PG., 3, 824 C. —God is above the Ideas, *De div. nom.*, V, 8; PG., 3, 824 B.—God knows all things as the cause of all being and of all knowledge, *De div. nom.*, VII, 2; PG., 3, 869 B C.

[52] *De div. nom.*, V, 6; PG., 3, 820-821. —God as love is the unifying force of all, *De div. nom.*, IV, 12; PG., 3, 709 D.—On the ecstatic power of love, *De div. nom.*, IV, 13; PG., 3, 712.—Hence the return of all things to God, *De div. nom.*, IV, 14; PG., 3, 712-713.

[53] God is the One, *De div. nom.*, I, 5; PG., 3, 593 B.—God is the supreme and all-inclusive unity, *De div. nom.*, I, 4; PG., 3, 589. II, 11; PG., 3, 649 B.—God is the One who is above unity, *De div. nom.*, II, 1; PG., 3, 637 A.—Not to know God is the highest knowledge of God, *De div. nom.*, VII, 3; PG., 872 B.—*De mystica theologia*, II; PG., 3, 1025 and V; PG., 3, 1045-1048.

[54] *De div. nom.*, I, 3; PG., 3, 589.

[55] MAXIMUS THE CONFESSOR (or of Chrysopolis, now Scutari) born *ca.* 580, died Aug. 13, 662.—Works in PG., 90-91. Notes or commentaries on Denis, PG., 4,

15-432. Commentaries *On Several Difficult Passages in Denis and Gregory* (Nazianzenus), PG., 91, 1031-1060; *Ambiguities in Saint Gregory the Theologian* (Nazianzenus) PG., 91, 1061-1418. Less important, his short treatise *On the Soul* handles the questions that "are usually asked" on this matter: existence of the soul, substantiality, incorporeity, immortality, rationality.—BIBLIOGRAPHY, up to 1908, O. Bardenhewer, *Patrology*, 576-580. J. Draeseke, *Maximus Confessor und Johannes Scotus Erigena*, TSK., 84 (1911) 20-60, 204-229. V. Grumel, art. *Maxime de Chrysopolis*, DTC., 10 (1928) 448-459. J. Pegon, *Maxime le Confesseur, Centuries sur la Charité*, Introduction and French translation, Paris, 1945. H. Urs von Balthasar, *Liturgie cosmique. Maxime le Confesseur*, Paris, 1947. I. H. Dalmais, *La théorie des "logoï" des créatures chez S. Maxime le Confesseur*, RSPT., 36 (1952) 244-249. I. Hausherr SJ., *Philautie. De la tendresse pour soi à la charité selon saint Maxime le Confesseur*, Roma, 1952.

[56] On the sources of Maximus Confessor, see Viller, *Aux Sources de la spiritualité de saint Maxime*, RAM., 1 (1930) 156-184, 239-268, 331-336: stresses the influence of Evagrius Ponticus (an Origenist, *ca.* 345-399; O. Bardenhewer, *Patrology*, 309-310).—H. Urs von Balthasar, *Das Scholienwerk des Johannes von Scythopolis*, Scholastik, 15 (1940) 16-39. The author notes that John of Scythopolis uses the words *eidè* and *ideai* to designate the divine Ideas (in which he differs from Maximus): pp. 31-32. On the philosophical formation of John, pp. 35-36.

[57] All the following references are to the commentaries of Maximus on the *Divine Names*, PG., 4. God is beyond the reach of geometrical and of dialectical methods, 185 B. He is the object of an un-knowledge which is loftier than knowledge, 216-220; cf. 224 D.—God is above being: 185 C—188 A; 316-320 (Exod, 3, 14); 412 B C. God is "nothing," 204 D— 205 A. God is an unthinkable Thought; hence he is "infinite": 189-192 and 369 D. God is the absolutely simple unity: 189 B C.—On the infinity of God: *Ambigua*, PG., 91, 1232 B.

[58] *Ambigua*, PG., 91, 1036.—Motion and rest in God, *Div. Names*, PG., 4, 323 A

D. Cf. 256 C-257 D, and 333 C D.—To move is to know: *Coel. hierar.*, PG., 4, 73 A B.

[59] *Ambigua*, PG., 91, 1077 C-1085 A.— On the divine Ideas: *Div. Names*, PG., 4, 260 C and 329-332. Cf. *Ambigua*, PG., 91, 1085 A C.—Simplicity of the divine wisdom, *Coel, hier*, PG., 4, 109 A B.— Multiplication in God, *Div. Names*, PG., 4, 232 B-233 A. Cf. 240 B D.—How things emanate from God: *Div. Names*, PG., 4, 320 B-322 B. Cf. 324 A D, and 305 C-309 B C. *Coel. hier.*, PG., 4, 101 B. *Eccl. hier.*, PG., 4, 172-173 (against Origen).—Evil is non-being, *Div. Names*, PG., 4, 273 B-275 C and 292 B.—Matter is non-being, but not evil: *Div. Names*, PG., 4, 297 C-300 D.—Nature as divine art, *Div. Names*, PG., 4, 296 B. Cf. 301 C D.—All that is not God is finite: 1180 B-1188 C.—Against the pre-existence of souls, *Ambigua*, PG., 91, 1326 D-1336 B. —Against that of bodies, *Ambigua*, PG., 91, 1336 C-1341 C.

[60] *Ambigua*, PG., 91, 1072 A-1085 A. Cf. 1154 A C; 1304 D-1308 C; 1309 A-1312 B; 1358 D-1361 A.

[61] AENEAS OF GAZA (Syria) *ca.* 460/530) has written the dialogue: *Theophrastus, or On the Immortality of the Soul and the Resurrection of the Body*. Printed in PG., 85, 871-1004; re-edited by J. Fr. Boissonade, Paris, 1836.—On his doctrine, see G. Schalkhauser, *Aeneas von Gaza als Philosoph* (Inaug.-Dissert.), Erlangen, 1898. The main topics touched by Aeneas are: Against the transmigration of souls, PG., 85, 877 C-900 C.—Against the pre-existence of souls, 900 C-905 B.—How man is responsible for his own destiny, 916 A-941 A. —Why God still creates souls, 945 B-950 A.—Immortality of rational beings, 949 B-952 A.—Definition of the soul, 952 A B.—Matter is created (against Plotinus), 958 C-965 B.—Goodness of the works of God, 966 C-974 B.—On resurrection, 974 C-1001 B.

[62] ZACHARIUS RHETOR (or Zacharius Scholasticus), Bishop of Mitylene (Lesbos) died before 553. His dialogue: *Ammonius* (or *De mundi opificio*), is found in PG., 85, 1012-1144; reedited by J. Fr. Boissonade, Paris, 1836. Develops in a more rhetorical way than the dialogue of Aeneas, the Christian notion of creation, and justifies it against the objections of the neoplatonists.—BET., 3832 (Syriac chronicle).

[63] JOHANNES PHILOPONUS (or Johannes Grammaticus, John the Grammarian); dates of birth and of death unknown; he certainly lived in the sixth century and seems to have died about 580.—WORKS. Two of his theological writings are of philosophical interest: 1, *De opificio mundi libri* VII, ed. by G. Reichardt, Leipzig, Teubner, 1897; 2, *De aeternitate mundi contra Proclum*, ed. by H. Rabe, Leipzig, Teubner, 1899. His commentaries on Aristotle have been published in the *Commentaria in Aristotelem Graeca*, ed. by the Berlin Academy: vol. XIII, *In Categorias, In Analytica Priora, In Analytica Posteriora.*—vol. XIV, *In Meteora, De generatione et corruptione, De generatione animalium* (Michael of Ephesus).— vol. XV, *De anima.*—vols. XVI—XVII, *In libros Physicorum.*—The *De anima* published in vol. XV differs from the Greek text translated into Latin by William of Moerbeke about 1268; the third Book, at least, should be read in its mediaeval Latin translation, which represents the authentic work of Philoponus: M. de Corte, *Le commentaire de Jean Philopon sur le Troisième livre du "Traité de l'Ame" d'Aristote*, Liège, 1934 (includes the commentaries on ch. IV-VIII in their mediaeval Latin translation). A. Mansion, *Le texte du "De intellectu" de Philopon corrigé à l'aide de la collation de Mgr Pelzer*, MAP., 325-346 (emendations to M. de Corte's edition). —BIBLIOGRAPHY. Theological writings, O. Bardenhewer, *Patrology*, 544. Philosophical writings, Ueberwegs, *Grundriss*, I, 643; II, 123. On the scientific doctrines of Philoponus, P. Tannery, *Notes critiques sur le traité de l'astrolabe de Philopon*, Revue de Philologie, 12 (1888) 60-73. P. Tannery, *Sur la période finale de la philosophie grecque*, Revue philosophique, 42 (1896) 272-275. P. Duhem, *Le système du monde*, I, 313-321, 351-356, 361-371; II, 494-501.—BET., 2270 (astrolabe).

[64] The more interesting of these two treatises is the second one, *On the Eternity of the World;* Latin translation by G. M. Montagnensis, *Libri duodeviginti Adversus totidem Procli successoris rationes de mundi aeternitate*, Venice, 1551. In the Greek original and in the Latin

translation, the text is divided into eighteen questions, each of which is subdivided into chapters. God is infinite, as appears from the infinity of his action, I, ch. 2-3 (Aristotle); the relation of light to the sun is not that of the world to God, ch. 6-8; the Ideas are in God, II, ch. 5 (Plotinus); why God has not always exercised his power, III, ch. 2 (uses the twofold distinction of act and potency in Aristotle); on God's immutability, IV, ch. 2 (Aristotle versus Proclus); on divine providence, IV, ch. 14 (Plato); the existence of the world adds nothing to the perfection of God, IV, ch. 17 (Plotinus); on eternity and time, V, ch. 4; the world has been produced, VI, ch. 7 (Plato), cf. ch. 12-13, 18, 19, 20; Plato should not be preferred to truth, IX, ch. 1 (Aristotle); on Plato's errors, IX, ch. 3, 4; that matter and material forms are created, IX, ch. 13, 15, 17; on the unity of prime matter, XI, ch. 1-8; Plato does not say that matter is eternal, XI, ch. 13; it is false that all that is produced presupposes a matter, XII, ch. 1, 3; on the relation of the world to its intelligible model, XV, ch. 3; on the unity of the divine will, XVI, 1-2, 4; cf. XVIII, ch. 2; Plato has often followed the fables of the poets rather than philosophical reasons, XVIII, 8 and 10.

[65]Commentary on *De amina*, Bk. III, ch. 5; ed by M. de Corte, 29-38.—On the immortality of the soul, 41-42.

[66] Criticism of Aristotle's notions of "place" and of "emptiness," Duhem, *Le système du monde*, I, 313-320.—On the motion of projectiles, Duhem, *Le système du monde*, I, 380-384 (Philoponus as forerunner of XIV-century dynamics and thereby of modern science).—On possible forerunners of Philoponus on this point, same work, I, 385-388.—On the influence of Philoponus, P. Duhem, *Etudes sur Léonard de Vinci*, II, 189-193 (Nicolas de Cues); III, 34, 62 (Buridan), 256 (Ramus).

[67] JOHN DAMASCENE (John of Damascus, Johannes Damascenus). Dates of birth and death unknown; entered the monastery of St. Saba (Jerusalem) after 730; was ordained a priest in the same monastery and probably died there. His main work is *The Source of Knowledge,* whose third part: *Exact Exposition of the Orthodox Faith* was called *De fide ortho-*doxa by the Scholastics. Text in PG., 94, 517-1228. Bibliography up to 1928 in GDP. 668-669.—The *De fide orthodoxa* became known to the Latins through its translation (*ca.* 1148-1150) by Burgundio Pisano: L. Callari, *Contributo allo studio della versione di Burgundio Pisano del "De orthodoxa fide" di Giovanni Damasceno,* Atti del Reale Istituto Veneto di scienze, lettre ed arti, Venice, 1941, 217-218, 236-239. A partial Latin translation, by Cerbanus has preceded that of Burgundio; R. L. Szigeti, *Translatio latina Joannis Damasceni (De orthodoxa fide l. III, c. 1-8) saeculo XII in Hungaria confecta,* Budapest, 1940; probable date of the transl., 1134-1138. Text more easily accessible in E. M. Buytaert, *The Earliest Latin Translation of Damascene's De orthodoxa fide III, 1-8,* Franciscan Studies, 11 (1951) 49-67. Cf. N. M. Haring SAC., *The First Traces of the So-called Cerbanus Translation of St. John Damascene De fide orthodoxa, III, 1-8,* MS. 12 (1950) 214-216.

On the doctrine: J. Langen, *Johannes von Damascus,* Gotha, 1879. J. H. Lupton, *St. John of Damascus,* London, 1884. V. Ermoni, *Saint Jean Damascène,* Paris, 1904 (selected texts in French transl.). M. Jugie, art. *Jean Damascène (saint),* DTC., 8 (1924) 663-751 (excellent).—Engl. transl. NPN., 9; N. Y. 1899.

[68] This first part is often called *Dialectica;* its correct title is *Philosophical Chapters.* It is a short encyclopedia that makes claim to no originality (PG., 94, 533 A). Definition and division of philosophy (ch. 3; PG., 94, 533-536). Being, substance and accident (ch. 4; PG., 94, 536-540). The rest of these chapters gives a summary exposition of the main notions studied in logic: genus and species, difference, predication, etc. Entity (*ousia*) and nature are defined first according to the "philosophers beyond the pale," next according to the "Holy Fathers" (ch. 30; PG., 94, 589-596); cf. ch. 39, on substance, and ch. 40, on nature (PG., 94, 605-608). On person, ch. 43, PG., 94, 613. After a study of the categories (ch. 49-59), John of Damascus concludes by a short exposition of the syllogism: ch. 64; PG., 94, 653-657.

[69] The notion of heresy, wider than it now is, includes the doctrines of the Platonists, Stoics and Epicureans, PG., 94, 684.

⁷⁰ Unless otherwise indicated, the following references are to *De fide orthodoxa*, I, PG., 94.—Attributes of God: uncreated, immutable, infinite, etc., ch. 2, 792-793.—Demonstration of his existence from the mutability of things, from their conservation, from their order (against Epicurus), ch. 3, 794-797.—Infinity and incomprehensibility of God, ch. 4, 797 B C, 800 B; ch. 9, 836 (God is "He Who Is," i.e., an infinite ocean of being).—Oneness of God, ch. 5, 800-801. —The names of God say either what he is not, or a certain relation to what is not God, ch. 9, 833 B-836 A; ch. 12, 844-845. —A more complete demonstration of the oneness of God is to be found in the *Dialogue Against the Manicheans*, PG., 94, 1505-1584.

⁷¹ The following references are to *De fide orthodoxa*, II; PG., 94: cosmography (heaven, light stars, air, waters, seas, earth, earthly paradise), ch. 5-11; PG., 94, 880-917.—Man, created innocent of sin and free; ch. 12, 924 A.—The soul, whose purest part is the mind (ch. 12, 924 B), is incorporeal by the grace of God (926 A); its faculties, 928 B-929A; and ch. 18-21.—The footnotes to the text printed in Migne are full of references to the patristic sources of John Damascene. These references are useful to place his work in its proper light. The *De fide orthodoxa* does not represent a sudden invasion of theology by philosophy, but a moment in the continuous development of Christian speculation.

⁷² The will (*thélèsis*) is defined in accordance with Nemesius as a natural, vital and rational appetite: II, 22; PG., 94, 944 B. Its act is volition (*boulèsis*). Its object is the end, not the means, 945 A B. These are the object of deliberation, followed by a judgment of the intellect and concluded by a decision. Then the will makes its choice (*proairesis*). There is an appetite in beasts, but since it is not rational, it is not free; hence it is not a

will: 945 B C. In God, there is a will, but no deliberation, 945 C D. (On these distinctions, cf. 948 C-949 A).—On "voluntary" and "non-voluntary," II, 24, PG., 94, 952-956. On free choice (*liberum arbitrium*) ch. 25-28, 956-961. On providence and predestination ch. 29-30, 964-979. Most of these notions are borrowed from Nemesius, Maximus or Gregory Nazianzenus rather than directly from Aristotle. John Damascene is here collecting and ordering philosophical notions scattered throughout the writings of his predecessors.—O. Lottin, PEM., 393-424.

⁷³ On the so-called "Platonism of the Fathers," see R. Arnou, S.J., *Platonisme des Pères*, DTC., 12 (1925) 2258-2392 (excellent); to be completed by the selected texts edited and annotated by the same author: *De "platonismo" Patrum*, Pontificia Universitas Gregoriana, Rome, 1935.—See also J. Stiglmayr, *Kirchenväter und Klassizismus*, Freiburg i. Breisg., 1913. R. Klibanski, *The Continuity of the Platonic Tradition During the Middle Ages, Outline of a Corpus Platonicorum Medii Aevi*, London, 1939. General views on the question in E. Gilson, *Le christianisme et la tradition philosophique*, RSPT., 1941/42, pp. 249-266. It would not be difficult to write a chapter on the "anti-Platonism" of the Fathers. Most of them have denied, against Plato, that matter is eternal; that God is a mere "demiurge," not a true creator; that the Ideas are eternal entities subsisting in themselves apart from God; that human souls are immortal by nature; that souls pre-exist to bodies; that there is a transmigration of the soul from body to body, etc. Naturally, since Plato himself has not always said the same things, for instance in the *Phaedo* and in the *Timaeus*, a Greek Father of the Church could sometimes hesitate in his judgment or even in his interpretation, but, by and large, they have less followed Plato than reacted to him in a predominantly Christian way.

PART THREE

CHAPTER III.   END OF THE LATIN PATRISTIC AGE

⁷⁴ MARTIANUS CAPELLA, not a Christian, wrote between 400 and 439 his *De nuptiis Mercurii et Philologiae*, or *The Marriage of Mercury and Philology*. Ed.

by Ad. Dick, *Martianus Capella*, Leipzig, Teubner, 1925. This allegorical treatise has been widely spread in mediaeval schools. See, M. Guggenheim, *Die Stel-*

lung der liberalen Künste oder encyklischen Wissenschaften im Altertum, Zürich, 1893. G. Meier, *Die sieben freien Künste im Mittelalter,* Einsiedeln, 1885. P. Monceaux, *Les Africains,* Paris, 1894, 445-458. —Martianus' treatise deals with the "encyclopaedic arts" (*disciplinas cyclicas,* IX, ed. A. Dick, p. 534). Grammar, lib. III; Dialectics, lib. IV; Rhetoric, lib. V (the future *Trivium*); Geometry, lib, VI; Arithmetic, lib. VII; Astronomy, lib. VIII; Music (*Harmonia*), lib. IX (the future *Quadrivium*). On the history of the Trivium and Quadrivium, see St. d'Irsay, *Histoire des Universités françaises et étrangères des origines jusqu'à nos jours,* 2 vols., Paris, 1933, 1935; I, 34-38. Powicke and Emden, *Rashdall's Mediaeval Universities,* Oxford Press, 1936, v. I, 34-37; especially 34, note 2.

[75] FAUSTUS OF RIEZ (Faustus of Reii) now Riez (Provence), born in Brittany, abbot of Lérins (433), Bishop of Riez (452); exiled *ca.* 478 for his opposition to Arianism; returned to Riez in 485; date of death unknown. Ancient edition PL., 58, 783-890 and 53, 681-683; critical edition by Aug. Engelbrecht, *Fausti Reiiensis, praeter sermones pseudo-Eusebianos, Opera,* CSEL., Wien, 1891, vol. XXI.—O. Bardenhewer, *Patrology,* 600-603. A. Koch, *Der hl. Faustus, Bischof von Riez, eine dogmengeschichtliche Monographie,* Stuttgart, 1895. A. C. Elg, *In Faustum Reiensem studia,* Upsala, 1937. M. Chastaing, *Descartes, Fauste de Riez et le problème de la connaissance d'autrui,* Rencontres, 30 (1949), Paris, Editions du Cerf, 187-211. J. Huhn, *De ratione fidei als ein Werk des Faustus von Reji,* TQ., 130 (1950) 176-183 (not in PL.). *Epistola,* ed. Engelbrecht, 171-178; corporeity of angels, 178-180; God alone is incorporeal, 180-181; the source of Faustus is Cassian, *Collationes* VII, 13; ed. Petschenig, CSEL., II, 192.—Cf. *Epistola* 5, ed. Engelbrecht, 188, 18-189, 19. On *spiritus* and *anima,* 191, 10-193, 4.

[76] CLAUDIANUS MAMERTUS, a priest of Vienne (France) died *ca.* 474. *De statu animae,* PL., 53, 697-780; better text in A. Engelbrecht, *Claudiani Mamerti opera,* CSEL., Wien, 1885, vol. XI.—A. C. Germain, *De Mamerti Claudiani scriptis et philosophia,* Montpellier, 1840. R. de la Broise, *Mamerti Claudiani vita ejusque doctrina de anima hominis,* Paris, 1890. M. Schulte, *Die Schrift des Claudianus*

Mamertus, Presbyters zu Vienna, De statu animae, im Auszuge mit kritischen Bemerkungen, Dresden, 1883. F. Zimmermann, *Des Claudianus Mamertus Schrift De statu animae libri tres,* DTF., II. Serie, I (1914) 238-255, 333-368, 470-495. F. Böhmer, *Der lateinische Neuplatonismus und Neupythagorismus und Claudianus Mamertus in Sprache und Philosophie,* Leipzig, 1936; cf. R. Beutler, Gnomon, 13 (1937) 552-558.

[77] The following references indicate the book and the chapter in the text of the *De statu animae,* followed by the pages in Engelbrecht's edition; for instance, I, 3; 26, signifies: Bk. I, ch. 3; page 26.— On the possibility of incorporeal creatures, I, 10-11; 50-52.—The soul must be incorporeal because it is an image of God, I, 5; 40.—On the difference between "incorporeal" and "invisible," I, 6; 41-44. —And between *incorporeum* and *incorporatum,* II, 3; 106.—Matter is not nothing, III, 7; 165-166.

[78]*De statu animae,* I, 14; 58-59.

[79] *De statu animae,* I, 16; 61-62. This introduces an analysis of three kinds of motion: *stabilis motus,* which is that of God creating and conserving the world; *inlocalis motus,* the non-local motion, which is that of the soul moving its body in time without itself being moved in space; *localis motus,* the local motion of bodies in both time and space: I, 18; 64-68. God escapes all the categories of Aristotle; the soul is subjected to the category of quality, not of quantity: I, 19-20; 68-71.—Life is incorporeal even in corporeal beings, I, 21; 74.—Following Augustine, Claudianus proves the immateriality of the soul by the vastness of memory, I, 22; 80-81; then by the nature of intellection, I, 23; 81-83; then by the resemblance of the soul to God, I, 26; 94-97. Cf. II, 2; 103-104 and III, 11; 172-176. Note, III, 12; 176-178, the curious doctrine of those who said that the soul was incorporeal to itself, but corporeal to God.

[80] Claudianus praises the soul of Plato, too great to be corporeal, II, 7; 122.— Definition of the soul as immortal and cause of motion (from *Phaedrus,* 245 C) II, 7; 123. Long quotation from *Phaedo,* 66 B-67 A: II, 7; 125-127 (Claudianus mentions *Laches, Protagoras,* the *Banquet,*

Alcibiades, Gorgias, Crito, Timaeus, as other sources of the same doctrine: II, 7; 127-128).

[81] *De statu animae,* Epilog.; 196. Cf. II, 2; 103.

[82] BOETHIUS. Manlius Severinus Boethius, born *ca.* 480; studied philosophy in Athens; minister to King Theodoric (510); disgraced for political reasons, sentenced to death and executed in 524 or 525. The *Consolation of Philosophy* was written by Boethius while he was in jail.—On his philosophical formation, R. Bonnaud, *L'éducation scientifique de Boèce,* Speculum 4 (1929) 198-206.

The writings of Boethius are divided into four groups:

1) Logic: two commentaries on the *Isagoge* of Porphyry, one on the translation by Marius Victorinus, another on a new translation by Boethius; translation of Aristotle's *Perihermeneias* (*De interpretatione*), with two commentaries, one for beginners, another one for advanced readers; translations of Aristotle's *Prior Analytics, Posterior Analytics, Sophistic Arguments* and *Topics.* These four translations will remain unknown up to the middle of the twelfth century; after their discovery, they will constitute the "new logic" (*logica nova*) as opposed to the "old logic" (*logica vetus*).—2) Sciences: the *Arithmetic* (*Institutio arithmetica*) and the *Music* (*Institutio musica*) are adaptations of Greek originals by Nicomachus of Gerasa; he certainly wrote a *Geometry,* after Euclid, but the treatise now printed under his name is perhaps not the true one (MAN., I, 28).—3) The *Consolation of Philosophy* (quoted as CP.,) certainly authentic and his masterpiece; although strictly philosophical, its Christian inspiration cannot be doubted (Scripture, Origen, Augustine are used, though not quoted).—4) Theological tractates: *De sancta Trinitate, Utrum Pater et Filius et Spiritus Sanctus de divinitate substantialiter praedicentur. De persona et duabus naturis in Christo. Quomodo substantiae, in eo quod sint, bonae sint cum non sint substantialia bona* (commonly called, after Boethius himself, PL., 64, 1311 A: *De Hebdomadibus*). The authenticity of these treatises is generally accepted since the discovery of a text of Cassiodorus attributing four of them to Boethius (MAN., I, 35).— Spurious works: *On Catholic Faith* is doubtful, E. K. Rand, *Der dem Boethius zugeschriebene Traktat De fide catholica,* Jahrbücher für klassische Philologie, 26, 1901, Supplementband; in his later edition of the text (Loeb Clas. Libr. I, 52) Rand has withdrawn his own objections, but without decisive reasons. The *De unitate et uno* belongs to Gundissalinus: P. Correns, *Die dem Boethius zugeschriebene Abhandlung des Dominici Gundissalvi de Unitate,* Münster i. W., 1891 (Beiträge, I, 1). The *De definitione* seems to belong to Marius Victorinus: H. Usener, *Anecdota Holderi,* Bonn, 1877, 59-66.

EDITIONS. Uncritical edition of the complete works in PL., 63-64. The Latin translations of *Analytica priora, Analytica posteriora, Topica, Sophistici elenchi* (PL., 64, 639-672; 609 ff; 1007 ff) cannot be safely used under their present form: M. Grabmann, *Aristoteles im zwölften Jahrhundert,* MS., 12 (1950) 124. On the contrary, the text of the *Posterior Analytics,* as printed in the Basel edition of 1546, is the translation by Boethius, not by James of Venice: C. H. Haskins, *Studies in the History of Mediaeval Science,* Cambridge, Mass., 1924, pp. 231-232.—*Arithmetic, Music, Geometry,* G. Friedlein, Leipzig, 1867. *Perihermeneias,* C. Meiser, Leipzig, 2 vols., 1877, 1880. *In Isagogen Porphyrii Commenta,* Schepss & Brandt, CSEL., 48, Wien, 1906.—*De consolatione philosophiae,* A. a Forti Scuto (Fortescue) London, 1925. English transl. of the *Consolation* by H. R. James, London-New York, 1906 (New Universal Library). English transl. of Bk. IV-V by A. C. Pegis, *The Wisdom of Catholicism,* 161-202.—*Theological Tractates,* text and English transl. by H. F. Stewart and E. K. Rand, London—New York, 1918 (Loeb Classical Library). R. McKeon, *The Second Edition of the Commentaries on the Isagoge of Porphyry,* in *Selections,* N. Y. 1928, I, 70-99.—BET., 705-717.

BIBLIOGRAPHY. L. Cooper, *A Concordance of Boethius. The Five Theological Tractates and the Consolation of Philosophy,* Cambridge (Mass.) 1928.—Aug. Hildebrand, *Boethius und seine Stellung zum Christentum,* Regensburg, 1883. K. Bruder, *Die philosophische Elemente in der "Opuscula sacra" des Boethius,* Leipzig, 1928. H. J. Brosch, *Der Seinsbegriff bei Boethius,* Innsbruck, 1931. R. Carton, *Le christianisme et l'augustinisme dé Boèce,* Mélanges augustiniens, Paris, Rivière, 1931, 243-299. On his Greek sources: J. Bidez, *Boèce et Porphyre,* Revue belge de philologie et d'histoire, 1 (1923) 189-201. P. Courcelle, *Boèce et l'Ecole d'Alexandrie*, Mélanges de l'Ecole française de Rome, 52 (1935) 185-223; *Les lettres grecques en Occident de Macrobe à Cassiodore*, Paris, 1943, pp. 257-312. Influence of Boethius: H. R. Patch, *The Tradition of Boethius. A Study of His Importance in Mediaeval Culture*, New York, 1935. P. Courcelle, *Etudes critiques sur les commentaires de Boèce (IXe-XVe siècles)*, AHDL., 13 (1939) 5-140.—Patristic origin of the literary "consolation" form, Ch. Favez, *La consolation latine chrétienne*, Paris, 1937 (Cyprian, Ambrose, Jerome, Paulinus of Nola).—MAN., I, 22-36. M. Cappuyns, art. *Boèce*, DHGE., 9 (1936) 348-380.

[83] *In lib. de Interpretatione II;* PL., 64, 433. Cf. Adelard of Bath, *De eodem et diverso*, ed. H. Willner, Münster i. W., 1903, pp. 11-13 (Beiträge, IV, 1).—Allegorical description of philosophy, *De consolatione philosophiae* (henceforward to be quoted as *CP.*) I, pros. 1; PL., 63, 587-590. Cf. E. Male, *L'art religieux du XIIIe siècle en France*, 4 ed. Paris, 1919, 112-117. M.-T. d'Alverny, *La Sagesse et ses sept filles*, in Mélanges Félix Grat, Paris, 1946, pp. 245-278 (iconography). Definition of philosophy: *In Porphyr. ed. I*, PL., 64, 10-11.—Division of philosophy, *ibid.*, 11 A-12 B.—On the three kinds of beings, *ibid.*, 11 B-C.—On the *Quadrivium: De Arithmetica*, PL., 63; 1079. Cf. 1081 C-D.

[84] *In Porphyr. I*, PL., 64; 73 C-75 A. —See J. Mariétan, *Le problème de la classification des sciences d'Aristote à saint Thomas*, Paris, 1901; pp. 63-76.

[85] *In Porphyrium ed. II*, I; PL., 64; 82 A-B. After defining these problems, Boethius attempts to solve them (83 A) and he finally approves Aristotle, not that he agrees with him, but because the *Isagoge* is an introduction to Aristotle's doctrine: 86 A.

[86] *CP.*, V, pros. 4; PL., 63, 849 A-850 B. —Cf. "our Plato," *CP.* I, pros. 3; PL., 63, 606 A. Also III, pros. 9; PL., 63; 757 A. The following poem (9) expresses in Platonic terms a Christian view of the divine providence: *ibid.*, 758-763; But Boethius also says "my Aristotle."

[87] It is a common notion (Stoic influ-

ence) that God is good, because: "nihil Deo melius excogitari queat . . ." *CP.*, III, pr. 10; PL., 63, 765.—God is the perfect form of the good, III, pr. 10; 764 A.—Beings inferior in perfection presuppose a being perfect in the same genus: *ibid.*, 764-765. (See Anselm's proofs in the *Monologium*, I, PL., 158; 144-146. The parallelism is striking: no regression to infinity, PL., 158; 149 A. Impossibility of positing two Gods: *CP.*, 766 B-767 A, and Anselm, *Monol.*, III; PL., 158, 147 B).—Definition of beatitude: "statum bonorum omnium congregatione perfectum": *CP.*, III, pr. 2; 724. Cf. III, 8; 752 A. Taken up by Thomas Aquinas, *Sum. theol.*, I, 26, 1, ad 1m.—God is beatitude itself, *CP.*, III, pr. 10; 765-767.—Man's beatitude is his divinisation, III, pr. 9; 767. Cf. IV, pr. 3, 798 B.—Another reason to posit God is that there must be in the world a unifying principle: *CP.*, III, pr. 12; 778. Cf. Wil. of Conches and Honorius of Autun in G. Grunwald, *Geschichte der Gottesbeweise im Mittelalter bis zum Ausgang der Hochscholastic* (Beiträge, VI, 3), 67-69. The proof goes back, through Chalcidius, to Plato, *Timaeus*, 32 C.—The good is also the one, III, pr. 11; 772 A-774 C.— God rules the world by his wisdom, *CP.*, III, pr. 12; 780 A (cf. Wisd. 8, 1).— God cannot be described in terms of categories, *De Trinitate*, IV and V, PL., 64; 1252-1254.—God known and named from his works, especially as prime immovable mover, *CP.*, III, metr. 9; 758. (refers his reader to Parmenides, III, pr. 12; 781 B). —And as providence; fate is subjected to providence: it is the order inherent in things, IV, pr. 1; 831 A-832 A.—Human freedom; its relation to providence; its degrees, V, pr. 2; 834 A-837 A.—Providence and future contingents, V, pr. 3; 838 B—842 B. Cf. pr. 6; 858-862. All these themes will reappear in Anselm of Canterbury.

[88] *De Trinitate*, Prooemium, PL., 64, 1249 B. Anselm may have remembered the example set up by Boethius, when he decided not to quote Scripture even in theology.

[89] *In Porphyrium ed. I*, PL., 64, 11 C. Cf. *CP.*, III, metr. 11, and pr. 12; 775-778. Albert the Great has attributed to Boethius the doctrine of the pre-existence of souls, in his *De anima*, III, tr. 2, c. 10.

[90] Allegory of the "wheel of fortune," *CP.*, II, pr. 1; 662 (Cf. E. Male, *L'art religieux du XIIe siècle en France*, 4 ed. Paris, 1919, 117-122). Also II, pr. 2, 666-668.—On providence and freedom see note 87.—Man endowed with a will, *CP.*, III, pr. 11; 774 A.—Definition of eternity, *CP.*, V, pr. 6; 858.—Sanctions, *CP.*, IV, pr. 3; 800 A. Cf. metr. 3, 801-803. Besides these moral sanctions, there are other ones: *CP.*, IV, pr. 4; 806. Let us remember the secret character which Boethius still attributes to the truths of revelation: *Quomodo substantiae . . .*, PL., 64; 1311 A.

[91] The forms that are in matter do not deserve the title of forms; they are images of the true forms: *De Trinitate*, II; PL., 64, 1250 (cf. Gilbert's commentary, PL., 64; 1266 CD).—On "nature" as cause of motion in bodies, *De persona et duabus naturis*, I; PL., 64, 1342 AB.—On "esse" and "quod est," *Quomodo substantiae* (alias *De hebdomadibus*) PL., 64, 1311 BC. *De Trinitate*, I, PL., 64, 1249 CD. Cf. II, 1250 B, and 1250 C. —See M.-D. Roland-Gosselin, *Le De ente et essentia de S. Thomas d'Aquin*, Paris, 1926, 142-145.

[92] *Quomodo substantiae . . .*, PL., 64, 1311 AB. This is the model of the *Regulae de sacra theologia* of Alanus de Insulis (Alan of Lille). Alanus expressly refers to Boethius in his *Regulae*, PL., 210; 622 A.—The last sentence of our chapter refers to PL., 64; 1302 C: «Fidem, si poteris, rationemque conjunge».—On this problem in general, A. J. MacDonald, *Authority and Reason in the Early Middle Ages*, Oxford Univ. Press, 1933 (from Boethius to Abélard).

[93] CASSIODORUS, born in Calabria *ca.* 477, retired from the court of King Theodoric to the monastery of Vivarium *ca.* 540; died *ca.* 570. Works in PL., 69-70. Bibliography in O. Bardenhewer, *Patrology*, 636-637. GDP., 671. Cf. A. Van de Vyver, *Cassiodore et son oeuvre*, Speculum, 6 (1931) 244-292. P. Courcelle, *Les Lettres grecques en Occident de Macrobe à Cassiodore*, Paris, 1943: *L'hellénisme au service de la culture monastique: Cassiodore*, pp. 312-388.—MAN., I, 36-52. BET., 818 (letters).

[94] The *De anima* is found in PL., 70, 1279-1308. It deals with "the substance of the soul and its powers" (1279 D).—The soul, which knows the universe, should not be allowed to ignore itself, 1280 D-1281 A (from Cassiodorus on a commonplace statement).—Pseudo-etymological definitions of *anima, animus* and *mens.* Their distinction. *Animus* and *mens* are the more excellent parts of the soul. *Spiritus* properly designates God. The soul (*anima*) is "a spiritual substance" that no loss of blood can destroy: I, 1282-1283. —Definition of the soul: an immaterial substance, created by God, vivifying its body, rational and immortal, yet able to turn towards good or evil, II, 1283 A B. —Its "quality" is analogous to light, III, 1287-1289.—It has no *forma* (i.e. figure), IV, 1289 A.—Its faculties (*virtutes*) VI, 1291-1292.—Prudence of Augustine in not determining the mode of its creation, VII, 1292-1293.—The soul is seated in the head, VIII, 1293-1295.—Description of the body, IX, 1295-1298.—The evil man, X, 1298-1299.—The good man, XI, 1299-1301.—On future life, XII, 1301-1307.— On Cassiodorus' *De anima*, MAN., 41-42.

[95] The *Institutiones,* or *De institutione divinarum litterarum* of Cassiodorus are found in PL., 70, 1105-1150, immediately followed by the *De artibus ac disciplinis liberalium litterarum*, 1149-1218. Cassiodorus would have liked to do at Vivarium what had been done in Syria at Nisibis: 1105 D.—Unity of the two parts of his work, 1108 B C.—Follows in the wake of Cassian's *Collationes* and of Augustine's *De doctrina christiana,* 1108 B D. The first Book analyses the parts of Scripture (ch. 1-16);—list of the Christian historians and Doctors (ch. 17-23; note ch. 23 on his master the monk Denis the Small (Dionysius Parvus), P. Courcelle, *Les Lettres grecques . . .*, 313-316); detailed advice on the various occupations of monks (ch. 28-32; note ch. 29, on the monastery of Vivarium).—The II Bk., *De artibus . . . ,* is a text-book for beginners in the study of liberal arts, or "secular studies" (PL., 70, 1149 D). Note the various definitions of philosophy, 1167 D; its division, 1167-1168; the definition of dialectics borrowed from Varro, 1168 A; dialectics is already more developed than the other liberal arts: 1167-1203. Geometry is disposed of in less than four columns of Migne; Astronomy in less than three.

[96] ISIDORE OF SEVILLE, died in 636. Works PL., 81-84. *Etymologiae*, ed. W.

M. Lindsay, 2 vols., Oxford, 1911. Bibliography in GDP., 671, and O. Bardenhewer, *Patrology*, 663-664.—MAN., I, 52-70.

[97] MARTIN OF BRACARA, also called "Martinus Dumiensis," or "Martinus Bracarensis"; Abbot and Bishop of Dumio, apostle of the Arian Sueves of Spain; died in 580. Works scattered in PL., 72, 73, 74, 84, 130. The three more interesting of his writings, from the point of view of Seneca's influence, are the *De paupertate,* the *Liber de moribus,* and the *Formula vitae honestae;* these can be easily found in the third volume of the works of Seneca ed. by Fr. Haase, Leipzig, 1895; Appendix, 458-475. *De ira,* PL., 72, 41-48.—J. Madoz, *Martin de Braga, En el XIV centenario de su advenimiento a la Peninsula (550-1950)*, Estudios ecclesiasticos, 25 (1951) 219-242 (life and works). MAN., I, 109-118.

[98] GREGORY THE GREAT, born *ca.* 540; monk in the Benedictine monastery of Monte Celio, then its abbot (*ca.* 585), he was consecrated Pope on Sept. 3, 590. "He laid the foundations of the mediaeval Church and of the political power of the papacy. Gregory believed, to the extent that this belief was compatible with his conviction that the end of the world was at hand, that the future belonged to the Teutonic peoples. He helped them to establish a new order amidst the surrounding chaos. Clausier rightly says that Gregory and the middle ages were born on the same day" (O. Bardenhewer, *Patrology,* 651).—Works in PL., 75-79.—Bibliography in O. Bardenhewer, *Patrology,* 655-657; MAN., I, 92-106; H. Dudden, *Gregory the Great,* London, 1905; H. H. Howart, *St. Gregory the Great,* London, 1912; P. Batiffol, *S. Grégoire le Grand,* Paris, 1928.—The *Pastoral Care,* English transl. by H. Davis, Westminster (Maryland), 1950.—BET., 1780-1785.

[99] *Moralia in Job,* PL., 75, 509-1162, and 76, 9-782. English transl. by J. H. Parker *Morals on the Book of Job,* Oxford, 3 vols., 1844-1850.

[100] *Epistola 54;* PL., 77, 1171-1172.—Note, however, that despite what Gregory has said, what he has done may have favored, at least up to a point, the spreading of classical culture. J. Spörl, *Gregor der Grosse und die Antike,* in K. Schmidthis, Christliche Verwicklichung (to R. Guardini), Rothenfels a. M., 1935, pp. 198-211.

[101] *In lib. Regum,* I, 30; PL., 79, 355-356.—*Moralia in Job,* Praef., PL., 75, 516 B.—On Gregory and mediaeval mysticism, F. Lieblang, *Grundfragen der mystischen Theologie nach Gregors des Grossen Moralia und Ezechielhomilien,* Freiburg i. Br., 1934.

PART FOUR

FROM SCOTUS ERIGENA TO SAINT BERNARD

CHAPTER I. SCOTUS ERIGENA

[1] MEDIAEVAL CIVILIZATION. Von Eicken, *Geschichte und System der mittelalterlichen Weltanschauung,* 3 ed. 1917. M. de Wulf, *Civilization and Philosophy in the Middle Ages,* Princeton, 1922.—Classical background: M. Roger, *L'enseignement des lettres classiques d'Ausone à Alcuin,* Paris, 1905. A Gwynn, *Roman Education from Cicero to Quintilian,* Oxford, 1926. H. O. Taylor, *The Classical Heritage of the Middle Ages,* 3 ed. New York, 1929. H. I. Marrou, *Histoire de l'éducation dans l'Antiquité,* Paris, 1948.—Influence: *The Legacy of the Middle Ages,* Oxford, 1926. —Art and Letters: R. Focillon, *Art d'Occident. Le moyen âge roman et gothique,* Paris, 1938. E. de Bruyne, *Etudes d'esthétique médiévale. I, De Boèce à Jean Scot Erigène. II, L'époque romane. III, Le XIIIe siècle,* 3 vols. Brugge, 1946; *L'esthétique du moyen âge,* Louvain, 1947 (a digest of the preceding work). Sciences: A. C. Crombie, *Augustine to Galileo. The History of Science A.D. 400-1650,* Falcon Press, London, 1952.

ANGLO-SAXON CIVILIZATION. A Brooke, *English Literature from the Beginning to the Roman Conquest,* London, 1908.— A. R. Benham, *English Literature from Widsith to the Death of Chaucer,* New Haven, 1916.—R. W. Chambers, *On the Continuity of English Prose from Alfred to More and his School,* London, 1932. —A. F. Leach, *The Schools of Mediae-*

val England, London, 2 ed. 1916.—Fr. Raphael, *Christian Schools and Scholars*, London, 1924.—A. H. Thompson (edit.), *Bede, His Life, Times and Writings*, Oxford, Clarendon Press, 1935. H. M. Gillett, *Saint Bede the Venerable*, London, 1935. M. T. A. Carroll, *The Venerable Bede: His Spiritual Teachings*, Washington, 1946.—Several translations of the letters of St. Boniface, by E. Kylie, London, 1911; see BET., 744-746.—Transl. of the poems of Aldhelm, Bishop of Shelborne (640?-709) by J. H. Pitman, Yale Univ. Press, New Haven, 1925.—Carolingian civilization: E. Patzelt, *Die karolingische Renaissance. Beiträge zur Geschichte der Kultur des frühen Mittelalters*, Wien, 1924.

MEDIAEVAL PHILOSOPHY. Bibliographical complement to M. de Wulf's *Histoire . . .*, in F. Van Steenberghen, *Philosophie des Mittelalters*, Bern, 1950.—Introductions: B. Hauréau, *De la philosophie scolastique*, 2 vols., Paris, 1850; *Histoire de la philosophie scolastique*, 3 vols., Paris, 1872 and 1880; still important. A. Stöckl, *Geschichte der Philosophie des Mittelalters*, 3 vols., Mainz, 1864-1866; remarkable for its clarity. R. L. Poole, *Illustrations of the History of Mediaeval Thought*, London, 1884. F. Picavet, *Esquisse d'une histoire générale et comparée des philosophies médiévales*, 2 ed. Paris, 1907; stresses the dominating influence of neoplatonism. Fr. Ueberwegs, *Grundriss der Geschichte der Philosophie*, vol. III, 11 ed. by B. Geyer: *Die patristische und scholastische Philosophie*, Berlin, 1928; an absolutely necessary book which contains an immense wealth of bibliographical information up to its own date. E. Bréhier, *La philosophie au moyen âge*, Paris, 2 ed. 1949. P. Vignaux, *La pensée au moyen âge*, Paris, 1938. M. de Wulf, *Histoire de la philosophie médiévale*, 6 ed., 3 vols., Louvain, 1934, 1936, 1947; completes the bibliographies of Ueberweg after 1928; English transl., London and New York; I, 1935; II, 1938. D. J. B. Hawkins, *A Sketch of Mediaeval Philosophy*, London, 1946. E. Gilson, *The Spirit of Mediaeval Philosophy*, New York, Scribner's, 1948; a philosophical survey of the problems. F. Copleston, *A History of Philosophy*, vol. II, *Mediaeval Philosophy from Augustine to Scotus;* N.Y. Philosophical Library, 1952; vol. III, *Ockham to Suarez*, Westminster, 1953. C. B. Burch, *Early Medieval Philosophy*, Columbia University, N.Y., 1951 (Erigena, Anselm, Abe-

lard, Bernard of Clairvaux). A. Forest, E. Van Steenberghen & M. de Gandillac, *Le mouvement intellectuel du XIe au XIIIe siècle*, Paris, 1951 (in Fliche and Martin, *Histoire de l'Eglise*, vol. 13). A choice of texts in English translation is found in R. McKeon, *Selections from Medieval Philosophers*, 2 vols. in the Philosophy Series of the Modern Student's Library, C. Scribner's, N.Y. (1923-1930), Vol. I, *From Augustine to Albert the Great;* vol. II, *From Roger Bacon to William of Ockham.*—History of the scholastic method: M. Grabmann, *Die Geschichte der scholastischen Methode*, 2 vols. Freiburg i. Br., 1900, 1910. —Generally speaking, all the recent histories of philosophy include a history of mediaeval philosophy.—Five German histories of philosophy have been recently published: J. Fischl, *Geschichte der Philosophie. I, Altertum und Mittelalter*, Graz-Wien, Pustet, 1947. H. Meyer, *Geschichte der abendlandischen Weltanschauung. III, Die Weltanschauung des Mittelalters*, Würzburg, Schöning, 1948. J. Hirschberger, *Geschichte der Philosophie. I, Altertum und Mittelalter*, Freiburg i. Br., Herder, 1949. K. Vorländer, *Geschichte der Philosophie. I, Altertum und Mittelalter . . .* 9 ed. revised by E. Metzke, Hamburg, Meiner, 1949 (the part dealing with the middle ages has been checked by M. Grabmann). K. Schilling, *Geschichte der Philosophie. I, Die alte Welt. Das christlich-germanische Mittelalter*, 2 ed., München-Basel, Reinhardt, 1951.—On these works, see H. D. Saffrey OP., in Bulletin Thomiste, 8 (1951) 194-196, to which we are indebted for this information.

ALCUIN is more important as a founder of Western civilisation than as a philosopher. Works in PL., 100 and 101. Literary history, MAN., I, 273-288.—*Dialectica*, PL., 100, 949-976. *Rhetorica*, in W. S. Hornell, *The Rhetoric of Alcuin and Charlemagne*, Latin and English transl., Princeton, 1941. *De anima ad Eulaliam virginem*, PL., 101, 639-647 (see K. Werner, *Der Entwicklungsgang der mittelalterlichen Psychologie von Alcuin bis Albertus Magnus*, Wien, 1876. E. Seydl, *Alcuins Psychologie*, JPST., 26 (1910-1911) 34-55. Alcuin's poems, in Monumenta Germaniae Historica, Series Lat. poet., I, 169-235 and IV, 2-3, 903-910. Letters of Alcuin, same coll., Series Epist. Karolini Aevi, II, 1-493. The statement of the *Chronicle of St Gall* is found in the same coll., Series Scriptores, II, 731.—On Alcuin, C. J. B. Gaskoin, *Alcuin, His Life and His Work,* London, 1904. G. F. Brown, *Alcuin of York,* London, 1908. E. M. Wilmot-Buxton, *Alcuin,* London, 1922. E. Gilson, *Les idées et les lettres,* Paris, J. Vrin, 1932, 171-196. A. J. Kleinclausz, *Alcuin,* Paris, 1948. E. S. Duckett, *Alcuin, Friend of Charlemagne,* New York, 1951.—Iconography, M. Th. d'Alverny, *La Sagesse et ses sept filles* . . . in Mélanges Félix Grat, Paris, 1946, I, 245-278. L. Wallach, *Charlemagne's De litteris colendis and Alcuin, a Diplomatic-Historical Study,* 26 (1951) 288-305.

² FREDEGISUS, *Epistola de nihilo et tenebris,* PL., 105, 751-756.—An anonymous letter, addressed to King Louis the Pious and to Einhard, contains some elementary notions concerning the image of the Trinity in the human soul: Monumenta Germaniae Historica, Epistolae Karolini Aevi, III, 615-616.—MAN., I, 459-461.

³ AGOBARD, Archbishop of Lyons, *Contra objectiones Fredegisi,* PL., 104, 159-174; and Mon. Germ. Hist., Epist. Karolini Aevi, III, 210-221. The answers of Agobard make Fredegisus appear as having raised difficulties from the point of view of the compatibility of grammatical correctness with theological rectitude. He seems to have been a predecessor of the XI-century dialecticians.—MAN., I, 380-390. J. A. Cabaniss, *Agobard of Lyons,* Speculum, 26 (1951) 50-76.

⁴ HRABANUS MAURUS (784-856), a German disciple of Alcuin, was mainly a theologian. Yet his treatise on the education of clerics (*De clericorum institutione*) has played an important part in the transmission of the educational ideal of Saint Augustine to the middle ages (*De doctrina christiana*). His encyclopedia, *De universo,* deals at one and the same time with the nature of things, the properties of their names and their mystical signification. It is an ample repertory of allegorical interpretations. Works in PL., III. See D. Turnau, *Rabanus Maurus praeceptor Germaniae,* Munich, 1900. —MAN., I, 288-302.—The German monk Brunn, usually called CANDIDUS OF FULDA (MAN., I, 660-663), author of the *Dicta Candidi de imagine Dei* (complete text in B. Hauréau, *Hist. de la philos. scolast.,* I, 134-137, notes), dealt in this short treatise, with the Augustinian problem of the image of the Trinity in the soul, and with the conditions of the applicability of the categories to God, according to the pseudo-Augustinian *Categoriae decem.* Its last paragraph contains the first dialectically developed proof of the existence of God that we come across in the modern part of the middle ages. The universe is divided into three classes: that which merely is, that which is and lives, that which, over and above being and living, is intelligent. These three classes are hierarchized from the least to the more perfect. Let man, who is at the peak of this hierarchy on account of his intellect, and who knows he is more perfect and more powerful than the rest, ask himself if he is all-powerful? Since he cannot do all he wants to, he is not. Man must therefore acknowledge above himself an omnipotent power which dominates at the same time what is, what lives, and what has intellectual knowledge. This omnipotence is God. The authorship of Candidus of Fulda is not absolutely certain. This short treatise might be the work of another Candidus, Wizo, a pupil of Alcuin (MAN., I, 662).—RATRAMNUS OF CORBIE (d. after 868), wrote a *De anima* and a *De quantitate animae* (MAN., I, 417) wherein he criticized the opinion held by MACARIUS SCOTUS, that "all men are one man as to substance"; to which Ratramnus objects that, "if such is the case, the result is that there is only one man and only one soul." Obviously, his adversary was in favor of the reality of universals (*genera* and *species*) outside of the mind: *Liber de anima ad Odonem Bellovacensum,* ed. by D. C. Lambot, 1952.—On the Irish (Scotus) Macarius, MAN., I, 290, 414-415.— The author and date of the treatise *De mundi coelestis terrestrisque constitutione* are still unknown. It is printed among the apocryphal works ascribed to the Venerable Bede (PL., 90, 881-910). It is therefore not certain that its developments concerning the nature of the human soul (900-901), the origin of souls (901-902), the world-soul (902-903), and again the true nature and origin of souls (903-904), should be dated from the IXth century. Concerning matter (*hyle*) and the Ideas (904-907).—Ph. Delhaye, *Un plaidoyer pour l'âme universelle au IXe siècle,* Mélanges de Science Religieuse, 4 (1947), 155-182; same author, *Une con-*

troverse sur l'âme universelle au IXe siècle, Lille, 1950 (Analecta mediaevalia Namurcensia).

⁵ SCOTUS ERIGENA (Johannes Scotus Erigena, Eriugena, John the Scot). Born in Ireland *ca.* 810, John went to France about 840-847, where he lived and taught at the court of Charles the Bald. Wrote a treatise on predestination (*De praedestinatione*) against Gottschalk (851); his own position was condemned by the Council of Valence (855), then by the Council of Langres (859). John seems to have either completed his study of the Greek language at Paris, or perhaps even to have learned it there. He translated into Latin the writings attributed to Denis, part of the commentaries of Maximus Confessor to Denis and the *De hominis opificio* of Gregory of Nyssa. His main works are: his long treatise *On the Division of Nature* (*De divisione naturae, Perifision*), his commentary on the *Celestial Hierarchy* of Denys and a commentary on the Gospel of Saint John (incomplete). The end of his life is obscure. John died *ca.* 877.—On the legend of the foundation of the abbey of St. Denys, near Paris, by the Areopagite, R. J. Lörentz, *La légende de S. Denys l'Aréopagite*, Analecta Bollandiana, 69 (1951) 217-237. This legend appears for the first time in 827.—On GOTTSCHALK (Godescalc), F. Picavet, *Les discussions sur la liberté au temps de Gottschalk, de Raban Maur, d'Hincmar et de Jean Scot*, Paris, 1896. E. Dinkler, *Gottschalk der Sachse . . .* Stuttgart, 1936. C. Lambot OSB., *Oeuvres théologiques et grammaticales de Godescalc d'Orbais. Textes en majeure partie inédits*. Louvain, 1945 (fundamental).—MAN., I, 568-574.

The works of Erigena are found in PL., 132: *De divisione naturae*, 441-1022. The hitherto missing part of the commentary on the *Celestial Hierarchy* has been found and published by H. F. Dondaine OP., AHDL., 25-26 (1950-1951) 245-302. C. E. Lutz, *Johannis Scoti Annotationes in Marcianum*, Cambridge (Mass.) 1939. H. Sylvestre, *Le commentaire inédit de Jean Scot Erigène au Mètre IX du Livre III du De Consolatione philosophiae de Boèce*, RHE., 47 (1952) 5-43.—The authenticity of some commentaries on the opuscles of Boethius is doubtful: E. K. Rand, *Johannes Scotus*, Munich, 1906; cf. RNSP., 36 (1934) 67-77. Of no less doubtful authenticity, but interesting in

itself: E. T. Silk, *Saeculi noni auctoris in Boetii Consolationem philosophiae commentarius*, Roma, American Academy, 1935; cf. B. M. Peebles, Speculum, I, (1925) 106-141.—Engl. transl. of *De divisione naturae*, IV, 7-9, in McKeon, *Selections*, I, 106-141.—MAN., I, 323-339.

BIBLIOGRAPHY. F. Staudenmaier, *Johannes Scotus Erigena und die Wissenschaft seiner Zeit*, Frankfurt a.M., 1834 (vol. I only has been published). Saint-René Taillandier, *Scot Erigène et la philosophie scolastique*, Strasbourg, 1843. Brilliantov, *The Influence of Eastern Theology on the West in the Work of John Scotus Erigena*, St. Petersburg, 1898; in Russian. Studies; by F. Dzäseke (GDP., 694) among which: *Johannes Scotus Erigena und dessen Gewährsmänner in seinem Werke De divisione naturae lib.* V, Leipzig, 1902. Same author: *Gregorios von Nyssa in den Anführungen des Johannes Scotus Erigena*, TSK., 1909, 530-576; *Maximus Confessor und Johannes Scotus Erigena*, TSK., 1911, 20-60, 204-230. M. Jacquin, *Le néoplatonisme de Jean Scot*, RSPT., 1 (1907) 674-685; *Le rationalisme de Jean Scot*, RSPT., 2 (1908) 747-748; *L'influence doctrinale de Jean Scot au début du XIIIe siècle*, RSPT., 4 (1910) 104-106. A. Schneider, *Die Erkenntnislehre des Johannes Erigena*, 2 vols. Berlin, 1921. H. Dörries, *Zur Geschichte der Mystik. Erigena und der Neuplatonismus*, Tübingen, 1925. H. Bett, *Johannes Scotus Erigena. A Study in Mediaeval Philosophy*, Cambridge, 1925. M. Cappuyns, *Jean Scot Erigène, sa vie, son oeuvre, sa pensée*, Paris, 1933 (necessary; extensive bibliography, XII-XVII). W. Seul, *Die Gotteserkenntnis bei Johannes Scotus Erigena unter Berücksichtigung ihrer neuplatonischen und augustinischen Elemente*, Bonn, 1932 (Inaug.-Dissert.). H. F. Dondaine, *Saint Thomas et Scot Erigène*, RSPT., 35 (1951) 31-33 (quotations of Erigena borrowed by Thomas from Albert who had attributed them to Maximus Confessor). M. Del Prà, *Scoto Eriugena ed il neoplatonismo medievale*, Milan, 1941. H. F. Dondaine, *Cinq citations de Jean Scot chez Simon de Tournai*, RTAM., 17 (1950) 303-311.

Problems studied over extended periods: J. Mariétan, *Problème de la classification des sciences d'Aristote à saint Thomas*, Paris, 1901. A. Faust, *Der Möglichkeitsgedanke*, Systemgeschichtliche Untersuchungen; 2 Teil: Christliche Philosophie, Heidelberg, 1932 (Augustine,

John Scotus, Peter Damiani, Anselm, P. Lombard, Albert the Great, Thomas, Scotus, Nicholas of Cues; useful analytical tables). F. J. Von Rintelen, *Der Wertgedanke in der europäischen Geitesentwicklung;* I Altertum und Mittelalter, Halle an der Saale, 1932.

On the origins of the influence of Denys in Western Europe, L. Levillain, *Etudes sur l'abbaye de Saint Denis à l'époque mérovingienne,* Paris, 1921. G. Théry, *Contribution à l'histoire de l'aréopagitisme au IXe siècle,* Le moyen âge, 26 (1923) 111-153; *Scot Erigène traducteur de Denys,* Bulletin Du Cange, 1931, 185-278 (important); *Scot Erigène introducteur de Denys,* NS., 7 (1933) 91-108; *Etudes Dionysiennes, I: Hilduin traducteur de Denys,* Paris, 1932.

Scientific notions in Erigena, P. Duhem, *Le système du monde,* III, 44-62. E. von Ehrhardt-Siebold & R. von Ehrhardt, *The Astronomy of Johannes Scotus Erigena,* Baltimore, 1940; same authors, *Cosmology in the "Annotationes in Marcianum." More light on Erigena's Astronomy,* Baltimore, 1940 (despite what has been said about it, there is no heliocentrism in Erigena).

[6] *In evang. Joann.,* PL., 122, 300 A C. Cf. 338 D-339 A.—See G. Brunhes, *La foi chrétenne et la philosophie au temps de la Renaissance carolingienne,* Paris, 1903.

[7] *In prol. evang. Joann.,* PL., 122, 284-285. Following Augustine, Erigena quotes Is. 7, 9, as if the text said: "Nisi credideritis, non intelligetis," whereas the correct translation should be: "If you will not believe, you shall not continue," that is: "Nisi credideritis, non permanebitis."

[8] *De divisione naturae,* I, 71; PL., 122, 516. Cf. I, 64; 509. I, 67; 511-512. II, 20; 556 B.

[9] *In evang. Joann.,* PL., 122, 333 C-334 A. Note the forceful expressions: "Human nature which naturally desires the source of reason"; "Jesus . . . asks from the primitive Church . . . the drink of faith, through which men believed in Him; He asks from nature the drink of reason, through which its creator and redeemer is investigated."—On the symbolic meaning of the well, 334 D.

[10] *In prol. evang. Joannis,* PL., 122, 290 B. This light, of course, is Christ.

[11] Compare Erigena, *De praedestinatione,* I, 1, PL., 122, 357-358, with Augustine (quoted by Erigena himself) *De vera religione,* V, 8; PL., 34, 126. Also *De divisione naturae,* I, 69; PL., 122, 513, with Augustine, *De ordine,* II, 9, 26; PL., 32, 1007: with respect to authority, reason is posterior in time, but anterior by nature.

[12] A detailed exposition of his doctrine on this point should include the texts where John defines his attitude toward the Fathers of the Church. Their opinions must be accepted with respect (*De div. nat.,* II, 16; PL., 122, 548 D. IV, 14; 804 C-805 A). But, in fact, the authority of the Fathers is that of the rational truth which they have discovered and transmitted to us concerning the object of faith (*De div. nat.,* III, 1; 619 B). Consequently, we are not bound to their authority against the light of natural reason, which must always have the last word in these matters. Besides, true authority cannot contradict true reason, nor conversely, since their common source is the divine Wisdom (*De div nat.,* I, 66; PL., 122, 511 B). B. Hauréau, *Hist. de la philosophie scolastique,* Paris, 1872; I, 153: rationalistic interpretation explainable by the personal convictions of the author, pp. II-III. Christian interpretation: Peder Hjolt, *Johannes Scotus Erigena, oder von dem Ursprung einer christliche Philosophie und ihrem heiligen Beruf,* Köpenhagen, 1823.

[13] *Hier. Coelest.,* VII, 2; PL., 122, 184-185. *De praedestinatione,* I, 1; 358 A. *De div. nat.,* II, 1; 526 A C. On the Greek origin of these notions, G. Théry, in Bulletin du Cange, 6 (1931) 220-224.

[14] *Hier. Coel.,* II, 3; PL., 122, 154-156. *De div. nat.,* I, 14; 459-463. I, 15; 463-464. I, 45; 487 B. I, 73; 518-519. Denis is expressly quoted as source of the doctrine, I, 14; 461 B.

[15] God alone has no principle: *De div. nat.,* I, 11; PL., 122, 451-452. III, 23; 688 C.—On the various names given to Ideas, II, 2; 529 B. II, 36; 615 D-616 A.

[16] God has "willed" and "pre-formed" the Ideas: *De div. nat.,* II, 2; PL., 122,

529 C. The Ideas have been *conditae* and *formatae:* II, 15; 547 B. God has *made* them: II, 19; 553 A. II, 36; 616 A ("Pater in Filio fecit").

[17] *De div. nat.,* II, 21; PL., 122; 561 D-562 A. Inasmuch as all things have been created by God in their Ideas, the universe can be said to be eternal in the Word of God: III, 8; 639 C.—On the distinction between "eternal" and "coeternal," see Denis, *De div. nom.,* ch. 10; PL., 122; 1164 B C. The authority of Denis has been influential on this point. Revived by Bernard of Chartres in the XII century (John of Salisbury, *Metalogicon,* IV, 35; Webb ed., 206); rejected by Hugh of St. Victor (*De sacramentis,* I, 4, 26; PL., 176, 246) the doctrine will be officially condemned in 1225 and 1241.

[18] For instance, Erigena sometimes says that the Word himself is created (*De div. nat.,* III, 21; PL., 122, 685 D) but this only means that the Word is "made" in all the creatures which are "made in him." In another text, Erigena states with precision that the Ideas are not strictly creatures: "As a matter of fact, the term creature properly signifies the begotten beings which, according to their respective species, visible or invisible, follow, so to speak, the movement of time. As to what is established before all times and all places, because it is beyond times and places, it is not properly called "creature," even though, taking the part for the whole, creature is the name given to the universality of beings established after God (*De div. nat.,* V, 16; PL., 122, 887 D-888 A). But this merely means that the term "creature" does not *properly* apply to Ideas, it does not mean that they are not "made," which is the root of the whole difficulty.

[19] Definition of "theophany," *De div. nat.,* I, 7; 446 C.—Sources in Gregory and Maximus, I, 9; 449-450.—Synonym: "divinae apparitiones," *De div. nat.,* II, 23; 577 A. Cf. *Hier. Coel.,* I, 2; 132 C.—Theophanies invisible to angels, I, 7; 446 C and I, 8; 448 B; not seen in beatific vision, I, 8; 448 C and I, 10; 450 C D.

[20] Creation of Ideas as God's self-creation, *De div. nat.,* III, 23; 689 B.—On the procession of creatures, V, 15; 887 A. III, 23; 689 B C. II, 36; 616 D-617 A. —Operation of the Holy Ghost, II, 22-23;

564 C-568 A.—Cf. P. Duhem, *Le système du monde,* V, 65-75.

[21] *Hier. Coel.,* I, 1; 129 B C. A "stone" is a "light" for what it can teach us about God. Cf. the typical formula, *ibid.* D: "Hinc est, quod universalis hujus mundi fabrica maximum lumen fit, ex multis partibus veluti ex multis lucernis compactum, ad intelligibilium rerum puras species revelandas et contuendas mentis acie, divina gratia et rationis ope in corde fidelium sapientum cooperantibus."—Other metaphors to the same effect are found in *De div. nat.,* III, 4; 632-634.—On sensible illumination in particular, see I, 75; 520-521. V, 11; 882 C D.

[22] Erigena interprets in this sense the famous text of St. Paul (Rom. 1, 20): "Invisibilia ejus . . ." etc., which he comments on with the text of James, in *Hier. Coel.,* I, 1; 129. —On the correspondence between the notions of illumination and of participation: *Hier. Coel.,* VIII, 1; 196 A. IX, 3; 217 A D.—On the three worlds, *In prol. evang. Johan.* PL., 122; 293-294. Cf. *De div. nat.,* IV, 5; 755 B.—Pantheistic formula: *De div. nat.,* III, 19; 678 C. Let us remember that God creates himself in the sense that he "reveals" himself, and also that Erigena has in mind Coloss., 1, 16 and 3, 11.—The notion of "creation from nothing" (*ex nihilo*) can receive different interpretations in the doctrine of Erigena. The more Erigenian one is that things have been created from that nothingness which God is inasmuch as he is no creature either real or possible: *De div. nat.,* III, 5; 634 C D. III, 19; 680-681. III, 22; 686-688.—On the time of creation, *In prol. evang. Joan.,* 287 C. *De div. nom.,* III, 15; 665-666.

This notion of creation accounts for some of the so-called "pantheistic" formulas of Erigena. In fact, creatures are not God, but they are in virtue of God, who is the form of all things (i.e., the form by which they are): *De praedestinatione,* II, 3; 362. God is the entity (*essentia*) of all things, in this sense that they exist by him only: *De div. nat.,* I, 12; 453-454. I, 71; 516 C. I, 72; 518 B (source of the formula in Denis, as quoted by Erigena, I, 71; 516 C). This brings back paradoxical statements to the effect that God and creature are one and the same thing, because creatures have no being of their own apart from being his manifestations (justified again in his mind by Coloss. I, 16-17): *De div nat.*, I, 71; 516 C. III, 17; 678 C.

[23] *De div. nat.*, I, 13; 455 C. I, 8; 448 B C.

[24] *Hier. Coel.*, VII., 2; 198 B C. Ibid., 199 B C. Cf. XV, 1; 253 A.—On the beauty of the cosmos, *Hier. Coel.*, IX, 2; 211-212. IX, 3; 217 A D. XIII, 3; 237-238.—Extension of the notion of illumination to other beings, *In prol. evang. Joann.*, 290 A-291 A. This is the reason why John is the theologian *par excellence, ibid.* 285 C.

[25] *De div. nat.*, II, 1; 523. II, 7; 533. II, 10; 537. II, 14; 542-545. IV, 9; 777 B-778 B. IV, 12; 799 A B. IV, 16; 817 A-818 B. IV, 7-8; 765 C-775 B. V, 32; 949 A.

[26] *De div. nat.*, IV, 7; 765-766. IV, 8; 774 C-775 B. Cf. I, 50; 492-493. V, 14; 886 B C.

[27] In God, every corporeal being is intelligible *qua* substance: *De div. nat.*, I, 49; 492 C. III, 27; 703 A C.—Next it is intelligible *qua* essence and nature: V, 3; 867 A.—Next, *qua* quantity: I, 50; 492-493. I, 53; 495-497.—Next, as a whole made up of these intelligible elements: I, 53; 495-497. III, 14; 664 A. III, 29; 706 C D, and by their elementary qualities: III, 32; 711 D-714 B. Cf. P. Duhem, *Le système du monde*, V, 54-55.—In short, matter is a concourse of intelligible accidents (*consursus accidentium*), I, 34; 479 B. I, 53; 497 A. I, 57; 501 A. I, 58; 501 C. I, 60; 503 B. V, 15; 887.

[28] *De div. nat.*, IV, 9; 775 C-780 A. V, 23; 906 D-907 A (the history of creation, as told by Scripture, is for Erigena the history of the fall of man: remember Origen).—Bodies as coagulated intelligible elements: V, 15; 887 A.—Erigena takes up the Augustinian doctrine of the "seminal reasons": III, 28; 704 C-705 B. Cf. IV, 5; 749 D-750 B.—Conciliation between his cosmogony and the text of Genesis: II, 20; 554-560. III, 31; 708-710.

[29] Erigena strives to avoid both Gnosticism and Origenism: *De div. nat.*, II, 12; 540 B.

[30] *De div. nat.*, III, 23; 689 C D. Cf. the striking formula: "Ut enim per sen-

sum pervenitur ad intellectum, ita per creaturam reditur ad Deum," op. cit., III, 35; 723 C. Parallelism with the symbolical meaning of Scripture, *Hier. Coel.*, I, 3; 142 A and II, 1; 146.

[31] Trinity in the human soul, *De div. nat.*, II, 24; 579-580. Sources in Augustine: II, 31; 603 A C, and V, 31; 942 A. Sources in Gregory of Nyssa, IV, 11-12; 787 D-802 A. Image of the Trinity in sense, reason and intellect: II, 23; 572 C (cf. Maximus, *Ambigua*, VIII, in Erigena's translation, 1219 C).—Simplicity of the soul and diversity of its functions, IV, 5; 754. Cf. III, 37; 733 D-734 A; and *In evang. Joannis*, 336 B C.—The doctrine of sensation recalls that of Augustine: a vital function exercised by the soul on behalf of the body: II, 23; 573 A C. II, 24; 581 C.—On the errors of senses: III, 35; 725 B. IV, 10; 784 A.

[32] *De div. nat.*, II, 23; 578 A D. This is an important description of the way the human soul is essentially orientated toward God. Cf. II, 23; 574 D-575 D.

[33] On divine love as source of motion, *Hier. Coel.*, II, 4; 163 A. VII, 2; 180 D. Cf. *De praedestinatione*, II, 3; 362 B.—Informity as motion, *De div. nat.*, II, 15; 547 B.—Starting point of the return to God, *De div. nat.*, III, 4; 632 C. III, 20; 683 A C. V, 7; 875. V, 8; 876 A.

[34] On resurrection (better studied by the Greeks than by the Latins), *De div. nat.*, V, 23; 899 A. Cf. 902 C D; 904 B C.—Its nature, *De div. nat.*, V, 8; 876 A.—Reunion of sexes, II, 6; 532-533. V, 20; 893 C.—Third stage of the return, V, 8; 876 A. V, 39; 1020-1021.— Fourth and fifth stages, II, 11; 539-540. V, 8; 876 B. —The world of matter returns to the intelligible world, IV, 8; 774 B. V, 20; 893-894. V, 25; 913 D-914 A.—Earthly paradise and its non-local nature, IV, 16; 822 and IV, 21; 841-842.—That bodies are of intelligible nature, V, 8; 879 A. V, 12; 885 A C.

[35] Role of grace in the universal return to God, *De div. nat.*, V, 38; 1001 B. Cf. V, 36; 978 D-979 B.—Grace of Christ, V, 20; 984 A. V, 39; 1020 B.—Special return through grace, V, 39; 1020 C-1021 B.

[36] Equivalence of "deification," "beatification" and "return to God," *Hier.*

Coel., IX, 4; 222 D-223 A.—Cf. *In Prol. evang. Joan.,* 285-286. *De div. nat.,* V. 38; 1015 C.—Source of the doctrine, *Hier. Coel.,* I, 3; 141 C. Cf. Maximus Confessor, *Ambigua,* II; in Erigena's own translation 1208 B.—Intrinsic invisibility of God, *De div. nat.,* I, 8; 448 B C. I, 13; 456 A. V, 23; 905 C.—That beatitude entails no confusion of natures, *De div. nat.,* V, 8; 879 B-880 A. V, 9-13; 881-885. V, 20; 893-894. Cf. Bernard of Clairvaux, *De diligendo Deo,* X, 28; W. W. Williams ed., p. 50. Also Eadmer, *Liber de sancti Anselmi similitudinibus,* 67; PL., 159; 640-641. E. Gilson *Maxime, Erigène, S. Bernard,* ADGM., I, 188-195.—Cf. supra, pp. 87-88.

[37] *De div. nat.,* V, 3; 867 B D, and 868 B. V, 27; 926 D-927 C. V, 35; 954 D-955 B. V, 37; 984 B-989 B. This text (986 D and 989 B) implies that a lively controversy opposed him to some of his contemporaries on this point, perhaps on account of *De praedestinatione,* XVI; 417-425. Nevertheless in this latter work Erigena seems to admit some sort of corporeal punishment (XIX; 436-438), a position which the *De divisione naturae* rejects as impossible. After the return of human bodies to their intelligible causes, there will be nothing left to suffer corporeal punishment: *De div. nat.,* V, 30; 938 D. Since nature is good in itself, even the substance of the demons (V, 28; 934 B), or that of eternal fire (*De praedestinatione,* XVII, 8; 429-430), no nature will be punished as such (*Hier. Coel.,* VII, 2; 204-205), but every sinner will be punished within the confines of his own evil will: *De div. nat.,* V, 29; 936 C (follows St. Ambrose).

[38] *De div. nat.,* V, 37; 989 A. Cf. *De predestinatione,* XVII, 9; 430 B. In *evang. sec. Joannem,* 321 B C.

[39] Erigena has been considered a rationalist: C. B. Schlueter, in PL., 122; 101 ff. This interpretation has been refuted by Jacquin, OP. in RSPT., 2 (1908), 747-748.—B. Hauréau, *Histoire de la philosophie scolastique,* I, 159, and M. de Wulf, *Histoire de la philosophie médiévale,* 5 ed., I, 130, considered him a pantheist; but M. de Wulf has modified this conclusion in the 6th ed. of his history (1934), I, 138.—On the other hand, without turning Erigena into a pantheist, H. Bett maintains that, according to him, the universe was a "necessary" development of God (*Johannes Scotus Erigena,* 95), while G. B. Burch, in *Early Mediaeval Philosophy* (New York, 1951, pp. 18-19) still favors the pantheistic interpretation of the doctrine. We do not know of a single text where Erigena said that the universe follows "with necessity" from the divine nature. As to his pantheism, he himself repeatedly denies that God is all things, or that all things are God. Cf. the excellent remarks of P. Duhem, *Le système du monde,* V, 61-65. Of course, it is all a question of definitions, but if "pantheism" means a doctrine in which the universe shares in the being of God, there can be no pantheism in a doctrine according to which God is non-being. Let us remember, however, that such discussions are more philosophical than historical, because they presuppose an agreement on the meaning of some philosophical notions. At any rate, the doctrine of Erigena was condemned time and again in the middle ages: in 1210, Peter of Corbeil (CUP., I, 70) condemns the doctrine of Amaury of Bènes; see M.-T. d'Alverny, *Un fragment du procès des Amauriciens,* in AHDL., 18 (1950-1951) pp. 325-336, especially pp. 335-336. In 1225 the Bishop of Paris, William of Auvergne obtains the condemnation of the *De divisione* (CUP., I, 106-107, note 1; Alexander of Hales, *Summa,* ed. Quaracchi, II, 547). Condemnation renewed in 1241 (CUP., I, 170-171; St. Bonaventure, *In Sent.,* II, 93, 2, 3, ed. Quaracchi, II, 547). After their first publication by Th. Gale (1681) the writings of Erigena were put on the Index (1684): *Index librorum prohibitorum,* Rome, 1924, p. 90.

PART FOUR

CHAPTER II. SAINT ANSELM OF CANTERBURY

[40] The study of liberal arts continues in various monasteries, particularly in the field of humanities (grammar) and of logic.

I HUMANITIES. Manitius, *Bildung, Wissenschaft und Literatur im Abendlande von 800 bis 1100,* Crimitschau, 1925; *Handschriften antiker Autoren in mittelal-*

terlichen Bibliothekskatalogen, Leipzig, 1935. E. Norden, *Die antike Kunstprosa vom 6ten Jahrhundert vor Christus bis in die Zeit der Renaissance,* 2 vols. Leipzig, 1909. L. Friedländer, *Das Nachleben der Antike im Mittelalter,* in *Erinnerungen, Reden und Studien,* Strasburg, 1905, pp. 272-391.

[1] SERVATUS LUPUS (Loup de Ferrières), elected Abbot of Ferrières in 840; died in 860. His letters betray his keen interest in literary studies: see Loup de Ferrières, *Correspondance,* ed. by L. Levillain, 2 vols. Paris, 1927. P. von Severus, *Lupus von Ferrières . . . ,* Münster i. W., 1940. MAN., I, 483-490.

[2] SMARAGDUS, Abbot of St. Mihiel, on the River Meuse, *ca.* 819, a grammarian, author of a *Liber in partibus Donati.* Favored Church Latin against the purists who were trying to maintain the rights of classical Latin. Exemplifies the general fact that the assimilation of classical grammar by Christians has raised the same problems as the assimilation of logic. See Ch. Thurot, *Notices et extraits de divers manuscrits pour servir à l'histoire grammaticale du moyen âge,* Paris, 1868. MAN., I, 461-468.

[3] HADOARD, a librarian, compiler of a collection of texts drawn from the philosophical treatises of Cicero. He may have used a similar collection, probably French in origin, known by the title of *Sententiae philosophorum.* See MAN., I, 478-481.

II LOGIC. See A. Van de Vyver, *Les étapes du développement philosophique du haut moyen âge,* Revue Belge de philologie et d'histoire, 8 (1929), 425-442.

[1] HEIRIC OF AUXERRE (about 841-876), a Latin poet; compiled a collection of extracts from classical Latin authors; wrote several grammatical commentaries. As a logician, Heiric wrote glosses on the pseudo-Augustinian *Categoriae decem.* The influence of Scotus Erigena is visible in these glosses, particularly where they deal with the notion of "nature." Other texts, ascribed to Heiric by Hauréau (*Hist. de la philos. scolast.,* I, 186-187), sound more Aristotelian; they place reality in singular substances only, but their authenticity is not certain.—On a contemporary of Heiric, wrongly considered as his pupil, see A. Van de Vyver, *Hucbald*

de Saint-Amand, écolâtre, et l'invention du nombre d'or, Mélanges Auguste Pelzer, Louvain, 1947, pp. 61-79.

[2] REMIGIUS OF AUXERRE (about 841-908), the most famous among Heiric's pupils, succeeded his master at Auxerre, whence he was called to Rheims and then to Paris. Author of commentaries on the grammars of Donatus, Priscian, Phocas and Eutyches, as well as on Persius and Juvenal. As a theologian, Remigius wrote marginal glosses on pseudo-Augustinian *Dialectica,* commentaries on Martianus Capella, on the *De consolatione philosophiae* and on the theological tractates of Boethius. The influence of Erigena's *De divisione naturae* is so obvious in his commentaries on the tractates of Boethius that some scholars have attributed them to Erigena himself. See Hauréau, *Histoire,* I, 199-206. P. Courcelle, *Etude critique . . . ,* in AHDL., 14 (1939), 56-65. MAN., I, 504-519.

[3] ABBO OF FLEURY (d. 1004), a Benedictine monk at Fleury-sur-Loire (now Saint-Benoit-sur-Loire). His teaching marks an advance in the knowledge of Aristotle's logic. The oldest known mediaeval manuscripts containing the *Prior Analytics* and the *Posterior Analytics* in Latin translation were written in the second half of the tenth century and come from Fleury-sur-Loire. On Abbo, see the pioneering work of A. Van de Vyver, *Les oeuvres inédites d'Abbon de Fleury,* RB., 47 (1935) 125-169. MAN., I, 664-672.

[4] GERBERT, a monk at Aurillac, spent three years in Northern Spain, whence he is supposed to have brought back some knowledge of Arabic science; head of the school of Rheims; Abbot of Bobbio (982), Archbishop of Rheims (991), and finally (999) Pope under the name of Sylvester II (the first French Pope); died in 1003. Author of a *Geometria* and of a *Liber de astrolabio* (astronomy). His biographer Richer describes as follows the program of his teaching in logic: a textual explanation of Porphyry's *Isagoge* in the two translations of Victorinus and of Boethius; then an explanation of the *Categories* of Aristotle, of the *Perihermeneias* and of the *Topics,* with Boethius' commentaries on this latter work. Gerbert has left us an example of the dialectical school treatment of a proposition in his opuscule *De rationali et ratione uti.* His

letters bear witness to his interest in books and are a valuable source of information concerning the intellectual life of his times.—Works in PL., 139. More recent editions, A. Olleris, *Oeuvres de Gerbert* . . . , Clermont-Ferrand, 1867. J. Havet, *Lettres de Gerbert (983-997)* . . . , Paris, 1889. N. Bubnov, *Gerberti opera, mathematica (972-1003)* . . . , Berlin, 1899.—F. Picavet, *Gerbert, un pape philosophe d'après l'histoire et d'après la légende*, Paris, Leroux, 1897. A. Fliche, *Un précurseur de l'humanisme au Xe siècle, le moine Gerbert (pape Silvestre II)*, Quelques aspects de l'humanisme médiéval (Association G. Budé-Montpellier), Paris, 1943.—MAN., II, 729-742.

[41] The commonly received distinction between "dialecticians" and "anti-dialecticians" is only acceptable with the reservations that should attend all classifications. All these writers knew dialectics; not one of them ever said that the dialectical use of natural reason was evil in itself, but two problems did arise in connection with the use of dialectics; first, was it lawful for a *monk,* who had renounced the world, to pursue secular learning? Next, was it lawful for a Christian to submit the mysteries of faith to the rules of logical reasoning? The so-called "dialecticians" are those who were accused of overindulging in dialectics by the so called "anti-dialecticians."

Among the dialecticians: BERENGAR OF TOURS (d. 1086), who applied dialectics and elementary philosophical notions to the explanation of the Eucharist: *Berengarii Turonensis De Sacra Coena adversus Lanfrancum,* ed. A. F. and F. Th. Vischer, Berlin, 1834. Why not use reason everywhere, since it is by the gift of reason that man was made in the image of God? Now reason says that accidents cannot subsist apart from substance; since the accidents of bread subsist after the consecration, its substance must needs remain. Hence Berengar's conclusion that the effect of the consecration is to add, to the subsisting form of the bread, another form, which is that of the body of Christ beatified.—MAN., II, 103-124. M. Cappuyns, art. *Bérenger de Tours,* DHGE., 8 (1934) 385-407. M. Matronola, *Un testo inedito di Berengario di Tours e il concilio romano del 1079,* Milan, 1936. G. Morin, *Bérenger contre Bérenger,* RTAM., 4 (1932) 109-133; *Lettre inédite*

de Bérenger de Tours à l'archevêque Josselin de Bordeaux, RB., 44 (1932) 220-226. J. R. Geiselman, *Ein neuentdecktes Werk Berengars von Tours über das Abendmahl?* TQ., 118 (1937) 1-31, 133-172. Introductory, A. J. McDonald, *Berengar and the Reform of Sacramental Doctrine,* London, 1930.—Covering the problem of faith and reason over a long period: Th. Heitz, *Essai historique sur les rapports entre la philosophie et la foi de Bérenger de Tours à S. Thomas d'Aquin,* Paris, 1909. J. M. Verweyen, *Philosophie und Theologie im Mittelalter,* Bonn, 1911. W. Betzendörfer, *Glauben und Wissen bei den grossen Denkern des Mittelalters. Ein Beitrag zur Geschichte des Zentralproblems der Scholastik,* Gotha, 1931 (from John Scotus Erigena and Anselm to Duns Scotus and Ockham).

Berengar's adversary, the Italian LANFRANC (1010-1089), who died Archbishop of Canterbury, was no systematic opponent of logic. Dialectics, he says, does not contradict the mysteries of God (PL., 150; 158). He only objects to the indiscrete application of logic to the interpretation of these mysteries. Yet, he will reproach his pupil Anselm of Canterbury with writing theological treatises without quoting Holy Scripture (PL., 158; 1139 A B). To each theologian, the proper use of dialectics was the one which he himself was making of it. On another Berengar, see supra: G. Morin, RTAM., 4 (1932) 109-133.

Among those who denounced, with more or less severity the excessive use of dialectics in theology let us quote: OTLOH OF SAINT-EMMERAM (1010-1070), author of an interesting autobiography: *Liber de tentationibus suis et scriptis,* PL., 146; 29-58) in which he regrets the time spent in secular studies that should be forbidden to monks. Against the monks who were putting Boethius above Sacred Scripture, *De tribus quaestionibus,* PL., 146; 60. MAN., II, 83-103.—MANEGOLD OF LUTTENBACH, in Alsatia, wrote about 1080 an *Opusculum contra Wolfelmum Coloniensem* (PL., 155; 150-176). He rejects the idea that Macrobius' commentary on *The Dream of Scipio* agrees, on the whole, with Christianity. Faith should not be submitted to dialectics. In his *De inventione rhetorica,* I, 29, 44, Cicero had quoted as an irrefutable proposition: *Si peperit, concubuit;* yet Christ was born of the Virgin Mary. We should not let worldly learning divert us from the profundity of revelation: PL., 155; 163 A. Cf. 153 C-155 C.—The typical representative of this tendency, and of the monastic *contemptus saeculi* in general, is Saint PETER DAMIAN (1007-1072). According to him, a monk needs no philosophy (*Dominus vobiscum*, PL., 145; 232-233). The library whose short catalogue he sketches in his *De ordine eremitarum* (PL., 145; 334 C D) contains no profane books. Had philosophy been necessary to save mankind, God would have sent philosophers to convert it, not fishermen (*De sancta simplicitate*, PL., 145; 697 B C). Some monks seem to prefer the rules of Donatus to those of Saint Benedict; yet, the first professor of grammar was the devil, who first taught Adam to decline *deus* in the plural (Gen. 3, 5). In his *De divina omnipotentia*, arguing against Saint Jerome on the strength of the principle that what is impossible in time is possible in eternity, Peter maintains that God can bring about that a past event did not happen (PL., 145, 618 B-620 C). Philosophy should serve Holy Scripture as a maid serves her mistress (PL., 145, 603); this text is one of the origins of the oft-quoted formula: "philosophy the handmaid of theology" (*philosophia ancilla theologiae*), which, however, is not found in Peter Damian; at least, not in so many words.

On this movement as a whole, J. A. Endres, *Forschungen zur Geschichte der frühmittelalterlichen Philosophie*, Münster i. W., 1915 (Beiträge, 17, 2-3).—On Lanfranc, A. J. Macdonald, *Lanfranc, a Study of his Life, Works and Writings*, Oxford, 1926.—On Peter Damian, essential texts in *S. Pier Damiani De divina omnipotentia ed altri opuscoli*, ed. P. Brezzi, Ital. transl. B. Nardi, Florence, 1943 (contains *De divina omnipotentia, De sancta simplicitate scientiae inflanti anteponenda, De perfectione monachorum, De vera felicitate ac sapientia*). J. A. Endres, *Petrus Damiani und die weltliche Wissenschaft*, Münster i. W., 1910 (Beiträge, 8, 3). O. J. Blum, OFM., *St. Peter Damian, His Teaching on the Spiritual Life*, Washington, 1947.

[42] ANSELM OF CANTERBURY (Anselmus Cantuarensis) born at Aosta (1033), studied under Lanfranc at the Benedictine abbey of Le Bec (now Bec-Helluin); Prior of the abbey, 1063; Abbot, 1078; Archbishop of Canterbury, 1093; died in

1109.—R. W. Church, *Saint Anselm,* London, 1905. J. Clayton, *Saint Anselm, a Critical Biography*, Milwaukee, 1933.— Essential for the history of philosophy, *Monologium; Proslogion* (so-called "ontological" argument); objections to the argument by a monk of Marmoutier, GAUNILO, *Liber pro insipiente;* reply of Anselm to Gaunilon in *Liber apologeticus ad insipientem.* Influential by his doctrine of the oneness of truth: *De veritate.* More strictly theological but containing many philosophical discussions: *De fide Trinitatis, De incarnatione Verbi, Cur Deus homo, De libero arbitrio, De concordia praescientiae Dei cum libero arbitrio.*—An alleged first redaction of the *Cur Deus homo* has been published by E. Druwé, SJ., *Libri sancti Anselmi "Cur Deus homo" prima forma inedita*, Roma, Univers. Gregor., 1933; this attribution has been opposed by J. Rivière, *Un premier jet du "Cur Deus homo"?* RSR., 14 (1934) 329-369.

EDITIONS. Migne PL., 158-159 (a reprint of the Gerberon edition; the text is quite reliable). Critical edition by F. S. Schmitt, *Sancti Anselmi Opera omnia:* I, Seckau, 1938; Edinburgh, 1946. II, Rome, 1940. III, IV, Edinburgh, 1946, 1949. V, London, 1951.—Separate editions: *Monologion,* F. S. Schmitt, Bonn, 1929. *Proslogion,* F. S. Schmitt, Bonn, 1929. *Cur Deus homo,* F. S. Schmitt, Bonn, 1929. *Epistola de Incarnatione Verbi,* F. S. Schmitt, Bonn, 1931. F. S. Schmitt, *Ein neues unvollendetes Werk des hl. Anselm von Canterbury*, Münster i. W., 1936 (Beiträge, 33, 3).—French transl., *Saint Anselme, oeuvres philosophiques*, by A. Rousseau, Paris, 1945. English transl., by S. N. Deane, Chicago, The Open Court Co., 1903 (*Proslogium, Monologion, Libellus* by Gaunilo and Anselm's reply). *Proslogion,* by A. C. Pegis, in *The Wisdom of Catholicism*, 202-228. *De veritate,* by R. McKeon, *Selections,* I, 150-184.

BIBLIOGRAPHY. Ch. de Rémusat, *Anselme de Cantorbéry, tableau de la vie monastique et de la lutte du pouvoir spirituel avec le pouvoir temporel au XIe siècle*, Paris, 2 ed. 1868. Van Weddingen, *Essai critique sur la philosophie de saint Anselme*, Bruxelles, 1875. E. Domet de Vorges, *Saint Anselme*, Paris, 1901. Collected essays by various authors in *La revue de philosophie*, 15, December, 1908. J. Fischer, *Die Erkenntnislehre Anselms von Canterbury*, Münster i. W., 1911 (Beiträge, 10, 3). Ch. Filliatre, *La philosophie de saint Anselme, ses principes, sa nature, son influence*, Paris, 1920. A. Koyré, *L'idée de Dieu dans la philosophie de saint Anselme*, Paris, 1923. H. Ostlender, *Anselm von Canterbury, der Vater der Scholastik*, Dusseldorf, 1927. A. Jacquin, *Les rationes necessariae de saint Anselme*, Mélanges Mandonnet, Paris, 1930; II, 67-78. K. Barth, *Fides querens intellectum. Anselms Beweis der Existenz Gottes in Zusammenhang seines theologischen Programms*, Munich, 1931. A. Wilmart, *Le premier ouvrage de saint Anselme contre le trithéisme de Roscelin*, RTAM., 3 (1931) 20-26. M. Losacco, *La dialettica in Anselmo d'Aosta*, Sophia, 1 (1933) 188-193. C. Ottaviano, *Le "rationes necessariae" in S. Anselmo*, Sophia, 1 (1933) 91-97. A. Antweiler, *Anselmus von Canterbury, Monologion und Proslogion*, Scholastik, 8 (1933) 551-560. A. Stolz, *Zur Theologie Anselms im Proslogion*, Catholica, 2 (1933) 1-21. F. S. Schmitt, *Der Ontologische Gottesbeweis Anselms*, TR., 32 (1933) 217-223. G. Capone Braga, *Varie forme dell'argomento ontologico*, Sophia, 2 (1933) 97-99. E. Gilson, *Sens et nature de l'argument de saint Anselme*, AHDL., 9 (1934) 5-51. A. Kolping, *Anselms Proslogion-Beweis der Existenz Gottes*, . . . , Bonn, 1939. M. Cappuyns, *L'argument de saint Anselme*, RTAM., 6 (1934) 313-330. A. Stolz, *"Vere esse" im Proslogion des hl. Anselm*, Scholastik, 9 (1934) 400-409; *Das Proslogion des hl. Anselm*, RB., 47 (1935) 331-347, *Anselm of Canterbury*, Munich, 1937, J. Marias, *San Anselmo y el insensato y otros studios de filosofia*, Madrid, 1944, pp. 5-32. A. Wihler, *L'argomento del Proslogion di S. Anselmo per l'esistenza di Dio*, Scuola cattolica, 70 (1942) 441-449. J. L. Springer, *Argumentum ontologicum. Existentieele interpretatie van het Godsbewijs in het Proslogion van S. Anselmus*, Assen (Holland) 1947. F. Spedalieri, *Anselmus an Gaunilo? seu de recta argumenti sancti doctoris interpretatione*, Gregorianum, 28 (1947) 55-77; same author, *De intrinseca argumenti S. Anselmi vi et natura*, Gregorianum, 29 (1948) 204-212. F. Bergenthal, *Ist der ontologische Gottesbeweis Anselms von Canterbury ein Trugschluss*, PJ., 59 (1949) 155-168. S. Vanni Rovighi, *S. Anselmo e la filosofia del sec. XI*, Milan, 1949. A. Cicchetti, *L'agostinismo nel pensiero di Anselmo d'Aosta*, Roma, 1951. T. Moretti-Costanzi, *L'ascesi di coscienza e l'argomento di S. Anselmo*,

Roma, 1951. M. T. Antonelli, *Il significato del Proslogion di Anselmo d'Aosta*, Rivista Rosminiana, 45 (1951) 260-268; 46 (1952) 35-43.
Literary history of early scholasticism, A. M. Landgraf, *Einführung in die Geschichte der theologischen Literatur der Frühscholastik*, Regensburg, 1948. J. de Ghellinck, *Le mouvement théologique du XIIe siècle*, Bruges, 1948.

[43] Unless otherwise indicated, all our references will be to Migne, PL., vol. 158. Only the number of the columns will be indicated. On the nature of the *Monologium*, 143 A. Cf. *Proslogion*, 223.—P. Vignaux, *Structure et sens du Monologion*, RSPT., 31 (1947) 192-212.

[44] Even this is a revealed truth which we have to believe: *Prosl.*, I; 227 C. Cf. Is. 7, 9.—On the Augustinian sources of the doctrine, A. Koyré, *L'idée de Dieu* . . . , 21-24.

[45] *Prosl.*, 1; 227 B. *Cur Deus homo*, I, 2; 362 B.—Love moves faith to seek understanding, *Monol.*, 77; 220-221. Hence the necessity of moral purification and of prayer: *Prosl.*, 1; 225-227. *De fide Trinitatis*, 2; 263. Cf. Augustine, *De Trinitate*, VIII, 4, 6; PL., 42; 951.—The understanding of faith stands midway between blind belief and the sight of God face to face. *De fide Trinitatis*, Praef., 261 A. There is in it an aspiration toward beatific vision: *Prosl.*, 26; 242 B.

[46] Some conclusions are more self-sufficient than others with respect to faith (Beurlier, *Les rapports de la raison et de la foi dans la philosophie de saint Bonaventure*, Revue de philosophie, 15 (1909), 722-723); yet Anselm's demonstrations are about faith, even that of the existence of God (*Liber apologeticus*, 8; 258), and he never introduced any distinction between his *rationes necessariae;* they all deal with the possibility of faith: *De fide Trinitatis*, 4; 272 C D.

[47] *Monol.*, 1; 145 A.

[48] *Monol.*, 1; 145 B-146 B.

[49] *Monol.*, 2; 146-147.

[50] *Monol.*, 4; 148-150. Cf. Thomas Aquinas, *Sum. theol.*, I, 2, 3, Resp.

[51] *Prosl.*, 2; 227-228.—The proofs of *Monologium* are too intricate, *Prosl.*, Prooem., 223 B C.—Efforts of Anselm to discover a new proof and how the devil attempted to suppress it: Eadmer, *Vita S. Anselmi*, I, 3, 26; PL., 158, 63.—The *Proslogion* applies the rule "faith seeking understanding": *Prosl.*, 1; 227 B.—Historical origins of the nominal definition of God: Augustine, *De libero arbitrio*, II, 2, 5; PL., 32; 1242. This text includes the words of the fool: II, 2, 6, PL., 32, 1243; the *nisi credideritis:* ibid., and the equivalent of the Anselmian definition: 14, 1248. Cf. Augustine, *De doctrina christiana*, I, 7, 7; PL., 34; 22.

[52] Objections of Gaunilon, *Liber pro insipiente*, 241-248; especially 8, 248 B, where his attitude is clearly defined; 4, 244-245 and 5; 246.—Answers of Anselm in *Liber apologeticus contra Gaunilonem:* appeal to Gaunilon's Christian faith, 1; 249 B. Not to have a distinct notion of God is different from having no notion of God, 1; 251 A, and 6; 256.—That, for a notion, to be is to be conceived: 2; 251 B. —That if such a being is possible, it exists: 1; 249 B C. Cf. E. Gilson, *Jean Duns Scot*, p. 142, and Malebranche, *Entretiens métaphysiques*, II, 5.—The comparison with an island is not valid: 3; 252 B. God is not a being "greater than all," but "a being than which no greater can be thought," 5; 254 B.—The argument of the *Proslogion* does not invalidate those of the *Monologium*: 8; 258 B, with quotation of Rom. 1, 20: "Invisibilia Dei . . . ," etc.—T. A. Audet, *Une source augustinienne de l'argument de saint Anselme*, Rencontres, 30 (1949) 105-142.

[53] God exists through himself in this sense that to be belongs to his essence as to shine belongs to light: *Monol.*, 6; 152-153.—Creation *ex nihilo*, 7; 154 C. Cf. 157 A B.

[54] On Ideas, *Monol.*, 9; 157.—On the Word, *Monol.*, 10; 159 B.—Existence of creatures in divine knowledge, *Monol.*, 11; 159 D-160 B. Cf. 19; 168-169.—Production of creatures by the Word: *Monol.*, 12; 160 C. Cf. 34; 189 A B.— Beings are more real in the divine thought than in themselves: *Monol.*, 36; 190 B.

[55] *Monol.*, 13; 160-161. Cf. 14; 161.

[56] *Monol.*, 15; 164 A. Cf., *Prosl.*, 5; 229. Also 6; 229-230.—On the divine attributes, *Prosl.*, 7-13; 230-234.—Simplicity of God, *Prosl.*, 12; 234. Cf. 18; 236-237, and 22; 238.—On eternity, *Prosl.*, 18-21; 236-238.

[57] *Monol.*, 67; 213 C.—On resemblance and participation, *Monol.*, 31; 184-185.

[58] On Roscelin, see p. 625.

[59] *De fide Trinitatis*, 2; 265 A C: "Illi utique nostri temporis dialectici, immo dialecticae heretici, qui nonnisi flatum vocis putant esse universales substantias . . ." etc.

[60] The truth of a proposition is its "rectitude": *De veritate*, 2; 470 A.—The rectitude of right thinking consists in thinking that what is, is, and that what is not, is not: 3; 471.—Rectitude, or truth, of the will: 4; 472 A.—Rectitude, or truth, of actions: 5; 472 C. Cf. John, 3, 21.— Rectitude, or truth, of things: 9; 478 A. It consists in their conformity to the supreme truth: 7; 475 C.—Hence the unity of truth in all things: 13; 486 A B.—The supreme truth belongs to no particular being; each and every thing is true insofar as it is conformable to it: 13; 486 C.

[61] On the three meanings of *voluntas*, see *liber de voluntate*: PL., 158; 487-490.—On the *affectiones* (inclinations or affections), 487 A-488 B.—On true justice, *De veritate*, 12; 483 B-484 A.

[62] An image of God, the rational soul can raise itself up to him through self-knowledge, *Monol.*, 66; 213 A.—Righteous living is a twofold effort to discover truth, goodness, justice, and to adhere to it. To adhere to it is to love it, that is to say, it is to love God: *Monol.*, 68; 214. To love God is to share in his own life and in his own beatitude: *Monol.*, 70; 216 C D, and the admirable conclusion of the *Proslogion*, 25-26; in Pegis, *Wisdom of Catholicism*, 225-228.

[63] *Liber de voluntate*, 488 C-489 A.

[64] *De libero arbitrio*, 2; 492 B. Cf. 515 C, 516 C.—On choice as a judgment, *De concordia praescientiae . . . Dei cum libero arbitrio*, 516 D.—Cf. Fr. Baeumker, *Die Lehre Anselms von Canterbury über den Willen und seine Wahlfreiheit*, Mün-

ster i. W., 1912. I. Choquette, *Voluntas, affectio and potestas in the Liber de voluntate of saint Anselm,* MS., 4 (1942), 61-81.—General history of the problem, O. Lottin, *Libre arbitre et liberté depuis saint Anselme jusqu'à la fin du XIIIe siècle,* PEM., I, 11-389.

[65] *De lib. arb.,* 3; 494 B. Cf. *De veritate,* 12; 480.

[66] *De lib. arb.,* 3; 494 C. Cf. 4; 495 C. The doctrine is summed up in 13; 505-506.

[67] On predestination, *Monol.,* 71-72; 217-218. Even this purely theological problem has philosophical implications: see *De concordantia praescientiae . . . ,* I, 1; 509 B, on the distinction between necessity and coercion; how divine foreknowledge entails necessity without coercion, I, 2; 510 C D; God foresees the necessary as necessary and the contingent as contingent, I, 3; 511 A B; cf. 512, A

B; since God is eternal, there is in him neither real pre-vision nor predestination, II, 2-3; 520; in restoring the rectitude lost by sinful will, God restores its liberty, III, 2-3; 522-524. The doctrine is summed up in III, 14; 540-541.

[68] H. Bouchitté, *Le rationalisme chrétien de saint Anselm,* Paris, 1842.—Anselm as "father of scholasticism": M. Grabmann, *Geschichte der schol. Meth.,* I, 58.

[69] G. Grunwald, *Geschichte der Gottesbeweise im Mittelalter bis zum Ausgang der Hochscholastik,* Münster i. W., 1907 (Beiträge, 6, 3). A. Daniels, *Quellenbeiträge und Untersuchungen zur Geschichte der Gottesbeweise im dreizehnten Jahrhundert, mit besonderer Berücksichtigung des Arguments im Proslogion des hl. Anselm,* Münster i. W., 1908 (Beiträge, 8, 1-2). Bibliography concerning the argument in J. Bainvel, DTC., I (1923) 1359-1360.

PART FOUR

CHAPTER III.   THE SCHOOL OF CHARTRES

[70] On the schools of Chartres: A. Clerval, *Les écoles de Chartres au moyen âge du Ve siècle au XVIe siècle,* Paris, 1895. R. L. Poole, *The Masters of the Schools at Paris and Chartres in John of Salisbury's Time,* Engl. Hist. Review, 35 (1920), 321-342. Edm. Faral, *Le manuscrit 511 du "Hunterian Museum" de Glasgow,* Studi medievali, 9 (1936), especially pp. 69-103.—Our main source of information concerning Chartres is John of Salisbury, PL., 199. Two excellent editions have been published by C. C. J. Webb, *Polycraticus,* Oxford, 1909, 2 vols., and *Metalogicon,* Oxford, 1929.—On the philosophical notions common to the masters of these schools: J. M. Parent, *La doctrine de la création dans l'école de Chartres,* Paris, J. Vrin, 1938. M. de Wulf, *Le panthéisme chartrain,* ADGM., I, 282-288. Tullio Gregory, *L'idea della natura nella scuola di Chartres,* GCFI. Fasc., 4 (1952) 433-442.

[71] BERNARD OF CHARTRES, chancellor of the schools. A lover of classical antiquity, he used to tell his pupils: "We are like dwarfs sitting on the shoulders of giants; we see more things, and more far-off ones,

than they did, not because our sight is better, nor because we are taller than they were, but because they raise us up and add to our height by their gigantic loftiness." J. of Salisbury, *Metal.,* III, 4; PL., 199; 900. Description of the way he used to teach humanities, *op. cit.,* I, 24; PL., 199, 854. Cf. Clerval, 225-226. (UNIV., 7-10). In philosophy, he was accounted the best Platonist of his time. He divided beings into those that truly *are,* and those that seem to be, but are not. The things that are truly real are three in number: God, the Ideas and matter. God is being itself, that is immutability. Ideas are the models of natural things (cf. Seneca, *Ad Lucilium,* 58). Being immutable and eternal, Ideas truly *are;* consequently, universals are real beings: "proprie et vere dicuntur esse universalia." God has always had the Ideas with him, yet, since they represent possible participations in the divine nature, Bernard used to call them eternal, but not "coeternal" (*Metal.,* IV, 35; PL., 199, 938-939. Cf. Scotus Erigena). In short, Ideas are "the first entities after God." Composite substances are not true beings; only their component elements, the Idea and matter (*yle,* see Chalcidius), are truly real. In four verses of a poem quoted by J. of Salisbury, Bernard had said: "The *what is* (i.e., Boethius' *quod est*) to which I attribute being is not the two-part compound made up of form involved in matter; the *what is* to which I attribute being, consists in each one of these parts; the one is called *idea* in Greek, the other *yle.*" Ideas, however, are not directly mixed up with matter; the begotten forms (*formae nativae*) which come forth from them order matter and make it susceptible of motion (of itself, matter is immobile); conversely, these native forms are somehow diversified by their contact with matter (*Metal.,* IV, 35; PL., 199, 938). Cf. Boethius, *De Trinitate,* II; PL., 64, 1250. Bernard was a true humanist; J. of Salisbury calls him "the most abundant source of Letters in modern times"; yet he seems to have played some part in the movement which was to turn grammar into a field of philosophical speculation. The reasons for it are obvious. In his *Categories,* Aristotle himself had dealt with notions common to both grammar and logic: what is a noun, a verb, etc.? Moreover, since the same professors who had to teach grammar often had to teach logic, it was inevitable that they should compare the grammatical definitions of some notions with their logical definitions. This was to lead to the "speculative grammar" of the XIIIth-century, whose influence can still be felt in many grammars up to our own day. Discussing the problem of the relation of words to their derivatives (white, whiteness, to whiten), Bernard conceived it as the progressive pollution of a virgin substance (whiteness), which soils itself in its act (it whitens), and finally corrupts itself by mixing with some material substance (white). In short, for this grammarian, the relation of the primitive word to its derivatives was of the same sort as the relation of the Platonic Idea to its participations. This same question, asked in Priscian's grammar, and already discussed by Boethius, has held the attention of several XIIth-century philosophers, Abélard among others.—On Bernard of Chartres: J. of Salisbury, *Metal.,* I, 24; II, 17; III, 2, 4; IV, 35, 36. *Polycrat.,* VII, 13. E. Gilson, *Le platonisme de Bernard de Chartres,* RNSP., 25 (1923), 5-19.—Cf. J. M. Parent, *La doctrine de la création . . . ,* 12-13.

On the general flowering of studies at that time: C. H. Haskins, *The Renaissance of the Twelfth Century,* Cambridge (Mass.), 1927. G. Paré, A. Brunet and P. Tremblay, *La Renaissance du XIIe siècle,* Paris, J. Vrin, 1933 (replaces the work of G. Robert, 1909). P. Delhaye, *L'organisation scolaire au XIIe siècle,* Traditio, 5 (1947) 211-263. W. A. Nitze, *The so-called Twelfth Century Renaissance,* Speculum, 23 (1948) 464-471. E. M. Sanford, *The Twelfth Century-Renaissance or Proto-Renaissance?,* Speculum, 26 (1951) 635-641.

[72] GILBERTUS PORRETANUS (Gilbert of la Porrée), born at Poitiers, about 1076, studied at Chartres under Bernard of Chartres; became professor at the same school, then its chancellor; professor at Paris in 1141; Bishop of Poitiers in 1142; died in 1154. His works include the *Liber sex principiorum* (authenticity extremely uncertain) and important commentaries on Boethius' tractates *De Trinitate* and *De duabus naturis.* Works published in PL., 64, 1255-1412, for the commentaries on Boethius, and 188, 1257-1270 for the *De sex principiis.* A crit. ed. of this treatise is to be found in the collection *Opuscula et Textus,* Münster i. W., VII: *Tractatus de sex principiis,* ed. Alb. Heysse, 1929; new ed. 1953. Writings: MAN., III, 210-215. Doctrine and influence: Berthaud, *Gilbert de la Porrée et sa philosophie,* Poitiers, 1892. M. Grabmann, *Geschichte der scholastischen Methode,* II, 408-438. A. Landgraf, *Untersuchungen zu den Eigenlehren Gilberts de la Porrée,* ZKT., 54 (1930) 180-213. A. Forest, *Le réalisme de Gilbert de la Porrée, dans le commentaire du De hebdomadibus,* RNSP., 36 (1934), 101-110. A. Hayen, *Le concile de Reims et l'erreur théologique de Gilbert de la Porrée,* AHDL., 10-11 (1935-1936) 29-102. M. H. Vicaire, *Les porrétains et l'avicennisme avant 1215,* RSPT., 26 (1937), 449-482. N. M. Haring, *The Case of Gilbert de la Porrée Bishop of Poitiers (1142-1154),* MS., 13 (1951), 1-40. Fr. Pelster, *Die anonyme Verteidigungsschrift der Lehre Gilberts von Poitiers im Cod. Vat. 561 und ihr Verfasser canonicus Adhemar von Saint-Ruf in Valence (um 1180),* Studia mediaevalia (Miscellanea Martin), Brugis (n.d.) 113-146. V. Miano, *Il commento alle lettere di S. Paolo di Gilberto Porretano,* SRHC., 171-199. N. M. Haring, *A Latin Dialogue on the Doctrine of Gilbert of Poitiers,* MS., 15 (1953) 243-

289.—On Gilbert's influence on Thomas Aquinas, A. Landgraf, *Porretanisches Gut beim hl. Thomas van Aquin*, APA., 6 (1939-1940) 214-225.—Influence of Chalcidius on Gilbert's terminology, E. Gilson, *Note sur les noms de la matière chez Gilbert de la Porrée*, Revue du moyen âge latin, 2 (1946) 173-176.

[73] So far, the oldest known attribution of the *Liber sex principiorum* to Gilbert is to be found in Albertus Magnus, whose attributions are not always safe. Moreover, the VIIIth Book of the present text does not seem to belong to the original treatise. The success of this work has been remarkable. It enjoyed the same authority as a work of Aristotle. Many commentaries have been written on it, one of them by Albertus Magnus. The oldest known of these commentaries is that of a professor at the Faculty of Arts of Paris, Nicholas of Paris. See M. Grabmann, *Aristoteles im zwölften Jahrhundert*, MS., 12 (1950), 131-132.

[74] Texts in Gilbert's commentary on Boethius' *De Trinitate*, PL., 64. On *subsistentia*, 1265 D; 1266 A; 1275 D.—On *subsistentia* and *substantia*, 1374 B D.— The *subsistentiae* are the being (*esse*) of their parts and, conversely, they are made up, not of their parts, but of the being of their parts: "unumquodque est ex partibus suis et est partes suae," 1271 C D.—It is both conjoined and disjoined, 1272 D.—For the same reason, some subsistents are made up of other subsistents, 1273 C.

[75] God, Ideas and matter, 1266 D; 1287 A; 1360 D; 1361 D; 1362 B C.—On Ideas, 1266 B D; 1274 D.—On form in general, including God, 1266 B C.—On engendered forms, images of Ideas, 1267 A; 1274 C; 1366 C.—On matter, 1265 D; 1269 B; 1361 B; 1367 B; 1399 C D (important).—Matter in Ideas, 1266 B and D.—Generic and specific substances, 1265 D-1266 A; 1269 B C.—Species, resemblance and conformity, 1262 B; 1264 A; 1294 A B.—On individuation, 1264 A D.—Conformity and individuality, 1371 B. And personality, 1294 A B.—Formation of concepts, 1374 C.

[76] God is being, *essentia*, 1269-1270; 1283 C; 1284 D; 1288 D; 1361 A.—*Essentia* and *essens*, 1280 D.—All being is *ex forma*, 1269 C.—In natural beings, all

that is, is through something else than itself, 1270 A-1271 A.—Unity of compound beings, 1271 B D; 1272 A; 1272 C. —What the commentary says about categories (1281-1282; 1285 C) does not seem to agree with the *Liber sex principiorum;* especially on the category of relation, 1291 D.

[77] There is no real distinction between God and his divinity; God is his own divinity, 1270 A. There are no parts in his being, 1270 D. God is through nothing else than his divinity, and his divinity is, because God is through his divinity, 1273 C D (see the objections of an anonymous commentator of Boethius, in J. M. Parent, *La doctrine de la création . . . ,* p. 202). There is in him no plurality of essences, 1273 D. God can be determined by no form, 1268 A. He is pure entity, and as Boethius says, the form of all things, but he himself has no forms, nor added natures, 1269 A D. This position, already familiar to Augustine, does not mean that God is the substantial form of things, but that all forms are what they are in virtue of the supreme formality, viz., essentiality, of God.—God is eternal, 1287-1288.—On the specificity of theological method, 1255 B D; 1256 B; 1257 D, and particularly 1268 C.—See his attack against a curious and, to the best of our knowledge, not yet identified heresy, 1397 C.

[78] Fragments of THIERRY OF CHARTRES' *De septem diebus* have been first published by B. Hauréau, *Notices et extraits . . . ,* Paris, 1890; I, 52-68. A new and better edition is to be found in W. Jansen, *Der Kommentar des Clarenbaldus von Arras zu Boethius De Trinitate*, Breslau, 1926, pp. 106-112. W. Jansen has joined to this commentary fragments of another one, the *"Librum hunc,"* which he considers a probable work of Thierry: pp. 3-25. The attribution is indeed probable. Clarenbaud, who claims Thierry for one of his masters, often follows the *"Librum hunc."* In neither one of these two works can we discover the so-called "pantheism of Chartres" which W. Jansen, after Clerval and Hauréau, seems to have found there (W. Jansen, p. 93). The text of *"Librum hunc,"* pp. 10-11, almost literally copied by Clarenbaud, p. 59, has no pantheistic connotations. The formula "Deus forma essendi est" is just a way of saying that what

is not God owes its being to God. See the commentary which follows this expression in the text: "God is entity itself, for he is the form of being, that is (the form) from which being is, since all things hold their being from God, who holds it from nothing" (ed. W. Jansen, p. 10). Even the words "Deus est omnia" (p. 21), when read in their context, simply mean that "the universality of things is in God," as the apostle John says (I, 4): "Omnia in ipso vita erant." To which the text immediately adds, that, although all things are in the divine wisdom, God himself is no one of those things. It would be a sophism, the author concludes, to make us say that God is either wood or stone, because we say that he is all things. M. de Wulf rightly refuses to read pantheism into such expressions (*Hist. de la phil. méd.*, 6 ed., I, 183). See, on this point, the excellent chapter of J. M. Parent, *La doctrine de la création* . . . , pp. 82-90, and, in the same volume, the anonymous commentary on Boethius *De Trinitate*, p. 195: God is "the true form and entity of all things . . . He is indeed the author of the being of all things." Cf. p. 109.—On God as *forma omnium rerum*, that is, the cause of their unity and being, see Augustine, *Sermo* 117, 2, 3; PL., 38, 663-664. On form as principle of unity, *De Genesi ad litt. liber imperf.*, 10, 32; PL., 34, 232-233—Ed. Jeauneau, *Un représentant du platonisme au XIIe siècle, maître Thierry de Chartres*, Mémoires de la Société archéologique d'Eure-et-Loir, 20 (1954) 3-12.

[79] Let us join to the name of Thierry of Chartres that of BERNARDUS SILVESTRIS, or Bernard of Tours, author of a *De mundi universitate sive Megacosmus et Microcosmus*, dedicated to Thierry. Ed. by C. S. Barach and J. Wrobel, *Bernardus Silvestris, De mundi universitate libri duo*, Innsbrück, 1876. Written in "chantefable" form, it is an allegory which describes the creation of nature and of man. The influence of the *Asclepius*, of Macrobius and of Chalcidius' commentary on the *Timaeus* is easily recognizable. See E. Gilson, *La cosmogonie de Bernardus Silvestris*, in AHDL., 3 (1928) 5-24). R. B. Wolsey, *Bernard Silvester and the Hermetic Asclepius*, Traditio, 6 (1948), 340-344. MAN., III, 205-209.—Another disciple of Thierry, whose identity is still unknown, called his master "the greatest philosopher of all Europe" (B. Hauréau, *Notices et extraits* . . . , I, 49). J. M. Parent has published his *Liber de eodem secundus* (*La doctrine de la création* . . . , pp. 208-213). Its editor rightly notes, in this short treatise, an obvious desire to justify the doctrine of Thierry by theological authorities, especially that of Augustine: pp. 210-212.—Entirely different from the *De mundi universitate* of B. Silvestris in its inspiration, but similar to it in its form (an imitation of Boethius) is the moralizing mixture of prose and verse *Petri Compostellani "De cosolatione rationis" libri duo*, ed. by P. Blanco Soto, Münster i. W., 1912 (Beiträge, 8, 4). The date seems to fall between 1140 and 1147 (p. 15). The content is often derived from Augustine, *De libero arbitrio*, chiefly Bk. III; see Soto's ed., pp. 134-149.—MAN., III, 198-202.

[80] WILLIAM OF CONCHES, born about 1080, at Conches in Normandy, studied at Chartres between 1110 and 1120; taught in Paris from 1120 up to the time of his death; died probably in Paris about 1154 (see H. Flatten, p. 9). A grammarian, he may be the author of an anonymous commentary on Priscian (H. Flatten, p. 12). As a philosopher he has left us an encyclopedia, *De philosophia mundi*, PL., 90; 1127-1178, among the works of Bede, and again 172; 39-102, among the works of Honorius Augustodunensis. Fragments of a commentary on the *Timaeus*, in J. M. Parent, *La doctrine de la création*, pp. 142-177 (replaces the old V. Cousin edition). Glosses on the *De consolatione philosophiae* in J. M. Parent, *La doctrine de la création* . . . , pp. 124-136. *Das Moralium dogma philosophorum des Guillaume de Conches*, ed. by J. Holmberg, Upsala, 1929. Fragments of the *Philosophia mundi* have been added to the already published text by C. Ottaviano, *Un brano inedito della "Philosophia" di Guglielmo di Conches*, Napoli, 1935.—P. Duhem, *Le système du monde*, III, 87-125. H. Flatten, *Die Philosophie des Wilhelm von Conches*, Koblenz, 1929. See also J. R. Williams, *Authorship of the Moralium dogma philosophorum*, Speculum, 6 (1931), 392-411. M. Grabmann, *Handschriftliche Forschungen und Mitteilungen zum Schrifttum des Wilhelm von Conches und zu Bearbeitungen seiner wissenschaftlichen Werke*, Mitt. Bayer. Akad. d. Wissens., Munich, 1935. P. Courcelle, *Etude*

critique des commentaires sur la Consolatio philosophiae, in AHDL., 13 (1939) 5-140. J. M. Parent, *La doctrine de la création . . .* , 48-54, 99-106. R.-A. Gauthier, *Pour l'attribution à Gauthier de Châtillon du Moralium dogma philosophorum,* RML., 7 (1951) 19-64. Ph. Delhaye, *Gauthier de Châtillon est-il l'auteur du Moralium dogma?* Lille, 1953.—MAN., III, 215-220.

The *De philosophia mundi* is an encyclopedia similar to those of Bede, of Honorius Augustodunensis, etc. Its plan is as follows: 1, Nature and division of philosophy; 2, God, angels, world-soul, human souls; 3, Elements, firmament, planets and their effects up to the moon; 4, Meteorology; 5, Geography; 6, Creation of man. His work was fiercely attacked by William of St. Thierry, who reproached him with granting too little to faith and too much to reason (*De erroribus Guillelmi de Conchis,* PL., 180, 333-340). In fact, the *Philosophia* is quite harmless and without much originality. Two points in it have attracted attention: his doctrine of the world-soul and his atomistic conception of matter. Walter of St. Victor attacked William on these points in his *Contra quatuor labyrinthos Franciae* (Flatten, 113, note 633). On the world-soul see the fragment published by C. Ottaviano, 46-52.

The glosses on the *Consolatio philosophiae* are not much more original. Let us note, however, his Christian atomism, in J. M. Parent, 132; his interpretation of the creation of the world in time, pp. 133-134 (Augustine, *Conf.,* XI, 13; PL., 32, 815).—The glosses on the *Timaeus,* on the contrary, are a typical illustration of the Chartres spirit: degrees of knowledge, ed. J. M. Parent, 145-146; on causality, 147; the divine essence is the efficient cause of the world, the divine wisdom is its formal cause, 152; why our reasons concerning God must be necessary, while our reasons concerning the world need not always be more than probable, 156; the final cause of the world is divine goodness, 157; a short interpretation of Genesis, 158-162; on the soul and its creation, 163-165; on the world-soul, 166-170; on matter (*yle*), 173-176; concerning elements, William refers readers to his *Philosophia,* 176.

The constant presence of the *Timaeus* in so many writings belonging to the school of Chartres raises once more the puzzling question: why did nobody attempt to find the other dialogues of Plato? Only two other ones were translated into Latin by Henricus Aristippus (d. shortly after 1162); both translations have been published: V. Kordeuter and C. Labowsky, *Meno, interprete Henrico Aristippo,* London, 1940; L. Minio-Paluello, *Phaedo, interprete Henrico Aristippo,* London, 1950. The influence of these two texts was hardly perceptible, even in the XIIIth century. The indirect influence of Plato has always been much more considerable, and, through the commentaries of Proclus, it will grow steadily from the end of the XIIIth century up to the XVth. For a general survey of the problem, R. Klibanski, *The Continuity of the Platonic Tradition,* London, 1939, pp. 51-53.

On the use made of Horace by William and others, M.-D. Chenu, OP., *Horace chez les théologiens,* RSPT., 24 (1935) 462-465; at that time, *ethicus* generally means "philosopher" as opposed to "sacred writer."

[81] CLARENBAUD OF ARRAS: Wilh. Jansen, *Der Kommentar des Clarenbaldus von Arras zu Boethius De Trinitate, ein Werk aus der Schule von Chartres im 12. Jahrhundert,* Breslau, 1926. The text of the commentary will be quoted from this edition. Our numbers will refer to the pages of Jansen's work which bear an asterisk. For a detailed analysis of the text, see Jansen, *op. cit.,* pp. 33-134.—On Clarenbaud's life, pp. 3-11. A pupil of Hugo of Saint Victor and of Thierry of Chartres, whom he calls "my venerable teachers" (*doctores*); Provost of Arras (1152), then archdeacon of the same church (1160); died after 1170. His commentary follows on many points the *Librum hunc,* which was probably written by his master, Thierry of Chartres: see W. Jansen, pp. 135-148.—MAN., III, 240-241. N. M. Haring, SAC, *A Hitherto Unknown Commentary on Boethius' De Hebdomadibus Written by Clarenbaldus of Arras,* MS., 15 (1953) 212-221.

[82] Division of philosophy, 26-27.—Object of theology, 27.—On intellectibility, 36-37; a divine element in human nature, 54; only faculty capable of knowing God, 88.—God is being, 58; pure formal act, immutable and eternal, 60.—Matter is pure possibility, 59-60.—Because God is pure of matter, and consequently of possibility, he is absolutely simple; the sim-

plicity of God (p. 90) is one of the leading themes of this commentary. An interesting passage is that where Clarenbaud stresses the distinction between "indifference" understood as meaning possibility, hence matter, and indifference understood as meaning "unity of substance" that is the positive simplicity of God, 44.

[83] In *De Trinitate,* 59. W. Jansen (p. 93) finds here a proof of the alleged pantheistic tendency of the School of Chartres.

[84] In *De Trinitate,* 45-46.

[85] In *De Trinitate,* 77-78.—Against Abélard, 48-49.

[86] In *Trinitate,* 42-43.—An anonymous witness to the diffusion of Platonism in the XIIth-century schools of theology has been discovered by M.-D. Chenu and studied by J.-M. Parent, *Un nouveau témoin de la théologie dionysienne au XIIe siècle,* ADGM., I, 289-309: text of the Prologue, pp. 305-309; relations to Erigena, Alanus de Insulis, etc., pp. 299-304.

[87] JOHN OF SALISBURY, born about 1125, studied in Paris, where he came in 1136; then in Chartres, then in Paris again. (UNIV., 11-14, 18-19.) He thus heard all the most famous masters of his own time and was able to become acquainted with their conflicting doctrines without taking sides in the controversy. A secretary to Thibald, Archbishop of Canterbury, then to Thomas Becket, John acquired in these functions the wide and intimate knowledge of court life which is apparent in his *Polycraticus.* Elected Bishop of Chartres, he died in 1180. His works comprise the *Metalogicon,* the *Polycraticus,* a philosophical poem entitled *Entheticus sive de dogmate philosophorum,* his *Historia pontificalis* and an interesting collection of letters, full of information on the history of his own times. Complete works in Migne, PL., 199. Separate and better editions: *Entheticus,* by C. Petersen, 1843; *Policraticus,* by C. C. J. Webb, 2 vols. Oxford, 1909; *Metalogicon,* by C. C. J. Webb, Oxford, 1929. On his life and doctrine, see: M. Demimuid, *Jean de Salisbury,* Paris, 1873. C. Schaarschmidt, *Joannes Saresberiensis nach Leben und Studien, Schriften und Philosophie,* Leipzig, 1862. L. Denis, *La question des universaux d'après Jean de Salisbury,* RSPT., 16 (1927) 425-434. H. Waddell, *John of Salisbury,* in *Essays and Studies by Members of the English Associations,* 13 (1928), Oxford, 1928, pp. 28-51. C. C. J. Webb, *John of Salisbury,* London, 1932 (a biography). H. Daniels, *Die Wissenschaftslehre des Johannes von Salisbury,* Kaldenkirchen, 1932. MAN., III, 253-264. —On XIIth-century humanism, C. H. Haskins, *The Renaissance of the Twelfth Century,* Cambridge, Harvard Press, 1927. G. Paré, A. Brunet, P. Tremblay, *La Renaissance du XIIe siècle,* Paris, 1933.

In praise of Antiquity, *Pol.,* 7, 1; PL., 199, 637 D. "Cicero noster," 638 C. Against absolute scepticism, *Pol.,* 7, 2; 638 D, 639, 640 A. Praise of Cicero's academism, 640 A B. Plato compared with Moses, 7, 5; 645-646. Aristotle is philosophy just as Virgil is poetry. The first principles are certain as well as their necessary consequences, 7, 7; 649-650. Religion too has its principles, 650 B C. The rest belongs in the order of probability, 650 D. On the attitude of true philosophers, 7, 8; 651-653 (contrasted with submission to authority, 7, 9; 653 D). How to philosophize, 7, 11; 661 A B. Against vain dialectics, 7, 12; 662-665.—Dialectics is the proper domain of the Philosopher, Aristotle, *Metal.,* 2, 16; 873. It is to philosophy what animal spirits are to the body, 2, 11; 869. Of itself, it begets nothing, 2, 17; 874-875 and 2, 20; 885 A.—Doctrines upheld by his contemporaries concerning the nature of universals: Walter of Mortagne (*unitas*), 2, 17; 874-875. Cf. 2, 20; 885 A. Bernard of Chartres, 2, 20; 885 A. Cf. 4, 35; 938. Gilbertus Porretanus (*conformitas*), 2, 17; 875. Joscelin of Soissons (*collectivitas*), 876. Anonymous dialectician (*maneries*), 876 A B. All say they are followers of Aristotle, 2, 19; 877. His own solution of the problem, 2, 20; 878 A C. Cf. 882 B C. Universals are the images left in our intellect by what actually existing things have in common. We conceive the models after the copies (actual beings). Our concepts are, so to say, shadows of reality, and when we try to grasp universals in themselves, they fade away like dreams, 2, 20; 878. John finds realism even in Roscelin and in Abélard, 888 C. We resort to universals in order to account for the fact that things resemble one another and, taken together, God, but they are an unnecessary hypothesis. God creates each thing directly with its form and its properties, 882 D; he creates things that resemble one another because they all resemble him. When did God create those so-called realities (885 A)? They are ghosts, fictions made by reason (*figmenta rationis*); in fact, they are chimeras, *monstra enim sunt,* 885 D. Cf. 888 B.

PART FOUR

CHAPTER IV. PETER ABÉLARD

[88] ROSCELIN, born at Compiègne (about 1050). Studied dialectics under a certain John, who taught that "the sophistic art" (i.e., logic) was about words (*esse vocalem*). About 1090, Roscelin himself was teaching logic and applying the dialectical method to matters of theology. Denounced by a monk of Bec, he was accused of teaching that, were it permitted by usage, one could say that there are three Gods (council of Soissons, 1092). Roscelin denied having ever taught that and he was not condemned. After staying in England for some time, he taught logic at Besançon, then at Loches, where Abélard was his pupil. Later on, he became a canon at Tours. The date of his death is unknown (after 1120).— On his life and work Fr. Picavet, *Roscelin philosophe et théologien d'après la légende et d'après l'histoire; sa place dans l'histoire générale et comparée des philosophies médiévales,* Paris, 1911. An appendix (pp. 112-143) contains the texts concerning Roscelin's life and doctrine, including his own Letter to Abélard (pp. 129-139), which is the only one of his works we still have.—On the history of the problem of universals, J. Reiners, *Der aristotelische Realismus in der Frühscholastik,* Bonn, 1907. Same author, *Der Nominalismus in der Frühscholastik,* Münster i. W., 1910 (Beiträge, 8, 5).

[89] Roscelin seems to have been reproached with theological consequences drawn by his adversaries from his logical positions. On the other hand, he had begun by attacking the consequences of Anselm's realism with respect to the formulation of the trinitarian dogma: if species are wholly present in individuals then the three persons are only one being and the Father as well as the Holy Ghost must have become incarnate together with the Son (John to Anselm, in Picavet, 113). To which Anselm rejoined that, if the three persons are three things, then, either Roscelin means to say that there are three Gods, or else he does not understand what he says (Picavet, 114; cf. the later testimony of Anselm, ibid. 118-119). In his *De fide Trinitatis,* ch. II, Anselm criticizes those dialecticians of his own times, or, rather "those heretics of dialectics who think that universal substances are nothing but emissions of voice," i.e., *flatus vocis* (text in Picavet, 119-120). Note that he quotes no text of Roscelin to that effect; it is not certain that Roscelin himself used this formula, it is only probable. To be known through its adversaries only is, for a doctrine, an unfortunate position. If he used it, Roscelin was probably restating in his own way what he had read in Priscian, *Institutionum grammaticarum,* lib. I, ch. 1 (ed. Hertz, I, 5): "Philosophi definiunt vocem esse aerem tenuissimum, vel suum sensibile aurium." Naturally, the definition of a "word," taken precisely as word, does not apply to its meaning, taken precisely *qua* meaning.

[90] I.—ADELHARD OF BATH, taught at Paris and at Laon, did extensive traveling in Italy and Greece, perhaps even Asia Minor. His *Quaestiones naturales,* mathematical treatises, a treatise in astronomy and a translation of Euclid constitute the scientific part of his work. The *De eodem et diverso* is his own contribution to philosophy. In this dialogue between Philosophy, which deals with the *idem,* or "identical" and "immutable," and Philocosmy, which deals with the *diversum,* or changing world of science, Adelhard anticipates the later well-known idea that Plato represents wisdom, while Aristotle represents science. All visible beings are united and simple in *Noys* (i.e., the *Nous*); the same are distinct and multiple in genera, species and individuals; it is all a question of points of view (*respectus*) on the same reality; the same beings can be considered by the intellect either as "the same" (intellectual contemplation), or as "different" (scientific

knowledge).—Text and study in H. Willner, *Des Adelard von Bath Traktat De eodem et diverso,* Münster i. W., 1903 (Beiträge, 4, 1). M. Müller, *Die Quaestiones naturales des Adelardus von Bath,* Münster i. W., 1934 (Beiträge, 31). F. Bliemetzrieder, *Adelhard von Bath. Eine kulturgeschichtliche Studie,* Munich, 1935 (a necessary starting point despite some confusion).

II.—WILLIAM OF CHAMPEAUX, born about 1070 at Champeaux (near Melun), studied in Paris under Manegold of Luttenbach and Anselm of Laon; rector of the schools of Paris (1103); after his difficulties with his pupil Abélard, he retires to the school of St. Victor (Paris); Bishop of Chalons-sur-Marne (1113) up to the time of his death (about 1121). —See E. Michaud, *Guillaume de Champeaux et les écoles de Paris au XIIe siècle d'après des documents inédits,* Paris, 1867. G. Lefèvre, *Les variations de Guillaume de Champeaux et la question des universaux,* Lille (Travaux et mémoires de l'Université de Lille, VI, 20), 1898: contains, pp. 21-79, forty-seven "sentences or questions" on theological matters which, added to the fragment already published by Migne (PL., 163, 1039-1040), make up the only now known texts of William. His glosses on *De interpretatione* are lost, so that we have no work of his concerning the doctrine of universals. The *De origine animae* ascribed to William (PL., 163 1043-1045) belongs to Anselm of Laon. The *Dialogus, seu altercatio cujusdam Christiani et Judaei de fide catholica,* PL., 163, 1045-1072, also ascribed to William, has not yet found its true author.—On the doctrine, B. Adloch, *War Wilhelm of Champeaux Ultrarealist?,* PJ., 22 (1909) 467-481. M. de Wulf, *Histoire . . . ,* I, 177-178. H. Weisweiler, *L'école d'Anselme de Laon et de Guillaume de Champeaux,* RTAM., 4 (1932) 237-269, 371-391; *Das Schrifttum der Schule Anselms von Laon und Wilhelm von Champeaux in deutschen Bibliotheken,* Münster i. W., 1936 Beiträge, 33, 1-2); *Die ältesten scholastiken Gesamtdarstellungen der Theologie. Ein Beitrag zur Chronologie der Sentenzenwerke der Schule Anselms von Laon und Wilhelms von Champeaux,* Scholastik, 16 (1941) 231-254, 351-368.—More general outlook, H. Dehove, *Qui praecipui fuerint labente XIIo saeculo ante introductam arabum philosophiam temperati realismi antecessores,* Lille, 1908.

[91] Gilbert of la Porrée had taught that accidents are not the cause of individuation, but its mark (*In Boeth. De Trinitate,* PL., 64; 1264 A D). This was consistent with his fundamental position that each man, for instance, is a man through his own "humanity," but some of his expressions seem to ascribe an individuating function to accidents (1264 D). At any rate, in doctrines where three men are men in virtue of one and the same "humanity," numerical distinction must be caused by the diversity of their accidents. See, for instance, Clarenbaud of Arras, in *Boeth. De Trinitate,* ed. Jansen, pp. 42-46. Also the anonymous commentary on Boethius *De Trinitate,* in J. M. Parent, *La doctrine de la création . . . ,* p. 204: "Accidentia enim ex quibus pluralitas et numerus contingit et quae variant subjecta . . ." etc.

[92] According to Abélard, William had begun by teaching that there are certain universal essences which are "in singulis individuis totas essentialiter" (V. Cousin, *Ouvrages inédits d'Abélard,* pp. 513-514). Then he taught that those essences are in individuals "indifferenter." In the only known text where William expresses himself on this problem, he says that this "indifference" is not really an identity, but a "resemblance," that is a nondifference: "Sed si veritatem confiteri volumus, non est eadem utriusque (sc. Petri et Pauli) humanitas, sed similis, cum sint duo homines": see G. Lefèvre, *op. cit.,* p. 14. Was this a third position? Or had it already been the meaning of what Abélard describes as his second one? Historians do not even all agree that Abélard succeeded in making him give up his first position: G. Lefèvre, pp. 11-13. Nor is this surprising. All these men were dialecticians. For them, an adversary had said all that it was possible to make him say. In fact, Abélard himself has recognized that where William said "indifferent," he meant "similar": "idem pro indifferenti, id est consimili, intelligunt." See R. McKeon, *Selections . . . ,* I, 228.

[93] PETER ABÉLARD (or Abailard) born at Pallet, in Britanny, about 1079; studied under Roscelin and William of Champeaux; opened a school of his own in Melun, then in Corbeil, near Paris; sickness obliged him to go back to Britanny for some time after which he returned

to Paris and studied rhetoric under his former master William of Champeaux, then theology under Anselm of Laon. After the episode of his love affair with Héloise and his mutilation, he took vows and continued his roving life, carrying his teaching and his restlessness with him into various monasteries (St. Denis, Paraclet, St. Gildas, Cluny) until his death which occurred in 1142.—On Abélard's life, see Ch. de Rémusat, *Abélard, sa vie, sa philosophie et sa théologie*, 2 vols., 2 ed. Paris, 1855. C. Ottaviano, *Pietro Abelardo, la vita, le opere, il pensiero*, Rome, 1931. J. K. Sikes, *Peter Abailard*, Cambridge, 1932. G. Frascolla, *Pietro Abelardo. I, Abelardo umanista e razionalista; II, Abelardo filosofo*, 2 vols. Pesaro, 1950, 1951.—On Héloise and Abélard's life: *Historia calamitatum*, ed. J. T. Muckle CSB, MS., 12 (1950), 163-213. English transl. by the same author: *The Story of Abélard's Adversities*, Toronto, 1954. Same author, *The Personal Letters Between Abélard and Heloise; Introduction, Authenticity and Text*, MS., 15 (1953) 47-94. Among many books on the subject, see Ch. Charrier, *Héloïse dans l'histoire et dans la légende*, Paris, 1933. E. Gilson, *Héloïse et Abélard*, Paris, J. Vrin, 1938; English transl. by L. K. Shook, Chicago, H. Regnery, 1951 (*Heloise and Abelard*). Cf. B. Schmeidler, *Der Briefwechsel zwischen Abaelard und Heloise dennoch eine literarische Fiction Abaelards*, RB., 52 (1940) 84-95; cf. MS., 15 (1953) 48, note 5.

[94] The Duchesne collective edition of Abélard has been reprinted in Migne, PL., 178. It still is indispensable, but it needs to be supplemented or corrected with the help of more recent publications: V. Cousin, *Ouvrages inédits d'Abélard*, Paris, 1836. V. Cousin, *Petri Abaelardi opera*, Paris, 2 vols., 1849 and 1859. R. Stöltzle, *Abaelards 1121 zu Soissons verurtheilter Tractatus de unitate et Trinitate divina*, Freiburg i. Br., 1891. B. Geyer, *Peter Abaelards philosophische Schriften*, Münster i. W., 1919, 1921, 1927, 1933 (Beiträge, 21). P. Ruf and M. Grabmann, *Ein neuaufgefundenes Bruchstück der Apologia Abaelards*, Munich, R. Oldenburg, 1930. H. Ostlender, *Peter Abaelards Theologia "Summi boni" zum ersten Male vollständig herausgegeben*, Münster i. W., 1939 (Beiträge, 35, 2-3); *Die Theologia "scholarium" des Peter Abaelard*, ADGM., I, 282-288.—English transl.,

R. McKeon, *The Glosses of Peter Abailard on Porphyry*, in *Selections*, I. 208-258. Cf. note 103.—BET., 1-4, 1976, 1980.

[95] The "old logic" (*logica vetus*) included the translations, by Boethius, of Aristotle's *Categories* and *Perihermeneias* (or *De interpretatione*); the two commentaries of Boethius on Porphyry's *Isagoge*, his commentary on the *Categories* and his two commentaries on the *Perihermeneias;* his own treatises *Introductio ad syllogismos categoricos, De syllogismo categorico, De syllogismo hypothetico, De divisione, De differentiis topicis* and his unfinished commentary on the *Topics* of Cicero.—The "new logic" (*logica nova*) added to the preceding treatises the following treatises of Aristotle: *Prior Analytics, Posterior Analytics, Topics, De sophisticis elenchis*, plus *the Liber sex principiorum* attributed to Gilbert of la Porrée.—Introduction to the problem: E. Franceschini, *Aristotle nel medio evo latino*, Padova, 1935. M. Grabmann, *Forschungen über die lateinischen Aristotelesübersetzungen des 12. Jahrhunderts*, Münster i. W., 1916 (Beiträge, 17, 5-6); same author, *Aristoteles im zwölften Jahrhundert*, MS., 12 (1950) 123-162. Less studied, but no less important than the transmission of Aristotle, is the transmission of the works of the Greek Fathers of the Church; covering the whole field, J. T. Muckle CSB., *Greek Works Translated Directly into Latin before 1350*, MS., 4 (1942) 33-42; 5 (1943) 102-114.

[96] The description of this position seems to fit the doctrine of Thierry of Chartres. As has been seen, Thierry has criticized Gilbert of la Porrée for having taught that each individual man is man through his own *humanitas*. The second position which Abélard will criticize is precisely that of Gilbert himself, as William of Champeaux had understood it. —Our present analysis follows, with many simplifications, the discussion of the problem in Abélard's glosses in Porphyry, ed. B. Geyer, I, 1-32. A translation of the whole text is to be found in R. McKeon, *Selections*, I, 208-258.

[97] Dialectically speaking, Abélard's argumentation is irrefutable, but he was attacking, in the person of William of Champeaux, a much better man, whose

existence he did not even know. Avicenna
(Ibn Sina), who died in 1037, had already developed a complete system of
metaphysics which, to a large extent, was
an application of the logical principle that
essences are "indifferent" to all their
possible determinations. On Avicenna, see
Part V, ch. 1.—Another solution of the
same problem refuted by Abélard is the
doctrine of the "collection." According to
its defender, Josselin of Soissons (d. 1151;
see J. of Salisbury, *Metalogicon*, II, 17),
who makes the best of expressions used
by Boethius, the reality of a universal
consists in this, that it is the "collection"
of its individuals: see the anonymous
treatise *De generibus et speciebus* (probably written by Josselin), published in
V. Cousin, *Ouvrages inédits d'Abélard,*
especially pp. 524-525. Abélard replies
that a collection cannot be predicated of
things. If the whole collection is predicated of each individual, the theory is
absurd. If, on the contrary, part of the
collection is predicated of one or more of
its individuals, then the collection is not
a universal, whose nature it is to be
predicable wholly of each individual. Besides, any universal is prior to its individuals, whereas a collection is posterior
to its parts. See the complete discussion
in McKeon, I, 228-230.—M. Grabmann,
*Ein Tractatus de Universalibus und andere
logische Inedita aus dem 12. Jahrhundert
im Cod. lat. 2486 der Nationalbibliothek
in Wien,* MS., 9 (1947) 56-70 (text of
the treatise).

[98] As will be seen, Abélard still maintains the existence of Ideas in the mind of
God, and consequently, of common conceptions whose objects are essences. But,
Abélard adds, these subsisting genera or
species can be ascribed to God, not to
man. See McKeon, I, 242.

[99] See McKeon, I, 242-243.

[100] On this distinction, see text in
McKeon, I, 243, with the ensuing effort
of Abélard to reconcile Aristotle and
Plato: 243-244.

[101] The detailed answers are given in
the text translated by R. McKeon, I,
250-254.—Concerning the fourth question,
Cf. Anselm, *De veritate,* 13; PL., 158;
485 B.

[102] A necessary tool for any research
work in the field of speculative grammar

is Priscian, *Institutionum Grammaticarum
libri XVIII,* ed. M. Hertz, Teubner, Leipzig, 1855 (this edition has been republished several times by Teubner). As a
general introduction to the problem, see
the pioneering work of M. Grabmann,
*Die Entwicklung der mittelalterlichen
Sprachlogik,* in *Mittelalterliches Geitesle-
ben,* München, 1936, I, 104-106. Also
M.-D. Chenu OP., *Grammaire et théologie aux XIIe et XIIIe siècles,* in AHDL.,
10 (1935-36) 5-28. In mediaeval texts,
"Priscianus major" designates the grammar of Priscian, Books I-XVI; "Priscianus minor" designates Books XVII-XVIII.
The introduction of grammatical reasonings into theological matters has raised
violent oppositions (see Chenu, art. cit.,
and Ch. Thurot, *Notes et extraits . . . ,*
Paris, 1868, pp. 81-82, 204, etc.). A typical
case of this opposition is that of Peter
Damian, *De perfectione monachorum,* XI;
PL., 145, 306-307); also *De sancta simplicitate,* III; PL., 145, 697. Cf. the
anonymous *Sententiae divinitatis,* ed. by
B. Geyer, Münster i. W. 1909 (Beiträge,
7, 2-3), text pp. 67-70, and the violent
reply of W. of St. Victor, op. cit., 191:
"Grammatica tua haec tecum sit in per-
ditionem!" Despite this opposition, grammatical reasoning was never to be wholly
given up by theologians.—In logic, Priscian himself had paved the way by stressing the ambivalent character of some
notions susceptible of logical as well as of
grammatical treatment, for instance: noun
and verb. He justifies the priority of the
noun over the verb by the priority of the
category of substance over that of action
and passion (*Inst. gramm.,* XVII, 14; II,
116). In the verb itself, he ascribes priority to the indicative mode because it
points out the "essence," or "substance"
of the thing (VIII, 63-64; I, 422. Also
VIII, 67; I, 423). On the reality of species, XVII, 35; II, 130. The problem of
the "consignification" of time by verbs
(Aristotle, *De interpretatione,* III) taken
up by Boethius (PL., 64, 306, and 427
A B), then by Abélard (in *De interpr.,*
ed. B. Geyer, 337 and 345), has been
integrated by Peter Helias with the more
general problem of the *modi significandi*
(see Ch. Thurot, *Notices et extraits . . . ,*
182-183). The problem of "denomination," that is of the nature of derivative
words, raised by Priscian (Bk. IV, especially I, 117) and discussed by Boethius
(*In Categ. Arist.,* I; PL., 64, 168 A B),
became tied up in his logic with the met-

aphysical notion of participation (Cf. Bernard of Chartres, Anselm of Canterbury, in Chenu, art. cit.); on the contrary, Abélard maintains that derived words do not participate in any essence signified by their common root, for the simple reason that there is no such essence (glosses on the *Categories*, in his *Logica*, ed. B. Geyer, 1223-1224). The problem of "enuntiation" and of the nature of the *enuntiabile* has given rise to considerable theological speculation, but it was, first of all, a grammaticological problem: see Abélard, *Logica* . . . , ed. B. Geyer, 327.

[103] The *Scito teipsum* of Abélard, i.e., *Know Thyself*, is to be found in PL., 178, 633-678, and, under a slightly more complete form, in V. Cousin, *Petri Abaelardi opera*, Paris, 1859, II, 594-642. English transl. by J. Ramsay McCallum, *Abailard's Ethics*, Blackwell, Oxford, 1935. —On Abélard's ethics, J. Schiller, *Abaelards Ethik im Vergleich zur Ethik seiner Zeit*, München, 1906. G. de Giuli, *Abelardo e la morale* GCFI., 1931, 33-44. Particularly: J. Rohmer, *La finalité morale chez les théologiens de saint Augustin à Duns Scot*, Paris, J. Vrin, 1939, ch. II and III. O. Lottin, *Le problème de la moralité intrinsèque, d'Abélard à saint Thomas d'Aquin*, RT., 39 (1934) 477-515 Ph. Delhaye, *Un cas de transmission indirecte d'un thème philosophique grec*, SRHC., pp. 145-167; *L'enseignement de la philosophie morale au XIIe siècle*, MS., 11 (1949) 77-99.

[104] Sin and disposition to evil, *Scito teipsum*, J. R. McCallum's transl., II, pp. 17-18. Definition of sin, III, p. 18-19. Sin cannot be defined in terms of "will," p. 22. The deed does not add anything to either merit or demerit, p. 22, p. 25. Original sin is not a sharing in the guilt of our first parents, but in the penalty attending their guilt, p. 27 (cf. *In Epist. Pauli ad Romanos*, PL., 178, 871; in McCallum, p. 2, note 1). Sin then consists in consent only, pp. 28-29, and p. 30. Application to the case of Abraham, p. 33. Abélard sums up his doctrine p. 34. On temptation as distinct from sin, pp. 35-36.

[105] On goodness and intention, ch. VII, McCallum transl., pp. 42-44; ch. XI, pp. 46-47.

[106] Nature of "good intention," ch. XII, pp. 47-48. No sin without contempt of God, ch. XIV, pp. 52-53. Mortal and venial sin, ch. XV, pp. 56-58. Difference between sin and guilt, ch. XIV, p. 55. Not sin, only guilt is prohibited by God, ch. XV, p. 56. Blasphemy against the Spirit the only unforgivable sin, ch. XXII, 72-73. Sin of the persecutors of Christ, ch. XIII, pp. 48-49 and ch. XIV, p. 55. —In saying that, for once, Abélard stopped short, we do not mean to say that, for once, his logic was at fault. Quite the reverse: it is Abélard's constant doctrine that some may have to endure punishments which they have not merited. His doctrine of original sin, which maintains that we share in its penalty without sharing in the sin, is a striking proof of such a possibility. Let us add the persecutors of Christ, the infants who die without baptism, many innocent persons afflicted through no fault of their own. Infidelity caused by ignorance is just one more case which verifies the same law. Even disbelief in the Gospel, in Christ or in the virtue of sacraments, may not be a sin, it nevertheless remains a reason for damnation: ch. XIV, pp. 52-53. The real difficulty was, for Abélard, to justify the application of sanctions to acts whose criminal nature cannot possibly be known. Only his dialectical treatment of the problem could lead him to maintain a personal culpability without personal responsibility.

[107] *Epitome theologiae christianae*, PL., 178, 1172 A.—Since the knowledge of God through natural reason is possible (Rom. I, 20), who would have ever reached it, if not the philosophers? (1172 A B). Cicero suggests that there is only one God (1712 C); many philosophers have established his attributes (1714-1715); some of them have had at least some intimations of the Trinity (1715 C), especially Plato (the Good, the *Nous*, the World Soul, 1144 A C); same doctrine in Mercurius Trismegistus (1141-1142). The whole *Timaeus* of Plato proves that the Holy Ghost is the origin of our souls; hence our duty to glorify God by imitating him (1151-1152). The same doctrine is confirmed by Macrobius (i.e., the *Dream of Scipio*, 1153-1159), as well as by the oracles of the Sibyl (1162 C), etc. On the quasi holiness of the great pagan philosophers: 1179 B C; the precepts of the Gospel are but a reformation

of the natural law already followed by the philosophers, 1179 D; hence those cities of philosophers, ruled by neighborly love and preluding to Christian monasteries, 1180 C (cf. 1184-1185; note, 1185 B, the appeal to the testimony of St. Jerome); some philosophers, like Socrates, died for truth (1190 B); Christians should feel ashamed rather than proud of their conduct when they compare their vices to the chastity of philosophers (1195-1201; obviously a condemnation of his own love affair with Heloise).

[108] On the contribution of Abélard to the method of theology and on the history of his controversies against Bernard of Clairvaux, the best starting point still is Emile Kaiser, *Pierre Abélard critique,* Fribourg (Switz.) 1901. In a rather literary spirit: P. Lasserre, *Un conflit religieux au XIIe siècle, Abélard contre saint Bernard,* Paris, 1930. G. Englhardt, *Die Entwicklung der dogmatischen Psychologie in der mittelalterlichen Scholastik vom Abaelardstreit (um 1140) bis zu Philipp dem Kanzler (gest. 1236),* Münster i. W., 1933 (Beiträge, 30, 4-6). J. Cottiaux, *La conception de la théologie chez Abélard,* RHE., 28 (1932) 247-295, 533-551, 788-828 (excellent). J. Rivière, *Les "capitula" d'Abélard condamnés au Concile de Sens,* RTAM., 5 (1933), 5-22. J. R. MacCallum, *Abélard's Christian Theology,* London, 1948.

PART FOUR

CHAPTER V. SPECULATIVE MYSTICISM

[109] BERNARD OF CLAIRVAUX, born near Dijon in 1091; educated at the school of St. Vorles; in 1112, entered the monastery of Citeaux; abbot of the monastery of Clairvaux in 1115; played an important part in many political transactions and exercised a powerful influence on princes as well as within the Church; preached the second crusade, which was to fail in 1149; died in 1153.—On Bernard's life, see E. Vacandard, *Vie de saint Bernard,* 2 vols. Paris, 1927. A. J. Luddy, *Life and Teachings of St. Bernard,* Dublin, 1927. Watkin Williams, *Saint Bernard of Clairvaux,* Manchester, 1935. General introduction, C. Butler, *Western Mysticism. The Teaching of SS. Augustine, Gregory and Bernard on Contemplation and the Contemplative Life,* 2 ed. London, 1951.

Among the works of St. Bernard, the most important ones for the study of his mystical doctrine are: the *De gradibus humilitatis et superbiae,* that is *The Degrees of Humility and Pride;* the *De diligendo Deo,* that is *On the Love of God;* the *Sermons on Canticles,* and parts of the treatise *On Consideration.* His treatise *De gratia et libero arbitrio,* that is *On Grace and Free Will* deals with the theological problem of the relations between grace, free will and liberty.

EDITIONS.—PL., 182-185. English transl. by S. J. Eales, 4 vols. London, 1889-1896; reprinted London, Burns and Oates, n.d. —Separate editions: *Sermones de tempore, de sanctis, de diversis,* Wien, 1891. *De diligendo Deo* and *De gradibus humilitatis,* in W. W. Williams and B. R. V. Mills, *Select Treatises of St. Bernard of Clairvaux,* Cambridge, 1926. *De conversione,* in W. Williams, *On Conversion,* London, 1938. English transl., G. Lewis, *Saint Bernard On Consideration,* Oxford, 1908. *Works,* translated by a Priest of Mount Melleray, 6 vols., Dublin, 1920-1925 (sermons on the Canticle of Canticles, *On Consideration*). *The Steps of Humility,* by G. B. Burch, Cambridge, Mass., 1940. *The Book of St. Bernard on the Love of God,* by E. G. Gardner, London, 1915 (with text); by T. L. Connolly, New York, 1937; by A. C. Pegis, in *The Wisdom of Catholicism,* New York, 1949, pp. 230-268, followed by the *Jesu dulcis memoria,* pp. 269-271. W. Williams, *Concerning Grace and Free Will,* London, 1920 (with extremely valuable footnotes).—BET., 624-656.

BIBLIOGRAPHY.—J. Ries, *Das geistliche Leben, in seinen Entwicklungsstufen nach der Lehre des hl. Bernard,* Freiburg i. Br., Herder, 1906 (very useful). J. Schuck, *Das religiöse Erlebnis beim hl. Bernard von Clairvaux, ein Beitrag zur Geschichte der christlichen Gotteserfahrung,* Würzburg, 1922 (excellent). *Saint Bernard et son temps,* Acts of the congress of the Association bourguignonne des Sociétés Savantes, Dijon, 1928, 2 vols. R. Linhardt, *Die Mystik des hl. Bernhard von Clairvaux,* München, 1028. W. Williams,

The Mysticism of St. Bernard of Clairvaux, London, 1931. P. Miterre, *La doctrine de saint Bernard*, Bruxelles, 1932. A. Wilmart, *Auteurs spirituels et textes dévots du moyen âge, Etudes d'histoire littéraire*, Paris, 1932. E. Gilson, *The Mystical Theology of Saint Bernard* (1934), transl. from the French by A. H. C. Downes, London, 1940. J. Weingartner, *Abälard und Bernhard. Zwei Gestalten des Mittelalters*, Innsbruck, 1937. O. Castrén, *Bernhard von Clairvaux. Zur Typologie des mittelalterlichen Menschen*, Lund, 1938. D. J. Baarslag, *Bernard van Clairvaux*, Amsterdam, 1941. J. Baudry, *Saint Bernard*, Paris, 1946. M. Standaert OCR., *Le principe de l'ordination dans la théologie spirituelle de saint Bernard*, Collectanea Ord. Cisterc. reform., 8 (1946) 178-216 (on the notion of order). J. Leclercq, *Saint Bernard et Origène d'après un manuscrit de Madrid*, RB., 59 (1949) 183-195; same author, *Textes sur Saint Bernard et Gilbert de la Porrée*, MS., 14 (1952) 107-128.—GDP., 707-708.

[110] First degree of humility, *De gradibus . . .*, I, 4; Mills transl., 29-34. Second degree, I, 5; Mills, 34-37. Third degree, I, 6; Mills, 37-40. On ensuing mystical experience, I, 7; Mills, 42-45.

[111] *De diligendo Deo*, 10; Pegis transl., 255-256. On the Greek antecedents of the notion of "deification," see M. Lot-Borodine, *La doctrine de la déification dans l'Eglise grecque jusqu'au XIe siècle*, RHR., 105 (1932), 5-43; 106 (1932), 525-574; 107 (1933), 8-55. On the doctrine itself, E. Gilson, *The Mystical Theol. of St. Bernard*, ch. V, pp. 119-152.

[112] *In Cant. Cant.*, Sermon 71, 9-10; PL., 183, 1125-1126. Translation in E. Gilson, *The Mystical Theol. of St. Bernard*, pp. 123-125.

[113] On the personal nature of mystical experience, see *Cant. of Cant.*, I, 11; PL., 183, 789. III, 1; PL., 183, 794.

[114] *In Cant. Cant.*, Sermon 82, 5-7; PL., 183, 1179-1181. The notion of divine resemblance in man introduces the notion of liberty. The image and likeness of the creator in man consists in three kinds of freedom: freedom from necessity (free choice), freedom from sin (freedom to choose according to right judgment); freedom from misery (freedom to enjoy what is freely chosen): *Concerning Grace and Free Will*, ch. 3; W. Williams' transl., pp. 14-17. Cf. ch. 9; pp. 46-51. Mystical experience is a temporary pledge of absolute freedom from misery, that is of eternal beatitude: ch. 8, pp. 43-45. Perfect freedom, perfect resemblance and perfect love are one, *De diligendo Deo*, ch. 11; Pegis transl., 257-260.

[115] That true love asks no reward but is always rewarded, *De diligendo Deo*, ch. 7; Pegis transl., pp. 246-247. On the doctrine of love, see *The Myst. theol. of St. Bernard*, pp. 87-89, and *De diligendo Deo*, ch. 12; Pegis transl., pp. 260-263.

[116] WILLIAM OF ST. THIERRY, born at Liège (date unknown), Abbot of St. Thierry from 1119 up to 1135; himself a Cluniac, he desired to become a Cistercian under the authority of St. Bernard; he finally resigned his functions and entered the Cistercian abbey of Signy; William died in 1148. Works in PL., 184: *Epistola aurea*, 307-354 (excluding Book III); English transl. by J. McCann, London, 1930. *De contemplando Deo*, 365-380; *De natura et dignitate amoris*, 379-407; the *Meditativae orationes*, 205-248, have been republished, with a French translation, by M.-M. Davy, Paris, J. Vrin, 1934. *De natura corporis et animae* PL., 180, 695-726. Other works listed in E. Gilson, *The Myst. Theol. of St. Bernard*, p. 199.—For a sketch of his mystical theology, ibid., 200-214.—A. Adam, *Guillaume de Saint-Thierry, sa vie et ses oeuvres*, Bourg-en-Bresse, 1923. A. Wilmart, *La série et la date des ouvrages de Guillaume de Saint-Thierry*, Revue Mabillon, 14 (1925), 157-167. L. Malevez, *La doctrine de l'image et de la connaissance mystique chez Guillaume de Saint-Thierry*, RSR., 23 (1933), 569-588. M.-M. Davy, *Les trois étapes de la vie spirituelle d'après G. de Saint-Thierry*, RSR., 23 (1933), pp. 569-588. M.-M. Davy, *Guillaume de Saint-Thierry, un traité De la vie solitaire*, 2 vols., Paris, J. Vrin, 1914 (text, French transl. and notes). J.-M. Déchanet, *Guillaume de Saint-Thierry. L'homme et son oeuvre*, Paris, 1942; *Guillaume de Saint-Thierry. Oeuvres choisies*, Paris, 1944; *Seneca Noster, Des Lettres à Lucilius à la Lettre aux Frères du Mont-Dieu*, Mélanges de Ghellinck, II, 753-766.—GDP., 708.

[117] ISAAC OF STELLA, Abbot of the French abbey of Stella; near Poitiers; an Eng-

lishman who once felt sorry not to have stayed at home (PL., 194, 1896 A B). *Epistola de anima*, PL., 194, 1875-1890. *Sermons*, PL., 194, 1689-1876.—GDP., 708.

Epistola de anima, soul and reason are one substance, 1877 A. Unity and trinity in the soul, 1877 B. And in things, 1887 B. Is illumined and illuminates, 1877 C; 1887 C-1888 D. Rationality, 1878 C. Affectivity, 1878 D-1879 A. Memory, 1879 D. Division of faculties, 1879 B C; 1884 C-1885 B. Sense knowledge, 1880 C-1881 A. Imagination, 1881 B C. Intelligence and mind, 1881 D. Capable of knowing all things, 1887 C. Perceives intelligible beings, 1885 B C. Sense and imagination at their best in physics, reason in mathematics, intelligence in divinity, 1886 D. The soul is finite, 1883 B-1884 C. Immortality of the soul, 1882 D-1883 B. The soul inheres in the body through a corporeal spirit, i.e., *sensualitas*, 1881 D; 1882 C. The soul as likeness of all things, 1886 A B. The golden chain of beings, 1885 C.

Sermones, man capable of deification, II, 1695, C. On the soul, VIII, 1716 C D. On his personal devil, XXXVIII, 1818 D-1819 C.—The meditation on the nature of God begins in *Sermon* XIX, 1752 C: being is first in reality; it comes before matter and form: "Quidquid igitur est, accepta essendi forma est, atque subsistit, ut hoc vel aliud esse, id est aliqua teneri specie possit. Omne enim quod est, ideo est, quia unum numero est . . ." etc. (see Thierry of Chartres). All that is, is either *per se* or *per aliud*. Prime substance is eminently *ens per se,* 1754 C. Second substances exist in prime substances only; yet complete being requires the existence of a second substance (i.e. species) in a prime substance, 1754 D. Thus, "substance" is as a matter naturally and causally anterior to all substances; it gives them to be (*quod est essentiae*) and to be what they are, that is, substances, 1755 A. Each and every substance is *a* substance, not substance itself. There must therefore be a kind of "supersubstance," which exists in itself and absolutely. Even if it does not exist, this absolute substance is at least conceivable, 1755 C. But what does exist? All that we know is made up of substance, which cannot exist without accidents, and of accidents which cannot exist without substance; or of matter which is nothing without form, and of form which cannot exist without matter;

how can being be made up of elements which, if taken apart, are nothing? (1755 D-1756 B). On the contrary, if there is a God, he is Being (Exod. 3, 14), 1756 A. True being is immutable, 1757 B C. Hence he is above all creatures, 1757 D. And one, principle, end of all things; creator of the universe and its preserver, XXI, 1758 D. Besides, if there never was a God, it was at least true that there was no God; hence truth was from all eternity, 1759 D. Thus, any denial of the existence of God provides a starting point to prove his existence, 1760 A. The nature of God is incomprehensible; nature of theological knowledge, XXII, 1762 A D. On unity, 1764 A D. On the Trinity, XXIII, 1766 B D; on eternity and immutability, 1767 B-1768 D. There was more in God than there is in creation; all was in his foreknowledge and he made all things good (*Genesis* and *Timaeus,* 1769 D); besides, God was light, and the property of light is to shine, XXIV, 1770 C-1771 B.—On these sermons, see P. Bliemetzrieder, *Isaac of Stella, sa spéculation théologique,* in RTAM., 4 (1932), 134-159.—The remarkable diffusion of Cistercian spirituality in England is attested by a striking document: C. H. Talbot, *A List of Cistercian Manuscripts in Great Britain,* Traditio 8, (1952) 402-418.

[118] ALCHER OF CLAIRVAUX, *De spiritu et anima,* in Migne, PL., 40, 779-832. On the authorship of the treatise, G. Théry, *L'authenticité du De spiritu et anima dans S. Thomas et Albert le Grand,* RSPT., 10 (1921), 373-377. When looking for the source of a psychological definition, it is often advisable to try the patchwork of Alcher. For instance, definition of *animus,* I, 781 (i.e., ch. I, col. 781). Definition of *anima,* 8, 784 and 13, 788-789; 24, 796-797 (on self-knowledge, 801); 43, 811-812. Definition of man as made up of two substances (from Gennadius), 3, 781. Definition of *spiritus,* 9, 784; 10, 785-786. Mind (*mens*) and its functions, 11, 786-787. Vital energy and animal life, 21-22, 795. Origin of the soul, 48, 814-815. Faculties of the soul, 37, 807-808. Sense knowledge, 23, 795-796 and 33, 802-803. Degrees of knowledge, 52, 817-818.—On the general problem of the classification of the powers of the soul, P. Michaud-Quantin, *La classification des puissances de l'âme au XIIe siècle,* Revue du moyen âge latin, 5 (1949) 15-34.

[119] GILBERT OF HOYT (Gillebertus de Hoilandia), in England (HLF., 15, 461-469), has written 84 sermons on the *Canticle*, which continue those of Bernard, from III, 1 up to V, 10 (PL., 184, 11-252); then seven tractates: *Tractatus ascetici* (PL., 184, 251-290) and four *Letters* (PL., 184, 289-298). Died in France, at the monastery of Rivour, in 1172. The literary influence of Bernard is visible everywhere in his works (*Cant. of Cant.* I, 2; 13 A. VI, 1; 38 D. IX, 8; 52 B C. XIV, 6; 71 D. XIX, 6; 100 C. XXXIX, 3-4; 204-206 (sums up the *De gratia* of Saint Bernard). In *Tractatus ascetici*, III, 4; 263 B C. Having no mystical experience of his own, he has decided to come down from mysteries to ethics (*de mysteriis ad mores descendere*), *In Cant. of Cant.*, II, 8; 22 A. Nevertheless he has interesting developments on the theme of mystical night: I, 2-5; 13-15. On mystical union, II, 4-6; 19-21. On faith and reason, IV, 2-7; 26-39. On philosophers, V, 2-3; 33. On deification, II, 4; 19 C ("et, si sic dici potest, non est nisi ipse"). Cf. XLIV, 4; 233 B (strong influence of Bernard) and *Tract. ascet.*, I, 6; 256 A. Love is to itself its own reward, *In Cant. Cant.* XIX, 2; 97 D.

On AELRED, see F. M. Powicke, *Ailred of Rievaulx and his Biographer Walter Daniel*, Manchester, 1922 (Text of biography, pp. 71-111). A. Wilmart, *Auteurs spirituels . . .*, pp. 287-297. Author of *Speculum caritatis*, about 1141-42; *Sermones de oneribus*, 1163-64; *De spirituali amicitia*, 1164-65, etc. Died in 1167. His best-known work is his *De spirituali amicitia liber* (PL., 195, 659-702), which is important for the history of the notion of friendship. His avowed intention was to rewrite the *De amicitia* of Cicero for the use of Christians (659 A; 661 D-662 B). On this part of his doctrine, see R. Egenter, *Gottesfreundschaft. Die Lehre von der Gottesfreundschaft in der Scholastik und Mystik des 12. und 13. Jahrhunderts*, Augsburg, 1928; pp. 233-237. E. Vansteenberghe, *Deux théoriciens de l'amitié au XIIe siècle, Pierre de Blois et Aelred de Riéval*, RSR., 12 (1932) 572-588. PETER OF BLOIS (1130-1200) wrote a treatise *De amicitia christiana* which has wrongly been ascribed to Cassiodorus. Text published by M.-M. Davy, *Un traité de l'amour au XIIe siècle: Pierre de Blois*, Paris, 1932. Egenter (op. cit. pp. 243-246), had already proved that Peter's work is largely copied from Aelred.

[120] HUGH OF ST. VICTOR (Hugo de Sancto Victore), PL., 175-177. New and better edition of the *Didascalion* (or *Didascalicon, De eruditione didascalica*) by C. H. Buttimer, *Hugonis de Sancto Victore Didascalion, de studio legendi, a Critical Text*, Washington, D.C., 1939 (necessary). The text of the Grammar has been recently published by J. Leclercq, *Le de Grammatica de Hugues de Saint Victor*, AHDL., 14 (1943-1945), 263-322.—On his life and doctrine, B. Hauréau, *Les oeuvres de Hugues de Saint-Victor, essai critique*, Paris, 1886. A. Mignon, *Les origines de la scolastique et Hugues de Saint Victor*, 2 vols., Paris, 1895. Otto Schmidt, *Hugo von St. Victor als Pädagog*, Meissen, 1893 (Inaug.-Diss.). H. Ostler, *Die Psychologie des Hugo von St. Victor*, Münster i. W., 1906 (Beiträge, 6, 1). F. Vernet, *Hugues de Saint-Victor*, DTC., 7 (1927) 240-308. J. de Ghellinck, *La table des matières de la première édition des oeuvres de Hugues de Saint-Victor*, Recherches de science religieuse, I (1910), 270-289, 385-396. G. Grassi-Bertazzi, *La filosofia di Hugo da San Vittore*, Rome, 1912. J. de Ghellinck, *Un catalogue des oeuvres de Hugues de Saint-Victor*, RNSP., 20 (1913) 226-232. A. Wilmart, *Opuscules choisis de Hugues de Saint-Victor*, RB., 45 (1933) 242-248. W. A. Schneider, *Geschichte und Geschichtsphilosophie bei Hugo von St. Victor*, Münster i. W., 1933. J. Kleinz, *The Theory of Knowledge of Hugh of Saint-Victor*, Washington, 1944. H. Weisweiler, *Die Arbeitsmethode Hugos von St. Victor*, Scholastik, 20-24 (1949), 59-87, 232-267. On the *Didascalicon* as a typical example of a XII-century introduction to philosophy, see R. W. Hunt, *The Introductions to the "Artes" in the Twelfth Century*, Studia mediaevalia (Miscellanea Martin), Bruggis (n.d.), pp. 85-112, especially p. 99. Besides Hugh, this study covers the doctrines of Boethius, Thierry of Chartres, Petrus Helias, Gundissalinus, William of Conches, an "Introduction to Astronomy" and anonymous Glosses on Priscian. M.-D. Chenu OP., *Théologie symbolique et exégèse scolastique aux XIIe-XIIIe siècles*, Mélanges de Ghellinck, II (1951) 509-526. H. Weisweiler SJ., *Zur Einflussphäre der "Vorlesungen" Hugos von St. Viktor*, Mélanges de Ghellinck, II (1951) 527-581. H. Weisweiler, *Die Pseudo-Dionysoskom-*

mentare *"In coelestem hierarchiam"* des Skotus Eriugena und Hugo von St. Viktor, RTAM., 19 (1952) 26-47.—English transl. by Roy J. Deferrari, *On the Sacraments of the Christian Faith,* Cambridge (Mass.) 1951.

ACHARD OF SAINT VICTOR, second abbot of the abbey (d. 1171): text of the treatise *De discretione animae, spiritus et mentis* in G. Morin OSB., *Un traité inédit d'Achard de Saint-Victor,* ADGM., 251-262. Cf. RB., 16 (1899) 218-219.

[121] H. of Saint Victor, *Didascalion,* ed. Buttimer: definition of philosophy, Bk. I, 2; 6-7, and Bk. II, 1; 23-25. Faculties of the soul, Bk. I, 3; 7-10. Also in Bk. I, objects of philosophy, 4, 10-11; division of philosophy, 5, 12; three orders of being (Boethius), 6, 12-14; on nature, 10, 17-18; on logic, 11, 18-22; cf. Bk. II. 29, 45-47.—In Bk. II: on theology, 2, 25; 18, 37. Mathematic (Boethius), 3, 25-27; 7, 30. On the *Quadrivium,* 6, 29-30; 15, 34. Mode of consideration proper to each science, 17, 35-36. Division of mechanics, 20-27, 38-44.—In Bk. III, authors, 2, 49-52. On the seven liberal arts, 3, 52-54, and 4, 54-55. They should be taught separately, 5, 55-57. Art of reading, 6-8, 57-59. Love of learning, 14, 64-67. Bks. IV-VI deal with the reading of Holy Writ.—On Hugh's so-called "theory of knowledge," and especially the doctrine of abstraction ascribed to him by some historians, see the excellent pages of Kleinz, 50-55 (with reference to Hugh's *De unione animae et corporis*). His conclusion, that Hugh "barely touched the real problem" (p. 61) seems to be justified.

[122] *De sacramentis,* in PL., 176, 173-618. Bk. I is an *Hexaemeron:* creation *ex nihilo.* 1, 187; God has created *materia informis* before informing it, 3, 188-189. Matter never wholly deprived of form, 4, 189. In what sense all things were created at a time, 5, 189-190, and 6, 190-192. On light, 8, 194 A. The first three causes: *potentia, sapientia, voluntas,* Bk. I, 2, ch. 6, 208 B. These are one and they are said of the substance of God, 7, 209 A. Existence of God, Bk. I, 3, ch. 7-9, 219 B D. On *mutatio ad formam,* 15, 221 D ("et non est forma aliquid omnino nisi dispositio partium in toto"); on *forma totius,* 221 D. Concerning the creation and nature of man, his intellect and will, see Bk. I, part 6 (creation of man) and part 7 (fall of man); scattered indications only.—On the last remark concerning the will of God, see *De sacramentis,* Bk. I, part 4, ch. 1; PL., 176, 233 D-235 A.

[123] I. RICHARD OF SAINT VICTOR, born in Scotland *ca.* 1123; Prior of the Abbey of St. Victor in Paris; died March 10, 1173. —Works in PL., 196; English transl. in BET., 3295.—On the doctrine: J. Ebner, *Die Erkenntnislehre Richards von St. Victor,* Münster i. W., 1907 (Beiträge, 19, 4). C. Ottaviano, *Riccardo di S. Victore, la vita, le opere, il pensiero,* Rome, 1933 (Mem. della R. Accademia dei Lincei, 4 (1933) 411-541). M. Lenglart, *La théorie de la contemplation mystique dans l'oeuvre de Richard de Saint-Victor,* Paris, 1933. A. E. Ethier, *Le De Trinitate de Richard de Saint-Victor,* Paris, J. Vrin, 1939. G. Dumeige, *Richard de Saint Victor et l'idée chrétienne de l'amour,* Paris, 1952. Classification of Richard's works, in C. Ottaviano, 423-426; psychological elements scattered through his works, ibid., 453-466; mystical speculation, ibid., 471-487.—The *De Trinitate* (PL., 196, 887-992) is an application of the *fides quaerens intellectum* (889 C); like Anselm before him, and Scotus after him, Richard aims to provide necessary reasons in favor of faith (I, 4; 892 C-893 A); after distributing all actual or possible being into three classes (eternal and by itself, neither eternal nor by itself, eternal but not by itself), Richard starts from indubitable sense experience (I, 7; 894 B. Cf. I, 11; 895 B), namely, the existence of things that are not by themselves, since they begin and end, in order to prove the existence of their cause, an eternal and self-subsisting being (I, 8; 894 D-895 A). The whole treatise deals with this eternal being: "Quidquid igitur in hoc opere de aeternis dicitur est ex intentione; quod vero de temporalibus, ex occasione" (I, 10; 895 D). This primordial substance is by itself in this sense that it is in virtue of its own power of existing. Note the curious reasoning: "nothing can be, without either having of itself the possibility of its existence, or else having received it from somewhere else. What cannot be, is not at all; in order then that something exists, it must receive its power to exist from the power of existing" (I, 12; 896 C). In this formula, as in the following one ("Ex essendi itaque potentia esse accipit omne quod in rerum

universitate subsistit") it is not easy to know if *potentia* designates a "power" or a "possibility." Here again, Richard evokes Duns Scotus. The following chapters establish the omnipotence of God, his oneness, the identity of his substance with his deity (I, 16; 898 B) and the other divine attributes.

II. Another Victorine, GODFREY OF St. VICTOR (d. 1194), is just beginning to receive some attention. Works in Migne PL., 196, 1417-1422. Introduction to his life and works in Philippe Delhaye, *Le Microcosmus de Godefroy de Saint-Victor. Etude théologique*, Lille, 1951. Biography, pp. 13-49; doctrine of the *Microcosmus*, pp. 53-177. Indications concerning the *Fons philosophiae* of Godfrey, pp. 181-218. The same historian has given a critical edition of the *Microcosmus* in *Godefroid de Saint-Victor, Microcosmus*. Lille, 1951. On the philosophical poem of Godfrey, *Fons philosophiae*, see A. Charma, *Godefroid de Breteuil, Fons philosophiae*, Caen, 1868. The *Fons philosophiae* seems to have been fiercely attacked by another Victorine, Walter of St. Victor, in his *Contra quatuor labyrinthos Francie;* the text of Walter has been published by P. Glorieux, AHDL., 19 (1953) 187-335.

In his *Microcosmus* (i.e., "man"), Godfrey intends to stress the dignity of human nature (ed. P. Delhaye, p. 32). Man is well defined *animal rationale*, but we should not add *mortale*, p. 35. On human nature as a *microcosmus*, p. 46. Godfrey's *In Hexaemeron* (pp. 47-264) provides him with a framework for the discussion of the particular problems he wants to introduce, either physical, or psychological, or ethical, or theological. All these different levels of explanation are present at one and the same time. The dominant authority is that of Scripture. A good instance of his general attitude is his treatment of the problem of the antipodes, pp. 66-68, which he sees to be connected with that of the unity of mankind; cf. Ph. Delhaye, *Le Microcosmus*, pp. 282-286.—General description of the liberal arts, pp. 81-88.—Ph. Delhaye has characterized the doctrine of Godfrey as "a Christian humanism" (*Le Microcosmus*, p. 93), which he rightly understands in this sense, that, in Godfrey's mind, the appreciation of the supernatural order entails no depreciation of the natural order.

III. On THOMAS GALLUS (*Vercellensis*),

G. Théry, *Thomas Gallus, aperçu biographique*, in AHDL., 14 (1939) 141-208. M.-T. d'Alverny, *Le second commentaire de Thomas Gallus, abbé de Verceil, sur le Cantique des Cantiques*, in AHDL., 13 (1940-1941) 391-401. E. von Ivanka, *Apex mentis* . . . , in ZKT., 72 (1950) 167-169.

[124] ALAN OF LILLE (Alanus de Insulis); PL., 210., *Ars predicatoria*, 111-198; *De fide catholica contra haereticos sui temporis*, 305-430; *De planctu naturae*, 431-482; *Anticlaudianus*, 485-576; *Regulae de sacra theologia*, 621-684.—Other editions: Th. Wright, *The Anglo-latin Satirical Poets and Epigrammatists of the XII century*, II, 268-522, London, 1872. J. Huizinga, *Ueber die Verknüpfung des Poetischen mit dem Theologischen bei Alanus de Insulis*, Amsterdam, 1932; edition of the *De virtutibus et vitiis* in appendix. O. Lottin, *Le Traité d'Alain de Lille sur les vertus, les vices et les dons du Saint-Esprit*, MS., 12 (1950), 20-56. —On the doctrine, M. Baumgartner, *Die Philosophie des Alanus de Insulis im Zusammenhang den Anschauungen des 12 Jahrhunderts dargestellt*, Münster i. W., 1896 (Beiträge, 2, 4). R. de Lage, *Alain de Lille, poète du XIIe siècle*, Paris, 1951. —English transl., *Anticlaudianus*, by W. H. Cornog, Philadelphia, 1935. *Planctus naturae*, by D. M. Moffat, New York (H. Holt) 1908.—If P. Glorieux is right in attributing to Alan of Lille a still unpublished *Summa* studied by J. M. Parent, the general interpretation of his work will have to be revised after the publication of this remarkable text. See J. M. Parent, OP., *Un nouveau témoin de la théologie dionysienne au XIIe siècle*, ADGM., 289-309; on the incomprehensibility of God, 295, 296; on theophanies, 296; equivocity of being, 297-298; influence of Denis and of Scotus Erigena, 300-302; analogies between this work and those of Alan of Lille, 302-303; text of the Prologue, 305-309.

[125] The VENERABLE PETER (Petrus Venerabilis), Abbot of Cluny, visited in 1143 the monasteries of his Order in Spain. He met in Toledo Archbishop Ramon of la Sauvetat and became interested in the work of the Toledan school of translations. Peter suggested that a translation of the Koran would help in the task of refuting the Mohammedan doctrines. The Koran was trans-

lated into Latin by Robert of Ketene, or Ketton (*Ketenensis,* not *Retinensis*) about the years 1141-1143. Peter himself then wrote his *Libri II adversus nefariam sectam saracenorum,* a refutation of Islam. On the early translations of the Koran, see the important study of M.-T. d'Alverny, *Deux traductions latines du Coran au moyen âge,* in AHDL., 22-23 (1947-1948), pp. 69-131. On this Robert and his collaborator Hermann of Dalmatia, see Ch. H. Haskins, *Studies in the History of Mediaeval Science,* 2 ed., 1927, pp. 43-66 and 120-123 (d'Alverny, p. 71, note 2). On the study of Islam in mediaeval Europe: U. Monneret de Villard, *Lo studio dell'Islam in Europa nel XII e nel XIII secolo,* Roma, 1944. On the life and works of the Venerable Peter: J. Leclercq, *Pierre le Vénérable,* Saint-Wandrille, 1946.

[126] The four parts of the *De fide catholica* are directed against the Albigenses, the Waldenses, the Jews and the Pagans. On the Manichean dualism of the Albigenses, I, 2-3; PL., 210, 308-309. Other doctrines are refuted in the same Part I, for instance: mortality of souls, I, 27; 328-329.

[127] *Regulae de sacra theologia,* PL., 210, 621-624.

[128] *De fide catholica,* I, 30; PL., 210, 332-333. Quotes "Mercurius in *Asclepio";* Mercurius *"in Aphorismis de essentia summae bonitatis";* Cicero's *Rhetorica;* Plato, who has given many proofs of the existence of God in the *Phaedo.*—On the methodological problem: M.-D. Chenu, *Un essai de méthode théologique au XIIe siècle,* RSPT., 24 (1935) 258-267.

[129] Text in Cl. Baeumker, *Das pseudohermetische "Buch der vierundzwanzig Meister" (Liber XXIV philosophorum).* See Part III, note 1. The title given by the mss. of Paris is: "Liber Termegisti de regulis theologiae."—On "Deus est sphaera infinita, cujus centrum est ubique, circumferentia nusquam" and its many quotations, p. 31, note 8.

[130] *Regulae* . . . , I, "Monas est qua quaelibet res est una," 623; 2, "In supercaelesti unitas, in caelesti alteritas, in subcaelesti pluralitas"; 3, "Monas gignit Monadem et in se suum reflectit ardorem," 624-625; 5, "Sola Monas est alpha et omega sine alpha et omega," 625-626; 7, "Deus est sphaera intelligibilis, cujus centrum ubique, circumferentia nusquam," 627; 11, "Omne simplex esse suum, et id quod est, unum habet," 628-629; 14, "Omne esse ex forma est," 629; 68, "Omnia in quantum sunt, bona sunt," 654-666; 99, on deification (*apotheosis*), 673-674; on unity as supreme cause, 125, 684.

[131] *Anticlaudianus,* PL., 210, 485-576. Liberal arts, II, 7—IV, 1. 505-521. Prudence and theology, V, 4-5, 532-535. Ecstasis, VI, 2, 541-543. On "Noys" and the work of creation, VI, 8; 548-550. Part played by arithmetic and music, VII, 2, 550-551; VII, 6, 554-556.

[132] E. Gilson, *Le moyen âge et le naturalisme antique,* AHDL., 7 (1932) 5-37.

[133] *De planctu naturae,* PL., 210, 431-482. On Nature, 446 C-451 B. Nature and God, 445 C-446 A. Cf. 453 A-454 B. Reason and faith, 446 A C.

[134] NICHOLAS OF AMIENS (Nicolaus Ambianensis). E. Amann, art. *Nicolas d'Amiens,* DTC., 11 (1931) 555-558.—The *Ars fidei catholicae,* or *Ars fidei* (PL., 210, 595-618) dedicated to Pope Clement III (1187-1191) was traditionally attributed to Alan of Lille until it was attributed to Nicholas of Amiens (together with a *Defensio fidei orthodoxae Gilberti Porretae*) by M. Grabmann, *Die Geschichte der scholastischen Methode,* II, 431-434 and 452-476. It has been recently restored to Alan of Lille by C. Balić, *De auctore operis quod "Ars fidei catholicae" inscribitur,* Mélanges de Ghellinck, II (1951) 793-814. According to the conclusions of C. Balić, the *Ars fidei catholicae* belongs to Alan of Lille, but Nicholas of Amiens has written a short treatise on the work of Alan (text in Balić, 802-814); title, *Scriptum Nicolai Ambianensis in "Artem fidei catholicae" Alani de Insulis.*

PART FIVE

CHAPTER I. ARABIAN PHILOSOPHY

[1] The oldest known Syriac text (after the translation of the Bible) is the *Book on the Laws of the Country*, a misleading title, usually replaced by a more suitable one: *Book on Destiny;* it is a dialogue between Bardesane (154-222) and his disciples.—On the Letter of the Stoic philosopher Mara, see R. Duval, 2 ed., 248-249. —On Ahouddemmeh (d. 575), author of a book of definitions and of treatises on logic, free will and human nature (microcosmus), R. Duval, 250.—On the school of Edessa and the spreading of Greek science and philosophy by the Syrian translators, see R. Duval, 254-272. —Two names of Syrian translators which not unfrequently occur in mediaeval texts are those of Johannitius (d. 873), that is Honein ben Ishaq, of Baghdad, author of many translations of Greek scientific works; and that of Constabulinus, Latin form of Costa ben Luca (864-923), author of a treatise on the distinction between "spirit" and "soul," translated into Latin by John of Spain (Johannes Hispanus) in the XIIth century: *De differentia spiritus et animae.*—On the school of Nisibis, J. Chabot, *L'école de Nisibe, son histoire, ses Statuts*, Paris, 1896.—On Syriac literature, see W. Wright, *A Short History of Syriac Literature*, London, 1894. Rubens Duval, *Anciennes littératures chrétiennes, II, La littérature syriaque*, 2 ed. Paris, 1900; 3 ed. 1907. A. Baumstark, *Die christlichen Literaturen des Orients*, 2 vols., Leipzig, 1911 (Goeschen Collection).—On the philosophical literature in Syriac and in Arabic, bibliography in GDP., 715-716.

[2] The so-called THEOLOGY OF ARISTOTLE seems to have been written in Syriac by the monk Johannân of Euphemia (A. Baumstark, *Die christl. Lit. des Orients*, I, 75). Translated into Arabic about 840 by the Christian Ibn Abdallah Naima, it was retranslated into Latin by the Dominican William of Moerbeke. Extracts in Munk, *Mélanges de phil. juive et arabe*, Paris, 1859 (reprinted Paris, J. Vrin, 1927, pp. 249 ff.). Arabic text by F. Dieterici, *Die sogenannte Theologie des Aristoteles . . .* , Leipzig, 1882. German transl. by F. Dieterici, *Die sogenannte Theologie des*

Aristoteles aus den arabischen Handschriften zum erstenmal herausgegeben, Leipzig, 1883. The mediaeval Latin translation was published under the title: *Sapientissimi philosophi Aristotelis . . . Theologia sive mystica philosophia secundum Aegyptios*, Rome, 1572. Critical edition by C. Vansteenkiste, see infra, p. 652, note 1, III. On the Greek source, see V. Rose's Introduction to his own edition of Plotinus' *Enneads* (Teubner). The confusion about the origin of the doctrine was already apparent in the *incipit* of the Arabic translation (Fr. Dieterici, p. 1): "The book of the philosopher Aristotle, which is called in Greek *Theology*, wherein the doctrine of divine government is expounded and explained by Porphyry of Tyr." Now Porphyry was not a disciple of Aristotle, but of Plotinus. Recent research has not added much to what was already known, it has rather curtailed it: L. Gardet, *La pensée religieuse d'Avicenne*, p. 23, n. 2.

[3] LIBER DE CAUSIS (Book on Causes, Liber Aristotelis de expositione bonitatis purae), excerpted by an unknown author from Proclus' *Elementatio theologica* (Elements of theology); translated into Latin, either from the Greek or from an Arabic compilation, by an unknown translator (perhaps Gerard of Cremona, d. 1187). Arabic text, and mediaeval Latin translation in O. Bardenhewer, *Die pseudo-aristotelische Schrift über das reine Gute, bekannt unter den Namen Liber de Causis*, Freiburg (Switz.) 1882. Already quoted by Alan of Lille under the title: *Aphorismi de essentia summae bonitatis*. Albert the Great knew that it was not a work written by Aristotle; Thomas Aquinas knew that its source was the *Elementatio theologica* (Thomas Aquinas, *In librum De causis*, Opera omnia, Fretté ed., XXVI, 515).—P. Duhem, *Le système du monde*, IV, 321-401. H. Bédoret, *L'auteur et le traducteur du Liber de Causis*, RNSP., 41 (1938) 519-533. P. Kraus, *Plotin chez les Arabes*, Bulletin de l'Institut d'Egypte, 23 (1940-1941) 263-295. M. Alonso, *El Liber de causis*, Al-Andalous, 9 (1944) 43-69; *Las*

fuentes literarias del Liber de causis, Al-Andalous, 10 (1945) 345-382. G. Doresse, *Les sources du Liber de Causis,* RHR., 13 (1946) 234-238. G. Théry, *Tolède . . .* , Oran, 1944. L. Gardet, *La pensée religieuse d'Avicenne,* p. 23, note 3. C. Vansteenkiste, *Notes sur le commentaire de saint Thomas du 'Liber de Causis'* Etudes et recherches, Paris-Ottawa, 8 (1952) 171-191.

[4] M.-M. Anawati, OP., *Avicenne et le dialogue Orient-Occident,* Revue des conférences françaises en Orient, 15 (1951) 202.

[5] On Arabian philosophy in general: T. J. de Boer, *Geschichte der Philosophie im Islam,* Stuttgart, 1901; English transl. by E. R. Jones, London, 1903. D. B. Macdonald, *Development of Muslim Theology, Jurisprudence and Constitutional Theory,* New York, 1903. M. Horten, *Die philosophischen Systeme der spekulativen Theologen im Islam,* Bonn, 1912. Carra de Vaux, *Les penseurs de l'Islam,* 5 vols., Paris, 1921-1926. De Lacy O'Leary, *Arabic Thought and its Place in History,* London, 1922. L. Gauthier, *Introduction à l'étude des philosophies musulmanes . . .* ; Paris, 1923 (generalities). M. Horten, *Die Philosophie des Islam in ihren Beziehungen zu den philosophischen Weltanschauungen des westlichen Orients,* Munich, 1924. L. Gauthier, *Scolastique musulmane et scolastique chrétienne,* Revue d'histoire de la philosophie, 1928, pp. 221-253 and 333-365. M. Horten, *Islamische Philosophie,* Tübingen, 1930. Ibr. Madkour, *L'Organon d'Aristote dans le monde arabe, ses traductions, son étude et ses applications,* Paris, 1934. G. Quadri, *La philosophie arabe dans l'Europe médiévale des origines à Averroès,* Paris, 1947 (transl. from the Italian original). L. Gardet and M.-M. Anawati, *Introduction à la théologie musulmane. Essai de théologie comparée,* Paris, 1948; on the "Kalâm," pp. 39-51.—On the influence of the Koran: J. Abd-el-Djalil, *Le Coran et la pensée musulmane,* En Terre d'Islam, 1939, 303-316. I.-K. Khalifé, *L'anthropologie philosophique du Coran,* ibid., 1943, 3-32. L. Gardet & Anawati, *Introduction . . .* , see note 5. L. Gardet, *La pensée religieuse d'Avicenne . . .* , 109-141. J. W. Sweetman, *Islam and Christian Theology. A Study of the Interpretation of Theologic Ideas in the Two Religions. I, Origins.*

I, *Preparatory Historical Survey of the Early Period.* 2, *The Theological Position at the Close of the Period of Christian Ascendancy in the Near East,* 2 vols., London, 1945, 1947.—GDP., 716-720.

[6] On ALKINDI, Albino Nagy, *Die philosophischen Abhandlungen des Ja'qub ben Ishaq al-Kindi zum ersten Male herausgegeben,* Münster i. W., 1897 (Beiträge, 2, 5). This work comprises the following treatises of Alkindi in their mediaeval translations: *De intellectu, De somno et visione, De quinque essentiis, Liber introductorius in artem logicae demonstrationis.*—See T. J. de Boer, *Zu Kindi und seiner Schule,* Archiv für Geschichte der Philosophie, 13 (1900), 153-178. H. Malter, *Al-Kindi, "the Philosopher of the Arabs,"* Hebrew College Annual, 1904, 55-71.—GDP., 720.

[7] ALFARABI. In German translation, Fr. Dieterici, *Alfarabis philosophische Abhandlungen, aus dem arabischen übersetzt,* Leiden, 1892; same author, *Der Musterstaat,* Leiden, 1900 (cf. L. Cheikho, *Traités inédits d'anciens philosophes arabes,* 2 ed., Beyrouth, 1911).—Latin translations, Cl. Baeumker, *Alfarabi über den Ursprung der Wissenschaften (De ortu scientiarum). Eine mittelalterliche Einleitungschrift in die philosophischen Wissenschaften,* Münster i. W., 1916 (Beiträge, 19, 3). E. Gilson, *Les sources gréco-arabes de l'augustinisme avicennisant,* AHDL., 4 (1930) 115-126 (*De intellectu et intellecto*). D. H. Salman, *Le Liber exercitationis ad viam felicitatis,* RTAM., 12 (1940) 33-48; same author, *Fragments inédits de la logique d'Alfarabi,* RSPT., 32 (1948) 222-225; same author, *The Mediaeval Latin Translations of Alfarabi's Works,* NS., 13 (1939) 245-261. Fr. Rosenthal & R. Walzer, *Alfarabius de Platonis philosophia,* London, 1943 (modern Latin transl.).—A. Birkenmajer, *Eine wiedergefundene Uebersetzung Gerhards von Cremona,* ADGM., 472-481: text of the *Distinctio sermonis Abunazar Alpharabii super librum "Auditus naturalis,"* pp. 475-481.—On the doctrine: M. Steinschneider, *Alfarabis des arabischen Philosophers Leben und Schriften,* Leipzig, 1869. Ibn Madkour, *La place d'Al Farabi dans l'école philosophique musulmane,* Paris, 1934. H. Bédoret, *Les premières traductions tolédanes de philosophie. Oeuvres d'Alfarabi,* RNSP., 41 (1938) 80-97.

R. Hammond, *The Philosophy of Al-farabi and its Influence on Mediaeval Thought,* New York, 1944. E. L. Fackenheim, *The Possibility of the Universe in al-Farabi, Ibn Sina and Maimonides,* American Academy for Jewish Research, New York, 1947. M. Cruz Hernandez, *El "Fontes Quaestionum . . . de Abu Nasr Al-Farabi,* AHDL., 18 (1950-1951) 303-323. A. Cortabarria, *Las obras y la filosofia de Alfarabi en los escritos de San Alberto Magno,* La Ciencia Tomista, 77 (1950) 362-387; 78 (1951) 81-103.— GDP., 291, and 720-721.

[8] AL ASH'ARI (873-935), a typical representative of the Motekallimun. Thomas Aquinas knew the essentials of his position through Moses Maimonides. The Ash'arites represented to him the philosophers who deprive nature of its efficacy: *Contra Gentiles,* III, 69.—On their atomism, Salomon Pines, *Beiträge zur Islamischen Atomenlehre,* Berlin, 1936.—On the school as a whole, detailed information is to be found in M. Horten, *Die philosophischen Systeme der spekulativen Theologen in Islam,* Bonn, 1912 (see index, under *Aschari,* p. 628 and *Aschariten,* p. 629). Cf. L. Gardet and M.-M. Anawati, *Introduction à la théologie musulmane,* pp. 52-66.

[9] Quoted by Djemil Saliba, *Etude sur la métaphysique d'Avicenne,* 84-85. Among the treatises of Alfarabi translated by Friedrich Dieterici (Leiden, 1892), particular attention should be paid to his *Harmony between Plato and Aristotle* (pp. 1-53) whose title is in itself a philosophical program. Alfarabi does not cheat; he quotes from Plato's *Phaedo* and *Republic,* and from Aristotle's *Organon* and *Nichomachean Ethics,* which all are authentic works. Moreover, he is well aware of discrepancies between the two doctrines; yet he considers the *Theology of Aristotle* as authentic and, consequently, instead of reconciling Aristotle with Plato, he actually reconciles Plotinus with Plato, which is a much easier thing to do. The blending of this composite philosophy with his own religion becomes apparent when Alfarabi deals with the problem of the origin of the world: "Aristotle recognized a creator, who has created the world from nothing" (p. 37). This applies even to matter. The contradiction which appears between the denial of Ideas in Aristotle's *Metaphysics* and their affirmation in the so called *Theology of Aristotle* was a harder nut to crack. Alfarabi envisages three possible solutions: 1, Aristotle contradicted himself, but this was impossible for so great a philosopher; 2, the *Theology* is a spurious work (which was the right hypothesis), but this is still more impossible, for his works are so well known that they could not have been falsified; 3, there is a deeper meaning which enables us to reconcile these two writings. And indeed, the criticism directed by Aristotle against Plato's Ideas does not mean that these do not exist, but that they do not subsist in themselves, outside of the divine mind.

[10] See the German translation of Alfarabi's treatise *On the Different Meanings of the Word Intellect in Aristotle,* in Fr. Dieterici, pp. 61-81: or its Latin translation in AHDL., 4 (1930), pp. 115-126. On the agent Intellect as giver of forms, Fr. Dieterici, p. 77; on its relations to God, p. 80.

Among the difficulties created for their readers by the special terminology of the Latin translations of Alfarabi and Avicenna, one or two at least can be easily eliminated. Imagination (*imaginatio*) or formation (*formatio*) signify: conception, that is, either the act of forming a concept (more exactly, a simple apprehension), or the product of this act, namely, the concept or simple apprehension itself. "Faith" (*fides*) signifies not religious belief, but the assent of the mind implied in a judgment. Another term for *fides* is *credulitas:* not "credulity," but intellectual assent. This is the meaning of the verb *credere* in the Latin translations of Aristotle himself: *pisteuein,* to give assent to. On the Stoic origin of these notions, M.-D. Chenu, *Notes de lexicographie philosophique médiévale. Un vestige de stoïcisme,* RSPT., 27 (1938) 63-68. P. Michaud-Quantin, *Aestimare et Aestimatio,* Archivum latinitatis medii aevi (Bulletin Du Cange) 22 (1952) 171-183.

[11] AVICENNA (Ibn Sina), born near Boukhara in 980 (Hegira, 370); an extremely precocious child, he assimilated successively the Koran, elementary arithmetic and geometry, logic, then medicine, which he learned from both books and practice. He then was 16 years old. After a year and a half devoted to free studies and meditations, he chanced upon the

treatise of Alfarabi *On the Intentions of Aristotle in His Book on Metaphysics.* This reading cleared up for him all the difficulties which he still found in the metaphysics of Aristotle. Avicenna wrote his first book at the age of 21. His whole life was devoted to the composition of poetic, scientific and philosophical writings, as well as to various teaching, legal and political activities. He died at Hamadân, in July, 1037, in his 58th year (Hegira, 428).

Bibliography in M.-M. Anawati, *La tradition manuscrite orientale de l'oeuvre d'Avicenne,* in Revue thomiste, 1951, pp. 415-440 (lists 276 authentic or spurious works). His famous *Canon* of medicine belongs to the history of sciences; it was translated into Latin by Gehrard of Cremona (XII cent.). On its history, see M.-M. Anawati, *Essai de bibliographie avicennienne,* Cairo, 1951 (in Arabic), p. 212. Of his many philosophical works only a few have been translated into Latin and made accessible to the mediaeval scholastics. The most important one is *The Healing* (Arabic, *al Shifa*), in four parts: logic, physics, mathematics, metaphysics (ed. of the Arabic text, vol. I, Logic: *Isagoge,* Cairo, 1952). It was translated into Latin by Dominicus Gundisalvi (Gundissalinus) and Ibn Daoud (Avendeath). This XII-cent. translation is incomplete. The mathematical part is left out; the logic represents but a small part of the original text; large sections of the physics have been suppressed. On the contrary, the *De caelo* does not seem to be authentic. Note that because the treatise on the soul came sixth in the complete work, it will often be called by the scholastics, *Liber sextus naturalium* (the sixth book of natural philosophy). Since it represents what the West has known of Avicenna's doctrine, our own exposition will chiefly rest on the *Shifa.* —The *Najat* (i.e., *The Cure*) is a shorter redaction of the *Shifa.* Although the scholastics did not know it, modern readers may use it instead of the longer redaction.—The only available editions of the mediaeval Latin translation of the *Shifa* are those of the XVth and XVIth centuries: *Metaphysica,* Venice, 1493. *Avicennae peripatetici philosophi ac medicorum facile primi Opera omnia . . . ,* Venice, 1495, 1508, 1546.—Modern translations of other works (unknown to the middle ages): P. Vattier, *La logique du fils de Sina . . . ,* Paris, 1659 (logical

section of the *Najat*). A. F. Mehren, *Traités mystiques d'Avicenne; texte arabe avec l'explication en français,* Leyde, 1889-1891. J. Forget, *Le livre des théorèmes et des avertissements d'Avicenne,* Leyde, 1892. Van Dyck, *Avicenna's Offering to a Prince, a Compendium on the Soul,* Verona, 1906. M. Horten, *Das Buch der Genesung,* Halle, 1907 (metaphysical and theological sections of the *Shifa*). Nematallah Carame, *Avicennae metaphysices compendium,* Rome, 1926 (metaphysical section of the *Najat*). H. J. Holmyard and D. C. Mandeville, *Avicennae de congelatione et conglutinatione lapidum,* Paris, 1927. M. A. Goichon, *Introduction à Avicenne: son Epitre des définitions,* Paris, 1933. M. A. Goichon, *Ibn Sina, Livre des directives et des remarques,* French transl. and notes, Beyrouth-Paris, 1951. Arthur J. Arberry, *Avicenna on Theology,* London, 1951 (see pp. 9-14, an English transl. of Avicenna's Autobiography, and its continuation pp. 15-24.

BIBLIOGRAPHY.—M.-M. Anawati, OP., *Essai de bibliographie avicennienne,* Cairo, 1950 (in Arabic). GDP., 721-722.—Prantl, *Geschichte der Logik im Abendlande,* II; 2 ed. pp. 325-367. B. Haneberg, *Zur Erkenntnislehre des Ibn Sina und Albertus Magnus,* Abhandlungen der bayer. Akad. der Wiss. (philos.-philolog. Klasse), XI, 1, München, 1866, pp. 189-267. H. Siebeck, *Zur Psychologie der Scholastik. Avicenna,* Archiv für Gesch. der Philosophie, 2 (1889), 22-28. Carra de Vaux, *Avicenne,* Paris, 1900. C. Sauter, *Avicennas Bearbeitung der aristotelischen Metaphysik,* Freiburg i. Br., 1912. E. Gilson, *L'étude des philosophies arabes et son rôle dans l'interprétation de la scolastique,* Proceedings of the Sixth International Congress of Philosophy (Harvard, Sept., 1926) Longman, Green, New York, 1927, pp. 592-596. Djémil Saliba, *Etude sur la métaphysique d'Avicenne,* Paris, 1927. M.-A. Goichon, *La distinction de l'essence et de l'existence d'après Ibn Sina (Avicenne),* Paris, 1937; *Lexique de la langue philosophique d'Ibn Sina (Avicenne),* Paris, 1938; *La philosophie d'Avicenne et son influence en Europe médiévale,* Paris, 1940 (2 ed. 1951). Moussa Amid, *Essai sur la psychologie d'Avicenne,* Genève, 1940. C. Smith SJ., *Avicenna and the Possibles,* NS., 17 (1943) 340-357 (important). B. H. Zedler, *Saint Thomas and Avicenna,* Traditio, 6 (1948) 105-159. M. Cruz Hernandez, *La metafisica de Avicenna,* Granada, 1949. G. Vajda, *Les notes d'Avicenne sur la "Théologie d'Aristote,"* RT., 51 (1951) 346-406; on the importance of these notes, L. Gardet, *En l'honneur du millénaire d'Avicenne*, ibid., 333-345. L. Gardet, *La pensée religieuse d'Avicenne (Ibn Sina)*, Paris, 1951. F. Rahman, *Avicenna's Psychology*, New York, 1952. E. Bloch, *Avicenna und die aristotelische Linke*, 1952.—On the Latin translations, H. Bédoret, *Les premières versions tolédanes de philosophie. Oeuvres d'Avicenne*, RNSP., 41 (1938) 374-400. M.-T. d'Alverny, *Les traductions latines d'Ibn Sina et leur diffusion au moyen âge*, Millénaire d'Avicenne, Congrès de Bagdad (20-28 mars 1952), Le Caire, 1952, pp. 59-69; cf. AHDL., 19 (1953) 337-358.—BET., 499-501.

[12] The Physics is the second part of Avicenna's *Shifa;* it comprises eight parts: 1, Generalities (*Sufficientia*, or *Communia naturalibus*, or *Communia naturalium*) ; 2, Heaven and the world, probably spurious; 3, On coming to be and passing away (*De generatione et corruptione*), not included in the 1508 ed.; 4, On elements, action and passion (*De actione et passione*), same remark; 5, On meteors (*De rebus congelatis*), same remark; 6, On the soul (*De anima*, or *Liber sextus naturalium*) ; 7, On plants (*De plantis*), not included in the 1508 ed.; 8, On animals (1, *De animalibus;* 2, *De partibus animalium*), translation ascribed to Michael the Scot by the 1508 edition. All the references included in our text are to this 1508 Venice edition. For instance, *Sufficientia*, I, 2, should be read: *Sufficientia*, Book I, chapter 2.—On the problem of the elements and of their subsistence in mixed bodies according to Avicenna, Anneliese Maier, *An der Grenze von der Scholastik und Naturwissenschaft*, Essen, 1943, 28-33; on the problem *de latitudine formarum*, op. cit., 31-32.—Avicenna's influence, A. Birkenmajer, *Avicennas Vorrede zum "Liber Sufficientiae" und Roger Bacon*, RNSP., 36 (1934) 308-320.

[13] ALGAZEL's exposition of Avicenna's philosophy (minus its logic) is to be found in *Algazel's Metaphysics, a Mediaeval Translation*, ed. J. T. Muckle, Toronto, 1933. See also Asin Palacios, *Algazel: dogmatica, moral, ascetica*, Saragossa, 1901. Carra de Vaux, *Gazali*, Paris, 1902. J. Oberman, *Der philosophische und religiöse Subjektivismus Ghazalis*,

Wien, 1921. M. A. Palacios, *La espiritualidad de Algazel y su sentido cristiano*, Madrid, 1924, 1925, 2 vols. A. J. Wensinck, *La pensée de Ghazzali*, Paris, 1940 (see p. 203 on the editions of the arabic texts). S. de Beaurecueil, *Ghazzali et saint Thomas d'Aquin*, in Bulletin de l'Institut français d'archéologie orientale du Caire, 46 (1947), 199-238 (existence of God) GDP., 722.—According to his exposition of Avicenna's doctrine (which he does not accept) everything that exists, is either possible or necessary. The possible only is through a cause; the necessary is in virtue of itself. One cannot say of it that it may be, but that it has to be; it is "sufficient to itself" (ed. Muckle, p. 46). The necessary being is the cause of all the rest. There is only one such being, which we call the First (*Primus*), or God. All the other beings are merely possible in themselves, but they become necessary in virtue of the necessity of the First, from which all possible effects are bound to follow in a necessary way (pp. 46-47). Being necessary, God is eternal in both his existence and his causality. Consequently he is eternally creating (*factor incessabilis sempiternus*, p. 50) and the universe is eternally being produced (*si fuerit (factor) eternus, erit factura eterna*, p. 51). The universe flows from the science and will of God as light flows from the sun (p. 61). The order of emanation is that of the astronomical world (p. 121). The lowest separate Intelligence is too weak a contemplation to beget another Intelligence, but it acts as *"dator formarum."* Hence, in sublunary matter, the eternal succession of corruptible beings, including man and his intellect. Intellectual knowledge comes to man from without, that is from the *Intelligencia agens*, or giver of forms (pp. 183-185).—On the origin and meaning of the term *anitas* (*annyya*) G. Vajda, *La philosophie et la théologie d'Ibn Caddiq*, AHDL., 17 (1949) 161, note 3; the question is still obscure.

[14] I. AVEMPACE (Ibn Badja), born at Saragossa, known as a mathematician, a physician, an astronomer and a philosopher. His logical treatises have not yet been published. Information about his doctrine in S. Munk, *Mélanges de philosophie juive et arabe*, 349-409. His noetic seems to have been known to the scholastics chiefly through Averroes.

II. ABUBACER (Abu Bekr ibn Thofaïl,

d. *ca.* 1185. See L. Gauthier, *Hajj ben Yakdhan, Roman philosophique d'Ibn Thofaïl, texte arabe et traduction française,* Alger, 1900; Spanish transl. by Fr. Pons, Zaragossa, 1900. Selections in English transl. by P. Brönnle, London, Orient Press, 1910.—English transl., BET., 45-48. —On the doctrine, L. Gauthier, *Ibn Thofaïl, sa vie et ses oeuvres,* Paris, 1909.

[15] IBN ROCHD (Averroes). Our references are to the edition of Aristotle's *Opera omnia,* Venetiis, apud Juntas, 1574, which includes the commentaries of Averroes. A table of the ten volumes is to be found in G. Quadri *La philosophie arabe,* pp. 201-203. Two volumes of a new edition of the *Averroes latinus* have been published: *Compendium librorum Aristotelis qui Parva Naturalia vocantur,* ed. A. L. Shields and H. Blumberg, Cambridge, Mass., 1949. *Commentarium magnum in Aristotelis De Anima libros,* by F. S. Crawford, Cambridge, Mass., 1953. The shorter exposition of the metaphysics (*Epitome*) is to be found in the Venice edition, v. VIII, in Latin translation (pp. 356-396). Spanish transl., by C. Quiros Rodriguez, *Averroes Compendio de metafisica,* Madrid, 1919. German transl., by S. Van den Bergh, *Die Epitome der Metaphysik des Averroes,* Leiden, 1924. On the doctrine, E. Renan, *Averroès et l'averroïsme, Paris,* 1852. L. Gauthier, *La théorie d'Ibn Rochd sur les rapports de la religion et de la philosophie,* Paris, 1909. M. Horten, *Die Metaphysik des Averroes,* Halle, 1912. Same author: *Die Hauptprobleme des Averroes nach seiner Schrift: Die Widerlegung des Gazali,* Bonn, 1913. P. Duhem, *Le système du monde,* IV, 496-575. Manuel Alonso, *Teologia de Averroes (estudios y documentos),* Madrid-Granada, 1947. L. Gauthier, *Ibn Rochd (Averroes),* Paris, 1948; Cf. Louis Gardet, Bulletin thomiste, 8 (1951) 248-252.—On the doctrine of the composition of material substances and its influence, A. Maier, *An der Grenze der Scholastik,* 33-90.

[16] The main treatise of Averroes on this problem exists in several translations: L. Gauthier, *Accord de la religion et de la philosophie, Traité d'Ibn Rochd (Averroës), traduit et annoté,* Algiers, 1905. M. J. Müller, *Philosophie und Theologie von Averroes,* Munich, 1859 and 1875 (German transl.). Moham. Jamil-ur-Rehman, *The Philosophy and Theology of Averroes,* Baroda, 1921 (English transl.). On the meaning of the doctrine, see L. Gauthier's book quoted note 15.

[17] Hyperbolic in expression as it is, the sincerity of Averroes' loyalty to Aristotle cannot be doubted. Aristotle has "invented" physics, since nothing that was written before him on the subject is worth reading; moreover, Aristotle has "terminated" physics, since no one of those who came after him has been able to add anything to it; in more than a thousand years no error of any size has been found in his writings; this is miraculous, and divine rather than human (*In Physic.,* Prolog., Venice, 1562, v. IV, p. 5 ro). This is not with him a feeling only, but a doctrine. Aristotle has never been wrong because, given his demonstrative method, he could not be wrong. True enough, some of his successors, for instance Galen in biology, may have added to what Aristotle knew, and for this they should be praised (*In de part. animal.,* III, 10; v. VI, p. 172 ro), but where they contradicted him, he was right and they were not. See the extraordinary statement: whatever Galen may have *seen* by anatomy (*per anatomiam*), it cannot possibly contradict the conclusions of Aristotle, for the simple reason that these "are universal demonstrations, taken from propositions that are natural, prime, universal and essential. Now it is a character of such demonstrations that no sense perception can ever contradict them." (*In de Part. animal.,* II, 7; v. VI, p. 139 ro). Against Avicenna and Galen, who dared to contradict Aristotle, *In VIII Physic.,* 4; v. IV, p. 424 vo. Against Nicholas of Damas, who thought that a better order than that of Aristotle's could be followed, *In Metaph.,* XII, Prooemium; v. VIII, p. 290 ro. The blending of philosophy with religion is equally damaging to both and ruins the doctrine of Aristotle, *In Physic.,* I, 3; v. IV, p. 36 vo (against Algazel).

[18] By "logical" method, we should not understand "dialectical" and merely probable, but, as far as it is possible to achieve it, the pursuit of necessary demonstrations, taken from universal and necessary principles. We have quoted texts related to biology (note 17), but the same kind of demonstrations applies to astronomy (*In de Coelo,* II, 1; v. V, p. 8 vo). It still more evidently applies

to metaphysics.—Against Avicenna's doctrine, that existence is accidental to essence and substance, the best text is: *Destructio destructionum philosophiae Algazelis,* disp. V; v. IX, pp. 77 vo-78 vo. As a necessary consequence, Averroes denies that the *esse* of God is his essence (since actual existence is nowhere distinct from actual substance), op. cit., disp. VIII, pp. 99 vo-100 vo. These positions will deeply influence scholastic theology. —Being is analogical, *In metaph.,* IV, 2, 2; v. VIII, p. 65 ro. It is one by nature, not by accident (against Avicenna), op. cit., IV, 2, 3; p. 67 ro. Cf. V, 6; pp. 110-115. Substance is also analogical, V, 8; p. 118. On accidents, necessary or separable, V, 30; p. 143 ro. The categories are the accidents of substance, VII, 1; p. 153 vo. Being is eminently substance, ibid., p. 154 ro. Substance is eminently form, ibid., p. 158 ro. Bodies are substance in virtue of their forms, ibid., pp. 158 vo-159 vo. Definitions are about substances, VII, 3; pp. 162 vo-163 ro. And especially about quiddities, or forms, as they are in actual beings (against Plato's separate Ideas), VII, 5; pp. 169 ro-170 ro. Cf. VII, 6; p. 172 ro, and VII, 8; pp. 177 vo-178 vo. All forms are not given to matter by a "giver of forms" (against Avicenna, and perhaps Themistius), VII, 10; pp. 181 ro-181 vo (note the conclusion concerning the reasons why theologians favor Plato). Cf. XII, 3; p. 304 ro and vo. Being *qua* being divides into potency and act, IX, 1; p. 225 vo-226 ro. On act, IX, 2, 1; p. 236 ro-237 ro. Act is prior to potency, IX, 2, 3; p. 239 vo-240 ro, and form to matter, ibid., 4, pp. 241 ro-244 vo.

[19] See the commentary of Averroes *In Praedicamenta,* I, 1; v. I, p. 24 vo. Cf. op. cit., II, 1; p. 29 ro-31 ro.

[20] *Epitome,* I; v. VIII, p. 358 ro and vo. —In view of what follows it is necessary to note the following points. 1) No mention is made by Aristotle of an efficient cause as distinct from the moving cause (*Metaph.,* V, 2, 1013 a 24-34); 2) this distinction has been made by Avicenna (*causa agens*); 3) the Latin text commented by Averroes and Averroes himself freely use *causa agens* as an equivalent for *causa efficiens;* 4) in Averroes, the *causa movens* is efficient inasmuch as it is cause of the generation by way of motion (*causa generans*); 5) the notion of efficient cause adds nothing to that of moving cause

("illud ex quo est principium motus, et est causa movens et agens," *In Phys.* II, 4; v. IV, p. 72 v E); 6) for this reason, Avicenna was wrong in imagining a production of all other beings by the Prime Cause, for indeed, since the separate substances are not in potency with respect to being, it is a mere imagination to speak of action, consecution, coming from, etc., with respect to such beings; there is no production of being there, except in the sense that intellect is cause of intellection ("causa et causatum secundum quod dicimus quod intellectus est causa intelligentis," *In Metaph.,* XII, ch. 4, text. 44; vol. VIII, p. 327 vo I-K); 7) again for the same reason, there is no sense in pretending, with Avicenna, that "from one single and simple being only one effect can follow," for indeed a multiplicity of intellections can follow from what is an Intelligence (ibid., 327 vo I-K); the Moderns (Avicenna) who say that a movent follows from another movent are mistaken about the nature of these separate beings which, since there is in them no potency, cannot be educed from potency to act; so, once more, such words as *consequitur, praecedit, provenit,* etc., simply do not apply to them (ibid., 328 ro D).

As Averroes sees it the problem is to know if the effect is latent in the nature of the generating cause, as those who do not understand the meaning of generation say it is (Plato, Themistius) or if it is educed by the cause from the potency of matter (Aristotle). Those who favor the first position divide into three groups: *a*) the supporters of the latency (*latitationem*) of forms in matter, according to whom the agent has nothing more to do than to extract and to disengage them from matter, so that, in fact, the agent cause is for them a moving cause; *b*) the supporters of creation properly so-called, according to whom the efficient causes create the whole being from nothing and without a pre-existing matter (all the theologians, or *loquentes,* either Moslems or Christians, perhaps the Christian philosopher John Philoponus according to Alpharabi in his treatise *On Transmuted Beings*); *c*) the mediating positions, which all agree that creation from nothing is impossible because generation presupposes a subject, namely, matter, and these, in turn, subdivide into three positions: Avicenna, according to whom the agent creates the form and

puts it in matter (the "giver of forms");
Themistius, and perhaps Alfarabi, who
distinguish between agent causes present
in matter and agent causes separated
from matter; Aristotle, according to
whom "the agent only makes the compound of matter and form, and makes
it by moving the matter, and transmutes
it until there arises from it what there
was in it that was in potency with respect to that form in act." Even the
position of Aristotle is a sort of mediation between intrinsecism (*latitatio*) and
extrincesism (*creatio*): it does not teach
the latency of forms, but their eduction
from potency to act; it does not teach
creation, for the Aristotelian agent does
not cause by introducing forms into matter from without ("non est agens quia
adducit in illam materiam aliquid extrin-
secum"), but because, by moving matter,
the Aristotelian form causes a form similar to itself to arise out of it. Averroes,
In Metaph., XII, 3, text. 17; Venice, 1574,
pp. 303 ro-305 vo. This important text
should be kept in mind while reading
Siger of Brabant and even Thomas Aquinas, *De veritate,* XI, 1.

The place assigned by Averroes to Avicenna is in keeping with his appreciation
of the general position of his predecessor
as a half-way house between philosophy
and theology: "The way he followed in
proving the first principle is the way of
the theologians and what he says is always found to be, so to say, between
the Aristotelians and the theologians," *In
Physic.,* II, 3, 22; Venice, 1562, pp. 56
vo-57 ro.

[21] Against Avicenna (whom Duns Scotus will support on this point) Averroes
maintains that physics (natural science),
not metaphysics, is qualified to determine
the existence of separate substances, particularly that of the First separate substance, namely, God (*In I Physic.,* ch. 5;
v. IV, p. 47 ro and vo). On the contrary,
the nature of God is studied by metaphysics: *In Metaph.,* IV, 2, 1; v. VIII,
p. 73 ro. Averroes likewise blames Avicenna for saying that physics has to learn
from metaphysics that bodies are composed of matter and form (ibid., p. 47
vo). On nature and its analogical meaning, *In II Physic.,* I, 3; v. IV, p. 49. *In V
Metaph.,* 4, 5; v. VIII, p. 107 vo-108 vo.
—Nature is matter, eternal and subject
of all forms, *II Physic.,* ch. 6 and 7; pp.
50 vo-51 ro.—Form too is nature, ibid.,

pp. 52-53.—Unlike mathematics, physics
considers matter together with form, ibid.,
II, 2, ch. 1; pp. 53 vo-55 vo, and ch. 3;
pp. 55 vo-57 vo.—On causes, II, 3, ch. 1;
pp. 59 ro-63 vo.—On chance, against Avicenna, II, 3, 2; p. 66 vo.—Importance
of final cause in both physics and metaphysics, II, 4, ch. 1; p. 75 vo.—After a
re-exposition of Aristotle's doctrines on
place and motion, Averroes establishes,
in Bk. VII, that all that which moves
is moved by another (VII, 1; pp. 306-
308), and that it is impossible for such
a series of causes to be infinite (VII,
2, 8; pp. 311-312). Since movement is
eternal (VIII, 1; pp. 338 ro-339 ro),
and necessary (against the theologians,
ibid., p. 341 vo), the first motion must
be a circular one (pp. 342 vo-343 ro).
Whatever the theologians may say, there
can be no beginning of movement, nor
of the world, because there can be no
new will of God (pp. 349 vo-350 ro).
Consequently, there must be a prime
mover, itself immobile (VIII, 2, ch. 1;
pp. 355 vo-356 vo; cf. VIII, 2, ch. 3, 36,
p. 375 ro and vo). There is only one
eternal, perpetual and immobile Prime
Mover (VIII, 2, ch. 5, 45; p. 385 ro and
vo). The Prime Mover has no quantity;
hence he is simple (VIII, 4, 78; pp. 423
vo-424 vo); and since he is moving during
an infinite time, his power is infinite
(VIII, 4, 79; pp. 425 vo-429 ro); cf. *In
XII Metaph.,* 3, 41; v. VIII, pp. 323 vo-
325 vo. Being immaterial, he is nowhere,
except in those places where his effects appear; in this sense, religions are right in
saying that God is in his heaven, because
the motion of heavens is his effect (*In VIII
Physic.,* loc. cit., 84; v. IV, p. 432 ro); cf.
In de Coelo, I, 6; v. V, p. 17 vo.
These positions will be taken up and
reinterpreted by Thomas Aquinas, just
as those of Avicenna will provide a starting point for Duns Scotus.

[22] Eternal action of the Prime Mover,
In Metaph., XII, 1, 30; v. VIII, pp. 314
vo-315 vo. Itself is immobile, XII, 2, 36;
pp. 318 ro-319 ro. The principle of the
movement of heaven is intellectual, ibid.,
37, p. 319 vo. Life, perfection and beauty
of the First Cause, XII, 3; pp. 322 ro-323
ro. How the other eternal and separate
Substances are moved by the first one,
XII, 4; pp. 326 vo-328 vo. On the various
astronomical systems, ibid., 45, pp. 329 ro-
334 ro. That celestial bodies have no souls
(against Avicenna), *De substantia orbis,*

1; IX, p. 5. On the noblest of all questions about God, namely, the nature and object of his knowledge, XII, 4, 51; pp. 335 ro-336 ro; and the nature of his knowledge of inferior beings, XII, 5, 1; pp. 337 vo-318 ro (note conclusion on God's general providence). In reading the metaphysical cosmography of Averroes, one should carefully keep in mind that, in his doctrine, the Prime Mover is the cause of the substance of the universe *qua* final moving cause only; God is the cause of the being of the world, not its "maker"; creation is to him a religious notion and, as such, it is extraneous to philosophy proper: *Destructio destructionum philosophiae,* disp. 4; see, v. IX, p. 69 ro, especially the striking formula: "agens motus est agens mundi": to cause movement is to cause the world. On the causality of the Prime Mover, the texts of Aristotle, Averroes and Avicenna quoted by Thomas Aquinas should be understood in terms of Christian creation.

[23] On this question, the best study we know is B. H. Zedler, *Averroes on the Possible Intellect,* Proceedings of the American Catholic Association, 25 (1951) 164-178.—Since it knows all things, the intellect is none of them, *In de anima,* III, 4; ed. F. S. Crawford, 385-386. As receptive of cognition, it is called "material," not because it is corporeal (which it is not) but because, like matter, it is pure potentiality (pp. 387-388). It is perhaps not a substance really separate from the agent Intellect; cf. Zedler, p. 168, note 25: every Intelligence, except the first one, is in potency with respect to intelligible forms and, to that extent, it is "material." This separate Intellect (both material and agent) is the same for all men, *In de Anima,* III, 5; 401-403. There is a continuity (*continuatio*) between this separate Intellect and the particular soul of every man. The contact is made possible by the imagination of man, in which a certain preparation is required in view of intellection, p. 405. Alexander of Aphrodisias was wrong in conceiving the material intellect as a preparation in a tablet instead of conceiving it as a tablet that has received this preparation 431: "O Alexander . . . Ego autem verecundor de hoc sermone . . ."; his crime was to not follow Aristotle: "Credo enim quod iste homo fuerit regula in natura et exemplar, quod natura invenit ad demonstrandum ulti-

mam perfectionem humanam in materiis," p. 433. In fact, imagination is the "passive intellect" of man (*intellectus passivus*). In this doctrine, for our own soul to abstract is to receive intelligibles from on high; hence the reception of intelligible forms in our own "passive intellect" from the separate Intellect is called "acquisition" (*adeptio,* to attain, attaining); in consequence of this acquisition, our passive intellect is in the condition of received, or acquired, intellection (*intellectus adeptus*). Naturally, all these expressions borrowed from sensible reality (potency, act, acquisition, etc.) are used equivocally when applied to the intellect.—Since they are separate substances (in fact, they make up the lowest one) the material and agent Intellects are eternal and therefore immortal (III, 4; p. 185 vo). Man only becomes similar to the separate substances to the extent that, through knowledge, he becomes somehow all things. For indeed beings are nothing else than the science God has of them, and his science of beings is their cause: ibid., p. 501.

A clear summary of Averroes' doctrine on this point is found in its commentary (*infra,* p. 798, note 71) by Cajetan of Thiene, *Expositio super libros De anima Aristotelis,* Venice, 1502, Lib. III, text. 6, dub.; fo 74 verso a: "The second opinion was that of Averroes, who posited the intellective soul as a form separated from matter in its being but appropriated to human bodies in operating. For indeed, in understanding, it depends on the human phantasm as on its proximate mover. Moreover, he asserted that there was only one single intellective soul in all human bodies, contiguous to them, assisting them as the Intelligence assists the sphere it moves, ungenerable and incorruptible. And he said that it was essentially composed of two indivisible substances, the one called agent intellect, the other one called possible intellect. And he said that the possible intellect has no other nature than potentiality and receptivity with respect to the intelligibles. As to the agent intellect, he wants it to be an active cause with respect to the species. By phantasm, he understands the act of three internal faculties ministering to the intellect, namely, the imaginative, the cogitative and the memory. He then affirms that the possible intellect is perfected by the agent intellect as matter is perfected by form; and that the agent intellect is a certain intelligible nature inferior in perfection to the heavenly Intelligences, but superior to the possible intellect. Moreover, he maintains that, besides the intellective soul, there is in man another soul, namely, the sensitive soul, educed from the potency of matter, generable and corruptible, and numerically multiplied. This soul is united with the human body in its being; it specifies the being of man; it is generable and corruptible." This represents the average position of the Latin Averroists from the XIIIth up to the XVIth century.-- On the Greek sources of the doctrine: P. Wilpert, *Die Ausgestaltung der aristotelischen Lehre vom Intellectus agens bei den griechischen Kommentatoren und in der Scholastik des 13. Jahrhunderts,* ADGM., 447-462.

PART FIVE

CHAPTER II. JEWISH PHILOSOPHY

[24] On the history of Jewish mediaeval Philosophy, GDP., 723-725. S. Munk, *Mélanges de philosophie juive et arabe,* Paris, 1859; photostatic reproduction, Paris, 1927. M. Eisler, *Vorlesungen über die jüdischen Philosophie des Mittelalters,* 3 vols, Wien, 1870, 1876, 1884. D. Neumark, *Geschichte der jüdischen Philosophie des Mittelalters nach Problemen dargestellt,* 2 vols, Berlin, 1907, 1910. J. Husik, *A History of Mediaeval Jewish Philosophy,* New York, 1916 (bibliography, pp. 433-437). G. Vajda, *Jüdische Philosophie* (bibliographical). G. Vajda, *Introduction à la pensée juive du moyen âge,* Paris, 1947; with an excellent bibliography to which we are indebted for part of the following notes. See particularly, pp. 213-214, the indications concerning doctrinal monographies (H. A. Wolfson, etc.) not indicated in our own text.—On the influence of Jewish philosophy, J. Guttmann, *Das Verhältnis des Thomas von Aquino zum Judentum und Jüdischen Literatur,* Göttingen, 1891. Same author, *Die Scholastik des XIIIen Jahrhunderts in ihren Beziehungen zum Judentum und zum jüdischen Literatur,* Breslau, 1902. J. Koch, *Meister Eckhart und die jüdische Religionsphilosophie des Mittelalters,* Jahresbericht der Schlesischen Gesellschaft für vaterländische Kultur, Breslau, 1928. E. S. Koplowitz, *Ueber die Abhängigkeit Thomas von Aquinas, von Boethius und R. Moses ben Maimon,* Kallmünz, 1935. K. Schubert, *Die Problemstellung in der mittelalterlichen jüdischen Religionsphilosophie vor Maimonides,* ZKT., 75 (1953) 55-81.

[25] On SAADIA BEN JOSEPH, besides G. Vajda, pp. 45-60 (bibliography, pp. 219-221), see J. Guttmann, *Die Religionsphilosophie des Saadia,* Göttingen, 1882.

H. Malter, *Saadia Gaon, His Life and Works,* Philadelphia, 1921. D. Neumark, *Saadia's Philosophy, Sources, Characters,* in *Essays in Jewish Philosophy,* 1929, pp. 145-218. M. Ventura, *La philosophie de Saadia Gaon,* Paris, 1934. I. Efros, *Saadia's Theory of Knowledge,* JQR., 33 (1942-1943), 133-170. H. A. Wolfson, *The Double Faith Theory in Clement, Saadia, Averroes and St. Thomas and its Origin in Aristotle and the Stoics,* JQR., pp. 213-264. A. Herschel, *The Quest for Certainty in Saadia's Philosophy,* JQR., pp. 265-313; to be completed by, *Reason and Revelation in Saadia's Philosophy,* JQR., 34 (1944), pp. 391-408. G. Vajda, *Le Commentaire de Saadia sur le Séfer Yecira,* Revue des Etudes Juives, 106 (1941-1945), 64-86. H. A. Wolfson, *The Kalam Arguments for Creation in Saadia, Averroes, Maimonides and St. Thomas,* American Academy for Jewish Research; Texts and Studies; vol. II, Saadia's Anniversary Volume, New York, 1943, pp. 197-245. Same author, *Atomism in Saadia,* JQR., 37 (1946), 107-124.

[26] ISAAC ISRAELI.—*Opera omnia Ysaac . . . ,* Lugduni, 1515. Edition of the best-known treatise of Isaac by J. T. Muckle, *Isaac Israeli. Liber de Definitionibus,* in AHDL., 11 (1937-1938) 299-340. On the doctrine: J. Guttmann. *Die philosophischen Lehren des Isaak ben Salomon Israeli,* Münster i. W., 1911 (Beiträge, 10, 4). H. A. Wolfson, *Isaac Israeli on the Internal Senses,* "Jewish Studies in Memory of G. A. Kohut," New York, 1935, 583-598.

The *Liber de definitionibus* has been for the middle ages an inexhaustible mine of information. On *anitas* and *quidditas,* ed. J. T. Muckle, 300-302. Definition and description of philosophy, 302-303. On the four causes (including the "efficient" cause), 303-305. Philosophy described as man's self-knowledge, 306. Description of Wisdom, 306-309. What the essence of Intelligence is, 309-311. Its three degrees: always in act, in potency, progressively passing from potency to act, 311-312. On the soul: "a substance united to a body"; this does not contradict the definition given by Aristotle; both teach that the soul is a substance and that it perfects a natural body, 312-313. Souls penetrate bodies as the light illuminates air, 313. Illumination of the world by the Intelligence, 316-317. Difference between *spiritus* and *anima*, 318-319. On nature, 320. On rational knowledge, 321-328, a long chain of definitions, some of which have been widely used; note, however, that the famous definition of truth attributed to Isaac: "adaequatio rei et intellectus" is not to be found in this treatise. Isaac defines truth: "Et sermo quidem dicentis: veritas est quod est, enuntiativus est naturae veritatis et essentiae ejus, quoniam illud sciendum quod est res, vera est; est veritas nonnisi quod est," pp. 322-323.—The true origin of the formula seems to have been ascertained by D. H. Pouillon, *Le premier traité des propriétés transcendentales,* RNSP., 42 (1939) 58-61. It is a sentence of Avicenna, *Metaph.,* I, 4: "veritas . . . intelligitur dispositio in re exteriore cum est ei aequalis." William of Auvergne quoted it several times in clearer terms: "et hoc (sc. intentio veritatis) ait Avicenna, est adaequatio orationis et rerum" (*De universo,* III-I, ch. 26, p. 749). And again: "adaequatio intellectus ad rem" (*De universo,* I, 10, 5; I, 14, 3). Cf. art. cit., p. 59.

[27] IBN GABIROL. The text of the *Source of Life,* in its mediaeval Latin translation, has been published by Cl. Baeumker, *Avencebrolis Fons Vitae ex Arabico in Latinum translatus ab Johanne Hispano et Dominico Gundissalino,* Münster i. W., 1892-1895 (Beiträge, 1, 2-4).—On his doctrine, see GDP., 726. S. Munk, *Mélanges . . . ,* pp. 5-306. J. Guttmann, *Die Philosophie des Salomon Ibn Gabirol,* Göttingen, 1889. D. Kaufmann, *Studien über Salomon Ibn Gabirol,* Budapest, 1899. M. Wittmann, *Die Stellung des hl. Thomas von Aquin zu Avencebrol,* Münster i .W., 1900 (Beiträge, 3, 3). Same author, *Zur Stellung Avencebrols im Entwicklungsgang der arabischen Philosophie,* Münster i. W.,

1905 (Beiträge, 5, 1). P. Duhem, *Le système du monde,* V, 3-75. K. Dryer, *Die religiöse Gedankenwelt des Salomon ibn Gabirol. Ein Beitrag zur Religionsgeschichte des jüdischen Mittelalters,* Leipzig, 1930. F. Brunner, *La Source de Vie,* livre III, Paris, 1950 (introduction to, and French translation of, Bk. III; list of variants borrowed from mss. not used by Baeumker, pp. 51-52). On Gabirol as source of the scholastic doctrine of the plurality of forms in composite substances, G. Théry, *L'augustinisme médiéval et le problème de la forme substantielle,* Acta hebdomadae augustinianae-thomisticae, Torino-Roma, 1931, pp. 140-200.—BET., 2067-2069, 2364; not the *Source of Life).*—On the influence of Gabirol on Jewish philosophy: G. Vajda, *La philosophie et la théologie de Joseph Ibn Caddiq,* AHDL., 17 (1949) 106-110.

[28] The division of the *Source of Life* arises from its very subject matter. The ultimate end of man is his supreme good, namely, knowledge (*scientia*). Through self-knowledge, man achieves the knowledge of all the rest, including the knowledge of the Prime Being, which is his mover and his cause. Unknowable in itself, because it is infinite, this being can be known from its creatures and, before anything else, from universal being (*essentia universalis*), whose two roots are matter and form (*materia universalis* and *forma universalis*). Everything is reducible to them, if not really, at least dialectically (I, 6, pp. 8-9). Hence the division of the work into five treatises: 1, matter, form, and their union in composite substances; 2, on matter as the subject of the corporeity of the world; 3, on simple substances; 4, on matter and form in simple substances; 5, on universal matter and universal form. Within this general frame, the reader should be ready for a free dialectical flow and a great many repetitions.—Our references are to the Baeumker edition: Treatise, article and page.

[29] A reductive analysis, which consists in mentally abstracting from given beings all their forms, uncovers two opposite principles: 1, universal matter, existing in itself, one in essence, in which all formal diversity subsists and, for this reason, giving to all things its essence and its name (I, 10-12, pp. 10-15); 2, universal form, whose properties are to subsist in a sub-

ject, to perfect the essence of that in which it subsists and to give it being: *dare ei esse* (I, 13, p. 16). Intelligence is the universal form of all things, and the forms of all things are the forms of Intelligence, V, 14, p. 282; V, 16, p. 286.

[80] Everything is made up of matter and form; bodies are such because their matter is subjected to the form "corporeity": *materia sustinens corporeitatem,* II, 1, p. 24. It is therefore correct to speak of a matter of corporeity: *materia corporeitatis.* II, 1, p. 23; but the expression "form of corporeity," although widely used, is not correct; corporeity itself is a form, IV, 81, p. 228. Even simple substances are made up of matter and form; composition and simplicity are not incompatible, III, 4, pp. 217-220; III, 7, pp. 226-228. Matter is a formless spiritual energy (*virtus*); the essence of form is a light adding to that in which it is its specific distinction, V, 4, p. 263. On matter, *hyle,* and substance, II, 11, p. 43. Since everything is made up of universal matter and universal form, there is matter even in Intelligences, II, 8, pp. 38-39; IV, 1, pp. 211-213; matter is cause of their diversity, IV, 3, pp. 215-217; V, 5, pp. 264-267. Prime matter, not being, is the *genus generalissimum,* V, 8, p. 271. Since it has being through form, matter itself only has being in potency, V, 10, pp. 274-277.—As far as we know, the formula *forma corporeitatis* does not occur in Gabirol; at any rate, his usual expression is *corporeitas;* on the contrary, *forma corporeitatis* is frequent in the Latin version of Avicenna, which is its probable origin. Naturally, this does not prevent Gabirol from being one of the origins, if not of the formula, at least of the doctrine. On its significance for scholasticism: B. Baudoux, *De forma corporeitatis scholastica,* Antonianum 13 (1938) 429-474.

[81] "Plurality of forms" is a later expression, used by historians to point out the position of Gabirol on this point. It means that, in his own description of composite beings, their inner structure appears as made up of forms hierarchically ordered according to their higher or lower degree of generality. These forms are distinguished by dialectical reasoning: (*resolutio* and *separatio,* II, 3, p. 28); inferior forms are *in* superior forms, III, 23, p. 133; III, 26, p. 142; they are

united in them as intelligible forms are united in the form of Intelligences, V, 18, p. 290. In this sense, *continentia* is a property of all forms; the higher the form, the more inferior forms it contains, IV, 15, p. 246. For the same reason, the more united it is, the more unifying a form is, III, 23, p. 123; III, 32, p. 154-155 (cf. later on, in Duns Scotus, the doctrine of the *continentia unitiva* in forms). Pp. 154-155 are full of justifications for the expression "plurality of forms"; for instance: "Formae substantiae compositae multae sunt" (p. 154); "formae substantiae compositae multae inventae sunt in forma substantiae simplicis" (ibid.); "unitas quae est in substantia simplici est debita causa collectionis multarum formarum in illa" (ibid.); "in unitate sunt multae formae" (p. 155) etc. Note that, in such a doctrine, far from endangering the unity of beings, the multiplicity of their forms flows from it. It should be so, since such is the general law of the universe: "Unitas est origo multiplicitatis per se."

[32] On this correspondence between modes of subsistence and places, II, 14, pp. 48-49. Place is either corporeal or spiritual, ibid., p. 49.

[33] The universe is the work of a Maker (*factor*), III, 2, p. 75. He only makes one simple substance, III, 2, p. 78. For Him to make is to create out of nothing (*ex nihilo*); but he creates simple entities only, what is composite is not really created, III, 3, p. 79. Intermediate beings between the Maker of the world and creature properly said are therefore composite. The Prime Maker is not in time, nor does he act in time, III, 5, p. 88; III, 7, p. 94. All that which begins to be was possible; it becomes necessary after it exists, III, 10, p. 100. The holy, supreme and universal Prime Maker creates out of his generosity; he is the source, and the container, of the forms that flow from him, III, 13, p. 107; III, 29, pp. 147-151. Simple and intelligible substances flow and act in a necessary way; their order is like the progressive spreading of sunlight, III, 16, pp. 112-113; IV, 14, pp. 242-245. Intelligible and spiritual substances contain in themselves all the forms scattered throughout the corporeal substances, III, 24, p. 136; III, 25, p. 138; III, 32, pp. 152-155. Only God creates, simple spiritual substances

only impress forms into matter, III, 25, p. 139. How this is possible, III, 34-35, pp. 158-161. How this explanation applies to the nine categories, III, 42, p. 172-174. On the three souls (animal, rational and intellectual), and on their operations, III, 46, pp. 181-190. The production of form in matter by God is like the projection of intellection, by the intellect, upon the known thing, or like the projection (*emissio*) of sensation, by sense, upon the perceived thing, V, 6, p. 267. According to Plato, forms are caused in the universal Intelligence by an intuition of the Will; in the Soul by an intuition of the universal Intelligence, and in natural substances by an intuition of the universal Soul, V, 17, pp. 289-290. V, 18, pp. 290-292.

[34] II, 13, p. 46. Cf. ibid. "Omnia quaecumque sunt coartata sub voluntate sunt et omnia pendent ex ea." The science of the will is the perfection of wisdom, V, 40, p. 329. It is the science of the reason why things exist, V, 40, p. 329; cf. II, 13, p. 45. Will cannot be described, except indirectly, as the divine virtue which makes matter and form, ties them together, and is in the whole universe as the soul is in its body, III, 38, p. 326. It is an efficient cause, IV, 20, p. 256. It is between the Prime Essence on the one hand and, on the other hand, prime matter and prime form, I, 7, pp. 9-10. While it is not acting, the will is identical with essence, IV, 19, p. 253; V, 37, p. 325. The will of God can do nothing contrary to his essence, V, 42, p. 335. Everything is submitted to the will of God, I, 2, p. 4; V, 39, p. 327. Cf. V, 41, p. 330; V, 40, p. 329. The will creates matter and form II, 13, p. 47; V, 36, p. 323. Matter and form are two branches of the will (*rami voluntatis*), I, 7, p. 10. On the difficulty and importance of the science of the will, V, 40, pp. 329-330.

[35] The temptation to mistake Gabirol for a Christian was almost irresistible in those passages where he identifies the will with a *"verbum agens"* and, therefore, with the creative energy of God, V, 36, pp. 322-323: "Verbum, id est voluntas, postquam creavit materiam et formam, ligavit se cum eis, sicut est ligatio animae cum corpore, et effudit se in illis et non discessit ab eis et penetravit a summo usque ad infimum."

[36] On IBN PAKUDA, see G. Vajda, *Introduction . . .* , pp. 85-94; on IBN CADDIQ, pp. 104-109; on ABRAHAM IBN DAOUD and early Jewish Aristotelianism, pp. 125-129. In his bibliography, Vajda refers to J. Guttman, *Die Religionsphilosophie des Abraham ibn Daoud*, Göttingen, 1879. The uncertainty still prevailing about the respective identities of Ibn Daoud and Dominicus Gundissalinus should be kept in mind.—On JUDA HALLEVI, G. Vajda, pp. 110-118; bibliography, pp. 226-227.

[37] MOSES MAIMONIDES (Moses ben Maimon).—*Le Guide des égarés*, text, French translation and notes, by Salomon Munk, 3 vols. Paris, 1856-1866. English transl. by M. Friedländer, 3 vols. London, 1881-1885; revised and republished in one volume, minus the notes, in 1904; sixth impression of this second edition, London, Routledge, 1936. The Latin mediaeval translation follows the Hebraic version of Juda-al Haziri. This Latin translation, probably made about 1240 in Toledo, has been printed, with omissions and modifications, by Giustiniani: *Rabbi Mossei Aegyptii Dux seu director dubitantium aut perplexorum*, Paris, 1520. It is sometimes quoted by the scholastics under the title of *Dux neutrorum*. GDP., 329-331.—On Maimonides, see GDP., 727. A. Rohner, *Das Schöpfungsproblem bei Moses Maimonides, Albertus Magnus und Thomas von Aquin*, Münster i. W., 1913 (Beiträge, 11, 5). By several authors, *Moses ben Maimon, sein Leben, seine Werke und sein Einfluss*, 2 vols., Leipzig, 1908 and 1914. L.-G. Lévy, *Maïmonide*, Paris, 1911; revised ed., 1932. Fr. Kuntze, *Die Philosophie Salomon Maimons*, 1913. M. T.-L. Penido, *Les attributs de Dieu d'après Maimonide*, RNSP., 26 (1924) 137-163. P. Duhem, *Le système du monde*, V, 170-201. An important series of studies by H. A. Wolfson, *Maimonides and Halevi*, JQR., 3, 2 (1912), pp. 297-337. *Maimonides on Internal Senses*, ibid., 25 (1935), pp. 441-467. *Note on Maimonides' Classification of the Sciences*, ibid., 26 (1937), pp. 369-377. *The Aristotelian Predicables and Maimonides, Division of Attributes*, Essays and Studies in Memory of Linda R. Miller, 1938, pp. 201-234. *The Amphibolous Terms in Aristotle, Arabic Philosophy and Maimonides*, HTR., 31 (1938), pp. 151-173. L. Roth, *Spinoza, Descartes and Maimonides*, Oxford, 1924. Z. Diesendruck, *Maimonides Lehre von der Prophetie*, in Jewish

Studies in Memory of Israel Abrahams, New York, 1927, pp. 74-134. Same author, *Die Teleologie bei Maimonides,* Hebrew College Annual, 1928, pp. 415-534. L. Strauss, *Philosophie und Gesetz, Beiträge zum Verständnis Maimunis und seiner Vorläufer,* Berlin, 1935. Abr. Heschel, *Maimonides, Eine Biographie,* Berlin, 1935; French transl., *Maïmonide,* Paris, 1936. M. Ventura, *Maïmonide, Terminologie logique,* Hebrew text and French transl., Paris, 1935. Collective work, *Maïmonide, sa vie, son oeuvre, son influence,* Les Cahiers juifs, 2 (1935), 16/17; extensive bibliography, pp. 141-151.—English transl., BET., 2793 (logic), 2801-2802 (*Guide*), 2805-2806 (*ethics*), 2807 (*selections*).

[38] Metaphysics is not accessible to all human minds whose inequality is an obvious fact (I, 31). Nobody should investigate what is beyond his intellectual powers (I, 32); many impediments prevent most men from studying philosophy, especially metaphysics (I, 34; all this doctrine reappears in Thomas Aquinas, *Contra Gentiles,* I, 1); but even those who do not know philosophy can learn, on the authority of Scripture, that there is a God, one, incorporeal, perfect and wholly unlike all that which can be said about him (I, 35). Theologians have not to teach philosophy nor natural science, but they can use it in order to show that religious faith is either true or, at least, rationally possible, II, 2. To mistake dialectical and merely probable conclusions for demonstrated truths is a grievous fault; no desire to justify religious belief can excuse this error; on the contrary, it does not give men philosophical certitude and it leads them to lose their religious faith, II, 16. For instance, creation in time is a fundamental belief in religion; all we can do is to demonstrate its rational "non impossibility."—For a comparison with Thomas Aquinas: P. Synave, *La révélation des vérités divines naturelles d'après S. Thomas d'Aquin,* MM., I, 327-370; reprints, pp. 366-370, the relevant text of Maimonides according to the Giustiniani edition of 1520.

[39] The doctrine that separate Intelligences inspire the souls of heavenly bodies with a desire to imitate their perfection, follows Alexander of Aphrodisias, *On the Origin of the Universe* (II, 3).

Description of the heavenly spheres; number of the separate Intelligences (nine, plus the *Intellectus agens*); compatibility of the doctrine with Scripture (II, 4 and 5). The only important difference is that the universe of philosophy is eternal, whereas that of Scripture is created, together with its spheres, their souls and the desire of these souls to imitate the perfection of God (II, 6. Cf. II, 10 and 11). How the agent Intellect actualizes our material intellect; God is the only intellect always in act, I, 68. On prophecy as an extreme case of the influence of God on the human intellect, II, 36 and 37.

[40] Maimonides has clearly seen that, just as the doctrine of the eternity of the world agrees with the Greek notion of necessity (II, 18), the doctrine of creation in time agrees with the Biblical notion of a world produced by a will following a design (II, 19) and in which a revelation and miracles are possible (II, 25). The question: "What is the purpose, or final cause of the universe and of man?" is meaningless in an eternal universe, but it has a meaning in a created one (III, 13). Read, in Friedländer's translation, pp. 272-277. This remarkable chapter, together with the following one, ch. 14, pp. 277-278 (on the exceeding smallness of man and of the earth in the universe) anticipates some well known pages of Pascal.

[41] The proof of the existence of God rests upon twenty-six propositions, each of which has been demonstrated by Aristotle and his disciples. Maimonides accepts them all, except the one which affirms the eternity of the universe: *Guide . . . ,* Bk. II, Introduction. The starting point of the demonstration is that motion requires a cause; now the series of its causes cannot be infinite; consequently, there must be a first cause. From this conclusion can be deduced, the eternity of God, his oneness, his incorporeality. The eternity of the world can be neither proved nor disproved (II, *Introduction,* prop. 26; p. 149); cf. Thomas Aquinas, *Contra Gentiles,* II, 32-38. For a full discussion of this point, see *Guide . . . ,* II, 13-21, followed by the demonstration of the superiority of the doctrine of the *creatio ex nihilo,* which, in Maimonides' mind, is identical with that of creation in time: II, 22-25. This demonstration, however, does not

intend to prove that the world has been created in time, but only that Aristotle has not proved the contrary, that it is rationally possible, and even more probable than the eternity of the world: II, 18, end of the chapter. On the contrary, there is nothing in religious faith against the idea that the world shall never be destroyed: II, 27; many passages in the Bible are rather in favor of the indestructibility of the universe, II, 28.

⁴² There is no resemblance at all between God and his creatures, I, 35. Moreover, being absolutely one, he excludes multiplicity and has no attributes, I, 50. Actually existing distinct attributes of God would be several Gods, I, 51. Cf. I, 52. The variety of God's actions does not imply a variety of attributes, I, 53 and 54. In things, existence is an accident of essence (cf. Avicenna); not so in God, who exists without having the attribute of existence; the same remark applies to his unity, I, 57. When attributes de not denote an action of God, but his essence, the negative attributes are the only true ones, I, 58. We only know that God is, and that he is unlike anything else. On the "Tetragrammaton," I, 62. Through Moses, God has revealed his existence to men; in Exod., 3, 14, God has said that he is "the existing being which is the existing being," that is absolute existence, I, 63. E. Gilson, *Maïmonide et la philosophie de l'Exode* MS. 13 (1951) 223-225.

⁴³ According to Maimonides, the divine providence is no object of strict demonstration; after discussing four different theories, he states his own, which is that of the religious Law: man is perfectly free; the eternal will of God is that man should act according to his own choice, within the limits of his power; accordingly, the providence of God extends, in this sublunary world, as far as human individuals only. It does not extend to irrational beings whose acts are not free (III, 17). The providence of God entails his omniscience, III, 21. Note that

God does not derive his knowledge from its objects; he knows them as their creator. Even when we do not know why God has made things as they are, we are sure that he has done nothing purposeless, and that all that he had made is good, III, 25; cf. Gen. I, 31.

⁴⁴ The views of Maimonides on the subject still deserve the attention of historians. According to him, the origin of Moslem theology lies in the efforts of the Greek and Syrian Christian scholars to defend their faith against objections raised by Greek philosophers, or drawn from their works. Such was, for instance, the intention of John Philoponus (Johannes Grammaticus). When these Christian writings were translated into Arabic, the Moslem theologians adopted their conclusions and, later on, they added to them many doctrines of their own in order to justify Islamic dogmas (1, 71), as if we should adapt the properties of things to our opinions, instead of adapting our opinions to the properties of things (ibid., p. 110).

Of the theology of the As'harites, which represented for him Moslem theology, Maimonides provides a detailed analysis. The doctrine rests upon twelve main propositions, such as: All things are made up of atoms; Void exists; Time is made up of time-atoms; of itself, no accident can last longer than one time-atom, etc. (I, 73; p. 120). For the justifications of these propositions, see I, 74. Thomas Aquinas will know this doctrine through Maimonides, and it will represent to him the position of those who deprive natural beings of their own efficacy: *Contra Gentiles,* III, 69, "Quidam etiam Loquentes (i.e., Mutakallemin) in Lege Maurorum . . ." Cf. Averroes, *In IX Metaph.,* text. 7, and *In XII Metaph.,* text. 18. What matters here is the spirit that animates the refutation of this doctrine by Maimonides: the fact that certain arguments favor our religious belief in the all-powerfulness of God does not make them to be *philosophically* true. Hence they should be disregarded by theologians.

PART SIX
EARLY SCHOLASTICISM

CHAPTER I.   GRECO—ARABIAN INFLUENCES

[1] I.—THE TOLEDO SCHOOL.—A. G. Palencia, *Los Mozarabes de Toledo en los siglos XII y XIII,* 4 vols., Madrid, 1926-1930. A. G. Palencia, *El arzobispo Don Raimundo de Toledo,* Barcelona-Madrid, 1942. H. Bédoret, *Les premières traductions tolédanes de philosophie,* in RNSP., 41 (1938) 80-97; *Les premières versions tolédanes de philosophie.* Oeuvres d'Avicenne, in RNSP., 41 (1938) 374-400. D. Salman, *The Mediaeval Latin Translations of Alfarabi's Works,* in NS., 13 (1939) 245-261. M. Alonso, *Notas sobre los traductores toledanos Domingo Gundissalvo y Juan Hispano,* Al-Andalus, 8 (1943) 155-188. G. Théry, *Tolède, ville de la renaissance médiévale, point de jonction entre la philosophie musulmane et la pensée chrétienne,* Oran, 1944. M. Alonso, *Hermann de Carintia: De essentiis,* Miscellanea Comillas, 5 (1946) 7-107. M.-T. d'Alverny and G. Vajda, *Marc de Tolède, traducteur d'Ibn Tumart,* Al-Andalus, 17 (1952) 99-148; includes, with other texts, the translation of Ibn Tumart's (*Habentometus*) treatise *De unione Dei* (269-279). M.-T. d'Alverny, *Notes sur les traductions médiévales des oeuvres philosophiques d'Avicenne,* AHDL., 19 (1952) 337-358.

IBN DAOUD (Avendeath), probably identical with the Jewish philosopher Abraham Ibn Daoud (he calls himself "philosophus Israelita"); studied at Cordova during many years (1148-1180), then moved to Toledo where he shared in the work of the translators. There is no evidence that he became a convert to Christianity.

JOHN OF SPAIN (Johannes Hispanus, Hispanensis, Hispalensis) is a name that seems to apply to two successive collaborators of Gundissalinus: first, the John of Spain who collaborated on the translations of Algazel and of the *Fons vitae* of Gabirol; secondly, another John, translator of scientific works (including the *De spiritu et anima* of Costa ben Luca, or Constabulinus) an author of treatises on astrology (active about 1130-1155). All this information is subject to revision according to the new discoveries which will certainly be made.

II.—INTRODUCTION OF ARISTOTLE. *Aristoteles latinus . . . ,* by G. Lacombe, A. Birkenmajer, M. Dulong and A. Franceschini (Corpus philososophorum medii aevi, I), Rome, 1939.—More general: C. H. Haskins, *Studies in the History of Mediaeval Science,* Cambridge (Mass.) 1924. A. Birkenmajer, *Le rôle joué par la médecine et les naturalistes dans la réception d'Aristote aux XIIe et XIIIe siècles,* La Pologne au VIe congrès international d'histoire des sciences historiques d'Oslo, 1928 (Warsaw, 1930). D. A. Callus OP., *Introduction of Aristotelian Learning to Oxford,* PBA., 29 (1943). F. Van Steenberghen, *Siger of Brabant . . . ,* Louvain, 1942. II, pp. 389-408: *L'entrée d'Aristote à Paris.*—M. Bouyges SJ., *Annotations à l'Aristoteles Latinus relativement au Grand Commentaire d'Averroes sur la Métaphysique,* RMAL., 5 (1949) 211-232.

III.—LIBER DE CAUSIS, see Part V, note 3. We are following the text of Bardenhewer. Another edition of the Latin version is found in R. Bacon, *Opera hactenus inedita . . . ,* ed. Steele, vol. 16, pp. 167-187. Uncritical editions are found in all the editions of Thomas Aquinas' commentary on the *Liber de causis.*—The Latin translation of the *Elements of Theology* has been published by C. Vansteenkiste, *Procli "Elementatio theologica" translata a Guilelmo de Moerbeke (Textus ineditus),* Tijdschrift voor Philosophie, 13 (1951) 263-302, 491-531.

[2] DOMINICUS GUNDISSALINUS (Dominic Gundisalvi, i.e., son of Gonzalez), a canon of Segovia, resided in Toledo during part of his life. His activity is now being placed in the second half of the twelfth century. With Ibn Daoud (Avendeath), probably under the authority of John, Archbishop of Toledo (1151-1166) he translated the *Liber sextus naturalium* (or *De anima*) of Avicenna. In collaboration with a certain Johannes, called "magister" by good and ancient manuscripts, he also translated the *Logic* and the *Metaphysics* of Algazel as well as the *Fons Vitae* of Gabirol. On account of similarities in vocabulary and style, he is also credited

with the translations of the *Metaphysics* of Avicenna and of a chapter of the *Posterior Analytics* of Avicenna included by Dominicus in his own *De divisione philosophiae*. — Other possible attributions: translations of Alfarabi, *De intellectu; Fontes quaestionum, De scientiis* (used by Dominicus in his *De divisione*), *Liber excitativus ad viam felicitatis;* Alkindi, second redaction of the *De intellectu;* Isaac Israeli, *Liber de definitionibus.*

On his treatise *On the Division of Philosophy:* L. Baur, *Dominicus Gundissalinus De divisione philosophiae,* Münster i. W., 1903 (Beiträge, 4, 2-3); text 1-124; positions of Avicenna on the question, 124-142; excellent history of the "Introductions to Philosophy" from Gundissalinus up to the end of the middle ages, 316-397.—Cl. Baeumker, *Dominicus Gundissalinus als philosophischer Schriftsteller* (1908) reprinted in *Studien und Charakterristiken* . . . , Münster i. W., 1927, 255-275 (Beiträge 25, 1-2). P. Alonso, *Las fuentes literarias de Domingo Gundisalvo,* Al-Andalus, 11 (1947) 209-211. A. H. Chroust, *The Definitions of Philosophy in the "De divisione philosophiae" of Dominicus Gundissalinus,* NS., 25 (1951) 253-281.—More general: A. Schneider, *Die abendländische Spekulation des zwölften Jahrhunderts in ihrem Verhältnis zur aristotelischen und jüdisch-arabischen Philosophie,* Münster i. W., 1916 (Beiträge, 17, 4).

[3] Text in Menéndez Pelayo, *Historia de los heterodoxos Españoles,* Madrid, 1880, I, 691-711. Critical edition in G. Bülow, *Des Dominicus Gundissalinus Schrift . . . De Processione mundi herausgegeben und auf ihre Quellen untersucht,* Münster i. W., 1925 (Beiträge, 24, 3). Despite its many borrowings from Avicenna and Gabirol, this treatise is of very good philosophical quality and its influence may have been wider than we suppose. Thomas Aquinas seems to have both read and reinterpreted its proofs of the existence of God by the Prime Mover (Bülow's ed. pp. 4-5 and 18-19); by efficient causality, 5-7; by possibility and necessity, 7-10.—On creation, 20-22 and 36; on *forma et esse (si omne esse ex forma est, forma utique non est esse. —Cum enim forma in materiam advenit, necesse est ut esse in actu sit),* p. 27; on matter as being in potency, 27-28; on unity as form, 29-31; matter eternal in the divine mind, 33-34; beginning of its

formal being *(formale esse),* 34; creation of matter, 37-38; definition of creation: *exitus formae ab ejus (creatoris) sapientia et voluntate* . . . , 40; three degrees of form: *spiritualis, corporalis, media (media,* i.e., unitas, substantialitas etc.) 42-43; conspectus of the way things proceeded from God: "Sic igitur processit totius mundi constitutio de nihil esse ad possibiliter esse, de possibiliter esse ad actu esse, et de actu esse ad corporeum et incorporeum esse; et hoc totum simul, non in tempore," p. 54.

[4] Text in G. Bülow, *Des Dominicus Gundisalvi Schrift von der Unsterblichkeit der Seele,* Münster i. W., 1903 (Beiträge, 2, 3). An appendix shows how deeply indebted to Gundissalinus William of Paris (or of Auvergne) was for his own treatment of the same question. The source of Gundissalinus himself is not known. His arguments will be endlessly reproduced: independence of the intellect from the body, immateriality of the soul as form, natural desire, union of the soul with the Source of life, etc.

[5] Text in PL., 63, 1075-1078. Critical edition by P. Correns, *Die dem Boethius fälschlich zugeschriebene Abhandlung des Dominicus Gundissalinus De Unitate,* Münster i. W., 1891 (Beiträge, 1, 1); on the doctrine, 39-49. This very short treatise is also very compact; it follows the style of Boethius, often its very doctrine, and it is full of aphorisms which have been frequently quoted by the successors of Gundissalinus.

[6] Text in J. T. Muckle, CSB., *The Treatise De anima of Dominicus Gundissalinus,* MS., 2 (1940), 23-103; introduction by E. Gilson, 23-27. On the nature of the doctrine, R. de Vaux, *Notes et textes sur l'avicennisme latin aux confins des XIIe et XIIIe siècles,* Paris, J. Vrin, 1934. D. A. Callus, OP., *Gundissalinus' De anima and the Problem of Substantial Form,* NS., 13 (1939) 338-355.

[7] E. Gilson, *Les sources gréco-arabes de l'augustinisme avicennisant,* AHDL., 4 (1930) 142-149. Latin text in Avicenna's 1508 edition, 64 v-67 v, under the title: *Liber Avicennae in primis et secundis substantiis et de fluxu entis;* re-edited by R. de Vaux, *Notes et textes . . . ,* Paris, 1934. M. Alonso, *El Liber de causis primis et secundis et de fluxu qui consequitur*

eas, Al-Andalus, 9 (1944) 419-440.—The passage of Augustine usually quoted in such works is that of *Soliloquies,* I, 6, 2; PL., 32, 875. The history of the progressive rediscovery of the philosophical elements contained in the works of St. Augustine, between the end of the XIIth century and the middle of the XIIIth century, remains to be written.

[8] Historical background: P. Alphandéry, *Les idées morales des hétérodoxes latins au début du XIIIe siècle,* Paris, 1903. E. Broekx, *Le Catharisme,* Louvain, 1916. S. Runciman, *The Mediaeval Manichee,* Cambridge, 1947. Söderberg, *La religion des Cathares,* Upsala, 1949. See particularly the treatise published by A. Dondaine OP., *Un traité manichéen du XIIIe siècle, le "Liber de duobus principiis" suivi d'un fragment de rituel cathare,* Rome, 1939 (bibliography on Catharism, 16, note 7). This treatise establishes the existence of a straight Manichaean theology dominated by the philosophical notion of a God submitted to strict necessity. If God is both good and swayed by his own absolute necessity, then the only explanation for the presence of evil is the existence of a second principle of the universe: the principle of evil. This is a treatise written by a theologian invoking the authority of Scripture and fully aware of the fact that he is going against the opinion of "almost all the religious" (p. 81).—On the Manichaean system of JOHN OF LUGIO, A. Dondaine, 31-33; on RAINERIUS SACCONI, a Manichaean for seventeen years who died a Dominican (after 1262) op. cit., 57-61. His own *Summa* of the doctrine of the Cathars (1250) is found in Martène and Durand, *Thesaurus novus anecdotorum,* V, 1761-1776; A. Dondaine, 64-78.

AMAURY OF BENE: Cl. Baeumker, *Contra Amaurianos. Ein anonymer, warscheinlich dem Garnerius von Rochefort zugehöriger Traktat gegen die Amalrikaner aus dem Anfang des XIII Jahrhunderts,* Münster i. W., 1926 (Beiträge, 24, 5-6). C. Capelle, *Autour du décret de 1210: III, Amaury de Bène, étude sur son panthéisme formel,* Paris, 1932. M.-Th. d'Alverny, *Un fragment du procès des Amauriciens,* AHDL., 25-26 (1950-1951) 325-336.—See note 13.

[9] DAVID OF DINANT. G. Théry OP., *Autour du décret de 1210: I, David de Dinant, Etude sur son panthéisme maté-*

rialiste, Paris, 1925; *Autour du décret de 1210:* II, *Alexandre d'Aphrodise,* Paris, 1926. R. Arnou SJ., *Quelques idées néoplatoniciennes de David de Dinant,* Philosophia perennis (Festgabe Geyser) Regensburg, 1930, I, 115-127. Al. Birkenmajer, *Découverte de fragments manuscrits de David de Dinant,* RNSP., 35 (1933) 220-229.

[10] M.-T. d'Alverny, *Les pérégrinations de l'âme dans l'autre monde d'après un anonyme de la fin du XIIIe siècle,* AHDL., 13 (1942) 239-299.—On the late twelfth-century and early thirteenth-century syncretism, M.-D. Chenu, *Le dernier avatar de la théologie orientale,* MAP., 159-181: note, p. 166, n. 7, the remarks concerning the *Liber de diversitate personae et naturae* (cf. C. H. Haskins, *Studies in the History of Mediaeval Science,* Cambridge, Mass., 1924, p. 211) and concerning the *Liber de vera philosophia* (p. 166, n. 8). P. Fournier, *Etudes sur Joachim de Flore,* Paris, 1909.

[11] M. and Ch. Dickson, *Le cardinal Robert de Courson. Sa vie,* in AHDL., 9 (1934), 53-142. GLOREP., I, 237. A master in theology at Paris before 1200, Robert has left a still unpublished *Summa theologiae* (about 1204).

[12] E. Gilson, *La philosophie au moyen âge,* Paris, 1922; I, 126-140. M. Grabmann, *I Papi del Duecento e l'aristotelismo,* 2 vols., Roma, 1941, 1946. Especially vol. I (1941), *I divieti ecclesiastici.* M. Grabmann, *Aristoteles im Werturteil des Mittelalters,* MG., II, 62-102. A. Chollet, art. *Aristotélisme,* DTC., 1 (1923) 1869-1887.

[13] CUP., 11; v. I, p. 70. This is the text excommunicating Amaury of Benes.—UNIV., 26-27.

[14] CUP., 20; v. I, pp. 78-79.—M. Bouyges, *Connaissons-nous le Mauricius Hyspanus interdit par Robert de Courçon en 1215?* RHE., 29 (1933) 637-658.

[15] CUP., 72; v. I, pp. 129-131: an extremely interesting document, in which it is expressly stated (p. 131) that the books of natural science forbidden in Paris could be freely studied in Toulouse. On the Roman authority behind this move, M. Grabmann (following A. Mas-

novo), *I divieti ecclesiastici* . . . , I, 92-93.—See UNIV., 32-35.

[16] CUP., 79; I, 136-139 (UNIV., 35-39). On the projected correction of the scientific treatises of Aristotle, op. cit., 87; I, 143-144 (UNIV., 39-40).

[17] Around the year 1263, Manfred, King of Sicily, gave to the University of Paris a collection of philosophical and scientific manuscripts containing works of Aristotle and of Arabian authors. By that time, such a gift raised no problem: *Chartularium*, 394; I, 435-436. It is to be noted, however, that as late as 1276, it still was forbidden to lecture on any other subject than grammar or logic in a private room; see CUP., 468; I, pp. 538-539.

[18] At that date, the prescribed readings included the *De anima, Libri physicorum, De generatione et corruptione, De coelo et mundo, Parva naturalia, Metaphysica,* even "aliquos libros mathematicos," etc., CUP., III, 145. Engl translation in UNIV., 244-247.

[19] These very general indications should not be understood as a classification properly so-called. Philosophies and theologies are not individuals susceptible of forming species, as is the case with plants and animals. Augustinism, Averroism, Thomism, Scotism, are so many words pointing to groups of facts that are not definable in terms of genus and of specific difference. Description applies to them better than definition.

PART SIX

CHAPTER II. UNIVERSITIES AND SCHOLASTICISM

[20] H. Denifle, *Die Universitäten des Mittelalters bis 1400,* Berlin, 1885. H. Rashdall, *The Universities of Europe in the Middle Ages;* new ed. by F. M. Powicke and A. B. Emden, 3 vols., Oxford, 1936. Stephen d'Irsay, *Histoire des universités françaises et étrangères des origines à nos jours,* v. I, Paris, 1933 (vol. II, deals with post-mediaeval universities). The main documents are to be found in H. Denifle and E. Chatelain, *Chartularium Universitatis Parisiensis,* 4 vols., Paris, 1889-1897, completed by *Auctuarium Chartularii universitatis parisiensis,* Paris, 1933 and following years. P. Glorieux, *Répertoire des maîtres en théologie de Paris au XIIIe siècle,* 2 vols., Paris, 1933-1934; v. I has a general introduction on the organization of teaching at the university, pp. 11-26. Additions and corrections in V. Doucet, *Maîtres franciscains de Paris,* AFH., 27 (1934), 531-564. M. Toulouse, *La Nation Anglaise-Allemande de l'Université de Paris des origines à la fin du XVe siècle,* Paris, 1939. P. Kibre, *The Nations in the Mediaeval Universities,* Cambridge, Mass., 1948. Ch. Thouzellier, *L'enseignement et les universités,* in Fliche and Martin, *Histoire de l'Eglise,* 10 (1950) 341-386; see n. 22. A. L. Gabriel, *The Preparatory Teaching in the Parisian Colleges during the XIVth Century,* extract from the Revue de l'Université d'Ottawa, Oct.-Dec., 1951; *Robert de Sorbonne,* op. cit., 1953.

On Bologna; Fr. Ehrle, *I piu antichi statuti della facoltà teologica dell' Università di Bologna,* Bologna, 1932. On Oxford; Strickland-Gibson, *Statuta antiqua universitatis Oxoniensis,* Oxford, 1931. F. Pelster, *Oxford University Customs,* OTT., 25-72.

[21] Programs of studies, CUP., I, 78-79; I, 137; See UNIV., 27-30. Robert Grosseteste invites the Oxonian masters to follow the Parisian program for theology, I, 169. Against the reading of Scotus Erigena, I, 106-107.—Honorius III on Paris as center of theological studies, I, 90-93; cf. Alexander IV, I, 279; organization of the Dominican and Franciscan centers of studies, I, 95-96, 108, 112, 153. —Gregory IX warns the theologians against overindulgence in philosophy, I, 114-116.—Universal validity of the Parisian degrees, II, 54-55.—On the controverted date of the organization of the university as a formally constituted corporation: G. Post, *Parisian Masters as a Corporation* (1200-1246), Speculum 9 (1934) 421-445.—General survey: P. Glorieux, *La Faculté de Théologie de Paris et ses principaux docteurs au XIIIe siècle,* RHET., 52 (1946) 241-264.—Mention is often made of a *magister in curia.*

He simply was a master teaching at the convent of his own Order situated in the city where the pope happened to reside: R. Creytens, *Le "Studium Romanae Curiae" et le Maître du Sacré Palais*, AFP., 12 (1942) 1-83; especially 18-34.

[22] A. Pelzer, *Répertoires d'incipit pour la littérature latine philosophique et théologique du moyen âge*, Roma, 1951. P. Glorieux, *La littérature quodlibétique de 1260 à 1320*, 2 vols., Paris, 1925, 1933. F. Stegmüller, *Repertorium Commentariorum in Sententias Petri Lombardi*, 2 vols., Würzburg, 1947. P. Glorieux, art. *Sentences (commentaires sur les)*, DTC., 14 (1939) 1860-1884.—Specimens of Academic Sermons, M.-M. Davy, *Les sermons universitaires de 1230-1231. Contribution à l'étude de la prédication médiévale*, Paris, 1931. P. Glorieux, *Sermons universitaires parisiens de 1267-1268*, RTAM., 16 (1949) 40-71; see p. 70, note 24. F. Pelster, *Sermons and Preachers at the University of Oxford in the years 1291-1293*, OTT., 149-213.—On the technique of the Quodlibetal question, P. Glorieux, *Le Quodlibet et ses procédés rédactionnels*, DTP., 42 (1939) 61-93; *Où en est la question du Quodlibet?* RMAL., 2 (1946) 405-414. On the XII-cent. origins of the "disputation," A. M. Landgraf, *Zur Technik und Ueberliefe-*

rung der Disputation, CF., 20 (1950) 173-188 (note the role of the *notarii*, or reporters).—On the fabrication of manuscripts: J. Destrez, *L'outillage des copistes du XIIIe siècle et du XIVe siècle*, ADGM., 19-34.—Methodology: P. Glorieux, *Pour jalonner l'histoire littéraire du XIIIe siècle*, ADGM., 482-502.—Traductions: G. Théry OP., *Notes indicatrices pour s'orienter dans l'étude des traductions médiévales*, Mélanges J. Maréchal, II (1950) 297-315.

[23] List of definitions of "scholastic" and "scholasticism" in M. de Wulf, *Histoire de la philosophie médiévale*, 6 ed., 1934; I, 15, n. 2; same author, *Notion de la scolastique médiévale*, RNSP., 18 (1911) 177-196. Excellent remarks in M.-D. Chenu, OP., *Introduction à l'étude de S. Thomas*, 51-60.—General interpretations of the history of mediaeval philosophies: F. Van Steenberghen, *L'interprétation de la pensée médiévale au cours du siècle écoulé*, SRHC., 25-39. Cf. E. Gilson, same volume, 133-142.—On the rise of modern intellectual nationalism, G. Zeller, *Les rois de France candidats à l'empire. Essai sur l'idéologie impériale de la France*, Revue historique, 173 (1934) 273-311. H. Kampf, *Pierre Dubois und die geistigen Grundlagen des französischen Nationalbewusstsein um 1300*, Leipzig, 1935.

PART SIX

CHAPTER III. EARLY THIRTEENTH-CENTURY THEOLOGIANS

[24] PETER OF POITIERS, glosses on P. Lombard, PL., 211, col. 789-1279. In critical edition: *Sententiae Petri Pictaviensis*, Bk. I, ed. P. S. Moore and M. Dulong, Notre Dame, Ind., 1943. Bk. II, ed. P. S. Moore, J. N. Garvin and M. Dulong, Notre Dame, Ind., 1950. The *Allegories on the Tabernacle of Moses*, also in critical edition: *Petri Pictaviensis Allegoriae Super Tabernaculum Moysi*, ed. P. S. Moore and J. A. Corbett, Notre Dame, Ind., 1938. On the life and works of Peter, Philip S. Moore, *The Works of Peter of Poitiers, Master in Theology and Chancellor of Paris (1193-1205)*, Notre Dame, Ind., 1936.—The mention made of Aristotle's *Metaphysics* (P. S. Moore, *The Works . . .*, p. 164, note 38) does not necessarily imply that Peter himself has read it. The glosses on the *Sentences* are still written in the traditional twelfth

century style; they really are glosses, not a commentary divided into questions and articles. Cf. O. Lottin, *Le Prologue des Gloses sur les Sentences attribuées à Pierre de Poitiers*, RTAM., 7 (1935), 70-73. Peter is mentioned several times in A. M. Landgraf, *Das Problem Utrum Christus fuerit homo in triduo mortis in der Frühscholastik*, MAP., 109-158.

[25] SIMON OF TOURNAI, J. Warichez, *Les Disputationes de Simon de Tournai, Texte inédit*, Louvain (Spicilegium sacrum Lovaniense), 1932. H. Weisweiler, *Maître Simon et son groupe De sacramentis*, Louvain (Spic. sac. Lovan.), 1937. On Simon's knowledge of the works of Aristotle: see *Physics, On the Soul and Metaphysics*, in J. Warichez, op. cit., p. XXIV.

[26] WILLIAM OF AUXERRE. *Summa super*

quatuor libros sententiarum, usually called *Summa aurea,* Paris, 1500, 1518; Venice, 1591. A critical edition is announced. Fragments in A. Daniels, *Beiträge und Untersuchungen . . . ,* 25-27.— On the doctrine, A. Landgraf, *Beobachtungen zur Einflussphäre Wilhelms von Auxerre,* ZKT., 51 (1928) 53-64. C. Ottaviano, *Guglielmo d'Auxerre* (d. *1231*). *La vita, le opere, il pensiero,* Roma, 1930 (still the best introduction). P. Mandonnet, *La date de la mort de Guillaume d'Auxerre* (3 nov. 1231), AHDL., 7 (1932) 39-46. R. M. Martineau, *Le plan de la Summa aurea de Guillaume d'Auxerre,* Ottawa, 1937. O. Lottin, PEM., I, 63-96; 484-490. II, 75-82, 123-134, 409, 520-525. III, 23-31, 70-71, 209, 257-259, 318 (psychological and ethical problems). H. Pouillon, *La beauté, propriété transcendentale chez les Scolastiques,* AHDL., 15 (1946) 266-273. The question of the *Summa* devoted to the problem of the existence of God is an early instance of the use of philosophy made by a Parisian master. William lists four arguments without wondering whether or not they are philosophically compatible: necessity of a prime cause (Avicenna), argument *per fluxum rerum* (Gundissalinus), argument by the supreme good (Boethius), Anselm's argument by the notion of God. Theology is an "art," or a "science," because it argues from principles, which are the articles of faith (Ottaviano, op. cit., 39, note 75); but it can use philosophy to its own end; hence the preceding proofs of the existence of God. On the divine Ideas, identical with God and the eternal ordering in his mind of the things to be made, ibid., 74-75. Ideas are the intelligible world, 76. Things flow from God immediately, but through his will, and they are created from nothing (78-79), it is false to say that from one God only one creature can flow, otherwise God would be "unipotent," not "omnipotent" (text in Ottaviano, 81, n. 164). Against the anthropomorphic nature of Plato's demiurge, 82. Even matter is created, 85. The acquisition of knowledge is described in accordance with the doctrine of Augustine, 95; abstraction is possible owing to the intrinsic indifference of essences to either singularity or universality (Avicenna), 98-100. Individuation is caused by accidents, 101-103. On William as witness to the survival of the twelfth-century dispute between *reales* and *nominales* (realists and nominalists), 104-106. The distinction of

essence and existence (pp. 112-113) seems to be studied again, not in the spirit of the metaphysical distinction of Boethius, but with a purely theological intention. William is an ancestor of the theologians to whom this distinction merely means that created beings owe their existence to God: "Et ideo cum dicitur, Quaelibet creatura est, sic ponitur duplex esse, scilicet esse creatum quod est in creatura, et esse divinum ut a quo est illud esse" (112, n. 292) this distinction of *esse* and *quod est* is, in fact, a distinction between God and his creatures.

[27] PHILIP THE CHANCELLOR (Philippus Cancellarius), died 1236. Not to be confused with PHILIP OF GREVES (H. Meylan, *Les Questions de Philippe le Chancelier,* Positions des thèses de l'Ecole Nationale des Chartes, Paris, 1927, pp. 89-94). The *Summa de bono* of Philip the Chancellor is still unpublished except a section of the first part: L. W. Keeler, *Ex Summa Philippi Cancellarii Quaestiones de anima,* Münster i. W., 1937; on the mss., Introduction, 13-15.—On the doctrine: P. Minges, *Philosophiegeschichtliche Bemerkungen über Philipp von Grève,* d. *1236* (read: *the Chancellor*), PJ., 27 (1914) 21-32. O. Lottin, *Le créateur du traité de la syndérèse,* RNSP., 29 (1927) 197-220, text of the treatise; cf. PEM., 138-157; *L'influence littéraire du Chancelier Philippe sur les théologiens préthomistes,* RTAM., 2 (1930) 311-326; *La pluralité des formes avant saint Thomas,* RNSP., 34 (1932) 449-467; *La composition hylémorphique des substances spirituelles, les débuts de la controverse,* RNSP., 34 (1932) 21-41. H. Pouillon, *Le premier traité des propriétés transcendentales. La Summa de bono du chancelier Philippe,* RNSP., 42 (1939) 40-77. L. Keeler, *The Dependence of R. Grosseteste's De anima on the Summa of Philip the Chancellor,* NS., 11 (1937) 197-219.—Hylomorphic composition of souls: L. Keeler, *Ex Summa . . . ,* pp. 21-22. Cf. E. Kleinadam, *Das Problem der hylomorphen Zusammensetzung der geistigen Substanzen im 13. Jahrhundert behandelt bis Thomas von Aquin,* Breslau, 1930 (Inaug.-Diss.).

Directed against Manichaeism and its dualism of good and evil, this *Summa* is a clear instance of a philosophical development prompted by a theological motive. An analysis of the treatise on the transcendentals is found in H. Pouillon, *Le premier traité . . ,* pp. 42-71.—

The questions of the *Summa* that deal with the soul are known thanks to their publication by L. W. Keeler (in *Opuscula et textus,* XX, Münster i. W.). The soul is an "incorporeal substance ruling a body" (Nemesius?); it is "an incorporeal substance, sharing in reason, apt to rule a body" (*De spir. et anima,* Alcher of Clairvaux) it is "an incorporeal substance perceptive, at the lowest level, of the illuminations coming from the First" (Alfred of Sareshel, *De motu cordis*). All this is justifiable by the teaching of Augustine (whom Philip considers the author of the *De spir. et anima*). Since God alone is simple, and since the soul is passive as well as active (agent intellect and possible intellect), it has matter and form (for matter is the passive principle, form the active principle). Moreover, since the *quod est* of the soul is not its *quo est,* it must have matter and form (Keeler, 21-22). Again, since the philosophers have posited a spiritual matter and a spiritual form, spiritual substance must have both (Gabirol and *Liber de causis,* art. 8); cf. p. 23, n. 2. Some say that the rational soul, the sensitive soul and the vegetative soul are three distinct substances, yet they make up one soul because the rational soul is the perfection of the other ones. Thus do two light beams unite without ceasing to be, on account of the quasi-spirituality of their nature (pp. 32-33). This solution is mentioned by John of la Rochelle, Albert the Great, Buckfield, Fishacre, etc. Others say that there is only one soul in man, namely, the rational soul, and that vegetative, sensitive and rational are three powers rooted in one substance (p. 34). Philip seems to favor the latter solution (p. 39). Unibility to a body is the difference between souls and angels; souls are the perfections of their bodies (pp. 46-47). The soul is "ita substantia quod perfectio," which distinguishes it from the simple forms given to prepared matter by the "giver of forms" (p. 51). It is created by God, like the angels, so as to show that it is not a mere form, but a substance (p. 52). Proofs of the immortality of the soul, from "the golden chain of Pythagoras" (order of the universe, pp. 53-56); and from its powers and operations: a spiritual substance (pp. 56-57), it operates without bodily organs, it is able to know incorruptible beings (Augustine, pp. 56-58), it comprehends truth, which is immortal (Augustine, *Solilo-*

quies, II, 13, 24) and it grasps intelligible truth as angels do (p. 59), it knows itself directly (authority: Aristotle, *De anima,* III, 4, 429 b 9!) as a separate substance (*substantia separata intelligitur esse, scil. individua et immortalis*), p. 61. Philip affirms that, according to Aristotle, even the possible intellect is separable from matter and incorruptible, p. 63. Reason (*rationale*) is corruptible, because it belongs to the composite. The intellect is not corruptible, p. 66. Meanings of "nature," pp. 71-72. Presence of the soul to the body (Augustine, *De quantitate animae*), pp. 73-78. Since the soul is not only a form, but a substance, it "coexists" with the body, p. 80: note the difficulty arising from the thesis of Augustine, *De imm. animae,* X, 17, PL., 32, 1030, that the soul is not in the body as a form is in matter; the soul coexists with its body as its perfection; cf. p. 83. The *medium* of their union is the spirit, p. 87. By and large, and considered in its essential positions, this psychology represents fairly well what will remain the common doctrine of many theologians up to the rise of Thomism.

[28] WILLIAM OF AUVERGNE.—Born about 1180, at Aurillac (Auvergne, France). Studies at Paris; master in theology in 1223. In April 1228, being still a deacon, he is ordained a priest and consecrated as Bishop of Paris by Pope Gregory IX. Died on March 30, 1249. GLOREP., I, 315-320.—The true title of William's main work was *Magisterium divinale;* on its plan, J. Kramp, *Des Wilhelms von Auvergne "Magisterium divinale,"* Gregorianum, 1 (1920) 538-616; 2 (1921) 42-103, 174-195. Its parts have been printed, under their own particular titles: *De Trinitate, De universo, De anima, De immortalitate animae,* in the collective edition: Guillelmi Alverni . . . *Opera omnia,* 2 vols. Paris, 1674. Another part of the *Magisterium* has been published by J. R. O'Donnell, *Tractatus magistri Guillelmi Alvernensis "De bono et malo,"* MS., 8 (1946) 245-299.

BIBLIOGRAPHY. N. Valois, *Guillaume d'Auvergne . . . , sa vie et ses ouvrages,* Paris 1880.—On the doctrine, M. Baumgartner, *Die Erkenntnislehre des Wilhelm von Auvergne,* Münster i. W., 1895 (Beiträge, 2, 1). St. Schindele, *Beiträge zur Metaphysik des Wilhelm von Auvergne,* Munich, 1900 (Inaug.-Dissert.). P. Duhem, *Le système du monde,* III, 249-260;

V, 261-303. M. D. Roland-Gosselin, *Le "De ente et essentia" de saint Thomas d'Aquin,* Paris, 1926, pp. 72-74 and 160-166. J. Lingenheim, *L'art de prier de Guillaume d'Auvergne,* Lyon, 1934. Amato Masnovo, *Da Guglielmo d'Auvergne a san Tommaso d'Aquino,* 3 vols., Milano, 2 ed., 1945, 1946. E. Gilson, *La notion d'existence chez Guillaume d'Auvergne,* AHDL., 15 (1946) 55-91. A. Masnovo, *Guglielmo d'Auvergne e la Providenza divina,* ADGM., 503-524.—GDP., 730-731.

²⁹ Unless otherwise indicated, our references are to the *Opera omnia.*—On faith and reason, *De Trinitate,* Prolog., v. II, p. 1. His intention is to persuade philosophers; hence his constant use of philosophical arguments: "ex toto cum ipsis agendum suscepimus"; cf. the *Contra Gentiles.* The philosophical and demonstrative method is that of logic, ibid.—On William's knowledge of Arabic scientists and philosophers, R. de Vaux, *Notes et textes sur l'Avicennisme latin,* 18-22; 22-30 (William and Avicenna); 30-38).

³⁰ On the meaning of *ens* and *esse;* on the distinction between being by essence and being by participation; being by participation is accidental (cf. Algazel, *Metaphysics,* ed. T. J. Muckle, p. 53), a thesis which William combines with that of Boethius on *esse* and *quod est,* in *De Trinitate,* ch. I; v. II, pp. 1-2. Cf. *De universo,* P. I, ch. 1, a. 3; v. I, p. 594, and P. II, 2, ch. 2, a. 8; v. I, p. 852.

³¹ The demonstration of the existence of God rests upon the necessity there is to posit a being by substance in order to account for the existence of beings by accident; the series of causes can be neither circular, nor infinite, *De Trinitate,* ch. 2; II, pp. 2-3.

³² True being is by substance; its existence is inconceivable, *De Trinitate,* ch. 2, II, p. 2. It is simple (i.e., without accidents), ch. 3; II, p. 4. It is one, singular, and separated from all the rest, ch. 4; II, pp. 4-5. Its true name is HE WHO IS, ch. 4; II, pp. 5-6 (Exod. 3, 13-14). Hence it is God, who is essence by himself, yet has no quiddity, ch. 4; II, p. 6: "Item non habet (ens) quidditatem nec definitionem"; cf. Avicenna, *Metaph.,* VIII, 4; fol. 99 v b, and Thomas Aquinas, *De ente et essentia,* ch. 6. Note the pre-

Scotist remark; "per se impressum est intellectui nostro inquantum est ens, inquantum autem Deus et Dominus, non est ex primis impressionibus, et hic est modus quo errant imperiti intellectu circa ipsum" (ibid.). The deep-seated relation there is, in such doctrines, between God as pure being and the immediate evidence of our notion of being is here apparent.

³³ See the penetrating study of B. J. Muller-Thym, quoted Part X, ch. 1, note 21; infra, p. 756.

³⁴ In accordance with this general position, creation is the gift of existence granted by the Being by essence, or substance, to beings by accident. Using the terminology of Gabirol's *Fons vitae,* William says of Being by essence that he is the source of being (*fons primus essendi;* this is true of both essence and existence: "si autem ens ab ente, et esse ab esse." The universe flows from God like a stream: "universum est fluxus et exuberantia esse ejus" (*esse* is a genitive case). Again: "Omnia inquantum sunt ejus fluxus, sunt exuberantia primi purissimi hujus fontis, et intantum posuerunt multi de nobilioribus philosophorum omnia bona, inquantam scilicet de purissimo fonte esse (genit. case) defluunt." The "possibility" of the universe receives this flux: "implet possibilitatem universi affluentia et vehementia primi et fontalis esse, pro capacitate receptibilium magis aut minus influens . . ." etc. *De Trinitate,* ch. 5; v. II, p. 6. Secondary being is "caused"; its other names are, "derivatum, datum, sive receptum, vestitum, debitum, subditum," etc., ibid. Of itself, the universe is only "potential"; hence it requires for its cause a necessary being, "necesse per semetipsum," "necesse esse," "prohibens suum non esse," "non cessans esse," ibid., p. 7. Being necessary, this essence is also "true," ibid. As to caused being, since it has not its own existence in virtue of its essence, it is "false" being ("esse falsum, esse indigentiae, esse potentiale, esse fluens, esse pendens"); the conjunction of its possibility with its actual existence is itself potential, op. cit., ch. 6; v. II, p. 7. Cf. "ens potentiale est non ens per essentiam . . . ," ch. 6; p. 8. Its potentiality is "filled up" by the First essence, ibid., p. 8 (refers to Scripture, Jerem. 23, 24: "do not I fill heaven and earth, saith the

Lord?"). God is to beings as the soul is to body, ch. 7; p. 9. To sum up, there are sixteen notions proper to the Prime being: verissime esse, essentiale esse, esse sufficientiae, esse necesse, actuale purum esse veritatis, esse fixum, esse non causatum, esse primitivum, esse fontale, esse absolutum, esse omnino liberum, esse spoliatum et nudissimum (esse simplex, esse irresolubile et omnium resolutionem praebens), esse inadunatum (purum et solitarium), esse dativum. (St. Schindele, *Beiträge zur Metaphysik* . . . , p. 55, rightly compares with Bonaventure, *Itinerarium,* V, 3-8.). In short, the universe is a hierarchical order of participations: ch. 8; v. II, p. 8.

[35] Once more, the notion of creation invites us to philosophize about what is beyond mere philosophy, *De Trinitate,* ch. 8; v. II, p. 9. God is both the "creator" and the "artist" who made the world. As creator, he acts by his power (*potentia*), which is a beam issuing from his being, the cause of his operations: "exuberantia vel radius ipsius esse, de quo exeunt operationes," ibid. Matter is not possibility itself (against Gabirol, *Fons vitae,* V, 34 and V, 42); it is not the relation of possibility to its cause, ibid., p. 10; the being of matter is the subject in which its potency with respect to act does actually reside. Definition of the divine power: "Prima igitur et perfecta potentia est quae per se potest super utrumque oppositorum et quae totam suam operationem fluit (active verb) de se sola, et per se solam, quae fortitudine sua nec cogi nec prohiberi potest," ch. 9, p. 11. Its *fortitudo* and its *amplitudo* make it to be an *omnipotentia,* ibid. Since it can produce any one of two opposites, the power of God is attended by a will (*voluntas*) capable of choice (*electio*). This, in turn, implies that God has knowledge and, therefore, a reason. His will is cause of itself (*causa suiipsius*). These three principles, namely power, wisdom and will, are the causes of all that is, and they are one with the very essence of the creator, ibid., pp. 12-13. How the divine will, itself eternal, produces new beings, ch. 11; pp. 15-16. Note, in this chapter, the intrinsic insufficiency of secondary beings and causes; these are "windows" for the divine illuminations: "viae quaedam et fenestrae mediae naturae sunt, *non causae,* nisi aliquantulum abusive accipimus nomen causae," ibid.,

p. 16. Cf. ch. 12; pp. 16-17, where Gabirol is called "unicus omnium philosophorum nobilissimus" (also *De universo,* I, 1, 26; v. II, p. 16: Gabirol as a Christian). The mark of the divine generosity is that beings are bound to communicate their own being (through causality) in order that other things may exist, ibid., p. 16. To sum up, the universe is like a book in which the will of God can be read, ch. 13; v. II, p. 17. Only God is a true cause: "solus est veri nominis causa," ch. 12, p. 17. Ch. 14, p. 17, begins the exposition of the mystery of the Trinity.—On the intrinsic fecundity of being, see *De bono et malo,* in MS., 8 (1946), p. 258.

[36] All our references are to *De anima,* vol. II of the *Opera omnia.* The *De anima* of William is divided into chapters, themselves subdivided into parts. Definition of the soul by Aristotle, *De anima,* ch. I, part 1; vol. II, p. 65. Not the soul, but man, is human nature I, 2; 66. III, 11; 101-102. The soul cannot doubt its own existence, I, 4; 68; III, 12-13; 102-104. It is a substance, I, 5; 68-71. Incorporeal, II, 3; 75; II, 6; 77-78; II, 13-14, pp. 83-85; III, 1-2, pp. 86-87. Indivisible, II, 10; 80-81. One soul in each body, IV, 3; 106-108. Created by God, V, 2, pp. 113-114. Endowed with a free will, II, 14; 85-86. And with powers which, like that of God (III, 5; 90-91) are one with its essence, III, 6; 91-93.

[37] Man knows through his own intellect, which is like a spider, V, 7; 122. Our intellect produces intelligible forms, V, 8; 122-124. It governs the other powers, V, 14; 135-136. It knows sensible things, V, 17; 141-142; to what end, V, 18-19; 142-144. Cf. VII, 1; 203-204. Against those who swallow what the philosophers say concerning the two intellects, VII, 3; 105-107. No agent intellect within the soul between the intelligibles and the possible intellect, VII, 4; 207-209 (cf. later on the position of Peter of Trabes). No agent intellect outside of the soul, VII, 5, p. 210. Both principles and essences are known through the natural presence of the Intelligible World to our intellect: "creator ipse liber est naturalis et proprius intellectus humani," VII, 6; 211-212; cf. VII, 7; 213. Our knowledge of effects through causes, VIII-IX; 213-216. On the speculative in-

tellect, X; 216-217. On *intellectus adeptus*, XI; 217-218. On the prophetic intellect, XII; 218-219. On synderesis, XIII; 219-220. On conscience, XIV; 220-221. The end of the *De anima* deals with the condition of souls after death.—Other considerations on the soul in *De bono et malo*, MS., 8 (1946), pp. 274-277; on intellectual knowledge, 279-280; 289-290.

[38] ADAM PULCHRAE MULIERIS. His *Memoriale rerum difficilium* has been published under the title: *De Intelligentiis*, by Cl. Baeumker, *Witelo, ein Philosoph und Naturforscher des XIII Jahrhundert*, Münster i. W., 1908 (Beiträge, 3, 2): *Zur Frage nach Abfassungszeit und Verfasser des irrtümlich Witelo zugeschrieben Liber de Intelligentiis*, Miscellanca Ehrle, Rome, 1924, I, 87-102.

[39] EARLY ENGLISH SCHOLARS. — Recent research has stressed the importance of some early English scholars, especially in the field of natural science. Among them: 1.—ALEXANDER NECKHAM (*Nequam*), 1157-1217, author of a *De naturis rerum et de laudibus divinae sapientiae*, ed. M. Th. Wright, London, 1863. He now passes for an "ardent Aristotelian" (D. A. Callus, *Introduction* . . . , 9). Apart from his personal feelings toward Aristotle, and judging him from his work, Alexander is a representative of the allegorical interpretation of nature popular in the middle ages. See, however, his attacks against the dialectical vanities of the Parisian schools, pp. 302-307. This does not make him a scientist. Besides, he freely recognizes that the world center for liberal arts and theological studies is Paris, just as Italy (Bologna) is the center for Civil Law, p. 311. A different Alexander may appear when the still unpublished thesis of R. W. Hunt, *Alexander Neckam* is printed (D. A. Callus, op. cit., p. 9). GDP., 731.

2.—ALFRED OF SARESHEL (*Alfredus Anglicus*), author of a treatise on the movement of the heart, dedicated to his friend Neckham (d. 1217) and, therefore, probably anterior to this date. Text in C. Baeumker, *Des Alfred von Sareshel (Alfredus Anglicus) Schrift De motu cordis*, Münster i. W., 1923 (Beiträge, 23, 1-2). Cf. A. Pelzer, *Une source inconnue de Roger Bacon, Alfred de Sareshel, commentateur des Météorologiques d'Aristote*, AFH., 12 (1919) 44-67. G. Lacombe, *Alfredus Anglicus in Metheora*, ADGM.,

463-471. D. A. Callus, *Introduction* . . . , 10-12. By his glosses on Aristotle's *Meteors* and on *De plantis*, Alfred was a precursor in the field of natural science. "It is tempting to venture the supposition that these glosses represent his lectures at Oxford; but not the slightest evidence has so far come to light to support such a presumption," D. A. Callus, op. cit., p. 11. Cf., p. 4: "It would be rash to assume that Aristotle's writings were taught in the schools as soon as they were translated."—English transl. of the *Quaestiones naturales*, by H. Gollancz, London, Milford, 1920.

3.—DANIEL OF MORLEY. — Contemporary with Neckham, but in a much higher scientific class, left the schools of Paris and went to Toledo in order to study under "the most learned philosophers in the world" (D. A. Callus, op. cit., p. 8). Author of a *Philosophy*, or *Book on Superior and Inferior Natures* (at the request of John of Oxford, Bishop of Norwich, 1175-1200, ibid.). Text in K. Sudhoff, *Daniels von Morley "Liber de naturis superiorum et inferiorum"* . . . , Archiv für die Geschichte der Naturwissenschaften und der Technik, 8 (1918) 1-40. C. Singer, *Daniel of Morley, an English Philosopher of the XIIth Century*, Isis, 3 (1920-1921) 263-269. The best introduction, from the point of view of doctrinal history, is: M. Müller, *Die Stellung des Daniel von Morley in der Wissenschaft des Mittelalters*, PJ., 41 (1928) 301-337 (dates the work *ca.* 1189). T. Silverstein, *Daniel of Morley, English Cosmogonist and Student of Arabic Science*, MS., 10 (1948) 179-196.

4.—BARTHOLOMEW OF ENGLAND (Bartholomeus Anglicus OFM.), author of an encyclopedia *De proprietatibus rerum*, written *ca.* 1250: A. Schneider, *Metaphysische Begriffe des Bartholomaeus Anglicus*, Festgabe-Baeumker, 1913, 139-179. Th. Plassmann OFM., *Bartholomaeus Anglicus*, AFH., 12 (1919) 68-109; was influenced by Grosseteste, p. 92. Cf. E. Gilson, *La philosophie au moyen âge*, pp. 401-412, on the corresponding recession of literary studies in the thirteenth century.

[40] 1. JOHN BLUND. On the origins of learning at Oxford, D. A. Callus, *Introduction* . . . , PBA., 29, no date (1943): introduction of Aristotle, p. 7; teaching of Edmund Rich (Saint Edmund of Abingdon) first at Paris, then at Oxford, 13-14 (GLOREP., I, 261-262); on John Blund, 17-23 (GLOREP., I, 302-303). All

these masters taught in Paris before teaching in Oxford.—Callus reports Blund as having been "a true Aristotelian" who denied the plurality of forms (op. cit., 26). In fact, in his questions *De anima* (Cambridge, St. John's 120, folios 123 r-155 v), Blund upholds the view that "the name *soul* points out the genus of the soul, both sensitive and rational, and that there is in man only one soul in which there is vegetative life (*vegetatio*), sense and reason" (f. 125 v a). It is an incorporal substance. At this early date, Blund argues against the composition of matter and form in the rational soul. If the form of a thus composed soul is animated, then it itself must have a soul, etc.; if it is not animated, then the matter of the soul is not animated; from the composition of two non-animated components, no soul can arise. Again, if the soul is a composite substance, then it is divisible, corruptible and not immortal (149 v a). If these questions were written at Oxford, their date should be after 1230; if they date from Blund's Parisian teaching (before 1229) his Aristotelianism is still more remarkable.

2. ADAM OF BUCKFIELD (Bockfeld, identified by some with Adam of Bouchermefort): A. Pelzer, *Une source inconnue de Roger Bacon . . .*, AFH., 12 (1919) 44-67. Fr. Pelster, *Adam von Bocfeld (Bockingfold) ein Oxforder Erklärer des Aristoteles um die Mitte des 13. Jahrhunderts. Sein Leben und seine Schriften*, Scholastik, 11 (1936) 196-224. D. Salman, *Notes sur la première influence d'Averroès*, RNSP., 40 (1937) 209-212. M. Grabmann, *Mitteilungen über Werke des Adam von Bocfeld im Mss. quart. 906 der Preussischen Staatsbibliothek in Berlin. Ein Beitrag zur Geschichte der vorthomistische Aristoteleserklärung im 13. Jahrhundert,* DTF., 17 (1939) 5-29 (especially p. 26, excellent text on the blending of Aristotle and Augustine on illumination); cf. MG., II, 138-182. D. A. Callus OP., *Two Early Oxford Masters on the Problem of the Plurality of Forms. Adam of Buckfield—Richardus Rufus of Cornwall,* RNSP., 42 (1939) 411-445. S. H. Thomson, *The Works of Magister Adam de Bocfeld (Bouchermefort),* Medievalia et Humanistica, 2 (1944) 55-87. A. Pelzer upholds the identity of Buckfield and Bouchermefort, op. cit., 197-201. —On the simplicity or multiplicity of the soul, text in D. A. Callus, *Two Early English Masters,* 436, 438 ad 4m. Three

souls can be one as the light of three candles can blend into one single light; yet these three lights do not lose their distinction since each candle continues to cast its own shadow, 437-438. The commentary on *De anima* is written "by mode of question." From the fragment published by D. A. Callus it seems to be, at least on these points, rather more personal than his commentary on the *Metaphysics* (Balliol, 241), which supposes a certain acquaintance with Avicenna and Algazel, but follows the method of Averroes (by mode of exposition). Its author had the text of Averroes at hand. Adam notes that, according to Aristotle himself, the Philosopher "understood the truth absolutely, or for the most part, to the extent that it is possible to human nature." This is borrowed from Averroes, whose authority is constantly being quoted: "ut vult Commentator," "ut dicit Commentator," etc. The commentary on the first Book contains a complete demonstration of the impossibility of an infinite series in any one of the four kinds of causes. It is a well prepared explanation of the text of Aristotle in view of its public "reading" by a good professor.—Another treatise, perhaps of English origin, written about 1230, has been published by D. A. Callus, *The Powers of the Soul. An Early Unpublished Text,* RTAM., 19 (1952) 131-170. The anonymous author refuses to posit a separate agent Intellect illuminating the soul (*sufficit intellectus agens, qui est lumen interius, cum intellectu possibili*), p. 156. D. A. Callus considers this treatise as the source of John of La Rochelle on this point; the dates Callus suggests for the treatise (between 1220 and 1230) seem surprisingly early for such a clear cut position; but, of course, actual history is full of unexpected things.

[41] ROBERT GROSSETESTE.—LIFE. H. R. Luard, *Roberti Grosseteste Episcopi Quondam Lincolniensis Epistolae,* London 1861 (some dates corrected by S. H. Thomson, *The Writings . . . ,* pp. 192-213). F. S. Stevenson, *Robert Grosseteste, Bishop of Lincoln,* London, 1889. B. C. Boulter, *Robert Grosseteste, The Defender of Our Church and Our Liberties,* London, SPCK., 1936 (Anglican).—WORKS. L. Baur, *Die philosophischen Werke des Robert Grosseteste, Bischopf von Lincoln,* Münster i. W., 1912 (Beiträge, 9).—BIB-

LIOGRAPHY. GDP., 731-732. S. H. Thomson, *The Writings of Robert Grosseteste, Bishop of Lincoln, 1235-1253,* Cambridge Univ. Press, 1940: on Grosseteste's translations of John Damascene, Maximus Confessor and Dionysius, pp. 42-58; commentaries on Dionysius, John Damascene and Aristotle (logic, physics, astronomy, ethics) pp. 78-88; philosophical and scientific works, pp. 89-120.—On the doctrine, with some unpublished fragments: G. V. Lechler, *Robert Grosseteste,* Leipzig, 1867. J. Felten, *Robert Grosseteste, Bischof von Lincoln,* Freiburg, 1887. Friedr. Vogelsang, *Der Begriff der Freiheit bei Robert Grosseteste,* Gütersloh, 1915. L. Baur, *Die Philosophie des Robert Grosseteste,* Münster i. W., 1917 (Beiträge, 18, 4-6: a general survey of the doctrine by the editor of the philosophical works). P. Duhem, *Le système du monde,* V, 341-358. A. Pelzer, *Les versions latines des ouvrages de morale conservés sous le nom d'Aristote en usage au XIIIe siècle,* RNSP., 23 (1921), 316-341, 378-412. F. Pelster, *Zwei unbekannte Traktate des Robert Grosseteste,* Scholastik, 1 (1926) 572-573. F. M. Powicke, *Robert Grosseteste and the Nicomachean Ethics* (PBA., 16), London, 1930. A series of contributions by S. H. Thomson, *The De anima of Robert Grosseteste,* NS., 7 (1933), 201-221; *The 'Notule' of Grosseteste on the Nicomachean Ethics* (PBA., 19), London, 1933; *The text of Grosseteste's De cometis,* Isis, 1933, 19-25; *Grosseteste's Topical Concordance of the Bible and the Fathers,* Speculum, 9 (1934) 139-144; *The Summa in VIII libros Physicorum,* Isis, 1934, pp. 12-18. L. M. Friedman, *Robert Grosseteste and the Jews,* Harvard Press, 1934. G. B. Phelan, *An Unedited Text of Robert Grosseteste on the Subject-Matter of Theology,* RNSP., 36 (1934), 172-179 (from the Hexameron). E. Franceschini, *Roberto Grossatesta, vescovo di Lincoln e le sue traduzione latine,* Atti del Reale Istituto Veneto di Scienze, Lettere ed Arti, 93, II (1933-1934) 1-138; *Grosseteste's Translation of the Prologos and Scholia of Maximus to the Writings of the Pseudo-Dionysius Areopagita,* JTS., 34 (1933) 355-363. J. C. Russell, *The Preferments and "adjutores" of Robert Grosseteste,* HTR., 26 (1933) 161-172. L. W. Keeler, *The Dependence of R. Grosseteste's De anima on the Summa of Philip the Chancellor,* NS., 11 (1937), 197-219 (on *forma corporeitatis* and *forma situalis,* p. 218). L. E. Lynch, *The Doctrine of Divine Ideas and Illumination in Robert Grosseteste,* MS., 3 (1941), 161-173. U. Gamba, *Il commento di Roberto Grossatesta al 'De mystica theologia,'* Milano, 1942 (with text). J. T. Muckle, *The Hexameron of Robert Grosseteste, The First Twelve Chapters of Part Seven,* MS., 6 (1944), 151-174 (with text); *Robert Grosseteste's Use of Greek Sources in his Hexameron,* Medievalia et Humanistica, 3 (1945), 33-48. D. A. Callus, *The Oxford Career of R. Grosseteste,* Oxoniensia, 10 (1945) 42-72. D. A. Callus, *The Date of Grosseteste's Translations and Commentaries on Pseudo-Dionysius and the Nicomachean Ethics,* RTAM., 14 (1947) 186-210. J. T. Muckle, *Did Robert Grosseteste attribute the Hexameron of the Venerable Bede to St. Jerome?,* MS., 13 (1951), pp. 242-246. D. A. Callus, *The Summa theologiae of Robert Grosseteste,* in *Studies . . . presented to F. M. Powicke,* Oxford, 1948, pp. 180-208 (there is no such *Summa,* but R. G. may have thought of writing one; texts from his *Quaestiones theologiae,* 194-208). A. C. Crombie, *Robert Grosseteste and the Origins of Experimental Science* (1100-1700), Oxford, 1953 (bibliography, 320-352).—In Actes du XIe Congrès international de philosophie, Bruxelles: D. A. Callus, *Robert Grosseteste's Place in the History of Philosophy,* 12 (1953) 161-165. P. Michaud-Quantin, *La notion de loi naturelle chez Robert Grosseteste,* 12 (1953) 166-170. A. C. Crombie, *Robert Grosseteste on the Logic of Science,* 12 (1953) 171-173.

The three treatises, *De veritate, De veritate propositionis, De scientia Dei,* are found in English translation, in R. McKeon, *Selections . . . ,* I, 263-287. The *De luce,* in C. C. Riedl, *Robert Grosseteste On Light,* Marquette Univ. Press, Milwaukee, 1942.

ALHAZEN (965-1038), author of an extremely influential treatise on optics (*Perspectiva,* or *De aspectibus*), translated about the end of the twelfth century, is constantly used by the thirteenth-century scholastics. On his psychology of sense perceptions and its influence, Cl. Baeumker, *Witelo . . . ,* 225-234. H. Bauer, *Die Psychologie Alhazens auf Grund von Alhazens Optik dargestellt,* Münster i. W. 1911 (Beiträge, 10, 5).

[42] Grosseteste's treatise *De artibus liberalibus,* ed. L. Baur, pp. 1-10, is less a classification of sciences than a demon-

stration of the usefulness of the liberal arts. What he says on the universality of music and on the various classes of numbers is inspired by Augustine, *De musica,* I, 4; I, 8-13; VI, 5-8. All the liberal arts are subservient to a higher discipline, Ethics. The practical trend of the doctrine is strongly marked.—Note, p. 2, line 29 to p. 3, line 17, the precise description of a sound vibration.

[43] Light is what some (i.e., Gabirol) call corporeity. It is a form; *De luce,* transl. Clare C. Riedl, p. 10 (Latin original in L. Baur, p. 51 ff.).

[44] *De luce,* Riedl transl., p. 11. See the next paragraph, concerning the infinites of various orders, pp. 11-12. Grosseteste thinks that such is the meaning of atomism (p. 12), a doctrine which he does not consider contradictory with that of Aristotle.

[45] *De luce,* Riedl transl., p. 15. On the distinction of *lux* and *lumen,* op. cit., p. 15. On the finiteness of motion and time (against Aristotle), *De finitate motus et temporis,* ed. L. Baur, pp. 101-106; especially p. 105, lines 12-35. Cf. op. cit., p. 147, lines 23-25, and p. 150, lines 3-9.

[46] See the remarkable treatise *De lineis, angulis et figuris,* ed L. Baur, pp. 59-60. Cf.: "Omnes enim causae effectuum naturalium habent dari per lineas, angulos et figuras," op. cit., p. 60.

[47] *De natura locorum,* ed. L. Baur, pp. 65-66. Every operation of nature proceeds in the shortest, simplest and best possible way, *De iride,* p. 75; cf. *De lineis,* pp. 60-63. Heat is a motion of disaggregation in matter, *De calore solis,* pp. 80-81. On the production of sounds, *De artibus liberalibus,* pp. 7-8. The fundamental reason why everything can be accounted for by means of geometry is that physical motion is, in itself, nothing else than the self-multiplying energy of light; and the same remark applies to corporeal and natural appetites: *De motu corporali,* p. 92, lines 6-19. Cf. the striking text in *De lineis,* p. 60, lines 16-29. Naturally, the use of geometrical explanations does not exclude observations nor experiments. On the contrary, experiments are necessary everywhere, ed. cit., p. 36, line 15; pp. 74, 75, 79, 80 (*ratione et experimento*), 82, 83, 84 and, especially, p. 88,

lines 30-34. Roger Bacon has added very little to Grosseteste on these points.

[48] On man conceived as a *microcosmus,* ed. cit., p. 59, lines 4-16. Following the example of Augustine, Grosseteste considers God as the supreme form, hence as the sole form of all things; see his letter to Adam Rufus on the question, *De unica forma omnium,* ed. L. Baur, pp. 106-111. Cf. Augustine, *De lib. arb.,* II, 16, 44—17, 45; *Conf.,* XI, 30, 40 and XII, 2, 3. This does not mean that God is in things in the same way as form is in matter, but, rather, that God is "ipsa formositas et speciositas" (p. 108, lines 19-23). God is not form as part of created substances, but as their ideal model and exemplar.—Since there is only one form, there is only one truth for all things, namely, God (John, 14, 6). This conclusion is established in Grosseteste's *De veritate* (ed. L. Baur, pp. 130-143; cf. Anselm's dialogue, same title), where, for the first time, an extensive use is made of the Augustinian doctrine of the divine illumination. This does not happen in reaction against Aristotle, but as an independent development, in the line of Saint Anselm. We do not see the light of God, but we see truth in his light, which is one: *De veritate,* pp. 138, l. 24-139, l. 27; p. 141, lines 13-33.

[49] R. Grosseteste, *In Aristotelis Posteriorum Analyticorum libros,* Venice, 1537. An extremely interesting example of a Platonizing interpretation of Aristotle. From the very beginning (*Omnis doctrina et omnis disciplina . . . ,* fo. 2 r a), Augustine is present: "Sed verus doctor est qui interius mentem et intellectum illuminat, et veritatem ostendit." The blending of Augustine with Greco-Arabian influences is evident in Bk. I, chapt. 7, fo. 8 r a which deals with the cognition of the incorruptible. Universals are the principles of knowledge and they can be known by a pure intellect, separated from images, contemplating the Prime Light, which is the Prime Cause; thus, the uncreated reasons of things, eternally subsisting in the Prime Cause, are the principles of knowledge. These are the reasons of the things to be created and their formal exemplary causes; they are creative and it is these causes which Plato called Ideas and "archetypal world." They are causes of both being and knowledge. When a pure intellect can steadily

intuit these Ideas, it very truly and most manifestly knows created things; it even knows the Prime Light itself: "et non solum res creatas, sed ipsam lucem primam in qua cognoscit cetera." Grosseteste presently adds that, since it is not pure enough immediately to intuit the Prime light, our intellect has to receive frequent irradiations from a separate Intelligence, which is full of forms and imparts them both to things and to intellects: "multotiens recipit irradiationem a luce creata quae est Intelligentia, et in ipsis descriptionibus quae sunt in intelligentia cognoscit res posteriores, quarum formae exemplares sunt illae descriptiones." This higher mode of knowledge does not exclude the cognition of things in themselves: "Quarto modo cognoscitur res in sua causa formali quae est in ipsa, a qua ipsa est hoc quod est," etc. This latter type of cognition is the one Aristotle has in mind.

[50] See the decisive text Bk. I, ch. 14, commenting upon the well-known statement of Aristotle, where a sense is lacking, a science is necessarily lacking. For a disciple of Augustine, this was a crucial test. Grosseteste answers, 1, that any science is possible without the help of sensations, and indeed, God knows all, including singulars, without the help of sense knowledge; 2, that the separate Intelligences, seeing everything in the light of God, singulars as well as universals, know all without the help of sense knowledge; 3, that this would be true of the human intellect also, if its higher part, "intelligence" were not depressed and obscured by the weight of the human body: "et similiter pars suprema animae humanae, quae vocatur intelligentia, *et quae non est actus alicujus corporis,* nec egens in sua operatione propria instrumento corporeo, si non esset mole corporis obnubilata et aggravata, ipsa per irradiationem acceptam a lumine superiori haberet completam scientiam sine corporis adminiculo, sicut habebit cum anima fuerit exuta a corpore, et sicut habent forte aliqui absoluti ab amore et phantasmatibus rerum corporalium," etc. Hence, for man, the necessity of abstract knowledge, which is here described as an awakening of the soul under the impact of repeated sense impressions caused by external things. The result of our comparative judgments is "abstraction," an operation whichs yields

what Grosseteste calls an "experimental universal principle," *principium universale experimentale* (ibid., fo 17 v a). This completely elaborated doctrine cannot be understood as a reaction against the Aristotelianism of Albertus Magnus nor of Thomas Aquinas. It represents the effort of an older doctrinal complex to survive in the teeth of the very letter of Aristotle.—Cf. op. cit., Bk. I, ch. 17, fo 21 r a, and fo. 23 r b-23 v a. On universals, Bk. 1, ch. 18, 24 v a-25 r a.—On Grosseteste's interpretation of the agent intellect, see R. Bacon, *Opus majus,* Part II, ch. 5, Burke transl., vol. I, p. 46, and *Opus tertium,* ed. J. S. Brewer, pp. 74-75. William of Auvergne, Grosseteste and Adam of Marsh, are quoted by Bacon as agreeing on this point: the agent intellect is no part of the human soul.

[51] An outstanding personality, Grosseteste was seen by his contemporaries as the center of a group of friends, mostly English, who were either his friends or friends of his friends (Salimbene, *Chronica,* in Monumenta Germaniae Historica, Scriptores, 32, p. 234). Among them, Adam de Marisco (Adam of Marsh), whose writings have not yet been identified.—F. Ruello, *Un commentaire dionysien en quête d'auteur,* AHDL., 19 (1952) 141-181.

THOMAS OF YORK, OFM., (d. about 1260) author of a yet unpublished *Sapientiale.* Undoubtedly important as it is, this work will perhaps suffer a little from having been somewhat overpraised before its publication. Its main interest is that it bears witness to the survival, about 1256, of the late twelfth-century doctrinal complex born of the combined influences of Augustine, Gabirol and the so-called "light metaphysic." In fact, it seems to be, for the most part, a compilation, with these two reservations however: 1, that it is a philosophical one, and, so to say, a kind of *speculum* (like those of Vincent of Beauvais) dealing with philosophical problems; 2, that this compilation is directed in its choice by definite doctrinal preferences which give it a sort of doctrinal unity. Pending its publication, information about its content may be found in: M. Grabmann, *Die Metaphysik des Thomas von York,* Beiträge, Supplementband I. Münster i. W., 1913, pp. 181-193. Ephrem Longpré, *Thomas d'York, OFM., la première somme métaphysique du XIIIe siècle,* AFH., 19 (1926), 875-

920. *Thomas d'York et Matthieu d'Aquasparta. Textes inédits sur le problème de la création,* AHDL., 1 (1926-1927) 269-293. F. Treserra, *Entorn del Sapientiale de Tomas de York,* Criterion, 5 (1929) 5-45, 158-180. D. Sharp, *Franciscan Philosophy at Oxford in the Thirteenth Century,* Oxford, 1930, 49-112. D. A. Callus, *Introduction of Aristotelian learning,* pp. 34-35.
The clearest survey of Thomas of York's metaphysical positions is in F. Treserra, *De doctrinis metaphysicis Fratris Thomae de Eboraco OFM (Oxoniae magistri an. 1253),* AST., 5 (1929) 33-102. Since God alone is one, his first effect must be a twofold one (Gundissalinus, Gabirol), 6. These are potency and act, matter and form (Gabirol) 6-7. A third created principle is privation (Aristotle, Averroes) 8-11. Matter blended with privation leads to the matter-mutability of Augustine, 13, 15-16. Matter has its Idea in God, 17-18 (Gabirol, Gundissalinus). The divisions of common matter follow the divisions of forms, 19-20. On hylomorphism; John Damascene and Augustine are for, Denis and Hugh of St. Victor are against (p. 20); Thomas himself is for it, 21-27. There is no contradiction between the doctrine of the "giver of forms" (Plato) and that of the eduction of forms from matter (Aristotle); text of this surprising conciliation, 33-36. Light-metaphysics, 37. The union of matter and form is due to the cause of beings, namely the Will (Gabirol), 38-40. This composition of matter and form, and of *esse* and *id quod est,* leads to a distinction of *ens* and *esse.* This *esse* is the act of *ens;* it is not accident, nor substance, or, rather, substantial (*ut forma*). In God alone *esse* and *id quod est* are identical. In creatures, *esse* belongs to the compound of matter and form. It is the mark of its non-necessity, 41. Individuation by matter and form, 42. Plurality of forms and seminal reasons, 44. Necessary and possible (Avicenna), 44-46 (*anitas* and *quidditas*). Efficient cause, 48-49. Good and evil, 51-53. Eighteen proofs of the existence of God, 54-57. Attributes of God (oneness, simplicity, list of definitions of God including the "intelligible sphere" of Hermes Trismegistus, immutability), 57-62. Creation of the world in time, 63-64. Thomas of York is well acquainted with the new Aristotelianism of Albert and Thomas, but he wholly favors "the ancient Augustinian Scholasticism" (Treserra, p. 65).

[52] The text of the *Summa philosophiae* wrongly ascribed to Grosseteste, is printed in L. Baur, *Die philosophische Werke des Robert Grosseteste,* Münster i. W., 1912 (Beiträge, 9). Fragments transl. into English by R. McKeon, in *Selections* I, 290-314. C. K. McKeon, *A Study of the 'Summa philosophiae' of the Pseudo-Grosseteste,* New York, Columbia Press, 1948 (useful analysis).

PART SEVEN

THEOLOGY AND LEARNING

CHAPTER I.   ALBERT THE GREAT

[1] ALBERT THE GREAT. — BIOGRAPHICAL. Paulus de Loe, *De vita et scriptis Alberti Magni,* Analecta Bollandiana, 19 (1900) 257-284; 20 (1901) 273-316; 21 (1902) 361-371. Fr. Pelster, *Kritische Studien zum Leben und zu den Schriften Alberts des Grossen,* Freiburg i. Br., 1920. C. H. Scheeben, *Albert der Grosse, zur Chronologie seines Lebens,* Vechta, 1931. Th. M. Schwertner OP., *St. Albert the Great,* New York, 1932. Mary-Albert, *Saint Albert the Great,* Oxford, 1948.—On his writings: Fr. Pelster, *Zur Datierung einiger Schriften Alberts des Grossen,* ZKT., 47 (1923) 475-482. C. H. Scheeben, *Les écrits d'Albert le Grand d'après les catalogues,* RT., 36 (1931) 260-292. P. G. Meersseman, *Introductio in opera omnia B. Alberti Magni,* C. Beyaert, Bruges, 1931 (fundamental).—EDITIONS. Reprint of the 1651 Jammy edition: *Alberti Magni Opera omnia,* ed. Borgnet, Paris, Vivès, 1890-1899; 38 vols.—In critical edition, P. de Loë, *B. Alberti Magni commentarii in librum Boethii de divisione,* 1913. *Albertus Magnus De animalibus lib. XXVI,* ed. H. Stadler, Münster i. W., 2 vols. 1916 and 1920 (Beiträge, 15 and 16). New critical edition of the complete works: *Alberti Magni . . . Opera omnia,* vol. 28, *De bono,* Münster i. W., 1951; vol. 19, *Postilla super Isaiam,* Münster i. W., 1952.—GLOREP., I, 62-77.—Engl. transl., *On the Intellect and the In-*

telligible, I, 1-8; II, 1-5; III, 1-3, in R. McKeon, *Selections*, I, 368-375.
BIBLIOGRAPHY. — Fundamental: M.-H. Laurent and M.-J. Congar, *Essai de bibliographie albertinienne*, in *Le bienheureux Albert le Grand*, RT., 36 (1931) 422-468; biography, works, and studies on the doctrine.—Bibliography up to 1928 by J. Koch in GDP., 739-742.
A. Stöckl, *Geschichte der Philosophie des Mittelalters*, II, Mainz, 1865, pp. 352-421. C. Prantl, *Geschichte der Logik im Abendlande*, III, Leipzig, 1867, pp. 89-107. B. Haneberg, *Zur Erkenntnislehre des Ibn-Sina und Albertus Magnus*, Abhandlungen . . . der bayer. Akad., 11 (1866) 189-268. J. Bach, *Des Albertus Magnus Verhältnis zu der Erkenntnislehre der Griechen und Römer, Araber und Juden, Ein Beitrag zur Geschichte der Ethik*, Wien, 1881. W. Feiler, *Die Moral des Albertus Magnus. Ein Beitrag zur Geschichte der Ethik des Mittelalters*, (Inaug.-Dissert.), Leipzig, 1891. A. Schneider, *Die Psychologie Alberts des Grossen nach den Quellen dargestellt*, 2 vols., Münster i. W., I, 1903; II, 1906 (Beiträge, 4, 5-6). J. Mariétan, *Problème de la classification des sciences d'Aristote à S. Thomas*, Paris, 1901, pp. 156-175. P. Mandonnet, art. *Albert le Grand*, DTC., I (1903), 666-675; and DHGE., I (1912), col. 1515-1524. H.-D. Noble, *Note pour l'étude de la psychophysiologie d'Albert le Grand et de saint Thomas. Le cerveau et les facultés sensibles*, RT., 13 (1905), 91-101. A. Mansion, *L'induction chez Albert le Grand*, RNSP., 13 (1906) 115-134, 246-264. H. Fronober, *Die Lehre der Materie und Form nach Albert dem Grosse, nach der Quellen bearbeitet*, (Inaug.-Dissert.), Breslau, 1909. J. Verweyen, *Das Problem der Willensfreiheit in der Scholastik*, Heidelberg, 1909, pp. 112-127. A. Horwath, *Albert der Grosse und der hl. Thomas von Aquin als Begründer der christlichen Philosophie*, DTF., 3 (1916) 591-636. M. Mastrorilli, *La filosofia naturale di Alberto Magno*, Naples, 1922. Tusquets y Terrats, *Metafisica de la generacion*, Miscellanca Tomista, Barcelona, 1924, pp. 326-360. O Lottin, *La syndérèse chez Albert le Grand et S. Thomas d'Aquin*, RNSP., 30 (1928) 18-44. G. S. Busnelli, *L'origine dell'anima razionale secundo Dante e Alberto Magno*, Civiltà cattolica, 80 (1929) 289-300; 81 (1930) 97-107, 229-237, 336-347. W. Arendt, *Die Staats- und Gesellschafslehre Alberts des Grossen,*

Jena, 1929. E. Kleineidam, *Das Problem der hylemorphen Zusammensetzung der geistigen Substanzen im 13. Jahrhundert bis Thomas von Aquino*, (Inaug.-Dissert.), Breslau, 1930, 51-57. H. Kuhle, *Die Lehre Alberts des Grossen von der Transzendentalien*, in *Philosophia Perennis* (Festgabe-Geyser), Regensburg, 1930, pp. 129-147. E. Barbado, *Relations entre la physionomie, le tempérament et le caractère d'après le B. Albert et la science moderne*, RT., 36 (1931) 314-351. H.-D. Simonin, *La doctrine de l'amour naturel de Dieu d'après le B. Albert le Grand*, RT., 36 (1931) 361-370. G. Théry, *L'augustinisme médiéval et l'unité de la forme substantielle*, APA., Torino, 1931, pp. 164-169. M.-M. Gorce, *Le problème des trois Sommes: Alexandre de Hales, Thomas d'Aquin, Albert le Grand*, RT., 36 (1931) 293-301. A. Delorme, *La morphogénèse d'Albert le Grand dans l'embryologie scolastique*, ibid., pp. 352-360. J. Goergen, *Des hl. Albertus Magnus Lehre von der göttlichen Vorsehung und dem Fatum, unter Besonderer Berücksichtigung der Vorsehungs-und Schicksalslehre des Ulrich von Strassburg*, Vechta i. Oldbg., 1932. Collective work (Masnovo, B. Geyer, F. Pelster, E. Ruffini, M. Grabmann, O. Lottin, etc.), *Alberto Magno, Atti della settimana albertina*, Roma, Pustet, 1932. H. C. Scheeben, *Albertus Magnus*, Bonn, 1932 (biographical). A. Masnovo, *Ancora Alberto Magno e l'averroismo latino*, RFNS., 24 (1932) 317-326. K. Schmieder, *Alberts des Grossen Lehre vom natürlichen Gotteswissen*, Freiburg i. Br., 1932. R. Meister, *Zur Formulierung des Universalienproblem bei Albertus Magnus*, Wiener Studien, 50 (1932) 160-165. U. Dähnert, *Die Erkenntnislehre des Albertus Magnus gemessen an den Stufen der "abstractio,"* Leipzig, 1933. O. Lottin, *Saint Albert le Grand et l'Ethique à Nicómaque*, ADGM., 611-626. F.-M. Henquinet, *Vingt-deux questions inédites d'Albert le Grand dans un manuscrit à l'usage de saint Thomas d'Aquin*, NS., 9 (1935) 283-328. B. Geyer, *Die Albert dem Grossen zugeschriebene Summa Naturalium (Philosophia Pauperum)*. Münster i. W., 1938 (Beiträge, 35, 1; attributes this *Summa* to Albert of Orlamond). A. Hufnagel, *Die Wahrheit als philosophisch-theologisches Problem bei Albert dem Deutschen*, Bonn, 1940. W. Gorman, *Albertus Magnus on Aristotle's Second Definition of the Soul*, MS., 2 (1940) 223-230. D. Siedler, *Intellektualismus und*

Voluntarismus bei Albertus Magnus, Münster i. W., 1941 (Beiträge, 36, 2). E. Gilson, *L'âme raisonnable chez Albert le Grand,* AHDL., 14 (1943-1945) 5-72. V. J. Bourke, *The Provenance of the De apprehensione Attributed to Albertus Magnus,* Speculum, 18 (1943) 91-98.— Two collective publications: *Serta Albertina,* Angelicum, 21 (1944), 22 studies on Albert as a scientist; *Studia Albertina* (Festschrift f. Bernhard Geyer), Beiträge, Supplementband IV, Münster i. W., 1952, 23 studies on Albert the Great, among which: *Der Geist als höherer Teil der Seele nach Albert dem Grossen,* by A. J. Backes, 52-67; *Zur Frage der anfangslosen und zeitlichen Schöpfung bei Albert dem Grossen,* by J. Hansen, 167-188; *Die ursprüngliche Einteilung des Sentenzenkommentars Alberts des Grossen,* by A. Heidl, 189-201; *Der Person-Problem bei Albertus Magnus,* by A. Hufnagel, 202-233; *Die frühscholastischen Vorarbeiten zum Kommentar Alberts des Grossen zu 3, dist. 38, a. 6,* by A. M. Landgraf, 319-342; *Die Bedeutung Alberts des Grossen für die Aufrollung der fundamentaltheologischen Fragen,* by A. Lang, 343-373; *Zum Fortleben Alberts des Grossen bei Heymeric von Kamp und Nikolaus von Kues,* by R. Haubst, 420-447. M. Grabmann, *Albertus Magnus Theologe Philosoph und Naturforsher,* PJ., 61 (1951) 473-480.—O. Lottin, PEM., 210-221, II, 430-463 (Albert and Thomas Aquinas); 470-473 (*Summa de bono*), 572-578 (*Summa de creaturis*); III, 309, 540-550 (reason and morality).—P. Duhem, *Le système du Monde,* V, 412-468.

² See P. Mandonnet, *La date de naissance d'Albert le Grand,* RT., 36 (1931) 233-256; followed by M. H. Laurent, *Les grandes lignes de la vie du bienheureux Albert,* pp. 257-259. According to M. H. Laurent, p. 257, the *Summa de creaturis,* still partly unpublished, was written during the years 1228-1233. The philosophical encyclopedia was begun at Paris, in 1245, and continued during the following years. The commentaries on Dionysius the Areopagite and on the *Nicomachean Ethics* date from Albert's second teaching at Cologne (1248). The *De unitate intellectus,* against Averroes, dates from 1256. His last work seems to be the unfinished *Summa theologiae.* More recent conclusions in O. Lottin, *Problèmes concernant la "Summa de creaturis" et le Commentaire des Sentences*

de Saint Albert le Grand, RTAM., 17 (1950) 319-328. (Commentary begun *ca.* 1243-1244; Books 1, 2, 3, completed after 1246; Book 4, in 1249; *Summa de creaturis* before 1243.

³ In his philosophical encyclopedia, Albert has several times warned his readers that all the doctrines he was reporting should not be considered as expressing his own thought. Texts in P. G. Meersseman, *Introductio.,* pp. 6-9. —Roger Bacon has several times protested against the title of "author" given to Albert by his contemporaries (*pro auctore allegatur*). Albert, Bacon says, has adopted in his books the style of an author (*per modum authenticum scripsit libros suos*). Hence, his "authority." A text of Bonaventure shows that there was then a clear distinction between the "scribe" (*scriptor*), who was a copyist; the "compiler" (*compilator*), who added to what he was borrowing, but not enough to make it his own; the commentator (*commentator*), who added to the text only what was needed in order to make it intelligible; and finally the "author" (*auctor*), who principally intended to express his own ideas, although he might incidentally quote other writers in support of his own opinions: St. Bonaventure, *In I Sent.,* Prooemium, qu. 4, Resp. (Quaracchi, minor ed., I, p. 12).— On the distinction between "authors" and "masters," M.-D. Chenu OP., *Authentica et Magistralia, deux lieux théologiques aux XIIe-XIIIe siècles,* DTP., 28 (1925) 257-285.

⁴ Unless otherwise indicated, our references, will be to the Borgnet (Vivès) edition.—Albert states his intentions at the beginning of his exposition on *Physics,* Bk. VIII. Yielding to the repeated request of the brothers of his Order, who desired an explanation of Aristotle's *Physics,* he will follow the order and the sense of the doctrine and say what he will deem necessary in order to explain and to prove its doctrine, but without ever mentioning its text ("ita tamen quod textus ejus nulla fiat mentio"). Moreover, he will add digressions in order to remove occasional difficulties and to supply what may be lacking in the text of Aristotle; simple titles indicate that the chapter exists in Aristotle, whereas any chapter whose title includes the word "digression" is a personal contribution of

Albert: "Following this method, we will write the same number of books as Aristotle, and with the same titles; and we shall even add the missing parts of his unfinished books, or the books which are missing because Aristotle himself did not write them or, if he did, because they did not come to us" (B. 3, 1: i.e., ed. Borgnet, vol. 3, p. 1.). In short, Albert is writing a paraphrase with explanatory and complementary digressions. The true extent to which he blended Platonism with Aristotelianism is difficult to ascertain, the more so as Albert himself does not seem to have had a perfectly precise notion of their distinction. On this problem: L. Gaul, *Alberts des Grossen Verhältnis zur Plato. Eine literarische und philosophiegeschichtliche Untersuchung,* Münster i. W., 1913 (Beiträge, 12, 1). H. Stadler, *Irrthümer des Albertus Magnus bei Benützung des Aristoteles,* Archiv für Geschichte der Naturwissenschaften und der Technik, 6 (1913) 387-393. More indications in RT., 36 (1921) 457-459.

[5] Albert follows the doctrine of Boethius on the distinction of *quod est* and *quo est,* or *esse.* The *quo est* is the form of the whole (*forma totius*). See *Summa theologiae,* Part II, tr. 1, q. 3, a. 2; B. 32, pp. 36-37. This was the commonly received position among the theologians (P. W. Nash SJ., *The Meaning of Est in the Sentences (1152-1160) of Robert of Melun,* MS., 14 (1952) 129-142. In some texts Albert uses a language more similar to that of Thomas Aquinas; for instance: "cum esse sit actus essentiae," or "esse uniuscujusque est actus formae ultimae," etc., *De unitate intellectus contra Averroistas,* V; B. 9, 452-453; yet, even there, what Albert means to say is that *esse* is an effect of the formal cause: ibid., B. 9, 454; cf. *In de praedicamentis,* II, 8; B. I, 181-182.—M. Grabmann, *Ein dem hl. Albertus Magnus zugeschriebener Traktat "De quidditate et esse" (Codd. 1, Admont 487, Vat. 806). Untersuchung und Ausgabe,* DTF., 20 (1942) 116-156. Probably spurious and of little importance except concerning the terminology of the problem.

[6] In Albert's doctrine, the expression "form of the whole" (*forma totius*) has two different meanings. First, the form alone, which is the formal essence of the thing, as "humanity" is the form of the human being, man; as such, it is not predicated of that whose form it is, because no being that has a form is its own formal essence: "man" is not "humanity"; secondly, the whole itself, whose form it is ("totum esse dicens cujus est forma"). In this second sense, it is called "form of the whole" because *qua* form, it gives *esse* to the whole being whose form it is. In saying that "Peter is a man," I point to the fact that "man" is the form of the whole composite being which this particular man, Peter, is: *De praedicabilibus,* II, 8; B. 1, p. 38.

[7] The demonstration of the existence of God accepted by Albert is Aristotle's proof of the existence of a Prime Cause, as exposed in the paraphrase on *Metaphysics,* Bk. XI, tr. 2, a. 5-6; B. 6, pp. 617-620.

[8] On the notion of the soul, *Summa de creaturis,* II, 4, 1, B., 35, 34-35. The starting point is Avicenna, quoted in full by Albert. The word "soul" does not designate the essence of the soul; the definition of the soul by Aristotle does not say what it is, except as the source and cause of voluntary acts: "et sic affirmatur esse ejus ex hoc quod habet aliquod accidens: quod tamen accidens valet ad certificandum ejus essentiam et ad cognoscendum quid sit." Hence the definition of the soul is a twofold one: "ita anima dupliciter potest diffiniri, scilicet secundum quod est anima, id est actus corporis et motor, et secundum quod est substantia quaedam contenta secundum seipsam in praedicamento substantiae."—The difference between souls and angels is that: "anima inclinatur ad corpus ut actus, angelus autem non." (p. 34). Albert does not deny that the intellective soul is the form of the body; he says that to define it as a form is not to define its substance; hence he also maintains that, on two accounts, "melius dicitur actus vel perfectio quam forma" (ad 6m, p. 35). One reason is that a form cannot subsist without its matter, whereas there are "perfections" which can subsist without it: "Perfectio autem quaedam bene est sine perfecto secundum suam substantiam, sicut nauta sine navi" (ibid.). Another reason is that "form" points out perfection with respect to matter only, whereas "perfection" points out that which perfects the thing in all respects.—Same position in *De anima,* II, 1, 1; B. 5, p. 193. II, 1, 3, pp. 197-198. II, 1, 4, pp.

198-199. II, 1, 6, pp. 205-206. *Liber de unitate intellectus,* ch. 6, B. 9, p. 463. It is substantial to the soul to be the form of the body, but its substance is not to be a form.—On this point, Albert thinks that the worst masters have been the Latins, *De anima,* III, 2, 1; B. 5, p. 330 (*in istarum quaestionum determinatione omnino abhorremus Doctorum Latinorum verba*).—G. Meersseman, *Die Einheit der menschlichen Seele nach Albertus Magnus,* DTF., 10 (1932) 213-226; extracts from the lectures of Albert on the *Nicomachean Ethics.* A. C. Pegis, *St. Thomas and the Problem of the Soul in the Thirteenth Century,* Toronto, 1934, pp. 77-120: many excellently chosen texts.

On the scholastic origin of the expressions "primary and secondary qualities" and "tabula rasa" (used by Locke), Cl. Baeumker, *Zur Vorgeschichte zweier Lockescher Begriffe,* Archiv für Geschichte der Philosophie, 21 (1908) 296-298, 516-517.—Concerning *tabula rasa,* Albert the Great, *De anima,* III, 2, 17; Bonaventure, *II Sent.* d. I, p. 2, a. 1, q. 2, ad 2, 3; Thomas Aquinas, *Sum. theol.,* I, 79, 2.— More general, A. Tellkamp, *Das Verhältnis J. Lockes zur Scholastik,* Veröffentlichungen des Katholischen Instituts für Philosophie (Albertus-Magnus-Akademie) zu Köln, vol. II, 2.

[9] The agent intellect and the possible intellect are two powers inherent in the human soul. Both are separated from matter, but not from the soul. On the other hand, most of the modern Peripatetics agree that there is a separate Intelligence giving forms to matter and knowledge in intellects (*De unitate intellectus contra Averroem,* II; B. 9, pp. 439-440); this is an invention of the Arabs (ibid., IV, p. 445). On this point Averroes is wrong like the rest of them, but while all the others have been mistaken concerning the mutual relations of the two intellects, Averroes was right. Consequently, Albert takes up the two intellects just about as he finds them in Averroes, and reinstates them in the individual human soul. Nothing throws a more vivid light on Albert's intellectual temper than his attitude on this point. A correct description of the relationship of the two intellects is so important to him, that he considers the rest comparatively unimportant: "Nos autem dissentimus in paucis ab Averroe . . .", *De anima,* III, 3, 11; B. 5, p. 385. And

again: "Nos autem in dictis istis nihil mutamus nisi hoc quod etiam Aristoteles mutasse videtur, quoniam dixit quod in omni natura in qua est patiens, est etiam et agens, et ita oportet in anima esse has differentias," ibid., pp. 385-386. Cf. *De unitate intellectus,* VI; B. 9, pp. 463-464. This does not forbid us to posit God as a universal agent intellect. Albert ascribes to the human intellect an active power of its own, but he submits the whole soul of man to the higher illuminating influence of a separate substance, which is God. With respect to God, the human soul, including its intellective powers, is "possible," that is, in potency to a higher illumination. The same dual position is to be found in Roger Bacon. The formula (God is the separate Intellect) was so commonly received that even Thomas Aquinas will pay it at least lip service, in *Summa theologiae,* I, 79, 4: «Sed intellectus separatus (Thomas does not say *agens*) secundum nostrae fidei documenta, est ipse Deus, qui est creator animae, et in quo solo beatificatur.»

[10] The hierarchy of the intellects described by Alfarabi and Avicenna is accepted by Albert as a technical development of the doctrine of Denis on the divine illumination. With this reservation, it is to be found, complete, in Albert's *De unitate intellectus,* ch. VI; B. 9, p. 464: by contemplating itself, the speculative intellect achieves the awareness of its beauty; it sees itself in the light of the Intelligences; it knows itself as necessary in its Prime Cause and, by the same token, it contacts the root of immortality and of eternal blessedness (Alfarabi): "et sic continuabitur radici immortalitatis et felicitatis aeternae." Albert himself subscribes to this doctrine "Et hoc est quod verius de intellectu dici potest, et de natura ipsius . . ." (p. 464). He then refers to what he has already written on the subject in his own *De intellectu et intelligibili,* where God is the Prime Intelligence and source of all forms (II, 2; B. 9, pp. 505-506); the prime cause of intelligible being ("primum agens esse intelligibile," II, 3; pp. 507-508). On the acquired intellect (*intellectus adeptus,* II, 8; pp. 514-516); the assimilative intellect (*intellectus assimilativus:* "quo homo quantum possibile sive fas est proportionaliter surgit ad intellectum divinum, qui est lumen et causa omnium" (II, 9; p. 516); this also is the pure

and holy intellect (*mundus et sanctus*), as Avicenna says, or, according to Aristotle, the divine intellect (*intellectus divinus*, I, 3, 3; p. 501 and II, 10, pp. 518-519). Same doctrine in *De causis et processu universitatis*, II, 2, 20; B. 10, pp. 509-510. A text of the *Commentary on the Sentences* clearly shows that Albert added a divine illumination over and above the natural light of the agent intellect. In order to know, man needs "a more abundant light than that of the agent intellect, such as a beam of the divine light or of an angelic revelation." In short, in a sense, every true cognition presupposes a sort of grace, *Sent.*, I, 2, 5; B. 25, 59-60. This important text calls for several remarks. 1, it has never been withdrawn nor corrected by Albert; 2, it deals with natural cognitions; 3, after listing the four conditions for natural knowledge (possible intellect, agent intellect, thing offered by imagination, principles) it adds that "the light of the agent intellect is *not* sufficient by itself without an application of the light of the uncreated Intellect"; 4, this application produces a twofold intellectual light (by "conjunction" of our agent intellect with the light of the uncreated Intellect, i.e., the "Interior Master" of Augustine); it sometimes produces a threefold intellectual beam (agent intellect, angelic intellect, uncreated intellect); 5, Albert expressly refers to the agreement of Denis and Augustine on this point; 6, he does not consider this a position borrowed from any philosopher; on the contrary, he says that *even* some philosophers agree on this point, for indeed: a) some of them call this the "continuation of the intellects" and they say that nothing is seen except in the Prime Light; b) at least one of them (Avicenna) says that even habitual cognitions cannot be known in act without a turning of our intellect to the light of the uncreated intellect (op. cit., p. 60). Incidentally, this is a clear instance of what we call a doctrinal complex, since it includes Augustine, Denis, Alfarabi and Avicenna.

[11] This text is important concerning the doctrine of intellectual abstraction. There are other ones, which differ according to the point of view adopted by Albert in each case. For instance, in *De unitate intellectus contra Averroem*, Albert intends to give a correct interpretation of this operation as Aristotle himself understood it; it is the true explanation of abstraction: "Et iste pro certo fuit intellectus Aristotelis in verbis suis de intellectu, et solus iste est verus et nullus alius" (op. cit., ch. VI; B. 9, p. 464). The operation is as follows: 1, because every intellectual nature holds its necessity from its prime cause, and its possibility from itself (Avicenna), the agent Intellect can turn upon itself (*De causis*) and in doing so, it lets the light of the Prime Cause (Denis) penetrate its own potentiality. Some call *intellectus formalis* the possible intellect thus informed by the light of the agent intellect (ibid., p. 464; cf. *De intellectu et intelligibili*, II, 5; B. 9, pp. 510-511). The agent intellect sheds upon the sensible and imaginary forms an abstracted light; this begets a species, or "intention," received in the possible intellect, and this intention of the form (rather than the form) conveys it to the possible intellect in a state of abstraction. Intentions are the forms and perfections of the possible intellect, which is, so to say, their "place" (locus), or container. "The species penetrates and perfects the possible intellect by the virtue of the agent intellect"; at that moment, the "universal intention" and the possible intellect are actually one: loc. cit., p. 464.—G. C. Reilly, *The Psychology of St. Albert the Great Compared with that of St. Thomas*, Washington, 1934. G. de Mattos, *L'intellect agent personnel dans les premiers écrits d'Albert le Grand et de Thomas d'Aquin*, RNSP., 43 (1940) 145-161.

[12] The problem of the composition of the *Summa theologiae* of Albert has not been solved. The best study of the question is that of Hubert Neufeld, *Zum Problem des Verhältnisses der theologischen Summe Alberts des Grossen zur theologischen Summe Alexander von Hales*, FS., 27 (1940) 22-56, 65-87; conclusions, pp. 83-84. It appears: 1, that Albert has borrowed from Alexander (and others) a large part of his material: order of the questions, objections, quotations, etc.; 2, that even when the framework of a question is borrowed from some other work, Albert always goes his own way and teaches his own doctrine. The question raised by Gorce (*Le problème des trois Sommes: Al. de Hales, Thomas d'Aquin, Albert le Grand*, RT., 36 (1931) 293-301), is different: why did Albert write another *Summa* after that of Thomas Aquinas?

The question only arises for those who imagine Albert as a late convert to Thomism. Few men have more consistently accumulated new learning than Albert; but few men seem to have more consistently adhered to their early doctrinal attitudes than he did. Augustine (*Soliloquies*), Denis and Maximus the Confessor, the *Liber de causis,* Boethius, Anselm, Richard of St. Victor, Alfarabi, Avicenna, Gabirol, Averroes and, of course, through the Arabs, Aristotle, provided him with the bulk of his material. The connecting link between his theology and the use he made of his immense philosophical learning, seems to have been Denis.

On the relation between the *Summa* and the Commentary of Albert on the *Sentences:* H. Kühle, *Zum Problem der "Summa theologica" und des "Sentenzenkommentars" Albert des Grossen,* ADGM., I, 591-610. O. Lottin, *Commentaire des Sentences et Somme théologique d'Albert le Grand,* RTAM., 8 (1936) 117-153.

[13] Albert the Great does not think that the philosophers have known the notion of creation understood as a production *ex nihilo:* "Philosophi non cognoverunt creationem secundum quod est actus creantis," *Summa theologiae,* II, tr. 1, q. 4, a. 1, partic. 1; B. 32, p. 59. On the other hand, he refuses to consider the philosophers as having denied creation; they simply never thought of it. Consequently, their own descriptions of the formation of the world are not necessarily in contradiction with Christian revelation. Albert may well have admitted as true a large part of his *De causis et processu universitatis.* This important treatise probably represented to him what science and philosophy can say concerning the way God created the world. God is the necessary being (*De causis . . .* , I, 1, 10; B. 10, pp. 380-383) in which the question *an est* does not even arise (I, 1, 8, p. 377). He is a universal agent intellect (*intellectus universaliter agens*), that is "a being whose light is the cause of existence for all that is" (I, 2, 1, p. 388). He also is a will, a truth which, among all philosophers, Gabirol alone has known (I, 3, 4, p. 405; cf. I, 4, 8, p. 430: Gabirol "specialem sibi fingens philosophiam."). The origin of the world therefore was a flowing of beings out of God (*fluxus est emanatio formae a primo fonte, qui omnium formarum est fons et origo*) caused by his intellect and his will (I, 4, 1; p.

411). In order to account for the way it happened, let us suppose with all philosophers, except Gabirol, that from one cause only one effect can follow: "Supponentes autem propositionem quam omnes ante nos Philosophos supposuerunt, scilicet quod ab uno simplici immediate non est nisi unum secundum naturae ordinem" (I, 4, 8, p. 428). All we have to do after this is to follow the order of generation of the Intelligences, spheres, and souls, or quasi souls (I, 4, 7; p. 424) of the spheres as Avicenna and other philosophers have described it (p. 428). The insertion of such a cosmogony in the general frame of the biblical narrative was certainly not impossible; only, this means that Alfarabi's and Avicenna's cosmogonies have been integrated by Albert in his doctrine; it does not turn them into personal contributions of his own.

[14] In the texts which express Albert's own doctrine, the universally acting Intellect is God. This position is already present in Albert's paraphrase on the *Categories.* According to him, the universal can be considered either in the soul, or in itself, or in singulars. In all three cases, it is the same universal seen in three different ways under the light of the Prime Intelligence: *De praedicabilibus,* II, 6; B. 1, pp. 35-36. This agent Intelligence (God) is the prime cause of universals either in themselves, or in the soul, or in singulars: ibid., II, 7; pp. 36-37. The Avicennian doctrine of simple natures is related to the same divine light, ibid., IX, 3; pp. 146-148. On the three states in which universals are to be found: *De intellectu et intelligibili,* I, 2, 2; B. 9, pp. 492-493.

The remark of Grabmann quoted at the end of this chapter is found in his article *De theologia ut scientia argumentativa secundum S. Albertum Magnum et S. Thomam,* Angelicum, 13 (1937) 52. The objection of Albert Lang (Beiträge, Supplementband IV, p. 351, n. 40) is irrelevant to the precise point which Grabmann had in mind. Albert has certainly been an initiator. In at least one case we know for sure that he went over from the psychological notion of time upheld by Augustine (time is in the soul) to the physical notion of time upheld by the Arabian philosophers (*Phys.* IV, tr. 3, cap. 6; B. 3, 318). This is typical of Albert's true originality. He has substituted the philosophical material borrowed from Aristotle for the Augustinian philosophical material borrowed from Plotinus. On some points he has even enriched this new philosophical and scientific erudition. Yet, when all is said and done, Grabmann seems to be right in suggesting that Albert's intention was to defend theology rather than to renew it and this is the reason why, important as it is, his work implies no renovation of the

philosophical notions of being, of man or of God.—These remarks are offered as so many invitations to personal reflection, not as historically demonstrable conclusions.—On the problem in the thirteenth and fourteenth centuries: J. N. Espenberger, *Grund und Gewissheit des übernatürlichen Glaubens in der Hoch- und Spätscholastik*, Paderborn, 1915.

PART SEVEN

CHAPTER II. ROGER BACON

[15] ROGER BACON OFM.—On Bacon's life and works: Stewart C. Easton, *Roger Bacon and His Search for a Universal Science*, Oxford, 1952; Th. Crowley, *Roger Bacon, The Problem of the Soul in His Philosophical Commentaries*, Louvain-Dublin, 1950, ch. I, *Bacon's Life and Works*, pp. 17-78. Both works contain extended bibliographies.

The writings of Bacon are divided into two groups: his commentaries on Aristotle and the various expositions of his views on the restoration of Christian wisdom.

I. The commentaries have been edited by Robert Steele, *Opera hactenus inedita fratris Rogeri Baconis*, Oxford, Clarendon Press, 1905 and following years. I, *Metaphysica Fratris Rogeri (De viciis contractis in studio theologiae)*, not dated, belongs in the second category of Bacon's writings; II-IV, *Liber primus communium naturalium; Liber secundus communium naturalium*, 1905, 1911, 1913; V, *Secretum Secretorum cum glossis et notulis Fratris Rogeri*, 1920; VI, *Compotus Fratris Rogeri*, 1926 (spurious); VII, *Quaestiones supra undecimum prime philosophie Aristotelis*, 1926; VIII, *Quaestiones supra libros quatuor Physicorum Aristotelis*, ed. F. Delorme, 1928; IX, *De retardatione accidentium senectutis cum aliis opusculis de rebus medicinalibus*, edd. A. G. Little and E. Withington, 1928; X, *Quaestiones altere supra libros prime philosophie*, 1930; XI, *Quaestiones supra quatuor libros prime philosophie*, 1932, pp. 1-170, and *Quaestiones supra librum des plantis*, pp. 173-252; XII, *Quaestiones supra Librum de causis*, 1935; XIII, *Quaestiones altere supra libros octo Physicorum Aristotelis*, ed. F. Delorme, 1935; XIV, *Liber de sensu et sensato, Summa de sophismatibus et destruccionibus*, 1937;

XV, *Summa grammatica, Summulae dialectices*, 1941; XVI, *Communia mathematica Fratris Rogeri*, I and II, 1940.— The *Compotus*, vol. VI, belongs to Gilles of Lessines, OP. (*Aegidius de Luxinis*); see F. Delorme, Antonianum, 11 (1939) 313-322.—To be added: E. Nolan and S. A. Hirsch, *The Greek Grammar of Roger Bacon, and a Fragment of his Hebrew Grammar*, Cambridge, 1902. S. H. Thomson, *An Unnoticed Treatise by Roger Bacon on Time and Motion*, in Isis, 27 (1937) 219-224. F. Delorme, *Le prologue de R. Bacon à son traité De influentiis agentium*, Antonianum, 18 (1943), 81-90.

II. The works related to the reformation of theological teaching are still to be critically edited, but their present editions are more than sufficient for a general appreciation of his thought. The main work is: *Opus majus*, ed. J. H. Bridges, Oxford, 1897-1900, 3 vols. The complete text of Part VII (*Moralis philosophia*) incompletely published by Bridges, is found in F. Delorme and E. Massa, *Rogeri Baconis Moralis philosophia*, Turici, 1953.—Other treatises to the same purpose: *Fr. Rogeri Bacon Opera quaedam hactenus inedita*, ed. J. S. Brewer, London, 1859 (*Rerum Britannicarum Medii Aevi Scriptores*), contains: I, *Opus tertium;* II, *Opus minus;* III, *Compendium philosophiae;* IV, *De secretis operibus artis et de nullitate magiae*. Supplements to the text of the *Opus tertium*, in P. Duhem, *Un fragment inédit de l'Opus tertium de Roger Bacon, précédé d'une étude sur ce fragment*, Quaracchi, 1909. A. G. Little, *Part of the Opus tertium of Roger Bacon, Including a Fragment Now Printed for the First Time*, Aberdeen, 1912. For the *Compendium*, see *Fr. Rogeri Bacon Compen-*

dium studii theologia, ed. H. Rashdall, Aberdeen, 1911.—English translation of the *Opus majus,* by R. B. Burke, *The 'Opus majus' of Roger Bacon,* 2 vols. Philadelphia, 1928. BIBLIOGRAPHY. E. Charles, *Roger Bacon, sa vie, ses ouvrages, sa doctrine,* Bordeaux, 1861. Cl. Baeumker, *Roger Bacons Naturphilosophie, insbesondere seine Lehre von Materie und Form,* FS., 3 (1916) 1-40, 109-139. P. Duhem, *Le système du monde,* V, 375-511. R. Carton, *L'expérience physique chez Roger Bacon,* Paris, 1924; *L'expérience mystique de l'illumination intérieure chez Roger Bacon,* Paris, 1924; *La synthèse doctrinale de Roger Bacon,* Paris, 1924.—Studies on Bacon by H. Hoffmans, *Une théorie intuitioniste de la connaissance au XIIIe siècle,* RNSP., 13 (1906) 371-391; *La synthèse doctrinale de Roger Bacon,* RNSP., 14 (1907) 106-124; *La genèse des sensations d'après Roger Bacon,* RNSP., 15 (1908) 474-498; *La sensibilité et les modes de la connaissances d'après Roger Bacon,* RNSP., 16 (1909) 32-46; *L'intuition mystique et la science,* RNSP., 16 (1909) 370-397; *L'expérience chez Roger Bacon,* RNSP., 27 (1925) 170-190. —H. Höver, *Roger Bacons Hylomorphismus als Grundlage seiner philosophischen Anschauungen,* Limburg, 1912. A. Pelzer, *Une source inconnue de Roger Bacon. Alfred de Sareshel commentateur des Météorologiques d'Aristote,* AHF., 12 (1919) 44-67. E. Lutz OFM., *Roger Bacon's Contribution to Knowledge,* New York, J. F. Wagner, 1936. J. A. Sheridan, *Expositio plenior hylemorphismi Fr. Rogeri Baconis,* Analecta Gergoriana (Philos. XVII) Rome, 1938. G. Théry, *Note sur l'aventure "Bélénienne" de Roger Bacon,* AHLD., 25-26 (1950-1951) 129-147 (in this study, note that, on p. 142, "scholares" should be translated by "pupils," not "fellow-students"; p. 144, instead of "cui fuit," read "cui fui"; then there is no "aventure Bélénienne" left). Th. Crowley, *Roger Bacon and Avicenna,* Philosophical Studies, 2 (1952) 82-88.— GDP., 760-761.

[16] It is certain that matter is common "sicut genus generalissimum compositum" (II, 57). It is also certain that Bacon has identified matter with what Gundissalinus had already called the *possibilitas essendi* (*De processione mundi,* ed. G. Bülow, p. 25; quoted by Th. Crowley, *Roger Bacon . . . ,* p. 99, note 72). The

interpretation submitted by Crowley seems therefore irrecusable and we can find no better one. Nevertheless, Gundissalinus does not say that matter is the *possibilitas essendi* itself, but that "possibilitas essendi non est nisi ex materia," which is easier to understand and, at any rate, different.

[17] On this point, see Th. Crowley, *Roger Bacon . . . ,* pp. 108-110. Referring to X, 284, Crowley remarks that, in this doctrine, "the extramental reality, the individual thing in nature, is, to a certain extent, a veritable *arbor porphyriana*" (p. 107; confirmed by Bacon, *Opera Inedita;* II, 87-89). As to the plurality of forms: "The lower forms are not expelled by the advent of higher forms but persevere in the composite and are principles of operations within it" (pp. 106-107). The pages 109-110, on the progressive actualization of matter by forms are no less excellent and should be quoted in full, up to their conclusion: "The substantial form, in Bacon's theory, is one, but its unity is a unity of composition and not a unity of simplicity." Incidentally, this is the reason why Bacon could not have accepted the composition *ex esse et ente,* even under its Boethian form (Th. Crowley, p. 87); otherwise each formal *quo est* would have determined a distinct being.

[18] For a contrary interpretation of Bacon's doctrine on this point, see Th. Crowley, *Roger Bacon . . . ,* p. 176: "Abstraction is described by Bacon along strictly Aristotelian lines." Compare this conclusion with the text of R. Bacon himself: "Alius est intellectus creatus materiae transmutabili conjunctus, scilicet corpori, et hic est duplex: quidam est agens, scilicet una pars intellectus elevata ad superiora contemplandum, et haec vocatur intellectus agens, et haec non intelligit per administrationem sensuum, sed per exempla sibi innata, confusa tamen; et quantum ad hanc partem non suscipit intellectus lassitudinem, languorem in intelligendo, et hic est intellectus agens qui remanet in anima quando a corpore separata est. Alter est intellectus possibilis, scilicet altera pars intellectus vel rationis quando ratio se inclinat ad inferiora, et hic intelligit per administrationem sensuum de quo dicitur 'nichil est in intellectu quin prius fuerit in sensu'; de quo dicitur 'omne nostrum intelligere est cum continuo et tempore.' Et hic lassitudinem,

et fatigationem, languorem suscipit in consecutione intelligendi; sed non agens, quamvis idem sint in substantia, quia intelligere agentis non est mensuratum a tempore." (VII, 110). The following page, speaking of the various meanings of "exemplar," mentions the fact that "aliud est innatum, et hoc est duplex; quoddam confusum in intellectu animae scilicet agente, aliud est distinctum ut est in intelligentiis" (VII, pp. 111-112). These are the very innate *exemplaria* which we find at work in the text VIII, 31, quoted by Th. Crowley himself (p. 176, note 40): "et tunc intellectus agens cujus creata sunt exemplaria, irradiat super phantasmata, ipsa a conditionibus materialibus abstrahens in intellectu possibili reponendo."

[19] Bacon ascribes to the human soul an intellect of its own; it is no less certain that, in comparison with God, man only has a possible intellect whose agent intellect is God: "Nam ponitur quod agens (intellectus) sit pars animae, quod est improbatum in 2a Parte *Primi Operis*, deinde in hoc *Tercio opere* explanavi hoc, et solvi objectiones contrarium (sic ed.). Dato vero quod solum sit intellectus possibilis in homine, adhuc est labor quasi infinitus circa ejus partes" (III, 298). This text refers to *Opus majus*, II, 5; Bridges ed., III, 47; and to *Opus tertium*, Brewer ed., pp. 74-75. To confuse these two issues is to create a maze of contradictory texts.

[20] For a witness to the survival of the problem, Ign. Brady OFM., *The Liber de Anima of William of Vaurouillon OFM.*, MS., 10 (1948) 225-297, 11 (1949) 247-307; especially, 10, 254-256.

[21] "Cause, or principle, is understood in a twofold way. In a first way, as principles of being. And this again in a twofold way: first, inasmuch as they are principles of being *qua* being, and this is how they are considered by the theologian or the metaphysician; secondly, inasmuch as they are principles of changing being, and this is how they are considered by the philosophy of nature. In a second way they are considered as principles of cognition, and, this time, in a three-fold way: 1, according to probability, by the logician; 2, according to truth and necessity, by the demonstrator; 3, in a tentative way, by him

who wants to ascertain what another man knows or does not know." XI, 106.

[22] On the nature of Ideas: X, 71-94. This text incidentally deals with the problem of the nature of universals. On universals, II, 92-107 and XI, 151-159.

[23] Bacon does not fit any classification. On the one hand, he teaches that all learning, including philosophy and natural science, is contained in Holy Scripture and revelation; consequently, he is an extreme traditionalist. On the other hand, he feels convinced that the progressive development of this revealed wisdom is far from having reached its term; consequently, he is a progressive. In fact, long before Francis Bacon, Roger Bacon has taught that the more modern men are, the more learning and perspicacity they have: *quanto juniores tempore, tanto perspicaciores (De vitiis,* I, 5). Hence his repeated criticism of the laziness of his contemporaries, coupled with his constant glorification of the ancient philosophers (*De vitiis,* I, 11-37). The first four obstacles to be removed from the path to learning are: 1, blind belief in authority (*Opus majus,* I, 2); 2, the fact that men are imitating each other, although there are thousand falsehoods for one truth (ibid., I, 3); 3, the reign of prejudice (ibid., I, 4), for "authority merely entices, habit binds, popular opinion makes men obstinate and confirms them in their obstinacy" (I, 4; transl. Burke, I, p. 10); 4, the worst of these causes of error, namely, pride, which leads men to conceal their own ignorance and to make an ostentatious display of a mock learning (Ibid., I, 9). The same doctrine reappears in the *Compendium studii theologiae,* Brewer ed., p. 393 ff. His personal attacks against Alexander of Hales, Albert the Great, the two mendicant Orders and what he scornfully calls the *vulgus* of philosophers and theologians, could not fail to render him unpopular with his contemporaries.

[24] *Opus majus,* II, 1; Burke, I, 36.

[25] *Opus majus,* II, 5; Burke, I, 43-48. On Alfarabi and Avicenna, p. 44. On Aristotle, interpreted according to Avicenna, p. 45. On the opinion of W. of Auvergne, p. 46. On the authority of Augustine "in his *Soliloquies* and elsewhere," p. 47. This text of *Opus majus* clearly shows the true meaning of Bacon's objections

to Avicenna. Augustine has said that God alone is the first source of all our illuminations; as Bacon himself recalls it, Augustine says that God is the sun whose light we receive; as to the angels, all they can do is to open the window in order to let the light pass (p. 47). Such is the reason why Bacon rejects the "giver of forms" of Avicenna. If there is a giver of forms, it is God.

[26] The science of mathematics is wholly distinct from the pseudoscience which bears the same name and, being a superstition, is no part of philosophy (XVI, 2). No science is more perverted than mathematics by the common causes of error, XVI, 5-6. Why the "philosophantes Christiani et theologi" should study science and know it better than the Pagans, especially mathematics, XVI, 8-11. It precedes all sciences and is common to all, XVI, 11-17. These references are to *Communia mathematica,* ed. Steele, vol. XVI.

[27] On PETER OF MARICOURT: E. Schlund, *Peter Peregrinus von Maricourt, sein Leben und seine Schriften, Ein Beitrag zur Roger Baco-Forschung,* in AFH., 4 (1911) 436-455, 633-643; 5 (1912) 22-40. Bibliography, pp. 438-439.GDP., 760.

[28] Grammar and even logic are but accidental parts of philosophy, whereas mathematics is the gate and key to all the other sciences (*Opus majus,* IV, 1, 2; Burke, I, p. 118). Every science needs mathematics (IV, 2, 3; Burke, I, 121-127). Bacon then once more develops his theory of the geometrical laws of the propagation of physical forces (*species*); these laws also apply to the activity of the soul, for indeed, all substances are active, and the soul is a substance (IV, 2, 1; I, p. 130). On the physical (although not perceptible) nature of the *species, Opus majus,* IV, 4; Burke, II, pp. 462-463. On the nature of their propagation or multiplication, which takes so short a time that it is practically instantaneous (*Opus majus,* V, 7, 3; II, p. 470 and V, 9, 3; II, p. 486). On the incorporeal nature of the *species* (op. cit., V, 9, 4; II, pp. 489-490). Naturally, the *species* of light multiplies much more rapidly than the other ones. Bacon finds no difficulty in showing the necessity of mathematics for the science of the ecclesiastical calendar (*computus*), but he extends its applications to biblical chronology, to the mystery of the Trinity, to the horoscopy of the various religions, and practically to everything.

[29] Experiment is twofold in kind, external and internal. External experiment is gained through sense knowledge; internal experiment is purely spiritual; in fact, it is the divine illumination. Since men hold philosophy from revelation, the grace of faith and the divine illuminations are experiments of great help not only in matters spiritual, but in the sciences of nature and in philosophy as well (*Opus majus,* VI, 1; Burke, II, p. 583). Bacon includes in his comprehensive notion of experimental knowledge even the seven gifts of the Holy Ghost, ibid., pp. 586-587.

Physical experiment remains, however, the dominant interest in R. Bacon. Speaking of it under the name of "experimental science" (*scientia experimentalis*), Bacon ascribes to it three main prerogatives: 1, it tests by means of experiment the conclusions of the other sciences (*Opus majus,* VI, 2; Burke, II, pp. 587-588); 2, in every particular science, it reveals to us facts that are neither principles nor conclusions and which could not be known otherwise (VI, 2; II, pp. 615-627); 3, it enables us to investigate certain problems and to form certain conclusions which lie entirely outside of the boundaries of all the other sciences: for instance, the foreknowledge of future events and the engineering of extraordinary machines whose effects would give the Church victory over the enemies of the faith, or, at least, help her to convert unbelievers VI, 2; II, pp. 627-634). See a quasi prophetic page, *Opus majus,* V, 3, 4; Burke, II, p. 582.

[30] The true meaning of Bacon's doctrine cannot be correctly appreciated apart from his fundamental notion of the *respublica fidelium.* All his philosophical works were written in view of theology, and all his theology was intended to supply the doctrine required for a universal extension of the Church. E. Gilson, *Les métamorphoses de la Cité de Dieu,* Louvain-Paris, 1952, pp. 75-109.

[31] On this problem see the pioneering work of Martin Grabmann, *Die Entwicklung der mittelalterlichen Sprachlogik,* MG., I, 104-146. On the later development of the problem: G. Wallerand, *Les*

oeuvres de Siger de Courtrai, Louvain, 1913. H. Roos, *Die Modi significandi des Martinus de Dacia,* ch. IV, pp. 72-120.

[32] L. J. Paetow, *The Arts Course at Medieval Universities with Special Reference to Grammar and Rhetoric,* Champaign (Illinois), 1910. Same author, *The Battle of the Seven Arts,* Berkeley University, 1914 (study, French text and English translation). Paetow has excellently described the transformation which then turned grammar into a science. We know of no more typical illustration of the thirteenth-century notion of teaching (*doctrina*) than the gloss of one of the new grammatical textbooks quoted by Paetow: Priscian is not a complete grammarian because he contents himself with saying what the correct constructions are

without assigning their causes (*unde multas constructiones dicit, quarum tamen causas non assignat*); consequently, since he does not assign the causes, he does not "teach" (*non docet*). There is no *doctrina* where there is no demonstration by causes.—M. Grabmann, *Der Kommentar des seligen Jordanus von Sachsen (d. 1327) zum Priscianus minor,* AFP., 10 (1940) 5-19.

[33] St. Easton, *Roger Bacon . . . ,* p. 45, note 3, rightly observes that it is not a tenable position to classify the faculty of arts as Aristotelian and the faculty of theology as Augustinian in the 1220's and 1230's. Contrarywise to what Easton says, without quoting any text, we do not remember having ever upheld this position.

PART SEVEN

CHAPTER III. MIDDLE THIRTEENTH-CENTURY LOGICIANS

[34] The history of the faculties of arts, and of logic in particular, has been renewed for this period by the pioneering work of M. Grabmann. General survey of the results: R. Martin, *Travaux récents relatifs à la Faculté des Arts aux XIIIe-XIVe siècles,* RNSP., 31 (1935) 356-368. M. Grabmann, *Bearbeitungen und Auslegungen . . . ,* and *Mittelalterliche lateinische Aristotelesübersetzungen . . . ,* see note 35.—Rules for determinations in Arts, 1252: UNIV., 52-56; courses in Arts, 64-66.

Among many still little studied masters: BERNARD OF SANCIZE, commentary on *Isagoge;* WILLIAM OF SAINT AMOUR, master of arts 1236-1347, well-known adversary of the Mendicant Orders, author of commentaries on the two *Analytics;* ROBERTUS DE AUCUMPNO, MATTHEW OF ORLEANS, ROBERT OF PARIS, etc.

JOHN LE PAGE (Johannes Pagus, Pagius), Fr. Pelster, *Literaturgeschichtliches zur Pariser Theologischen Schule aus den Jahren 1230-bis 1256,* Scholastik, 5 (1930) 46-78. M.-D. Chenu OP., *Maîtres et bacheliers de l'université de Paris vers 1240,* Etudes d'histoire littéraire et doctrinale du XIIIe siècle, Paris, 1932, 11-39. E. Franceschini, *Giovanni Pago: Le sue "Rationes super Predicamenta Aristotelis" e la loro posizione nel movimento aristotelico del secolo XIII,* Sophia, Palermo,

1934 (we have not seen this study). H. Roos, *Die Modi significandi,* p. 117.

NICHOLAS OF PARIS, M. Grabmann, *Die logischen Schriften des Nikolaus von Paris und ihre Stellung in der Aristotelischen Bewegung des XIII Jahrhunderts,* MG., I, 222-348; *I divieti ecclesiastici . . . ,* I, 128-129. H. Roos, *Die Modi significandi,* p. 117.

JOHN SACKVILLE (Johannes de Siccavilla), an English master at the Faculty of Arts of the University of Paris, died in England after 1292; author of a still unpublished treatise *De principiis naturae,* written between 1260 and 1270. See M. Grabmann, *Die logischen Schriften . . . ,* MG., I, 235 (the proposed date, 1236, is most unlikely). Sackville has inserted in his treatise a short excursus on logical "supposition." The treatise itself deals with the principles of nature, especially matter and form. Sackville follows Averroes in his interpretation of Aristotle; the text of the Commentator is often inserted in that of Sackville who takes sides with Averroes against Avicenna "always found to stand midway between the Peripatetics and the theologians (*loquentes*)." John denies the hylomorphic composition of separate substances; these are not simple, however, being composed of genus and difference. Sackville does not conceal the fact that

Aristotle does not always agree with the teachings of Christian truth (eternity of motion), but his attitude is different from that of Siger, not only in degree but in kind. Sackville has literary ambitions; he often writes as a clumsy John of Salisbury interested in physics instead of dialectics; there is no trace of Averroistic dogmatism in this treatise; rather, while refusing to subscribe to any skepticism, Sackville declares his intention to write about philosophy rather in the inquiring mood of the Academicians than in a spirit of contention. Everybody should examine such problems and feel free to draw his own conclusions. Even when they erred, our predecessors should be thanked for having helped us in discovering truth. This sounds quite different from the Averroistic contention that the conclusions of Aristotle are "hardly refutable."—A critical edition of the text is being prepared by Fr. Giguère OP.

[35] On the history of logic, besides the classical work of Prantl, see M. Grabmann, *Mittelalterliche lateinische Aristotelesübersetzungen und Aristoteleskommentare in Handschriften Spanischer Bibliotheken,* Sitzungsberichte . . . , München, 1928, pp. 51-63; *Bearbeitungen und Auslegungen der aristotelischen Logik aus der Zeit von Peter Abaelard bis Petrus Hispanus,* Abhandlungen der Preussichen Akad. d. Wissenschaften, (Philos.-Philolog.-und histor,-Klasse), 1927, 5; *Kommentare zur Aristotelischen Logik aus dem 12. und 13. Jahrhundert im Ms. lat. fol. 624 der Preussischen Staatsbibliothek in Berlin. Ein Beitrag zur Abaelardforschung,* same series, 1938, 18; *Eine für Examinazwecke abgefasste Quästionensammlung der Pariser Artistenfakultät aus der ersten Hälfte des 13. Jahrhunderts,* MG., II, 183-199; *Mitteilungen aus Münchener Handschriften über bisher Unbekannte Philosophen der Artistenfakultät,* MG., II, 225-238; *Methoden und Hilfsmittel des Aristotelesstudiums im Mittelalter,* Sitzungsberichte . . . , München, 1939, 5.

A synthesis of the problems related to the influence of Aristotle in the thirteenth century Parisian schools is to be found in F. Van Steenberghen, *Aristote en Occident. Les origines de l'aristotélisme parisien,* Louvain, 1946 (separate reprint of part of his major work on Siger of Brabant, Louvain, 1931: see bibliography to Siger). On logic, see the useful introduction by Phil. Boehner, OFM., *Medieval Logic. An Outline of Its Development from 1250 to ca. 1400,* Univ. of Chicago Press, 1952.

The document mentioned in our text is M. Grabmann, *Eine für Examinazwecke abgefasste Quaestionensammlung . . . ,* 1934. A table of its content is in F. Van Steenberghen, *Siger de Brabant . . . ,* Louvain, 1942, II, 416. It should be kept in mind that, according to this handbook, both the *Metaphysica vetus* and the *Metaphysica nova* were on the program. Moreover, the discussion of ethical problems provided opportunities to deal with metaphysical and psychological questions: O. Lottin, *Psychologie et morale à la Faculté des Arts de Paris aux approches de 1250,* RNSP., 42 (1939) 182-212.

[36] On WILLIAM OF SHERWOOD, Prantl, *Geschichte der Logik,* III, pp. 10-24. Text of the *Introductiones* in M. Grabmann, *Die Introductiones in logicam des Wilhelm von Shyreswood (d. nach 1267),* in Sitzungsberichte . . . , München, 1937, 10. J. R. O'Donnell, *The Syncategoremata of William of Sherwood,* MS., 3 (1941) 46-93. Three other treatises are considered by Grabmann as probable works of William: *De insolubilibus, Petitiones contrariorum* and *Obligationes.*—A treatise *de insolubili* deals with propositions that are self-destroying (cf. Boehner, p. 18): "I am not speaking" is an *insolubile.*— A treatise *De obligatione,* or *De arte exercitiva,* deals with obligatory rules of logical consecution from initial positions, especially in dialectical disputations (Boehner, pp. 14-15).

[37] The "syncategoremata" or "conpraedicativa" are words that are always joined with subjects or predicates, but do not point out something which either the subject, or the predicate, actually is. For instance, in "white man," white points to something that the subject is, namely, white. "White" then is not a syncategorema. But in "any man runs," the word "any" does not point out something that man is; it does not even mean that man is a universal; it then is a syncategorema. In this case, "any" signifies the subject "man," taken as indifferent to whatever individual we may care to consider. Such syncategoremata are "all" (O'Donnell ed., pp. 48-54), "whole" (pp. 54-56), "none" (pp. 56-58), "nothing" (pp. 58-59), then "neither one," "besides," "alone," "only,"

etc. Despite the contrary opinion, "est" (is) is not a syncategorema (pp. 70-71). Note the remark, p. 71, that when "est" is *tertium adjacens* (as in "man is animal"), it is not a predicate, it merely indicates composition. Some terms, like "necessarily" and "contingently" may be either "categoremata" or "syncategoremata" (pp. 73-75). This doctrine is completed by an examination of the conjunctive or disjunctive syncategoremata (definitions p. 79), such as "if," "unless," "and," "or," etc. This kind of discussion clearly shows the intimate relation there is between speculative grammar (or logic of language) and straight logic.—On the meaning of the notion of "syncategorema" taken it itself, see Ph. Boehner, *Medieval Logic*, pp. 19-26.

[38] *Introductiones* . . . , ed. Grabmann, p. 56.—Rhetoric teaches to speak well, logic teaches to speak the truth. It chiefly is about syllogism (*est de syllogismo principaliter,* p. 30); hence the plan of the work: from sound to word, then to noun and verb, then to sentence (*oratio*), then to enunciations, propositions, categories and syllogisms. On *verbum rectum* (present indicative) and *obliquum* (any other form), p. 32. On the six modes: true, false, possible, impossible, contingent, necessary, and on modal propositions, pp. 40-45. On authority as a logical *locus*, p. 68.—A particularly important part of the treatise deals with the properties of terms: signification, supposition, copulation and appellation. Signification means the presentation of any notion (*forma*) to the intellect. Supposition means *suppositio,* that is, the act of subsuming an intellection under another one (*Suppositio . . . est ordinatio alicujus intellectus sub alio,* p. 74). Copulation consists in adding an intellection to another one; any copulating term (*copulans*) is the name of an accident (p. 81). Appellation is the aptness of a term, (due to its meaning) to be said of something by means of the verb "is" (p. 74). The more controverted of these problems, in mediaeval logic, was to be that of "supposition." From the treatise of William, it appears that the controversy was already active in his own times. He himself distinguishes material supposition (the term stands for itself: e.g., man is a monosyllable, man is a noun); formal supposition (the term stands for its meaning: e.g., "man is a

rational animal"). Formal supposition itself is divided into two classes: simple supposition (the notion of the term stands for a meaning: e.g., man is a species); personal supposition (the notion of the term stands for a thing, a substance: e.g., "man runs," i.e., running is in man through a particular man who runs), p. 75. Another division of formal supposition is into common (*communis*) which uses a common term, as "man runs"; and into discrete (*discreta*) which uses a discrete term: "Socrates runs." Personal supposition is divided into determinate or confused. It is determinate (*determinata*) when what is said can be explained by a single case: "man runs" is only true of one single running man. Personal supposition is confused (*confusa*) when the term stands for several beings: for instance, "animal." Again, confused personal supposition can be mobile, when the supposition of the term can be restricted from a more general to a less general object: if "every man is an animal," then Socrates is an animal; or else confused personal supposition can be immobile, when such particularization is impossible: from "only every man runs," one cannot infer "hence, only Socrates runs" (pp. 75-76). Lastly, there can be a confused distributive supposition, when the term stands for any one of many: e.g., in "man is an animal," man stands for any individual man. *Nota bene:* what makes supposition to be "personal" is not the fact that what is being "supposed" (i.e., subsumed under the term) is an individual, a concrete person; rather, it is the fact that what is being subsumed is a thing which carries the form signified by the term. Now this happens even with proper names when they signify a substance with a certain quality. For instance, when I say: "Socrates runs," Socrates stands for an individual being; but when I say: "Socrates is predicable of only one being," Socrates stands for the form signified by the name (p. 76).—In his study of the three modes of equivocation, William uses the following examples: "All bishops are priests; now these asses are bishops; hence these asses are priests." Example of the second: what runs has feet; now the Seine River runs; hence the Seine River has feet" (p. 87). This second example is what invites historians to believe that William taught his *Introductiones* in Paris. The argument is valid, as Grabmann says, if some Parisian scribe, copying the text in Paris, did not substitute the name of the Seine for that of another river (p. 17). These substitutions of local names for foreign ones are frequent in mediaeval manuscripts.

[39] Little is known about LAMBERT OF AUXERRE. In his notice on Lambert's works, Prantl (*Geschichte der Logik*, III, p. 25), who follows Lebeuf, *Mémoires concernant l'histoire ecclésiastique et civile d'Auxerre*, II, pp. 493 ff., considers him younger than William of Sherwood and older than Peter of Spain. He places his logic about the middle of the thirteenth century. Analysis of the treatise, pp. 27-32. On *suppositio* in Lambert, some information p. 31. Our own quotations are borrowed from the texts of Lambert published by Grabmann in his *Handschriftliche Forschungen* on Peter of Spain (see note 40) pp. 46-48. On the known manuscripts and the division of the treatise, pp. 35-36.

[40] PETER OF SPAIN, born in Lisbon, Portugal, between 1210 and 1220, was really a Portuguese. He studied at the cathedral school of Lisbon, then at the Faculty of Arts of the University of Paris. He may have studied under William of Sherwood *ca.* 1240. In Siena, Italy, in 1245. Dean of the Church of Lisbon (1261). Physician of Pope Gregory X (1272). Archbishop of Braga, then Cardinal of Tusculum (1273). After attending the Council of Lyons (1274), he was elected Pope under the name of John XXI (1276). One of his first acts was to commission Etienne Tempier, Bishop of Paris, to investigate and to report to him the errors which, once more, were then invading the University (Jan. 18, 1277). After their condemnation by Tempier (March 7, 1277), Pope John XXI implemented it by appropriate measures (April 28, 1277). Fatally injured by the collapse of a roof at his Viterbo palace, he died a few days later (May 20, 1277). His death occurred, Bartholomew of Lucca observes, at the very time when "quaedam fulminaverat contra religiosos" (*Historia ecclesiastica*, Bk. XXIII, ch. 21).—The medical writings of Peter of Spain are listed in M. Alonso, *Scientia libri de anima*, pp. 7-12. The treatises VI-XIII of his logical textbook have been published, with English translation, by J. P. Mullally, *The Summulae logicales of Peter of Spain*, Notre Dame (Ind.), 1945. For a complete edition of the Latin

text, see J. M. Bochenski, OP., *Petri Hispani Summulae Logicales*, Rome, Marietti, 1947. Other still unpublished logical treatises are: *Tractatus majorum fallacium* and *Syncategoremata*. A treatise on the soul and commentaries on the *De anima* of Aristotle have been published by M. Alonso, *Pedro Hispano, Scientia libri de Anima*, Madrid, 1941; *Pedro Hispano. Obras filosoficas, vol. II, Commentario al De anima de Aristoteles*, Madrid, 1944; vol. III, *Expositio libri de anima, De morte et vita, De causis longitudinis et brevitatis vitae, Liber naturalis de rebus principalibus*, Madrid, 1952.

BIBLIOGRAPHY. T. y J. Carrera y Artau, *Historia de la filosofia española*, I, Madrid, 1939, pp. 101-144. K. Prantl, *Geschichte der Logik*, III, pp. 33-75. M. Grabmann, *Handschriftliche Forschungen und Funde zu den philosophischen Schriften des Petrus Hispanus, des späteren Papstes Johannes XXI* (d. 1277), in Sitzungsberichte . . . , München, 1937; *Die Lehre vom Intellectus possibilis und intellectus agens im Liber de Anima des Petrus Hispanus des späteren Papstes Johannes XXI*, AHDL., 12-13 (1937-1938), 167-208: contains the concluding chapters of the *De anima*. The historical introduction is important; note, pp. 180-181: "A large part of the arguments formulated in the *Summa contra gentiles* (II, 74-78) against the Avicennian doctrine of the agent intellect, could be directed just as well against Petrus Hispanus."—It should be remembered that the authentic meaning of the doctrine in Aristotle himself still remains an open question. On the mediaeval treatment of the problem: M. Grabmann, *Mittelalterliche Deutung und Umbildung der aristotelischen Lehre vom "nous poietikos" nach einer Zusammenstellung im Cod. B III 22 der Universitätsbibliothek Basel*, Sitzungsberichte . . . , Munich, 1936, 4. On the meaning of the problem, P. Wilpert, *Die Ausgestaltung der aristotelischen Lehre . . .*, ADGM., I, 447-462.—M. Martins, *Os Commentários de Pedro Hispano ao Pseudo-Dionisio Areopagita*, Revista Portuguesa di Filosofia, 8 (1952) 295-314.

[41] The treatise of Peter of Spain is typical of the new logical teaching and very different from the commentaries on the logic of Aristotle (Averroes-Thomas Aquinas type) or even of their paraphrases (Avicenna-Albert the Great type). In the edition of J. M. Bochenski, the work

of Peter is divided into twelve short treatises (or *summulae*): 1, Propositions; 2, Predicables (genus, species, difference, proper, accident, etc.); 3, Categories; 4, Syllogisms; 5, Topics; 6, Suppositions; 7, Sophisms; 8, Relatives ("who," "he," etc.); 9, Amplifications (*De ampliationibus*); 10, Appellations; 11, Restrictions; 12, Distributions. The additional treatise on the *Exponibilia,* published by J. P. Mullally (pp. 104-129), is considered spurious by J. M. Bochenski, ed. cit., p. XXIII. On the treatises on "Suppositions," "Ampliations," etc., see Ph. Boehner, "The New Elements of Scholastic logic," in *Medieval Logic,* pp. 6-18.

⁴² "Signification" is the conventional meaning attached to a word in order to point out a certain thing. "Supposition" is the meaning of a substantive term, taken with its signification, when it stands for something: "Suppositio est acceptio termini substantivi pro aliquo" (Bochenski, pp. 57-58). Supposition may be "common," when the term is common, e.g., "man." It may be "discrete," when the term is discrete, e.g., "Socrates." Common supposition is "natural" when a common term stands for all its particulars; e.g., "man" stands for all possible particular men. It is "accidental" when the common term stands for particulars specified by an added term; e.g., in "man is," man stands for any actually existing man. Accidental supposition itself may be either simple or personal. In simple supposition the term stands for the whole thing which it designates; e.g., in "man is a species," "man" stands for the whole species. In personal supposition the common term stands for particular things; e.g., in "man is running," the term "man" can supposit for nothing else than some running man. Again, personal supposition is either determinate, or it is confused (i.e., indeterminate). If it is determinate, then the common term necessarily stands for some particular being; such was the case in the preceding example, "man is running," that is: some man, a man, is running. If the personal supposition is confused, the term stands for many particulars because it is qualified by some sign of universality; e.g., in "every man is an animal," the term "man" stands for many men owing to its qualification by the universal sign "every." In this latter case, the term can "movably" stand for (if every man is an animal, then Plato is an animal), or it can stand for in an immovable way (from "every man is an animal," it does not follow that "hence, *every* man is *this* animal"). See Bochenski, pp. 58-60.

⁴³ Another *Commentary on the De anima of Aristotle,* also published by M. Alonso (Madrid) 1944, is attributed to Peter of Spain in the Cracow manuscript Univ., ms. 726. It is an incomplete work, made up of a series of questions on the text of the *De anima,* I and II. Whereas the *Scientia de anima* does not quote a single proper name, this commentary is full of them (Alfarabi, Avicenna, Averroes, Gabirol, Ibn Daoud, etc.). It is verbose and repetitious. Unlike Peter of Spain, its author is less interested in physiology and biology than in determining, time and again, the respective competencies of logic, natural science and metaphysics with respect to psychology. His own positions are not always clear. Like most of his contemporaries, the author defines the soul, first as a complete substance, then as act of the body (553, 617-618, 683); it has no root in its body (667); it is to it as the pilot is to his ship (669); when it comes to giving a clear cut definition of the soul-body relation, the author offers a choice of opinions and invites every one to choose the one he prefers ("Quilibet autem eligat positionem quam decernit elegantiorem," 580). He uses the Avicennian argument of the "floating man," but in order to prove that there is "in us" an intellective soul (622-623). His doctrine of the two intellects in us resembles that of Peter (and of many others, including Bacon and Albert the Great), but it is not presented exactly as in the *Scientia de anima* (comment., 294-297). Although this treatise has its own points of interest, we cannot help doubting its authenticity. Incidentally, the fact that one manuscript attributes it to Peter of Spain can hardly pass for a proof. It only witnesses to the personal conviction of the scribe who copied it. And perhaps to even less than that.

⁴⁴ This is a remarkable statement. Peter does not reduce the separate Intelligence to the God of Saint Augustine; he states its existence and its illuminating functions just as they are described in Avicenna. To our personal knowledge, this is the only known case of straight "Latin Avi-

cennism" (R. de Vaux, *Notes et textes ... ,* Paris, 1934). The vague allusion to the "prime cause" which follows this statement does not imply its identification with the separate Intelligence of the lowest order that is here in question. The "commentary" attributed to Peter of Spain does not help on this point. On the contrary, it develops at great length the doctrine of the "universal Intellect moving all things" (the *intelligentia universaliter agens* of Albert the Great), which is upheld, under various forms, by many masters of those times (371, 435-436), but the separate Intelligence of Peter does not appear in the commentary. The possible objection, that the place for it was in Book III, is not very impressive, for the author of these questions has found a way to describe the relations of the two intellects, possible and agent, long before the end of Bk. II. To repeat, we do not deny the authenticity of the commentary, we doubt it.

[45] Another still little known late thirteenth-century master is HENRY OF BRUSSELS. B. Hauréau, *Henri de Bruxelles, religieux de l'abbaye d'Affighem,* in HLF., 27 (1887) 105-108; *Notices et extraits,* 35 (1906) 213-219. M. Grabmann, *Die Aris-* *toteleskommentare des Heinrich von Brüssel und der Einfluss Alberts des Grossen auf die mittelalterliche Aristoteleserklärung,* Sitzungsberichte, 1943, 10; Munich, 1944; life, 29-39 (began to teach shortly before 1289; perhaps rector in 1307); Commentaries on *Topics* (6-11), on *Metaphysics* (11-15), on *Posterior Analytics* (15-17); Quodlibetal questions in natural philosophy by Henry of Brussels, Henricus Alemanus, Johannes Vate, Wericus (17-24). Specimens of topics for disputed questions on *Physionomia,* "Utrum homines rufi sint fideles"; on *Problemata,* "Utrum ebrius bibens oleum fit sobrius"; on *De animalibus,* "Utrum tigris magis debeat stare supra unum pedem quam supra duos." A very remarkable question, especially since it belongs in *Historia animalium,* is "Utrum monachi debeant esse pinguiores quam alii." Between those who think that mediaeval masters only asked silly questions, and those who think they never asked silly questions, there is room for an intermediate opinion. Mediaeval masters sometimes asked foolish questions, but they asked quite a few important ones. At any rate, the preceding questions were simply intended to provide material for practical drill in dialectics.—Fragments of the commentaries, pp. 68-92.

PART EIGHT
THE GOLDEN AGE OF SCHOLASTICISM

CHAPTER I. THE FRANCISCAN SCHOOL

[1] ALEXANDER OF HALES. Alexandri de Hales OFM., *Summa theologica,* ad Claras Aquas (Quaracchi), 4 vols., I, 1924; II, 1928; III, 1930; IV, 1948 (in two parts). On the problem of authenticity, V. Doucet, ed. cit., *Prolegomena ad Summam Halesianam,* IV.—Same author, *The History of the Problem of the Authenticity of the Summa,* Franciscan Studies, 7 (1947) 26-41, 274-312; *De "Summa Fratris Alexandri Halensis" historice considerata,* RFNS., 40 (1948) 1-44. F. Henquinet, *Fr. Considerans, l'un des auteurs jumeaux de la Summa Fratris Alexandri primitive,* RTAM., 15 (1948) 76-96.—Authentic questions of Alexander have been discovered: F. M. Henquinet, *Les questions inédites d'Alexandre de Hales sur les fins dernières,* RTAM., 10 (1938) 56-78, 153-172; *De 107 quaestionibus* *halesianis cod. Tudertin. 121,* Antonianum, 13 (1938) 335-366, 489-514; *Le commentaire d'Alexandre de Hales sur les Sentences enfin retrouvé,* Miscellanea G. Mercati, Città del Vaticano, 1946, pp. 359-382 (Studi e Testi, 122). V. Doucet, *A New Source of the "Summa Fratris Alexandri." The Commentary on the Sentences of Alexander of Hales,* Franciscan Studies, 6 (1946) 403-417.—Publication of the oldest among these authentic texts: *Magistri Alexandri de Hales Glossa in Quatuor Libros Sententiarum Petri Lombardi,* I, Quaracchi-Florence 1951; II Quaracchi-Florence, 1952 (glosses on *Sentences* I and II).—Bibliography: I. Herscher, *A Bibliography of Alexander of Hales,* Franciscan Studies, 5 (1945) 435-454. Introduction to the doctrine of the *Summa:* Ph. Boehner OFM., *The System*

of Metaphysics of Alexander of Hales, Franciscan Studies, 5 (1945) 366-414. E. Bettoni, *Il problema della cognoscibilità di Dio nella scuola francescana (Alessandro d'Hales, S. Bonaventura, Duns Scoto)*, Padova, 1950. Cf. J. Rohmer, AHLD., 3 (1928) 106-120. C. Bérubé, *La connaissance intellectuelle du singulier matériel au XIIIe siècle*, Franciscan Studies, 11 (1951) 157-201 (from Alexander of Hales to Henry of Ghent).—V. Doucet, AFH., 27 (1934) 534-538.

An important witness to the influence of Alexander of Hales is the Franciscan ODO RIGAUD (Eudes Rigaud, Odo Rigaldus, d. 1275). His treatise *On the Powers of the Soul* has long been attributed to Albert the Great (O. Lottin, PEM., I, 498-499).—F. M. Hcnquinet, *Les manuscrits et l'influence des écrits théologiques d'Eudes Rigaud OFM.*, RTAM., 11 (1939) 324-350; *Le commentaire d'Eudes Rigaud sur le IVe livre des Sentences*, CF., 10 (1940) 481-493. V. Doucet, *Alexandri de Hales Summa theologica, IV, Prolegomena*, 228-234. O. Lottin, *Une question disputée d'Odon Rigaud sur le libre arbitre*, RT., 36 (1931) 886-895; cf. 34 (1929) 234-248; *Un Commentaire sur les Sentences tributaire d'Odon Rigaud*, RTAM., 7 (1935) 402-405; PEM., *passim*, particularly 149-181, 220-222, 447-450, 494-500; II, 196-202, 449-450, 473-479, 561-563; III, 85-89, 159-161, 215-225, 294-295, 388-397, 435-437, 594-597, 713-720. B. Pergamo OFM., *Il desiderio innato del soprannaturale nelle questioni inedite di Odone Rigaldo OFM.*, arcivescovo di Rouen (d. 1275), Studi Francescani, 33 (1936) 76-108. F. Pelster, *Beiträge zur Erforschung des schriftlichen Nachlasses Odo Rigaldis*, Scholastik, 11 (1936) 518-542.—V. Doucet AFH., 27 (1934) 541-542. GLOLIT., 2, 289.

² Imperfect but useful edition of John's *Summa* by Teofilo Domenichelli, *La "Summa de anima" di Frate Giovanni della Rochelle*, Prato, 1882. Manuscripts of the works attributed to John, including the *Summa de anima*, in Part. Minges, *De scriptis quibusdam Fr. Joannis de Rupella OFM., (d. 1245)*, AFH., 6 (1913), 597-622; according to Minges, the text of Domenichelli is spurious from p. 299 line 26 up to the end (p. 605).—On the doctrine: H. Luguet, *Essai d'analyse et de critique sur le texte inédit du Traité de l'âme de Jean de la Rochelle*, Paris, 1875; *Johannis de Rupella ex libro hactenus*

inedito cui "Summa de anima" titulus inscribitur psychologicam doctrinam depromptsit H. Luguet, Paris, 1875 G. Manser, *Johann von Rupella, Ein Beitrag zu seiner Characteristik mit besonderer Berücksichtigung seiner Erkenntnislehre*, JPST., 26 (1912) 290-324; *Die Realdistinctio von Wesenheit und Existenz bei Johannes von Rupella*, RT., 19 (1911) 89-92. Parth. Minges, *Zur Erkenntnislehre des Franziskaners Johannes de Rupella*, PJ., 27 (1914) 461-477; *Die psychologische Summe des Johann von Rupella und Alexander von Hales*, FS., 3 (1916) 365-378. J. Rohmer, AHDL., 3 (1928) 120-141. O. Lottin, *Alexandre de Hales et la Summa de vitiis de Jean de la Rochelle*, RTAM., 1 (1929) 240-243; *Alexander de Hales et la Summa de anima de Jean de la Rochelle*, RTAM., 2 (1930) 396-409. F. M. Henquinet, *Ist der Traktat De legibus et praeceptis in der Summa Alexander von Hales von Joh. von Rupella?*, FS., 26 (1939), 1-22, 234-258. C. Fabro, *La distinzione tra "quod est" e "quo est" nella Summa de Anima di Giovanni de la Rochelle*, DTP., 41 (1938) 508-522. H. Pouillon, *La beauté . . .*, AHDL., 15 (1946) 274-277. D. H. Salman, *Jean de la Rochelle et les débuts de l'Averroisme latin*, AHDL., 16 (1947-1948) 133-144. — Literary history, V. Doucet, *Alexandri de Hales Summa theologica*, vol. IV, Quaracchi, 1948: *Prolegomena*, 211-228; and AFH., 27 (1934) 539-541.

³ All the references in notes 3 and 4 are to Bk. I of the *Summa*. The prologue begins with a prayer in the twelfth century Cistercian style, which soon leads to the already scholastic division of the subject matter: *primo quaerendum an sit anima, secundo, quid sit* (ed. Domenichelli, p. 102). The existence of the soul as a spiritual substance is proved by the argument of Avicenna: a man suddenly created without sensations, external or internal, would not know that he has a body; yet he would know himself as a spiritual being; hence his soul is incorporeal (ch. I, p. 104). Moreover, the soul is receptive of the divine illumination (quotes Augustine, *Soliloquies*); so, in itself, it is a substance, both incorporeal, intellectual, and able, after the Intelligences, to perceive the divine illumination (III, p. 107). With respect to its body, it is form; the Aristotelian definition of the soul thus completes its Augustinian

and Avicennian definitions (V, pp. 110-111). John justifies seven different definitions. The soul is not composed of matter and form, but of *quod est* and *quo est* (XIII, pp. 118-121). Being an incorporeal substance, it is simple, at least as to its essence (XXIII, pp. 134-135) and in comparison with all that is not God. On the other hand, it has multiplicity with respect to its operations; so the soul is one substance in three powers: the vegetative, the sensitive and the rational powers (XXIV, pp. 135-138). In this sense, it is an image of God (XXVII, pp. 143-145). John deals at great length with this Augustinian problem (XXXI-XXXIII, pp. 152-160).

⁴ Unlike an angel, a soul has an essential aptness to be united to a body, whose form it is; yet, there are intermediaries between body and soul (XXXV, pp. 161-163). These are the powers of the soul, which are intermediate between its essence and its operations (XXXVI, p. 163-165). Moreover, the body itself contains a still more noble nature than that which is to be found in corporeal animals, namely "light"; more precisely, the light of the empyrean heaven which, because it is as near being spiritual as a body can be, disposes the human body to receive the noblest life, namely, rational life (XXXVIII, p. 174). At any rate, since it is of the essence of the soul to be united to a body, to be in it is for the soul neither misery nor a punishment (XXXIX, pp. 175-176). Besides moral reasons, there are direct arguments in favor of the immortality of the soul; since it is immaterial, the soul cannot suffer a division of matter from form, and since it is simple, there can be in it no disintegration of parts; moreover, since its being does not depend on that of the body, the absence of the body cannot corrupt the being of the soul (XXXVIII, p. 172; XLII, pp. 179-184; XLIII, pp. 184-189). While they are being united, however, there is between soul and body a sort of solidarity (*colligatio*) which explains how the body, which is a corporeal substance, can act upon an incorporeal substance such as the soul: XLII, pp. 193-194.

⁵ All the following notes refer to Bk. II of the *Summa;* only chapters and pages are indicated.—As has been said, the essence of the soul is not identical with its powers (several positions discussed, I, pp. 217-220). The distinction of the powers of the soul is due to their own nature, but it is known from both their objects and their operations (II, pp. 220-223). John classifies the powers of the soul according to the doctrine of a treatise *De anima et spiritu,* which he ascribed to Saint Augustine, although it was the work of the Cistercian monk Alcher of Clairvaux (i.e., *De spiritu et anima*). For more precisions, he resorts to John Damascene. Because he then follows Alcher, John introduces the highest power of the soul, *intelligentia,* in ch. IV, p. 227, after which, following Damascene, he studies sensations (V, pp. 228-230), imagination (VI, 230-231), the cogitative, or *opinio* (VII, 231), memory (VIII, 231-232), the mind or *mens* (IX, pp. 232-235), passions (X, pp. 235-239), the will and free will (XI-XV, pp. 239-245). After exploiting this material borrowed from John Damascene, our author goes over practically the same problems a second time, following now the teaching of the "philosophers," especially of Avicenna (XVI-XXXIII, pp. 245-283). This, however, does not prevent him from blending, even there, Augustine and Damascene with philosophers properly so-called, as happens in ch. XXXV, pp. 284-288. The nature of abstraction is first described, in a general way, as a stripping of forms from their individuating accidents (pp. 286-288), but, at the moment of describing the nature of the intellect, John has to face the psychology of Avicenna, with its well-known classification of the intellects, from the *intellectus materialis* to the *intellectus accommodatus* and the *intellectus agens* (XXXVI, pp. 288-290). There, blending together the gospel of Saint John (I, 9), Augustine (*Soliloquies* I, 8, 15; PL., 32, 877) and Denis the Aeropagite, he observes that an angel could be posited as the agent Intellect of our possible intellect; but he rejects this solution and identifies the agent Intellect with the higher part of our own created intellect (XXXVII, p. 290-294). Our agent intellect is a nature substantially identical with the divine light of which the Psalmist says (Ps. 4, 7): "The light of thy countenance . . .", etc. (XXXVIII, p. 295). Cf. Thomas Aquinas, *Summa theologiae,* I₁ 79, 4, Resp.

⁶ *Summa de anima,* II, ch. 35, p. 286. —On psychological and moral problems

omitted from this book, O. Lottin, PEM., I, 401, 443, 474, 493; II, 86, 357; III, 35, 76, 177, 182, 293, 375.

[7] SAINT BONAVENTURE. OFM.—Born in 1221 at Bagnorea, near Viterbo (Italy), entered the Franciscan Order about 1238; studied under Alexander of Hales at the University of Paris, where he himself taught from 1248 to 1255. His commentary on the *Sentences* of Peter Lombard dates from these years (1250-1255). He was appointed to his chair of theology the same day as Thomas Aquinas, on October 23, 1256. For local reasons, the University deferred their accession to the degree of Doctor and their right officially to occupy their chairs until October, 1257. By that time, Bonaventure had already been named General Minister of his Order and was never to resume his teaching activities. He died toward the end of the Council of Lyons, July 15, 1274, the same year as Thomas Aquinas.—WORKS. Main works: *Commentary on the Sentences* (1250-1255), *Itinerarium mentis in Deum, Breviloquium, Collationes in Hexaemeron;* several important disputed questions should also be consulted. Standard edition: *S. Bonaventurae . . . Opera omnia,* Quaracchi, 10 vols., 1882-1902. The commentary on the *Sentences,* minus the notes, has been reprinted in 4 vols., Quaracchi, 1934 ff. Also separately published: *Tria Opuscula,* Quaracchi, 3 ed., 1911 (*Breviloquium, Itinerarium mentis in Deum, De reductione artium ad theologiam*).—*Collationes in Hexaemeron,* Quaracchi, 1934 (in another redaction than that of the *Opera omnia*).—*Questions disputées "De caritate, "De novissimis,"* ed. P. Glorieux, Paris, 1950.—Engl. transl. of *Sent.,* I, 3, 1, in R. McKeon, *Selections,* II, 118-148.—BET., 720-742.

BIBLIOGRAPHY. GDP., 735-738.—G. Palhoriès, *Saint Bonaventure,* Paris, 1913 (with French transl. of the *Itinerarium*). E. Lutz, *Die Psychologie Bonaventuras,* Münster i. W., 1909 (Beiträge, 6, 4-5): B. Luyckx, *Die Erkenntnislehre Bonaventuras,* Münster i. W., 1923 (Beiträge, 23, 3-4). E. Gilson, *La philosophie de saint Bonaventure,* Paris, 1924 (English transl., 1938); 2nd ed., Paris, 1943. J. M. Bissen, *L'exemplarisme divin chez saint Bonaventure,* Paris, 1929. J. Rohmer, *Sur la doctrine franciscaine des deux faces de l'âme,* AHDL., 2 (1927) 73-77; *La théorie de l'abstraction dans l'Ecole franciscaine d'Alexandre de Hales à Jean Peckham,*

AHDL., 3 (1928) 141-161. B. Rosenmöller, *Die religiöse Erkenntnis nach Bonaventura,* Münster i. W., 1925 (Beiträge, 25, 3-4). C. J. O'Leary, *The Substantial Composition of Man according to St. Bonaventure,* Washington, 1931. J. Kaup, *Zur Konkurslehre des Petrus Olivi und des hl. Bonaventura,* FS., 19 (1932) 315-326. E. Szdzuj, *St. Bonaventure et le problème du rapport entre l'âme et le corps,* France Franciscaine, 15 (1932) 283-310. F. Immle, *Gott und Geist. Zusammenwirken des geschaffenen und des ungeschaffenen Geistes im höheren Erkentnisakte nach Bonaventura,* Werl i. W., 1934; *Die Unsterblichkeit der Seele bei den Franziskanertheologen des 13 Jahrhunderts,* FS., 24 (1937) 284-294. L. Jessberger, *Das Abhängigkeitsverhältnis des hl. Thomas Aquinas von Albertus Magnus und Bonaventura im dritten Buche des Sentenzenkommentars,* Würzburg, 1936 (Inaug.-Diss.). F. Tiniviella OFM., *De impossibili sapientiae adeptione in philosophia pagana juxta "Collationes in Hexaemeron" S. Bonaventurae,* Antonianum, 11 (1936) 27-50, 135-186, 277-318. P. Robert OFM., *Hylémorphisme et devenir chez S. Bonaventure,* Montréal, 1936. J. Bittremieux, *Distinctio inter essentiam et esse apud S. Bonaventuram,* Ephemerides theologicae Lovanienses, 14 (1937) 302-307. H. Legowicz, *Essai sur la philosophie sociale du docteur Séraphique,* Fribourg (Suisse), 1937. E. Longpré OFM., art. *Bonaventure,* DHGE., 9 (1937) 741-788. C. M. O'Donnell, *The Psychology of St. Bonaventure and St. Thomas Aquinas,* Washington, 1937. S. Clasen, *Der hl. Bonaventura und das Mendikantentum. Ein Beitrag zur Ideengeschichte des Pariser Mendikantenstreites (1252-1272),* Werl i. W., 1940. L. Veuthey, *S. Bonaventurae philosophia christiana,* Rome, 1943 (bibliography pp. XV-XXI). M. M. de Benedictis, *The Social Thought of Saint Bonaventure,* Washington, 1946. R. Lazzarini, *San Bonaventura, filosofo e mistico del Cristianesimo,* Milano, 1946. Z. Alszeghy, *Grundformen der Liebe. Die Theorie der Gottesliebe bei dem hl. Bonaventura,* Roma, 1946. A. Sépinski, *La psychologie du Christ chez saint Bonaventure, Paris,* 1948. I. Hilsop, OP., *Introduction to St. Bonaventure's Theory of Knowledge,* Dominican Studies, 2 (1949) 46-55. F. Copleston, II, 250-292. A. Pisvin OFM., *L'intuition sensible selon S. Bonaventure,* SRHC., 367-378. T. Szabó, OFM., *De distinctionis formalis origine Bonaven-*

turiana . . . , SRHC., 381-445. A. de Villamonte, *El argumento de "Razones necessarias" en San Buenaventura*, Barcelona, Estudios Franciscanos, 1952. G. Bonafede, *Il pensiero francescano nel secolo XIII*, Palermo, 1952. L. Veuthey, *Le problème de l'existence de Dieu chez saint Bonaventure*, Antonianum, 28 (1953) 19-38. R. Messner, *Ueber die Gegenwartsbedeutung der Erkenntnislehre Bonaventuras und Ockham*, Antonianum, 28 (1953) 131-147. —On the usual expression "Franciscan school," E. Gilson, *La philosophie franciscaine*, Saint François d'Assise, Paris, 1927, 148-175. On such denominations in general, M. Thiel, OSB., *Ueber die Aufteilung der christlichen Philosophie nach verschiedenen Ordensideale*, DTF., 23 (1945) 345-378; Dominicans, 357-358; Franciscans, 358-361; Jesuits, 361-362; Benedictines, 363-378.—On the attitude of the Franciscan school toward Aristotelianism: B. Nardi, *L'aristotelismo della scolastica e i Francescani*, SRHC., 609-626. —On the doctrinal schools: L. Veuthey, OFM. Conv., *Les divers courants de la philosophie augustino-franciscaine au moyen-âge*, SRHC., 629-652; favors the following classification: 1) Franciscan Augustinism with St. Bonaventure; 2) Christian Aristotelianism with Albert the Great and St. Thomas; 3) Averroistic Aristotelianism with Siger of Brabant; 4) scientific Augustinism with Roger Bacon and the Oxford school. This is one among many equally acceptable classifications.

[8] References to *Itinerarium, De reductione* and other short treatises are to the minor editions of Quaracchi; all the other ones refer to the *Opera omnia*, Quaracchi, 1882-1902.— *In Hexaemeron*, II, 14; V, 386. Cf. *Itinerarium*, II, 12; p. 313. In creatures, to be images of God, or vestiges, is not accidental, but substantial, *II Sent.*, 16, 1, 2, fund. 4; II, 397.

[9] "Shadow," "vestige" and "image" are not always classified in the same way. This freedom is characteristic of symbolic theology. See *I Sent.*, 3, 1, un., ad 4m; I, 73. For a general table, see E. Gilson, *The Philosophy of Saint Bonaventure*, London and New York, 1938, p. 515.

[10] *I Sent.*, 3, 1, 1, ad 5m; I, 69. Refers to Augustine, *De Trinitate*, IX, II, 16; PL., 42, 969.

[11] *I Sent.*, 8, 1, 1, 2, Concl.; I, 153. Cf. *De mysterio Trinitatis*, I, 1, 22; V, 47.

[12] *De mysterio Trinitatis*, I, 1, 29; V, 48.

[13] Hugh of St. Victor, *De sacramentis*, I, 3, 1; approved by Bonaventure, *I Sent.*, 8, 1, 1, 2, Concl.; I, 154. *De mysterio Trinitatis*, I, 1, fund. 2; V, 15.

[14] *II Sent.*, 25, 2, un., 6, Concl.; II, 623. Cf. *Itinerarium*, II, 4; pp. 305-306. *De reductione artium ad theologiam*, 8; p. 374.

[15] *II Sent.*, 7, 2, 2, 1, Concl.; II, 198 and note 3. Cf. 24, 1, 2, 4, Concl.; II, 569, and ad 5m, 571-572. *In Hexaemeron*, VII, 2; V, 365. *De donis Spiritus Sancti*, IV, 2; V, 474.

[16] *Sermo IV de rebus theologicis*, 18-19; V, 572.

[17] *De scientia Christi*, IV, ad 22m; V, 26. On divine illumination, *De scientia Christi*, IV, Concl.; V, 23. *In Hexaemeron*, II, 10; V, 338. The plenary effect of divine illumination is mystical contemplation. The names given by Bonaventure to the mystical powers of the soul will be picked up by Eckhart (*apex mentis*, etc.). They came to Bonaventure from Thomas Gallus. On their Greek origin, E. van Ivanka, *Apex mentis, Wandering und Wandlung eines stoischen Terminus*, ZKT., 72 (1950) 123-176.

[18] The Index of the Quaracchi edition of Bonaventure's commentary on the *Sentences* lists more than one thousand references to the works of Aristotle (vol. X, pp. 266-267) covering the whole range of Aristotle's writings from the *Organon* up to the *Problemata*.—On our own interpretation of the attitude of Bonaventure toward Aristotle: *La philosophie de saint Bonaventure*, 3 ed., Paris, 1953, p. 12, p. 133, p. 153, pp. 158-159.

[19] Definition of creation, *II Sent.*, 1, 1, 1, 2, Concl.; II, 22. *Breviloquium*, II, 1, 3; ed. min., 61. The notion of creation unknown to Aristotle, *II Sent.*, 1, 1, 1, 1, Concl.; II, 16-17, and dist. 1, dubium 2m; II, 37. At a later date, *In Hexaemeron* VI, 4; V, 36. Against the eternity of the world, *II Sent.*, 1, 1, 1, 2; the arguments of Bonaventure in favor of the creation of the world in time (*II Sent.*, 1, 1, 1, 2)

are criticized by Thomas Aquinas, *Summa theologiae*, I, 46, 2.

[20] *In I Sent.*, 8, 2, un., 2, Concl.; I, 168 and *II Sent.*, 3, 1, 1, 1, Concl. 1; II, 90-91. Creatures are composed of *ens* and *esse*, because, apart from God, all that is "receives its existence (*esse*) from somewhere else"; consequently, "nothing is its own being." This is not the doctrine of the composition of *esse* and *essentia* we will meet in the doctrine of Thomas Aquinas. See G. P. Klubertanz SJ., *Esse and existere in St. Bonaventure*, MS., 8 (1946) 169-188.

[21] *II Sent.*, 3, 1, 1, 1, Concl. 3a; II, 91.

[22] *II Sent.*, 3, 1, 2, 3, Concl.; II, 109-110. Cf. 18, 1, 3; II, 441.

[23] Hylomorphic composition of the soul, *II Sent.*, 17, 1, 2, Concl.; II, 414-415. Consequently the soul is a distinct substance, mainly owing to its form, *II Sent.*, 3, 1, 2, 3, fund. 3; II, 108; its individuation results from the whole compound, *II Sent.*, 18, 2, 1, ad 1m; II, 447.—On the history of the problem, E. Kleineidam, *Das Problem* . . . , Breslau, 1930. O. Lottin, *La composition hylémorphique des substances spirituelles*, RNSP., 34 (1932) 21-41 (early history of the problem; Roland of Cremona, Philip the Chancellor, A. of Hales, Odo Rigaud; on Bonaventure, p. 40).

[24] *II Sent.*, 17, 2, 2, ad 6m; II, 423. *In Hexaemeron*, II, 2; V, 336: "To say that the ultimate form is added to prime matter . . . without any intermediate form, is insane." The language is harder than it was in 1250, but it is the same position.—Several different interpretations of Bonaventure's general attitude with respect to Aristotle are found in: I. Squadrini, *S. Bonaventura philosophus christianus*, Antonianum, 16 (1941) 103-130, 205-252. P. Robert, *Le problème de la philosophie bonaventurienne*, Laval théologique et philosophique, 6 (1950) 161, and 6 (1951) 57, 58 additional note. F. Van Steenberghen, *Siger de Brabant* . . . , considers that, "in philosophy, Augustinism is one of the sources of his (Bonaventure's) thought, but a secondary one as compared with Aristotelianism," p. 464; accordingly, "in philosophy (not in theology) the doctrine of Bonaventure is an authentic *Aristotelianism*" (sic, italics

not ours); it is "a neoplatonizing Aristotelianism," p. 464; finally, it is "an eclectic and neoplatonizing Aristotelianism at the service of an Augustinian theology," p. 464. A. Da Vinca, OFM., Cap., *L'aspetto filosofico dell'aristotelismo di S. Bonaventura*, CF., 19 (1949) 5-44 (does not consider Bonaventure an Aristotelian).

[25] EUSTACHIUS OF ARRAS OFM., bishop of Coutances, d. 1291. He has left sermons, *Quodlibeta*, and perhaps a commentary on the *Sentences*. Three Questions have been published in *De humanae cognitionis ratione anecdota quaedam*, Quaracchi, 1883, pp. 183-195. See also P. Glorieux, in France Franciscaine, 13 (1930) 125-171; GLOREP., II, 78-82; GLOLIT., II, 77 81. An impressive witness to the reality of the Franciscan school is the ms. studied by V. Doucet, *Quaestiones centum* . . . , AFH., 26 (1933) 183-202, 474-496; cf. AFH., 27 (1934) 547.

Eustachius distinguishes between the "general" and the "special" influence of God. Under his special influence, the soul of some men immediately attains to the immediate intuition of the divine essence (*De humanae cognitionis ratione* . . . , p. 184). The general influence of God does not suffice to achieve this result without the added influence of divine "rules," in whose light we judge things without seeing the uncreated Truth itself: "per istas regulas vel irradiationes mentis directivas judicat mens de omnibus et tamen non videt illam Veritatem increatam, cujus sunt expressae similitudines," pp. 186-187. Through species, the substantial forms of things are presented by the senses to the intellect which receives them as possible intellect and sees them as agent intellect. Since it is an active power with a twofold virtue, or force (*vis*), the intellect "acts upon these species, and forms them and makes them intelligible in act," p. 191. Knowledge and love are *habitus* connatural to the soul. They are consubstantial with the soul and emanate from its substance in which they are rooted. Otherwise, the soul could not act through them nor direct itself toward its end, which is God (p. 193). Everything Eustachius says is confirmed by the authority "egregii Doctoris Augustini," p. 194.—Introduction to the history of the problem: M. Grabmann, *Zur Erkenntnislehre der älteren Franziskanerschule*, FS., 4 (1917) 105-

118; documents interesting for the speculative background of this historical problem, pp. 119-126.

[26] WALTER OF BRUGES OFM., Bishop of Poitiers (1279), died in 1307. On his unpublished works, GLOREP., II, 84-86. A series of 22 Questions has been published by E. Longpré, *Quaestiones disputatae du B. Gauthier de Bruges*, Louvain, 1928. On the unprinted parts of his commentary on Peter Lombard, A. Pelzer, *Le commentaire de Gauthier de Bruges sur le quatrième livre des Sentences*, in RTAM., 2 (1930) 327-334. E. Longpré, *Le commentaire sur les Sentences du B. Gauthier de Bruges (1225-1307)*, Etudes d'histoire doctrinale et littéraire du XIIIe siècle, Paris, 1932, 5-24; *Questions inédites du commentaire sur les Sentences de Gauthier de Bruges*, AHDL., 7 (1932) 251-275.

The 22 Questions published by E. Longpré are devoted to ethical problems and moral theology. This seems to have been the center of his speculative interests. Note the questions III-VI, particularly interesting concerning his doctrine of the will. Walter stresses the fact that the will, inasmuch as it is deliberative, is not necessitated by the desirable object offered to it by reason (p. 39). Following mainly Augustine, Anselm and Bernard of Clairvaux, he strongly stresses the radical independence of the will (p. 51) and its ruling authority (pp. 60-61). The three questions extracted from his commentary on the *Sentences,* Bk. I, and published by the same historian give a better idea of the place of Walter in the theological movement of his time. His proofs of the existence of God follow the ways of the efficient cause (following Algazel, *Metaphysics,* I, 5), of the moving causes (he does not quote Aristotle, but Boethius, *De consolat. philos.,* IV, prosa 6), of the connection and ontological indigence of things (quotes Plato, *Timaeus*), and of the universal order (AHDL., 7 (1932) 260-261.) In what sense the existence of God is demonstrable, and in what senses it is not, pp. 263-264 (note, p. 263, n. 2, the Augustinian and Bonaventurian flavor of the doctrine). The soul is composed of form and of spiritual or intelligible matter; Walter affirms this on the authority of "philosophers" and of "saints," that is, on the one side, Aristotle (sic), Avicenna and Gabirol, and, on the other side, Au-

gustine, Damascene and Boethius. Moses Maimonides and the *Liber XXIV philosophorum* are less easy to classify (p. 270). Note, p. 271, n. 1, the text of William of La Mare in which the same position is maintained. In William, matter is the cause of the possibility of non-existence to be found in all creatures, hence their composition "quae est ex actu existendi et potentia ad non esse."—R. Hofman, *Die Gewissenslehre des Walter von Brügge OFM., und die Entwicklung der Gewissenslehre in der Hochscholastik,* Münster i. W., 1941 (Beiträge, 36). Particular studies: E. Longpré, *Gauthier de Bruges OFM. et l'Augustinisme franciscain au XIIIe siècle,* Miscellanea Ehrle, I, Rome, 1924, 190-218. S. Belmond, *La preuve de l'existence de Dieu d'après Gauthier de Bruges,* RFNS., 25 (1933) 410-425.

[27] MATTHEW OF AQUASPARTA OFM.— Born *ca.* 1240; studied at Paris (in 1268 or slightly earlier), became a master at the same university (1275-1276), then taught at Bologna and succeeded John Peckham as a master in theology at the Pontifical Curia (1279). General Minister of the Franciscan Order (1287-1289). Cardinal (1288), he carried out several diplomatic missions up to the time of his death (Rome, October 29, 1302). These dates are those of a career contemporary with the incipient post-Thomistic doctrinal controversies. GLOLIT., II, 194-198. GLOREP., 102-107.—Texts in A. Daniels, *Quellenbeiträge und Untersuchungen,* 52-63 (*Sent.* I, dist. 2). M. ab Aquasparta, *Quaestiones disputatae selectae;* I, *Quaestiones de fide et de cognitione,* Quaracchi, 1903; vol I also contains *Tractatus de excellentia sacrae scripturae,* pp. 1-22; *Sermo de studio sacre scripturae,* pp. 22-36; *De aeterna processione Spiritus Sancti,* pp. 429-453. II, III, *Quaestiones disputatae de Gratia,* Quaracchi, 1935 (important Introduction by V. Doucet). *Quaestiones de Christo,* Quaracchi, 1914; E. Longpré, *Thomas d'York et Mathieu d'Aquasparta. Textes inédits sur le problème de la création,* AHDL., 1 (1926-1927) 293-308. L. Amoros, *La teologia como ciencia practica en los tiempos que preceden a Escoto,* AHDL., 9 (1934) 261-303. Engl. transl. of *Disp. Quest. I On Knowledge,* McKeon, *Selections,* II, 240-302.—On his doctrine: GDP., 761-762. I. Jeiler, *Dissertatio . . . ,* in *De humanae cognitionis ratione,* Quaracchi, 1883. M. Grabmann, *Die phi-*

*losophische und theologische Erkenntnis-
lehre des Kardinals Matthaeus ab Aquasparta*, Wien, 1906. E. Longpré, art.
Matthieu d'Aquasparta, DTC., 10 (1928)
375-389. H. D. Simonin, *La connaissance
humaine des singuliers matériels d'après
les maîtres franciscains au XIIIe siècle*,
MM., 1930, II, 289-303. A. C. Pegis,
*Matthew of Aquasparta and the Cogni-
tion of Non-Being*, SRHC., 463-480. J.
Auer, *Die Entwicklung der Gnadenlehre
in der Hochscholastik, mit besonderer
Berücksichtigung des Kardinals Matteo
d'Aquasparta. I, Das Wesen der Gnade*,
Freiburg i. Br., 1942. Cf. J. Rohmer,
AHDL., 3 (1928) 161-177.

[28] Judging from the specimen published
by Aug. Daniels, the proofs of the existence of God alleged in the *Sentences* are
sketchy. Matthew argues from the "origin, the multitude, the order and the
movement" of beings (A. Daniels, pp.
55-56). In qu. III, where he asks if the
existence of God is an "indubitable truth,"
he resorts to Augustine's *Soliloquies*, I,
8 (PL., 32, 877) and to Anselm's *Proslogion* in order to establish that God cannot be conceived as non-existing. Yet this
is not given as a proof; it follows the
proofs already given. Pages 60-63 contain
interesting combinations of Anselm and
Bonaventure (or Augustine); cf. Daniels,
pp. 159-161. All the theologians who admit the presence in man of an innate
idea of God do not use it as a proof of
God's existence; some of them resort to
it in order to prove that, once acquired
by demonstration, this truth becomes a
sort of self-evident notion.

[29] The soul is the act and perfection
of the body, and not only the soul, but
the intellect (*Quaestiones de fide et cognitione*, pp. 425-426); to actuate the body
"is not the prime being of the soul, otherwise it would have no being once separated from the body" (p. 392, ad 12);
nevertheless, separated from its body, it
does not exist in a condition that perfectly suits its nature (pp. 425-426). On
the *colligantia* between soul and body,
Qu. de Christo, p. 62, ad 16.

[30] See, *Qu. de fide*, p. 409, ad 14, where
Matthew concedes to Avicenna (*Metaph.*,
IX, 2) that "the intellect seeks pure goodness," but adds that, because the philosophers have had a taste of divine contemplation, and no taste of divine love,
they mentioned the speculative felicity
only, not the affective one.

[31] On the various doctrines concerning
the nature of the human intellect (Alexander, Themistius, Avicenna, Avempace
and Alfarabi), *Qu. de fide*, pp. 348-350.
Matthew considers them as refuted by
Averroes, but what interests him are the
positions of the theologians indulging in
philosophy. Some of them take up the
division of Averroes: *intellectus possibilis,
speculativus, agens* and *adeptus*. The possible intellect and the agent intellect are
powers connatural to the human soul;
they are separated, but the agent intellect
still more so than the possible intellect.
This position is that of great men in
philosophy and theology (Albert the
Great?), yet it is not too safe (p. 351);
for so long as the soul is in its body, it
cannot unite with the separate substances;
now this should be possible according to
this position. Let us maintain, with Augustine, that we can know the existence
of such substances, not their nature (pp.
352-353).

[32] The ambiguity of the twofold meaning of *intellectus* (understanding or the
understood) is often a cause of obscurity
in such texts: "illa species . . . tunc est
quodammodo apta intellectui, et dicitur
esse *intentio intellecta in potentia* a Com-
mentatore (Averroes). Intellectus agens,
quo est omnia facere, transformat eam in
intellectum possibilem et facit eam intel-
lectam actu; et illud vocat Philosophus
abstrahere," p. 287. The main point is
that the soul undergoes nothing from
sensible bodies, "sed potius facit ex illis
et de illis, et format sibi species aptas et
proportionatas secundum exigentiam or-
ganorum et virium, quousque det sibi esse
intelligibile et coaptet eam et formet sive
transformet eam in intellectum possibilem,
quo est omnia fieri," p. 287. Cf. pp. 288-
291, including the doctrine of the "con-
nexio potentiarum et virtutum."—On the
fundamental activity of the intellect, F.
Prezioso, *L'attività del soggetto pensante
nella gnoseologia di Matteo d'Aquasparta
e di Ruggiero Marston*, Antonianum, 25
(1950) 259-326.

[33] Since, according to Avicenna, essences
are indifferent to existence and non-existence ("quidditas indifferenter se habet ad
esse et non-esse") the intellectual cognition of non-existents is possible (*Qu. de*

fide, p. 231); the quiddity then is the object of the intellect. Yet, this object would be just a concept; in order to avoid this consequence, Matthew resorts to theology (p. 231) and assigns to the intellect for its object "the quiddity conceived by our intellect, but related to the art, that is to an eternal exemplar, inasmuch as, touching our mind, it acts as a mover," p. 233. The Augustinian doctrine of the divine illumination follows. The divine ideas are not the sole cause of intellectual knowledge (against Plato), but they cause it (against Aristotle); following Bonaventure, Matthew posits the divine Ideas as the "objectum motivum" (p. 254) which, acting upon the data of sense knowledge (a necessary element), makes us see the immutable truths. We *see by* this divine light, we do not *see it* (p. 254). A detailed examination of these texts would confirm that, about 1270, Thomas Aquinas already had adversaries well informed of his positions; for instance, p. 251, Thomas is certainly one of the "philosophantes" in question. — Against the separate Intelligence of Avicenna, p. 278. That we know singulars (against Thomas, p. 308) through singular species and universals through universal species, pp. 309-310 (On this point, cf. Roger Bacon, *Opus tertium,* ch. 35, Brewer ed., p. 115). That the soul knows itself and its *habitus,* if not at the beginning of its knowledge, at least after it has gone beyond phantasms, pp. 329-334.

³⁴ See especially, *Quaestiones de Christo,* qu. IX, where Matthew discusses the question: is there only one *esse* in Christ? Matthew answers in the affirmative. He avails himself of this occasion to restate the doctrine of the plurality of forms. One could not wish for a clearer statement of the relation between the two positions: plurality of forms, plurality of *esse.* In doctrines like these, in which *esse* does not mean the "act of being," but just entity, several substantial forms entail several *esse.* This, Matthew says, is the common opinion of the Parisian Masters: "Quilibet homo, quamvis unus homo sit, tamen in uno et eodem homine sunt plura esse, quia plures formae substantiales perficientes secundum diversos gradus essendi, et per quas reponitur in diversis generibus gradatim ordinalis, secundum communem sententiam Magistrorum Parisiensium," p. 167. The contrary opinion (Thomas Aquinas, *Summa theologiae,* III, 17, 1 and 2) has been condemned by the Parisian Masters as unsound and not agreeing with faith, pp. 168-169. And indeed, there was at that time (1270) a strong opposition against the doctrine of the unity of the substantial form in composite substances, especially man.

³⁵ BARTHOLOMEW OF BOLOGNA OFM.; GLOREP., II, 108-109. V. Doucet, AFH., 27 (1934) 550. E. Longpré, *Bartolommeo di Bologna,* Studi Francescani, 1923, 365-384. Studied philosophy and taught Theology at the University of Paris. Succeeded Matthew of Aquasparta as master in theology at Bologna (1282). History loses his trace after 1294. His 35 *Quaestiones disputatae* are dated about 1277, at Paris (Glorieux, p. 108). The *De luce* has been published by Squadrani, *Tractatus de luce Fr. Bartholomei de Bononia,* Antonianum 7 (1932) 201-238, 337-376, 465-494. The text of the Questions has been published by M. Mückshoff, *Die Quaestiones disputatae de fide des Bartholomaeus von Bologna OFM.,* Münster i. W., 1940 (Beiträge, 24, 4). We have not been able to find this volume, probably destroyed during the last war.

A little-studied Franciscan of the same period, and apparently of the same school, or group, is the elusive WILLIAM OF FALGUIÈRES OFM. (Guillelmus de Falgario). On his life and works, GLOLIT., II, 125-127; GLOREP., II, 112-113. V. Doucet, AFH., 27 (1934) 550; his identification with PETER OF FALCO OFM., suggested by P. Glorieux (France Franciscaine, 12 (1929) 257-289) has been opposed by A. Théry OFM., *De vita et operibus Petri de Falco,* Sophia, 8 (1940) 28-45 and by A. Heysse OFM., *Pierre de Falco ne peut être identifié avec Guillaume de Falegar OFM.,* AFH., 33 (1940) 241-267.

³⁶ ROGER MARSTON OFM.—On his life and works, see the introduction to his Disputed Questions: *Fr. Rogeri Marston OFM., Quaestitiones disputatae,* Quaracchi, 1932 (life, VIII-XXXIV, writings, XXXV-LI, doctrine, LI-LXXIX). — Extract from *Quodlibet II,* qu. 22, in Roberto Zavalloni, *Richard de Mediavilla . . . ,* pp. 180-199.—A. G. Little, OTT., 93-95. GLOLIT., II, 264-269. BIBLIOGRAPHY.—F. Pelster, *Roger Marston OFM.,* (d. *1303*) *ein englischer Vertreter des Augustinismus,* Scholastik, 3 (1928) 526-

556. E. Gilson, *Roger Marston, un cas d'Augustinisme avincennisant*, AHDL., 8 (1952) 37-42; *Sur quelques difficultés de l'illumination augustinienne*, RNSP., 36 (1934) 321-331. J. Cairola, *L'opposizione a S. Tommaso nelle Quaestiones disputatae di Ruggero Marston*, SRHC., 449-460. P. A. Faustino Prezioso, *L'attività del soggetto pensante nella gnoseologia di Matteo d'Acquasparta e di Ruggiero Marston*, Antonianum, 25 (1950), reprint pp. 1-69 (excellent; note Marston's criticism of Henry of Ghent's rejection of intelligible species, 36-42; against Giles of Rome, 42-44; influence of Marston's noetic, 45-50).

[37] References to *Quaestiones disputatae*, Quaracchi, 1932.—Roger opposes to the *Sancti* the *theologi philosophantes* (the philosophizers), p. 360. This distinction is seldom taken in a sense favorable to the "philosophizing theologians." (E. Gilson, *Les Philosophantes*, AHDL., 19 (1952) 135-140).—Matter has its own being (p. 208). Whether or not the soul has matter is not clear in his texts; he does not seem to commit himself, pp. 361, 364. United to a body, the soul exists *per se* and, consequently, it is immortal, p. 361. Even if it had matter, it would still be immortal (ibid.). There are "rationes seminales" in natural beings (an incidental statement), p. 173, ad 22m. The supreme power of the soul is the intellect, which is both passive and active, pp. 325, ad 8; 348, ad 11m, etc. Its passive power is the possible intellect, p. 387; its active and illuminating power is the agent intellect, which acts upon the phantasms as light upon colors; it purifies them and enables them to "multiply" up to the possible intellect; apart from Aristotle, no philosopher has ever made this distinction (pp. 386-387); it does not seem to agree with the intention of Augustine (p. 387), whose doctrine of sensation Roger maintains (pp. 387-396), together with the Augustinian doctrine of the divine illumination: Alfarabi, Avicenna, perhaps Aristotle himself, posit the agent Intellect as a separate substance (p. 258); in Aristotle's *De anima*, III, 5, it is said that the agent Intellect is eternally knowing all things by actual knowledge; this, which applies to God alone, agrees with the Catholic truth and the doctrine of Augustine, so it should not be denied (p. 258). Nevertheless, this language is philosophical, and if we say that "the agent Intellect . . . is a separate substance, namely, God himself" (p. 259), we should understand it in the sense of Augustine's doctrine of the divine illumination (important text, p. 260). Man knows all in a light derived from the eternal light, which the soul sees in itself, and which is distinct from the light of its own agent intellect, pp. 252-258. Against those who garble the texts of Augustine (probably Thomas Aquinas) see his indignant reaction, pp. 255-256; p. 262: "Sic igitur . . . , and p. 273, "Haec idcirco dixerim. . . ." On the internal difficulties met by the Franciscan school concerning the natural or supernatural nature of the divine illumination, E. Gilson, *Sur quelques difficultés . . .* , p. 329, n. 7. Note that the problem was not simply to choose between a "general" and a "special" illumination, but between a "grace" and a "natural gift."

[38] PETER OLIEU OFM (*Petrus Joannis Olivi*), born at Sérignan (France) about 1248; entered the Franciscan Order about 1260 (he heard Saint Bonaventure in 1268); had to retract 22 propositions concerning monastic poverty (1283); after years spent in controversies on the subject, he died at Narbonne, March 14, 1298. On life and works: GLOLIT., II, 205-211; GLORER., II, 127-134. V. Doucet, AFH., 27 (1936) 555-556; 28 (1935) 156-197, 408-442. The main published texts are: *Petri Joannis Olivi Provencalis Quodlibeta*, Venice, 1509 (we have not seen this edition). B. Jansen, *Petrus Johannis Olivi OFM., Quaestiones in IIm librum Sententiarum*, 3 vols., Quaracchi, 1922, 1924, 1926; a model edition with perfect doctrinal tables (III, 583-617). D. Laberge, *P. Joannis Olivi tria scripta ejus apologetica*, in AFH., 28 (1935) 115-155. F. Delorme, *Fr. Petri Joannis Olivi tractatus "De perlegendis philosophorum libris,"* Antonianum, 16 (1941) 31-44. Abbreviations of some questions of Olieu (*Memoralia P. J. Olivi*) in F. Delorme, *Vitalis de Furno Quodlibeta tria*, 249-260.

On his philosophical doctrines: GDP., 763; especially a series of studies by Bern. Jansen, SJ., *Die Lehre Olivis über das Verhältnis von Leib und Seele*, FS., 5 (1918) 153-175, 233-258; *Die Erkenntnislehre Olivis*, Berlin, 1921 (bibliography, IX-XIII); *Die Unsterblichkeitsbeweise bei Olivi und ihre philosophiegeschichtliche Bedeutung*, FS., 9 (1922) 49-69; *Die Seelenlehre Olivis und ihre Verurteilung auf dem Wiener Konzil*, FS., 21 (1934) 297-314; *Der Augustinismus des Petrus Johannis Olivi*, ADGM., 878-895.—J. Koch, *Der Sentenzenkommentar des P. J. Olivi*, RTAM., 2 (1930) 290-310. L. Jarraux, *Pierre Jean Olivi, sa vie, sa doctrine*, Etudes franciscaines, 45 (1933) 129-153, 277-298, 513-529. F. Callaey, art. *Olieu ou Olivi*, DTC., 11 (1931) 982-991. P. G. Ricci, *Pietro Olivi e la pluralità delle forme sostanziali*, Studi Francescani, 8, (1936) 225-239; *Pietro Olivi e l'unità sostanziale dell'uomo*, Studi Francescani, 9 (1937) 51-65. L. Seidel, *Natur und Person. Metaphysische Probleme bei Petrus Olivi*, Würzburg, 1938. B. Echeverria, *El problema de l'alma humana en la Edad Media. Pedro de Olivi y la definicion del Concilio de Vienne*, Buenos Aires, 1941. O. Lottin, PEM., II, 254-260.

On the question whether the doctrine of Olieu himself was condemned at the Council of Vienne, the negative is upheld by L. Jarraux OFM., *Pierre Jean Olivi*, op. cit., p. 528, and in the fundamental study of E. Müller OFM., *Das Konzil von Vienne 1311-1312. Seine Quellen und seine Geschichte*, Münster i. W., 1934. The contrary view, more generally accepted, finds justifications in J. Koch, *Das Gutachten des Aegidius Romanus über die Lehren des Petrus Johannis Olivi. Eine neue Quelle zum Konzil von Vienne* (1311-1312), Scientia sacra, Theologische Festgabe—K. J. Schulte, Cologne, 1935, pp. 142-168; B. Jansen, *Ein neues gewichtiges Zeugnis über die Verurteilung Olivis*, Scholastik, 10 (1935) 406-408. L. Amorós, *Aegidii Romani impugnatio doctrinae Petri Johannis Olivi an. 1311-1312, nunc primum in lucem edita*, AFH., 27 (1934) 399-451; there is little doubt that the doctrine of Olieu himself was then condemned.

[39] The composition of matter and form in angels and souls is maintained by Olieu, even at this late date, as the "more common opinion," *Quaestiones*, Quaracchi ed., I, 304-330. His authorities on this point are Aristotle (sic), Augustine and Boethius "christianissimus theologus": I, 318-320, and I, 325-327. He does not quote Gabirol. Olieu's position implies that matter is an act, or an "actuality" distinct in itself from the other kind of art called "form," I, 305-306. On the universality of the composition of matter and form, including souls, pp. 315-316.— On the plurality of forms in man. II, 29-

35; note the concluding remark: "therefore I simply hold that, in the human body, besides the soul, there are other forms really different from the soul, and I even believe that all the formal degrees which are in it contribute to constituting one perfect form, the principal and, so to say the form and root of all the other forms, being the one that comes last," p. 35.—That the intellectual soul of man is not the form *per se* of the body, II, 104-126. Note, p. 111, that "if the soul, or the intellective form, is the form of the body, it cannot possibly be intellectual, and free, and immortal and separable from the body." This union is a "consubstantial," yet not a "formal" one; it is intimate and very strong, yet not "immediate," II, 537.—Incidentally, let us note that Olieu is an interesting witness to the disputes concerning the composition of *esse* and essence. To posit the essence as in potency to *esse*, its act, is "absurd," I, 152. The distinction of Boethius between *esse* and *quod est* is not absurd, but it simply points out the composition of matter and substantial form, I, 154. Olieu's case is a timely warning for us to remember that the Thomistic composition of essence and existence will meet a two-fold opposition coming from two opposite quarters: the Aristotelians, who could find no room for it in the metaphysics of Aristotle, and their adversaries, the representative of the traditional theology, who did not need it. Olieu belongs in the latter group. Another "Augustinian" witness to this type of opposition is the anonymous author studied by G. Engelhardt, *Die Lehrrichtung des Cod. Par. Bibl. nat. 16407. Ein Beitrag zum Augustinismus der Hochscholastik*, ADGM., 792-825, particularly 813. To this theologian, the composition of essence and existence means nothing: "Sed hoc nihil est." This document is extremely interesting.

[40] The main texts of Olieu on this point are to be found in his *Quaestiones de Deo cognoscendo*, published by B. Jansen in Appendix to vol. III, pp. 455-554. In qu. II, after maintaining the doctrine of Augustine against those among the "magni" (i.e., Thomas Aquinas, *Sum. theol.*, I, 84, 5, Resp.), who pretend that, on this point, he was a Platonist (I, 503), Olieu adds that, in so far as he himself is concerned, he adheres to it under certain conditions: 1, the divine ideas should not

be said to be the "forms" of our intellect; 2, they should not be posited as representing to us intelligible objects as immediately "seen" and "known". So much for the object of cognition, and now for its mode: 3, the divine light should not be considered a "natural" principle of cognition, either total or partial and instrumental; 4, the intellect itself should not be deprived of its natural aptitude to grasp absolutely certain truth; 5, we should also beware not to posit the knowledge of all things as innate in the human intellect. Conclusion (III, 512-513): "Not knowing how to explain away these difficulties, I merely present them as errors to be avoided, for indeed, although the said position is in itself famous and sound, it might become very dangerous if these points were not carefully observed. For this reason, I hold the said position taken in itself, because it is that of very famous men, and I leave it to their wisdom to deal with the aforesaid difficulties." Some say that Olieu was giving up the doctrine without daring to say so; but he was giving up the doctrine of the *rationes seminales* without hesitating to say so (I, 515-551); moreover, he explicitly says he maintains it, only he does not fully know on what grounds. He is a puzzled man.—His short treatise "On the Reading of the Books of the Philosophers" is exactly in the spirit of the last writings of Saint Bonaventure; see Antonianum, 16 (1941) 37-44.

⁴¹ The solidarity of the powers of the soul is not a theory proper to Olieu, but he has made it his own by his treatment of it: II, 546-547; III, 30-39; III, 274-275. On Olieu's doctrine of motion, B. Jansen, *Olivi der älteste scholastische Vertreter des heutigens Bewegungsbegriffs*, PJ., 33 (1920) 137-152.—On the history of the condemnations of Olieu and his successors, L. Amorós OFM., *Series condemnationum et processuum contra doctrinam et sequaces Petri Joannis Olivi (e cod. Vat. Ottob. lat. 1816)*, AFH., 24 (1931) 495-512.

⁴² PETER OF TRABES OFM.—Born at Trabes, near Bazas, France (*Petrus de Trabibus*) is still little known and deserves to be more closely studied.—GLOLIT., II, 229-232. E. Longpré, *Pietro de Trabibus, un discepolo di Pier Giovanni Olivi*, Studi Francescani, 19 (1922) n. 3, extract 1-24; same author, *Nuovi documenti per la storia dell' Agostinismo Francescano*, Studi Francescani, 1923, 314-350 (see pp. 329-350, questions by an alleged disciple of Peter of Trabes, more Augustinian than his master: 332-336; Alfarabi and Avicenna support Augustine, p. 336). B. Jansen, *Petrus de Trabibus, seine spekulative Eigenart oder sein Verhältnis zu Olivi*, Festgabe Clemens Baeumker, Münster i. W., 1923, 243-254. A. Ledoux, *Petri de Trabibus OFM., Quaestiones duo de aeternitate mundi*, Antonianum, 6 (1931) 137-152. A. Teetaert, art. *Pierre de Trabes*, DTC., 12 (1933) 2049-2064. M. Schmaus, *Des Petrus de Trabibus Lehre über das göttliche Vorauswissen und die Prädestination*, Antonianum 10 (1935) 121-148. O. Lottin, PEM., II, 254-260. G. Gàl, *Commentarius Petri de Trabibus in IV libros Sententiarum Petro de Tarantasia falso inscriptus*, AFH., 45 (1952) 241-278.

Peter rejects the composition of essence and *esse* "tanquam ex diversis naturis" (Jansen, 247). *Esse* adds nothing real to essence, but only "alium modum significandi et dicendi." Same remark concerning individuation; its cause is the cause of its existence; it adds nothing to the essence, "cujus individuatio dicitur esse" (ibid., cf. Olieu, whose doctrine will be rejected by Duns Scotus on this point). The human soul is a compound of matter and form; it contains several forms; the intellectual soul communicates with the body, but it is not its act (Jansen, 250-251). Peter seems to reduce the seminal reasons of Augustine to an active potentiality of matter (ibid., 251-252). Concerning the divine illumination, he acknowledges that the works of Augustine are full of it; he himself accepted it for a time, then he gave it up (see Olieu), at least in its strict interpretation, and simply maintained that God gives our intellect both being and light (ibid., 248). But his position remains very different from that of Thomas Aquinas. To Peter, since we should not unnecessarily add philosophy to the teaching of the "Saints," there is no reason to speak of a "possible" intellect nor of an "agent intellect". Our intellect is an active possibility (*possibilitas activa*). It can form intelligible species of singulars or of universals according to its needs, and it can do this without having to receive sensible species from outside. This is the teaching of Augustine and of the Saints whose authority theologians and Christians should prefer to that of pagan philosophers (*Studi Francescani,* pp. 12-16). Against the distinction: possible-intellect, agent-intellect, op. cit., 19-21. Difficulties of Augustinian illumination, op. cit., 22.— On his opposition to the Averroistic doctrine of the unity of the intellect, see Cr. Krzanic, *Grandi lottatori contro l'averroismo,* in RFNS., 22 (1950) 203-206.

[43] VITAL DU FOUR OFM (or vidal, *Vitalis de Furno*), birth date unknown; entered the Franciscan Order, taught theology at Paris (1292-1295, probably), then at Montpellier (1295-1297) and at Toulouse (1300); Cardinal-priest (1312) and Cardinal-Bishop (1321); died August 16, 1327. On his life and works, see HLF., 36 (1927) 295-305. GLOLIT., II, 280-283; GLOREP . . . , II, 137-140. V. Doucet, AFH., 27 (1934) 556-557.—F. Delorme, *Autour d'un apocryphe scotiste,* France Franciscaine, 8 (1925) 279-295: restores to Vital the partial authorship of the pseudo-Scotist *De rerum principio.* Same author: *L'oeuvre scolastique de maître Vital du Four d'après le ms. 95 de Todi,* France Franciscaine, 9 (1926) 421-471. Texts in: F. Delorme, *Le cardinal Vital du Four. Huit questions disputées sur le problème de la connaissance,* AHDL., 2 (1927) 151-337. E. Longpré, *Pour la défense de Duns Scot,* RFNS., 18 (1926) 32-42: ascribes to Vital the *De rerum principio,* printed in several editions of Duns Scotus, for instance, *Opera omnia,* ed. Wadding, vol. III. P. Glorieux, *Pour en finir avec le De rerum principio,* AFH., 31 (1938) 225-234. F. Delorme, *Vitalis de Furno SRE. Card. Quodlibeta tria,* Roma, 1947 (Spicilegium Pontif. Athen. Antoniani V): on the life and works of Vital, Preface, pp. V-XXXII.

No distinction between existence and essence; refutation of the position of Thomas Aquinas, in AHDL., 2 (1927), 274-281. On the contrary: "esse non dicit aliquid absolutum additum essentiae creaturae ut ab ea differens et ei per creationem inhaerens ut forma materiae per generationem, sed est idem re absoluta cum essentia" (281). Existence is essence itself as related to its efficient cause (281). Their distinction is one of reason only (282-283). When we know a non-existing thing, which is possible, the object is not non-being, which is impossible; it is the object as known by the intellect; in other words, it is the being of essence (*esse*

essentiae), that is the being of what can be made after the model of its exemplar in God (293-294).—The following references are to *De rerum principio,* in Duns Scot, *Opera omnia,* Paris, 1891-1895, vol. IV, pp. 267-471. The first number, indicating the Question, will enable the reader to find the text in any one of the two other editions: *Opera omnia,* Lyon, 1639, III, pp. 1-207; or, separately, Quaracchi, 1910. Proofs of God's existence by causality (Avicennian type but with an added pre-Scotist structure), qu. I, art. 2-4. God can directly produce many beings (against Avicenna), II, 1-4; 279-289. God acts by his free will, III, 3, 2; 301-302; against Avicenna, IV, 302-326. God alone can create (against Avicenna, Alfarabi, Themistius etc.,) VI, 334-346. Matter has actual entity (quotes Augustine, *Conf.,* XII, 3 and XIII, 33) VII, 346-349; VIII, 364 ff. There is matter in angels and souls, I, 1, 3, 268; VII, 2, 349-364. Prime matter is one and the same for all beings, VIII, 4, particularly 378: "Ego autem ad positionem Avicembroni redeo . . . ;" as for me, I go back to the position of Gabirol; this statement, bitterly reproached to Duns Scotus, who never made it, will probably sound harmless now that its author is merely Vital du Four. The intellective soul is the true and specific form of the body, LX, 2, 2, 406-436; but it is not as intimately united to it as the sensitive soul, 415, 418; it is not the form of the organic body *qua* organic, 423-426. The soul is identical with its powers, but it contains a plurality of forms, XI, 3, 468-482; cf. 466. Since essence and being of existence are one in nature, wherever there is a being of essence there is a being of existence: "ubicumque reperitur ratio essentiae ibi reperitur et esse existentiae," XXV, 712. Incidentally, this is the reason why there are several *esse existentiae* in Christ, 713.

The *Quodlibeta tria* published by Ferd. Delorme confirm what could be learned from the *De rerum principio:* essence is individual by itself, without any addition, p. 21; the soul is one with its powers, 28-29; on the unity of matter and the universal composition of matter and form, he refers to *De rerum principio,* VIII, 4 (ed. Fernandez) and it is noteworthy that his authorities on this point are Boethius and Denis, not Gabirol, p. 90; souls as substances and souls as forms, pp. 114-115 (quoted as an opinion held by some to justify the inequalities between souls, but he himself prefers to assert that souls are created unequal in themselves, not on account of their union with more or less perfect bodies, pp. 122-123); souls are not individuated by their bodies, p. 124; that only God can create, pp. 128-134 (note, p. 130 a clear reference to *De rerum principio*); maintains "seminal reasons" against Olieu, pp. 134-149; (note, p. 145, the connection with the problem of essence and existence); on the eduction of forms from matter, against Olieu, pp. 149-162; on the instantaneous propagation of light and its difficulties, pp. 163-173; that heavy bodies move faster when they approach the center of the earth, pp. 174-177.—If the *Memoralia Vitalis de Furno,* published by Delorme, are to be trusted, they raise a curious question. how is it that, in this summary, Vital is supposed to have affirmed the real distinction of essence and existence (p. 247)? He denies it everywhere else.

44 The following references are to the *Quaestiones* published by Fr. Delorme in AHDL., 2 (1927); only the pages are indicated.—The intellectual soul is present to all the senses (165); although its proper object is the universal, it can contract and particularize itself; it knows whiteness in sight, sound in hearing, etc. (168); hence its cognition of the singular, owing to its accidental contraction and determination by sense perception (171). Against Giles of Rome and Thomas Aquinas, Vital maintains that our intellectual cognition of the singular is a direct apprehension of its existence (176). The object of the intellect is the "actualitas existentiae rei sensibilis per sensationem" (181; note the term "sensatio"). It implies an "experimentatio de actualitate rei" (181). The intellect knows the singular before the universal (183).— Concerning the cognition of universals Vital sharply criticizes the usual interpretation of abstraction (177-178; 196-198). The possible intellect and the agent intellect are one and the same power (197); the process of abstraction is as follows: "The intellect gathers the species of the universal thing from all these species, namely: from that of the sensation, from the species of the sensible thing as it is in sense, then as it is in imagination; for indeed, sensation itself is immediately known, and since the intellect is a reflecting and comparing power, it knows the quiddity in the sensation as universal or, if it knows the particular thing by a species which it gathers from sense or from imagination, it immediately considers that thing under the aspect of universality; thus, in understanding this color, it understands absolute color through the species of color produced in it. By the virtue of the (agent) intellect, the intelligible species can be multiplied in the (possible) intellect from the species that is in sense as well as from the species that is in imagination" (211). The intelligible species does not act upon the intellect, it is produced by it (224); the soul receives the sensible species from things, and, to that extent, the act of intellection is indirectly caused by them 227).

45 Intuitive cognition of the soul by itself, as to its existence and essence (241-243). This intuitive cognition is accessible to a morally purified soul, according to Matthew of Aquasparta and Augustine (243-252); on this "sensus interior," p. 243. The divine light is not a seen object, it is the cause why we see the truth (331). It moves and it sharpens our intellect (332) without inhering in it as if it were one of its dispositions. It is a "ratio cognoscendi ut forma et species non inherens, sed mentem immutans ad intelligendum" (334); it is for our intellect an exemplar (334) which, together with the intelligible species abstracted from sense, makes up a perfect cause of true cognition. This solution, together with the notion of the intimate presence of the divine light to the soul, is borrowed from Henry of Ghent (335-336). One of the many sources of Vital du Four is the little studied Franciscan RAYMOND RIGAUT (master in theology at Paris about 1287/1288; d. 1296): GLOLIT., II, 240-251. GLOREP., II, 124. V Doucet, AFH., 27 (1934) 555. List of his Disputed Questions and of his Quodlibet in F. Delorme, *Quodlibets et Questions disputées de Raymond Rigaut, maître franciscain de Paris, d'après le Ms. 98 de la Bibl. Comm. de Todi,* ADGM., 826-841; text of the Prologue to Quodlibet VIII, 841.

46 RICHARD OF MEDIAVILLA OFM. Called Richard of Middleton by those who consider him an Englishman, and Richard of Menneville, Moyenville etc., by those who consider him a Frenchman. Bachelor in theology at Paris in 1283; full professor 1284-1287; IV Books on the *Sentences* completed after 1294; date of death unknown. GLOREP., II, 120-123. V. Doucet, AFH., 27 (1934) 554-555. W. Lampen, *De manuscriptis Richardi de Mediavilla OFM.,* Antonianum 16 (1941) 45-52.

WRITINGS. *In IV libros Sententiarum,* Venice, 1507-1509; Brescia, 1591. *Quaestiones quodlibetales,* Venice, 1507, 1509; Paris, 1510, 1519, 1529; Brescia, 1591.— *Quaest. disput. 13,* in *De humanae cognitionis ratione,* 221-245.—*Quaestio Fratris Richardi De gradu formarum,* in R. Zavalloni, *Richard de Mediavilla et la controverse sur la pluralité des formes,* Louvain, 1951, pp. 35-169, 173-180.— BIBLIOGRAPHY. GDP., 762-763, E. Hocedez, *Richard de Middleton, sa vie, ses oeuvres, sa doctrine,* Louvain (fundamental). Particular studies: W. Witterbruch, *Die Gewissenstheorie bei Heinrich of Ghent und Richard von Mediavilla,* Elberfeld, 1929. P. Rucker, *Der Ursprung unserer Begriffe nach Richard von Mediavilla,* Münster i. W., 1934 (Beiträge, 31, 1). J. Reuss, *Die theologische Tugend der Liebe nach der Lehre des Richard von Mediavilla,* FS., 22 (1935) 11-43, 158-198. O. Lottin, PEM., II, 247-249.—The abovementioned work of Zavalloni is a necessary complement to Hocedez; chronological table, 505-507; extensive bibliography, 508-538; text of a question tentatively attributed to Richard, *De unitate formae;* the question *De gradu formarum* is one of the origins of the discussions on the possibility and nature of variations of degree within one and the same order of forms; physics, metaphysics and theology were all interested in the question.

[47] The necessary texts are to be found in *De humanae cognitionis ratione . . .* pp. 221-245. The position of Richard is stated with perfect limpidity: 1) even if things are true by reason of their exemplars in God, one can know their truth without knowing their relation to their exemplar in God, p. 225; 2) what is naturally known is known in a "natural" light; we should carefully avoid introducing a supernatural light in this process, p. 226; now every natural power should be able to perform its natural operations, and since the natural operation of an *intellectus* is *intelligere,* our intellect must be able to perform this operation, pp. 226-227; there are only three ways to prove

the contrary: by the authority of Sacred Scripture, whose texts are distorted in order to make them prove it (Ps. 12, 4; 35, 9; John, 1, 9; 8, 12), pp. 227-228; or by experience, but what experience proves is that every man is capable of some natural knowledge without any illumination; or by reasoning, but no convincing demonstration of this position has ever been found, p. 228; 3) we must distinguish between the absolute truth of a thing: its conformity to its model in an intellect on which it depends; and its relative truth: its conformity to the model it has in a created intellect on which it does not depend. Now we are not talking about absolute truth, which is in the mind of God alone; the truth at stake is that which is in created intellects and in created things, pp. 228-229; 4) absolute truth is distinct, intuitive, immediate and clear; our own knowledge is general, discursive, mediate and obscure, pp. 230-233; 5) we have no intuitive knowledge of intelligible truth, we do not "see" it, pp. 233-234; 6) we only can know intelligible truth in general, mediately and obscurely, by investigating it as the cause of its effects; to conclude: "we can grasp some created truth in the natural light, because the natural light itself is impressed by God in our intellect; and one can adapt to this the words of the Psalmist: *The light of thy countenance O Lord, is signed upon us* (4, 7), for it can be called the light of eternal truth, since it comes in us directly from the eternal truth. So we can say that we can naturally understand some created truth in the eternal light, as in the reason which makes us know it, because we understand it by means of the natural light impressed in us by eternal truth," p. 235. It is impossible not to remember Thomas Aquinas, *Summa theologiae,* I, 84, 5, Resp.: "For the intellectual light itself, which is in us, is nothing else than a participated likeness of the uncreated light, in which are contained the eternal exemplars. Whence it is written, Ps. 4, 6, . . ." etc. Thomas Aquinas died ten years before Richard was made a full professor of theology. The *Summa* seems have done its work, at least on this point, in the mind of Richard.—On the act of abstraction itself, there is nothing in the text we have analyzed, and Hocedez seems to have found very little, except metaphors, *Richard de Middleton,* pp. 147-148. Even here, however, Richard does not accept

Thomism without some Augustinian scruples. In saying that we can know "aliquod verum," "aliquod verum creatum," and even the eternal truth in a weak and confused way, he gives his reader the impression that, as he himself understands it, natural knowledge cannot pretend to the certitude it would have if it really did receive a supernatural illumination. We would not dare to attribute to him this intention if others (William of Ware for instance, see note 56) had not criticized him on this very point.

[48] E. Hocedez, op. cit., pp. 149-152. This indirect cognition of the singular is very different from the doctrine, classical in the Franciscan school, according to which we know the universal in a universal species and the singular in a singular species. Hocedez is right in saying that Richard is trying to follow Thomas without completely giving up the Franciscan tradition.

[49] Being is analogous, Hocedez, p. 183. Good is better than being, p. 185. God can be demonstrated from his effects; the argument of Saint Anselm is not conclusive, pp. 188-189. Existence is not an accident added to essence (against Avicenna seen by Thomas Aquinas); and it is not the act of essence, because, in order to be added to essence, it has to be, and since it could not be without being actuated by another *esse*, we would have to go *in infinitum*. What existence adds to essence can be nothing else than a relation; Hocedez, pp. 189-190. Like Vital du Four, Richard defines it as the relation of the creature to the cause which gives it its existence. Like Olieu and Vital du Four, Richard is a witness to the controversy concerning the composition of *essentia* and *esse*. Its origin is not Henry of Ghent (Hocedez, p. 397), but, rather, the very author of the distinction, namely, Thomas Aquinas. See P. Mandonnet, *Les premières disputes sur la distinction réelle*, RT., 18, (1910), p. 748); 1276 is about the time when the distinction became a controversial issue. Concerning Richard's own position see texts in Hocedez, pp. 397-401: Richard substantially agrees with Henry of Ghent; on the position of Giles of Rome, pp. 402-407.

[50] On the hylomorphic composition of angels, texts in Hocedez, pp. 190-191 and p. 257. On the debate then in progress on this question, see the remarkable Appendix VII, in Hocedez, pp. 454-477, with the respective contributions of Henry of Ghent, Giles of Lessines and Giles of Rome to the controversy. A useful chronological table of the relevant writings, from 1275 up to 1288, follows in Appendix VIII, pp. 478-479.

[51] Richard distinguishes between a matter which is *res pure possibilis,* and the matter which receives forms and is part of the composite. The first matter has no actuality of its own, but the second one has an inferior actuality, so much so that God could miraculously make it subsist apart from its form, pp. 191-192. Theological reasons are backing this position. The first matter (pure possibility) is between actuality and nothingness. An extraordinary sentence says that it is transmuted into form: "Quod quidem principium pure possibile transmutatur in ipsam formam" (p. 193). Cf.: "Res pure possibilis transmutabilis in formam," ibid. It is not the matter of the composites, it is its potency. This, as Hocedez has clearly seen, enables Richard to find an answer to the question: in what sense are forms educed from the potency of matter? (Hocedez, pp. 195-199). The "thing purely possible transmutable into form" looks like a substitute for the seminal reasons.—On the plurality of forms in man, texts in Hocedez, pp. 200-204; in Zavalloni, pp. 343-374; text of Richard, op. cit., 68-110. On the transition from Richard to Duns Scotus, Zavalloni, pp. 374-381.

[52] E. Hocedez, p. 162. See P. Duhem, *Léonard de Vinci, ceux qu'il a lus, ceux qui l'ont lu,* II, 368-372, 411-412; III, 274-275; *Le système du monde,* III, 484-488, and the penetrating remark of Hocedez, p. 161, that "it is in order to save the omnipotence of God that Richard has formulated his thesis on the infinite." On the possibility for God to impart to the farthest heaven a movement of translation, and on the laws of motion, Hocedez, pp. 163-167.—On the void and on infinite space, A Koyré, *Le vide et l'espace infini au XIVe siècle,* AHDL., 17 (1949) 67-75.

[53] Hocedez, p. 386. At the time of Richard, the Franciscan school finds itself challenged by new doctrines, including Thomism; it is on the defensive and must

often consent to yield some ground, but the school is not dead:

I. GONSALVUS HISPANUS (Gonsalvus of Balboa, de Valle Bona), master of Duns Scotus at Paris, d. 1313. GLOREP., II, 194-195. His *Conclusiones Metaphysicae Aristotelis* have been published under the name of Duns Scotus (Wadding, IV, 463-495; Vivès. VI, 601-667). Fr. Gonsalvi Hispani OFM., *Quaestiones disputatae et de Quodlibet,* by L. Amorós OFM., Quaracchi, 1925; excellent introduction, pp. LXV-LXXVI.—Gonsalvus upholds hylomorphism in both angel and man; matter is the same in all beings in which there is matter (*Qu.,* 11, pp. 213-216). Plurality of forms in man (*Qu.,* 14, 282). There is in man a *forma mixti* (*Qu.,* 14, 286-290). Extension of the plurality of forms to all other beings (*Qu.,* 14, pp. 290-305). Identity of the powers of the soul with its essence (*Qu.,* 10, pp. 165-171). Against the separate Intellects of Averroes (*Qu.,* 13, pp. 257-258); Gonsalvus grants to the soul a possible intellect but posits the agent Intellect as separate. This is "Platonis opinio et Augustini et Avicennae"; but Avicenna identifies this separate Intellect with an Intelligence inferior to God, which is wrong, whereas Plato and Augustine identify the agent Intellect with God, which is right. They do not use the expression *intellectus agens,* but they say "light" (p. 258). Objection: but then the *moderni doctores* contradict Augustine in agreeing to attribute an agent intellect to the human soul (*cum ergo doctores moderni concorditer ponant*); answer: "Besides the particular light of the soul called agent intellect, the moderns posit a universal uncreated light *illuminating every man that comes into this world,* and therefore they do not contradict Augustine," p. 259. Besides, this is the position of Aristotle, p. 262. These two intellects (agent and possible) are one single power of the soul, p. 265. The will is not determined by the intellect (*Qu.,* 3, pp. 30-41); it can act against the judgment of the intellect at all times (*Qu.,* 8, pp. 124-131; recalls the articles condemned in 1277). Freedom is in the will (*Qu.,* 12, pp. 230-242). The will is more noble than the intellect (*Qu.,* 4, pp. 52-67). Except the divine illumination understood under this somewhat crude form, all these positions, slightly modified, will survive in the Scotist school.

II. Another representative of the first Franciscan school, successor of Gonsalvus Hispanus as General Minister of the Franciscan Order in 1313, is ALEXANDER OF ALESSANDRIA (d. 1314). His commentary on the *Metaphysics* of Aristotle has been printed at Venice, in 1572, under the name of Alexander of Hales. His commentary on the *De anima,* Oxford, 1481. Commentary on the *Sentences* (2 redactions, before 1303 and after 1309), his *Quodlibet* and a *Summa questionum fr. Bonaventurae in IV libros Sententiarum,* are still unpublished. GLOLIT., II, 55-56; GLOREP., II, 199-202. V. Doucet, AFH., 27 (1934) 558-561.—A short fragment in *De humanae cognitionis . . . ,* Quaracchi, 1883, pp. 219-220, identifies the agent intellect of man with the eternal light of God: "Dicendum quod si eamdem veritatem cognoscimus, hoc non est nisi eadem luce aeterna, non per eamdem vim creatam, sed increatam. Ista lux aeterna in anima dicitur intellectus agens, licet cum hoc anima habeat aliquam lucem creatam." His doctrine of the intellect is said to resemble that of Peckham. On this little studied theologian, see L. Veuthey OFM., *Alexandre d'Alexandrie, maître de l'Université de Paris et ministre général des Frères Mineurs,* Etudes Franciscaines 43 (1931) 145-176, 319-344; 44 (1932), 21-42, 193-207, 321-336, 429-467 (good doctrinal introduction). Alexander has been identified as the source of Suarez's distinction of essence and existence: Corn. Fabro, *Una fonte antitomista della metafisica suareziana,* DTP., 50 (1947) 57-68. A rather passionate reply by R. Cenal, *Alejandro de Alejandria: su influjo en la metafiscia de Suarez,* Pensiamento, 4 (1948) 91-122, establishes the fact that many so-called "Thomists" have forsaken the position of Thomas on this crucial point, a point which C. Fabro has certainly no intention to deny.—On the formal distinction, B. Jansen. *Beiträge zur geschichtliche Entwicklung der Distinctio formalis,* ZKT., 53 (1929) 532-544.

[54] WILLIAM OF WARE ofm (*Guarro, Warro*), dates of birth and death unknown; certainly a Franciscan; seems to have been one of the teachers of Duns Scotus at the University of Paris about 1293.—GLOREP., II, 144-145. V. Doucet, AFH., 27 (1934) 558. H. Klug, *Zur Biographie der Minderbrüder Johannes Duns Scotus and Wilhelm von Ware,* FS., 2 (1915) 377-385. A. Daniels, *Zu den Beziehungen zwischen Wilhelm von Ware*

und Johannes Duns Scotus, FS., 4 (1917) 221-238. Fr. Pelster, *Handschriftliches zu Scotus mit neuen Angaben über sein Leben,* FS., 10 (1923) 2-6.—Texts in A. Daniels, *Quellenbeiträge und Untersuchungen . . . ,* 90-104 (proofs of the existence of God). Same author, *Wilhelm von Ware über das menschliche Erkennen,* in Festgabe Cl. Baeumker, Beiträge, Suppl. I, Münster i. W., 309-318 (intellectual knowledge). P. Muscat, *Guillelmi de Ware quaestio inedita de unitate Dei,* Antonianum, 2 (1927) 335-350. Ath. Ledoux, *De gratia creata et increata juxta Quaestionem ineditam Guillelmi de Ware,* Antonianum, 5 (1930) 148-156. A theological question on the immaculate conception is found in *Fr. Gulielmi Guarrae . . . Quaestiones disputatae de Imm. Conc. B. M. Virginis,* Quaracchi, 1904, 1-11.—On the doctrine: E. Longpré, *Guillaume de Ware,* La France Franciscaine, 6 (1922) 1-22. H. Spettmann, *Die philosophiegeschichtliche Stellung des Wilhelms von Ware,* PJ., 40 (1927) 401-413; 41 (1928) 42-49. J. Lechner, *Beiträge zum mittelalterlichen Franziskanerschrifttum, vornehmlich der Oxforder Schule des 13/14 Jahrh., auf Grund einer Florentiner Wilhelm von Ware-Hs.,* FS., 19 (1932) 1-12. E. Magrini, *La produzione letteraria di Guglielmo di Ware,* Miscellanea Francescana 36 (1936) 312-322, and 38 (1938) 411-429. J. Lechner, *Die mehrfachen Fassungen des Sentenzenkommentars des Wilhelm von Ware OFM.,* FS., 31 (1949) 14-31.

[55] On the existence of God, see William's *Quaestiones super libros Sententiarum,* qu. XIV; text in Aug. Daniels, *Quellenbeiträge und Untersuchungen . . . ,* pp. 90-104. The proofs are given following six ways: movement (Aristotle and Averroes), order of causes (Aristotle), order of the universe (Aristotle and Damascene), imperfection of beings (Anselm, *Monolog.,* I), possibility and necessity (R. of S. Victor, *De Trinit.,* I, 8, and Avicenna), presence of immutable truths in our minds (Augustine). Following an already Scotist order, William then proves the infinity of God (as pure act), p. 93, whence his omnipotence follows, pp. 93-95. Note, however, that the argument he uses p. 94 (there is an infinite distance from non-being to actual being) will be rejected by Scotus. On God's existence as a *per se nota* proposition, 98-104.—On the question of the oneness of God, William is of opinion that it cannot be

demonstrated without presupposing faith: "sola fide tenetur unum esse Deum," Muscat, Antonianum, 1927, 348. Arguing against some theologians, he observes that if their reasons prove the oneness of God, they prove as well that there cannot be three persons in the Trinity, p. 349. According to P. Muscat, many successors of William have subscribed to his conclusion: John Rodington, Joachim de Alta Villa, OC., Henricus de Oyta, Ockham. Rich. Swineshead, Joh. de Bassolis, Adam Wodham, Peter of Ailly, Robert Holkot, etc. It would be interesting to verify this list and to know if William has extended his criticism to other points.

[56] A. Daniels has published qu. XIX of the commentary of William on the *Sentences.* His argument follows the same line as that of Richard of Mediavilla: "Sicut natura non deficit in necessariis" as Augustine and Aristotle say "sic nec Deus," op. cit., p. 313. Yet, the next argument seems to be directed, among other men (Henry of Ghent?) against Richard, who had distinguished between two cognitions of truth: an imperfect one, for which natural light suffices, and a perfect one, which requires a divine illumination (pp. 313). William's own conclusion is that our natural light enables us to know, not only "certain things" with certitude (see Richard), but all things: "Unde concedendum quod anima potest videre aliqua, imo omnia naturaliter cognoscibilia mediante lumine naturali sine aliquo lumine supernaturali, subposita divina influentia generali," p. 316. This confirms the restrictive interpretation of the conclusion of Richard suggested by us in note 47. At the very moment he leaves Augustine and goes over to Thomas, William finds a consolation in defending Augustine against Thomas; compare William, p. 318, and Thomas, *Sum. theol.,* I, 84, 5, Resp. If, William says, Thomas had taken the Retractations of Augustine into account, he would have known that, at the end of his life, Augustine has given up the doctrine of the divine illumination. In short, Augustine died a Thomist.— With respect to the nature of the soul, William denies the existence of a spiritual matter and, consequently, the hylomorphic composition of angels and souls (see H. Spettman, PJ., 1928, 42-43).—On the unity of the powers of the soul with its substance, pp. 44-45.—On the primacy of nobility of the will in William of Ware

(his so-called "voluntarism") op. cit., pp. 46-49.

On another Franciscan master, contemporary with William, namely JOHN OF MURRO, see GLOREP., II, 125-126. E. Longpré, *L'oeuvre scolastique du cardinal Jean de Murro OFM.* (d. *1312*), MAP., 467-492. O. Lottin, PEM., III, 513-514, 648-649, notes. Against the attribution to Murro of the Commentary on the *Sentences*, Paris Nat. Lat. 16407: O. Lottin, *Le Commentaire des Sentences de Jean de Murro est-il trouvé?*, RHE., 44 (1949) 153-172.

[57] RAMON LULL (*Lullus, Lullius*) birth date unknown (1232/1235?) born at Palma de Mayorca, of a Catalan family; attached to the courts of Jaime I of Aragon, then of Jaime II of Mayorca, married in 1256 and lived a free courtly life up to the time of his "conversion" (1262). From that time on he devoted himself to the missionary work which became his main interest in life. All his activities were related to it: foundation of the college of Miramar (Mayorca); missionary work in Asia (1279), in Armenia (1302), in Africa (1280, 1293, 1306, 1314); last, not least, the writing of an incredible number of Catalan and Latin works (including those related to the "Great Art") all of them concerned with the propagation of the faith. His reputation was such that, without having obtained any degree in theology at the University of Paris, he was permitted to teach his doctrine there three times (1287-1289, 1297-1299, 1309-1311). After a last missionary voyage to Africa, during which he was tortured for the faith, he died on the ship (1316) on his way back to Mayorca. Lull is said to have joined the Third-Order of Saint Francis in 1292. The relics of Blessed Ramon Lull are the object of public veneration in the church of San Francisco de Palma in Mayorca. Incidentally, the American city of San Francisco derives its name from this church and the adjoining Franciscan monastery, whose missionaries were its first founders. See GLOREP., II, 146-191. E. Longpré, art. *Raymond Lulle*, DTC., 9 (1926) 1072-1141. E. A. Allison Peers, *Ramon Lull, A Biography*, London, 1929 (fundamental). A necessary document is the short anonymous *Vida coetania*, ed. F. de Moll, Palma de Mallorca, 1935.—Still deserving to be consulted, E Littré *Raymond Lulle*, HLF., 29 (1835) 1-386;

pages 1-67 are a biography of Lull by B. Hauréau.

WRITINGS. B. *Raymundi Lulli . . . Opera . . .*, by Y. Salzinger, 8 vols., Mainz, 1721-1742; on the history of this edition, A. Gottron, FS., 3 (1916) 214-235, 379-396.—Separate works: *Liber de Immaculata Beatissimae Virginis Conceptione*, ed. J. Avinyó, Barcelona, 1901. *Declaratio Raymundi per modum dialogi edita contra aliquorum philosophorum et eorum sequacium opiniones erroneas et damnatas a venerabili patre et domino episcopo Parisiensi: seu liber contra errores Boethii et Sigerii*, in Otto Keicher, *Raymundus Lullus und seine Stellung zur arabischen Philosophie*, Münster i. W., 1909 (Beiträge, 7, 4-5). C. Ottaviano, *L'ars compendiosa de R. Lulle*, Paris, 1930.—F. Stegmüller, *De ostentione per quam fides catholica est probabilis et demonstrabilis;* P. Gàlscécs, *De vita divina;* J. Giers, *De Deo majore et de Deo minore;* S. Galmès, *Ars infusa*, in Studia monographica, Lullist School of Medieval Studies, VII-VIII, Mallorca, 1952. Letter of Lull to the University of Paris urging the study of Oriental languages, UNIV., 125-127.—The Catalan writings of Lull are mainly concerned with contemplative and mystical life; bibliography in Allison Peers, 425-426; English translations, p. 426. Fr. Sureda Blanes, *Bases criteriologicas del pensamiento Luliano,* (Mallorca?) 1935; bibliography, 23-35. M. Battlori, *Introducción bibliografica a los estudios lulianos*, Palma de Mallorca, 1945. Bibliographical bulletin: *Studia monographica et recensiones*, School for Lullist Studies, Palma de Mallorca, 1947 ff.

BIBLIOGRAPHY. For E. Longpré and A. Peers, see *supra*. GDP., 758-759. T. and J. Carreras y Artau, *Historia de la Filosofia Española. Filosofia cristiana de los siglos VIII al XV*, I, Barcelona, 1935. J.-H. Probst, *Caractère et origines des idées du Bx Raymond Lulle (Ramon Lull)*, Toulouse, 1912; *La mystique de Raymond Lulle et l'Art de Contemplacio*, Münster i. W., 1914 (Beiträge, 13, 2-3). Fr. Sureda Blanes, *El beato Ramon Lull. Su epoca, sus obras, suas empresas*, Madrid, 1934. E. W. Platzeck, *Die Lullsche Kombinatorik. Ein erneuter Darstellungs-und Deutungsversuch mit Bezug auf die gesamteuropäische Philosophie*, FS., 34 (1952) 32-60.

[58] O. Keicher (*Raymundus Lullus . . . ,*

pp. 62-71) rightly stresses the importance of Averroism as a determining factor of Lull's attitude concerning the relation of reason and faith. See the text where a Saracen king answers the Christian missionary: "I do not want to exchange belief for belief, but for understanding," p. 63, n. 2. Again: "A clever man is more likely to be led to truth by reasons than by faith and authorities," p. 64, n. 2. Again: "It is better for a man to demonstrate the truth to the intellect of his adversary than to force him to confess it without having been conducted to it and convinced of it," p. 64, n. 4. Nevertheless, Lull never thought that the mysteries of faith could be really demonstrated; like all theologians of his time, he wanted to support them by reasons and to show that none of them could be demonstrated to be false.

[59] Lull's *Declaratio per modum dialogi* (ed. O. Keicher) is explicitely directed against the 219 articles condemned by E. Tempier in 1277 (op. cit., p. 95). The stage is set in a forest near Paris and Socrates obviously represents the "philosophers" who maintained that these propositions were true according to philosophy (94-95). Hence the 219 chapters of the dialogue, each of which answers one of the 219 condemned propositions. Ramon begins by enumerating the "principles" of his "table" and persuades Socrates to accept the rules of his own recently discovered method of discussion. Then he defines what he calls "the common opinions of all the great philosophers," and, first of all: "That God exists, that he is the prime cause and that the whole world is his effect in its universality as well as in each one of its parts," etc. (98-99). When Socrates is not fully convinced, for instance concerning the Trinity, Ramon refers him to one of his other works. (cf. ch. XVI, p. 118) in which, however, he does not pretend that he has convinced Socrates of the necessity of faith; Socrates simply answers that he will try to see if his intellect assents to Ramon's words and if he feels love for them in his will, p. 120. Nevertheless, ch. XXXVI, Ramon considers Socrates as bound by an assent he has not given, op. cit., p. 138.

[60] This is the eighth rule of the *Ars Magna* (O. Keicher, p. 99). Socrates assents to it, as to many other ones, and

he could not do differently, since everything Ramon has said is evident, p. 101. Some among the answers of Ramon throw a vivid light on the reasons for the condemnation of certain articles. For instance: VII, "That the human intellect is not the act of the body, except as the pilot is that of his ship," etc.; because this favors the doctrine of the separate agent intellect (pp. 110-111). XI, "That man is man apart from the rational soul"; same reason (pp. 113-115). XIII and XIV, likewise condemned as threatening the substantial unity of man (pp. 116-117). XXIII, "That God cannot give felicity to a man without giving it to another man"; rejected as presupposing that beings flow from God with necessity. XXVII, "That God could not make more than one soul"; same answer (pp. 130-131). XLIX, "That God could not move the heavens by a straight motion, because, otherwise, there would be a void left"; his own answer to this article (p. 143) remarkably illustrates what has been said in this chapter about Richard of Middleton. On several other points (chapters, 70, 87, 118 (separate agent intellect), 168 (continence not necessary), the explanations provided by Socrates help in ascertaining the meaning of the condemned propositions in the minds of the "philosophers." Ramon's remark (p. 220) on the "venerabiles domini mei theologi sive doctores in theologia, qui sunt columnae sanctae fidei christianae," vividly illustrate the remarks of M.-D. Chenu, *Introduction* . . . , 18-19, on the new status acquired in the Church by the theologians. In the twelfth century, the sentence of Ramon could not have been written. The answer of Socrates: "Let us go to Paris and present our book to these venerable Masters, so that it be corrected by them" (p. 221) is little more likely in the mouth of an Averroist than in that of the real Socrates. But what Ramon himself desired was to reconcile the masters of the two faculties, that is, the *venerabiles magistri regentes Parisius in philosophia* and their colleagues in the Faculty of Theology. This seems to have been for him one more personal mission to fulfill: "quia bonum zelum habui et multum desidero magnam concordantiam esse inter dominos meos magistros in theologia et in philosophia," p. 221.

[61] An important witness to the later influence of R. Lull is the *Liber creatura-*

rum of Ramon Sibiude (Raymond Sebond, Raymond de Sebonde) published at Deventer under the title *"Theologia naturalis"* (about 1484), but written at the University of Toulouse in 1436. It was translated into French by Montaigne, in whose *Essays* the well-known *Apologie de Raymond Sebond* is included. The so-called "skepticism" of Montaigne is partly due to the fact that, having translated a theology in which, after the Lullist manner, practically all dogmas are more or less demonstrable, he felt justified in showing that, even in the order of natural knowledge, we believe many things just about as unbelievable as most of the Christian dogmas; in fact, at least in his

Apologie, the attitude of Montaigne is a rational scepticism redeemed by a religious fideism, itself a reaction to what was improperly called the "Christian rationalism" of R. Lull.—On Ramon Sibiude, G. Compayré, *De Ramundo Sebundo et de Theologiae naturalis libro,* Paris, 1872. J.-H. Probst, *Le lullisme de Raymond de Sebonde,* Toulouse, 1912. J. Coppin, *Montaigne traducteur de Raymond Sebond,* Lille, 1925. T. Carreras Y Artau, *Origenes de la filosofia de Raimundo Sibiuda (Sabunde),* Barcelona, 1928. M. Dorer, *Montaignes Apologie des Raimund von Sabunde und ihre Bedeutung für den Skeptizismus,* PJ., 40 (1927) 414-422, and 41 (1928) 71-82.

PART EIGHT

CHAPTER II. SCHOLASTIC THEOLOGIANS IN ENGLAND

[62] RICHARD FISHACRE OP. On his life and works, F. Pelster, *Das Leben und die Schriften des Oxforder Dominikanerlehrers Richard Fishacre,* in ZKT., 54 (1930) 515-553. D. E. Sharp, *The Philosophy of Richard Fishacre* (d. *1248*), NS., 7 (1933) 281-297. For the question published by A. Daniels, see note 64. More general points of view adopted in: R. M. Martin, *La question de l'unité de la forme substantielle dans le premier collège dominicain à Oxford (1221-1248),* RNSP., 22 (1920) 107-112. O. Lottin, *La notion du libre arbitre dans la jeune école dominicaine d'Oxford,* RSPT., 24 (1935) 268-283: Fishacre, 269-275; Kilwardby, 275-283 (important fragments of unpublished works by these masters).

[63] In his commentary on the *Sentences,* Richard maintained the hylomorphic composition of angels and souls (D. Sharp, art. cit., pp. 287-288); on "seminal reasons," pp. 295-296, a position which, D. Sharp rightly says, does "violence both to Augustine and to Aristotle" (p. 296); on intellectual cognition in the divine light, pp. 288-293; on the existence of God, pp. 293-294; on the relations of intellect and will, pp. 294-295; divine knowledge of singulars, p. 296.—Man is neither soul nor body, he is a substantial composite of both; note here a distinct reaction against Avicenna's (and Augustine's) definition of man as being primarily a soul (p. 284). Concerning the unity of

the soul, he distinguishes three positions: 1, the three souls are one substance and only differ as to operation; 2, the human soul is one single substance, but it has different forms mutually ordered and related; 3, there are three substances, causes of their respective operations, yet these three substances make up one soul, as the hand is one although made up of nerves, bones and flesh (p. 285). He does not "dare" to choose between these three opinions (p. 286). Although it seems to be implied by most of his positions, Richard does not explicitly recognize the "form of corporeity," op. cit., p. 286.—Another text, published by Stegmüller in connection with questions by Robert Kilwardby, introduces an interesting distinction between two kinds of memory: 1, the memory of sensible species and images preserved in the possible intellect; 2, the *habitus* of the intelligible forms which, in us, is that of the agent intellect. For this second memory, Fishacre refers to Augustine, *Retract.,* I, 9; *De Trinitate,* X, 8 and XIV, 5. This doctrine will be developed by his pupil Kilwardby, who will also maintain, with Fishacre, that to know and to love are one and the same act of the soul; text in AHDL., 10-11 (1936) 334-335. This position agrees with the oneness of the substantial form of the soul, but it does not prevent the same masters from teaching the hylomorphic composition of the soul, the plurality of souls within man, and, consequently, the plurality of forms.

[64] Judging from the question published by Aug. Daniels, *Quellenbeiträge und Untersuchungen* . . . , 22-24, Fishacre proves the existence of God as the supreme good, cause of all finite good (Boethius); then as the non-caused cause of all; then he posits God's existence as self-evident (Anselm) and, finally, as evidently known from the mere existence of truth (Augustine): if God is not, it is true to say that "God is not"; hence some truth exists; if this truth is eternal, then it is God; if it is not eternal, then its opposite, "God is" has been eternally true (pp. 23-24).

[65] RICHARD RUFUS OFM. (Richard of Cornwall). On his life and works, A. G. Little, *The Franciscan School at Oxford in the XIIIth century*, AFH., 19 (1926) 803-874, particularly 841-845. Several contributions by Fr. Pelster, *Zu Richardus Rufus de Cornubia*, ZKT., 48 (1924) 625-629; *Der älteste Sentenzenkommentar aus der Oxforder Franziskanerschule*, Scholastik, 1 (1926) 50-80; *Roger Bacons "Compendium studii theologiae" und der Sentenzenkommentar des Richardus Rufus*, ibid., 4 (1929) 410-416; *Neue Schriften des englischen Franziskaners Richardus Rufus von Cornwall*, ibid., 8 (1933) 561-568, 9 (1934) 256-264; *Quästionen des Franziskaners Richardus Rufus de Cornubia (um 1250) in Cod. VII C. 19 der Nationalbibliothek Neapel und Cod. 138 der Stadtbibliothek Assisi*, ibid., 14 (1949) 215-233; *Die älteste Abkürzung und Kritik vom Sentenzenkommentar des hl. Bonaventura. Ein Werk des Richardus Rufus*, Gregorianum, 17 (1936) 195-223. *Der Oxforder Theologe Richardus Rufus OFM. über die Frage: "Utrum Christus in triduo mortis fuerit homo,"* RTAM., 16 (1949) 259-280; *Richardus Rufus Anglicus OFM. (c. 1250) ein Vorläufer des Duns Scotus in der Lehre der priestlicher Lossprechung*, Scholastik, 25 (1950) 549-552.—Willibrord Lampen, *De Fr. Richardo Rufo Cornubiensi*, in AFH., 21 (1928) 403-406. F. M. Henquinet, *Autour des écrits d'Alexander de Hales et de Richard Rufus*, Antonianum, 11 (1936) 187-218. D. A. Callus, *Two Early Oxford Masters*, RNSP., 42 (1939), 424-432, 439-445; *Introduction of Aristotelian Learning to Oxford*, pp. 36-37.

[66] Fragments of Richard's works have been published by O. Lottin, PEM., I, 185-198, 454-459; II (1948) 303-312.

D. A. Callus, *Two Early Oxford Masters*, pp. 439-445. Fr. Pelster, *Der Oxforder Theologe*, 275-280.

[67] According to Augustine, the soul is one substance; but "philosophy" affirms the contrary" (cf. Aristotle, *De gener. animalium*, II, 3, 736 a 36-b 5) "Thus there seems to be complete contradiction between philosophers and theologians" (text in D. A. Callus, *Two Early Oxford Theologians*, 439, 441). "What should I say here?" (p. 441). "Some hold these (philosophical) opinions and do not worry much about the authorities of the Saints when these deal with natural beings and with philosophical matters, but only in those cases when the Saints speak of things that belong to faith. In these latter cases, it is the Holy Ghost that speaks in the Saints; consequently, in such matters, the Saints cannot err. In natural sciences, however, the Saints speak as men. Consequently it is not to be wondered that, in these matters, something escaped their sight" (p. 442). He himself feebly favors a compromise between philosophers and theologians: the sensitive and the vegetative are in man in a twofold way: first, as powers of the soul and numerically one with its substance; secondly, as distinct substances (and not simply powers) coming from matter and making man an imperfect animal to be further perfected by the rational soul with its powers. Here, however, Richard wonders if this position can be reconciled with that of Hugh of St. Victor (PL., 175, 418 D-419 C) and of Augustine, D. A. Callus, op. cit., pp. 443-444. The sources of Richard are (ibid., p. 431) Philip the Chancellor, John of La Rochelle, Fishacre, "and above all the anonymous commentary on the *De anima* in Merton College, ms., 272, ff.211 rb-212 va." The conclusion of Richard on this point is: I do not conclude.

[68] On Richard's hylomorphism, Fr. Pelster, Scholastik, 8 (1933) 562-563. In another passage, he calls his adversary "fly foot" (*pes muscae*); op. cit., 567.

[69] ROBERT KILWARDBY OP (d. 1279). Most of his published texts are included in studies on his life and doctrine: GDP., 764. L. Baur, *Dominicus Gundissalinus De divisione philosophiae*, 369-375. Letter to Peter of Confians, Fr. Ehrle, *Der Augustinismus und der Aristotelismus in der*

Scholastik gegen Ende des 13. Jahrhunderts, ALKM., 5 (1889) 614-632. Cf. Al. Birkenmajer, *Vermischte Untersuchungen,* Münster i. W., 1932, 36-69. (Beiträge, 20, 5.) M.-D. Chenu, *Le De spiritu imaginativo de Robert Kilwardby,* RSPT., 15 (1926) 507-517; *Le De conscientia de Robert Kilwardby,* RSPT., 16 (1927) 318-326; *Les réponses de saint Thomas et de Kilwardby à la consultation de Jean de Verceil, 1271,* MM., 1930, I, 191-222; *Le traité De tempore de R. Kilwardby,* ADGM., 1935, 855-861; *Aux origines de la "science moderne,"* RSPT., 29 (1940) 206-217. F. Stegmüller, *Les questions du Commentaire des Sentences de Robert Kilwardby,* RTAM., 6 (1934) 55-79, 215-228; *Robert Kilwardby OP. über die Möglichkeit der natürlichen Gottesliebe,* DTP., 38 (1935) 306-319. D. E. Sharp, *Further Philosophical Doctrines of Kilwardby,* NS., 9 (1935) 39-65 (quotations from the Commentary); *The 1277 Condemnation of Kilwardby,* NS., 8 (1934) 306-318. Fr. Stegmüller, *Der Traktat des Robert Kilwardby OP. De imagine et vestigio Trinitatis,* AHDL., 10 (1935-1936) 324-407. E. M. F. Sommer-Seckendorff, *Studies in the Life of Robert Kilwardby OP.,* Roma, 1937. D. A. Callus, *The Condemnation of St. Thomas at Oxford,* Oxford, 1946, pp. 12-18; *The "Tabulae super originalia Patrum" of Robert Kilwardby OP.,* in *Studia Mediaevalia* (Miscellanea Martin), 1948, 243-270. Cf. *New Manuscripts of Kilwardby's Tabulae super originalia Patrum,* Dominican Studies, 2 (1949) 38-45.

[70] The list of the commentaries on Aristotle ascribed to Kilwardby has not yet been critically established; see, however, valuable information on this point in Stegmüller, RTAM., 6 (1934) 57-60; list of the questions contained in the *Commentary on the Sentences,* ibid., 61-79 and 215-228. Cf. E.M.F. Sommer-Seckendorff, *Studies . . . ,* 14-15.

[71] On this treatise, see D. E. Sharp, *The "De ortu scientiarum" of Robert Kilwardby,* NS., 8 (1934) 1-30. E. M. F. Sommer-Seckendorff, Historisches Jahrbuch, 55 (1955) 312-324 (Festgabe-H. Finke). Also the older study of L. Baur, see n. 69. It is a classification of sciences in the tradition of the Victorines and of Gundissalinus. Mechanical arts are included in the classification (cf. Bonaventure, *De reductione artium . . .*). The

general division of philosophy is as follows: I, Philosophy of divine things: natural, mathematical, metaphysical; II, Philosophy of human things: 1) Practical philosophy, that is, *a*) Ethics, personal, familial or public; *b*) Mechanical arts; 2), Logic.

[72] Kilwardby prohibited the teaching at Oxford of fourteen propositions pertaining to grammar and logic, among which: 6, that necessary truth requires the constancy of its object (wrong, since the divine cognition of contingents is necessarily true); 7, that there can be no demonstration except about existing beings (wrong, since demonstrations about non-existing essences are possible); 8, that every true proposition concerning the future is necessary (wrong, unless one takes into account the free decision of God to create a contingent). The sixteen following propositions (in "natural philosophy") concern the human soul and the seminal reasons; on these, see note 73. Text of the prohibition in CUP., I, 558-559; cf. D. Sharp, *The 1277 Condemnation by Kilwardby,* NS., 8 (1934) 307-308, n. 2.

[73] The answer of Robert to Peter of Conflans limits itself to seven (out of the sixteen) condemned articles to whose prohibition Peter had taken exception. All these, Robert says, are both scientifically false and religiously untenable. He deals with them successively, but they all are related to the problem of the "seminal reasons." Robert sees no difficulty in reconciling this Augustinian doctrine with Aristotle if it is admitted that, according to the Philosopher, there is in matter something of the form, in short an "active potency" (text in Ehrle, 618). Whether this active potency is called "seminal reason" or not is of no importance. On the strength of this position, Robert Kilwardby successively maintains that: 1, in passing away the form is not corrupted into pure nothingness (because, since corruption is the opposite of generation, if the corruption of a form were an annihilation, its coming to be would be a creation); 2, there is an active potency in matter; for indeed, there are three matters, *a*) a matter common to both corporeal and spiritual substances; *b*) a matter common to both sublunary bodies (*recta:* i.e., moving along straight lines) and heavenly bodies (*circularia:* i.e., bodies whose natural motion is a circular

one); c) a matter common to terrestrial elements and to their compounds (Ehrle, 616-617; compare the first matter with the "pure possibility" of Richard of Mediavilla): the first two matters are studied in metaphysics, the third one in physics (note, p. 620, *Denique verba . . .*), that Peter of Conflans himself seemed to grant the presence of a pseudo-Aristotelian inchoation of active form in matter); 3, privation is not pure nothingness; it is one of the principles of generation, hence it cannot be nothing; 4, the generation of animals is not like the transformation of elements, otherwise dreadful moral consequences would follow (p. 622) and the transmigration of human souls could be maintained (p. 623; the "unreadable" word mentioned by Ehrle probably is *compares*); 5, there is in the embryo and in man only one substance, not several: because the three souls are essentially distinct, and "their primordial reasons have been inherent in the matter of transmutable things from the very beginning, so that, in consequence, they arise out of the works created by God, in virtue of his government of the world during the course of centuries" (p. 627). Naturally, the human soul is a single substance, yet it is composed of parts, as the Philosopher and Augustine agree (p. 628); 6, the vegetative, the sensitive and the intellective souls are distinct substances: this is made evident by what precedes, and, besides, God alone is simple. The 7th article, unknown to Ehrle, has been published by A. Birkenmajer, *Der Brief Robert Kilwardby an Peter von Conflans und die Streitschrift des Aegidius von Lessines,* Münster i. W., 1922, pp. 60-64 (Beiträge, 20, 5). Kilwardby says that the so-called doctrine of the unity of form ("positio de unitate formae") is something unheard of to him and which he does not understand. It seems to mean that, on its arrival, the latest form takes up and exercises the operations formerly produced by the preceding ones, which are totally corrupted (Birkenmajer, 60). This is visibly false, since we see that, in any human body, flesh, bones, nerves, blood, eye, foot, all have their own forms (ibid., 60). Again, if this were true, "nothing would be composed except of matter and form" (ibid., 61). After accumulating arguments, both philosophical and theological (the body of Christ after his death and the Eucharist, 62-63), he concludes

with an excellent re-exposition of the doctrine of the plurality of forms, ibid., 63-64. This seventh point is the object of the discussion of Giles of Lessines in his own treatise *De unitate formarum.* See Part IX, ch. 4, note 90. A large number of variants and corrections to the text of the Letter published by Ehrle is to be found in A. Birkenmajer, op. cit., pp. 49-64.

[74] What is known of the other writings of Kilwardby confirms the stability of the positions upheld in the answer to Peter of Conflans: hylomorphism (Sharp, NS., 9 (1935), 41, 47-52); self-individuation of the composite (ibid., 53-54); reduction of the powers of the soul to its substance: Stegmüller, AHDL., 10-11 (1936) 365; on the unity of knowledge and love, or *aspectus* and *affectus,* ibid., 370-374; active nature of sense knowledge, ibid., 401, and Chenu, RSPT., 15 (1926) 510-511; on the two memories: that of Aristotle for received sensible species and that of Augustine for intelligible species, ibid., 366, 377-380, 394, the divine illumination being unknown to Augustine, Sharp, NS., 9 (1935) 42-43. The doctrine of the memory of the past species (Aristotle) should be related to that of imagination (the *spiritus imaginativus*), Chenu, RSTP., 15 (1926) 509-510.

[75] P. Duhem, *Etudes sur Léonard de Vinci . . . ,* II, 411-412.

[76] P. Duhem, op. cit., III, p. xi.

[77] M.-D. Chenu, *Les réponses de saint Thomas et de Robert Kilwardby . . . ,* MM., I, 191-222.

[78] John Peckham ofm. (d. 1292). GLOLIT., II, 173-180. GLOREP., II, 87-98: biography, 87; scientific writings (including the *Perspectiva communis*), 87-88; commentary on *I Sent.,* 88 *h.* Cf. V. Doucet, AFH., 27 (1934) 548-549. Correspondence of Peckham: *Registrum epistolarum fr. Johannis Pecham,* ed. C. T. Martin, London, 3 vols. 1882-1885. —H. Spettmann, *Johannis Pechami Quaestiones tractantes de anima,* Munster i. W., 1918 (Beiträge, 19, 5-6); *Die Psychologie des Johannes Pecham,* Münster i. W., 1919 (Beiträge, 20, 6). More texts in *De humanae cognitionis ratione (Quodl.,* III, 4) 179-182; H. Spettmann, DTF., 5 (1927) 327-345; A. Daniels, *Quellenbei-*

träge . . . , 41-50. Kingsford, Little and Tocco, *Johannis Peckham* . . . *tractatus tres,* British Society of Franciscan Studies, II (1910) 121-147. *Summa de ente et essentia,* ed. F. Delorme, Studi Francescani, 25 (1928) 61-71. F. Delorme, *Johannis Pecham, Archiepiscopi Cantuarensis, Quodlibetum Romanum,* Roma, 1938. G. Melani, *Tractatus de anima Johannis Pecham,* Firenze, 1949; Appendix: *In I Sent.,* d. 3, 9. 3. *Arithmetica mystica,* ch. 1-5. Question *On the Root of Constancy (Postilla Super Cantica).* Florentine *Quodlibet,* quaest. 2-3, 5-6.

BIBLIOGRAPHY.—H. Spettmann, *Quellenkritisches zur Biographie des Johannes Peckham,* FS., 2 (1915) 170-207, 266-285; *Der Ethikkommentar des Johannes Peckham,* Beiträge, Supplementband II, 1923, 221-242; *Der Sentenzenkommentar des Franziskaner-Erzbischofs Johannes Peckham (d. 1292),* DTF., 5 (1927) 327-345; *Pechams Kommentar zum IV. Buch der Sentenzen,* ZKT., 52 (1928) 64-74. E. Gilson, *Pourquoi saint Thomas* . . . , AHDL., I (1926) 99-104. D. E. Sharp, *Franciscan Philosophy* . . . , 175-207. A. Callebaut, *Jean Peckham OFM., et l'Augustinisme,* AFH., 18 (1925) 441-472. A. Teetaert, art. *Pecham,* DTC., 12 (1933) 100-140. V. Doucet, *Notulae bibliographicae de quibusdam operibus fr. Joannis Peckham,* Antonianum, 8 (1933) 307-328, 425-459; texts.—On the Oxford controversies and condemnations, F. Ehrle, *John Peckham über den Kampf des Augustinismus und Aristotelismus im XIII Jahrhundert,* ZKT., 13 (1889) 172-193. P. Glorieux, *Comment les thèses thomistes furent proscrites à Oxford,* RT., 32 (1927) 259-291. M. D. Knowles, *Some Aspects of the Career of Archbishop Peckham,* English Historical Review, 58 (1942) 1-18, 178-201. D. A. Callus, *The Condemnation of St. Thomas at Oxford,* London, 1946; on Knapwell's reaction, 32-38. D. L. Douie, *Archbishop Peckham,* Oxford, 1952; on the Oxford condemnations, ch. VII, pp. 272-301.

[79] J. Peckham, *Registrum epistolarum* . . . , III, 871, 901-902. This text, together with the collection of Disputed Questions *De humanae cognitionis ratione* (which could be made much longer than it is) should dispose of the opinion that the problem of human knowledge was not a living issue, in the thirteenth century. Its properly metaphysical connotations have been masterfully summed up by Thomas Aquinas in his *De veritate,* q. 11, a. 1, Resp.

[80] The positions of Peckham conform to the *theologia communis* of the thirteenth century.—MATTER, can be created apart from form, *Quodl. rom.,* ed. Delorme, 2-5; created common to spiritual and to corporeal beings, *Qu. de anima,* ed. H. Spettmann, 8.—SOUL, its hylomorphic composition, *Qu. de anima,* 49-50; is a rational substance, *Tract. de anima,* 14, p. 47; the noblest of all spiritual forms, it is immortal, 15, pp. 48-51; cf. *Qu. de anima,* 23, 26 (ad 13m, noteworthy). Only one soul, ibid., 36; yet with a threefold substance, ibid., 37; presupposes corporeity as form of the body, *Quodl. rom.,* 63-64; united to the body through vital spirits, *Tract. de anima,* VII, 5, p. 27; its powers are rooted in its essence, op. cit., p. 44: "Sed sciendum . . ."; the sensitive soul and its actions, sensation as an act, Florentine *Quodlibet,* II, in Melani, *Tract. de anima,* 147-149; Avicennian division of the intellects, G. Melani, in *Tract. de anima,* 86-87; on sensible and intelligible species, *Qu. de anima,* 84-87; on the self-knowledge of the soul by mode of presence, not of form, *Quodl. romanum,* 69-70.—GOD, on the demonstrations of the existence of God, *In I Sent.,* d. 2, q. 1, in Aug. Daniels, *Quellenbeiträge* . . . , 41-50. The being of God is object of faith, but his existence is naturally known to man (ref. to Damascene, I, 1); this natural knowledge is confirmed by arguments drawn from creatures, but these arguments do not prevent it from being held by faith (p. 45). Moreover, since God is his own being, he cannot be conceived as non-existent, pp. 49-50.—A detailed study of Peckham's doctrinal positions remains a much needed desideratum.

[81] "The agent intellect of which the Philosopher speaks is in no way part of the soul; rather, as I believe, it is God, who is the light of minds . . . ," etc., in *Johannis Pechami qu. de anima,* ed. H. Spettmann, p. 73. Against Avicenna and Averroes, 49-52, 65. Against Thomas Aquinas, 66. For Augustine, 66-68.— *Quodlibetum romanum.* ed. F. Delorme, 11-13; note, p. 13: "However, this does not exclude the created light of the natural intellect. . . ."—*Tractatus de anima,* ed. G. Melani, ch. III, 9-12 (about 1271-1279, strictly Augustinian); historical commentary by Melani, pp. 109-115.

Cf. Appendix I, the question *I Sent.*, d. 3, q. 3, pp. 131-138.

[82] For a striking specimen of this curious complex, see the *Arithmetica mystica*, in G. Melani, *Tractatus de anima*, Appendix II, pp. 138-144. It is strongly influenced by the *De musica* of Augustine, and Peckham does not forget the presence of the Platonic definitions of the soul (p. 144): a substance full of numbers, or, rather, a self-moving number: *Laws*, X, 895-896; *Phaedrus*, ch. 24.

[83] SIMON OF FAVERSHAM. F. M. Powicke, *Master Simon of Faversham*, Mélanges

Ferd. Lot, Paris, 1925, 649-658. C. Ottaviano, *Le "Questiones super libro Predicamentorum" di Simone di Faversham, dal. ms. Ambrosiano C. 161, Inf.*, Memorie della Reale Accademia dei Lincei, ser. 6, vol. 3, fasc. 4; *Le opere di Simone di Faversham e la sua posizione nel problema degli universali*, Archivio di Filosofia, 1931, 15-29. M. Grabmann, *Die Aristoteleskommentare des Simon von Faversham (d. 1306), handschriftliche Mitteilungen*, Sitzungsberichte . . . , Munich, 1933, n. 3. D. Sharp, *Simonis de Faversham (c. 1240-1306) Quaestiones super tertium de Anima*, AHLD., 9 (1934) 307-368.—A. G. Little, OTT., 262-265.

PART EIGHT

CHAPTER III. SAINT THOMAS AQUINAS

[84] Plato, *Alcibiades*, 129 E. Plotinus, *Enneads*, I, 1, 3. Augustine, *De quantitate animae*, XIII, 22; PL., 32, 1048, popularized in the middle ages by the pseudo-Augustinian *De spiritu et anima*, I, PL., 40, 781. Another text, quoted by Philip the Chancellor and other theologians, denies that the soul is in the body as a form is in matter: *De immortalitate animae*, X, 17; PL., 32, 1030. This alone was an invitation not to define the soul as being, *in itself*, the form of its body. It also favored the doctrine of the plurality of forms. On this question: G. M. Manser, *Augustins Philosophie . . .*, DTF., 10 (1932) 19-20. J. Müller, *Ist die Lehre von der Mehrheit der substantiellen Formen augustinisch?*, DTF., 20 (1942) 237-252.

[85] The thread that runs unbroken throughout this whole tradition (including Albert the Great) is the text of Augustine's *Soliloquies*, I, 8, 15; PL., 32, 877. It still reappears, as late as the fifteenth century, in the *Liber de anima* of William of Vaurouillon OFM., (d. 1463); ed. Ign. Brady, in MS., 11 (1949) 294.

[86] P. Mandonnet has given a description of mediaeval Augustinism, or rather of its "general physiognomy": absence of a formal distinction between the domains of theology and of philosophy, attribution of a positive actuality to prime matter, seminal reasons, universal hylomorphism, plurality of forms (P. Mandonnet, *Siger of Brabant*, Louvain, 1911, pp. 55-57).

M. de Wulf (*Le traité de unitate formae de Gilles de Lessines*, Louvain, 1901, 16-19) considers as Augustinian the following positions: primacy of good and of will, substantial independence of the soul with respect to the body, seminal reasons, active nature of sense cognition. He denies the Augustinian character of the doctrine of divine illumination as taught by Bonaventure and Matthew of Aquasparta; he maintains that their notion of matter is more directly related to the doctrine of Aristotle. Such controversies are mostly about names.

[87] D. A. Callus, *The Condemnation . . .*, p. 4.

[88] *Sum. theol.*, II-II, 188, 5, ad 3m. On the authority of Augustine, *De musica* VI, conclusion; PL., 32, 1194.

[89] On the nature of theology and its relations to philosophical sciences, the fundamental text is *Summa theologiae*, Part I, qu. 1. The interpretation of these deceptively simple articles has given rise to many controversies. The ancient commentators, especially Bañez, should be consulted. In recent times: M.-D. Chenu, *La théologie comme science au XIIIe siècle*, 2 éd., Paris, J. Vrin, 1943. Against the first article of Chenu on the question, AHDL., 2 (1927) 31-71: J.-Fr. Bonnefoy, *La nature de la théologie selon saint Thomas d'Aquin*, Ephemerides theologicae Lovanienses, 14 (1937) 421-446, 600-631; 15 (1938) 491-516; published

separately, Paris, J. Vrin, 1939. R. Gagne-
bet, *La nature de la théologie spécula-
tive,* RT., 44 (1938). 1-39; 213-255, 645-
674. G. F. Van Ackeren, *Sacra doctrina.
The Subject of the First Question of the
Summa Theologica of St. Thomas Aquinas,* Roma, Catholic Book Agency, 1952
(extensive bibliography, pp. 123-128): a
clear introduction to the problem.—More
general approach to the problem in A. R.
Motte OP., *Théodicée et théologie chez
saint Thomas d'Aquin,* RSPT., 26 (1937)
5-26.—On the variations of the meaning
of "philosophy" in the middle ages up
to Thomas Aquinas, E. R. Curtius, *Zur
Geschichte des Wortes Philosophie im
Mittelalter,* Romanische Forschungen, 57
(1943) 290-309.—Incidentally, the true
title of the *Summa* is not *Summa theologica* but *Summa theologiae,* A. Walz
OP., *De genuino titulo "Summae theologiae,"* Angelicum, 18 (1941) 142-151.

[90] Thomas Aquinas has clearly distinguished philosophy from theology; see
Contra Gentiles, II, 4. Philosophy considers things in themselves, theology
considers them as images of God; philosophy considers things from the point
of view of their own natures, theology
considers them as related to God; last
not least, even when they consider the
same things, philosophy argues from
their proper causes, theology argues from
the Prime Cause. For instance, the theologian can argue either from revelation, or from what is due to the glory of
God, or again from the divine omnipotence, which is infinite. In arguing from
the Prime Cause, the theologian changes
philosophy into theology as water was
changed into wine at the marriage feast
in Cana of Galilee (*In Boethium De Trinitate,* II, q. 3, ad 3m). Nevertheless,
what is naturally accessible to the human
intellect does not cease to be purely rational in becoming theological; the theologian can, from time to time, "proceed
from the principles of human philosophy"
(*Contra Gentiles,* II, 4) just as a metaphysician sometimes argues from the principles of lower sciences. In doing so, the
metaphysician does not cease to deal with
metaphysics; likewise, the theologian
does not cease to deal with theology even
while proceeding from the principles of
philosophy in view of theological ends.
The theologian does not then attempt the
contradictory task of deducting philosophical conclusions from revealed prem-

ises, but he uses philosophical sciences as
handmaids in view of divine revelation.
In this sense, that is, as seen in the light
of revelation, the philosophical sciences
are included under the formal object of
theological knowledge; they then become
revelabilia.—This notion of theology differed from that of Roger Bacon, who had
protested against the inclusion of philosophical data in theology (*Opus minus,*
ed. Brewer, 322-323); it has been directly
opposed by Albert the Great (*Summa
theologiae,* I, 1, 3, 2; Borgnet, 31, 16-17);
even in our own days it remains open to
divergent interpretations.—On the problem, distinct from the preceding one,
of the object of metaphysics: M. de
Andrea, OP., *Soggetto e oggetto della
metafisica secondo S. Tommaso,* Angelicum, 27 (1950) 165-195. J. D.-D. Robert
OP., *La métaphysique science distincte de
toute autre discipline philosophique . . . ,*
DTP., 50 (1947) 206-222.

[91] Thomas Aquinas, *Summa theologiae,*
I, 1, 1. *Contra Gentiles,* I, 4. On the
reasons why few men, if any, can reach
the whole metaphysical truth without any
divine help, P. Synave, *La révélation des
vérités naturelles d'après saint Thomas
d'Aquin,* MM., I, 327-370.

[92] *Summa theologiae,* I, 1, 3, ad 3m.
Cf. "Sacred doctrine, being one, extends
to things which belong to the different
philosophical sciences, because it considers in each the same formal aspect,
namely, so far as they can be known in
the divine light," op. cit., I, 1, 4, Resp.
To be "divino lumine cognoscibilia" is
the formal reason and the very definition
of the "revelabilia." Consequently, all the
philosophical arguments used by the theologian are integrated by him in theology
without losing their essential rationality.
The unity of theology is one of order:
all its parts are related to the end of
revelation as to their final cause and
consequently, they are all seen in the
light of revelation. This is to say that
there are no *a priori* limits to the amount
of natural learning which the theologian
may deem it fit to integrate in his work.
He assumes what pertains to natural
knowledge "to the extent that either it is
presupposed for the grace of God or is
relatable to it," Bañez, *In I Sum. theol.,*
ed. Luis Urbano, I, p. 31-32. Cf. John
of Saint-Thomas, *Cursus theologicus,*
Paris, 1931; vol. I, p. 381: the philo-

sophical elements included in theology are like bodily organs included under the formal unity of one and the same soul.

[93] The novelty of the teaching of Thomas Aquinas is not an historical inference; his own contemporaries have either admired it or resented it; at any rate, they have felt it. Writing later, his biographer William of Tocco has vividly rendered this feeling: "In his teaching, he (Thomas) was raising new questions, finding a clear and new way of answering them, and introducing new reasons in his answers, so that, in hearing him teach new things and solve difficulties by new reasons, nobody could doubt that God was enlightening, by the rays of a new light, this man whose judgment began at once to be so sure that he did not hesitate to teach and to write the new opinions with which God had vouchsafed newly to inspire him," *Acta SS.,* March 7, n. 15 (quoted by Fr. Ehrle, *Der Augustinismus . . .* , p. 608, and many times after him). Anybody knowing how theologians feel about "novelty," will appreciate this testimony at its full value. Wherever Christian dogma is concerned, the teaching of Thomas is identically the same as that of Augustine, but the philosophical framework of the two theologies is different.—M.M. Gorce OP., *L'essor de la pensée au moyen âge. Albert le Grand—Thomas d'Aquin, Paris,* 1933. A. C. Pegis, *Saint Thomas and the Greeks,* 2 ed. Marquette Univ. Press, Milwaukee, 1943.

[94] See the testimony of Humbert of Romans, General Minister of the Dominican Order (1254-1263), written shortly before the Council of Lyons, that is, about 1273: "Item philosophia sic conculcata est per viros quosdam catholicos excellentis ingenii qui omnia quae apud eam sunt investigaverunt et multo clarius quam ipsi philosophi plura intellexerunt propter divinam scientiam quam habuerunt, et in iis pluribus eos illuminaverunt, quod non solum non rebellat philosphia fidei catholicae, sed redacta est quasi tota in obsequium ejus." Humbert of Romans, *Opus tripartitum,* II, 5; ed. by R. Brown, appendix ad *Fasciculum rerum expetendarum et fugiendarum,* London, 1669, II, 187. Quoted by Leclercq, RSR., 21 (1947) 149. —In accordance with this text, one should not forget that even the elementary notions of physical substance, of matter and

of form, above all of potency and act, have not the same sense in Aristotle and in Thomas Aquinas, because his own notion of being is other than that of Aristotle. One cannot go from the physics of Aristotle to the metaphysics of Thomas Aquinas; the fact that so many interpreters of Thomas Aquinas have deemed it possible to do so accounts to a large extent for the more or less Aristotelianized brands of Thomism which have never ceased to prosper.—On the commentators of the *Summa,* see the useful list established by Ant. Michelitsch, *Kommentatoren zur Summa theologiae des hl. Thomas von Aquin,* DTF., 3 (1916) 260-291.

[95] THOMAS AQUINAS OP.—I, LIFE. Born at Roccasecca, near Aquino (Italy) in 1225. Oblate at the abbey of Monte Cassino (1230-1239). Student at the newly founded University of Naples; joins the Dominican Order (1244); student at the Dominican College of Paris (1245-1248), under Albert the Great whom he follows to Cologne (1248-1252). *Baccalarius biblicus* at Paris (1252-1254); then *Sententiarius* (1254-1256); master in theology (1256). Teaches theology in Paris from 1256 to 1259. Goes to Italy, where he teaches theology in various cities (Anagni, Orvieto, Rome, Viterbo, from 1259 to 1268). Recalled to Paris in January 1268, he resumes his teaching at the university up to 1272. In October, 1272, Thomas undertakes the organization of the Dominican college at the University of Naples. Dies at Fossanova, March 7, 1274, on his way to the Council of Lyons. —G. K. Chesterton, *St. Thomas Aquinas,* London, Hodder and Stoughton, 1933. P. Mandonnet, *Chronologie sommaire de la vie et des écrits de saint Thomas d'Aquin,* RSPT., 9 (1920) 142-152. Cf. *Bibliographie thomiste,* pp. IX-XI. GLOREP., I, 85.

II. WRITINGS.—No writing of Thomas Aquinas is completely irrelevant to the study of philosophy. Nevertheless, if he reads them in view of ascertaining the personal contribution of their author to the evolution of philosophical thought, their historian should probably attach particular importance to the following ones: 1) Interpretation of Aristotle, as found in the following commentaries: *Perihermeneias and Posterior Analytics; Physics, De caelo et mundo, De genera-*

tione et corruptione, Meteorologicorum, De generatione et corruptione, De anima, De memoria et reminiscentia, De sensu et sensato, In libros Ethicorum, In libros Politicorum (Books I, II and the first six lectures of Book III; completed by Peter of Auvergne): 2) Interpretation of neoplatonism, as found in the following commentaries: *In librum de Causis, In Dionysium De divinis nominibus, in librum Boethii De hebdomadibus, In librum Boethii de Trinitate;* 3) The new metaphysical notion of being, as found in the following opuscules: *De ente et essentia, De substantiis separatis;* 4) Opuscules dealing with particular philosophical problems: *De differentia verbi divini et humani, De unitate intellectus, De regimine principum ad regem Cypri* (up to Part II, ch. 4), *De aeternitate mundi contra murmurantes, De principio individuationis, De principiis naturae, De natura materiae et dimensionibus interminatis* (doubtful), *De mixtione elementorum, De occultis operationibus naturae, De motu cordis, De instantibus;* to which should be added a group of opuscules in logic: *De demonstratione, De fallaciis, De natura generis, De propositionibus modalibus, De quatuor oppositis;* 5) The great theological syntheses: *Commentarium in quatuor libros Sententiarum Petri Lombardi, Summa contra Gentiles, Compendium theologiae, Summa theologiae* (up to Part III, qu. 90, art. 4); 6) The important collections of *Quaestiones Quodlibetales* and of *Quaestiones disputatae* devoted to the discussion of particularly important problems; among those which it is advisable to study: *Quaestiones disputatae de potentia, Qu. disp. de malo, Qu disp. de anima, Qu disp. de virtutibus in communi, Qu disp. de veritate* (exceptionally important).—We have intentionally refrained from giving chronological indications; despite the assurance of each scholar, the dates of these writings are far from safe. At any rate, except in case of research work on a very precise point, it should suffice to know that the *De ente et essentia* is one of the earliest works of Thomas (*ca.* 1256), that the order of the great doctrinal syntheses is as follows: *Sentences* (*ca.* 1254-1257), *Summa contra Gentiles* (*ca.* 1258-1264), *Compendium theologiae* (*ca.* 1260-1266), *Summa theologiae* (*ca.* 1266-1273). If we keep in mind that the mass of the commentaries on Aristotle are dated by scholars between 1261 and 1273, while the

Disputed questions extend over practically the same dates (*De veritate*, 1256-1259; *De potentia*, 1265-1268; *De spiritualibus creaturis*, 1268; *De anima*, 1269; *De malo*, 1269-1272, it becomes obvious that Thomas has simultaneously pursued his three main tasks. His gigantic intellectual production extends from about 1253 to 1274; in other words, it covers about twenty-one years.—On all questions of authenticity and dates, consult M. Grabmann, *Die Werke des hl. Thomas von Aquin, Eine literarhistorische Untersuchung und Einführung*, Münster i. W., 1949 (Beiträge, 22, 1-2, 3 ed.).—On a recent problem of authenticity: A. Fries CSR., *Thomas und die Quaestio "De immortalitate animae,"* DTF., 31 (1953) 18-52.

III. EDITIONS. *Opera Omnia*, Parmae, 1862-1870, 25 vols. (Piana edition); photostatic reproduction, New York, Musurgia, 1948-1950. *Opera omnia*, by Fretté and Maré, Paris, Vivès, 1871-1880, 34 v. *Opera omnia*, Romae, 1882 ff., 16 vols. published (1953); the best edition to date (Leonine edition). — Separate editions: *Summa contra Gentiles*, Marietti, Torino-Roma, 1934 (text of the Leonine edition). —*Summa theologiae* (text of the Leonine) Taurini Marietti, 1948, 4 vol. Another ed. Ottawa, 1941 ff.; Piana text, excellent notes.—*Scriptum super Sententiis Magistri Petri Lombardi*, ed. M. F. Moos, Paris, Lethielleux, 1947 ff.; 4 vols.— *Quaestiones disputatae*, ed. R. Spiazzi, Taurini, Marietti, 1949, 2 vols.—*Quaestiones Quodilebetales*, ed. R. Spiazzi, Taurini, Marietti, 1949.—*In XII libros Metaphysicorum* . . . , ed. R. Spiazzi, Taurini, Marietti, 1950.—*In Aristotelis libros De sensu et sensato, De memoria et reminiscentia* . . . , ed. R. Spiazzi, Taurini, Marietti, 1949.—*In Aristotelis librum De anima* . . . , ed. A.-M. Pirotta, 3 ed. Taurini, Marietti, 1948.—*In librum beati Dionysii De divinis nominibus* . . . , ed. C. Pera, hist. introduct., P. Caramello; doctr. synthesis, C. Mazzantini; Taurini, Marietti, 1950.—*In X Libros Ethicorum Aristotelis ad Nichomachum expositio*, ed. R. Spiazzi, Taurini, Marietti, 1949.—*In libros Politicorum Aristotelis expositio*, ed. R. Spiazzi, Taurini, Marietti, 1951. *In de Coelo et mundo, De generatione et corruptione, Meteorologicorum expositio*, ed. R. Spiazzi, Taurini, Marietti, 1952. *In octo libros De physico auditu sive physicorum Aristotelis commentaria*, ed. A.-M. Pirotta, Taurini, Marietti, 1953.—*De ente*

et essentia, often republished separately:
M.-D. Roland-Gosselin, OP., *Le "De ente
et essentia," texte établi d'après les manuscripts parisiens, Introduction, Notes et
Etudes historiques,* Paris (Bibliothèque
thomiste, VIII) 1926; ed. C. Boyer,
Gregor-Univ., Rome, 1933; ed. L. Baur,
Münster i. W., 1933.—*Opuscula philosophica et theologica,* ed. P. Mandonnet,
Paris, Lethielleux, 1927, 5 vols. New ed.
by Perrier, 1 vol. published, ibid.—Doctrinal tables: *Indices in Summa theologiae
et in Summa contra Gentiles S. Thomae
Aquinatis,* Torino, Marietti, n.d.; reprint
of the tables of the Leonine edition, vol.
XVI.

IV. ENGLISH TRANSLATIONS.—BET.,
3644-3666 a.—*English Translation of St.
Thomas Aquinas,* TMS., 26 (1948-1949)
78-81; 27 (1949-1950) 244-245.—*Summa
theologiae,* by the Fathers of the Dominican Province, New York, Benzinger, 20
vols. 1911-1923. *Summa contra Gentiles,*
4 vols. New York, Benziger, 1923.—*Basic
Writings of Saint Thomas Aquinas,* edited,
annotated, with an Introduction by A. C.
Pegis, 2 vols., 1097 and 1172 pages, New
York, Random House, 1944; abridgment of same, *Introduction to St. Thomas
Aquinas,* New York (The Modern Library) 1948.—*On Being and Essence,* by
A. Maurer CSB., Toronto, 1949.—*Compendium of theology,* by C. Vollert, St.
Louis, 1947.—*De principiis naturae,* Lat.
and Engl., by R. J. Henle and V. J.
Bourke, St. Louis, 1947.—*On Kingship to
the King of Cyprus,* by G. B. Phelan and
I. Th. Eschmann, Toronto, 1949.—Selected
Political Writings, by A. P. d'Entrèves
and J. G. Dawson.—*The Division and
Methods of the Sciences. Quest. V and VI
of . . . Commentary on the De Trinitate
of Boethius . . . ,* by A. Maurer, CSB., Toronto, 1953.—*The Trinity and The Unicity
of the Intellect,* by R. E. Brennan, St.
Louis, 1946.—Disputed Questions: *On the
Power of God,* 3 vols. London, 1932-
1934; 1 vol., Westminster, Newman Press,
1952.—*The Soul,* by J.-P. Rowan, St.
Louis, Herder, 1949—*On Spiritual Creatures,* by M. G. Fitzpatrick and J. J.
Wellmuth SJ., Marquette Univ. Press,
1949.—*Aristotle's De anima in the Version of W. of Moerbeke and the Commentary of St. Thomas Aquinas,* by K.
Foster and S. Humpfries, London, Routledge and Kegan Paul, 1951.—*Truth,* by
R. Mulligan, Chicago, Regnery, vol. I,
1952, vol. II, 1953 (will include three volumes). — *The Philosophy of Teaching*

. . . , by M. H. Mayer, Milwaukee,
Bruce, 1929.

V. BIBLIOGRAPHY. P. Mandonnet and
J. Destrez, *Bibliographie thomiste,* Kain
(now Paris) 1921 (Bibliothèque thomiste,
I). Continued by *Bulletin Thomiste,* see
supra; Bibliographical sources. V. J.
Bourke, *Thomistic Bibliography,* St. Louis
University Press, 1945 (completes Man-
donnet for the years 1920-1940).—Intro-
ductions, L. Schütz, *Thomas Lexicon
. . . ,* 2 ed., Paderborn, 1895; photostatic reproduction, New York, n.d. (ex-
tremely useful). R. J. Deferrari, Sister
M. Inviolata Barry, *A Lexicon of St.
Thomas Aquinas based on The Summa
Theologica and Selected Passages of His
Other Works,* Wash. D.C., 1948. A.-D.
Sertillanges OP., *Saint Thomas d'Aquin,*
Paris, 2 vols. 1910. Same author, *Les
grandes thèses de la philosophie thomiste,*
Paris, 1928. C. M. Manser, *Das Wesen
des Thomismus,* Freiburg (Switz.), 3
ed. 1949. E. Gilson, *Le Thomisme. In-
troduction à la philosophie de saint
Thomas d'Aquin,* 5 ed., Paris, J. Vrin,
1948. M. C. D'Arcy, *Thomas Aquinas,*
London, 1931. M. Grabmann, *Thomas
von Aquino. Eine Einführung in seine
Persönlichkeit und Gedankenwelt,* 7 ed.,
Munich, 1946. M.-D. Chenu, *Introduction à l'étude de saint Thomas d'Aquin,*
Paris, 1950. G. Smith SJ., *Natural Theology,* New York, Macmillan, 1951 (an
excellent introduction to the metaphysics of Saint Thomas).—G. Geenen, art.
Thomas d'Aquin (saint), DTC., 15
(1946) 618-761. R. Garrigou-Lagrange,
art. *Thomisme,* DTC., 15 (1946) 823-
1023.—On the Aristotelian background of
Thomism, J. Owens, CSSR., *The Doctrine
of Being in the Aristotelian "Metaphysics." A Study in the Greek Background
of Mediaeval Thought,* Pont. Instit. of
Medieval Studies, Toronto, 1951. Cf. MS.,
11 (1949) 239-245.—On the place of
Thomism in history and its comparison
with both Averroism and Augustinism,
L.-B. Gillon OP., art. *Signification historique de la théologie de saint Thomas,*
DTC., 15 (1946) 651-693.—F. Copleston,
A History of Philosophy, II, 312-434.

[96] *C.G.,* I ,20, 4. This text applies to
every actual being. In the preceding para-
graphs, struggling for words to express
the permanency of heavenly bodies,
Thomas has spoken several times of their
existential act as of a "quasi active
power," very different from the passive

potentiality with respect to being attributed by Averroes to matter; Thomas calls this "active power to be" a *virtus essendi*. He even generously credits Aristotle with this notion; and we would not deny that it is in Aristotle, but it is not there in the same sense. This *virtus essendi* is entirely different from the *potentia ad esse* which characterizes matter.—On the notions of being and *esse* in Thomas Aquinas, K. Feckes, *Das Opusculum des hl. Thomas von Aquin De ente et essentia*, ADGM., 667-681. E. Gilson, *Being and Some Philosophers*, 2 ed. Toronto, Pont. Inst. of Mediaeval Studies, 1952. A different redaction of the same work exists in French: *L'être et l'essence*, Paris, 1948. J. de Finance, *Etre et agir dans la philosophie de saint Thomas*, Paris, 1945. M.-D. Roland-Gosselin, *De distinctione inter essentiam et esse apud Avicennam et D. Thomam*, Xenia thomistica, 1925, III, 281-288. On the general method applied by Thomas, excellent remarks in J. Isaac, OP., *La notion de dialectique chez saint Thomas*, RSPT., 34 (1950) 481-506.

[97] "There is something, namely God, whose essence is its own *esse*, and this is the reason why there are certain philosophers who say that God has no essence, because his essence is nothing else than his own *esse*," *De ente et essentia*, ch. VI; cf. CG., I, 21. Among these philosophers one at least is known: Avicenna, followed by William of Auvergne. —A. Forest, *La structure métaphysique du concret selon S. Thomas d'Aquin*, Paris, 1931. J. Maritain, *Sur la doctrine de l'aséité divine*, MS., 5 (1943) 39-50.

[98] *S.T.*, I, 3, 4, ad 2m. *De potentia*, 7, 2, ad lm. Cf. E. Gilson, *Le thomisme*, 5 ed., Paris, 1948, 138-139. E. L. Mascall, *He Who is*, New York, 1943.

[99] *S.T.*, I, 13, 5. *C.G.*, I, 33. J. Habbel, *Die Analogie zwischen Gott und Welt nach Thomas von Aquin*, Regensburg, 1928. M. T.-L. Penido, *Le role de l'analogie en théologie dogmatique*, Paris, 1931, pp. 11-78. J. Maritain, *Distinguer pour unir, ou les degrés du savoir*, Paris, 1932; Annex II, *De l'analogie*, pp. 821-826. C. Ryan, OP., *God and Analogy*, Blackfriars, 25 (1944) 137-143. E. L. Mascall, *Existence and Analogy*, New York, 1949. J. F. Anderson, *The Bond of Being. An Essay on Analogy and Existence*, St. Louis, 1949.

[100] On the alleged proof of the existence of God in *De ente et essentia:* F. Van Steenberghen, *Monographies sur les philosophies du moyen âge*, RNSP., 40 (1937) 123-126; *La composition constitutive de l'être fini*, RNSP., 41 (1938) 489-518; *Le problème philosophique de l'existence de Dieu*, RPL., 45 (1947) 5-20, 141-168, 301-313 (especially 301-308); *Le problème de l'existence de Dieu dans le De ente et essentia de Saint Thomas d'Aquin*, Mélanges de Ghellinck, II (1951) 837-847.

[101] *C.G.*, I, 13. *S.T.*, I, 2, 3. *Compendium theologiae*, I, 3. Collected texts: J. A. Baisnée SS., *St. Thomas Aquinas' Proofs of the Existence of God Presented in Their Chronological Order*, Philosophical Studies in Honor of . . . Ign. Smith OP., Newman Press, Westminster (Maryland) 1952, 29-64.—E. Rolfes, *Die Gottesbeweise bei Thomas von Aquin und Aristoteles*, 2 ed., Limburg, 1926. R. Arnou, SJ., *De quinque viis sancti Thomas ad demonstrandum Dei existentiam apud antiquos Graecos et Arabes et Judaeos praeformatis vel adumbratis*, Roma, Univ. Gregoriana, 1932; 2 ed. 1949. M. Bouyges, *Exégèse de la "tertia via" de saint Thomas*, Revue de philosophie, 32 (1932) 113-146. O. Bonamartini, *La "quarta via" di. S. Tommaso d'Aquino*, Scuola cattolica, 60, 1 (1932) 17-24. H. Meyer, *Thomas Aquinas als Interpret des aristotelischen Gotteslehre*, ADGM., I, 682-687. J. Paulus, *Le caractère métaphysique des preuves thomistes de l'existence de Dieu*, AHDL., 9 (1934) 143-153. A. R. Motte, OP., *A propos des "cinq voies,"* RSPT., 27 (1938) 577-582. P. Muniz, OP., *La "quarta via" di Santo Tomás para demostrar la existencia de Dios*, Revista de Philosophia, 3 (1944) 385-433; 4 (1945) 49-101. M. A. Donovan, *The Henological Argument for the Existence of God in the Works of St. Thomas Aquinas*, Notre Dame (Ind.), 1946. E. G. Jay, *The Existence of God. A Commentary on St. Thomas Aquinas' Five Ways of Demonstrating the Existence of God*, London, SPCK., 1946. M. Bouyges SJ., *Pour l'interprétation des "quinque viae" de saint Thomas d'Aquin*, Recherches de science religieuse, 36 (1949) 593-601. H. Holstein, SJ., *L'origine aristotélicienne de le "tertia via" de saint Thomas*, RPL., 48 (1950) 354-370; cf. H.-D. Simonin, OP.,

in Bulletin Thomiste, 8 (1951) 237-241. A. Boehm, *Autour du mystère des "quinque viae" de saint Thomas d'Aquin*, RSR., 24 (1950) 217-234. W. Bryar, *St. Thomas and the Existence of God. Three Interpretations*, Chicago, 1951. J. Owens, *The Conclusion of the prima via*, TMS., 30 (1952-1953) 33-53, 109-121, 203-215.

[102] *S.T.*, I, 3, 1-3. *C.G.*, I, 20.

[103] *S.T.*, I, 3, 4. *C.G.*., I, 21.

[104] *S.T.*, I, 3, 4, ad 2m. *C.G.*, I, 22.

[105] Simplicity of God, *S.T.*, I, 3, 7. *C.G.*, I, 18.—Perfection, *S.T.*, I, 4, 1-2. *C.G.*, I, 28.—Infinity, *S.T.*, I, 7, 1-2. *C.G.*, I, 43.

[106] *CG.*, I, 30-36. *S. T.*, I, 13, 5.—God as the supreme good, *S.T.*, I, 6, 2.—On the controverted question of our knowledge of the divine attributes, E. Gilson, *Le thomisme*, 140-174.—J. Bittremieux, *Similitudo creaturarum cum Deo fundamentum cognoscibilitatis Dei*, DTP., 43 (1940) 310-323. A. Horwath, OP., *Der thomistische Gottesbegriff*, DTF., 18 (1940) 141-210; *Der analytische Wert des Gottesbegriffes*, DTF., 18 (1940) 449-494; *Die einzelnen Arten der Theologie in ihrem Verhältnis zum Gottesbegriff*, DTF., 19 (1941) 36-48. Ch. Journet, *Connaissance et inconnaissance de Dieu*, Lyon, 1943.

[107] See note 106.

[108] On the notion of participation: L.-B. Geiger, *La participation dans la philosophie de saint Thomas*, Paris, 1942. Cornelio Fabro, *La nozione metafisica di partecipazione*, Roma, 1950. C. A. Hart, *Participation in the Thomistic Five Ways*, NS., 26 (1952) 267-282.—Consequences for the philosophy of nature: J. M. Marling, *The Order of Nature in the Philosophy of St. Thomas Aquinas*, Washington, 1934. A. C. Pegis, *A Note on St. Thomas, Summa theologica, I, 44, 1-2*, MS., 8 (1946) 159-168.

[109] *S.T.*, I, 47, 1. *C.G.*, II, 39-45.—J. Benes, *Valor "possibilium" apud S. Thomam, Henricum Gandavensem, B. Jacobum de Viterbo*, DTP., 29 (1926) 612-634; 30 (1927) 94-117, 333-355.

[110] On the divine ideas, *S.T.*, I, 15, 1-3, and I, 44, 3. *C.G.*, I, 47-55. *De veritate*, qu. III, 1-8.

[111] God can create, *S.T.*, I, 45, 2. Only God can create, I, 45, 5. Cf. *C.G.*, II, 16-21. This entails the all-powerfulness of God, *C.G.*, II, 22. Thus understood, creation, that is the free gift of being, is the proper effect of God, who is the pure act of being, *S.T.*, I, 8, 1, Resp. Since creation is free, there is no way to prove either that it has been eternal, or that the world has had a beginning; on the first point, Thomas opposes Averroes and his followers who thought they could demonstrate the eternity of the world; on the second point, he opposes the Augustinians who thought they could demonstrate that the eternity of a *created* world was impossible. See the opuscule of Thomas *De aeternitate mundi contra murmurantes*, and *C.G.*, II, 31-38. Th. Esser, *Die Lehre des heil. Thomas von Aquin über die Möglichkeit einer Anfangslosen Schöpfung*, Münster i. W., 1895. A. Rohner, *Das Schöpfungsproblem bei Moses Maimonides, Albertus Magnus und Thomas von Aquin*, Münster i. W., 1913 (Beiträge 11, 5). For a free restatement of the problem in the spirit of Thomas Aquinas: A.-D. Sertillanges, *L'idée de création et ses retentissements en philosophie*, Paris, 1945; justified remarks in J. de Blie, *A propos de l'éternité du monde*, Bulletin de littérature ecclésiastique, 47 (1946) 162-170. J. F. Anderson, *The Cause of Being*, St. Louis, 1953.—On causality, G. Schuleman, *Das Kausalprinzip in der Philosophie des heiligen Thomas von Aquin*, Münster i. W., 1915 (Beiträge, 13, 5). F. Beemelmans, *Zeit und Ewigkeit nach Thomas von Aquin*, Münster i. W., 1914 (Beiträge, 17, 1).—H. A. Wolfson, *The Meaning of "ex nihilo" in the Church Fathers, Arabic and Hebrew Philosophy, and St. Thomas*, Studies in Honor of J. D. M. Ford, Harvard Univ. Press, 1948, pp. 355-370.—On the problem of evil: J. Maritain, *Saint Thomas and the Problem of Evil*, Milwaukee, Marquette University Press, 1942. Th. Deman, OP., *Le mal et Dieu*, Paris, 1943.

[112] *C.G.*, IV, 7. Cf. *In librum Dionysii de divinis nominibus*, I, 1; ed. C. Pera, p. 9, n. 29.—On evil as a privation of goodness and, therefore, of being, *S.T.*, I, 48, 1 and 3. *C.G.*, III, 8-14. *Qu. disp. de malo*, I, 1-2. *In librum Dionysii de divinis nominibus*, IV, lect. 15; ed. C. Pera, pp. 169-178. Through Denis, the doctrine can

be traced back to Proclus, Plotinus and Plato.

[113] On angels, against hylomorphism, *S.T.*, I, 50, 2. *C.G.*, II, 50-51. *Qu. disp. de spiritualibus creaturis*, 1. *De ente et essentia*, ch. V (against Gabirol).—Their specific distinction, *S.T.*, I, 50, 4. Cognition in angels, *S.T.*, I, 54, 1-5 and I, 55, 1-3. In what sense the study of angels belongs in metaphysics, *In Boethium de Trinitate*, V, 4, ad 3m.

[114] The human soul is both a substance and a form (*forma et hoc aliquid*); it is an individual substance whose proper nature it is to be a form, Disp. quest. *De anima*, art. 1; *S.T.*, I, 75, 2. It is not man (Thomas knows the only text of Augustine that can be quoted to that effect: *De civ. Dei*, XIX, 3; PL., 41, 626; cf. Thomas Aquinas, *S.T.*, I, 75, 5); it is incorruptible, *S.T.*, I, 75, 6; it is united with the body as its form, I, 75, 1; hence the intellective soul of man cannot be a separate substance, Qu. disp. *De anima*, art. 2; this notion of the soul entails the rejection of hylomorphism with respect to spiritual substances, *S.T.*, I, 76, 1, end of the answer; against the plurality of souls, I, 76, 3; against the form of corporeity, I, 76, 4; unity and distinction of the powers of the soul, I, 77, 1-5.—Historical antecedents, O. Lottin, PEM., I, 427-466, simplicity of the soul; 463-479, oneness of the soul in man; 483-502, identity of the soul with its faculties. —History of the doctrine: A. C. Pegis, *St. Thomas and the Problem of the Soul in the Thirteenth Century*, Toronto, 1934; *Some Permanent contributions of Medieval Philosophy to the Notion of Man*, Transactions of the Royal Society of Canada, III, 2; 45 (1952) 67-78.—On human nature, J. Maritain, *The Humanism of St. Thomas Aquinas*, Twentieth Century Philosophy, New York, 293-311. G. Klubertanz, SJ., *The Philosophy of Human Nature*, St. Louis, 1951.— J. Bobik, *La doctrine de Saint Thomas sur l'individuation des substances corporelles*, RPL., 51 (1953) 5-41.—Transition to ethics: A. C. Pegis, *Matter, Beatitude and Liberty*, The Thomist, The Maritain Volume, 1943, 265-280.

[115] *De ente et essentia*, V, 5. *De substantiis separatis*, VI (*Opuscula*, Mandonet ed., I, 97).—M. Grabmann, *Die Schrift "De ente et essentia" und die Seinsmetaphysik des hl. Thomas von Aquin*, ADGM., I, 314-331.—Comparison with Plato's ontology and noetic, A. C. Pegis, *Cosmogony and Knowledge*; I, *St. Thomas and Plato*, Thought, 18 (1943) 643-664; II, *The Dilemma of Composite Essences*, 19 (1944) 269-290; III, *Between Thought and Being*, 20 (1945) 473-498.

[116] *Qu. disp. De potentia*, VII, 2, ad 2m. *C.G.*, II, 54. *S.T.*, I, 3, 4 and I, 5, 3. To the studies quoted in the bibliography, add A. Maurer, *Form and Essence in the Philosophy of St. Thomas*, MS., 13 (1951) 165-176.—The notion of act of being, is a point on which Thomas Aquinas has met a persistent opposition even within his own school: "Et hoc est quod saepissime D. Thomas clamat, *et Thomistae nolunt audire*, quod esse est actualitas omnis formae vel naturae . . ." etc., Bañez, Commentary on *Summa theologiae*, I, 3, 4, ed. Luis Urbano, Madrid, 1934, I, 141. The notion itself has sometimes been held responsible for this resistance: "Es ist aber, wie zugestanden werden muss die thomistische Lehre eine nicht jedem Verständnis liegende Lehre; sie erheischt spekulative Tiefe." G. von Holtum, OSB., *Zur thomistischen Lehre vom realen Unterschied zwischen Wesenheit und Dasein in den Geschöpfen*, DTF., 3 (1916) 303. Since some theologians are not Thomists the German sentence had better stay untranslated. M. Feigl, *Der Begriff des Wesens und die Verschiedenheit von Wesen und Sein nach "De ente et essentia" des hl. Thomas von Aquin*, PJ., 55 (1942) 277-299.

[117] On the passivity of sense knowledge, *S.T.*, I, 78, 3 (this eliminates the Augustinian doctrine of sensation as an act of the soul). The intellect is not the soul but one of its powers, *S.T.*, I, 79, 1. It is, in a way, a passive power, I, 79, 2. Nevertheless, there is an agent intellect, I, 79, 3. This intellect is in the soul, I, 79, 4; the position of Aristotle is that the agent intellect is comparable to light, whereas that of Plato is that it is comparable to the sun; note the remarkable conclusion: "But the separate intellect, according to the teaching of our Faith, is God himself, who is the soul's creator, and only beatitude. . . . Therefore the human soul derives its intellectual light from him, according to Ps. 4, 7, *The light of thy*

countenance, *O Lord, is signed upon us."*
In short, Thomas does not refuse to speak
of a separate intellect, provided that:
1, it be God; 2, that its illumination
of the soul be identified with the creation, in man, of the natural light of reason. The verbal nature of this concession
is verified by *S.T.*, I, 84, 5, where the
Augustinian doctrine of the divine illumination, *understood in its Augustinian
sense,* is eliminated. On the individuality
of the agent intellect, I, 79, 5. On intellectual cognition by mode of abstraction
from images, I, 85, 1 and 2. *C.G.*, II, 77.
The abstractive nature of human knowledge applies even to our cognition of the
soul, *S.T.*, I, 87, 3. *De veritate*, X, 8.—
One of the most perfect texts of Thomas
concerning his own interpretation of the
divine illumination is *In Boethium De
Trinitate,* I, 1.—D. Lanna, *La teoria della
conoscenza in S. Tommaso d'Aquino,*
Firenze, 1913 (bibliography). M. Baumgartner, *Zur thomistischen Lehre von
den ersten Prinzipien der Erkenntnis,*
Festgabe Hertling, Freiburg i. Br., 1913,
241-260. Same author, *Zum thomistischen
Wahrheitsbegriff,* in Baeumker Festgabe,
Münster i. W., 1913, 241-260. A. Hufnagel,
*Intuition und Erkenntnis nach Thomas
von Aquin,* Münster i. W., 1932. A. Gar-
deil, *La perception de l'âme par elle-
même d'après saint Thomas,* Mélanges
thomistes, 219-236. E. Gilson, *Réalisme
thomiste et critique de la connaissance,*
Paris, 1938. G. B. Phelan, *Verum sequitur
esse rerum,* MS., 1 (1939) 11-22. G. van
Riet, *L'épistémologie thomiste,* Louvain,
1946. E. J. Ryan, *The Role of the Sensus
communis in the Psychology of St.
Thomas,* Carthagena (Ohio) 1951. G.
P. Klubertanz, *The Discursive Power.
Sources and Doctrine of the Vis Cogita-
tiva According to St. Thomas Aquinas,*
St. Louis, 1952 (extensive bibliography on
the noetic of Thomas Aquinas, 331-346).
P. Hoenen, *Reality and Judgment According to St. Thomas,* Chicago, 1952.—
On the notion of "mental word": B. Lon-
ergan SJ., *The Concept of Verbum in
the Writings of St. Thomas Aquinas,*
Theological Studies (Baltimore): 7 (1946)
349-392; 8 (1947) 35-79, 404-444; 10
(1949) 3-40, 359-393.

[118] General structure of the world, *C.G.*,
III, 1. Everything acts in view of an
end, III, 2 (either known or not known).
This end is the good, III, 3. Consequently, it is God (III, 17), who, since he
himself *has* no end, *is* the ultimate end
of all beings and operations, III, 18. For
all things to act in view of God is to
assimilate themselves to God, that is to
make themselves as similar to him as is
compatible with their natures (*Deo as-
similari*); they resist corruption because
they love to be: now God is *Esse;* they
operate in view of some good: now God
is *Bonum,* III, 19. Natural causality is
an effort (conscious or not) to imitate
the creative fecundity of the supreme
Esse, III, 21. To sum up, things imitate
God to the extent that they are and that
they cause; this is, for them, to participate in the divine being, in the divine
goodness and therefore in the divine will,
III, 22. This applies to beings deprived
of knowledge, III, 24. As to intellectual
substances, their end is to know God by
means of their intellect (*intelligere Deum*)
III, 25. Consequntly, man's felicity cannot consist in an act of the will, but in
an act of the intellect, III, 26. The cognition of God by faith is not sufficient
to give beatitude, III, 40. Even if it were
possible to us, the cognition of the separate Intelligences (III, 45), or the self-
knowledge of the soul by intuition of its
own essence (III, 46) would not give us
full beatitude. Only the intellectual cognition of God can fulfill our obscure
desire, and since such cognition is not
possible in this life (III, 47-48), man
must order all his activities in view of
another life. In this sense, nature is ordained to grace, which radically transcends it. — All human operations are
caused by both intellect and will; will
is the natural appetite of an intellectual
being; it necessarily wills the good in
general (*S.T.*, I, 81, 1), but not what is
not the absolute good, *S.T.*, I, 82, 2.
Since the good cannot be desired unless
it be known, the intellect is more noble
than the will, *S.T.*, I, 82, 3. Morality consists in ordering all human acts in view
of the true good, which is the true end,
I-II, 18, 4-7; and this not only as a
general intention but taking account of
all the circumstances that determine any
particular act, I-II, 18, 10. Where practical reason is wrong, the will is wrong,
I-II, 19, 6. The goodness of intention
determines that of the will (I-II, 19, 7)
in this sense that, if the intention is
wrong, the will is wrong, but wrong decisions of the will can be made even
with a good intention, I-II, 19, 8.—
Among countless contributions to a widely

discussed problem, L. E. O'Mahony, *The Desire of God in the Philosophy of St. Thomas Aquinas,* London, 1929. St. Vallaro OP., *De naturali desiderio videndi essentiam Dei et de ejus valore ad demonstrandam possibilitatem ejusdem visionis Dei quidditativae,* Angelicum, 11 (1934) 133-170.—B. J. Diggs, *Love and Being. An Investigation into the Metaphysics of St. Thomas Aquinas,* New York, 1947. Ch. Hollencamp, *Causa causarum. On the Nature of Good and Final Cause,* Québec, Université Laval, 1949 (important for the history of Thomism).

[119] The act by which we will a means is not the same as the act by which we will the end (*S.T.,* I-II, 8, 3), but intention runs through the will of the means and that of the end, I-II, 12, 3. Choice (*electio*) is an act of the will preceded by rational cognition, I-II, 13, 1. It is the choosing of means in view of the willed end, I-II, 13, 3. It is proper to human acts, I-II, 13, 4. Deliberation (*consilium*) is a rational inquiry into the best means to achieve a willed end, I-II, 14, 2 and 4. Consent (*consensus*) is the approval given by our appetitive power to the rational conclusion of deliberation (I-II, 15, 1) concerning the appropriate means in view of a willed end, I-II, 15, 3. The will can sway the acts of reason, I-II, 17, 6.—The texts of Thomas Aquinas on voluntary action sometimes refer to a work of Aristotle called *On Good Fortune;* many other masters, for instance Duns Scotus, have quoted it. It is a Latin translation of Aristotle's *Ethica Eudemica,* Bk. VII, ch. 14, joined to a Latin translation of *Magna Moralia,* Bk. II, ch. 8, and circulated under the common title, *Liber de bona fortuna.* See Th. Deman, *Le Liber de bona Fortuna dans la théologie de saint Thomas d'Aquin,* RSPT., 17 (1928) 38-58.—On the history of the doctrine before Thomas Aquinas (Alexander Neckham, John Blund, Alexander of Hales) and on its influence (Giles of Rome, anonymous commentaries on *Ethics*), O. Lottin, PEM., III, 606-675.—Selcted texts and commentaries in E. Gilson, *Moral Values and the Moral Life,* translated by L. R. Ward CSC., Saint Louis, 1941.

[120] On moral habits (*habitus*), *S.T.,* I-II, 49, 2 and 4. Intellectual and moral virtues, *S.T.,* I-II, 58, 2.—P. de Roton, *Les Habitus, leur caractère spirituel,* Paris, 1934.

[121] On intellectual virtues, *S.T.,* I-II, 58, 4-5. Cf. E. Gilson, *Wisdom and Love in Saint Thomas Aquinas, Marquette Press,* Milwaukee, 1951. L. B. Geiger OP., *Le problème de l'amour chez saint Thomas d'Aquin,* Montréal, 1952, pp. 56-67.

[122] *S.T.,* I-II, 64, 1, ad 1.

[123] Divine law, natural law, human law, *S.T.,* I-II, 90, 1-4 and 91, 1-5. For a detailed study of these different types of law, I-II, 93 (eternal law), I-II, 94 (natural law), I-II, 95 (human law). On human law and personal moral conscience, I-II, 96, 1-6.—For a modern appreciation of the doctrine, Huntington Cairns, *Legal Philosophy from Plato to Hegel,* Baltimore, 1949, pp. 163-204. Origins, meaning and influence of the doctrine, O. Lottin, PEM., II, 11-100.

[124] ETHICS. A. G. Sertillanges OP., *La philosophie morale de saint Thomas,* Paris, 1916. J. Pieper, *Die ontische Grundlage des sittlichen nach Thomas Aquinas,* Münster i. W., 1929. M. Wittmann, *Die Ethik des hl. Thomas von Aquin in ihrem systematischen Aufbau dargestellt und in ihren geschichtlichen, besonders in den antiken Quellen erforscht,* Munich, 1935. On practically all problems related to the ethics of Thomas Aquinas in relation with its historical environment, consult O. Lottin, *Psychologie et morale aux XIIe et XIIIe siècles,* especially vols. II-III, Louvain, 1948-1949; cf. R. Gauthier, *Bulletin Thomiste,* 8 (1947-1953) 60-86. H. V. Jaffa, *Thomism and Aristotelianism. A Study of the Commentary by Thomas Aquinas on the Nicomachean Ethics,* Chicago, Univ. of Chicago Press, 1952.—V. J. Bourke, *Ethics. A Textbook in Moral Philosophy,* New York, Macmillan, 1951. SOCIOLOGY. R. Linhardt, *Die Sozialprinzipien des hl. Thomas von Aquin . . . ,* Freiburg i. Br., 1932. E. Kurz, *Individuum und Gemeinschaft beim hl. Thomas von Aquin,* Munich, 1932. L. Lachance, *Le concept de droit selon Aristote et saint Thomas,* Paris, 1933. C. Riedl, *The Social Theory of St. Thomas Aquinas,* Philadelphia, 1934. I. Th. Eschmann OP., *Bonum commune melius est quam bonum unius. Eine Studie über den Wertvorrang des Personalen bei Thomas*

Aquinas, MS., 6 (1944) 62-120; *Studies on the Notion of Society in St. Thomas Aquinas*, MS., 8 (1946) 1-42; 9 (1947) 19-55. M. L. Martinez, *Distributive Justice according to St Thomas*, TMS., 24 (1946-1947) 208-223. J. T. Delos, *La sociologie de S. Thomas et le fondement du droit international*, Angelicum, 22 (1945) 3-16.

POLITICAL PHILOSOPHY. M. Demongeot, *Le meilleur régime politique selon S. Thomas d'Aquin*, Paris, 1928. H. Gmür, *Thomas von Aquino und der Krieg*, Leipzig, Teubner, 1933. J. L. Lagor, *La phi-*

losophie politique de saint Thomas, Paris, 1949.

ECONOMICS. A. Horwath, *Eigentumsrecht nach dem hl. Thomas von Aquin*, Graz, 1929. A. Rohner, *Naturrecht und positives Recht*, DTF., 12 (1934) 59-83. R. Brunet SJ., *La propriété privée chez saint Thomas*, NRT., 61 (1934) 914-927, 1022-1041. E. Welty OP., *Vom Sinn und Wert des menschlichen Arbeit aus der Gedankenwelt des hl. Thomas Aquinas*, Heidelberg, 1946. A. F. Utz, *Aushöhlung oder Dynamik des Eigentumsbegriffes?* DTF., 25 (1947) 243-254.

PART NINE

THE CONDEMNATION OF 1277

CHAPTER I. LATIN AVERROISM

[1] AVERROISM. E. Renan, *Averroès et l'Averroisme*, Paris, 1852 (often reprinted and still useful). M. Grabmann, *Neuaufgefundene Werke des Siger von Brabant und Boetius von Dacien*, Sitzungsberichte, Munich, 1924; *Der lateinische Averroismus des 13. Jahrhunderts und seine Stellung zur christlichen Weltanschauung*, Sitzungsberichte, Munich, 1931, 2. M.-M. Gorce, art. *Averroisme*, DHGE., 5 (1931) 1032-1091.—On the discovery of Averroes by the Latins, P. Mandonnet, *Siger de Brabant . . .*, I, 240-243. R. de Vaux, *La première entrée d'Averroès chez les Latins*, RSPT., 22 (1933) 193-245. See following note.

[2] On the earliest efforts to interpret the texts of Averroes, besides Mandonnet, see D. Salman, *Note sur la première influence d'Averroès*, RNSP., 40 (1937) 203-212. The influence of Averroes extends much farther than Averroism. As *the* Commentator of Aristotle, Averroes has influenced all the scholastics. Even Thomas Aquinas (*the* Expositor) will often have Averroes at hand while writing the *Contra Gentiles* (especially on the intellect) and his own commentaries on Aristotle. Proofs are to be found in Klubertanz, *The Discursive Power*, St. Louis, 1952, 196-201.

[3] See above, Part VII, p. 285, and p. 670, note 9.

[4] Thomas Aquinas is said to have been the first to use the name "Averroists": "Sed quia . . . Averroistae . . . accipere

volunt intentionem fuisse, quod intellectus non sit anima quae est actus corporis . . . ," *De unitate intellectus*, Keeler ed., 17, pp. 12-13. See, however, M. Bouyges SJ., *Attention à Averroista*, RMAL., 4 (1948) 173-176, calling attention to the fact that "Averroista" may mean Averroes, not Averroist. The sentence could therefore mean: "But because . . . they want the intention of Averroes to have been . . ." Another reading of the same text runs as follows: "Averroes . . . voluit." The treatise is certainly directed against several supporters of the doctrine but there is no certitude that the word "Averroistae" was coined at that time. It became common at a later date. Niphus (Nifo) in his *De intellectu* (1492): "Vir gravis (i.e., Siger) sectae Averroisticae fautor," B. Nardi, *Sigieri di Brabante*, p. 20; cf. "magni Averroistae," "Averrois sectatores," pp. 17-19.—Against this appellation, F. Van Steenberghen, *Siger de Brabant . . .*, II, 493-497; R.-A. Gauthier, *Trois commentaires "averroistes" . . .*, AHDL., 16 (1947-1948) 334-336.

[5] D. Salman, *Albert le Grand et l'Averroisme latin*, RSPT., 24 (1935) 38-64; especially 48-49; against the interpretation of Masnovo, 52-56. F. Van Steenberghen rightly remarks, however, that the treatise of Albert "betrays a certain uneasiness in the philosophical world about 1256," *Siger de Brabant*, II, 472. The very fact that Albert undertook his work on the order of Pope Alexander IV (*ad praeceptum Domini Alexandri papae*) confirms the existence of that uneasy

feeling. In favor of Masnovo's position: P. Mazzarella, *Il "De unitate" di Alberto Magno e di Tommaso d'Aquino in rapporto alla teoria averroistica. Concordanze, divergenze, sviluppi,* Napoli, 1949.

[6] On this condemnation, see ch. II, pp. 403-404.

[7] SIGER OF BRABANT.—LIFE. Dates of birth and death unknown. Master of Arts at the University of Paris in 1266. Involved in the condemnation of thirteen propositions by Etienne Tempier, Bishop of Paris, on December 10, 1270. Second warning issued, this time, by the Faculty of Arts, April 1, 1272. On May 7, 1275, the pontifical legate Simon of Brion attempts a conciliation within the Faculty; Peter of Auvergne is appointed as Rector of the University. On March 7, 1277, condemnation of 219 propositions; Siger of Brabant and Bernier of Nivelles are summoned to appear before the French inquisitor, Simon du Val (November 23, 1277); at that time, the two masters had already left France. Siger seems to have died at Orvieto, before 1285. A letter of John Peckham, dated November 10, 1284, shows that, at that date, Siger was already dead.

EDITIONS.—Cl. Baeumker, *Die Impossibilia des Siger von Brabant. Eine philosophische Streitschrift aus dem 13. Jahrhundert zum ersten Male vollständig herausgegeben und besprochen,* Münster i. W., 1898 (Beiträge, 2, 6). P. Mandonnet, *Siger de Brabant et l'averroisme latin,* vol. II, *Quaestiones logicales, Quaestio utrum haec sit vera: homo est animal nullo homine existente?, Quaestiones naturales, De aeternitate mundi, Impossibilia, Quaestiones de anima intellectiva,* plus treatises by various authors, Louvain, 1908. M. Grabmann, *Neuaufgefundene "Quaestionen" Sigers von Brabant zu den Werken des Aristoteles, (Clm. 9559),* Miscellanea Ehrle, Roma, 1924, I, 103-147 (extracts from Questions on *Metaphysics* and *Physics*). F. Stegmüller, *Neugefundene Quaestionen des Siger von Brabant,* RTAM., 3 (1931) 158-182 (text of five questions on ethics). F. Van Steenberghen, *Siger de Brabant d'après ses oeuvres inédites. I, Les oeuvres inédites,* Louvain, 1931: *Sigeri de Brabantia Quaestiones de anima;* pp. 163-334, detailed study of the still unpublished works attributed to Siger of Brabant. R. Barsotti, *Sigeri de Brabantia De ae-*

ternitate mundi, Münster i. W., 1933. A third edition of the same treatise by W. J. Dwyer, *L'opuscule de Siger de Brabant "De aeternitate mundi,"* Louvain, 1937 cf. *Le texte du De aeternitate mundi de Siger de Brabant,* RNSP., 40 (1937) 44-66. Ph. Delhaye, *Siger de Brabant. Questions sur la Physique d'Aristote,* Louvain, 1941. C. A. Graiff, *Siger de Brabant. Questions sur la Métaphysique,* Louvain, 1948.— A set of four questions on Bk. III *De anima* is contained in an Oxford ms., Merton College, cod. lat. 292, 357 v-364 r; extracts in F. Van Steenberghen, *Siger de Brabant,* I, 164-177.

BIBLIOGRAPHY. — GDP., 757-758. Cl. Baeumker, *Die Impossibilia des Siger von Brabant. Eine philosophische Streitschrift aus dem XIII Jahrhundert . . . ,* Münster i. W., 1898 (Beiträge, 2, 6, 1898). P. Mandonnet, *Siger de Brabant et l'averroisme latin au XIIIe siècle. Etude critique et documents inédits,* Fribourg (Suisse) 1899; 2 ed. in 2 vols. Louvain, 1908, 1911. On the controversy Baeumker-Mandonnet concerning the nature of the *Impossibilia,* P. Mandonnet, *Autour de Siger de Brabant,* RT., (1911) 314-337, 476-502. Nobody now admits that the *Impossibilia* was directed against Siger (Baeumker); it is a work by Siger (Mandonnet). Another target of Mandonnet's criticism was Fr. Bruckmüller, *Untersuchungen über Sigers (von Brabant) Anima intellectiva,* Munich, 1908.—A second phase of the problem began with M. Grabmann's *Neuaufgefundene Werke . . .* (see note) in which writings whose authenticity is not certain (Questions on *De anima* and on *Physics*) were attributed to Siger. The controversy is still open. M. Grabmann, *Die Lehre des hl. Albertus Magnus vom Grunde der Vielheit der Dinge und der lateinische Averroismus,* MG., 1936, II, 285-312. J. P. Muller, *Philosophie et foi chez Siger de Brabant. La doctrine de la double vérité.* Studia anselmiana 7-8 (1938) 35-50. B. Nardi, *Il preteso tomismo di Sigieri di Brabante,* GCFI., 17 (1936) 26-35; *Ancora sul preteso tomismo di Sigieri di Brabante,* GCFI., 18 (1937) 160-164; *S. Tommaso d' Aquino, Trattato sull'unità dell' intelletto contro gli Averroisti,* Florence, 1938 (important commentaries); *Sigieri di Brabante nel pensiero del Rinascimento italiano,* Roma, 1945 (new information); *Note per una storia dell 'averroismo latino, I, Controversie Sigeriane,* Rivista di storia della filosofia, 2 (1947) 19-25;

II, *La posizione di Alberto Magno di fronte all 'averroismo,* ibid., 2 (1947) 197-220; III, *Egidio Romano e l'averroismo,* ibid., 3 (1948) 8-29; IV, *Sigieri di Brabante e Maestro Gosvino de la Chapelle,* ibid., 3 (1948) 120-122. Anneliese Maier, *Nouvelles Questions de Siger sur la Physique d'Aristote,* RPL., 44 (1946) 497-513. J. J. Duin, *Les commentaires de Siger de Brabant sur la Physique d'Aristote,* RPL., 46 (1948) 463-480. A. Maier, *Les commentaires sur la Physique d'Aristote attribués à Siger de Brabant,* RPL., 47 (1949) 334-350. A. Maurer CSB., *Another Redaction of the Metaphysics of Siger of Brabant?* MS., 11 (1949) 224-232; *Siger of Brabant and an Averroistic Commentary on the Metaphysics in Cambridge, Peterhouse Ms 152,* MS., 12 (1950) 233-235. F. Van Steenberghen, *Siger of Brabant,* TMS., 29 (1951) 11-27. A. Maurer, *Siger of Brabant's De necessitate et contingentia causarum and Ms Peterhouse 152,* MS., 14 (1952) 48-60 (new text). W. Dunphy, *The Similarities Between Certain Questions of Peter of Auvergne's Commentary on the Metaphysics and the Anonymous Commentary on the Physics attributed to Siger of Brabant,* MS., 15 (1953) 159-168.
A Siger of Brabant different from our own will be found in the works of F. Van Steenberghen, *Siger de Brabant d'après ses oeuvres inédites,* RNSP., 32 (1930) 403-423; *Les oeuvres et la doctrine de Siger de Brabant,* Bruxelles, 1938; *Siger de Brabant d'après ses oeuvres inédites;* vol. II, *Siger dans l'Histoire de l'Aristotélisme,* Louvain, 1942; partly reprinted, minus many notes, under the title: *Aristote en Occident. Les origines de l'Aristotélisme parisien,* Louvain, 1946. Historical research, not dialectical controversy, will settle the question.—See B. Nardi, GCFI., 1943, 85-89.

[8] Questions on *Metaphysics,* Graiff ed., pp. 4-5, 7-8, 8-9, especially the commentary, pp. 183-191. This is not a matter of doctrine, but of language. Averroes usually gives metaphysics the name of its highest part because metaphysics is true theology.

[9] God knowable from his effects, Graiff, 84. God as moving cause, 53-56. God as final cause, 62-64. God as *ratio essendi* of all that is, 23-25. Cf. Siger, *Impossibilia,* Mandonnet ed., II, 74-77.

[10] Text in Graiff, 42-45.

[11] Graiff, 95: "Sexto intelligendum quod Avicenna, Aristoteles, fides et Proclus volunt quod una sit causa effectiva omnium." Again, 99: "Attendamus ergo plures vias, Aristotelis, Avicennae, Procli et aliorum ad illud probandum." Note, in both cases, the perhaps significant substitution of Proclus for Averroes. In Averroes and Siger, however, "efficient" cause means "moving" cause, and the First moves as "final" cause, that is as desired. For this reason, Siger says that, in caused beings, "participation" is "imitation," Graiff, 161; imitation and similitude, 109, lines 44-46; "participation by imitation," 85, lines 18-21.

[12] Proclus is regularly invoked in matters involving the causality of the Prime Being: 45, 46, 49, 95, 99, 103, 111, 112, 335; this is especially true with respect to efficient causality. On Siger's own position, 95-96, 98-103, 108-112.

[13] Against the separate Ideas of Plato; if they did exist, they would be gods, Graiff, 113-114, 114-117. There are ideas, but they are in God, 152. The divine thought knows an infinity of objects; his "species intelligendi" in his own essence; he knows all that flows from him, 71-73 (Incidentally, Siger has clearly seen that, in the world of Plato, there is no room left for an agent intellect nor for abstractive cognition, 129). As will be seen, this leaves open another question: what beings does God cause, strictly speaking, and, consequently, what beings does his self-knowledge necessarily include?

[14] Graiff, 60-62.

[15] From non-being, no becoming is possible, Graiff, 136. Pure non-being cannot be transmuted into being, because any transmutation demands a transmutable subject; now pure non-being is no subject, 136-137. Siger notes, however, that, on this point, Aristotle is begging the principle of his demonstration; he does not consider that an object B, for which there is no matter out of which it could be made, can nevertheless be more than pure non-being to the extent that it is in the power of its cause. From the point of view of its cause, it is possible, which is to be more than nothing, 138-139; cf. from a different point of view, 50 (against

Avicenna). This, however, is what Aristotle takes for granted; he is not speaking of the production of beings, but of their generation; now, obviously, generation cannot be out of nothing, 136-137. Eternal and incorruptible beings do not have to be produced; corruptible beings are always generated out of something; that is what philosophy says; "it is not good to conceal philosophy; consequently the intention of Aristotle on this point should not be concealed, although it be contrary to truth (*licet sit contraria veritati*)." On this point "nobody should attempt to investigate by reason what is above reason, *nor to refute reasons to the contrary*. But since a philosopher, however great he is, may always err in many matters, no one should deny the Catholic truth on account of some philosophical reason, even though he does not see how to refute it," Graiff, 140. Note two points: Siger does not know how to refute Aristotle because, starting as he does from absolute non-being, the notion of a generation out of nothing is a contradiction in terms: Graiff, 136, lines (85)-(88); secondly, the doctrine of Aristotle should not be concealed by masters, since it is their job to explain his books to students, 140, lines (19)-(20).—Cf. p. 153: creation *ex nihilo* is a contradictory notion; to say that Aristotle says this is not to say that it is true; nor does Aristotle himself prove this, he postulates it. The same interpretation is applied to the problem of the eternity of the intellective soul, in *Quaest. de anima intellectiva*, V; Mandonnet, *Siger de Brabant* . . . , II, 160-162: "Diceret aliquis. . . ."

[16] Fundamental text in W. J. Dwyer, *L'opuscule de Siger de Brabant De aeternitate mundi*, Louvain, 1937. This opuscule really is a Question. Siger proves that, taken collectively, the human species is only caused by generation of individuals from matter. Consequently (since its existence presupposes that of matter) it cannot have proceeded immediately from God, p. 28. The philosophers consider the human species to be both sempiternal and caused, p. 29. Its whole reality is the sempiternal succession of human individuals, pp. 29-30. Besides, the very notion that the human "species" could have begun by the production of one "individual" is an arbitrary one; those who maintain this should first prove that an individual has not been generated before

this one and so on to infinity, p. 32. The eternity of the species does not imply the existence of an eternally subsisting separate substance, man. Universals, qua universals, are no substances; they only exist in the intellect which abstracts them from singulars. Themistius calls them "concepts," p. 34-36. No universal precedes abstraction, p. 37; universals are things conceived in a universal way, p. 38. Concerning the possible beginning of time, and consequently of beings, let us note that if the universality of beings had not always existed (as is said by certain poets, theologians and philosophers) potency would have preceded act; if, then, there was potency, there was time (otherwise, potency could not be there "before" act); now, another act was required to actuate this potency (otherwise, nothing would have ever existed), and so on to infinity, pp. 43-44; cf. 45-46. In the last analysis, all this follows from the fact that the Prime Mover itself is eternally in act; so there must be eternally moved things. Consequently, "what has been before comes back specifically the same (n.b. not individually); opinions, laws, religions and other things revolve here below because of the revolutions of the higher beings (i.e., celestial substances), although, on account of its antiquity, the memory of the circulation of some beings was lost," p. 42. To which Siger immediately adds: "We are saying these things following the opinion of the Philosopher, we are not affirming them as true."

[17] Graiff, 72-73.

[18] Graiff, 190.—On the analogy of being, 108.—See the article of W. Dunphy quoted *infra*, note 127, p. 749.

[19] Albert the Great, *De causis et processu universitatis*, I, 1, 8; Borgnet, X, 377. On the notion of being, Armand Maurer, *Esse and Essentia in the Metaphysics of Siger of Brabant*, MS., 8 (1946) 68-85. This excellent article contains the text of the relevant Question of Siger, with the necessary references and a doctrinal study. The position of Siger in the Question *Utrum haec sit vera . . .* , is analyzed pp. 83-84.—The text of the same question is included in C. A. Graiff, 11-22.

[20] Siger, ed. Maurer, p. 70.

[21] Siger, ed. Maurer, pp. 70-71. The references to Avicenna are given in note 21. —For a perfectly correct interpretation of the famous text of Aristotle, *Post. Anal.*, I, 10, 76 b 35, see the text of Siger, in Graiff, 86.

[22] Maurer, p. 71. See, notes 25, 26, references to William of Auvergne and to Avicenna.

[23] Maurer, p. 71. A further criticism (Siger, in Maurer p. 74) is directed against Thomas Aquinas, *Sum. theol.*, I, 50, 2, ad 3m, or *Cont. Gent.*, II, 52. Cf. Maurer, MS., 12 (1950) 234.

[24] Maurer, p. 84, n. 58.

[25] Ibid.

[26] See the treatise of Siger, *On the Necessity and Contingency of Causes,* Mandonnet, op. cit., II, 111-128. The order of causes is as follows: 1, The Prime Cause, which immediately and necessarily causes the first separate Intelligence; 2, The same Prime Cause, as causing universally and necessarily all the other separate Intelligences, not immediately, but through the first one and according to their order: "because from one simple being, only one effect can follow immediately, and not many, except in a certain order" (p. 112); 3, The same Prime Cause as necessary but mediate cause of all the future positions occupied by the celestial bodies in virtue of the movement caused in them by the Prime Cause (in other words, the Prime Cause is the necessary, though mediate, cause of all the motions of celestial bodies, including their conjunctions, divisions, etc.); 4, The celestial bodies necessarily cause what happens in this sublunary world, but the dispositions of matter sometimes interfere with the causal necessity of the constellations, whose causality can thus be neutralized; 5, The particular and inferior causes, whose causality extends to few effects, some necessary, some common, some accidental (p. 113). The general conclusion of Siger, that not all future events are necessary before they happen (p. 114), means that all events are either necessary or accidental, not that some of them are free. "All effects . . . result from the Prime Cause as from a non-impedable cause," but "since it produces inferior effects through mediate causes, and not immediately," these effects result from sometimes impedable causes; whence accidents follow in the universe. All events would be necessary if all accidents followed from non-impedable causes, and if they all could be accounted for by a cause which, uniting and combining accidents, prevented them from being rare happenings (p. 115). The core of the matter is that, since the Prime Cause produces only one effect necessarily and immediately, there can be no more liberty in the universe than there is in the act in virtue of which it exists. There is human free choice precisely because there are accidental discontinuities in the chain of causal necessity; deliberation (*consilium*) always is about impedable future events. "The liberty of the will in its works should not be understood in this sense, that the will itself is the prime cause of its volitions and of its operations, as if it were able to move toward either one of two opposites without itself being moved" (p. 118). Against this position, Siger replies that "the liberty of the will consists in this, that although it is sometimes moved by certain movers, when these movers cannot be impeded, nevertheless, the nature of the will is such, that the moving action of all its possible movers can be impeded, because it wills according to the judgment of reason, which knows opposites" (p. 118). The existence of chance, or hazard, itself due to that of impedable causes (*causae impedibiles*) is the primary condition for the possibility of free choice: if there were no impedable causes, deliberations would be vain, the will itself would be necessitated so that there would be no free will (p. 119).— The positions of the Questions on *Metaphysics* are substantially the same: the corruptible cannot be the immediate effect of the incorruptible, Graiff, 154-156; from the Prime cause only one effect can immediately follow, 302-305: the first twenty lines of the copy followed by Graiff have been deleted by mediaeval censorship.

[27] In the *De necessitate et contingentia causarum,* providence is identified with the "practical reason" of God, itself defined as "the intellection of the connection and order of causes with respect to their effects," Mandonnet, *Siger of Brabant,* II, 122. Siger posits chance, or hazard, as the foundation for the very possibility of liberty. There is no chance (or accident) in the divine order, which is

that of intelligible necessity. Where there is no intelligible necessity, there is no truth. Consequently, since God knows nothing that is not necessary and true (that is himself and what flows from him in a necessary way) there can be in him no foreknowledge nor providence concerning contingents. If it sounds unpleasant to hear that there can be something which escapes the foreknowledge and providence of God, let us say that the infallible intellect of God does not know all future events as necessary in virtue of his self-knowledge, but in virtue of the knowledge he has of their causes (p. 123). In short, Siger is against those who deny that there is contingency in the world; there is nothing in the passive potency of matter that is not first in the active potency of the Prime Mover; but matter endures in time, and since the dispositions of passive matter required for a certain effect are not always present when the active cause is present, or vice versa, the possible effects of even a non-impedable cause do not always happen (p. 125); consequently, because of matter, some events are fortuitous "non simpliciter sed in respectu."—The only way not to get lost in the maze of Siger's arguments is to keep in mind his fundamental principle: in the Prime Cause, all is necessary; its self-knowledge is necessary and, given its object, it is about the necessary. Since all the rest is necessary only in virtue of the necessity of God, there is contingency in the world to the extent that there is only one unconditionally necessary being. As Prime Cause, God is cause of even contingents, but indirectly, and as cause of their causes. Consequently, his cognition of contingents is his cognition of that which, in their causes, is necessary in virtue of his own necessity. Such is the reason why, on this question, the authentic position of Siger is that there is in God no cognition of such events, except the cognition which is the intellection of himself and of his own substance. "Now, such an infallible and always true cognition of future events need not impose on them any necessity, so that we must say (*ita quod dicendum est*) of any future contingent, that it is not foreseen nor foreknown by God that it will take place, since only that which is true is foreseen and foreknown by God," Mandonnet, op. cit., p. 123. Cf. in the Questions on *Metaphysics*, Graiff, 308-309; Siger specifies that special interven-

tions of the divine will are possible, but, since such events cannot be foreseen, they escape scientific cognition; man cannot investigate the will of God, Graiff, 363, lines 75-79.—The newly discovered redaction of the Questions on the *Metaphysics* published by A. Maurer, MS., 14 (1952) 48-60, develops substantially the same solution of the problem of causal necessity and contingency as the text published by Mandonnet; it is, however, more careful in its wording.

[28] According to Siger, if the human intellect, taken as a power of the soul, could not understand a separate substance such as the separate agent Intellect, then the separate Intelligences could not know God. If God cannot be known by one intellective power, he cannot be known at all. His next argument seems to be a justification of Averroes by means of Proclus: if the intellect which is man's soul cannot understand God, no other Intelligence can; hence no Intelligence can understand itself; hence all Intelligences are absolutely unknown. For indeed, they are not known by the First, who knows nothing outside of himself; nor by ourselves or by themselves; in short, they are not known at all, "which entails that nature has acted in vain. This is what Siger says in his treatise *De intellectu* . . . , which was sent to Thomas in answer to his treatise against Averroes," B. Nardi, op. cit., p. 22 (Cf. Ferrariensis, commentary on *Contra Gentiles,* III, 45; Leonine edition, XIV, 119). Note that Siger has written a *De intellectu* in answer to Thomas Aquinas, and that this treatise was different from the Questions published by Mandonnet. According to B. Nardi, the *De intellectu* of Siger must have been written before the Questions published by Mandonnet, see op. cit., p. 33.—For the seven positions listed in our text, see B. Nardi, op. cit., p. 47.—M. Chossat, *Saint Thomas et Siger de Brabant,* Revue de Philosophie, 24 (1914) 553-575; 25, pp. 25-53. F. Van Steenberghen, *Les oeuvres et la doctrine* . . . , 64-75.

[29] In his *Sigieri di Brabante,* B. Nardi has established the existence of another lost treatise of Siger, the *Liber de felicitate.* In this treatise *On happiness,* Siger distinguished between two positions of the question, according as "felicity formally is the agent Intellect," or that "felicity

formally is God." The first position is that of all the Peripatetics (Alexander, Themistius, Simplicius, Averroes, Avicenna, Alfarabi, Avempace, etc.) The second, still more obviously a mediation than the one concerning the agent Intellect, seems to have been that of Siger. According to it, "all the Intellects are beatified by a felicity that is numerically one," namely by God who is felicity itself. "The intellect of man is beatified by the essence of God, in the same way as God is beatified by the essence of God. Consequently the felicity by which God is blessed is numerically the same as that by which other beings are blessed; for indeed God is felicity both to himself and to all the rest." In this text, however, as Nifo reports it (B. Nardi, op. cit., p. 26), the agent Intellect is explicitly called God. Siger seems to have desired to posit God as the ultimate beatitude of man (Christian position) without giving up his position concerning the separate Intellect. So he adds: "The copulation of the intellective power of the Moon, and others, with the agent Intellect, that is the divine Intellect, differs from the copulation of the agent Intellect (i.e., God) with our own intellective power. The former is absolutely eternal in itself, both simply and relatively; whereas the copulation of the agent Intellect with the rational soul is eternal in a certain way, but in another way it is new, as will be explained later on," p. 26. In these passages, Siger is dealing in a philosophical way with the problem (raised by Aristotle) of the felicity which man finds in the cognition of God. He is opposing the doctrine of Thomas (*Sum. theol.*, I, 12, 6), but Thomas was speaking of the eternal vision of God by individual men, whereas Siger is speaking of the philosophical beatification of man mentioned by Aristotle: "Siger believes that the Intellect cannot ever be happy in itself, without some individual man being happy in some part of the world: for indeed all that is in the Intellect, *qua* Intellect, is in some man," p. 29. Cf. the 36th proposition condemned in 1277: "That in this mortal life we can understand God by his essence," Nardi, p. 37, n. 2.—For the three positions listed in our text, see B. Nardi, op. cit., pp. 46-47.

[30] In his *De intellectu* (1492), reporting the position of Siger, Nifo observes: "This is how he mediates between the Latins and the Averroists: from the Averroists, he borrows the indivisibility, the immateriality and the oneness of the intellect; as to the Latins, he borrows from them that the intellect is the form that constitutes man in his specific being, and this one man in his particular being as such; so that it gives both individual being and specific being," B. Nardi, *Sigieri di Brabante*, p. 19. The mediating nature of this position appears in the following passage of Nifo, where he calls Siger the founder of the sects of the Averroists: the intellect is the direct and immediate act and form of "human nature" in general; as to Socrates or Plato (i.e., individual men) it is their form and perfection in an accidental way only, that is, "only by its copulation with intentions in imagination," op. cit., p. 20. So far as we can see, the concession made by Siger to the Latins was a rather verbal one. The more so as Averroes, himself following Plotinus, had already posited the intellect as the soul of man, despite its substantial separation from the human composite. The whole interpretation of Averroes himself should be examined anew in the light of the texts of Aristotle, *De anima*, II, 1 412a 19-21; III, 4, 429a 10 ff., commented by Plotinus, *Enneads*, IV, 7, 8 (Bréhier ed., IV, 203-204). Plotinus observes that the intellect is not a perfection in the sense described by the Aristotelian definition of the soul. If the word is to be used in connection with the intellect, which is immortal, it is "perfection" (*entelekheia*), for the Aristotelians themselves, in another sense than what they call the human soul. This is identically the problem Siger is here dealing with. Apart from any mediation between the Latins and the Greeks, the problem was intrinsic to the position of the Greeks. Cf. the interesting "Averroistic" question published by F. Van Steenberghen, *Un commentaire averroïste, anonyme et inédit, du Traité de l'âme*, ADGM., 842-854; especially 851-852.

[31] The *Quaestiones de anima* (Mandonnet, *Siger de Brabant* . . . , II, 145-171), define the soul as that by which the animated boly has life (q. I, p. 146). It is the prime act, form and perfection of a natural body able to live (q. 2, p. 147). Since intellection is no operation of the body, the question arises whether the intellective soul is the perfection and form of the body (q. 3, pp. 150-157).

The leading men in philosophy (*praecipui viri in philosophia*), namely, Albert and Thomas, say that the substance of the intellective soul is united to the body, but that the intellective power of this soul is separated from the body (p. 152). The reason given by Albert is that, in man, the vegetative, sensitive and intellective powers belong to the same soul; now the first two powers are forms of the body; consequently, etc. (p. 152). But Aristotle and Themistius deny that these three powers belong to the same soul: "Now what concerns us is only the intention of the philosophers, especially Aristotle, even though the opinion of the Philosopher does not agree with truth, and revelation has given us, concerning the soul, information which natural reason cannot conclusively justify." Whereupon, quoting against Albert one of Albert's own remarks, Siger shoots this Parthian shaft: "But we are not now concerned with God's miracles, since we are talking in a natural way about natural things," (p. 154; cf. Albert, *De generatione et corruptione,* I, 1, 22; Borgnet, IV, 363). The position of Thomas Aquinas is that intellection is an operation, not of the intellect alone, but of man; now this requires that the intellect be the act and perfection of the body. To which Siger replies that this is not the question; first, because it will be shown that, in fact, the intellect can be separate and nevertheless be the act and perfection of the body; secondly, if what Thomas says is true, any material part of the composite should be said to have intellectual knowledge (p. 154). The common objection to these two positions is that if a substance is united to matter, no power of that substance can be separated from matter (p. 152).—The position of Siger is a twofold one: 1, the intellective soul is separated from the body in being (*separata in essendo*); 2, the intellective soul is united to the body in its operation (*unita in operando*). This is the very reverse of the position of Thomas Aquinas. Intellection belongs, not only to the intellect, but to man, because, when it operates, the intellect does so within the body of man (*operans intrinsecus ad corpus per suam naturam*); now, such "intrinsic operators," and even movers, are called by philosophers the forms and perfections of what they move or of the beings within which they operate; consequently, separated from the body of man

in being, the intellect is united to it in its operating (pp. 154-155). Cf. p. 156: "Ad ultimum . . ." Such a separate substance is immortal in the future (q. 4, pp. 157-158) ; it has always existed in the past, that is, it has eternally been caused (q. 5, 158-161); nevertheless, according to the opinion of Averroes (and perhaps of Aristotle), the only way to maintain that it is immortal even *qua* act and perfection of the body, is to say that, since the species man is eternal, the separate Intellect is always the act and perfection of some human body (pp. 162-163). Its immortality is one with the eternity of the species. Naturally, this does not mean that individual souls are immortal and totally separable from their individual bodies. The problem of future rewards and punishments immediately arises, but Siger's intention is not "to investigate the truth about the soul, it is to ascertain the opinion of the Philosopher about it," (p. 163). In point of fact, divine Providence does not let good go unrewarded, nor evil unpunished: "to him who does good, the good deed itself is a reward . . . just as to evildoers, evil and vicious deeds themselves are punishments" (p. 163). For man to act according to virtue is true felicity. — The following question is answered in the same spirit: "investigating the doctrine of the philosophers rather than truth, and proceeding philosophically," we must say that the intellective soul is not multiplied with the multiplication of bodies, although, since infallible revelation teaches the contrary, it is true that the intellective soul is so multiplied (p. 164); Siger has long hesitated on the position of Aristotle on this point, which is one more reason why he should adhere to faith (p. 169).—On moral sanctions, see a much more elaborate text in *Impossibilia,* Mandonnet, op. cit., II, 86-90.—Albert and Thomas are also named in *Impossibilia,* II, pp. 84-85. Compare Siger, *Impossibilia,* II, 91: "Intelligendum est . . ." and Thomas Aquinas, *In Sent.,* I, 19, 5, art. 1, ad 7m; Mandonnet ed., I, p. 97.

[32] The views of Siger on philosophical knowledge in general offer nothing particularly original (see Graiff, 35-41). So far as we know, nobody has ever denied that Siger admitted the possibility of philosophical truth; what has been said is that every time the conclusions of philosophy contradict some theological position, Siger

refrains from saying that the conclusions of philosophy are true. Unless he were deliberately lying, which is possible but cannot be proved, Siger must have thought that certain conclusions could be philosophically irrefutable without being true. E. Gilson, *Etudes de philosophie médiévale*, Strasbourg, 1921, 59; *Reason and Revelation in the Middle Ages*, New York, 1938, 57; *Dante the Philosopher*, London-New York, 1948, 308-316; *La philosophie au moyen âge*, Paris, 1944, 562.

[33] Rather than "Averroism" which he finds inexact and confusing, F. Van Steenberghen favors the following appellations: *radical Aristotelianism;* then *heterodox Aristotelianism;* then *neoplatonizing Aristotelianism;* finally, *an heterodox neoplatonizing Aristotelianism influenced by both Averroism and Thomism;* see *Siger de Brabant . . .* , Louvain, 1942, 690-700. The conclusion that Siger was no Averroist had already been maintained by F. Bruckmüller, *Untersuchungen . . .* , 168-170; but F. Van Steenberghen goes further than this purely negative conclusion. In his own view, Siger found himself, in 1277, in the company of Thomas Aquinas, among the victims of that "inconsiderate act, prompted by the panic of the theologians, and perhaps also by the growing success of Aristotelianism"; this accounts for the glorification of Siger by Dante, for indeed Dante "may have known the true physiognomy of Siger, the head of the Aristotelian school, an admirer and even a disciple of Thomas Aquinas, an obedient son of the Church despite the intellectual crisis which set him at grips with the theologians and with the Bishop of Paris." (*Les oeuvres et la doctrine de Siger de Brabant*, p. 183).

[34] BOETIUS OF SWEDEN OP (Boetius de Dacia).—Life and works: P. Doncoeur, *Notes sur les averroistes latins. Boèce le Dace*, RSPT., 4 (1910) 500-511. M. Grabmann, *Neu aufgefundene Werke . . .* J. Nordström, *Bidrag rörande Boetius de Dacia*, Sartrych ur Samlaren, Uppsala, 1927. P. Mandonnet, *Note complémentaire sur Boèce de Dacie*, RSPT., 22 (1933) 246-250. M. Grabmann, *Die Opuscula De summo bono sive de vita philosophi und De sompniis des Boetius von Dacien*, AHDL., 6 (1931) 287-317; reprinted in MG., I (1936) 200-204 (text of the two treatises). F. Van Steen-

berghen, art. *Boèce de Dacie*, DHGE., 9 (1936) 381-382. M. Grabmann, *Die Sophismataliteratur des 12. und 13. Jahrhunderts, mit Textausgabe eines Sophisma des Boetius von Dacien . . .* , Münster i. W. (Beiträge, 36, 1) 1940.
MARTIN OF DENMARK (Martinus de Dacia), d. 1304.—M. Grabmann, *Texte des Martinus von Dacien zur Frage nach der Unterschied von essentia und existentia*, Miscellanea J. Gredt, Roma, 1938, 7-17 (SA., 7-8). H. Roos SJ., *Die Modi significandi des Martinus de Dacia. Forschungen zur Geschichte der Sprachlogik im Mittelalter*, Münster i. W., 1952 (Beiträge, 37, 2).—The meaning of Dacia is a twofold one. Applied to members of a mendicant Order, it designates the whole northern province of the Order (Boetius, born in Sweden, but OP., was of the Dominican province of Dacia); applied to a member of the secular clergy (Martin of Dacia), it designates Denmark.

[35] The same sincere religious feeling was already present in Averroes himself; for instance *De substantia orbis*, ch. 2, end (Venice, 1573, vol. IX, 8 v). It is more strongly marked than in those of the works of Aristotle which we know. See Averroes, *Tractatus de animae beatitudine*, Venice, 1573, vol. IX, 148-155. The second chapter of this treatise shows the religious implications of the problem of the intellect, on which Averroes admits that Aristotle did not express himself clearly (p. 149 r).

[36] JAMES OF DOUAI, see M. Grabmann, *Jacob von Douai, ein Aristoteleskommentator zur Zeit des hl. Thomas von Aquin und des Siger von Brabant*, MAP., 389-413. Describes the Questions of James on the *De anima* and publishes extracts related to the problem of the intellect. Two other masters seem to have exhibited Averroistic tendencies: GILES OF ORLEANS, author of commentaries on Aristotle's *Ethics*, M. Grabmann, *Die lateinische . . .* , 46-51; ANTHONY OF PARMA, a commentator of the same work, M. Grabmann, op. cit., 55-60.

[37] M. Grabmann, *Der lateinische Averroismus . . .* , anonymous commentary on Aristotle's *Ethics* (Erfurt, F 13), 37-46. R. A. Gauthier, *Trois commentaires "averroistes" sur l'Ethique à Nicomaque*, AHDL., 16 (1947-1948) 187-336. The

conclusion of this remarkable study (335-336) raises problems of general interest. It will be usefully compared with the

texts published by O. Lottin, PEM., III, 630-648 and with his own conclusions, 648-650.

PART NINE

CHAPTER II. THE THEOLOGICAL REACTION

[38] Bonaventure, *Collationes de decem praeceptis,* II, 28; Quaracchi, V, 515. Cf. Jules d'Albi, *Saint Bonaventure et les luttes doctrinales de 1267-1277,* Tamines (Belgium) 1923, p. 148. The general thesis of the author is that Bonaventure was the initiator of the anti-Averroistic campaign which culminated in the condemnation of 1277. Judging from the now known facts, the thesis is correct. On the contrary, Jules d'Albi's treatment of the position of Thomas Aquinas is open to discussion.

[39] *Collationes,* II, 25; Quaracchi, V, 514.

[40] *De donis Spiritus Sancti,* VIII, 15-16; Quaracchi, V, 497-498.

[41] *In II Sent.,* 1, 1, 1, 2, Concl.; Quaracchi, II, 22. *Breviloquium,* II, 1, 3; min. ed., p. 61.

[42] CUP., I, 486-487.—UNIV., 80-81; cf. 85-86.

[43] The *De unitate intellectus* of Thomas Aquinas is to be found, besides the Perrier edition of the *Opuscula* (I, 71-120), in an excellent edition by L. W. Keeler, Roma, Pont. Univ. Gregoriana, 1936. Thomas has written this treatise against some Averroists whom he does not name. If the words he ascribes to his adversary (Perrier, 55, p. 119; Keeler, 122, p. 78) have been written by Siger, they belong to one of his lost writings. But his adversary may have been another Averroist. On the contrary, the Questions of Siger's *De anima* are posterior to the *De unitate intellectus* of Thomas Aquinas and partly directed against it: M. Chossat, *Saint Thomas et Siger de Brabant,* Revue de Philosophie, 24 (1914) 553-575; 25 (1914) 25-53.

Assuredly, the reaction of Thomas was also theological (see Keeler ed., 122, pp. 78-80); but in dealing with philosophers, his method was distinctly philosophical. He met squarely the Averroistic issue in establishing that, on this crucial

point, the "Commentator" of Aristotle had really been his "perverter," 121, pp. 77-78 (*philosophiae peripateticae perversorem*). His strong point was that his adversaries had no right to oppose, on this issue, *all* the Greeks to all the Latins, since neither Aristotle, nor Theophrastus, nor Themistius (to say nothing of Plato) can be said to have taught that the possible intellect was a separate substance (Keeler, 121, pp. 77-78). Read the belligerent conclusion, Keeler, 124, p. 80.

A secular master at the University of Paris, GERARD OF ABBEVILLE (Gerardus de Abbatisvilla, d. 1272) has left still unpublished quodlibetic questions; one of them, directed against the oneness of the agent intellect, is found in M. Grabmann, *Quaestio Gerardi de Abbatisvilla (d. 1272) de unitate intellectus contra monopsychismum averroisticum,* APA., 7 (1941) 1-18. —GLOREP., I, 356-360.

[44] The *Collationes in Hexaemeron* have been published in two distinct reportations; the substance of the doctrine is the same but the division and the wording of the text are different: see *Opera omnia,* Quaracchi, V, 327-454, and *Collationes in Hexaemeron et Bonaventuriana quaedam selecta,* Quaracchi, 1934. Our references will be to the latter edition.—On the three central errors, I, 3, 1, pp. 91-93. This text is followed, pp. 93-103, by a long development on the illumination of moral virtues, which constantly opposes theological truth to the doctrine of the philosophers in general. Jules d'Albi has made an extensive use of sermons of Bonaventure whose interest is undeniable, but whose exact dates have not yet been established with certainty: *Saint Bonaventure et les luttes doctrinales . . . ,* pp. 190-213. These sermons are certainly relevant and all belong in the period which extends from 1266 to 1270 or slightly later.

[45] *In Hexaemeron,* III, 7, 8-12; pp. 215-216.—In order to understand the protest of Siger against the theologians who

thought that the intention of the Philosopher should be concealed, see Bonaventure's candid statement, *In Hexaemeron,* I, 3, 1, 5, p. 92: "It is more prudent to say that Aristotle did not think that the world was eternal, whether he himself thought so or not, because he was so great that all would follow him and affirm that he said so. All the light spread by what precedes would be extinguished. Let us follow him in the truth he said, not in those things in which he was obscure, which he did not know or which he concealed." By adding Thomas to the group, we obtain three different attitudes: 1, Siger: let us say that Aristotle says what he does say, even though his conclusions are hardly refutable; 2, Thomas: let us say that Aristotle says what he does say, but let us first make sure that he said it and let us not conclude, from the sole fact that he said it, that it is true; 3, Bonaventure: let us be careful not to affirm that Aristotle said anything which contradicts faith, even if he said it, because too many men would follow him in his error.

[46] Giles of Rome, *Errores philosophorum,* Critical text with notes and introduction by Joseph Koch. English transl. by J. O. Riedl, Milwaukee, 1944. An older edition of the text is to be found in P. Mandonnet, *Siger de Brabant,* under the title *De erroribus philosophorum,* II, 1-25. It successively lists: 1, the errors of Aristotle (ch. I-III); 2, of Averroes (ch. IV-V); 3, of Avicenna (ch. VI-VIII); of Algazel (ch. VIII-IX); of Alkindi (ch. X-XI); of Maimonides (ch. XII). The conclusion (ch. XIV) is a short prayer to God by the author of this treatise written "in detestation of those who contradict" God and who oppose what Giles holds to be the sole true and Catholic faith.

[47] Albertus Magnus, *De quindecim problematibus,* in Mandonnet, *Siger de Brabant . . . ,* II, 29-52. The short letter of Giles of Lessines is printed at the beginning of Albert's answers. The answers of Albert are those of a theologian who still belongs to the traditional school. For instance, he still maintains that the intellective soul of man is to the Intelligence of the tenth sphere in the same relation as this Intelligence is to the higher ones; the *intellectus adeptus* and the *intellectus in habitu,* received by the soul as lights coming to it from the Intelligences are implied in the formula he uses: "ita in anima sunt lumina intelligentiarum *adepta* et *possessa* ab illustratione intelligibilium," Mandonnet, II, 33. Same page, bottom, this illumination is still called the root of immortality: *radix immortalitatis.* His conclusion is that what the Parisian masters teach is "absurd," "ridiculous," and that it proceeds either from ignorance or, surely, from hatred against faith (p. 45). The Aristotle he opposes to Averroes still is, on the whole, that of Alfarabi and Avicenna. — F. Van Steenberghen, *Le "De quindecim problematibus" d'Albert le Grand,* MAP., pp. 415-439; favors the dates 1273-1276 rather than 1270.

[48] Letter of John XXI to Tempier, CUP., 1, 541. Cf. P. Mandonnet, *Siger de Brabant . . . ,* I, 213.

[49] A. Callebaut, *Jean Peckham et l'augustinisme. Aperçus historiques (1263-1285),* AFH., 18 (1925) 441-472. According to the text of this document, published for the first time by Callebaut, John XXI commanded that the "authors, inventors and promoters" of the condemned errors be sent to him as rapidly as possible, p. 460. In fact, both Siger and Boethius of Sweden, willingly or not, went to the Pontifical Curia. This capital document proves that far from blaming Tempier, the Pope acted as though he approved of the condemnation.

[50] The text of the condemnation has been published in CUP., I, 543-558. There is hardly any order in the list of the propositions; they have been reprinted, in a more systematic order by Mandonnet, *Siger de Brabant,* II, 175-181. Our references will be to Mandonnet.—The introduction expressly denounces some men "studying in Arts at Paris and overstepping the limits of their own Faculty," who presume to treat and to discuss in schools, as open to discussion (*dubitabilia*), the propositions listed in the document. "For indeed they say that these things are true according to philosophy, but not according to the Catholic faith, as though there were two contrary truths . . ." etc., p. 175.—P. Glorieux, art. *Tempier (Etienne),* DTC., 15 (1946) 99-107. GLOREP., I, 362-363.

[51] The *Liber de amore,* or *De deo amoris,* has been identified by Denifle and

Chatelain, in CUP., I, p. 557, note 8, as the work of Andreas Capellanus familiar to students of courtly love. The discovery has been made again by M. Grabmann, *Das Werk De amore des Andreas Capellanus und das Verurteilungsdekret des Bischofs Tempier von Paris vom 7 März 1277*, Speculum, 7 (1932) 75-79.—On the condemned propositions traceable to Andreas Capellanus: A. J. Denomy, *The De amore of Andreas Capellanus and the Condemnation of 1277*, MS., 8 (1946) 107-149, 300-301.—English transl. only in *Andreas Capellanus. The Art of Courtly Love, with Introduction, Translation and Notes*, by J. J. Parry, New York, Columbia Univ. Press, 1941.

[52] The list of the Thomistic propositions involved in the condemnation is longer, or shorter according as it is compiled by a Franciscan or by a Dominican. P. Mandonnet OP., counts about twenty of them: 1) *Oneness of the world:* That the Prime Cause cannot make several worlds (Mandonnet's list, 27), That if there were a separate substance moving nothing, it would not be included in the universe (50); 2) *Individuation:* That God cannot multiply individuals in a species without matter (42), That, since Intelligences have no matter, God cannot make several Intelligences of the same species (43), That forms only receive division owing to matter (110), That God could not make souls many in number (115), That individuals of the same species differ by the sole position of matter (116); 3) *Relations of separate Substances to the physical world:* That separate Substances do not change in their operation, because their appetition is one (52), That an Intelligence, or an Angel, or a separate soul, is nowhere (53), That separate Substances are nowhere as to their substance (54), That separate Substances are somewhere by their operation, etc., (55); 4) *Intellect:* That the fact that we understand better or less well comes from the passive intellect, which he says to be a sensitive power—Error, because this is to posit one single intellect in all men, or equality in all souls (146); That it is not fitting to posit some intellects as more noble than others, because since this diversity cannot originate in their bodies, it would necessarily originate in their intelligences, and thus more noble and less noble souls would necessarily belong in diverse species, like the Intelligences.—Error, because

thus the soul of Christ would not be more noble than the soul of Judas (147); 5) *Will:* That the cognition of contraries is the sole cause why the rational soul can will opposites, and that a power simply cannot will opposites except by accident and by reason of another one (162); That the will firmly pursues what is firmly believed by reason, and that it cannot abstain from what reason prescribes: to be thus necessitated is not coercion, it is the nature of the will (163); That while passion and particular cognition (*scientia*) are actually present, the will cannot act against them (169). —The list could be made shorter, or longer, because these propositions cannot always be found literally in Thomas Aquinas, at least not without important qualifications, while others could just as well be added, with the same reservation. The general impression is that Tempier asked various masters to bring him lists of suspicious propositions, after which, without examining them too closely, he did a scissors and paste job.—On the still confused question of the possible influence of the Condemnation on the origins of modern science, see the pertinent and humorous remarks of A. Koyré, *Le vide et l'espace infini au XIVe siècle*, AHDL., 17 (1949) 45-91; especially 45-52.—Related to the same period: M.-T. d'Alverny, *Un témoin muet des luttes doctrinales du XIIIe siècle*, AHDL., 17 (1949) 223-265 (censured texts of the anonymous Arabian treatise *De causis et proprietatibus elementorum*, 228; *Liber XXIV philosophorum*, 230-240; Alfarabi, *Liber excitationis ad viam felicitatis*, 240-245; even the *Quaestiones naturales* of Adelard of Bath, 246-247).

[53] Mandonnet, *Siger de Brabant . . .*, prop. 180-184; II, p. 189. These strictly anti-Christian propositions have not yet been discovered in any writing; it is possible that such things were said rather than written.

[54] The 1277 list includes the 1270 list, with many additions, and it is not always easy to say with certitude who, in the mind of the theologians, was behind each proposition. In many cases, however, it is possible. Following the order of Mandonnet: 9, That in this mortal life we can know God by essence (Siger); 10, That all that we can know of God is that he is, or his existence (probably Thomas Aqui-

nas); 13-15, That God does not know other beings and has no immediate knowledge of contingents (Siger); 20, That God necessarily produces what immediately follows from him (Siger); 22, That God cannot be the cause of a new fact, and that he cannot produce something in a new way (Siger); 33, That the Prime Cause can immediately cause only one single effect (Siger); 64, That God is the necessary cause of the motion of superior bodies and of conjunctions and divisions in stars (Avicenna); 69, That God cannot produce the effect of a secondary cause without this secondary cause itself (Averroes); 80, That the argument of the Philosopher demonstrating that the motion of heaven is eternal is not sophistical, and that it is surprising that men of profound intellect do not see this (perhaps Thomas, *De aeternitate mundi,* 9; Perrier ed., I, p. 59); 95, That, in order that all effects be necessary with respect to the Prime Cause, it is not enough that the Prime Cause be not impedable; it is also required that the intermediate causes be not impedable (Siger); 99, That there are several Prime Movers (probably Siger); 108, That God only is the efficient cause of what has being in the potency of matter (Averroes); 117, That the intellect of all men is numerically one, although it is always united to a certain body (Siger); 123, That the intellect only is the form of the body as the pilot is the form of his ship, and that it is not the essential perfection of man (note the possible danger of falling from the soul-substance into the separate Intellective soul); 133, That the soul is inseparable from the body (Averroes, but does not apply to the separate Intellect); 140, That the agent Intellect is not united to our possible intellect; that the possible Intellect is not united to us by essence, and that, if it were united to us as a form, it would be inseparable from the body (Averroes, Siger); 153, That the will and the intellect are not moved to their acts by themselves, but by an eternal cause, namely, celestial bodies (Averroes); 172, That felicity is obtained in this life, not in another one (Averroes, Siger); 189, That creation *ex nihilo* is impossible, although the contrary must be held by faith (Siger).—Siger practically always presupposes Averroes, and often Aristotle. To say that the authors of the condemnation had Averroes or Siger in mind (and sometimes perhaps Thomas Aqui-

nas), does not mean that Siger, and still less Thomas, would have recognized these propositions as a faithful rendering of their authentic positions: but a great many of them can be safely traced to Siger and Averroes.

[55] F. Ehrle, *Beiträge zur Geschichte der mittelalterlichen Scholastik. II, Der Augustinismus und Aristotelismus in der Scholastik gegen Ende des dreizehnten Jahrhunderts,* ALKM., 5 (1889) 603-635; *Der Kampf um die Lehre des hl. Thomas in den ersten fünfzig Jahre nach seinem Tode,* ZKT., 37 (1913) 266-318; *L'agostinismo e l'aristotelismo nella Scolastica del secolo XIII,* Xenia thomistica, Rome, 1925; III, 14-21, 38-76, 517-588. — P. Mandonnet, *Premier travaux de polémique thomiste,* RSPT., 7 (1913) 46-70, 245-262.—M. Grabmann, *Hilfsmittel des Thomasstudiums aus alter Zeit . . . ,* DTF., 1 (1923) 13-43, 97-122, 373-380; *Die Italienische Thomistenschule des 13. und beginnenden 14. Jahrhunderts,* MG., I, 332-391; *Forschungen zur Geschichte der ältesten deutschen Thomistenschule des Dominikanerordens,* MG., I, 392-431; *Einzelgestalten aus der mittelalterlichen Dominikaner-und Thomistentheologie,* MG., II, 512-613; *Das Weiterleben und Weiterwirken des moraltheologischen Schrifttums des hl. Thomas von Aquin im Mittelalter,* DTF., 25 (1947) 3-28. F. Pelster, *List of Questions im MS Assisi 158,* OTT., 104-132.

PETER OF TARANTASIA OP (Petrus de Tarantasia, Pope Innocent V), d. 1316.— *Innocentii Quinti in quattuor libros Sententiarum commentaria,* Toulouse, 1649-1652. Fragments on the existence of God in A. Daniels, *Quellenbeiträge und Untersuchungen . . . ,* 68-71. Turinaz, *Un pape savoisien,* Nancy, 1901.—GLOREP., I, 107-112. V. Doucet, AFH. 26 (1933) 208-210. Collective work: *Beatus Innocentius V (Petrus de Tarentasia OP). Studia et documenta,* Roma, 1943; according to H.-D. Simonin (*Les écrits de Pierre de Tarentaise,* op. cit., 163-335) his commentary on the *Sentences* (ca. 1257-1259) shows Peter hesitating between Bonaventure and Thomas Aquinas; same interpretation in B. Smeraldo, *Intorno all'opuscolo IX di S. Tommaso d'Aquino. Pietro di Tarantasia. Ha errato in teologia?* Roma, 1945 (answer: no; he was worthy of becoming a pope). See, however, G. Gàl, Part VIII, note 42. O. Lottin, *A propos du Commentaire des*

Sentences de Pierre de Tarentaise, RTAM., 13 (1946) 86-98. R. Martin OP., *Pour une réédition critique du commentaire de Pierre de Tarentaise sur le Livre des Sentences de Pierre Lombard,* Miscellanea-Alb. de Meyer, Louvain, 1946, I, 590-602. M.-H. Laurent, *Le bienheureux Innocent V (Pierre de Tarentaise) et son temps,* Città del Vaticano, 1947 (Studi e Testi). P. Glorieux, *Questions nouvelles de Pierre de Tarentaise,* RTAM., 14 (1947) 96-106.—O. Lottin, PEM., *passim* and particularly, II, 58-63, 92-94, 236-241, 393-394; III, 46-47, 233-234, 417-418, 462-464, 720-721.

PART NINE

CHAPTER III. PHILOSOPHICAL CONTROVERSIES

[56] See the official price lists for booksellers at the University of Paris, CUP., I, 644-650 (list of 1275) also in UNIV., 112-117; II, 107-112 (list of 1304).

[57] P. Glorieux, *Les premières polémiques thomistes; I, Le "Correctorium Corruptorii QUARE, édition critique,* Kain (Belgium), 1927. Contains the text of William of la Mare and the answers of a Thomist, probably Richard Clapwell (Knapwell). —W. OF LA MARE, an English Franciscan, master in theology at Paris (*ca.* 1274-1275); died about 1285. GLOLIT., II, 117-118. GLOREP., II, 99-101. V. Doucet, AFH., 27 (1934) 549. E. Longpré, DTC., 8 (1925) 2467-2470. William's criticism of Thomas (*Correctorium*) was officially adopted by the General Chapter of the Franciscan Order at Strasbourg in 1282. On his unpublished 25 Disputed Questions, GLOREP., 99; consult E. Longpré, France Franciscaine, 1922, 289-306, and F. Pelster, RTAM., 3 (1931) 397-411. Over and above the two already known redactions (objections are usually directed against the second redaction), the complete text of a third redaction (anterior to 1284-1285) has been discovered by R. Creytens, *Autour de la littérature des correctoires,* AFP., 12 (1942) 313-330.—On the controversies about human knowledge, A. Hufnagel, *Studien zur Entwicklung des thomistischen Erkenntnisbegriffes im Anschluss an das Correctorium "Quare,"* Münster i. W., 1935 (Beiträge, 31, 4).—On the controversies about freedom, O. Lottin, *Les fondements de la liberté humaine; I, De 1250 à la condamnation de 1270; II, De la condamnation de 1270 à celle de 1277; III, Après la condamnation de 1277,* PEM., I, 225-389 (Thomas Aquinas, Walter of Bruges, William of La Mare, Matthew of Aquasparta, Henry of Ghent, Peter of Falco, William of Hothun, Richard of Mediavilla, Marston, Quidort, Giles of Rome, Godfrey of Fontaines, Thomas of Sutton, Nicholas Trivet).

[58] On the attribution to Richard Clapwell of the reply to William of la Mare, P. Glorieux, *Les premières polémiques . . . ,* pp. XLIV-LV. Glorieux considers this attribution as highly probable, not to say certain. On the contrary, F. Pelster, *Zur Datierung der Schriften des Johannes von Paris* OP. (that is, John Quidort), DTF., 30 (1952) 417-438, attributes the *correctorium Quare* to Thomas of Sutton (p. 420) and considers it posterior to 1286; the *correctorium Sciendum* is attributed to Robert of Orford; the *correctorium Circa* to John Quidort. If and when P. Glorieux agrees with F. Pelster, what we are attributing to Clapwell on the ground of the *correctorium Quare* should be attributed to Sutton.

Richard Clapwell (Klapwell, Knapwell, Clapoil, etc.) OP., an English master in theology, progressively adopted the positions of Thomas Aquinas and opposed their condemnation by Peckham in 1286 (P. Glorieux, op. cit., LII-LIV); date of death unknown. On the "difficult" and "hesitant" conversion of Clapwell to Thomism attested by his *Notabilia:* D. L. Douie, *Archbishop Peckham,* p. 281.— M.-D. Chenu OP., *La première diffusion du thomisme à Oxford,* AHDL., 3 (1928) 185-200. F. Pelster, *Richard von Knapwell OP., seine Quaestiones disputatae und sein Quodlibet,* ZKT., 52 (1928) 473-491; *Die Sätze der Londoner Verurteilung von 1286 und die Schriften des Magister Richard von Knapwell OP.,* AFP., 16 (1946) 83-106.—On the English theologians of this period in general, many notices in A. G. Little and F. Pelster SJ., *Oxford Theology and Theologians ca. A.D. 1282-1302,* Oxford, Clarendon Press, 1934; quoted in this book as OTT.

Cf. V. Doucet, AFH., 27 (1934) 274-280. On a probable collaborator of Clapwell, WILLIAM OF MACCLESFIELD OP. (d. 1303), OTT., 270-275.

[59] *Correctorium,* 4, pp. 25-26. Cf. 79, pp. 326-327; 97, pp. 389-390.

[60] On the distinct idea of each genus, *Correctorium,* 4, p. 26, "Praeterea . . ." Cf. 81, pp. 329-330; note, in this latter text, that the Ideas are the "substantial forms" of things.—On the plurality of forms; connection between hylomorphism and the plurality of forms, 12, p. 64; on the essence of matter as distinct from the essence of form, 27, pp. 114-115; on the plurality of forms in man (otherwise there would be in man no forms of elements, nor of the mixed body, which means the end of the study of medicine; still worse, one and the same form would give both corporeal being and spiritual being), 31, pp. 130-131; connection between the plurality of forms and seminal reasons (Augustine, Ambrosius *In Hexaemeron,* III, 8, PL., 42, 976, Macrobius, Aristotle and Averroes, *sic*), 85, pp. 351-353; connection with the problem whether the *esse* of the soul is communicated to the body, which is to forget that, in the composite, each part has its own being, 86, p. 362; the soul is not immediately united to corporeal matter, 90, p. 373; besides, this position has been condemned by the masters as erroneous, pp. 372-374; on the contrary, the soul is composed of matter and form (references to Augustine p. 376) 91, pp. 375-378; cf. 113, pp. 419-420 (note, p. 420 the connection with the problem of the immortality of the soul). The only quotation of Gabirol contained in the whole *Correctorium* is not made by William, but by Clapwell, p. 152.

[61] This controversial literature adds little to our knowledge of either Thomism or Augustinism, but it is of invaluable help in revealing the dialectical structure of the two doctrines.

[62] On the presence of future contingents to God, 3, pp. 18-81; note, p. 21, the pertinent answer of Clapwell, that Thomas does not teach that time is already present in eternity, but that all the successive moments of time have in eternity the same presence which each one of them has in time (*Cont. Gent.,* I, 66).

The problem has connections with the divine Ideas and seminal reasons, p. 19, and with the whole cosmogony in both doctrines: the non-eternity of creation is demonstrable, at least by reduction of the contrary to absurdity, 6, pp. 31-34; 7, pp. 40-43; 109, 411-412.

[63] Hylomorphic composition of angels, in Themistius and others, Glorieux, *Correctorium,* 54-55. Clapwell restates the Thomistic composition of essence and existence, p. 55, ad 8m.

[64] *Correctorium,* pp. 49-50.

[65] *Correctorium,* p. 50: "Dicendum ergo. . . ."

[66] *Correctorium,* art. 10; texts of Augustine quoted pp. 49 and 50. His other authorities are Boethius, *De Trinitate,* 3; PL., 64, 1250) and pseudo-Boethius (Gundissalinus) *De unitate et uno,* PL., 64, 1077.—It has recently been said that the influence of Gabirol was neither deep nor enduring (R. Zavalloni, *Richard de Middleton* . . . , p. 422). To limit ourselves to hylomorphism, let us note that, rightly or wrongly, Thomas Aquinas considered Gabirol as responsible for this doctrine (*Sum. theol.,* I, 50, 2), and even as its founder (*De ente et essentia,* 5). At a still later date, Vital du Four did not hesitate to write: "Ego autem ad positionem Avecembroni redeo . . ." Nevertheless, there is truth in Zavalloni's remark. It seems that at a certain date, and perhaps during Vital du Four's own life time, the Augustinians began to drop Gabirol and to substitute for his authority on hylomorphism, those of Augustine, Boethius and Denis. To what extent they were justified in involving Boethius and Denis in this controversy is another question.

[67] JOHN QUIDORT OP (John of Paris, *Joannes Dormiens, Surdus, Soardus,* etc.), French, entered the Dominican Order at an unknown date; seems to have lectured on the *Sentences* long before being made a licentiate; the reportation of his Commentary on Lombard precedes his answer to the *Correctorium* of William of La Mare (1280/1285?); licentiate and master in theology at the University of Paris (1304); *Quodlibetum* in 1304-1305 (A. Heiman); treatise on Transsubstantion, theological censure by a board of

censors under the presidency of Giles of Rome, suspension of his teaching activity (1305); appeal to the pope and death in 1306.—GLOREP., I, 189-193 and II, 508. GLOLIT., II, 182-183. M. Grabmann, *Le Correctorium Corruptorii du dominicain Jean Quidort de Paris*, RNSP., 19 (1912) 404-418; *Studien zu Johannes Quidort von Paris O. Pr.*, Sitzungsberichte, Munich, 1922, 3. J. Leclercq OSB., *Jean de Paris et l'ecclésiologie du XIIIe siècle*, Paris, 1942. Corrections to W. of La Mare in J. P. Muller, *Le Correctorium Corruptorii "Circa" de Jean Quidort de Paris*, (SA., 12-13) Rome, 1941. Same author, *Der Tractatus de formis des Johannes Quidort von Paris*, DTF., 19 (1941) 195-210; *La thèse de Jean Quidort sur la béatitude formelle*, MAP., 493-511; *Les critiques de la thèse de Jean Quidort sur la béatitude formelle*, RTAM., 15 (1948) 152-170 (P. of Auvergne, Harvey Nedellec, John of Pouilly, M. Eckhart). F. Pelster, *Ein anonymer Traktat des Johannes von Paris OP., über das Formenproblem in Cod. Vat. lat. 862*, DTF., 24 (1946) 3-28: analysis, 22-28; John strongly maintains the oneness of the substantial form.—O. Lottin, PEM., I, 300-302; II, 264-267; III, 472-476, and *passim*.—Studies on Quidort's *De adventu Christi* by D. Planzer, AFP., I, 1931, 76-81, and A. Wachtel, FS., 25 (1938) 370-378 (R. Bacon source of Quidort).

[68] On this incident, P. Glorieux, *Un mémoire justificatif de Bernard de Trilia*, RSPT., 17 (1928) 405-426. The same historian established later on that this writing belongs to John Quidort: *Le mémoire justificatif de Bernard de Trilia*, RSPT., 19 (1930) 469-474 (cf. J. Koch, ibid., pp. 464-468). The propositions were essentially theological; list in Glorieux, *Un mémoire*, 407-413 (except 12, 13, 14, in which philosophical notions are involved). The document is interesting as an instance of denunciation of a master by auditors whom he has neither seen nor heard and whose accusations he has not even been given to read. All that he can do is to refer his judges to his "reportation of St. Victor," which he seems to consider accurate.

[69] The treatise *On Transubstantiation* (*De transubstantiatione panis et vini in sacramento altaris*) was published by the Protestant theologian Petrus Alix, *Determinatio de modo existendi corpus Christi in sacramento altaris alio quam sit ille quem tenet ecclesia*, London, 1686. Since W. Münscher (1834) John Quidort has been made a forerunner of Luther's "impanation" theory (M. Grabmann, *Studien*, 14, n. 1). H. Weisweiler, *Die Impanationslehre des Johannes Quidort*, Scholastik, 6 (1931) 161-195. The prologue to an unpublished answer to Quidort is to be found in Grabmann, pp. 15-16. The philosophical origin of the new interpretation of the dogma is expressly marked and the position of Quidort is summed up in clear terms (p. 16); the philosophical intentions are confirmed in Grabmann, op. cit., pp. 17-18; on its later refutations (Hervaeus Natalis, Durand of St. Pourçain, Petrus de Palude, Thomas of Strassburg and John Baconthorp) p. 19. The new position of Quidort was that, in transubstantiation, the bread becomes the body of Christ, not by mode of conversion, but by mode of assumption of the humanity of Christ.

[70] On Quidort's *Quodlibetum*, M. Grabmann, *Studien*, 35-41. A complete transcription of the 10 Questions has been made by Ambrose J. Heiman, *The Esse of Creatures in the Doctrine of Jean Quidort. Study and Texts*, Ph.D. Thesis, Toronto, 1949. On Quidort's commentary on Peter Lombard, M. Grabmann, *Studien*, 41-57. The texts relevant to the doctrine of being have been transcribed by Heiman, op. cit. All our references to these texts will be borrowed from this transcription.

[71] On the divine knowledge of future contingents, 24-30; divine Ideas, 33-47; if the present universe could be better than it is, 38-39; faith and reason, 41-47 (eternity of the world, 44-47); species and individual in separate substances, 49, 158-163.

[72] Art. 26, pp. 138-139; matter has no distinct Idea in God, 143; connection with the problem of the unity of the form, ibid.

[73] Against the hylomorphic composition of souls, art. 27, pp. 146-155; incidentally, on intelligible species and abstraction, 151-155.

[74] Rejection of hylomorphism in angels, art. 9, pp. 53-63. The following lines are a fair sample of the degree of pre-

cision with which John defines his position on this point: "Angels are simple forms by privation of composition of matter and form, but they are composed by composition with something else, that is with existence (*esse*), with the powers flowing from the form they are and with their accidents. They are even composed of certain things, namely, of genus and difference. Or else one could say that he (Thomas) calls simple a form, or act, that is in potency with respect to nothing, like God. Now, although the form of an angel has no matter, it is in potency with respect to many things," etc., p. 59.

[75] Quidort distinguishes between two philosophical positions (and errors): 1) some beings have existence formally in virtue of their essences, for instance, if Aristotle has taught that separate substances necessarily exist in virtue of their formal essences, just as a man is necessarily a man in virtue of his essence; 2) some beings are their own being *consecutive*, that is, because their existence flows from their form, so that these can lose existence if they lose their form, not otherwise. The second position is that of the Platonists: Proclus, *Elementatio*, 46. In fact, Quidort is arguing against Avicenna in maintaining that "no thing can formally have necessary existence by another" (*Quod.* I, 2). Whether Avicenna ever said "formally" is another question. Formulated in these terms, however, the proposition becomes self-contradictory. To be "formally-necessary-by-another" is an impossibility. Quidort's interpretation of Aristotle ("Quod Aristoteles posuit . . .") is excellent and shows what progress was then being made in the correct historical understanding of the Philosopher by the Aristotelians as well as of Augustine by the Augustinians.

[76] Quidort affirms the distinction of essence and existence, but he must have understood it in a peculiar way, for he draws from it consequences which would have surprised Thomas Aquinas. For instance: God could produce matter without form or quiddity: "and thus matter will be a being, but not any specified being (*aliquod ens*); and I say that this is possible, if essence is really different from existence, as I believe it is," *Quodl.*, I, 7 ("Et hoc dico possibile si essentia differt ab esse realiter, sicut credo"). Conversely, although it is the act of all ex-

istents, *esse* is in itself indeterminate to genus or species. It is reduced to the genus or species of the thing whose act it is. Consequently, "God can create this *esse*, which is other than essence, and he can confer upon it being by itself or entity (*esse per se vel entitatem*), and thus it will exist apart from essence (*et sic erit separatum ab essentia*); yet, it cannot be separated from essence by the divine power qua *esse* or act, but as to that which it is (*sed secundum id quod est*)," *Quodl.*, I, 7. In other words, Quidort imagines the act of being as that whose existential nature it is to be the existential act of existing things. There is an entity of existence, so much so that God could create it apart, although God cannot create the act of being of an essence apart from the essence whose act it is. John says that existence is an "accident" of essence, in the Avicennian sense in which "all that which happens to something is an accident" (*In II Sent.*, "Utrum in rebus creatis differant essentia et esse realiter vel sint idem secundum rem"). To him, the distinction means that no created being holds its existence from its essence. Existence does not flow from the intrinsic principles of the essence, it comes to it from without.—P. Glorieux, *Jean Quidort et la distinction réelle de l'essence et de l'existence*, RTAM., 18 (1951) 151-157. J. P. Muller, *A propos du mémoire justificatif de Jean Quidort*, RTAM., 19 (1952) 343-351 (text pp. 344-345) A. J. Heiman, CPPS., *Essence and Esse According to Jean Quidort*, MS., 15 (1953) 137-146.

[77] Art. 30, pp. 170-185. The philosophical arguments are borrowed from Plato's *Timaeus* and from Aristotle, 176-181. We do not find in the *Correctorium* the verbal appeasements given in *Quodl.*, 10 to the supporters of the form of corporeity.—References to a long treaty of Quidort on the plurality of forms are given p. 176 and p. 249. According to Muller (DTF., 19 (1941) 195-210) this was the treatise printed under the name of Nedellec in the edition of his *Quodlibeta Undecim*, Venice, 1513. According to Pelster, DTF., 94 (1946) 3-28, it was the *De unitate formarum* contained in the ms. *Vat. lat. 862*. The problem has not yet been solved: see note 67.

[78] John Quidort is against the plurality of forms. Unless we misinterpret his me-

andering discussion (I *Quodl.*, 10), his intention is both to prove that the rational soul is immediately united to the body (not through intermediate forms) and to say it in such terms that there still seems to remain a form of corporeity. The christological problems connected with this notion (for instance: after the death of Christ, if there is no form of corporeity, was the dead body still the body of Christ?) invited both parties to the controversy to be either firm or prudent on this issue. Question 10 affirms that the soul is the immediate form of body, flesh, eye, spleen and other parts; so there is no need for a distinct form of corporeity; but it can be said that, since it needs corporeal organs to sway the body, inasmuch as it is the form of these organs, the soul itself is the form of corporeity. In Quidort's doctrine, the distinction of organs does not arise from distinct substantial forms, but from the more or less complex organic structures (*contemperamentum*) of the various parts of the body actuated by one and the same substantial form.

[79] On the *Quodlibetum,* M. Grabmann, *Studien,* 35-41. On the Commentary on Peter Lombard, 41-57. From what Grabmann says concerning Quidort's interpretation of the distinction of essence and existence (p. 45) there is no reason to suppose that his "real" distinction went beyond the distinction between created and uncreated being. According to Quidort, Grabmann says, existence does not flow from the inner essence of being: "It happens to essence in a quasi-accidental way," p. 45. On the problem of the relation of the soul to its powers, pp. 51-52. Suggestive remarks of Quidort on Augustine's noetics (no agent intellect in Augustine) p. 54. Against Avicenna, he maintains that each man has an agent intellect of his own, but that, instead of flowing from the essence of the soul, like the other powers, it is given to the soul by a loftier agent, just about as moonlight is a light in the moon, but not from the moon. As supporting this position, Quidort names "many great" men, among whom Peter (of Auvergne), Albert (the Great) and Roman (of Rome); this, Grabmann rightly observes, is not a Thomistic position, p. 55.—Incidentally, we fail to see in what sense the doctrine developed by Quidort in his treatise *On the Power of the King and of the Pope*

(Leclercq ed., 173-260) can be said to agree with the views of Thomas Aquinas on the question. Quidort teaches that, in case the pope proves unworthy, the king can depose him, and, if the pope refuses to comply, the king "can make the people do something that will cause the pope to give in," or even make the people depose him (op. cit., p. 214, lines 21-24). Quidort euphemistically calls this an indirect excommunication of the pope by the prince; it is: "to depose him *per accidens.*" He seems to have anticipated the modern doctrine of the "indirect" power of the popes over the temporal, p. 216, line 3; cf. p. 254, lines 3-7 and 22-27.

[80] RAMBERT OF BOLOGNA, OP.—Italian, Dominican, master in theology at Paris about (1292/1299; Bishop of Castello, 1303; died in 1308; buried in San Zanipolo, Venice). GLOREP., I, 170-171. J. P. Muller, *Rambert de'Primadizzi de Bologne, Apologeticum veritatis contra Corruptorium,* édition critique (Studi e Testi, 108), Città del Vaticano, 1943. Excellent biographical introduction. Notes the unusual title of the work (as a *Correctorium*) and the discussions directed by Rambert, not only against William, but also against Henry of Ghent (p. XXVIII), Richard of Mediavilla (p. XXX) and Giles of Rome (pp. XXX-XXXI). The supposed allusion to Siger of Brabant might apply to one of the many masters of arts who had then adopted the philosophical positions of Thomas Aquinas.—A possible answer to our remarks concerning the distinction of essence and existence in Rambert is that his discussion is about angels and that his *Apologeticum* stops before dealing with the composition of man. But we are merely asking a question. Rambert quotes Boethius in support of his own position, p. 127. He uses *compositio quae est ex essentia et esse* (p. 128, line 5), he plays around with the formula, p. 129, lines 19-22, but goes back to Boethius in his explanation of it, p. 130, lines 2-18. Cf. p. 155, "Quamvis autem . . ." P. 176, Rambert once more returns to Boethius. Which Boethius? Boethius himself or that of Thomas Aquinas? We have no clear answer to the question.

[81] There would be no point in giving here the last conclusions of the last scholars who dealt with the question. The

work is in progress and only results which can be considered highly probable have been reported. The authors of two answers to the *Correctorium* of William are certain: John Quidort (*Correctorium "Circa"*) and Rambert de'Primadizzi (*Apologeticum*) ; another one is probable: Richard Clapwell (*Correctorium "Quare"*), but this work has long been ascribed to Giles of Rome; a fourth writing of the same family is tentatively ascribed to Tortocollo (Colletorto) or ROBERT OF ORFORD, OP. (see OTT., 98-99): *Correctorium "Sciendum,"* still unpublished; the fifth one, also unpublished (*Correctorium "Quaestione"*) is attributed either to William of Macklefield (or Macclesfield) or to Hugh of Billom.—On the question: R. Creytens, *Autour de la littérature des Correctoires,* AFP., 12 (1942) 313-330. R. Zavalloni, *Richard de Mediavilla . . . ,* 225-231. According to D. L. Douie (*Archbishop Peckham,* 281) the *Sciendum* "is certainly the work of Robert of Orford, at that time still a student in theology." Cf. F. Pelster, *Thomas of Sutton und Robert of Orford, OP.,* Gregorianum, 24 (1943) 135-170.

PART NINE

CHAPTER III, 1. THE PLURALITY OF FORMS

[82] On the main controversial themes in the last years of the century: A. Dondaine, *Un catalogue de dissensions doctrinales entre les maîtres parisiens de la fin du XIIIe siècle,* RTAM., 10 (1938) 374-395.

[83] Roger Marston, *Quaestiones disputatae,* VI, 116-117. Callebaut, *Jean Peckham . . . ,* 448. R. Zavalloni, *Richard de Mediavilla . . . ,* 215, n. 6.

[84] R. Zavalloni, op. cit., 215, n. 7. In Peckham, *Registrum epistolarum,* III, 871.

[85] J. Peckham, *Registrum epistolarum,* III, 866. CUP., I, 625. R. Zavalloni, op. cit., 219, n. 22.

[86] At that time, the Dominican Order had already decided to defend the doctrine of Thomas Aquinas: "Two Visitors were sent over to England by the General Chapter of 1278 to punish those who *in scandalum ordinis* showed disrespect to the teaching and memory of the *Venerabilis patris fratris Thomae de Aquino.* Since then the English Province had been won to the side of the *Doctor Communis,* and, with the rest of the Order, followed his doctrine consistently," D. A. Callus, *The Condemnation . . . ,* 33-34. Clapwell (Knapwell) did this as best he could, with moderation and in his own personal way (Callus, 34-36). He was personally involved in the new condemnation of the doctrine by Peckham (op. cit., 36, n. 1). Text of the articles condemmed in 1286: J. Peckham, *Registrum epistolarum,* III, 921-923; reproduced by R. Zavalloni, op. cit., 220, n. 25. The "heretical" propositions are related to the body of Christ during the three days he was dead (*in triduo mortis*), but they all follow from the oneness of the substantial form in man, *Registrum,* III, 923.

[87] GILES OF ROME (Aegidius Romanus). Born about 1247; entered the Order of the Hermits of St. Augustine; studied at Paris under Thomas Aquinas (1269-1272); bachelor in theology, 1276; was involved in the condemnation of 1277 and interrupted his teaching; General Vicar of his Order, 1285; resumed his teaching at Paris as master in theology, 1285-1291; his doctrine became the official doctrine of his Order, 1287; General Minister, 1292; Archbishop of Bourges, 1295; attended the Council of Vienne, 1311; died at Avignon, December 22, 1316.—GLOLIT., II, 99-101. GLOREP., II, 293-308. On the probable motives of Giles' condemnation, E. Hocedez, *La condamnation de Giles de Rome,* RTAM., 4 (1932) 34-58. V. Doucet, AFH., 27 (1934) 587.

WORKS.—No collective edition; ancient editions listed in GDP., 532-533. GLOREP., II, 294-308. Commentaries on Aristotle: *Expositio in artem veterem* Venice, 1507, 1582; *Prior Analytics,* Venice, 1499, 1504, 1516, 1522. *Posterior Analytics,* Venice, 1488, 1495, 1500, 1513, 1530; *Physics,* Padua, 1483, 1493, Venice, 1491, 1496, 1502; *De generatione et corruptione,* Venice, Naples, 1480, Venice, 1493, 1498, 1500, 1518, 1520, 1555, 1567; *De anima,* Venice, 1496, 1499, 1500; *Quaestiones metaphysicales,* Venice, 1499, 1501, 1552; *Super authorem Libri de Causis, Alfarabium,* Venice, 1550; *De bona fortuna,* Venice, 1496, 1551. *De esse et essentia, de mensura angelorum et de cognitione angelorum,* Venice, 1503. *De formatione corporis humani,* Paris, 1515, 1551; Venice, 1524, 1528; Rimini, 1626. Commentary on the *Sentences,* ed. by A. de Aguilar, 5 vols., Cordova, 1707 (question on the existence of God in Aug. Daniels, *Quellenbeiträge,* 72-78). *Quodlibeta,* Venice, 1496, 1502, 1504; Louvain, 1646. *Operum D. Aegidii Romani,* vol. I, Rome, 1555 (*De peccato originali, Theoremata quinquaginta de Corpore Christi, Hexameron*) The *Hexameron,* separately, Padua, 1549. The 1500 Venice edition of the commentary *De anima,* also contains the *De intellectu possibili* and the important *De gradibus formarum.* Recently reprinted and essential: Edg. Hocedez, *Aegidii Romani Theoremata de esse et essentia,* text with critical and historical introduction, Louvain, 1930. English transl. by M. V. Murray SJ., *Theorems on Existence and Essence,* Milwaukee, 1952. These *Theoremata* should not be confused with the Questions *De esse et essentia* listed *supra* (Venice, 1503).—The question published by G. Bruni, *Una inedita Quaestio de natura universalis di Egidio Romano,* Naples, 1935, 26-43, seems to be spurious (J. Koch, *Giles of Rome, Errores philosophorum,* XXIX, note 62).—G. Bruni, *Quaestiones a fratre Aegidio Romano Paduae disputatae in capitulo generali OESA. 1281,* Analecta augustiniana, 17 (1939-1940) 125-157; *Aegidii Romani Quaestiones I-II circa unionem numeralem substantiarum,* ibid., 197-245.

BIBLIOGRAPHY.—K. Werner, *Die Scholastik des späteren Mittelalters,* III, Wien, 1883. N. Mattioli, *Studio critico sopra Egidio Romano,* Roma, 1896. P. Mandonnet, *La carrière scolaire de Gilles de Rome (1276-1291),* RSPT., 4 (1910) 480-499. G. Boffito, *Saggio di Bibliografia Egidiana,* Florence, 1911. S. Makaay, *Der Tractat des Aegidius Romanus über die Einzigkeit der substantiellen Form,* Würzburg, 1924. R. Egenter, *Die Erkenntnisphyschologie des Aegidius Romanus,* Regensburg, 1926. Edg. Hocedez, *Gilles de Rome et saint Thomas,* MM., I, 385-409; *Gilles de Rome et Henri de Gand sur la distinction réelle, 1276-1287,* Gregorianum, 8 (1927) 358-384; *La condamnation de Gilles de Rome,* RTAM., 4 (1932) 34-58. P. Vollmer, *Die göttliche Mitwirkung bei Aegidius Romanus,* DTF.,

6 (1928) 452-470; *Die Schöpfungslehre des Aegidius Romanus,* Würzburg, 1931. G. Bruni, *Catalogo dei mss. di Egidio Romano,* RFNS., 22 (1930) 230-249; 23 (1931) 410-441; *Sulli scriti di Egidio Romano,* Archivio di Filosofia, 1931, 32-51; *The "De differentia Rhetoricae, Ethicae et Politicae" of Aegidius Romanus,* NS., 6 (1932) 1-18; *Egidio Romano anti-Averroista,* Sophia, 1933, 208-219; *Egidio Romano e la sua polemica antitomista,* RFNS., 26 (1934) 239-251; *Catalogo critico delle opere di Egidio Romano,* La Bibliofilia, 1934, 8-110; 1935, 247-306; *Di alcune opere inedite e dubbie di Egidio Romano,* RTAM., 7 (1935) 174-196. D. Gutiérrez, *Ultimas investigaciones acerca de los escolasticos agustinos. Egidio Romano (1243-1316),* Religion y Cultura, 27 (1934) 161-178. J. Koch, *Studien zur handschriftlichen Ueberlieferung des Tractatus De erroribus philosophorum,* Münster i. W., 1935 (Beiträge, Suppl. III, 3) 862-875; *Das Gutachten des Aegidius Romanus über die Lehren des Petrus Johannis Olivi,* Scientia Sacra (Festgabe Schulte), 1935, 142-168; *Giles of Rome, Errores philosophorum,* critical text and English transl., by J. O. Riedl, Milwaukee, 1944. G. Bruni, *Incerti auctoris impugnationes contra Aegidium Romanum contradicentem Thomae super Primum Sententiarum,* Typ. Vaticana, 1942 (Bibliot. Augustiniana, I, 1). J. Paulus, *Les disputes d'Henri de Gand et de Gilles de Rome sur la distinction de l'essence et de l'existence,* AHDL., 15 (1940-1942) 323-358. A. Trape, *Il concorso divino nel pensiero di Aegidio Romano,* Tolentino, 1942. F. Richeldi, *Il commento di Aegidio Romano al libro III delle Sentenze di Pietro Lombardo,* Modena, n.d. D. Gutierrez, *Notitia antiquae scholae aegidianae,* Analecta augustiniana, 18 (1941-1942) 39-67. B. Nardi, *Egidio Romano e l'Averroismo,* Rivista di Storia della Filosofia, 1947, 197-220; 1948, 1-22 (important text of Giles on the interpretation of Averroes' noetic, pp. 4-5). P. W. Nash SJ., *Giles of Rome on Boethius' "Diversum est esse et id quod est,"* MS., 12 (1950) 57-91; *Giles of Rome Auditor and Critic of St. Thomas,* TMS., 28 (1950) 1-20.

[88] The necessary starting point, on this question, remains E. Hocedez, *Richard de Middleton,* especially its invaluable Appendices; to be completed by R. Zavalloni, *Richard de Mediavilla,* especially pp.

221-225, 231-241. The essential texts marking the evolution of Giles on this point are quoted in Zavalloni, pp. 273-275, notes.

[89] Text in Edg. Hocedez, *Richard de Middleton*, 459-460. Cf. R. Zavalloni, op. cit., 276-278 and notes. On the reasons which may account for the doctrinal shyness of Giles on this point, Hocedez, 473-477. Hocedez considers the concluding sentence of the *De gradu formarum* as the deepest remark ever made during the course of the controversy: "To wish to posit many forms is to wish to philosophize in a way that is neither human nor Aristotelian, since Aristotle has said that our science comes from sense knowledge and that we must rise from the sensible up to the intelligible, whereas they want to philosophize in a way that is not that of man, but of Plato, who wanted to descend from the intelligible to the sensible," 477. On some oppositions of Giles to Thomas, see the defense of Thomas against Giles published by G. Bruni, *Incerti auctoris impugnationes . . .* , Vaticano, 1942.—On the new type of composition (*ex* and *huic*), *Theoremata de esse et essentia*, XV, Hocedez ed., 98-99; prudent reservation concerning plurality in man on account of the 1277 condemnation, *Theorema* XIV, 90; how this invites Giles to posit in man a form of the part without, however, positing two forms, 113-116. See note 106.

[90] GILES OF LESSINES, OP. Born at Lessines (Belgium) about 1230; a Dominican; studied under Albert the Great (after 1262), then at Paris; a bachelor in theology he never became a master; died after 1304: GLOREP., I, 127-128. Author of treatises *On the Essence, Movement and Signification of Comets* (after October 1264), *On Geometry, On Usury* (printed among the opuscules attributed to Thomas Aquinas). Giles wrote the already-mentioned letter to Albert the Great (Mandonnet, *Siger*, II, 29-30) whose answer makes up the treatise *De quindecim problematibus* (op. cit., II, 30-52). The only important work of Giles is his treatise on the oneness of the substantial form, published by M. de Wulf, *Le traité "De unitate formae" de Gilles de Lessines,* texte inédit et étude, Louvain, 1901. P. Mandonnet, *Gilles de Lessines et son "Tractatus de crepusculis,"* RNSP., 22 (1920) 190-194. Lynn Thorndike, *A History of Magic . . .* , II, 453. M. Grabmann, *Aegidius von Lessines*, MG., 1936, II, 512-530. E. Hocedez, *La date du De usuris de Gilles de Lessines,* Ephemerides theologicae Lovanienses, 1926, 508-512. E. Hocedez, *Richard de Middleton*, 454-477. R. Zavalloni, *Richard de Mediavilla,* 278-282. M. Grabmann, *Eine dritte Handschrift des Traktates "De unitate formae des Aegidius von Lessines OP.,* (*Cod. Erlangen 207*), DTF., 26 (1948) 324-330: confirms the early conclusion of de Wulf that the treatise was directed against Kilwardby.

[91] Directed against Kilwardby, the *De unitate formae* of Giles of Lessines is divided into three parts: 1) exposition of the doctrine of the plurality of forms; 2) true nature of form and of its relation to matter; 3) demonstration of the oneness of the substantial form. Beings arise when forms are received by matter; form is the actuating part of every material thing; the prime act of every thing is its specifically determined being; consequently, form gives being: *forma dat esse* (De Wulf ed., 19; cf. Boethius, *De Trinitate*, 2; PL., 64, 1250). It is not easy to determine the meaning of *esse* in Giles of Lessines; see 32, 53, 92. One text, however, can be read in a genuinely Thomistic sense: "Esse autem compositorum non potest dici compositum ex pluribus actibus essendi, quia partes compositi, secundum quod sunt partes, non habent aliud esse quam totius compositi . . .", 98. *Actus essendi* is almost a proof. Nevertheless, he calls form "act" because it is a principle of external operations according to species, 19. The essence of form is simple, 22-23. To posit it as dual is a contradictory notion: humanity cannot be made up of corporeity and spirituality, 23-24. If the essence of form had composition of potency and act, it would be a principle made up of principles, or else it would be two forms, 24-25, 98. If there is only one form, the soul is immediately united with matter, 28-30; nevertheless, it is separable from matter, 32-35. All forms are educed from the potency of matter (46); exception should be made only for the rational soul, 48-49; Aristotle himself makes this exception (*Metaph.*, XII, 3, 1070a 25-26). The essence of the soul is simple; its powers and operations proceed from it, 50-51, 90. Matter and form are the only two principles of being, 63. The name of

Thomas Aquinas is not mentioned in the treatise.

[92] R. Zavalloni, *Richard de Mediavilla,* 283-286.

[93] THOMAS OF SUTTON, OP. English, Dominican, master in theology at Oxford in 1300. He maintained the doctrine of Thomas Aquinas against two successive generations of opponents: 1) the representatives of the late thirteenth century Augustinism: *De productione formae substantialis, Contra pluralitatem formarum, Quodlibeta* I, II; 2) the new theology of John Duns Scotus, *Quodlibeta* III, IV, *Quaestiones disputatae, Liber propugnatorius,* probably in 1311. The career of Sutton seems to be the first one during which Thomism found itself confronted with Duns Scot. The *De pluralitate formarum* of Sutton is included in many editions of the *Opuscula* of Thomas Aquinas. F. Pelster, *Thomae de Sutton OP. Quaestiones de reali distinctione inter essentiam et esse,* Münster i. W., 1929. M. Schmaus, *Der Liber propugnatorius des Thomas Anglicus und die Lehrunterscheide zwischen Thomas von Aquin und Duns Scotus; II, Die trinitärischen Lehrdifferenzen,* Münster i. W., 1930 (Beiträge, 29). F. Pelster, *Thomistische Streitschriften gegen Aegidius Romanus und ihre Verfasser: Thomas von Sutton und Robert von Orford,* Gregorianum, 24 (1943) 135-170.—A. G. Little, OTT., 281-282. BIBLIOGRAPHY. F. Ehrle, *Thomas de Sutton, sein Leben, seine Quodlibet und seine Quaestiones disputatae,* Festschrift G. von Hertling, Kempten, 1913, 426-450; fragments and titles of the Questions. F. Pelster, *Thomas von Sutton OP., ein Oxforder Verteidiger der Thomistischen Lehre,* ZKT., 46 (1922) 212-253, 361-401; *Schriften des Thomas von Sutton . . . ,* ZKT., 47 (1923) 483-494; *Thomas von Sutton OP. als Verfasser zweier Schriften über die Einheit der Wesenform,* Scholastik, 3 (1928) 526-556; *Thomas von Sutton und das Correctorium "Quare detraxisti,"* MAP., 441-466. D. E. Sharp, *Thomas of Sutton O.P.,* RNSP., 36 (1934) 332-354; 37 (1934) 88-104, 219-233. P. Glorieux, art. *Sutton (Thomas de),* DTC., 14 (1941) 2867-2873. O. Lottin, *Thomas de Sutton OP. et le libre arbitre,* RTAM., 9 (1937) 281-312. H. Pouillon OSB., *Les Questions sur la Métaphysique de Thomas de Sutton OP.,* Mélanges de Ghellinck, II (1951) 937-950; if this text really belongs

to Sutton, he began by denying the distinction of essence and existence (p. 948) which he was to uphold later on.

[94] *De pluralitate formarum* (Th. Sutton) in *Thomae Aquinatis Opuscula omnia,* P. Mandonnet ed. Paris, 1927, V, 308-346. Sutton neither quotes nor names Thomas Aquinas; he announces no intention of supporting his doctrine, but only the doctrine of the unity of the form. Part I draws arguments from the nature of "physical" beings. There can be only one form in one being, 309-310; this is true of even the human soul, immediate act of its body (311-312); it can be its act because a more perfect substantial form always contains the less perfect one, "and more," 314. Part II, takes its arguments from metaphysics, that is from the fact that it is of the essence of the substantial form to constitute being (*constituit ens simpliciter*), 320. Being, *ens,* is the individual subsistent: *quod est hoc aliquid et subsistens,* 320. Such being can have only one form, 320-321. What is added to it is accidental to it; since substance is the receiver of *esse* (existence?), to which it is as potency is to act, Sutton seems to conceive *esse* as accidental to substance: *omne quod advenit rei subsistenti tanquam ipsam informans, accidens est,* 321. Being is substance; a form acquires existence when it is produced, or begotten, by its cause; for it to lose being is to corrupt or to be destroyed, 322. Consequently, the plurality of forms turns the substantial form into an accident of an already constituted substance; it turns substantial being into accidental being, generation into alteration, etc., 322. The argumentation is directly based upon Averroes, 322-328, thus unconsciously paving the way to the later difficulties of Cajetan concerning the demonstrability of the immortality of the soul. Part III draws arguments from the unity of beings; one single thing demands one single substantial form, 329; confirmed by Averroes, 330-331. Answers to philosophical difficulties: elements in mixed beings, embryogeny; answers to theological difficulties: transmission of original sin, body of Christ, 332-346 (interesting remarks, 343-344). As it stands, the treatise represents the doctrine of Aristotle revised by Thomas Aquinas minus the ultimate metaphysical justifications for its Thomistic revision. The inclusion of this treatise among the works of Thomas Aquinas was

an explainable error, but a significant one from the point of view of the history of the Thomistic school.

[95] GODFREY OF FONTAINES. Born at Liège (Belgium); studied at Paris; master in theology 1285-1304; after this date Godfrey pursued an ecclesiastical career and died in 1306. Many of the manuscripts owned by Godfrey are in the Bibliothèque nationale, Paris; most of them bear marginal annotations from his hand. His *Scholia* on the *Contra Gentiles* and on the first Part of the *Summa theologiae* are still unpublished. Three Disputed Questions *De virtutibus* are also waiting for publication. The main work of Godfrey, his *Quodlibeta*, extended from 1285 up to 1297. The whole series has been published by M. de Wulf, A. Pelzer, J. Hoffmans, O. Lottin, in Les Philosophes Belges, 2-14, 1904-1937; the last volume includes three *Quaestiones ordinariae* of Godfrey.—GLOREP., I, 396-399.

BIBLIOGRAPHY. M. de Wulf, *Un théologien-philosophe du XIIIe siècle. Etude sur la vie, les oeuvres et l'influence de Godefroid de Fontaines*, Bruxelles, 1904; *Histoire de la philosophie en Belgique*, Bruxelles, 1910, 80-116; *L'intellectualisme de Godefroid de Fontaines d'après le Quodl. VI, qu. 15*, Baeumker-Beiträge, Supplementband I, Münster i. W., 1913, 287-296. A. Pelzer, *Godefroid de Fontaines. Les manuscripts de ses quodlibets conservés à la Vaticane et dans quelques autres bibliothèques*, RNSP., 20 (1913) 365-388, 491-532. M. H. Laurent, *Godefroid de Fontaines et la condamnation de 1277*, RT., 13 (1930) 273-281. P. Glorieux, *Un recueil scolaire de Godefroid de Fontaines* RTAM., 3 (1931) 37-53. J. Hoffmans, *La table des divergences et innovations doctrinales de Godefroid de Fontaines*, RNSP., 36 (1934) 412-436. O. Lottin, *Le libre arbitre chez Godefroid de Fontaines*, RNSP., 40 (1937) 213-241. G. de Lagarde, *La philosophie sociale d'Henri de Gand et de Godefroid de Fontaines*, AHDL., 13 (1943-1945) 73-142. O. Lottin, *Le thomisme de Godefroid de Fontaines en matière de libre arbitre*, RNSP., 40 (1937) 554-573. E. Hocedez, *Une question inédite de Pierre d'Auvergne . . .* , RNSP., 36 (1934) 355-386 (influence of Peter of Auvergne on Godfrey). O. Lottin, PEM., II, 269-270.

[96] Before reporting the hesitations of Godfrey, let us recall his question: "If a master in theology should speak against a doctrinal decision made by a bishop in case he believes the contrary is true?" His answer is, no. One must never say what is false, but one must not always say what one knows to be true, unless, of course, the truth at stake be necessary for salvation. This does not prevent the condemnation or excommunication of a true or probable opinion by a bishop from being wrong, but it forbids private persons to disobey a prelate of the Church; *Quodl.* VII, 18, 401-403. This does not facilitate the interpretation of texts written by Godfrey on an article condemned by Bishop Tempier. He himself distinguishes three interpretations of the plurality of forms: 1) there are in man as many forms as there are genera and differences (Gabirol), to which he opposes Averroes, *De substantia orbis*, I, where the Commentator says that, according to Aristotle, there cannot be more than one substantial form in one subject; 2) there are in man several forms, because he is a mixture of elements and, consequently, he must have several forms, to which Godfrey answers that, in such a being, the forms of the elements remain virtually present in the whole; 3) a third way is to posit several forms in man alone, and only two (Henry of Ghent), a material form for matter, and an immaterial form which actuates the body together with the material form, but Godfrey cannot see how *two* substantial forms can make up *one* being. There are difficulties on both sides; the main one is common to both positions, namely: how can the soul, a spiritual, simple, unextended and indivisible substance, have union with a material and extended body? (*Quodl.* II, 7, 123-124). This is so hard to understand that the philosophers who posited only one form have imagined the most different explanations for the possibility of intellectual knowledge. Absolutely speaking, there is more probability on the side of the oneness of the substantial form; the maximum of improbability rests with the doctrine that posits a plurality of forms in all beings; the doctrine which ascribes only one form to all beings, with the sole exception of man (two forms) is less probable than the first one and more probable than the second one (II, 7, 124).—*Esse* comes through form; since there can be only one *esse* in a given being, there can be only one form, III, 4, 187; this is proved by Averroes, *Metaph.,*

IV, 2, where he shows that the noun "being" primarily points out substance, ibid., 189.—The controversy about the oneness of the substantial form, which is a philosophical question, is reduced to faith on account of its connection with man, especially Christ, III, 5; 197; on the danger in condemning some positions in England and not in Paris, 205-208. Cf. C. J. Jellouschek, *Quaestio Magistri Joannis de Neapoli OP.: "Utrum licite possit doceri Parisius doctrina fratris Thomae quantum ad omnes conclusiones eius"...*, Xenia Thomistica, III, Romae 1925, 73-104.

[97] *Quodl.* X, 10, p. 347. R. Zavalloni, op. cit., 301, n. 13.

[98] "Therefore, as an opinion at least probable and not contradicting, so far as I can see, what must be held as certain by faith, it can be maintained that there is only one form in man, without however blaming the other position, nor considering it impossible or erroneous," II, 7, p. 125. In other words: "I wish to affirm that there is only one form in beings other than man; nevertheless, I am prepared to hold determinately that there are several forms in man, if other and stronger reasons are offered, or if the Church determines that something that has not yet been determined concerning the body of Christ should be held, or anything else on account of which one must posit several forms in man," II, 7, p. 126. The Questions of Godfrey witness to the trouble created in the minds of some masters by the condemnations of 1277.

The rest of the psychology of Godfrey, where no dogma is at stake, is an Aristotelianism strongly influenced by Averroes, in this sense at least that it is a stricter Aristotelianism than that of Thomas Aquinas. Every man has his own possible intellect and his own agent intellect. No divine illumination is added to the natural light of man (*Quodl.* IX, 19). The agent intellect is a light created by God with the intellect; it operates no transmutation, but, as the sun has only to shine in order to make colors visible, so also the agent intellect has only to illumine the phantasms in order to make what they represent appear to the possible intellect without individuating determinations. This is called abstraction (VI, 15, 251-252). Note, however, that even here, Godfrey presents this doctrine as "more probable" than the one which, on the authority of Augustine, considers the light of the intellect as requiring a supplement of divine light in order to achieve certain and immutable cognition, p. 253. Unlike Thomas Aquinas (*Sum. theol.*, I, 85, 1, 4m) Godfrey denies that the agent intellect does anything in the phantasms; it just illumines them and reveals their intelligible content, V, 10, 35-40. Godfrey extends this passivity from the intellect to the will. Understanding is more noble than love, VI, 10, 182-218. The will has no self-determining spontaneity: the act of the intellect is determined by its object and the act of the appetite is the determined object which is its active and moving cause (*secundum rationem causae moventis et agentis*), VI, 11, 221. The will produces no determination in any power of the soul unless reason has first conceived that this determination should be made, ibid., 222. It has no dominion over the intellect as to the determination of its acts, ibid. What is true of the speculative intellect is no less true of the practical intellect, 223-224. The passivity of the will is complete; it seems hardly an exaggeration to attribute to Godfrey a sort of intellectualistic determinism. The will is never moved by itself, neither as to the exercise of its act nor as to its determination. In ultimate analysis, these two come to the same, XV, 2, 11.

PART NINE

CHAPTER III, 2.   EXISTENCE AND ESSENCE

[99] M. Chossat, *L'Averroisme de saint Thomas. Note sur la distinction d'essence et d'existence à la fin du XIIIe siècle*, Archives de philosophie, 9 (1932) 129-177. Incidentally, to speak of "Averroism of Thomas Aquinas" is misleading, because to posit an act of the form was the most radically un-Averroistic move Thomas Aquinas could have made. By making it, he replaced the universe of Aristotle and Averroes with a new one.— Introductory: S. Schindele, *Aseität Gottes,*

Essentia und Existentia im Neuplatonismus, PJ., 22 (1909) 3-19, 159-170; *Zur
Geschichte der Unterscheidung von Wesenheit und Dasein in der Scholastik,* Munich,
1900.

[100] M. Grabmann, *Circa historiam distinctionis essentiae et existentiae,* APA.,
1935, 61-76; *Doctrina sancti Thomae de
distinctione reali inter essentiam et esse
ex documentis ineditis saeculi XIII illus-
tratur,* Acta Hebdomadae Thomisticae,
Roma, 1924, 131-190.—On the general
problem raised by the notion of "Thomism," see the pertinent remarks of Corn.
Fabro, *Per una storia del Tomismo,* Sa-
pienza, 1 (1951) 1-16.—On the theological
problem of the oneness of *esse* in Christ,
which so often entails discussions concerning both the oneness of the substantial form and the relation of existence to
essence, see the useful collection of texts
by E. Hocedez, *Quaestio de unico esse in
Christo a doctoribus saeculi XIII disputata,* Romae, Univ. Greg., 1933 (Albert
the Great, Robert of Tortocollo, Ulrich of
Strasbourg, Bernard of Auvergne, Henry
of Ghent, Godfrey of Fontaines, etc.).—
On an otherwise little-known supporter of
the Thomistic distinction against Henry
of Ghent, HUMBERT OF PRULLY, see M.
Grabmann, *Humberti de Prulliaco* (d.
1298) *O. Cist., Abbatis de Prulliaco,
Quaestio de esse et essentia, utrum differunt realiter vel secundum intentionem
. . . ,* Angelicum 17 (1940) 352-369. The
text of this question fails to convince us
that Humbert discussed the problem in
a deep and sagacious way (M. Grabmann,
p. 358); one may even wonder if Humbert has understood the Thomistic meaning of the distinction.—The oldest known
commentary on the *De ente et essentia*
is that of ARMAND OF BELVEZER (Armand
de Beauvoir, Armandus de Bellovisu),
d. *ca.* 1334.—M. H. Laurent OP, *Armand
de Belvézer et son Commentaire sur le
"De ente et essentia,"* RT., 35 (1930)
426-436; mentions two printed editions:
Padua, 1486 and Venice, 1496; considers
Armand, at that date, a faithful disciple of Thomas Aquinas (p. 436).—Cf.
P. Glorieux, RTAM., 6 (1934) 94-96.
F. Stegmüller, RTAM., 7 (1935) 86-91.
K. Feckes, *Das Opusculum des hl. Thomas
von Aquin "De ente et essentia" im
Lichte seiner Kommentare,* ADGM., 667-
687, especially 668-669. HLF., 36, 265-
295 and 647.

[101] Edg. Hocedez, *Aegidii Romani Theoremata de Esse et Essentia,* Louvain, 1930.
Our very translation of the title is a
betrayal. *Esse* may mean existence, or
being, or to be, etc. It often connotes two
or three notions. It should likewise be
kept in mind that, when a Latin writer
says "aliquid," "aliud," we must translate
these words by "something," "another
thing"; to us, "aliquid aliud" means
"something else," whereas, to be correct,
we should never use "thing" where there
is no "res" in a Latin text. The intrinsic
difficulties of the doctrine are not alle-
viated by the differences in the languages.
—On the theology and philosophy of the
school of the Hermits of Saint Augustine,
Karl Werner, *Der Augustinismus in der
Scholastik des späteren Mittelalters.* Wien,
1883; on the Augustinism of the school,
ch. II, 9-17; Giles of Rome, III, 18-33
(intellect and abstraction according to
Giles); IV, 33-58 (epistemology); V, 58-
100 (metaphysics of being, causality, creation, essence and existence, matter, form,
Aristotelian causality (91, n. 1), motion,
time; VI, 100-148 (cosmology and anthropology: angels, the world, man, the
human soul, intellect and will); VII, 148-
170 (God); XI, 213-232 (ethics and
sociology). Werner has probably overstressed the Augustinian character of the
doctrines at stake, but the many texts
which he has quoted should be taken into
account. To study Giles and his school,
including Gregory of Rimini, as a sort of
doctrinal unit, is a method which has its
own dangers, but it has not yet been
proved that Werner had given a distorted
image of historical reality on this point.

[102] Edg. Hocedez, op. cit., Introduction,
15-16, note. The quoted text is borrowed from the *Theoremata de corpore
Christi,* prop. XXIX. On the form "theorema," used by Giles under the influence of Proclus (*Elementatio theologica*),
16-17.

[103] Giles of Rome, *Quodl.* VII; Hocedez,
Introduction, 13. — Creation reveals the
distinction of essence and existence just
as generation reveals the distinction of
matter and form, 19. Created being participates in being, that is it takes part
in being (*participare: partem capere*);
what participates does not receive the
fullness of the whole; consequently, it is
"limitated," "particularized." 17. This applies to existence, which should be con-

ceived apart from form and as a distinct participation. In Giles, being is caused by form (*ens* is caused by the form, not, as in Thomas, by *esse*): "quaelibet forma dat rei quod sit ens," 78; a thing is *ens* through that which makes it to be the substance it is, 80. This is what makes it necessary to add to it existence: "Every thing is being (*ens*) by its essence; nevertheless, since the essence of a created being is not a complete act, but is in potency with respect to existence, essence is not sufficient for the thing actually to exist, unless some existence (*aliquod esse*) be superadded to it as an act and complement of essence. Consequently, things exist in virtue of existence super-added to essence or nature," 83. "The actuality which belongs to essence is too small to suffice to make essence exist as one amongst natural beings," 21. This is the core of the argumentation: "For if essence were in itself so actual and complete that, without any addition, it could exist and be a being in nature, then such an essence could not possibly not exist," 21-22. For this reason, the notion of a created being not composed of essence and existence is self-contradictory; remember that the whole argument presupposes creation, 22. As an interpretation, let us add that it also seems to presuppose that existence is a supplement of actuality in the same line as that of essence, which already causes "being." This is the reason why its composition with essence does not give rise to a third being, 132-134. See note 107.

[104] N. Del Prado, *De veritate fundamentali philosophiae christianae,* Fribourg (Switz.) 1911. R. Garrigou-Lagrange OP., *Les XXIV thèses thomistes pour le trentième anniversaire de leur approbation,* Angelicum, 22 (1945) 17-30; cf. RPST., 3 (1909) 308-313.

[105] "And just as matter and quantity are two things, so also essence and existence are two really different things (*essentia et esse sunt duae res realiter differentes*)," 134; "res realiter differens," 111; "sic forte diceret aliquis quod essentia et esse non sunt duae res," 127, etc. —A remarkable consequence of the new notion of existence is that, in this doctrine, existence can become a principle of individuation. Giles might be the author of the individuation by *esse* criticized by Duns Scotus.—Joh. Assenmacher, *Die Ge-*

schichte des Individuationsprinzips in der Scholastik, Leipzig, 1926, pp. 49-51. The texts quoted in the notes (*Quodlibeta,* ed. Coninck, Louvain, 1646) belong to Giles of Rome, and not, as Assenmacher imagines, to Giles of Lessines.

[106] This curious position, foreign to the doctrine of Thomas Aquinas, is a necessary moment of Giles' own doctrine. In corporeal creatures, the cause of being is form (see note 103); so a substance is a being apart from existence; consequently, in a corporeal creature, the real essence is already a compound of matter and form: it includes the form of the matter, or substantial form (*forma partis*) and the form of the whole: humanity, including matter and form, or body and soul (*forma totius*). There is, therefore, in every corporeal creature, a twofold existence (*esse*). First, an existence which flows from the substantial form and gives *esse* to its matter; since this gives to matter a share in the being of form, it makes it to be a being; on the other hand, since it does not give matter existence, it only gives it a certain mode of existence (*modus essendi*). Secondly, there is existence properly speaking, which is one for the whole being and makes it to be an actually existing being. This was made necessary by the proposition: "the being (*esse*) caused by the form of the whole is a thing (*res*) different from the form itself," 101. If the essence is not a being in its own right, it is not a thing, and then "essence and existence are not two really different things," 133. On the twofold *esse* (that is, *esse* plus *modus essendi*), and why it does not give rise to a third thing, 101-102. Thus we really have two things. These doctrinal distinctions, which modern history rightly considers important, did not always interest the mediaeval masters; an anonymous commentator quoted by Grabmann (*Circa historiam* . . . , 66-67) says that, since Thomas posits existence as an addition to essence, he agrees with Giles; they only differ *in modo ponendi*. Grabmann tentatively places this text about 1276. Cf. 68-69.

[107] Given that there are created beings, their nature, precisely *qua* created, demands that they be compounds of essence and existence. Before reading any one of these demonstrations, it should be remembered that, in this doctrine, existence is

not limited by essence (as it is in the doctrine of Thomas Aquinas); on the contrary, God creates limited or partial existences in order to prevent certain forms from being infinite. See the formulation of his problem: "to show that, however immaterial and separated (from matter) a form may possibly be, it is not its own existence; rather, it is really different and distinct from its own existence," 23. Giles develops three proofs of the distinction. First, since created nature can be or not be, it is in potency with respect to existence; now potency is really distinct from act; consequently what creation adds to essence in order to make it exist must be really distinct from it, 24. Secondly, the distinction is necessary to insure the limitation of created natures, at least in the case of separate substances; for indeed, these forms are not limited by any matter; if therefore they did not receive an existence really different from their substantial being, they would be existence itself (being really one with these forms, their existence would be as unlimited as they themselves are); they would then be self-existing beings, that is pure and infinite being, 24-25. Thirdly, if it were its own existence, a creature would be wholly simple, because, as Boethius says (*De Hebdomadibus*, 5; PL., 64, 1311 B): existence itself does not participate in anything; consequently, if a creature were existence itself, it would participate in nothing; it would be simple and immutable; it would not be a creature at all, 25-26. Another set of demonstrations, 66-74. Note, p. 74, the deep remark that, in Aristotle, forms *qua* forms are necessary beings; their possibility with regard to existence or non existence comes to them from matter; this is the reason why, in his doctrine, the separate substances are necessary beings by their own natures, 74-76. The only way to prevent such substances from being necessary is to create in them an existence really other than their essence. This limitation of essence by existence does not prevent Giles, in his commentary on the *De causis* and obviously under the influence of Proclus, from likening God to an ocean of existence, which fills up finite vessels according to their respective capacities: Hocedez, Introduction, 71-73.

[108] The influence of Proclus, everywhere visible in Giles, has not yet been fully investigated; on his commentary on the *Liber de causis,* Hocedez, Introduction, 71-72; on his own understanding of the notion of participation, 72-73; on his opposition to Thomas concerning abstraction and the agent intellect, 77-82.—Influence of Giles, 82-100.—On Thomism as a historical enigma: how is it that there have been centuries of discussion about the true meaning of the Thomistic distinction of essence and existence, while there has never been any doubt concerning the meaning of the distinction in Giles of Rome, 100-116.

1) JAMES OF VITERBO (Jacobus de Viterbo, Capocci) born *ca.* 1255, entered the Order of Saint Augustine, succeeded Giles of Rome as master in theology at Paris (1293/1300); Archbishop of Naples, 1302; died March 17, 1308. GLOREP., II, 309-312.—M. Grabmann, *Doctrina S. Thomae . . . ,* 162-176; *Die Lehre des Jakob von Viterbo* (d. 1308) *von der Wirklichkeit des göttlichen Seins,* MG., II, 490-511. See particularly the remarkable Question analyzed by Grabmann: If God is being (from *Quaestiones de praedicamentis in divinis*), in which James opposes the negative answer given to the question by Eckhart and makes an excellent survey of the controversy on essence and existence. He himself tones down the expressions used by Giles; the composition is not one of "thing and thing"; actual being is an essence plus what makes it exist.—O. Lottin, PEM., III, 482-486.

2) AUGUSTINE OF ANCONA (Augustinus Triumphus, Agostino Trionfo), 1243-1328, Hermit of Saint Augustine; read the *Sentences* at Paris, 1303-1304; probably master in theology at the same university about 1314-1316. Best known for his writings in political philosophy and theology. GLOREP., II, 321-327. On his theological writings, M. Schmaus, *Die Gotteslehre des Augustinus Triumphus nach seinem Sentenzenkommentar,* ADGM., 896-929; important fragments, 929-935; fragments from the *Sentences* of Giles of Rome, 938-939, 943. Note the important text concerning the meaning of *esse* as applied to God, 940-941, and on God as "esse omnium," not formally, but causally, 942 (cf. Bernard of Clairvaux, Thomas Aquinas, etc.). M. Grabmann, *Der Metaphysikkommentar des Augustinus Triumphus von Ancona* (d. *1328*), Scholastik, 16 (1941) 11-23: Augustine a pupil and disciple of Thomas Aquinas. Unpublished works, J. Kürzinger, *Ein Handschrift zum*

Klagenlieder des hl. Thomas von Aquin, Biblica, 1942, 306-317 (ms. attribution to Augustine); *Handschriften philosophischer Werke des Augustinereremiten Augustinus Triumphus de Ancona,* PJ., 53 (1940) 355-361.

3) THOMAS OF STRASBOURG, born at Haguenau (Alsatia), died in Wien, 1357. A Hermit of Saint Augustine, Thomas appears, in his commentary on the *Sentences,* rather bewildered by the number of contradictory positions from which to choose. His general intention is to follow Aristotle wherever he does not contradict faith. His historians show him standing in favor of a moderate "realism" equally opposed to "conceptualism" and to "nominalism." N. Paulus, *Der Augustinergeneral Thomas von Strassburg,* Rixheim (Alsatia), 1926; *Die Pariser Doktorpromotion des Thomas von Strassburg,* Archiv für elsässische Kirchengeschichte, 2 (1928) 444-446. B. Lindner, *Die Erkenntnislehre des Thomas von Strassburg OESA.,* Münster i. W., 1930 (Beiträge, 27, 4-5). J. L. Shannon OSA., *Good Works and Predestination according to Thomas of Strassburg OSA.,* Westminster (Maryland) 1940.—The book of B. Lindner contains comparisons between the positions of Thomas of Strasbourg and those of Thomas Aquinas, Godfrey of Fontaines, Henry of Ghent, Scotus, Durandus of St. Pourçain, Gregory of Rimini, Giles, Aureoli, Ockham, etc. Interesting study of the problem of the existence of God, 83-110; text 131-134. Opposition to the "conceptualism" of Peter Auriol, 111-128.

On the history of this religious Order, J. F. Ossinger, *Bibliotheca Augustiniana,* Ingolstadt, 1768 (full of information about the writers of the school). E. A. Van Moe, *Recherches sur l'histoire des Ermites de Saint Augustin,* Revue des Questions historiques, 1932, 275-316. M. Th. Disdier, art. *Ermites de Saint Augustin,* DHGE., 5 (1931) 499-595. Founded in 1254, it counted among its masters, besides Giles of Rome, James of Viterbo (d. 1308), Angelo de Camereno (d. 1314), Agostino Trionfo (d. 1328), Prosper of Reggio Emilia (d. 1333): see GLOREP., II, 309-332. For the later history of the school, see Ossinger, op. cit. The influence of the doctrine of Giles extends up to the seventeenth century, when Raphael Bonherba (d. 1681) attempted to find in Giles of Rome a conciliation between Thomism and Scotism: *Disputationes phi-*

losophiae in quibus omnes philosophicae inter D. Thomam et Scotum controversiae principaliter cum doctrina nostri Aegydii Columnii illustrantur, Palermo, 1671. In the eighteenth century: Aug. Arpe, *Summa totius theologiae Aegydii Columnii,* Bologna, 1701; Franciscus ab Annuntiatione, who died in 1720, still published a *Philosophia ad mentem doctoris fundatissimi B. Aegydii Columnii;* the seventeenth century was a much more "scholastic" age than it is commonly believed to have been.

[109] On Sutton, see note 93. We are quoting from Fr. Pelster, *Thomae de Sutton O.P. Quaestiones de reali distinctione inter essentiam et esse,* Münster i. W., 1928.—Sutton seems to have first considered the distinction of essence and existence as unimportant; the text published by Pelster, and which we are taking into account, shows him completely won over to this fundamental Thomistic position.—On the early indifference of Sutton to the problem, text in Fr. Pelster, *Thomas of Sutton . . . ,* ZKT., 46 (1922) 374-375.

[110] Text in Pelster, op. cit., 45 and 50. In Giles of Rome, *Theoremata,* XII; Hocedez, 67-70. In what sense Thomas Aquinas had used the same argument, J. Isaac OP., *La notion de dialectique chez saint Thomas,* RSPT., 34 (1950) 481-506; cf. Bulletin Thomiste, 8 (1951) 53-58.

[111] Thomas of Sutton, *Quaestiones,* 52-53: existence is an absolute, it cannot be a relation, cf. 50-51.—On the existential meaning of the verb *is,* 53-54. —No intermediate difference between real difference and difference of reason, 24-25. —Notion of *esse* (existence), *Quaestiones,* 28, lines 16-18; 33, lines, 22-31; 47, lines 24-26. "Esse in Deo est quid absolutum sicut essentia," 52-53.

[112] Against Giles of Rome, 55-57.

[113] *Quaestiones,* 29-30.

[114] *Quaestiones,* 30.

[115] *Quaestiones,* 22-23.

[116] Sutton's use of *res, realis,* etc., creates a non-Thomistic atmosphere; strictly speaking, existence is no form, unless,

calling all actuality a form, we say that existence is form: *est enim actualitas rei,* 6m, 35; strictly speaking, *esse* is no *res,* nor is it an essence, but it is the *realis actualitas essentiae,* 7m, 35. All these formulas betray a mind expressing Thomistic notions in a language slightly different from that of Thomas Aquinas. On the crucial point of the limitation of existence by essences, Sutton is completely faithful to Thomas, ad 13m, 37-38. Cf. ad 20m, 41-42; ad 23m, 45; ad 25m, 46-47.

Other slight differences with Thomas Aquinas seem to obtain in Sutton's noetic. According to him, "the intellect does not cause, either as efficient cause or as formal cause, the assimilation which is intellection." The agent intellect is act, and it illumines, but it causes nothing. Sutton's notion of the will is a similar one. Starting, like Godfrey of Fontaines, from the Aristotelian principle that all that is in motion is moved by another, he infers that "the will must necessarily be said to be, not an act, but a pure potency that has no activity in itself." This is equally true as to the production of the act and as to its determination; in the first case, the will is moved by its desire of the good in general; in the second case, it is moved by a particular good. What is true is that, under this general motion by the good, the will moves itself to elicit such and such a particular act; yet, it does not move itself "effectively" (*effective*), but, rather, "consecutively" (i.e., in consequence of its general motion by the good). Sutton seems to go a little less far than Godfrey of Fontaines on this point, for he posits the root of the freedom of the will in its power "to move the intellect to judge." The will moves the intellect to form judgments about the means without which it could not reach its end. More research work is required to determine the exact relations of Sutton to Thomas and to Godfrey on this point. See D. E. Sharp, *Thomas of Sutton* . . . , RNSP., 36 (1934) 332-354; 37 (1935) 88-104, 219-233.

[117] BERNARD OF TRILLIA, OP., d. August 4, 1292. GLOREP., I, 155-157; GLOLIT., I, 101-104. V. Doucet, AFH., 26 (1933) 208-210. G. André, *Les Quodlibeta de Bernard de Trillia,* Gregorianum, 11 (1921) 226-264 (especially 249-254). M. Grabmann, *Doctrina S. Thomae* . . . , Acta Hebdomadae Thomisticae, Rome, 1924, 159-162;

Bernhard von Trillia OP. (d. *1292*) *und seine Quaestiones de cognitione animae conjunctae corpori et de cognitione animae separatae,* DTF., 13 (1935) 385-399. P. Duhem, *Le système du monde,* III, 363-383. P. Bayerschmidt, *Die Seins-und Formmetaphysik,* 149-151. Bernard likewise followed Thomas on the unity of the substantial form and, generally speaking, on all questions related to the problem of intellectual knowledge.

BERNARD OF AUVERGNE OP. (d. after 1307). Also considered a supporter of Thomism, including the real composition. GLOREP., I, 172-173. A polemist, Bernard wrote treatises *Contra dicta Henrici de Gandavo ubi impugnat Thomam, Improbationes contra Godefridum de Fontibus, Impugnationes contra Jacobum de Viterbio.* On his doctrinal positions, M. Grabmann, *Bernhard von Auvergne OP.* (d. *nach* 1304) *ein Interpret und Verteidiger der Lehre des hl. Thomas von Aquin aus alter Zeit,* MG., II, 547-558. On his defense of the real composition, M. Grabmann, *Doctrina S. Thomae de distinctione reali,* Rome, 1924, 131-190. P. Bayerschmidt, *Die Seins-und Formmetaphysik,* 159-164.

[118] On Godfrey of Fontaines, see note 95. On the non-indifference of the essence of creatures to being and to non-being, *Quodl.,* II, 2, 53-68. On the three conditions of essence according to Avicenna, 59. Three possible solutions, 60. Against the real distinction, 60. Indifference to existence is impossible, 61. Impossibility of an eternal quidditative being of creatures without positing an efficient cause before the formal cause, II, 2, 67-68. Cf. II, 3, 68-80.

[119] No being of essence without a being of existence, III, 1, 156-177. Probably against Thomas Aquinas, 158, 159, 171-172. No real distinction, 160. "Esse dicit idem re quod essentia vel ens," 160. Such distinctions are abstractions, 164-165.

[120] No necessary connection between creation and the distinction of essence and existence, 175-176. Creation of essence before existence is impossible, III, 2, 177-178.

[121] There has not been, even among the Dominicans, the unanimous agreement imagined by earlier historians. See J. Krauss, *Die Stellung des Oxforder Domi-*

nikaner Lehrers Crathorn zu Thomas von Aquin, ZKT., 57 (1933) 66-68.

[122] The letter of the masters of arts of the University of Paris on the occasion of the death of Thomas Aquinas is a clear proof of the fact (CUP., I, 504-505; UNIV., 98-100). The main point is not the regrets it expresses, but, rather, what it says concerning the efforts made by the faculty to obtain the return of Thomas Aquinas to the University of Paris. Text in Al. Birkenmajer, *Der Brief der Pariser Artistenfakultät über den Tod des hl. Thomas von Aquino,* Vermischte Untersuchungen, Münster i. W., 1922 (Beiträge, 20, 5), 1-32; especially p. 3: "quem vivum non potuimus rehabere." Same author: *Neues zu dem Brief der Pariser Artistenfakultät über den Tod des heiligen Thomas von Aquin,* Xenia Thomistica, III, Roma, 1925, 57-72. Still more decisive proofs in O. Lottin, *Saint Thomas à la faculté des arts de Paris aux approches de 1277,* RTAM., 16 (1949) 292-313.

[123] On the position of Giles of Lessines, see note 91. Among other masters usually considered Thomists:

THOMAS OF CLAXTON OP.—M. Grabmann, *Thomae de Claxton OP. (ca. 1400) Quaestiones de distinctione inter esse et essentiam reali atque de analogia entis,* APA., 8 (1943) 92-153. Maintains the Thomistic distinction on the ground that essence is to existence as matter is to extension, 107-108. Otherwise, creation would be impossible, 108-109. Against the univocity of being, 132-133, 137-143.

WILLIAM OF PETER OF GODIN OP (Guilelmus Petri de Godino), d. 1306; P. Fournier, *Le cardinal Guillaume de Peyre de Godin,* Bibliothèque de l'Ecole des Chartes, 1925, 100-121; HLF., 37 (1938) 146-153. M. Grabmann, *Einzelgestalten,* MG., II, 559-576; author of a *Lectura Thomasina* (p. 567-575), followed in a ms. by an anonymous treatise in which the real composition is denied ("essentia et esse non differunt realiter," 568); perhaps written under the influence of Harvey of Nedellec who also opposed the real composition (568-569). William himself supports the real composition: text in Grabmann, *Doctrina S. Thomae* . . . , Acta hebdomadae Thomisticae, Romae, 1924, 181-182. O. Lottin, PEM., III, 476-479.

JOHN OF STERNGASSEN OP. (Joannes Coloniensis), after Henry of Ghent and John Quidort: A. Landgraf, *Johannes Sterngasse OP. und sein Sentenzenkommentar,* DTF., 4 (1926) 40-54, 207-214, 327-350, 467-480. M. Grabmann, *Forschungen* . . . , MG., I, 392-404; John belongs to the neoplatonizing direction of the German Dominican school, but Grabmann includes him among the Thomists; see p. 395 the passage in which John rejects the real composition (perhaps that of Giles of Rome), and, p. 399, the text in which he rejects even that of Thomas Aquinas; note, p. 400, his invective against Durand of St. Pourçain: "Durandus is a petty pilferer (*quidam latrunclus*) of Peter of Auvergne, as all Frenchmen generally are, because they are men without any invention." In the light of thirteenth century philosophical production, John was not far wrong. This time, however, he was out of luck because this was a case of a Frenchman robbing another Frenchman. To even up the situation, let us mention another Dominican, NICHOLAS OF STRASSBURG, accused of having, although a German, plagiarized a Frenchman: H. Denifle, *Der Plagiator Nikolaus von Strassburg,* ALKG., 4 (1888) 312-329. The victim was John Quidort. Nicholas taught the immediate *concursus divinus* (text in Grabmann, 403-404) but there is no evidence that he related this authentically Thomistic position to the "act of being."—P. Bayerschmidt, *Die Seinsund Formmetaphysik,* 179-180.

JOHN OF LICHTENBERG (Joannes Picardi de Lucidomonte, de Lucemberg), died after 1313: M. Grabmann, MG., I, 410-420. Has left a penetrating discussion of the problem of essence and existence (416-420); he subscribes to the distinction for four reasons: 1) all that is not included in the quiddity, or essence, makes composition with it (Avicenna); 2) if essence is its own existence, it is God (Thomas); 3) if existence means essence, these propositions: Man is, or roses are, predicate an essential predicate, from which difficulties follow; 4) if essence is really identical with existence, then, since Christ has two natures, he would have two existences (p. 419).

Among the Dominican masters, Grabmann observes that BOMBOLOGNUS OF BOLOGNA was no Thomist (MG., I, 340). He upheld hylomorphism on the authority of Gabirol.—ROMANO OF ROME, d. 1273, taught at Paris under Thomas Aquinas and was his successor at that university

(MG., I, 340-346; DTF., 19 (1941) 166-194. O. Lottin, CSB., PEM., III, 235-239, 418-421, 465-467).—HANNIBALDUS DE HANNIBALDIS, OP., a Thomist in a broad sense of the term; Grabmann, MG., I, 437. A. Duval, *Annibal des Annibaldi,* in Catholicisme, Hier, Aujourdhui, Demain, 2 (1948) 597; d. 1272 or 1273.— REMIGIO DE'GIROLAMI, d. 1319, pupil of Thomas Aquinas and master of Dante (Grabmann, MG., I, 361-369) favors a real composition. On his social doctrines: R. Egenter, *Gemeinnutz vor Eigennutz* . . . , Scholastik, 12 (1934) 79-92.—ADE-NULF VON ANAGNI, M. Grabmann, *Adenulf of Anagni, Propst von Saint-Omer* (d. *1290) ein Freund und Schüler des hl. Thomas von Aquin,* Traditio, 5 (1947) 269-283.

[124] I.—HARVEY OF NEDELLEC, OP. (Hervaeus Natalis, Hervé Nédélec), Dominican, was teaching at Paris in 1303, master in theology in 1307. Harvey supported the doctrine of Thomas, first against Henry of Ghent and James of Metz, then against Scotus, Durand of St. Pourçain and Peter Auriol. General Minister of the Dominican Order, 1318, Harvey promoted the canonization of Thomas Aquinas (1323) and died on August 7th in the same year. HLF., 34, 308-351. GLOREP., I, 199-206. V. Doucet, AFH., 26 (1933) 211-212. The commentary on the *Sentences* has been published at Paris, 1647. *Quaestiones Quodlibetales,* Venice, 1513. Several treatises are still waiting for their publication: *Tractatus de formis; De quatuor materiis* (list of chapters, RSPT., 18 (1929), 291-295); *De aeternitate mundi; De materia coeli; De cognitione primi principii;* for his controversy with Durandus, GLOREP., 201 *g,* 203 *v, w,* and 204, *x, y;* against James of Metz, 200 *e.* E. Elter, *Un ouvrage inconnu de Hervé Nédellec,* Gregorianum, 4 (1923) 211-240: not philosophical (*De jurisdictione, De exemptione*). Capital for the history of the notion of theology: Eug. Krebs, *Theologie und Wissenschaft nach der Lehre der Hochscholastik,* Münster i. W., 1912 (Beiträge, 11, 3-4): Part II, *Defensa doctrinae D. Thomae* by Hervaeus Natalis, or *De causis theologiae,* 1-112, with important historical notes.— BIBLIOGRAPHY. Biographical, A. de Guimarães, *Hervé Noel* (d. *1323*). *Etude biographique,* AFP., 8 (1938), 5-81. C. Jellouschek, *Verteidigung der Möglichkeit einer Anfangslosen Weltschöpfung bei*

Hervaeus Natalis, Joannes a Neapoli, Gregorius Ariminensis und Joannes Capreolus, JPST., 26 (1912) 155-187, 325-367. W. Schöllgen, *Das Problem der Willensfreiheit bei Heinrich von Ghent und Hervaeus Natalis,* Abhandlungen aus Ethik und Moral, Düsseldorf, 1927. R.-M. Martin, *La table des matières de l'ouvrage "De quatuor materiis" d'Hervé de Nédellec OP.,* RSPT., 18 (1929) 291-295. J. Santeler, *Der kausale Gottesbeweis bei Herveus Natalis, nach dem ungedrucktem Traktat "De cognitione primi principii,"* (Philosophie und Grenzwissenschaften, III, 1), Innsbruck, 1930. A. Fries, *Quaestiones super quartum librum Sententiarum Hervaeo Natali vindicatae,* Angelicum, 13 (1936) 498-533. C. Vollert SJ., *Hervaeus Natalis and the Problem of Original Justice,* Theological Studies, 3 (1942) 231-251.

Among the "doctrinal peculiarities" by which Harvey differs from Thomas, M. de Wulf (*Histoire,* III, 59) counts his rejection of the "real distinction of essence and existence." Another one is his insistence on the distinction between the "subjective being" of the act of knowing (as a psychological fact) and the "objective being" of the thing as an object of cognition. Harvey situated the reality that answers universals (general concepts) in a "real conformity" obtaining between the individuals that belong to the same species; this invited him to attribute a certain numerical unity to the species. Individuation is not accounted for by quantified matter (Thomas), nor by "hecceity" (Scotus); the external cause for the distinction of individuals is their efficient cause; the internal cause for it is essence itself, which individualizes its own accidents. All these positions are typical of the early fourteenth century. The effort of Harvey to prove the existence of God even if the series of the causes is infinite also betrays a preoccupation common at a time when the possibility of an actually given infinite was beginning to be envisaged. Speaking in a general way, it is worthy of note that to be a "Thomist" cannot mean quite the same thing for a commentator of Thomas and for a theologian engaged in controversies with his contemporaries, which was the case of Harvey. But, for this very reason, one should carefully read a theologian before describing him as "an outstanding Thomist" who "defended the philosophy of Aquinas with reliability and measure against Henry of Ghent, Scotus . . ." etc. (M. Grabmann, *Die Lehre des hl. Thomas von Aquin von der Kirche als Gotteswerk,* Regensburg, 1903, pp. 33-35).

II.—JOHN OF NAPLES (Johannes de Neapoli), master in theology at Paris (1315), supported the position of Thomas Aquinas against Durand of St. Pourçain. *Quaestiones variae 42 Parisiis disputatae,* Naples, 1618. C. J. Jellouschek, *Quaestio magistri Johannis de Neapoli OP.: Utrum licite possit doceri Parisius doctrina Fr. Thomae quantum ad omnes conclusiones ejus,* Xenia Thomistica, III, (1925) 73-104. Pr. Stella SDB., *Zwei unedierte Artikel des Johannes von Neapel über das Individuationsprinzip,* DTF., 29 (1951) 129-166. On his questions and quodlibets, J. Koch, *Durandus . . .* , 285-314. M. Grabmann, MG., I, 374-382. P. M. Schaff, art. *Jean de Naples,* DTC., 8 (1924) 793-794. C. J. Jellouschek, *Johannes von Neapel und seine Lehre vom Verhältnisse zwischen Gott und Welt,* Wien, 1918.—The texts published by Pr. Stella invite us to qualify the title of defender of "pure Thomism" against Durand (M. de Wulf, *Histoire . . .* , III, 65). The principle of individuation is not a secondary point in metaphysics; John of Naples rejects individuation by quantified matter and upholds the solution proposed by Henry of Ghent: individuation by double negation (*Quodl.* III, 5; Stella ed. p. 154). In fact, John thinks everything is individuated by the very fact that it is a being: "individuation adds nothing positive over and above the reality and entity of the thing" (ibid.). His third reason in favor of his own position is of far-reaching significance: according to Aristotle, universals only exist in the intellect; consequently, what exists outside of the intellect is bound to be singular: "Si ergo universalitas convenit rebus ab alio scilicet ab intellectu . . . ergo per oppositum individuatio non convenit rei ab alio sed a se ipsa" (ibid.). The cause of a being is the cause of its individuality, because actual being is individual by itself. Since universality belongs to things in virtue of something else (the intellect) singularity belongs to them by themselves: "cui competit universalitas solum ab alio, illud quantum est ex se non habet universalitatem" (*Quodl.* VII, 6; Stella ed., p. 162). This "pure Thomism" could easily be purified. In his excellent introduction, Pr. Stella notes the literal identity of one of John's statements with a conclusion of Roger Bacon: "Frustra quaeritur quid est principium et causa individuationis, sed magis deberet quaeri quid est principium universalitatis" (p. 162). Pr. Stella's concluding remark (p. 150) is that John follows the speculative stream which, born of G. of Fontaines, runs through Peter of Auvergne and James of Metz up to Durand. Beyond Durand, there is Ockham.—This John of Naples (Giovanni Regina) must not be confused with another one (John Cataldi, d. after 1465 at Montpellier), T. Käppeli, *Note sugli scrittori domenicani di nome Giovanni di Napoli,* AFP., 10 (1940) 40-76.

[125] PETER OF LA PALU OP. (Petrus de Palude), master in theology (1314), General Minister of the Order (1317), Patriarch of Jerusalem (1329), died in 1342. Commentary on the *Sentences,* Paris, 1518. M. Grabmann, *Petri de Palude OP. (d. 1342) quaestio: Utrum Deus immediate agat in omni actione?,* APA., 6 (1940) 41-58. See, p. 46: "Quidam tamen" and "Alii vero dicunt" (opinions reported by Durand); p. 53, "Tertia opinio est, quae videtur esse fratris Thomae, et est vera, si bene intelligatur . . . Ergo in omni re Deus est causa intimius et immediatius operans quam aliqua creatura." (refers to *De causis,* 54); his own opinion ("quarta opinio") agrees with the third opinion (Thomas) as to the conclusion, but for reasons that are different (56-58) and do not make use of the *esse* of Thomas Aquinas. The constant adversary of Peter is Durand of St. Pourçain: J. Koch, *Durandus . . .* , 22-31; 272-279.—Life and works, P. Fournier, *Pierre de la Palu,* HLF., 37 (1938) 39-84. The problem of the divine co-operation with creatures is discussed by another little-known Dominican who wrote in the first half of the fourteenth century, HENRY OF LÜBECK; M. Grabmann, MG., I, 421-428. Texts in *Henrici de Lübeck OP., Quaestiones de motu creaturarum et de concursu divino,* ed. F. Mitzka, Münster i. W., 1932.

NICHOLAS TRIVET OP. (Trevet, Treveth), English, master in theology (probably at Oxford); taught in Oxford (1314) and in London (1324); died after 1330. A. G. Little, OTT., 283-285. Fr. Ehrle, *Nikolaus Trivet, sein Leben, seine Quodli-*

bet und Quaestiones ordinariae, Festgabe-Baeumker, 1-63 (Beiträge, Supplement-band II). M. Schmaus, *Nicolai Trivet Quaestiones de causalitate Dei et concurso divino,* DTP., 35 (1932) 185-196. On the rejection of the real composition, texts in Ehrle, art. cit., 28, notes 2 and 3. Nicholas accepts a real distinction, but not in the same sense as Thomas Aquinas. On the oneness of the form, 32, n. 1. On transubstantiation, against John Quidort, 33-41; list of the questions, 52-62. In agreement with his hesitations concerning the "act of being" of Thomas Aquinas, Trivet has his doubts concerning the immediacy of the *concursus Dei.* In Thomas Aquinas, *esse* (existence) is the proper term of the creative act of God; it is therefore more intimate to any being than all the rest and, consequently, through *esse,* God is immediately concurring with all that any being is or does. The Thomistic "immediatus concursus Dei" stands and falls with the Thomistic act of being. Before rejecting the immediate co-operation of God, Durand of St. Pourçain will intelligently begin by denying the Thomistic principle: "Existence (*esse*) is more intimate than that whereby it is determined." See J. Stufler, *Bemerkungen zur Konkurslehre des Durandus von St. Pourçain,* AGDM., 1086-1087; on Giles of Rome, 1087-1089.—Positions similar to that of Trivet have been held by the otherwise unknown English master KYKELEY: M. Schmaus, *Kykeley, cuiusdam adhuc ignoti auctoris anglici ineunte XIV. florentis, Quaestio de cooperatione divina,* Bohoslovia, 10 (1932) 193-228 (text). On the possible identity of Kykeley with a certain Kirkebi, OTT., 267-269.

[126] BERNARDUS LOMBARDI OP., born in Provence, read the *Sentences* at Paris in 1327-1328; traditionally considered a Thomist. In fact, his doctrine has been little studied. P. Fournier, *Bernard Lombardi,* HLF., 37 (1938) 517-522. J. Koch, *Durandus de S. Porciano . . . ,* 314-340 (biographical, 314-315); on his attitude toward Thomas Aquinas and his defense of the Thomistic composition of essence and existence, 330 (cf. M. Grabmann, *La scuola tomistica . . . ,* RFNS., 15 (1923) 152, including the oft-quoted text of Bernard: "In ista quaestione erunt duo articuli: primus de hoc, quod quaeritur, an in creaturis differat esse et essentia; secundus, an in Deo sint idem. Quantum

ad primum in genere est duplex modus dicendi: Primus est doctoris sancti Thomae, qui ponit quod in omnibus citra Deum differt esse ab essentia; secundus est omnium aliorum concorditer Parisiensium, qui dicunt oppositum." In general, Bernard stands halfway between Thomas and Durand, 330; on his evolution toward Thomas, 331; on his *Quodlibet* I, 332-340: polemic against Peter Auriol and others (339).—T. Käppeli, *Kurze Mitteilungen über mittelalterliche Dominikanerschriftsteller,* AFP., 10 (1940) 283-296; Bernard Lombardi, Robert Kilwardby, Roland of Cremona, Eckhart, etc.

[127] PETER OF AUVERGNE, rector of the University of Paris in 1275; master in theology, 1296-1302; Bishop of Clermont, 1302; died September 25, 1304. GLOREP., I, 412-417; GLOLIT., 257-263. A series of articles by Edg. Hocedez, *La théologie de Pierre d'Auvergne,* Gregorianum, 11 (1930) 526-552; *Les Quaestiones in Metaphysicam de Pierre d'Auvergne,* Archives de philosophie, 9 (1932) 180-234; *La vie et les oeuvres de Pierre d'Auvergne,* Gregorianum, 14 (1933) 3-36; *Une question inédite de Pierre d'Auvergne sur l'individuation,* RNSP., 36 (1934) 355-386; *La philosophie des Quodlibets de Pierre d'Auvergne,* ADGM., II, 779-791. F. Segarra, *Un precursor de Durando, Pedro d'Auvergne,* Estudios ecclesiasticos, 12 (1933) 114-124. O. Lottin, PEM., II, 269-270. W. Dunphy, *The Similarities Between Certain Questions of Peter of Auvergne's Commentary on the Metaphysics and the Anonymous Commentary on the Physics attributed to Siger of Brabant,* MS., 15 (1953) 159-168.

The doctrine of Peter of Auvergne has been described as "the impressive continuation and completion of the interpretation of Aristotle by his great and intimately beloved master, Thomas Aquinas," MG., 310. According to Hocedez, (*La philosophie . . . ,* 791 and n. 57) the philosophy of Peter is rather Aristotelian. He rejects the composition of essence and existence, art, cit., 780, n. 12. Actual existence is identical with the actuality of the form, 780-781. Essence has its own being, which is indifferent to existence and to non-existence, 781. Prime matter is pure potentiality, 781-782. No hylomorphism, 783 in angels. Individuation by the form; quantity is the principle of numerical unity, 785. Like Godfrey of Fontaines, the condemnation of 1277 makes him hesitate to affirm the oneness of the form in man, 786. Every man has his own agent intellect; yet, "to produce intelligibles in act is not properly an action of the intellectual light that is in the soul, but rather, of a separate intellect," 789, n. 44. On the self-determination of the will, Peter agrees with Thomas Aquinas, 789-790. What prevented him from being a complete Thomist was his Aristotelianism.

[128] G. Wallerand, *Henri Bate de Malines: "Speculum divinorum et quorumdam naturalium,* Louvain, 1941; *Henri Bate de Malines et saint Thomas d'Aquin,* RNSP., 36 (1934) 387-411. Al. Birkenmajer, *Henri*

Bate de Malines, astronome et philosophe du XIIIe siècle, Cracovie, Imprimerie de l'Université, 1923 (La Pologne au Congrès international de Bruxelles).—Henry opens with the problem of sensation, whence he goes on to the possible intellect, the agent intellect, matter, the relations of intellect and body, the plurality of intellects, the divine Ideas, the structure of the human body, its generation, the operations of the soul, on the intellect and the intelligible, wakefulness, sleep and dreams, meteors, natural or supernatural apparitions, weather, movement, the celestial bodies that cause it, the Prime Principle. In his effort to reconcile Aristotle and Plato, Aristotle is often sacrificed.

PART TEN

FOURTEENTH-CENTURY SCHOLASTICISM

CHAPTER I. ALBERTISTS AND NEOPLATONISTS

[1] Albertus Magnus, *Sum. theol.,* II, 12, 69, 2, 12; Borgnet ed., vol. 18, p. 348.— The main positions of Albert the Great concerning the intellective soul should be kept in mind while reading the works of his successors. They are summarized in his treatise, *On the Intellect and the Intelligible,* Borgnet, 9, 477-521. There are intelligible forms in intellectual souls because they flow into these souls in virtue of the light of an agent Intelligence (II, 1; Borgnet, 504). These forms flow from the separate Intelligence which is the form of the world (*forma mundi*), II, 2, 505-506. Some ask the question (Augustinians): how can the forms of material things act upon the soul, which is a nobler substance than they are? This betrays their ignorance of natural philosophy. The forms of material things act upon the soul inasmuch as they themselves act under the light of the agent Intelligence. This light is *in* them. Had the Stoics (i.e., the Platonists) known this, they would not have posited separate forms, II, 3, 506-508. Description of the successive conditions of the possible intellect: possible, formal, in act (*in effectu*), acquired (*adeptus*), assimilative (*assimilativus*), II, 4-9, 508-517. Note, p. 516, that the *intellectus assimilativus* extends from its own light to the light of the Intelligence and from the light of the

Intelligence to that of God (cf. Ulrich of Strasbourg). The remarks concerning the *intellectus sanctus* should also be noted in view of Ulrich of Strasbourg; the saintliness of intellect is the purity it achieves by turning away from matter; this is to pursue beauty and, consequently, to achieve purification, II, 10, 518. Divine illumination and prophecy (II, 11, 519-520). Reduction of all things to the divine light (II, 12, 52-521).—All these positions agree with those of Albert in his thelogical writings; the fact that Ulrich will accept even the boldest ones (*intellectus assimilativus*) confirms the conclusion that Albert himself held them to be as many philosophically true conclusions. The mystical possibilities included in the doctrine of the soul of Albert and in his noetic have been examined by M. Grabmann, *Der Einfluss Alberts des Grossen auf das mittelalterliche Geistesleben, Das Deutsche Element in der mittelalterlichen Scholastik und Mystik,* MG., II, 324-412; particularly 360-394: Ulrich of Strasbourg, 370; Eckhart and Tauler, 371-372; etc. Still unknown territories are revealed by the list of names contained in G. M. Löhr, *Zur Geschichte der Kölner Dominikanerschule im 14. Jahrhundert,* DTF., 23 (1945) 57-84; 54 notices on diverse masters; *Zur Geschichte der Kölner Dominikanerschule im 15. Jahrhun-*

dert, ibid., pp. 287-300, 427-445; on the distribution of masters and candidates by theological schools, pp. 294-295.

[2] HUGH RIPELIN OP (Hugh of Strasbourg), author of the *Compendium theologiae* printed among the works of Albert the Great, *Opera omnia*, Borgnet, 34, 1-306. History of the text, M. Grabmann, *Mitteilungen über scholastische Funde in der Bibliotheca Ambrosiana zu Mailand*, TQ., 93 (1911) 536-550.—This *Compendium* is a clear summary of the main theological positions of Albert, with a minimum of philosophy. The existence of God is mainly held on faith, or as a sort of immediate evidence; sketchy proof by causality, I, 1, pp. 3-4. There is only one supreme Good (against Manichaeism; theme *De bono*, Albert, Hugh, Ulrich), I, 3, pp. 5-6. The essence of God is infinite *negative*, I, 15; 17. Incomprehensibility of God (Bernard, Denis), I, 16, pp. 17-19, and 24, pp. 27-28. Eternity, immutability, simplicity and transcendency of God, I, 18-21, pp. 20-25. Divine Ideas, I, 25, pp. 28-29. Omnipotence, I, 27, pp. 30-31. Divine will, I, 32, pp. 35-37. Creation of the world (*hexameron*), II, 1-10, pp. 40-49. Difference between angels and souls (*unibiles corpori*), II, 11, 49-50. Twofold definition of the soul, in itself and as ruler of the body, II, 29, pp. 60-61. Let us follow the definition given by the Saints and the Catholic masters: "a spiritual and rational substance, created out of nothing in view of imparting life to the human body," II, 30, pp. 61-62. It is called *anima* inasmuch as it "animates"; it is called mind inasmuch as it remembers (*mens: meminit*), II, 31, p. 62. In man, the three souls are one essence and three powers, II, 32, p. 62. Sense and imagination, II, 34-41, pp. 63-69. Intellectual knowledge: *intellectus adeptus* and *in effectu* as degrees of perfection of the possible intellect, II, 44, pp. 69-70. Possible intellect and agent intellect, II, 46, pp. 71-72. On intellectual memory, II, 40, pp. 66-67 (on the historical significance of this notion in general, M.-D. Chenu, *La première diffusion du Thomisme* . . . , AHDL., 3 (1928) 193-196: *memoria intellectiva* and *abditum mentis*). On the human will, II, 50, p. 73. Free choice, II, 56, pp. 76-78. Immortality of the soul, II, 55, pp. 76-77. Human body (physiognomy) II, 68-69, pp. 79-82. On man as a whole, 60-61, pp. 82-83.—On Hugh of Strasbourg as the absolutely certain author of the *Compendium*, M. Grabmann, *Studien über Ulrich von Strassburg*, MG., I, 174-185.

[3] ULRICH OF STRASBOURG OP (Ulrich Engelberti), contemporary with Thomas Aquinas; taught at the Dominican convent of Strasbourg, then at Paris, where he died *ca.* 1278. GLOREP., I, 148-151. Letters of Ulrich have been published by H. Finke, *Ungedruckte Dominikanerbriefe des 13. Jahrhunderts*, Paderborn, 1891, 78-104. Only fragments of his main work have been published: J. Daguillon, *Ulrich de Strasbourg. La "Summa de bono." I. Introduction et édition critique, Paris*, 1930. Same author: Bk. VI, tr. 4, ch. 7-11, in La vie spirituelle, Paris, ed. du Cerf, 1926, Supplement, 19-37, 89-102, 56-57. M. Grabmann, *Des Ulrich Engelberti von Strassburg OP. (d. 1277) Abhandlung De pulchro. Untersuchungen und Texte* (Bk. II, tr. 3, ch. 4), Sitzungsberichte, Munich, 1926. G. Théry, *Originalité du plan de la Summa de Bono d'Ulrich de Strasbourg*, RT., 27 (1922) 376-397.— BIBLIOGRAPHY. M. Grabmann, *Studien über Ulrich von Strassburg*, MG., 1926, I, 147-221. A. Stohr, *Die Trinitätslehre Ulrichs von Strasburg mit besonderer Berücksichtigung ihres Verhältnisses zu Albert dem Grossen und Thomas Aquinas*, Münster i. W., 1928 (Beiträge, zur Theologie, 13). J. Koch, *Neue Literatur über Ulrich von Strassburg*, TR., 1930, 433-439. H. Weisweiler, *Eine neue Ueberlieferung der Summa de Bono Ulrichs von Strassburg*, ZKT., 59 (1935) 442-446. C. J. Fagin, *The Doctrine of the Divine Ideas in the "Summa de Bono" of Ulrich of Strasbourg, Text and philosophical introduction* (De bono, II, 5), Univ. of Toronto-Abstract, 1948. Fr. Lescoe, *The Theory of the First Principle in the Summa de Bono of Ulrich of Strasbourg, Philosophical Study and text* (De bono, IV, 1) Univ. of Toronto-Abstract, 1949. F. J. Collingwood, *The Theory of Being in Summa de Bono (Bk. II)* of *Ulrich of Strassburg: Philosophical Study and Text*, Univ. of Toronto-Abstract, 1952. A Fries, *Die Abhandlung "De anima" des Ulrich Engelberti OP.*, RTAM., 17 (1950) 328-331. L. Thomas (C. J. Fagin), *Ulrich of Strasbourg: his Doctrine of the Divine Ideas*, TMS., 30 (1952-1953) 21-32.

[4] On theology *qua* science, *Summa,* I, 2, 3 and 4; Daguillon ed., 33-38.

[5] God escapes human understanding, Matt. 11, 27. If any philosopher says this in the same terms as John, he has borrowed them from him; for instance, Plato, *Timaeus* 40d; Hermes Trismegistus, *Logos Stileos;* at any rate, the philosophers have known the names of the Father and the Son, not their nature; as to the Holy Ghost, even the name remained unknown to them, I, 1, 2, pp. 6-10. The existence of God is known by a sort of natural instinct; the agent intellect is a natural image of God in us; this is the reason why, as soon as we look at creatures, we know there is a God; the existence of God is a kind of *per se notum,* I, 1, 3; pp. 10-13. I, 1, 5, pp. 14-16.

[6] The degrees of perfection of the possible intellect are introduced in the fifth "way" leading to the existence of God, I, 1, 7, pp. 19-21: *possibilis, in effectu, adeptus, sanctus* (that is, pure of materiality and of all impurity pertaining to matter), *assimilatus,* p. 19. Through the light of the "assimilated intellect" (that is: made, or become similar to . . .) the light of the separate substances enters the soul; this gives rise to the "divine condition of the intellect" (*intellectus divinus*), because, in this light, we know God (John, I, 9). This light is the perfection of the intellect; it is a single light made up of three lights: that of the agent intellect of man, that of the separate Intelligence, and the divine light. By this compound light we know not only *that* God is, but even *what* God is, at least so far as the quiddity of a thing can be known through the species and likeness that represents it, pp. 19-20. This is emphatically not to know God by his essence, but it is more than to know him by mode of abstraction only; it is to know God by his image and resemblance impressed in our intellect, p. 20. Ulrich makes it clear that he is here talking about natural knowledge apart from either faith or grace, p. 21. This natural resemblance to God accounts for what the philosophers have known of God, as can be gathered from Plato, Aristotle, Epicurus (according to Cicero, *De natura deorum,* I, 16, 43, and I, 17, 45), the *Book on Causes,* Avicenna, etc. Ulrich, I, 1, 8, pp. 21-26.

[7] Ideas are one with the divine essence.

They are the forms of the things to be created. "The ideas are completely practical" (C. J. Fagin). There is an idea of prime matter, and even of material privation. In this sense, God is the formal cause of all things. The action of the First Cause is like that of light: "diffusio hujus lucis et formalitatis"). Form is the cause of matter; consequently, God is the First Idea, or Form, which is the cause of all. Plato was right in saying that all the primordial Ideas are essentially one Idea, and, therefore, that the First Idea (i.e., God) is an intelligible world (*mundus intelligibilis*). All the forms come to things through the movers of the heavenly spheres, whose energy comes from their information by the light of the first Intellect. They owe to God both to be and to be causes, M. Grabmann, *Studien über Ulrich von Stassburg,* MG., I, 210-212; texts quoted in footnotes.

[8] The first created thing is being (*Book on Causes*). This common being (*esse commune*) is the universal stuff out of which all things have been formed. It alone is created, all the rest arises by way of "formation." Of itself, it is completely formless and indeterminate, but since a multitude of determinate forms may come out of it, it cannot be matter, it must needs be an Intelligence. It resembles the human intellect in potency with respect to all forms: "All creatures participate in it and so do not participate in the substance of God" (F. J. Collingwood, *The Theory of Being* . . . , p. 3). This diffusive creation of beings accounts for the resemblance of creatures to the Good; "by similitude creatures are the very *esse divinum* itself; for, inasmuch as the image of a thing is in a certain way that thing, the creature by its similitude is the divine being itself," F. J. Collingwood, ibid. According to the same historian, this synthesis of creation and emanation might be a personal contribution of Ulrich and set him apart in the doctrinal tradition initiated at Cologne by St. Albert the Great (ibid., p. 4). On the relation of the first created being (already blended with non-being) to God, M. Grabmann, *Studien* . . . , 204-205. Note the text quoted p. 205, n. 13, which says that the first created being is an Intelligence in the sense, not of an "intellectual substance," but of a form produced by the light of the agent intellect (*intel-*

lectus agentis). A certain obscurity concerning the meaning of the doctrine will subsist at least until the publication of Ulrich's text.

[9] DIETRICH OF VRIBERG (of Vrieberg, von Freiburg).—Eug. Krebs, *Meister Dietrich (Theodoricus Teutonicus de Vriberg). Sein Leben, seine Werke, seine Wissenschaft*, Münster i. W., 1906 (Beiträge, V, 5-6). M. de Wulf, *Un scolastique inconnu de la fin du XIIIe siècle*, RNSP., 13 (1906) 434-441. L. Gauthier, *Un psychologue de la fin du XIIIe siècle, Thierry de Fribourg*, Revue Augustinienne, 15 (1909) 657-673; 16 (1910) 178-206, 541-566. E. Krebs, *Le traité "De esse et essentia" de Thierry de Fribourg*, RNSP., 18 (1911) 511-536. J. Würschmidt, *Theodoricus Teutonicus de Vriberg, De iride et radialibus impressionibus*, Münster i. W., 1914 (Beiträge, 12, 5-6). A. Birkenmajer, *Drei neue Handschriften der Werke Meister Dietrichs*, Vermischte Untersuchungen, 70-90. Fred. Stegmüller, *Meister Dietrich von Freiberg über die Zeit und das Sein*, AHDL., 13 (1942) 153-221; includes the opuscules *De tempore* and *De mensuris durationis*. P. Duhem, *Le système du monde*, III, 383-396. GLOREP., I, 162-165. G. della Volpe, *Eckhart o della filosofia mistica*, Roma, 1952, pp. 82-86.
List of the writings of Dietrich in E. Krebs, *Meister Dietrich . . .*, Part II, 4-9. Analysis and fragments, 10-116 (extremely useful for the unpublished works); complete text of the treatise on the intellect and the intelligible (*Tractatus de intellectu et intelligibili*), 119-206; *Tractatus de habitibus*, 207-215.

[10] M. Grabmann, *Die Proklosübersetzungen des Wilhelm von Moerbeke und ihre Verwertung in der lateinischen Literatur des Mittelalters*, MG., II, 413-423; date of the translation, 415-416. On William's translation of Proclus' commentaries on *Timaeus* and *Parmenides*, A. Birkenmajer, *Vermischte Abhandlungen . . .*, Münster i. W., 1922, 8-13, 16-19. R. Klibansky, *Ein Proklosfund und seine Bedeutung*, Sitzungsberichte, Heidelberg, 1928-1929, 5; Heidelberg 1929.—On the vocabulary of W. of Moerbeke's translation of Proclus: Cl. Vansteenkiste, *Procli Elementatio theologica translata a Guilelmo de Moerbeke. Notae de methodo translationis*. Tijdschrift voor Philosophie, 14 (1952) 503-546.—English transl. by Th.

Taylor, *The Commentaries of Proclus on the Timaeus of Plato . . .*, 2 vols. London, 1820.—Among the witnesses to the influence of the translation of Proclus' *Elements of Theology*, Grabmann quotes, p. 420, William of Leus (Guillelmus de Levibus, Guillaume de Leux), Dominican, master in theology at Narbonne (1296), Carcassonne (1300), Toulouse (1303), d. after 1311. See A. Pelzer, *Guillaume de Leus (de Levibus) frère prêcheur de Toulouse*, ADGM., 1065-1079: title of the questions of his commentary on the *Liber de Causis*, 1074-1075; on William's commentary on the *Sentences*, I-III, 1075-1076.

[11] G. F. Böhringer, *Die deutschen Mystiker des 14. und 15. Jahrhunderts*, Zürich, 1835. C. Greith, *Die deutsche Mystik im Predigerorden*, Freiburg i. Br., 1861. W. Preger, *Geschichte der deutschen Mystik im Mittelalter*, Leipzig, 1881. H. Denifle, *Ueber die Anfänge der Predigtweise der deutschen Mystiker*, ALKG., 2 (1886) 641-652. F. Pfeiffer, *Deutsche Mystiker*, Göttingen, 1907. J. Zahn, *Einführung in die deutsche Mystik*, Paderborn, 1918. C. Boeckl, *Die Bedingtheiten der deutschen Mystik des Mittelalters*, ADGM., 1011-1020. M. David-Windstosser, *Deutsche Frauenmystik im Mittelalter*, 1918 (Sammlung Kösel). M. Grabmann, *Die Deutsche Frauenmystik des Mittelalters. Ein Ueberblick*, MG., I, 469-488. J. Ancelet-Hustache, *Les "Vitae sororum" d'Unterlinden. Edition critique . . .*, AHDL., 5 (1930) 317-509. G. M. Gieraths, *Johannes Nider OP. und die "deutsche Mystik" des 14. Jahrhunderts*, DTF., 30 (1952) 321-346.

[12] E. Krebs, *Meister Dietrich . . .*, 61.

[13] Dietrich restates the fundamental propositions of Proclus, *De intellectu . . .*, I, 6, 125-126; this proposition concerning the One (Proclus, 20) is of great importance with respect to Eckhart; note, p. 126, in complete agreement with Plotinus: the first principle is above even unity.

[14] Our scrupulous historical distinctions are foreign to the perspective of Dietrich. Concerning the overflowing of things from God, a sure sign of truth is the agreement there is between all the great philosophers: Aristotle, Plato, the Platonist Proclus, Avicenna and his abbreviator Algazel. All affirm that things flow from God

according to a definite order, *De intellectu,* I, 11, 132. Augustine fully agrees
with Proclus on this point, I, 9, 130.
Creation is an external manifestation, or
freely willed expression of the inner
"transfusion" and fecundity of the divine
being, ibid.

[15] *De intellectu* . . . , I, 11, 132.

[16] Instead of positing the agent intellect
as flowing from the essence of the soul
and causing its intellectual operations,
Dietrich posits it as the cause of the very
essence of the soul; it is in the soul as
the heart is in the living being, II, 2,
135-136. From this important consequences follow; the soul is a certain
"withinhood" (*quaedam intraneitas*) that
is not conjoined to the body as its form;
it performs even its sensitive operations,
as Augustine says it does (II, 3, 136-137);
this is the meaning of the doctrine of
the *quaedam intraneitas* to be found *in*
the soul, II, 4, 137; as a whole, it is
united to the body as its form, but Augustine says there is in it something
(*mens*), a certain "withinhood," "a certain qualitative and substantial mode,"
according to which the soul "is not united
to the body," II, 5, 137-138. Cf. II, 8,
10, 140-143.

[17] The agent intellect is numerically one,
II, 13, 144-145. Its individuation is in
it in an inchoative way; it belongs in a
complete way to the whole essence of the
soul and to the whole man, II, 19, 149.
Hence, the whole is one by essence, ibid.
Cf. II, 27, 156-158. This is in keeping
with the classical Plotinian scheme: an
Idea begets an Intelligence, which begets
a soul, which begets a corporeal being.
—How the agent Intellect came into
being, II, 32, 162-163 and 34, 164-165.
On the stability and unity of its intuitive
knowledge, II, 36, 166-167; II, 37, 167-
168. The latter text refers to Augustine,
De immortalitate animae, 4, 6; *Conf.* X,
10; *De Trinitate,* XIV, 21, 40 (*abstrusior
profunditas*), and XIV, 7, 9 (*abditum
mentis*); this secret recess of the mind is
the agent intellect, in which the spirit of
man finds eternal things which it itself
cannot possibly produce, Dietrich, *De intellectu,* II, 37, 168. The possible intellect
is an accident, not a substance; nevertheless, since conceptional being" (*ens
conceptionale*) is the first intention of
being and, as such, is distinct from noth-

ingness, the possible intellect, which posits
things in their conceptional being, has
the modality of substance (*modus substantiae*) without itself being a substance,
III, 8, 176-177. Against Averroes, III,
10-14, 178-181. Notion of known object
in general, III, 17, 184-185. That all
is known in the light of the Prime
Truth, III, 18-21, 185-188 (according to
Augustine). Recapitulation of the doctrine, III, 34, 200-203. In what sense the
intellect is, and again is not, eternal, III,
38, 205-206.

[18] *De visione beatifica,* analyzed by
Krebs, Part II, 70-82. This important text
begins by positing the three authorities
on which the doctrine rests: Augustine,
Denis, Proclus. The *abditum mentis* of
Augustine dominates the treatise. We beg
to quote the Latin original for the main
positions because their translation cannot
do them full justice: 1) "Abditum mentis
secundum Augustinum, quod est intellectus agens in sua essentia, est vere substantia," 71; 2) First proof: "Abditum
mentis (quod est intellectus agens) semper stat in lumine actualis intelligentiae
et semper actu intelligit," 72; 3) Second
proof; "Abditum mentis tali intellectione
se ipsum intelligit per suam essentiam,"
73; 4) Third proof: "Intellectus per
essentiam est exemplar quoddam et similitudo entis in eo, quod ens et omnia intelligit," 73; 5) Fourth proof: "Intellectus
per essentiam et semper in actu, qualis
est intellectus agens, sicut se ipsum, sic
omnia alia intelligit per suam essentiam
eodem modo quo se intelligit, et eadem
simplici intellectione," 74. The comparison with divine knowledge is to be found
in the immediately following lines. Consequently, the *abditum mentis* is no accident, it is a substance, as had been taught
by all the Peripatetics (Alexander, Alfarabi, Avicenna and Averroes) but, above
all, by Augustine, 74.—This hidden recess
of the mind is the image of God in us;
it is "capax Dei"; always turned toward
God whose emanation it is; it also is
that by which man can be united to
God in the beatific vision, 76; it is "quoddam pelagus totius intellectualitatis," 77.

[19] Being (*ens*) signifies the essence of
that of which it is predicated, Dietrich,
De esse et essentia, Krebs ed., RNSP.,
1911, p. 520. To have existence is to be
a being. Entity belongs to all that is a
being, 521. Being expresses concretely

what entity expresses abstractly. They really predicate the same thing. Not so with "what" and "whatness" (*quid* and *quidditas*). The "what" signifies the whole essence of the thing, taken in the concrete; the "whatness" (*quidditas*) only signifies the formal element by which the thing is what it is, 522. Essence and existence signify the same things as being and entity, that is to say the whole essence of the thing; their sole distinction is *in modis dicendi;* what existence signifies by mode of act, essence and entity signify by mode of habitual and quiet possession, 525; that existence (*esse*) signifies the whole essence of the thing, is proved by both reason and authority. In fact, the first reason of Dietrich is an authority: "Prima rerum creatarum est esse" (*De causis,* 4): consequently, *esse* signifies the whole essence of the thing and not existence considered as an accident: "Therefore, existence is identically the essence of the thing, nor can it be said that the essence is something into which existence can be infused or instilled," 526. His whole argumentation rests upon the assumption that there is nothing more noble than essence; consequently, since creation is the noblest of actions, its term must be the noblest of effects; now, this effect is *esse;* consequently, *esse* must needs mean essence: "Ergo esse est idem quod essentia," 526; "Esse significat totam essentiam cujusque rei," 527. Dietrich then argues from Boethius to the same effect, 528-530; then from Aristotle, and even from Augustine. Part II is entirely directed against the sophistic reasons of those who maintain the real distinction of essence and existence. No being can be understood apart from its existence, 532. This is so true that, if man does not exist, even the proposition "man is man" becomes false. To say that man is man if there is no man is just as false as to say: man reasons, if there is no man, 533; "homo est homo" signifies "homo hominat," which is false if there is no man, 533.

[20] BERTHOLD OF MOSBURG (of Mosburch); his unpublished commentary is to be found in ms. Vat. lat. 2192. Berthold calls Proclus "the most excellent disciple of Plato," on the same rank as Plotinus. On the use made of Proclus by Nicholas of Cues, R. Klibanski, *Ein Proklosfund* . . . , 25-29: M. Grabmann, *Die Proklosübersetzungen* . . . , MG., II, 421.

[21] MASTER ECKHART, OP. H. Denifle, *Meister Eckharts lateinische Schriften und die Grundanschauung seiner Lehre,* ALKM., 2 (1886) 417-652; (text of prologues to *Opus tripartitum, Opus propositionum, Opus expositionum,* Commentaries on Genesis, Exodus, Ecclesiasticus, Wisdom); *Das Cusanische Exemplar lateinischer Schriften Eckeharts in Cues,* 673-687. G. Théry, *Edition critique des pièces relatives au procès d'Eckhart, contenues dans le manuscrit 33b de la bibliothèque de Soest,* AHDL., 1 (1926) 129-268. Fr. Pelster, *Ein Gutachten aus dem Eckehart-Prozess in Avignon,* ADGM., 1099-1108; text 1109-1124. GLOREP., I, 180-185.—Intended editions of the complete works: Eckhart, *Die deutschen und lateinischen Werke,* Stuttgart, 1936 ff. R. Klibanski, *Super oratione dominica;* II, H. Bascour, *Opus tripartitum;* III, A. Dondaine, *XIII Quaestiones Parisienses,* 1934, 1935, 1936.—Meister Eckhart, *Die lateinischen Schriften:* I, 1, *Prologi; Exp. libri Genesis et Exodi.* I, 2; *Exp. libri Exodi.* III, 1-4, *In Johannem.* IV, 1-3, *Sermones.* V, *Opera minora,* 1-2. To be continued. W. Kohlhammer, Stuttgart.—Partial editions. Still necessary: F. Pfeiffer, *Deutsche Mystiker des 14. Jahrhunderts,* II, Leipzig, 1857. G. Théry, *Le commentaire de Maître Eckhart sur le Livre de la Sagesse,* AHDL., 3 (1928) 325-443 and 4 (1929) 233-392. E. Longpré, *Questions inédites de maître Eckhart OP. et de Gonzalve de Balboa O.F.M.,* RNSP., 29 (1927) 69-85. J. Quint, *Deutsche Mystikertexte des Mittelalters,* Bonn, 1929. B. Geyer, *Magistri Echardi quaestiones et sermo Parisienses,* (Floril. patrist., 25) Bonn, 1931. French transl., *Maître Eckhart, Traités et sermons,* transl. by F. A(ubier), introd. by M. de Gandillac, Paris, 1942. English transl., C. de B. Evans, *Meister Eckhart,* London, 1924 (transl. of Pfeiffer's edition, minus some texts).—BIBLIOGRAPHY. O. Karrer, *Meister Eckhart, das System seiner religiöse Lehre und Lebenweisheit,* Munich, 1926. M. Grabmann, *Neuaufgefunden Pariser Quaestionen Meister Eckharts und ihre Stellung in seinem geistigen Entwicklungsgange,* Munich, 1927 (Abhandlungen d. Bayer. Akad., 32, 7). J. Koch, *Meister Eckhart und die jüdische Religionsphilosophie des Mittelalters,* Jahresbericht der Schlesischen Gesellschaft für vaterländische Kultur, 1928. G. della Volpe, *Il misticismo speculativo di maestro Eckhart nei suoi rapporti storici,* Bologna, 1930. E.

Mugler, *Die katholische Kirche und Meister Eckhart,* Stuttgart, 1931. K. Weiss, *Die Seelenmetaphysik des Meister Eckhart,* Stuttgart, 1934. A. Dempf, *Meister Eckhart. Eine Einführung in sein Werk,* Leipzig, 1934. H. Bascour, *La double rédaction du premier commentaire de Maître Eckhart sur la Genèse,* RTAM., 7 (1935) 294-320. H. Piesch, *Meister Eckharts Ethik,* Luzern, 1935 (2 ed., 1948). G. Théry OP., *Le "Benedictus Deus" de Maître Eckhart,* Mélanges de Ghellinck, II (1951) 905-935. W. Bange, *Meister Eckharts Lehre vom göttlichen und geschöpflichen Sein . . . ,* Limburg an der Lahn, 1937. O. Bolza, *Meister Eckehart als Mystiker. Eine religionspsychologische Studie,* München, 1938. B. J. Muller-Thym, *The Establishment of the University of Being in the Doctrine of Meister Eckhart of Hochheim,* New York, 1939 (important). H. Ebeling, *Meister Eckharts Mystik. Studien zu den Geisteskämpfen um die Wende des 13. Jahrhunderts,* Stuttgart, 1941. G. Faggin, *Meister Eckhart e la mistica tedesca preprotestante,* Milano, 1946. J. M. Clark, *The Great German Mystics, Eckhart, Tauler and Suso,* Oxford, 1949 (bibliography, 110-117). M. A. Lücker, *Meister Eckhart und die Devotio moderna,* Leiden, 1950. Galvano della Volpe, *Eckhart o della filosofia mistica,* Roma, 1952.

[22] Eckhart, *Quaestiones Parisienses,* I, B. Geyer ed., 5-12; Klibansky ed., 1-10. Eckhart is full of *verbal* contradictions. Before deciding that they are real ones, it is advisable to consider the question with utmost care. For instance, in his *Opus propositionum,* the first proposition is: "Esse Deus est" (*Opus tripartitum,* Bascour ed., 20); again: "Only God is properly being," 21. The language is certainly different from that of the *Quaestiones Parisienses,* but there is no contradiction between saying that, as Intellect, God is above being, and saying that God is being; the two questions are different. Intellect, *qua* intellect, is nothing of what it knows; consequently, it is no being; in God, from whom all being comes, there is no being: "ratio entis non invenitur"; "in intellectu non invenitur ratio entis": Klibansky ed., 14 and 13; these two propositions are equivalent.—Eckhart accepts the oneness of the substantial form, *Quaest. Paris.,* Klibansky, 31. On the problem of essence and existence, the

position of Eckhart is much less clear; naturally, he agrees that the existence of creatures is not included in their essence; he also uses the Boethian distinction of *quo est* and *quod est;* Wilhelm Bange (*Meister Eckharts Lehre . . . ,* 132-140) does not quote a single text going beyond the classical formula: the substantial form gives existence and subsistence to the compound. Keeping in mind that many texts of Eckhart are still unknown, it can be said that the Thomistic composition of essence and existence does not seem to fit his principles.

[23] On the relation of the notion of being to the theological interpretation of the Trinity, W. Bange, *Meister Eckharts Lehre . . . ,* 105-113. On the relation of the Word to the Father, Commentary on the Gospel of St. John, in Evans transl., 396-397; note, 396, the eternal creation in God. The Dionysian origin or inspiration of the doctrine is visible in the treatise on John's saying: "I saw the Word in God," Evans, 377-382: the transcendent nothingness of God is the being of all things, 380-381. Cf. 388, 390-396. The treatise *On the Kingdom of God* (added by Evans to Pfeiffer) expresses in simple terms the relation of the Godhead to being and to the Persons: "The Godhead in itself is motionless unity and balanced stillness and is the source of all emanations. Hence I assume a passive welling-up. We call this first utterance *being,* for the most intrinsic utterance, the formal assumption in the Godhead is being: *being* as essential *word.* God is being, but being is not God," Evans transl., I, 267.—G. della Volpe, *Eckhart . . . ,* ch. IX, pp. 137-182.

[24] M. Grabmann, *Neuaufgefundene . . . ,* 80-81. This doctrine of the anteriority of the One with respect to being is the root of the boldest assertions of Eckhart concerning the intellective soul of man. Since intellect is not being (except as its cause) it cannot possibly be created. This is not a psychological question, it is a metaphysical one. Many of the obscurities and inconsistencies attributed to Eckhart might well arise from the difficulty which some of his historians find in following his Plotinian dialectic. Naturally, those who begin by assuming that Eckhart was fundamentally a Thomist cannot expect to find much consistency in his

writings. His thought is difficult to follow, his expressions are often obscure, but we do not think that Eckhart, when met on his own doctrinal ground, is inconsistent.

²⁵ M. Grabmann, op. cit., 80.

²⁶ The condemned propositions are often typical of Eckhart's own positions and methods: 1) creation is an eternal act on the part of God; consequently, on the part of God, creation is eternal. Passive creation (i.e., on the part of the created world) is not eternal, but began with the world, F. Pelster, ADGM., 1109-1110; 2) it can be conceded that the world is eternal (on the part of God, since God created the world in his Son, or Word, who is eternal); 4) there is in the soul something that is uncreated and uncreatable; if the whole soul were that, the whole soul would be uncreated and uncreatable; and that is the intellect, ibid., 1111; 5) God is neither good, nor better, nor best; consequently I say the wrong thing every time I say that God is good, just as though I called black that which is white, ibid., 1112; 6) all creatures are a pure nothingness; and I am not saying that they are not much, but that they are a pure nothing, ibid., 1112; 7) in every act, even in a bad one, and I mean even a sinful one, the glory of God is manifested and shines equally, ibid., 1113; 13) God loves souls, not their external works, ibid., 1114; 15) those who do not pursue things, nor honors, nor usefulness, nor sanctity, nor reward, nor the kingdom of heaven, but have renounced all these things, even what they own, in these men God is being honored, ibid., 1115 (from a sermon); 17, 18) if a man is good, or if his soul is noble, he is the only begotten Son of God whom God has begotten from all eternity, ibid., 1117, and 1117-1121; 23) God is one in all possible ways and in all respects, so that there is in him no multiplicity either in his intellect or outside of it; he who sees distinction, or duality, does not see God; for indeed God is one, outside of number and above number, nor does he add up with anything; consequently no distinction can either be, or be understood, in him, ibid., 1121; 27) a good man wants his will so to conform to the will of God that he himself wills all that which God wills; and since God wills me to sin from time

to time, I cannot want not to have committed sins; and this is true penance, ibid., 1123; 28) if a man had committed a thousand mortal sins, and if this man were in the right disposition, he should not will not to have committed these sins: ibid., 1123.—On the *abditum mentis*, or "ground" of the soul, F. Pfeiffer, *Meister Eckhart*, Evans transl., I, 4-6; active and passive intellect, I, 14-18; the perfect man can drop all outward disciplines, I, 19; absolute stillness is best of all, 23; man may have the filial nature of the Son of God, I, 32-34; 123-125; on the "citadel" of the soul, I, 36-37: it is the "tabernacle" of the soul, or a "spark," 37-38; its divine nature, I, 84, 86, 88-89; 117; 153; 164 (creation, the Son, the soul); 175; 201-202; 209-210; 212; 239 (condemned proposition); Things are nothing, I, 109. The fundamental notion of analogy which justifies this assertion is found in H. Denifle, ALKG., 2 (1886) 586, 588-589. In God there is neither being, nor good, nor better, nor best, 211 (condemned proposition); man as the only-begotten son, 238 (condemned proposition). With respect to the notion of "noble man" and his unity with God (condemned proposition), II, 78-86; the soul is one with God, and not simply united to him, II, 89.

²⁷ The sermons and spiritual treatises of Eckhart are full of these doctrines. Any reader is bound to meet them if he opens, practically at random, the Evans translation of the texts published by Pfeiffer. Incidentally, it is not easy to find more beautiful texts to read. Among the treatises, we recommend: *The Nobility of the Soul*, I, 279-288 (on divine unity, 285); *The Rank and Nature of the Soul*, 288-306; *The Soul's Perfection*, 306-308; the confession of Sister Katrei, 317-320, and passim up to 334; *Detachment*, 340-348, cf. 356-363; proximity of the soul to God, 367. In the *Sayings*, 10, p. 420; 17, p. 421; 44, p. 428-429; 50, p. 432; 52, pp. 432-433; 59, pp. 435-436; 61, p. 436; 68, p. 438.

²⁸ JOHN TAULER OP. *Opera omnia*, Paris, 1623. F. Vetter, *Die Predigten Taulers*, Berlin, 1910. French transl., *Les sermons de Tauler, traduction sur les plus anciens manuscrits alemands*, by Hugueny, Théry, Corin, 3 vols., Paris, 1927-1935 (the first volume contains historical and doctrinal

introductions). A. L. Corin, *Sermons de Tauler et autres écrits mystiques,* 2 vols., Liège, 1924, 1929. G. Siedel, *Die Mystik Taulers,* Leipzig, 1911.—BET., 3573-3579. HENRY SUSO OP. K. Bihlmeyer, *Heinrich Seuse, Deutsche Schriften,* 2 vols., Stuttgart, 1907. X. de Hornstein, *Les grands mystiques allemands du XIVe siècle, Eckhart, Tauler, Suso,* Luzern, 1929. R. Zeller, *Le bienheureux Henri Suso,* Paris, 1922. J.-A. Bizet, *Henri Suso et le déclin de la scolastique,* Paris, 1946 (bibliography). J. M. Clark, *The Great Mystics,* Oxford, 1949, 55-74.— From the point of view of the history of philosophy, Suso does not appear to us as requiring a special treatment. Even in his *Book of Truth,* his positions are a weaker restatement of those of Eckhart. His doctrinal positions are summarized by J.-A. Bizet, *Henri Suso . . . ,* 301-378. Cf. S. Hahn, *Heinrich Susos Bedeutung als Philosoph,* Beiträge, Supplementband, 1913, 347-356. — French transl., J. Ancelet-Hustache, *Le bienheureux Henri Suso,* Paris, 1943 (selected writings). B. Lavaud OP., *L'oeuvre mystique de Henri Suso.* I, *La vie;* II, *Livret de l'éternelle sagesse;* III, *Livret de la vérité, Livret des lettres;* IV, *Grand livre des lettres, Sermons, Livret d'amour,* Fribourg (Switzerland), 4 vols., 1946-1947. —BET., 3538-3540.

[29] Tauler, *Sermon* 64, 2; Hugueny, *Sermons de Tauler,* I, 78-79. No text indicates that Tauler accepted the position of Eckhart on the uncreated nature of

this "spark," or "ground," or "citadel" of the soul.

[30] On the *Gemüt,* or fundamental disposition of the will, Tauler, *Sermons,* 64, 6-7 and 66, 5: Hugueny, *Sermons de Tauler,* I, 80-82.

[31] Tauler, *Sermon* 60, 4; Hugueny, *Sermons de Tauler,* I, 90-92.

[32] RUYSBROECK, *Oeuvres de Ruysbroeck l'Admirable,* Traduction du Flamand par les Bénédictins de Saint-Paul de Wisques, Bruxelles-Paris, Vromant, 6 vols., 1915, 1917, 1920, 1928, 1930, 1938. W. de Wreese, *Jean de Ruysbroeck,* Biographie nationale de Belgique, 20 (1908-1910) 507-591. A. Wautier d'Aygalliers, *Ruysbroeck l'Admirable,* Paris, 1923. G. Dolezich, *Die Mystik Jan van Ruysbroecks,* Breslau, 1926. *Jan van Ruusbroec, Leven, Werken,* collected essays published by the *Ruusbroec* Society of Antwerp, Mechlin-Amsterdam, 1931 (bibliography, 325-395). Special number dedicated to Ruysbroeck by *Ons geestelijk Erf,* 6 (1932) 3 and 4. L. Brigué, art. *Ruysbroeck,* DTC., 14 (1938) 408-420. J. Kuckhoff, *Johannes von Ruysbroeck der Wunderbare,* Munich, 1938.—English transl., *The Adornment of the Spiritual Marriage, The Sparkling Stone, The Book of Supreme Truth,* by C. A. Wynschenk, Intr. and notes by Evelyn Underhill, New York, E. P. Dutton, 1916. *The Book of the Twelve Béguines . . . ,* by J. Francis, London, J. M. Watkins, 1913 (ch. I-XIII). *The Kingdom of the Lovers of God,* by T. A. Hyde, New York, E. P. Dutton, 1919. BET., 2237-2243.

PART TEN

CHAPTER II, 1. THE SECOND AUGUSTINIAN SCHOOL

[33] M. Grabmann, *Der Benediktinermystiker Johannes von Kastl, der Verfasser des Büchleins De adhaerendo Deo,* MG., I, 489-524. On the still unpublished chapters of the treatise, 509-510; *Spiritualis philosophia,* 510-513; *De lumine increato,* 516-524.

[34] *Imitation of Christ,* I, 1, 7-10; I, 2, 4-8; I, 3, 3, 6 (*et quid curae nobis de generibus et speciebus?*), 13, 23-31. See the letters of Gerrit Groot (1340-1384) published by Wilhelm Mulder, *Gerardi*

Magni Epistolae, Antwerp, 1933. Thomas A. Kempis (1380-1471) often considered the author of the *Imitation,* has left us an interesting biography of Groot: *Vita Gerardi Magni,* in his *Opera omnia,* Cologne, 1759. On this "devout humanism," E. Gilson, *La philosophie au moyen âge,* 2 éd., 1944, 741-754.—BET., 2108-2132 (*Imitation of Christ*); 3630-3643 (Thomas a Kempis).

[35] Augustine, *De diversis quaestionibus 83,* qu. 9, PL., 40, 13. In Henry of Ghent,

Summa I, art. 1, q. 2. In reaction against Henry of Ghent on this point, Duns Scotus, *Opus Oxoniense*, I, 3, 4.

[36] There was no skeptical school in the fourteenth century. We do not even know of any isolated master whose last word in philosophy was anything like the "What do I know?" of Montaigne. The difference is striking with the late fifteenth century and the early sixteenth century, when skeptics will be met everywhere. There has been no mediaeval skepticism, properly speaking. The work of Sextus Empiricus: *Pyrrhonian Hypotyposes*, was translated, perhaps as early as the end of the twelfth century; this Latin translation, preserved in the library of St. Victor, has never been published. It is remarkable that, so far, nobody has ever found any evidence that any mediaeval master made use of the various skeptical arguments it contained (Ch. Jourdain, *Sextus Empiricus et la philosophie scolastique*, Paris, 1858). Jourdain, who discovered this unknown translation almost a hundred years ago, has noted the fact that Henry of Ghent, whose initial question is precisely that of the Pyrrhonians: "Does man know something?" (*Sum. theol.*, I, 1, 1) borrows his skeptical arguments from other sources: Cicero, his refutation by Augustine and even the refutation of Protagoras by Aristotle, *Metaph.*, VII, 3 (Ch. Jourdain, op. cit., 14-17: even Walter Burleigh, *Lives of the Philosophers and Poets*, will still ignore Pyrrho). Our own point is different. It is the fact that, for the first time, a *Summa* opens with the question: Does man know something? This, which is new, marks the moment when, *for theological reasons*, some masters became aware of the problem raised by the skepticism of the New Academy. Like Matthew of Aquasparta, Henry of Ghent will grant, to put it more bluntly than they did, that skepticism cannot be completely refuted on the ground of natural knowledge alone. This is precisely one of the fundamental points on which he will be opposed by Duns Scotus.

[37] HENRY OF GHENT. *Summa quaestionum ordinariorum Henrici a Gandavo*, Paris, 1520. Same work: *Magistri Henrici Goethals a Gandavo Summa . . .* , Ferrariae, 1646. Reprint of the 1520 edition, vol. I and II, St. Bonaventure, N.Y., 1953. —*Quodlibet magistri Henrici Goethals a Gandavo*, Paris, 1518; Venice, 1608 and

1613.—Philosophical works (authentic or not): *Magistri Henrici Gandavensis philosophicarum tripartitio doctrinarum et rationum*, Bologna, 1701.—GLOREP., I, 387-391.

BIBLIOGRAPHY.—GDP., 764-765. Paulus XXII-XXXII; Bayerschmidt, VIII-XVI. Fr. Huet, *Recherches historiques et critiques sur la vie, les ouvrages et la doctrine de Henri de Gand . . .* , Gand, 1838. M. Schwartz, *Henri de Gand et ses derniers historiens*, Mémoires . . . de l'Académie de Belgique, X, 1859. K. Werner, *Heinrich von Ghent als Repräsentant des christlichen Platonismus im 13. Jahrhundert*, Denkschrift der königl. Akad. der Wissensch., Wien, 1876. F. Ehrle, *Beiträge zu den Biographien berühmter Scholastiker*, I, Heinrich von Ghent, ALKG., I, 1885, 365-401, 507-508. M. de Wulf, *Etudes sur Henri de Gand*, Louvain, 1894. G. Hageman, *De Henrici Gandavensis quem vocant ontologismo*, Münster i. W., 1898. J. Lichterfeld, *Die Ethik Heinrichs von Ghent in ihren Grundzügen*, Erlangen, 1906 (Inaug.-Diss.). P. Duhem, *Etudes sur Léonard de Vinci*, II, Paris, 1909, 446-455. R. Braun, *Die Erkenntnislehre Heinrichs von Ghent*, Fribourg (Switz.) 1916. GDP., 498-502. J. Paulus, *Henri de Gand. Essai sur les tendances de sa métaphysique*, Paris, J. Vrin, 1938. P. Bayerschmidt, *Die Seins-und Formmetaphysik des Heinrich von Ghent in ihrer Anwendung auf die Christologie. Eine philosophie-und dogmengeschichtliche Studie*, Münster i. W., 1941 (Beiträge, 36, 3-4) supplies a large amount of new historical information. J. Paulus, *Les disputes d'Henri de Gand et de Gilles de Rome sur la distinction de l'essence et de l'existence*, AHDL., 13 (1940-1942) 323-358. G. de Lagarde, *La philosophie sociale d'Henri de Gand et de Godefroid de Fontaines*, AHDL., 14 (1943-1945) 73-142. A. Maurer, *Henry of Ghent and the Unity of Man*, MS., 10 (1948) 1-20. Th. Nys, *De Werking van het menselijk verstand volgens Hendrik van Gent*, Leuven (Louvain) 1949; cf. J. Paulus, RPL., 47 (1949) 493-496. On the possibility of empty space, A. Koyré, *Le vide et l'espace infini*, 52-67.—F. Copleston, *A History . . .* , II, 465-475.

[38] Henry of Ghent, *Summa theologiae*, I, art. 1, qu. 1 and qu. 2. The first question asks if knowledge is possible (*de possibilitate sciendi*); the second asks how

one knows (*de modo sciendi*). The position of Henry is far removed from skepticism. He maintains with Augustine, and against the skeptics of the Academy, that man can have true knowledge because he can know things such as they are without error or deception. No sincere truth can be expected from sense knowledge alone, but it can be expected from reason judging sense knowledge in the pure light of eternal truth. To say the contrary is to vilify human nature and especially the rational soul. God has created it capable of exercising its own natural operations. Nevertheless, to know the true about a thing is not to know the truth of that thing; in other words, to know what is true about a thing is not to know the truth which enables us to form true judgments about that thing. Animals truly perceive men, they do not know any truth about man. So also, when it follows true sense knowledge, the intellect says true things about objects known such as they are, but it does not yet grasp their truth. It is doubtful that man can know truth about any thing by his own natural powers alone and without some special divine illumination (*ex puris naturalibus . . . scrire aliquid sine omni speciali illustratione divina*). What of truth can be gathered from sense by the intellect does not deserve to be called "science." Now, in his present condition, man cannot attain by his sole natural powers the rules of eternal truth so as to know pure truth in them. The rational soul has been created able to see them, but it cannot now see them unless God shows them to its intellect; and God shows them to whom he pleases: "sed illas (regulas) Deus offert quibus vult, et quibus vult subtrahit." Conclusion: "Absolute ergo dicendum quod homo sinceram veritatem de nulla re habere potest ex puris naturalibus ejus notitiam acquirendo, sed solum illustratione luminis divini; ita quod licet in puris naturalibus constitutus illud attingat, tamen illud ex puris naturalibus naturaliter attingere non potest, sed libera voluntate quibus vult seipsum offert."

[39] Henry of Ghent, *Summa theologiae,* I, 2, f. 7, vM. This is a simple corollary of the doctrine of the divine illumination as Henry understands it. However we may look at the abstract notion drawn from sense data by our intellect, we cannot see in it any certain and infallible truth, because it is not there (*Sum. theol.,* I, 2, f. 8); it only is in the "exemplar of the uncreated light and truth"; consequently, those to whom it is given to contact this truth, can have a knowledge of some certain and infallible truths, op. cit., I, 2, f. 8. The texts in which Henry says that the principles of scientific cognition are acquired in a purely natural way do not mean that the divine illumination is not required for such knowledge; on the contrary, it is required for natural knowledge precisely *qua* natural I, 2, f. 82. Note that this position simply develops one of the conclusions of Matthew of Aquasparta: the proper object of infallible natural cognition is neither the concept alone, nor the quiddity alone, nor the eternal exemplar directly seen; it is "the quiddity conceived by our intellect, but related to the eternal exemplar or art," *De humanae cognitionis . . . ,* p. 118. Matthew expressly declares in the same text that since the principles of philosophy do not provide an adequate answer to the problem, he must resort to theological principles, ibid. In both cases natural knowledge alone is at stake. Henry calls this type of divine illumination: "communem illustrationem a divino exemplari," *Sum.,* I, 2, f. 7 v. Without original sin, this illumination would have always been present to all men; Plato was under the illusion that men still were in their primitive state of innocence; hence his conclusion that God necessarily illumines the soul; in fact, God grants this light according to his will, *Sum.* I, 2, f. 82 M.

[40] J. Paulus, *Henri de Gand et l'argument ontologique,* AHDL., 10 (1935-1936) 265-323. Text in Aug. Daniels, *Quellenbeiträge und Untersuchungen . . . ,* 79-81 Stresses the natural knowledge present in the heart of man (Damascene), the manifestation of God's existence by creatures (Augustine), the hierarchy of beings (Augustine, *De Trinitate,* XV, 4; PL., 42, 1061). Henry expressly denies that the existence of God is known by itself; however certain it may be, the existence of God is a conclusion (this should dispose of the "ontologism" of Henry).

[41] M. de Wulf, *Etudes sur Henri de Gand,* 128, n. 3, defends Henry of Gnent against the accusation of ontologism (natural intuition of the divine Being through

the notion of being). We are simply stressing the fact that, in Henry's doctrine, the *primum cognitum* is a notion of the divine being which, without being an intuition of God, is known, when clearly seen, in the light of God.

[42] An excellent text on this problem is *Quodl.*, III, q. 9, ed. 1518, fol. 60-65. The starting point is the definition of essences by Avicenna; *humanitas* or *equinitas* are neither universal nor singular but indifferent to both. As such, they have a being of essence (*esse essentiae*). All things either made, or apt to be made, have eternally this being of essence either in the divine intellect or in reality: "Sic habent omnia facta et factibilia ab aeterno vel in intellectu vel in re extra."

[43] Henry of Ghent, *Quodl.* V, q. 1.—On the controverted question, if God knows by a single Idea the individuals of one and the same species, *Quodl.* II, q. 1. The problem is tied up with the possibility for God, who is one, to create immediately a plurality of effects (against Avicenna): *Quodl.* IX, q. 2, folio 344. In this question Henry takes up again the doctrine of divine knowledge. God knows: first, his own essence, which is the *objectum primarium* of the divine intellect; secondly, what Henry calls its *objectum secundarium*, that is, what is other than God. This secondary object itself is known by God in a twofold way: a) cognition of the creature as it is in God (*id quod ipsa est in Deo*); b) cognition of the being which the creature has outside of God (*cognoscendo de ipsa id quod ipsa habet esse in seipsa aliud a Deo, quamvis no habeat esse extra ejus notitiam*). The ideas are exemplary forms: "non sunt nisi respectus quidam quibus ipse ut forma exemplaris relative se habet ad essentias rerum extra . . ." As known by God in their Ideas, things have in Him an "esse diminutum"; they exist in Him "in esse cognito"; they have in Him the being of essence that can be turned into a being of actual existence, which is the perfect mode of being: "Sic enim ista . . ." His authorities are Plato, *Timaeus* and Augustine. But one should remember that the non-coeternity of the divine Ideas is expressly taught by Denis: "Oportet itaque non simpliciter coaeterna Deo, qui est ante aeternum, aestimari, quae aeterna dicta sunt," *De div. nom.*, X, Pl., 122, 1164 B C.

[44] From the point of view of Henry of Ghent, the problem does not make sense. In God, every creature has its own being of essence, but, naturally, not its being of existence, so it can have no composition of essence and existence in God. In itself, it has the same being of essence which God eternally knew he would create outside of his own intellect. Its actual existence precisely consists in being a created essence; in other words, its existence is its essence after it has been created: *Quodl.* I, q. 9: "Et sicut est de isto radio . . ." To which Henry immediately adds: "It is surprising that some theologians cannot see what the philosophers have seen, especially since reason proves it to be true." Consequently, there is no distinction of essence and existence in created beings. "Esse" is not "res aliqua super essentiam creaturae." If *esse* is added to essence, is it a substance or an accident? It cannot be an accident because, before its creation, there is no essence to receive existence. In fact, existence is not an extrinsic participation by mode of inherence, it is produced by creation. Strictly speaking, only God is his own existence. Creatures are not their own existence in the same sense; what is true is that creatures are not really distinct from their own *esse*. Their existence does not happen to their already existing essence (in God, it has no existence of its own); it is "an effect of the creator in that which receives being." Nevertheless, since an essence as such is something else than an existing essence, their distinction in our mind is not only of reason, it is that of two notions (*non solum ratione differunt sed etiam intentione*). This means that it takes two distinct concepts to signify an essence and an existent.

[45] Henry of Ghent, *Quodl.* V, q. 8.

[46] "Materia nominat substantiam quamdam absolutam inquantum materia est, differentem per essentiam a quacumque forma et a qualibet dispositione formali; et est fundamentum susceptivum omnium," *Quodl.* IV, q. 14. There are seminal reasons in it: "Semen autem proprie appellatur . . ." ibid. On this point, however, Henry is full of hesitations.— Matter is not merely a certain potentiality, *Quodl.* I, 10 (quotes *Timaeus, Confessiones,* Avicenna): "Quia igitur materia non est ita prope nihil nec ita in potentia quin

sit aliqua natura et substantia quae est capax formarum differens per essentiam a forma; nec habet esse suum quo est quid capax formarum a forma, sed a Deo, et immediatius quam ipsa forma, ita quod ipsarum formarum productio quodammodo magis proprie poterit dici formatio quaedam de materia quam creatio; non est dicendum, propter debile esse et potentiale materiae, quod omnino possibilitas esse ejus simpliciter dependeat a forma, sed magis e converso. Immo ipsa est susceptibilis esse per se tanquam per se creabile et propriam habens ideam in mente creatori."

[47] With reference to those beings whose *quod est* is distinct from their *quo est*, Henry says that: "loquendo de tali esse, ea sunt diversa quorumcumque essentiae sunt diversae," *Quodl.* I, 10.

[48] "In omnibus aliis ab homine debemus negare formarum substantialium pluralitatem," *Quodl.*, IV, 13. One natural generation terminates at only one form, but, precisely, the human soul is not the term of a generation, but of a creation. There must be both generation of a man and creation of a soul. The term of the generation of man, *qua* generation, must needs be another form than the intellective soul: "Sic ergo a priori . . ." ibid. This form is the form of the body. In other words, man can be neither wholly created nor wholly generated. Two distinct productions have for their terms two distinct forms. This other form is a substantial form.

[49] Henry of Ghent, *Quodl.* XI, q. 5; XI, q. 6; XIII, 8; XIV, 6.

[50] On the difference between intellect and "memory," *Quodl.* IV, 8; V, 25.

[51] *Sum. theol.*, 45, 2, f. 17 r. *Quodl.* XII, q. 26. On judgment as occasion for free choice, *Quodl.* I, 16; III, 17. The expression "causa sine qua non," to which Scotus will object, is in *Quodl.* XII, q. 26.—Cf. W. Witterbruch, *Die Gewissentheorie bei Heinrich von Gent und Richard von Mediavilla,* Elberfeld, Wuppertal, 1929.

[52] Before the spreading of Scotism, however, Henry found a defender against Duns Scotus, even in the Franciscan Order. See RICHARD OF CONINGTON, who

taught at Oxford, then at Cambridge and died in 1310. Some of his positions show him hesitating between Henry and Duns Scotus. V. Doucet, *L'oeuvre scolastique de Richard de Conington* OFM., AFH., 29 (1936) 396-442: text of *Quodl.*, qu. I. On FRANCIS OF MARCHIA, (Franciscus de Marchia, de Esculo, de Pignano, Rubei, Rubeus de Apiniano) died after 1344: Fr. Ehrle, *Der Sentenzenkommentar Peters von Candia,* 253-260. V. Doucet, AFH., 29 (1936) 404-405, 409.

[53] JOHN OF RODINGTON, OFM., (d. *ca.* 1348). C. Michalski, *Les sources du criticisme* . . . , Cracovie, 1924; *Le criticisme* . . . , Cracovie, 1924, 77 ff. J. Lechner, *Johannes von Rodington, OFM., und sein Quodlibet de conscientia,* ADGM., 1125-1168; characters of his positions, 1160; fragments 1162-1167. Bruno Nardi, *Soggetto e oggetto del conoscere nella filosofia antica e medievale,* Roma, 1952: Appendice, 70-92, *Il dubbio iperbolico e Giovanni di Rodinton,* text of *Sent.,* I, 3, 3: 74-92.

[54] Text in B. Nardi, *Soggetto e oggetto* . . . , 74-92. An excellent collection of skeptical arguments. Probability is accessible to philosophers; exidence is accessible in mathematics while our intellect is seeing it; the question is: is there such evidence as is so necessary that absolutely no doubt can possibly arise about its truth? Sensation as such cannot be deceptive because it entails no judgment and, consequently, neither truth nor error. On the contrary, judgments based upon sense knowledge are deceptive (p. 77); true enough, reason can correct them (pp. 78-79: a stick looks broken in water, etc.) but then cognition becomes intellectual. Now, "the intellect can have no natural cognition of anything without being able to doubt that it knows it," p. 80. The devil can make a thing look like another one, now God is no less powerful than the devil. God cannot deceive man, because to deceive is to intend evil, but he can make man see something that does not exist, or he can make a thing look different from what it is, pp. 80-81. God can make the terms of a proposition seem to signify something else than what they mean, p. 81. For these reasons, and many other ones (pp. 81-83) it can be said that man can reach the first two degrees of cognition (probability and

mathematical evidence while it lasts) but not the third one (absolute certitude, proof against all possible objections), pp. 84, 85. Assuredly, there remains the Augustinian cognition in the eternal "reasons," but Augustine can always be interpreted (p. 86): for instance, it can be said that he was talking according to Plato, not according to truth; or that, once formed, such propositions are only certain for a few people who have a special illumination from God (pp. 86-87). At any rate, the divine Ideas are in the mind of God, not of man, p. 87. As to the so-called certitude we have of our own existence, life or thought, it is no more safe against all objections than the other certitudes, since the arguments against them drawn from dreams and from in-

sanity need to be refuted, p. 88. In what dispositions man should study, pp. 88-92.

[55] Text in B. Nardi, op. cit., p. 92.—J. Lechner, who has studied Rodington from the point of view of the problem of moral conscience, concludes that John had a leaning toward "ethical positivism somewhat in the sense of John of Mirecourt" (p. 1160). In the same article, information about little-known masters of the fourteenth century, Richard of Killington (ADMG., 1135-1136), Robert Eliphat OFM., (ADGM., 1136-1137), Francis of Perugia (Franciscus de Perusio OFM., ibid., 1137).

[56] C. Michalski, *Les courants critiques* . . . , 209-214.

PART TEN

CHAPTER II, 1. JOHN DUNS SCOTUS AND HIS SCHOOL

[57] JOHN DUNS SCOTUS. *Opera omnia,* Lyon, 1639; 12 vols., usually called Wadding edition. Reprinted in the so-called Vivès edition, Paris, 1891-1895 (adds to Wadding the probably spurious *De perfectione statuum*). These two editions contain other spurious works; it is particularly important to know that the *De rerum principio* does *not* belong to Scotus (see: Vital du Four). Countless interpreters of Scotism have been misled by this time-honored false attribution. The treatise *De primo principio* is authentically Scotist, at least as to its content and inspiration. Listed according to their importance, the main writings of Duns Scotus are: *Opus Oxoniense,* critical edition, Joannis Duns Scoti OFM., *Opera omnia,* published by the Scotist Commission under the direction of C. Balić, 2 vols. published: Prologue, Bk. I, up to dit. 2, part 2, q. 1-4. This is the *Ordinatio,* by Scotus himself, of his Oxonian lectures on the *Sentences.* His lecture notes (*Lectura prima*) are still unpublished.— *Reportata Parisiensia,* reportation of his Parisian lectures on the *Sentences;* the text printed by Wadding blends different reportations, but it represents the actual teaching of Duns Scotus.—*Quaestiones Quodlibetales,* almost always the perfect and final expression of the doctrine of Duns Scotus on every point touched in these questions.—*Quaestiones subtilissimae*

in Metaphysicam, authentic except perhaps the last two books (E. Longpré, *La philosophie* . . . , 28-29); important but badly edited.—*Tractatus de primo principio,* recently re-edited by M. Müller, Freiburg i. Br., 1941; Latin text and English transl., by Evan Roche, OFM., Saint Bonaventure (N.Y.) 1949. English transl. of *Sentences* I, 3, 4, R. McKeon, *Selections,* II, 313-350.

BIBLIOGRAPHY. U. Smeets, *Lineamenta bibliographica* . . . , intr. by C. Balić, Roma, 1942. Partial bibliographies in C. R. S. Harris, *Duns Scotus* . . . , II, 313-360. E. Bettoni OFM., *Vent'anni di studi scotisti (1920-1940),* Quaderni della Rivista di Filosofia neoscolastica, Milano, 1943: M. Grajewski OFM., *Scotistic Bibliography of the Last Decade (1929-1939),* Franciscan Studies, 22 (1941) i, pp. 73-78; 2, pp. 55-72; 23 (1942) 61-71, 158-173.—General introductions: P. Minges, *J.D. Scoti doctrina philosophica et theologica,* 2 vols. Quaracchi, 1908; 2 ed. 1930 (generally excellent but sometimes misleading because it still accepts the authenticity of the *De rerum principio*). B. Landry, *La philosophie de Duns Scot,* Paris, 1922 (often misleading for the same reason). Against Landry: E. Longpré, *La philosophie du Bienheureux Duns Scot,* Paris, 1924. P. Tochowicz, *Joannis Duns Scoti de cognitionis Dei doctrina,* Fribourg (Switz.) 1926. C. R. S.

Harris, *Duns Scotus,* 2 vols. Oxford, 1927 (with unpublished texts; sometimes misled by the *De rerum principio*). D. E. Sharp, *Franciscan Philosophy at Oxford,* Oxford, 1930, 277-368. E. Gilson, *Jean Duns Scot. Introduction à ses positions fondamentales,* Paris, J. Vrin, 1952 (the conclusions in English transl., by G. P. Klubertanz SJ., TMS., 1952, 237-245); cf. C. Balić OFM., *Circa positiones fundamentales I. Duns Scoti,* Antonianum 28 (1953) 261-306. E. Gilson, *Les maîtresses positions de Duns Scot d'après le Prologue de l'Ordinatio,* Antonianum, 28 (1953) 7-18. E. Bettoni, *De argumentatione Doctoris Subtilis quoad existentiam Dei,* Antonianum, 28 (1953) 39-58. F. Copleston, *A History . . .* , II, 426-551.

[58] The notion of "infinite being" is not the object of metaphysics but of theology: *Opus Oxoniense* (or *Ordinatio*), Prol., q. 3, a. 4, n. 12 (Wadding). This is the simplest concept of God accessible to us, ibid. n. 17. The proper object of metaphysics is not "infinite being" but, rather, "being *qua being*," at least to the extent that we know it from the data of sense knowledge: *De anima,* XXI, 2-3 (Scotist work even if Scotus himself did not write it); on the possible reasons for this limitation of our present knowledge of being, *Op. Ox.,* I, d. 3, q. 3, a. 4, n. 24. —E. Bettoni, *L'ascesa a Dio in Duns Scoto,* Milano, 1943, 83-84. E. Gilson, *Jean Duns Scot,* 56-71. E. W. Platzeck, *De infinito secundum metaphysicam theologicam affirmativam necnon negativam respectu analogiae entis,* Antonianum, 28 (1953) 111-130.

[59] Univocity of Being, a fundamental position in Scotism: *a*) general notion of "common being" (*ens commune*) and its relation to the Avicennian doctrine of the *natura communis,* E. Gilson, *Avicenne et le point de départ de Duns Scot,* AHDL., 2 (1927) 89-149. Many other theologians had accepted this position before Duns Scotus: Matthew of Aquasparta, Henry of Ghent etc; *b*) notion of univocal being, "In order to avoid contention about univocity (*univocatio*), I call univocal a concept that is so one that its unity suffices to make it contradictory to affirm it and to deny it, at one and the same time, of one and the same thing; it should also suffice, as a syllogistical middle term, to justify the conclusion that the extremes united to-

gether on account of the unity of this term are not equivocally united," *Op. Ox.,* I, d. 3, q. 2, a. 4, n. 5; cf. I, d. 8, q. 3, n. 14.—On this all-important problem, Tim. Barth OFM., *De fundamento univocationis apud Joannem Duns Scotum,* Romae, 1939; *Zum Problem der Eindeutigkeit . . . ,* PJ., 55 (1942) 300-321. C. L. Shircel, *The Univocity of the Concept of Being in the Philosophy of Duns Scotus,* Washington, 1942. Although the main feature of the Scotist school seems rather to have been the "formal distinction," the univocity of being has never ceased to be studied after Scotus. See, for instance, M. Schmaus, *Die Quaestio des Petrus Sutton OFM., über die Univokation des Seins,* CF., 3 (1933) 5-25. T. Barth. *De univocationis entis scotisticae intentione principali necnon valore critico,* Antonianum, 28 (1953) 72-110. E. Bettoni, *Punti di contatto fro la dottrina bonaventuriana dell' illuminazione e la dottrina scotista dell' univocità,* SRHC. 519-532.

[60] On infinity as an "intrinsic mode" of being, *Quodl.* V, 3-4. *Op. Ox.,* I, d. 3, q. 1, a. 4, n. 17. Because infinity is a mode of being, intrinsic to it, and not an attribute determining if from without, the concept of "infinite being" is as simple as a completely determinate concept may be. It is not the concept of being plus something else, it is the concept of a certain manner of being a "being." Such is the reason why no concept could be more fittingly posited as the object of our theology. On the Scotist notion of God, see the excellent study of J. Klein, *Der Gottesbegriff des Johannes Duns Scotus,* Paderborn, 1913.

[61] Duns Scotus does not say that physical demonstrations cannot lead to the existence of God; he only says that the God whose existence they conclude to is but the author of the physical universe. Moreover, since the existence of the created world is contingent, proofs based upon its actual existence share in the contingency of their empirically given starting point. His attitude with respect to this problem is related to the choice he has made between the Avicennian and the Averroistic notion of the object of metaphysics. According to Averroes, the existence of God is proved in physics; according to Avicenna, it is proved in metaphysics. On this point, Scotus says,

"Averroes is wrong and Avicenna is right," *Op. Ox.,* Prol., I, q. 3, a. 1, n. 3. *Reportata Parisiensia,* Prol., I, q. 3, a. 1. *Qu. in Metaphysicam,* VI, q. 4, n. 3.— Consequences concerning the demonstrations of the existence of God, *Qu. in Metaph.,* VI, q. 4, n. 2-3. *Rep. Paris.,* I, d. 8, q. 3, n. 10. Cf. E. Bettoni, *L'ascesa a Dio,* pp. 13-16.

[62] The *De primo principio* contains a perfect exposition of the Scotist demonstrations of the existence of God; transl. Evan Roche, Saint Bonaventure, N.Y., 1949. Order of the demonstration, *Op. Ox.,* I, d. 2, q. 2, a. 1, n. 11. Demonstration, *Op. Ox.,* I, d. 2, q. 2, a. 1, nn. 12-19. Demonstration of the infinity of the Prime Being, ibid., a. 2, nn. 20-35.

[63] The formal distinction was to become, perhaps still more than the univocity of being, the distinctive mark of the Scotist school in the middle ages. It has been diversely interpreted:—Formal distinction in God, *Op. Ox.,* I, d. 2, q. 4, a. 5, n. 41-45. It subsists under the infinity of the divine essence, *Op. Ox.,* I, d. 8, q. 4, a. 3, n. 17. Cf. I, d. 2, q. 7, nn. 43-44. General notion: there is formal distinction where there is no formal identity; two things are formally distinct when one of them is not included in the formal notion of the other one; in other words, it is a non-identity. The formal distinction is weaker than the real distinction, because it entails no distinction in actual existence; but it is stronger than the modal distinction, because it entails a distinction between two formally distinct essences, or quiddities: *Op. Ox.,* I, d. 2, q. 7, n. 44. See P. Minges, *Die distinctio formalis des Duns Scotus,* TQ., 90 (1908) 409-436. On the origins of the distinction, B. Jansen, *Beiträge zur geschichtlichen Entwicklung der distinctio formalis,* ZKT., 53 (1929), 317-344, 517-544.

[64] The presence of contingency and of freedom in the world presupposes the presence of both in the Prime Cause of the world, *Op. Ox.,* I, d. 39, q. unica, n. 14. The source of the possibles is the divine intellect, *Op. Ox.,* I, d. 43, q. unica, nn. 3-5. The first object of the divine intellect is the divine essence, the secondary object of the divine intellect is the essence of the things that can be created, *Quodl.,* XIV, 15-17. The divine will plays no part in this twofold operation; it in-tervenes with respect to the choice of the possibles to be created, because their existence is contingent; since this choice is free, the will of God has no "cause," *Quodl.* XVI, n. 9, 15, 16. There is no voluntarism in the theology of Duns Scotus, unless, of course, one calls a doctrine a "voluntarism" because it teaches that the will of God is free with respect to the *existence* of all contingents. But then, all Christian theologians should be considered voluntarists.—On the divine foreknowledge of the future contingents, H. Schwamm, *Das göttliche Vorherwissen bei Duns Scotus und seinen ersten Anhängern,* Innsbruck, 1934. (attributes to Duns Scotus the doctrine of the predeterminating decrees: examines the positions of R. Cowton, Alex. of Alexandria, Antonius Andreas, Francis of Mayronnes, William Alnwick, John of Bassoles, John of Ripa, etc.).—There is some disagreement between the interpreters of Duns Scotus as to what extent his ethics is affected by the absolute freedom of God with respect to contingents; on this point, moderate interpretations are found in J. Klein, *Der Gottesbegriff des Johannes Duns Scotus vor allem nach seiner ethischen Seite betrachtet,* Paderborn, 1913. F. Schwendinger, OFM., *Metaphysik des Sittlichen nach Johannes Duns Scotus,* Wissenschaft und Weisheit, 1 (1934) 180-210; 2 (1935) 18-50, 112-135; 3 (1936) 93-119.

[65] As secondary objects of the divine intellect, the possibles are called Ideas, *Op. Ox.,* I, d. 35, q. unica, n. 12. Their production by the divine intellect follows the process already described, ibid., n. 10; cf. *Rep. Par.,* I, d. 36, q. 2, n. 34. The Ideas are the quiddities of things having the being of known objects in the divine intellect, *Op. Ox.,* ibid., n. 12. Since they have no actual existence of their own outside of the divine mind, they are no creatures; they have not even the "being of essence" attributed to them by Henry of Ghent; their only being is that which belongs to an object of cognition in the intellect (of an *objectum cognitum*); since its whole being is to be known, the Idea only exists with relation to the knowing intellect, so that its being is "relative" (*secundum quid*), not actual (*ens diminutum*). Yet it is not a pure nothingness. This doctrine has an immediate repercussion on the noetic of Duns Scotus, for he strongly maintains, against

Henry of Ghent, the reliability of sense cognition; consequently he denies the necessity of any Augustinian illumination to insure the possibility of absolutely certain natural knowledge, but he adds that the general motion of our intellect by the divine light is its motion by these "intelligible quiddities." The divine intellect has pure and simple being; these quiddities only have in it a "relative being" (*secundum quid*), namely, an "objective being," or being of known object (*esse objectivum*); the same quiddities "move our intellect to the knowing of sincere truths," *Op. Ox.*, I, d. 36, q. unica, n. 10. There is therefore a trace of the Augustinian cognition "in rationibus aeternis" left in the noetic of Duns Scotus. This distinction will become a center of active controversies. W. Alnwick will deny it as unintelligible; Francis of Mayronnes and John of Ripa will reinforce it and consequently ascribe more entity to the Ideas; outside of the school, it will be judged as an attempt to subordinate the Ideas to God: ROBERT WALSINGHAM (Carmelite, d. after 1312): B. M. Xiberta, *De scriptoribus scholasticis saeculi XIV ex Ordine Carmelitarum*, Louvain, 1931, pp. 128-129.— Origin of the notion: A. Maurer, CSB., *Ens diminutum: a Note on its Origin and Meaning*, MS., 12 (1950) 216-222; cf. M. Hubert OP., Bulletin Thomiste, 8 (1951) 243.

[66] On the formal distinction, see note 63.

[67] The noetic of Duns Scotus is in sharp reaction against the doctrine of Henry of Ghent. The reliability of sense knowledge is firmly maintained against Henry; as a consequence, the Augustinian illumination can be, if not eliminated, at least reduced to the general influence of the divine Ideas upon the human intellect: *Op. Ox.*, I, d. 3, q. 4, a. 5. This is one of the most perfect questions ever written by Duns Scotus. — Intellectual cognition requires the possible intellect, the agent intellect, an object and the species; intellection consists in the production, by the agent intellect, of a "representative being" endowed with actual existence, which formally represents the universal *qua* universal. This form is the intelligible species. Received in the possible intellect, it causes intellection: *Op. Ox.*, I, d. 3, q. 6, n. 8. Cf. *Rep. Par.*, I, d. 3, q. 4, n. 4. Cf. P. Minges, *J. D. Scoti doctrina*, I,

146-181. J. Kraus, *Die Lehre des Johannes Duns Scotus der natura communis*, Paderborn, 1927. H. Klug, *Die Lehre des sel. Duns Scotus über die Seele*, PJ., 36 (1923) 131-144; 37 (1924) 57-75. O. Lacombe, *La critique des théories de la connaissance chez Duns Scot*, RT., 35 (1930) 24-47, 144-157, 217-235. S. Belmond, *Le mécanisme de la connaissance d'après Duns Scot*, France Franciscaine, 13 (1930) 285-323. T. Barth, *Duns Scotus und die ontologische Grundlage unserer Verstandeserkenntnis*, FS., 33 (1951) 348-384.—Duns Scotus has sharply contrasted intuitive cognition, whose proper object is the existing singular perceived as existing, and abstractive cognition whose proper object is the quiddity, or essence, of the known thing: *Op. Ox.*, II, d. 3, q. 9, n. 6. In Duns Scotus, the intuition of a nonexisting thing is a contradiction, *Rep. Par.*, III, d. 14, q. 3, n. 12: "Contradictio est igitur, quod sit cognitio intuitiva in genere proprio, et quod res non sit." Many texts collected in S. J. Day, *Intuitive Cognition, a Key to the Significance of the Latter Scholastics*, Saint Bonaventure, N.Y., 1947. E. Gilson, *Jean Duns Scot*, pp. 425-427, 430-431, 548. P. C. Vier OFM., *Evidence and its Function according to John Duns Scotus*, Saint Bonaventure, N.Y., 1951.

[68] Matter is created, and since it can be the term of an act of creation it must be "a reality distinct from the form" and something "positive," *Op. Ox.*, II, d. 12, q. 1, n. 11; Scotus refers to Augustine, *Confessions*, XII, 7, 7. Besides, if matter had no reality of its own, distinct from the form, there would only be one principle of generation and, consequently, no generation, *Op. Ox.*, ibid., nn. 13, 16. Since it has its own entity, matter has its own existence; without ever discussing the problem in itself, Duns Scotus denies the composition of essence and existence, *Op. Ox.*, IV, d. 11, q. 3, n. 46. The *esse* superadded to essence appears to him as a "fiction." The finite being is in virtue of its composition of matter and form. In man, the prime form of matter is the form of corporeity; the other forms (vegetative, sensitive, intellective) are all one substantial form without losing their formal distinction in the unity of the highest one (intellective soul). Here, as in other similar cases, the distinction of formal entities within one and the same whole does not prevent it from preserving the

unity of its actual being: *Op. Ox.*, ibid., n. 47. See B. Baudoux OFM., *De forma corporeitatis scotistica*, Antonianum, 13 (1938) 429-474. E. Gilson, *Jean Duns Scot*, 497, n. 2.—Duns Scotus refuses to add an act of being to the actual existent, but he, too, adds something to the form in order fully to constitute the singular. He adds to it its individuating principle (hecceity). This principle cannot be found in matter: since matter has its own entity and its own individuating principle, it cannot individuate other beings. This principle cannot be a form: since forms, as essences, are indifferent to both singularity and universality, they cannot cause individuation. It is, in the form, not an added form, but the ultimate reality of the form. It is an "ultimate difference" of formal being, beyond the order of formal being: *Op. Ox.*, II, d. 3, q. 6, nn. 11-13. Note that, like the quiddity, this "hecceity" is in itself indifferent to both existence and non-existence. It is, in created being, the ultimate determination and actuality which perfects its entity. E. Gilson, *Jean Duns Scot*, 451-466; on the unity of compound being in Scotism, 467-477. J. Klein, *Materie und Form. Pluralität der Formen. Das Compositum. Das Individuelle . . .*, FS., 19 (1932) 40-51. P. Stella SDB., *La critica all' ilemorfismo universale in Duns Scoto*, SRHC., 535-559.

[69] The will can be considered from two points of view: *a*) its nobility; it is a more noble power of the soul than the intellect: *Rep. Par.*, IV, d. 49, q. 2, n. 11-12; the reason for this is theological, namely, the primacy of the virtue of charity; *b*) its nature; following his general distinction between natures, Duns Scotus maintains that just as the intellect is ultimately the cause of its act, the will is ultimately the cause of its volition; in flat contradiction with Godfrey of Fontaines, Duns Scotus maintains the radical activity of the will as cause of its volitions, *Op. Ox.*, II, d. 25, q. unica, n. 20-23.—J. Auer, *Die menschliche Willensfreiheit im Lehrsystem des Thomas von Aquin und Johannes Duns Scotus*, Munich, 1938.
This doctrine of the spontaneity of the will should perhaps be related to the Scotist interpretation of the fall of bodies (*Op. Ox.*, II, 2, 10), considered by A. Maier as a turning point in the history of the problem (*An der Grenze . . .*, 163) and which ascribes to falling bodies an inner principle of motion as cause of their fall.

[70] *Quodl.* IX. *Rep. Par.*, IV, d. 43, q. 2, 16-17. The text of *Quodl.* IX, 15-17 is important to establish the significance of the acceptance or rejection of the notion of "act of being" with respect to the demonstrability, or indemonstrability of the immortality of the soul. On the predecessors of Duns Scotus on this point (R. Grosseteste, Thomas of York, Roger Bacon). S. Rovighi, *L'immortalità dell'anima nei maestri francescani del Secolo XIII*, Milan, 1936. Cf. Z. van de Voestyne OFM., in AFH., 29 (1936) 257-260. F. Immle, FS., 24 (1937) 284-294.

[71] On the meaning of this term, and of a related one: M.-D. Chenu, *Sufficiens*, RSTP., 22 (1933) 250-259. Th. Deman, *Probabilis*, ibid., 260-290. On a text of Thomas (*probabiliter*), 277, n. 1. Since *probable* entails the notion of proof (to be susceptible of it), *probabiliter* may mean "convincingly" (286-287); on the other hand, to the extent that it is tied up with a certain notion of scientific demonstration, *probable* points out an opinion that deserves to be tested (288-289) by the intellect on its way to demonstrated certitude. These thirteenth-century meanings of the term are still valid in the fourteenth century. One should content oneself with probability "only in those cases when the object, although perfectly knowable, is also perfectly inaccessible" (289). The difference consists in this, that the list of merely probable conclusions (from the point of view of rational and philosophical demonstrability) became much longer in the fourteenth century than it was in the thirteenth century.

[72] Attributed to Duns Scotus in the Wadding edition, the *Theoremata* have been denounced as spurious by several historians in the twentieth century. Their two main objections can no longer be upheld as valid, for indeed manuscript evidence does exist in favor of the authenticity and the doctrine itself is not Ockhamist: E. Gilson, *Les seize premiers Theoremata et la pensée de Duns Scot*, AHDL., 12-13 (1938) pp. 5-86. C. Balić is more positive still: "The treatises *De primo principio* and *Theoremata* are noth-

ing else than two excerpts from the *Opus Oxoniense,* sketched by Scotus and completed by others." *De critica textuali Scholasticorum scriptis accommodata,* Roma, 1945, 288-289, 293-297. G. Gal, *De Johannis Duns Scoti "Theorematum" authenticitate ex ultima parte operis confirmata,* CF., 20 (1950) 5-50: an examination of the last seven *Theoremata* confirms the Scotist origin of the treatise; conclusion: "The doctrine contained in these theorems is the authentic doctrine of Scotus," p. 48.

[73] ANTONIUS ANDREAS (Antoni Andreu OFM., d. *ca.* 1320), perhaps the redactor of the remarkable Questions *De anima* commonly attributed to Duns Scotus. Author of logical commentaries: *Expositiones super artem veterem et super Boetium De divisionibus,* Venice, 1508, 1517. *Quaestiones Antonii Andreae super XII libr. metaphysicae,* Venice, 1514, 1523: a remarkably clear statement of the main metaphysical positions of Duns Scotus. *De tribus principiis rerum naturalium,* Venice, 1489.—B. Hauréau, *Histoire de la philosophie scolastique,* II, 2, Paris, 1880, 345-355. Marti de Barcelona, *Fra Antoni Andreu OM, "Doctor dulcifluus,"* Criterion, 1929, 321-346. M. Bihl, art. in DHGE., II (1914), 1633-1634; works and editions.

Another direct pupil of Duns Scotus at Paris (1303-07) has been discovered: ANFREDUS GONTERI: V. Doucet, *Der unbekannte Skotist des Vat. lat. 1113, Fr. Anfredus Gonteri OFM.,* FS., 25 (1938) 201-240; texts pp. 227-239. If these texts really belong to Anfred, the formation of what was to become the special dialect of the Scotist school took place at a very early date. Anfred says that there is in God only one being of essence and of actual existence, but "tria esse personalia divina," p. 229. Again: "ista distinctio provenit ex natura divinitatis fundamentaliter et radicaliter, et non actualiter, complete et formaliter," p. 229. This is not the language of Scotus, but of Scotism. Date of the commentary, *ca.* 1325.

[74] FRANCIS OF MAYRONNES OFM., d. *ca.* 1325.—*Praeclarissima . . . Scripta . . . Francisci de Mayronis,* Venice, 1520 (commentary on the *Sentences, Quodlibeta, Tractatus formalitatum, De univocatione entis,* etc). P. Duhem, *François de Mayronnes et la rotation de la terre,* AFH., 6 (1913) 23-25. Ch.-V. Langlois, *Fran-*

çois de Mayronnes, Frère Mineur, HLF., 36 (1924-1927) 305-342 and 652. Bart. Roth, OFM., *Franz von Mayronis und der Augustinismus seiner Zeit,* FS., 22 (1935) 44-75; *Franz von Mayronis OFM., Sein Leben, seine Lehre vom Formalunterschied in Gott,* Werl i. W., 1936 (fundamental). F. Claessens, *Liste alphabétique des manuscrits de François de Mayronnes,* La France Franciscaine, 22 (1939), 57-68.

Roth has rightly stressed the opposition there was between the "Prince of the Scotists" and Duns Scotus on the problem of the divine Ideas (p. 563). See the remarkable objections of William of Vaurouillon (Vorilongus) against Mayronnes. Obviously, Mayronnes had increased the ontological density of the Ideas. He thinks they should be worshiped as objects of beatific fruition (no, William answers, one does not worship *entia rationis*) ; he adds that if they were merely secondary objects of the divine intellect, they could not be eternal; thirdly, if they only were secondary objects of the divine intellect, God could not be *sapiens* by his Ideas. Mayronnes attributed to the Ideas an *esse essentiae* (Henry of Ghent) whose cognition in God is a "secondary object" of the divine intellect (Duns Scotus). This tendency to strengthen the distinction between God and his Ideas will reappear in John of Ripa.

[75] JOHN OF BASSOLES OFM., d. July 4, 1333.—*Joannis de Bassolis in IV Sententiarum libros,* Paris, 1516-1517. Ch.-V. Langlois, *Jean de Bassoles,* HLF., 36 (1924-1927) 349-355. P. Duhem, *Etudes sur Léonard de Vinci,* II, 373-378. C. Michalski, *Les courants critiques et sceptiques . . . ,* 221-224. E. d'Alençon, art. *Bassoles (Jean de),* DTC., 2 (1923) 475.—Doctrine practically unknown.

[76] WILLIAM OF ALNWICK OFM., d. 1333, A. Ledoux, *Guilelmi Alnwick Quaestiones disputatae de esse intelligibili et de Quolibet,* Quaracchi, 1937. M Schmaus, *Guilelmi de Alnwick OFM. doctrina de medio quo Deus cognoscit futura contingentia,* Bogoslovni Vestnik, 1932, 201-225. M. Bihl, art. *Alnwick,* DHGE., II, 662. V. Doucet, *Descriptio codicis 172 bibliothecae communalis Assisiensis.* AFH., 25 (1932) 257-274, 378-389, 502-524 (*Sentences* of W. Alnwick).

William should not be confused with

another Alnwick: MARTIN OF ALNWICK (Martinus Anglicus), also an English Franciscan: J. Lechner, *Beiträge zum Schrifttum des Martinus Anglicus (Martin of Alnwick)* OFM., FS., 19 (1932) 1-12.

ROBERT COWTON OFM., whose commentary on the *Sentences* is slightly later than that of Scotus, was an Oxford master; his doctrine has not been studied yet. Like Alnwick and many of their contemporaries, he was concerned, besides the usual theological problems, with the question of divine foreknowledge, whose answer is intimately tied up with the problem of predestination. Aristotle, Averroes and the Averroists had maintained that since future contingent events have no necessity, they cannot be objects of true and necessary cognition; on the contrary, Christian theologians had to maintain that God foreknows all future events, even contingent ones. The possibility of such foreknowledge could be explained either by the infinity of God's science, or by the infinity of his power and will (if God predetermines, he also knows his own "predetermining decrees"). The present tendency, among historians of theology, is to look to Duns Scotus for the origin of the doctrine of the "predetermining decrees": Pelster, ZKT., 46 (1922) 386; H. Schwamm, *Robert Cowton OFM., über das göttliche Vorherwissen,* Innsbruck, 1931. M. Schmaus, *Uno sconosciuto discepolo di Scoto intorno alla prescienza di Dio,* RFNS., 24 (1932) 327-355.

[77] I. WALTER OF CHATTON, a Franciscan who lectured at Oxford (1320-1330), is just beginning to emerge from complete obscurity owing to the first publication of one of his texts by E. Longpré, *Gualterio di Catton, un maestro francescano,* Studi Francescani, 9 (1935) 101-114. D. Douie, *Three Treatises on Evangelical Poverty: De paupertate evangelica,* AFH., 24 (1931) 36-58, 210-240. GDP., 588-589. L. Baudry, *Gauthier de Chatton et son Commentaire sur les Sentences,* AHDL., 18 (1943) 337-369; texts 358-368: stresses the explicit opposition of Chatton to Ockham, 345-346; dates suggested: 1322-1323, p. 353, for a first redaction; the date of the second redaction is unknown, p. 354; the published fragments are definitely Scotist in inspiration: God is the Infinite Being, 358-359: interesting remark on the demonstrability of the existence of an infinite and absolutely

prime being, 359; Chatton holds that the existence of God (a single and absolutely Prime Cause) can be proved with evidence by natural reason, but not with an evidence capable of convincing all opponents, 365, 368. Influence of Ockham admitted by L. Baudry, op. cit., 356 and by J. J. O'Callaghan, *Walter of Chatton's Doctrine of Intuitive and Abstractive Knowledge, Study and Text* (Univ. of Toronto Doctorate-Abstract) 1949: Chatton maintains against Ockham the Scotist interpretation of intuitive knowledge, not, however, without "giving proof of the doubts raised by the probing criticism of Scotus' acute critic, William of Ockham." The commentary on the *Sentences* of Chatton, Prol., qu. 2, art. 2, proves against Auriol that the intuition of a non-existing object is naturally impossible; it clearly shows that the possibility of any naturally certain knowledge is at stake in this controversy; if God causes in us such an intuition (as he can do) he places us in a condition of invincible error, ad 2m. "At Oxford, about 1320-1330, Chatton was introducing his students to the opinions mainly of Scotus and Ockham. His commentary was designed to direct their loyalties to Scotus and to guide them in a systematic rejection of Ockham." But, O'Callaghan concludes, some of his students may have preferred the positions to their refutations. Cf. L. Baudry, *Guillaume d'Occam,* Appendix I, pp. 250-253.

II. WALTER BURLEIGH (Burlaeus OFM., d. after 1343), wrote a *De vitis et moribus philosophorum* inspired by Diogenes Laertius, ed. H. Knust, Tübingen, 1886; commentaries on the *logica vetus,* Venice, 1485; on the *Posterior Analytics,* Venice, 1537, 1559 (together with the commentary of Grosseteste); *Summa totius logicae,* Venice, 1508; on *Physics,* Venice, 1509, 1524; on *Ethics,* Venice, 1500, 1521; *De intentione et remissione formarum,* Venice, 1519; *De materia et forma,* Oxford, 1500. Other works are indicated in A. Niglis, *Siger von Courtrai* (Inaug.-Dissert.), Freiburg i. Br., 1903: *De puritate artis logicae, Obligationes* (Prantl, IV, 40), *Sophismata, Insolubilia* III, 443), *De potentiis animae, De fluxu et refluxu maris Anglicani.* Very little is known about Burleigh's philosophical positions. Duhem has called attention to his doctrine of the reality of empty space; he is known to have opposed Ockham and the "moderns" (i.e., the nominalists), but our only information concerning the precise nature of his opposition is still limited to the notes on Burleigh in Michalski, II, IV, V, and to the articles of L. Baudry, *Les rapports de Guillaume d'Occam et de Walter Burleigh,* AHDL., 9 (1934) 155-173. S. H. Thomson, *Walter Burley's Commentary on the Politics of Aristotle,* MAP., 1947, 557-578. We are better informed about his logic owing to the recent publication of his *De puritate artis logicae,* ed. Ph. Böhner, St. Bonaventure, N.Y., 1951: the first part of this logic, containing Burleigh's doctrine of "supposition," is not included in this publication; information about it in Ph. Böhner, *Medieval Logic,* 44-51; on his realism of universals, pp. 48-49.— C. Michalski, *La physique nouvelle,* 95-102, 120-125. A. Koyré, *Le vide et l'espace infini* . . . , AHDL., 17 (1949) 75-80.

On the English Franciscan group: J. Lechner, *Beiträge zum mittelalterlichen Franziskanerschrifttum, vornehmlich der Oxforder Schule des 13. und 14. Jahrhunderts,* FS., 19 (1932) 99-127; *Kleine Beiträge zur Geschichte des englischen Franziskanerschrifttums in Mittelalter,* PJ., 53 (1940) 374-385.—JOHN OF READING, E. Longpré, *Jean de Reading et le Bx Jean Duns Scot. L'école franciscaine d'Oxford au début du XIVe siècle,* La France Franciscaine, 7 (1924) 99-109.— WILLIAM OF NOTTINGHAM, E. Longpré, *Le commentaire sur les Sentences de Guillaume de Nottingham OFM.,* AFH., 22 (1929) 232-233; C. Balić, RTAM., 11 (1930) 171-187. L. Meier, *Wilhelm von Nottingham* (d. 1336) *ein Zeuge für die Entwicklung der distinctio formalis an der Universität Oxford,* Philosophia Perennis (Festgabe Geyser) 1930, I, 247-266. M. Schmaus, *Guillelmi de Nottingham OFM., doctrina de aeternitate mundi,* Antonianum, 7 (1932) 139-166 (*Sent.* II, 1, 3); *Neue Mitteilungen zum Sentenzenkommentar Wilhelms von Nottingham,* FS., 19 (1932) 195-223 (texts).— HUGH OF NEWCASTLE (Hugo de Novo Castro), commented on the Sentences between 1307 and 1317: HLF., 36 (1924-1927) 342-349. L. Amoros, *Hugo von Novo Castro OFM. und sein Kommentar zum ersten Buch der Sentenzen,* FS., 20 (1933) 177-222. E. Auweiler, *De codice Commentarii in IV librum Sententiarum Fr. Hugonis de Novo Castro Washingtonii servato,* AFH., 28 (1935) 570-573.—JOHN OF WALSHAM, F. Pelster, *Die Quästionen des Johannes von Walsham OFM.,* FS.,

34 (1952) 129-146; dated *ca.* 1350. In the same article, information concerning Thomas of York, Roger Marston, Thomas of Bungay, Walter of Knolle, Adam of Hoveden, Richard of Conington, Robert of Worstede, Bartholomew of Stalham, John of Lipenho, Henry of Costenhey, Robert of Halifax, all Oxonian masters.

III. THOMAS BRADWARDINE, d. 1349 *De causa Dei adversus Pelagium et de virtute causarum ad suos Mertonenses Libri tres,* London, 1618. *Tractatus de proportione velocitatum,* Paris, 1495; Wien, 1515. *De arithmetica speculativa,* Paris, 1516. *De geometria speculativa,* Paris, 1516.—On the doctrine, K. Werner, *Die Scholastik des späteren Mittelalters; III, Der Augustinismus* . . . ; B., *Der scholastische Augustinismus und Antipelagianismus,* 234-331 (the best introduction to Bradwardine): scholastic masters generally forget grace, 238 (*De causa Dei,* I, 35); unitarian notion of Christian Wisdom (cf. R. Bacon), including the prophets and the philosophers, 244 (*De causa Dei,* Pref., and I, 1, coroll. 32); God as supreme Good and pure Act, 244-247 (Anselm; Hermes, *Liber XXIV philosophorum*); the first simple principle is: *God;* the first complex principle is: *God is,* 257 (*De causa Dei,* I, 11); freedom of the divine will with respect to natural law, 262-264 (*De causa Dei,* I, 21); omnipotence of the divine will, 267-270 (*De causa Dei,* I, 28-34); limitations of human free choice, 271-275 (*De causa Dei,* II, 2-6, 29-32); against Averroistic necessity, approval of the condemnation of 1277, 275-276 (*De causa Dei,* III, 2, 4); limitation of theological determinism, 278-285; relation to Anselm, 288-293 (note, *De causa Dei,* III, 28: "Secundum probabilem logicam modernorum Oxoniae . . . , etc.); relation to Thomas Aquinas, 293-298; to Scotus, 298-300; opposition of contemporaries to the doctrine; influence on John of Mirecourt, John Baconthorp and Wyclif, 300-306. Cf. S. Hahn, *Thomas Bradwardinus und Seine Lehre von der menschlichen Willensfreiheit,* Münster I. W., 1905 (Beiträge, 5, 2). J. F. Laun, *Recherches sur Thomas de Bradwardin précurseur de Wiclif,* Revue d'Histoire et de philosophie religieuses (Strasbourg) 9 (1929) 217-233. B. M. Xiberta, *Fragments d'una qüestio inèdita de Tomàs Bradwardin,* ADGM., 1935, 1169-1180. E. Stamm, *Tractatus de continuo von Thomas Bradwardina,* Isis, 1936, 13-32. A. Koyré, *Le vide et l'espace*

infini . . . , AHDL., 17 (1949) 80-91. E.
A. Moody, *The Medieval Science of
Weight (Scientia de ponderibus)* . . .
Madison, Univ. of Wisconsin Press, 1952;
pp. 285-291, Thomas Bradwardine's discussion of Proposition One of the *Liber
de ponderibus.*

IV. JOHN WYCLIF (1320-1384), taught
at Oxford. A religious reformer, he nevertheless took an interest in philosophical
problems. Thirty-five volumes of Latin
works of the reformer published by the
Wyclif Society (1882-1924). History of
philosophy must take into account his
Trialogus, ed. Lechler, Oxford, 1869; *De
compositione hominis,* ed. R. Beer, Lon-
don, 1884. *De ente predicamentali,* ed.
R. Beer, London, 1891. *De ente,* ed. M. H.
Dziewicki, London, 1909. *Summa de ente,
I, tr. 1 and 2,* ed. S. H. Thomson, Ox-
ford, 1930.—BIBLIOGRAPHY. G. Lechler,
John Wycliffe and his English Precursors,
London, 1873 (transl. from the German,
Leipzig, 1873). S. H. Thomson, *The
Order of Writing of Wyclif's Philosophi-
cal Works,* Českou Minulosti, Homage V.
Novotny, Prague, 1929, 146-166; *A Lost
Chapter of Wyclif's Summa de ente,* Spec-
ulum, 4 (1929) 339-346. I. H. Stein,
*Another "lost" Chapter of Wyclif's Summa
de ente,* Speculum, 8 (1933) 254-255;
S. H. Thomson, *The Philosophical Basis
of Wyclif's Theology,* The Journal of Re-
ligion, 1931, 86-116. H. B. Workman,
John Wyclif, Oxford, 1926. Fr. Ehrle,
*Der Sentenzenkommentar Peters von Can-
dia,* 119-123. J. F. Laun, *Die Prädestina-
tion bei Wyclif und Bradwardin,* in H.
Bornkamm, *Imago Dei,* Giessen, 1932, pp.
63-84 (Wyclif inherited from Bradwardine his doctrine of predestination). A.
Du Pont Breck, *The Manuscripts of John
Wyclif's "De Trinitate,"* Mediaevalia et
Humanistica, 7 (1952) 56-70.

Those who speak formally, as perfect
philosophers, conceive well the formal
distinction between divine Ideas ("Illi
autem qui loquuntur formaliter sicut per-
fecti philosophi, satis concipiunt distinctionem formalem hujusmodi idearum"),
J. Wiclefi, *Dialogorum Libri* IV, Frankfurt, 1753, I, 8, *De Ideis,* p. 22. Everybody would understand the doctrine of
the divine Word (John) and of the
divine Ideas (Augustine) were it not for
the general corruption of Scripture by
the ignorance of grammar and of logic
now prevailing, p. 23. The logic to be
followed is that of Scripture, I, 9, p. 25.
The Idea is essentially the divine nature;

formally it is the reason (*ratio*) according to which God knows creatures, p.
25; Augustine has well shown that everything was created according to its own
reason, pp. 25-26. Quotes Grosseteste, p.
27. (There is no excessive realism in this
doctrine of Ideas; on the contrary, ch. I,
10 begins to introduce theological considerations about the efficacy of the divine
power which might raise difficulties, even
with Augustine.) The series of Ideas is a
limited one, since there is a "prime Idea,
which is the Idea of substance, or of
analogical being," I, 11, pp. 30-31; Avicenna and many more ancient philosophers, "whom we call heretics," p. 33;
consequences for the Eucharist, ibid. Predestination, II, 14, pp. 73-75.—This *Trialogus* shows the invasion of theology by
grammar and dialectic; Wycliff opposes
them on their own ground. As to its general philosophical positions, the *Trialogus*
agrees with the *Summa de ente.* It represents a fourteenth-century Augustinism:
God is the prime and simple affirmation
accompanying every truth, so that it is a
formal contradiction that anything be, or
may be, if there is no God (*Trialogus,*
I, 1, Frankfurt ed., I, 1, p. 3; cf. *Summa
de ente,* ed. Thomson, being *in communi*
is inseparable from existence; if I know
that this is, I know that being is, pp.
1-2 and 4; common being is first known,
p. 18; it is eternal and non-caused; it
includes all the ideal reasons called universals; in this work, the definition of
Ideas prepares Wyclif's theology of predestination, p. 40). Theory of the three
"suppositions" (*pure significativa:* points
out an external thing; *pure materialis:*
points out the term itself or a similar
one; *mixta,* points out indiscriminately
both the term itself and the external
thing), *Trialogus,* I, 3, p. 7. Universals
are really *in* singulars; where there is a
singular, there is a universal; the *Doctores signorum* are wrong on this point.
Scripture does not deal with signs, but
with things; "ille praecipuus philosophus
Moyses" does not write about concepts,
but about real beings (*Summa,* pp. 47-49).
Universals are real: "Certum est igitur
. . . quod sunt universalia ex parte rei,
quia nemo est quin prius naturaliter cognoscit hominem esse quam quemcumque
singularem esse" (*Summa,* pp. 53-54; cf.
55; 59, lines 16-21; 61, "cum omne universale sit singulare et e contra . . ."");
multiplication of universals, quotes Grosseteste, p. 65. Prime matter is a "material

essence"; Augustine says it is neither something nor nothing (*Trialogus,* II, 4, p. 44). Hierarchy of the forms (*Trialogus,* II, 4, pp. 44-45). The person does not change, whatever changes may happen in its body, because the soul, which is its intellective essence, remains the same (*Trialogus,* II, 5, p. 46). The Brothers consider heretical the doctrine of the plurality of forms, yet it is a possible position if the forms are mutually subordinated (*Trialogus,* II, 8, pp. 47-48). The possible intellect and the agent intellect are enough without adding others; Averroes was wrong and we should not palliate his error by saying that God is the agent Intellect (*Trialogus,* II, 9, p. 61). Reaffirmation of the divine Ideas (*Summa,* pp. 68-70). Against the modern logicians who say that only negative propositions can be necessary (*De ente,* pp. 72-76). On the contrary, the existence of God is known as a necessary truth because he himself is necessary (*Summa,* pp. 78-79). Reference to Avicenna and Anselm's *Proslogion.* Proof of God's existence by the beauty and order of the world (*Summa,* pp. 84-86). References to Augustine and Anselm's *Monologion.* Simplicity (pp. 87-88), transcendency (pp. 88-90) and ineffability of God (pp. 89-91). God is most principally known by intuitive cognition: "vocatur autem notitia intuitiva notitia sensus de veritate objective sibi praesenti sine distinctiori notitia prius cogniti a qua sensus elicit illam notitiam discursive," *Summa,* p. 109. This does not mean that we have an intuition of God in himself, but he is the immense book of life in which all truths are included; to acquire any new knowledge about anything is to acquire a new knowledge about God, pp. 108-111. —Wyclif certainly was a "realist" (i.e., not a nominalist, or Ockhamist); his sympathy went to the metaphysics of the formal distinction, but his metaphysics of being is not that of Scotus. On the reality of universals, "Jeronimus recommendavit Wikleph maxime" (Fr. Ehrle, *Der Sentenzenkommentar,* 122, note). See J. Loserth, *Wiclif and Huss,* London, 1884. J. Kvačala, *Hus und sein Werk,* Jahrbücher für Kultur und Geschichte der Slaven, 8 (1932) 58-82, 121-142. S. H. Thomson, *Four unpublished Questions of John Hus,* Medievalia et Humanistica, 7 (1952) 79-88. The third Question was written in 1409. Our only reason for not speaking of Huss as of a scholastic theologian is that we have not been able to see his commentary *Super IV Libros Sententiarum,* whose copies, owing to the present situation in Europe, are not easily available.

[78] JOHN OF RIPA OFM (Johannes de Ripa, Johannes de Marchia, not to be confused with Francis de Marchia), H. Schwamm, *Magistri Joannis de Ripa OFM. doctrina de praescientia divina. Inquisitio historica,* Roma, Pont. Univ. Gregoriana, 1930. A. Combes, *Jean de Vippa, Jean de Rupa, ou Jean de Ripa?,* AHDL., 14 (1939) 253-290; *Jean Gerson commentateur dionysien. Pour l'histoire des courants doctrinaux à l'Université de Paris à la fin du XIVe siècle,* Paris, 1930: Appendice XVII, 608-687; *Un inédit de saint Anselme? Le traité De unitate divinae essentiae et pluralitate creaturarum d'après Jean de Ripa,* Paris, 1944.

The problem of the nature of the divine Ideas is connected in John of Ripa with his Scotist formalism, as can be seen from his question *In I Sent . . .* dist. 8, art. 2. Every essential perfection which can be communicated to creatures has a distinct formative reason in the divine essence. The divine essence is anterior to its essential perfections. Since God is infinite, the immensity of the distinction between two of these essential perfections is "immense," or, rather, infinite. Since the intensity of a formal distinction is proportional to the intensity of the formal being which belongs to its terms, just as it is infinite between divine formal perfections, it is finite between created and finite perfections. In order to account for the divine cognition of future contingents, we must introduce in God a *ratio intrinseca contingens* for each contingent truth (Schwamm, p. 21, concl. 8). This is in God a *ratio cognitiva* (p. 22, concl. 9). Each one of these reasons is a *complexum significabile* (an *incomplexum significabile* is a simple term: v. g. Antichrist; a *complexum significabile* is a proposition: v. g. Antichrist will come; cf. H. Elie, *Le complexe significabile,* Paris, J. Vrin, 1937). Since the number of possible creatures is infinite, these complex cognitive reasons are infinite in number; only, since the formal distinction of Scotus does not break up the real identity of being, the divine unity is safe (Schwamm, p. 35). Thus we have: 1) the essence of God; 2) the formal distinctions between the "essential reasons" in God; 3) the "rationes" of the individuals as such, that is, reasons that are incommunicable in virtue of their individual nature (*rationes incommunicabiles*) and to which, consequently, no "ideas" can answer in the divine essence; God knows these individual reasons as deriving from his Ideas in an indirect way only and in consequence of his will (Schwamm, pp. 39-40); 4) to conclude, God knows contingents *qua* contingents, and not in virtue of ideas proper to them (individualities as such have no ideas, i.e., ideal *forms*), but simply by knowing his own will whose free choice makes some of them to be true, Schwamm, p. 47. The formal distinction introduced by John of Ripa between God and his Ideas goes far beyond the "esse secundum quid" attributed to them by Duns Scotus. John reproaches Scotus with not having resorted to his own formal distinction. The pseudo-Anselmian treatise he quotes profusely goes still further than John of Ripa; it posits the divine Ideas as created.—The conclusions of H. Schwamm concerning the doctrine of the divine foreknowledge of future contingent events should be related to his former conclusions concerning William Alnwick OFM., and Robert Cowton OFM. Note, however, that the Scotist origin of the doctrine has been questioned by M. Schmaus in his study of William Alnwick.

The controversy concerning the divine Ideas conceived as creatures goes back to Scotus Erigena. Formally condemned January 23, 1225, CUP., I, 107, note 1; cf. Alexander of Hales, *Summa*, Quaracchi, II, p. 52. On January 13, 1241, new condemnation of the proposition: "There are many eternal truths that are not God," CUP., I, 170-171; cf. Bonaventure, *In II Sent.*, 23, 2, 3, Quaracchi, II, 547; in 1243 and 1256, the General Chapters of the Dominican Order prescribed to delete these errors from all copy books, CUP., I, 172, note 1. So it still was circulating. The puzzling *De unitate divinae essentiae et pluralitate creaturarum*, whose fragments were discovered in John of Ripa by A. Combes and whose text was discovered by M.-T. d'Alverny (who is preparing its publication) is anonymous. Its author, called Venerabilis Anselmus, seems to be Achard of Saint Victor (see *supra* note 120, p. 634). He distinguishes the absolutely prime form (divine essence); the created form in the divine mind ("forma creata . . . prout est objective in divina mente"); the forms created in space and time. Note that this author is avoiding the term Idea; he says "forms," "exemplars." Eternally formed in God, they are inferior to him; all things are in him *per propriam creationem* before being created in themselves.

PART TEN

CHAPTER III. THE DISINTEGRATION OF SCHOLASTIC THEOLOGY

[79] JAMES OF METZ OP (Jacobus Metensis), GLOREP., I, 197-198. J. Koch, *Jakob von Metz OP., der Lehrer des Durandus de S. Porciano*, AHDL., 4 (1929-1930) 169-232; cf. Bulletin Thomiste, 1931, 327-333. P. Fournier, HLF., 37 (1938) 513-515.—For this period it is necessary to consult the series of contributions by C. Michalski: I, *Les courants philosophiques à Oxford et à Paris pendant le XIVe siècle*, Bulletin de l'Académie polonaise des sciences et des lettres, Classe d'Histoire et de Philosophie, 1920, pp. 59-88, Cracow, 1921. II, *Les sources du criticisme et du scepticisme dans la philosophie du XIVe siècle*, La Pologne au Congrès international de Bruxelles, pp. 241-268, Cracow, 1924. III, *Le criticisme et le scepticisme dans la philosophie du XIVe siècle*, Bulletin de

l'Académie polonaise . . . , 1925, pp. 41-122, Cracow, 1926. IV, *Les courants critiques et sceptiques dans la philosophie du XIVe siècle*, Bulletin de l'Académie polonaise . . . , 1925, pp. 192-242, Cracow, 1927. V, *La physique nouvelle et les différents courants philosophiques au XIVe siècle*, ibid., Cracow, 1928. VI, *Le problème de la volonté à Oxford et à Paris au XIVe siècle*, Commentariorum societatis philosophicae Polonorum, II, Lemberg, 1937, 233-365. We numbered these publications so as to facilitate further references.

On the early lists of condemned errors, J. Koch, *Philosophische und theologische Irrtumslisten von 1270-1329*, MM., II, 305-329. K. Michalski, *La révocation par Frère Barthélemy, en 1316, de 13 thèses incriminées*, ADGM., 1091-1098; notes the similarity of some condemned propositions with those upheld later on by Ockham, Holcot and John of Mirecourt; text of the retraction, 1097-1098. J. Koch counts 16 theological trials attended by condemnations between 1270 and 1329. —For the statement quoted at the beginning of this chapter: "Die Scholastik wird erst nach Thomas interessant," see Hans Mayer, *Ehrenrettung des Duns Scotus*, PJ., 50 (1937) 399-400; quoted by P. Bayerschmidt, *Die Seins-und Formmetaphysik*, 336. A dialectical refutation of this remark is easy, but one must have personally gone through the whole history of what comes before Thomas Aquinas in order to realize its true meaning. Unfortunately this personal experience is not transmissible by means of words.—For the letter of Pope Clement VI, see CUP., III, 588.—Growing mistrust of fourteenth-cent. theologians with respect to philosophy: J. Leclercq, *La théologie comme science d'après la littérature quodlibétique*, RTAM., 11 (1939) 351-374: P. of Auvergne, James of Thérines, G. of Fontaines, Robert Holcot (texts).

[80] DURAND OF SAINT POURÇAIN OP (Durandus de Sancto Porciano). The printed editions contain the third and last redaction of his commentary on the Sentences: *Durandi a Sancto Porciano in Sententias theologicas Petri Lombardi Commentariorum libri quatuor*, Paris, 1508 . . . , 1550; Lyon, 1533 . . . 1595; Venice, 1571, 1586. J. Koch, *Durandi de S. Porciano OP. Quaestio de natura cognitionis et Disputatio cum anonymo quodam necnon Determinatio Hervaei Natalis OP.*, Münster i. W., 2 ed. 1935. Same author, *Durandus de Sancto Porciano Tractatus de habitibus, q. 4: De subjectis habituum, addita quaestione critica anonymi cujusdam*, Münster i. W., 1930.—BIBLIOGRAPHY. J. Koch, *Die Jahre 1312-1317 im Leben des Durandus de Sancto Porciano OP.*, Miscellanea Fr. Ehrle, I, 265-306; *Die Verteidigung der Theologie des hl. Thomas von Aquin durch den Dominikanerorden gegenüber Durandus de S. Porciano OP.*, Xenia Thomistica, Romae, III, 327-362. J. Koch, *Durandus de S. Porciano OP., Forschungen zum Streit um Thomas von Aquin zu Begin des 14. Jahrhunderts; I Teil, Literargeschichtliche Grundlegung*, Münster i. W., 1927 (Beiträge, 26, 1) ; fundamental for the history of the whole period; chronology of Du-

rand's works, 389-394; biography, 395-436. P. Fournier, HLP., 37 (1938) 1-38. J. Stufler, *Bemerkungen zur Konkurslehre des Durandus von St. Pourçain*, ADGM., 1080-1090. J. Müller, *Quaestionen der erste Redaktion von I und II Sentenzen des Durandus de Sancto Porciano in einer Hs. der Biblioteca Antoniana in Padua*, DTF., 19 (1941) 435-440. J. Koch, *Zu der Durandus-Hs. der Biblioteca Antoniana in Padua.* DTF., 20 (1942) 409-414.

[81] The only available redaction of the commentary on the *Sentences* is the third one, carefully revised by Durand and very moderate in comparison with the preceding ones. J. Koch places its redaction between 1317 and 1327 (p. 391). Until the first two redactions are published, we cannot follow the evolution of his thought or, at least, of his language. J. Koch (pp. 83-84) says that "the third redaction is full of compromises." Of the Augustinian system of psychology contained in the first redaction, the third redaction only contains ruins. It is no wonder that Durand has influenced his contemporaries chiefly by the first redaction of his commentary (p. 84). The main problems with which Durand concerns himself are essentially philosophical: "Theology is, to Durand, as to most of his contemporaries, applied philosophy" (p. 192). We shall follow the selection of problems made by J. Koch and complete his information by our own reading of the commentary on the *Sentences*. Any information related to the first two redactions will be borrowed from J. Koch. This great scholar should not be made responsible for our own historical interpretations of certain texts. The edition we are quoting is that of Venice, 1571.

[82] Joseph Koch interprets the position of Durand on this point as an effort to save the reality of relation without turning it into a distinct thing in the compound: op. cit., p. 193. His answer to this problem is by no means nominalistic (p. 108). On the contrary, Durand maintains, even in God, a real distinction between essence and relation; they differ "realiter, id est ex natura rei." In his desire to save the objective validity of the category of real relation, he resorts to a *distinctio formalis ex natura rei* similar to that of Duns Scotus (J. Koch, p. 108). The formula quoted by J. Koch from the first

redaction: "Relatio est alia res a suo fundamento et tamen non facit compositionem," p. 193, confirms this interpretation. This was to Durand the most important problem in metaphysics (ibid.). The third redaction of the commentary contains an ontology which provides the metaphysical background for this doctrine of relation.—Being belongs to all that is, and it belongs to all "according to a certain common reason"; consequently, existence cannot differ really from being; since it is a transcendental, to say being is to say *esse;* now all transcendentals predicate the essence of the things of which they are predicated, and nothing superadded, *ergo* . . . , I Sent., 8, 2, n. 16. The distinction of essence and existence is between *modi significandi,* ibid., n. 15. Those who posit an eternal *esse essentiae* (Henry of Ghent) cannot avoid the conclusion that Ideas are created, ibid., n. 13 (note the part played by Henry in the revival of the old problem of the creation of Ideas). His own conclusion: "Esse actualis existentiae non est aliud quam esse actu ens," ibid., n. 16. *Esse* is not a name proper to God, it is appropriated to him, I, 8, 1. n. 7. The science of God is both universal and particular, I, 35, 4, n. 8. On the divine Ideas, I, 36, 3, n. 8. An Idea is the created thing as secondary object of the divine intellect, n. 10-13; and I, 36, 4, nn. 4-6. Matter cannot be pure nothingness, II, 1, 1, nn. 9-10. On the *rationes primordiales* (divine Ideas), *rationes obedientiales* (potentiality of created being with regard to all that is not self-contradictory), *rationes seminales* (active and passive virtues attributed by God to things according to their species), II, 18, 2, nn. 13-16.

[83] Positively no hylomorphic composition of the soul, *I Sent.,* 8, 2, 2, n. 4. The soul is the immediate form of the body, yet it is separable from it, I, 8, 3, n. 14. It is ingenerable and incorruptible, II, 18, 3, n. 4; although we should not worry much about what Aristotle says, let us note that he himself seems to have considered the soul incorruptible in both being and operation, ibid., n. 6. Souls are created unequal in natural perfections, II, 32, 3, nn. 4-7; but equal as to their essences, ibid., nn. 8-10. The vegetative and generative powers of the soul are one with its essence, I, 3, 2, n. 18-19; but not the sensitive

powers, n. 30, nor the intellective power, n. 42. Intellect and will are not absolutely different, but only with respect to their acts, I, 3, 4, n. 8. The only reason to posit an agent intellect would be to account for what it does either in the phantasm or in the possible intellect; since it does nothing in either one, there is no reason to posit it, I, 3, 5, n. 4.— On the psychology of Durand, see Karl Werner, *Die nominalisierende Psychologie der Scholastik des späteren Mittelalters,* Sitzungsberichte Königl. Akad. d. Wiss., philos.-histor. Klasse, Wien, 99 (1882) 213-254.

[84] Text in *Durandi de S. Porciano OP., Quaestio de natura cognitionis,* ed. J. Koch; 1 ed. Münster i. W., 1929; 2 ed., 1935. These texts represent the first redaction of Durand's commentary. Durand lists five reasons for not adding the operation to the intellect: the operation of the form cannot be distinct from the form. Otherwise the operation itself would be prime act; feeling and understanding are immanent operations and no such operation is more than verbally distinct from the operating form; even God could not make sensation or intellection exist apart from either sense or intellect, etc. —Durand has summed up the Scotist distinction between abstractive and intuitive knowledge (but he seems to have had still another theologian in mind), Prol., 3, n. 7. He himself says that intuitive cognition always comes first, n. 10; but this problem does not seem to have detained his attention.

[85] "Nihil est principium individuationis nisi quod est principum naturae et quidditatis," II, 3, 2, n. 14. The principle of individuation cannot be quantity, ibid., 8-13. Being is individual because it is being: "esse individuum convertitur cum ente accepto secundum reale," n. 15. Socrates is an individual, from without, by his causes; from within, by "haec materia et haec forma"; naturally, its matter and its form are individual for the same reason: they are, n. 15. The decisive reason is that "it is a fiction to posit an agent intellect, and it is futile to say that universality is caused in things, because universality cannot be in things, but singularity only" ("universalitas non potest esse in rebus, sed solum singularitas"), II, 6, 7, n. 8. This entails the conclusion that, since

there is nothing universal in things, the prime known object is the singular, ibid., nn. 6-12. This is, of course, an Aristotelian thesis, *De anima,* I, 1, 402b, 7-8; and it is interpreted following the authority of Averroes (*intellectus est qui facit universalitatem in rebus*); only, like John of Naples, Durand concludes that since there is nothing universal in things, the problem of individuation does not arise, a consequence which many Aristotelians had not deduced from this principle.

[86] There is no reason to posit an agent intellect, I, 3, 5, n. 4. If there were one, it could not act on the phantasm. First, not by impressing anything on it, because, if it did, its action would become corporeal as the phantasm itself is, n. 5. Secondly, not by abstracting anything from it, because, while it is present to the intellect, the phantasm remains intact, nothing is removed from it nor transferred from it to the possible intellect (n. 7); as to saying that this abstraction is merely one of reason (not a real one), it is impossible, because the agent intellect does not know the phantasms; its action is not a cognition. Since then its action on the phantasms can be neither real nor of reason, it does not exist; then there is no reason to posit an agent intellect, n. 7. Cf. n. 13. Likewise, the agent intellect does not act in the possible intellect. We do not posit an agent sense, why should we posit an agent intellect? n. 17. Were it objected that the agent intellect and the phantasm co-operate in acting in the possible intellect (n. 21), the answer would be that this is begging the question. Our own question is: what reasons are there to posit such an intellect? If the phantasms suffice to move the possible intellect, there is no reason to posit such an intellect, n. 23. What the sense can do, the possible intellect is able to do too, n. 26. Averroes was wrong on this point, n. 17; and we should not worry about what Aristotle has said, but about truth, n. 29. For similar reasons, we should not posit species either sensible or intelligible; if there were species, we would see them and we would know them; the notion of an object of cognition that we do not know does not make sense. We see colors, not species; we know things, not species; so species should not be posited, II, 6, 6, nn. 10-14.—The true answer of Durand

to the problem is to be found in the first redaction: *Quaest. de natura cognitionis,* ed. J. Koch, where the Augustinian background of the doctrine is clearly visible. Durand upholds the Augustinian doctrine of sensation as an act of representative imitation performed by the soul: Augustine, *De musica,* VI, 5, PL., 32, 1168. Similarly, the object is only for the intellect the cause *sine qua non* of intellectual cognition. It does not actuate the possible intellect. What actuates it is its Cause. Confronted with the phantasm, it conceives an intelligible just as sense produces its sense perception.—Durand does not criticize Thomas Aquinas more systematically than any other theologian with whom he does not agree, at least in the third redaction of his commentary. Nor was he a voluntarist. First, he denies any absolute distinction between intellect and will, I, 3, 4, n. 8. As to the freedom from coercion (*a coactione*) the intellect is as free as the will, II, 14, 3, n. 13-14. As to free choice (*libertas arbitrii*) which is but the power of choosing between two opposites, even there, the intellect is free more principally than the will, ibid., n. 15; cf. n. 17. Election is not the prime act of free choice; rather, it is the concluding judgment determining the election, n. 18. On the goodness of moral acts, II, 38, 1-4. Beatitude consists in an operation of the intellect: "est operatio solius intellectus praecise," IV, 49, 4, n. 11. Cf.: "nulla autem perfectio nobis melior est voluntatis actu, quam actus intellectus, ergo actus voluntatis est propter actum intellectus," n. 14, and n. 15. On the immediate nature of the beatific vision, without either species representing the divine essence or created light elevating the intellect, IV, 49, 2, n. 24; this is not impossible, since "omnis potentia habet proportionem cum omni eo quod cadit sub ratione sui subjecti; Deus autem cadit sub ratione entis, quae est formalis ratio objecti intellectus," n. 29.

[87] J. Koch, *Durandus de S. Porciano,* 410-417.

[88] On the first list, July 3, 1314; J. Koch, *Die Jahre 1312-1317* . . . and *Durandus de S. Porciano* . . . , 200-203. On the list of 235 articles, ibid., pp. 203-208. List of John of Guevara, ibid. 208-210.

[89] J. Koch, *Durandus de S. Porciano . . .* , 285-314; especially the notes.

[90] A. Pelzer, *Les 51 articles de Guillaume Occam censurés en Avignon en 1326,* RHE., 18 (1922) 240-270. See the remarks of Fr. Ehrle, *Der Sentenzenkommentar Peters von Candia,* p. 91; and the reflections of J. Koch about these remarks, *Durandus de S. Porciano,* pp. 170-171. Apart from the general problem, J. Koch observes that since Durand came in contact with Ockhamism at a time when the last redaction of his own commentary was nearly completed (1326) the question whether Durand was influenced by Ockham should be answered in the negative.

[91] PETER AURIOL OFM (Petrus Aureoli): *Commentariorium in I Sententiarum pars prima, auctore Petro Aureolo Verberio OM.,* Romae, Typographia Vaticana, 1596. *In II Librum Sententiarum,* Romae, A. Zanetti, 1605. On the life of Auriol: N. Valois, HLF., 33 (1906) 479-489: life and works. R. Dreiling, *Der Konzeptualismus . . .* , 1-53. V. Doucet, AFH., 27 (1934) 562-564. BIBLIOGRAPHY: GLOREP., II, 244-248. GDP., 769 R. Dreiling, *Der Konzeptualismus in der Universalienlehre des Franziskanerbischofs Petrus Aureoli (Pierre d'Auriole).* Münster i. W., 1913 (Beiträge II, 6). Am. Teetaert, art. *Pierre Auriol,* DTC., 12, (1935) 1810-1881 (bibliography, 1879-1881). P. Vignaux, *Justification et prédestination au XIXe siècle. Duns Scot, Pierre d'Auriole et Grégoire de Rimini,* Paris, 1934, ch. II, pp. 43-95; *Note sur la relation du conceptualisme de Pierre d'Auriole à sa théologie trinitaire,* Annuaire de l'Ecole pratique des Hautes Etudes (Science religieuses) 1935. R. Schmücker, *Propositio per se nota, Gottesbeweis und ihr Verhältnis nach Petrus Aureoli,* Werl i. W., 1941. P. Vignaux, *Le nominalisme au XIVe siècle,* Montréal, 1948. F. Prezioso, *La teoria dell'essere apparente nella gnoseoolgia di Pietro Aureolo,* Studi Francescani, 22 (1950) 15-43. Ph. Boehner, *Notitia intuitiva of non existents according to Peter Aureoli,* Franciscan Studies, 8 (1948) 388-416.

Recently reprinted: *Peter Auroli Scriptum super primum Sententiarum,* by E. M. Buytaert, St. Bonaventure (N.Y.), 1953. Includes the text of the Prologue and the Distinction I. The table of the 75 questions, published pp. 13-124, provides a great deal of information concerning the positions of Auriol.—Part played by metaphysics in theology, 77-79, pp. 154-155 (he who proves the existence of God is metaphysician rather than theologian; "et si Aristoteles habuisset occasiones hujusmodi, non dubium quod ad eas multo excellentius ascendisset."); on the proper role of probability in theology, 111, p. 164. Intuitive cognition is possible without the presence or existence of; its object (against Scotus); this is proved by "the experience of the five" (*experientiae quinque*), to which we should adhere more than to any logical reasons (81, p. 198): "experience teaches that intuitive (cognition) and eyesight (*visio sensitiva*) do not necessarily require the presence (of the object)." Visual illusions (Augustine), 82, pp. 198-199. Dreams (Averroes), 83, p. 199, etc. What nature or deception can do, God can do it *multo fortius,* 88, p. 200 (cf. Rodington). And let us not argue that those people do not "see," but simply believe they see (89, p. 200): to this decisive objection, Auriol's answer already is that of Ockham's: "There is no act in the seeing power that does not share in the *specific nature* of sight," 90, p. 200. If it is seeing, then it is seeing, whether there be a seen thing or not; note the repeatedly conjoined authorities: Augustine and Averroes: "Sed hujusmodi actus sunt in oculo, ut expresse dicit Augustinus et Commentator," 90, p. 200. True and false inhere in the same cognition (*eidem notitiae numerali*), 91, p. 200. Consequently God can cause such an objectless intuition without contradiction, 93, p. 201. This is expressly against Scotus, 102, p. 203. Intuitive cognition then is such, not because the thing is, but because it makes the thing appear to be, "quoniam realem existentiam ejus (objecti) et actualem positionem facit apparere, esto etiam quod non sit," 109, p. 205. Intellectual intuition is possible, 117, p. 208.—Object of theology: "ratio deitatis ut concepta per analogiam a viatore," 85, p. 314; extension of the object of theology, 92-93, pp. 316-317.—Word (*vox*) as expressive of the concept is the subject of logic, 106-118, pp. 321-324 (that is, words, and not second intentions).—Auriol's objections are directed against Thomas, Scotus, Henry of Ghent, Henry of Harclay, Gerald of Bologna, etc.

[92] JAMES OF ASCOLI (Jacobus de Esculo), still unstudied. *Quaestiones disputatae* and *Quodlibet* in ms. Vat. lat. 1012.—

GLOREP., II, 236-237. V. Doucet, AFH., 27 (1934) 562.

[93] Texts in Dreiling, *Der Konzeptualismus* . . . , p. 40, note 1; p. 42, notes 1 and 2, where Auriol states that neither faith nor reason can oblige us to think that "a soul is the perfection of its body as its configuration is the form of wax." —Concerning the perplexities of Auriol on this point, A. Baldissera, *La definizione del Concilio di Vienne (1311): "Substantia animae rationalis seu intellectivae vere ac per se humani corporis forma" nella interpretazione di un contemporaneo*, RFNS., 34 (1942) 212-232.

[94] If the soul is the actuating principle of matter, as other forms are, its separability becomes miraculous: "Fides tamen tenet quod anima separatur et ideo difficile est videre quomodo possit fieri, si ponatur pura actuatio materiae sicut aliae," Dreiling, op. cit., p. 43, note 3. Cf. "Fidei autem sententia inconcusse tenenda est, quod anima hominis est immortalis et quoad intellectum et voluntatem, et quia ita est nobis communis animi conceptio et veritas per se nota, sed propter quid invenire, non est sic facile. Adducuntur ad hoc rationes diversae quae parum concludunt. . . . Nunc pono meas. Nescio si concludunt," Dreiling, op. cit., p. 201, note 1. This recourse to a sort of probabilism is frequent in Auriol. Creation, which never entered the mind of the philosophers, is nevertheless more probable than any other interpretation of the causality of the First Cause: text in Dreiling, pp. 200-201, notes. The omnipotence of God, already tied up with this problem in the mind of Duns Scotus, is not strictly demonstrable, etc.

[95] See the fundamental text in Dreiling, op, cit., p. 40, note 2. Auriol naturally refers to Averroes, but the Commentator had not attempted to deduce, from the *continuatio* between the separate Intellect and the "passive Intellect" of every man, the substantial unity of each man with the separate Intellect.

[96] "Multitudo ponenda non est, nisi ratio evidens necessaria illud probet aliter per pauciora salvari non posse," Dreiling, op. cit., p. 205, note 4. This "principle of economy" (which is essential to scientific method itself at all times) is not proper to Auriol. Duns Scotus, Durand

of St. Pourçain and many others were then using it; Ockham is going to use it so often that it has been called "Ockham's razor," but Ockham did not invent it. The reason for its growing popularity, as we are approaching the Ockhamist reformation, is the growing unpopularity of metaphysical Platonism under all its forms. Before Ockham, Auriol has shaved off intelligible species, all the intellects other than the agent intellect and the possible intellect, all the Scotist "formalities," etc. His anti-Scotism finds here its inspiration. The primacy of nobility of the singular over the universal entails the primacy of sense experience over abstract reasoning. This is another point where the influence of Averroes is manifest in Auriol's doctrine. He himself quotes the Commentator as his authority on this point. Of course, beyond Averroes, this empiricism is one of the constitutive elements of the philosophy of Aristotle. It is here conflicting with another no less Arisotelian element, the dialectical one: "Prima quidem via experientiae, cui adhaerendum est potius quam quibuscumque logicis rationibus . . . ," etc. Dreiling, op. cit., p. 196, note 1; cf. notes 2-6.

[97] A singular being is a being indivisible into other beings of the same nature. What is the cause of individuation? The question is senseless, because everything is individual from the very fact that it is: "realiter quaestio nulla est, cum quaeritur quid addit individuum ad rationem speciei, quoniam omnis res, eo quod est, singularis est, ut eo ipso quod est indifferens et communis ratio, est concepta. Ideo quaerere aliquid per quid res, quae extra intellectum est, est singularis, nihil est quaerere," Dreiling, op. cit., p. 160, note 1.

[98] The similarity there is between the qualities of certain individuals is the sole reality that can be attributed to the genus or to the species; it is therefore the sole content of the concept. Note, in the texts quoted by Dreiling, the recourse to Averroes, p. 141, note 1. "Everything is singular and its concept is singular," ibid. A general concept is an entirely different concept from that of a singular; it is "another" concept (not the same more or less modified); it is not the concept of a real being but of qualitative resemblances

between certain beings. Aristotle and Averroes agree that beings of first intention are substances, whereas beings of second intention (universals) are "qualities." Naturally, the question remains: what is that resemblance? Or, what is its cause? The only answer of Auriol is, that there always can be another thing like the particular one we know: "Intelligit Commentator, quod omnis res eo quo existit, est particularis; eo autem ipso quod potest habere secum comparticipem, fundat *quemdam conceptum similitudinarium* illis. Solum enim illud habet conceptum similitudinarium, quod potest plurificari," Dreiling, p. 142, note 4. The ultimate foundation for universality then is the possibility that several similar beings be created by God. On the process of formation of general concepts by a repetition of similar particular impressions, text p. 143, note 1. Cf. p. 161-163. This is not a question of individuation, but of multiplication, p. 163, note 1.

[99] Extensive fragments quoted by Dreiling, op. cit., 104, note 2; 108, note 1; 112, note 1; 114, notes 1 and 2; 116, note 3.—On the doctrine of the divine Ideas presupposed by this noetic, pp. 82-84.

[100] Dreiling, who has so intelligently and diligently studied the doctrine of Auriol, would oppose this conclusion. To him, "the rejection of any realistic interpretation of universal concepts" appears as characteristic of Auriol, p. 119.

[101] HENRY OF HARCLAY, d. 1317. F. Pelster, *Heinrich von Harclay, Kanzler von Oxford, und seine Quästionen*, Miscellanea Ehrle, I, Rome, 1924, 307-355. Joh. Kraus, *Die Universalienlehre des Oxforder Kanzlers Heinrich von Harclay in ihrer Mittelstellung zwischen skotistischen Realismus und Ockhamistischen Nominalismus*, DTF., 10 (1932) 36-58, 475-508; 11 (1933) 76-96, 288-314; many texts quoted in the notes,—Refutation of Scotus by Harclay, J. Kraus, op. cit., p. 54, notes 1 and 2. Harclay quotes the famous formula of Aristotle: "Animal autem universale aut nihil aut posterius est" (*De anima*, I, 1, 402b, 7-8), with its commentary by Averroes: the definitions of genus and species "are not the definitions of universal things existing outside of the soul; they are definitions of particular things outside of the intellect; it is the intellect which makes universality in them," pp. 57-58, note. Accordingly, "Omnis res posita extra animam est singularis eo ipso," p. 78. It can be said to be universal because: "est universalis quod non est aliud nisi quod confuse et indistincte est cognoscibilis," p. 79, note 1. As a cognition, a universal concept is the concept of a singular confusedly known, p. 82, note 1. "Animal significat Socratem confuse intellectum," p. 84, note. The commonness of a concept is its confusion; its "supposition" is indeterminate, p. 87. It is the work of the agent intellect, which makes it (*fingit*, fabricates, imagines); it is, so to speak, a true figment (*figmentum philosophicum*), p. 88, note 3; cf. pp. 91-93, notes. William Ockham has rejected the position of Harclay in his own commentary on the *Sentences*, I, d. 2, q. 7; yet, this position is so close to that of Ockham that the exposition of Harclay by Ockham has sometimes been mistaken for an exposition of Ockham's doctrine by himself: J. Kraus, p. 290, note 1 (reproduces the text of Ockham). There are so many similar positions, all moving toward Ockhamism, that the same text has been interpreted as exposing the doctrine of the fourteenth-cent. Carmelite Guy Terrena.

[102] WILLIAM FARINIER, OFM. E. Longpré, *Les questions disputées de Guillaume Farinier OFM., ministre général de l'Ordre (1348-1357) et cardinal (1356-1361)*, La France Franciscaine, 5 (1922) 434-437. Johan. Kraus, *Die Universalienlehre des . . . Heinrich von Harclay*, DTF., 11 (1933) 301-305. William opposes the Scotist "hecceity," as well as the quiddity, or common nature of Avicenna and Scotus: no specific unity *ex parte rei*, pp. 302-303; he defines the universal a "similitudinarius conceptus" whose unity is that of a concept, not of a thing (p. 304). This definition presupposes that certain things imitate other ones: "inter ignem et ignem est major imitatio *ex natura rei* quam inter ignem et aquam. Unde unus ignis particularis imitatur seipso alium ignem particularem plus quam imitetur aquam. Nec oportet propter hoc quod conveniant in aliquo tertio nisi in aptitudine, quia sunt apti facere unum conceptum," p. 304, note 3. Supposition, p. 305, note 4. Comparison of Harclay with Ockham, p. 299-300 (J. Kraus considers Harclay a realist); position of W. Farinier, pp. 304-305.

[103] GERARD OF BOLOGNA. On the Order of the Carmelites, their schools and studies, GLOREP., II, 334-335. B. M. Xiberta, *De institutis Ordinis Carmelitarum quae ad doctrinas philosophorum et theologorum sequendas pertinent,* in Analecta Ordinis Carmelitarum, 6 (1929) 337-379. Same author, *De scriptoribus scholasticis saeculi XIV ex Ordine Carmelitarum,* Louvain, 1931. B. M. de la Croix, *Les Carmes aux Universités du moyen âge,* Etudes Carmélitaines, 12(1932) 82-112.—On Gerard of Bologna (d. 1317): GLOREP., II, 336-337. B. M. Xiberta, *De summa theologiae M. Gerardi Bononiensis,* Analecta Ordinis Carmelitarum, 2 (1923) 1-54; same author, *De scriptoribus . . . ,* 74-110 (on this *Summa theologiae,* P. Glorieux, II, p. 337 c;* the commentary on the *Sentences* published at Venice in 1622 under the name of Gerard belongs to Michel of Bologna). Fragments of the *Quodlibeta* in B. Hauréau, *Hist. de la philos. scol.,* II, 2, Paris 1880, pp. 267-272; see p. 272, the rejection of the intelligible species. Opposes Thomas Aquinas, Scotus, Henry of Ghent. Against the real composition of essence and existence as well as the formal distinctions of Scotus.

[104] GUY TERRENA (Guiu de Terena, Gui Terré), d. 1342.—GLOREP., II, 339-343. B. M. Xiberta, *De magistro Guidone Terreni . . . ,* Analecta Ord. Carm., 5 (1924) 113-206; *De doctrinis theologicis magistri Guidonis Terreni,* ibid., 233-376; *La metafisica i la psicologia del mestre Guiu de Terrena . . . ,* Anuari de la Societat Catalana de Filosofia, I (1923) 165-212. J. Kraus, *Die Universalienlehre . . . ,* DTF., 11 (1933) 305-309: excellent texts on the non-existence of universality, p. 307, notes; no common nature, but a "convenientia realis," a "major conformitas" or "minor conformitas" between really distinct individuals, p. 308, notes 1 and 2. As J. Kraus aptly says, all these masters refuse actual being to "universality" but they desire to attribute a content to "universals."

PART ELEVEN
THE MODERN WAY

CHAPTER I. WILLIAM OF OCKHAM

[1] L. Lachance, *Saint Thomas dans l'histoire de la logique,* Publications de l'Institut d'Etudes médiévales d'Ottawa, I, Paris, J. Vrin, 1932, 61-103. The *Summa totius logicae,* included among the spurious works of Thomas Aquinas, and sometimes attributed without decisive reasons to Giles of Rome, bears witness to the penetration of the metaphysic of Thomas (or of Giles) into logic: it mentions a distinction of essence and existence; on the doctrine, C. Prantl, *Geschichte der Logik,* III, 250-257.

The history of logic in the fourteenth century is complicated by at least two elements foreign to logic properly so-called: grammar and metaphysics.

I. GRAMMAR. Mediaeval "grammar" (*grammatica*) essentially consisted in the teaching of the usual Latin grammars of Priscian and Donatus as an introduction to the reading of the Latin classical writers. Since classical Latin differed from the Latin of the Bible, conflicts soon arose between some grammarians impatient with Biblical Latin and some theologians: M.-D. Chenu, *Grammaire et théologie aux XIIe et XIIIe siècles,* AHDL., 10-11 (1936), 5-28.

Other problems arose in consequence of questions asked by the classical grammarians themselves. For instance, Priscian had said that "the property of the name is to signify substance with quality"; and that "the property of the verb is to signify an action performed, or undergone, or both, by means of modes, of forms and of tenses . . ." etc. (Priscian, *Institutionum grammaticarum,* II, 18; ed. M. Hertz, Teubner, 1855; I, 55). Four categories of Aristotle are involved in these definitions: substance, quality, action, passion. Moreover, Priscian is there using the notion of "signification," which raises the question of the meaning of "meaning." The problem of *significatio* was to become one of the central problems discussed by logicians. Again, Priscian found himself confronted with words, indispensable to common language, that do not signify any "thing" nor any "action." These are always used in connection with significative words; so they themselves do not signify, but they con-signify. These are the *consignificantia*, which we already met under their Greek name: *syncategoremata* (Priscian, *Institutiones*, II, 15; I, 54). The two problems of *signification* and of *consignification* were inseparably tied together, as can be seen from the grammatical description of the verb. It signifies when used in the indicative; in fact, "it signifies the substance or the essence of the thing" (Priscian, VIII, 63-64; I, 422); when used in the infinitive, it is just a noun (VIII, 43; I, 408. Cf. VIII, 48; I, 412). In all other tenses, it consignifies time. Many philosophical questions arose from these notions: Aristotle, *On Interpretation*, III, 16; Boethius, PL., 64, 306; Abélard, ed. Geyer, pp. 336, 337, 345, etc.—The notion of "denomination" (Aristotle, *Categories*, I, *paronuma*), to which Priscian devoted the whole Bk. IV of his *Institutions* (prudence is the denominative from "prudent," ed. Hertz, I, 117), was taken up by Boethius (PL., 64, 168 A-B), and then, of course, by all logicians (cf. Abelard, ed. Geyer, 122 ff.).

This intrusion of logic into grammar was resented by a few "humanists" but welcomed by many other grammarians, the more so as, most of the time, the same men were equally competent in both disciplines. There is a visible continuity from the definition of "word" (*vox*) by Priscian (I, 1; Hertz, I, 5) to its nominalistic interpretation by Abelard (ed. Geyer, 37-38; 124-125). Grammar is nominalistic by definition; a logician can carry its nominalism from grammar to logic, then to metaphysics. In the fourteenth century, at the same time when grammar was invading metaphysics through logic, metaphysics invaded grammar. This movement, visible ever since the twelfth century, gave rise to "speculative grammar" (*grammatica speculativa*). Its two characters are: 1) to be an abstract speculation about the classification and functions of words in language; 2) to be, in virtue of its very abstraction, independent from the grammars of particular languages. He who knows, in this way, the grammar of one single language, knows the grammar of all languages because "grammar is substantially one and the same in all languages, despite its accidental variations" (R. Bacon, in Wallerand, p. 43, note 6). On the history of this movement, Ch. Thurot, *Notices et*

extraits de divers manuscrits latins pour servir à l'histoire des doctrines grammaticales du moyen âge, Paris, 1868. G. Wallerand, *Les oeuvres de Siger de Courtrai,* Louvain, 1913 (very important). M. Grabmann, *Die Entwicklung der mittelalterlichen Sprachlogik,* MG., I, 104-146; one of the more original contributions of this admirable historian.—On Thomas of Erfurt, long mistaken for Duns Scotus, M. Heidegger, *Die Kategorien—und Bedeutungslehre des Duns Scotus,* Tübingen, 1916. M. Grabmann, *Thomas von Erfurt und die Sprachlogik des mittelalterlichen Aristotelismus,* Sitzungsberichte, Munich, 1943, 2. S. Buchanan, *An Introduction to the De modis significandi of Thomas of Erfurt,* Philosophical Essays for A. N. Whitehead, London, 1936, 67-89.

II. METAPHYSICS. With metaphysics, it is no longer a question of influence; it is almost everywhere present in logic. Aristotle had been the first to bring it to bear upon his own answers to many logical problems. The philosophical question set aside by Boethius at the beginning of his commentary on Porphyry's *Isagoge* acted as a provocative statement. With Roscelin, Abélard and their successors, the philosophical problem of the nature of universals came in the foreground. From the thirteenth century on, it gave a particular importance to the problem of "supposition." Ockham will interpret his logic in terms of his own answer to this philosophical problem. The confusion of the orders of logic and metaphysics, denounced later on by John Gerson, will be so complete that even the excellent historian of mediaeval logic, Carl Prantl, in his *Geschichte der Logik,* has had to resort, in countless cases, to the metaphysical writings of mediaeval logicians in order to define their respective doctrines of supposition, denomination, etc.

A particularly important notion, on account of its constant collusion with metaphysics, is that of "sentence" (grammar: *oratio*, Priscian, ed. Hertz, I, 53), called, in logic, an "enunciation" (Aristotle, *Categories*, II, a "verbal complex"; *On Interpretation*, IV) and, especially since Boethius, an *enuntiativa oratio* (PL., 64, 168-169). Only such enunciations can be true or false. Aristotle had raised the question: can enunciations concerning the future be either true or false? It naturally invaded theology under a new form: can God himself know true or false enunciations with respect to contingent future events? (Peter Lombard, *Sent.*, I, 41, 3). The foreknowledge of God was at stake. Hence the growing importance attached by logicians to the notion of *enutiabile*, i.e., that which is the object of a possible enunciation. On the history of this notion, H. Elie, *Le complexe significabile;* see *supra*, p. 722, n. 78.

III. ORIGINS OF MODERN PHYSICS. The pioneering work of P. Duhem (*Le système du monde*, IV, ch. 9, pp. 91-183) has initiated a new type of research more directly concerned with the history of science than with the history of theology and philosophy. Nevertheless, on two points at least, these two histories are inseparable: the speculation on the magnitude, or intensity, of forms, which, connected with the theological problem of the degrees of virtue (esp. charity), gave rise to an abundant literature; secondly, the speculation on the infinite, whose theological import becomes evident after 1277, and which opened the way to new physical notions. In both cases, the physics of Aristotle provided a starting point. How is a quantitative variation possible within a form whose nature it is not to be susceptible of more or less? Is an actually infinite quantity possible? Can it be demonstrated that there is an infinitely powerful cause? These problems, already known to many thirteenth-century theologians, have been still more widely discussed in the theologies of the fourteenth century. On their own side, the masters of arts have ceased to content themselves with teaching the letter of the *Physics* of Aristotle, and their doctrines concerning the structure of the universe and the nature of motion then began to attest a certain originality. The best work in this field is now being done by A. Maier, *Die Anfänge des physikalischen Denkens im 14. Jahrhundert,* Philosophia Naturalis, 1 (1950) 7-35. Covering the whole problem: Anneliese Maier, *Das Problem der intensive Grösse in der Scholastik (de intensione et remissione formarum)*, Leipzig, 1939; *Die Impetustheorie der Scholastik,* Wien, 1940; *An der Grenze von Scholastik und Naturwissenschaft, Studien zur Naturphilosophie des 14. Jahrhunderts,* Essen, 1943; *Die Vorläufer Galileis im 14. Jahrhundert. Studien zur Naturphilosophie der Spätscholastik,* Roma, 1949. R. Masi, *Nota sulla storia del prinzipio d'inerzia,* RFNS., 40 (1948) 121-133.

[2] The logic of Aristotle provides a complete equipment in nominalistic arguments for anybody desiring to turn logic into metaphysics. Individuals are not predicable of a subject; nothing that is predicable of a subject is an individual. Substance, in the primary and fundamental sense of the word, is the individual man or horse; species and genus are secondary beings (beings of second intention). If there were no primary substances, or beings (individuals) nothing else would exist. We speak of secondary beings (genus or species) as though they were individuals, but they are not: Aristotle, *Categories*, 1a 21-2b 21; 3b 10-4a 21. Note the explicit remark of Aristotle that the relation of speech to thought is a philosophical problem which he has already discussed in his *De anima*. In this treatise, Aristotle says that sensation bears upon the singular, science upon universals, and that universals are, somehow, in the soul, whereas sensation deals with what is outside of the soul, II, 5, 417b, 19-28. In his metaphysics, universals are no beings (*ousiai*, entities), III, 6, 1003a, 8; being belongs to individuals, VII, 13, 1038b, 22-23; nothing that is universal has entity, 1038 b, 34-35: all the refutation of Plato's doctrine of Ideas is a consequence of this metaphysical position; X, 2, 1053b, 16-20: universals do not exist, they are predicables, etc. At the same time, Aristotle upheld a metaphysics of forms according to which the form (*morphe*) is eminently being and entity in the composite, VII, 3, 1029a, 29-32. There was a tension between these two elements; Aristotle is equally at the origin of the so-called "moderate realism" of Thomas Aquinas (in metaphysics) as at the origin of the so-called "nominalism" of Ockham. A powerful influence in favor of the logical interpretation of Aristotle was Averroes; the tension in his doctrine was the same ("sequitur quod forma sit magis substantia quam compositum," *In Metaph.*, VII, 1; Venice, 1524, p. 18 r); but he provided the Latins with striking formulas: "Universale enim non habet esse nisi secundum quod est scientia, idest secundum quod est in anima," *Metaph.*, I, 4, n. 27; f. 18 r. One had to choose among three ways: going back to Plato's Ideas; positing the mental nature of universals while maintaining the reality of the specific forms in concrete substances; denying all reality to specific

forms on the ground that such forms would be, after all, nothing more than concrete universals. This third decision is what is more or less properly called nominalism.

³WILLIAM OCKHAM OFM., d. ca. 1350.—Editions listed GDP., 572. *Guilhelmi de Ockam anglici super quatuor libros sententiarum subtilissimae quaestiones earumdemque decisiones,* Lugduni, 1495 (includes the probably spurious *Centiloquium theologicum*). *Quodlibeta septem,* Paris, 1487; Strasbourg, 1491 (the Strasbourg edition includes the *De sacramento altaris et de corpore Christi*). *Expositio aurea . . . super artem veterem,* with questions by Albertus parvus de Saxonia, Bologna, 1496. *Summa totius logicae,* Paris, 1488; Bologna, 1498; Venice, 1591; Oxford, 1675; Rome, 1637. *Summulae in libros Physicorum,* Rome, 1637.—Modern editions: Commentary on the *Sentences,* first question of the Prologue, *Ordinatio, quaestio prima principalis Prologi,* ed. Ph. Böhner, Paderborn, 1939; *Ordinatio,* d. 2, q. 8, NS., 16 (1942) 224-240; *Ordinatio,* d. 36, q. 1, Review of Metaphysics, 1 (1948) 74-78; *Quodlibeta,* II, 7, ibid., 1 (1948) 79-81; *Reportatio,* qq. 14-15, Traditio, 1 (1943) pp. 245-275; *Tractatus de successivis* (attributed to Ockham) St. Bonaventure, N.Y., 1944; *Tractatus de praedestinatione et de praescientia Dei et de futuris contingentibus of William Ockham,* St. Bonaventure, N.Y., 1945; *William Ockham, Summa logicae. Pars I,* St. Bonaventure, N.Y., 1951.—Not by Ockham, but a faithful digest of his doctrine: L. Baudry, *Le Tractatus de principiis theologiae attribué à Guillaume d'Occam,* Paris, 1936. M. Grabmann, *Quaestio de universali secundum viam et doctrinam Guilelmi de Ockham,* Münster i. W., 1930.—Engl. transl. of selections from *The Seven Quodlibeta,* R. McKeon, *Selections,* II, 360-421. *De sacramento altaris,* Latin and English, by T. B. Birch, 1930.
BIBLIOGRAPHY. GDP., 781-782. G. M. Manser, *Drei Zweifler am Kausalprinzip . . . ,* JPT., 27 (1912) 405-437. F. Federhofer, *Die Philosophie des Wilhelm von Ockham im Rahmen seiner Zeit,* FS., 12 (1925) 273-296; *Die Psychologie und die psychologischen Grundlagen der Erkenntnislehre des Wilhelm von Ockham,* PJ., 39 (1926) 263-287. F. Hochstetter, *Studien zur*

Metaphysik und Erkenntnislehre Wilhelms von Ockham, Berlin, 1927. Leipzig, 1927. P. Vignaux, art. *Nominalisme,* DTC., II (1931) 717-784; art. *Occam,* DTC., 11 (1931) 523-528 (both important). S. U. Zuidema, *De philosophie van Occam in zijn Commentar op de Sententien,* Hilversum, 1936, 2 vols.; even those who do not read Dutch can use vol. II, made up of quotations from the commentary on the *Sentences.* G. Giacon, *Guglielmo di Occam,* 2 vols. Milano, 1941. G. Martin, *Wilhelm von Ockham, Untersuchungen zur Ontologie der Ordnungen,* Berlin, 1949. L. Baudry, *Guillaume d'Occam. Sa vie, ses oeuvres, ses idées sociales et politiques. I, L'homme et les oeuvres,* Paris, 1950, fundamental (cf. P. Böhner, Franciscan Studies, 11 (1951) 305-316). M. de Gandillac, *Ockham et la via moderna,* in A. Fliche and V. Martin, *Histoire de l'Eglise,* Paris, 13 (1951) 417-473. O. Fuchs, *The Psychology of Habit According to William Ockham,* St. Bonaventure, N.Y., 1952.—Noetic: P. Böhner, *The Realistic Conceptualism of William Ockham,* Traditio, 4 (1946) 307-336. J. Salamucha, *Die Aussagenlogik bei Wilhelm Ockham,* FS., 32 (1950) 97-134.—Philosophy of nature: S. Moser, *Grundbegriffe der Naturphilosophie bei Wilhelm von Ockham,* Innsbruck, 1932.—Extensive bibliography covering the years 1919-1949 by V. Heinck, FS., 32 (1950) 164-183.

⁴A. Pelzer, *Les 51 articles de Guillaume Occam censurés en Avignon, en 1326,* Revue d'histoire ecclésiastique, 18 (1922) 240-270. J. Koch, *Neue Aktenstücke zu dem gegen Wilhelm Ockham in Avignon geführten Prozess,* RTAM., 7 (1935) 353-380; 8 (1936) 79-93, 168-197.
The origin of the trial seems to have been a denunciation of Ockham's teaching by the successor of Harclay as Chancellor of the University of Oxford, JOHN LUTTERELL. This theologian attacked the doctrine of Ockham in a *Libellus* where the new interpretation of universals, together with the correspondingly new interpretations of the logical *suppositio,* were severely criticized from the point of view of realism. This treatise was written about 1324. F. Hoffmann, *Die erste Kritik des Ockhamismus durch den Oxforder Kanzler J. Lutterell,* Breslau, 1941.

⁵ Being is the object of metaphysics, God is the object of theology, but meta-

physics can demonstrate, *demonstratione quia,* many theological conclusions about God. The same intellectual *habitus* can be metaphysical and theological, just as the same man can be part of the people and part of the army, I *Sent.,* Prol., 1, ed. Böhner, p. 13. The main conclusions of Ockham are: 1) In our present condition, with respect to the same object seen under the same aspect, our intellect can have two simple cognitions specifically distinct, the one intuitive, the other abstractive; 2) this twofold cognition is possible with respect to God under the proper reason of Deity; 3) each one of these two cognitions is separable from the other one; 4) whence there follows that an abstractive notion of the Deity is possible to man in this life; op. cit., 14-15. The whole epistemology of Ockham is directly or indirectly involved in these questions.

[6] "Notitia evidens est in plus quam scientia, intellectus vel sapientia, quia propositio aliqua contingens potest evidenter cognosci, et tamen illa notitia nec est scientia nec est intellectus nec aliquis illorum habituum quos ponit Philosophus 6 Ethicorum," *Sent.,* Prol., I, 1, ed. Böhner, p. 8.—Definition of an evident cognition: "the cognition of a true proposition which can be sufficiently caused, immediately or mediately, by the simple apprehension of its terms," ibid.

[7] S. Day, *Intuitive Cognition. A Key to the Significance of the Later Scholastics,* Saint Bonaventure, N.Y., 1947 (Duns Scot and Ockham). Ph. Böhner, *Notitia intuitiva of non existents according to William Ockham,* Traditio, 1 (1943) 223-275. Objections in A. C. Pegis, *Concerning William of Ockham,* Traditio, II (1944) 465-480. Reply: Ph. Böhner, *In propria causa. A reply to Prof. Pegis* . . . , Franciscan Studies, 5 (1945) 37-54. Additional remarks: A. C. Pegis, *Some Recent Interpretations of Ockham,* Speculum, 23 (1948) 458-463. Some obscurity arises from the complexity of the point at stake. All theologians agree that God can create in any intellect a cognition which, although no actual being answers it in reality, will be perceived as an intuition: miraculous apparitions are possible *de potentia Dei absoluta.* The real question is: can it be said that what then invincibly appears as an intuition *is* an intuition? Scotus denies it: "contradictio est igitur quod sit cognitio intuitiva in genere proprio, et quod res non sit," *Rep. Par.,* III, 14, 3, n. 12. If it is self-contradictory, God cannot produce it even *de potentia absoluta.* Ockham does not think it is self-contradictory: "notitia abstractiva et intuitiva non differunt quia abstractiva potest esse indifferenter existentis et non existentis, praesentis et non praesentis (non-existence or absence come to the same), intuitiva autem existentis et praesentis realiter, quam differentiam ponunt aliqui ubicumque loquuntur de ista materia," *Sent.,* Prol., I, 1, Böhner, p. 26. What Ockham denies here is exactly the position of Scotus and of the Scotists maintained, against Ockham, by Walter of Chatton: "Ergo sequitur corollarium quod verum dicunt, ponentes quod Deus non potest facere intuitionem sine praesentia rei," *Sent.,* II, Prol., 2, 3, Sol. (quoted from the unpublished thesis of J. J. O'Callaghan). A notion which was contradictory in Scotus, and which ceased to be contradictory in Ockham, cannot have been the same notion.

[8] Ockham grants the Scotist distinction of abstractive knowledge for the cases when the cognition is a natural one, not when its cause is supernatural; see the decisive text of the *Reportatio* published by Böhner, Traditio, 1 (1943) 249: "Et ideo differentiae quas dat Johannes (Scotus) . . ." In Ockham's own noetic, the cognition of an existent is not intuitive for the reason that its object actually exists, but rather because, whether its object exists or not, it is by itself an intuitive cognition. The essential moment of the answer is: "Unde absolute loquendo non necessario requiritur ad cognitionem intuitivam alia praesentia, nisi quod possit actum intuitivum terminare," p. 249. This is the very essence of Ockham's noetic. Intuition and abstraction differ *by themselves,* and not by their objects nor by their causes: "Ideo dico quod notitia intuitiva et abstractiva seipsis differunt et non penes objecta, nec penes causas suas quascumque quamvis naturaliter notitia intuitiva non possit esse sine existentia rei . . . ," *Sent.* Prol., I, 1; ed. Böhner, p. 28.—*Quodl.,* I, 15; V, 5; V, 6 (on the intuition of non-existents), and the theological censure of 1326, RHE., 18 (1922) 255-256.

[9] Intuitive cognition yields propositions known by themselves; if I see Socrates, I know with evidence that "Socrates is

white"; if I imagine him as white while he is not there (abstractive knowledge) I do not know evidently that Socrates is white, "et ideo non est propositio per se nota," *Sent.*, Prol., I, 1, ed. Böhner, p. 9. This evidence is purely sensible in its terms, but the intellect is required to form the judgment, p. 21; the evidence of the judgment is caused by the intuitive cognition of its terms, p. 22. No contingent truth can be known by abstractive knowledge, p. 25. Intuitive cognition as origin of experiential cognition, p. 25 (Aristotle, *Metaph.*, I, 1, 980a 27-981a 22). Against the distinction as understood by Scotus, pp. 26-27. In fact, Ockham interprets the Scotist distinction in a sense foreign to the mind of Scotus. In Scotism, abstractive cognition is the apprehension of a "common nature," or real quiddity, endowed with its formal being of essence, which is metaphysically indifferent to existence; in Ockhamism, where there are no essences, this cognition abstracts from existence because it deals with mental signs of possible sense perceptions, as the cognition one has of an object in its absence. The mental images of green or red are abstract cognitions.—J. Rohmer, *L'intentionalité des sensations de Platon à Ockham*, RSR., 25 (1951) 5-39.

[10] *Sent.* Prol., I, 1, ed. Böhner, p. 29. We are witnessing the first appearance, in Ockham, of the theological *locus* by the absolute omnipotence of God (*de potentia Dei absoluta*). Ockham resorts to it as to a theological experiment every time he wants to show that, in fact, two things are absolutely distinct, which is but another way of saying that they are two. They are distinct, Ockham will then say, since God could destroy the one without destroying the other. What matters, philosophically speaking, is his conception of a world made up of ontological "absolutes," through which the omnipotent will of God circulates without ever having to overcome any ontological necessity.—God has an intuitive knowledge of non-existing things, p. 29. God can cause in us the sight of a color that is not there, p. 29. Intellectual intuition is frequent: for instance, "I know," pp. 29-30. Scotus was right on the possibility of an intuition of intelligible objects, p. 32.—Essential texts on the distinction of intuitive and abstractive knowledge, p. 43, l. 58—p. 44, l. 72 (note: *seipsis distinguuntur formali-*

ter); ad 2m, p. 49; ad 7m, p. 50; ad ultimum, pp. 50-51.

[11] Aristotle (*Metaph.*, I, 1053b, 21) had said that nothing universal can possibly be a being (*ousia*, entity). Thomas Aquinas had rightly deduced from this principle that all that is in an individual is individuated (*De ente et essentia*, Roland-Gosselin ed., p. 27, l. 5). The main difference between this Aristotelianism and that of James of Naples and of other so-called Thomists is that, to them, all that was in an individual was itself individual by right. The intrinsic singularity of the component elements then accounts for the singularity of the whole. To say, with Thomas, that "Quicquid in eo (Socrate) est, est *individuatum*," is not at all to say, with Roger Bacon, "Quicquid est in singulari, est *singulare*" (Roland-Gosselin, op. cit., p. 27, note). Ockham decidedly follows this second direction. All that which is outside of an intellect is individual by the very fact that it is real, and not by reason of any individuating principle added to, or included in, its actual being: "quaelibet res extra animam seipsa est singularis; ita quod ipsa sine omni addito est illud quod immediate denominatur ab intentione singulari . . . et ita quaelibet res extra animam seipsa erit haec. Nec est quaerenda aliqua causa individuationis, nisi forte causae extrinsecae et intrinsecae quando individuum est compositum; sed magis esset quaerenda quomodo possibile est aliquid esse commune et universale," *Sent.*, I, 2, 6, Q. This last remark had already been made by Roger Bacon and by the "Thomist" John of Naples (Johannes de Neapoli). In Ockham himself the immediate consequence of what precedes is that universality has no real existence outside of the mind: "illud quod est universale et univocum non est aliquid realiter ex parte rei, distinctum formaliter ab individuo," ibid., R. Incidentally, this text establishes the radical opposition of Ockham to the Scotist univocity of common natures. These cannot be univocal, since they do not exist.—Interesting suggestions in N. Picard, *Notae de loco et momento historico philosophiae Guillelmi de Ockham*, Antonianum, 19 (1944) 87-104.

[12] *Summa logicae*, I, 14; ed. Böhner, pp. 44-45. *Sent.*, I, 2, 8, E.

[13] The commentary on the *Sentences*, I, 2, 8, offers a choice of two interpretations

of the nature of the universal: 1) it is a figment (*quoddam fictum*) which has no other being than that of an object of cognition (*esse objectivum*) and which the intellect makes in the mind as a likeness of the thing outside of the mind (Durand of St. Pourçain, William of Auvergne, Augustine); this *abstractio* should rather be called a *fictio;* 2) the universal is a certain quality subjectively existing in the mind, and which holds from nature the same aptitude to signify that words receive from voluntary institution, I, 2, 8, Q. In short, according to this second explanation, universals are concepts themselves with their subjective reality of qualities of the mind. Ockham does not choose between these two interpretations because, since neither one attributes to the universal any extra-mental reality, both are acceptable to him. Nevertheless, yielding to the spirit of his own doctrine, he decided later on in favor of the second solution. A decisive text is *Quodl.* IV, 19. Ockham defines the concept of prime intention: "nomen mentale praecise natum esse extremum propositionis et supponere pro re quae non est signum, sicut conceptus hominis, animalis substantiae, corporis. Et breviter: omnia nomina mentalia quae naturaliter significant res singulares quae non sunt signa." The "second intention" is a concept that signifies first intentions, that is, the naturally signifying intentions (the species "man" signifies the concept of man, which signifies this singular man). Note "nomen mentale" as another name for the concept of first intention: hence the apellation of "nominalism" often used to designate Ockham's doctrine. He then exposes the doctrine of first and second intentions conceived as "quaedam entia ficta quae tantum sunt objective in mente et nullibi subjective," (*Quodl. IV,* 19). After refuting this hypothesis, because this objective being is superfluous, Ockham concludes: "Ideo dico quod tam intentio prima quam secunda est vere actus intelligendi, quia per actum potest salvari quicquid salvatur per fictum." Hence two consequences: 1) since second intentions are acts signifying first intentions, first and second intentions are really distinct (*realiter distinguuntur*); 2) since they are qualities subjectively existing in the mind, both first and second intentions are real beings: "tam intentiones primae quam secundae sunt vere entia realia, et sunt vere qualitates subjective existentes

in anima," ibid., end of the question. Thus, those who call Ockham a "nominalist," do not betray his intention since he himself calls his concepts "mental names"; on the other hand, to attribute to him a realism of concepts would also be justified since his concepts of prime intention are qualities subjectively existing in the mind, signifying singulars outside of the mind. The main point to remember, in order not to betray him, is that, if his concepts are names, they are *natural names,* not conventional ones: "A fourth opinion could be that nothing can be universal in virtue of its own nature, but only by institution, as a word (*vox*) is universal, because it is not in the nature of a thing to supposit (*supponere,* stand for) for another thing, nor to be truly predicated of another thing, which words are not, except by voluntary institution. In this view, all universals would be predicable of things and universal by institution, just as words are. But this does not seem to be right, because then nothing would be a species or genus in virtue of its own nature, nor conversely, and then God or a substance outside of the soul could be something universal just as well as something that is in the soul, which does not seem to be true," *Sent.,* I, 2, 8, R.

[14] *Summa logicae,* I, 15; Böhner ed., p. 48.—The logic of Ockham is as full of philosophy as any other one. The notion that he attempted to purify logic of Platonism is quite correct, but just like that of his predecessors, his logic is the logic of his philosophy (and conversely). In his *Summa logicae* (I, 15, p. 47) all his authorities against the reality of universality are borrowed, not from the logic of Aristotle or Averroes, but from their *Metaphysics.*—The easiest way to understand Ockham on this question is to adopt his own point of view. According to him, he was the first not to attribute *any* reality to universality in things, *Sent.,* I, 2, 7, B: "My conclusion on this point is that *all* those I have seen agree in saying that the nature on account of which something is somehow universal, at least in potency and incompletely, is really in the individual, although some say that it is really distinct from it, others that it is there only formally, still others that it is in no way really distinct from it, but only by a distinction of reason, or by the consideration of the intellect." After

restating four solutions of the problem (including those of Thomas and Scotus Ockham concludes: "Hoc modo dico quod omnis res positiva extra animam eo ipso est singularis," ibid., F. Against the *equinitas* of Avicenna, I, 2, 6, KK-LL; the whole q. 6 is directed against the "common nature" of Duns Scotus; cf. q. 5. This refutation of Scotus is naturally directed against the possibility of concepts univocal to God and creatures, I, 2, 4.

[15] See text in the preceding note.

[16] *Summa logicae,* I, 16, ed. Böhner, pp. 49-51 (against the Scotist essences); I, 17, pp. 52-56 (against various other positions). The doctrine of a real resemblance superadded to similar things is found ad 2m, p. 53.

[17] On relation, *Summa logicae,* I, 49, ed. Böhner, p. 141, l. 37-142, l. 55. Cf. *Sent.,* I, 30, 1, R.—P. Doncoeur, *Le nominalisme de Guillaume d'Occam. La théorie de la relation,* RNSP., 23 (1921) 5-25. L. Baudry, *A propos de la théorie occamiste de la relation,* AHDL., 9 (1934) 199-203. G. Martin, *Ist Ockhams Relationstheorie Nominalismus?* FS., 32 (1950) 31-49. G. A. Mohan OFM., *The Quaestio de relatione attributed to Ockham,* Franciscan Studies, 11 (1951) 273-303.

[18] *Summa logicae,* I, 64, ed. Böhner, pp. 177-179. Cf. I, 65, pp. 179-181 and the following chapters from 66 up to 77. On his own reinterpretation of "confuse" and "distributive" suppositions, I, 73-75, pp. 204-208.
A refutation of Ockham's logic was undertaken by an otherwise little known realist, RICHARD OF CAMPSALL: *Logica Campsale valde utilis et realis contra Ocham.*—E. A. Synan, *Richard of Campsall, an English Theologian of the Fourteenth Century,* MS., 14 (1952) 1-8. Born 1280/1290, died 1350/1360; the authorship is not considered certain by E. A. Synan, who is preparing an edition of the text.

[19] In a universe where universality has no reality in things, it cannot be abstracted from singulars, so we need no agent intellect to perform abstraction; if universals are really present in things, we still need no agent intellect to abstract them (Plato), *Sent.* II, 14-15, XX. What they call agent intellect is just the soul naturally producing its concept, ibid., SS. Neither Aristotle nor Averroes says anything about the agent intellect making the understood in potency an understood in act, ibid., TT. There is no distinction in the soul between possible intellect and agent intellect; no more than between intellect and will, II, 24, K, and Q (against their separation from man by Averroes: "et ipse in hoc negandus est a Christianis"). This would be multiplying beings without necessity, ibid. The agent intellect is the soul itself causing intuitive or abstractive intuition, ibid., R. As a matter of fact, discounting all the authorities of the Saints as well as of the philosophers, there is no reason to posit an active intellect; a passive one would do just as well, II, 25, A. To conceive is a natural and vital operation entirely accountable for by the intellect and the activity of the thing. Its mental products are "fabricationes," *Sent.,* I, 7, 1, N.

[20] "Dico quod natura occulte operatur in universalibus (cf. *Liber sex principiorum,* I, 4; ed, D. Van Den Eynde, p. 10); non quod producat ipsa universalia extra animam tanquam alia realia, sed quia, producendo cognitionem suam in anima, quasi occulte saltem immediate vel mediate producit illa modo quo nata sunt produci. Et ideo omnis communitas isto modo est naturalis, et a singularitate procedit, nec oportet illud, quod isto modo fit a natura, esse extra animam, sed potest esse in anima," *Sent.,* I, 2, 7, CC. L. Baudry observes that the criticism of the theory of the *fictum* (mental picture representing the thing) by Walter of Chatton may have decided Ockham to give it up (*Guillaume d'Occam,* 70-72, notes). It is at least certain that, in his own *Sentences,* Prol., q. 2, Chatton has criticized the doctrine of Auriol (art. 2) and the doctrine of Ockham (art. 3). In art. 3, ad 2m, Chatton exposes the two solutions; then he concludes: "Ita rem esse in anima est cognitionem esse in anima, qua posita, res denominatur cognita extrinseca denominatione. . . . Isto modo visio diceretur quoddam esse rei visae. Iste intellectus potest concedi, qui vellet; tamen cum isto stat quod non sit ibi ens objectivum distinctum a visione et visibili," (quoted from the unpublished thesis of J. J. O'Callaghan).

[21] *Sent.*, I, 2, 9a: whether some universal is univocal to God and creature. Something may be univocal to God and creature, even a universal, provided it has no reality on the part of things. Scotus first proves that the concept of being (not to speak of other ones) is univocal to God and to creatures, ibid., B. Ockham reports the definition of univocity given by Scotus (*Op. Ox.*, I, 3, 2, n. 5), but he does not accept it in the same sense. According to Ockham, the conclusion of Duns Scotus is true, in this sense that being is indeed univocal to God and to creatures, but it is false in what it says, "that being is common and univocal to certain things, but not to all existents in reality," ibid., C. The fact that Ockham is extending the univocity of being to all existents *a parte rei*, should warn his reader that he is talking about a univocity entirely different from that of Scotus, and opposed to it. He is denying the univocity ascribed by Scotus to the metaphysical concept of being, conceived as a common entity; he is affirming the univocal predicability of being with respect to irreducibly distinct singulars. No two beings have anything real in common. Consequently, the word answering this concept is predicated univocally of things that are not univocal in reality. The reason for this is a universal one: "quia universaliter nihil quod est a parte rei est univocum quibuscumque," ibid., U (cf. note 25).

[22] On the common concept of being: "Uno modo accipitur hoc nomen *ens,* secundum quod sibi correspondet unus conceptus communis omnibus rebus praedicabilis de omnibus in quid illo modo, quo transcendens potest in quid praedicari," *Summa logicae,* ed. Böhner, I, 38, p. 98.—Against our interpretation: M. C. Menges OFM., *The Concept of the Univocity of Being regarding the Predication of God and Creature According to William Ockham,* St. Bonaventure, N.Y., 1952.

[23] "Tamen non obstante quod sic sit unus conceptus communis omni enti, tamen hoc nomen *ens* est aequivocum, quia non praedicatur de omnibus subjicibilibus quando significative sumitur (text: *sumuntur*) secundum unum conceptum, sed sibi diversi conceptus correspondent, sicut super Porphyrium declaravi," *Summa logicae,* I, 38; ed. Böhner, p. 99. The reading *sumitur,* which seems preferable, is attested by several manuscripts, p. 100, note 37 (on their respective value, p. xiii). One fails to see how Ockham could have thought differently; since nothing exists that is not singular, every signification is a personal supposition for a singular; hence it is equivocal by its own nature.

[24] Properly speaking, Ockham says, there only is univocity in words; precisely because there is nothing really common in beings, no concept can be properly called univocal: "Circa primum dico *quod univocum proprie accipitur pro voce univoca,* quia accipitur secundum quod distinguitur contra aequivocum vel denominativum, et isto modo nihil est quaerere an ens dicat conceptum univocum Deo et creaturae," *Sent.* I, 2, 9, K. "Primo ergo videndum est de univoco secundum quod improprie dicitur de conceptu," ibid. Nothing could be more clear than this was in his own mind: "nullus conceptus unus praedicabilis de pluribus, sive per se primo modo, sive secundo modo, sive per accidens, sive necessario, sive contingenter, est conceptus univocus, *quia nullus conceptus predicabilis de pluribus est conceptus proprius uni rei, de illa praedicabilis et non de alia*" I, 2, 9, L. Cf. ibid., N; and again: "nullum univocum est de essentia univocatorum suorum," ibid., O. The usual formula of Ockham: a single concept common to God and creature, and predicable of both *in quid* (ibid., P), is a *substitute* for the univocity which cannot be properly attributed to concepts, but only to words.

[25] "Universaliter nihil quod est a parte rei est univocum quibuscumque," *Sent.,* I, 2, 9, U; Menges, *The Univocity . . . ,* p. 96, n. 95. Cf. "ita dico in proposito quod nihil a parte rei est univocum quibuscumque individuis, et tamen est aliquid praedicabile in quid de individuis," *Sent.,* I, 2, 7, X.—In a doctrine where being *qua* being is a "mental name," there is little to be said about it. Ockham rejects (naturally) the distinction of essence and existence. *Esse* is sometimes used as a noun (essence) and sometimes as a verb (existence), but, in both cases, it signifies identically the same thing. His favorite target, on this point, is the doctrine of the indifference of essence with respect to existence or non-existence (Avicenna). A non-existing essence cannot be indif-

ferent, because it is nothing: *Quodl.*, II, 7.

[26] *Sent.*, Prol. III, 9, F and L.

[27] There are causes and effects, there is no such thing as causality, because it would be a "real relation." The relation of causality is nothing outside of the two absolute things called cause and effect. If efficient causality were something else than the thing, it would have to be either anterior to the effect, or simultaneous with it, or posterior to it. It cannot be anterior, because there is no causality so long as there is no effect; it cannot be simultaneous with the effect, since once the effect is there, it is too late for the cause to produce it; it can still less be posterior to the effect, for if it were, the effect would have existed before being produced by its cause *Quodl.*, VI, 12. We know there is a cause when we know there is an effect, and vice versa. How do we know this? "The definition of the efficient cause is, to be that whose existence or presence is followed by something," *Quodl.*, IV, 1. And what is it "to effect"? "It is nothing else than that the effect exists at the presence of the thing," *Quodl.*, II, 9; cf. ibid. "quando effectus natus est naturaliter causari et esse ad praesentiam agentis, *tunc efficere non est aliud quam effectum sic esse.*" Carefully note the significance of the formula: to "effect" (to exercise efficient causality) reduces itself to the fact that the effect is present when its cause is present. Ockham does not doubt the existence of causes and effects; only, they are empirically given to him in sensible experience; like concepts in the mind, causes are works of nature; like all such works, these are submitted to the free will and to the absolute power of God. This does not prevent them from following a generally regular course (how to ascertain causes by the methods of presence and absence, *Sent.*, I, 1, 3, N), but it makes it impossible strictly to demonstrate that something is a cause: "non potest demonstrari quod aliquis effectus producitur a causa secunda . . . ; ideo non est mirabile si non potest demonstrari quod aliquid sit causa," *Sent.*, II, 4-5, I.

[28] All agree that God is the absolutely Prime Being; consequently, to prove that there is such a Prime Being is to prove that there is a God; it remains, then, to prove that there is only one, *Sent.*, I, 2, 10, B.—I). On the first point, Ockham relates the Scotist proof by the "effectibility" of being and the impossibility of going to infinity in the series of causes; a series of essentially ordered causes is impossible, ibid., D. But this notion of essentially ordered causes raises many difficulties (as it should in a doctrine where essences have no actual reality), ibid., K-M. The reason proving the primacy of an efficient cause is sufficient, and it is the reason of all philosophers; yet "the primacy of the Efficient seems to be more evidently proved by the conservation of reality by its cause than by its production, in the sense in which a thing is said to receive being immediately after not being. The reason for this is that it is difficult or impossible to prove against the philosophers that a series of things of same nature is not infinite; one of them can exist without the other one, as when they posited a begetting man before a begotten man and so on to infinity. It is likewise difficult to prove, about production, that a man cannot be produced by another man as by his total cause. And if these two were true, it would be difficult to prove that this process to infinity is impossible unless there is one single everlasting being on which the whole infinity is hanging." Let us rather prove that, since what is being caused is being conserved by that which causes it, at least so long as it continues to be, there must be a Prime Conserving Cause of what actually exists; ibid., O.—II). There is only one single absolutely Prime Being; the reason given by Scotus to this effect is valid; at least, it is probable, although it does not prove conclusively: "Haec ratio est probabilis, quamvis non demonstret sufficienter," ibid., P.—See Fr. Bruckmüller, *Die Gotteslehre Wilhelms von Ockham,* Munich, 1911. H. Becker, *Gottesbegriff und Gottesbeweis bei Wilhelm von Ockham,* Scholastik, 3 (1928) 369-393.

As is often the case, the Questions are more radical than the Commentary, or, rather, they more clearly reveal the import of the conclusion. Ochham's main concern is to make clear that the Prime Cause whose existence can be proved is *not* the infinite being proved by Duns Scotus. If God is defined an infinite being, or a being than which no greater can be nor be conceived, then "it cannot be known with evidence that God is," *Quodl.,* I, 1. The infinity of God can be proved from no finite effect, *Quodl.,* II, 2 and III, 1. The *Quodl.,* VII, 17-23, is directed against this position of Duns Scotus.—Ph. Böhner, *Zu Ockham's Beweis der Existenz Gottes,* FS., 32 (1950) 50-69. —On the possibility of actual infinity, Annaliese Maier, *Diskussionen über das aktuell Unendliche in der ersten Hälfte des 14. Jahrhunderts,* DTF., 25 (1947) 147-166, 317-337.

²⁹ *Quodl.* I, 1. Two definitions of God: 1) God is something better and more noble than anything else; 2) God is a being than which nothing better, higher (*prius*) or more perfect exists. In the first sense, one cannot prove that there is only one God, because one cannot even prove there is a God. If it were possible to prove the existence of such a God, the conclusion that there is only one God could be demonstrated. Such is not the case. On the contrary, we can prove the existence of a God in the second sense (as, in fact, Aristotle did), but then there is no evident demonstration that there is only one such God: "Sciendum tamen est quod potest demonstrari Deum esse accipiendo Deum secundo modo prius dicto, quia aliter esset processus in infinitum nisi esset aliquid in entibus quo nihil esset prius et perfectius; sed ex hoc non sequitur quod possit demonstrari quod tantum unum est tale, sed hoc fide tantum tenemus."—Scotus proves the oneness of God by the infinity of his intellect; but this is held on faith, it cannot be evidently demonstrated, op. cit., I, 1.

³⁰ The fact that there is contingency in things does not prove that there must be contingency in the Prime Cause (against Scotus), *Sent.,* I, 43, 1; on the contrary, it cannot be demonstrated by natural reason that, just as effects necessarily flow from the perfection of the sun, so also many effects do not necessarily flow from the divine being, so that these effects can be otherwise than as they are, ibid., M. An "immediate" cause is any cause whose presence is attended by an effect and whose absence is attended by the absence of the effect; every real cause is an immediate cause, *Sent.,* I, 45, 1, D. God is the cause of certain things, namely, the separate Intelligences, but it cannot be demonstrated that he is the cause of *all* things (including

corruptible ones), nor that he created them anew and contingently, *Sent.,* II, 6, B. So it cannot be proved that God is the immediate efficient cause of all things, *Quodl.,* II, 1; especially not of corruptible ones, II, 6; "God is the cause mediate or immediate of all things," and although this cannot be demonstrated, it can be the object of persuasion by authority and reason, *Quodl.,* III, 3. *Sent.,* I, 43, 1, L-O. It is still less demonstrable that God acts in view of an end offered to his will: "et ideo not potest probari quod tale agens agat propter finem," *Quodl.,* IV, 2.

³¹ It can be proved by natural reason that we have a soul similar to that of all other animated beings, that is, an extended form, generable and corruptible, but that we have a soul both incorporeal and immortal is something we only know by faith, *Quodl.,* I, 10. The sensitive soul and the intellectual soul are really distinct in man, but this is hard to prove because it cannot be deduced from evident premises. The sensitive soul and the form of corporeity are really distinct in animals as well as in man, only this is not easy to demonstrate, *Quodl.,* II, 10.

³² The question of knowing why certain acts are meritorious while others are not, leads Ockham sometimes to strange conclusions because supernatural merit hangs of the free will of God, to whose omnipotence Ockham sets no limits. But this is outside of natural and philosophical ethics. Positive ethics, which hangs on the decisions of positive law established by the jurists, is no object of science: "But the non-positive moral discipline is a demonstrative science, because a knowledge which syllogistically deduces conclusions from principles, or from things known by experience, is demonstrative. Now moral science is such a knowledge; therefore etc. The major is manifest. The minor is proved because there are in moral philosophy many principles known by themselves. For instance, that the will must conform to right reason. And that all avoidable evil should be avoided. Likewise, many principles are known there by experience, as is evident to those who follow it. Moreover, I say that this science is more certain than many other ones, for the reason that everybody can have a more certain experience of his own acts than of other things. From which it appears that this

science is most useful and evident," *Quodl.*, II, 14. This is in agreement with the possibility of an intuitive cognition of our own inner acts, *Quodl.*, I, 14; this text is a good example of psychological observation, including that of subconscious states which, up to then, had not attracted much attention.

[33] God has knowledge, not in virtue of his immateriality (for an immaterial form knowing nothing is not a contradictory notion) but because it is his nature to know: *Sent.* I, 35, 1, C. In God, science is his own essence, ibid., D. There is no distinction of reason between it and the divine essence because they are strictly the same thing, ibid., E. Three conclusions cannot be demonstrated by natural reason: 1) that God knows nothing outside of himself; 2) that God knows all things outside of himself; 3) that God knows something outside of himself. Concerning this third conclusion, however, Ockham thinks it can be proved to be probable, although not so as to convince an obstinate opponent (*protervus*). God is the prime object of God's cognition, *Sent.*, I, 35, 3, K. Supposing he knows something else, there is no reason to posit distinct relations of reason between him and the intelligibles, *Sent.*, I, 35, 4, E-F (an important text). Ideas have no subjective and real being in God, "and nevertheless they are in him objectively, as objects known by him, *because the Ideas are the things themselves producible by God*," *Sent.*, I, 35, 5, G. Consequently: "the Ideas of all producible things are distinct, just as the things themselves are distinct from one another," ibid. Thirdly, there are distinct Ideas of matter, form and, universally speaking, of all the essential and integral parts of beings. Fourthly, the Ideas are ideas of individuals, not of species, because only singulars are producible outside of the mind, and nothing else. Fifthly, there are no Ideas of genera, differences nor of any other universals. Manifestly, since an infinity of things are producible by God, he has an infinity of Ideas of this infinity of singulars, ibid. God does know the other beings by the ideas he has of them; they are neither his very intellect, nor an intermediary object between God and what he knows; he knows them as objects terminating his intellection, ibid., H. "Ipsae ideae sunt ipsamet cognita a Deo alia a Deo," ibid. Since they have no

subjective being, they have no eternal being; they are eternal *qua* eternally known, ibid., K—L. This divine cognition is practical, *Sent.*, I, 35, 6, D. It is the same thing to say that the perfections of creatures are contained in God and to say that creatures themselves are contained in God, *Sent.*, I, 36, 1, E—Several propositions concerning the Ideas were censured at Avignon in 1326, as philosophically false, not as heretical, RHE., 18 (1922) 264. Cf. art., 43, p. 268. Just as our agent intellect does not produce the intelligible being of its objects, God neither creates nor produces from eternity any intelligible objects; he just knows them (against the "diminished" being of the Scotist Ideas, I, 36, 1, Q); even in God universal objects have no being, *Sent.*, I, 36, 1, R. In this view, since Ideas have no being of their own, "stone," "man," etc., have not *been* from all eternity; and since every cognition is the cognition of something, there has been no "known being" of creatures so long as they were not created. Before the creation of the world, there was divine cognition, but there was for God no creatures to be known: "cognitio divina potest esse sine esse cognito creaturae, et ita fuit de facto ante mundi creationem, quia tunc fuit cognitio divina, et tunc non fuit esse cognitum creaturae, quia illud esse cognitum creaturae est ipsa creatura (i.e., it has no being of its own apart from the creature that is-being-known), vel esse existere creaturae, et sic est idem realiter cum creatura, et ideo sicut verum fuit dicere quod creatura vel lapis non fuit ab aeterno, et ita verum est dicere quod esse cognitum non fuit ab aeterno, "*Sent.*, 1, 36, 1, X. Hence the radical destruction of Avicennian and Averroistic necessity: "God does not necessarily will the intelligible being of the creature," ibid., BB. All the following texts should be read: CC, DD, FF, with the radical conclusion: the intelligible being of creatures is not more necessary in itself than their actual being is, GG. The Avicennian essences are not being subjected to God, they are being suppressed.

[34] This important point belongs in the history of theology *qua* theology. Read, on this question, R. Guelluy, *Philosophie et théologie chez Guillaume d'Ockham,* ch. V, especially pp. 248-258.

[35] Ghelluy's dispassionate interpretation of Ockham's theology, rooted in a deep

understanding of his philosophy, rightly concludes: "What is proper to Ockham is not to have said that theology, such as we can make it, is not a science, it is *the explanation of this position he provides,* in saying that a quidditative concept proper to the thing is the only one that certainly contains a real quiddity (*quid rei*) and that, in consequence, the notions which express the divine attributes, or those that befit creature as well as its creator, have but *a nominal definition,*" p. 258 (italics ours), This is, indeed, the whole point.

[36] Ockham has, in fact, elaborated a noetic of the concept which made a scientifically conceived theology a contradiction in terms.—A. Lang, *Die Wege der Glaubensbegründung bei den Scholastikern des 14. Jahrhunderts,* Münster i. W., 1931 (Beiträge, 1931, 1-2). P. Vignaux, *Sur Luther et Ockham,* FS., 32 (1950) 21-30.

[37] L. Baudry, *Le Tractatus de principiis theologiae attribué à G. d' Occam,* Paris, J. Vrin. Authenticity not established, but not chronologically impossible (the treatise was written before 1350, p. 13); Baudry does not consider it authentic, pp. 15-16. The two "principles of theology" are: 1) that God can make all that which it is not contradictory to make (divine omnipotence); 2) that beings should not be multiplied without necessity (Ockham's razor). The main consequences are: no distinction of essence and existence; no "being of essence"; no eternal essences in God (Ideas); no such being in things, so all that is real is singular; no principle of individuation; no formal distinctions in things; act and potency, privation, negation, relation, all relations, are just the singular substance of the thing; motion is the mobile thing; so are time, number, dimensions etc.; truth is the true proposition itself; intellection is about singulars not about a "common nature" that does not exist; distinction between intuitive and abstractive cognition; the intuition of what does not exist is possible (since God has eternally intuited non-existing singulars); intuitive cognition comes first; from the cognition of a being we cannot infer any other still unknown being; from the cognition of a cause, we cannot infer not actually intuited effects; we cannot form any abstract concept proper to God, because we have no intuition of him.

See L. Baudry, Introduction, pp. 18-27; consequences concerning logic, pp. 27-30; Ockham's doctrine is a reaction against the necessitarianism condemned in 1277: "In short, his philosophy is an anti-Averroistic philosophy," p. 42.—This treatise can safely be read by those who desire a short cut to Ockhamism, which it exposes with fidelity, order and clarity. We are indebted to it for calling to our attention at least one point that had escaped us while reading Ockham: there is no reason to conceive celestial bodies as made up of another matter than that of the four elements; the main objection to the contrary, namely their incorruptibility, has no weight in the mind of a theologian, p. 138, n. 41. We have long believed and taught that this was one of the great discoveries made by Galileo.

[38] GABRIEL BIEL (d. 1495), *Epitome et Collectorium ex Occamo super quatuor libros sententiarum,* Tübingen, 1495, 1501, 1512; with the supplement by W. Steinback, Paris, 1521; Basel, 1512; Lyon, 1514.—C. Ruch, art. *Biel,* DTC., II (1910) 814-825. E. Bonke, *Doctrina nominalistica de fundamento ordinis moralis apud Gulielmum de Ockham et Gabriel Biel,* C F., 1944, 57-83. In his Prologue Biel announces his intention to write an abridgment of Ockham's commentary (hence the title, *epitome*) but also to fill up the gaps where Ockham says little or nothing, and, in order to do so, to collect the opinions of other masters on these questions (hence the second title, *collectorium*). In the first Question of his Prologue, reprinted by Ph. Böhner (*W. Ockham Quaestio prima,* pp. 53-63), Biel writes: "Ad illud pro captu meo respondeo, prout intelligo, quia hunc modum loquendi Doctoris non accepto . . ." p. 60. He can see the weak points of the doctrine: can we have an intuitive cognition of the non-existence of an object? "Hoc frequenter dictum est a Doctore, sed non probatum, nec per experientiam notum," p. 63. Then he proves it in his own way, and the demonstration deserves to be read. The *Epitome* has been widely read, especially in Germany. In some universities (Wittenberg and Erfurt) the "moderns" were called *Gabrielistae;* it is by his reading of Peter of Ailly and of Biel that Luther was introduced to the "sect of Ockham." By that time, however, Ockhamism was way beyond Ockham. On the position of Biel himself: C. Feckes, *Die Rechtfertigungs-*

lehre des Gabriel Biel und ihre Stellung innerhalb der nominalistische Schule, Münster i. W., 1925.

[39] CENTILOQIUM THEOLOGICUM, attributed to Ockham in the edition of his commentary on the *Sentences,* Lyon, 1495. Authenticity rejected by Fr. Böhner, *The Centiloquium attributed to Ockham,* Franciscan Studies (1941) n. 1, 58-72; n. 2, 35-54; n. 3, 62-70; (1942) 49-60, 146-157, 251-301. Same author: *The Medieval Crisis of Logic and the Author of the Centiloquium attributed to Ockham,* Franciscan Studies, 25 (1944) 151-170. Its authenticity is considered doubtful by L. Baudry, *Guillaume d'Ockham,* 270-271, 286-287; it is maintained by E. Iserloh, *Um die Echtheit des Centiloquium. Ein Beitrag zur Wertung Ockhams und zur Chronologie seiner Werke,* Gregorianum, 30 (1949) 78-103, 309-346—The attribution or non-attribution of this work to Ockham does not modify the general interpretation of the doctrine. The impossiblility of proving the existence of God by a finite series of causes, which it denies, is likewise denied in the *Sentences* of Ockham (the *Centiloqium* does not speak of the proof by the conservation of the world); the *Centiloqium* and Ockham agree to consider as simply probable the oneness of God, the intensive infinity of God's power, his absolute omnipotence, etc.

[40] The terminology is very confused on this point and gives rise to many verbal controversies. Prantl has critized the appellation "nominalist" and the label "nominalism" applied to Ockham (*Geschichte der Logik,* IV, 147 ff.); historically speaking, Ehrle says that the followers of Ockham were first called "terminists" by their adversaries, the realists (Gerson, *De modo significandi,* in *Opera,* ed. Dupin, IV, 819); then came "nominalists" *(nominales),* which was in fact an old appellation; then "conceptualists," and, much more recently, "conceptualists," F. Ehrle, *Der Sentenzenkommentar . . . ,* pp. 106-108. Since no single term can sufficiently define a doctrinal position, the simplest appellation might well be "Ockhamism;" at any rate, there is no doubt that almost every one of Ockham's philosophical positions is affected by his fundamental denial of the reality of universality under any form.—As has already been noted, the appellation had been common in the

twelfth century; it never completely disappeared in the thirteenth century: F. Pelster, *Nominales und reales im 13. Jahrhundert,* Sophia, 1946, 154-161.

[41] Statement of September 25, 1339, CUP., II, 485. Statement of December 29, 1340, CUP., II, 505-507; UNIV., 195-197 *(de reprobatione quorumdam errorum Ockhanicorum).* In the fifteenth century, Ockhamism was to become in France a quasi-political problem; by that time, the University of Paris had lost its autonomy and been subjected to the authority of the French king and of the parliament. This enabled the Thomists to obtain, March 1, 1474, an edict of banishment against the Nominalists. The texts concerning the banishment are published in Ehrle, *Der Sentenzenkommentar,* 305-321. The Nominalists replied by a collective manifesto; text in Ehrle, 322-326. This document addressed in 1474 to King Louis XI, begins by a definition of the words Nominalists and Realists: those who do not posit as many beings as there are terms, and those who do: "Anno 1473 illi doctores Nominales dicti sunt qui non multiplicant res principaliter signatas per terminos secundum multiplicationem terminorum; Reales autem, qui e contra res multiplicatas esse contendunt secundum multiplicationem terminorum." (Ehrle, 322). English transl. in UNIV., 355-360.

[42] ADAM WODHAM OFM (Wodeham, Goddam) d. 1358. Editions, GDP., 587. Fr. Ehrle, *Der Sentenzenkommentar,* 96-103. On the 1512 edition of the commentary by Johannes Major, 96, note 7; notice of Major on Wodham, 98, note 3; text of the Preface of Wodham to Ockham's logic, 100-101. On Wodham as "imitator" of Ockham, 79, note 4 (Peter of Candia).

[43] ROBERT HOLKOT OP. (d. 1349). Editions, GDP., 588. *Super quatuor libros Sententiarum quaestiones, Quaedam conferentiae, De imputabilitate peccati, Determinationes quarumdam aliarum quaestionum,* Lyon, 1497, 1510, 1518. P. Duhem, *Etudes sur Léonard de Vinci,* 2 ser., Paris, 1909, 399-403 (on the infinite). Michalski, *La physique nouvelle,* 102-111, 125-133 J. C. Wey CSB. *The Sermo finalis of Robert Holkot,* MS., 11 (1949) 219-223.—Similar positions have been found by Michalski (op. cit., pp.

133-137) in the commentary on the *Sentences* (dated 1367) by the Cistercian GOTTSCHALK OF POMUK. His theological probabilism resembles that of Ockham.— We have already noted the extremist position of the English Dominican CRATHORN, OP., *Quaestiones de universalibus magistrorum Crathorn OP., anonymi OFM., Joannis Canonici OFM*, ed J. Kraus, Münster i. W., 1937. J. Kraus, *Die Stellung des Oxforder Dominikanerlehrers Crathorn zu Thomas von Aquin*, ZKT., 57 (1933) 66-88 (Crathorn was at Oxford what Nicholas of Autrecourt was at Paris, the "Hume of the Middle Ages." p. 88). On JOANNES CANONICUS OFM (John Marbres) whose text has been published by J. Kraus. L. Baudry, *En lisant Jean le Chanoine*, AHDL., 9 (1934) 175-197.

44 GREGORY OF RIMINI OSA., d. 1358 (Gregorius Ariminensis). The commentary on the *Sentences*, Books I and II is found in ancient editions: *Lectura in primum et secundum librum sententiarum*, Paris, 1494, 1562. K. Werner, *Die Augustinische Psychologie in ihre mittelalterlich-scholastischen Einkleidung uns Ausgestaltung*, Sitzungsberichte, Wien, 1882, 449-452, 488-494; *Die Scholastik des späteren Mittelalters*, III (*Der Augustinismus in der scholastik des späteren Mittelalters*), Wien, 1883, 84-100. P. Duhem, *Etudes sur Léonard de Vinci*, 2 ser., Paris, 1909, 385-399 (on the infinite). J. Wursdörfer, *Erkennen und Wissen nach Gregor von Rimini. Ein Beitrag zur Geschichte der Erkentnistheorie des Nominalismus*, Münster i. W., 1917 (Beiträge, 20, 1). P. Vignaux, *Justification et prédestination au XIVe siècle. Duns Scot, Pierre d'Auriole et Grégoire de Rimini*, Paris, 1934, pp. 141-175. M. Schüler, *Prädestination, Sünde und Freiheit bei Gregor von Rimini*, Stuttgart, 1934.

45 JOHN OF MIRECOURT Cist. (Joannes de Mirecuria), on his still unpublished works, F. Ehrle, *Der Sentenzenkommentar*, 103-106. Text of the 1347 condemnation in CUP., II, 610-614. C. Michalski, *Die vielfachen Redaktionen einiger Kommentare zu Petrus Lombardus*, Miscellanea Ehrle, I, 226-236. F. Stegmüller, *Die zwei Apologien des Jean de Mirecourt*, RTAM., 5 (1933) 40-78, 192-204.

46 The text of the justification, by John of Mirecourt, of the propositions con-

demned in 1347, is published in A. Birkenmajer, *Ein Rechtfertigungsschreiben Johanns von Mirecourt*, in *Vermischte Untersuchungen*, 91-128. The propositions themselves suffer from a certain lack of theological seriousness. They show how deeply the logic of the Faculty of Arts had invaded the Faculty of Theology.

47 NICHOLAS OF AUTRECOURT (Nicolaus de Ultricuria). The treatise *Exigit ordo executionis* in J. R. O'Donnell, *Nicholas of Autrecourt*, MS., I (1939) 179-280.—On the doctrine, G. M. Manser, *Drei Zweifler am Kausalprinzip im XIV Jahrhundert*, JPT., 37 (1912) 301-305; same author, *Die Geistekrise des XIV Jahrhunderts*, Freiburg i. Br., 1915. H. Rashdall, *Nicholas de Ultricuria, a Mediaeval Hume*, Proceedings of the Aristotelian Society, 8 (1907) 1-27. J. Lappe, *Nicolaus von Autrecourt, Sein Leben, seine Philosophie, seine Schriften*, Münster i. W., 1908 (Beiträge, 6, 2). P. Vignaux, art. *Nicolas d'Autrecourt*, DTC., 11, (1931) 562-587. J. R. O'Donnell, *The Philosophy of Nicholas of Autrecourt and his Appraisal of Aristotle*, MS., 4 (1942) 97-125. J. R. Weinberg, *Nicolaus of Autrecourt, A Study in Fourteenth-Century Thought*, Princeton, 1948. M. Dal Pra, *Nicola di Autrecourt*, Milano, 1951. E. Maccagnolo, *Metafisica e gnoseologia in Nicolò d' Autrecourt*, RFNS., 45 (1953) 36-53.

48 RICHARD BILLINGHAM, Fr. Ehrle, *Der Sentenzenkommentar . . .* , 202-204.

49 RICHARD BRINKEL OFM, as quoted by Peter of Candia: Fr. Ehrle, *Der Sentenzenkommentar . . .* , 68-69; "ex logica Brinchil," 71; information on Brinkel, 277-278. GDP., 594.

50 JOHN BURIDAN (Johannes Buridanus) d. after 1358.—Editions, GDP., 595, and E. Faral, *Jean Buridan*, 499-593. *Summulae* or *Compendium logicae* with the commentary of Johannes Dorp, Paris, 1504; Oxford, 1637; London, 1740. *Quaestiones super octo Physicorum libros*, Paris, 1509, 1516. *Quaestiones in libros de anima*, Paris, 1516; *Parva naturalia*, in *Quaestiones et decisiones physicales . . . Alberti de Saxonia, Thimonis, Buridani . . .* , Paris, 1516, 1568. *In Metaphysicam Aristotelis quaestiones*, Paris, 1518. *Quaestiones super decem libros Ethicorum Aristotelis ad Nicomachum*, Paris,

1513, 1518; Oxford, 1637. *Quaestiones in libros Politicorum Aristotelis,* Paris, 1500; Oxford, 1640. *Quaestiones super libros IV De caelo et mundo,* ed. E. A. Moody, Cambridge (Mass.), 1942.

Necessary starting point: Edm. Faral *Jean Buridan, maître ès arts de l'Université de Paris,* HLF., 38 (1949) 462-605; same author, *Jean Buridan. Notes sur les manuscrits, les éditions et le contenu de ses oeuvres,* AHDL., 15 (1946) 1-53. On the doctrine: C. Prantl, *Geschichte der Logik,* IV, Leipzig, 1870, 14-38. P. Duhem, *Etudes sur Léonard de Vinci,* 2 series, 379-384, 420-423, 431-441; 3 series, 1-259; 279-286; 350-360 (also on Oresme). J. Bulliot, *Jean Buridan et le mouvement de la terre,* Revue de Philosophie, 14 (25) 5-24; texts and French transl. H. Bascour, art. *Buridan,* DHGE., 10 (1938) 1370-1375. E. A. Moody, *John Buridan and the Habitability of the Earth,* Speculum, 16 (1941) 415-425. L. Thorndike, *Buridan's Questions on the Physiognomy Ascribed to Aristotle,* Speculum, 18 (1943) 99-103. C. Michalski, *Les courants critiques . . . ,* 202-209, 238-242; *La physique nouvelle,* 113-117, 114-149. The influence of Buridan went far beyond what we can imagine. The "Answer" of the masters of Cologne to the Princes, December 24, 1425, stresses the fact that realism used to be the common doctrine in universities "before Buridan" (*ante Buridanum*), before "the age of Buridan" (*ante saeculum Buridani*); text in Fr. Ehrle, *Der Sentenzenkommentar Peters von Candia,* pp. 283-284.

[51] On the notion of physical substance in Buridan and Albert of Saxony, A. Maier, *An der Grenze . . . ,* Index of proper names, 381-382. The research work initiated by Duhem and whose present development is remarkable should not obscure two facts. First, the late mediaeval physicists are still struggling with the Aristotelian notion of physical qualities and their efforts to apply measurement to these qualities, under the form of intensities, could not lead to decisive scientific results; the importance of Descartes' criticism of qualitative physics can here be seen in its true light. Secondly, the notion of physics still remains tied up with the Aristotelian tenet that scientific knowledge deals with the universal only; this point can be clearly seen in Buridan's *Quaestiones de caelo et mundo,* ed. E. A.

Moody, 3-7.—Metaphysics is wisdom; unlike theology, which deals with faith and argues from revelation; metaphysics argues from natural reason only, *In Metaph.,* I, 2. In *Metaph.,* lib. IV, qq. 8-9, Buridan establishes that existence (*esse*) and essence are identical in reality and only differ in reason; existence is the thing known as present; essence is the same thing known apart from the fact that it is either existent or present. The truth of the mental proposition is the mental proposition itself, *In Metaph.,* II, 1. Genera and species are, in the first place, terms existing in the mind, then the words, spoken or written, signifying them, op. cit., VI, 1.—Since it seems impossible to avoid the animal, let us recall that the origin of the problem illustrated by Buridan's ass has been traced, long ago, to Aristotle, *De caelo* II, 13, 295 b, 32: M. Baumgartner, *Ueberwegs Grundriss,* 10 ed., Berlin, 1915, p. 621. See, same page, information about the "pons asinorum."

[52] ALBERT OF SAXONY, d. 1390.—Editions, GDP., 596. *Quaestiones subtilissimae Alberti de Saxonia super libros Posteriorum,* Venice, 1497. *Logica Albertuttii . . . ,* Venice, 1522. *Sophismata Alberti de Saxonia,* Paris, 1489. *Tractatus obligationum, Insolubilia,* Paris, 1490, 1495. His Questions on the Logic of Ockham are found in Ockham, *Expositio aurea,* Bologna, 1496. *Subtilissimae quaestiones super octo libros Physicorum,* Venice, 1504, 1516. *Quaestiones in libros de caelo et mundo,* Venice, 1520. *Quaestiones in libros De generatione,* Venice, 1504, 1505, 1518 (includes the commentaries of Giles of Rome and of Marsilius of Inghen). A. Dyroff, *Ueber Albertus von Sachsen,* Baeumker-Festgabe, Münster i. W., 1913, 330-342. G. Heidingsfelder, *Albert von Sachsen. Sein Lebensgang und sein Kommentar zur Nikomachischen. Ethik des Aristoteles,* Münster i. W., 1926 (Beiträge, 22, 3-4).—Cf. C. Prantl, *Geschichte der Logik,* IV, 60-88. P. Duhem, *Etudes . . . ,* II, 379-384, 420-423, 431-441; III, 1-259, 279-286, 350-360; same author, *Le système du monde,* IV, 124-142.

[53] NICHOLAS ORESME d. 1382.—Editions, GDP., 595-596. *Traictie de la première invention des monnaies de Nicole Oresme,* ed. M. L. Wolowski, Paris, 1864. A. J. Menut, *Nicolas Oresme. Le Livre des*

Ethiques d'Aristote, New York, 1940. A. J. Menut and A. J. Denomy CSB., *Maistre Nicole Oresme, le Livre du Ciel et du Monde, Text and Commentary,* MS., 3 (1941) 185-280; 4 (1942) 159-297; 5 (1943) 167-333.—On the doctrine, P. Duhem, *Etudes sur Léonard de Vinci* . . . , 3rd series, 346-405, 481-492. E. Bridey, *La théorie de la monnaie au XIVe siècle, Nicole Oresme,* Paris, 1906. E. Borchert, *Die Lehre von der Bewegung bei Nicolaus Oresme,* Münster i. W., 1934 (Beiträge, 31, 5); *Der Einfluss des Nominalismus auf die Christologie der Spätscholastik nach dem Traktat "De communicatione idiomatum" des Nicolaus Oresme,* Münster i. W., 1940 (Beiträge, 35 4-5). Anneliese Maier, *La doctrine de Nicole d'Oresme sur les "configurations intensionum,"* RSPT., 32 (1948) 52-67. G. W. Coopland, *Nicole Oresme and the Astrologers: A Study of His Livre de Divinacions,* Harvard University Press, 1952.—On Oresme's disciple PETER OF CEFFONDS, C. Michalski, *La physique nouvelle* . . . , 155 (on Oresme, 150-155).

⁵⁴ MARSILIUS OF INGHEN, d. 1396.—Editions, GDP., 603-604. *Quaestiones super quatuor libros Sententiarum* Argentorati, 1501. *Marsilii de Inguen textus dialectices* . . . , in the editions of the *Summulae* of Peter of Spain, Wien, 1512, 1516. *Expositio super libros Priorum,* Venice, 1516 (together with the commentary of Giles of Rome). *Egidius cum Marcello et Alberto* (of Saxony) *De generatione,* Venice, 1518. *Abbreviationes libri Physicorum,* Venice, 1521.—G. Ritter, *Studien zur Spätscholastik, I, Marsilius von Inghen und die Okkamistische Schule in Deutschland,* Heidelberg, 1921; *II, Via antiqua und via moderna auf den deutschen Universitäten des XV Jahrhunderts,* Heidelberg, 1922 (important for the history of the diffusion of Ockhamism). Cf. C. Prantl, *Geschichte der Logik,* IV, 94-103. Fr. Pelster, *Der Heidelberger Magister artium und Baccalarius theologiae Heilmann Wunnenberg als lehrer des Marsilius von Inghen und Erklärer der Sentenzen,* TQ., 1944, 83-86.

⁵⁵ HENRY OF HAINBUCH (of Langestein) d. 1397.—Editions, GDP., 604; on his unpublished works, O. Hartwig, *Leben und Schriften Heinrichs von Langenstein,* Marburg, 1858. H. Pruckner, *Studien zu den astrologischen Schriften des Heinrich von Langenstein,* Leipzig, 1933.

⁵⁶ HENRY TOTTING OF OYTA (d. 1397). Fr. Ehrle, *Der Sentenzenkommentar Peters von Candia,* p. 141, refers to the work of G. Sommerfeldt, in Mitteilungen des Instituts für österreich. Geschichtforschung, 25 (1904) 576-604; see the long note of Ehrle, op. cit., p. 141, n. 10. On Henry Pape, ibid., p. 142, under the year 1369, and p. 143, end of note 10. A. Lang, *Henrici Totting de Oyta, Quaestio de sacra scriptura,* Münster i. W., 1932, biography of Henry in the Preface; same author, *Henrici Totting de Oyta Quaestio de veritatibus catholicis,* Münster i. W., 1933; *Heinrich Totting von Oyta* . . . , Münster i. W., 1937 (Beiträge, 33, 4-5).

⁵⁷ SWINESHEAD (Swynshed, Suiseth, Suincet), a fellow of Merton College, 1348.—Ricardi Suiseth Anglici, *Calculationes,* Venice, 1520. His Questions on the *Sentences* do not seem to have been studied. C. Prantl (*Geschichte der Logik,* p. 90) barely mentions his name. On his scientific ideas, P. Duhem, *Etudes sur Léonard de Vinci,* 3rd series, Paris, 1913, 413-420, 451-460. C. Michalski, *Le criticisme et le scepticisme,* 38-39, 79-80. A. de Poorter, *Un recueil peu connu de Questions sur les Sentences,* RNSP., 33 (1931) 487-491.

⁵⁸ WILLIAM HEYTISBURY, a fellow of Merton College in 1370, *Tractatus Gulielmi Hentisberi* . . . , Venice, 1494 (with commentaries by Cajetan of Tiene). C. Prantl, *Geschichte der Logik,* IV, 90-93. P. Duhem, *Etudes sur Léonard de Vinci,* 3rd series, Paris, 1913, 406-408, 468-471.

⁵⁹ RICHARD FITZ RALPH (Siraph, Armaghanus). Biographical: A. Gwynn, *Richard Fitz Ralph, Archbishop of Armagh.* Studies, 22 (1933) 389-405, 591-607; 23 (1934) 395-411; 24 (1935) 25-42, 558-572; 25 (1936) 81-96; 26 (1937) 50-67. Indications concerning the doctrine in C. Michalski, *Le criticisme et le scepticisme,* 52-53, 73-74.

⁶⁰ JOHN BACONTHORP Carm.—Editions, GDP., 613. *Joannis Baconis Commentaria seu Quaestiones super quatuor libros Sententiarum,* Milan, 1510; Venice, 1527; Paris, 1518; with the *Quaestiones Quodlibetales,* Cremona, 1618. *Compendium legis Christi cum quodlibetis,* Venice, 1527. —K. Werner, *Der Averroismus* . . . , 231-265.—B. M. Xiberta, *Le thomisme de l'Ecole Carmélitaine,* MM., I, 441-448.

Chrysogone du Saint-Sacrement, *Maître Jean Baconthrop. Les sources, la doctrine, les disciples,* RNSP., 34 (1932) 341-365.

On the Carmelite school: B. M. Xiberta OC., *De scriptoribus scholasticis saeculi XIV ex ordine Carmelitarum,* Louvain, 1931 (Biblioth. de la Revue d'hist. ecclés., VI); *Guiu Terrena Carmelita de Perpinyà,* Barcinone, 1932; *Methodus historico-critica et auctores scholastici Ord. Carmeli,* SRHC., 585-594. A. G. Little, OTT., 276-277.

[61] THOMAS WILTON (Thomas Anglicus), C. Michalski, *La lutte pour l'âme à Oxford et à Paris au XIVe siècle,* Proceedings, Seventh International Congress of Philosophy, Oxford, 1931, 508-515; *Le criticisme et le scepticisme,* 49-52.

PART ELEVEN

CHAPTER III. THE SECOND AVERROISM

[62] JOHN OF JANDUN (Johannes de Janduno). d. 1328.—Editions, GDP., 613. *Quaestiones in XII libros metaphysicorum,* Venice, 1525, 1553, 1560, 1586. *Quaestiones in libros Physicorum,* Venice, 1575, 1596; Paris, 1506. *Quaestiones in libros de Coelo et Mundo,* Venice, 1501 . . . 1552, 1589. *Quaestiones in libros de anima,* Venice, 1473 . . . 1561, 1587. *Quaestiones super Parvis Naturalibus,* Venice, 1505, 1589. *Quaestiones in Averroem De substantia orbis,* Venetiis, 1481 . . . 1514, 1552, 1589.—K. Werner, *Der Averroismus* . . . , 265-268. E. Gilson, *La doctrine de la double vérité,* Etudes de philosophie médiévale, Strasbourg, 1921, 51-75. J. Rivière, art. *Jean de Jandun,* DTC., 8 (1924) 764-765. Konst. Michalski, *Dysputa miedzy Janem z Jandun* (d. *1328*) *a Bartlomiejem z Bruges* (d. *1356*), Collectanea theologica, 17 (1936) 317-325 (summed up in French, pp. 325-326; note the discovery of a treatise *De specie intelligibili* by John of Jandun).

John of Jandun is often mistaken for JOHN OF GHENT (Joannes de Gandavo) a master in theology at Paris *ca.* 1303. The name printed on some editions of John of Jandun: Joannes de Janduno Gandavensi, does not make sense: Jandun and Ghent are both in Belgium, but they are not the same city.

[63] Like all the Averroists, John of Jandun rejects the distinction of essence and existence. In his *Metaphysics,* lib. IV, qu. 3, John discusses the problem at great length. Naturally, he refutes Avicenna by the reasons of Averroes. Thomas Aquinas (*opinio antiqui Expositoris in suo tractatu De ente et essentia*) is then refuted on the strength of the typically Aristotelian argument: "in separate substances being is subsisting by itself, and not truly participated, because it is essentially identical with essence," text in M. Grabmann, *Circa historiam* . . . , 74.

[64] This is a clear allusion to the classical text of Gregory the Great, *In Evangel.,* II, hom. 26; PL., 76, 1197. Cf. Thomas Aquinas, *Summa theologiae,* I, I, 8, obj. 2a.—Apart from his dialectical irony, we find no proof of religious incredulity in John of Jandun. Since, however, the origins of this attitude are often traced back to the thirteenth and fourteenth centuries, see L. Massignon, *La légende des trois imposteurs,* Revue d'histoire religieuse, 82 (1920) 74-78. J. Presser, *Das Buch "De tribus impostoribus"* Amsterdam, 1926. M. Esposito, *Una manifestazione d'incredulità religiosa: il detto dei "Tre impostatori" et la sua transmissione da Federico II a Pomponazzi,* Archivo storico italiano, 16 (1931) 3-48.

[65] MARSILIUS OF PADUA, d. between 1336 and 1343.—Texts in C. W. Previte-Orton, *The Defensor Pacis of Marsilius of Padua,* Cambridge Univ. Press, 1928. R. Scholz, *Marsilius von Padua, Defensor pacis* (Fontes Juris Germanici Antiqui) Hannover, 2 vols., 1932-1933.—On the doctrine, G. de Lagarde, *La naissance de l'esprit laïque, II, Marsile de Padoue ou le premier théoricien de l'Etat laïque,* Saint - Paul - Trois - Châteaux (Drome) France, 1934; same author, *Marsile de Padoue et Guillaume d'Ockham,* RSR., 17 (1937) 168-185, 428-454. R. Scholz, *Marsilius von Padua und die Genesis des modernen Staatsbewusstseins,* Historische Zeitschrift, 1937, 88-103. C. W. Previte-Orton, *Marsilius of Padua,* Proceedings of the British Academy, 1935, 137-183. A. Checchini, *Interpretazione storica di*

Marsilio da Padova, Padua, 1942. G. Miglio, *Questioni Marsiliane,* RFNS., 38 (1946) 26-37. A. Gewirth, *Marsilius of Padua, The Defender of Peace.* Vol. I: *Marsilius of Padua and Medieval Political Philosophy,* New York, 1951.

[66] PETER OF ABANO, d. *ca.* 1315.—Editions, GDP., 613. *Conciliator differentiarum philosophorum et praecipue medicorum,* Venice, 1476 . . . 1565. *Expositio problematum Aristotelis,* Mantua, 1475; Padua, 1482. — On the doctrine, Bruno Nardi, *La teoria dell'anima secondo Pietro d'Abano,* Milano, 1912; *Intorno alle dottrine filosofiche di Pietro d'Abano,* Milano, 1921. L. Norpoth, *Zur Bio-Bibliographie und Wissenschaftslehre des Pietro d'Abano, Mediziner, Philosophen und Astronomen in Padua,* Kyklos, 3 (1930) 292-353. B. Nardi, *Saggi di filosofia dantesca,* Milan, 1930 (Dante and Pietro d'Abano). C. Giacon, *Pietro d'Abano e l'Averroismo padovano,* Società Italiana per il progresso delle scienze (Venice, 1937), Roma, 1938; II, 334-339. Erm. Troilo, *Aristotelismo e averroismo padovano,* Padova, 1939; same author, *Per l'averroismo padovano o veneto,* Venice, 1940.

[67] TADDEO OF PARMA, S. Vanni Rovighi, *La psicologia averroisticca di Taddeo di Parma,* RFNS., 33 (1931) 504-517. M. Grabmann, *Studien über den Averroisten Taddeo da Parma (ca.* 1320), MG., II, 1936, 239-260. S. Vanni Rovighi, *Le "Quaestiones de Anima" di Taddeo da Parma* (text and introduction) Milano, 1951; see especially qu. III, which identifies the rational soul with a separate Intelligence.

[68] ANGELO OF AREZZO, M. Grabmann, *Der Bologneser Averroist Angelo d'Arezzo (ca.* 1325) MG., II, 261-271.

[69] GENTILE OF CINGOLI, M. Grabmann, *Gentile da Cingoli, ein italienischer Aristoteleserklärer aus der Zeit Dantes,* Sitzungsberichte, 1940, 9; Munich, 1941.

[70] PAUL OF VENICE (Paolo Nicoletti da Udine, Paolo Veneto) d. 1429. *In libros de anima explanatio,* Venice, 1504; *Summa philosophiae naturalis,* Venice, 1503.— E. Renan, *Averroes . . . ,* 344-346. K. Werner, *Die Augustinische Psychologie . . . ,* 486. C. Prantl, *Geschichte der Logik,* IV, 118-140. F. Momigliano, *Paolo Veneto e le correnti del pensiero religioso*

e filosofico del suo tempo (1372-1429), Atti dell' Accademia di Udine, 1905-1907. P. Gothein, *Paolo Veneto e Proscodimo dei Conti, maestri padovani di Lodovico Foscarini,* Rinascita, 1942, 236-243.

On the Averroistic movement in the fifteenth and sixteenth centuries, besides the already quoted work of E. Renan: L. Mabilleau, *Etude historique sur la philosophie de la Renaissance en Italie,* Paris, 1881. H. Busson, *Les sources et le développement du rationalisme dans la littérature française de la Renaissance (1533-1601),* Paris, 1922.—The center of the controversy remains the notion of the intellective soul. Is it, as Alexander Aphrodisiensis says it is, united with matter, extended as matter is, individuated by it, educible from it, generable and corruptible? Or is it, according to Averroes, separated from matter, one in all men, ungenerable and incorruptible? The "opinion of faith" agrees with Alexander that it is united with matter and multiplied by it; the same *opinio fidei* agrees with Averroes that it is unextended, incorruptible and not educible from the potency of matter; the opinion of Aristotle is what one makes it to be. On Pietro Pomponazzi (Petrus Pomponatius, 1462-1525), pupil of Nicoletti Vernias, see G. Heidingsfelder, *Zum Unsterblichkeitsstreit . . . ,* ADGM., 1267-1270; his controvery with Caspar Contarini (1483-1542), art. cit., 1271-1276; controversy of Bartholomew of Spina OP., against both Pomponazzi and Cajetan, art. cit., 1280-1286. Text of the treatise which was at the center of the controversy: Pietro Pomponazzi, *De immortalitate animae,* ed. by G. Gentile, Messina-Roma, 1925.

[71] CAJETAN OF THIENE (Gajetanus de Thienis), born at Gaeta, 1387; died at Padova, July 18, 1465. List of writings (after S. D. Valsanzibio): *Recollectae super Regulas Hentisberi* (in *Tractatus Guilelmi Hentisberi De sensu composito et diviso . . . ,* Venice, 1494). *Recollectae super Sophismatibus Hentisberi,* Papiae, 1483 (Pavia). *Recollectae super Consequentias Strodi* (in *Alexandri Sermonetae . . . ,* Venice, 1488, 1507). *Expositio super Consequentias Ricardi de Ferabrich* (in *Consequentiae Strodi cum commento Alexandri Sermonetae, Declarationes Gaetani in easdem consequentias, Dubia magistri Pauli pergulensis, Obligationes ejusdem Strodi, Consequentiae Ricardi de Ferabrich, Expositio Gaetani super eas-*

dem, Venice, 1507). *Complementum Quaestionis Messini de Coderonco De motu locali*, no edition known to us. All the preceding works written 1422-1430. — *Quaestiones duodecim philosophicae*, no edition known to us. *Recollectae super octo libros Physicorum Aristotelis*, Venice, 1496 (*ca.* 1436). *Super libros de caelo et mundo Aristotelis expositio*, Venice, 1502 (*ca.* 1443). *Quaestio de sensu agente*, Venice, 1514. *Quaestio de sensibilibus communibus*, Venice 1514. *Quaestio de perpetuitate intellectus*, Venice, 1514. *Expositio super libros De anima Aristotelis*, Venice, 1514 (*ca.* 1443).—Valsanzibio also attributes to Cajetan: *Tractatus de reactione* (1449-1453), *Commentaria in libros metheorum Aristotelis* (1460-1461), *Tractatus de intensione et remissione formarum* (1460-1461); tables of mss. 45-57.
Silvestro da Valsanzibio OFMC., *Vita e dottrina di Gaetano di Thiene, Filosofo dello Studio di Padova (1387-1465)*, Verona, 1948: List of Cajetan's main positions in psychology and noetic, 183-186. According to Valsanzibio, Cajetan followed a predominantly Albertino-Thomistic line of thought (p. 199); he rejected the eternity of the world, the oneness of the agent intellect (*similis figmento*), the negation of Providence, etc. In short, Cajetan was "a moderate Aristotelian Scholastic," p. 199.

[72] NICOLETTO VERNIAS (Vernia Nicoletto), Vernias Nicolettus Theatinus, *Quaestio an ens sit totius naturalis philosophiae subjectum*, Venice, 1500; *Contra perversam Averroys opinionem de unitate intellectus: et de animae felicitate quesliones . . . Eiusdem etiam de gravibus et levibus questio subtilissima*, Venice, 1504. —B. Nardi, *Le opere inedite del Pomponazzi. II, La miscredenza e il carattere morale di Nicoletto Vernia*, GCFI., 29 (1950) 103-118. Biographical: P. Ragnisco, *Nicoletto Vernia. Studi storici sulla filosofia padovana nella seconda metà del secolo decimo quinto*, Venice, 1891; *Do-*

cumenti inediti e rari intorno alla vita e agli scritti di Nicoletto Vernia e di Elia del Medigo, Padova, 1891.—On the controversy concerning the immortality of the human soul: G. Heidingsfelder, *Zum Unsterblichkeitsstreit in der Renaissance (Petrus Pomponatius, d. 1525)*, ADGM., 1265-1286.

[73] On these facts, consult the already quoted work of Gehrard Ritter, *Studien zur Spätscholastik*, 2 vols., Heidelberg, 1921, 1922.

[74] PETER OF AILLY (*Petrus de Alliaco*) d. 1420.—Editions, GDP., 603. *Quaestiones super primum, tertium et quartum Sententiarum*, Venice, 1500; see Tschackaert, *Peter von Ailly . . .*, Gotha, 1877, p. 349. *Destructiones modorum significandi. Conceptus et insolubilia secundum viam nominalium magistri Petri de Allyaco*, no date. *Tractatus exponibilium magistri Petri de Allyaco*, Paris, 1494. *Tractatus et sermones*, Douai, 1634; this edition includes the *De anima*, separately printed, Paris, 1505.—On the doctrine, C. Prantl, *Geschichte der Logik*, IV, 103-118. K. Werner, *Die nominalisierende Psychologie . . .*, 302-327. L. Salembier, *Petrus de Alliaco*, Lille, 1886; same author, *Bibliographie des oeuvres du cardinal Pierre d'Ailly*, Besançon, 1909; same author, art. *Ailly*, DTC., 1 (1909) 642-654. E. Hartmann, *Die sinnliche Wahrnemung nach Pierre d'Ailly*, PJ., 16 (1903) 36-48, 139-148. G. M. Manser, JPT., 37 (1912) 293-300. E. Buron, *Ymago mundi . . .*, 3 vols., Paris, 1930. L. Salembier, *Le cardinal Pierre d'Ailly*, Mons-en-Bareul, 1932. M. Patronnier de Gandillac, *Usage et valeur des arguments probables chez Pierre d'Ailly*, AHDL., 8 (1933) 43-91. E. Vansteenberghe, *Un "programme de vie" de la fin du moyen âge. Le "De exercitio proficiencium" de Pierre d'Ailly*, ADGM., II, 1231-1246; text, pp. 1238-1242 (Latin), 1243-1246 (old French).

PART ELEVEN

CHAPTER IV. JOURNEY'S END

[75] JOHN GERSON, d. 1429.—Editions, GDP., 603. *Johannis Gersonii Opera omnia . . .*, ed. M. L. Ellies du Pin, Antwerp, 1706, 5 vols., reproduces the 1606 Paris edition.—On the doctrine,

J. B. Schwab, *Johannes Gerson*, Würzburg, 1858. J. Seltzenberger, *Die Mystik des Johannes Gerson*, Breslau, 1928. J. L. Connolly, *John Gerson, Reformer and Mystic*, Louvain, 1928. A. Combes, *Jean*

Gerson commentateur dionysien, Paris, 1940 (excellent introduction to the position of Gerson, 421-472) ; *Jean de Montreuil et le Chancelier Gerson,* Paris, 1942 ; *Essai sur la critique de Ruysbroek par Gerson,* Paris, 1945. E. Vansteenberghe, *Quelques écrits de Jean Gerson* (textes inédits et études), RSR., 13 (1933) 165-185, 393-424; 14 (1934) 191-218, 370-395; 15 (1935) 532-566; 16 (1936) 33-46; *Un traité inconnu de Gerson sur la doctrine de Raymond Lulle,* 16 (1936) 441-473. W. Dress, *Die Theologie Gerson. Eine Untersuchung zur Verbindung von Nominalismus und Mystik im Spätmittelalter,* Gütersloh, 1931. Against W. Dress, see J. B. Monnoyeur OSB., *La doctrine de Gerson, augustinienne et bonaventurienne,* Etudes Franciscaines, 46 (1934) 690-697. P. Glorieux, *Le Commentaire sur les Sentences attribué à Jean Gerson,* RTAM., 18 (1951) 107-108: is the work of a Franciscan, perhaps John Regis; dates, 1369-1370; *La vie et les oeuvres de Gerson. Essai chronologique,* AHDL., 25-26 (1950-1951) 151-152. J. Schneider, *Die Verpflichtung des menschlichen Gesetzes nach Johannes Gerson,* ZKT., 75 (1953) 1-54.

[76] I. CAPREOLUS (Johannes Capreolus) born *ca.* 1380 at Rodez (France), taught the *Sentences* at Paris (1408-1411), then at Toulouse, died at Rodez, 1444. His main work is his *Defensiones (Libri IV defensionum theologiae divi Thomas de Aquino)* ; modern edition, Paban and Pègues, *Joannis Capreoli Defensiones theologiae . . . ,* Tours, 7 vols., 1899-1908. John is often honored by the title of "Prince of the Thomists." His questions on the doctrine of Thomas reveal a supporter able to defend his master against his adversaries (Scotus, Auriol, Durand, John of Ripa, etc.) and incidentally against some of the so-called Thomists who often took liberties with his doctrine. His text is an abundant source of information concerning the positions of early fourteenth-century theologians whose doctrines are not well known. Capreolus is the first interpreter of Thomas whose intention it was to restate the Master's own doctrine, such as it is found in his writings. M. Grabmann, *Johannes Capreolus OP., der Princeps Thomistarum (d. 7 April 1444) und seine Stellung in der Geschichte der Thomistenschule,* DTF., 22 (1944) 85-109, 145-170. U. Degl' Innocenti, *Il principio d'individuazione e Giovanni Capreolo nel V Centenario della sua morte,* APA., 10 (1945) 147-196.

II. DOMINIC OF FLANDERS. Dominici de Flandria OP., *D. Thomae Aquinatis fidelissimi interpretis in libros Metaphysicae Aristotelis secundum expositionem ejusdem Angelici Doctoris lucidissimae atque utilissimae Quaestiones,* Cologne, 1621. L. Mahieu, *Dominique de Flandres (XVe) siècle, Sa métaphysique,* Paris, 1942. U. Schikwoski, *Dominicus de Flandria OP.* (d. 1479). *Sein Leben, seine Schriften, seine Bedeutung,* AFP., 10 (1940) 169-221.—On the composition of essence and existence, Mahieu, 139-150; Dominic quotes Giles of Rome and Armand of Belvezer in favor of Thomas Aquinas; his opposition to the "ficti Thomistae" who consider existence an accident, p. 142.

III. CAJETAN (Thomas de Vio, Cajetanus), born Febr. 20, 1468; entered the Dominican Order in 1484; studied at Naples, Bologna and Padua. Professor of metaphysics at Padua where he maintained the positions of Thomas Aquinas against Trombetta, professor of Scotist metaphysics since 1468, and against various Averroists (Vernias, Niphus, Pomponazzi). Taught theology at Pavia (1497-1499). General minister of the Dominican Order (1508). Cardinal (1517). Died Oct. 10, 1534.—The commentary of Cajetan on the *Summa theologiae* of St. Thomas Aquinas, printed in several editions of the *Summa* (including the Leonine edition) is still generally considered as the standard interpretation of Thomism. In fact, Cajetanism has largely superseded Thomism in the teaching of the schools; Cajetan's own doctrine is much more Aristotelian than that of Thomas Aquinas.—Philosophical works: commentaries *In de ente et essentia D. Thomae Aquinatis,* ed. M.-H. Laurent, Turis, 1934; *In de anima Aristotelis,* ed. I. Coquelle, Rome, I, 1938; II, 1939; *In Porphyrii Isagogen,* ed. I. M. Marega, Rome, 1934; *In Praedicamenta Aristotelis,* ed. M-H. Laurent, Rome, 1939; *De nominum analogia. De conceptu entis,* ed. P. N. Zammit, revised by P. H. Hering, Rome, 1952; English transl. by E. A. Bushinski and H. J. Koren, *The Analogy of Names and The Concept of Being,* Duquesne University Press, 1953.—Introductory, *Cajetan,* RT., 17 (1934-1935), special number of the Revue Thomiste: M.-J. Congar, *Bio-bibliographie de Cajetan,* 3-49. M.-H. Laurent, *Quelques documents des archives vati-*

canes (1517-1534), 50-148; Fr. Stegmüller, *Tolet et Cajétan*, 358-370; M.-M. Gorce, *Cajetan précurseur de Catharin et de Bañes*, 371-399; M.-H. Laurent, *Les premières biographies de Cajétan*, 446-448 (Leander Alberti); 449-454 (Bartholomew Spina); 456-490 (J.-B. Flavio); 491-493 (Ant. Fonseca OP.); 494-503 (Seb. of Olmeda, 494-503).—On the opposition of Cajetan to the demonstrability of the immortality of the human soul: Lateran Council, 1512; Mansi, *Amplissima collectio*, 32, col. 843.

BIBLIOGRAPHY. P. Mandonnet, art. *Cajetan*, DTC., 2 (1923) 1313-1321. M. Grabmann, *Die Stellung des Kard. Cajetan in der Geschichte des Thomismus und der Thomistenschule*, Angelicum, 11 (1934) 547-560. S. Bersani, *De mente cardinalis Cajetani circa vim conclusionum quinque viarum*, DTP., 36 (1933) 429-434. A. F. Claverie, *Le commentaire de la Somme théologique*, RT., 17 (1934-1935) 275-296. M. J. Congar, *Le rôle des images dans l'abstraction intellectuelle selon Cajétan*, ibid., 225-245. S. Alvarez, *De diversitate et identitate analogica juxta Cajetanum*, La Ciencia Tomista, 49 (1934) 310-329; 50 (1935) 5-14. R. Fei, *Fra Tommaso Gaetano l'uomo delle singolare opinioni*, RFNS., 27, Suppl. (1935) 127-147. R. Garrigou-Lagrange, *De personalitate juxta Cajetanum*, Angelicum, 11 (1934) 407-424; *L'éminence de la déité, ses attributs et les personnes divines selon Cajétan*, RT., 17 (1934-1935) 297-318. C. Mazzantini, *A proposito della critica del Gaetano alla distinctio formalis di Scoto nel Commentarium al De ente et essentia*, RFNS., 27 (1935) 17-19. J. Messaut, *L'immanence intellectuelle d'après Cajétan*, RT., 17 (1934-1935) 133-224. E. Moran, *Circa humanae animae subsistentiam Cajetani elucubratio quaedam*, Angelicum, 11 (1934) 539-546. A. Oddone, *La dottrina dell'analogia nell'opuscolo De nominum analogia del Card. Gaetano*, RFNS., 27 (1935) 5-16. T. L. Penido, *Cajétan et notre connaissance analogique de Dieu*, RT., 17 (1934-1935) 149-192. A. Gazzana SJ., *La materia signata di S. Tommaso secondo la diversa interpretazione del Gaetano e del Ferrarese*, Gregorianum, 24 (1940) 78-85. G. Heidingsfelder, *Zur Aristotelesdeutung in der Renaissance*, PJ., 53 (1940) 386-396. H. Gazzana SJ, *De formali constitutivo personae juxta Cajetanum (recens quaedam controversia)* Gregorianum, 27 (1946) 319-326. G. Giacon, *La seconda scolastica*,

I, I grandi commentatori di San Tommaso, Milan, 1944. U. Degl' Innocenti, *Animadversiones in Cajetani doctrinam de corporum individuatione*, DTP., 51 (1948) 3-18. J. F. Groner SJ, *Kardinal Cajetan. Eine Gestalt aus der Reformationszeit*, Louvain, 1951. E. Gilson, *Cajétan et l'existence*, Tijdschrift voor Philosophie, 15 (1953) 267-286; *Note sur le "revelabile" selon Cajétan*, MS. 15 (1953) 199-206.

On AMBROGIO CATARINO POLITO, (Ambrosius Catharinus Politus) the sometimes excessive, yet not always wrong, adversary of Cajetan: Jos. Schweitzer, *Ambrosius Catharinus Politus (1484-1553) ein Theologe des Reformationszeitalters. Sein Leben und seine Schriften*, Münster i. W., 1910 (Reformationsgeschichtliche Studien und Texte, 11-12), particularly pp. 43-79.

[77] PETER TARTARET (Tateret, Petrus Tartaretus), Rector of the University of Paris, 1490.—Editions, GDP., 612-613. Petrus Tartaretus, *In universam philosophiam opera omnia*, Venice, 1623. Commentaries on the *Quodlibeta* of Scotus, Paris, 1519; on *Opus Oxoniense*, Paris, 1520; reprinted together, Venice, 1580, 1583, 1607.—C. Prantl, *Geschichte der Logik*, IV, 204-209. A. Renaudet, *Préréforme et humanisme à Paris pendant les premières guerres d'Italie (1494- 1517)*, Paris, 1916.

Mauritius a Portu (d. 1513), Francis Lychetus (d. 1520), Hugh Cavellus (d. 1626), are represented by their commentaries and notes on Duns Scotus in the Wadding and Vivès editions of his *Opera omnia*. The commentary of Lychetus on the *Opus Oxoniense* is an excellent guide to the study of Scotism. On Mauritius a Portu (O' Fihely) a master at Padua in 1491, see the article of E. Longpré, DTC., 10 (1928) 404-405.—Just as the future progress of our understanding of Thomism now demands an extensive historical study of the Thomistic school of disciples and commentators, so also the doctrinal interpretation of Scotism will not progress without a detailed study of his school, including his sixteenth- and seventeenth-century interpreters. The works, printed but hard to find, of Macedo, Mastrius, Hauzeur and others, should be given in the future more recognition than they have hitherto received from historians.

New material on a fifteenth-century

Franciscan master in S. Clasen, *Walram von Siegburg OFM. und seine Doktorpromotion an der Kölner Universität (1430-1435)*, AFH., 45 (1952) 323-396 (text).

[78] SECOND ALBERTISM. A movement distinct from the school of Cologne, despite the fact that it returned to Cologne as to its natural place after beginning at Paris. It added a new opposition to Thomism within the group of the Realists. G. Meersseman, *Les origines parisiennes de l'albertisme colonais*, AHDL., 7 (1932) 121-142; *Geschichte des Albertismus. I, Die Pariser Anfänge des Kölner Albertismus*, Paris, 1933 (fundamental, contains the text of the *De ente et essentia* by John of Maisonneuve, pp. 91-191); *La lutte entre Thomistes et Albertistes parisiens vers 1410. Une voix Thomiste*, DTP., 40 (1937) 397-403.— JOHN OF MAISONNEUVE (Johannes de Nova Domo) conceives existence as a kind of fluid that fills up essences but is not really distinct from them. For Albert the Great versus Thomas on this point, 108-112. Form of the whole and form of the part (Gilbert of la Porrée) 149-157. Note the expression "vultus naturae" (the face of nature) 110, 124, 130, 131; John defines it, p. 126, as "the possibilities of all things" ("Voco autem naturae vultum rerum omnium possibilitates"). The source quoted by John (110, line 12) is Denis, to whom it is attributed several times by Albert the Great (Meersseman, op. cit., 110, note to 12-13). It has not yet been found in Denis himself. It will reappear under different forms in seventeenth-century philosophies.

This Parisian neo-Albertism migrated to Cologne *ca.* 1422. Its leader in this city was HEYMERICUS OF CAMPO (d. 1460). The controversy between Thomists and Albertists lasted at Cologne during the whole lifetime of Heymeric.—Heymericus de Campo, *Problemata inter Albertum Magnum et Sanctum Thomam ad utriusque opinionem multum conferentia*, Cologne, 1496.—G. Meersseman, *Geschichte des Albertismus. II, Die ersten kölner Kontroversen*, Rome, 1935.

The University of Louvain, whose origins are related to Cologne by some of its early masters, was divided by a controversy which lasted from 1465 to 1473. A master of arts, PETER OF RIVO, upheld the doctrine, correct according to the teaching of Aristotle, that propositions concerning future contingents are neither true nor false; a master in theology, HENRY OF ZOEMEREN, maintained the theologically correct proposition that, since divine foreknowledge is possible, such propositions must be either true or false. In the course of the controversy, Rivo accused Zoemeren of perjury for teaching conclusions contrary to those of Aristotle whose doctrine he had sworn to follow (text in L. Baudry, p. 296). Peter of Rivo signed a retraction in 1473, but he did not modify his position. He signed a second one in 1476.—Texts and historical introduction in L. Baudry, *La querelle des futurs contingents (Louvain 1465-1475). Textes inédits*, Paris, 1950. The statute of the University of Louvain (1447) prescribed the distinction between the teaching of philosophy and the teaching of theology; concerning philosophy, it prohibited the teaching of Aristotle according to the interpretation of Wyclif, Ockham, their disciples or other suspects; it prescribed to keep faith with the text of Aristotle as interpreted by Averroes (except where Averroes contradicts faith), or by Albert the Great, Thomas Aquinas, Giles of Rome, or any other master unanimously accepted by the faculty. This formula: "Averroes, ubi contra fidem non militat," describes rather well the kind of Aristotelianism which was then steadily gaining ground in the schools.—Note, pp. 71-72, 79, the use made of Cicero's *De fato* and, consequently, of Chrysippus and Epicurus. All the information added by Themistius to the text of Aristotle concerning the attitude of the non-Aristotelian Greek schools (Stoics, Megarics, Epicureans) with respect to this problem is beginning, in the fifteenth century, to be enriched by the text of Cicero.—On the transition to the fourteenth-century controversies on future contingents (Molina, Bañez, etc.) see Fr. Stegmüller, *Zur Prädestinationslehre des jungen Vasquez*, ADGM., II, p. 1289, n. 4; p. 1294, n. 14; freedom of indifference, 1296, n. 18.

[79] JOHN MAIR (Johannes Major), text in H. Elie, *Le traité "De l'infini" de Jean Mair. Nouvelle édition avec traduction et annotations*, Paris, J. Vrin, 1938. Reprints the *Propositum de infinito* first published in the commentary of John on the *Summulae* of Peter of Spain (1506); additions to it in John's commentary on the *Sentences* (I, dist. 44; edit. 1510,

1519, 1530). Note the answers of John, a supporter of the possibility of actual infinity, to the objections of his pupil and adversary on this point, Louis Coronel. John Mair is considered a terminist. A long list of practically unknown late masters is found in the article of H. Elie, *Quelques maîtres de l'Université de Paris vers l'an 1500*, AHDL., 25-26 (1950-1951) 193-243; pupils of John Mair, 212-228; pupils of his pupils, 228-236.

[80] NICHOLAS OF CUES (Nicolaus Cusanus, de Cusa). *Nicolai de Cusa Opera*, critical edition of the complete Latin works, Meiner, Leipzig, 1934 and ff., seven volumes published to date (1953), including, I, *De docta ignorantia* (1932), II, *Apologia doctae ignorantiae* (1932, we are quoting from this edition); *Directio speculantis seu de non aliud*, 1934; *Idiota, De sapientia, De mente, De staticis experimentis* (1937); *De beryllo* (1940); *De catholica concordantia* (no date).—A different series is: *Cusanus Texte; I. Predigten;* I., *Dies Sanctificatus*, by E. Hoffman and R. Klibanski, Heidelberg, 1929 (Sitzungsberichte, 1928/29, 3); 2/5. *Vier Predigten im Geiste Eckharts*, by J. Koch, Heidelberg, 1937 (Sitzungsberichte, 1936/37, 2).—A reprint of the Paris 1514 edition has been published by A. Petzelt, *Nicolaus von Cues*, Stuttgart, vol. I, 1949 (includes *De docta ignorantia, De conjecturis, De Deo abscondito, De quaerendo Deum, De filiatione Dei, De dato Patris luminum, De Genesi, Apologia doctae ignorantiae, Idiota, De sapientia, De mente).—English transl., The Vision of God (De visione Dei)*, by E. G. Salter, London-Toronto, Dent; N.Y. E. P. Dutton, 1928. French transl., M. de Gandillac, *Oeuvres choisies*, Paris, 1942.—BIBLIOGRAPHY. The classical introduction is E. Vansteenberghe, *Le cardinal Nicolas de Cues*, 1921. On the doctrine, Lenz, *Die docta ignorantia* . . . , Wurzburg, 1923. J. Hommes, *Die philosophischen Grundlehren des N. Cusanus* . . . , München, 1926. M. de Gandillac, *La philosophie de Nicolas de Cues*, Paris, 1941; German translation, after revision by the author, 1952. Important biographical notes in J. Koch, *Nicolaus von Cues und seine Umwelt*, Heidelberg, 1948.—P. Rotta, *Il cardinale Nicolò di Cusa*, Milan, 1928. B. Jansen, *Nicolaus Cusanus, philosophus antinomiarum*, Gregorianum 11 (1930) 380-397. H. Bett, *Nicholas of Cusa*, London, 1932. P.

Mennicken, *Nikolaus von Kues*, Leipzig, 1932. J. Neuner SJ, *Das Gottesproblem bei Nikolaus von Cues*, PJ., 46 (1933) 331-343. H. Rogner, *Die Bewegung des Erkennens und das Sein in der Philosophie des Nikolaus von Cues*, Heidelberg, 1937. R. Lazzarini, *Il "De ludo globi" e la concezione dell'uomo del Cusano*, Roma, 1938. M. Feigl, *Vom incomprehensibiliter inquirere Gottes im I Buch von De docta ignorantia des Nikolaus von Cues*, DTF., 22 (1944) 321-338. P. Wilhert, *Das Problem der coincidentia oppositorum* . . . , J. Koch, *Nikolaus, von Cues als Mensch*, in *Humanismus, Mystik und Kunst in der Welt des Mittelalters*, ed. by J. Koch, Leiden-Cologne, 1953.

[81] JOHN WENCK OF HERRENBERG, Rector of the University of Heidelberg in 1435, 1444, 1451; his opuscule against Nicholas of Cues has been discovered and published by E. Vansteenberghe, *Le "De ignota litteratura" de Jean Wenck de Herrenberg contre Nicolas de Cues*, Münster i. W., 1910 (Beiträge, 8, 6). After observing how hard it is to refute a man who believes in the coincidence of opposites (p. 21), John reduces the positions of Nicholas to the already censured doctrine of Eckhart (pp. 19, 24-26, 30) and proceeds to a theological condemnation rather than to a philosophical refutation.

[82] This is one of the main reasons why the sixteenth-century Renaissance was a continuation of the Christian civilization of the middle ages. The so-called "discovery" of classical Latin literature was the discovery of the Latin classics preserved by the mediaeval masters of Grammar; Petrarch's career covers the fourteenth century: he is contemporary with Ockham (E. Gilson, *La philosophie au moyen âge*, 720-730); the same remark applies to Boccaccio (1313-1375); as to the discovery of Plato, who was just as much of a Greek as Aristotle, but no more, it gains momentum with the translations of the Dialogues by Leonardo Bruni Aretino (1369-1444; op. cit., 736-738). Even Marsilio Ficino, commonly hailed in histories of literature as the herald of the Platonism of the Renaissance, was a continuator of the progressive rediscovery of Greek thought which is one of the fundamental elements of the history of Christian philosophy in the middle ages. Moreover, he was full of scholastic theology. His historians are beginning to realize that

this is true of his early writings; see the remarkable article by P. O. Kristeller, *The Scholastic Background of Marsilio Ficino, with an Edition of Unpublished Texts,* Traditio, 2 (1944) 257-318. Compare Ficino's *Theologia Platonica de immortalitate animorum,* dedicated to Lorenzo de Medici (1449-1492), with the *Summa contra Gentiles* of Thomas Aquinas: Ficino, Bk. II, ch. 4; *CG.* I, 43.—Bk. II, 5; *CG* I, 15.—Bk. II, 6-9; *CG.* I, 44-49. We fully agree that Ficino intended to be a Platonist; our only point is that, in trying to make Plato *Christianae veritati simillimum,* he was simply continuing the history of Christian thought in the middle ages.

G. Toffanin, *Storia dell' Umanesimo dal XIII al XVI secolo,* Napoli, 1933. N. Sapegno, *Il Trecento,* Milano, 1934. E. Gilson, *Les Idées et les Lettres,* Paris, 1932, 171-196; *Philosophie médiévale et humanisme,* in *Héloise et Abélard,* 1 ed. only, Paris J. Vrin, 1938, 225-245; *Le moyen âge et le naturalisme antique,* ibid., 183-224, and AHDL., 7 (1932) 5-37. A. J. Festugière OP., *Studia Mirandulana,* AHDL., 7 (1932) 143-250; text of the *De ente et uno,* 208-224; French transl. 225-250. English transl. by V. M. Hamm,

Marquette University Press, 1943. The *De ente et uno* of Pico della Mirandola (1491) is the only fragment that is left of his unfinished *Symphonia Platonis et Aristotelis.* On the fundamental agreement between Ficino and Pico della Mirandola ("sublimem Picum complatonicum nostrum") see the important Preface of Ficino to his own translation of Plotinus: "Totus enim ferme terrarum orbis a Peripateticis occupatus in duas plurimum sectas divisus est, Alexandricam (Alex. of Aphrodisias) et Averroicam . . ." AHDL., 7 (1932) 190, note. Plato and Plotinus are called upon, once more, to stop the spreading of a flood of impiety which "the mere preaching of faith" is unable to contain.

[88] H. Heimsoeth, *Die sechs grossen Themen der abendländischen Metaphysik und der Ausgang des Mittelalters,* 2 ed., Berlin, 1934. E. Gilson, *The Unity of Philosophical Experience,* New York, 1937; *Being and Some Philosophers,* 2 ed., Toronto 1952; *Les recherches historico-critiques et l'avenir de la scolastique,* Antonianum, 26 (1951) 40-48. A. D. Sertillonges, *Le christianisme et les philosophies,* 2 vols. Paris, 1939, 1942.

I

INDEX OF AUTHORS

Abbo of Fleury, 316, 614.
Abélard (Peter Abailard, Abailardus), 145,
  150, *153-163*, 164, 169, 231, 306, 316,
  475, 480, 541, 605, 607, 624, 625, *626-
  630*, 678, 781, 804.
Aboudemmeh, 637.
Abra, 579.
Abraham, 13, 33, 229, 265, 629.
Aboul—Abbas, 181.
Abubacer (Abu Bekr ibn Thofaïl), 217,
  641, 642.
Achard of Saint Victor, 634, 773.
Adam, 3, 58, 78, 80, 124, 616.
Adam Dorp, 528.
Adam of Buckfield, (Bockfeld, Boucher-
  mefort), 261, 389, 662.
Adam of Hoveden, 770.
Adam of Marsh (Adam de Marisco), 265,
  309, 355, 665.
Adam Pulchrae Mulieris, 259, 661.
Adam Rufus, 664.
Adam Wodam (Godam), 500, 699, *793*.
Adelard of Bath (Adelhard, Adelhardus),
  154, 260, 604, *625-626*, 728.
Adenulf of Anagni, 747.
Adhemar of Saint-Ruf, 620.
Adimantus, 590.
Aegidius of Rome, see Giles of Rome.
Aelred of Rievaulx, 169, 633.
Aeneas of Gaza, 89, 599.
Agar, 33.
Agobard of Lyons, 112.
Ailly (Peter of), see Peter of Ailly.
Alan of Lille (Alanus de Insulis), *172-
  178*, 182, 236, 259, 265, 328, 351, 432,
  434, 605, 624, 635, 636.
Al' Ashari, 184, 639, 651.
Alberic of Trois-Fontaines, 241.
Albert of Helmstedt, A. of Ricmestorp,
  see Albert of Saxony.
Albert of Orlamond, 667.
Albert of Saxony (Albertus Parvus, Al-
  bertutius), *516-517*, 518, 519, 520, 528,
  783, 794, 795, 796.
Albert the Great (Albertus Magnus),
  61, 85, 89, 169, 186, 205, 216, 217, 225,
  239, 241, 242, 243, 249, 252, 254, 266,
  267, 274, 275, *277-294*, 295, 296, 300,
  302, 304, 307, 312, 314, 315, 320, 322,
  323, 331, 346, 360, 362, 364, 374, 381,
  387, 389, 392, 393, 397, 405, 409, 426,
  429, 431, 432, 433, 434, 435, 437, 438,
  441, 442, 443, 446, 498, 499, 528, 534,

607, 621, 637, 639, 640, 649, 665, *666-
  673*, 670, 675, 680, 682, 683, 686, 689,
  708, 709, 713, 717, 720, 724, 734, 737,
  741, 750, 751, 752.
Al Bitrogi (Alpetragius, Anavalpetra),
  281.
Alcher of Clairvaux, *168-169*, 632, 658.
Alcinous (Platonist), 564.
Alcuin, 111, 139, 169, 267, 607.
Aldhelm, 607.
Alexander IV, 655, 717, 754.
Alexander V (Peter of Candia), 470.
Alexander of Alessandria, 698, 705.
Alexander of Aphrodisias, 62, 90, 99, 181,
  182, 183, 184, 186, 219, 235, 242, 243,
  284, 436, 527, 645, 689, 723, 798, 804.
Alexander of Hales (Al. Halensis), 252,
  266, 267, 274, 293, 294, 296, *327-329*,
  353, 359, 528, 613, 667, 675, 682, 683,
  685, 687, 698, 703, 716, 718, 719, 773.
Alexander Neckham (Neckam, Nequam),
  260, 661, 716.
Alexander Sermoneta, 798.
Alfano, Alfanus, 584.
Alfarabi, 183, *184-187*, 190, 216, 235, 236,
  253, 265, 269, 278, 284, 285, 297, 308,
  341, 392, 431, 436, 638, 639, 643, 652,
  653, 670, 671, 672, 675, 689, 691, 694,
  723, 728, 754.
Alfonso IX (King of Spain), 249.
Alfred (King of England), 106, 108, 605.
Alfred of Sareshel (Alfredus Anglicus),
  235, 260, 658, 661, 674.
Alfred (?), 266.
Algazel (Al Gazzali), 127, 211, 216, 226,
  235, 236, 265, 269, 291, 435, 531, 532,
  641, 642, 652, 662, 688, 727, 753.
Alhazen, Alhacen (Ibn al Haitam), 341,
  435, 663.
Alkindi, 179, 183-184, 186, 236, 284, 638,
  653, 727.
Amaury of Bène, 240, 243, 244₁ 531,
  654.
Ambrose, 9, 55, 70, 114, 267, 589, 590, 604,
  613, 731.
Ammonius Saccas, 35, 36, 37, 39, 61, 63,
  94, 569, 570, 585.
Anastasius the Librarian, 127.
Anaxagoras, 539, 540.
Andrew Capellanus (Andreas, André le
  Chapelain), 406, 727.
Anfredus Gonteri, 768.
Angelo de Camereno, 744.

II

INDEX OF HISTORIANS

Diels, H., 25, 564.
Diesendruck, Z., 649.
Dieterici, F., 637, 639.
Diggs, B. J., 716.
Diller, H., 576.
Dinkler, E., 594.
Disdier, Th., 744.
Dobler, E., 584.
Dobschütz, E. von., 552.
Dodds, M., 560, 561, 591.
Dolezich, G., 758.
Döllinger, I., 565.
Domanski, B., 584.
Dombrowski, H., 557.
Domenichelli, T., 682, 683.
Domet de Vorges, E., 616.
Doncoeur, P., 725, 787.
Dondaine, H. F., 597, 609, 654, 735, 755.
Donini, A., 564.
Donovan, M. A., 712.
Dorer, M., 702.
Doresse, G., 637.
Dörries, H., 609.
Doucet, V., 655, 682, 683, 687, 688, 691, 696, 698, 706, 729, 745, 747, 762, 768, 777.
Douie, D. L., 706, 730, 735, 769.
Doutreleau, L., 570.
Downes, A. H., 631.
Dräseke, J., 598, 609.
Dreiling, R., 777, 778.
Dress, W., 800.
Druwé, E., 616.
Dubarle, A. M., 591.
Duchesne (Mgr. L.), 19, 560, 562.
Duckett, E. S., 608.
Dudden, H., 589, 606.
Dufourcq, A., 561, 562.
Duhem, P., 349, 357, 467, 519, 520, 552, 586, 587, 591, 599, 600, 610, 611, 613, 637, 642, 647, 649, 658, 663, 668, 673, 674, 697, 705, 745, 753, 758, 759, 769, 782, 793, 794, 795, 796.
Duin, J. J., 719.
Draeseke, J., 598.
Dulong, M., 652, 656.
Dumeige, G., 634.
Duncker, L., 561.
Dunphy, W., 719, 720, 749.
Durand, 654.
Duval, A., 747.
Duval, R., 637.
Dwyer, K., 647.
Dwyer, W. J., 718, 720.
Dyroff, A., 795.
Dziewicki, M. H., 771.

Eales, S. J., 630.
Easton, B. S., 564.
Easton, S. C., 673.

Ebeling, H., 756.
Eberhard, A., 558.
Ebner, J., 634.
Echeverria, B., 692.
Edouard d'Alençon, 768.
Efros, I., 646.
Egenter, R., 633, 736.
Ehrhard-Siebold, E., and R. von Ehrhard, 610.
Ehrle, Fr., 655, 661, 688, 703, 706, 729, 738, 748, 759, 762, 771, 774, 779, 793, 794, 795.
Eibl, H., 595.
Eicken, H. von., 606.
Eisler, 646.
Elg, A. C., 602.
Elie, H., 772, 782, 802, 803.
Ellies du Pin, M. L., 799.
Elter, E., 747.
Emden, M., 602, 655.
Emmenegger, E., 580.
Endres, J. A., 616.
Engelbrecht, A., 602.
Engelhardt, C., 692.
Entrèves, A. P., 711.
Erbmann, H. G., 561.
Ernesti, K., 566.
Ernst, W., 568.
Eschmann, I. Th., 711, 716.
Esposito, M., 797.
Esser, G., 574.
Esser, Th., 713.
Ethier, A. E., 634.
Evans, A. P., 550, 553.
Evans, C. de B., 755, 756.
Eynde, D. van den., 575, 787.
Eyssenhardt, Fr., 586.

Fabro, C., 683, 698, 713, 741.
Fackenheim, E. L., 639.
Faggin, G., 756.
Fagin, C. J., 751, 752.
Fairweather, W., 570.
Falls, T. B., 555.
Faral, E., 619, 794, 795.
Farrar, C. P., 550, 553.
Faust, A., 609.
Favez, Ch., 604.
Faye, F. de., 34, 562, 569, 570, 571.
Feckes, K., 712, 741, 792.
Feder, A. L., 555.
Federhofer, F., 783.
Feigl, M., 714, 803.
Feiler, W., 667.
Felten, J., 663.
Ferrar, W. J., 579.
Ferretti, G., 589.
Festugière, A. J., 576, 577, 586, 804.
Figgis, J. N., 595.
Filliatre, Ch., 617.